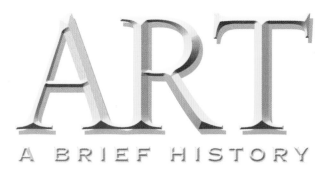

ART
A BRIEF HISTORY

On the cover and title page: Pierre Auguste Renoir (1841–1919). *Luncheon of the Boating Party*, 1880–81 (detail used on cover, full image on title page). Oil on canvas. 51 ¼ x 69 ⅛ inches (130.2 x 175.6 cm). Acquired 1923. The Phillips Collection, Washington, D.C.

Upper Saddle River, NJ 07458

ART
A BRIEF HISTORY
SECOND EDITION

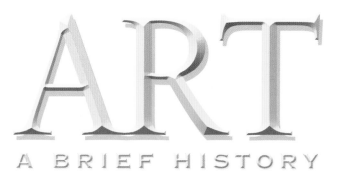

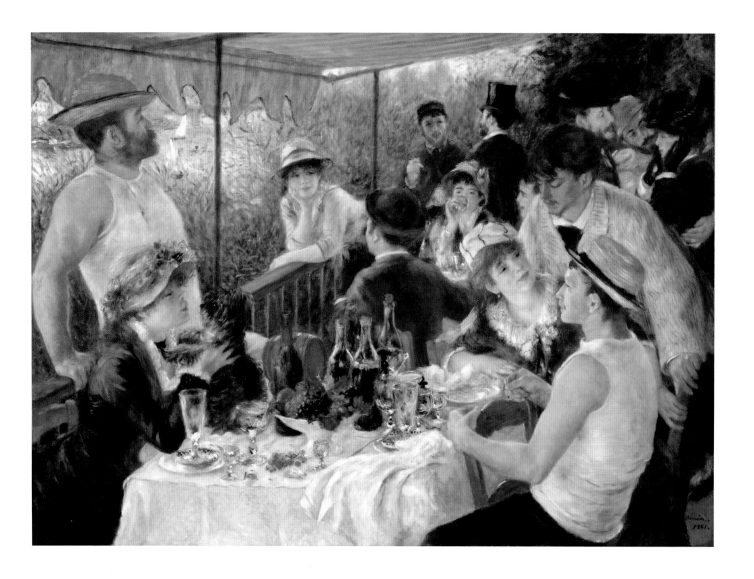

MARILYN STOKSTAD

EMIRITA
The University of Kansas

Library of Congress Cataloging-in-Publication Data

Stokstad, Marilyn, (date)
   [Art History]
   Art : a brief history / Marilyn Stokstad;
   with contributions by Stephen Addiss ... [et al.].— 2nd ed.
   p. cm.
   Includes bibliographical references and index.
   ISBN 0-13-183689-7 (hc) — ISBN 0-13-182769-3 (pbk.)
     1. Art—History. I. Addiss, Stephen, (date) II. Title.

   N5300.S923 2003
   709—dc21

                                                            2002044807

Editorial Director: *Charlyce Jones Owen*
Executive Editor: *Sarah Touborg*
Managing Editor: *Julia Moore*
Project Manager and Developmental Editor: *Cynthia Henthorn*
Project Editor: *Holly Jennings*
Editorial Assistants: *Doria Romero, Heather King*
Project Assistant: *Sasha Anderson*
Media Editor: *Anita Castro*
Design Concept: *Design 5 Creatives*
Design and Production: *Thomasina Webb of Octavo Editions*
Cover Design: *Kathryn Foot*
Photo Editing, Rights and Reproduction: *Susan Wechsler and Jennifer Sanfilippo of PhotoSearch, Inc.*
Illustrator: *John McKenna*
Indexer: *Corinne Ferrara*
Director of Production and Manufacturing: *Barbara Kittle*
Prepress and Manufacturing Manager: *Nick Sklitsis*
Prepress and Manufacturing Buyer: *Sherry Lewis*
Senior Marketing Manager: *Christopher Ruel*
Marketing Assistant: *Kimberly Daum*

On the cover and page iii: Pierre Auguste Renoir (1841-1919). *Luncheon of the Boating Party*,
1880-81. Oil on Canvas. 51 1/4 x 69 1/8 inches (130.2 x 175.6 cm). Acquired 1923.
The Phillips Collection, Washington, D.C.

This book was set in 10/12.5 ITC Officina Serif by Octavo Editions. It was printed and bound in Japan
by Toppan Printing Co., Ltd. The cover was printed by Toppan Printing Co., Ltd.

© 2004 by Pearson Education
Upper Saddle River, New Jersey 07458

Printed in Japan
10 9 8 7 6 5 4 3 2

ISBN 0-13-182769-3

Pearson Education Ltd., London
Pearson Education Australia Pty, Limited, Sydney
Pearson Education Singapore, Pte. Ltd.
Pearson Education North Asia Ltd., Hong Kong
Pearson Education Canada, Ltd., Toronto
Pearson Education de Mexico, S.A. de C.V.
Pearson Education—Tokyo, Japan
Pearson Education Malaysia, Pte. Ltd.
Pearson Education, Upper Saddle River, New Jersey

Preface to *Art: A Brief History*

Over the many years that I have taught the history of art, I have become convinced that the first goal of an introductory course should be to create an educated, enthusiastic public for the arts. I firmly believe that everyone can and should enjoy their introduction to art history. Only then will people come to appreciate the visual arts as inspired, tangible creations of human skill and imagination.

When an art history book responds to the needs of its audience, that book can make a great difference in the role art assumes in the lives of individuals. All of us—authors and publishers—have tried to make the book from which this work is derived, *Art History*, a sensitive, accessible, engaging, and comprehensive book. Now in its second edition, *Art: A Brief History* preserves these goals and many of the features of *Art History*, while offering a more abbreviated and slightly more popular account.

Art: A Brief History is contextual, in the best sense of the term. This book, like *Art History*, balances formalist analysis with contextual art history to support the needs of a diverse and fast-changing student population. Throughout the text we treat the visual arts not in a vacuum but within the real-world contexts of history, geography, politics, religion, and culture. We carefully define the parameters—social, religious, political, and cultural—that either constrained or liberated individual artists. And bearing in mind that there is no substitute for experiencing works of art firsthand, we have whenever feasible included works on view in many different museums and collections around the United States, including college and university museums.

Art: A Brief History is wide-ranging and inclusive. We have reached beyond the West to the arts of other regions and cultures, presenting a global view of art through the millennia. We regard art as more than painting, sculpture, and architecture, and so we include drawings, photographs, works in metal and ceramics, textiles, and jewelry. We pay due respect to the canon of great monuments in the history of art, but we also treat artists, including women and minorities, and artworks not previously acknowledged in surveys. We incorporate the best and most up-to-date scholarship, including recent discoveries (the prehistoric paintings of Chauvet cave in southern France, for example), and bring new works to the forefront (the World Trade Center *Tribute in Light Memorial*, for example).

This book is a pleasure to read and use. As in the previous edition, the text carries the central narrative of *Art: A Brief History*, while set-off boxes present interesting and instructive material that enriches the text. A number of **critical issues** boxes focus on thought-provoking concepts such as the use of the idea of the "mainstream" as an art historical label and the way the titles given to works of art, such as "Venus," may affect our perception of them. Other boxes provide insights into contextual influences, such as women as art patrons, the lives of major religious leaders, and the intersection of art and politics. **Elements of Architecture** boxes explain basic architectural forms and terminology. **Technique** boxes explore how artworks have been made, from prehistoric cave paintings to Renaissance frescoes to photographs. Finally, *Art: A Brief History* includes a **rich illustration program** of 687 photographs—most in full color—as well as 70 original line drawings (including architectural plans and cutaways) that have been universally acclaimed in *Art History*.

What's New

We have strengthened the pedagogy of *Art: A Brief History*. Every chapter opens with a visually dramatic two-page spread called **Looking Forward** whose engaging text peaks the student's interest in the material to come. Centered on an image that exemplifies the key concepts of that chapter, each Looking Forward alerts the student to significant points in the narrative to follow. The illustrated **Closer Look** boxes found in each chapter provide an in-depth examination of a single work of art, demonstrating the variety and richness of art history as revealed by a specific artist, culture, and time. The Closer Look essays also amplify the student's understanding of art history by presenting different ways to explore and appreciate art.

Placed at the end of related groups of chapters ("cultural clusters"), the seven **Looking Back** double-page spreads are packed with useful teaching tools that reinforce and augment what the student has just read: **illustrated timelines** offer a visual chronology of the artworks, cultures, and/or movements in a cluster of chapters; **illustrated maps** put the artworks in their geographical contexts; and **concise essays** weave the unifying and connecting threads of the preceding chapters.

This edition has an inviting new design and new photographs and line art. Color is used throughout the new design to make the book highly navigable and enticing. Recently cleaned and/or restored works of art and architecture have been rephotographed and are now illustrated in their new states. Among the new images of buildings, fresco cycles, panel and easel paintings, and architectural freestanding sculpture are New York's Metropolitan Museum of Art's Archaic Greek *Kouros*, an interior view of the Dome of the Rock in Jerusalem, and Raphael's *School of Athens*.

Content has been significantly revised and expanded. In response to political events and student interest, the material on Islamic art has been expanded to a full chapter, resulting in a beneficial reorganization of the chapters on medieval art. The last four chapters of the book, covering art from the late eighteenth to the twenty-first century, have been completely revised. The **bibliography** and **glossary** have been updated and the invaluable **Starter Kit** expanded.

A complete ancillary package is available for *Art: A Brief History*. This package includes videos, an interactive CD-ROM with 1,000 images for study and presentation, a Student Study Guide, an Instructor's Manual with Computerized Test Bank, and the publication *A Prentice Hall Guide to Evaluating Online Resources: Art*. Ask your Prentice Hall sales representative about custom slide sets to accompany this edition.

Art: A Brief History is also supported by the most effective art textbook interactive website available today at www.prenhall.com/stokstad.

In Gratitude

Art: A Brief History represents the cumulative efforts of a distinguished team of scholars and educators. Even in a book of this size, single authorship is no longer a fully responsible proposition. Our world has become too complex, our coverage too wide, and our research on art too sophisticated to entrust the world's art to a single author. An individual view of art may be very persuasive—even elegant—but it remains personal. Now, however, we no longer look for a single "truth," nor do we venerate a static canon of artworks. *Art: A Brief History* incorporates the work of the original team of scholar-teachers, all with independent views and the ability to treat the art they write about on its own terms and in its own cultural context. The overarching viewpoint—the controlling imagination—is mine, but *Art History*, from which this book is derived, would not have been successful without the work of the distinguished contributing authors Stephen Addiss, David Cateforis, Chu-tsing Li, Marylin M. Rhie, and Christopher D. Roy.

Finally, *Art: A Brief History* would have been impossible without the invaluable assistance and advice of scores of other scholars and teachers who have generously answered my questions, given their recommendations on organization and priorities, and provided specialized critiques. They are listed in my acknowledgments. I am especially grateful to my colleagues at the University of Kansas, Amy McNair and Marsha Haufler, for their expert advice on aspects of Asian art; Marni Kessler and Charles Eldredge for modern art; and Sally Cornelison for Italian art. Jonathan Bloom of Boston College provided invaluable help and advice on Islamic art, and Roger Ward of the Norton Museum of Art worked with me on the Renaissance and Baroque periods in Europe. Reed Anderson significantly updated the bibliography. Margaret Oppenheimer labored to condense the revised edition of *Art History* into the original edition of *Art: A Brief History*, and Cynthia Henthorn and Holly Jennings contributed their editorial expertise to this new edition. As always Julia Moore played her role as creative and constructive "trailboss." To all these friends I offer my sincere thanks.

Acknowledgments to *Art: A Brief History*

This edition is dedicated to all my students and to my sister, Karen L. S. Leider, and my niece, Anna J. Leider.

*A*rt: A Brief History is a concise version of *Art History*, which was first published in 1995 by Harry N. Abrams, Inc., and Prentice Hall, Inc. This new edition reflects the changes made in the second edition of *Art History*. Everyone who contributed to the original and revised editions of *Art History* deserves to be recognized and thanked for step-parenting *Art: A Brief History*.

Again I worked with my editors at Abrams and Prentice Hall, Julia Moore and Cynthia Henthorn, to create a book that would incorporate effective pedagogical features into a shortened narrative. Art historian Cynthia Henthorn deftly managed the project; she and Holly Jennings diligently edited the manuscript and contributed fresh ideas and writing, all to the book's lasting benefit. They were ably supported by the skillful editorial assistance of Doria Romero and Heather King. John McKenna's drawings have brought information and clarity to the discussions of architecture, and designer Thomasina Webb of Octavo Editions showed a disciplined creativity in the intelligent, approachable design and layout of this book. She was supported by the masterful talents of Emily Baerga and Monica Ponomarev. Much appreciation goes to Christopher Ruel, Marketing Manager for Art and Music at Prentice Hall, and the entire Humanities and Social Sciences team at Prentice Hall. My research assistants at the University of Kansas, Ted Meadows and Reed Anderson, have earned my everlasting gratitude. So do all my former graduate teaching assistants at the University of Kansas. To all of you, my heartfelt thanks.

Many people reviewed the original edition of *Art History* and their work continues to be reflected in subsequent editions. Margaret Oppenheimer helped me condense *Art History* into the first edition of *Art: A Brief History*. Colleagues wrote chapters for the original book: Stephen Addiss, Chu-tsing Li, Marilyn M. Rhie, and Christopher Roy. For the second edition of *Art: A Brief History*, Jonathan Bloom has helped me revise and expand a chapter on Islamic Art, and David Cateforis thoroughly revised the chapters on modern art. Paul Rehak and John Younger answered my questions on the art of the classical world. Nancy Corwin has been an essential resource on the history of craft, and Jill Leslie Furst assisted on the chapters on the art of Pacific cultures and the art of the Americas. Jean Middleton James, a friend from Carleton College days, has read every word in every version of the book.

Others who have tried to keep me from errors of fact and interpretation—who have shared ideas and course syllabi, read chapters or sections of chapters, and offered suggestions and criticism—include: Barbara Abou-el-Haj, SUNY Binghamton; Roger Aiken, Creighton University; Molly Aitken; Anthony Alofsin, University of Texas, Austin; Christiane Andersson, Bucknell University; Kathryn Arnold; Julie Aronson, Cincinnati Art Museum; Larry Beck; Evelyn Bell, San Jose State University; Janetta Rebold Benton, Pace University; Janet Berlo, University of Rochester; David Binkley, The National Museum of African Art, Smithsonian Institution; Sara Blick, Kenyon College; Suzaan Boettger; Judith Bookbinder, University of Massachusetts, Boston; Marta Braun, Ryerson Polytechnic University; Elizabeth Gibson Broun, Smithsonian American Art Museum; Claudia Brown, Arizona State University; Glen R. Brown, Kansas State University; Maria Elena Buszek, Kansas City Art Institute; Robert G. Calkins, Cornell University; April Clagget, Keene State College; William W. Clark, Queens College, CUNY; John Clarke, University of Texas, Austin; Jaqueline Clipsham; Ralph T. Coe; Robert Cohon, The Nelson-Atkins Museum of Art; Bradford Collins, University of South Carolina; Alessandra Comini, Southern Methodist University; Sally Cornelison and Susan Craig, University of Kansas; Charles Cuttler; Patricia Darish; James D'Emilio, University of South Florida; Lois Drewer, Index of Christian Art; Susan Earle, Edmund Eglinski, and Charles Eldredge, University of Kansas; James Farmer, Virginia Commonwealth University; Grace Flam, Salt Lake City Community College; Patrick Frank, University of Kansas; Mary D. Garrard,

American University; Paula Gerson, Florida State University; Walter S. Gibson; Dorothy Glass, SUNY Buffalo; Stephen Goddard, University of Kansas; Randall Griffey, The Nelson-Atkins Museum of Art; Cynthia Hahn, Florida State University; Marsha Haufler, University of Kansas; Sharon Hill, Virginia Commonwealth University; John Hoopes, University of Kansas; Carol Ivory, Washington State University; Marni Kessler, University of Kansas; Alison Kettering, Carleton College; Wendy Kindred, University of Maine at Fort Kent; Alan T. Kohl, Minneapolis College of Art; Ruth Kolarik, Colorado College; Carol H. Krinski, New York University; Aileen Laing, Sweet Briar College; Janet Le Blanc, Clemson University; Charles Little, The Metropolitan Museum of Art; Laureen Reu Liu, McHenry Country College; Loretta Lorance; Brian Madigan, Wayne State University; Janice Mann, Bucknell University; Judith Mann, St. Louis Art Museum; Richard Mann, San Francisco State University; James Martin, The Nelson-Atkins Museum of Art; Elizabeth Parker McLachlan, Rutgers University; Amy McNair, University of Kansas; Gustav Medicus, Kent State University; Tamara Mikailova, St. Petersburg, Russia, and Macalester College; Vernon Minor, University of Colorado, Boulder; Anta Montet-White; Anne E. Morganstern, Ohio State University; Winslow Myers, Bancroft School; Lawrence Nees, University of Delaware; Amy Ogata, Cleveland Institute of Art; Judith Oliver, Colgate University; Edward Olszewski, Case Western Reserve University; Sarah Orel, Truman State University; Sara Jane Pearman, The Cleveland Museum of Art; John G. Pedley, University of Michigan; Michael Plante, H. Sophie Newcomb Memorial College; John Pultz, University of Kansas; Eloise Quiñones-Keber, Baruch College and the Graduate Center, CUNY; Virginia Raguin, College of the Holy Cross; Nancy H. Ramage, Ithaca College; Ann M. Roberts, University of Iowa; Lisa Robertson, The Cleveland Museum of Art; Barry Rubin, Talmudic College of Florida; Charles Sack, Parsons, Kansas; Jan Schall, The Nelson-Atkins Museum of Art; Diane Scillia, Kent State University; Tom Shaw, Kean College; Pamela Sheingorn, Baruch College, CUNY; Rachel Smith, Kansas City Art Institute; Lauren Soth, Carleton College; Anne R. Stanton, University of Missouri, Columbia; Michael Stoughton; Thomas Sullivan, OSB, Benedictine College (Conception Abbey); Pamela Trimpe, University of Iowa; Richard Turnbull, Fashion Institute of Technology; Elizabeth Valdez del Alamo, Montclair State College; Lisa Vergara; Monica Visoná, Metropolitan State College of Denver; Roger Ward, Norton Museum of Art; Mark Weil, Washington University, St. Louis; David Wilkins, University of Pittsburgh; Marcilene Wittmer, University of Miami; and Ann S. Zielinski.

Work began on this book while I was a resident at the American Academy in Rome, an ideal place for study and writing set in one of the most visually stimulating places in the Western world. Special thanks are due the director, Lester Little and the many scholars who patiently answered my questions. Many friends, as well as colleagues, have endured my enthusiasms and despairs, but I extend my special thanks to Katherine Giele, Nancy and David Dinneen, Anta Montet-White, Charlie and Jane Eldredge, and Katherine Stannard. Of course, my very special thanks go to my sister, Karen Leider, and my niece, Anna Leider.

Finally, Paul Gottlieb, who was for many years president of Harry N. Abrams, Inc., had faith in my projects from the beginning. Paul died in the spring of 2002, before this book was finished, but his love of beautiful books continues to inspire many of us. If the arts are the ultimate expression of human faith and integrity as well as creativity, then writing and producing books about art—and in so doing to introduce new viewers to the creativity, courage, and vision that artists express—remains a worthy undertaking.

Marilyn Stokstad
Lawrence, Kansas
Winter 2003

Brief Contents

Preface   *v*
Acknowledgments   *vi*
Starter Kit   *5*
Use Notes   *12*

Introduction   13
1   **Art Before the Written Word**   30
2   **The Art of Mesopotamia and Egypt**   42
3   **Early Asian Art**   66
4   **Art of the Aegean World**   88
5   **The Spread of Greek Art and Culture**   118
6   **Art of the Roman Republic and Empire**   136
7   **Jewish, Early Christian, and Byzantine Art**   164
8   **Islamic Art**   188
9   **Later Asian Art**   208
10   **Early Medieval and Romanesque Art**   232
11   **Gothic Art**   256
12   **Early Renaissance Art**   286
13   **Art of the High Renaissance and Reformation**   314
14   **Baroque and Rococo Art**   350
15   **Art of the Americas**   384
16   **African Art**   402
17   **Neoclassicism, Romanticism, and Realism**   416
18   **Later Nineteenth-Century Art in Europe and
the United States**   440
19   **Modern Art: Europe and North America
in the Early Twentieth Century**   466
20   **Art Since 1945**   498

Glossary   *530*
Selected Bibliography   *538*
Index   *546*
Credits   *557*

Contents

Preface v
Acknowledgments vi
Starter Kit 5
Use Notes 12

Introduction 13

1 Art Before the Written Word 30
   CLOSER LOOK 32
Upper Paleolithic Art 32
   THE POWER OF NAMING 34
   TECHNIQUE: *PREHISTORIC WALL PAINTING* 35
   THE MEANING(S) OF PREHISTORIC PAINTING 36
Art in the Neolithic Period 36
Megalithic Architecture 38
Bronze Age Europe 40
Early Art Outside Europe 41

2 The Art of Mesopotamia and Egypt 42
Early Neolithic Communities 44
Mesopotamia 45
   ORIGINS OF WRITING 45
   CLOSER LOOK 48
Egypt 52
Early Dynastic and Old Kingdom Egypt 52
   THE FIBER ARTS 53
   MUMMIES 55
   ELEMENTS OF ARCHITECTURE: *MASTABA TO PYRAMID* 56
   EGYPTIAN SYMBOLS 57
The Middle Kingdom 58
The New Kingdom 59
The Late Period 65

3 Early Asian Art 66
The Indian Subcontinent 68
   BUDDHISM 69
   ELEMENTS OF ARCHITECTURE: *STUPAS* 71
   BUDDHIST SYMBOLS 73
   HINDUISM 76
China 76
   CONFUCIANISM 78
   THE SILK ROAD AND THE MAKING OF SILK 80
   CALLIGRAPHY 81
   CLOSER LOOK 82
Japan 82
LOOKING BACK 1 ESSAY, MAP, TIMELINE 86–87

4 Art of the Aegean World 88
The Cycladic Islands 91
Minoan Crete 91
Mycenaean (Late Bronze Age) Civilization 95
   MYTHOLOGY 96

The Emergence of Greek Civilization 98
The Geometric Style 99
The Archaic Period 99
   ELEMENTS OF ARCHITECTURE: *THE GREEK ARCHITECTURAL ORDERS* 100
   GREEK GODS 100
   CLOSER LOOK 104
The Early Classical or Transitional Period 105
The "Golden Age" of Art 108
Late Classical Art of the Fourth Century BCE 114
   WOMEN ARTISTS IN ANCIENT GREECE 116

5 The Spread of Greek Art and Culture 118
The Etruscans 121
The Scythians 124
The Neo-Babylonians 125
The Persians 125
   CLOSER LOOK 126-27
The Hellenistic Greeks 129
   ELEMENTS OF ARCHITECTURE: *THEATERS* 129
   APHRODITE'S ARMS 130

6 Art of the Roman Republic and Empire 136
   ROMAN COUNTERPARTS OF GREEK GODS 138
The Republican Period 139
   ELEMENTS OF ARCHITECTURE: *ARCH AND VAULT* 141
   CLOSER LOOK 142
The Early Empire 143
The Empire 145
   ELEMENTS OF ARCHITECTURE: *ROMAN ARCHITECTURAL ORDERS* 147
The "Good Emperors" 152
Lands Outside the Roman Empire 157
The Late Empire 158
LOOKING BACK 2 ESSAY, MAP, TIMELINE 162–63

7 Jewish, Early Christian, and Byzantine Art 164
Judaism 166
   ICONOGRAPHY OF THE LIFE OF JESUS 168-69
Early Christianity 169
   ELEMENTS OF ARCHITECTURE: *BASILICA-PLAN AND CENTRAL-PLAN CHURCHES* 171
   SAINT PETER'S, NOTRE-DAME, AND SANTA MARIA MAGGIORE 171
   CLOSER LOOK 174
Early Byzantine Art 175
   ELEMENTS OF ARCHITECTURE: *PENDENTIVES AND SQUINCHES* 175
   THE DEPICTION OF SPACE 178
   CHRISTIAN SYMBOLS 180

Later Byzantine Art   181

8 Islamic Art   **188**
Art During the Early Caliphates   190
   ISLAM AND THE PROPHET MUHAMMAD   191
   ELEMENTS OF ARCHITECTURE: *MOSQUE PLANS*   193
   CLOSER LOOK   196
Later Islamic Art   197
The Mughal Empire   204
The Ottoman Empire   205

9 Later Asian Art   **208**
The South Asian Subcontinent   210
Rajput Painting   213
   INDIAN PAINTING ON PAPER   214
   CLOSER LOOK   214
China   215
   TECHNIQUE: *FORMATS OF CHINESE PAINTING*   220
Japan   221
   WRITING, LANGUAGE, AND CULTURE   222
LOOKING BACK 3   ESSAY, MAP, TIMELINE   230–31

10 Early Medieval and
   Romanesque Art   **232**
Early Medieval Art in the British Isles
   and Scandinavia   234
Carolingian Art   236
   THE MEDIEVAL SCRIPTORIUM   237
Painting in Christian Spain   239
The Ottonian Period   240
The Romanesque Period   245
Architecture and Mural Painting   245
   CLOSER LOOK   247
Sculpture   248
Books and Embroidery   251
Castles and Churches in England and Normandy   253
   ELEMENTS OF ARCHITECTURE: *RIB VAULTING*   255

11 Gothic Art   **256**
Gothic Art in France   259
   ELEMENTS OF ARCHITECTURE: *THE GOTHIC CHURCH*   262
   TECHNIQUE: *STAINED-GLASS WINDOWS*   264
   CLOSER LOOK   265
Castles   272
Gothic Art in England   273
Gothic Art in the Germanic Lands   275
Gothic Art in Italy   276
Sculpture   276
   TECHNIQUE: *CENNINI ON PANEL PAINTING*   279
Italian Panel and Mural Painting   279
LOOKING BACK 4   ESSAY, MAP, TIMELINE   284–85

12 Early Renaissance Art   **286**
Renaissance Art in the Low Countries   288
   TECHNIQUE: *PAINTING ON PANEL*   288
   TECHNIQUE: *RENAISSANCE PERSPECTIVE SYSTEMS*   289
   CLOSER LOOK   294
Flemish-Influenced Art Outside the Low Countries   294
   WOMEN ARTISTS IN THE LATE MIDDLE AGES
   AND THE RENAISSANCE   295
Renaissance Art in Italy   296
Architecture and Sculpture   297
Painting   303
Printmaking in Renaissance Europe   312
   TECHNIQUE: *WOODCUTS AND ENGRAVINGS ON METAL*   312

13 Art of the High Renaissance
   and Reformation   **314**
Italian Art   316
   THE VITRUVIAN MAN   316
   ELEMENTS OF ARCHITECTURE: *SAINT PETER'S*
   BASILICA   326
Venice and the Veneto   328
   WOMEN PATRONS OF THE ARTS   329
   CLOSER LOOK   332
Mannerism in Italy and France   334
   ELEMENTS OF ARCHITECTURE: *PARTS OF THE*
   CHURCH FACADE   340
German and English Art   341
The Reformation and the Arts   343
Netherlandish and Spanish Art   346

14 Baroque and Rococo Art   **350**
Art for the Counter-Reformation Church: Italy   352
Art for the Secular State: France   358
   GRADING THE OLD MASTERS   360
The Habsburg Empire in Spain and Flanders   362
   ELEMENTS OF ARCHITECTURE: *THE BAROQUE*
   CHURCH FACADE   365
   CLOSER LOOK   368
Protestant England   369
The Protestant Netherlands   371
   TECHNIQUE: *WOODCUTS AND ENGRAVINGS ON METAL*   372
   SCIENCE AND THE CHANGING WORLDVIEW   376
The Rococo Style   378
Art and Science   380
LOOKING BACK 5   ESSAY, MAP, TIMELINE   382–83

15 Art of the Americas   **384**
Mesoamerica   387
South America: The Central Andes   391
   ELEMENTS OF ARCHITECTURE: *INCA MASONRY*   392
The Aftermath of the Spanish Conquest   393
North America   394

The Southeast and the Southwest   394
The Eastern Woodlands and the Great Plains   397
    TECHNIQUE: *BASKETRY*   397
The Northwest Coast   398
    CLOSER LOOK   399

16 African Art   **402**
    THE MYTH OF "PRIMITIVE" ART   405
**African Art in the Modern Era: Living
Traditions and New Trends**   408
    CLOSER LOOK   409
LOOKING BACK 6 ESSAY, MAP, TIMELINE   414–15

**17 Neoclassicism, Romanticism,
     and Realism**   **416**
Neoclassicism and Its Heritage   418
Portrait Painting   419
    FORTY YEARS OF REVOLUTION: 1775–1815   419
    ART ACADEMIES IN THE EIGHTEENTH CENTURY   422
Moralized Genre Painting   422
Neoclassical Architecture in England and
North America   424
    CLOSER LOOK   425
Neoclassical Painting in France   427
Romanticism   429
Romantic Landscape Painting   433
    "AM I NOT A MAN AND A BROTHER?"   433
Early Photography   434
    TECHNIQUE: *HOW PHOTOGRAPHY WORKS*   436
Naturalism and Realism in Europe   436
Painting in the United States   438

**18 Later Nineteenth-Century Art in
     Europe and the United States**   **440**
Architecture   442
Academic Art   444
Reactions Against the Academy   445
Art Nouveau   447
    JAPONISME   448
Art in the United States   449
Impressionism   451
    ARTISTIC ALLUSIONS IN MANET'S ART   453
Later Impressionism   455
Post-Impressionism   457
    TECHNIQUE: *LITHOGRAPHY*   462
    CLOSER LOOK   463
Late-Nineteenth-Century French Sculpture   464

**19 Modern Art: Europe and North
     America in the Early Twentieth
     Century**   **466**
Early Modern Tendencies in Europe   468

Expressionism   469
    MODERNISM   469
    "PRIMITIVISM" AND MODERNITY   470
Expressionist Movements   471
Cubism   475
Responses to Cubism   478
Modernist Tendencies in the United States   479
Art After World War I   481
Architecture Between the Wars   483
    ELEMENTS OF ARCHITECTURE: *THE INTERNATIONAL
    STYLE*   485
Dada and Surrealism   486
    SUPPRESSION OF THE AVANT-GARDE IN GERMANY   487
    CLOSER LOOK   489
    ELEMENTS OF ARCHITECTURE: *THE SKYSCRAPER*   490
Art in North America Between the Wars   492
The United States   492
The Harlem Renaissance   494
Mexico   495
Canada   497

20 Art Since 1945   **498**
The "Mainstream" Crosses the Atlantic   500
    THE IDEA OF THE MAINSTREAM   503
Assemblage and Pop Art   505
    THE HIGH/LOW MYTH OF MODERNISM   506
    CLOSER LOOK   508
    APPROPRIATION   510
Minimalism/Post-Minimalism and Op Art   510
Conceptual and Performance Art   511
The Rise of American Craft Art   512
Late Modernism/Postmodernism   513
Architecture   513
Earthworks and Site-Specific Art   515
Feminist Art   516
Pluralism   518
    DECONSTRUCTION   522
Art With Social Impact   522
Installation and Video Art   523
Public Memory and Art: The Memorial   525
LOOKING BACK 7 ESSAY, MAP, TIMELINE   528–29

Glossary   *530*
Selected Bibliography   *538*
Index   *546*
Credits   *557*

STARTER KIT

This Starter Kit contains basic information and concepts that underlie and support your study of art history. It's like those small boxed tool sets intended for people who are moving into their own place for the first time and don't own the simplest tools they need to install and repair things. The implements in the Starter Kit are specifically for use in "installing" knowledge about art. The tools are the vocabulary and principles used to classify, describe, and experience art objects. The reason for putting them in one place at the beginning of the book is to make the Starter Kit an easy-to-find reference resource for terms you will encounter again and again when reading *Art: A Brief History* and in encountering art directly. Terms that appear in SMALL CAPITAL LETTERS are "tool words."

Julia Moore

Let us begin with basic properties of art. In concrete terms, a work of art is said to have two components: FORM and CONTENT. Artworks are also described and categorized according to STYLE and MEDIUM.

FORM

The term *form* refers to purely visual elements of art and architecture, which include LINE, COLOR, TEXTURE, SPATIAL ATTRIBUTES, and COMPOSITION. These are known as formal elements. When art historians use the terms *formal* and *formalist* they mean "relating to form."

LINE is an element—usually drawn or painted—made by a more-or-less continuous mark. It is probably the most basic visual element. Line can be clearly visible, or it may be implied, as when the movement of the eyes over the surface of the work of art follows a path that replicates a line or lines.

The outline, edge, or silhouette of an object is perceived as line, and it is this "line" that defines shape. Line can be angular (or geometric), curvy (called curvilinear), delicate, assertive, solid, or sketchy. In art historical writing, the word linear describes the artist's reliance on line to give form to the image.

COLOR has several attributes. These include, HUE, VALUE, and SATURATION.

HUE is what we think of when we hear the word color. Red, yellow, and blue are primary hues (colors) because the secondary colors of orange, green, and purple are made by combinations of red and yellow, yellow and blue, and red and blue, respectively. Red, orange, and yellow are regarded as warm colors, colors that advance toward us. Green, blue, and purple, which seem to recede, are called cool colors. The word *PALETTE* refers to the general range of colors used in a work. So a painting in greens, blues, and purples can be described as being of a cool palette. The use of more than one color is POLYCHROMY (meaning "many color").

VALUE is the relative degree of lightness or darkness of a given color and is created by the amount of light reflected from an object's surface. A dark green has a deeper value than a light green, for example. In black-and-white reproductions of colored objects, you see only value, and some artworks—for example, a drawing made with black ink—possesses only value, not hue or saturation and is MONOCHROMATIC ("one color").

SATURATION, also referred to sometimes as INTENSITY, is a color's quality of brightness or dullness. A color described as highly saturated looks vivid and pure; a hue of low saturation may look muddy.

TEXTURE, another attribute of form, is the tactile (or touch-perceived) quality of a surface. It is described with words like *smooth, polished, rough, grainy, pitted, oily,* and the like. Texture relates to two aspects of an art object: the texture of the artwork's actual surface and the texture of the implied but imaginary surface of the object that the work represents.

SPATIAL ATTRIBUTES include the following SPACE, MASS, and VOLUME.

SPACE is what contains objects. It may be actual and three-dimensional, as it is with sculpture and architecture, or it may be represented illusionistically, as it is when artists represent recession into the distance on two-dimensional, flat surfaces (walls, paper, or canvas for the most part) by various means described below under Composition.

MASS and **VOLUME** are properties of three-dimensional things. Mass is matter—whether sculpture or architecture—that takes up space; it can be solid or hollow. Volume is the space organized by mass, whether by enclosing it or partitioning it.

COMPOSITION is the organization, or arrangement, of form in a work of art. The possibilities for composing any subject are nearly endless, and the choices an artist makes about how to position various elements usually reflect the tastes of the time when and the place where the work of art was created as well as the artist's personal sensibilities. In very general terms, compositions may be characterized as balanced, static, asymmetrical, dynamic, and the like.

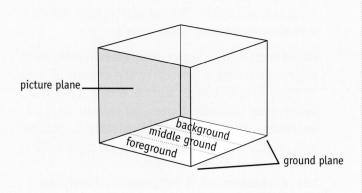

A specialized aspect of composition is PICTORIAL DEPTH (spatial recession), in which the three-dimensional world is represented in two dimensions on a flat surface, or PICTURE PLANE. The area "behind" the picture plane is called the PICTURE SPACE and conventionally contains three "zones": FOREGROUND, MIDDLE GROUND, and BACKGROUND. Perpendicular to the picture plane is the GROUND PLANE.

Various techniques for conveying a sense of pictorial depth have been devised and preferred by artists in different cultures and at different times. A number of them are diagrammed on page 7. In Western art, the use of various systems of PERSPECTIVE has created highly convincing illusions of recession into space. In other cultures, perspective is not the most favored way to treat objects in space.

CONTENT

Content is a term that embraces non-formal aspects of works of art, aspects that impart meaning. Content includes SUBJECT MATTER, which is, quite simply, what the artist is representing, even when what we see are strictly formal elements—for example, lines and colors without recognizable imagery. REPRESENTATIONAL ART and NONREPRESENTATIONAL ART (or NONOBJECTIVE) ART are terms used to indicate whether subject matter is or is not recognizable. David Smith's *Cubi XIX*, seen in figure 5, is an example of nonrepresentational art.

Content also includes the ideas contained in a work. Content may reveal the social, political, and economic CONTEXTS in which a work was created, the INTENTION of the artist, the RECEPTION of the work by the beholder (the audience), and ultimately the MEANINGS of the work of art to both artist and audience.

The study of subject matter is ICONOGRAPHY (literally, "the writing of images"). The iconographer asks, What are we looking at? Because so many artists have used visual SYMBOLS to represent or identify concepts and ideas, iconography includes the fascinating study of symbols and their meanings.

STYLE

STYLE is a word used in art history to mean an artwork's predominant visual characteristics, the combination of form and content that makes a work distinctive. Style can indicate the approximate date of a work of art (period), can locate it geographically (place), and can even identify the maker (person). (These are popularly known as the three "Ps" of style.)

STYLISTIC ANALYSIS is one of art history's most developed activities, because it is how art historians identify works that are unsigned or whose history is unknown and how they group and classify artworks. This book will help sensitize you to distinctions of style. For example, you can learn the ways in which French paintings in the Baroque style (see fig. 14-9) are distinguishable from Italian Baroque paintings (see fig. 14-7), or how to recognize the difference between Greek and Roman portrait heads (see figs. 4-37, 6-15). ARTISTIC STYLES fall in three major categories: PERIOD STYLE, REGIONAL STYLE, and FORMALIST STYLE.

PERIOD STYLE describes the common traits detectable in works of art and architecture from a certain time (and, usually, culture). For example, Roman portrait sculpture is distinguishable according to whether it was created during the Roman Republican era, the height of the Empire, or the late Empire (see Chapter 6).

REGIONAL STYLE refers to stylistic traits that persist in a geographic region. An art historian whose specialty is medieval art can recognize French style through many successive periods, even though individual objects

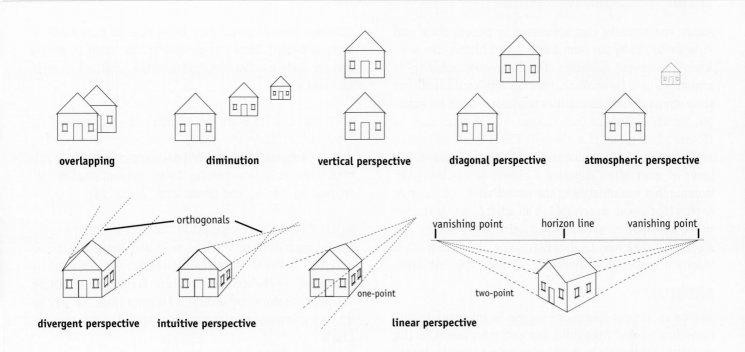

Techniques for depicting recession in space

The top row shows several comparatively simple devices, including OVERLAPPING, in which partially covered elements are meant to be seen as located behind those covering them, and DIMINUTION, in which smaller elements are to be perceived as being farther away than larger ones. In VERTICAL and DIAGONAL PERSPECTIVE, elements are stacked vertically or diagonally, with the higher elements intended to be perceived as deeper in space. Another way of suggesting depth is through ATMOSPHERIC PERSPECTIVE (see fig. 12-8), which depicts objects in the far distance, often in bluish gray hues, with less clarity than nearer objects and treats sky as paler near the horizon than higher up. In the lower row, DIVERGENT PERSPECTIVE, in which forms widen slightly and lines diverge as they recede in space, was used by East Asian artists (see Chapters 3 and 9). INTUITIVE PERSPECTIVE, used in some late medieval European art (see Chapters 11 and 12), takes the opposite approach: Forms become narrower and converge the farther they are from the viewer, approximating the optical experience of spatial recession. LINEAR PERSPECTIVE, also called SCIENTIFIC, MATHEMATICAL, ONE-POINT, and RENAISSANCE PERSPECTIVE, is an elaboration and standardization of intuitive perspective and was developed in fifteenth-century Italy (see fig. 12-28). It uses mathematical formulas to construct illusionistic images in which all elements are shaped by imaginary lines called ORTHOGONALS that converge in one or more VANISHING POINTS on a HORIZON LINE. Linear perspective is the system that most people living in Western cultures think of as perspective. Because it is the visual code they are accustomed to reading, they accept as "truth" the distortions it imposes. One of these distortions is FORESHORTENING, in which, for instance, the soles of the feet in the foreground are the largest elements of a figure lying on the ground.

may appear to the untrained eye to have been created in, say, Germany or the Low Countries (see Chapters 10 and 11).

FORMALIST STYLE is not a common term in the literature of art, but it is a convenient way to present stylistic traits that are grounded in formal considerations. REALISM, NATURALISM, IDEALIZATION, and EXPRESSIONISM are often-found names for styles.

REALISM is the attempt to depict objects as they are in actual, visible reality. Figure 2, *Flower Piece with Curtain*, is a good example of realism.

NATURALISM is a style of depiction in which the physical appearance of the rendered image in nature is the primary inspiration. A work in a naturalistic style resembles the original, but not with the same exactitude and literalness as a work in a realistic style. The *Medici Venus* (see fig. 7) is naturalistic in this sense.

IDEALIZATION strives to realize in visual form a concept of perfection embedded in a culture's value system. The *Medici Venus* (see fig. 7) just cited as naturalistic is also idealized.

EXPRESSIONISM refers to styles in which the artist uses exaggeration of form and expression to appeal directly to the beholder's subjective emotional responses. The Hellenistic sculpture *Laocoön* (see fig. 24) is expressionistic.

Artists and artworks that are related by period, place, and style are linked by the term SCHOOL. In art history, the word *school* has several meanings. The designation *school of* is sometimes used for works that are not attributable but that show strong stylistic similarities to a known artist for example, school of Rubens (see Chapter 14). A term such as *Sienese school* means that the work shows traits common in art from Siena, Italy, during the period being discussed. *Follower of* most often suggests a second-generation artist working in a variant style of the named artist. *Workshop of* implies that a work was created by an artist or artists trained in the workshop of an established artist. *Attributed to*, like a question mark next to an artist's name, means that there is some uncertainty as to whether the work is by that artist.

MEDIUM

MEDIUM or MEDIUMS (the plural we use in this book to distinguish the word from print and electronic media) is the material or materials from which an object is made. Broader even than medium is the distinction between art forms that are TWO-DIMENSIONAL and THREE-DIMENSIONAL.

Two-dimensional arts include PAINTING, DRAWING, the GRAPHIC ARTS (also called PRINTS), and PHOTOGRAPHY. In short, these are arts that are made on a flat surface. Three-dimensional arts are SCULPTURE, ARCHITECTURE, and many DECORATIVE and FUNCTIONAL ARTS.

The visual arts' traditional mediums have been the so-called fine arts of painting, drawing, graphic arts, sculpture, and architecture. As the study of art history has become more inclusive, other mediums have come within its sphere: photography and the ephemeral arts, furniture, works of ceramic and glass, metalwork, fiber arts, folk and vernacular art, as well as works that mix mediums. More recently, the study of popular arts, often referred to as visual culture, is emerging as a dimension of art history.

PAINTING includes WALL PAINTING (see fig. 1-6) and FRESCO (see fig. 19), ILLUMINATION (the decoration of books with paintings; see fig. 20), PANEL PAINTING (painting on wood panels; see fig. 11-27) and painting on canvas (see fig. 15), MINIATURE PAINTING (small-scale painting), and HANDSCROLL (see fig. 9-18) and HANGING SCROLL (see fig. 9-8) painting. Paint is pigment mixed with a liquid vehicle, or binder. Various kinds of paint and painting are explained throughout this book in "Technique" boxes.

DRAWING encompasses SKETCHES (quick visual notes for larger drawings or paintings), STUDIES (more carefully drawn analyses of details or entire compositions), DRAWINGS as complete artworks in themselves, and CARTOONS (full-scale drawings made in preparation for work in another medium, such as fresco). Drawings are essentially linear in nature and are made with such materials as ink, charcoal, crayon, and lead pencil.

GRAPHIC ARTS are the printed arts—images that are reproducible. They are usually works of art on paper. The graphic arts traditionally include WOODCUT (see fig. 9-24), WOOD ENGRAVING, ETCHING (see fig. 19-3), DRYPOINT, METAL ENGRAVING (see fig. 12-29), and LITHOGRAPHY (see fig. 26).

SCULPTURE was regarded as the most important medium for most of history and in most non-Western cultures, although in the Western tradition it has been eclipsed by painting since the sixteenth century. Perhaps its attraction lies in its absolute physicality; it takes up space the way we do, and it is made of materials that appeal to our sense of touch.

SCULPTURE is three-dimensional art that is categorized in a number of ways: as ADDITIVE or REDUCTIVE or ASSEMBLED; FREESTANDING or RELIEF; independent or ARCHITECTURAL; MONUMENTAL or SMALL SCALE.

ADDITIVE sculpture is created with a malleable material that can be built up and shaped, or modeled. Such materials include terra cotta and other clays, plaster and stucco, gesso, and wax. Often these materials are used to make molds, so that metals in a molten (liquefied) state can be CAST to create the final image (see "Lost-Wax Casting," page 10).

REDUCTIVE sculpture is CARVED: the image takes shape as the sculptor removes or carves away material (see fig. 13). Stone and marble, wood, ivory, even precious stones are carved. Some materials, such as wax or plaster, can be worked both additively and reductively. ASSEMBLED sculpture is put together from preexisting parts (see fig 12). Independent sculpture is FREESTANDING. It is very often referred to as SCULPTURE IN THE ROUND (see fig. 12-11). In contrast, in RELIEF sculpture (see fig. 4-30), the images remain part of the original material, the ground. Relief sculpture projects from the ground. HIGH RELIEF sculpture projects far; LOW RELIEF sculpture is only slightly raised; and SUNKEN RELIEF, found mainly in Egyptian art (see fig. 2-31), is carved into the surface, with the highest part of the relief being the flat ground.

ARCHITECTURAL sculpture is often created in relief and is integrated into the design and decoration of a building. MONUMENTAL refers to large-scale sculpture or pieces that give an impression of grandeur. SMALL SCALE implies a work significantly smaller than lifesize.

MIXED MEDIUM includes categories such as COLLAGE (see fig. 19-11) and ASSEMBLAGE (see fig. 20-9), in which two or more mediums are combined to create the artwork. One of the mediums may be paint, but it does not have to be.

EPHEMERAL ARTS include such chiefly modern categories as performance art, Happenings, earthworks, cinema, video art, and computer art (see Chapter 20). Common to all of them is the temporal aspect of the work: The art is viewable for a finite period of time, then disappears forever; is in a constant state of change; or must be replayed to be experienced again.

ARCHITECTURE is three-dimensional, highly spatial, functional, and closely bound with technology and materials. An example of the relationship among technology, materials, and function is how space is spanned (see "Space-Spanning Construction Devices," page 11). Several types of two-dimensional graphic devices are commonly used to help enable the visualization of a building. These architectural graphics include PLANS, ELEVATIONS, SECTIONS, and CUTAWAYS.

> **PLANS** depict a structure's masses and voids, presenting a view from above—as if the building had been sliced horizontally at about waist height.
>
> **ELEVATIONS** show exterior sides of a building as if seen from a moderate distance without any perspective distortion.
>
> **SECTIONS** reveal a building as if sliced through the middle from top to bottom.
>
> **CUTAWAY DRAWINGS** show both inside and outside elements from an oblique angle.

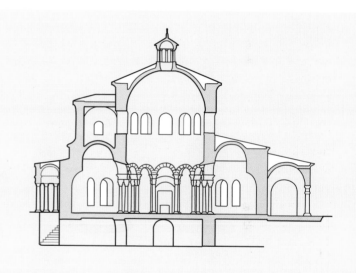

elevation

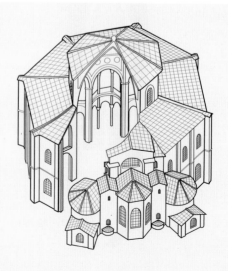

section

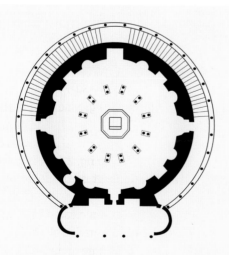

plan

cutaway drawing

TECHNIQUE
Lost-Wax Casting

The lost-wax casting process (also called *cire perdue*, the French term) has been used for many centuries. It probably started in Egypt. By 200 BCE the technique was known in China and ancient Mesopotamia and was soon after used by the Benin peoples in Africa. It spread to ancient Greece sometime in the sixth century BCE and was widespread in Europe until the eighteenth century, when a piece-mold process came to predominate. The usual metal is bronze, an alloy of copper and tin, or sometimes brass, an alloy of copper and zinc.

The progression of drawings here shows the steps used by Benin sculptors (see also fig. 16-3). A heat-resistant "core" of clay approximating the shape of the sculpture-to-be (and eventually becoming the hollow inside the sculpture) was covered by a layer of wax about the thickness of the final sculpture. The sculptor carved the details in the wax. Rods and a pouring cup made of wax were attached to the model. A thin layer of fine, damp sand was pressed very firmly into the surface of the wax model, and then model, rods, and cup were encased

in thick layers of clay. When the clay was completely dry, the mold was heated to melt out the wax. The mold was then turned upside down to receive the molten metal, which for the Benin was brass, heated to the point of liquification. The cast was placed in the ground. When the metal was completely cool, the outside clay cast and the inside core were broken up and removed, leaving the cast brass sculpture. Details were polished to finish the piece of sculpture, which could not be duplicated because the mold had been destroyed in the process.

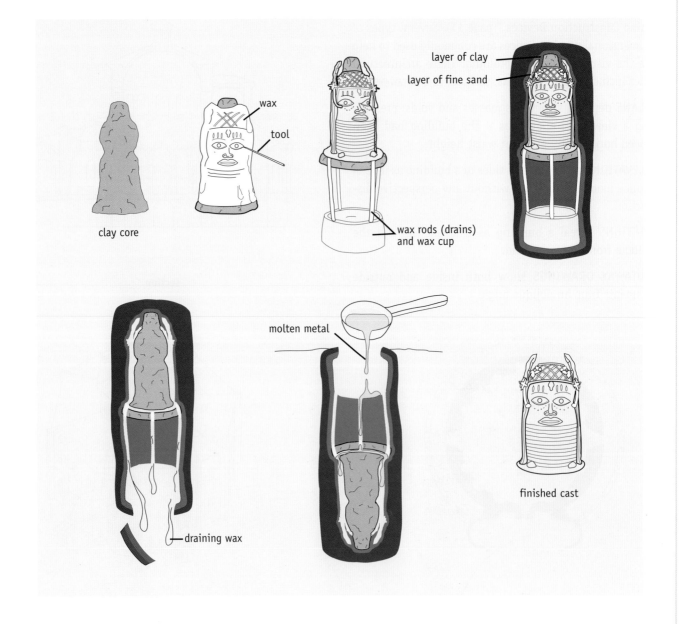

clay core

wax

tool

layer of clay

layer of fine sand

wax rods (drains) and wax cup

molten metal

draining wax

finished cast

Elements of Architecture

SPACE-SPANNING CONSTRUCTION DEVICES

Gravity pulls on everything, presenting great challenges to the need to cover spaces. The purpose of the spanning element is to transfer weight to the ground. The simplest space-spanning device is post-and-lintel construction, in which uprights are spanned by a horizontal element. However, if not flexible, a horizontal element over a side span breaks under the pressure of its own weight and the weight it carries.

Corbeling (see fig. 4-9), the building up of overlapping stones, is another simple method for transferring weight to the ground. Arches, round or pointed, span space. Vaults, which are essentially extended arches, move weight out from the center of the covered space and down through the corners (see fig. 10). The cantilever (see fig. 19-25) is a variant of post-and-lintel construction. When concrete is reinforced with steel or iron rods, the inherent brittleness of cement and stone is overcome because of metal's flexible qualities. The concrete can then span much more space and bear heavier loads. Suspension works to counter the effect of gravity by lifting the spanning element upward. Trusses of wood or metal are relatively lightweight spanners but cannot bear heavy loads. Large-scale modern construction is chiefly steel frame and relies on steel's properties of strength and flexibility to bear great loads. The balloon frame, an American innovations, is based in post-and-lintel principles and exploits the lightweight, flexible properties of wood.

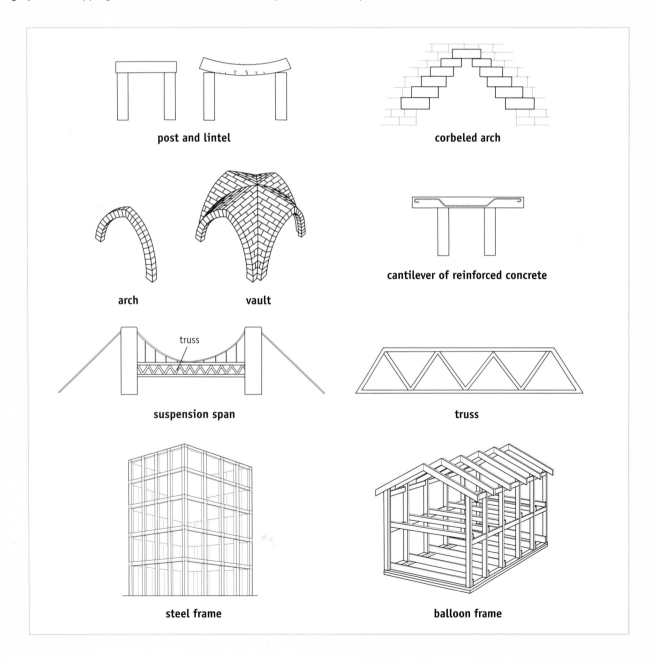

post and lintel

corbeled arch

arch

vault

cantilever of reinforced concrete

truss

suspension span

truss

steel frame

balloon frame

Use Notes

The various features of this book reinforce each other, helping you to become comfortable with terminology and concepts specific to art history.

Starter Kit and Introduction The Starter Kit is a concise primer of basic concepts and tools. The outside margins of the Starter Kit pages are tinted to make them easy to find. The Introduction that follows these Use Notes is an invitation to the pleasures of art history.

Captions There are two kinds of captions in this book: short and long. Short captions identify information specific to the work of art or architecture illustrated:

> artist (when known)
> title or descriptive name of work
> date
> original location
> material or materials a work is made of
> size (height before width) in feet and inches,
>> with centimeters and meters in parentheses
> present location (if moved to a museum or other site)

Dimensions are not given for architecture, for most wall painting, or for architectural sculpture. Some captions have one or more lines of small print below the identification section of the caption that gives museum or collection information.

Long captions contain information that complements the main text.

Definitions of Terms You will encounter the basic terms of art history in three places:

IN THE TEXT, where words appearing in boldface type are defined, or used in context, on first use; some terms are explained more than once, especially those that experience shows are hard to remember.

IN BOXED FEATURES on techniques and other subjects and in Elements of Architecture boxes, where labeled drawings and diagrams visually reinforce the use of terms.

IN THE GLOSSARY at the end of the volume, which contains all the words in **boldface** type in the text and boxes. The Glossary begins on page 530, and the outside margins are tinted to make the Glossary easy to find.

Looking Forward Every chapter opens with a Looking Forward essay centered on an image that is representative of key points and important concepts emphasized in that chapter. Looking Forward functions to alert you to what to watch for in the narrative text that follows.

Closer Look In boxes titled Closer Look, a single work of art, which is discussed in the narrative text, is examined in greater detail. Closer Look essays show you various ways to explore works of art.

Looking Back Every two-, three-, or four-chapter "cultural cluster" concludes with an essay, timeline, and map that bring together important issues common to the preceding group of chapters; a visual chronology of the artworks, cultures, and/or movements in that cluster; and a map to put these subjects in their geographical contexts. The seven Looking Back double-page spreads are extremely condensed overviews of major periods and cultures.

Boxes Special material that complements, enhances, explains, or extends the text is set off in three types of tinted boxes. Elements of Architecture boxes clarify specifically architectural features, such as "Space-Spanning Construction Devices" in the Starter Kit (page 11). Technique boxes (see "Lost-Wax Casting," page 10) describe the way in which a given type of artwork is created. Other boxes treat special-interest material related to the text.

Selected Bibliography The Selected Bibliography, at the end of this book beginning on page 538, contains books in English, organized by general works and by chapter, that are basic to the study of art history today.

Dates, Abbreviations, and Other Conventions This book uses the designations BCE and CE, abbreviations for "before the Common Era" and "Common Era," instead of BC ("before Christ") and AD ("Anno Domini," "the year of our Lord"). The first century BCE is the period from 99 BCE to 1 BCE; the first century CE is from the year 1 CE to 99 CE.

> *Circa* ("about" or "approximately") is used with dates and abbreviated to "c." in the captions, when an exact date is not known.

> An illustration is called a "figure," or "fig." Figure 6-25 is the twenty-fifth numbered illustration in Chapter 6. Figures 1 through 27 are in the Introduction.

> When introducing artists, we use the words *active* and *documented* with dates—in addition to "b." (for "born") and "d." (for "died"). "Active" means that an artist worked during the years given. "Documented" means that documents link the person to the date.

> Accents are used for words in Spanish, Italian, French, and German only.

> With few exceptions, names of museums and other cultural bodies in Western European countries are given in the form used in that country.

Titles of Works of Art Most paintings and sculpture created in Europe and the United States in the last 500 years have been given formal titles, either by the artist or by critics and art historians. Such formal titles are printed in italics. In other traditions and cultures, a single title is not important or even recognized. In this book we use formal titles of artworks in cases where they are established and descriptive titles of artworks where titles are not established. If a work is best known by its non-English title, such as Manet's *Le Déjeuner sur l'Herbe* (*The Luncheon on the Grass*), the original language precedes the translation.

Introduction

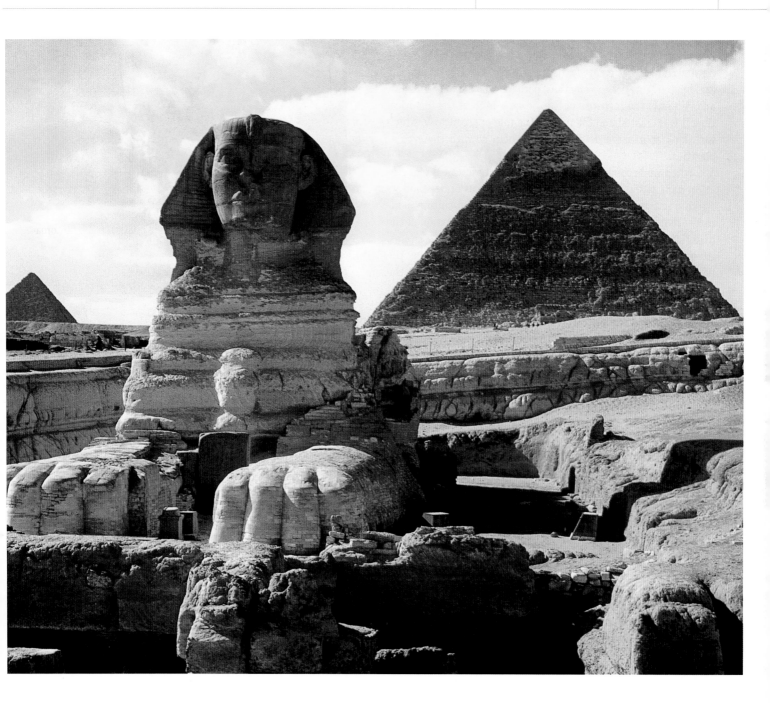

Crouching in front of the pyramids of Egypt and carved from the living rock of the Giza plateau, the Great Sphinx is one of the best-known monuments in the world (fig. 1). By placing the head of the ancient Egyptian king Khafra on the body of a huge lion, the sculptors joined human intelligence and animal strength in a single image to evoke the superhuman power of the ruler. For some 4,600 years the Sphinx has defied encroaching desert sands and other assaults of nature; today it also must withstand the human-made sprawl of urban Cairo and the impact of air pollution. The Sphinx, in its majesty, symbolizes mysterious wisdom and dreams of permanence, of immortality. But is such a monument a work of art? Does it matter that the people who carved the Sphinx—unlike today's independent, individualistic artists—followed time-honored, formulaic conventions and the precise instructions of their priests? No matter how viewers of the time may have labeled it, today most people would answer, "Certainly it is art. Human imagination conceived this amazing creature, and human skill gave material form to the concept of man-lion. Using imagination and skill to create huge, simplified shapes, the creators have defined the idea of awesome grandeur and have created a work of art." *But what is art?*

What Is Art?

The answer to this seemingly simple question is in fact multifaceted. Common definitions of art usually refer to the product of some combination of skill, training, and observation. But the definition of art also depends upon what is created, when it was created, how it was created, the intention of the creator and the anticipated "role" of the creation, perhaps who commissioned it, and certainly the response of the viewer—both at the historical time it was created and today. It is the role of art history, which we'll look at in more detail below, to help us with these complexities.

When we become captivated by the mysteriousness of a creation such as the Sphinx, art history can help us understand its striking imagery and meaning; the artwork's total cultural context—that is, the social, economic, and political situation of the historical period in which it was produced; the belief systems, rituals, and myths (the philosophy and religion) of the time; the relationships to other arts (music, drama, literature, dance); the technology making the art possible. Art history, unlike other humanistic studies, remains grounded in material objects that are the tangible expression of the ideas—and ideals—of a culture. Thus, art history is distinctive because it puts the primary focus on the art object even as it explores the context of its culture, because art does not simply reflect history but also participates in it. Art historians know, for example, that someone had to learn to read Egyptian hieroglyphs to tell us that we are looking at the face of a king on the Sphinx. By studying the translations of these hieroglyphs, they could study the historical period in which it was made and learn about the king's earthly power, the culture's belief in an afterlife, and the overwhelming cultural importance of ceremony—all defined and expressed by the monumental Sphinx.

Works of exceptional physical beauty—however *beauty* may be defined—can speak to us over great expanses of time and space, but the study of art history can greatly enhance our experience of art by helping us to formulate the kinds of questions that enable us to appreciate for ourselves the material culture of our own and other times. But while grappling with the question of what art is, we are inevitably drawn into another question whose answer is almost always culturally specific: *What is beauty?*

What Is Beauty?

Historically, beauty has quite literally been "in the eye of the beholder." Beauty has been expressed in a variety of **styles**, or manners of representation. Styles of beauty vary from time to time and place to place. People in some societies have valued styles of art that are realistic, or **naturalistic**—art that has a surface reality because the artists appear to have recorded, with greater or lesser accuracy, exactly what they saw. Naturalism and **abstraction**—the transformation of visible forms into patterns that suggest the original—are opposite approaches to representing beauty. In abstraction through **idealization**, for example, artists represent beauty not as it is but as they think it *should* be. So what is beauty? The way that various peoples have represented beauty can tell us a great deal about their cultures and values.

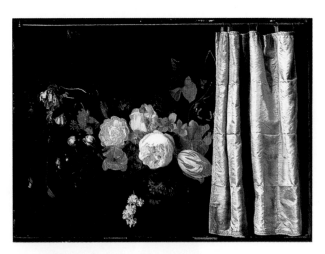

2 | **Adriaen van der Spelt** and **Frans van Mieris**. *Flower Piece with Curtain.* 1658. Oil on panel, 18¼ x 25¼" (46.5 x 64 cm). The Art Institute of Chicago
Wirt D. Walker Fund

NATURE OR ART?

Beauty can be expressed in many ways—in the natural beauty of flowers or in the created beauty of a painting of those flowers (fig. 2). In the ancient world, the Greek philosopher Aristotle (384–322 BCE) evaluated works of art on the basis of *mimesis* ("imitation"), that is, how faithfully artists recorded what they saw in the natural world. But we need to be aware that when artists working in a naturalistic style make images that seem like untouched snapshots of actual objects, their skill can also render lifelike such fictions as a unicorn or the Wicked Witch of the West—or a being with the body of a lion and the head of a king.

Like many people today, ancient Greeks enjoyed the work of especially skillful naturalistic artists (the Greek word for art, *tekne*, is the source of the English word *technique*; the word *art* comes from the Latin word *ars*, or "skill"). Their admiration for naturalistic depiction is illustrated in a famous story about a competition between rival Greek painters named Zeuxis and Parrhasios in the late fifth century BCE. Zeuxis painted a picture of grapes so accurately that birds flew down to peck at them. Then Parrhasios took his turn, and when Zeuxis asked his rival to remove the curtain hanging over the picture, Parrhasios gleefully pointed out that the curtain was his painting. Zeuxis agreed that Parrhasios won the competition since he, Zeuxis, had fooled only birds but Parrhasios had tricked an intelligent fellow artist. In the seventeenth century, painter Adriaen van der Spelt (1630–1673) and his artist friend Frans van Mieris (1635–1681) paid homage to the story of Parrhasios's curtain with their painting of blue satin drapery drawn aside to show a garland of flowers (fig. 2). More than a *tour de force* of eye-fooling naturalism, the work is an intellectual delight. The artists not only re-created Parrhasios's curtain illusion but also included a reference to another Greek legend, which was popular in the fourth century BCE, that told of Pausias, who painted the exquisite floral garlands made by a young woman, Glykera. This second story raises the troubling and possibly unanswerable question of who was the true artist—the painter

3 | **Edward Weston.** *Succulent.* 1930. Gelatin silver print, 7½ x 9½" (19.1 x 24 cm) Collection Center for Creative Photography The University of Arizona, Tucson
© 1981 Center for Creative Photography, Arizona Board of Regents

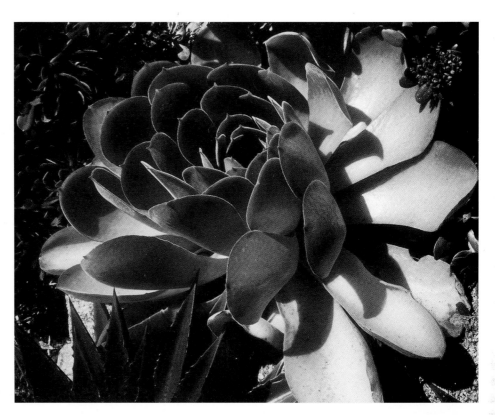

who copied nature in his art or the garland maker who made works of art out of nature. The seventeenth-century patrons—the people who bought such paintings, knew those stories and appreciated the artists' classical references as well as their skill in drawing and manipulating colors on canvas.

The flower garland also symbolizes the passage of time and the fleeting quality of human riches. The brilliant red and white tulip, the most desirable and expensive flower of the time, symbolizes wealth and power. Yet insects creep out of it, and a butterfly—fragile and transitory—hovers above the flower. Today, after studying the painting in its cultural context, we, too, understand that it is much more than a simple flower piece, the type of still life with flowers popular in the Netherlands in Van der Spelt's and Van Mieris's time.

Just as Dutch flower pieces were ideal representations of nature then, so today modern photography seems like a perfect medium for expressing the natural beauty of plants, especially when they are selected and captured at perfect moments in their life cycles. In his photograph *Succulent*, Edward Weston (1886–1958) did just that by using straightforward camera work, without manipulating the film in the darkroom (fig. 3). Aristotle might have appreciated this example of *mimesis*, but Weston did more than accurately portray his subject; he made photography an **expressionistic** medium by perfecting the close-up view to evoke an emotional response in th viewer. He argued that although the camera sees more than the human eye, the quality of the image depends not on the camera, but on the choices made by the photographer-artist.

Many people even today think that naturalism represents the highest accomplishment in art. But not everyone agrees. First to argue persuasively that observation alone produced "mere likeness" was the Italian master Leonardo da Vinci (1452–1519), who said that the painter who copied the external forms of nature was acting only as a mirror. He believed that the true artist should engage in intellectual activity of a higher order and attempt to capture the inner life—the energy and power—of a subject. In the twentieth century, Georgia O'Keeffe (1887–1986), like Van der Spelt and Weston, studied living plants; however, when she painted the canna lily she, like Leonardo, sought to capture the flower's essence (fig. 4). By painting the canna lily's organic energy, she created a new abstract beauty, conveying in paint the pure vigor of its life force.

Furthest of all from naturalism or the Greek concept of mimesis are the pure geometric creations of polished stainless

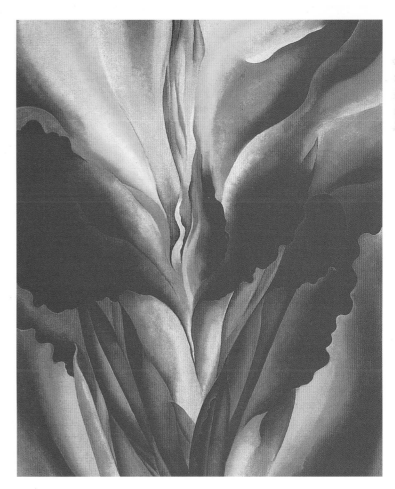

4 | **Georgia O'Keeffe.** *Red Canna.* 1924. Oil on canvas mounted on Masonite, 36 x 29⅞" (91.44 x 75.88 cm). The University of Arizona Museum of Art, Tucson

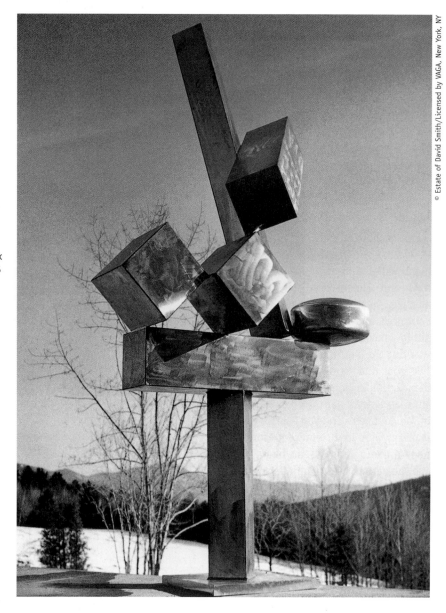

5

David Smith
Cubi XIX. 1964
Stainless steel
9'5³/₈" x 1'9³/₄" x
1'8" (2.88 x 0.55
x 0.51 m). Tate
Gallery, London

steel made by David Smith (1906–1965). His *Cubi* works, such as the sculpture in figure 5, are usually called **nonrepresentational** art—art so abstract that it does not represent the natural world. With works like *Cubi XIX*, it is important to distinguish between **subject matter** and content, or meaning. Abstract art has both subject matter and meaning. Nonrepresentational art does not have subject matter but it does have meaning, which is a product of the interaction between the artist's intention and the viewer's interpretation. Some viewers may see *Cubis* as giant excrescences, for example, mechanistic plants sprung from the core of an unyielding earth, a reflection of today's mechanistic society that challenges the natural forms of trees and hills. Because meaning can change over time, one goal of contextual art history, which this book exemplifies, is to identify the factors that produce a work, to determine what it probably meant for the artist and the original audience, and to acknowledge that no interpretation is definitive. Again, such visions are in the "eye of the beholder."

THE IDEA OF THE IDEAL

In contrast to Aristotle, an earlier Greek philosopher, Plato (428–348/7 BCE), had looked beyond nature for a definition of art. In his view even the greatest work of art was only a shadow of the material world, several times removed from reality. Physical beauty for Plato's followers depended on the harmony created by symmetry and proportion, on a rational, even mathematical, view of the world. The contemplation of such ideal physical beauty eventually leads the viewer to a new kind of artistic truth to be found in the realm of pure idea. Let us take a simple example from architecture: the carving at the top of a column called the capital. A popular type, known as the Corinthian order, which first began to appear in ancient Greece about 450 BCE, has an inverted bell shape surrounded by acanthus leaves (fig. 6). Although inspired by the appearance of natural vegetation, the sculptors who carved the leaves have eliminated blemishes and arranged the leaves symmetrically. In short, they have created ideal leaves by first looking at nature and then carving

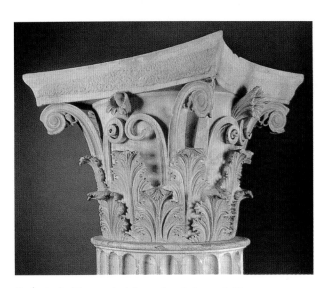

6 | **Corinthian capital from the *tholos* at Epidaurus.** C. 350 BCE. Archaeological Museum, Epidaurus, Greece

the essence of the form, the Platonic ideal of foliage. No insect has ever nibbled at such a timelessly perfect, ideal leaf.

To achieve Plato's ideal images and represent things "as they ought to be" in a triumph of human reason over nature, the sculptors eliminated all irregularities and instead sought perfect balance and harmony. The term *classical*, which refers to both the period in ancient Greek history when this type of idealism emerged and to the art of ancient Greece and Rome in general, has come to be used broadly as a synonym for the peak of perfection in any period. Classical sculpture and painting established ideals that have inspired Western art ever since.

For all recorded times and in most places, one of the subjects artists have frequently chosen to express the sense of beauty is woman. We can see how the different concepts of art and beauty we have mentioned play out by comparing the way that three different arts, in three different ages and parts of the world, have depicted women.

BEAUTIFUL WOMEN

Classical idealism pervades the image of Venus, goddess of love, even in a Roman copy of a Greek statue like the *Medici Venus* (fig. 7). Clearly the artist had the skill to represent a woman as she actually appeared but instead chose to generalize her form and adhere to the classical **canon** (rule) of proportions. In so doing, the sculptor has created a universal image, an ideal woman rather than a specific woman.

Very different from the classical ideal is the abstract vision of woman seen in a woodblock print by Japanese artist Kitagawa Utamaro (1753–1806). His *Woman at the Height of Her Beauty*

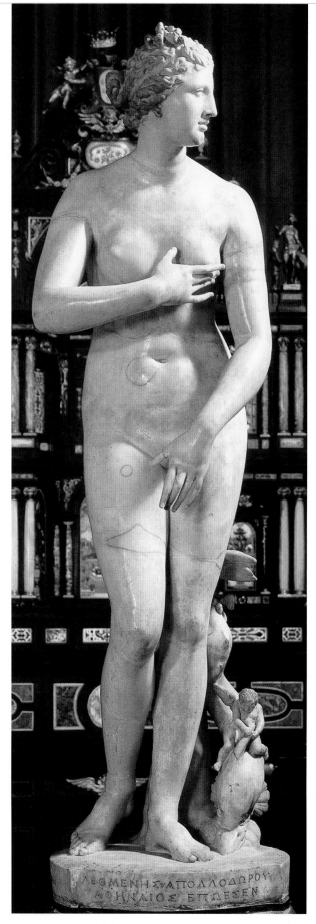

7 | *Medici Venus.* Roman copy of a 1st-century BCE Greek statue. Marble, height 5' (1.53 m) without base. Galleria degli Uffizi, Florence, Italy

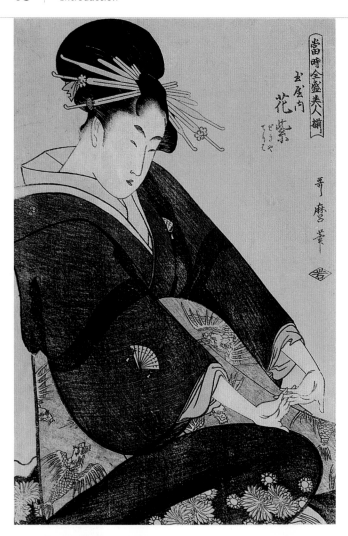

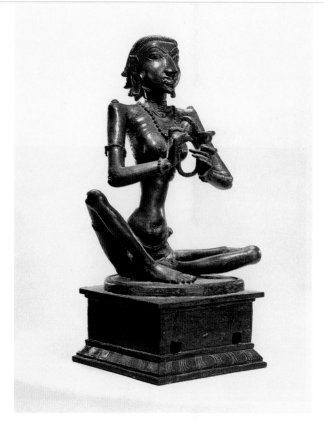

9 | ***Punitavati (Karaikkalammaiyar),*** Shiva saint, from Karaikka, India. 15th century. Bronze, height 16¼" (41.3 cm). The Nelson-Atkins Museum of Art, Kansas City Missouri
Purchase: Nelson Trust (33-533)

8 | **Kitagawa Utamaro.** ***Woman at the Height of Her Beauty***
Mid-1790s. Color woodblock print, 15⅛ x 10" (38.5 x 25.5 cm)
Spencer Museum of Art, The University of Kansas, Lawrence
William Bridges Thayer Memorial

(fig. 8) reflects a complex society regulated by convention and ritual in its stylization. Simplified shapes suggest underlying human forms, although the woman's dress and hairstyle defy the laws of nature. Rich textiles turn her body into an abstract pattern, and pins hold her hair in elaborate shapes. Utamaro rendered the decorative silks and carved pins meticulously, but he depicted the woman's face with a few sweeping lines. The elaboration of surface detail combined with an effort to capture the essence of form is characteristic of the abstract art of Utamaro's time and place.

How different from either of these ideas of physical beauty can be the perception and representation of spiritual beauty. A fifteenth-century bronze sculpture from India represents Punitavati, a beautiful and generous woman who was deeply devoted to the Hindu god Shiva. Abandoned by her miserly husband because she gave food to beggars, Punitavati offered her beauty to Shiva. Shiva accepted her offering and, in taking her loveliness, turned her into an emaciated, fanged hag (fig. 9). According to legend, Punitavati, with clanging cymbals, provides the music for Shiva as he keeps the universe in motion by dancing the cosmic dance of destruction and creation. The

bronze sculpture, although it depicts Punitavati's hideous appearance realistically, is beautiful both in its formal qualities as a work of art and in its message of generosity and sacrifice.

BEAUTY IN ARCHITECTURE

The ways that artists depict beauty in their representations of nature and human beings may seem obvious. But how does an artist represent beauty in architecture?

For thousands of years, people have sought to build what they hoped would be magnificent and permanent structures—buildings such as the Cathedral of Saint James in Santiago de Compostela, Spain (fig. 10). In the twelfth century, the author of a guidebook for pilgrims going to the shrine of the saint described the perfection of the building: its fine construction, spaciousness, and proportions ("In the church there is indeed not a single crack, nor any damage to be found; it is wonderfully built, large, spacious, well-lighted; of fitting size, harmonious in width, length, and height; held to be admirable and beautiful in execution"); its form ("And furthermore it is built with two stories like a royal palace"); and its effect on visitors ("For he who visits the galleries, if sad when he ascends, once he has seen the preeminent beauty of this temple, rejoices and is filled with gladness"). After nearly a thousand years, the building continues to shelter and dignify the rituals of the Christian religion and to affirm the ancient guidebook's evaluation of its beauty—its ability to bring pleasure to the senses, mind, and spirit.

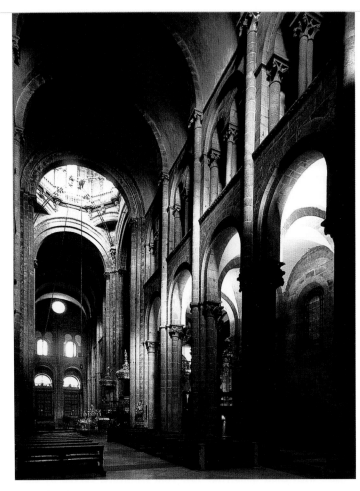

10 | **Cathedral of Saint James, Santiago de Compostela,** Spain
1078–1122. View toward the crossing
Achim Bednorz, Cologne

outsiders who do not know—or care—about their intended use and original significance.

Rituals are part of all belief systems, including religions such as Christianity. For Catholic Christians, a complex rite enacted at a consecrated altar changes ordinary wine into the blood of Christ; for Protestants, the wine remains the symbol of that blood; but for both, communication between God and humans becomes possible through the ritual enactment of Jesus' Last Supper with his friends and disciples. The chalice, the vessel for the sacramental wine, plays a central role and today is usually seen as a ritual object. But if a chalice is taken from its place on the altar and set in a different context, it may just as well be viewed purely as a work of art.

Much of the art that moves us most deeply today was originally created as an expression of spiritual experience and an object of devotion. Consider, for example, the *Chalice of Abbot Suger* (fig. 11). In twelfth-century France, Abbot Suger, head of the monastery dedicated to Saint Denis near Paris, found an ancient vase in the storage chests of the abbey. He ordered his goldsmiths to add a foot, a rim, and handles as well as semiprecious stones and medallions to the vase, turning it into a chalice to be used at the altar of the church that was the birthplace of Gothic architecture. Today Suger's chalice no longer functions in the liturgy of the Mass. It has taken on a new secular life,

11 | **Chalice of Abbot Suger,** from Abbey Church of Saint-Denis France. Composite of elements from Ptolemaic Egypt (2nd–1st century BCE) and 12th-century France. 1137–40. Cup: sardonyx; mounts: silver gilt, adorned with filigree, semiprecious stones, pearls, glass insets, and opaque white glass. 7$^{1}/_{2}$ x 4$^{1}/_{4}$" (19 x 10.8 cm). National Gallery of Art, Washington, D.C.

Why Do We Need Art?

The person who wrote of a building bringing gladness to the viewer reminds us of the importance of beauty in human life. Biologists account for the human desire for art in other terms. They explain that human beings have very large brains that demand stimulation. Curious, active, and inventive, we humans constantly explore, and in so doing invent things that appeal to our senses—fine arts, fine food, fine scents, and fine music. So far, we have mostly considered art in terms of seeking beauty, but there are other reasons deeply rooted in the human experience that create needs for art. For one, humans also speculate on the nature of things and the meaning of life. Visually and verbally, we constantly communicate with each other; in our need to understand and our need to communicate, the arts serve a vital function.

ART AND THE SEARCH FOR MEANING

Throughout history, art has played an important part in our search for the meaning of the human experience. In an effort to understand the world and our place in it, people create rituals that they believe will provide links with unseen powers and also with the past and the future. Believers employ special apparatus in their rituals, such as candles, incense, statues, masks, and various containers. But these utensils are works of art in the eyes of

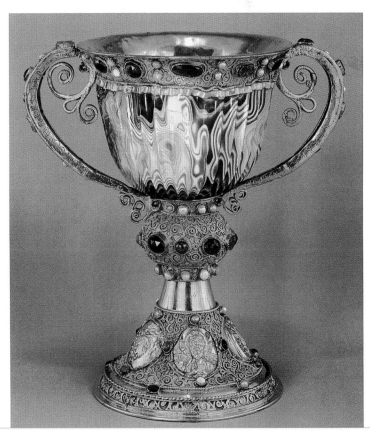

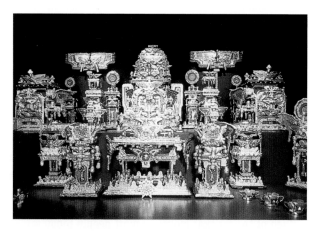

12 | James Hampton. *Throne of the Third Heaven of the Nations' Millennium General Assembly.* c. 1950–64. Gold and silver aluminum foil, colored Kraft paper, and plastic sheets over wood, paperboard, and glass, 10'6" x 27' x 14'6" (3.2 x 8.23 x 4.42 m). Smithsonian American Art Museum, Smithsonian Institution, Washington, D.C.

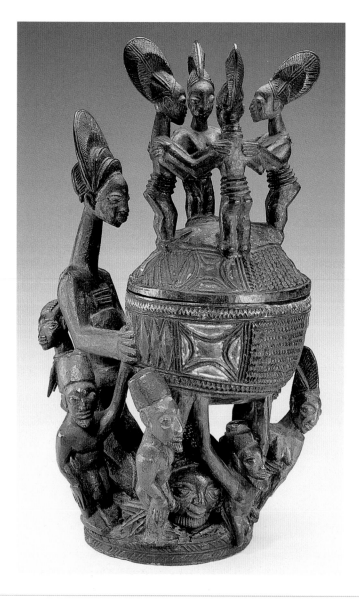

enshrined as a precious work of art in a museum. Instead of linking the congregation with God, now it links the modern viewer with the past, the Middle Ages of some 850 years ago.

Profoundly stirring religious art continues to be made, however. James Hampton's *Throne of the Third Heaven of the Nations' Millennium General Assembly* (fig. 12) is such a work, called by the art critic Robert Hughes the "finest piece of visionary art produced by an American." Hampton (1909–1964) worked as a janitor to support himself while, in a rented garage, he built this monument to his faith. In rising tiers, thrones and altars have been prepared for Jesus and Moses, with references to the New Testament on the right and to the Old Testament on the left. Hampton labeled and described everything, even inventing his own language to express his visions. On one of many placards he wrote his credo: "Where there is no vision, the people perish" (Proverbs 29:18). Yet he made this fabulous assemblage out of discarded furniture, flashbulbs, Kraft paper, and all sorts of refuse tacked together and wrapped in gold and silver aluminum foil and purple tissue paper. How can such worthless materials be turned into such an exalted work of art? Today we recognize that the genius of the artist transcends any material.

Works of art from many cultures may speak to us across the vastness of time and space. The Yoruba people of Africa, like people in other times and places, have used art objects to communicate with their gods (fig. 13). This sculpture, carved by the Yoruba master Olówè of Isè (d. 1938), may seem to be just a woman with a child on her back holding an ornate covered cup, but like Suger's chalice, this cup has an importance not immediately apparent to the outsider. It is a divination bowl, made to hold the objects used in ceremonies in which people call on the god Olodumare (or Olorun) to reveal their destiny. The child suggests the life-giving power of women and the idea that all creation rests on women's energy. Men and women help the woman support the bowl, and more women link arms in a ritual dance on the cover. The richly decorative and symbolic wood carving, even when isolated in a museum case, reminds us of those people seeking to learn from Olodumare, the god of destiny, certainty, and order.

Like the divination bowl, many of the expressions that we regard as art were originally meant for other purposes; some were intended to achieve social, political, and educational ends.

ART AND THE SOCIAL CONTEXT

The visual arts are among the most sophisticated forms of human communication, at once shaping and being shaped by their social context. Artists may unconsciously interpret their times, but they may also be enlisted to consciously serve social ends in ways that range from heavy-handed propaganda to subtle suggestion. From ancient Egyptian priests to elected

13 | Olówè of Isè. *Divination bowl.* c. 1925. Wood and pigment diameter 25 1/16" (63.7 cm). National Museum of African Art Smithsonian Institution, Washington, D.C.
Bequest of William A. McCarty-Cooper, 91-10-1

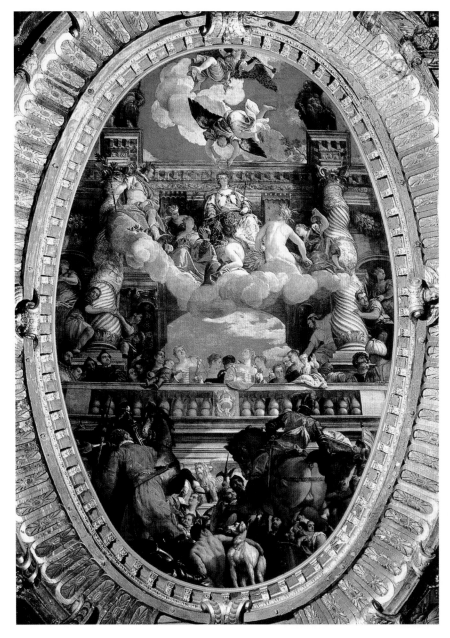

14

Veronese. *The Triumph of Venice,* oil on canvas in the Council Chamber Palazzo Ducale Venice, Italy c. 1585

officials today, religious and political leaders have understood the educational and motivational value of the visual arts.

How governments—that is, civic leaders—can use the power of art to strengthen the unity that nourishes society was well illustrated in sixteenth-century Venice. There, city officials ordered Veronese (Paolo Caliari, 1528–1588) and his assistants to fill the ceiling of the Council Chamber in the ruler's palace with a huge and colorful painting, *The Triumph of Venice* (fig. 14). Their contract with the artist survives, proclaiming their intention. They wanted a painting that showed their beloved Venice surrounded by peace, abundance, fame, happiness, honor, security, and freedom—all in vivid colors and idealized forms. Veronese complied by painting the city personified as a mature, beautiful, and splendidly robed woman enthroned between the towers of the arsenal, a building where ships were built for world-wide trade, the source of the city's wealth and power. Veronese painted enthusiastic crowds of cheering citizens, while personifications of Fame blow trumpets and Victory crowns Venice with a wreath. Supporting this happy throng, bound prisoners and piles of armor attest to Venetian military power. The Lion of Venice—the symbol of the city and its patron, Saint Mark—oversees the triumph. Veronese has created a splendid propaganda piece as well as a work of art. Although Veronese created his work to serve the purposes of his patron, his artistic vision was as individualistic as that of James Hampton, whose art was purely a form of self-expression.

Who Are Artists?

We have focused so far on works of art. But what of the artists who make them? How artists have viewed themselves and been

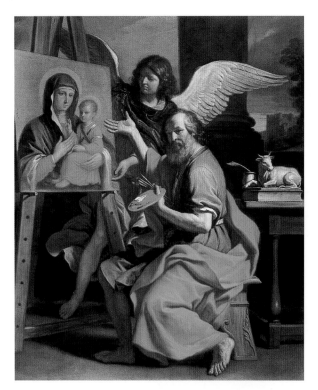

15 | Il Guercino. *Saint Luke Displaying a Painting of the Virgin.* 1652-53. Oil on canvas, 7'3" x 5'11" (2.21 x 1.81 m).
The Nelson-Atkins Museum of Art, Kansas City, Missouri. Purchase (F83-55)

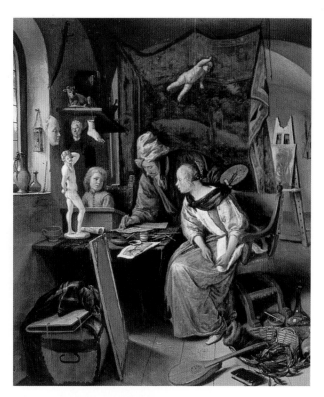

17 | Jan Steen. *The Drawing Lesson.* 1665. Oil on wood 19³/₈ x 16¹/₄" (49.3 x 41 cm). The J. Paul Getty Museum Los Angeles, California

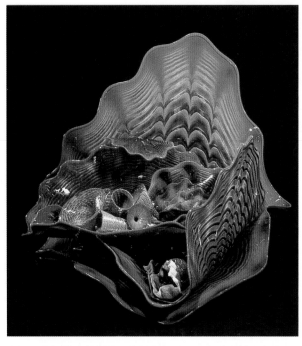

16 | Dale Chihuly. *Violet Persian Set with Red Lip Wraps* 1990. Glass, 26 x 30 x 25" (66 x 76.2 x 63.5 cm) Spencer Museum of Art, The University of Kansas Lawrence

Peter T. Bohan Acquisition Fund

viewed by their contemporaries has changed dramatically over time. In western art, artists were first considered artisans or craftspeople. Ancient Greeks and Romans, for example, considered artists to rank among the skilled workers; they admired the creations, but not the creators. People in the Middle Ages went to the opposite extreme and attributed especially fine works of art to angels or to Saint Luke. Artists continued to be seen as craftspeople—admired, often prosperous, but not particularly special—until the Renaissance, when artists such as Leonardo da Vinci proclaimed themselves to be geniuses with singular God-given abilities.

A little after Leonardo's declaration, the Italian painter Il Guercino (Giovanni Francesco Barbieri, 1591–1666) synthesized the idea that saints and angels make art with the concept that human painters have unique gifts. In his painting *Saint Luke Displaying a Painting of the Virgin* (fig. 15), Guercino portrays the evangelist who was regarded as the patron saint of artists because, Christians widely believed, he himself had painted a portrait of the Virgin Mary holding the Christ Child. In Guercino's work, Luke, seated before just such a painting and assisted by an angel, holds his palette and brushes. A book, a quill pen, and an inkpot decorated with a statue of an ox (Saint Luke's symbol) rest on a table, reminders of his status as an evangelist. Guercino seems to say that if Saint Luke is a divinely endowed artist, then surely all other artists share in this special power and status. This image of the artist as an inspired genius has largely continued into the twenty-first century.

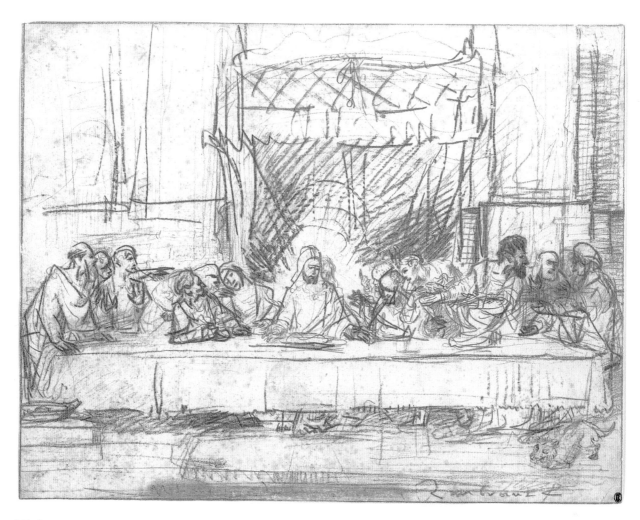

18 **Rembrandt van Rijn.** *The Last Supper,* after Leonardo da Vinci's fresco. Mid-1630s. Drawing in red chalks, 14³⁄₈ x 18³⁄₄" (36.5 x 47.5 cm). The Metropolitan Museum of Art, New York
Robert Lehman Collection, 1975 (1975.1.794)

Because art is often a communal creation, we sometimes need to use the plural of the word: *artists*. Even after the idea of "specially endowed" creators emerged, numerous artists continued to see themselves, as they had in many historical periods, as craftspeople led by the head of a workshop, and oftentimes artwork continued to be a team effort. In the eighteenth century, for example, Utamaro's color woodblock prints (see fig. 8) were the product of a number of people working together. Utamaro painted pictures for his assistants to transfer to blocks of wood. They carved the lines and areas to be colored, covered the surface with ink or colors, and then transferred the image to paper; nevertheless, Utamaro—as the one who conceived the work—is the "creative center."

The same spirit is evident today in the complex glassworks of American artist Dale Chihuly (b. 1941). His team of artist-craftspeople is skilled in the ancient art of glassmaking, but Chihuly remains the controlling mind and imagination. Once created, many of his multipart pieces are transformed every time they are assembled; they take on a new life in accordance with the will of every owner. The viewer/owner thus becomes part of the creative team. Made in 1990, *Violet Persian Set with Red Lip Wraps* (fig. 16) has twenty separate pieces, and the person who assembles them determines the composition. Artist and patron consequently unite in an ever-changing act of creation.

Whether artists work individually or communally, even the most brilliant ones typically spend years in study and apprenticeship. In his painting *The Drawing Lesson*, Dutch artist Jan Steen (1626–1679) takes us into an artist's studio where two people—a boy apprentice and a young woman—are learning the rudiments of their art. The pupil has been drawing from sculpture and plaster casts because women were not permitted to work from nude models (fig. 17). *The Drawing Lesson* records contemporary educational practice and is a valuable record of an artist's workplace in the seventeenth century.

Even mature artists considered among history's greatest continued to learn from each other. Before Rembrandt van Rijn (1606–1669), for example, painted *The Last Supper* (fig. 18), he carefully studied Leonardo da Vinci's late-fifteenth-century painting of the same subject (fig. 19; see page 24). Since he never went to Italy, Rembrandt could only have known the

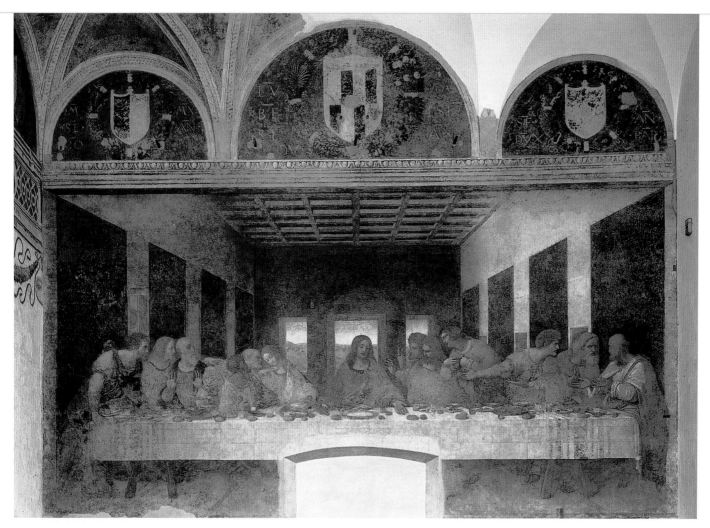

19 | **Leonardo da Vinci.** *The Last Supper,* wall painting in the refectory, Monastery of Santa Maria delle Grazie, Milan, Italy. 1495–98. Tempera and oil on plaster, 15'2" x 28'10" (4.6 x 8.8 m)

Italian master's great mural painting from a print. Rembrandt copied the image in hard red chalk, and also made detailed studies. Later he reworked the drawing in a softer chalk, assimilating Leonardo's lessons but revising the composition and the mood of the original. With heavy overdrawing, Rembrandt re-created the scene, shifting Jesus' position and expression. With a few strokes and smudges of chalk, he created a composition that now reflected the Baroque style of his time: classical symmetry has given way to asymmetry; shadows loom; highly expressive figures fill a compressed space. The drawing is more than an academic exercise; it is a sincere tribute from one great master to another. Rembrandt must have been pleased with his version of Leonardo's masterpiece because he signed his drawing boldly in the right-hand corner.

What Is a Patron?

As we have seen, the person or group who commissions or supports a work of art—the patron—can have significant impact on it. The Sphinx (see fig. 1) was "designed" by the conventions of priests in ancient Egypt; the content of Veronese's *Triumph of Venice* (see fig. 14) was determined by that city's government; Chihuly's glassworks (see fig. 16) are assembled according to the collector's specifications, desires, wishes, or whims. Although some artists work independently, hoping to sell their work on the open market, throughout art history both individuals and institutions have acted as patrons of the arts. Patrons very often have been essential factors in the development of arts, but all too often have been overlooked when we study the history of art. Today, not only individuals but also museums, other institutions, and national governments (for example, the United States, through the National Endowment for the Arts) provide support for the arts.

INDIVIDUAL PATRONS

People who are not artists often want to be involved with art, and patrons of art constitute a very special audience for artists. Many collectors truly love works of art, but some who collect art do so to enhance their own prestige, creating for themselves an aura of power and importance. Patrons vicariously participate in the creation of a work when they provide economic support to the artist. Such individual patronage can spring from a cordial relationship between a patron and an artist, as is evident in an early-fifteenth-century manuscript illustration in which the author, Christine de Pisan, presents her work to Isabeau, the

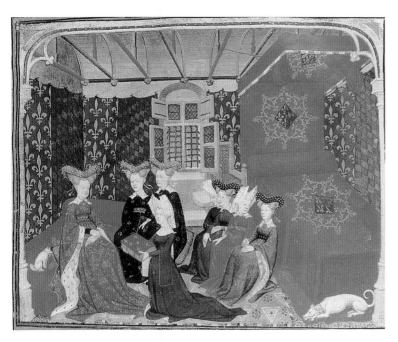

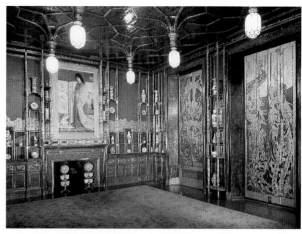

20 | ***Christine Presenting Her Book to the Queen of France.*** 1410–15 Tempera and gold on vellum, image approx. 5¹/₂ x 6³/₄" (14 x 17 cm). The British Library, London
MS. Harley 4431, folio 3

21 | **James McNeill Whistler. *Harmony in Blue and Gold.*** The Peacock Room, northeast corner, from a house owned by Frederick Leyland, London 1876-77. Oil paint and metal leaf on canvas, leather, and wood, 13'11⁷/₈" x 33'2" x 19'11¹/₂" (4.26 x 10.11 x 6.83 m).
Freer Gallery of Art, Smithsonian Institution, Washington, D.C. Gift of Charles Lang Freer, F1904.61

Queen of France. Christine, a widow who supported her family by writing, hired painters and scribes to copy, illustrate, and decorate her books. She especially admired the painting of a woman named Anastaise, whose work she considered unsurpassed in the city of Paris. Queen Isabeau was Christine's patron; Christine was Anastaise's patron; and all the women seen in the painting were patrons of the brilliant textile workers who supplied the brocades for their gowns, the tapestries for the wall, and the embroideries for the bed (fig. 20).

Relations between artists and patrons do not always prove to be as congenial as Christine portrayed them. Patrons may change their minds and sometimes fail to pay their bills. Artists may ignore their patron's wishes, to the dismay of everyone. In the late nineteenth century, the Liverpool shipping magnate Frederick Leyland asked James McNeill Whistler (1834–1903), an American painter living in London, what color to paint the shutters in the dining room where he planned to hang Whistler's painting *The Princess from the Land of Porcelain*. The room had been decorated with expensive embossed and gilded leather and finely crafted shelves to show off Leyland's blue-and-white porcelain. Whistler, inspired by the Japanese theme of his own painting as well as by the Asian porcelain, painted the window shutters with splendid turquoise, blue, and gold peacocks. But he did not stop there. While Leland was away, Whistler painted the entire room, covering the gilded leather on the walls with turquoise peacock feathers (fig. 21). Leyland was shocked and angry at what seemed to him to be wanton destruction of the room. Luckily, he did not destroy Whistler's "Peacock Room" (which Whistler called simply *Harmony in Blue and Gold*), for it is an extraordinary example of total interior design.

INSTITUTIONAL PATRONAGE: MUSEUMS AND CIVIC BODIES

From the earliest times, people have gathered and preserved precious objects that conveyed the idea of power and prestige. Today both private and public museums are major patrons, collectors, and preservers of art. Curators of such collections acquire works of art for their museums and often assist patrons in obtaining especially fine pieces, although the idea of what is best and what is worth collecting and preserving changes from one generation to another. For example, the collection of abstract and nonrepresentational art formed by members of the Guggenheim family was once considered so radical that few people—and certainly no civic or governmental group—would have considered the art worth collecting at all. Today the collection fills more than one major museum.

Frank Lloyd Wright's Solomon R. Guggenheim Museum (fig. 22; see page 26), with its snail-like, continuous spiral ramp, is a suitably avant-garde home for the collection in New York City. Sited on Fifth Avenue, beside the public green space of Central Park and surrounded on the other three sides by relentless quadrangles of the city buildings, the Guggenheim Museum challenges and relieves the inhumanity of the modern city. The Guggenheim Foundation recently opened another home for art, in Bilbao, Spain, designed by Frank Gehry, a leader of the twenty-first-century avant-garde in architecture (see fig. 20-24). As both Guggenheim museums show, such structures can do more than house collections; they can be works of art themselves.

Civic sponsorship of art is epitomized by the citizens of fifth-century BCE Athens, a Greek city-state where the people practiced an early form of democracy. Led by the statesman and general Perikles, the Athenians defeated the Persians, then rebuilt

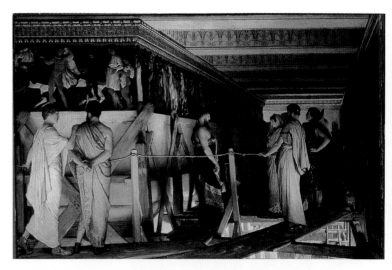

23 | Lawrence Alma-Tadema. *Pheidias and the Frieze of the Parthenon, Athens.* 1868. Oil on canvas, 29³/₅ x 42¹/₃" (75.3 x 108 cm). Birmingham City Museum and Art Gallery, England
118–23

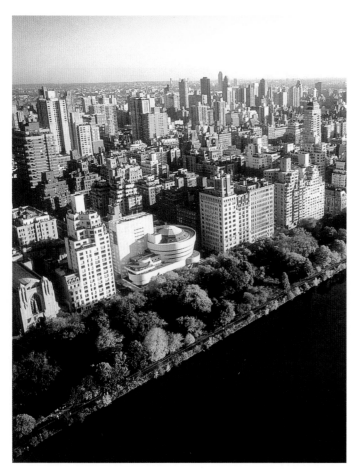

22 | Frank Lloyd Wright. Solomon R. Guggenheim Museum New York City. 1956–59. Aerial view

Athens's civic and religious center, the Acropolis, as a tribute to the goddess Athena and a testament to the glory of Athens (see fig. 4-28). In figure 23, a nineteenth-century British artist, Sir Lawrence Alma-Tadema, conveys the accomplishment of the Athenian architects, sculptors, and painters, who were led by the artist Pheidias. Alma-Tadema imagines the moment when Pheidias showed the sculpted and painted frieze at the top of the wall of the Temple of Athena (the Parthenon) to Pericles and a privileged group of Athenian citizens—his civic sponsors. We can also see civic sponsorship today in the architecture, including the museums, of most modern national capitals and in the wide variety of public monuments around the world.

What Is Art History Today?

Compared to art itself, art history as a field of study is a relatively recent phenomenon; many art historians consider the first art history book to be the 1550 publication *Lives of the Most Excellent Italian Architects, Painters, and Sculptors*, by the Italian artist and writer Giorgio Vasari. As the name implies, art history combines two very different special studies—the study of an individual work of art outside time and place (formal analysis and even art appreciation) and the study of art in its historical context (the primary approach taken in this book). The scope of art history is immense. It shows how people have represented their world and how they have expressed their ideas and

ideals. As a result, art history today draws on many other disciplines and diverse methodologies.

Art history as a humanistic discipline adds theoretical and contextual studies to the formal analysis of works of art. Art historians draw on biography to learn about artists' lives; social history to understand the economic and political forces shaping artists, their patrons, and their public; and the history of ideas to gain an understanding of the intellectual currents influencing artists' work. They also study the history of other arts—including music, drama, and literature—to gain a richer sense of the context of the visual arts. Their work results in an understanding of the **iconography** (the narrative and allegorical significance) and the context (social history) of the artwork.

Today art historians study a wider range of artworks than ever before, and many reject the idea of a fixed canon of superior pieces. The distinction between elite fine arts and popular utilitarian arts has become blurred, and the notion that some mediums, techniques, or subjects are better than others has almost disappeared. This is one of the most telling characteristics of art history today, along with the breadth of studies it now encompasses and its changing attitude to challenges such as preservation and restoration.

At the most sophisticated level, the intense study of individual art objects is known as **connoisseurship**. Through years of close contact with and study of the formal qualities that make up various styles in art, the connoisseur learns to recognize authenticity and quality. The connoisseur places an unknown work with related pieces, attributing it to a period, a place, and even to an artist. Today such experts also make use of all the scientific tests available to them, but ultimately they depend on their visual memory and their skills in formal analysis.

Such intense study of the history of art is also enhanced by the work of anthropologists and archaeologists, who study the wide range of material culture produced by a society. Archaeologists sometimes have the excitement of finding new and won-

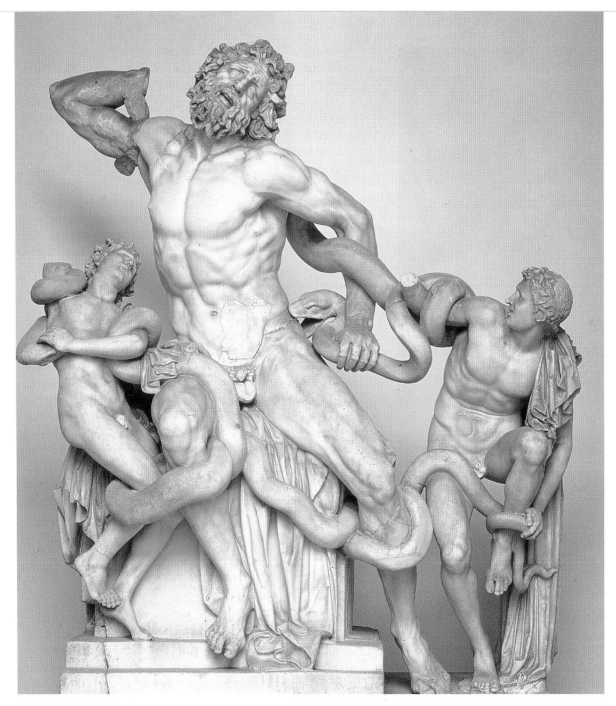

24

Hagesandros Polydoros, and **Athanadoros of Rhodes.** *Laocoön and His Sons,* as restored today Perhaps 2nd or 1st century BCE but probably a Roman copy of the 1st century CE Marble, height 8' (2.44 m). Musei Vaticani, Museo Pio Clementino Cortile Ottagono Rome, Italy

derful objects as they excavate a site. They do not, however, single out for special attention individual works of perceived excellence, produced for an elite culture.

Even as methodological sophistication and technological advances soar in art history today, art historians and other viewers are faced with some special challenges of interpretation, especially regarding works that have been damaged or restored. As we try to understand such works of art, we must remain quizzical and flexible; damaged artworks may have had large parts replaced—the legs of a marble figure or a section of wall in a mural painting, for example. Many of the works seen in this book have been restored, and many have recently been cleaned. Let's look more closely at some of the challenges those issues pose to art historians today.

DEFENDING ENDANGERED OBJECTS

Art historians must be concerned with natural and human-caused threats to works of art. In some cases, the threats result from well-meaning actions. The dangers inherent in restoration, for example, are blatantly illustrated by what happened during two restorations, hundreds of years apart, of the renowned sculpture *Laocoön and His Sons*, (figs. 24, 25; see page 28).

Laocoön was a priest who warned the Trojans of an invasion by the Greeks in Homer's account of the Trojan War. Although he told the truth, the goddess Athena, who took the Greeks' side in the war, dispatched serpents to strangle him and his sons. A tragic hero, Laocoön represents a virtuous man destroyed by unjust forces. In the powerful ancient Greek sculpture, his features twist in agony, and the muscles of his and his sons' superhuman torsos

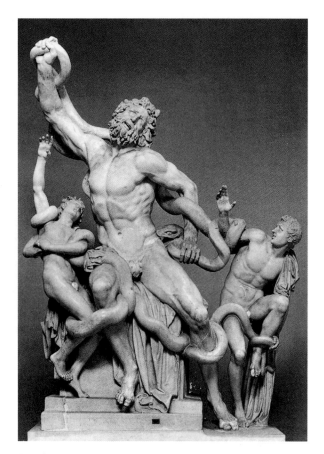

25   **Hagesandros, Polydoros,** and **Athanadoros of Rhodes**
Laocoön and His Sons, an incorrect earlier restoration
Perhaps 2nd or 1st century BCE, but probably a Roman
copy of the 1st century CE. Marble, height 8' (2.44 m)
Musei Vaticani, Museo Pio Clementino, Cortile Ottagono
Rome

continues to this day. Objects of cultural and artistic value are being poached from official and unofficial excavation sites around the world, then sold illegally.

In industrialized regions of the world, emissions from cars, trucks, buses, and factories accrue in corrosive rain that damages and sometimes literally destroys the works of art and architecture on which it falls. For art, however, war is by far the most destructive of all human enterprises. History is filled with examples of plundered works of art that, as spoils of war, were taken elsewhere and paraded and protected. But countless numbers of churches, synagogues, mosques, temples, and shrines have been burned, bombed, and stripped of decoration in the name of winning a war or confirming an ideology. So much has been lost—especially in modern times, with weapons of mass destruction—that is absolutely irrecoverable.

Individuals are sometimes moved to deface works of art, but nature itself can be equally capricious: floods, hurricanes, tornadoes, avalanches, mudslides, and earthquakes all damage and destroy priceless treasures. For example, an earthquake on the morning of September 27, 1997, convulsed the small Italian town of Assisi, where Saint Francis was born and where he founded the Franciscan order. It shook nearly to pieces the thirteenth-century Basilica of Saint Francis of Assisi—one of the richest repositories of Italian Gothic and Early Renaissance wall painting—causing great damage to architecture and paintings.

In all the examples mentioned, art historians have played a role in trying to protect the treasures that are the cultural heritage of us all. But they play another role that also affects our cultural heritage: helping to increase our understanding of the social and political factors that contribute to the artwork's context.

UNCOVERING SOCIOPOLITICAL INTENTIONS

Because art history considers the role and intention of artists, art historians have explored—but not always discovered—whether the sculpture of Laocoön, for example, had a political impact in its own time. As we have seen, artists throughout history have been used to promote the political and educational agendas of powerful patrons, but modern artists are often independent-minded, astute commentators in their own right. Art history needs to look at these motivations too. For example, among Honoré Daumier's most powerful critiques of the French government is his print *Rue Transonain, Le 15 Avril 1834* (fig. 26). During a period of urban unrest, the French National Guard fired on unarmed citizens, killing fourteen people. For his depiction of the massacre, Daumier used lithography—a cheap new means of illustration. He was not thinking in terms of an enduring historical record, but rather of a medium that would enable him to spread his message as widely as possible. Daumier's political commentary created such horror and revulsion that the government ordered all copies of the print to be gathered up and destroyed. As this example shows, art historians need to consider not just the historical context but also the political content and the medium of a work of art to have a complete understanding of it.

Another, more recent, work with a powerful sociopolitical message is a reminder to those of us in the twenty-first century

and arms extend and knot as they struggle. When the sculpture was discovered in Rome in 1506, artists such as Michelangelo rushed to see it, and it inspired many artists to develop a heroic style. The pope acquired it for the papal collection, and it can still be seen in the Vatican Museums.

In piecing together the past of this one work, we know that mistakes were made during an early restoration. The broken pieces of the *Laocoön* group first were reassembled with figures flinging their arms out in the melodramatic fashion seen in figure 25—this was the sculpture the Renaissance and Baroque artists knew. Modern conservation methods, however, have produced a different image and with it a changed mood (see fig. 24). Arms turn back upon the bodies, making a compact composition that internalizes the men's agony. This version speaks directly to a self-centered twentieth century. We can only wonder if twenty-fifth-century art historians will re-create yet another *Laocoön*.

Restoration of works like *Laocoön* is intended to conserve precious art. But throughout the world, other human acts intentionally or mindlessly threaten works of art and architecture—and this is not a recent problem. Egyptian tombs were plundered and vandalized many hundreds of years ago—and such theft

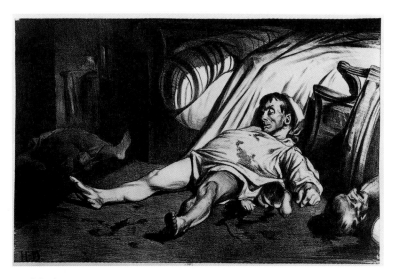

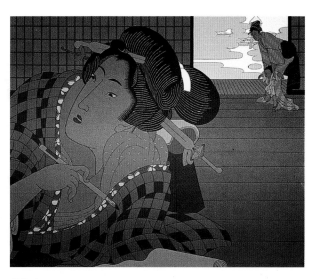

26 | Honoré Daumier. *Rue Transonain, Le 15 Avril 1834*
Lithograph, 11 x 17³/8" (28 x 44 cm). Bibliothèque Nationale
Paris

27 | Roger Shimomura. *Diary (Minidoka Series #3).* 1978
Acrylic on canvas, 4'11⁷/8" x 6'1/16" (1.52 x 1.83 m)
Spencer Museum of Art, The University of Kansas
Lawrence

who may not know or may have forgotten that American citizens of Japanese ancestry were removed from their homes and confined in internment camps during World War II. Roger Shimomura (b. 1939) in 1978 painted *Diary*, recalling his grandmother's record of the family's experience in one such camp in Idaho (fig. 27). Shimomura has painted his grandmother writing in her diary, while he (the toddler) and his mother stand by an open door—a door that does not signify freedom but opens on to a field bounded by barbed wire. In this painting—a commentary on twentieth-century discrimination and injustice—Shimomura combines two formal traditions—the Japanese art of color woodblock prints and American Pop art—to create a personal style that expresses his own dual culture.

Art historians must examine such sociopolitical factors as critical aspects of the historical context of works of art. But what is our responsibility as viewers?

What Is the Viewer's Responsibility?

We as viewers enter into an agreement with artists, who in turn make special demands on us. We re-create the works of art for ourselves as we bring to them our own experiences, our intelligence, even our prejudices. Without our participation, artworks are only chunks of stone or painted canvas. But we must also remember that styles change with time and place. From extreme realism at one end of the spectrum to entirely nonrepresentational art at the other—from Van der Spelt and Van Mieris's *Flower Piece with Curtain* (see fig. 2) to Smith's *Cubi XIX* (see fig. 5)—artists have worked with varying degrees of naturalism, idealism, and abstraction. The challenge for the student of art history is to discover not only how but also why those styles evolved, and ultimately what of significance can be learned from that evolution.

Our involvement with art may be casual or intense, naive or sophisticated. At first we may simply react instinctively to a painting or building or photograph, but this level of "feeling" about art—"I know what I like"—can never be fully satisfying. Because as viewers we participate in the re-creation of a work of art, its meaning changes from individual to individual, from era to era. Once we welcome the arts into our lives, we have a ready source of sustenance and challenge that grows, changes, mellows, and enriches our daily experience. The Starter Kit, which begins on page 5, introduces us to many of the tools of art history, but no matter how much we study or read about art and artists, eventually we return to the contemplation of an original work itself, for art is the tangible evidence of the ever-questing human spirit.

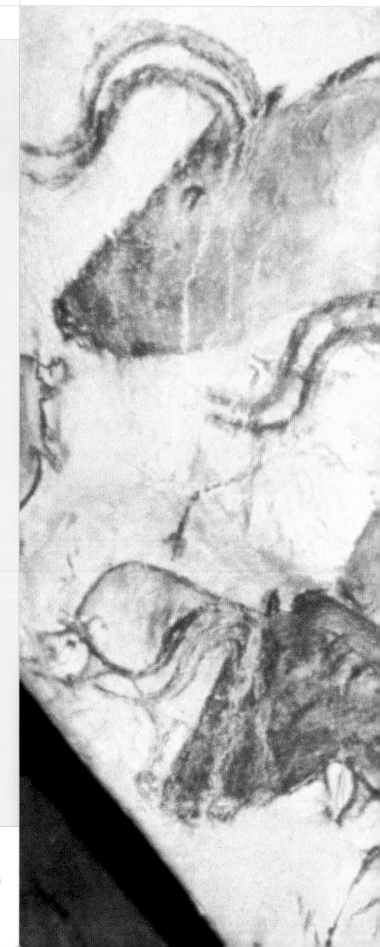

When the intrepid swimmers exploring the Mediterranean coast near Cassis, France, followed an underwater tunnel and emerged into a cave, they entered an almost unimaginably ancient world. What they found astounded them—and fascinates us—for the walls and ceiling of the cave held paintings and engravings that record herds of animals seen 30,000 years ago. If at times only in photographs, today we are looking at the roots of our culture, some of the very first images of the history of art.

Scholars of prehistory—archaeologists and anthropologists—study every aspect of material culture, while art historians usually focus on those things that to twenty-first century eyes seem superior in craft and beauty. But 30,000 years ago our ancestors were not making "works of art." People pounding (flaking) flints made arrows or scrapers, not sculptures, however beautiful the forms of these tools appear to us today. The creation of the images we see on the Chauvet cave walls must have seemed vitally important to their makers in terms of everyday survival. What we perceive as "art" was a matter of necessity to these ancient image makers.

Images of horses, aurochs (extinct ancestors of domestic cattle), even rhinos cover the cave walls. The animals are easily identifiable, for the painters represent the essence of well-observed animals—their meat-bearing flanks, their four powerful legs, and two dangerous horns. What a leap of intelligence and imagination we witness here. The painters have turned their memories of moving, three-dimensional figures into fixed, two-dimensional images. Without written words and using only the formal language of line and color, they seem to communicate with us. But what are they saying?

We wonder why these early humans made these paintings. Were they recording an event such as a hunt or a successful roundup? Could the images have played a role in the education or initiation of the young? Perhaps the paintings express beliefs, a spirit world, a complex ritual. Could the makers have been trying to control the forces of nature through their art? Do they recall a shaman's voyage? Could it be that the act of painting itself was important as a ritual, regardless of the image? We have no answers, only questions. Perhaps the value in our study of these mysterious images is their ability to lead us to speculate on what it means to be human.

Wall painting with four horses, Chauvet cave
Vallon-Pont-d'Arc, Ardèche gorge, France
c. 28,000 BCE. Paint on limestone. (See page 35.)

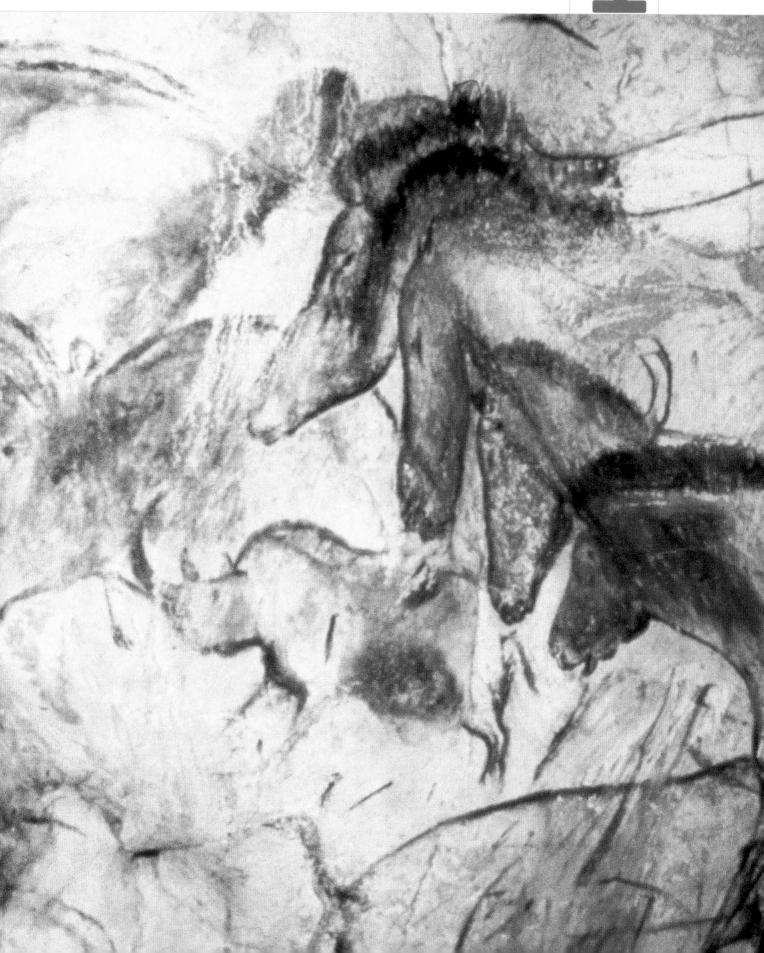

Archaeological evidence indicates that the earliest upright human species came into being about 4.4 million years ago in Africa. How and when modern humans evolved is the subject of lively debate, but it seems that the hominids called *Homo sapiens* (wise humans) appeared about 200,000 years ago and that the species to which we belong, *Homo sapiens sapiens*, evolved about 120,000 to 100,000 years ago. From Africa, modern humans spread across Asia, into Europe, and finally to Australia and the Americas. Among these people were those whom today we call artists (see Map 1, pages 86–87).

Scholars began to study prehistory systematically—that is, to examine the thousands of years of human civilization before the invention of written historical records—less than 200 years ago. Struck by the wealth of stone tools, weapons, and figures found at ancient living sites, nineteenth-century archaeologists named the whole period of early human development the Stone Age. Today's researchers further divide the time span into the Paleolithic, or Old Stone Age (from the

1-1 | ***Lion-Human,*** from Hohlenstein-Stadel, Germany c. 30,000–26,000 BCE. Mammoth ivory, height 11⅝" (29.6 cm). Ulmer Museum, Ulm, Germany

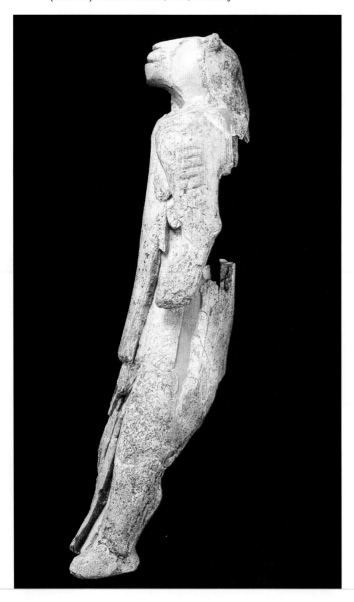

CLOSER LOOK

Elegant and remote yet warmly human, the *Woman from Brassempouy* (fig. 1-2) seems to contemplate her world with equanimity, her once-painted pupils made sightless by more than 24,000 years of lying in the soil of central France. The subtle arch of her brows, the graceful lines of her neck and nose, even the neat pattern of her hair or headdress capture the living presence of a mature young woman. Her image in ivory by a long-dead sculptor still speaks to us of our essential humanity, of our need to make images of ourselves and our kind, of our status as the only creatures who both make useful tools (the great apes do that too) *and* create works of art. We make things of beauty, however we may define such elusive concepts as "art" and "beauty."

We do not know what moved someone to carve this piece, of which only the head survives. Perhaps the maker associated the woman with spiritual or magical powers: ancestor, goddess, or perhaps a ruler of the natural world or of the spirit world of the hereafter. Perhaps she ensured her tribe's continuity as a fertility figure controlling the abundance of nature; perhaps she presided over some dark unknown world.

Our speculations are fruitless, for the *Woman from Brassempouy* and her kin left no written record to share with us their thoughts and deeds. She is indeed prehistoric. And therein lies part of our fascination with this art. Whereas new studies of physical remains—from fossils to Stone Age hunting sites—tell us about the physical life, appearance, and capabilities of our distant ancestors, only their painting and sculpture—what we choose to call art—can lead us to some understanding of their creative, spiritual, and intellectual life. We begin our study of the history of art with many great questions and a mission of understanding.

Greek *paleo*, "old," and *lithos*, "stone"), which has Lower (earliest), Middle, and Upper phases; and the Neolithic, or New Stone Age (from the Greek *neo*, "new").

Upper Paleolithic Art

Our hunter-gatherer ancestors lived in small nomadic groups and created works of art and architecture as early as the Upper (later) Paleolithic period (c. 42,000–8000 BCE). During this time, the glaciers of the last ice age still covered northern stretches of Europe, North America, and Asia. Some of the most ancient examples of Paleolithic art are small figures, or figurines, of people and animals, made of bone, ivory, stone, and clay. An early and puzzling example is a human figure with a feline head (fig. 1-1), made about 30,000 to 26,000 BCE.

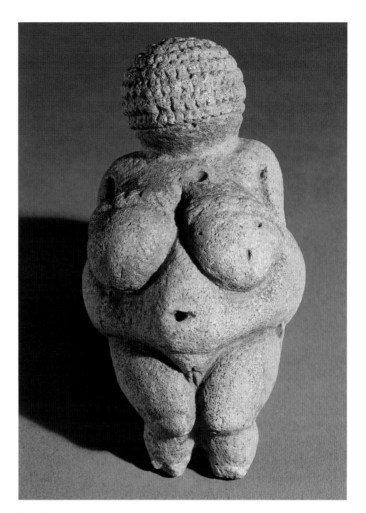

1-3 | ***Woman from Willendorf,*** Austria. c. 22,000–21,000 BCE
Limestone, height 4³/₈" (11 cm). Naturhistorisches Museum
Vienna

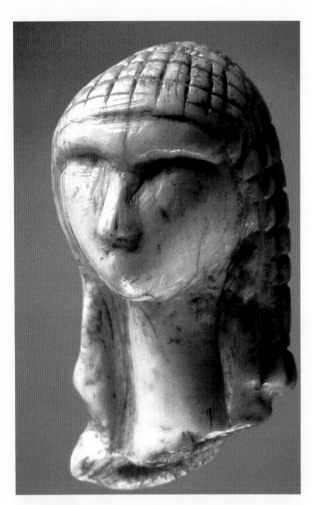

1-2 | ***Woman from Brassempouy,*** Grotte du Pape, Brassempouy
Landes, France. c. 22,000 BCE. Ivory, height 1¼" (3 cm)
Musée des Antiquités Nationales, St.-Germain-en-Laye

Archaeologists excavating at Hohlenstein-Stadel, Germany, found broken pieces of ivory from the tusk of the now-extinct woolly mammoth, which they realized were parts of an entire figure. Nearly a foot tall, this remarkable statue surpasses in size and complexity most early figurines. Instead of copying what he or she saw in nature, the sculptor created a unique, imagined creature, part human and part beast. Was it intended to represent a person wearing a lion mask and taking part in some ritual? Was it a shaman who has taken the appearance of his animal guardian? One of the few indisputable things that can be said about the *Lion-Human* is that it shows the sculptor's highly complex thinking and creative imagination: the ability to imagine and represent a creature never before seen in nature.

Paleolithic sculptors depicted women more frequently than other subjects. The carver of the *Woman from Brassempouy* (fig. 1-2) captured the essence of a head, that is, what psychologists call the "memory image"—those generalized elements that reside in our standard memory of a human head. An egg shape rests atop a long neck: a wide nose and a strongly defined browline suggest deep-set eyes, and an engraved squared patterning may be hair or a headdress. This is an example of **abstraction**: the reduction of shapes and appearances to basic yet recognizable **forms** that are not intended to be reproduced as if replicating nature exactly. The result in this case looks uncannily modern to the contemporary viewer. Today, when such a piece is isolated in a museum case—or as a book illustration—we enjoy the ivory head as an aesthetic object, but we lose its cultural context.

Another early female figurine, the *Woman from Willendorf* (fig. 1-3), dates from about 22,000–21,000 BCE (see "The Power of Naming," page 34). Carved from limestone and originally colored with red ocher, the statuette's swelling, rounded forms make it seem much larger than its actual 4³/₈-inch height. The sculptor exaggerated the figure's female **attributes**, giving it pendulous breasts, a big belly with a deep navel

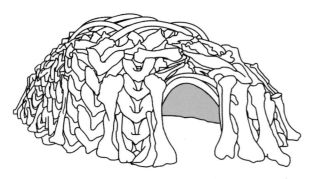

1-4 **Reconstruction drawing** of mammoth-bone house from Ukraine c. 16,000–10,000 BCE

(a natural hole in the stone), wide hips, dimpled knees and buttocks, and solid thighs. Sculptures of women, from slender adolescents to old women, have been found at dozens of sites from France to Ukraine. By carving a woman with a well-nourished body, the artist expresses the condition of health, which could guarantee both longevity and the ability to produce strong children for the survival of the clan.

Whatever their original significance, Paleolithic works of sculpture show an aesthetic sense and the ability to pose and solve problems. Both of these faculties are among the characteristics unique to human beings. Similar talents are revealed in structures of the period. Their builders sometimes seem to have had a feel for what we now call architecture—enclosure of spaces with some measure of aesthetic intent—rather than simple building construction.

Some well-preserved examples of Upper Paleolithic dwellings have been found in Russia and Ukraine. The people of those treeless grasslands built settlements of up to ten houses using the bones and hide of the woolly mammoth (fig. 1-4). One such village, dating from 16,000–10,000 BCE,

---

THE POWER OF NAMING

Figures such as the Woman of Willendorf (see fig. 1-3) are sometimes termed "goddess" or "Venus" figurines: this statuette, discovered near Willendorf, Austria, was originally called the "Venus of Willendorf." Because Venus was the Roman goddess of love and beauty, the use of this name sent a message that the statuette was associated with religious belief, that it represented an ideal of womanhood, and that it was one in a long line of images of "classical" feminine beauty. Yet there is no proof that figures such as the Woman from Willendorf had any religious associations. They can be interpreted as representations of actual women, fertility symbols, expressions of ideal beauty, erotic images, ancestor figures, or even dolls meant to help young girls learn women's roles. Given the diversity of ages and physical types represented, it is possible that they were any or all of these.

Our ability to understand and interpret works of art creatively is easily compromised by distracting labels. Even knowing that the figure was once labeled the "Venus of Willendorf" influences the way we look at it. The tradition of a name, no matter how guided by an era's cultural conventions, makes it extremely difficult to challenge accepted belief. Calling a prehistoric figure a "woman" instead of "Venus" frees us to think about it in new and different ways.

---

was discovered near the Ukrainian village of Mezhirich. Its turf-and-hide-covered houses were cleverly constructed with dozens of skulls, shoulder blades, pelvis bones, jawbones, and tusks. The largest house was an impressive 24 by 33 feet, and inside, archaeologists found fifteen small hearths containing ashes and charred bones left by its last occupants. Clearly, life revolved around the hearth, the source of light and heat.

Cave and rock paintings from the Upper Paleolithic period provide another means of connection to our early ancestors. Rock art survives in many places around the world, but the oldest known examples come from Australia and western Europe, beginning around 30,000 BCE. In Australia, the hunter-gatherer ancestors of today's Aborigines practiced both rock painting and rock engraving (pecking designs into rock with stone tools). They sometimes returned to a single location over many centuries to renew a fading painting or add new images. The ritual of making the painting may have been more important than the finished work. An ornately decorated rock surface, located on the northern coast of Australia in Oenpelli, Arnhem Land, contains two superimposed **compositions** (fig. 1-5). The first, painted around

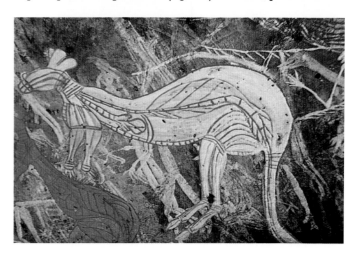

1-5 *Mimis and Kangaroo*, prehistoric rock art, Oenpelli, Arnhem Land, Australia. Older painting 16,000–7000 BCE. Red and yellow ocher and white pipe clay

16,000–7000 BCE, shows the skinny, sticklike humans that later Aborigines believed had been painted by *mimis* (ancestral spirits). Long after this imagery was abandoned, the figures were painted over with a kangaroo image in the so-called **x-ray style**, in which the bones and internal organs are drawn inside the silhouetted outline of the animal. Bark painters in Australia today still use the x-ray style.

In European caves, people began to paint, carve, and model images about 30,000 years ago. They produced many cave paintings in southern France and northern Spain between about 28,000 and 10,000 BCE. Artists painted images of animals, such as wild horses, bison, mammoths, aurochs (ancestors of domestic cattle), and a few people; many handprints; and hundreds of **geometric** markings, such as **grids**, circles, and dots. In some caves, painters decorated not only large caverns but also tiny chambers and recesses whose natural surfaces inspired images resembling **low-relief sculpture**. They worked in the light of

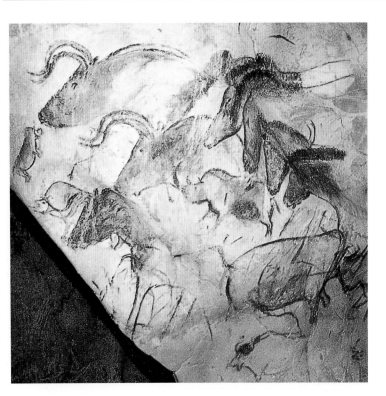

1-6 | **Wall painting with four horses,** Chauvet cave, Vallon-Pont-d'Arc Ardèche gorge, France. c. 28,000 BCE. Paint on limestone (See pages 30–31.)

TECHNIQUE
Prehistoric Wall Painting

In a dark cave, working by the light of an animal-fat lamp, an artist chews a piece of charcoal to dilute it with saliva and water. Then he blows out the mixture on the surface of a wall, using his hand as a stencil. Cave archaeologist Michel Lorblanchet is showing us how the original artists of a cave painting at Pech-Merle in France created a complex design of spotted horses. By turning himself into a human spray can, he can produce clear lines on the rough stone surface much more easily than he could with a brush. To create the line of a horse's back, with its clean upper edge and blurry lower one, he blows pigment below his hand; to capture its angular rump, he places his hand vertically against the wall, holding it slightly curved; to produce the sharpest lines, such as those of the upper hind leg and tail, he places his 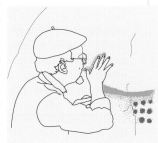 hands side by side and blows between them. The forelegs and the hair on the horses' bellies he executes with finger painting, and a hole punched in a piece of leather serves as a stencil for the horses' spots. It takes Lorblanchet only thirty-two hours to reproduce the Pech-Merle painting of spotted horses, his speed suggesting that a single artist created the original (perhaps with the help of an assistant to mix pigments and tend the lamp).

small stone lamps fueled by animal fat, using red and brown pigments ultimately derived from manganese dioxide (see "Prehistoric Wall Painting," right).

The oldest securely dated European cave paintings are found in the Chauvet cave in southeastern France, which was discovered in 1994 (fig. 1-6). These paintings were made around 28,000 BCE, which seems remarkable given the accomplished appearance of the animals depicted. It is impossible to know whether the horses shown here represent the beginnings

of early painting or some other stage in early artistic development. Because we have no records predating this time, we have no way of knowing whether early artists had actualy been practicing for thousands of years. The significance of such cave paintings is unknown, but many theories have been suggested (see "The Meaning(s) of Prehistoric Paintings," page 36).

The best-known cave paintings remain those at Lascaux, in southern France (fig. 1-7). The Lascaux paintings of cows, bulls, horses, and deer date from about 15,000–13,000 BCE. The animals

1-7 | **Hall of Bulls,** Lascaux caves. c. 15,000–13,000 BCE. Paint on limestone

Discovered in 1940 and opened to the public after World War II, the prehistoric "museum" at Lascaux soon became one of the most popular tourist sites in France. Too popular, for many visitors sowed the seeds of the paintings' destruction in the form of heat, humidity, exhaled carbon dioxide, and other contaminants. The cave was closed to the public in 1963 so that conservators might battle with an aggressive fungus that had attacked the paintings. Eventually they won, but instead of reopening the site, the authorities created a facsimile of it. Visitors at what is called Lascaux II may now view copies of the painted images without harming the precious originals.

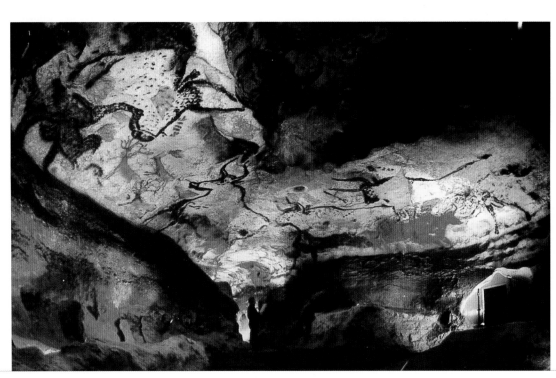

THE MEANING(S) OF PREHISTORIC PAINTINGS

Why did people thousands of years ago paint images on cave walls and ceilings? Anthropologists and art historians have put forward countless theories to explain this early artistic activity, often telling us as much about themselves and their times as about the art. Here are two early theories.

In the nineteenth century, the idea that human beings have an inherent desire to decorate themselves and their surroundings—an innate "aesthetic sense"—found ready acceptance. Some artists at the time promoted the idea of "art for art's sake," believing that people create works of art for the sheer love of beauty. However, the effort and organization required to accomplish the great paintings of Lascaux suggest that their creators were motivated by more than simple pleasure.

Early in the twentieth century, scholars rejected the idea of "art for art's sake" as a dated, romantic explanation. Led by Salomon Reinach, who believed that art fulfills a social function, they proposed that prehistoric cave paintings might be the end products of rites performed to enhance the fertility of the animals on which people depended for food. In 1903 Reinach proposed that cave paintings were expressions of "sympathetic magic." He suggested that the painters may have thought that producing a picture of a bison lying down would ensure that hunters found their prey asleep, or that the symbolic killing of the picture of a bison would guarantee the hunters' triumph over the beast itself.

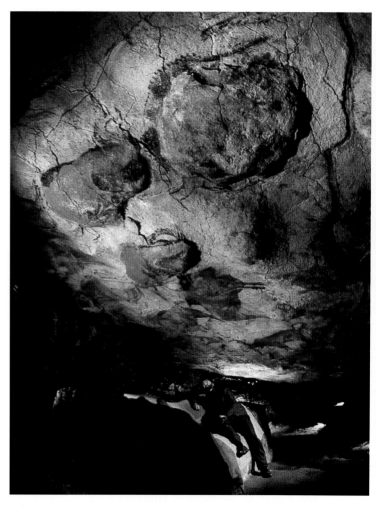

1-8 | ***Bison,*** on the ceiling of a cave at Altamira, Spain. c. 12,000 BCE. Paint on limestone, length approx. 8'3" (2.5 m)

No one knew of the existence of prehistoric cave painting until one day in 1879, when a young girl exploring with her father on the family estate in Altamira crawled through a small opening in the ground and found herself in a cave chamber whose ceiling was covered with painted animals. Her father searched the rest of the cave, then told authorities about the remarkable find. Few people believed that these amazing works could have been done by "primitive" people, and the scientific community declared the paintings a hoax. They were accepted as authentic only in 1902, after many other cave paintings, drawings, and engravings had been discovered at other spots in northern Spain and France.

appear singly, in rows, face-to-face, tail-to-tail, and even painted on top of one another. As in other caves, horns, eyes, and hooves are shown as seen from the front, while heads and bodies are rendered in profile. The artists used the contours of the rock as part of their compositions. This sculptural dimension is seen perhaps most clearly in photographs of the cave ceiling at Altamira, Spain (fig. 1-8).

Pottery cooking vessels, which first appeared in the Paleolithic period, also display the artistry of early humankind. Recent scientific dating methods have shown that Japanese potters made the oldest-known fired pottery vessels more than 12,000 years ago. The people of the Japanese Jomon culture who made the cooking pots, or *fukabachi*, decorated virtually all their ceramic **wares**, even utilitarian cooking vessels like this one (fig. 1–9). They pressed slender ribs of clay onto the body of the pot in a diamond pattern, set off above and below with bands of horizontal grooves. The round base of the vessel was probably buried in sand to steady it when cooking food over an open fire. Beginning about 7500 BCE, potters decorated *fukabachi* with *jomon*, or marks of cords pressed into damp clay, a pottery style that gives the Jomon period its name.

Art in the Neolithic Period

Fundamental social and cultural changes mark the beginning of the Neolithic period. These include the development of organized agriculture; the practice of animal husbandry (the maintenance of herds of domesticated animals); and the foundation of permanent, year-round settlements. These shifts, which took place as the Ice Age ended, occurred in some regions earlier than others and first in the Near East, where farmers began

to cultivate native grains about 9000 BCE. The transition from the Paleolithic to the Neolithic began later in Europe, around 8000 BCE; about 7000 BCE in China; about 3000 BCE in Africa south of the Sahara; and later yet in most parts of the Americas, where widespread human occupation had only begun around 10,000 BCE. The Neolithic period ended with the introduction of metalworking—the Bronze Age—around 3400 BCE in the Near East, about 2300 BCE in Europe, and about 1500 BCE in China. In other parts of the world, this Paleolithic-Neolithic-Bronze Age chronology based on technological development in Europe and Asia is irrelevant. For example, people in Africa south of the Sahara moved straight from the Neolithic to the Iron Age without an intervening Bronze Age. In Australia, the

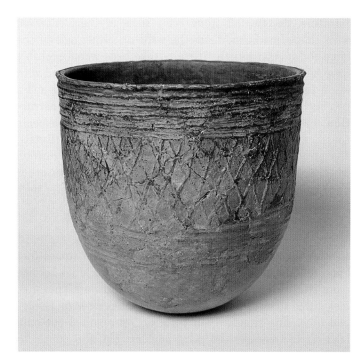

1-9 **Jomon vessel.** c. 10,000 BCE. Ceramic, reconstructed from sherds. Height 8⅝" (21.9 cm); mouth diameter 9¼" (23.5 cm). Yamato-shi Board of Education, Kanagawa-ken

The archaeologist's best friend is the potsherd, or piece of broken pottery. Ceramic vessels are easily broken, yet the fragments are almost indestructible. The discovery of early sherds at a site marks the time when people in the region first began producing ceramics. Pottery styles, like automobile designs and fashions in clothing, change over time. Archaeologists are able to determine the chronological order of such changes. By matching the potsherds excavated at a site with the types in this sequence, they can determine the relative date of the site.

hunter-gatherer culture developed by the Aborigines was so efficient and appropriate for the environment that the Aborigines never adapted Neolithic agriculture and the domestication of animals, even though they knew of these practices through contacts with Papua New Guinea.

Much of what we know of Neolithic life comes from ancient art and architecture. At Cogul, in the province of Lérida in Catalonia, the broad surfaces of a rock shelter are decorated with elaborate narrative scenes involving dozens of small figures— men, women, children, animals, even insects (fig. 1-10). They date from between 4000 and 2000 BCE. No specific landscape features are indicated, but occasional painted patterns of animal tracks give the sense of a rocky terrain, like that of the surrounding barren hillsides. In the detail shown here, a number of women are seen gracefully strolling or standing about, some in pairs holding hands. The women's small waists are emphasized by large, pendulous breasts. They wear skirts with scalloped hemlines revealing large calves and sturdy ankles, and all of them appear to have shoulder-length hair. An animal is also represented in motion; it leaps forward with fully extended legs. (The pose is called the "flying gallop.") Unnatural as it is, this pose has been the conventional way to indicate speed from prehistory to modern times.

These **wall paintings** contain so much information that it is tempting to imagine them as records of daily life. But like all early art, they probably served a greater social function. Perhaps they had an educational or religious use, for in some places the images were repainted many times. People were still coming to the sites in Roman times when, scribbling on the walls, they left **graffiti**.

A Neolithic settlement preserved in the sea sands at Skara Brae, in the Orkney Islands off the northern coast of Scotland,

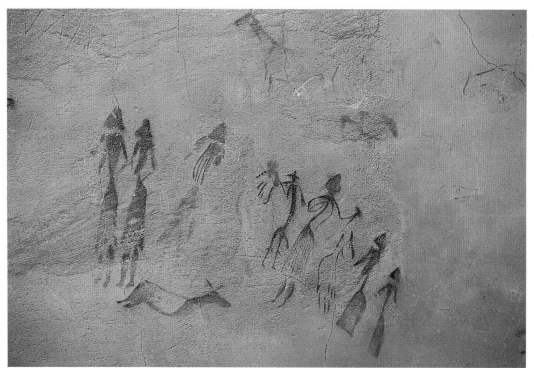

1-10

People and Animals detail of rock-shelter painting in Cogul Lérida, Spain c. 4000–2000 BCE Museo Arqueológico Bareclona

gives a vivid picture of life in an early village (fig. 1-11). The excavated village (built over time, and as we see it by 3100 BCE) consists of a compact cluster of stone dwellings linked together by covered passageways. The largest house measures 20 x 21 feet, the smallest 13 x 14 feet. The interiors, such as the one shown (fig. 1-12), were equipped with space-saving, built-in

furniture. Rectangular stone beds, some of them engraved with simple markings, flank the walls on either side of the large rectangular hearth. These boxlike beds would probably have been filled with heather "mattresses" and covered with warm furs. On the back wall is a sizable storage niche and a two-shelf cabinet erected using **post-and-lintel construction**. In this building system, two or more vertical elements (posts) are used to support a bridging horizontal one (**lintel**). The structural principle has been used throughout history, whether for simple framing elements like these shelves or for huge stone monuments such as Stonehenge or the later temples of Egypt (Chapter 2) and Greece (Chapter 4).

MEGALITHIC ARCHITECTURE

Massive tombs and monuments built from huge stones first appeared in the Neolithic period, as human societies became more stratified and complex. These structures are known as megalithic architecture, after the Greek terms *mega* for "large" and *lithos* for "stone." Their construction required not only laborers to transport the giant boulders but also people to devise methods to shape and align them. Could we consider them to be the predecessors of artists and engineers? These structures also called for powerful political and religious leaders to dictate a society's need for such edifices, as well as a co-ordinated workforce to build them.

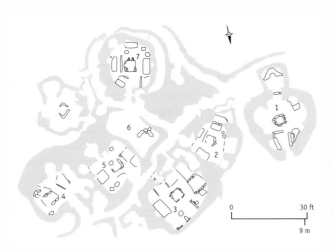

1-11 | **Plan,** village of Skara Brae, Orkney Islands, Scotland
By c. 3100 BCE

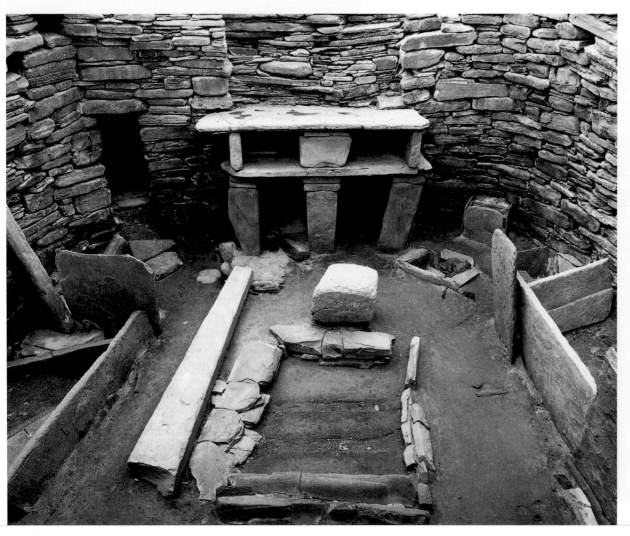

1-12

House interior Skara Brae (house 7 in fig. 1-11)

Many megalithic tombs are preserved in Europe, where they were used for both single and multiple burials. In the simplest type, the **dolmen**, a tomb chamber was formed of huge upright stones supporting one or more tablelike rocks, or **capstones**. Smaller rocks and dirt were mounded on top of the chamber to form an artificial hill called a **cairn**.

Elaborate burial sites, called **passage graves**, had one or more corridors leading into a large room at the cairn's center. Many still command the landscape in Ireland. One example (fig. 1-13) discovered at Newgrange, Ireland, was constructed around 3000 to 2500 BCE. Rings, spirals, diamond shapes, and other **linear** designs enrich the stones at its entrance and along its entrance passageway. These patterns must have been marked out using strings or compasses, then carved by pecking at the rock surface with tools made of antlers and hard stones. A cairn that measured about 280 feet in diameter concealed the tomb chamber and passage. The ritual use of the tomb/cairn is still a mystery; however, some powerful solar symbolism must have

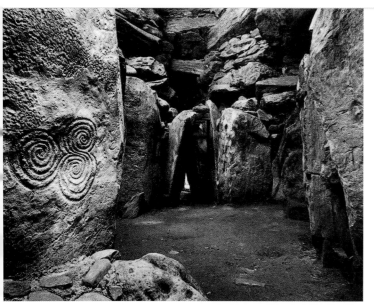

1-13 | **Tomb interior** with engraved stones, Newgrange, Ireland
c. 3000–2500 BCE

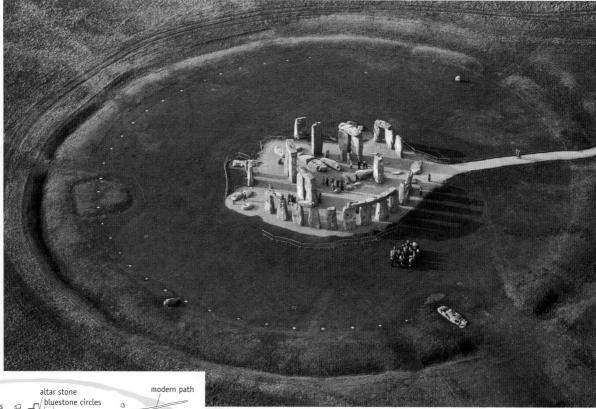

1-14

| (*right*)
Stonehenge
Salisbury Plain
Wiltshire, England
c. 2750–1500 BCE

1-15

| (*below*)
Diagram of Stonehenge showing elements discussed in text

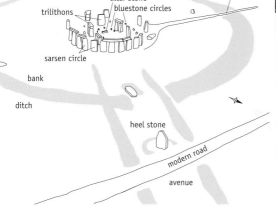

altar stone
bluestone circles
trilithons
modern path
sarsen circle
bank
ditch
heel stone
modern road
avenue

played a part. The builders oriented the passage to the rising sun in midsummer, at which time the sun shines through a semi-concealed opening down the length of the passage to the tomb chamber and falls on a shallow, scooped out, platterlike stone.

Besides tombs, Neolithic and post-Neolithic cultures built megalithic monuments and sculptures for ritual purposes that are still not fully understood by today's scholars. The best-known megalithic monument, and another solar structure, is Stonehenge in southern England (figs. 1-14, 1-15). Its name comes from the word ***henge,*** meaning a circle formed by stones or wooden posts, often surrounded by a ditch with built-up embankments. While Stonehenge is not the largest such circle from the Neolithic period, it is the most complex. Reworked over at least four major building phases between about 2750 and 1500 BCE, Stonehenge must have had extraordinary social and symbolic importance in its region.

The main elements of Stonehenge are illustrated in the accompanying aerial photograph and diagram. The earliest circle was a ditch with a 6-foot embankment, about 330 feet in diameter, with a surrounding circle of white chalk marks in the earth. A single 35-ton sarsen (sandstone) megalith, known today as the "heel stone," was moved from quarries 23 miles away and placed outside the circles. Later generations added a more complex structure. They built a ring of gray sarsen uprights about 20 feet tall and topped by a continuous lintel. Inside the sarsen circle they placed a ring of smaller bluestones, made of a bluish dolerite that they transported from Welsh quarries 150 miles away. These circles surround a horseshoe-shaped arrangement of five trilithons, or pairs of unlinked stones topped by lintels, and a second horseshoe of bluestones. The largest of the trilithons stood 24 feet high. At the very center of this complex lies the so-called altar stone. The actual role of this stone is unknown; designating it as an **altar** with religious connotations is a modern presumption. We have seen the problems modern labels or titles can present as discussed in "The Power of Naming," page 34. The opening of the horseshoe focuses on the "heel stone," which stands outside the henge to the northeast and connects to the opening by a causeway.

One aspect of this megalithic monument more than any other has captured the public's imagination. Anyone standing at the exact center of Stonehenge on the morning of the summer solstice 4,000 years ago would have seen the sun rise directly over the heel stone. Even today, the midsummer sunrise inspires hundreds of people to gather at Stonehenge. Given the relationship between the monument's orientation and the sun, some scholars think it may have been a kind of observatory that helped astronomers to track cosmic events. Aside from its possible astronomical significance, anthropologists suspect that Stonehenge was an important site for major public ceremonies, possibly planting or harvest rituals.

BRONZE AGE EUROPE

Neolithic culture persisted in northern Europe until about 2000 BCE. Metals had made their appearance about 2300 BCE, although gold and copper had been used in southern Europe and the Near East much earlier. The period that follows the introduction of metalworking is commonly called the Bronze Age. A remarkable sculpture found in Denmark depicts a horse pulling a wheeled cart laden with a large, upright disk, thought to represent the sun (fig. 1-16).

A widespread sun cult seems to have existed in the north, as our discussion of Stonehenge suggests. The horse, with its

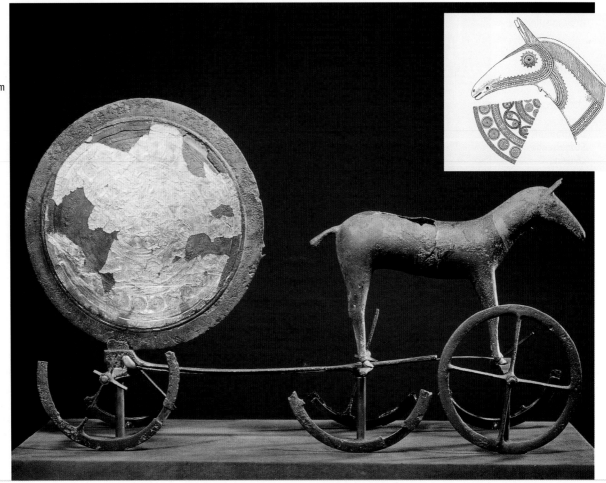

1-16

Horse and Sun Chariot from Trundholm Zealand Denmark c. 1800–1600 BCE Bronze Length 23¼" (59.2 cm) National Museum Copenhagen

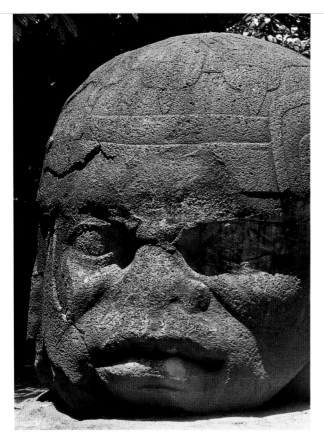

1-17 | **Colossal head (no. 4),** from La Venta, Mexico. Olmec culture, c. 900–500 BCE. Basalt, height 7'5" (2.26 m) La Venta Park, Villahermosa, Tabasco, Mexico

gleaming load, could have been rolled from place to place in a ritual reenactment of the sun's passage across the sky.

The *Horse and Sun Chariot* dates from between 1800 and 1600 BCE. The valuable materials from which the sculpture was made attest to its importance. The horse, cart, and disk were cast in bronze and delicately engraved with an abstract design of concentric rings, zigzags, circles, spirals, and loops. A thin sheet of beaten gold was then applied to the bronze disk and pressed into the **incised** patterns. The continuous and curvilinear patterns suggest the movement of the sun itself.

EARLY ART OUTSIDE EUROPE

Megalithic art was not limited to Europe. The Olmec peoples in the area that is now southern Mexico near the Gulf coast quarried and carved stone of a massive size. With basalt transported from the Tuxtla Mountains to an area near the Gulf coast, the La Venta Olmec carved heads that are up to 12 feet tall and 20 tons in weight (fig. 1-17). Dating from about 900 to 500 BCE, these heads represent men wearing close-fitting caps with chin straps, and large, round earplugs. Each face is different, suggesting that the heads may represent specific individuals. At present, most scholars consider them to be portraits of rulers. Obviously,

1-18 | **Ancestor figures (*moai*)** Ahu Nau Nau, Easter Island Polynesia c. 1000–1500 CE, restored 1978. Volcanic stone (tufa), average height approx. 36' (11 m)

the difficulty of transporting these boulders (it might have taken up to 200 people to drag the quarried stone) indicates strong motivation. They may have floated the raw basalt along the Gulf coast and navigable streams and rivers. Scholars do not know whether the driving force behind such arduous labor was religious in nature. As with Stonehenge, large groups of people united to accomplish a common goal.

Regardless of geographic location, megalithic sculpture offers some of the greatest art historical conundrums. For instance, many modern people have wondered about the towering stone figures known as *moai* that were erected on Easter Island (fig. 1-18), which lies in the Pacific Ocean. The figures' original meaning has been lost over the centuries, but they may have been island guardians or memorials to dead chiefs. Carved from a yellowish brown volcanic stone called tufa, they have coral and stone eyes and red tufa topknots. Not only do the figures stand some 36 feet tall; their topknots alone can measure up to 9 feet. The figures stand along the coast, facing toward the island's interior. The remains of nearly 1,000 *moai* have been found, including some unfinished examples discovered in quarries where they were being made. All probably date from around 1000 to 1500 CE. After that period, either warfare or neglect (perhaps resulting from political or religious change) caused many of the *moai* to be knocked down and destroyed.

It is so tempting to see history, and art history, as a series of cumulative developments: this perspective goes hand in hand with the notion that human beings have always strived toward ever-more perfect expressions of artistic and cultural values. Yet there is much evidence to the contrary—history does not unfold in neatly packaged categories—and nowhere is the notion of systematic human improvement shakier than when dealing with prehistoric periods and cultures.

Around the globe, many cultural transitions occurred at the same time in geographically unrelated and unconnected places. Conversely, some of the same changes have happened on very different timetables from place to place. Considering how little we know about early art and architecture, we must be prepared to revise our theories and change our ideas as new evidence comes to light.

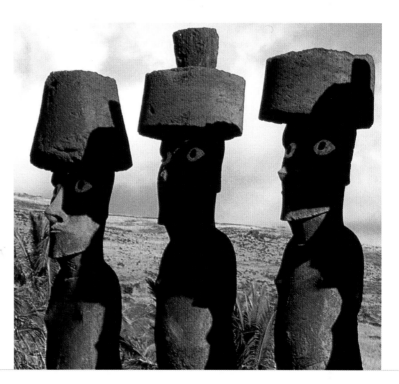

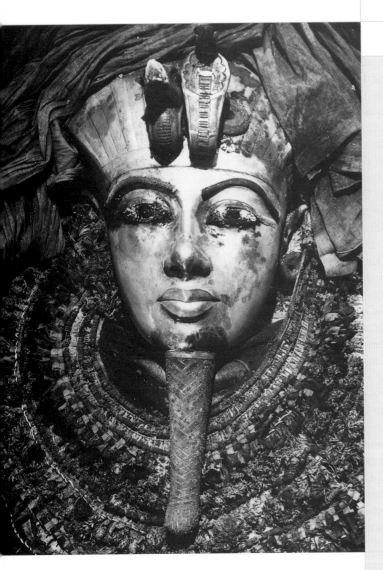

(*above*) **Funerary mask of Tutankhamun** (ruled 1336/35–1327 BCE), from the tomb of Tutankhamun, Valley of the Kings, Deir el-Bahri, Egypt Photographed the day it was discovered—October 28, 1925 (See pages 63–65.)

(*right*) **Funerary mask of Tutankhamun as it appears today** Gold inlaid with glass and semi-precious stones, height 21¼" (54.0 cm). Egyptian Museum, Cairo (See pages 63–65.)

taring serenely from his tomb, the young ruler Tutankhamun dazzles us with his royal splendor. Entombed in fine linen wrappings and decked with garlands of flowers, his head masked in gold, he looks ready to confront the gods of Egypt and to answer the questions set forth in the Book of the Dead. The British archaeologist Howard Carter's dramatic discovery of the king's tomb in 1922 established the "romance of archaeology" in the public mind. Now the more than 3,500 items from Tutankhamun's tomb are the centerpiece of the Egyptian National Museum in Cairo.

Why are we so mesmerized by the art of Egypt? The reason may lie in our fascination with ancient people's struggle to create an explanation for the transition between life and death and an eternal hereafter. Or it may be simply the elegant style and the exquisite craftsmanship of Egyptian art.

As fragile humans we observe nature's relentless cycle of birth, death, and rebirth, and we come to realize that for all our ingenuity we cannot escape death. Yet our imaginations recoil at the idea of our own extinction. Through the centuries people have lived with the hope or expectation of a life after death. Ancient Egyptians, from their narrow river valley, observed the constant regeneration of the land through yearly floods. They could easily believe such regeneration could be granted to human beings, or at least to their rulers, who became gods on earth. They thought of the afterlife as a continuation of the life they knew, so they made elaborate efforts to preserve their bodies forever. Through the arts, they equipped the dead magnificently for life in the hereafter. The Egyptians sought security for the body and spirit through all eternity, and their art served these beliefs and ideals.

The enchantment of Egyptian art is also aesthetic. Look into Tutankhamun's eyes. They are beautifully formed, simple shapes. Black discs set in white, they are energized by tiny touches of red at the corners, yet their dark outline lacks the natural detail of lashes. Capturing fleeting moments like the flutter of lashes in the blink of an eye is of no interest to a people concerned with timeless and eternal visions. Because of such concerns, Egyptian artists emphasized clarity of line and color, simplified forms, and the reduction of nature to elemental geometric shapes, thus establishing an unsurpassed standard of technical and aesthetic excellence.

The Art of Mesopotamia and Egypt

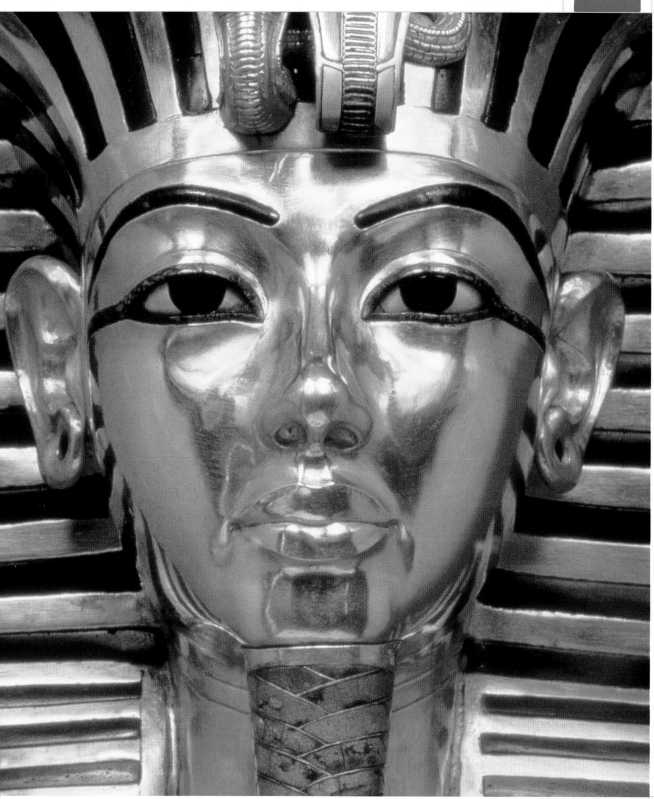

Earth's great river valleys nourished and united people: water and waterways made possible agriculture and a settled way of life. The Tigris and Euphrates Rivers in Mesopotamia (which means "between the rivers") and the Nile in Egypt—and, as we shall see, the Indus and the Yellow Rivers in Asia, the Danube in Europe, and the Mississippi in North America—were the most important waterways. The rivers also formed transportation corridors linking the farmers along the banks (see Map 1, pages 86–87).

More than 5,000 years ago, men and women in the ancient Near East and Egypt laid the foundations for western civilization. Political and religious hierarchies evolved as people banded together in community projects: digging irrigation and drainage ditches, planting and reaping crops, storing and distributing the harvest. The families and clans that had come together in communities eventually created cities, places known today by such fabled names as Jericho and Babylon, Memphis and Thebes. By about 3500 BCE, rulers, priests, and laborers—and eventually artists—lived and worked together in real cities in the service of the community and of gods and goddesses. The objects we now call art include weavings, ceramics, **monumental** sculpture, and statuettes. About 500 years later, another important breakthrough occurred in the ancient Near East. Around 3000 BCE, Sumerian artists became expert metalworkers. They created bronze, a hard, strong alloy of tin and copper. The Mesopotamian Bronze Age replaced the Stone Age a thousand years before this development occurred in northern Europe (see fig. 1-16).

In some ways, life in Mesopotamia and Egypt followed similar courses. People farmed in both the valleys of the Tigris and the Euphrates in Mesopotamia and along the Nile in Egypt. In both places, agriculture became the basis of wealth. Community leaders consolidated their power until kingship became the dominant form of government. Religion played a central role in government and daily life. People worshiped many gods and goddesses, each of whom had different powers and features. Rulers often identified closely with the gods, sometimes through symbolic marriage to a god or goddess. The responsibilities of rulers included ceremonial as well as political duties. The priests who honored and communicated with the gods joined the rulers to mediate between these deities and the people. Some individuals, freed from the necessity of daily work in the fields, became administrative assistants to these intermediaries, and eventually people settled into stratified social groups.

These complex, hierarchical societies could no longer depend on oral communication. People needed records, and this led to the development of writing—first, simple **pictographs** and then a complex standardized system of **hieroglyphic** or **cuneiform** signs. Today, these records, and the history and literature that were soon recorded, help us to interpret the visual arts that were produced at that time.

In other ways life and culture in Mesopotamia and Egypt differed. Mesopotamia's wealth and agricultural resources, as well as its few natural defenses, made its people vulnerable to repeated invasions and to internal conflicts between rival powers. Over the centuries, the balance of power in Mesopotamia shifted between north and south and between local powers and outside invaders. The rise and fall of cities like Babylon, Nineveh, and Ur have given Mesopotamia a varied and rich concentration of archaeological remains. Its art and architecture continued to be based on the earliest Sumerian traditions but changed subtly with each successive culture.

In contrast, mountains and deserts protected the Nile Valley. With only a few interruptions, Egypt remained a unified state for some 3,000 years. This cohesion made possible an unprecedented continuity in artistic and cultural development. Strikingly, Egypt's resources were directed toward the decoration and outfitting of tombs. Since the Egyptians imagined life after death as a continuation of earthly life, much of what we know about ancient Egypt today we owe to their funerary art.

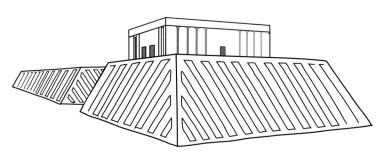

2-1 | **Reconstruction drawing** of the Anu Ziggurat and White Temple, Uruk (modern Warka, Iraq). c. 3100 BCE

Early Neolithic Communities

The world's first settled farming communities emerged in an area of the ancient Near East long referred to as the Fertile Crescent. Rising along the Mediterranean coast through modern Jordan, Israel, Lebanon, and Syria, the "crescent" arched into central Turkey and descended along the plains of Mesopotamia through Iraq and western Iran to the Persian Gulf. Agriculture first began in this region around 9000 BCE; farming villages formed nearly four thousand years later.

One of the earliest Near Eastern cities, Jericho, located in the West Bank territory, was home to about 2,000 people by around 7000 BCE. Its houses, made of mud brick (bricks shaped from clay and dried in the sun), covered 6 acres, an enormous size for that time. Ain Ghazal (Spring of Gazelles), located just outside present-day Amman, Jordan, was even larger. The settlement, dating from about 7200 to 5000 BCE, occupied 30 acres on a slope that was shaped into terraces stabilized by stone retaining walls. Its houses may have resembled the adobe pueblos that native peoples in the American Southwest began to build more than 7,000 years later (see fig. 15-21). The concentration of people and resources in cities such as Jericho and Ain Ghazal was an early step toward the formation of larger city-states that first arose in Mesopotamia and later became common in the ancient Near East.

Mesopotamia

The prosperous Mesopotamian cities and their surrounding territories developed around 3500 BCE into independently governed city-states. Eventually the most powerful city-states absorbed their neighbors to form larger kingdoms and empires.

One powerful cluster of cities in the southern region was known collectively as Sumer. The Sumerians have been credited with many "firsts": inventing the wagon wheel and the plow, casting objects in copper and bronze, and—perhaps the Sumerians' greatest contribution to later civilizations—inventing a system of writing known as cuneiform script between 3300 and 3000 BCE (see "Origins of Writing," right).

In architecture, the Sumerians' most imposing buildings were **ziggurats,** stepped pyramidal structures with a temple or shrine on top. Towering over the flat plains, ziggurats proclaimed the wealth, prestige, and stability of a city's rulers and glorified its gods. The peoples of the ancient Near East were polytheistic; they worshiped many gods and goddesses, attributing to them power over human activities and the forces of nature. Each city had one special protective deity for whom the people worked and from whom they received benefits. Religious specialists, eventually developing into a priest class, controlled rituals and sacred sites, ensuring that the gods were honored properly. Temple complexes—clusters of religious, administrative, and service buildings—stood in each city's center.

Two large temple complexes at Uruk (modern Warka, Iraq), mark the first independent Sumerian city-state. One complex was dedicated to Inanna, the goddess of fertility, the other probably to the sky god Anu. The Anu Ziggurat, built up in stages over the centuries, ultimately rose to a height of about 40 feet. Around 3100 BCE, the people of Uruk built a temple of whitewashed brick on its top. Modern archaeologists call it the White Temple (fig. 2-1).

Courtyards and interior walls in both the Inanna and the Anu compounds were decorated with **cone mosaics,** a decoration apparently invented at Uruk (fig. 2-2). Artisans pressed

2-2 | **Illustration of the technique of cone mosaic**

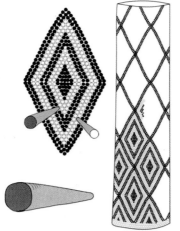

ORIGINS OF WRITING

The Sumerians developed the first known system of writing when they created records on clay tablets in the late third millennium BCE. The earliest preserved tablets, dating to around 3300 BCE, bear an accounting system for products traded at the city of Uruk. The symbols, which were drawn in the wet clay with a pointed tool, are simple pictures, or **pictographs**, that represent a thing or concept. The head of a bull, for example, means "bull." Between 2900 and 2400 BCE, the symbols evolved from pictures into phonograms—representations of the sounds of syllables in the Sumerian language—thus becoming a true writing system. During the same centuries, scribes (specialists in writing and maintaining records) developed a writing instrument called a **stylus**, shaped like a triangular wedge. Mesopotamian writing is termed **cuneiform** (from the Latin "wedge-shaped") after the shape of the marks made by the stylus.

Ancient Egypt developed three types of writing. The earliest system employed symbols called **hieroglyphs**. Like cuneiform, these were either pictographs or phonograms. Later, scribes evolved **hieratic** writing, a shorthand version of hieroglyphs. The simplified forms, used for record keeping, correspondence, and manuscripts of all sorts, could be written quickly in script on scrolls made of papyrus (a plant that grew along the Nile). The third type of Egyptian writing came into use only in the eighth century BCE, as written communication ceased to be restricted exclusively to priests and scribes. It was less formal and was easier to master, and the Greeks referred to it as demotic writing (from *demos*, "the people").

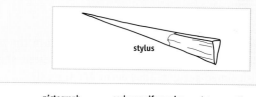

stylus

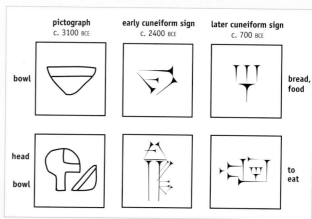

	pictograph c. 3100 BCE	early cuneiform sign c. 2400 BCE	later cuneiform sign c. 700 BCE	
bowl				bread, food
head bowl				to eat

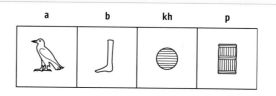

a	b	kh	p

Four hieroglyphs with the sounds they represent. Used in combinations, such phonogramic hieroglyphs were especially useful in rendering foreign names.

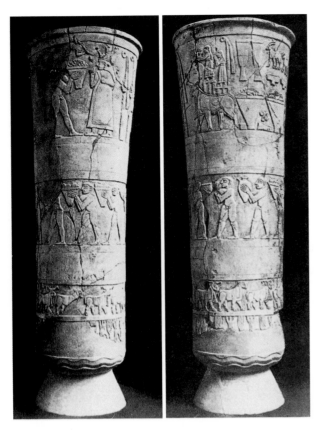

2-3 | **Carved vase** (two views), from Uruk (modern Warka Iraq). c. 3500–3000 BCE. Alabaster, height 36" (91 cm). Iraq Museum, Baghdad

stands in front of her shrine, indicated by two reed door-poles. Through the doorway her wealth is displayed, and behind the priest come others bearing offerings. Plants and animals in horizontal bands decorate the base of the vase. Medical historians have identified the plants as the pomegranate and the now-extinct silphium, plants used by early people as fertility symbols and to control fertility. The scene is usually interpreted as the ritual marriage between the goddess and a human to ensure the fertility of crops, animals, and people, and thus the continued survival of Uruk.

The ziggurat reached its final form (about a thousand years after the completion of the White Temple) in Ur, a city on the Euphrates south of Uruk. The people of Ur built a mud-brick ziggurat dedicated to the moon god Nanna, also called Sin (fig. 2-4). Here three staircases converge at an imposing entrance gate atop the first platform. Each platform is angled outward from top to base, probably to prevent rainwater from forming puddles and eroding the pavement. The first two levels of the Nanna Ziggurat and their retaining walls were reconstructed in recent times, but little remains of the upper level and the temple. Such temples were known as "the offering table of heaven" and "the waiting room of the gods," but we know nothing of the rituals performed in them.

Sculpture during this period was associated with religion, and large statues were commonly placed in temples as objects of devotion. In addition, individual worshipers set up votive figures—small statues that they sometimes identified as portraits of themselves. Apparently, anyone who could afford to might commission a **votive** figure and place it in the god's shrine. A simple inscription might identify the figure as "one who offers prayers." Larger inscriptions might recount all the things accomplished in the god's honor.

Marble votive statues dating from about 2900 to 2600 BCE (fig. 2-5) were found in the ruins of a temple at Eshnunna (modern Tell Asmar, Iraq). The carvers, following the conventions of Sumerian art—that is, traditional ways of representing forms—simplified the faces, bodies, and dress to emphasize the cylindrical shapes of the figures. The men in this group wear

thousands of baked clay cones like thumbtacks into the wet plaster walls so that the flat colored "heads" created shimmering, multicolored designs. They decorated the exterior surfaces of ziggurats with paint and patterns of plain or colored bricks.

Inanna had her devotees in Uruk. A tall vase of carved alabaster (a fine, white stone), found near her temple, shows her accepting an offering from a naked priest (fig. 2-3). Inanna

2-4 | **Nanna Ziggurat,** Ur (modern Muqaiyir, Iraq). c. 2100–2050 BCE

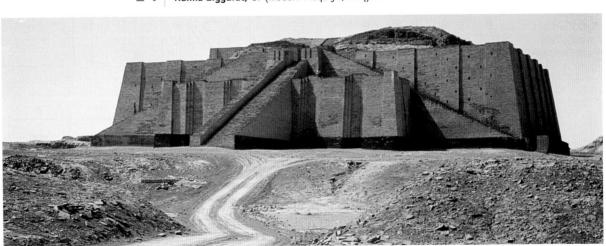

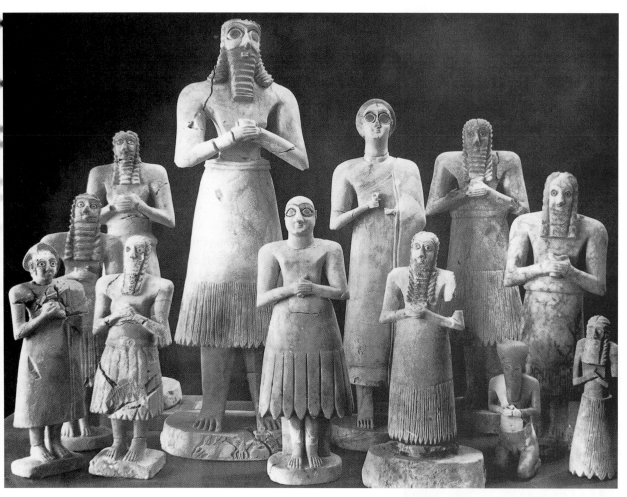

Votive statues from the Square Temple Eshnunna (modern Tell Asmar, Iraq) c. 2900–2600 BCE. Limestone alabaster, and gypsum, height of largest figure approx. 30" (76.3 cm) The Oriental Institute of the University of Chicago; Iraq Museum Baghdad

sheepskin kilts, while the tall female figure to the right of center wears a dress wrapped diagonally to expose one breast. Some of the figures hold small vessels, probably similar to those that human visitors used during ritual activities. The statues' wide, staring eyes indicate communication between the votive figures and the god of the temple. The figures stand at respectful attention for all eternity.

The artists of Ur became accomplished in many arts—music, storytelling (which later became literature), work in precious materials, as well as stone sculpture and architecture. They used great skill to make a superb lyre (c. 2680 BCE), a kind of harp (fig. 2-6), one of two found in the tomb of Queen Pu-abi of Ur. Archaeologists have restored the lost wooden parts of the lyre and reassembled the surviving pieces. On one end of the sound box, surmounting the inlaid shell images of animals (fig. 2-7; see page 48), sits the head of a magnificent bearded bull created out of gold and the semiprecious gemstone lapis lazuli.

2-6

Bull lyre, from the tomb of Queen Pu-abi, Ur (modern Muqaiyar, Iraq). c. 2680 BCE. (Detail shown in Figure 2-7. See page 48.) Wood with gold, lapis lazuli, and shell, reassembled in modern wood support.

University Museum, University of Pennsylvania, Philadelphia (T4-29)

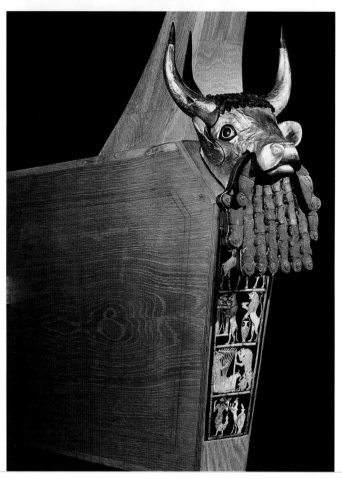

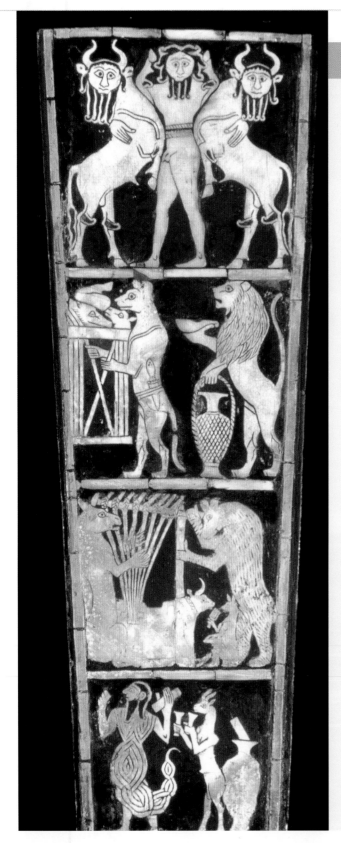

As in the animal fables of the legendary Greek author Aesop, the animals in the panels that decorate a very early (c. 2680 BCE) harp from Sumer (fig. 2-7) personify humans: a donkey, assisted by a bear, plays the harp, accompanied by a fox with a rattle; a lion and a wolf, imitating the upright posture of humans, march in stately procession carrying offerings. The top and bottom registers—bands—are particularly intriguing, because they seem to illustrate scenes that are found in the *Epic of Gilgamesh*, a 3,000-line epic poem that is Sumer's great contribution to world literature. What is especially interesting is that the poem was first written down nearly 700 years after the harp was decorated, suggesting a very long oral tradition.

The *Epic of Gilgamesh* probes the question of mortality, or immortality. Its hero undertakes a voyage to the netherworld, the Land of No Return, and declares it a bad place. In the depths of the ocean, Gilgamesh encounters scorpion-men, like the one pictured in the lowest register of figure 2-7. Gilgamesh's story also expresses the heroic aim to understand surroundings that were hostile and a longing to find meaning in human existence. The almost-human, bearded figure in the top register masterfully controls two rearing human-headed bulls—a recurring theme in art of the ancient Near East. So vivid were the imagined hybrid ancestors' strange adventures with fabulous friends and adversaries that early Mesopotamians actually thought they might have to confront these composite creatures during their lifetimes. (Other early civilizations also had human-animal composite power figures: sphinxes in Egypt; human-headed bulls and lions in Akkadia, Babylonia, and Assyria; and cat-faced humans in Japan, to name three.) About 3300 BCE, Sumerians invented markings to keep records, to make lists, and eventually to write stories. We can study the **iconography**, or imagery, of Sumerian works of art with some confidence, for beginning with inscribed clay tablets and decorated seals from Sumer we are no longer dealing with the speculations of prehistory.

2-7 | **Mythological figures,** detail of the sound box of the bull lyre from the tomb of Queen Pu-abi, Ur (modern Muqaiyir, Iraq) c. 2680 BCE. Wood with shell inlay, 12¼ x 4½" (31.1 x 11 cm) University Museum, University of Pennsylvania, Philadelphia

Sumerian temple staff and merchants not only invented cuneiform writing, they developed flat stamps and more elaborate cylinder-form seals for securing and identifying documents and signaling property ownership. **Cylinder seals**, usually less than 2 inches high, were made of hard and sometimes semiprecious stones with designs **incised** (cut) into the surface.

Rolled across a damp clay surface, the seal leaves a mirror image of its design that cannot be easily altered once dry. The seals were used for signing documents or marking container lids or storage-room doorways. One fine example shows an "animal combat" theme (fig. 2-8). The scene in figure 2-8 includes rearing lions fighting with a human-headed bull and a stag on the left,

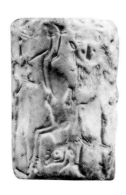
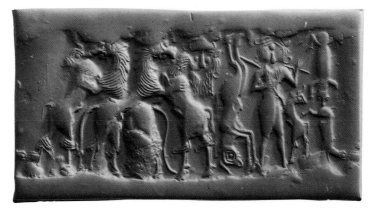

2-8 | **Cylinder seal** from Sumer and its impression. c. 2500 BCE. Marble, height approx. 1³/₄" (4.5 cm)
The Metropolitan Museum of Art, New York
Gift of Walter Hauser, 1955 (55.65.4)

The distinctive design on the stone cylinder seal on the left belonged to its owner, like a coat of arms in the European Middle Ages or a modern cattle-rancher's brand. When rolled across soft clay applied to the closure to be sealed—a jar lid, the knot securing a bundle, or the door to a room—the cylinder left a raised image, or band of repeated raised images, of the design. Sealing discouraged unauthorized people from secretly gaining access to goods or information.

and a hunter on the right—perhaps a spoils-of-the-hunt depiction or an example of the Near Eastern practice of showing leaders protecting their people.

Such animal and human combats remind us that kings were expected to protect their people from both human and animal enemies. They also intervened with the gods to exert control over the natural world. The Akkadians, warring invaders who settled the area north of Uruk near modern Baghdad, are an example of such a hostile group. Unlike the Sumerians, the Akkadians spoke a Semitic language (a language in the same family as Arabic and Hebrew). Under the powerful military and political figure Sargon I (ruled c. 2332–2279 BCE), they conquered the Sumerian cities and brought most of Mesopotamia under their control. Sargon I even elevated himself to the status of a god, setting a precedent followed by later Akkadian rulers. Soon after, the Akkadians adopted Sumerian culture.

The *Stela of Naramsin,* from about 2254–2218 BCE (fig. 2-9), commemorates a military victory of Naramsin, Sargon's grandson and successor. The king, wearing the horned crown associated with deities, stands above his soldiers and fallen foes near the top of the stone. The shape of the **stela** (upright stone slab) is used as a dynamic part of the composition. Its pointed shape accommodates the carved mountain within it. Naramsin is also larger than the other figures. In the art of many peoples, greater size is an indication of greater relative importance. Art historians call this convention **hieratic scale**.

The Akkadian empire fell around 2180 BCE to the Guti, a mountain people from the northeast. For a brief time the Guti controlled most of the Mesopotamian plain, except for the city-state of Lagash, which remained independent under its ruler, Gudea. The tradition of votive statues continued in the art of Lagash, about 2100 BCE. Gudea presented votive statues of himself, made of a hard, durable stone called diorite, to many temples he built or restored. The cuneiform inscription on the statue shown here

2-9 | *Stela of Naramsin.* c. 2254–2218 BCE. Limestone, height 6'6" (1.98 m). Musée du Louvre, Paris

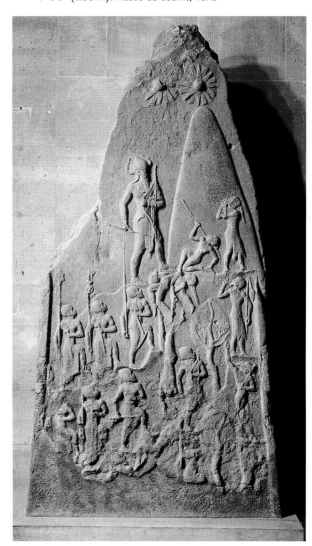

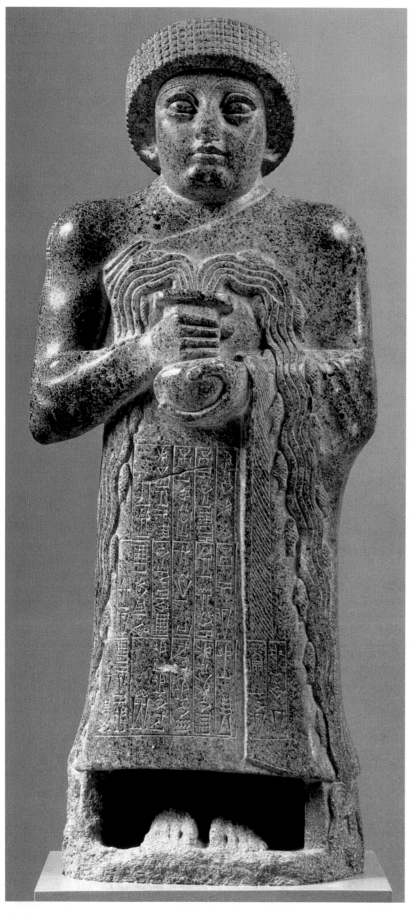

2-10 | **Votive statue of Gudea,** from Lagash (modern Telloh, Iraq). c. 2120 BCE Diorite, height 29" (73.7 cm). Musée du Louvre, Paris

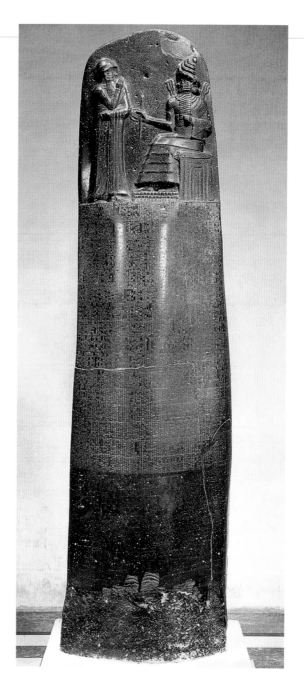

2-11 | **Stela of Hammurabi,** from Susa (modern Shush, Iran). c. 1792–1750 BCE. Basalt, height of stela approx. 7' (2.13 m), height of relief 28" (71.1 cm). Musée du Louvre, Paris

In the introductory section of the stela's long cuneiform inscription, Hammurabi declared that with this code of law he intended "to cause justice to prevail in the land and to destroy the wicked and the evil, that the strong might not oppress the weak nor the weak the strong." Most of the 300 or so entries that follow deal with commercial and property matters. Only sixty-eight relate to domestic problems, and a mere twenty deal with physical assault. Punishments depended on the gender and social standing of the offender.

(fig. 2-10) relates that Gudea dedicated himself, the sculpture, and the temple in which the sculpture resided to the goddess Geshtinanna, the divine poet and interpreter of dreams. Gudea is shown clothed in a long garment similar to that worn by the female votive figure from Eshnunna (see fig. 2-5). He holds a vessel from which life-giving water flows in two streams filled with leaping fish.

The land between the rivers remained a much fought-over prize. Periods of political turmoil and stable government alternated until the Amorites, a Semitic-speaking people from the Arabian Desert to the west, moved into the area and reunited Sumer under Hammurabi (ruled 1792–1750 BCE). Their capital city was Babylon, and its residents were called Babylonians.

Among Hammurabi's achievements was a written legal code that recorded the laws of his realm and the penalties for breaking them. The code is incised in cuneiform script on a stela, under a portrait of the ruler depicted standing before the supreme judge, the sun god Shamash (fig. 2-11). As in the *Stela of Naramsin,* the relative importance of the figures is indicated by hieratic scale. Hammurabi, the earthly law enforcer, is smaller than Shamash, who wears a four-horned headdress that marks him as a deity. Rays of light rise from the god's shoulders as he holds a rod and ring, Babylonian symbols of justice and power.

Around 1400 BCE, a people called the Assyrians rose to dominance in northern Mesopotamia. Known for their military prowess, they controlled most of Mesopotamia by the end of the ninth century BCE. By the early seventh century BCE, they had extended their influence as far west as Egypt. Strongly influenced by Sumerian culture, the Assyrians adopted the ziggurat form and preserved Sumerian texts. The most complete surviving version of the *Epic of Gilgamesh,* the best-known literary work of ancient Sumer, was found in the library of the powerful Assyrian king Assurbanipal (ruled 669–c. 627 BCE).

The Assyrians built fortified cities and vast palaces decorated with wall paintings and stone reliefs. The capital at Dur Sharrukin (modern Khorsabad, Iraq), built by Sargon II (ruled 721–705 BCE), featured a walled citadel, or fortress, containing 200 rooms, 30 courtyards, and an immense ziggurat. Inside the citadel, a palace complex was raised on a fortified platform about 52 feet high. Deep inside it, the king's throne room was protected by a stone gate carved with colossal guardian figures, such as the human-headed lion illustrated here (fig. 2-12). These hybrid creatures, ranging from 13 to 16 feet tall, also flanked the gates of the citadel.

Assurbanipal, king of the Assyrians three generations after Sargon II, had his own capital at Nineveh (modern Kuyunjik,

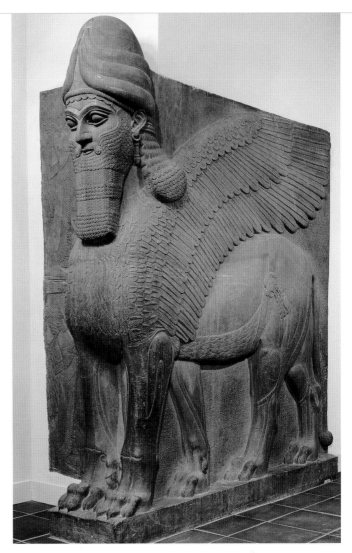

2-12   *Human-Headed Winged Lion (Lamassu),* from the palace of Assurnasirpal II, Nimrud. 883–859 BCE. Limestone, height 10'2" (3.11 m). The Metropolitan Museum of Art, New York
Gift of John D. Rockefeller, Jr., 1932 (32.143.2)

Iraq). His palace was decorated with panels of alabaster, carved with a pictorial narrative in low relief. One panel shows the king and queen in a pleasure garden (fig. 2-13). The ruler, reclining on a couch, and his queen, seated, are surrounded by servants bringing trays of food and whisking away flies. The king has taken off his rich necklace and hung it on his couch, and he has

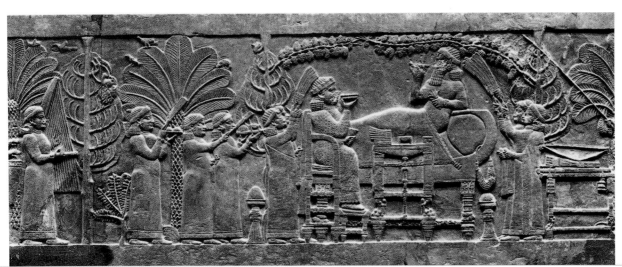

2-13

Assurbanipal and His Queen in the Garden from the palace at Nineveh (modern Kuyunjik, Iraq) c. 647 BCE Alabaster Height approx. 21" (53.3 cm) The British Museum London

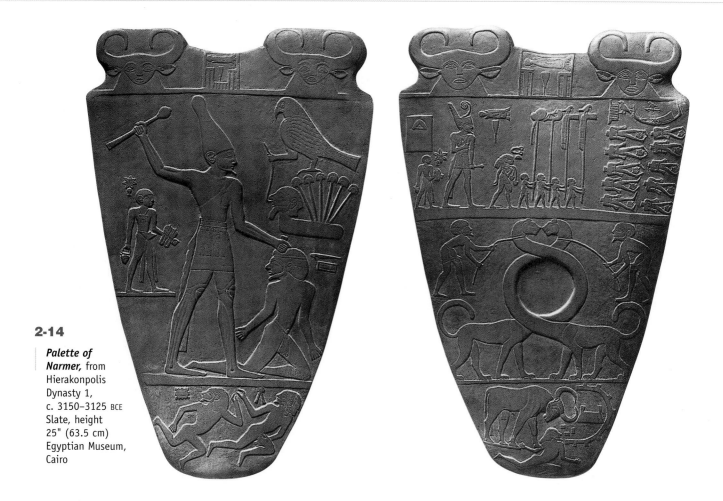

2-14

Palette of Narmer, from Hierakonpolis
Dynasty 1,
c. 3150–3125 BCE
Slate, height
25" (63.5 cm)
Egyptian Museum,
Cairo

laid aside his weapons, seen on the table behind him. This tranquil domestic scene is actually a victory celebration. A grisly trophy, the upside-down severed head of his vanquished enemy, hangs from a tree at the far left.

Assurbanipal's conquests, which stretched as far as Egypt, were short-lived. Soon after his reign, the Assyrians succumbed to internal weakness and external enemies, and by 600 BCE their empire had collapsed. Before another century passed, Mesopotamia was absorbed by the Persian Empire under Cyrus II, called the Great (ruled 559–530 BCE). Under Persian rule, Mesopotamia became part of an empire that eventually stretched from India to Egypt.

Egypt

While city-states such as Sumer began to develop in Mesopotamia, a rich civilization arose in Egypt in the fertile valley and delta of the Nile. The Predynastic period, which lasted roughly from 4500 to 3300 BCE, was a time of social and political transformation when Egypt was unified under a succession of powerful families or dynasties.

An Egyptian priest and historian named Manetho drew up a list of rulers in the third century BCE. He based his work on temple records and inscriptions written in hieroglyphs or hieratic writing (see "Origins of Writing," page 45). Manetho grouped the kings into thirty dynasties that ruled the country between its unification around 3150 BCE and its conquest by Alexander the Great of Macedonia in 332 BCE. Egyptologists have since grouped

these dynasties into larger time spans reflecting broad historical developments. The Early Dynastic period (c. 3150–2700 BCE, Dynasties 1–2) was followed by three major periods: the Old Kingdom (c. 2700–2190 BCE, Dynasties 3–6), the Middle Kingdom (c. 2040–1674 BCE, Dynasties 11–14), and the New Kingdom (c. 1552–1069 BCE, Dynasties 18–20). These phases alternated with politically turbulent intermediate periods. After the conquest of Egypt by Alexander the Great, and Macedonian rule (332–305 BCE), Greek Ptolemaic rulers (fifteen rulers in succession were named Ptolemy) reigned until the country became part of the Roman Empire in 31 BCE. The line ended with the famous queen, Cleopatra.

EARLY DYNASTIC AND OLD KINGDOM EGYPT

With the start of the Early Dynastic period, Egypt became a consolidated state along the banks of the Nile River. According to Egyptian tradition, the country had previously evolved into two kingdoms, Upper Egypt in the south and Lower Egypt in the north. (Upper and Lower Egypt refer to the flow of the Nile, not their position on modern maps.) An Upper Egyptian ruler, referred to in an ancient document as "Menes king–Menes god," finally conquered Lower Egypt and merged the lands into a single kingdom.

This legendary king-god Menes may have been an actual king named Narmer (Dynasty 1, ruled c. 3150–3125 BCE), known from a famous stone plaque, the *Palette of Narmer* (fig. 2-14), found in the temple of Horus at Hierakonpolis. **Palettes,** flat

THE FIBER ARTS

Fragments of fired clay impressed with cloth have been dated to 25,000 bce, showing that fiber arts, including various weaving and knotting techniques, vie with ceramics as the earliest evidence of human creative and technical skill. Since prehistoric times, weaving appears to have been women's work—probably because women, with primary responsibility for child care, could spin and weave in the home no matter how frequently they were interrupted by the needs of their families. Men, as shepherds and farmers, produced the raw materials for spinning and, as merchants, distributed the fabrics not needed by the family. Early Assyrian cuneiform tablets preserve the correspondence between merchants traveling by caravan and their wives, who were running the production end of the business back home and complaining about late payments and changed orders. It is no coincidence that the woman shown spinning in the fragment from Susa is important-looking and adorned with many ornaments. She sits barefoot and cross-legged on a lion-footed stool covered with sheep-skin, spinning thread with a large spindle. A fish lies on an offering stand in front of her, together with six round objects (perhaps fruit). A young servant stands behind the woman as she works, fanning her.

The production of textiles is complex. First thread must be produced. Fibers gathered from plants (such as flax for linen cloth or hemp for rope) or from animals (wool from sheep, goats, and camels or hair from humans and horses) are cleaned, combed, and sorted. Only then can they be twisted and drawn out under tension—that is, spun—into the long, strong, flexible fibers needed for textiles or cords. Spinning tools include a long, sticklike spindle to gather the spun fibers, a whorl (weight) to help rotate the spindle, and a distaff (a word still used to describe women and their work) to hold the raw materials. Because textiles are fragile and rapidly decompose, the indestructible stone- or clay-fired spindle whorls are usually the only surviving evidence of thread making.

Weaving begins on a loom. Warp threads are laid out at right angles to weft threads, which are passed over and under the warp. In the earliest, vertical looms, warp threads were hung from a beam, their tension created either by wrapping them around a lower beam (a tapestry loom) or by tying them to heavy stones (a warp-weighted loom, such as what the woman from Susa would have used). Although weaving was usually a home industry, in palaces and temples slave women staffed large shops, specializing as spinners, warpers, weavers, and finishers.

The fiber arts also include various nonweaving techniques—cording for ropes and strings; netting for traps, fish nets, and hair nets; knotting for macramé and carpets; sprang (a looping technique like cat's cradle); and single-hook work or crocheting (knitting with two needles came relatively late).

Early fiber artists depended on the natural color of their materials and on natural dyes from the earth (ochers) and from plants (madder for red, the herb woad, or indigo, for blue, and safflower and saffron crocus for yellow). Egyptians seem to have preferred white linen for their garments, elaborately folded and pleated. Minoans created multicolored patterned fabrics with fancy edgings. Greeks perfected pictorial tapestries. The people of the ancient Near East used woven and dyed patterns and developed knotted pile (the so-called Persian carpet) and felt (a cloth of fibers bound by heat and pressure, not spinning, weaving, or knitting).

Woman Spinning, from Susa (modern Shush, Iran). c. 8th–7th century BCE. Bitumen compound, 3⅝ x 5⅛" (9.2 x 13 cm) Musée du Louvre, Paris

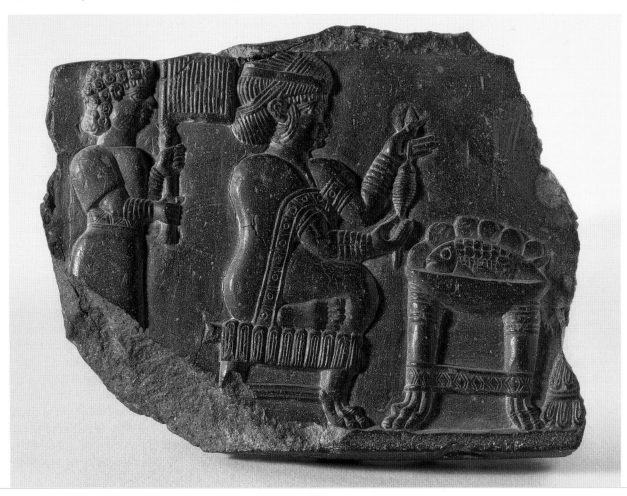

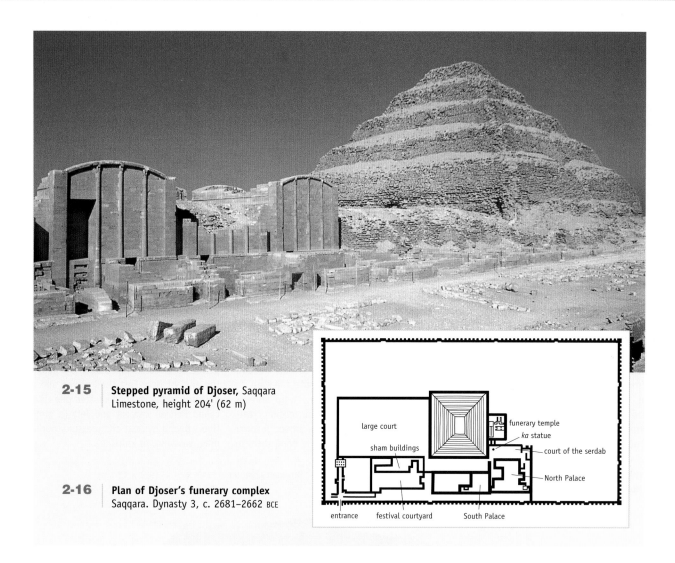

2-15 | **Stepped pyramid of Djoser,** Saqqara
Limestone, height 204' (62 m)

2-16 | **Plan of Djoser's funerary complex**
Saqqara. Dynasty 3, c. 2681–2662 BCE

large court

sham buildings

funerary temple
ka statue
court of the serdab

North Palace

entrance   festival courtyard   South Palace

stones with a circular depression on one side, were used to grind paint that was applied around the eye to reduce the glare of the sun. The *Palette of Narmer* has the same form as these common objects but is much larger and may have been a votive offering.

King Narmer dominates the scene on the palette, and his name appears at the top in pictographs, or picture writing: a horizontal fish (*nar*) above a vertical chisel (*mer*). Following the convention of hieratic scale, he is shown larger than the other human figures on the palette to indicate his importance. On one side of the palette (fig. 2-14, left; see page 52), Narmer, wearing the White Crown of Upper Egypt (see "Egyptian Symbols," page 57), holds the hair of a captive who may be the conquered ruler of Lower Egypt. On the other side of the palette (fig. 2-14, right; see page 52), Narmer is shown at the top left wearing the Red Crown of Lower Egypt, making it clear that he rules both lands now. The decapitated bodies of Lower Egyptian warriors have been placed in two neat rows, their heads between their feet.

Many of the figures on the palette are shown in poses that would be impossible to assume in real life. Heads are shown in profile, to best capture the subject's identifying features, while eyes, most expressive when seen from the front, are rendered in frontal view. The shoulders are represented frontally, but the hips, legs, and feet are drawn in profile. These conventions of Egyptian painting and relief sculpture were followed especially in the depiction of royalty and other dignitaries, while persons of lesser social rank tended to be represented slightly more **naturalistically** (compare the figure of Narmer with those of his standard-bearers in figure 2-14, right; see page 52).

Central to ancient Egyptian belief was the idea that every human being had a life force—the *ka*, or spirit. The *ka* lived on after the death of the body, forever engaged in the activities it had enjoyed during its earthly existence. The *ka* needed a body to live in, however, such as a carved likeness of the deceased and/or his or her actual corpse, preserved by mummification (see "Mummies," right).

The need to fulfill the requirements of the *ka* led not only to the creation of *ka* statues, but also to the development of elaborate funerary rites and tombs filled with supplies and furnishings that the *ka* might require throughout eternity. In the Early Dynastic period, the most common type of tomb structure in Egypt was the **mastaba**, a flat-topped, one-story building with slanted walls erected above an underground burial chamber. The kings of Dynasties 3 and 4, the first dynasties of the Old Kingdom, devoted huge sums to the construction of extensive funerary complexes. These structures tended to be grouped together

MUMMIES

No actual ancient recipes for preserving the dead have been found, but the basic process can be gleaned from several sources, including images found in tombs, the descriptions of later Greek writers, scientific analysis of mummies, and modern experiments. The process was roughly as follows.

The dead body was taken to a mortuary, a special structure used exclusively for embalming. Under the supervision of a priest, workers removed the brain, generally through the nose, and emptied the body cavity through an incision in the left side. They then placed the body, together with its major internal organs, in a vat of natron, a naturally occurring salt. It was left to steep in this solution for a period of a month or more. This caused the skin to blacken, so once the workers had retrieved a body from the vat and carefully dried it, they often dyed it to restore something of its color, using red ocher for a man, yellow ocher for a woman. They then packed the body cavity with clean linen, provided by the family of the deceased and soaked in various herbs and ointments. They wrapped the major organs in separate packets, either putting them in special containers to be placed in the tomb chamber or stuffing them back into the body.

The tedious ritual of wrapping the body could now begin. They first wound the trunk and each of the limbs separately with cloth strips, then wrapped the whole body in a shroud. They then wound it in additional strips of cloth, layer after layer, to produce the familiar mummy shape. The linen winders often inserted good luck charms and other small objects among the wrappings. If the family happened to have furnished a Book of the Dead, a selection of magic spells meant to help the deceased survive a "last judgment" and win everlasting life, it was tucked in between the mummy's legs.

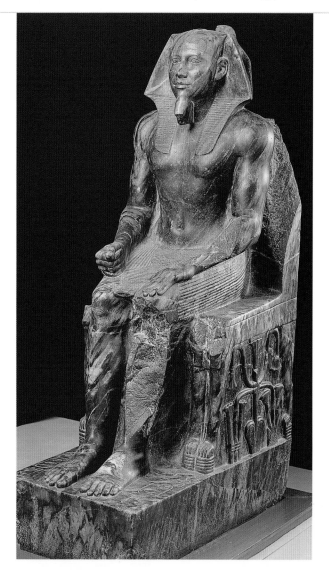

2-17 | *Khafre*, from Giza. Dynasty 4, c. 2570–2544 BCE. Diorite Height 5'6⅛" (1.68 m). Egyptian Museum, Cairo

in a **necropolis**—literally, a city of the dead—at the edge of the desert on the west bank of the Nile. The land of the dead was believed to be situated in the direction of the setting sun. Two of the most extensive of these early necropolises are those at Saqqara and Giza, near modern Cairo.

For his tomb complex at Saqqara, King Djoser (Dynasty 3, ruled c. 2681–2662 BCE) commissioned the earliest truly monumental architecture in Egypt. The designer of the complex, a man called Imhotep, laid out Djoser's tomb as a stepped pyramid consisting of six mastabalike elements placed on top of each other, and originally covered with a limestone facing, or **veneer** (fig. 2-15). Although the final structure superficially resembles the ziggurats of Mesopotamia, it differs in both concept and purpose. It is built of finely cut stone, not mud brick; it rises in stages and does not have ramps; and it protects a tomb. From its top, a 92-foot shaft descended to a granite-lined burial vault. Adjacent to the stepped pyramid, a funerary temple was used for continuing worship of the dead king, and sham buildings—simple masonry shells filled with debris—represented chapels, palaces with courtyards, and other structures (fig. 2-16). Designed as a miniature replica of the king's earthly realm, these buildings were intended for the use of his *ka* in the hereafter.

In three-dimensional sculpture, artists were capable of carving lifelike figures. Nevertheless a rigidly frontal, simple conception continued to control the sculpted forms. Egyptian sculpture is rectilinear and blocklike, in contrast to the cylindrical forms of early Mesopotamian sculpture. An over-lifesize statue of the Old Kingdom, the Dynasty 4 King Khafre (ruled c. 2570–2544 BCE), represents the ruler enthroned and protected by the falcon-god Horus (fig. 2-17). Horus merges with the king's headdress as he protectively enfolds the king's head at the back with his wings.

In this statue from his valley temple, Khafre wears the traditional royal costume: a short kilt, a false beard symbolic of kingship, and a linen headdress with an *uraeus*, the cobra symbol of the sun god Ra. The symbols of united Egypt, the lotus and papyrus, decorate the throne. Like the votive statue of Gudea of Lagash (see fig. 2-10), this statue was carved in hard graywacke, ensuring that the figure would last for eternity.

A double portrait of Khafre's son and daughter-in-law, King Menkaure (ruled c. 2533–2515 BCE) and Queen Khamerernebty

Elements of Architecture

MASTABA TO PYRAMID

As the gateway to the afterlife for Egyptian kings and members of the royal court, the Egyptian burial structure began as a low rectangular **mastaba** with an internal room and chapel. Later, mastaba forms of decreasing size were stacked over an underground burial chamber to form the stepped pyramid. The culmination of the Egyptian burial chamber is the pyramid—not below ground—with false chambers, false doors, and confusing passageways to foil potential tomb robbers.

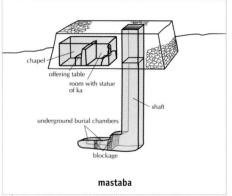

mastaba

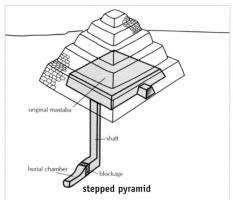

stepped pyramid

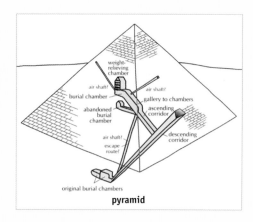

pyramid

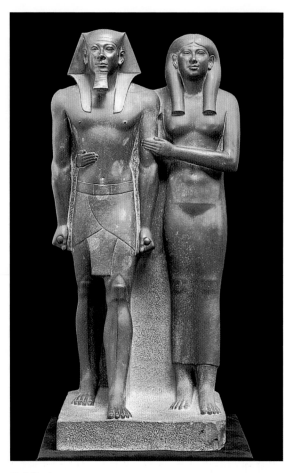

2-18 | ***Menkaure and His Wife, Queen Khamerernebty*** from Giza. Dynasty 4, c. 2515 BCE. Graywacke with traces of red and black paint, height 54½" (142.3 cm). Museum of Fine Arts, Boston

Harvard University–MFA Expedition

(fig. 2-18), was discovered in the funerary temple built by Menkaure. The figures, carved from a single block of stone, are visually joined by the queen's symbolic gesture of embrace. The king, depicted in accordance with cultural ideals as an athletic, youthful figure nude to the waist, stands in a typically Egyptian balanced pose with one foot in front of the other, his arms straight at his sides and his fists clenched. His equally youthful queen mimics his striding pose with a smaller step forward, her sheer, tight-fitting garment revealing the curves of her body.

The architectural form most closely identified with Egypt is the true pyramid with a square base and four sloping triangular sides (see "Mastaba to Pyramid," above). Egypt's most famous funerary structures are the three Great Pyramids at Giza (fig. 2-19; see also fig. 1), part of tomb complexes built by the Dynasty 4 kings Khufu (ruled c. 2601–2578 BCE), Khafre (ruled c. 2570–2544 BCE), and Menkaure (ruled c. 2533–2515 BCE). The oldest and largest of the Giza pyramids is that of Khufu, which covers 13 acres at its base and rises to a height of about 450 feet even in its deteriorated state. It was originally finished with a sheath of polished limestone that lifted its apex some 30 feet above the present summit, to roughly the height of a modern-day, 48-story skyscraper.

Next to each of the pyramids was a funerary temple connected by a causeway, or elevated road, to a valley temple on the bank of the Nile (fig. 2-20). When a king died, his body was ferried across the Nile from the royal palace to his valley temple, where it was received with elaborate ceremony. It was then carried up the causeway to his funerary temple and placed in its chapel, where further rites took place. Finally, the body was entombed in a well-hidden vault inside the pyramid.

Tombs of royalty and wealthy individuals were often decorated on the interior with paintings and reliefs. These images frequently show the dead person going about the duties and pleasures of earthly life. The paintings might also have symbolic

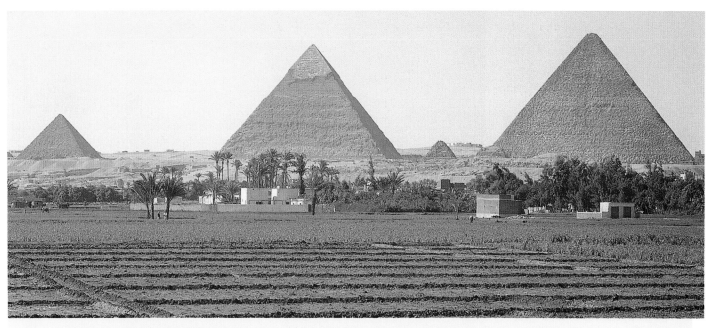

2-19 | **Great Pyramids,** Giza. Dynasty 4, c. 2601–2515 BCE. Erected by (from left) Menkaure, Khafre, and Khufu
Granite and limestone, height of pyramid of Khufu 450' (137 m)

The designers of the pyramids tried to ensure that the king and the tomb "home" would never be disturbed.
Khufu's builders placed his tomb chamber in the very heart of the mountain of masonry, at the end of a long,
narrow, steeply rising passageway, sealed off after the king's burial by a 50-ton stone block. Three false
passageways, either deliberately meant to mislead or the result of changes in plan as construction progressed,
obscured the location of the tomb. Despite such precautions, early looters managed to penetrate to the tomb
chamber and make off with Khufu's funeral treasure.

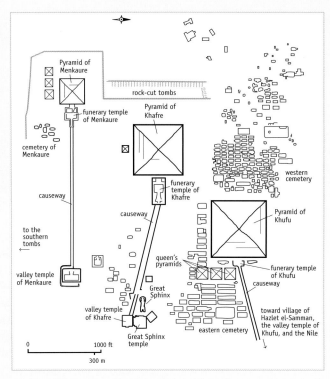

2-20 | **Plan of the funerary complex,** Giza

EGYPTIAN SYMBOLS

Crowned figures, symbolizing kingship, are everywhere in
Egyptian art. The false beard of a dead king is long, braid-
ed, and ends in a knob. A living king is portrayed with a
shorter, squared-off beard (see fig. 2-17). The cobra, "she
who rears up," was equated with the sun, the king, and
some deities.

The god Horus, king of the earth and a force for good, is
represented most characteristically as a falcon. Horus's eyes
(*wedjat*) were regarded as symbolic of the sun and moon. The
wedjat here is the solar eye. The *ankh* is symbolic of everlasting life. The scarab (beetle) was associated with the
creator god Atum and the rising sun.

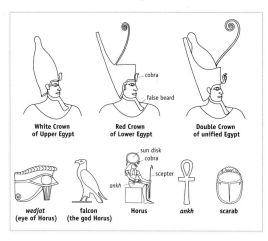

2-21 | ***Ti Watching a Hippopotamus Hunt.*** Tomb of Ti, Saqqara Dynasty 5, c. 2510–2460 BCE Painted limestone relief, height approx. 45" (114.3 cm)

This relief forms part of the decoration of a mastaba tomb discovered by the French archaeologist Auguste Mariette in 1865. Among Mariette's many other famous finds was the statue of Khafre (see fig. 2-17). A pioneer Egyptologist, Mariette was a man of great heart, intellect, and diverse talents. It was he who provided the composer Giuseppe Verdi with the scenario for the opera *Aida*, set in ancient Egypt. He pressed the Egyptians to establish the National Antiquities Service to protect, preserve, and study the country's art monuments. In gratitude, they later placed a statue of him in the new Egyptian Museum in Cairo. At his death, his remains were brought back to his beloved Egypt for burial.

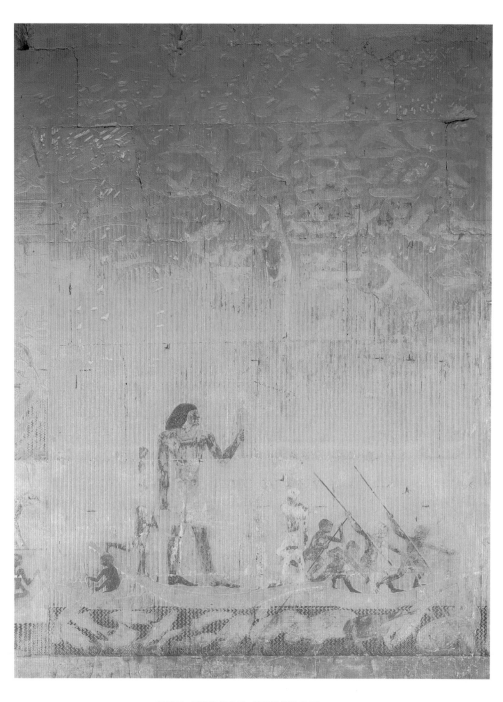

or religious meanings. A scene in the mastaba of a Dynasty 5 government official named Ti shows him supervising a hippopotamus hunt from a shallow boat (fig. 2-21). As dictated by Egyptian hieratic scale, Ti stands much larger than his men. Space is indicated in registers, with the nearest elements at the bottom of the composition. The river is seen from above, a band of parallel wavy lines below the boats. The fish, a crocodile, and hippopotamuses are shown in profile for easy identification. The boats skim the surface of the water unhampered by the papyrus stalks, shown as parallel vertical lines. The hunt had symbolic value: the companions of Seth, god of darkness, were believed to disguise themselves as hippopotamuses, so depictions of such hunts illustrate not only the valor of the deceased and the eradication of a troublesome beast that destroyed crops, but also the triumph of good over evil.

THE MIDDLE KINGDOM

During the Middle Kingdom, political authority became less centralized. Provincial governors claimed increasing power, limiting the king's responsibilities to national concerns such as the defense of Egypt's frontiers, the control of water, and related matters such as agricultural wealth and trade. Cities along the Nile grew up along the river's banks, with long streets laid out parallel to the river (that is, running north and south) and short crossing streets leading in from the water. This grid pattern became the first rational city plan. At Kahun, for example, archaeologists found the rectangular blocks formed by the streets further subdivided into lots for houses much like modern cities. The size of the houses and the arrangement of the rooms indicate three distinct economic and social levels within the population, each having its own quarter:

the governmental and ceremonial center with the palace of the king, the quarter with large dwellings probably for court officials and priests, and a large district with smaller mud-brick homes for the workers.

During Dynasties 11 and 12, wealthy members of the nobility and high-level officials commissioned labor-intensive rock-cut tombs that proclaimed their status. The tombs were carved out of faces of cliffs, and the walls were commonly painted with scenes of daily life. The Dynasty 12 tomb of a local lord named Khnumhotep in the necropolis at Beni Hasan on the east bank of the Nile has a painting in which two men picking figs compete for the fruit with three baboons seated in the trees (fig. 2-22). Like the hunters in the Old Kingdom relief of Ti, and the standard-bearers of Narmer, these active farmworkers are shown with their shoulders in profile, not in the unnatural pose prescribed for royalty.

There is little indication of how ancient Egyptians viewed the artists who created portraits of kings and nobles and recorded so many details of contemporary life, but they must have been admired and respected. Some certainly had a high opinion of themselves, as we learn from an inscription on the tombstone of a Middle Kingdom sculptor: "I am an artist who excels in my art, a man above the common herd in knowledge. I know the proper attitude for a statue [of a man]; I know how a woman holds herself, [and how] a spearman lifts his arm. . . . There is no man famous for this knowledge other than I myself and my eldest son" (cited in Montet, page 159).

The patron's and the artist's desire for clarity permeates Egyptian art. A pectoral, or chest ornament on a necklace (fig. 2-23), also made during Dynasty 12 (c. 1895–1878 BCE), incorporates clearly recognizable human and animal imagery. The pectoral suggests the splendor of royal dress and tomb furnishings during this period. Executed in gold and inlaid with perfectly cut and fitted semiprecious stones, it was discovered in the funerary complex of Senwosret II (Dynasty 12, ruled c. 1895–1878 BCE), in the tomb of the king's daughter Sithathoryunet. Two Horus falcons and coiled cobras of the sun god Ra support a **cartouche**—an oval figure or tablet—enclosing the hieroglyphs (symbols) of the king's name. Around their necks, the cobras wear the *ankh,* the symbol of life. Below, a male figure helps to support a double arch of notched palm ribs, a hieroglyph meaning "millions of years." Decoded, the pectoral's combination of images yields the message: "May the sun god give eternal life to Senwosret II."

THE NEW KINGDOM

During the New Kingdom, Egypt prospered both politically and economically, its kings surpassing in wealth and power the Mesopotamian rulers. One of the most dynamic kings of Dynasty 18, Tuthmose III (ruled 1479–1425 BCE), even extended Egypt's influence along the eastern Mediterranean coast as far as modern Syria. Tuthmose III was the first ruler to refer to himself as "pharaoh," a term that simply meant "great house." (Egyptians used it in the same way that people in the United States speak of "the White House" when they really mean the current president.) The successors of Tuthmose III continued to use the

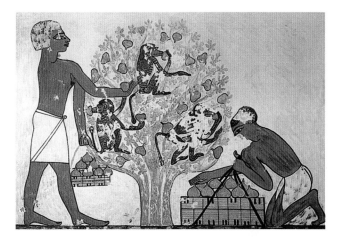

2-22 | *Harvest Scene,* tempera facsimile by Nina de Garis Davies of a wall painting in the tomb of Khnumhotep, Beni Hasan. Dynasty 12, c. 1928–1895 BCE

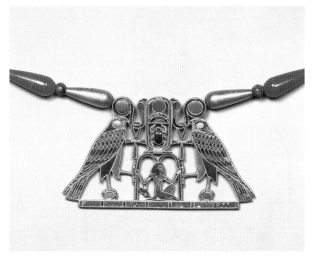

2-23 | **Pectoral with the name of Senwosret II** from el-Lahun. Dynasty 12, c. 1895–1878 BCE. Detail of a necklace. Gold and semiprecious stones, length 3¼" (8.3 cm) The Metropolitan Museum of Art New York
Purchase, Rogers Fund and Henry Walters Gift 1916 (16.1.3)

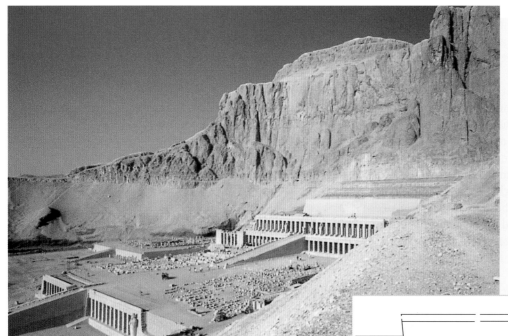

2-24

Funerary temple of Hatshepsut, Deir el-Bahri Dynasty 18, c. 1478–1458 BCE. At the far left are the ramp and base of the funerary temple of Mentuhotep I. Dynasty 11, c. 2009–1997 BCE

2-25 | **Plan of the funerary temple of Hatshepsut.** Deir el-Bahri

2-26 | **Plan of the Great Temple of Amun Karnak.** New Kingdom

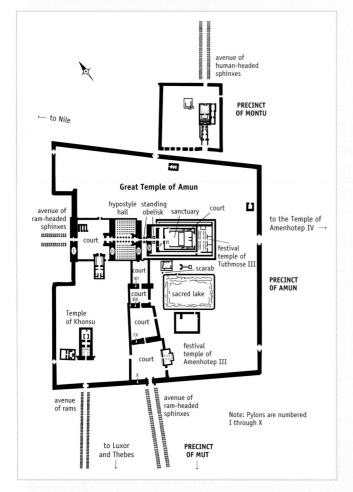

term, and it ultimately found its way into the Hebrew Bible—and modern usage—as the title for the kings of Egypt.

At the height of the New Kingdom, rulers undertook extensive building programs along the Nile. One of the most spectacular surviving architectural complexes is the funerary temple of the female ruler Hatshepsut (Dynasty 18, ruled c. 1478–1458 BCE). Like the temples adjacent to the Old Kingdom pyramids at Giza, the structure, located at Deir el-Bahri, across the Nile from the New Kingdom capital city of Thebes, was designed for funeral rites and commemorative ceremonies (fig. 2-24). Hatshepsut's actual tomb was hidden in the hills.

Magnificently positioned against high cliffs, Hatshepsut's temple was constructed on three levels, which were connected by ramps and adorned with rows of **columns**, or **colonnades** (fig. 2-25). The colonnade on the top level was fronted by colossal royal statues; behind it was a **hypostyle hall**, or vast column-filled space, with chapels to Hatshepsut, her father Tuthmose I, and the gods Amun and Ra-Horakhty. At the back of the hall, the temple's innermost sanctuary was cut deep into the cliff in the manner of Middle Kingdom rock-cut tombs. Rare myrrh trees brought from Nubia and pools of water decorated the temple's terraces, and an elevated causeway lined with sphinxes once connected the complex to a valley temple on the Nile.

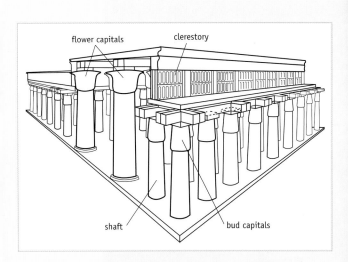

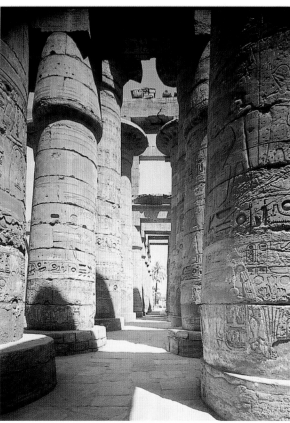

2-28

Hypostyle hall, Great Temple of Amun Karnak

2-27 | **Reconstruction drawing** of the hypostyle hall Great Temple of Amun, Karnak. Dynasty 19 c. 1294–1212 BCE

Other important New Kingdom building campaigns took place at Karnak, to the north of Thebes, and Luxor, to its south. Both sites had temple districts consecrated primarily to three Theban deities: Amun, his wife Mut, and their son Khonsu. At Karnak, remains of the Great Temple of Amun still dominate the landscape. Access to the heart of the temple, a sanctuary containing the statue of Amun, was through a series of **pylons** (massive gateways) and courtyards (fig. 2-26). The principal structure, a hypostyle hall, still amazes visitors by its overwhelming size.

The hypostyle hall (figs. 2-27, 2-28) was erected in the reigns of Dynasty 19 rulers Sety I (ruled 1294–1279 BCE) and his son Ramesses II (ruled c. 1279–1212 BCE), whom some believe to be the "pharaoh" of the biblical story of Moses and the Exodus. Known as the "Temple of the Spirit of Sety, Beloved of Ptah in the House of Amun," the hall may have been used for royal coronation ceremonies. Ramesses II referred to it in more mundane terms as "the place where the common people extol the name of his majesty." Extending 170 feet long and 340 feet wide, the hall roof was supported by 134 closely spaced columns, their **shafts** decorated with hieroglyphic inscriptions and images of kings and gods. The columns were topped with **capitals** shaped like lotus flowers or lotus buds, a flower symbolic of Upper Egypt.

Ramesses II, who constructed more temples than any other Egyptian king, also undertook a building campaign in the sacred district at Luxor. He enlarged the existing Temple of Amun, Mut, and Khonsu with the addition of a pylon and a **peristyle** court, or open courtyard ringed with columns and covered walkways (fig. 2-29). In front of his pylon stood two colossal statues of himself and a

2-29 | **Pylon of Ramesses II** with obelisk in the foreground, Temple of Amun, Mut, and Khonsu, Luxor. Dynasty 19, c. 1279–1212 BCE

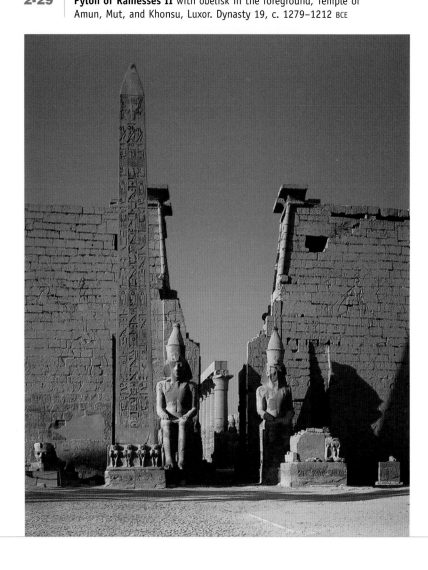

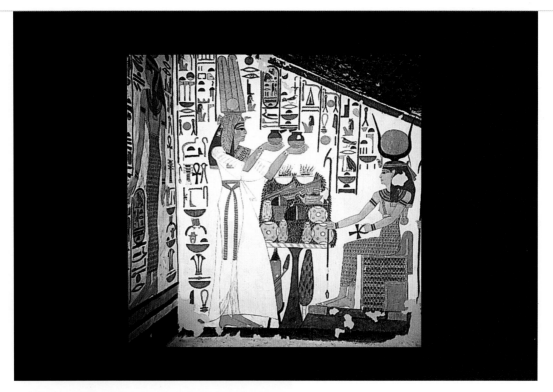

2-30   *Queen Nefertari Making an Offering to Isis,* wall painting in the tomb of Nefertari, Valley of the Queens near Deir el-Bahri. Dynasty 19, c. 1279–1212 BCE

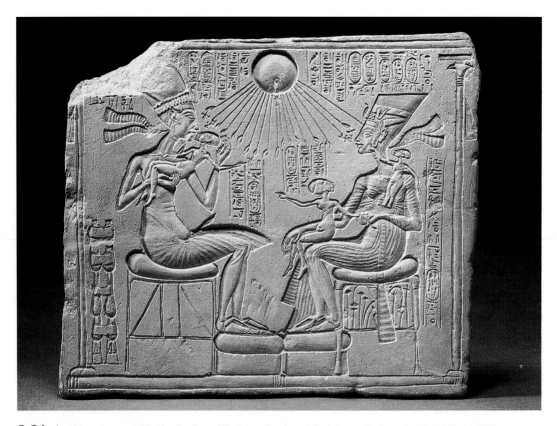

2-31   *Akhenaten and His Family,* from Akhetaten (modern Tell el-Amarna). Dynasty 18, 1348–1336/5 BCE Painted limestone relief, 12¼ x 15¼" (31.1 x 38.7 cm). Staatliche Museen zu Berlin, Preussischer Kulturbesitz, Ägyptisches Museum

Egyptian relief sculptors often employed the technique seen here, called sunken relief. In ordinary reliefs, the background is carved away so that the figures project out from the finished surface. In sunken relief, the original flat surface of the stone is the background, and the outlines of the figures are deeply incised, permitting the development of three-dimensional forms within them. If an ordinary relief became badly worn, a sculptor might restore it by recarving it as a sunken relief.

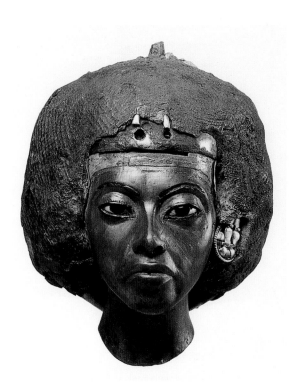

2-32 | ***Queen Tiy,*** from Kom Mendinet Ghurab (near el-Lahun). Dynasty 18, c. 1390–1352 BCE. Boxwood, ebony, glass, gold, lapis lazuli, cloth, clay, and wax Height 3¾" (9.4 cm). Staatliche Museen zu Berlin Preussischer Kulturbesitz, Ägyptisches Museum

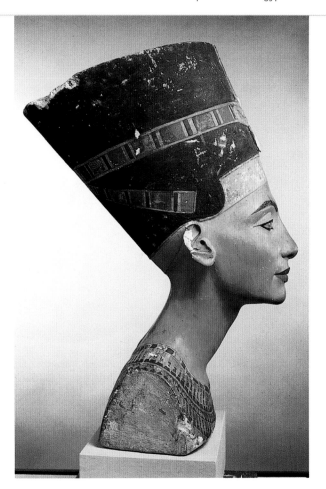

2-33 | ***Nefertiti,*** from Akhetaten (modern Tell el-Amarna) Dynasty 18, c. 1348–1336/5 BCE. Limestone, height 20" (51 cm). Staatliche Museen zu Berlin, Preussischer Kulturbesitz, Ägyptisches Museum

pair of **obelisks**—slender, slightly tapered shafts of stone capped by a pyramidal shape. The faces of the pylon are ornamented with reliefs detailing the king's military exploits.

The tomb of Nefertari, the best known of Ramesses II's eight wives, is among the wonders of the Valley of the Queens necropolis, near Deir el-Bahri. In one of the tomb's many beautiful, large-figured scenes, Nefertari offers jars of perfumed ointment to the goddess Isis (fig. 2-30). The queen wears the vulture-skin headdress of royalty, a royal collar, and a long, transparent white gown. The outline drawing and use of clear colors reflect traditional practices of depicting figures. The artists used particular care in placing the hieroglyphic inscriptions around these figures in order to create a harmonious overall design.

The veneration of traditional Egyptian deities, and especially the worship of the Theban gods Amun, Mut, and Khonsu, which spread throughout the country during the New Kingdom, was interrupted briefly during the reign of the unusual ruler Amenhotep IV (Dynasty 18, 1352–c. 1348 BCE). This king founded a new religion demanding belief in a single god, the life-giving sun disk Aten, and accordingly changed his own name to Akhenaten ("One Who Is Effective on Behalf of Aten"). Such concern for directness also found expression in art. In portraits of the king, such as a relief of him with his queen, Nefertiti, playing with three of their daughters (fig. 2-31), artists candidly emphasized his unusual physical characteristics—long, thin arms and legs, protruding stomach, and a thin neck supporting an elongated head. Above the royal couple, the sun god Aten is depicted as a solar disk sending down long rays ending in human hands. Some

of the hands hold *ankhs,* the symbol of life. The base of the queen's throne is adorned with the **stylized** symbol of a unified Egypt, which has led some historians to conclude that Nefertiti, who was sometimes called "the lady of the two lands," acted as coruler with her husband.

Akhenaten's mother, Queen Tiy, also played a significant role in affairs of state during his reign. Her personality emerges from a miniature portrait head that reveals the exquisite bone structure of her powerful face (fig. 2-32). One of Queen Tiy's formal titles, "The Woman Who Knows," here seems particularly apt. This portrait contrasts sharply with a head of Nefertiti, in which the heavy-lidded eyes and half smile divulge almost nothing about her personal qualities (fig. 2-33). Nefertiti's subjects referred to her as "Fair of Face," "Mistress of Happiness," and "Endowed with Favors," suggesting that she indeed possessed the great beauty seen in this sculpture, which is heightened by the artist's dramatic use of color.

Akhenaten's new religion outlived him by only a few years, and the priesthood of Amun quickly regained its former power. The young king Tutankhaten (ruled 1336/35–1327 BCE) returned to traditional religious beliefs, changing his name, which meant "Living Image of the Aten," to Tutankhamun, or "Living Image of Amun." He died at a young age and was buried in the Valley of the Kings near Thebes, a necropolis used by New Kingdom rulers.

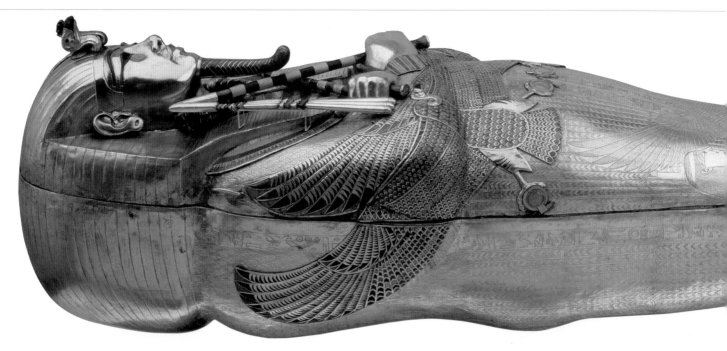

2-34 | **Inner coffin** of Tutankhamun's sarcophagus, from the tomb of Tutankhamun, Valley of the Kings. Dynasty 18, 1336/5–1327 BCE. Gold inlaid with glass and semiprecious stones, height 6'7/8" (1.85 m). Egyptian Museum, Cairo. (See pages 42–43.)

The English archaeologist Howard Carter had worked in Egypt for more than twenty years before he undertook a last expedition, sponsored by the wealthy British amateur Egyptologist Lord Carnarvon, after World War I. In November 1922 Carter discovered the entrance to the tomb of King Tutankhamun, the only Dynasty 18 royal burial place as yet unidentified. By November his workers had cleared their way down to its antechamber, which was found to contain unbelievable treasures: jewelry, textiles, gold-covered furniture, a carved and inlaid throne, four gold chariots, and other precious objects. In February 1923, they pierced through the wall separating the antechamber from the actual burial chamber, and in early January of the following year—having taken great care to catalog all the intervening riches and prepare for their safe removal—they finally reached the king's astonishing sarcophagus.

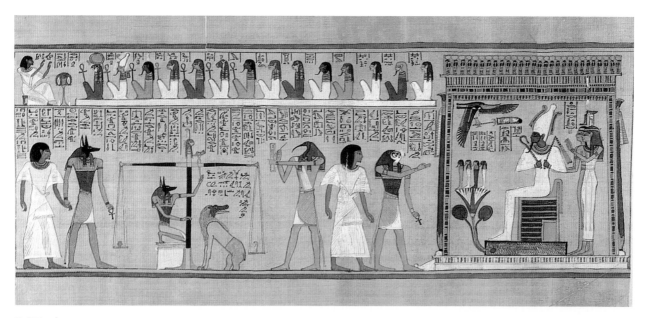

2-35 | *Judgment before Osiris,* illustration from a Book of the Dead. Dynasty 19, c. 1285 BCE. Painted papyrus, height 155/8" (39.8 cm) The British Museum, London

The sealed inner chamber of his tomb, discovered in 1922, was found to contain amazing treasures: jewelry, textiles, gold-clad furniture, a carved and inlaid throne, four gold chariots, and other precious objects. The king's body lay inside three nested coffins that identified him with Osiris, the god of the dead. The innermost coffin (fig. 2-34) of the **sarcophagus** (rectangular stone coffin), made of solid gold, is decorated with colored

enamelwork and semiprecious gemstones, as well as very finely incised linear designs and hieroglyphic inscriptions. The king holds a crook and a flail—agricultural harvest instruments associated with Osiris, a fertility and vegetation god who presided over the dead and the underworld.

Egyptian funerary practices revolved around Osiris, his resurrection, and a belief in the continuity of life after death by

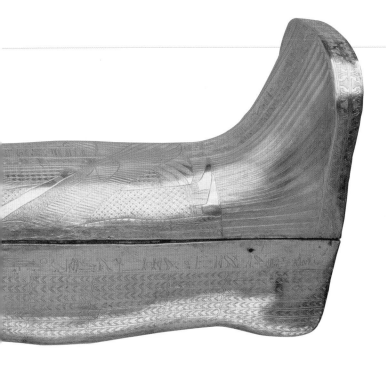

questioned by a delegation of deities about their behavior in life. Then their hearts, which the Egyptians believed to be the seat of the soul, were weighed on a scale against an ostrich feather, the symbol of Maat, goddess of truth. A monster Ammit, the "Eater of the Dead," waited beside the scale to devour those who tipped the balance.

These beliefs gave rise to additional funerary practices especially popular among the nonroyal classes. Family members commissioned papyrus scrolls containing magical texts or spells to help the dead survive and pass the tests (see "Mummies," page 55). Early collectors of Egyptian artifacts referred to such scrolls as Books of the Dead. A scene from a Dynasty 19 example, created for a man named Hunefer, shows him at successive stages in his introduction into the afterlife (fig. 2-35). At the left, Anubis leads him to the spot where he will weigh his heart in a tiny jar. After passing the test recorded by the ibis-headed god Thoth, Hunefer is presented by the god Horus to the enthroned Osiris, who holds his usual crook and flail. In the top register Hunefer kneels before the gods of Heliopolis, the sacred city of the sun god Ra.

Although we cannot know how Hunefer and other ancient Egyptians actually fared in the afterlife, the art produced to commemorate their lives and support them after death was a means to assure them of immortality.

THE LATE PERIOD

The Late Period in Egypt (c. 747–332 BCE) saw the country and its art in the hands and service of foreigners. In the eighth century, the Nubian leader Piye (747–716 BCE) from the Kingdom of Kush conquered Egypt and established capitals at Memphis and Thebes. The Nubians adopted Egyptian religious practices and architectural forms, including pyramids and sphinxes. The royal sphinx of King Taharqo (ruled c. 690–664 BCE) illustrates this continuity of tradition (fig. 2-36). Cobras rear up from the royal headdress, while the individual Nubian features of the king emerge from a lion's body and gaze out from a lion's mane. The sculpture combines the elegant simplified forms of Egyptian art with portraiture. The Nubians were followed by Assyrians, Persians, and Macedonians until the Ptolemies regained control of Egypt after the death of Alexander the Great in 323 BCE (see page 117). In 30 BCE the last Egyptian ruler, Cleopatra VII, died

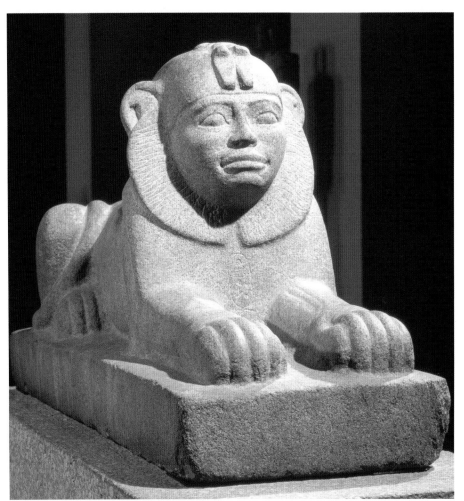

2-36 | **Sphinx of Taharqo,** from Temple T, Kawa, Nubia. Dynasty 25, c. 690–664 BCE. Height 29³/₈" (74.7 cm). The British Museum, London

Egyptians of all ranks. The dead were thought to undergo a "last judgment" consisting of two tests presided over by Osiris and supervised by Anubis, the overseer of funerals and cemeteries, represented as a man with a jackal's head. The deceased were first

a suicide and the Romans added Egypt to their empire. The creativity of the Egyptians over many centuries was acknowledged and admired by contemporary peoples—as it was by their eventual conquerors.

Soldiers, from the mausoleum of the first emperor of Qin, Lintong Shaanxi. Qin dynasty, c. 210 BCE Earthenware, lifesize (See pages 77–78.)

How can we understand the fierce determination and driving will that could lead a single man to conceive of himself as ruler of the world, a man who believed that his right to reign was bestowed by supernatural powers, that he was the son of heaven? Between 221 BCE when he brought the warring states under his control until his death in 210 BCE, Qin Shihuangdi turned his vast lands of China into a unified state. His tremendous actions were simple, direct, and brilliant. To govern the vast territory he created a bureaucracy—an intricate, hierarchal network—based on competence, not family heritage, and guided by a code of law. He united his lands with a common language and system of writing and more than 4,000 miles of roads. He brought prosperity by building canals and an irrigation system to increase agricultural production and by facilitating the ease of trade through uniform weights and measures. The modern name for the country—China—comes from Qin.

In life, a huge army defended the Qin Empire (historians write of 300,000 men). In death, an underground army with more than 8,000 terra-cotta figures stands in battle array and guards Qin Shihuangdi's tomb. Disciplined and alert, they remain poised to defend their emperor throughout eternity. According to early historians, his tomb beneath an earth mound at Lishan near modern Xi'an represented the universe with the heavens depicted on the ceiling and the earth with rippling rivers of mercury on the floor. The tomb also represented the success behind the bureaucratic universe Qin Shihuangdi had erected before he died.

How could such a vast project have been accomplished? The technical achievement of the artists and artisans is as amazing as the political organization that made the work possible and the worldview that inspired the art. Perhaps as many as a thousand potters molded and carved the clay, and eighty-five artists signed the figures—names like De, Chao, Wei, Yi, and Chong. By using standardized molds they mass-produced thousands of legs, torsos, arms, fingers, and even heads. They joined the prefabricated parts, and then modeled and carved them into individual, life-size figures. After the firing of the clay, the artists painted the figures and supplied them with real weapons of bronze and wood. Just consider the size of the kilns and the quantity of wood necessary to fire such vast numbers of clay figures let alone the organization of the labor force.

Standardization, mass production, and prefabrication of modular parts are associated with modern industrial society. Yet ancient cultures, from China to Egypt, fashioned intricate production systems for use in this world, as well as the next, centuries before Europe's Industrial Revolution in the eighteenth century. Here, within the earth at Lishan, we witness more than the confluence of power, art, and bureaucracy. Qin Shihuangdi's tomb represents the human drive for imposing order on chaos.

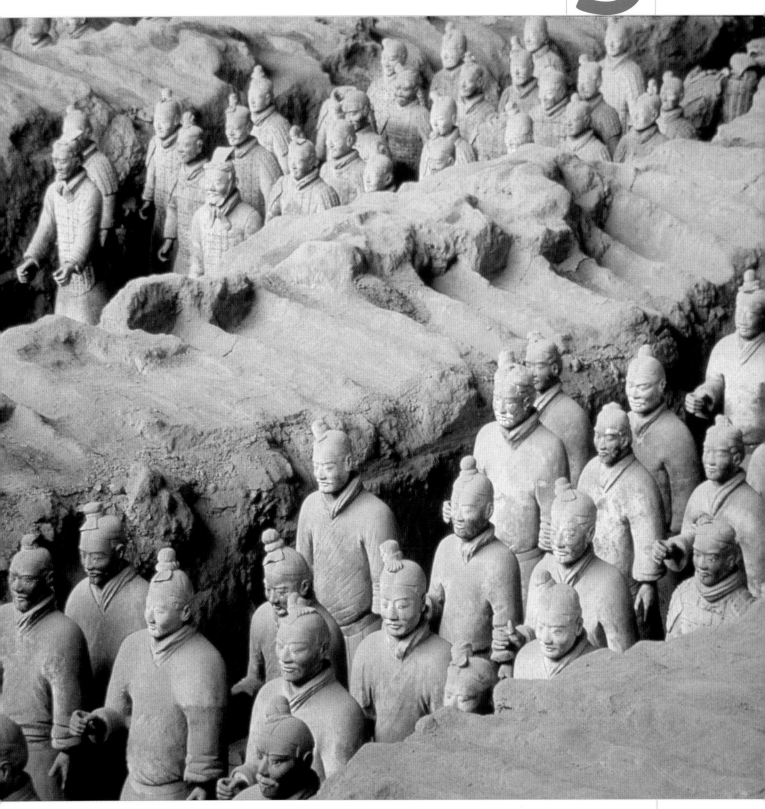

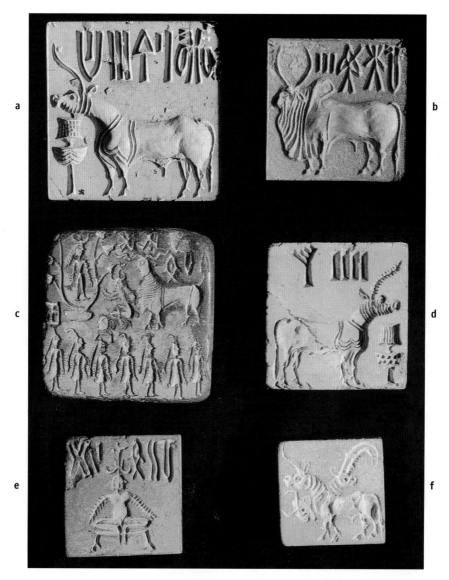

3-1 | **Seal impressions,** from the Indus Valley civilization: **a., d.** horned animal; **b.** buffalo; **c.** sacrificial rite to a goddess (?); **e.** yogi; **f.** three-headed animal. c. 2500–1500 BCE. Seals: steatite, each approx. 1¼ x 1¼" (3.2 x 3.2 cm)

Usually carved from steatite stone, seals were coated with alkali and then fired to produce a lustrous, white surface. A perforated knob on the back of each may have been for suspending them. The most popular subjects are animals, the most common being a long-horned bovine standing before an altarlike object (a, d). Animals on Indus Valley seals are often portrayed with remarkable naturalism, their taut, well-modeled surfaces implying their underlying skeletal structures.

The civilizations of South and East Asia, among the world's oldest, also rank among the most culturally rich. Together, the South Asian subcontinent and the East Asian countries of China and Japan witnessed the birth of six great, still-living religions and/or philosophies: Buddhism, Hinduism, and Jainism in India; Confucianism and Daoism in China; and Shinto in Japan. The eastward spread of Buddhism from India through Central Asia, to China, Korea, and Japan, united these regions culturally through its philosophy and art. At the same time, India, China, and Japan proudly point to the profound differences in their aesthetic traditions (see Map 1, pages 86–87).

The Indian Subcontinent

The South Asian, or Indian, subcontinent includes present-day India, southeastern Afghanistan, Pakistan, Nepal, Bangladesh, and the island of Sri Lanka. Throughout the history of the area, these places have been culturally linked. Differences in language, climate, and terrain within India have fostered distinct regional and cultural characteristics and artistic traditions. However, despite such regional diversity, several overarching traits tend to unite Indian art. Most evident is a distinctive sense of beauty, with voluptuous forms and a profusion of ornament, texture, and color. Visual abundance is considered auspicious, and it reflects a belief in the generosity and favor of the gods. Another characteristic is the pervasive symbolism that enriches all Indian arts with intellectual and emotional layers. Third, and perhaps most important, is an emphasis on capturing the vibrant quality of a world seen as infused with the dynamics of the divine. Gods and humans, ideas and abstractions, are given tactile, sensuous forms, radiant with inner spirit.

The earliest civilization of South Asia arose in the lower reaches of the Indus River (in present-day Pakistan and in northwestern India). This Indus Valley, or Harappan, civilization (after Harappa, the first discovered site) flourished from approximately 2600 to 1900 BCE, during roughly the same time as the Old Kingdom in Egypt and the dynasty of Ur in Mesopotamia. Indeed, with Egypt and Mesopotamia it is one of the world's earliest urban river-valley civilizations.

Stone seals offer an intriguing window on Indus Valley civilization (fig. 3-1). More than 2,000 small stone seals and impressions have been found. Many of the images carved on the seals suggest relationships with later South Asian culture. Seal (e) in figure 3-1, for example, depicts a man in the meditative posture associated in Indian culture with a yogi, one who seeks mental, physical, and spiritual purification and self-control. In seal (c), people in a procession walk single file under a kneeling worshiper and a figure, possibly a goddess, standing in a tree. This scene may offer some insight into the religious customs of Indus Valley peoples, whose deities may have been the prototypes of later Indian gods and goddesses. The function of the seals, beyond sealing packets, remains a mystery, and their pictographic script has yet to be deciphered.

Around 1500 BCE, after the Indus Valley civilization declined for unknown reasons, a seminomadic warrior people known as the Aryans entered India from the northwest, bringing with them an Indo-European language called Sanskrit and a hierarchical social order. The Vedic period that followed, named for the Vedas, a body of sacred writing, lasted from about 1500 BCE until the rise of the first unified empire in the South Asian subcontinent in the late fourth century BCE. The Vedic period is marked by the development of religiously sanctioned social classes or castes, which became hereditary, and by the beginnings of Buddhism, Hinduism, and Jainism—three of the four (the fourth is Islam) great religions of India. The metaphysical texts known as the *Upanishads* were also written during this period. Examining the meaning of earlier, more cryptic Vedic hymns, the *Upanishads* focus on the relationship between the individual soul and the universal soul, or *Brahman*. The *Upanishads* advanced concepts that became central to subsequent Indian philosophy, including the assertions that the material world is illusory and only the *Brahman* is real and eternal; that existence is cyclical; and that all beings are caught in a relentless cycle of birth, life, death, and rebirth. The goal of religious life is to attain *nirvana*—liberation from this cycle—by uniting our individual soul with the eternal, universal *Brahman*. These philosophical ideas are expressed in a more accessible and popular way in India's great literary epics, the *Mahabharata* and the *Ramayana*. Appearing toward the end of the Vedic period, these texts related stories of gods and humans that later became immensely important in Hinduism.

BUDDHISM

The Buddhist religion developed from the teachings of Shakyamuni Buddha (traditionally dated c. 563–483 BCE, though some scholars now put his death at c. 400 BCE), who lived and taught in the present-day regions of Nepal and northeast India. Born Prince Siddhartha Gautama in a small kingdom of the Shakya clan, he left his family and home at the age of twenty-nine to live as an ascetic in the wilderness. He was deeply troubled by the inevitable sufferings of the human condition—old age, sickness, and death—and the repetitions of these sufferings through the continual cycle of rebirth. But after six long years of meditation, while sitting under a pipal (bodhi) tree at Bodh Gaya, he attained complete enlightenment, or understanding of true reality.

In his teachings Shakyamuni Buddha expounded the Four Noble Truths, which are the foundation of Buddhism: (1) life is suffering; (2) this suffering has a cause, which is desire; (3) desire can be overcome and extinguished; and (4) the way to overcome desire is by following the eightfold path of right view, right resolve, right speech, right action, right livelihood, right effort, right mindfulness, and right concentration.

A buddha is not a god but rather one who sees the ultimate nature of the world and is therefore no longer subject to *samsara*, the cycle of birth, death, and rebirth. The early form of Buddhism, known as Theravada, stresses self-cultivation for the purpose of attaining *nirvana*, which is release from the wheel, or cycle, of *samsara*. In Mahayana Buddhism, which developed later and became popular in northern India, China, Korea, and Japan, the goal was expanded from attaining *nirvana* for oneself to the attainment of buddhahood for all beings. Compassion for all became a primary motivating force.

Mahayana Buddhism recognizes not only Shakyamuni Buddha but also numerous other buddhas, such as Maitreya, the Buddha of the Future, and Amitabha (called Amida in Japan), the Buddha of Infinite Light and Infinite Life (that is, incorporating all space and time). Mahayana Buddhism developed the concept of bodhisattvas, saintly beings on the brink of buddhahood who have vowed to help others become buddhas before crossing over themselves. The appearance of bodhisattvas in art is based on the princely image of Shakyamuni before he became the Buddha. They wear the princely garb of India, jewelry, and long hair. They are easily distinguished from buddhas, who wear a monk's robe, no jewelry, and have short hair.

The Buddhist and Jain religions arose in India with two great teachers, Shakyamuni Buddha (traditionally 563–483 BCE) and Mahavira (599–527 BCE). The Buddha, or "enlightened one," lived and taught in India (see "Buddhism," above). Both Shakyamuni Buddha and Mahavira espoused such basic Upanishadic tenets as the cyclical nature of existence and the desirability of escape from it. However, they rejected the authority of the Vedas and the hereditary class structure of Vedic society, with its powerful, exclusive priesthood. Buddhism and Jainism were open to all, regardless of social position.

Buddhism provided the impetus for much of the major art created between the third century BCE and the fifth century CE. Under the Maurya dynasty (c. 322–185 BCE), whose rule extended over all but the southernmost regions of the subconti-

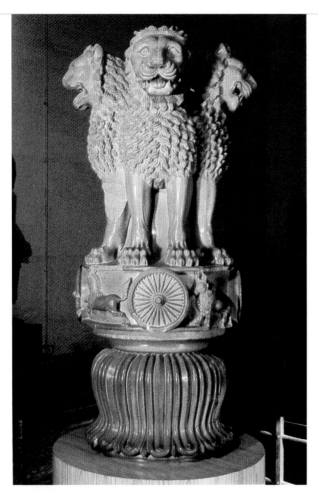

nent, Buddhism became the state religion. For many centuries, the painting and sculpture of India were associated with imperial sponsorship of the religion. The Mauryan lion capital, about 250 BCE, is a prime example of one emperor's promotion of Buddhism (fig. 3-2). This capital once topped a 50-foot-high pillar of highly polished sandstone located on the grounds of the monastery at Sarnath, site of the Buddha's first teaching. One of many so-called Ashokan pillars, it was erected by the king who first sponsored Buddhism as the state religion. The capital rises with a cushion of downturned lotus petals, on which rests a deep, round collar carved with four animals—lion, horse, bull, and elephant—alternating with four wheels called *chakras* (see pages 72, 73). Four lions stand back-to-back facing the four cardinal directions, emblematic of the universal nature of Buddhism. Their heraldic stance and the strong **stylization** of actual elements, such as leg tendons and veins, claws, manes, and toothy muzzles, endow them with almost supernatural presence. When India gained its independence in 1947, it made this capital the national emblem.

Between the second century BCE and the early first century CE, Buddhism continued as the main inspiration for art, and some of the most important and magnificent early Buddhist structures were created. Perhaps no early Indian monument is more famous than the Great Stupa at Sanchi in central India (fig. 3-3). **Stupas** derive from burial mounds and contain **relics**, that is, material remains associated with a holy person, within their solid, dome-shaped earthen core. The first Buddhist stupas, holding the remains of the Buddha after his cremation, were vener-

3-2 | **Lion capital,** from an Ashokan pillar at Sarnath, Uttar Pradesh India. Maurya period, c. 250 BCE. Polished sandstone, height 7' (2.13 m). Archaeological Museum, Sarnath

3-3

Great Stupa
Sanchi, Madhya
Pradesh, India
Founded 3rd
century BCE
Enlarged
c. 150–50 BCE

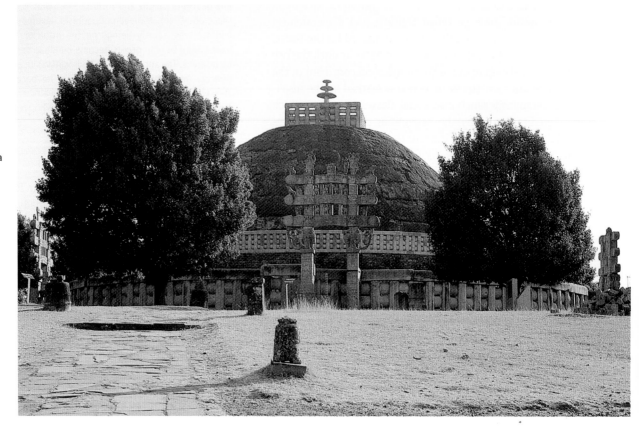

ated as his body and, by extension, his enlightenment and attainment of *nirvana*. Rituals of veneration included circumambulation, walking around the stupa in a clockwise direction, following the sun's path across the sky.

Originally built during the Maurya period and enlarged about 150 to 50 BCE, the Great Stupa at Sanchi was part of a large monastery complex crowning a hilltop. The stupa's brick dome, once covered with shining white plaster, is topped by a square stone railing defining the domain of the gods atop the cosmic mountain. The railing encloses the top of a mast bearing three stone disks, or "parasols," of decreasing size, which signal high rank and status. The mast itself is an ***axis mundi***, axis of the world, assumed to connect the cosmic waters below the earth with the celestial realm above it and to anchor everything in its proper place.

An 11-foot-tall stone railing, punctuated by four stone gateways, or **toranas** (fig. 3-4), rings the entire stupa. As in much religious architecture, the railing provides a physical and symbolic boundary between the inner, sacred area and the outer, profane world. Each gateway is decorated with a profusion of carved scenes of Buddha's life and past lives, as well as figural sculpture depicting such subjects as *yakshis*, female spirits associated with the beauty and fertility of nature. As in all known early Buddhist art, the Buddha himself is not shown in human form. Instead, he is represented by symbols such as his footprints, an empty "enlightenment" seat, or a stupa.

During the first century CE, the regions of present-day Afghanistan, Pakistan, and North India came under the control of the Kushans, a nomadic people from Central Asia. During this period Buddhism underwent profound change resulting in the development of a form of Buddhism known as Mahayana, or Great Vehicle (see "Buddhism," page 69). Closely related to this new movement was the appearance of the first Buddha images. The two earliest styles of Buddha images arose in Kushan-ruled areas: Gandhara in the northwest (present-day Pakistan and Afghanistan) and Mathura in central India. Slightly later, a third stylistic tradition, known as the Amaravati school after its most famous site, developed to the south in the region ruled by the Andhra dynasty.

In images from all three schools and throughout Asian art, the Buddha is readily recognized by certain visual characteristics. He wears a simple monk's robe, and because he had been a prince in his youth and had worn the customary heavy earrings, his earlobes are distended. The top of his head has a protuberance (*ushnisha*), which in images often resembles a bun or topknot, a symbol of his enlightenment. Between his eyes is the *urna*, a tuft of white hair.

Elements of Architecture

STUPAS

Stupas began in India as simple, solid dome-shaped structures containing Buddhist relics. Later, a multistoried form of the stupa developed in India's Gandhara region during the Kushan dynasty (c. 50–250 CE). As Buddhism spread northeastward along the Silk Road, the form of the multilevel stupa was merged with that of the watchtower of Han dynasty China, leading to the creation of multistoried masonry structures with projecting tiled roofs known as pagodas.

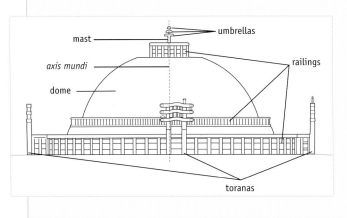

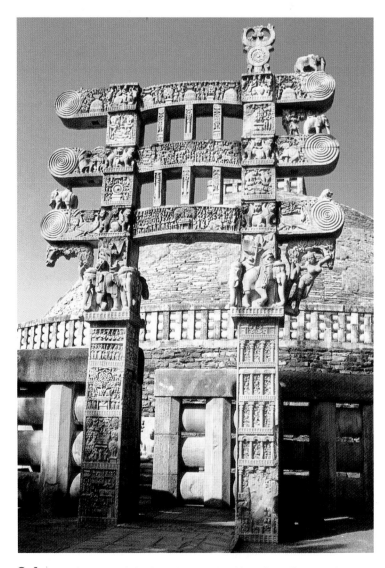

3-4 | **North torana** of the Great Stupa at Sanchi. Early Andhra period mid-1st century BCE. Stone, height 35' (10.66 m)

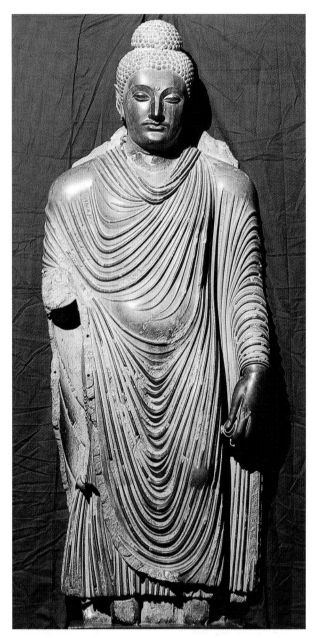

3-5 | *Standing Buddha,* from Gandhara (Pakistan)
Kushan period, c. 2nd–3rd century CE. Schist
Height 7'6" (2.28 m). Lahore Museum, Lahore

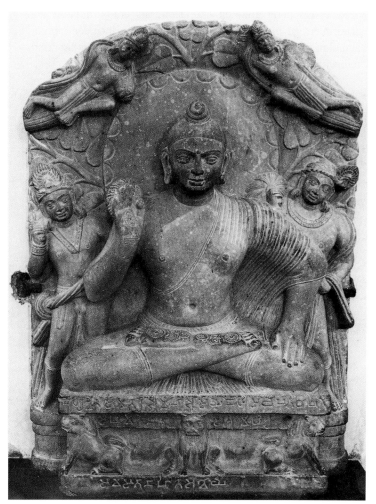

3-6 | *Buddha and Attendants,* from Katra Keshavdev, Mathura
Madhya Pradesh, India. Kushan period, c. late 1st–early
2nd century CE. Red sandstone, height 27¼" (69.2 cm)
Government Museum, Mathura

A typical image from the Gandhara school portrays the Buddha as a powerful, over-lifesize figure (fig. 3-5). His robe is carved in tight, riblike folds alternating with delicate creases, setting up a clear, rhythmic pattern of heavy and shallow lines. This complex fold pattern resembles the treatment of togas in some sculptural works from ancient Rome (see fig. 6-9), a stylistic influence resulting from this region's long history of contact with the Western world. The Gandhara style, transmitted across Central Asia, exerted a strong influence on portrayals of the Buddha in East Asia.

At Mathura, the image of Buddha developed within the indigenous sculptural tradition as represented by statues of *yakshas,* the native male nature deities. In one of the finest of the early Mathura images of Buddha (fig. 3-6), the robe is pulled tightly over the body, allowing the fleshy form to be seen as almost nude. The Buddha is seated in a yogic posture, and his right hand is raised in a **mudra**, or symbolic gesture, meaning "have no fear." His distinctive features and the impressions of *chakras,* or wheels, on his feet and right hand are all clearly visible. An ancient sun symbol, the *chakra* symbolizes both the various states of existence (the Wheel of Life) and the Buddhist doctrine (the Wheel of the Law). In the background are the branches of the pipal, or bodhi, tree, under which the Buddha was sitting when he achieved enlightenment.

Buddhism reached its greatest influence in India during the Gupta period (c. 320–500 CE), named for the founders of a dynasty that ruled much of India at that time. Some of the finest surviving artworks of the Gupta period are **murals** (wall paintings) from the Buddhist rock-cut temples and halls of Ajanta, in western India (see pages 73–74). From ancient times, caves, frequently the abode of holy ones and ascetics, were considered hallowed places in India. During the second century BCE, Buddhist

BUDDHIST SYMBOLS

A few of the most important Buddhist symbols, which have myriad variations, are described here in their most generalized forms.

Lotus flower: Usually shown as a white water lily, the lotus (Sanskrit, *padma*) symbolizes spiritual purity, the wholeness of creation, and cosmic harmony. The flower's stem is an ***axis mundi***.

Lotus throne: Buddhas are frequently shown seated on an open lotus, either single or double, a representation of *nirvana*.

Chakra: An ancient sun symbol, the wheel (*chakra*) symbolizes both the various states of existence (the Wheel of Life) and the Buddhist doctrine (the Wheel of the Law). A *chakra*'s exact meaning depends on its number of spokes.

Marks of *buddha*: A buddha is distinguished by thirty-two physical **attributes** (*lakshanas*). Among them are a bulge on top of the head (*ushnisha*), a tuft of hair between the eyebrows (*urna*), elongated earlobes, and thousand-spoked circles (*chakras*) on the soles of the feet.

Mandala: Mandalas are diagrams of cosmic realms, representing order and meaning within the spiritual universe. They may be simple or complex, three- or two-dimensional, and in a wide array of forms—such as an Indian stupa (see fig. 3-3).

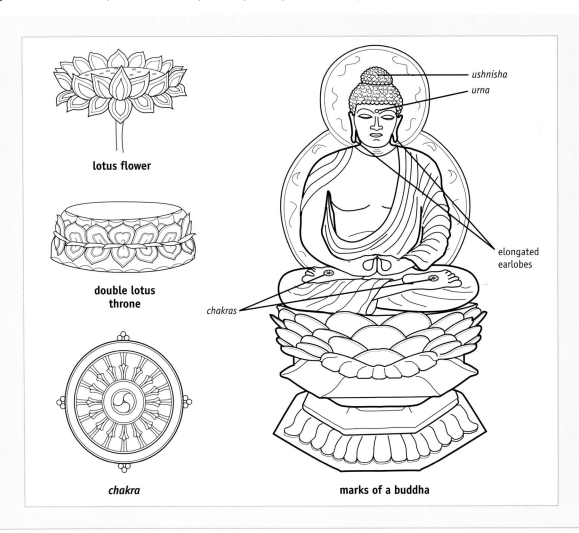

lotus flower

double lotus throne

chakra

ushnisha
urna
elongated earlobes
chakras

marks of a buddha

monks began to excavate two types of rock-cut halls out of the plateaus in the Deccan region. The type known as the *vihara* was used for the living quarters of the monks, and that known as *chaitya,* meaning "sacred," usually enshrined a stupa. Cave I at Ajanta, carved around 475 CE, is a *vihara* with monks' chambers around the sides and a shrine chamber in the back. Flanking the entrance of the shrine are **fresco** paintings of two **bodhisattvas,** beings who are in the process of becoming buddhas and who have reached a high level of spiritual attainment already. The bodhisattvas are distinguishable from Buddhas because the former

wears princely garments lavishly adorned with delicate ornaments and a crown festooned with pearls (fig. 3-7; see page 74), rather than the simple monk's robe. The graceful bending posture conveys his sympathetic attitude, while his spiritual power is suggested by his large size in comparison with the surrounding figures. In no other known example of Indian painting do bodhisattvas appear so magnanimous and graciously divine yet at the same time so human.

Even as Buddhism flourished, Hinduism, sponsored by Gupta monarchs, began the ascendancy that led to its eventual domi-

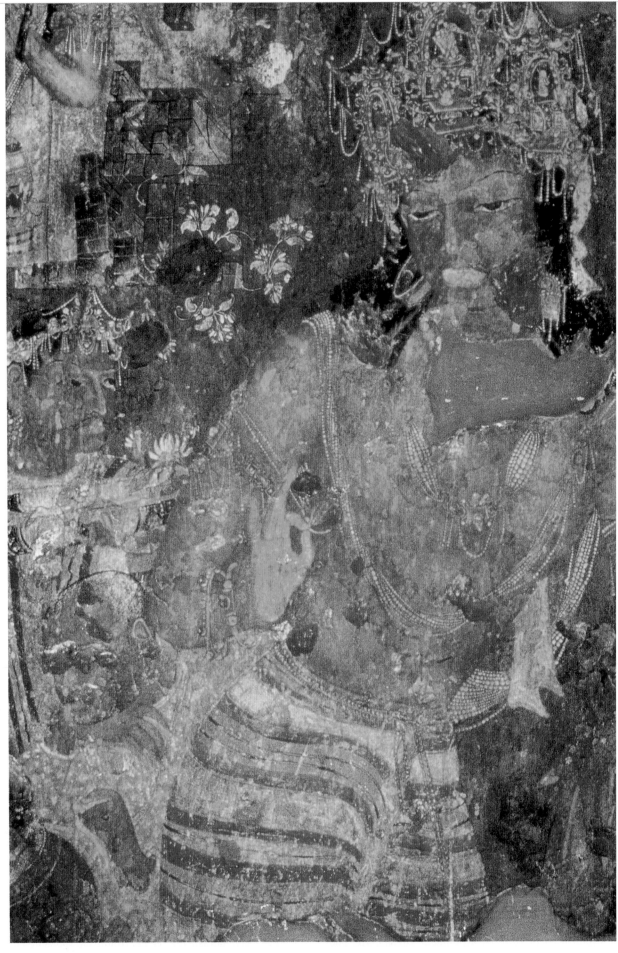

3-7 | *Bodhisattva,* detail of a wall painting in Cave I, Ajanta, Maharashtra, India. Gupta period, c. 475 CE

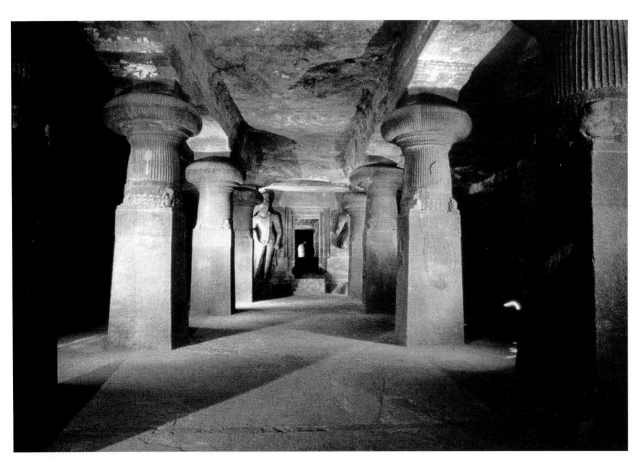

3-8   **Cave-Temple** of Shiva at Elephanta, Maharashtra, India. Mid-6th century CE. View along the east-west axis to the Shiva shrine

nation of Indian religious life (see "Hinduism," page 76). Hindu temples and sculpture of the Hindu gods rose with increasing frequency during the Gupta period and the post-Gupta era of the sixth to mid-seventh century.

In the mid-sixth century, a rock-cut cave-temple devoted to the major Hindu god Shiva was carved on the island of Elephanta, off the coast of Bombay in western India (fig. 3-8). Shiva (meaning "the auspicious one") exhibits a wide range of aspects or forms, both gentle and wild: he is the Great Yogi who dwells for vast periods of time in meditation in the Himalaya; he is also the husband par excellence who makes love to the goddess Parvati for eons at a time; he is the Slayer of Demons; and he is the Cosmic Dancer, who dances the destruction and re-creation of the world.

Many of these forms of Shiva appear in monumental relief panels adorning the cave-temple at Elephanta. A huge bust of the deity represents his Sadashiva, or Eternal Shiva, aspect (fig. 3-9). Carved out of the cave wall, three heads are shown resting upon the broad shoulders of the upper body. It is speculated that a fourth head may have been rendered in back, facing the stone wall. A four-faced Shiva (*chaturmuk*) is plausible in this setting and also a more common Hindu image. The heads summarize Shiva's fivefold nature as creator (back), protector (left shoulder), destroyer (right shoulder), obscurer (front), and releaser (top). On his left shoulder, his protector nature is depicted as female,

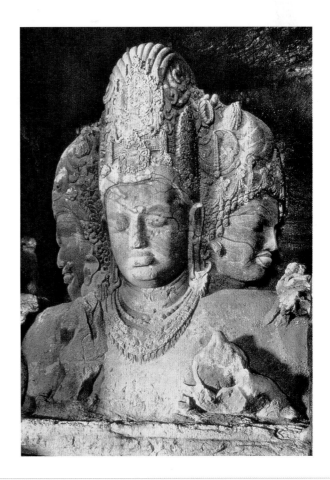

3-9   *Eternal Shiva,* rock-cut relief in the Cave-Temple of Shiva at Elephant Mid-6th century CE. Height approx. 11' (3.4 m)

HINDUISM

Hinduism is not one religion but many related beliefs and innumerable sects. It results from the mingling of Vedic beliefs (first appearing around 1500 BCE) with indigenous, local beliefs and practices. All three major Hindu sects draw upon the texts of the Vedas, which are believed to be sacred revelation set down about 1200–800 BCE. The gods lie outside the finite world, but they can appear in visible form to believers. Each Hindu sect takes its particular deity as supreme. By worshiping gods with rituals, meditation, and intense love, individuals may be reborn into increasingly higher positions until they escape the cycle of life, death, and rebirth, called *samsara*. The most popular deities are Vishnu, Shiva, and the Great Goddess, Devi. Deities are revealed and depicted in multiple aspects.

Vishnu is a benevolent god who works for the order and well-being of the world. He is often represented lying in a trance or asleep on the Cosmic Waters where he dreams the world into existence. His symbols are the wheel and a conch shell. A huge figure, he usually has four arms and wears a crown and lavish jewelry. He rides a man-bird, Garuda. Vishnu appears in ten different incarnations, including Rama and Krishna, who have their own cults. Rama embodies virtue, and assisted by the monkey king, he fights the demon Ravana. As Krishna, Vishnu is a supremely beautiful, blue-skinned youth who lives with the cowherds, loves the maiden Radha, and battles the demon Kansa (see fig. 9-5).

Shiva, Lord of Existence, embodies the entire universe; he is both creative and destructive, light and dark, male and female. His symbol is the lingam, an upright phallus, which is represented as a low pillar. As an expression of his power and creative energy, he is often represented as Lord of the Dance, dancing the Cosmic Dance, the endless cycle of death and rebirth, destruction and creation (see fig. 9-4). He dances within a ring of fire, his four hands holding fire, a drum, and gesturing to the worshipers. Shiva's animal is the bull. His consort is Parvati; their sons are the elephant-headed Ganesha, God of Prosperity, and the six-faced Karttikeya, God of War.

Devi, the Great Goddess, controls material riches and fertility. She has forms indicative of beauty, wealth, and auspiciousness, but also forms of wrath, pestilence, and power. As the embodiment of cosmic energy, she provides the vital force to all the male gods. Her symbol is an abstract depiction of female genitals, often associated with the lingam of Shiva. When armed and riding a lion (as the goddess Durga), she personifies righteous fury. As the goddess Lakshmi, she is the goddess of wealth and beauty. She is often represented by the basic geometric forms—squares, circles, triangles.

There are countless other deities, including Brahma, the creator, who once had his own cult. Brahma embodies spiritual wisdom. His four heads symbolize the four cosmic cycles, four earthly directions, and four classes of society: priests (brahmins), warriors, merchants, and laborers.

Central to Hindu practice are *puja* (forms of worship) and *darshan* (beholding a diety), generally performed to obtain a deity's favor and in the hope that this favor will lead to liberation from *samsara*'s endless cycle. Because desire for the fruits of our actions traps us, the ideal is to consider all earthly endeavors as sacrificial offerings to a god. Pleased with our devotion, he or she may grant us an eternal state of pure being, pure consciousness, and pure bliss.

with curled hair and a pearl-festooned crown. On his right, the wrathful destroyer nature wears a fierce expression, and in front, the god is shown in deep introspection, with the piled-up hair of a yogi. Indian artists often convey the many aspects or essential nature of a deity through multiple heads or arms. Their intent is to portray these additions with such convincing naturalism that we readily accept them. Here, for example, the artist has united three heads onto a single body so skillfully that we still relate to the statue as an essentially human presence.

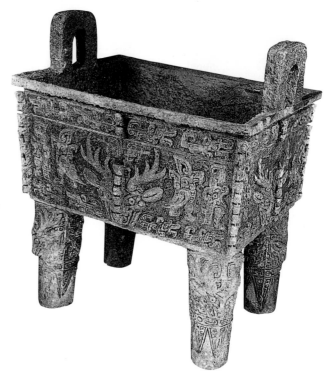

3-10 | *Fang ding,* from Tomb 1004, Houjiazhuang, Anyang, Henan Shang dynasty, Anyang period. c. 12th century BCE. Bronze Height 24½" (62.2 cm). Academia Sinica, Taipei, Taiwan

China

Among the cultures of the world, China is distinguished by its long, uninterrupted development, which has been traced back some 8,000 years. Even more remarkably, while rulers have come and gone, the country has been, with only a few breaks, unified since 221 BCE. Geographically, China is notable for its size, occupying a landmass slightly larger than the continental United States. Within its borders lives one-fifth of the human race.

The country's historical and cultural heart—sometimes called Inner China—is the land watered by its three great rivers, the Yellow, the Yangzi, and the Xi. Just as in South Asia, civilization first arose by the Indus River, and in Egypt by the banks of the Nile, Chinese towns and cities first emerged in the Neolithic period in fertile river valleys, especially around the deep southern bend of the Yellow River, nicknamed "China's Sorrow" because of its disastrous floods.

The first Chinese kingdoms date to the Bronze Age, which began in China before 1600 BCE. Traditional histories tell of three

Bronze Age dynasties: the Xia, the Shang, and the Zhou. Modern scholars once dismissed the Xia and Shang as legends, not actual civilizations, but recent archaeological discoveries have now established the historical existence of the Shang (c. 16th–11th century BCE), and point strongly to the historical existence of the Xia as well.

Shang kings ruled from a succession of capitals in the Yellow River valley, where archaeologists have found walled cities, palaces, and vast royal tombs. Society seems to have been highly stratified, with a ruling group that possessed the bronze technology needed to make weapons. They maintained their authority in part by claiming power as shamans, intermediaries between the supernatural and human realms. Nature and fertility spirits were also honored, and regular sacrifices were made to the spirits of dead ancestors so that they might help the living.

Bronze vessels are the most admired and studied of Shang artifacts. They were connected with shamanistic practices, serving as containers for ritual offerings of food and wine. The illustrated bronze *fang ding*, a square vessel with four legs (fig. 3-10), is one of the largest of hundreds of vessels recovered from royal tombs near the last of the Shang capitals, Yin (present-day Anyang). In typical Shang style its surface is decorated with a complex array of images based on animal forms. A large deer's head (*taotie*) adorns the center of each side; more deer appear on the legs; and the rest of the surface is filled with images resembling birds, dragons, and other fantastic creatures. Such images seem to be related to the hunting life of the Shang, but their deeper significance is unknown.

In the eleventh century BCE, the Shang were conquered by the Zhou from western China. During the Zhou dynasty (1100–256 BCE), a feudal society developed, with a king and his relatives ruling over numerous small states. The supreme deity became known as Tian, or Heaven, and the king ruled as the Son of Heaven. Tian remained the personal cult of China's sovereigns until the end of imperial rule in the early twentieth century.

Many of China's great philosophers lived during the Zhou dynasty, thinkers such as Confucius, Laozi, and Mozi. During the lifetime of Confucius (551–479 BCE)—a scholar born into an aristocratic family—warfare for supremacy among the various states of China had begun, and the traditional social fabric seemed to be breaking down. Looking back to the early Zhou dynasty as a golden age, Confucius thought about how a just and harmonious society could again emerge (see "Confucianism," page 78). He never found a ruler who would put his ideas into effect, but his philosophy, Confucianism, eventually became central to Chinese thought and culture.

Toward the middle of the third century BCE, the state of Qin (pronounced "chin," and the source for the English name "China") launched military campaigns that led to its triumph over the other Chinese states by 221 BCE. For the first time, China was united under a single ruler, the powerful emperor Shihuangdi, the first emperor of Qin (see page 66).

Anxious to ensure personal immortality, Shihuangdi built his own **mausoleum** (a building used as a tomb) at Lintong, near the city of Xi'an in Shaanxi Province. Archaeologists who began to excavate a pit near the tomb in 1974 were stunned by what they found: a vast underground army composed of more than 8,000 lifesize clay soldiers and horses standing in military formation ready for battle (fig. 3-11). The Chinese have not yet begun an archaeological excavation, but literary

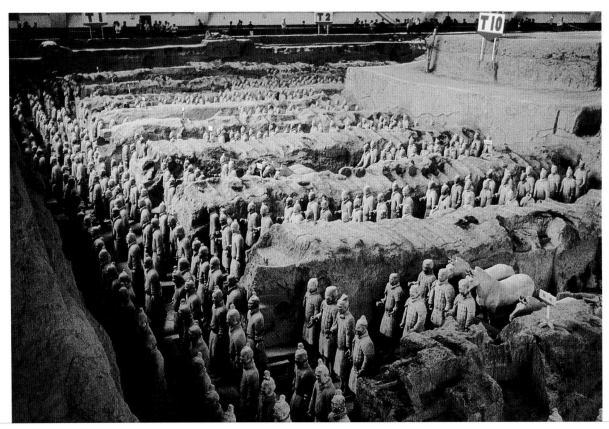

3-11

Soldiers, from the mausoleum of the first emperor of Qin, Lintong Shaanxi. Qin dynasty, c. 210 BCE. Earthenware lifesize. (See pages 66–67.)

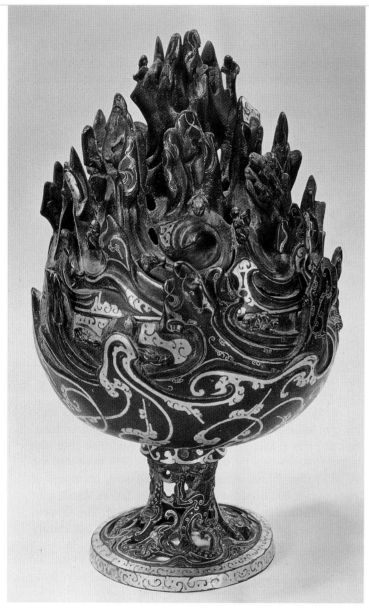

3-12 | **Incense burner,** from the tomb of Prince Liu Sheng Mancheng, Hebei. Han dynasty, 113 BCE. Bronze with gold inlay, height 10¼" (26 cm). Hebei Provincial Museum Shijiazhuang

Although harsh and repressive as rulers, the Qin emperors established a centralized bureaucracy and administrative framework, aspects of which are still used in China today. The country was divided into provinces and prefectures; the writing system and coinage were standardized; and forts on the northern frontier were connected to form the Great Wall. During the peaceful and prosperous Han dynasty that followed (206 BCE–220 CE), the country's borders were extended and secured. Chinese control over strategic stretches of Central Asia led to the opening of the famous Silk Road, actually a network of land and sea routes that linked China by trade to Europe.

Under the Han dynasty, the philosophies of Daoism and Confucianism flourished. Daoism emphasizes the close relationship between humans and nature. On the philosophical level, it is concerned with bringing the quiet and humble individual life into harmony with the *Dao*, or Way, of the universe. On a popular level Daoism developed into an organized religion, absorbing many traditional folk practices such as shamanism and the search for immortality.

A popular Daoist legend, which told of the Isles of the Immortals in the Eastern Sea, is depicted on a bronze incense burner from the tomb of Prince Liu Sheng, who died in 113 BCE (fig. 3-12). Gold **inlays** on the base outline the **stylized** waves of the sea. Above them rises the mountainous island, crowded with birds, animals, and people who have discovered the secret of immortality. The techniques used in the manufacturing of this piece represent the ultimate development of the long tradition of bronze casting in China.

In contrast to the metaphysical focus of Daoism, Confucianism is concerned with the human world, and its goal is the attainment of harmony. To this end, it offers an ethical system based on correct relationships among people. Attracted by this emphasis on social order and respect for authority, the Han emperor Wu (ruled 141–87 BCE) made Confucianism the official philosophy. It remained the state ideology of China until the end of imperial rule in the twentieth century and eventually assumed the form and force of a religion.

Confucian subjects appear frequently in Han art. Among the most famous examples are the reliefs from the Wu family shrines built in 151 CE in Jiaxiang. Carved and engraved in low relief on stone slabs, the scenes were meant to teach such basic Confucian tenets as respect for the emperor, filial piety, and wifely

sources suggest that the tomb itself may have been intended to reproduce the world as it was known to the Qin people, with stars overhead and rivers and mountains below.

CONFUCIANISM

Confucianism is based on the teachings of the Chinese scholar Confucius (551–479 BCE). His words have come down to us through a book known in English as the *Analects*, which records sayings of the great philosopher collected by his disciples and their followers. At the heart of Confucian thought is the concept of *ren*, or human-heartedness. *Ren*, which emphasizes morality and empathy as the basic standards for all human interactions, is most fully realized in the Confucian ideal of the *junzi*, or gentle-

man. Originally indicating noble birth, the term was redirected to mean one who through education and self-cultivation had become a superior person, right-thinking and right-acting in all situations.

Confucius also emphasized the importance of *li*, ritual or etiquette. The formalities of social interaction—scrupulous manners as well as ritual, ceremony, and protocol—choreographed life so that an entire society moved in harmony.

Both *ren* and *li* operated in the realm of

the Five Constant Relationships defining Confucian society: ruler and subject, parent and child, husband and wife, elder sibling and younger sibling, elder friend and younger friend. Deference based on age and sex is built into this view, as is the deference to authority that made Confucianism popular with emperors. Yet responsibilities flow the other way as well: the duty of a ruler is to earn the loyalty of subjects, of a husband to earn the respect of his wife, of age to guide youth wisely.

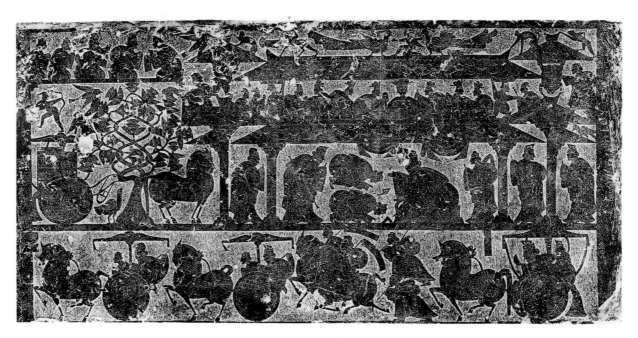

3-13 | **Detail** from a rubbing of a relief in the Wu family shrine (Wuliangci), Jiaxiang, Shandong. Han dynasty, 151 CE
Stone, 27¹/₂ x 66¹/₂" (70 x 169 cm)

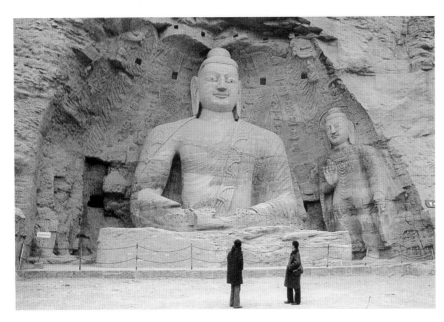

3-14 | **Seated Buddha**
Cave 20, Yungang
Datong, Shanxi.
Northern Wei
dynasty, c. 460 CE
Stone, height 45'
(13.7 m)

devotion. One relief (fig. 3-13) seems to depict homage to the first emperor of the Han dynasty, who is sheltered in a two-story building and distinguished by his larger size. The birds and small figures on the roof may represent mythical creatures and immortals, while to the left the legendary archer Yi shoots at one of the sun-crows. (Traditional myths tell how Yi shot all but one of the ten crows of the ten suns so that the earth would not dry out.) Across the lower register, a procession brings more dignitaries to the reception.

With the fall of the Han dynasty in 220 CE, China splintered into warring kingdoms. A period of almost constant turmoil broadly known as the period of the Northern and Southern Dynasties lasted until 579 CE. Many intellectuals turned to Daoism, which contained a strong escapist element. Yet ultimately it was a new system of belief, Buddhism, that brought the great-

est comfort to people of the time. Buddhism spread gradually north from India into Central Asia. With the opening of the Silk Road during the Han dynasty, it reached China (see "The Silk Road and the Making of Silk," page 80). To the Chinese of the post-Han period, beset by constant warfare and social devastation, Buddhism offered consolation in life and the promise of life after death.

The most impressive surviving works of Buddhist art from the Northern and Southern Dynasties period are hundreds of caves carved from the solid rock of cliffs. The rock-cut caves at Yungang in Shanxi Province, for instance, contain many impressive examples of early Chinese Buddhist sculpture. The monumental seated Buddha illustrated here was carved in the latter part of the fifth century (fig. 3-14). Because the front part of the cave has crumbled away, the 45-foot statue is now exposed to

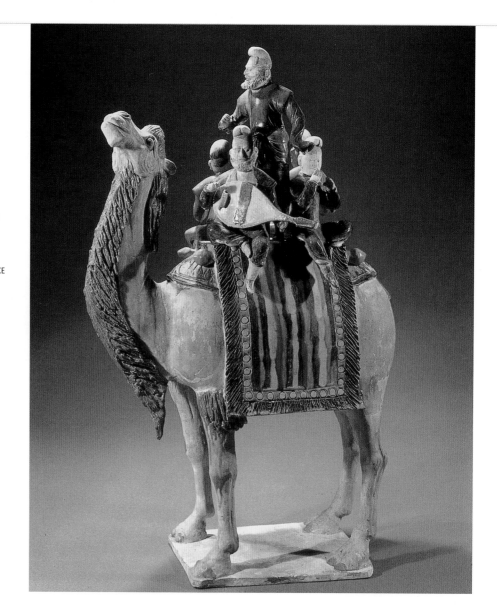

3-15 *Camel Carrying a Group of Musicians* from a tomb near Xi'an, Shanxi. Tang dynasty c. mid-8th century CE Earthenware with three-color glaze Height 26¹⁄₈" (66.5 cm) Museum of Chinese History, Beijing

THE SILK ROAD AND THE MAKING OF SILK

The fabled trade route between East Asia and the West, called the Silk Road, was a 5,000-mile-long network of caravan and sea routes stretching from Chang'an to the westernmost point of the Great Wall of China—then all the way to Rome. Caravans carrying Chinese luxury goods to the West—and bringing back gold in payment—passed through some of the most hostile regions in Asia and the Middle East, although no one caravan had to make the entire trip; goods were passed from trader to trader on both the overland and sea portions of the route. The Silk Road's importance fluctuated with the politics of the region, as did its safety. Only twice in its long history was it entirely open and comparatively safe.

One of the precious goods carried along the Silk Road, along with spices, was silk. The cultivation and weaving of silk had been a closely guarded secret in China since about 2640 BCE, and it was not until about 550 CE, when two Christian missionaries smuggled a few silkworm larvae to Constantinople, that the Chinese lost their virtual monopoly. From as early as the third century BCE, silk cloth was exported to Europe. It was treasured in Greece and Rome. In the sixth century CE, silk was a protected palace industry in the Byzantine Empire. Eventually, sericulture (the cultivation of silkworms) and luxury textile weaving took hold in southern Europe. For this and many other reasons, use of the Silk Road declined. By the sixteenth century, it was no longer in use.

the open air. The elongated ears, protuberance on the head (*ushnisha*), and monk's robe are traditional **attributes** of the Buddha. The masklike face, massive shoulders, and shallow, stylized drapery indicate a strong Central Asian influence.

In 589 CE a northern general reunified China and established a short-lived dynasty of his own, the Sui. The Sui paved the way for one of the greatest dynasties in Chinese history, the Tang (618–907 CE). Even today many Chinese living abroad still call themselves "Tang people." To them, Tang implies that part of the Chinese character that is strong and vigorous, noble and idealistic, but also realistic and pragmatic. Cosmopolitan and tolerant, the Tang Chinese were both self-confident and curious about the world. Many foreigners came to the splendid new capital, Chang'an (present-day Xi'an), and the Chinese depicted them in witty detail. A ceramic statue of a camel carrying a troupe of musicians reflects the Tang fascination with the "exotic" Turkic cultures of Central Asia (fig. 3-15).

Ceramic figurines produced by the thousands for tombs were decorated using a three-color **glaze**

CALLIGRAPHY

The emphasis on expressiveness and structural importance of brush-strokes finds its purest embodiment in calligraphy, the Greek word for "beautiful writing." Calligraphy is regarded as one of the highest forms of artistic expression in China. For more than 2,000 years, China's literati ("educated"), all of them Confucian scholars, have enjoyed being connoisseurs and practitioners of this abstract art. During the fourth century, calligraphy came to full maturity. The most important practitioner of the day was Wang Xizhi (c. 303–61 CE), whose works have served as models of excellence for all subsequent generations.

Calligraphy is based on combinations of strokes, executed with a brush and ink on paper, to create characters, as in Chinese writing, or letters, as in the Western alphabet. Chinese characters, unlike Western letterforms, evolved from pictographs. (A pictograph is a type of communication system of signs in which pictures—signs—representing an actual thing or concept are used to signify meaning.)

The art of calligraphy and its abstract features are devised through the stylization of strokes. Chinese calligraphic styles, from which Japanese and Korean calligraphy developed, are based on seven standard strokes, also known as the "Seven Mysteries," including a horizontal line, vertical line, dot, sharp curves curling either to the left or right, and diagonal strokes executed at various angles, sweeping downward either toward the left or right.

Several styles of calligraphy developed in Asia over the centuries, each with its own unique traits and purpose. Calligraphy used for meditation or poetry, for example, may appear far different than characters seen in bureaucratic documents or official seals. Depending on the intent of the calligrapher, the width and length of strokes may vary between styles as may the sharpness of edges and corners. (Compare, for example, the uniformly placed, compact characters with sharp strokes in figure 9-12 from China, to the fluidity and wild curls that comprise the elongated characters in figure 9-17 from Japan.) A single word can thus look very different from one calligraphic style to the next, depending on how the strokes in each character are formed through the control of the brush and concentration of the ink on the page.

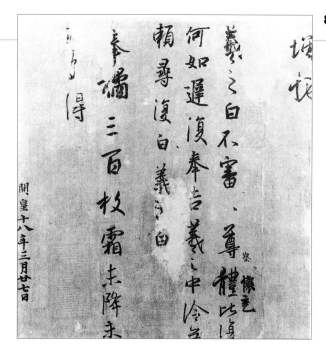

Wang Xizhi. Portion of a letter from the *Feng Ju* album
Six Dynasties period, mid-4th century CE. Ink on paper
9¹/₂ x 18¹/₂" (24.7 x 46.9 cm). National Palace Museum
Taipei, Taiwan

The stamped calligraphs that appear on Chinese artworks are seals—personal emblems. The use of seals dates from the Zhou dynasty, and to this day seals traditionally employ the archaic characters, known appropriately as "seal script," of the Zhou or Qin. Cut in stone, a seal may state a formal, given name, or it may state any of the numerous personal names that China's painters and writers adopted throughout their lives. A treasured work of art often bears not only the seal of its maker but also those of collectors and admirers through the centuries. In the Chinese view, these do not disfigure the work but add another layer of interest. This sample of Wang Xizhi's calligraphy, for example, bears the seals of two Song dynasty emperors, a Song official, a famous collector of the sixteenth century, and two emperors of the Qing dynasty of the eighteenth and nineteenth centuries.

technique that was a specialty of Tang ceramists. The glazes—usually chosen from a restricted palette of amber, yellow, green, and white—were splashed freely and allowed to run over the surface during firing to convey a feeling of spontaneity. Stylistically, the ceramic camel statue shows an interest in naturalistic gesture and expression, compared with the rigid, staring ceramic soldiers of the first emperor of Qin (see pages 66–67, 77–78, and fig. 3-11).

Buddhism flourished in China during the Tang dynasty. The early Tang emperors proclaimed a policy of religious tolerance, and virtually the entire country adopted the Buddhist faith. However, thousands of temples, shrines, and monasteries were destroyed and innumerable bronze statues melted down when Confucianism was reasserted during the ninth century and Buddhism was briefly persecuted as a "foreign" religion.

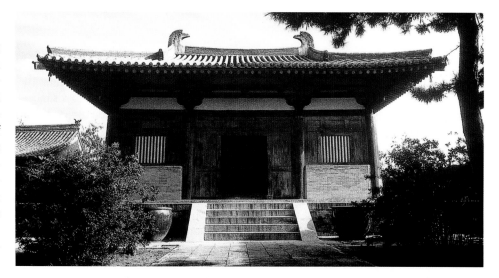

3-16 Nanchan Temple, Wutaishan, Shanxi. Tang dynasty, 782 CE

Nanchan Temple, located on Mount Wutai in the eastern part of Shanxi Province, is not only one of the rare wooden Buddhist structures surviving from the Tang dynasty but also the first important surviving example of Chinese woodframe architecture (fig. 3-16). Constructed in 782 CE, its curved and tiled

CLOSER LOOK

In Xi'an, the ancient capital of China, the Great Wild Goose Pagoda of the Ci'en Temple (fig. 3-17) rises majestically above small buildings and low foliage. Massive walls, punctuated by roof after horizontal roof, dominate the surroundings with grace and power. The temple was constructed in 645 CE for the famous monk Xuanzang on his return from a sixteen-year pilgrimage to India. At Ci'en Temple, Xuanzang taught and translated the Sanskrit Buddhist scriptures that he had brought back with him. His dedication to scholarship gave the temple special meaning for his students. Over the years, when students passed their official examinations, they went to the temple and inscribed their names, creating a veritable history of Chinese calligraphy.

Pagodas—towers associated with East Asian Buddhist temples—serve as reminders of the extent and influence of Buddhism. Like the stupas of South Asia, early East Asian pagodas were nearly solid, with small spaces for relics. In China the Buddhist mound-shaped stupa blended with the traditional Han watchtower to produce the multistoried pagoda. This transformation culminated in wooden pagodas with upward-curving roofs supported by elaborate bracketing much like their prototype found in the earlier Han watchtowers. Later pagoda examples often provided access to the ground floor and sometimes upper levels. Most pagodas were associated with Buddhism and retained the *axis mundi* masts of stupas. Built entirely of masonry, the Great Wild Goose Pagoda imitates the wooden architecture of its time. Although modified and

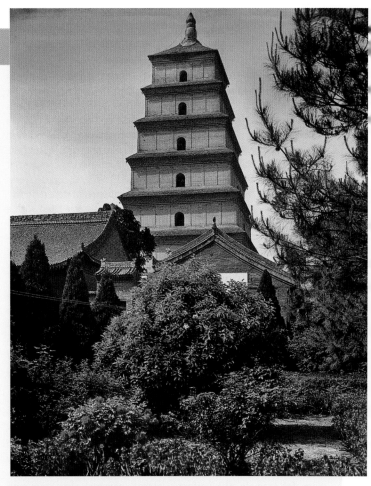

3-17 | **Great Wild Goose Pagoda** at Ci'en Temple, Xi'an, Shanxi
Tang dynasty, first erected 645 CE; rebuilt mid-8th century CE

repaired in later years (its seven stories were originally five, and a new finial has been added), the pagoda still preserves the essence of Tang architecture in its simplicity, symmetry, proportions, and grace.

roof has broad overhanging eaves supported by **brackets** (architectural supports projecting from the walls). Bracketing became a standard element of East Asian architecture, especially in palaces and temples. Also typical is the **bay** system of construction, in which a cubic unit of space, a bay, is formed by four posts and their lintels. To create larger structures, an architect multiplied the number of bays. Thus the three-bayed Nanchan Temple, modest in scope, gives an idea of the vast, multistoried, lost palaces of the Tang.

The Great Wild Goose Pagoda at the Ci'en Temple in Xi'an, the Tang capital, is another important monument of Tang architecture (fig. 3-17). The **pagoda**, or reliquary tower, originated in the Indian Buddhist stupa (see "Stupas," page 71). Chinese builders combined the idea of the stupa reliquary, which developed in India around the first century CE, with Han watchtowers to produce the tall pagoda.

Originally built of mud bricks between 645 and 652, and rebuilt at the beginning of the eighth century of brick with wooden floors and steps, the Great Wild Goose Pagoda imitates the forms of wooden architecture of the time. The walls are

decorated in low relief to resemble bays, and bracket systems are reproduced under the projecting roofs of each story. The pagoda helps us to visualize the splendor of Tang civilization and the architecture of the great cities of China.

Japan

Human habitation in Japan dates back at least 30,000 years, to a time when its islands were still linked to the East Asian landmass and the Sea of Japan was only a lake. Some 15,000 years ago, melting Ice Age glaciers caused the sea level to rise, creating the islands we know today. A distinctive Japanese culture began to emerge during the Jomon period (c. 12,000–300 BCE), which was remarkable for its creation of the world's earliest surviving fired pottery vessels (see fig. 1-9).

From ancient times, indigenous Japanese taste has been distinguished by a respect for and delight in natural materials. Wooden architecture such as Shinto shrines and farmhouses, for example, is often left unpainted, and ceramics frequently are only partly glazed in order to display all or some of their clay bodies. The Japanese aesthetic has a taste

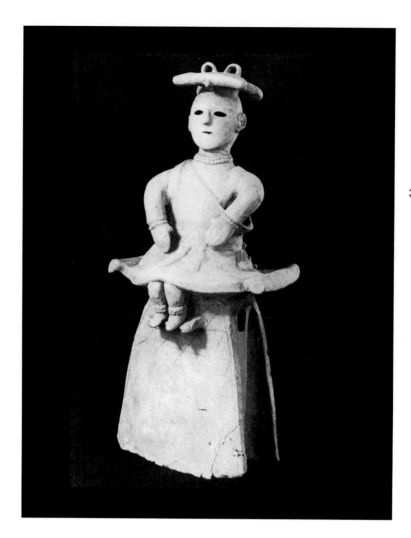

3-18 | *Haniwa*
from Kyoto
Kofun period
6th century CE
Earthenware
Height 27"
(68.5 cm) Tokyo
National Museum

for asymmetry, evidenced by paintings and prints that seem off-balance but are actually adroitly composed. In addition, a sense of humor and playfulness can surface in unexpected contexts, such as religious art of great power and depth. Finally, the Japanese have preserved their cultural heritage while welcoming and creatively transforming foreign influences—first from China and Korea and more recently from Europe and America.

Immigrants from Korea during the Yayoi (300 BCE–300 CE) and Kofun (300–552 CE) periods helped to transform Japan into an agricultural nation, where rice cultivation became widespread. The emergence of a class structure can be dated to the Yayoi period, as can the development of metal technology—first bronze and then iron.

The ensuing Kofun, or "old tombs" period, named for the large royal tombs that were built then, was distinguished by a pattern of veneration of leaders that grew into the beginnings of an imperial system. This system, still in existence today in Japan, eventually equated the emperor (or, very rarely, empress) with the all-powerful sun goddess.

When a Kofun emperor died, chamber tombs furnished with pottery and other grave goods were constructed. Tomb sites might extend over more than 400 acres, with artificial hills built over the tombs themselves. The hills were topped with hollow ceramic works of sculpture called **haniwa** to further distinguish the tomb sites.

The first *haniwa* were simple cylinders that may have held jars with ceremonial offerings. Gradually these cylinders came to be made in the shapes of ceremonial objects, houses, and boats, and later, birds and animals. Finally, *haniwa* in human shapes were crafted, of both sexes and all professions and classes. The *haniwa* illustrated here (fig. 3-18) has been identified as a seated female shaman. In early Japan, shamans acted as agents between the natural and supernatural worlds. Similarly, *haniwa* figures seem to have served as some kind of link between the world of the dead and the world of the living.

Haniwa figures may also reflect some of the beliefs of Shinto. Shinto, the indigenous religion of Japan, can be characterized as a loose confederation of beliefs in deities (*kami*). *Kami* were thought to inhabit many different aspects of nature, including

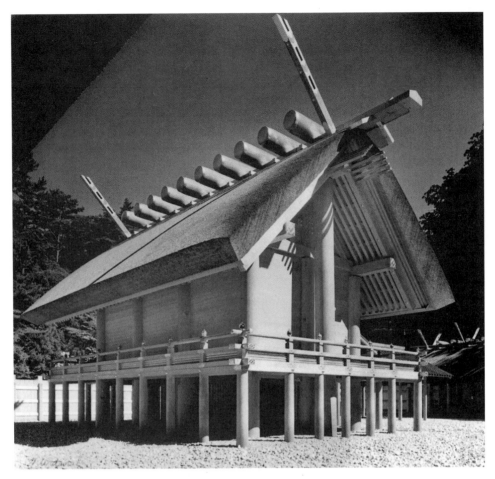

3-19 | **Inner Shrine,** Ise, Mie Prefecture. Early 1st century CE; rebuilt 1993

particularly hoary and magnificent trees, rocks, waterfalls, and living creatures such as deer. Shinto also represents the ancient Japanese belief in purification through the ritual use of water. In response to the arrival of Buddhism in Japan in the sixth century CE, Shinto became somewhat more systematized, with shrines, a hierarchy of deities, and more strictly regulated ceremonies.

One of the great Shinto sites is at Ise, on the coast southwest of Tokyo (fig. 3-19). The Inner Shrine is dedicated to the sun goddess, the legendary ancestor of Japan's imperial family. It was originally constructed in the early first century CE, and it has been ritually rebuilt at intervals over nearly 2,000 years. Stylistically and technically, the shrine is typical of Shinto architecture in the builder's use of wooden piles to raise the building off the ground, unpainted cypress wood as a construction material, and a thatched roof held in place by horizontal logs. These traditional features, which convey a sense of natural simplicity, ultimately derive from the architecture of ancient (first century CE) raised granaries used to store food. The Inner Shrine at Ise houses spiritual rather than corporal nourishment—a sword, a mirror, and a jewel—the three sacred symbols of Shinto.

Buddhism, introduced from China and Korea during the Asuka period (552–646 CE), soon coexisted with Shinto in Japan. During this time of intense cultural transformation, the Japanese also adopted a system of writing and a centralized governmental structure from China. Buddhism, which reached Japan in Mahayana form, with its many buddhas and bodhisattvas (see "Buddhism," page 69), soon became a state religion.

Buddhism introduced not only different gods but an entirely new concept of religion itself. Where Shinto had found deities in nature, Buddhism introduced a complex pantheon of anthropomorphic gods. The most significant surviving early Japanese temple is Horyu-ji (fig. 3-20), located on Japan's central plain not far from Nara. Founded in 607 CE and rebuilt after a fire in 670, Horyu-ji includes the oldest surviving documented wooden structure in the world.

The main compound of Horyu-ji consists of a rectangular courtyard surrounded by covered corridors. Only two buildings stand within the compound, a large *kondo,* or golden hall, and a slender, five-story pagoda. Both are Chinese-style woodframe buildings with tile roofs. The *kondo* is filled with Buddhist images and is used for worship and ceremonies. The pagoda also serves primarily as a **reliquary** (that is, it holds relics). Other monastery buildings, such as a repository for sacred texts and dormitories for monks, lie outside the main compound.

Among the many treasures preserved in Horyu-ji is a miniature shrine decorated with paintings in **lacquer** (a type of hard, glossy varnish) (fig. 3-21). It is known as the Tamamushi Shrine

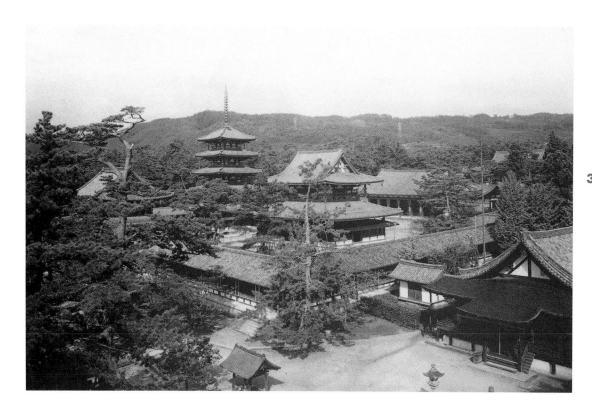

3-20 | **Main compound**
Horyu-ji, Nara
Prefecture
Asuka period
7th century CE

3-21 | *Hungry Tigress Jataka,* panel of the
Tamamushi Shrine, Horyu-ji. Asuka
period 7th century CE. Lacquer on
wood, height of shrine 7'7¾"
(2.33 m) Horyu-ji Treasure House

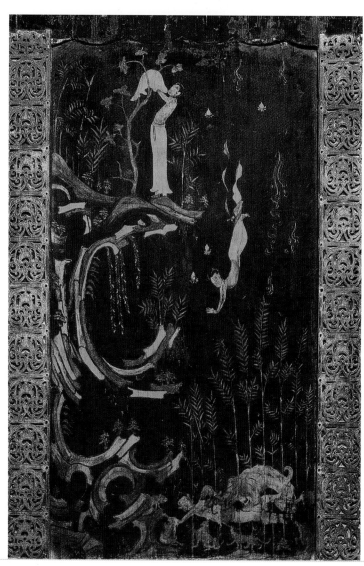

after the tamamushi beetle, whose iridescent wings were
originally affixed to the shrine to make it glitter. The
shrine may have been crafted in Korea or Japan, or perhaps
by Korean artisans working in Japan, testifying to the
international range of Buddhist art at this period.

The paintings ornamenting the Tamamushi Shrine are
among the few two-dimensional works of art to survive
from the Asuka period. The painting illustrated here tells
a story from a former life of the Buddha. In this painting,
he is shown nobly sacrificing his life in order to feed his
body to a starving tigress and her cubs. The tigers are at
first too weak to eat him, so he jumps off a cliff to break
open his flesh. The elegantly slender rendition of the Buddha's figure, shown three times in the three stages of the
story, and the abstract treatment of the cliff, trees, and
bamboo, represent a Buddhist style shared during this time
by China, Korea, and Japan.

During the seventh and eighth centuries Buddhism so
thoroughly permeated the upper levels of society that an
empress wanted to cede her throne to a Buddhist monk.
Her advisers intervened, but Buddhism remained the single most significant element in Japanese culture, comfortably coexisting with Shinto, just as it had with Hinduism
in India and with Confucianism and Daoism in China.

BCE 40,000	25,000	9000	4000	3000	2000

PREHISTORY IN EUROPE & AFRICA

Woman from Willendorf c. 22,000–21,000

Stonehenge c. 2750–1500

Horse and Sun Chariot c. 1800–1600

▲ UPPER PALEOLITHIC 40,000–8000   ▲ NEOLITHIC 8000   BRONZE AGE 2300–1000 ▲

MESOPOTAMIA & EGYPT

Palette of Narmer c. 3150–3125

Pyramids at Giza c. 2601–2515

Stela of Naramsin c. 2254–2218

Gudea c. 2120

▲ LAGASH 2150

EARLY NEOLITHIC 9000 ▲   SUMER 3500–2340 ▲ ▲ BRONZE AGE 3400   AKKAD 2340–2180 ▲ BABYLONIA 1792–1750 ▲

PREDYNASTIC PRE–3150 ▲ EARLY DYNASTIC 3150–2700 ▲   ▲ OLD KINGDOM 2700–2190

INDIA, CHINA, JAPAN

INDUS VALLEY CIVILIZATION 2700–1500 ▲   VEDIC PERIOD 1500–322 ▲

▲ NEOLITHIC c. 5000–2000 BCE   BRONZE AGE c. 1700–221

▲ JOMON c. 12,000–300 BCE

LOOKING BACK 1

Beginnings of Art

Long before men and women communicated through writing they made images and objects. The people who did so were not decorating cave walls or applying ornament to utensils in the sense that we use the words *decorating* and *ornament*. They believed that what they were doing was essential, perhaps even vital, to their very existence and that of their fellow humans.

When ritual action developed into religious ceremony, the arts became a means of communicating with the gods. As society became more highly stratified—as it did during the period covered in the preceding three chapters—priests and rulers led and governed, warriors defended the group and its fields and villages, artisans and farmers supplied basic material needs, and artists helped define and enhance the power of mortals as well as gods.

As we stand awestruck in front of Stonehenge in England, or the pyramids at Giza, or hundreds of terra-cotta figures in the emperor of China's ghostly army, we wonder how human beings could have imagined, and then achieved, these creations. People overcame enormous obstacles to move special stones to Stonehenge, and to cut, stack, and polish blocks into geometrically perfect pyramids at Giza. The Chinese emperor of Qin ordered an entire world for his tomb and a terra-cotta army, fully human in size and appearance, standing in timeless battle formation ready for action. Art substitutes for material reality, and power is expressed in the vastness of the projects.

These very ancient objects that we judge today to be especially fine, and call artworks, often appear simplified, geometric in appearance, and abstract in style. Representations of people and things are based on "memory images," that is, their makers, the artists, developed conventions and, eventually, rules for representing things and ideas. The artists created a symbolic visual language, a kind of conceptual art that communicated meaning to its audiences. To understand any symbolic language—whether composed of alphabets, shapes, hieroglyphs, or images—we too must learn the vocabularies and respect the rules. Our own preferences and prejudices are irrelevant to appreciating art of any era.

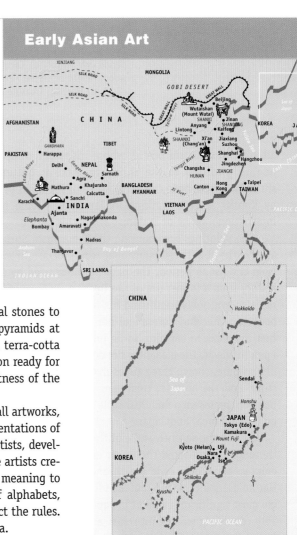

Early Asian Art

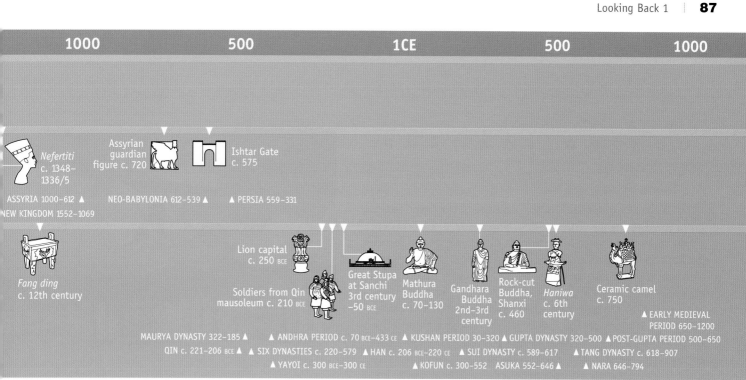

1000   500   1CE   500   1000

Nefertiti
c. 1348–
1336/5

Assyrian
guardian
figure c. 720

Ishtar Gate
c. 575

ASSYRIA 1000–612 ▲   NEO-BABYLONIA 612–539 ▲   ▲ PERSIA 559–331

NEW KINGDOM 1552–1069

Fang ding
c. 12th century

Lion capital
c. 250 BCE

Soldiers from Qin
mausoleum c. 210 BCE

Great Stupa
at Sanchi
3rd century
–50 BCE

Mathura
Buddha
c. 70–130

Gandhara
Buddha
2nd–3rd
century

Rock-cut
Buddha,
Shanxi
c. 460

Haniwa
c. 6th
century

Ceramic camel
c. 750

▲ EARLY MEDIEVAL
PERIOD 650–1200

MAURYA DYNASTY 322–185 ▲   ▲ ANDHRA PERIOD c. 70 BCE–433 CE   ▲ KUSHAN PERIOD 30–320 ▲ GUPTA DYNASTY 320–500 ▲ POST-GUPTA PERIOD 500–650

QIN c. 221–206 BCE ▲   ▲ SIX DYNASTIES c. 220–579   ▲ HAN c. 206 BCE–220 CE   ▲ SUI DYNASTY c. 589–617   ▲ TANG DYNASTY c. 618–907

▲ YAYOI c. 300 BCE–300 CE   ▲ KOFUN c. 300–552   ASUKA 552–646 ▲   ▲ NARA 646–794

Prehistoric, Mesopotamian, and Egyptian Art

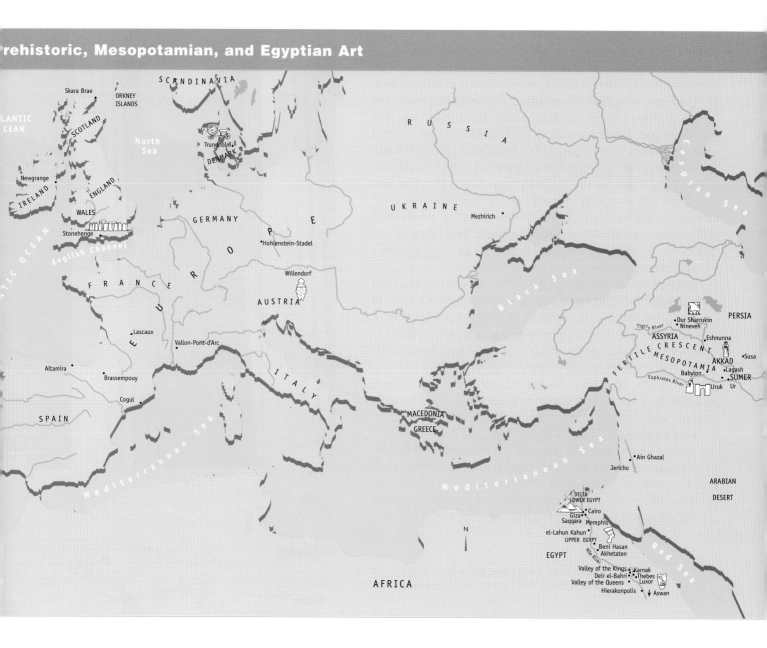

"Man is the measure of all things," said one of the Seven Sages of ancient Greece. For the first time we find a worldview dominated by human beings. To be sure, supernatural forces are at work and the gods meddle in, and often control, the affairs of men and women. But the Greek gods themselves have human forms and foibles.

In contrast to the autocratic civilizations of Egypt and China, Greek society focused on the individual—or at least on an elite group of men—a focus reflected in a new political system in which democracy replaced one-man, divine rule. This new view of society required a new art—an art centered in the material world but reflecting the philosophers' search for the human values of Truth, Virtue, and Harmony. Greek art and architecture established an ideal of earthly, physical, and visual perfection. Whether in sculpture, painting, ceramics, metalwork, or architecture, artists sought the essence of forms and combined close observation of nature with generalizations founded in the harmonious beauty of mathematics.

The Greek ideal seems encapsulated in Athens's Parthenon, the Temple of *Athena Parthenos* built nearly 2,400 years ago. The Parthenon rises triumphantly above the Acropolis summit, where it symbolizes Greek independence, self-confidence, and justifiable pride—through the excellence of its materials and craftwork, the rationality of its simple and elegant post-and-lintel structure, and the subtle yet ennobling messages of its sculpture. The great Athenian leader Perikles (c. 495–429 BCE) ordered the construction of this temple about 447 BCE, and it became Athens's most important center for civic and religious celebrations to honor the city's patron goddess.

Isolated like a work of sculpture, the Parthenon is the ideal Doric temple. The building is both an abstract form—a block of columns—and the essence of shelter, an earthly home for Athena. Over the centuries, different people living under a variety of circumstances have found that the temple could also express their ideals. They have responded to the Parthenon's harmonious proportions, subtle details, and rational relationship of part to part. As a symbol of the highest standards in art and politics, honesty, heroism, and civic virtue, the building has become a model for national monuments, government buildings, and even homes.

Ancient Greece continues to engage the imagination of twenty-first century artists and architects. They turn to its buildings and sculpture either to rebel against or to emulate the classical values embodied in its clean lines, simple forms, and mathematical ratios—even the very notion of perfectibility.

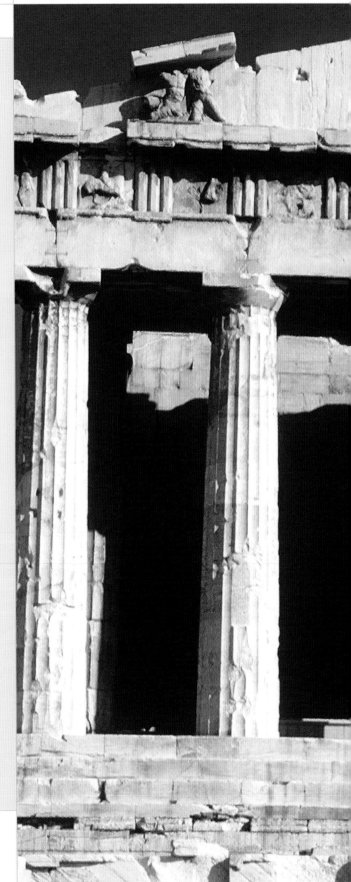

Kallikrates and **Iktinos. Parthenon.** Acropolis, Athens 447–438 BCE. View from the west. (See pages 109–11.)

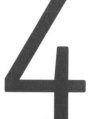
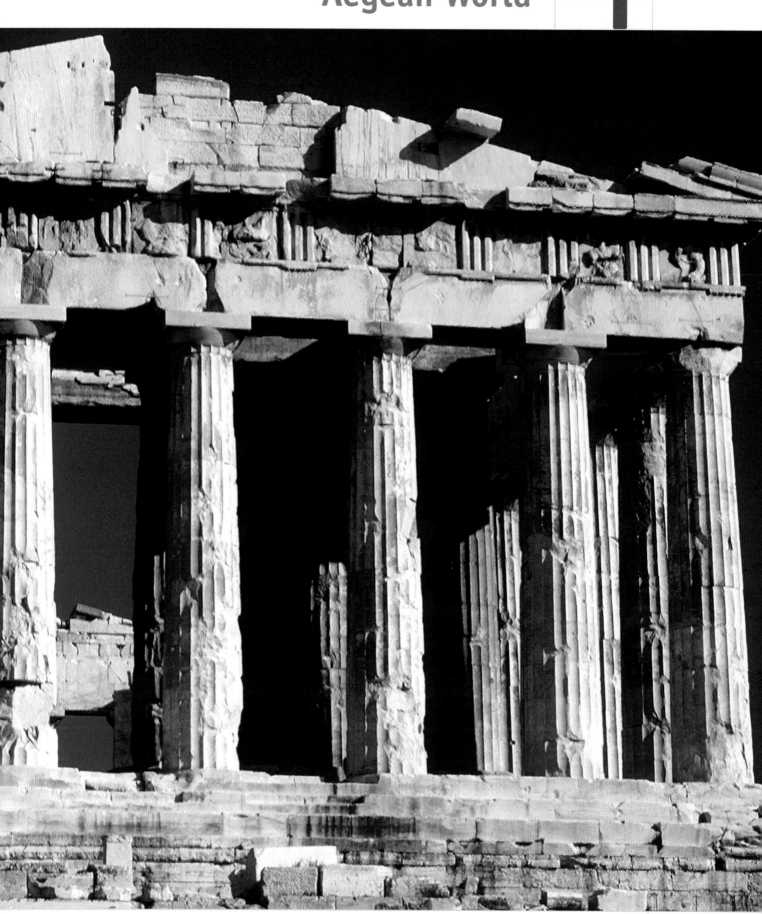

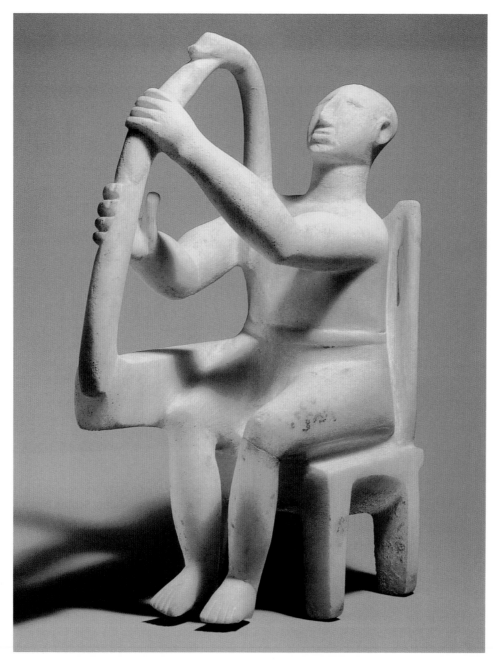

4-1 | ***Seated Harp Player,*** from Keros, Cyclades. c. 2800–2700 BCE. Marble, height 11¹/₂" (29.2 cm) The Metropolitan Museum of Art, New York
Rogers Fund, 1947 (47.100.1)

Natives of the islands and coast, the people of the Cyclades, Crete, and Greece, became seafaring and adventurous by necessity. They created visual arts of striking originality, beginning in the third millennium BCE and culminating in the Classical art of fifth-century BCE Athens. Most of the early civilizations we have already considered arose in fertile river valleys: the Tigris and Euphrates, the Nile, the Indus, and the Yellow Rivers. In the Aegean region, the surrounding seas provided the needed security and resources (see Map 2, page 163).

The Aegean region of Europe is an area composed of mainland Greece, a cluster of nearby islands in the Aegean Sea including the Cyclades, and the large southern island of Crete.

Cycladic peoples were established as early as 6000 BCE. Because they left no written records, the prosperous society they developed in the Bronze Age, about 3000 BCE, is obscure. Their art is one of our main sources of information about them.

South of the Cyclades, on the island of Crete, the culture now known as Minoan took shape at the beginning of the Aegean Bronze Age, which lasted from about 3100 BCE to 1100 BCE, and was marked technologically by the use of **bronze** to make weapons and tools. Strategically located, Minoan Crete became a great sea power, reaching its height between 1750 and 1470 BCE, the so-called New Palace period. Excavations in and around immense architectural complexes, built from about 1900 BCE, have revealed the richness of Minoan art and ceremony and have uncovered ceramics, sculpture, wall paintings, and spectacular craftwork in ivory and gold.

Minoan Crete declined after 1500 BCE, although the main center, Knossos, functioned until the mid-thirteenth century BCE. Dominance in the Aegean region then shifted to a mainland Greek culture known as Helladic and/or Mycenaean, after one of its major cities, Mycenae. The Mycenaeans, who spoke an early form of the Greek language, built fortified strongholds ruled by local princes or kings, warlords whose exploits were memorialized in later Greek epics such as the *Iliad* and the *Odyssey*.

The Aegean Bronze Age ended about 1100 BCE, when Mycenaean civilization collapsed for unknown reasons. A period of disorganization followed, and not until around 900 BCE did the inhabitants of the Aegean region begin to flourish again. These were the people who came to be called the Greeks. Linked by language—most spoke some form of Greek by then—they lived in self-sufficient, close-knit communities scattered throughout the region, which eventually developed into independently governed city-states.

For at least 700 years, the Greeks were unimaginably creative. We still credit them with groundbreaking experiments in science, mathematics, and herbal medicine; for the implementation of representative government, that is, democracy; and for an astounding legacy of art and architecture that influences the Western world to this day. The works of Greek poets, dramatists, and philosophers have endured for more than two millennia. Homer, Aeschylus, Sophocles, Euripides, and Plato are only a few of the Greek authors whose works are still studied today.

Greek philosophers sought to define the ideal community, the actions of responsible citizenship, and the meaning of a good life. They asked, What is the Good, the True, the Beautiful? Artists responded by trying to capture such intangible concepts as "truth" and "beauty" in the material forms of sculpture, architecture, and painting. "Know thyself" and "Nothing in excess" are maxims inscribed in the sun god Apollo's sanctuary at Delphi in the mountains above the Gulf of Corinth, and they seem to have been imprinted on the heart and hands of every Greek artist. Know thyself: study the world around you; observe the variety found in nature; focus on human beings, for the gods and goddesses have human form. Then attempt to simplify and clarify these impressions in order to capture the essence of life.

The Cycladic Islands

During the late Neolithic and early Bronze Ages, the people who lived on the Cycladic islands, like their contemporaries in the ancient Near East and Egypt (see Chapter 2) farmed, made utensils, and engaged in trade. They used local stone to build fortified towns and hillside burial chambers, and they produced ceramic pottery and clay figurines of humans and animals.

Human figurines made of a fine white marble, abundant especially on the islands of Naxos and Paros, have been unearthed in and around graves. A few male statuettes have been found, including depictions of musicians and acrobats. Now starkly white, originally they had painted faces and hair. They may have been used in religious or burial rituals since they have been found in graves.

The *Seated Harp Player* is fully developed **sculpture in the round** (fig. 4-1), yet its body shape is just as simplified as that of the female figurines. The figure has been reduced to its geometric essentials, yet with careful attention to those elements that best characterize an actual musician. The harpist sits on a high-backed chair with a splayed base, head tilted back as if singing, knees and feet apart for stability, and arms raised, bracing the instrument in one hand while plucking its strings with the other. So expressive is the pose that we can almost hear the song.

Minoan Crete

The culture of the island of Crete, called Minoan by twentieth-century archaeologists, came into being around 3000 BCE. The word *Minoan* comes from a much later Greek legend about King Minos of Crete, who was said to keep a human-eating monster called a Minotaur (half human and half bull) at the center of a labyrinth, or maze. (This legend inspired later artists as diverse as Titian and Picasso.)

Crete is the largest of the Aegean islands, 150 miles long and 36 miles wide. The earliest Minoans were self-sufficient agriculturally, producing grains, fruit, cattle, and sheep, which they traded for the copper and tin ores they needed to make bronze and for various luxury goods. Incredibly, the Minoan traders sailed to ports in places as distant as Egypt, the Near East, and Anatolia (western Turkey).

Relatively little is known about daily life during the Minoan period, although a number of written records have been found. The two earliest forms of Minoan writing, hieroglyphs and a script called Linear A, still defy translation, but the surviving documents in a later script, Linear B—a very early form of Greek imported from the mainland—have proved to be invaluable. The documents incorporating this script include administrative records and inventories: lists of animals, olive trees, chariots, and weapons. Minoan civilization remained very much a mystery until a British archaeologist, Sir Arthur Evans (1851–1941), excavated the buried ruins of an extraordinary palace complex at Knossos, on Crete's north coast, in the early twentieth century.

Great palace complexes such as Knossos dominated the architecture of Crete from roughly 1900 to 1300 BCE. Safeguarded by watchtowers and stone walls, they were simultaneously used as administrative, commercial, and religious centers. The builders devised an almost earthquake-proof flexible wall system of timber supports and braces with light, mud-brick fill. **Facades** and lower walls were faced with **dressed stone** (cut and highly finished).

After a major earthquake about 1750 BCE, several palaces, including Knossos, were repaired and enlarged. The resulting "new palaces"—multistoried, flat-roofed, and with many columns—were designed with staggered levels, open stairwells, and strategically placed air shafts and light wells to maximize air and light. Religious, residential, manufacturing, and warehouse areas surrounded a large, central courtyard.

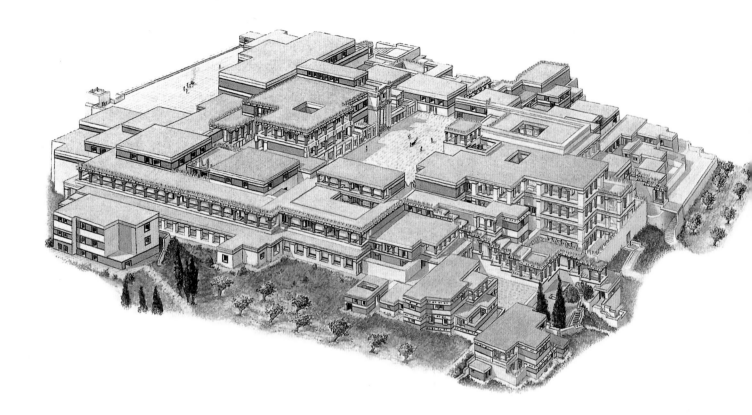

4-2 | **Reconstruction of the palace complex, Knossos,** Crete. Site occupied 2000–1375 BCE; complex begun in Old Palace period (c. 1900–1700 BCE); complex rebuilt after earthquakes and fires during Second Palace period (c. 1700–1450 BCE); final destruction c. 1375 BCE

During Knossos's heyday, the palace complex covered 6 acres (fig. 4-2). Its residential quarters had many assets: sunlit courtyards, richly colored murals, and an extraordinarily sophisticated plumbing system consisting of bathrooms and a network of terracotta pipes laid beneath the palace. Extensive workshops in and around Knossos and other complexes suggest that arts and crafts were officially sponsored. Huge storerooms point to the centralized management of trade in foodstuffs. In a single storeroom at Knossos, excavators found enough large ceramic jars to hold 20,000 gallons of olive oil.

The palace complexes in Crete included areas for ritual activities. Priestesses are believed to have overseen the worship of a goddess who controlled the natural world and who is associated with serpents, bulls, and the double ax. This Aegean deity may have inspired the later Greeks to venerate goddesses such as Artemis and Athena.

Like many other early cultures, Minoans may have associated their gods and god-rulers with powerful animals, especially the lion and the bull. Depictions of bulls appear often in Minoan art, rendered with an intensity not seen since the prehistoric cave paintings at Chauvet, Lascaux, and Altamira (see Chapter 1). While neither the images nor later myths offer any proof that the Minoans worshiped a bull god, the animals apparently were sacrificed; horn shapes decorated outdoor altars. They also figured in a rite called bull jumping practiced by men and women who must have been trained acrobats (see fig. 4-4).

Minoan wall painting displays elegant drawing, linear contours filled with bright colors, a preference for profile or full-faced views, and a stylization that turns natural forms into decorative patterns, yet keenly observes the appearance of the human body in motion. Those conventions can be seen in the vivid murals at Akrotiri, on the island Thera, an outpost of Minoan culture. One of the houses at Akrotiri has rooms dedicated to young women's initiation ceremonies. In the detail shown here, a young woman picks purple fall saffron crocus, valuable for its use as a yellow dye, as a flavoring for food, and as a medicinal plant to alleviate menstrual cramps (fig 4-3). The girl wears the typically colorful Minoan flounced skirt with a short-sleeved, open-breasted bodice, large earrings, and bracelets. She still has the shaved head, fringed hair, and long ponytail of a child. On another wall, not shown here, girls present their flowers to an older seated woman who is flanked by a monkey and a griffin (half lion–half eagle). Surely the woman is a goddess receiving her devotees, and the room had a special ceremonial use.

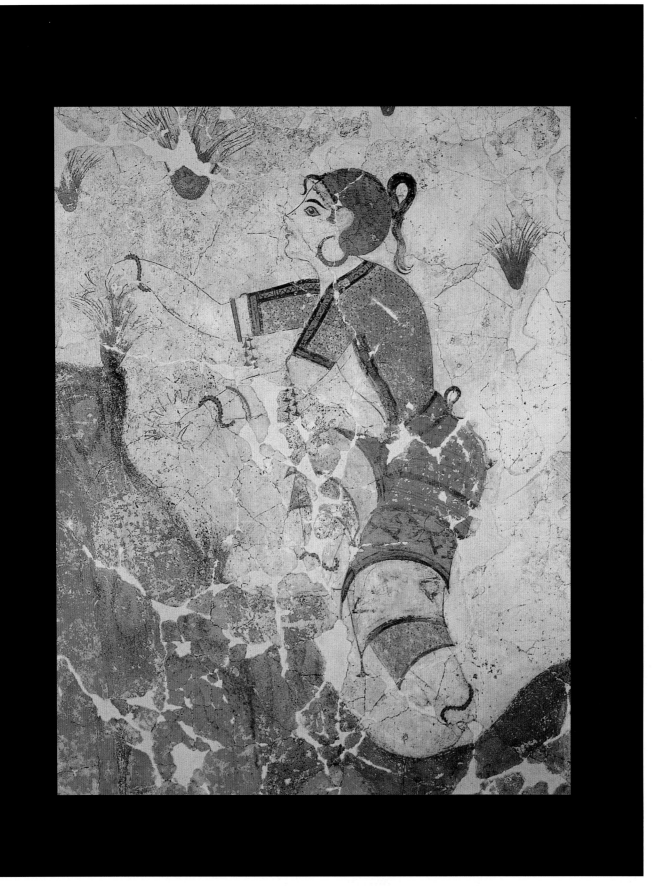

4-3 | ***Young Girl Gathering Crocus Flowers,*** detail of wall painting, Room 3 of House Xeste 3 Akrotiri, Thera. Second Palace period, c. 1700–1450 BCE

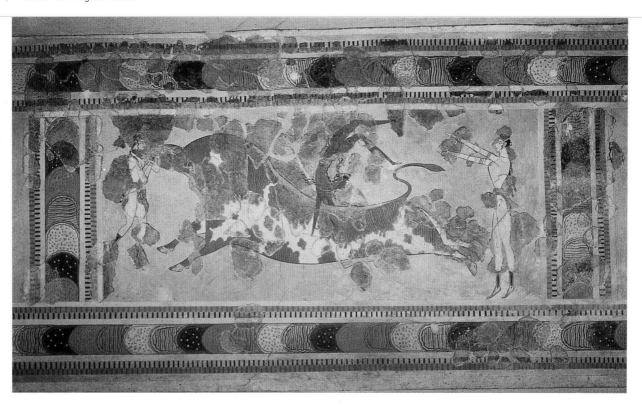

4-4 | ***Bull Jumping,*** wall painting with areas of modern reconstruction, from the palace complex, Knossos, Crete. c. 1550–1450 BCE Height approx. 24¹/₂" (62.3 cm). Archaeological Museum, Iráklion, Crete

Careful sifting during excavation preserved many fragments of the paintings that once covered the palace walls. The pieces were painstakingly sorted and cleaned by restorers and reassembled into puzzle pictures that still had more pieces missing than found. The next step was to fill in the gaps with colors similar to the original ones, but lighter and grayer in tone. It is therefore obvious which are the restored portions, but the eye can still read and enjoy the image.

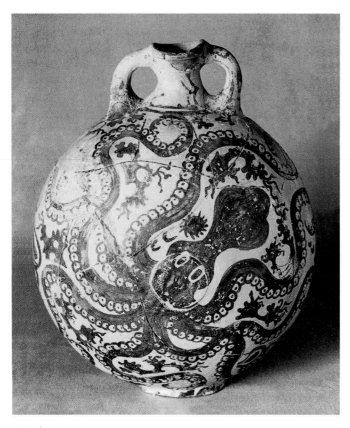

4-5 | ***Octopus Flask,*** from Palaikastro, Crete. c. 1500–1450 BCE. Ceramic Height 11" (28 cm). Archaeological Museum, Iráklion, Crete

The palace at Knossos also has wall paintings and painted low reliefs showing bulls. In one painting two women and a man engage in the dangerous ritual of bull jumping (fig. 4-4). (Minoan painters followed the convention of depicting figures with pale skin to represent women and dark skin to represent men.) The woman at the right is either beginning or finishing her vault, the man is in the midst of his, and the woman at the left grasps the bull by its horns, ready to leap. The painting may show an initiation or fertility ritual or it may honor a god or goddess by displaying human courage.

Painting on a smaller scale included decorating ceramics made in palace workshops, where the potter's wheel was in use from the early second millennium BCE. A striking vessel from the eastern site of Palaikastro, a bottle known as the *Octopus Flask,* dates about 1500–1450 BCE (fig. 4-5). The decoration with sea creatures and plants celebrates Cretan maritime power. Like microscopic life teeming in a drop of seawater, sea creatures float among an octopus's curling, sucker-covered tentacles. The painter captures the grace and energy of natural forms while presenting them as a stylized design in harmony with the vessel's shape.

The skills of Minoan artists, particularly those of metalsmiths, made their work highly sought after in mainland Greece. Jewelers became adept at decorating their goldwork with minute granules, or balls, of the precious metal fused to the surface, a technique known as **granulation**. This type of ornamentation is visible on a pendant perhaps made for a necklace in about

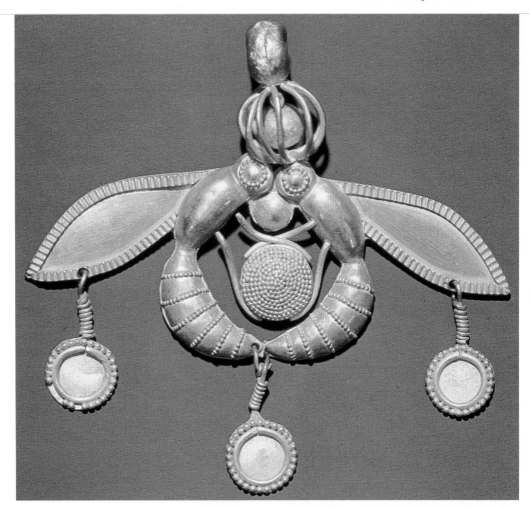

4-6 | (*right*) **Pendant** in the form of two bees or wasps from Chryssolakkos near Mallia, Crete c. 1700–1550 BCE Gold, height approx. 1¹³/₁₆" (4.6 cm) Archaeological Museum Iráklion, Crete

4-7 | (*below*) **Dagger blade** from Shaft Grave IV Grave Circle A, Mycenae Greece. c. 1600–1550 BCE Bronze inlaid with gold, silver, and copper, length 9³/₈" (23.8 cm) National Archaeological Museum, Athens

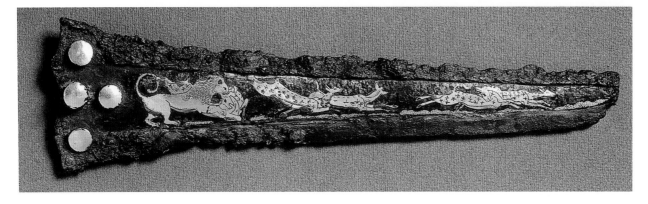

1700–1550 BCE (fig. 4-6). The artist arched a pair of bees or wasps around a granulated drop of honey. Their sleek bodies, decorated with parallel rows of granules, are framed by a single pair of outspread wings.

For reasons not entirely clear, Minoan civilization declined after about 1500 BCE, although Knossos continued as an administrative center until about 1250 BCE. Mainland Greece became the center of political power and cultural influence in the Aegean by 1400 BCE.

Mycenaean (Late Bronze Age) Civilization

Archaeologists have used the term *Helladic* (from *Hellas,* the Greek word for Greece) to designate the Bronze Age in mainland Greece. The Helladic period extends from about 3000 to

1000 BCE, overlapping with the Minoan chronology of Crete. (Like the time frames for Cycladic and Minoan cultures, dates continue to be debated.) Sometime in the early part of this period, Greek-speaking peoples invaded the mainland. They brought advanced metalworking, ceramic, and architectural techniques and displaced the indigenous Neolithic culture.

Life in fortified mainland Mycenaean strongholds such as Mycenae probably contrasted sharply with life in the open palace complexes on the island of Crete. The communities centered around strongholds controlled by local princes or kings. Evidence from shaft graves—deep vertical pits used for burial—dating from between 1600 and 1500 BCE, suggests a society that became increasingly wealthy and stratified. Magnificent swords, daggers, scepters, jewelry, and drinking cups mark the burials of an elite class of warriors (fig. 4-7).

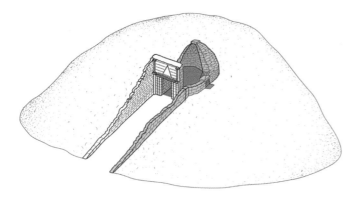

4-8 | **Cutaway drawing** of the beehive tomb called the Treasury of Atreus, Mycenae, Greece. c. 1300–1200 BCE

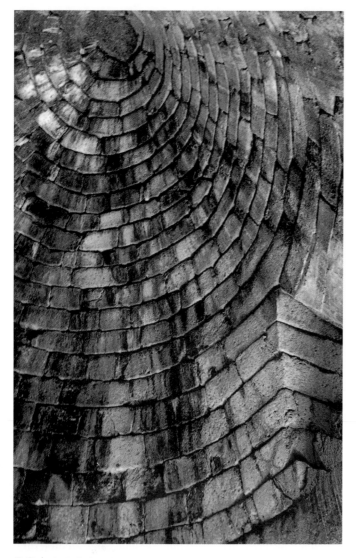

4-9 | **Corbeled vault,** interior of the so-called Treasury of Atreus. Stone Height of vault approx. 43' (13 m), diameter 47'6" (14.48 m)

Found in one of the shaft graves at Mycenae were three bronze dagger blades decorated with inlaid scenes. The Mycenaen artist cut shapes out of different-colored metals—copper, silver, and gold—then inlaid them in the bronze blades, then added the fine details in niello. In the *Iliad,* Homer's epic poem about the Trojan War written sometime before 700 BCE, the poet

MYTHOLOGY

Human beings are storytellers, and virtually every society has created its own *mythology* to give form to its gods and to explain the unexplained, including the origin of the universe, birth and death, and the existence of good and evil. Throughout the world, mythological characters and their stories are the most frequently represented subjects in the history of art. The main characters of Classical mythology—that of Greek and Roman civilizations—are gods and goddesses, demigods and demigoddesses, heroes and heroines, and monsters. The behavior, relationships, and attitudes of mythical characters mirror the nature and values of the society that created the myths.

Some myths seem to have originated in actual events. The Greeks' war against Troy in Asia Minor, for example, is now believed to have really happened more than 300 years before it was mythologized in the *Iliad* and the *Odyssey* by the legendary poet known as Homer in the eighth century BCE.

Homer tells of a ten-year siege by the Greeks of the city of Troy, which is generally believed to have stood on the site of Hissarlik, in modern Turkey. Inspired by the goddess Aphrodite, Paris, son of the Trojan king, abducted Helen, the most beautiful woman in the world and wife of King Menelaus of Sparta. King Menelaus and his brother King Agamemnon of Mycenae, both sons of Atreus, led the Greek troops in a siege of Troy. Human warriors, gods, and goddesses took sides in a ten-year war to avenge Menelaus and regain Helen. It is not clear whether Helen, Menelaus, Agamemnon, or Atreus really existed, or even if the Trojan War really took place, although the story probably had roots in some actual battle or raid. Ancient Greek historians, accepting the Trojan War as history, dated it anywhere from 1334 BCE to 1150 BCE, certainly long before Homer turned it into a legendary combat.

The story of the Trojan War was retold by the Roman poet Virgil (70–19 BCE) in his *Aeneid*, which he wrote to "prove" the lineage of Emperor Augustus back to the heroic era of ancient Greece. The *Aeneid* includes the story of Laocoön, the Trojan priest whose punishment from the gods was immortalized in a dramatic sculpture from the first century CE (see fig. 24).

describes similar decoration on Agamemnon's armor and Achilles' shield. The decoration on the blade shown here depicts a lion attacking a deer with four more terrified animals in full flight. Like the bull in figure 4-4 the animals spring forward in the "flying gallop" pose to indicate their speed and energy. The German archaeologist Heinrich Schliemann (1822–1890) excavated the shaft graves in 1876.

A tomb, popularly and incorrectly designated as the "Treasury of Atreus," built around 1300–1200 BCE (fig. 4-8), is close to the Trojan War in date, but is unlikely to be connected to Homer's kings of Mycenae. Other legends tell of a race of giants, the Cyclops, who moved the huge stones and gave the name **cyclopean** to the large-stone masonry seen in Mycenaean citadels and tombs. More than a hundred such tombs have been found on mainland Greece, nine of them, like this one, in the vicinity of Mycenae. They were constructed for members of Helladic ruling families and were used later than shaft graves.

An uncovered, walled passageway about 120 feet long and 20 feet wide led to the door of a conical structure, the **beehive-shaped** tomb. The circular main chamber, 43 feet high, is formed by a **corbeled vault:** a **vault** built up in regular **courses** (layers)

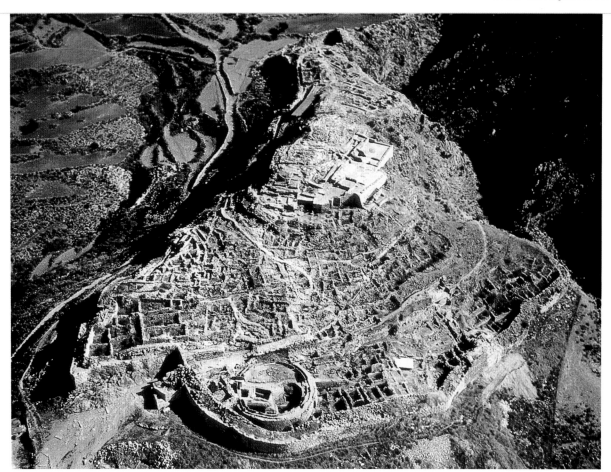

4-10 | **Mycenae,** Greece. c. 1600–1200 BCE

The citadel's hilltop position and fortified ring wall are clearly visible. The Lion Gate (see fig. 4-11) is at the lower left, approached today by a dirt path. The grave circle is at the lower center. The foundations of the palace are seen as a light rectangular area at the upper center.

4-11 | **Lion Gate,** Mycenae. c. 1250 BCE. Limestone relief, height of sculpture approx. 9'6" (2.9 m)

In this historic photograph, Heinrich Schliemann, director of the excavation, stands to the left of the gate and his second wife and partner in archaeology, Sophia, sits to the right.

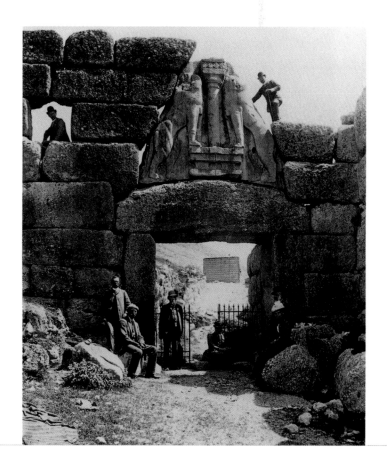

of dressed stone in overlapping and ever-decreasing rings carefully calculated to meet in a single **capstone** at the peak (fig. 4-9). The great size of the vaulted chamber—47 feet in diameter and 43 feet high—made the tomb the largest unobstructed interior space built before the Roman Pantheon (see fig. 6-24). Like the Neolithic passage graves constructed in western Europe (see fig. 1-13), the stone structure was covered by earth to form an artificial mountain.

Megalithic walls, broken by a monumental entrance and one or two secret emergency exits, encircled the Mycenaean fortress-palaces (fig. 4-10). The imposing Lion Gate (c. 1300–1200 BCE) led into the citadel of Mycenae (fig. 4-11). The gate consists of a **post-and-lintel** frame that once held massive wood and metal doors, topped by a **relieving arch**, in this case, a **corbel arch** spanning the open space with layers of stones, each layer projecting over the lower level. In the opening over the door, a pair of lions nearly 9 feet tall flank a Minoan-style column that may symbolize the king's inner retreat and audience chamber. The

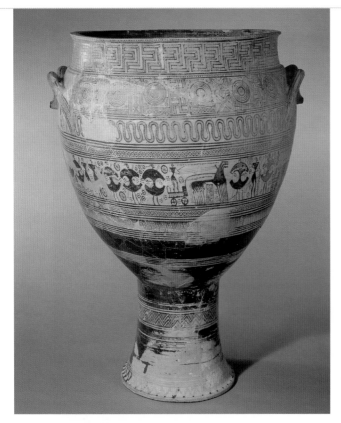

4-12 | **Krater,** attributed to the Hirschfeld Workshop, Athens c. 750–700 BCE. Terra cotta, height 4⁵/₈" (108 cm). The Metropolitan Museum of Art, New York

Rogers Fund, 1914 (14.130.14)

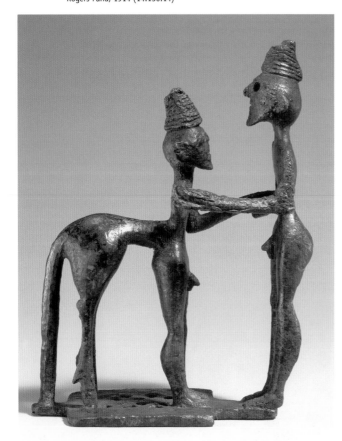

4-13 | ***Man and Centaur,*** perhaps from Olympia. c. 750 BCE Bronze, height 4⁵/₁₆" (11.1 cm). The Metropolitan Museum of Art, New York

Gift of J. Pierpont Morgan, 1917 (17.190.2072)

animals have lost their heads, but holes in the stones suggest the heads were removable and probably fashioned of some precious material. If they were indeed made of bronze or gold, they must have created an imposing presence. From this gate, a long, stone passageway pierces the citadel proper, at the center of which stood the king's palace.

Mycenaean civilization does not have a long history. By 1200 BCE, invaders are believed to have crossed into mainland Greece and taken control of the major cities and citadels. The period between about 1100 and 900 BCE became a "dark age" in the Aegean, marked by political and economic instability and upheaval and producing very little art. But a new culture emerged, one that looked back to the exploits of the Helladic warrior princes and the glories of a heroic age and at the same time formed the basis of a truly new Greek civilization.

The Emergence of Greek Civilization

In the ninth and eighth centuries BCE, the people we know as Greeks, the offspring of ancient inhabitants of the Aegean region and newer migrants, began to form independently governed city-states. Whenever possible, cities were built on a hilltop that could be fortified, an **acropolis** (*acro* means "high," and *polis* means "city"). Eventually the hill became a fortified religious sanctuary with the commercial, governmental, and domestic areas constructed in the plain or valley below. The most famous acropolis is in Athens.

As the population eventually outstripped crop yields, outlying colonies were established to alleviate food shortages. The new communities, like their Bronze Age predecessors, depended on trade with other regions to meet the needs of their growing populations. Many city-states developed merchant fleets that sailed across the Mediterranean and into the Black Sea. They too established colonies, some of which became influential commercial centers in their own right.

At first, aristocratic councils ruled the Greek city-states. Then, beginning around 700 BCE and extending into the sixth century BCE, self-appointed leaders called tyrants imposed a dictatorial form of rule, often with popular support. At their most beneficent, they fostered urban development at home and sought economic rather than military influence abroad.

The idea that all citizens should share in the rights and responsibilities of government began to emerge in the city-state of Athens in the sixth century BCE, although only a few privileged males were considered citizens. In the late sixth century, a leader called Kleisthenes, often called the father of democracy, instituted reforms that broadened the representative base of Athenian government. Although the system of rulership Kleisthenes developed was democratic in principle, it was open only to Athenian men. Women took no official part in government, nor did slaves or men born outside Athens.

Athens and the other Greek city-states, in spite of their rivalries, shared a common language and culture and developed a distinctively Greek art. Within a remarkably brief time Greek artists developed ideals of human beauty and architectural excellence that continue to have a profound influence today. From about 900 BCE to about 100 BCE, they explored new ideas and produced an impressive body of work with clear stylistic and technical characteristics. Periods of Greek art are named for these styles: Geometric, Archaic, and Classical.

THE GEOMETRIC STYLE

The Geometric style became widespread after about 900 BCE and lasted until about 700 BCE. An Athenian vase exemplifies the complex linear decoration of the Geometric style (fig. 4-12). Dated about 750 BCE, the vessel, a krater, was a grave marker made to hold offerings. Funerary rituals are recorded in two bands, or **registers**, of decoration. In the top register, the body of the deceased lies on its side on a platform. Accompanying figures with their hands on their heads may be tearing their hair with grief. Triangles were used to represent torsos; round dots stand for eyes in profile heads, and lines depicting arms and legs swell into bulging thighs and calves. Below, a procession of horse-drawn chariots and foot soldiers, who look like walking shields, recall the athletic competitions or funeral games held to honor dead men. Figures are neither in fully frontal nor in full-profile views but are subtly twisted.

Greek artists of the Geometric period also produced many small figurines of wood, ivory, clay, and especially cast bronze. A tiny bronze of this type, *Man and Centaur*, dates about 750 BCE (fig. 4-13). Like the painter of the vase from the Dipylon Cemetery (see fig. 4-12), the sculptor reduced the body parts to simple geometric shapes. Nevertheless the figures seem charged with energy. The identity of the two figures is unknown, but they might be the legendary hero Achilles and the centaur Chiron, his teacher. Figurines such as *Man and Centaur*, which possibly served as a votive offering, have been found in **sanctuaries**, sites sacred to one or more of the Greek gods.

THE ARCHAIC PERIOD

The Archaic period lasted from about 600 to 480 BCE. Although its name means "old" or "old-fashioned," the Archaic period was a time of great achievement. The poet Sappho on the island of Lesbos wrote poetry during the Archaic period. Her poetry would later inspire the geographer Strabo, near the end of the millennium, to write: "Never within human memory has there been a woman to compare with her as a poet." On another island, the legendary slave Aesop told animal fables of human folly that are still recounted today. Artists shared in the growing prosperity as city councils and wealthy individuals sponsored the creation of sculpture, fine ceramic wares, and civic buildings such as council chambers, public fountains (see fig. 4-21), and temples.

The earliest standing Greek temples date from the Archaic period. The temple was conceived both as an earthly home and as a treasury for gods and goddesses. It is in effect an idealized shelter. Generally temples have a main room, called the **cella** or **naos,** and a vestibule, called the **pronaos.** This room is surrounded by a single or double row of columns, known as a **peristyle** (see fig. 4-15). The platform or base of the building is called the **stylobate**. Architects developed systems of proportions and ornament known as *orders* for temple **plans** and **elevations**—the arrangement, proportions, and appearance

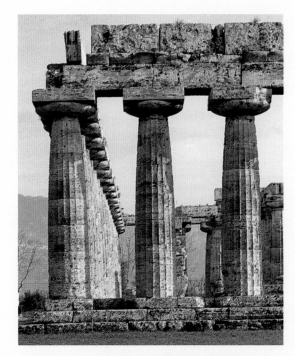

4-14 | **Corner view of the Temple of Hera I**
Paestum, Italy. c. 550 BCE

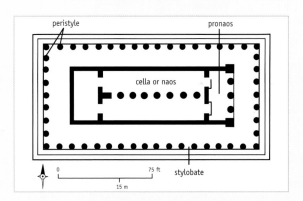

4-15 | **Plan of the Temple of Hera I,** Paestum

of the temple, especially the columns and the lintels. The posts and lintels we have seen up until now in the history of ancient architecture became **columns** and **entablatures** (see "The Greek Architectural Orders," page 100).

Buildings are often better preserved in outlying regions than in the homeland of a culture. A well-preserved Archaic period temple built about 550 BCE still stands at Paestum (Poseidonia), a Greek colony founded about 50 miles south of the modern city of Naples, Italy. Dedicated to Hera, queen of the gods, the temple (figs. 4-14, 4-15) is known today as Hera I to distinguish it from a second temple to Hera built adjacent to it about a century later. The builders used the **Doric order,** the earliest Greek order. Fluted columns without **bases,** resting directly on the **stylobate**, or floor of the temple, rise to

Elements of Architecture
THE GREEK ARCHITECTURAL ORDERS

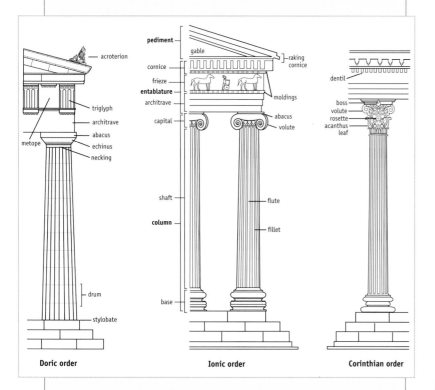

Doric order

Ionic order

Corinthian order

An *order* is a system of proportions derived from the diameter of a column shaft and used in the ensemble of entablature, capital, column, and base. No element of an order could be changed without producing a corresponding change in the other elements.

The Classical orders—columns with their entablatures—are comprised of a system of interdependent parts whose proportions are based on mathematical ratios. The three Classical Greek architectural orders are the Doric, the Ionic, and the Corinthian. The Doric and Ionic orders were well developed by about 600 BCE. The Doric order is the oldest and plainest of the three orders. The Ionic order is named after Ionia, a region occupied by Greeks on the west coast of Anatolia and the islands off that coast. The Corinthian order, a variation of the Ionic, began to appear around 450 BCE (see fig. 6). Later, the Romans appropriated the Corinthian order and elaborated it, as we shall see in Chapter 6.

The basic components of the Greek orders are the column and the entablature, which function as post and lintel. All types of columns have a shaft and a capital; some also have a base. Columns are formed of round sections, or drums, which are joined inside by metal pegs. The entablature consists of an architrave, frieze, and cornice.

Over the centuries, Western architects have invoked the Greek orders used for temple design to express rationality, restraint, and physical and moral perfection.

unadorned, cushionlike **capitals**, formed of a rounded **echinus** and a tabletlike **abacus**. The especially robust columns of Hera I, topped with widely flaring capitals, create an impression of great permanence and stability. But because the columns swell in the middle and contract toward the top (an attribute known as **entasis**) the building retains a sense of energy and upward lift. Above the columns, a horizontal entablature (composed of **architrave**, **frieze**, and **cornice**) and the triangular **pediments** (forming the triangular gable ends) support the temple's roof. In the frieze, flat panels (**metopes**) alternate with vertically grooved panels (**triglyphs**).

Sculpture or painting often decorated the metopes of the frieze and the pediments. Perhaps among the earliest surviving examples of Greek pedimental sculpture are fragments of the ruined Temple of Artemis on the island of Korkyra (Corfu), which date from about 600–580 BCE (fig. 4-16). The figures in this sculpture were carved in high relief on slabs, which were then installed in the pediment space. At the center is the snake-haired Medusa, a female monster who had the power to turn humans into stone if they looked upon her face (fig. 4-17). The hero Perseus avoided this fate by looking at her in the mirrorlike surface of his shield as he beheaded her. On either side of Medusa are her offspring: the flying horse Pegasus on the left (only part of his rump and tail remain) and the giant Chrysaor on

Greek Gods	
Zeus	king of the gods
Hera	Zeus's wife and sister, queen of the gods
Athena	goddess of wisdom and civilization
Ares	god of war
Apollo	god of the sun and reason
Aphrodite	goddess of love
Artemis	goddess of the moon and hunting
Hermes	messenger of the gods
Hades	god of the underworld
Dionysos	god of wine
Hephaistos	god of fire
Hestia	goddess of hearth and family
Demeter	goddess of agriculture
Poseidon	god of the sea
Eros	god of love
Although sometimes worshiped as a god, strictly speaking Herakles is a hero known for his physical strength.	

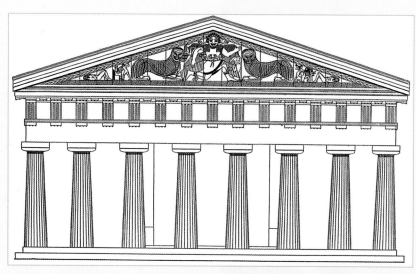

4-16   **Reconstruction of the west pediment of the Temple of Artemis,** Korkyra (Corfu), after G. Rodenwaldt. c. 600–580 BCE

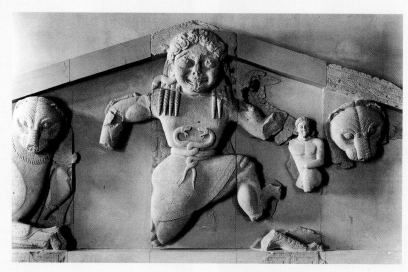

4-17   *Medusa,* fragments of sculpture from the west pediment of the Temple of Artemis, Korkyra. c. 580 BCE. Limestone, height of pediment at the center 9'2" (2.79 m). Archaeological Museum, Korkyra

the right. Flanking them are crouching felines and dying human warriors tucked into the corners of the pediment. Men, animals, and monster are all depicted in simple **volumetric** forms, once brightly painted in reds and blues.

In addition to carving sculpture for temple exteriors, artists of the Archaic period created freestanding statues. Usually lifesize or larger, most were made of white marble and originally were painted in bright, naturalistic colors. Some bore inscriptions indicating that they had been commissioned by individual men or women for a commemorative purpose. While some marked graves, most stood in sanctuaries, where they lined the sacred way from the entrance to the main temple in perpetual attendance on the god or goddess.

Traditionally, a female statue of this type is called a *kore* (plural, *korai*), Greek for "young woman," and a male statue is called a *kouros* (plural, *kouroi*), meaning "young man." The Archaic *korai*, wearing long, sleeveless garments and earrings, represented deities, priestesses, or nymphs. The *kouroi*, nearly always nude, have been variously identified as gods, warriors, and victorious athletes. Because the Greeks associated young athletic males with fertility and familial regeneration, the *kouroi* may also have been looked upon as symbolic ancestor figures.

A *kouros* dating from about 600 BCE (fig. 4-18; see page 102) exemplifies the early Greek ideal. Superficially reminiscent of standing males in Egyptian sculpture (see fig. 2-18), this young

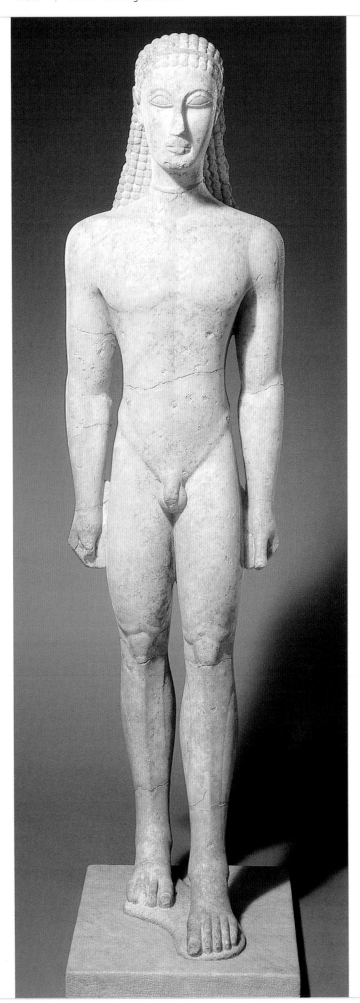

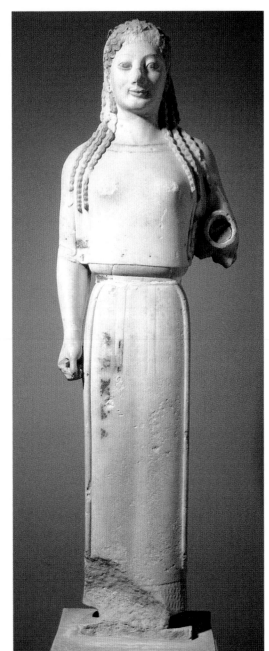

4-18 | *Kouros.* c. 600 BCE. Marble, height 6'4" (1.93 m)
The Metropolitan Museum of Art, New York
Fletcher Fund, 1932 (32.11.1)

Greek is shown frontally, arms at his sides, fists clenched, and one leg slightly in front of the other. Quite un-Egyptian, however, is the figure's athletic build. The sculptor removed the stone from around the body and between the legs, making the figure seem light and energetic. He depicted anatomy carefully, although tradition required that the ridges and grooves of bones and muscles form simple, balanced patterns. The eyes are relatively large and wide open, and the mouth forms a characteristic closed-lip smile, known as the **Archaic smile**, apparently used to enliven the expressions of figures. Unlike his partially clothed Egyptian counterpart, the young Greek wears only a ribbon around his neck and another band on his curly hair. Here nudity serves to remove the figure from a specific place, time, or social class.

4-19

Peplos Kore
from the
Acropolis
Athens
c. 530 BCE
Marble
Height 48"
(123 cm)
Acropolis
Museum
Athens

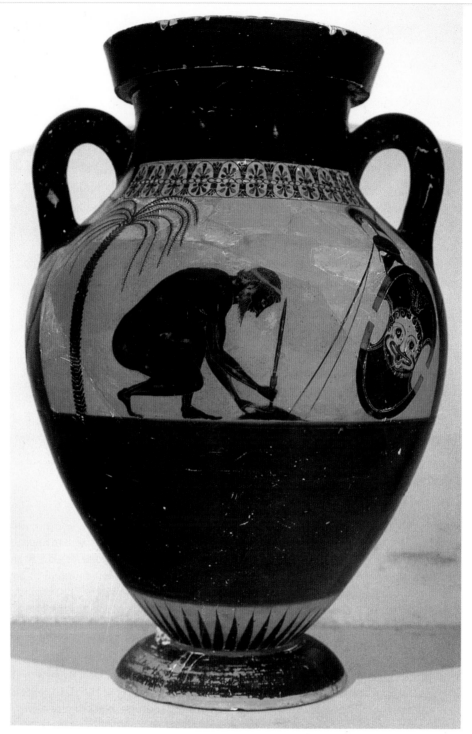

4-20

Exekias. *The Suicide of Ajax* black-figure decoration on an amphora c. 540 BCE Ceramic, height of amphora 27" (69 cm) Château-Musée Boulogne-sur-Mer, France

With remarkable rapidity, Greek sculptors perfected the art of creating lifelike human figures. The *Peplos Kore* (fig. 4-19), dated about seventy years after the youth, exhibits subtly rounded body forms. Her arms and head convey a greater sense of soft flesh covering a real bone structure. Her smile and hair seem almost natural, and color must have made her seem even more lifelike. She also once wore a metal crown and earrings. She wears the distinctive Athenian garment known as a *peplos*—a draped rectangle of woolen cloth, folded over the top, fastened at the shoulders, and belted to give a bloused effect. Traces of paint on the lower area of the sculpture suggest that the carved *peplos* may have been decorated with a pattern of rich embroidery.

In vase painting, artists presented not just a single figure, but a story, or narrative. Abandoning the narrow bands of decoration characteristic of the Geometric period (see fig. 4-12), vase painters, especially in Athens, gradually increased the size of figures until one or two scenes filled the body of the vessel. A mid-sixth-century BCE **amphora**—a large, all-purpose storage jar—illustrates this development (fig. 4-20). One side shows *The Suicide of Ajax*, an episode from the legends of the Trojan War. Ajax, a Greek warrior, was second only to Achilles in bravery. After the death of Achilles, the Greeks awarded the hero's armor to Odysseus rather than to Ajax; the latter, humiliated, committed suicide. With typical Greek restraint yet sense of drama, Exekias, the potter and painter

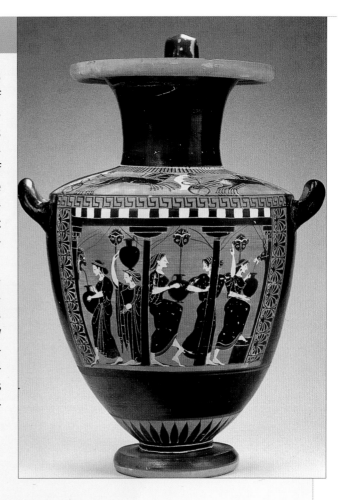

Throughout the ancient Greek world, archaeologists have unearthed thousands of ceramic vessels, a high proportion of them painted with complex designs depicting scenes from mythology or daily life. The hydria, or water jug, shown in figure 4-21, depicts Greek women performing a common chore: collecting water at a communal well. While earlier art historians tended to cite the fineness of vase painting as the height of Greek art, more recently scholars have pointed to the vessels' relevance as functional objects and as evidence of what subjects the Greeks cared about. Obviously, the Greek myths and legends were believed and enjoyed. The details of ordinary life were also considered worthy **subject matter**.

To meet the practical need for jugs, storage vessels, pitchers, and bowls, potters and painters produced them in great numbers, sometimes in a setting that would be called a small factory today. The wares were inexpensive to make and own. By comparison, few large-scale mural paintings survive intact, and only the most affluent Greeks could afford to commission them. The painters of large-scale murals were probably held in higher esteem than the painters of vases, in spite of the fact that these apparently common household objects often contain designs of infinite elegance and skill.

4-21   "A.D." Painter. *Women at a Fountain House,* black-figure decoration on a hydria. 520–510 BCE. Ceramic, height of hydria 20⅞" (53 cm). Museum of Fine Arts, Boston
William Francis Warden Fund

who signed this vase, captures the impending moment of tragedy rather than the instant of the hero's death. Ajax plants his sword upright in a mound of dirt so that he can fling himself upon it. Two in-curving elements—the tree on the left and the shield and helmet that the warrior has set aside on the right—echo the swelling shape of the amphora and the rounding of the hero's back. Thus the painter recalls a complex story in a single image, adding to its solemnity by creating a clear, easily understandable **composition**.

Exekias has used a technique known as **black-figure** painting. This technique became the principal mode of vase painting throughout Greece in the sixth century BCE. The painter used a **slip** (a mixture of clay and water) to silhouette figures against the reddish, unpainted clay of the background. Details are incised with a sharp tool inside the silhouetted shapes. The color contrast is created in the firing process.

Touches of white and reddish purple gloss, made of metallic pigments mixed with slip, enhance the black-figure decoration on some pieces, such as an Athenian **hydria**, or water jug, made about 510 BCE (fig. 4-21). Painted by an artist whom scholars named the "A.D." Painter, the hydria, as mentioned earlier, depicts women gathered at a communal fountain housed in a splendid Doric building. Columns with flaring Doric capitals support a brightly painted frieze. Water flows from carved animal-head water spouts. Three women fill hydrias like the one on which they are painted, while a fourth balances a jug on her head

for the trip home. A fifth woman appears to be waving to someone in greeting. The women's skin is painted white, a convention for female figures also found in Egyptian and Minoan art. Incised marks and touches of reddish purple gloss were used to create fine details in the architecture and in the figures' clothing and hair. In ancient Greece, communal fountains supplied water to the cities, and the daily meeting of the women at the fountain house provided opportunities for social interaction in a society that restricted most women to their homes.

In the last third of the sixth century BCE, painters were still creating handsome black-figure wares. Some painters turned away from this meticulous process to a new technique called **red-figure** decoration, so called because red figures stand out against a black background. In the red-figure technique, the painter covered the vase with slip but left figures unpainted to reveal the reddish body of the vessel. Instead of engraving details, the painter drew with a fine brush dipped in the slip. The result was a lustrous dark vessel with light-colored figures painted with dark-colored details (see fig. 4-23). The greater ease, speed, and flexibility of this technique led artists to adopt it quickly.

An early-fifth-century red-figure **kylix**, or two-handled drinking cup, displays the painter's virtuosity at adapting a scene to the shape of the vessel (fig. 4-22), as well as in the drawing of individual figures in action. The artist known as the Foundry Painter used the circular underside of the cup to illustrate the workings of a foundry for casting bronze figures. The walls of the pictured workshop are filled with tools and other paraphernalia: hammers, an ax and saw, molds of a human foot and hand, and several sketches. A seated worker attends to a furnace at left, while a second man, perhaps the supervisor (or is this another bronze figure like the *Young Warrior* from Riace, see figure 4-26) leans on a staff. A third worker assembles the already-cast parts of a figure; they are braced against a molded support. The painter has created a lively scene in an awkward space and also gives us insight into the working methods of sculptors using the cast-bronze **medium**.

THE EARLY CLASSICAL OR TRANSITIONAL PERIOD

Historically, the early fifth century BCE was marked by a series of invasions from Persia (see Chapter 5). The Greek cities banded together against their common foe, and by 479 BCE an

4-22 | **Foundry Painter.** *A Bronze Foundry,* red-figure decoration on a kylix from Vulci, Italy. 490–480 BCE. Ceramic diameter of kylix 12" (31 cm). Staatliche Museen zu Berlin, Preussischer Kulturbesitz, Antikensammlung

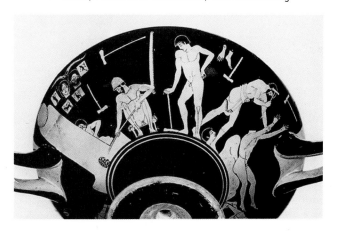

4-23 | **Pan Painter.** *Artemis Slaying Actaeon,* red-figure decoration on a bell krater. c. 470 BCE. Ceramic, height of krater 14⅝" (37 cm) Museum of Fine Arts, Boston
James Fund and by Special Contribution

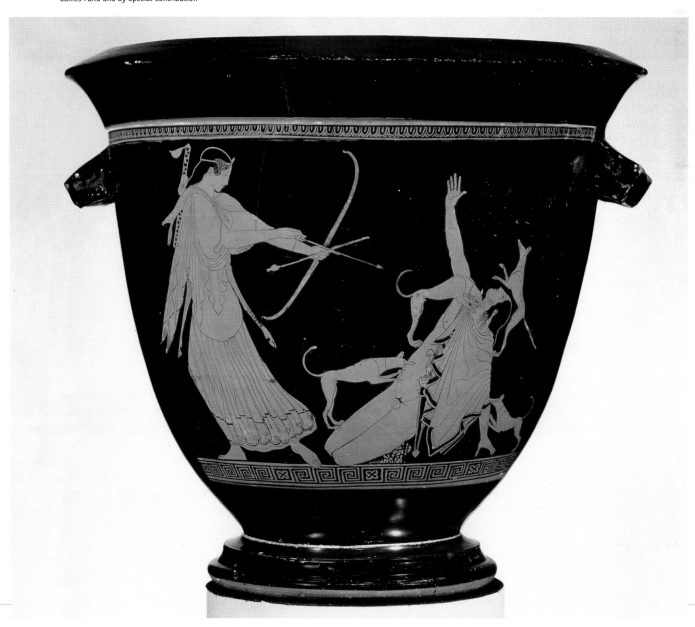

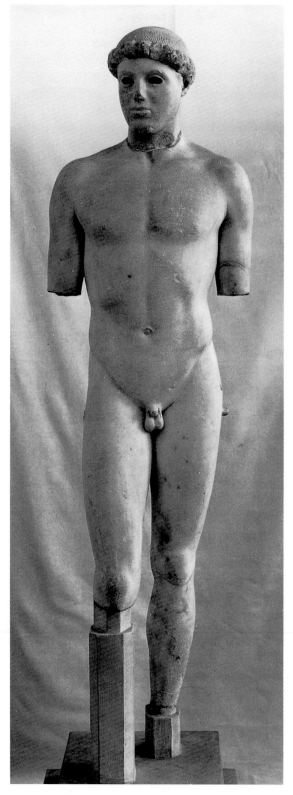

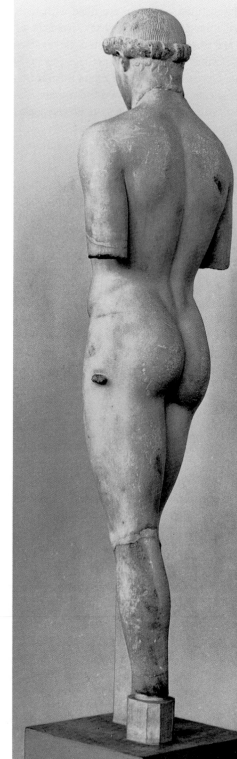

4-24

Kritios Boy. c. 480 BCE. Marble, height 33⁴/₅" (86 cm) Acropolis Museum Athens

When the *Kritios Boy* was excavated from debris at the Acropolis of Athens, the statue was thought by its finders to be by the Greek sculptor Kritios.

alliance of city-states led by Athens and Sparta had driven out the advancing Persians. Perhaps the Greeks' success against the Persians gave them a self-confidence that accelerated the development of their art. In any event within thirty years they created a new style. This period of marked change and evolution, called the Transitional or Early Classical period, lasted from the end of the Persian Wars to about 450 BCE.

A red-figured **bell krater** (bell-shaped bowl for mixing wine and water) shows the increasing **naturalism** (resemblance to visible nature) that differentiates the Early Classical from the Archaic style. Here, the painter, called the Pan Painter, depicted *Artemis Slaying Actaeon* (fig. 4-23; see page 105). When the hunter Actaeon accidentally saw the goddess Artemis taking her bath, she retaliated by causing his dogs to mistake him for a stag and to tear him apart. Here the hounds swarm over the fallen hunter, whom Artemis prepares to finish off with an arrow. The death seems melodramatic compared with the suicide of Ajax, but the Greek artist's sense of balance and order still successfully adjusts the actions of the figures to the vase shape.

In freestanding sculpture, the Greeks shifted in only a few generations from the rigid, frontal presentation of the human figure embodied in the Archaic *kouroi* to more natural, lifelike figures such as the so-called *Kritios Boy* (fig. 4-24). In contrast to the over-lifesize Archaic *kouroi* (see fig. 4-18), the *Kritios Boy* originally stood only a little over 3 feet tall. The solid, rounded body forms, broad facial features, and thoughtful expression—which lacks even a trace of the Archaic smile—give the figure an air of extraordinary solemnity. The easy pose contrasts markedly with the more rigid bearing of Archaic *kouroi*. The boy's weight rests on his left leg (the "engaged" leg), and his relaxed right leg bends slightly at the knee. The curve in his spine counters the slight shifting of his hips and the subtle drop of one shoulder. The sculptor captures the life and movement of the figure first implied in the Archaic *kouroi*.

The technique of modeling and **hollow-casting** bronze, developed at the end of the Archaic period, made possible more complex action poses, which would be difficult to carve in stone. A lifesize bronze *Charioteer* (fig. 4-25) illustrates the skill of Greek metalworkers. It was found in the Sanctuary of Apollo at Delphi together with fragments of a bronze chariot and horses. According to its inscription, the sculpture commemorates a victory by the driver sponsored by King Polyzalos of Gela (Sicily) in the Pythian Games (an event like the Olympics but held at Delphi and honoring Apollo) of 478 or 474 BCE. The idealized features of a handsome youth could almost be those of a particular individual. The single remaining hand and the feet are so realistic that they seem to have been cast from molds made from an actual person. The robe falls neatly into folds, yet the garment seems capable of swaying and rippling if the charioteer moved slightly or encountered a sudden breeze. The lifelike quality of the *Charioteer* calls to mind the claim by the Roman historian and naturalist Pliny the Elder (in the first century BCE), that three-time winners in Greek competitions had their features memorialized in statues.

A pair of over-lifesize bronze figures known as the *Riace Warriors* illustrate sculptors' skill in depicting the nude figure. Found by a diver on the seabed near Riace, a city on the southern coast of Italy, they may have been thrown from a sinking ship by sailors trying to lighten the load. One of the pair, the so-called *Young Warrior* (fig. 4-26; see page 108), dating from about 460–450 BCE, reveals a striking balance between anatomy based on arbitrary standards of perfection and details corresponding to visible nature. The athletic musculature suggests a youthfulness belied by the maturity of the heavy beard and almost haggard face. Minutely detailed touches, such as the swelling veins in the backs of the hands, contrast with the ide-

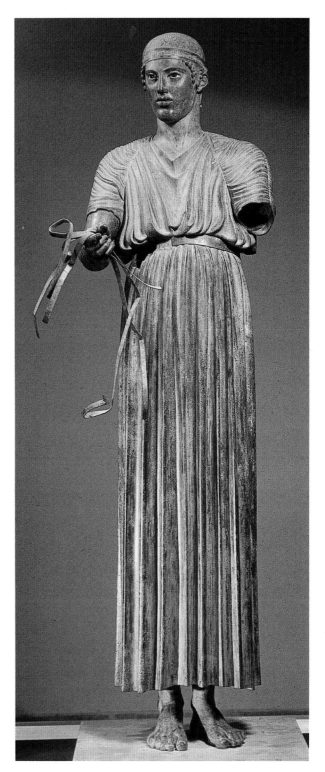

4-25 | *Charioteer,* from the Sanctuary of Apollo, Delphi. c. 470 BCE
Bronze, height 5'11" (1.8 m). Archaeological Museum, Delphi

The setting of a work of art affects our reaction to it. Today, this stunning figure is exhibited on a low base in the peaceful surroundings of a museum, isolated from other works and spotlighted for close examination. Its effect would have been very different in its original outdoor location, standing in a horse-drawn chariot atop a tall monument. Viewers in ancient times, exhausted from the steep climb to the sanctuary, possibly jostled by crowds of fellow pilgrims, could have absorbed only its overall effect, not the fine details of the face, robe, and hand visible to today's viewers.

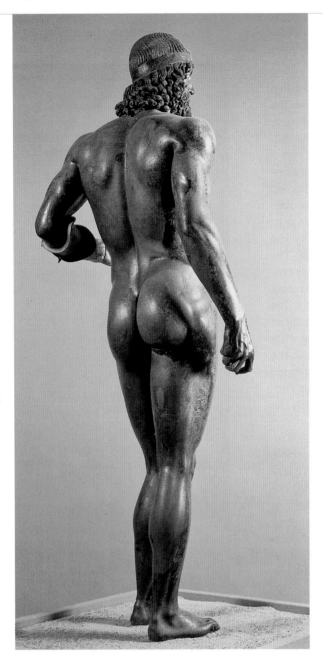

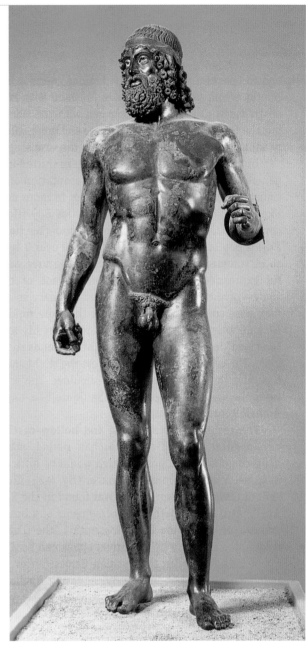

4-26

Young Warrior
found in the
sea off
Riace, Italy
c. 460–450 BCE
Bronze with
bone and glass
eyes, silver
teeth, and
copper lips and
nipples, height
6'8" (2.03 m)
Museo
Archaeològico
Nazionale
Reggio Calabria
Italy

alized smoothness of the rest of the body. The sculptor heightened the lifelike quality of the sculpture by adding eyes of bone and colored glass, silver plating on the teeth, and eyelashes and eyebrows of separately cast strands of bronze. Such intense study of the human figure prepared the way for the achievements of artists in the Classical period.

THE "GOLDEN AGE" OF ART

The Classical art of Greece dates about 450 to 400 BCE and is known also as the "Golden Age." Yet this period saw turmoil and destruction resulting from the Peloponnesian War: Sparta and Athens, without a common enemy, turned on each other. Sparta dominated the Peloponnese peninsula and much of the rest of mainland Greece, while Athens controlled the Aegean and became the wealthy and influential center of a maritime empire. Today we remember Athens for its cultural and intellectual brilliance and its experiments with democratic govern-

ment, which reached their zenith in the fifth century BCE under the charismatic leader Perikles.

The Acropolis of Athens, the hill that formed the city's ceremonial center, visually expressed the city's values and its civic pride. The Persians had destroyed the early buildings and statues in 480 BCE, so the Athenians rebuilt their monuments on the Acropolis during the second half of the fifth century BCE. According to Greek mythology, Athena, goddess of wisdom and civilization, claimed Athens as her city. Her temple, the Parthenon, dedicated to the Virgin Athena (*Athena Parthenos* in Greek), rose triumphantly over the city. It dominated the other structures on the hilltop site (fig. 4-27). The Parthenon was designed and built by the architects Kallikrates and Iktinos. The builders used the finest white marble everywhere on the building, even replacing the customary terra-cotta roof with marble slabs. The renowned sculptor Pheidias designed the sculptural decorations and in addition supervised the entire

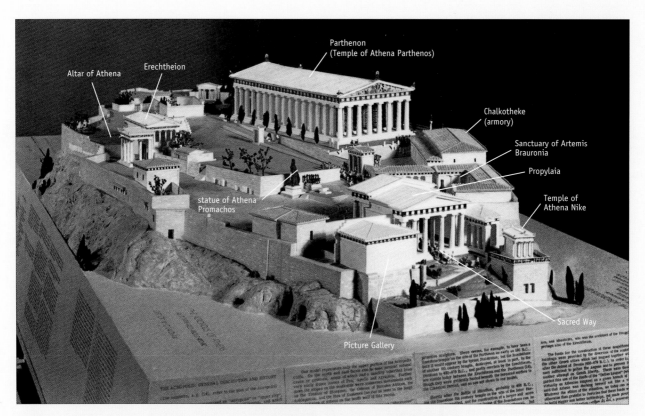

4-27   **Model of the Acropolis,** Athens. c. 400 BCE. With permission of the Royal Ontario Museum

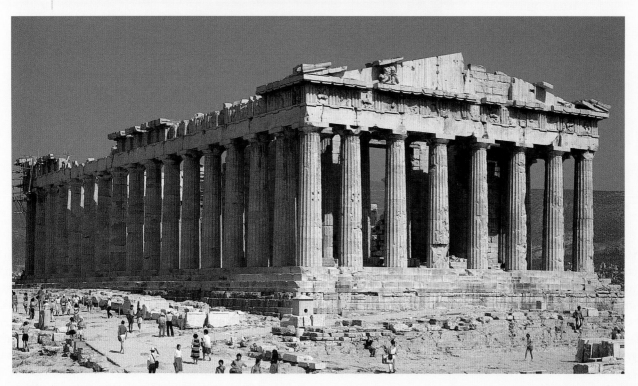

4-28   **Kallikrates** and **Iktinos. Parthenon,** Acropolis, Athens. 447–438 BCE. View from the northwest. (See pages 88–89.)

building project of the Acropolis. The building was completed in 438 BCE, and its sculpture, executed by Pheidias and other sculptors in his workshop, was finished in 432 BCE.

The Parthenon illustrates the refinement of Greek architecture in its structure and design (fig. 4-28). It follows the typical cella and peristyle plan and uses the Doric order. To counteract the optical illusions that would distort its appearance when seen from a distance, the architects made many subtle adjustments. Since long horizontal lines appear to sag in the center, the architects designed both the base of the

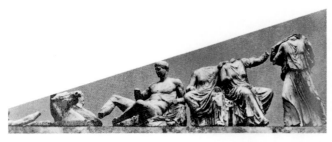
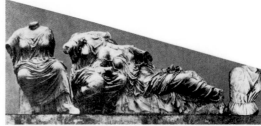

4-29 | **Photographic mock-up of the east pediment of the Parthenon** (using photographs of the extant marble sculpture of c. 438–432 BCE). The blank vertical spaces represent the missing sculptures

At the beginning of the nineteenth century, Thomas Bruce, the British earl of Elgin and ambassador to Constantinople, acquired much of the surviving sculpture from the Parthenon, which was being used for military purposes. He shipped it back to London in 1801 to decorate a lavish mansion for himself and his wife. By the time he returned to England a few years later, his wife had left him and the ancient treasures were at the center of a financial dispute. Finally, he sold the sculpture for a very low price. Referred to as the *Elgin Marbles*, most of the sculpture is now in the British Museum, including all the elements seen here except the torso of *Selene*, which is in the Acropolis Museum, Athens. The Greek government has tried unsuccessfully in recent times to have the *Elgin Marbles* returned.

4-30 | *Lapith Fighting a Centaur* metope relief from the Doric frieze on the south side of the Parthenon c. 440 BCE. Marble Height 56" (1.42 m) The British Museum London

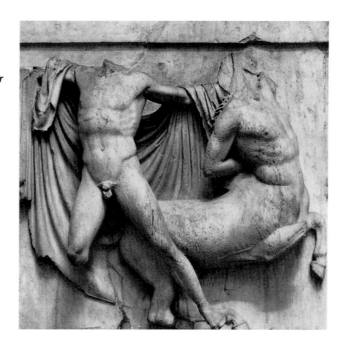

temple and the entablature to curve slightly upward toward the center. The columns have a subtle swelling, or entasis, and tilt inward slightly from bottom to top. In addition, corners are strengthened visually because the space between columns is less at the corners than elsewhere. These subtle modifications in the arrangement of elements give the Parthenon a buoyant organic appearance and prevent it from looking like a heavy, lifeless stone box. The building becomes, in effect, a gigantic marble sculpture.

Sculpture carved in the round filled the pediments of the Parthenon. The figures stood on the projecting shelves of the horizontal cornice—the top of the entablature—secured to the pediment wall with metal pins. Most of the works of sculpture have been damaged or lost over the centuries, but using the locations of the pinholes, scholars have determined the placement of the surviving statues and can infer the poses of the missing ones (fig. 4-29).

The figures on the east pediment illustrate the birth of Athena. The statues in the center of the composition, missing, probably showed Zeus seated on a throne, and standing next to him, Athena, who according to mythology had emerged fully grown from his head. Flanking the central figures were groups of goddesses, then single reclining male figures, and finally, in either corner, the sun god Apollo in his chariot and the moon goddess Selene in hers. The standing female figure left of center is Iris, messenger of the gods, already spreading the news of Athena's birth. The three female figures on the right side are perhaps Hestia (a sister of Zeus and the goddess of the hearth), Aphrodite (goddess of love), and her mother Dione (one of Zeus's many consorts). The sculptor, whether Pheidias or someone working in the Pheidian style, expertly rendered the human form beneath the draperies. The clinging fabric creates circular patterns rippling over torsos, breasts, and knees and uniting the three figures into a single mass.

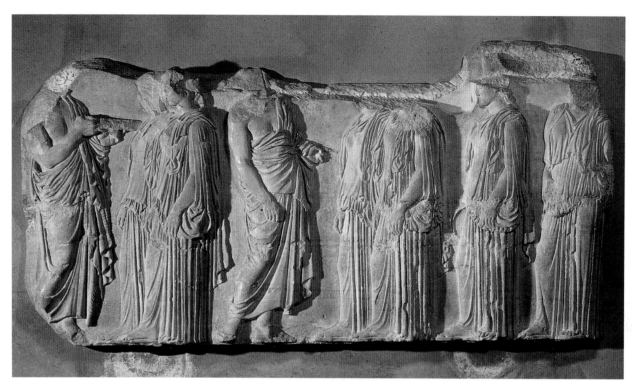

4-31 | *Marshals and Young Women,* detail of the *Procession*, from the Ionic frieze on the east side of the Parthenon. c. 438–432 BCE. Marble, height 43" (109 cm). Musée du Louvre, Paris

Originally, the white marble columns and inner walls supported bands of brightly painted low-relief sculpture (friezes). The Doric frieze of the Parthenon has carved metopes with scenes of victory. On the south side, the metopes depict the fight between the half-human centaurs and a legendary Greek tribe known as the Lapiths. The Lapith victory over the centaurs may have symbolized the triumph of reason over animal passions. In one relief (fig. 4-30), what should be a death struggle seems more like a choreographed, athletic ballet, displaying the Lapith's muscles and graceful movements against the implausible backdrop of his carefully draped cloak. In Greek art, a single image can stand for an entire historical episode.

Inside the Parthenon's Doric peristyle, an Ionic frieze (see "The Greek Architectural Orders," page 100) decorates the upper temple wall (fig. 4-31). Unlike the episodic Doric frieze, the Ionic frieze consisted of a continuous band of sculpture. Here the 525-foot-long frieze shows a procession, traditionally believed to celebrate the Great Panathenaic festival. In this procession, the women of Athens carried a new wool *peplos* to the Acropolis sanctuary to clothe an ancient wooden cult statue of Athena housed there. In the frieze, carefully planned rhythmic variations enliven the composition: the horses plunge ahead at full gallop; women proceed with a slow, stately step; parade marshals pause to look back at the progress of those behind them; and the gods and goddesses seated on benches await the arrival of the marchers.

The maidens who walk with such grace and dignity represent the Greek ideal of young womanhood, and their procession is an ideal procession outside time and place. Each figure fills the space, so maidens and marshals all have the same height. The marble sculpture of the frieze was originally painted in dark blue, red, and ocher, and details such as the bridles and reins on the horses were added in bronze (see fig. 23). To compensate for the dim lighting inside the peristyle, the top of the frieze band is carved in slightly higher relief than the lower part, tilting the figures outward to catch reflected light from the pavement. The procession of maidens attended by parade marshals, although only a fragment of the architectural decoration, provides an indication of the extraordinary quality of every detail of the temple.

Construction of another temple on the Acropolis, the Erechtheion (fig. 4-32; see page 112), began in the 430s BCE and continued until 405 BCE. Its precinct was thought to have been the site of a contest between Athena and the sea god Poseidon for patronage of Athens. The architect (believed to be Mnesikles) designed a temple with porches on three sides, the most famous of which is the Porch of the Maidens (fig. 4-33; see page 112). Six stately **caryatids** (carved figures functioning as columns) topped with simple Doric capitals stand on a high base and support an Ionic entablature, lightened by eliminating the frieze. Assuming a pose characteristic of Classical figures, each caryatid's weight is supported on one engaged leg, while the free leg,

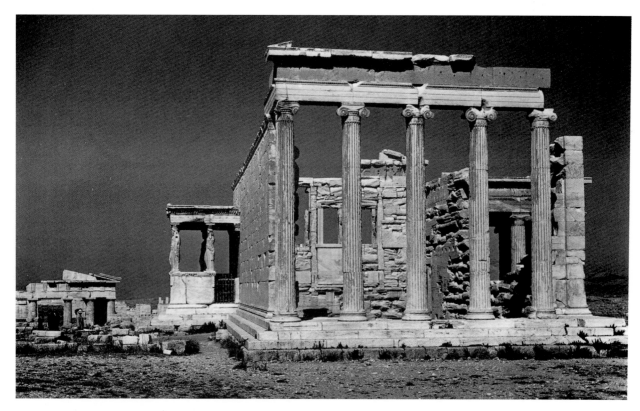

4-32 | **Mnesikles. Erechtheion,** Acropolis, Athens. c. 430–405 BCE. View from the east

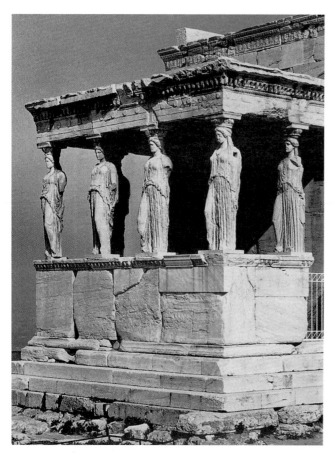

4-33 | **Porch of the Maidens** (Caryatid Porch) Erechtheion Acropolis, Athens. 421–405 BCE

bent at the knee, rests on the ball of the foot. The vertical fall of the drapery on the engaged side resembles the fluting of a column shaft and provides a sense of stability, whereas the bent leg gives an impression of relaxed grace and effortless support, like the entasis of the Doric shaft.

The building was constructed using the **Ionic order**, and the north and east porches of the Erechtheion epitomize the Ionic form. Taller and more slender in proportion than the Doric, the Ionic order also has richer and more elaborately carved decoration (see "The Greek Architectural Orders," page 100). The columns rise from molded bases and end in **volute** (spiral) capitals. The frieze consists of continuous moldings or bands of sculpture.

A second Ionic temple, dedicated to Athena Nike (Victory), stands near the entrance to the Acropolis precinct. A low wall faced with relief panels of Athena presiding over her winged attendants as they prepared for a victory celebration protects the viewer. The Victories contrast with the restrained caryatids of the Erechtheion. One of the most admired panels depicts Nike adjusting her sandal (fig. 4-34). The figure bends forward gracefully, causing her ample robe to slip off one shoulder. Her large wings, one open and one closed, effectively balance this unstable pose. Unlike the decorative swirls of heavy fabric covering the Parthenon goddesses or the weighty pleats of the robes of the Erechtheion caryatids, the textile covering this Nike appears delicate and light, clinging to her body like wet silk. The artist's vision, and the patron's wish, has changed dramatically since the creation of the *Peplos Kore* (see fig. 4-19).

Just as Greek architects defined and followed a set of standards for temple design, Greek sculptors sought an ideal **canon**

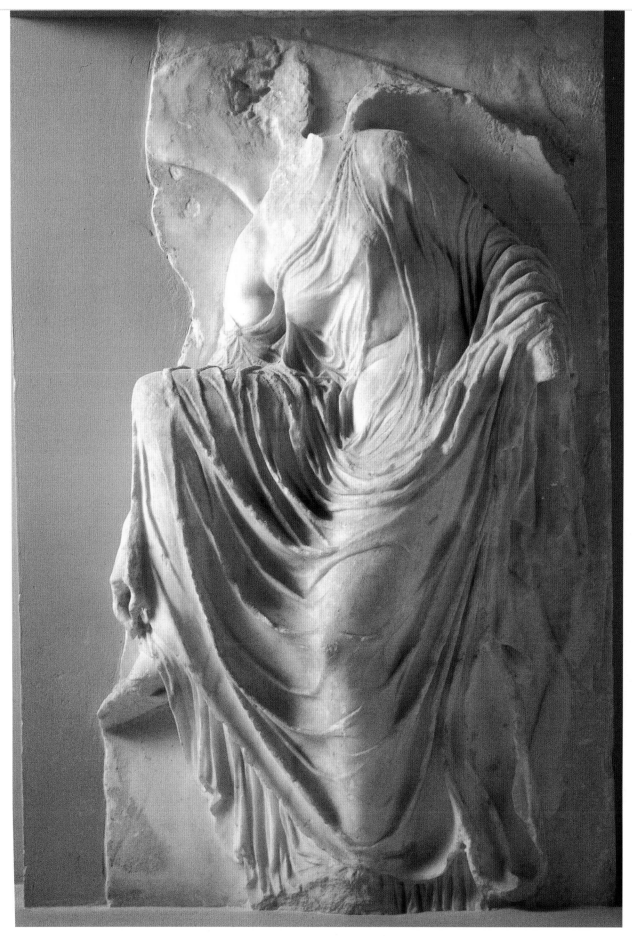

4-34 | *Nike (Victory) Adjusting Her Sandal,* fragment of relief decoration from the parapet (now destroyed). Temple of Athena Nike, Acropolis, Athens. 410–407 BCE. Marble, height 42" (107 cm). Acropolis Museum, Athens

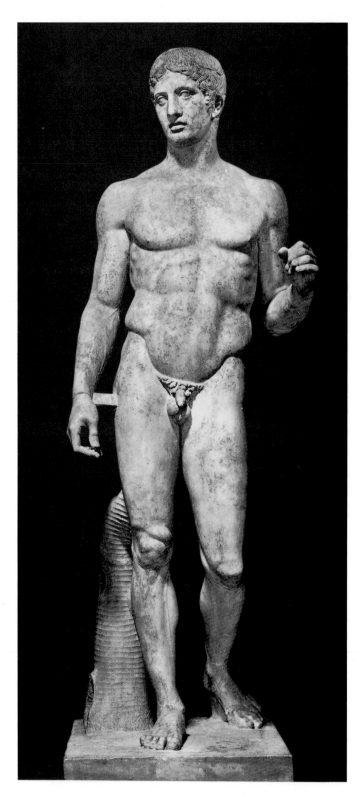

o4-35 Polykleitos. *Spear Bearer* (*Doryphoros*)
Roman copy after the original bronze of c. 450–440 BCE
Marble, height 6'6" (2 m). Museo Archaeològico
Nazionale, Naples, Italy

of proportions for human beauty. Studying human appearances closely, the sculptors of the Golden Age selected those attributes they considered the most desirable, such as regular facial features, smooth skin, and body proportions, and combined them into a single ideal of physical perfection. For example, a thousand like events must have been observed and distilled to achieve the rhythmic harmony presented in the *Procession* frieze, where each form is distinct and individual yet all are united into an utterly satisfying whole. This quest for the ideal can also be seen in the philosophy of Socrates (c. 470–399 BCE) and his disciple Plato (c. 429–347 BCE), both of whom argued that all objects in the physical world were reflections of ideal forms that could be discovered through reason.

About 450 BCE, the sculptor Polykleitos of Argos developed a set of mathematical rules for constructing the ideal human form, which he set down in a treatise, now lost, called *The Canon* (*kanon* is Greek for "measure," "rule," or "law"). To illustrate his theory, Polykleitos created a larger-than-lifesize bronze statue, the *Spear Bearer* (*Doryphoros*). The original statue has not survived, but later Roman artists made copies of it, such as the marble replica illustrated here (fig. 4-35). The pose is more dynamic than that of the *Kritios Boy* or the *Riace Warrior* of a generation earlier. The whole weight of the upper body is supported on the straight right leg; only the ball of the left foot touches the ground. This pattern of tension and relaxation is reversed in the arms, with the right arm relaxed and the left bent to support the weight of the (missing) spear. The tilt of the hipline is pronounced, and the head is tilted and turned toward the right. The young man appears to have paused for a moment, his body in perfect equilibrium, ready to step forward. Greek artists achieved such ideal figures through a combination of close observation of nature, seen in Transitional period art, and generalization based on ideal mathematical proportions. The resulting idealism for the human figure inspired artists and their patrons for centuries afterward.

LATE CLASSICAL ART OF THE FOURTH CENTURY BCE

In 404 BCE, the Peloponnesian War concluded with the defeat of Athens by Sparta. Athens never regained its dominant political and military status, yet Sparta failed to establish a lasting preeminence over the rest of Greece. The quarreling city-states finally fell under the dominance of Philip II of Macedonia in 338 BCE. After Philip's assassination two years later, his son, Alexander the Great, incorporated the Greek city-states into an empire.

4-36 | **Followers of Praxiteles.** *Hermes and the Infant Dionysos,* probably a Roman copy after an original of c. 300–250 BCE. Marble, with remnants of red paint on the lips and hair, height 7'1" (2.16 m) Archaeological Museum, Olympia

Discovered in the rubble of the ruined Temple of Hera at Olympia in 1875, this statue is now widely accepted as a very good Roman or Hellenistic copy. Support for this conclusion comes from certain elements typical of Roman sculpture: Hermes' sandals, which recent studies suggest are not accurate for a fourth-century BCE date; the supporting element of crumpled fabric covering a tree stump; and the use of a reinforcing strut, or brace, between Hermes' hip and the tree stump.

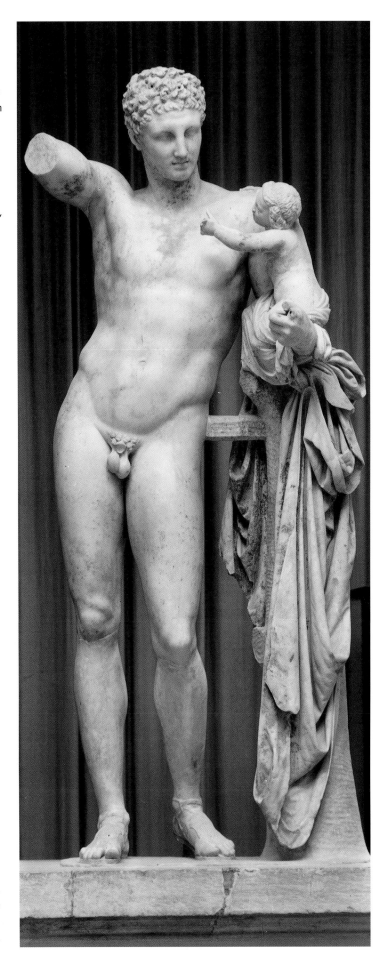

Remarkably, Greek art continued to evolve during this turbulent period. Architects preferred the elegant Ionic order and introduced the even more decorative **Corinthian order** (see "The Greek Architectural Orders," page 100; see also fig. 6). In their search for an ideal human form, sculptors, most notably Praxiteles and Lysippos in the fourth century BCE, developed a new canon of proportions for figures. Polykleitos's fifth-century BCE canon had produced a figure 6$\frac{1}{2}$ or 7 times the height of the head. Praxiteles, who worked in Athens from about 370 to 335 BCE or later, created figures about 8 or more "heads" tall. A marble sculpture of *Hermes and the Infant Dionysos* (fig. 4-36)—probably a Hellenistic or Roman copy but so fine that generations of scholars believed it to be an original statue by Praxiteles—has a smaller head and a more youthful and graceful body than Polykleitos's *Spear Bearer.* Its off-balance, S-curve pose contrasts sharply with that of the earlier work. The subject is less dignified: Hermes teases the infant god of wine with a bunch of grapes. Soft modulations in the musculature, deep folds in the draperies, and rough locks of hair create a sensuous play of light over the figure's surface.

Around 350 BCE Praxiteles created a daring statue of Aphrodite, the goddess of love. For the first time, a well-known Greek sculptor depicted a goddess as a completely nude woman (see fig. 7). The citizens of Knidos in Asia Minor purchased the sculpture and displayed it proudly in a shrine open on all four sides. The original sculpture is lost, but several versions survive in Roman copies, one that was once in the Medici collection. The goddess is preparing to take a bath. Her hands, posed in a gesture of modesty, paradoxically seem to emphasize her nudity. She leans forward slightly with one knee in front of the other in a seductive pose that emphasizes the swelling forms of her thighs, abdomen, and breasts. According to an old legend, Praxiteles' original statue depicted her so accurately

WOMEN ARTISTS IN ANCIENT GREECE

Although comparatively few artists in ancient Greece were women, there is evidence that women artists worked in many mediums. Ancient writers noted women painters—Pliny the Elder, for example listed Aristarete, Eirene, Iaia, Kalypso, Olympias, and Timarete. Helen, a painter from Egypt who had been taught by her father, is known to have worked in the fourth century BCE and may have been responsible for the original wall painting of *Alexander the Great Confronts Darius III* at the Battle of Issos (see fig. 5-19).

Greek women excelled in creating narrative or pictorial tapestries. They also worked in pottery-making workshops. The hydria here, dating from about 450 BCE, shows a woman artist in such a workshop, but her status is ambiguous. The composition focuses on the male painters, who are being approached by Nikes bearing wreaths symbolizing victory in an artistic competition. A well-dressed woman sits on a raised dais, painting the largest vase in the workshop. She is isolated from the other artists and is not part of the awards ceremony. Perhaps women were excluded from public artistic competitions, as they were from athletics. Another interpretation, however, is that the woman is the head of this workshop. Secure in her own status, she may have encouraged her assistants to enter contests to further their careers and bring glory to the workshop as a whole.

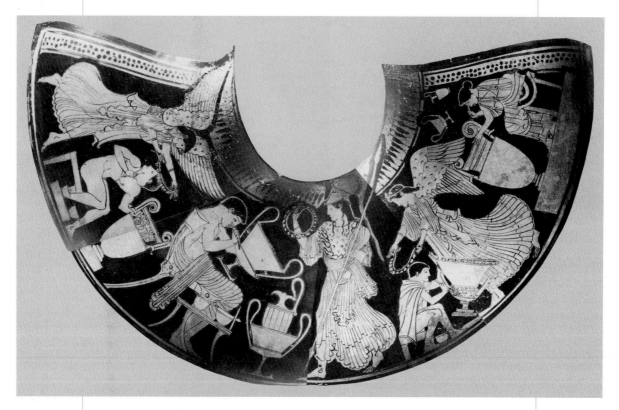

A Vase Painter and Assistants Crowned by Athena and Victories
composite photograph of the red-figure decoration on a hydria
from Athens. c. 450 BCE. Private collection

that Aphrodite herself made a journey to Knidos to see it and cried out in shock, "Where did Praxiteles see me naked?"

The other major sculptor of the fourth century BCE whose name and fame come down to us was Lysippos. He became famous for his monumental statues of Zeus. He also carved Alexander the Great standing and holding a scepter in the same way he is believed to have represented the king of the gods, though neither of these statues still exists. A marble head found at Perga-

mon (in Turkey), once part of a standing figure, is believed to come from one of several copies of Lysippos's portrait (fig. 4-37). According to the Roman historian Plutarch, the sculptor depicted Alexander with his head slightly turned and his face raised upward toward the sky, a description that fits this head well. The deep-set eyes are gazing upward and the low forehead is lined, as though the ruler, contemplating grave decisions, is waiting to receive divine advice.

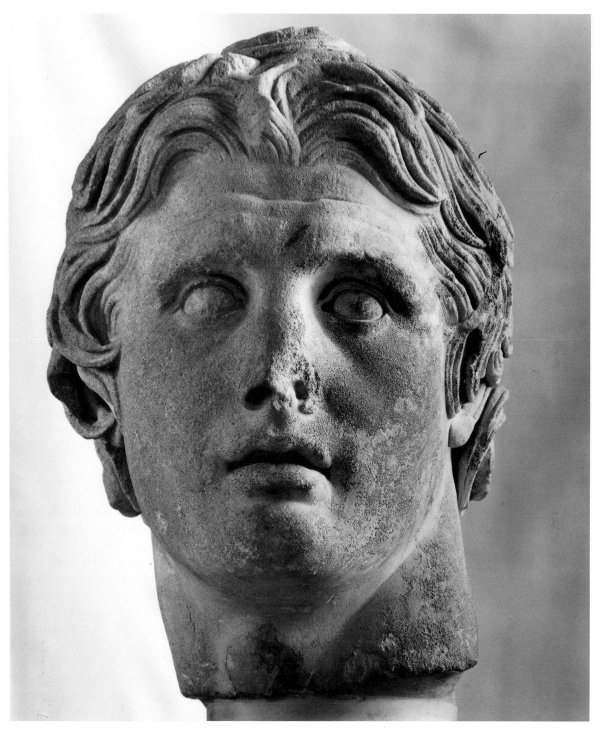

4-37   *Alexander the Great,* head from a Hellenistic copy (c. 200 BCE) of a statue possibly after a 4th-century BCE original by Lysippos. Marble fragment, height 16¹⁄₈" (41 cm). Archaeological Museum, Istanbul, Turkey

Alexander is typically portrayed in Greek art as young and godlike. After conquering an empire stretching from Greece south to Egypt, and as far east as India, he died of a fever in Babylon at the age of thirty-three in 323 BCE. Alexander's premature death, and the subsequent breakup of his vast empire, marks the end of the Classical period in Greek art.

(*front* and *side* views)
Nike (Victory) of Samothrace
from the Sanctuary of the Great
Gods, Samothrace. c. 190 BCE (?)
Marble, height 8' (2.44 m). Musée
du Louvre, Paris. (See pages 131,
133.)

Victory! Throughout history, warriors and athletes, leaders and mobs, men and women—shouting, dancing, embracing—have expressed the joy of winning. Yearning to capture that supreme yet fleeting sense of achievement, the victors have taken steps to make sure that their accomplishments would not be easily forgotten. In expressions intrinsic to the arts—songs, epic tales, and visible monuments such as stelae, huge freestanding arches, and memorials—the triumphant have chosen material objects to commemorate their successes and to guarantee their immortality.

In the late second century BCE, Greek artists personified victory as a supremely beautiful and powerful woman who swept through the air on the wings of an eagle, alighting at will to bestow the leafy crown of victory on a chosen mortal. Nowhere was she more magnificently portrayed than in Samothrace, a city on the coast of what is now modern Turkey. Here, to celebrate a naval victory, sculptors captured the goddess's idealized form in an imposing and subtly carved and polished marble sculpture.

The *Nike* (*Victory*) *of Samothrace* exemplifies the spread of Greek culture throughout the ancient world. Greek art and thought might be accepted, rejected, or modified, but it could not be ignored, not only in the wake of Alexander's triumphant armies late in the fourth century BCE, but also in the more mundane reality of seafaring merchants who carried the products of Greek artistry from the shores of the Black Sea to the Pillars of Hercules, where the Mediterranean Sea meets the Atlantic Ocean. The people with whom the Greek adventurers lived, fought, and traded had their own well-developed artistic traditions, but they adapted forms, techniques, and ideas from the Greeks, until a Hellenistic (that is, Greek-like) style emerged. In Italy skilled Etruscan bronze and terra-cotta workers were inspired by monumental Greek figure sculpture, but gave their adaptation of Greek forms an energetic realism which inspired later Roman art. In far off Russia and Ukraine, the Scythian herdsmen and farmers coveted Greek silver and gold jewelry and tableware, and they traded their grain and furs for magnificent showpieces. They ordered their own artists to create jewelry and weapons for themselves and showy harnesses for their horses. Far to the east, the powerful and sophisticated Persians built palaces with columned halls and refined low relief sculpture.

After Alexander's death in 323 BCE no single political center dominated the Hellenistic world. From Pergamon in Turkey to Alexandria in Egypt, as well as Athens and ultimately Rome, Greek art, architecture, literature, philosophy, and mathematics stimulated the diverse peoples touched by Alexander's march of conquest. They created a new Hellenized culture. Ultimately, Nike awarded the victor's wreath to the Greeks, not for their military might, but for their art and learning.

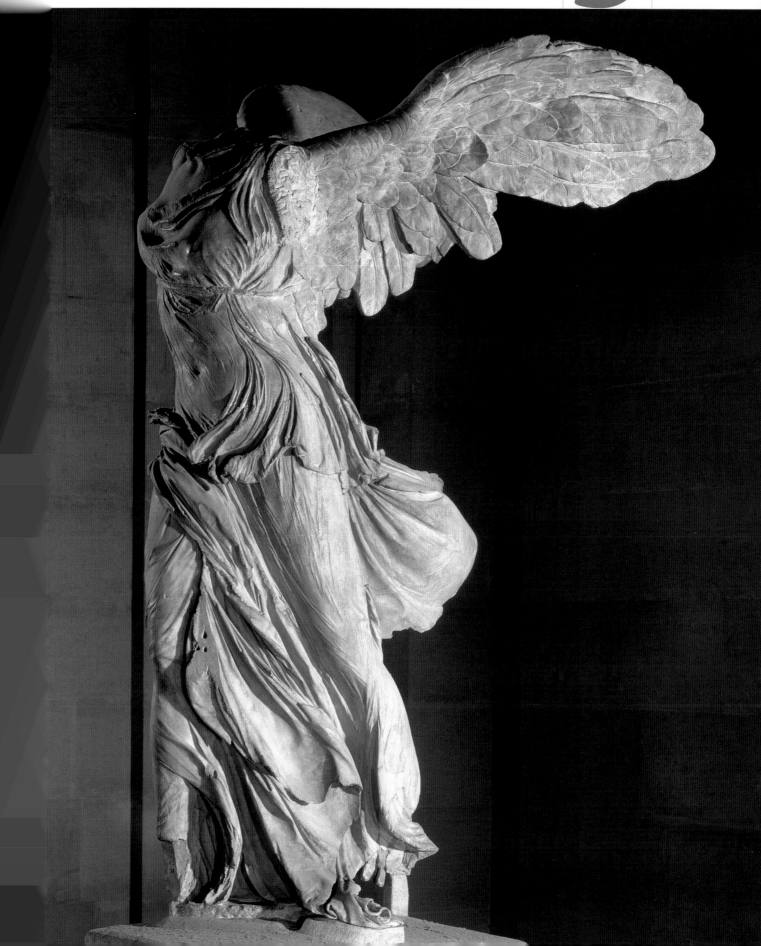

Alexander the Great (356–323 BCE) of Macedonia did not live to rule the lands he conquered. In fact, for much of the first millennium BCE, many states and kingdoms rose and fell, playing out a delicate balance of power (see Map 2, page 163).

In the western Mediterranean, the Etruscans controlled much of the Italian Peninsula from the seventh century BCE until the rise of Rome in the third century BCE. Renowned both as metalworkers and sailors, the Etruscans maintained close trading relationships with the Greeks and Phoenicians. The Phoenicians, based in the coastal area of modern Lebanon, sailed and traded as far as the western coast of Africa. They founded colonies in North Africa and Spain by the eighth century BCE. During the same period, the Greeks (see Chapter 4) ruled far-flung colonies, including southern Italy and Anatolia (western Asia Minor, forming modern Turkey). From coastal outposts in what is now the Crimean region of Ukraine, the Greeks also traded with the Scythians, nomadic horsemen who lived north of the Black Sea on the semi-arid, grass-covered plains, or steppes.

To the east, the Assyrian Empire in Mesopotamia remained a significant force until around 625 BCE (see Chapter 2). Harassed periodically by the Scythians, the Assyrians were overthrown in 612 BCE by an alliance of the southern Mesopotamian state of Babylonia (now Iraq) and an Iranian people known as the Medes. Neo-Babylonia—so-named because it recaptured the splendor that had marked Babylon twelve centuries earlier under Hammurabi—flourished for less than a century before being taken over by the Persians, vassals of the Medes who obtained their independence in 549 BCE.

Beginning in the mid-sixth century BCE, the Persians, who occupied an area that is now southwestern Iran, began a vigorous campaign of military expansion. Under a dynasty of kings known as the Achaemenids, the Persian Empire became the dominant power in an area reaching from Asia Minor to Bactria (modern Afghanistan). They also conquered Egypt, Arabia, and Syria and attempted, but failed, to overcome mainland Greece (as we learned in Chapter 4).

5-1 | ***She-Wolf.*** C. 500 BCE. Bronze, glass-paste eyes, height 33½" (85 cm). Museo Capitolino, Rome

Although this sculpture was almost certainly the work of an Etruscan artist, it has long been associated with Rome. According to an ancient Roman legend, twin infants named Romulus and Remus, who had been abandoned on the banks of the Tiber River by a wicked uncle and left there to die, were suckled by a she-wolf that had come to the river to drink. The twins were raised by a shepherd, and when they grew up, they decided to build a city near the spot where they had been rescued by the wolf. They quarreled, however, about its exact location. Romulus killed Remus and then established a small settlement that would become the great city of Rome, an event that, according to tradition, occurred in 753 BCE. The bronze twins were added to the sculpture during the Renaissance period.

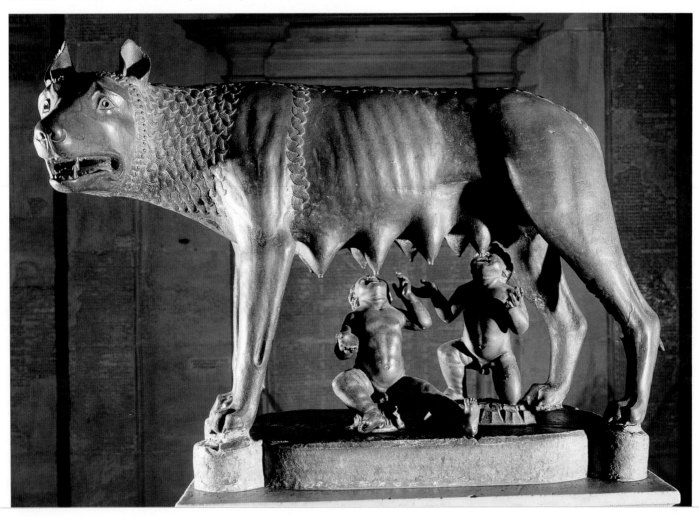

The vast region ruled by the Persians fell to Alexander the Great in the late fourth century BCE. Although his empire disintegrated, Alexander's lasting legacy can be seen in the impact of Greek culture far beyond its original borders. Under Alexander and his successors, non-Greek people produced Hellenistic ("Greek-like") art in Egypt, Asia Minor, and in the lands of the former Persian Empire.

The Etruscans

The boot-shaped Italian peninsula, shielded on the north by the formidable Alps, juts into the Mediterranean Sea, exposing its inhabitants in ancient times to the interplay among Near Eastern, Egyptian, and Greek civilizations. Etruscan society, deeply influenced by the Greek, emerged in the seventh century BCE in Etruria (modern Tuscany). The Etruscans may have descended from a people called the Villanovans, who had occupied the northern and western regions of Italy since the Bronze Age. The Etruscans reached the height of their power in the sixth century BCE, when they formed a loose federation of a dozen cities. The fertile soil of Etruria and its rich lodes of metal ore formed the basis of their wealth.

The skill of Etruscan bronzeworkers was widely known in ancient times. Only a few examples of large-scale cast-bronze sculpture in the round have survived the wholesale recycling of bronze objects over the centuries. One such sculpture, which dates to about 500 BCE, portrays a she-wolf with heavy, milk-filled teats—evidence that she has recently given birth (fig. 5-1). The sculpture may represent the legendary she-wolf who nurtured the twins Romulus and Remus, the founders of Rome. Remarkable realism combined with decorative stylization characterizes Etruscan art. In the sculpture of the wolf, the naturalistic rendering of the animal's body contrasts with the stylized rendering of the tightly curled ruff of fur around the neck.

Etruscan artists also excelled at making monumental terra-cotta sculpture, a task requiring great technical and physical skill. The artist had to construct the figures so that they would not collapse under their own weight while the raw clay was still heavy with moisture. In addition, the artist also had to regulate the **kiln** temperature during the long firing process. The lifesize sculpture of the god Apollo (fig. 5-2) was made about 500 BCE. The well-developed body and the "archaic smile" of this figure

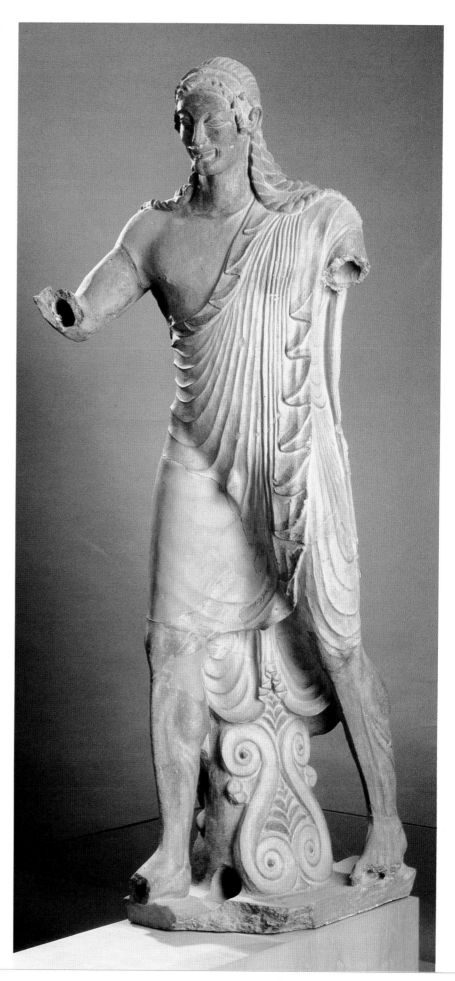

5-2 **Apollo,** from Veii. c. 500 BCE. Painted terra cotta Height 5'10" (1.8 m). Museo Nazionale di Villa Giulia, Rome

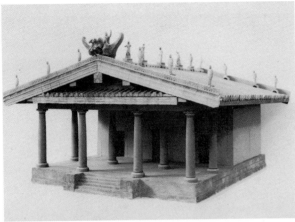

5-3 | (*left*) **Reconstruction of an Etruscan temple**
based partly on descriptions by Vitruvius
University of Rome, Istituto de Etruscologia e
Antichità Italiche

5-4 | (*below*) **Burial chamber,** Tomb of the Reliefs
Cerveteri. 3rd century BCE

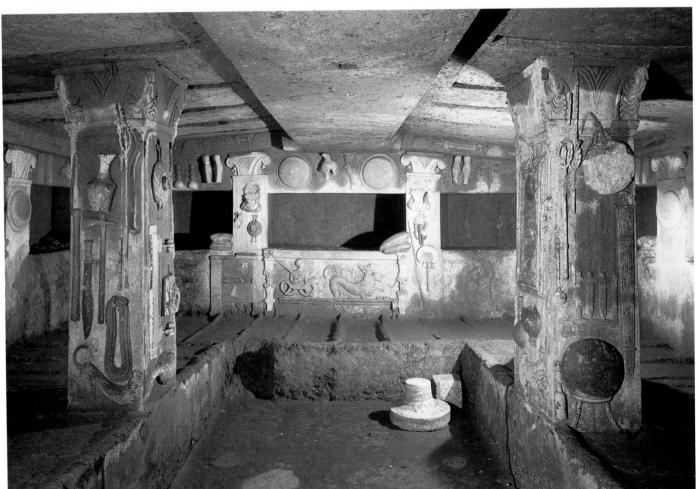

demonstrate that Etruscan sculptors knew Greek Archaic *kouroi*
and *korai* (see figs. 4-18, 4-19). But while the Greeks represented men nude, the Etruscans usually represented them partially
clothed. Here the figure of Apollo is partly concealed by a robe.
The striding pose has a vigor that contrasts with the quieter
stance of Archaic Greek figures (see Chapter 4). The figure was
originally placed along the roof ridge of an Etruscan temple at
Veii as part of a four-figure scene. Apollo looks as if he is step-
ping over the decorative scroll that actually helped support the
sculpture when it was atop a temple. This quality of energy
expressed in purposeful movement is characteristic of both
Etruscan sculpture and painting.

The scene from which this figure is drawn comes from Greek
mythology which the Etruscans incorporated into their religion.
Apollo fought with the hero Herakles for the possession of a deer
sacred to Artemis, goddess of the moon and of the hunt. Artemis
and Hermes watched over the struggle.

According to the Roman architect Vitruvius, Etruscan temples had only a superficial resemblance to those of the Greeks.
They used the post-and-lintel structure and gable roofs, but the
plan was different. The Etruscans built their temples on a high
base with a single flight of stairs leading to a columned porch.
The deep porch led in turn to a **cella**, which was divided into
three parallel rooms (fig. 5-3).

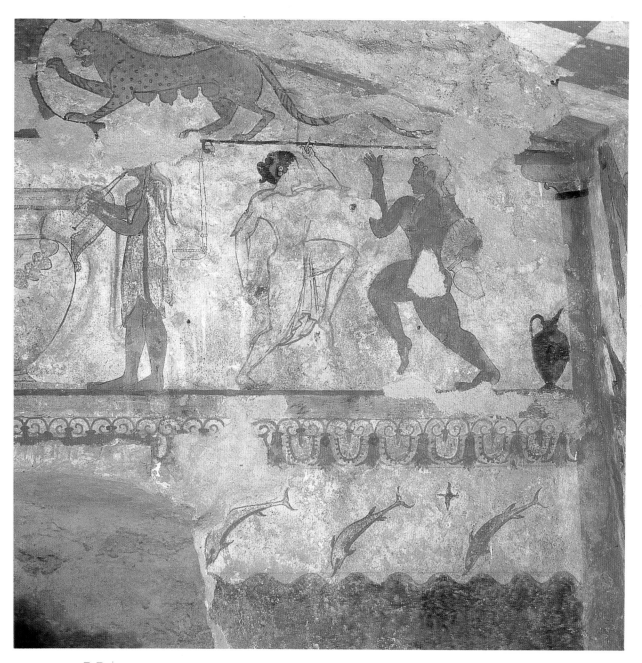

5-5 | *Musicians and Dancers,* detail of a wall painting, Tomb of the Lionesses, Tarquinia. c. 480–470 BCE

The typical Etruscan home was a rectangular mud-brick structure built either around a central courtyard or around an **atrium**, a room with a shallow indoor pool for drinking, cooking, and bathing, fed by rainwater through a large opening in the roof. The burial chamber of the Tomb of the Reliefs at Cerveteri was carved to imitate such a house in the third century BCE (fig. 5-4). Its walls were plastered and painted, and it was provided with a full selection of furnishings, some real, others simulated in **stucco**, a slow-drying type of plaster that can easily be modeled or molded.

Some tombs were painted not carved. In the Tomb of the Lionesses at Tarquinia, a detail of a frieze painted about 480–470 BCE shows a couple energetically dancing to the music of a double flute beneath a pediment ornamented with a leopardess (fig. 5-5). The woman is represented on equal footing with her male partner, suggesting that some women were well educated and active in Etruscan society. The immediacy of this wall painting is striking. The dancers and musicians seem to be performing for us, not enacting the formal rituals of a remote, long-dead civilization.

Sarcophagi (large carved tomb chests) also provided a domestic touch. Rather than a cold, somber memorial to the dead, sculpted figures of the dead recline comfortably on a terra-cotta sarcophagus made to look like a couch. Two happy

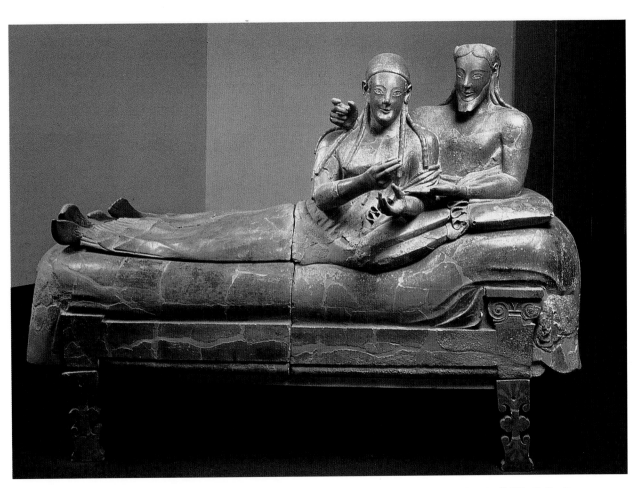

5-6 | **Sarcophagus,** from Cerveteri. c. 520 BCE. Terra cotta, length 6'7" (2.06 m). Museo Nazionale di Villa Giulia, Rome

individuals, with slanting almond eyes and benign smiles, seem to greet the viewer with lively gestures. Their conventionalized bodies are rendered in sufficient detail to convey contemporary hair and clothing styles (fig. 5-6). They might almost be attending a banquet or enjoying a performance of music or dance, convivial festivities recorded in paintings on tomb walls.

5-7 | **Scythian Stag,** shield plaque. Late 7th–early 6th century BCE Gold, length 12½" (31.7 cm). Hermitage Museum, St. Petersburg

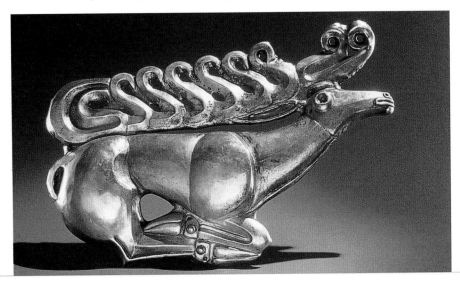

The Scythians

Burials also provide our best information about Scythian art. By the late seventh century BCE, the Scythians, who may have come originally from Siberia, settled north of the Black Sea in Russia and Ukraine. They bred cattle and horses on the grass-covered plains and sold livestock and grain to the Greeks and to Near Eastern kingdoms in Mesopotamia and Iran. In return, they received metal ores and textiles, gold- and silverwork, and other luxury goods.

Much of our knowledge of Scythian culture comes from burial mounds, known in Russian as *kurgans,* that the Scythians built for their rulers. The burial chamber beneath a *kurgan* was a large wood or stone structure, designed to shelter the ruler's body and those of his servants, horses, and concubines who were sacrificed and buried with him. Many tombs were furnished with valuable burial goods, especially vessels, jewelry, and weapons made of gold and silver.

The golden stag illustrated in figure 5-7, dating from the late seventh or the early sixth century BCE, was found in a *kurgan* at Kostromskaya, not far from the Black Sea. The tautly stretched neck and alert head belie the compact arrangement of the legs. Inlays, possibly of turquoise, once decorated the animal's eye and ear. This lavish work, made to decorate a warrior's shield, represents the **animal style** found across the steppes of Asia and eastern Europe. Birds and animals are commonly shown locked in combat or curled up with their legs under them. Characteristic features may be exaggerated, such as the antlers on this stag. Human figures are represented relatively infrequently in native Scythian art, but gold vessels and weapons of Greek workmanship, commissioned by Scythian customers, reveal aspects of daily life among the nomads of the steppes.

The Neo-Babylonians

In the seventh century BCE, the Scythian raiders joined the Medes from western Iran to invade the northern and eastern parts of Assyria. Meanwhile, in 615 BCE, the Babylonians, under a new royal dynasty, rebelled against Assyrian rule and formed a treaty with the Medes. In 612 BCE, they captured and sacked Ninevah, the capital of Assyria (see Chapter 2). When the dust settled, Assyria was no longer a power. The Medes controlled a large strip of land south of the Black and Caspian Seas, and the Neo-Babylonians dominated the lowlands of Mesopotamia.

The most famous Neo-Babylonian ruler was Nebuchadnezzar II (ruled 604–562 BCE). A great patron of architecture, he built temples throughout his realm and he transformed Babylon—the cultural, political, and economic hub of his empire—into one of the most splendid cities of its day. A broad avenue named May the Enemy Not Have Victory, also called the Processional Way because it was the route taken by religious processions honoring the city's patron god, Marduk, crossed the eastern sector of the city (fig. 5-8). Up to 66 feet wide at some points, the avenue was paved with large stone slabs. Colorful glazed bricks faced walls on both sides along the route. (When fired, glaze produces a shiny, waterproof surface.) The Processional Way ended at the Ishtar Gate, a main entrance to the city (fig. 5-9; see page 126). Named after the goddess known as Inanna in Sumer (see page 46) and Ishtar (see page 127) in the Semitic-speaking regions of Mesopotamia, the gate symbolized Babylonian power. Guarded by four **crenellated** (notched) towers, the glazed-brick gate was decorated with tiers of the dragons sacred to Marduk and the bulls with blue forelocks and tails associated with a number of other deities.

Now reconstructed in a Berlin State Museum, the Ishtar Gate is installed next to a panel from the wall of the throne room of Nebuchadnezzar's palace (seen on the right in fig. 5-9; see page

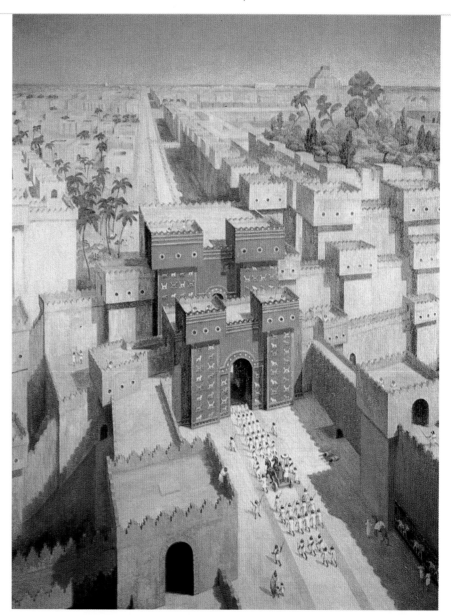

5-8 | **Reconstruction drawing of Babylon** in the 6th century BCE. The Oriental Institute of the University of Chicago

In this view, the palace of Nebuchadnezzar II, with its famous Hanging Gardens, can be seen just behind and to the right of the Ishtar Gate, to the west of the Processional Way. The Marduk Ziggurat looms up in the far distance on the east bank of the Euphrates. This structure was at times believed to be the biblical Tower of Babel—Bab-il was an early form of the city's name.

126). On this panel, lions made of molded and glazed brick walk in single file beneath stylized palm trees. Lions were often associated with royal power in the Near East, and in Mesopotamia the goddess Ishtar is sometimes shown on cylinder seals with her foot resting on a lion.

The Persians

When Cyrus the Great defeated the ancient country of Lydia's fabulously wealthy King Croesus (ruled 560–546 BCE) in 546 BCE, Persia gained control over its gold. (Croesus's name has come down to us in the lasting expression "rich as Croesus.") The Persians learned from the Lydians to mint coins in standard weights. One type of Persian coin, the gold daric, named for Darius and first minted during his reign, is among the most

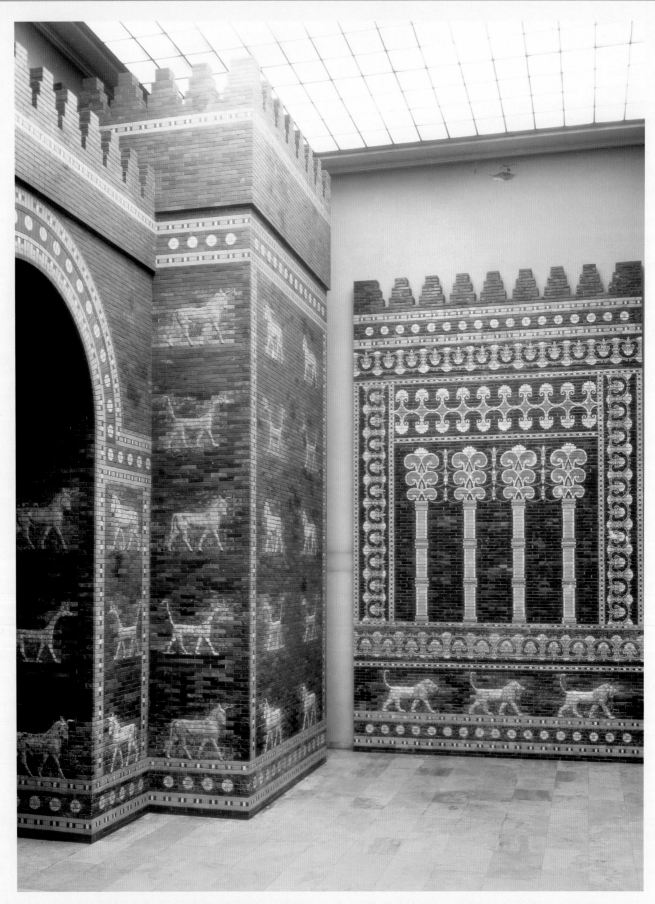

5-9 **Ishtar Gate and throne room wall,** from Babylon (Iraq). c. 575 BCE. Glazed brick. Staatliche Museen zu Berlin Preussischer Kulturbesitz, Vorderasiatisches Museum

Greek tales of the palaces, temples, and hanging gardens of ancient Babylon still fire the imagination, and biblical accounts of the tyranny and decadence of its rulers conjure up images of licentious splendor. The Jews had reason to record Babylonian faults, since twice—in 597 BCE and 587 BCE—Babylonian armies destroyed Jerusalem and its Temple and carried off the Jews into exile and captivity. In Babylon, one of these exiles, Daniel, survived death in the lions' den to tell his story. The "Babylonian Captivity" became a turning point in Jewish history, and the poetic lamentations of the prophets Isaiah and Ezekiel add to history's negative image of the Babylonians.

Babylon was a huge city covering over three and a half square miles on both sides of the Euphrates River in modern day Iraq. A moat, double walls, and gates with double towers defended the city. The northern gate in the royal sector was dedicated to Ishtar, the goddess of Love and War. A wide processional way running parallel to the river joined temples and palaces and ended at the northern palace complex.

The striding lions of the goddess Ishtar lined the avenue leading to the Ishtar Gate, and on the gate itself the bulls of Adad, the sky and weather god, alternate with dragons, sacred to the city god Marduk (fig. 5-9). Between 1905 and 1914 German archaeologists excavated the northern palace area. They recovered the brilliant glazed tile decoration of part of the Processional Way, the Ishtar Gate, and Nebuchadnezzar's throne room, which they shipped home and reassembled in a Berlin museum.

The technique of using glazed bricks to decorate the walls of the avenue, the gate, and important rooms in the palace required careful planning and great technical skill. Just one of the dragons, for example, required as many as seventy-five to eighty bricks. Since firing caused the bricks to shrink, each had to be slightly larger than the desired design, if they were to be reassembled into the correct pattern and fit the allotted space. To enhance the splendid effect, brilliantly colored glass-based glazes were applied to the reliefs.

The images on the throne room wall also recall Ishtar. An intricate design of striding lions, tall palm trees with blue fronds, white and yellow rosettes and palmettes covers the deep blue wall. In her early form as the Sumerian goddess Inanna (see fig. 2-3), Ishtar controlled ferocious lions, but she was also associated with date palms, seen here in very stylized form, in her role as protectress of the date storehouses. Date palms and lions reminded her devotees that she controlled both food and safety—the physical well-being and the survival of her people. In such a setting Nebuchadnezzar could have set up his golden idol, and Belshazzar could have used gold and silver vessels stolen from the Jewish Temple to serve wine at his infamous feast, causing Daniel to proclaim, "You have been weighed in the balance and found wanting!" Indeed Belshazzar's feast was his last, for the Persians entered the gates in 539 BCE—among them the Ishtar Gate—and destroyed Babylon that very night.

sought-after coins in the world today (fig. 5-10). Commonly called an archer, it shows the well-armed emperor wearing his crown and carrying a lance in his right hand and a bow in his left: he lunges forward as if he had just loosed an arrow from his bow. Besides their function as economic standard, coins also served as propaganda, carrying the ruler's portrait throughout the empire.

The Persians settled in southwestern Iran at the beginning of the first millennium BCE. Originally subservient to the Medes, the Persians obtained their independence in 549 BCE under a dynamic leader, Cyrus II, the Great (ruled 559–530 BCE). Cyrus led the Persians in an astonishing series of conquests. By the time of his death, the Persian Empire included Babylonia, vanquished by Persia in 539 BCE; and stretched from Iran into Anatolia. Cyrus's son Cambyses II (ruled 529–522 BCE) added Egypt and Cyprus to the empire. By the time Darius I (ruled 521–486 BCE) took the throne, he could boast: "I am Darius, great King, King of Kings, King of countries, King of this earth." Darius and his successors were known as the Achaemenid monarchs after a semi-legendary ancestor, Achaemenes. They ruled for nearly two centuries, expanding the Achaemenid Empire both eastward and westward.

An able administrator, Darius organized the Persian lands into twenty tribute-paying areas under Persian governors, and he often left local rulers in place. This practice, along with a tolerance for diverse native customs and religions, won the Persians the

5-10 | **Daric,** a coin first minted under Darius I of Persia 4th century BCE. Gold. Heberden Coin Room Ashmolean Museum, Oxford

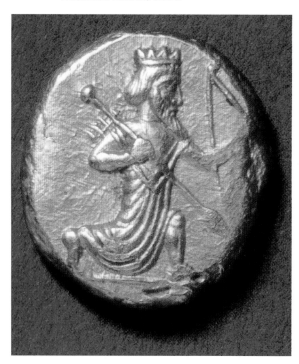

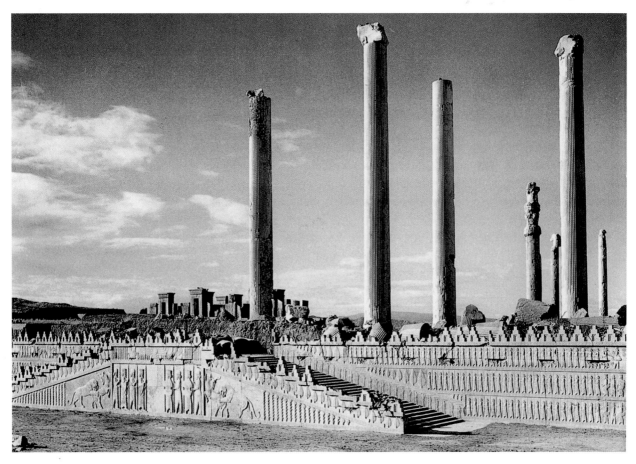

5-11 | **Apadana** (Audience Hall) of Darius I and Xerxes I, ceremonial complex, Persepolis, Iran. 518–c. 460 BCE

The ancient historian Cleiarchus of Alexandria relates that Alexander the Great and his troops accidentally torched the royal compound at Persepolis during a wild banquet in celebration of their victory over the Persians. It is more probable that Alexander had it destroyed deliberately. The site was never rebuilt, and its ruins were never buried. Scholars have been measuring, mapping, and studying what remains of the complex for generations. Various pieces of architectural ornament have been stripped from Persepolis for display in museums around the world.

loyalty of many of their subjects. Darius also developed a system of fair taxation, issued a standardized currency (see fig. 5-10), and improved communication throughout the empire.

Darius, like many powerful rulers, created monuments to serve as visible symbols of his authority. About 518 BCE, he began building a new capital in the Persian homeland, today known by its Greek name Persepolis. He imported materials, workers, and artists from all over his empire. The result was a new style of art that combined many different cultural traditions—Persian, Mede, Mesopotamian, Egyptian, and Greek.

In Assyrian fashion, the imperial complex at Persepolis was set on a raised platform, 40 feet high, and like Egyptian and Greek cities, it was laid out on a rectangular grid. The platform was accessible only from a single ramp made of wide, shallow steps to allow horsemen to ride up rather than dismount and climb on foot. Construction extended over nearly 60 years, and Darius lived to see the erection of only a treasury, the Apadana (Audience Hall), and a small palace for himself. His son Xerxes I (ruled 484–465 BCE) added a sprawling palace complex, enlarged the treasury building, and began a vast new public reception space, the Hall of 100 Columns.

Darius's Apadana (fig. 5-11), set above the rest of the complex on a second terrace, had a square hall large enough to hold several thousand people. The sides of the staircases and walls of the platform are covered with sculpture in low relief. On the walls, ranks of warriors seem ready to defend the palace, while on the staircase, lions attack bulls at each side of the Persian generals. These animal combats (a theme found throughout the Near East) emphasize the ferocity of the leaders and their men. Other reliefs throughout Persepolis depict displays of allegiance or economic prosperity. In one example, Darius holds an audience while his son and heir, Xerxes, listens from behind the throne (fig. 5-12). The Persian reliefs, like Greek friezes, were once brightly painted, and metal objects, such as Darius's crown, were covered in **gold leaf** (thin sheets of hammered gold).

At its height, the empire conquered by Darius and his successors extended from Africa to India. Only mainland Greeks successfully resisted the armies of the Achaemenids, and it was a Greek who ultimately put an end to their rule. In 334 BCE, Alexander the Great of Macedonia crossed into Anatolia and swept through Mesopotamia, defeating Darius III and sacking Persepolis in 331 BCE. The lands of Persia became part of the Greek world.

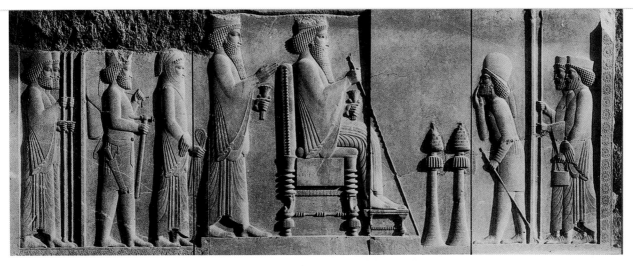

5-12 | ***Darius and Xerxes Receiving Tribute,*** detail of a relief from the stairway leading to the Apadana, ceremonial complex Persepolis, Iran. 491–486 BCE. Limestone, height 8'4" (2.54 m). Iranbastan Museum, Tehran

The Hellenistic Greeks

At his death in 323 BCE, Alexander left a vast empire with no administrative structure and no appointed successor. Almost immediately, his generals turned against one another, and local leaders tried to regain their lost autonomy. By the early third century BCE, three major powers had emerged out of the chaos, ruled by three of Alexander's generals and their heirs: Antigonus, Ptolemy, and Seleucus. The Antigonids controlled Macedonia and mainland Greece; the Ptolemies ruled Egypt; and the Seleucids controlled Anatolia, Syria, Mesopotamia, and Persia. Each of these regions followed a different political course, but they were unified artistically and culturally by the Greek ideas and art. This Hellenistic world lasted until the rise of Rome in the second and first centuries BCE.

Artists of the Hellenistic period had a vision discernibly different from that of their **Classical** Greek predecessors. Where earlier artists sought to capture the ideal and the all-encompassing in art, Hellenistic artists sought the individual and the specific. They turned increasingly from the heroic to the everyday, from aloof serenity to individual emotion, and from serious drama to melodramatic expression. They appealed to the senses through lustrous or glittering surface treatments and to the emotions by dramatic subjects and poses (see fig. 24). These tendencies, already seen in the fourth century BCE, became more pronounced in the Hellenistic period. Hellenistic artists also turned to the past, creating eclectic works by borrowing elements from earlier Classical styles. Not surprisingly, they often used the Corinthian order in architecture, preferring richly carved **acanthus** leaf capitals, to the severe Doric and elegant Ionic orders (see "The Greek Architectural Orders," page 100; and fig. 6).

Elements of Architecture

THEATERS

In ancient Greece, the theater offered more than mere entertainment; it was a vehicle for the communal expression of religious belief through music, poetry, and dance. During the fifth century BCE, the plays shown were primarily tragedies in verse based on popular myths and were performed at a festival dedicated to Dionysos. At this time, the three great Greek tragedians—Aeschylus, Sophocles, and Euripides—were creating the works that would define tragedy for centuries.

Because theaters were used continuously and were frequently modified over many centuries, no early theaters have survived in their original form. The largely intact theater at Epidauros, however, which dates from the early third century BCE, presents a good example of the characteristics of early theaters. A semicircle of tiered seats built into the hillside overlooked the circular performance area, called the orchestra, at the center of which was an altar to Dionysos. Rising behind the orchestra was a two-tiered stage structure made up of the vertical *skene* (scene)—an architectural backdrop for performances and a screen for the backstage area—and the *proskenion* (**proscenium**), a raised platform in front of the *skene* that was increasingly used over time as an extension of the orchestra. Ramps connecting the *proskenion* with lateral passageways (*parodoi;* singular *parodos*) provided access to the stage for performers. Steps gave the audience access to the fifty-five rows of seats and divided the seating area into uniform wedge-shaped sections. The tiers of seats above the wide corridor, or gangway, were added at a much later date. This design provided uninterrupted sight lines, good acoustics, and efficient crowd control for some 12,000 spectators. Greek theater plans have not been greatly improved upon since.

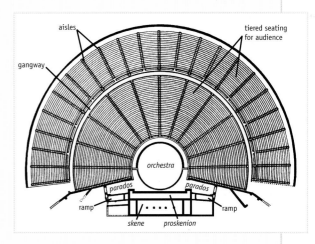

Plan of the theater at Epidauros

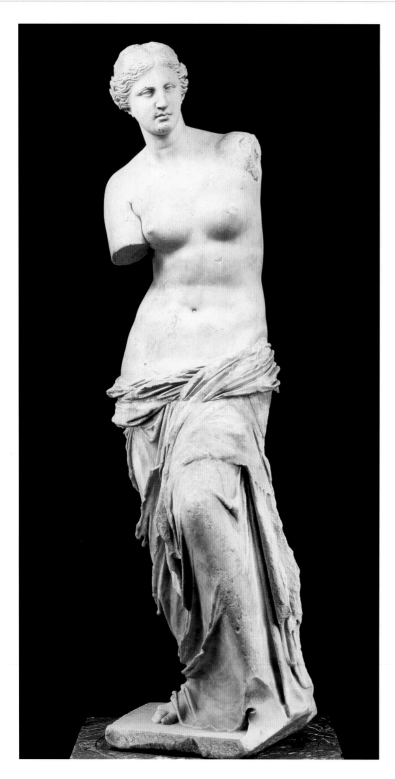

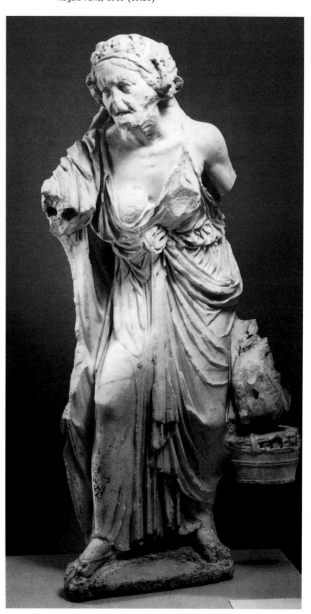

5-13 | (*left*) ***Aphrodite of Melos*** (also called *Venus de Milo*)
c. 150 BCE. Marble, height 6'10" (2.1 m)
Musée du Louvre, Paris

5-14 | (*below*) ***Market Woman.*** 1st century BCE. Marble
Height 49½" (125.7 cm). The Metropolitan Museum
of Art New York
Rogers Fund, 1909 (09.39)

APHRODITE'S ARMS

Aphrodite of Melos (see fig. 5-13), better known as the *Venus de Milo*, has traditionally been synonymous with female beauty in the Western world. Perhaps some of the figure's enduring hold is attributable to her very incompleteness. What was she doing, and where were her hands placed? Was she clutching the drapery slipping so seductively off her hips? Or was she temptingly holding out an apple in her right hand, as fragments of sculpture found near her suggest? When the sculpture was dug up in a field in 1820, many judged the loose fragments to be part of a later restoration and not part of the original statue.

The image of Aphrodite admiring herself in the highly polished shield of her lover, the war god Ares, became popular in the second century BCE. So this figure could have been holding a shield. If this were the case here, a shield would have been positioned at an angle to one side, and probably resting on the goddess' left thigh. Today many archaeologists compare the figure to the similar image of a Victory writing the name of a hero on a shield. These theories offer an explanation for the position of the shoulders, the pronounced S-curve of the pose, and the otherwise unnatural forward projection of the knee.

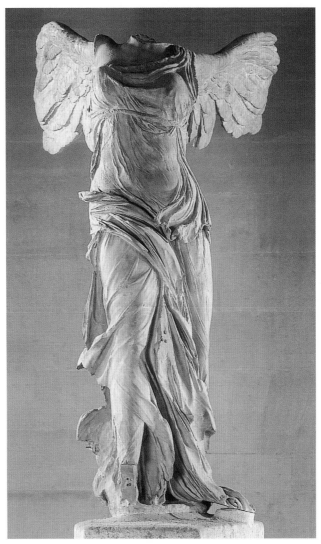

5-15 | ***Nike (Victory) of Samothrace,*** from the Sanctuary of the Great Gods, Samothrace. c. 190 BCE (?). Marble Height 8' (2.44 m). Musée du Louvre, Paris. (See pages 118–19.)

Many popular sculptors looked back especially to Praxiteles and Lysippos for their models. This renewed interest in the style of the fourth century BCE is exemplified by the *Aphrodite of Melos* (fig. 5-13), found on the Aegean island of Melos by French excavators in the early nineteenth century. The sculpture was intended by its maker to recall the *Aphrodite of Knidos* by Praxiteles, which exists only in later interpretations, including the *Medici Venus* (see fig. 7), and indeed the head, with its dreamy gaze, suggests Praxiteles' lost work. But the twisting stance and strong projection of the knee, as well as the rich, three-dimensional quality of the drapery, are typical of Hellenistic art of the third century BCE and later. Moreover, the sensuous juxtaposition of flesh with the texture of draperies, which seem about to slip off the figure, adds an insistent note of erotic tension that is thoroughly Hellenistic in concept and intent.

The idealized beauty of the *Aphrodite of Melos* contrasts sharply with the realistic depiction of an old woman carrying a basket, also made in the second century BCE (fig. 5-14). The disarray of her dress and her unfocused stare suggest that she represents an aging, dissolute follower of Dionysus, god of wine. We may assume that she is on her way to make an offering, since she seems to step out assertively into the space around her. The representation of people from all levels of society, as well as unusual physical types, became popular during the Hellenistic period.

Even more dramatic in its depiction of action is the *Nike (Victory) of Samothrace* (fig. 5-15; see pages 118–19). The wind-whipped robe and raised wings of this victory goddess indicate that she has just landed on the prow of the stone ship that formed the original base of the statue. The 8-foot-high Victory originally stood in a hillside niche high above the sanctuary of the Samothracian gods, perhaps drenched

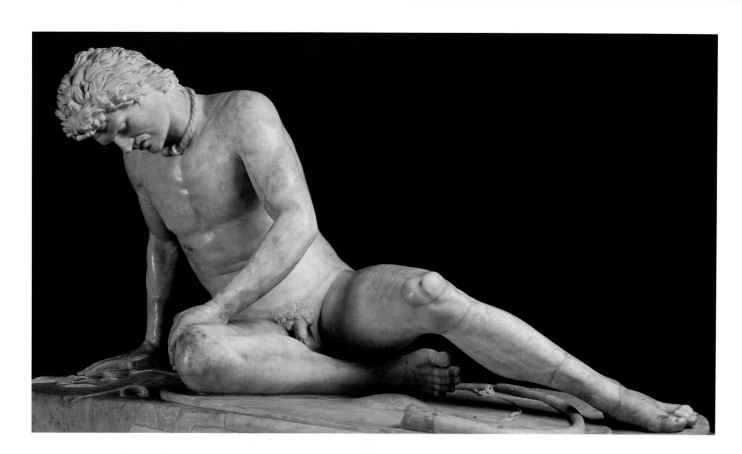

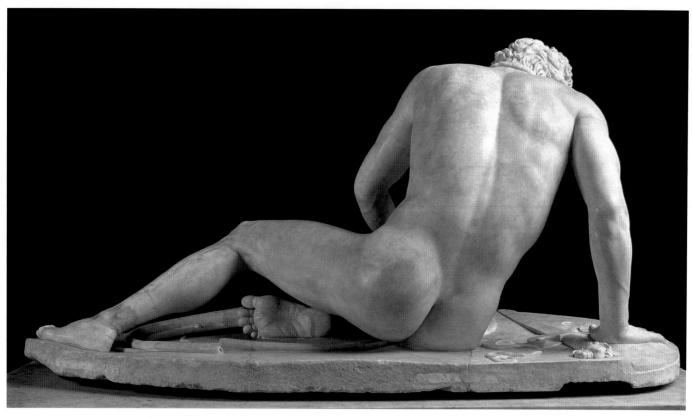

5-16 | **Epigonos (?).** *Dying Gallic Trumpeter,* Roman copy after the original bronze of c. 220 BCE
Marble, lifesize. Museo Capitolino, Rome

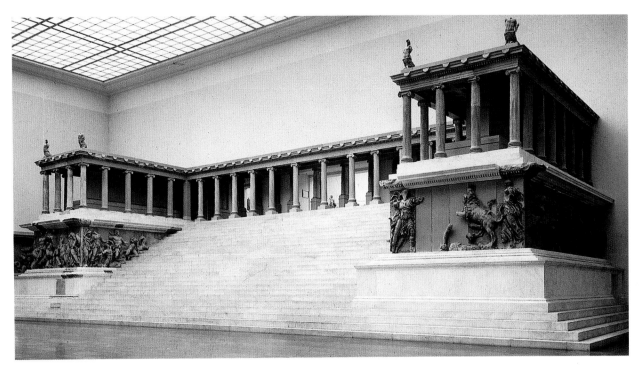

5-17 | **Reconstructed west front of the altar from Pergamon,** Turkey. c. 166–159 BCE. Marble
Staatliche Museen zu Berlin, Preussischer Kulturbesitz, Antikensammlung

with spray from a fountain. The fact that victory in real life does often seem miraculous makes this image of a goddess alighting suddenly on a ship breathtakingly appropriate for a war memorial.

Some of the best-known examples of Hellenistic art were made in the third and second centuries BCE in the kingdom of Pergamon, a Greek state on the west coast of Asia Minor. After gaining independence in the early third century BCE, Pergamon quickly became a leading center of the arts and the hub of a new sculptural style that had far-reaching influence. That style is illustrated by sculpture from a monument commemorating the victory in 230 BCE of Attalos I (ruled 241–197 BCE) over the Gauls, a Celtic people who invaded from the north. These figures, originally in bronze but known today from Roman copies in marble, were mounted on a large pedestal. One of them, with the name Epigonos inscribed on the base, shows the agonizing death of a wounded soldier-trumpeter (fig. 5-16). His wiry, unkempt hair and neck ring, or torque (reputedly the only item of dress the Gauls wore in battle), identify him as a "barbarian." But the sculpture also depicts

dignity and heroism in defeat, and the artist has sought to inspire the viewer's admiration and pity for his subject. The viewer experiences a sense of arrested motion seeing the trumpeter supporting himself on his right arm, struggling to remain upright. One can see that his elbow is buckling, his body about to collapse. This kind of deliberate attempt to elicit a specific emotional response in the viewer, "expressionism," became characteristic of Hellenistic art.

The style and approach seen in the monument to the defeated Gauls culminated in the frieze, which stretched around the base of a huge enclosure for an altar to Zeus on a mountainside at Pergamon (fig. 5-17). The frieze, which runs beneath the altar's Ionic colonnade, was probably executed during the reign of Eumenes II (197–159 BCE). It depicts the battle between the Gods and the Giants, a mythical struggle used by the Greeks as a metaphor for contemporary conflict—in this case, Pergamon's victory over the Gauls.

The panels, about 7¹/₂ feet high, show Greek gods fighting human-looking Giants and grotesque hybrids emerging from the bowels of the earth. In one section of the frieze, the goddess

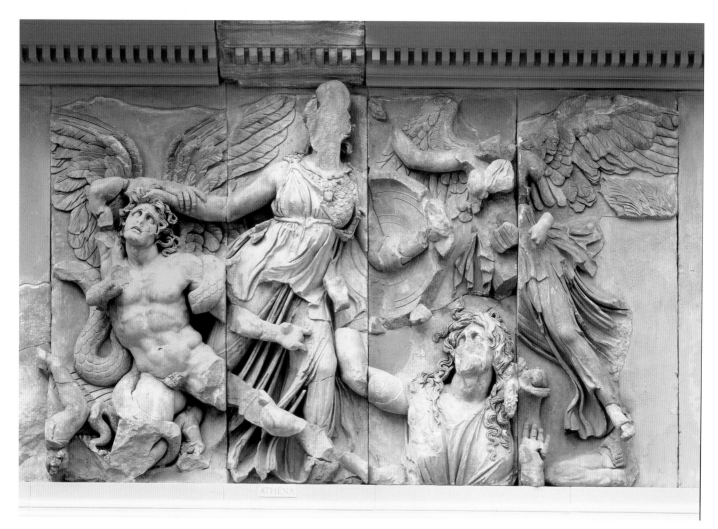

5-18 | **Athena Attacking the Giants,** detail of the frieze from the east front of the altar from Pergamon. Marble frieze height 7'6" (2.3 m). Staatliche Museen zu Berlin, Preussischer Kulturbesitz, Antikensammlung

Athena has forced a winged monster to his knees (fig. 5-18). Inscriptions along the base of the sculpture identify him as Alkyoneos, a son of the earth goddess Ge, who rises in maternal wrath from the ground on the right. At the far right, a winged Nike foretells the outcome of this struggle, as she is about to crown Athena the victor.

The Pergamon frieze is carved in high relief with deep **undercutting** that prompts dramatic contrasts of light and shade to play over the complex forms. Compositionally, the Pergamene sculptors sought to balance opposing forces in three-dimensional space along diagonal lines, whereas Greek artists of the fifth century BCE sought equilibrium and control through balanced horizontals and verticals. Some of the figures in the Pergamon frieze even crawl out of their architectural settings onto the steps, where visitors had to pass them on their way up to the shrine (see sculptural figures at far left, fig. 5-17). Many consider this theatrical and complex interaction of space and form to be a hallmark of the Hellenistic style, just as they consider the balanced restraint of the Parthenon sculpture to characterize the

Classical style. Similarly, the emotional composure admired in Classical art gives way in the Hellenistic period to extreme expressions of pain, stress, wild anger, fear, and despair. All of these emotions characterize the sculpture of *Laocoön and His Sons* (see fig. 24).

Hellenistic painting, like sculpture, reflects the new taste for dramatic narrative subject matter. Little remains of original Greek wall paintings, but in antiquity later patrons greatly admired Greek murals and commissioned copies in the form of wall paintings or mosaics. The second-century BCE mosaic illustrated in figure 5-19, showing a battle between Alexander the Great and Darius III of Persia, is a Roman copy of a wall painting of about 310 BCE. The historian Pliny the Elder attributed the original to a Greek painter named Philoxenos of Eretria; a recent theory claims it as a work of Helen of Egypt, one of a number of women painters recorded as having worked in ancient Greece. The **mosaic** was found in a home in the ancient Roman city of Pompeii, a city strongly influenced by Greek culture.

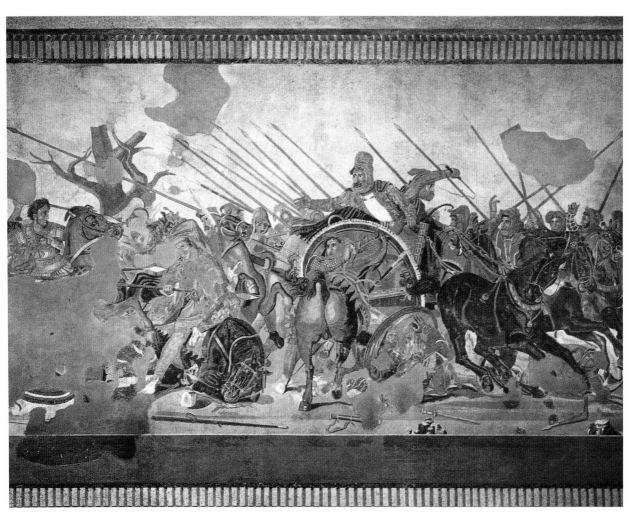

5-19 | *Alexander the Great Confronts Darius III at the Battle of Issos,* Roman mosaic copy after a Greek painting of c. 310 BCE, perhaps by Philoxenos or Helen of Egypt. Museo Archeològico Nazionale, Naples

The scene is one of violent action and radical **foreshortening,** both working to elicit the viewer's response to a dramatic situation. Astride a horse at the left, his hair blowing free and his neck bare, Alexander challenges the helmeted and armored Persian leader, who stretches out his arm in a gesture of defeat and apprehension as his charioteer whisks him back toward safety in the Persian ranks. Presumably in close imitation of the original painting, the mosaicist created the illusion of solid figures through **modeling,** mimicking the play of light on three-dimensional surfaces by highlighting protrusions and **shading** receding areas.

By the late first century BCE, the influence of Greek painting, sculpture, and architecture was paramount in communities such as the Roman city of Pompeii. As Romans conquered the lands around the Mediterannean Sea, they inherited the artistic legacy of the Hellenistic world. Roman patrons and artists were so enthusiastic about Greek art that they made replicas of Greek artworks and wrote careful descriptions of Greek buildings, paintings, and sculpture. The art of Rome, built on Greek foundations, is marked indelibly by this rich Hellenistic heritage.

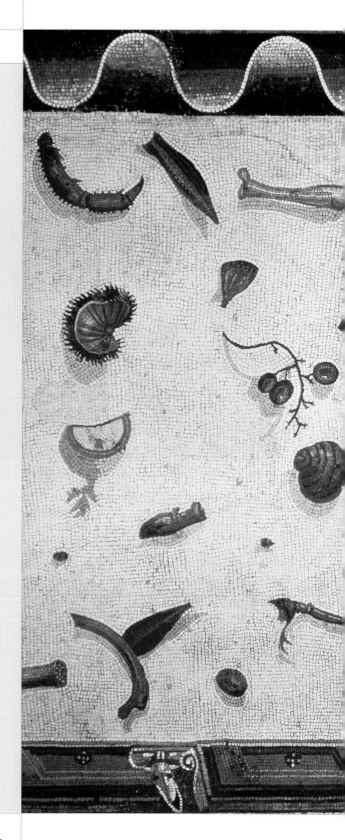

In his work of comic genius, the *Satyricon*, the first-century CE Roman satirist Petronius created one of the all-time fantastic dinner parties, Trimalchio's *Feast* (*Cena Trimalchionis*, Book 15). The newly rich Trimalchio entertains his friends at a lavish banquet where he shows off his extraordinary wealth, but also demonstrates his ignorance and boorish manners. When dishes are broken, Trimalchio orders his servants to sweep them away with the rubbish on the floor. In *The Unswept Floor* mosaic, the remains of fine food from just such a party litter the floor. The family and guests dining in this room would have seen the fictive remains of past gourmet pleasures—from lobster claws to cherry pits—under their couches.

If art reflects the ideals of a society, what does it mean that wealthy Romans commemorated their table scraps in mosaics of the greatest subtlety and skill? Is this a form of conspicuous consumption, proof positive that the owner of this house gave lavish banquets and hosted guests who had the kind of sophisticated humor that could appreciate Trimalchio's *Feast*? The Romans did in fact place a high value on displaying their wealth and taste in the semi-public rooms and gardens of their houses and villas. They did so through their possessions, especially their art collections. *The Unswept Floor* is just one of a very large number of Roman copies of great Greek mosaics and paintings, such as *Alexander the Great Confronts Darius III* (see fig. 5-19), and sculptures. Even Julius Caesar owned a version of the *Dying Gallic Trumpeter* (see fig. 5-16); a *Laocoön* (see fig. 24) belonged to Nero; and a copy of Polykleitos's *Spear Bearer* (see fig. 4-35) stood in the baths at Hadrian's Villa.

In the case of *The Unswept Floor*, Heraklitos, a second-century CE Greek mosaicist living in Rome (who signed his work), made this copy of an illusionistic painting by the renowned second-century BCE Pergamene artist Sosos. Guests could have displayed their knowledge of the notable precedents for the trash on the floor. The literary character of the imagery is emphasized by the inclusion of six actor's masks along one side of the room. The arrangement suggests that theatrical entertainment will follow the sumptuous feast.

Interest in history and literary allusions (as well as visual tricks and great skill in representing material objects) are characteristic of Roman art. For the first time in our study of art's history we see a material culture focus on the mundane concerns of prosperous families—not only on rulers or gods.

Heraklitos. *The Unswept Floor,* mosaic variant of a 2nd-century BCE painting by Sosos of Pergamon. 2nd century CE 13'3½" (4.05 m). Musei Vaticani Museo Gregoriano Profano, ex Lateranese, Rome. (See page 152.)

Art of the Roman Republic and Empire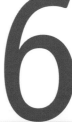

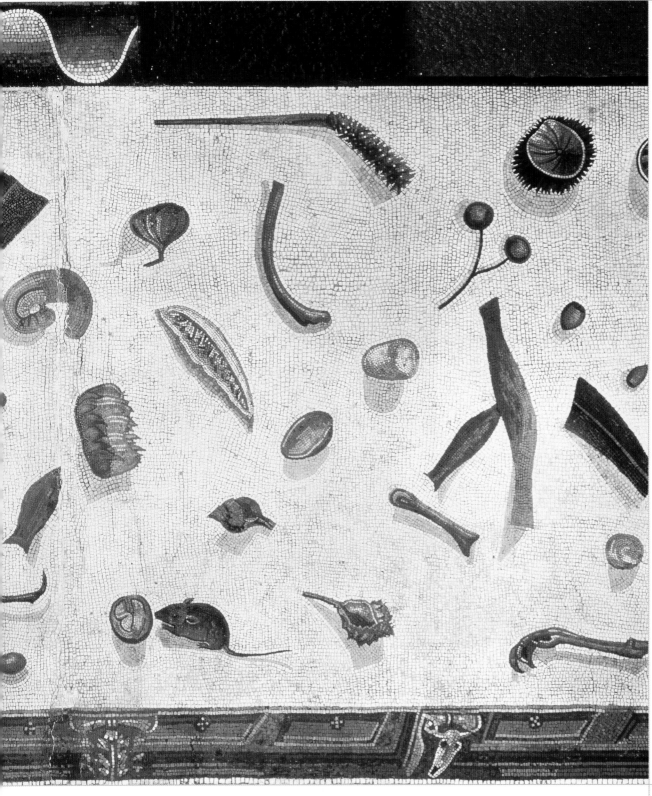

Roman Counterparts of Greek Gods

ROMAN NAME	GREEK GOD
Jupiter	Zeus
Juno	Hera
Minerva	Athena
Mars	Ares
Apollo; also Phoebus	Apollo
Venus	Aphrodite
Diana	Artemis
Mercury	Hermes
Pluto	Hades
Bacchus	Dionysos
Vulcan	Hephaistos
Vesta	Hestia
Ceres	Demeter
Neptune	Poseidon
Cupid or Amor	Eros
Hercules	Herakles

6-1

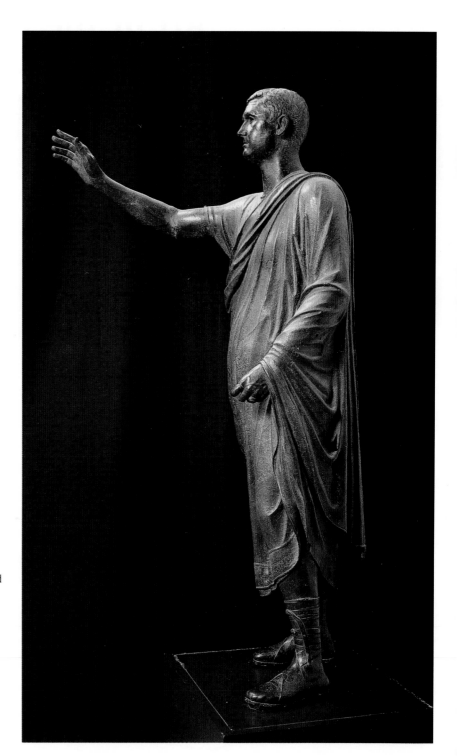

Aulus Metellus
found near
Perugia. Late 2nd
or early 1st
century BCE
Bronze, height
5'11" (1.8 m)
Museo
Archeològico
Nazionale
Florence

As early as the Iron Age, small groups of people who spoke a common language, Latin, settled in central Italy south of the Tiber River. They also built small settlements on seven hills near the Tiber. The villages eventually joined to become the city of Rome. By the sixth century BCE, Rome had developed into a major transportation and trading center. At this time central Italy was also home to the Etruscans (see Chapter 5). The Romans soon challenged the Etruscan presence, and by the first century BCE they ruled the peninsula. At the height of their power, Romans ruled all the lands around the Mediterranean Sea, which they proudly referred to as *mare nostrum*, or "our sea." In the early second century CE, the Roman Empire stretched east to the Euphrates River, south to Egypt, and northwest as far as Scotland (see Map 2, page 163).

To spur growth and simplify administration of the empire, the Roman government undertook building programs of unprecedented scale and complexity, constructing central administrative and commercial centers (**forums** and **basilicas**), racetracks, theaters, public baths, **aqueducts** to carry water, middle-class housing, and even entire new towns. To speed communication and facilitate commerce and the movement of troops, the Romans built a vast and sophisticated network of roads between their capital and the farthest reaches of the empire. Many modern European highways still follow the routes laid down by Roman engineers, and Roman-era foundations underlie the streets of many European cities.

Culturally, the Romans borrowed heavily from the Greek and Hellenistic world. They used Greek orders to decorate their architecture, imported Greek art, and employed Greek artists. Like the Etruscans, they adopted the Greek gods and heroes as their own, giving them Latin names (see "Roman Counterparts of Greek Gods," left). The sophisticated legal, administrative, and cultural systems that the Romans imposed on the people they conquered endured for some five hundred years in the West. In the eastern Mediterranean, **classical** traditions and styles survived into the fifteenth century as an important element of Byzantine art.

The Republican Period

Early Rome was governed by a series of kings and an advisory body called the Senate, made up of upper-class citizens. The last kings of Rome were overthrown in 509 BCE, marking the beginning of what is known as the period of the Republic (509 to 27 BCE). Sculptors of the Republican period sought to create believable images based on careful observation. The convention of rendering accurate and faithful portraits of individuals, called **naturalism**, may be derived from the practice of making death masks of deceased relatives. In any case patrons in the Republican period clearly admired **veristic** portraits, and it is not surprising that they often turned to skilled Etruscan artists to execute them. The lifesize bronze portrait of *Aulus Metellus*—the Roman official's name is inscribed on the hem of his garment in Etruscan letters (fig. 6-1)—depicts the man addressing a gathering, his arm outstretched and slightly raised, a pose expressive of authority and persuasiveness. The orator wears the folded and draped garment called a toga, characteristic of a Roman official. According to Pliny the Elder, large statues like this were often placed atop columns as memorials to the individuals portrayed.

Art and architecture during the Republic initially reflected both Etruscan and Greek influences. In religious architecture, the Romans favored urban temples set, in the Etruscan manner, in the midst of congested commercial centers. An early example is a small, rectangular temple built in the late second century BCE beside the Tiber River in Rome, perhaps dedicated to Portunus, the god of harbors and ports (figs. 6-2, 6-3). The structure rests on a raised platform, or **podium**. It has a rectangular cella and a colonnaded porch at one end approached by a broad stair. The Romans then applied the Greek Ionic order. However, in contrast to a Greek temple the Ionic columns are freestanding on the porch and **engaged** (attached to the wall) around the cella. The entablature above the porch columns continues around the cella as a frieze. This design was to become standard for Roman temples.

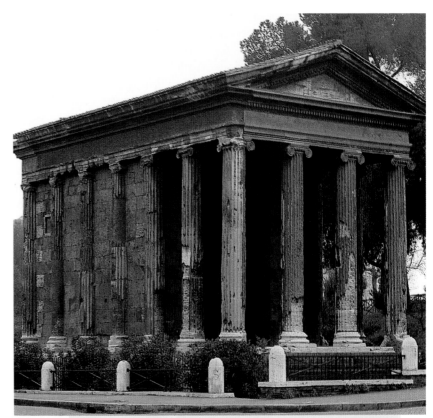

6-2 | **Temple perhaps dedicated to Portunus,** Forum Boarium (cattle market), Rome. Late 2nd century BCE

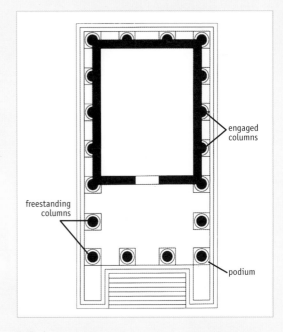

6-3 | **Plan of the temple perhaps dedicated to Portunus**

As city dwellers, Romans also devoted their ingenuity and resources to secular architecture. In large cities they built two- or three-story apartment buildings with shared walls, and in the towns, they lived in houses behind or above rows of shops. Wealthy people built gracious private residences with one or

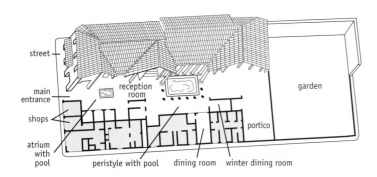

6-4 | **Reconstruction drawing and plan of the House of Pansa**
Pompeii. 2nd century BCE

more gardens (fig. 6-4). These large, elegant houses had rooms opening onto a central atrium, an unroofed space with a pool for catching the rainwater. In dry climates the rainwater coming through the open roof might instead be drained into a deep cistern.

Many fine examples of urban dwellings can be seen at Pompeii, near modern Naples. Located near Mount Vesuvius, Pompeii was buried in volcanic ash after the mountain's eruption in 79 CE and remained remarkably well preserved until its rediscovery in the eighteenth century. The "House of the Silver Wedding" is typical (fig. 6-5). Behind the atrium and its surrounding rooms lay a second open area, a peristyle court, an interior garden courtyard surrounded by a colonnaded walkway or **portico**. The more private family quarters, such as the bedrooms, dining room, and servants' quarters, were usually entered through the peristyle court.

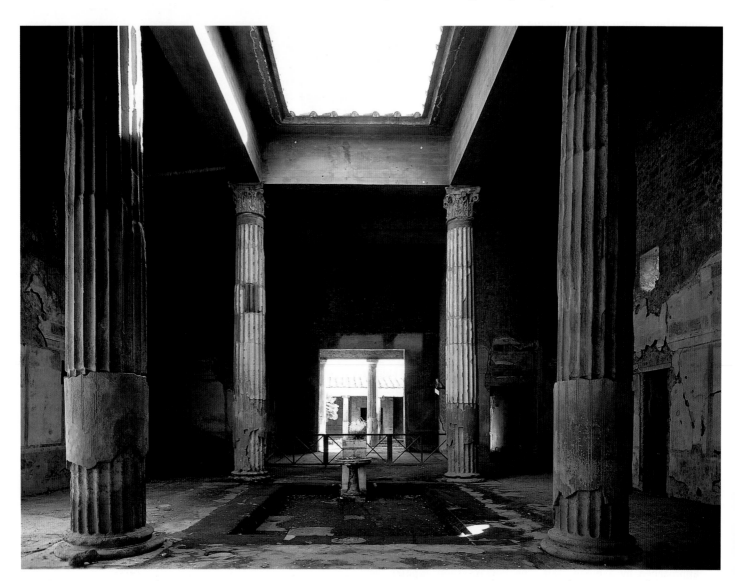

6-5 | **Atrium, House of the Silver Wedding, Pompeii.** Early 1st century CE

Ancient Roman houses excavated at Pompeii and elsewhere are usually simply given numbers by archaeologists or (if known) named after the families or individuals who once lived in them. This house received its unusual name as a commemorative gesture. It was excavated in 1893, the year of the silver wedding anniversary of Italy's King Humbert and his wife, Margaret of Savoy, who had supported archaeological fieldwork at Pompeii.

Public building projects to allow for the transport and storage of food and water also made possible the expansion of cities. In many areas of Europe and the Mediterranean, impressive examples of Roman engineering still stand. The Pont du Gard near Nîmes in southern France (fig. 6-6), spanning 900 feet, was designed to carry water over the Gard River. This aqueduct, as such structures with water conduits are called, was part of a system that brought water to Nîmes

Elements of Architecture

ARCH AND VAULT

The round arch is a basic unit of Roman architecture. It is designed to displace most of the weight of the masonry above it to its curving sides, and from there to the ground through supporting upright elements (**piers**, columns, or door or window **jambs**). In a succession of arches (an **arcade**), the space encompassed by each arch and its supports is called a **bay**. Wall areas adjacent to curves of an arch are called **spandrels**. In the illustration at right, arrows indicate the outward thrust and downward gravity pull (weight) of the arch or vault.

A round arch can be extended to form a **barrel vault**. A barrel vault is constructed in the same manner as a round arch, and the outward pressure exerted by its curving sides usually requires added support, called **buttressing**. When two barrel-vaulted spaces intersect each other at right angles, the result is a **groin vault**. The round arch and barrel vault were known and were put to limited use by the Mesopotamians and the Egyptians. They were employed more extensively by the Etruscans. But it was the Romans who realized the potential strength and versatility of these architectural elements and exploited them to the fullest degree.

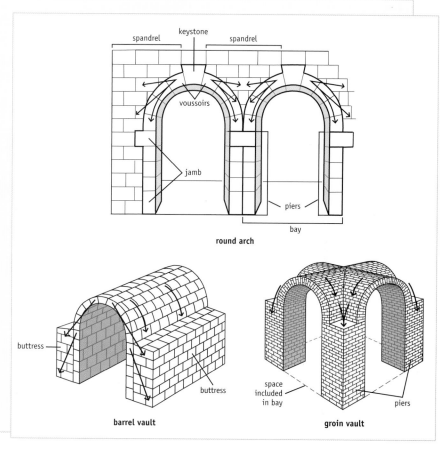

round arch

barrel vault

groin vault

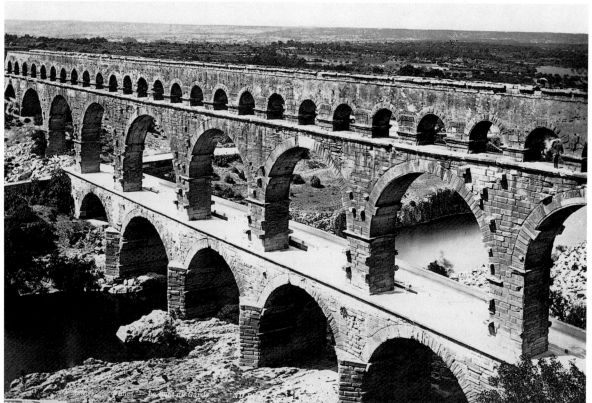

6-6

Pont du Gard Nîmes, France
Late 1st century BCE

CLOSER LOOK

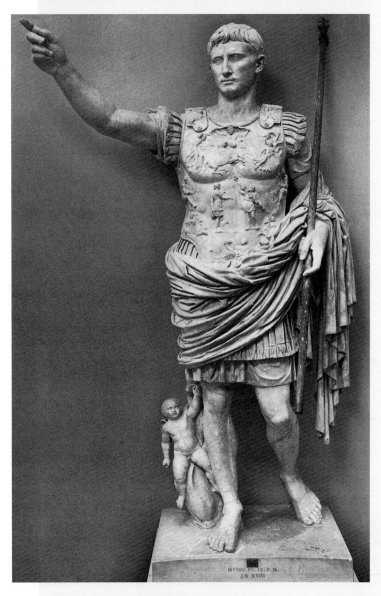

6-7 *Augustus of Primaporta.* Early 1st century CE (perhaps a copy of a bronze statue of c. 20 BCE). Marble, height 6'8" (2.03 m) Musei Vaticani, Braccio Nuovo, Rome

The first Roman emperor was born Gaius Octavius (Octavian) in 63 BCE into a minor branch of the Caesar family. When he was only eighteen years old, Octavian was adopted as son and heir by his brilliant great-uncle, Julius Caesar, who recognized qualities in him that would make him a worthy successor. That was in 45 BCE. Early in 44 BCE, Julius Caesar refused the Roman Senate's offer of the imperial crown, which amounted to his refusing to be the first Roman emperor. By March 15 of that year he was dead, murdered by a group of conspirators. Octavian stepped up. Over the next seventeen spectacular years, as general, politician, statesman, and public relations genius, Octavian vanquished warring internal factions and brought peace to fractious provinces. By 27 BCE, the Senate conferred on him the title Augustus (meaning "exalted, sacred"). For the West, Augustus defined the concepts of empire and imperial rule as he led the state and the empire for another forty-one years of peace and prosperity (the great *Pax Romana*, or Roman Peace) until his death in 14 CE.

The statue found in the villa of his wife, Livia, at Primaporta near Rome embodies the complex character and creative conservatism of the man (fig. 6-7). We see Augustus as he wanted to be seen and remembered, an image depicting him in his prime and inspired by heroic Greek figures like the *Spear Bearer* (see fig. 4-35). At the same time, the *Augustus of Primaporta* is one of the most successful imperial images of all time. The emperor extends his hand in an orator's gesture, as if convincing his people through his superior intellect rather than commanding them by force of arms. Yet imperial power is evident in the idealization of the figure, both in his bare feet, a sign of divine status, and in the parade armor, with its defeated "barbarians" and scenes of victory. Nonetheless, this convincing image is rendered with the skill in naturalistic representation demanded by Roman patrons and public. Augustus's staggering accomplishments are evoked through this work of art.

from springs 30 miles to the north. At the time it was built, probably about 20 BCE, the aqueduct could provide 100 gallons of water a day for every person in Nîmes.

The Pont du Gard was constructed of precisely cut stones from a nearby quarry. It consists of three **arcades** (a series of regularly spaced arched openings). The top arcade supports the water trough. The fundamental element of all three arcades is the round **arch** (see "Arch and Vault," page 141), formed by fitting together wedge-shaped pieces, called **voussoirs,** which are locked together at the top center by a final piece, called a **keystone**. A utilitarian structure, the aqueduct was left undecorated, and the projecting blocks that supported scaffolding during construction were left to provide easy access for repairs. The Pont du Gard nevertheless conveys a sense of proportion and rhythm: it harmonizes with its natural setting as it visually links the hilly riverbanks.

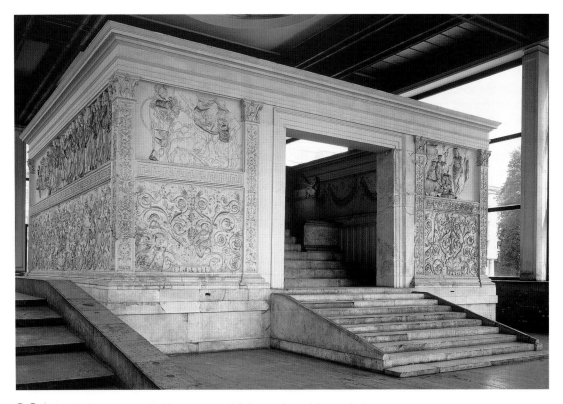

6-8 | **Ara Pacis.** 13–9 BCE. Marble, approx. 34'5" (10.5 m) x 38' (11.6 m). Rome

The altar stands at the top of the stairs, visible through the door in the enclosure wall.

The Early Empire

Rome's conquest of lands outside the Italian peninsula strained its political system, weakening the authority of the Senate and leading to a series of civil wars among powerful generals. In 46 BCE Julius Caesar emerged victorious over his rivals; he ruled Rome as dictator until his assassination in 44 BCE. After Caesar's death and a period of renewed fighting, his great-nephew and adopted son, Octavian, assumed power.

Although Octavian kept the forms of Republican government, he retained the real authority for himself, and his ascension marks the end of the Republic. Under Augustus Caesar, as Octavian was titled in 27 BCE, the Romans began to use imperial portraiture as political propaganda. An over-lifesize statue of the emperor, the *Augustus of Primaporta* (fig. 6-7), exemplifies this form of portraiture. Augustus wears a *cuirass* (body armor) and holds a commander's baton, but his feet are bare, suggesting to some scholars that the work was made after his death to commemorate his apotheosis, or elevation to divine status. Recently it has been suggested that the marble sculpture was made after Augustus's death in 14 BCE and copies an earlier bronze figure. After Augustus, Roman emperors were deified in part to unify the culturally diverse populations that had come under Roman rule. Worship of ancient gods was mingled with homage to past rulers and oaths of allegiance to the living ones.

Roman sculptors contributed unabashedly to imperial propaganda by recording contemporary events on commemorative arches, columns, and tombs. A monument erected by Augustus, the Ara Pacis, or Altar of Augustan Peace (fig. 6-8), was as famous in its day as the *Vietnam Veterans Memorial* is in ours (see fig. 20-42). The rectangular structure is a Roman adaptation of earlier Greek and Hellenistic altars. It was constructed in Rome between 13 and 9 BCE to memorialize Augustus's triumphal return to the city following the successful establishment of Roman rule in France and Spain.

Whenever a general or emperor returned to Rome after a significant campaign, he paraded through the city with his troops, captives, and booty in a victory celebration known as a "triumph." The route of the procession was ornamented with temporary structures such as **triumphal arches** and altars, which afterward might be re-created in stone as permanent memorials. The interior of the Ara Pacis enclosure wall, decorated with carved garlands suspended in **swags**, or loops, is a marble version of the flower-swagged temporary altar that would have been set up during Augustus's triumphal procession. Relief panels along the exterior of the north and south sides of the wall depict senators and members of the imperial family who would have attended the victory celebrations (fig. 6-9; see page 144). Unlike the Greek sculptors who created the procession on the frieze of the Parthenon (see fig. 4-31), the Roman sculptors of the Ara Pacis depicted actual individuals. They also attempted to suggest spatial depth by carving the closest elements in high relief and those farther back in increasingly lower relief. Using a device reminiscent of the Altar of Zeus at Pergamon (see fig. 5-18), the sculptors visually draw the spectator into the event by making the feet of the nearest figures project from the architectural **groundline** into our space.

During Rome's Republican period, a taste for strongly realistic portraiture developed, influenced by Etruscan models. The portraits in the Ara Pacis procession represent a continuation of that **naturalistic**, or realistic, tradition, in contrast to the *Augustus of Primaporta*, which displays a more **idealized** style of portraiture. The second foreground adult figure from the left in the detail shown in figure 6-9 is probably Augustus's second wife, Livia, who remained at his side for more than fifty years. She supported laws that favored marriage and family, provided increased legal protection for married women, and penalized bachelors, unmarried women, and childless wives or widows.

These laws made family life not only a desirable state but a patriotic duty and were aimed at increasing the Roman birthrate.

Because the marriage of Augustus and Livia was childless, the emperor's successor was Tiberius, one of Livia's two sons by her first marriage, to Tiberius Claudius Nero. A large onyx cameo (a gemstone carved in low relief) known as *Gemma Augustea* carries the scene of the **apotheosis** of Augustus after his death in 14 CE (fig. 6-10). The emperor, crowned with a victor's wreath, sits at the center right of the upper register. He has assumed the identity of Jupiter, king of the gods; an eagle, sacred to Jupiter, stands at his feet. Sitting next to him is a personification of Rome that has Livia's features. The sea goat in the roundel between them may represent Capricorn, the emperor's zodiac sign. Tiberius, the adopted son of Augustus, holds a lance and steps out of a chariot at the left. Returning victorious from the German front, he will assume the imperial throne as the designated heir of Augustus. Below this realm of godly rulers is the earth, where Roman soldiers are raising a trophy—a post or standard on which armor captured from the defeated enemy is displayed. The cowering, shackled barbarians on the bottom right

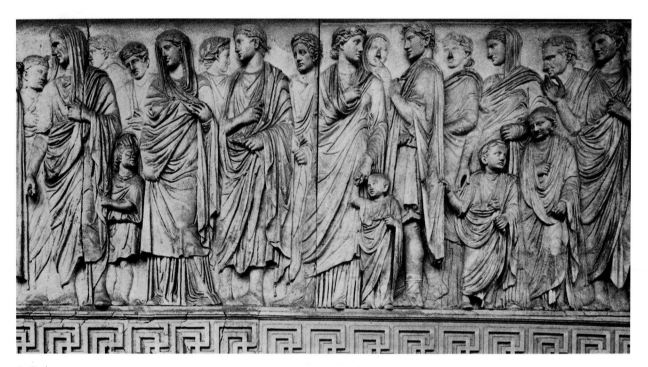

6-9 | *Imperial Procession,* detail of a relief on the Ara Pacis. Height 5'2" (1.6 m)

The middle-aged man with the shrouded head at the far left is Marcus Agrippa, who would have been Augustus's successor had he not died in 12 CE, the year after the Ara Pacis was dedicated. The bored but well-behaved youngster pulling at Agrippa's robe—and being restrained gently by the hand of the man behind him—is probably Agrippa's son, Gaius Caesar. The heavily swathed woman next to Agrippa on the right is probably Augustus's wife, Livia, followed by the elder of her two sons, Tiberius, who would become the next emperor. Behind Tiberius is Antonia, the niece of Augustus, looking back at her husband, Drusus, Livia's younger son. She grasps the hand of Germanicus, one of her younger children. Behind their uncle Drusus are Gnaeus and Domitia, children of Antonia's older sister, who can be seen standing quietly beside them. The depiction of children in an official relief was new to the Augustan period and reflects Augustus's desire to promote private family life.

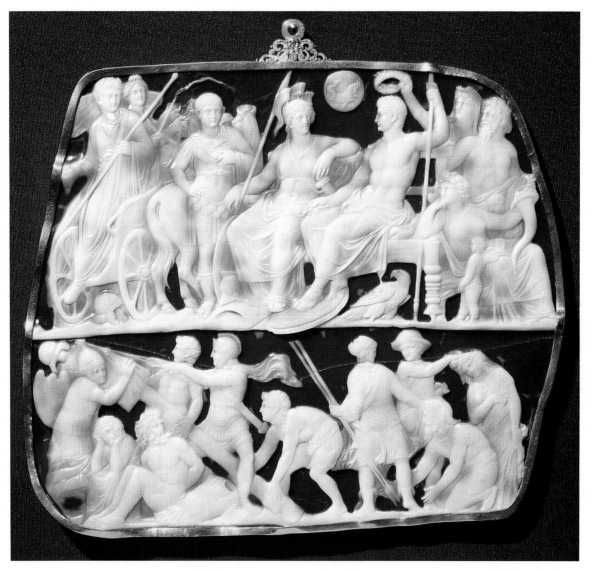

6-10 | *Gemma Augustea.* Early 1st century CE. Onyx, 7½ x 9" (19 x 23 cm)
Kunsthistorisches Museum, Vienna

wait to be tied to this trophy. The *Gemma Augustea* brilliantly combines idealized, heroic figures of a kind characteristic of Classical Greek art with recognizable portraits, the dramatic action of Hellenistic art, and a purely Roman realism in the depiction of historical events.

THE EMPIRE

The sequence of related rulers that begins with Tiberius is known as the Julio-Claudian dynasty (14–68 CE). It ended with the reign of the despotic and capricious emperor Nero. A powerful general named Vespasian seized control of the government after Nero's death. The dynasty he founded, the Flavian, ruled from 69 to 96 CE. The Flavian emperors, Vespasian (ruled 69–79 CE), Titus (ruled 79–81 CE), and Domitian (ruled 81–96 CE), restored imperial finances and stabilized the empire's frontiers.

The Colosseum (fig. 6-11; see page 146), one of Rome's most influential monuments, was built during the reign of Vespasian. Construction began in 72 CE, and the Colosseum was dedicated by Titus in 80 CE, after Vespasian's death. In this enormous entertainment center, Roman audiences watched blood sports and spectacles. These included animal hunts, fights to the death between gladiators or between gladiators and wild animals, performances of trained animals and acrobats, and even mock sea battles, for which the arena could be flooded by a built-in mechanism. The Flavians erected the structure to bolster their popularity in Rome, and its name then was the Flavian Amphitheater. (The name "Colosseum," by which it came to be known, derived from the Colossus, a bigger-than-life statue of Nero standing next to it.) The opening performance in 80 CE lasted 100 days, during which time, it was claimed, 9,000 wild animals and 2,000 gladiators died. The arena held about 45,000 spectators. For its ease of crowd movement and unobstructed views, the design of the Colosseum has never been improved upon. Architects still copy it today.

The Colosseum was built entirely of masonry—**concrete** faced with stone. Eighty barrel vaults over corridors and stairs radiate from the center and intersect the barrel ring vaults of the perimeter passageways to form groin vaults (see "Arch and Vault," page 141). These complex curved shapes could be formed

6-11 | **Colosseum,** Rome. 72–80 CE

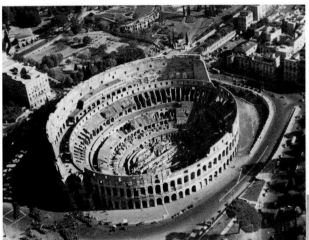

of concrete faster and more cheaply than of stone blocks that had to be cut by trained masons. The concrete consisted of stone rubble in a binder made from a natural cement and water. This rough but strong core was faced with finer, worked stone. (In very fine buildings, the core might be covered with a marble veneer or exterior facing.)

The curving outer wall of the Colosseum consists of three levels of arcade surmounted by a wall-like top, or **attic story** (fig. 6-12). Every arch in the arcades is framed by engaged columns, which support friezes marking the division between levels. Each level uses a different architectural order and becomes increasingly decorative as they rise. The ground floor is ornamented with columns in the Tuscan order (generally similar to the Greek Doric order except that the columns have bases). The Ionic order is used on the second level, the Corinthian on the third, and flat Corinthian **pilasters** (engaged shafts) adorn the fourth story. All of these elements are purely decorative and serve no structural function. The systematic use of the orders in a logical succession from sturdy Tuscan to decorative Corinthian follows a tradition inherited from Hellenistic architecture. It is still popular as a way of articulating and organizing the facades of large buildings.

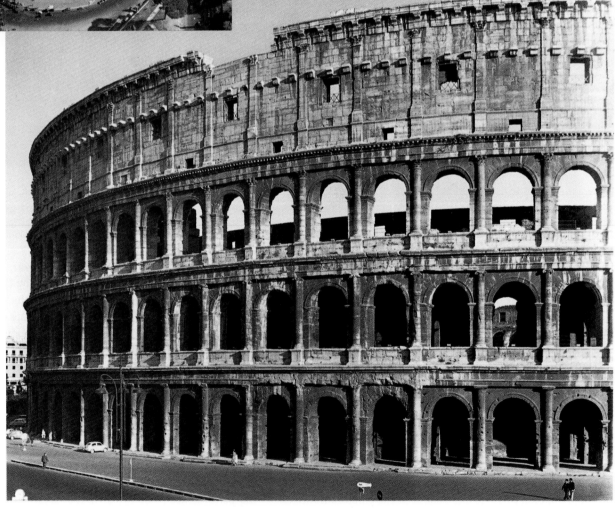

6-12 | **Colosseum**

When Domitian became emperor in 81 CE, he immediately commissioned a triumphal arch to honor his brother and deified predecessor, Titus (fig. 6-13). The Arch of Titus, which commemorates Titus's capture of Jerusalem in 70 CE, is essentially a free-standing gateway pierced by a barrel-vaulted passageway. The exterior of the arch is ornamented with engaged Composite columns. Originally the whole arch served as a giant base, 50 feet tall, for a statue of a four-horse chariot and driver, a typical Roman triumphal symbol.

Titus's capture of Jerusalem ended a fierce campaign to crush a revolt of the Jews in Palestine. His troops looted and destroyed the Second Temple of Jerusalem and carted off its sacred treasures. These spoils were displayed in Rome during Titus's triumphal procession. According to the Jewish eyewitness and historian Flavius Josephus, the prizes included "the law of the Jews," a gold table, and a seven-branched lamp stand, or menorah.

Elements of Architecture

ROMAN ARCHITECTURAL ORDERS

The Etruscans and Romans adapted Greek architectural orders to their own tastes and uses. For example, the Etruscans modified the Greek Doric order by adding a base to the column. The Romans created the **Composite order** by incorporating the **volute** and motif of the Greek Ionic capital and the acanthus leaves of the Corinthian order. The sturdy, unfluted **Tuscan order** combined the Greek Doric order and Etruscan models. In this diagram, the Roman orders are shown on **pedestals**, which consist of a **plinth**, a **dado**, and a **cornice**. The Romans often used the orders as applied (low relief) decoration on a wall.

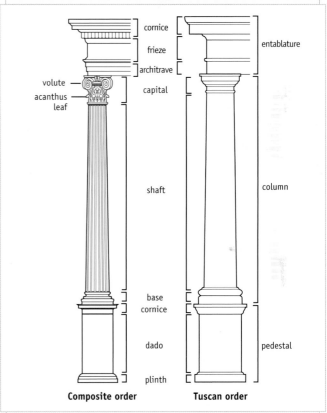

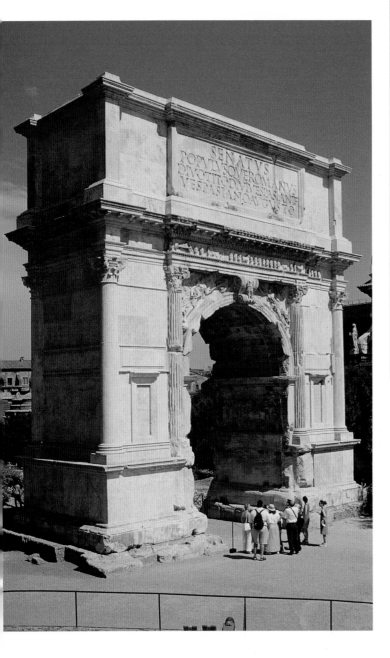

6-13 **Arch of Titus, Rome.** C. 81 CE. Concrete and white marble, height 50' (15 m)

The dedication inscribed across the tall attic story above the arch opening reads: "The Senate and the Roman People to the Deified Titus Flavius Vespasianus Augustus, son of the Deified Vespasian." The Romans typically recorded historic occasions and identified monuments with solemn prose and beautiful inscriptions in stone. The sculptors' use of elegant Roman capital letters—perfectly sized and spaced to be read from a distance and cut with sharp terminals (serifs) to catch the light—established a standard that calligraphers and alphabet designers still follow.

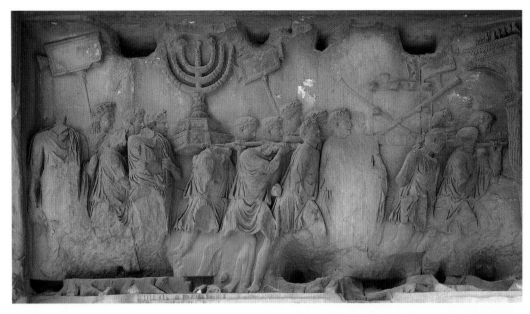

6-14 | *Spoils from the Temple of Solomon, Jerusalem,* relief in the passageway of the Arch of Titus. Marble Height 6'8" (2.03 m)

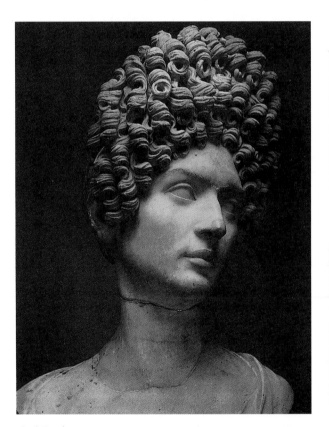 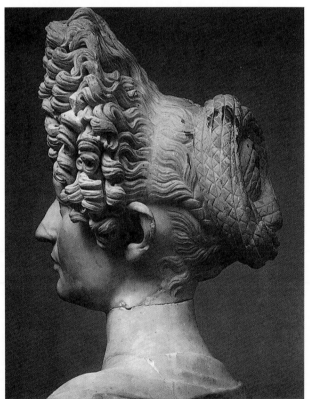

6-15 | *Young Flavian Woman.* c. 90 CE. Marble, height 25" (65.5 cm). Museo Capitolino, Rome

The typical Flavian hairstyle seen on this woman required a patient hairdresser handy with a curling iron and with a special knack for turning the back of the head into an intricate basketweave of braids. Male writers loved to scoff at the results. Martial described the style precisely as "a globe of hair." Statius spoke of "the glory of woman's lofty front, her storied hair." And Juvenal waxed comically poetic: "See her from the front; she is Andromache [an epic heroine]. From behind she looks half the size—a different woman you would think" (cited in Balsdon, page 256).

The reliefs on the inside walls of the arch depict Titus's soldiers carrying this booty through the streets of Rome (fig. 6-14). Viewing them, the observer can easily imagine the boisterous army on the march. The artist creates a window on the world through which we observe the crowd. The varying height of the relief elements creates the impression that the marchers

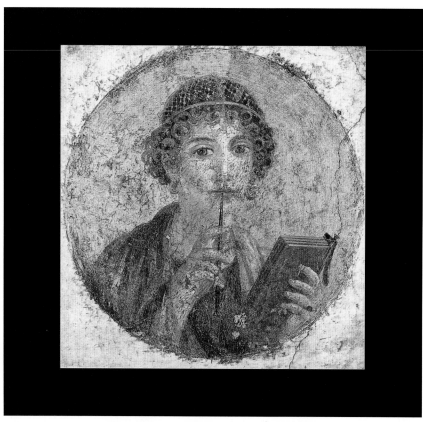

6-16 | ***Young Woman Writing,*** detail of a wall painting from Pompeii. Late 1st century CE. Diameter 14⅝" (37 cm) Museo Archeològico Nazionale, Naples

are moving toward the viewer and then turning to move away through a distant arch. Spatial relationships, achieved by rendering close elements in higher relief than those more distant, produce a sense of atmosphere. The mood and the illusion of space go beyond the formal solemnity and neutral background of the Ara Pacis.

The development of art in Rome depended on private as well as public patronage. For their homes, wealthy individuals might commission portraits in marble or bronze, or wall paintings, or mosaics. Roman patrons demanded likenesses in their portraits. However, sometimes they preferred some idealization of the sitter and at other times wanted an exact image. The portrait of a young Flavian woman, whose identity is not known (fig. 6-15), exemplifies the idealized portrait type, in the manner of the *Augustus of Primaporta* (see fig. 6-7). The well-observed, recognizable features—a strong nose and jaw, heavy brows, deep-set eyes, and a long neck contrast with the smoothly rendered flesh and soft lips. (The portrait suggests the retouched fashion photos of today.) The hair is piled high in an extraordinary mass of ringlets in the latest court fashion. Executing the head required skillfull chiseling and **drillwork**, a technique for rapidly cutting deep grooves with straight sides, as was done here to render the holes in the center of the curls. The overall effect, from a distance, is very lifelike. The play of natural light over the more subtly

sculpted surfaces gives the illusion of being reflected off real skin and hair.

Portraits, perhaps imaginary ones, were also popular in wall paintings. A late-first-century CE **tondo** (circular panel) from a house in Pompeii contains a portrait known as *Young Woman Writing* (fig. 6-16). Perhaps, like some Roman women, she was a professional writer. In a convention popular among women patrons, she is shown with the tip of a writing stylus raised to her lips. She holds a set of wood tablets coated with wax that were used in much the same way we might use a small chalkboard or pad of paper; letters engraved in soft wax with a stylus could be smoothed over and rewritten. When a text or letter was considered ready, it was copied onto expensive papyrus or parchment. As in a modern studio photograph, with its careful lighting and retouching, the young woman in this painting is portrayed in an idealized fashion.

At Pompeii, many wall paintings were preserved beneath the ashes from the volcano Vesuvius. In the earliest houses, artists created the illusion in paint that the walls were actually covered with thin slabs of colored marble set off by real architectural details such as plaster columns. In the first century BCE they extended the space of a room visually with painted scenes of figures on a shallow "stage" or with a landscape or cityscape seen close up. Architectural details were painted on rather than molded in plaster. Sometimes artists reemphasized the wall

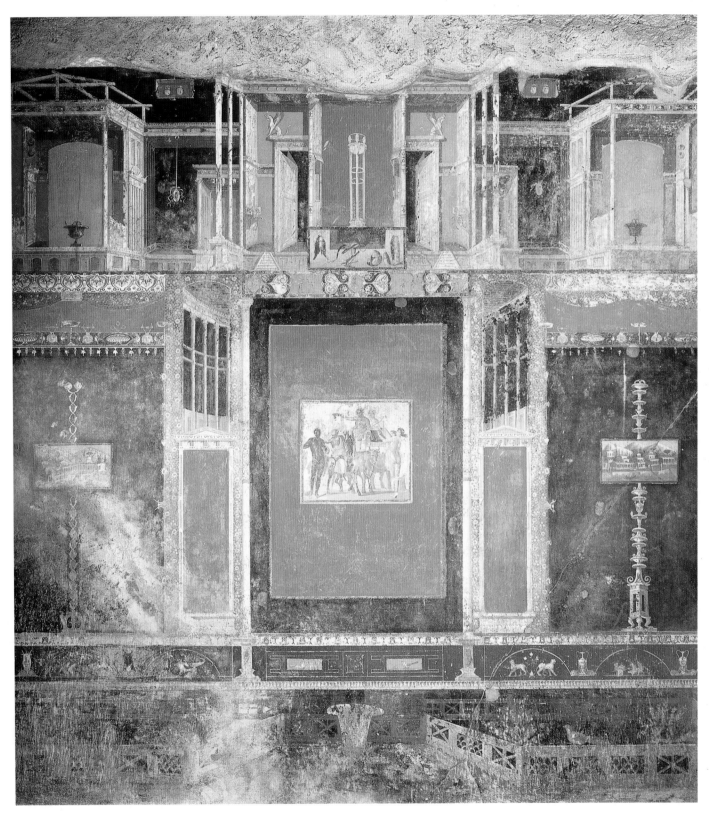

6-17 | **Detail of a wall painting in the House of M. Lucretius Fronto, Pompeii.** Mid-1st century CE

surface by painting it a solid color and decorating it with whimsical architecture. In these representations, delicate vignettes sometimes appear. By the first century CE, painters combined narrative paintings, especially mythological scenes, with ever more fantastic and realistic renderings of buildings.

Paintings dating to the mid-first century CE, found in the House of M. Lucretius Fronto in Pompeii, emphasize the walls in panels of black and red (fig. 6-17). Three rectangular pictures seem to be mounted on the panels, but they are actually painted on the wall. The artistic device of architectural illusionism can

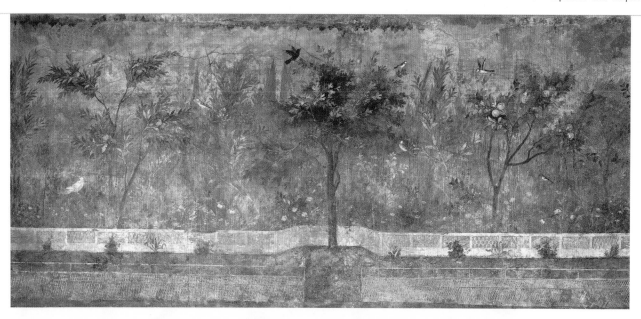

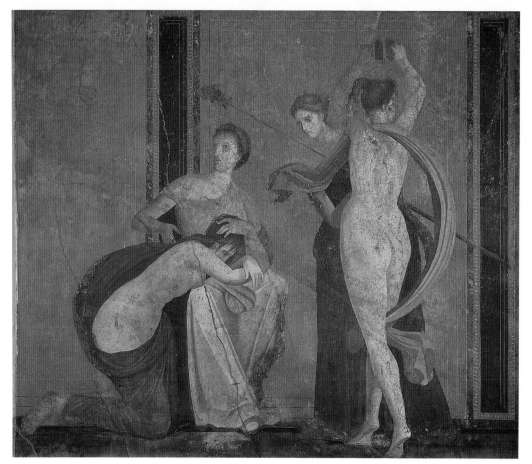

6-18 | (*above*) *Garden Scene*
detail of a wall painting
from the Villa of Livia at
Primaporta, near Rome
Late 1st century BCE
Museo Nazionale
Romano, Rome

6-19 | (*left*) *Initiation Rites of
the Cult of Bacchus (?)*
detail of a wall painting
in the Villa of the
Mysteries, Pompeii
c. 50 BCE

be seen in the simulated window openings protected by grilles and the suggestion of an upper level, but these elements show no logical layout or significant depiction of depth.

The dining room walls of the Villa of Livia at Primaporta exemplify yet another approach to creating a sense of expanded space (fig. 6-18). Instead of rendering a stage set or a cityscape, the artist "painted away" the wall surfaces to create the illusion of being on a porch or pavilion looking out over a low, paneled wall into an orchard of heavily laden fruit trees. These and the flowering shrubs are filled with a variety of wonderfully observed birds. In such paintings, the overall effect is one of wonder-invoking nature, an idealized view of the world, rendered with free, fluid brushwork and delicate color.

In addition to portraits and landscapes, other subjects that appeared in Roman art included historical and mythological scenes, and exquisitely rendered **still lifes** (compositions of inanimate objects). In the so-called Villa of the Mysteries at Pompeii (fig. 6-19), the rites of a mystery religion are per-formed. A reminder of the wide variety of religious practices tolerated by the Romans, the murals depict initiation rites—

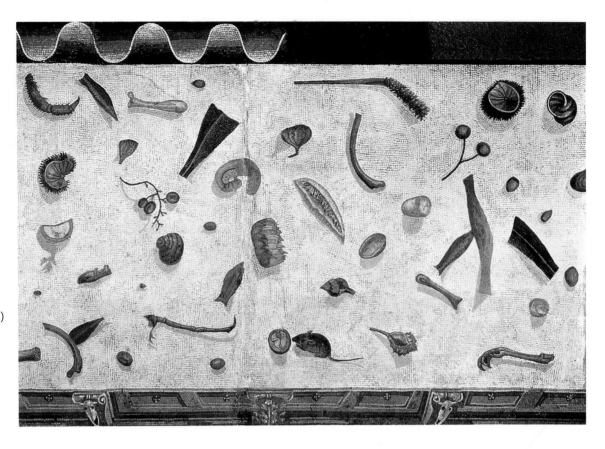

6-20

Heraklitos. *The Unswept Floor* mosaic variant of a 2nd-century BCE painting by Sosos of Pergamon. 2nd century CE. 13'3½" (4.05 m) Musei Vaticani Museo Gregoriano Profano, ex Lateranese, Rome (See pages 136–37.)

probably into the cult of Bacchus, who was the god of vegetation and fertility as well as wine. The action takes place on a shallow "stage" along the top of the **dado** (the lower part of a wall), with a background of brilliant, deep red (now known as Pompeian red) that was very popular with Roman painters. The scene unfolds around the entire room, depicting a succession of events that culminate in the acceptance of an initiate into the cult. In the portion of the room seen here, a winged figure (not seen in this illustration) whips a female initiate who lies across the lap of another woman, and a devotee dances with cymbals, perhaps to drown out the initiate's cries. According to another interpretation, the dancing figure is the initiate herself, who has risen to dance with joy at the conclusion of her trials. The whole scene may show a purification ritual meant to bring enlightenment and blissful union with the god.

Mosaics became popular as decoration for Roman floors and fountains, where durability and waterproofing were desired. Mosaic designs were created with pebbles or with small, regularly shaped pieces of colored stone, or marble, called **tesserae.** The tesserae were pressed into a kind of soft cement called **grout.**

So accomplished were some mosaicists that they could create works that looked like paintings. In fact, at the request of patrons, they often copied well-known paintings employing a technique in which very small tesserae created subtle shadings and color changes. In a work called *The Unswept Floor* (fig. 6-20; see pages 136–37), the Greek mosaicist Heraklitos (who worked in Rome) adapted the design of an earlier Hellenistic painter named Sosos. In Pergamon, in the

second century BCE, Sosos had created a large painting that included a **trompe l'oeil** ("fool the eye") representation of a floor littered with droppings from a table. Heraklitos's mosaic version, made three centuries later, shows a mouse among table scraps. Bones of fish and foul, fruit, and nuts are all re-created in meticulous detail, even to the extent of capturing the shadows they cast on the floor.

The "Good Emperors"

The arts flourished in Rome during the first and second centuries CE. Five very competent rulers succeeded the Flavians: Nerva (ruled 96–98 CE), Trajan (ruled 98–117 CE), Hadrian (ruled 117–138 CE), Antoninus Pius (ruled 138–161 CE), and Marcus Aurelius (ruled 161–180 CE). Known as the "Five Good Emperors," they oversaw a long period of stability and prosperity. Under Trajan, the empire reached its greatest extent, annexing Dacia (roughly modern Romania) in 106 CE and expanding the empire's boundaries in the Middle East.

Whether they were at home or abroad, Romans built roads, bridges, and cities. Projects such as the Imperial Forums in the capital were repeated throughout the empire on a smaller scale. A **forum**, the civic center, consists of a large open square generally surrounded by colonnades leading to a temple and sometimes a basilica.

In Trajan's Forum, the Basilica Ulpia, dedicated in 113 CE, was named for the family to which Trajan belonged. It was a large, rectangular building with a rounded extension, called an **apse**, at each end. A general-purpose administrative structure, a basilica could be adapted to many uses. The Basilica Ulpia was a court

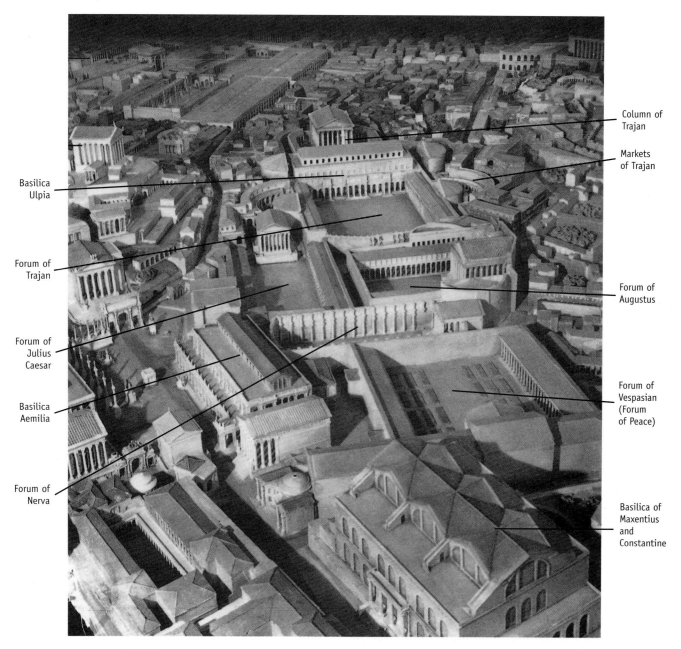

Basilica
Ulpia

Forum of
Trajan

Forum of
Julius
Caesar

Basilica
Aemilia

Forum of
Nerva

Column of
Trajan

Markets
of Trajan

Forum of
Augustus

Forum of
Vespasian
(Forum
of Peace)

Basilica of
Maxentius
and
Constantine

6-21 | **Model of the Forum Romanum and Imperial Forums, Rome.** c. 46 BCE–325 CE

of law. Other basilicas served as imperial audience chambers, army drill halls, and schools. The spacious and adaptable interior made the basilica form attractive to Christians, who would later appropriate it for churches.

Three basilicas can be seen in figure 6-21: the Basilica Aemilia, Basilica Ulpia, and the vaulted Basilica of Maxentius and Constantine. The Basilica Ulpia was entered through several doors on the long sides of the building facing the open square. The interior space was partitioned into a large central area bordered by two lower colonnaded **aisles**. This tall central space was able to accommodate a **clerestory**, or windowed wall area, that extended above the abutting aisle roofs and brought light into the interior. A timber-raftered roof covered the space. The semicircular vaulted apses at each end gave the building an overall

length of about 330 feet, and provided imposing settings for judges when the court was in session.

Beyond the Basilica Ulpia stood two libraries, one for Greek texts and the other for Latin. Trajan's tomb, surmounted by a column carved with reliefs depicting his victory over the Dacians, stood between the libraries. Later the complex was completed with a temple to the deified emperor. A great market was built into the hillside next to the square. The Forum of Trajan exemplifies the finest in imperial city planning, satisfying both the needs of the citizens and the imperial desire for impressive public works and propaganda.

Trajan's successor, Hadrian, was well educated and widely traveled. His admiration for Greek culture spurred new building programs throughout the empire. To the splendid architecture of

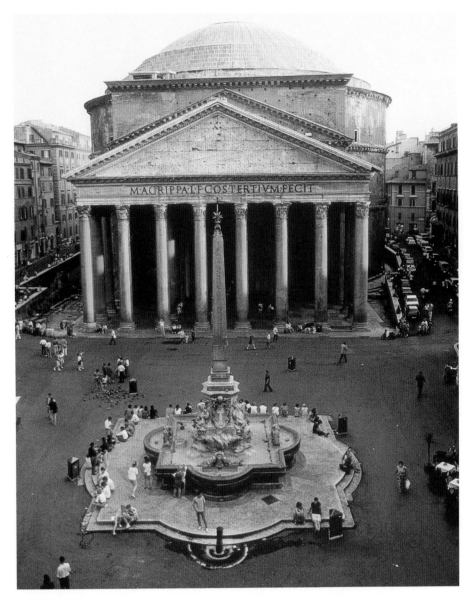

6-22 | **Pantheon**, Rome. 125–28 CE

It is not clear what the early Romans themselves thought of this architectural monument, so well known to travelers and students today, because it was rarely mentioned by any contemporary writers. An exception was Ammianus Marcellinus, who described it in 357 CE with restrained praise as being "rounded like the boundary of the horizon, and vaulted with a beautiful loftiness."

In the foreground of the photograph is a monumental fountain by G. della Porta, 1578. In 1711 Pope Clement XI added the obelisk (from the temple of Isis).

Rome itself he added the remarkable temple to the Olympian gods known as the Pantheon ("all the gods"), built between 125 and 128 CE (fig. 6-22). The entrance porch, made to resemble the facade of a typical Roman temple, was raised on a podium (now covered by centuries of dirt and street construction). Behind this porch, a giant **rotunda** (circular room) is surmounted with a huge, bowl-shaped dome, 143 feet in diameter and 143 feet from the floor at its summit (figs. 6-23, 6-24).

Although the Pantheon has inspired hundreds of copies, variants, and eclectic borrowings, only recently has the true complexity of its construction been fully understood. The cir-cular wall, or **drum**, of the rotunda, which supports and but-tresses the dome, is formed of brick arches and concrete. These structural elements are hidden beneath a marble veneer. Struc-turally a dome works as an arch pivoted 360° around the top of the drum. In the Pantheon the usual keystone is replaced by a central circular opening, or **oculus**, a daring concept. The repetition of square against circle, established on a large scale by juxtaposing the rectilinear portico against the circular rotunda, is found throughout the building's ornament. Seven niches, rectangular alternating with semicircular, originally held statues of the gods. The square, boxlike **coffers** (sunken

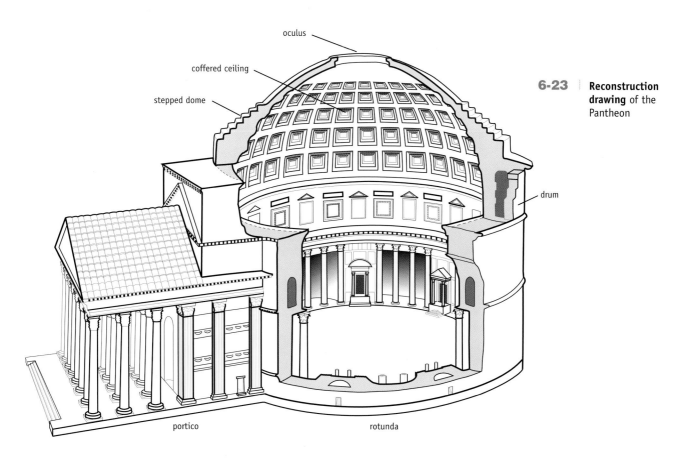

oculus

coffered ceiling

stepped dome

drum

portico

rotunda

6-23 | **Reconstruction drawing** of the Pantheon

6-24 | **Dome of the Pantheon** with light from oculus on its coffered ceiling

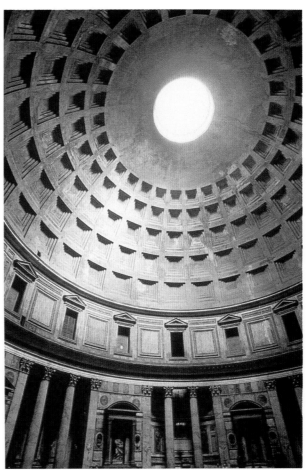

ceiling panels) inside the dome, which help lighten the weight of the masonry, may once have contained **gilded** bronze **rosettes** or stars suggesting the heavens.

Inside, the eye is drawn upward over the patterns made by the coffers to the light entering the 29-foot-wide oculus (see fig. 6–24). Clouds can be seen through this opening on clear days; rain falls through it on wet ones, then drains off as planned by the original engineer; and occasionally a bird flies through it. But the empty, luminous space also imparts a sense that one could rise buoyantly upward to escape the spherical hollow of the building and commune with the gods.

Hadrian used monumental sculpture as well as architecture to vaunt his accomplishments. Several large circular reliefs, or **roundels**—originally part of a monument that no longer exists—contain images designed to affirm his imperial stature and right to rule (fig. 6-25; see page 156). In the scene on the left, he demonstrates his courage and physical prowess in a boar hunt. At the right, in a show of piety and appreciation to the gods for their support of his endeavors, Hadrian makes a sacrificial offering to Apollo at an outdoor altar. The sculptors of these roundels included elements of a natural landscape setting but kept them relatively small, using them to frame the proportionally larger figures. The idealized heads, form-enhancing drapery, and graceful yet energetic movement of the figures owe a distant

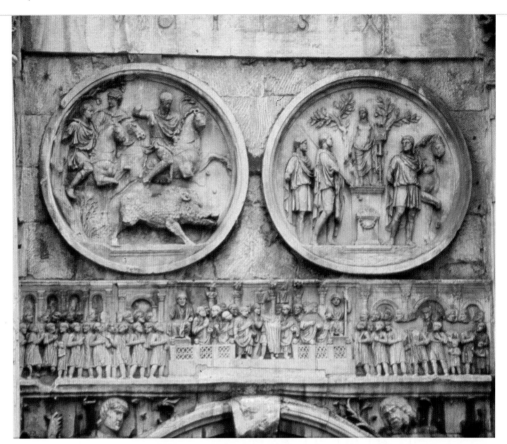

6-25 | *Hadrian Hunting Boar* and *Sacrificing to Apollo*
Roundels made for a monument to Hadrian and reused on the Arch of Constantine
Sculpture c. 130–38 CE
Marble, roundel diameter 40" (102 cm)

In the fourth century CE, Emperor Constantine had the roundels removed from the Hadrian monument, had Hadrian's head recarved with his own or his father's features, and placed them on his own triumphal arch (see fig. 6-33, page 161).

6-26 | *Marcus Aurelius.* 161–80 CE
Bronze, originally gilded
Height of statue 11'6" (3.5 m)
Capitoline Museum, Rome

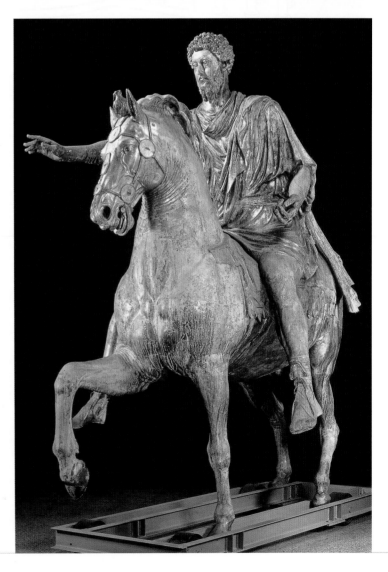

debt to the works of Praxiteles (see fig. 4-36) and Lysippos (see fig. 4-37), but the well-observed details of the features and the bits of landscape are typically Roman.

Hadrian's successor, Marcus Aurelius, was also renowned for both his intellectual and military achievements. In a gilded bronze equestrian statue, the emperor appears as a commander dressed in a tunic and short, heavy cloak (fig. 6-26). The raised foreleg of his horse is poised to trample a defeated foe (now lost). The emperor wears no armor and carries no weapons; like the Egyptian kings, he conquers effortlessly by the will of the gods. And like his illustrious predecessor Augustus (see fig. 6-7), he assumes a gesture symbolic of addressing an assembly. In a lucky error, or twist of fate, this statue came mistakenly to be revered during the Middle Ages as a portrait of Constantine, the first Christian emperor. Consequently, it escaped being melted down, a fate that befell many other bronze statues from antiquity.

Marcus Aurelius was succeeded by his son Commodus, a man without political skill, administrative competence, or intellectual distinction. During his unfortunate reign

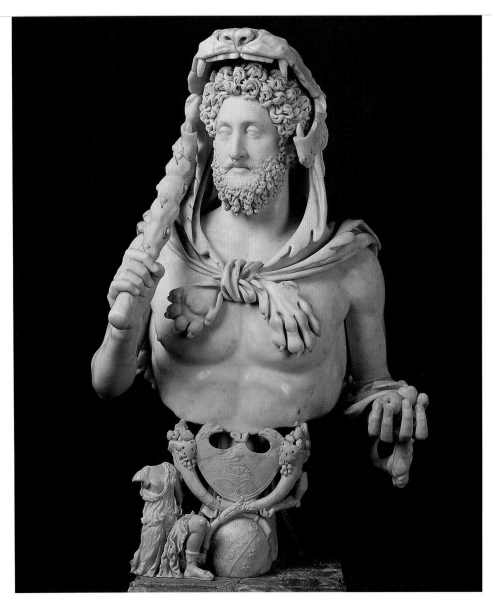

6-27 | ***Commodus as Hercules,*** from Esquiline Hill, Rome. c. 191–92 CE Marble, height 46½" (118 cm) Palazzo dei Conservatori, Rome

The emperor Commodus was not just decadent—he was probably insane. He claimed at various times to be the reincarnation of Hercules and the incarnation of the god Jupiter, and he even appeared in public as a gladiator. He ordered the months of the Roman year to be renamed after him and changed the name of Rome to Colonia Commodiana. When he proposed to assume the consulship dressed and armed as a gladiator, his associates, including his mistress, arranged to have him strangled in his bath by a wrestling partner. In this portrait, the emperor is shown in the guise of Hercules, adorned with references to the hero's legendary labors: his club, the skin and head of the Nemean Lion, and the golden apples from the garden of the Hesperides.

(180–192 CE), he devoted himself to luxury and frivolous pursuits. He did, however, attract some of the finest artists of the day for his commissions. A marble bust of Commodus posing as Hercules displays skillful chiseling and **drillwork** (fig. 6-27). With a drill, the sculptor hollowed out deep caverns with straight sides that look like dark lines at a distance—for example, the holes in Commodus's curls (see also fig. 6-15). With a combination of carving and drillwork, the sculptor exploited the play of light and shadow on the figure and brought out the textures of the hair, beard, and drapery. The portrait conveys the illusion of life and movement, but it also captures its subject's vanity and weakness through the grand pretensions of his costume.

Lands Outside the Roman Empire

Hadrian had consolidated the empire's borders and imposed far-reaching social, administrative, and military reforms. He ordered the construction of a monumental stone wall in England to protect his northern frontier. Known as Hadrian's Wall, this barrier stretches from coast to coast across a 73.5-mile-wide strip of England (fig. 6-28; see page 158). Some 8 to 10 feet thick and 20 feet high, it created a symbolic as well as a physical boundary between Roman territory and that of the Picts and Scots to the north. Towers were located at every mile mark. Seventeen larger camps housed auxiliary forces ready to respond to any trouble the sentries might spot. These camps were laid out in a grid pattern, like Roman cities, with main streets dividing them into blocks. In the center were the hospital, granaries, and the commander's house and administrative headquarters. Surrounding these structures were barracks. Similarly designed camps were built from one end of the Roman Empire to the other, wherever military troops were quartered.

During the first millennium BCE, Celtic peoples inhabited most of central and western Europe. Pushed westward by migrating people and then by Roman armies, they settled in the westernmost parts of Europe—Ireland, Cornwall, and Brittany. Their wooden buildings and sculpture and their colorful woven textiles have disintegrated, but protective **earthworks** such as embankments fortifying their cities and funerary goods such as jewelry, weapons, and tableware have survived. An **openwork** box lid illustrates the characteristic abstract Celtic

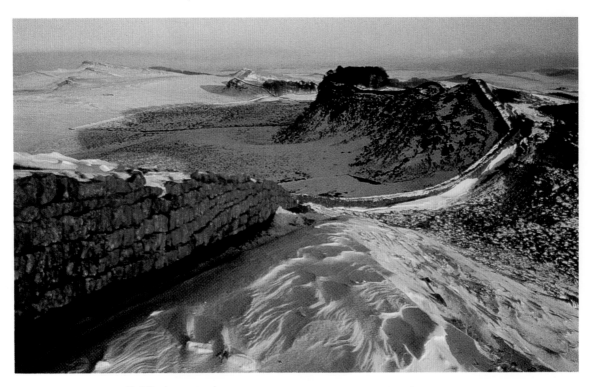

6-28 | **Hadrian's Wall,** seen near Housesteads, England. 2nd century CE

style (fig. 6-29). Solid metal and open space play equal roles in the pattern, which consists of a pair of expanding, diagonally symmetrical trumpet-shaped spirals surrounded by lattice. Shapes inspired by compass-drawn spirals, stylized vines, and serpentine dragons seem to change at the blink of an eye, for the artist has eliminated any distinction between figure and background. The openwork trumpets—the forms defined by the absence of material—catch the viewer's attention, yet at the same time the delicate tendrils of solid metal are equally compelling. In Celtic hands, pattern becomes an integral part of the object itself, not an applied decoration.

The Late Empire

The reign of Commodus marked the beginning of a period of political and economic decline. During the rule of the Severan emperors (193–235 CE) who succeeded Commodus, migrating peoples from the north and east began to cross Rome's frontiers, disrupting provincial government. Imperial rule became increasingly autocratic, and soon the army controlled the government.

During the turmoil of the third century, Roman artists lost interest in representing the natural world, emphasizing instead the symbolic or general characters of their subjects and expressing them in increasingly simplified, geometric forms. But the simplification of natural forms to geometric shapes, the disregard for normal human proportions, and the emphasis on message or idea are also characteristics of Roman art made by the end of the third century. By the beginning of the fourth century a new style of abstract art appeared in Rome.

The anarchy of the mid-third century ended with the rise to power of Emperor Diocletian (ruled 284–305 CE). This brilliant politician and general reversed the empire's declining fortunes, but he also initiated an increasingly dictatorial four-man government known as a Tetrarchy (two corulers and their assistants). In 305 CE Diocletian abdicated and forced his coruler, Maximian, to do so too. The orderly succession he had hoped for failed to occur, and a struggle for position and advantage almost immediately ensued. Two main contenders emerged in the Western Empire: Maxentius and Constantine, both sons of Tetrarchs. Constantine emerged victorious after defeating Maxentius at the Battle of the Milvian Bridge, at the entrance to Rome. According to tradition, Constantine had a vision the night before the battle in which he saw a flaming cross in the sky and heard these words: "In this sign you shall conquer." The next morning he ordered that his army's shields and standards be inscribed with the monogram *XP* (the Greek letters *chi* and *rho* for *Christos* or Christ, but also an abbreviation of the Greek word *chrestos*, meaning auspicious). Whatever his motivation, in 313 CE, Constantine issued the Edict of Milan granting freedom to all religious groups, not just Christians.

Maxentius's most impressive undertaking in Rome was a huge new basilica called the Basilica Nova, or New Basilica (fig. 6-30). Although Rome declined in importance, building did not end altogether. Maxentius (ruled 306–312 CE) ordered the repair of many buildings in Rome and had others built there during his short reign. Now known as the Basilica of Maxentius and Constantine because Constantine's architects modified and completed it, this was the last important imperial government building erected in Rome itself. It functioned, like all basilicas, as an administrative center and provided a magnificent setting for the emperor when he appeared as supreme judge. The monumental portrait of

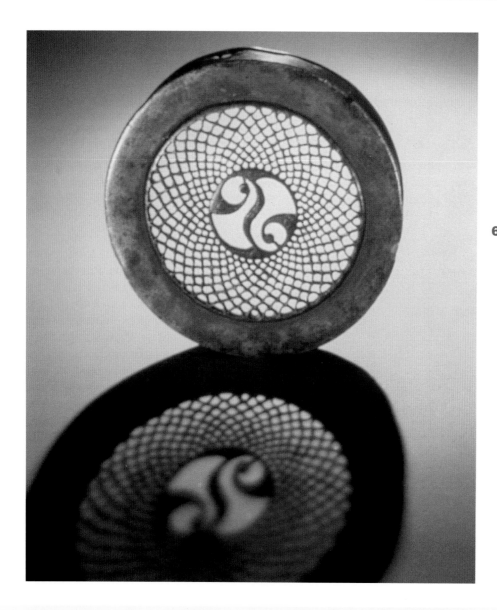

6-29 | **Openwork Box Lid.**
Cornalaragh, County Monaghan, Ireland. La Tène period c. 1st century BCE. Bronze, diameter 3" (7.5 cm).
Photo: National Museum of Ireland, Dublin

6-30 | **Plan and isometric reconstruction of the Basilica of Maxentius and Constantine,** Rome (constructed 306–13 CE)

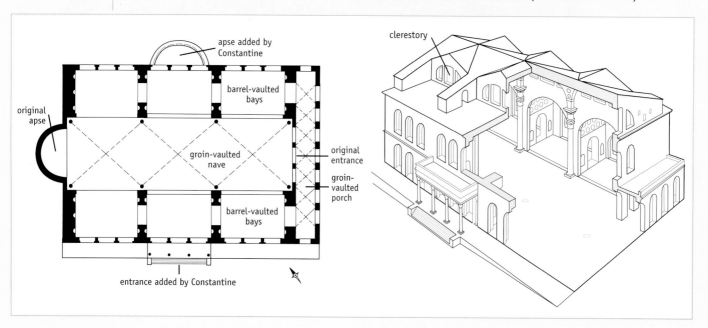

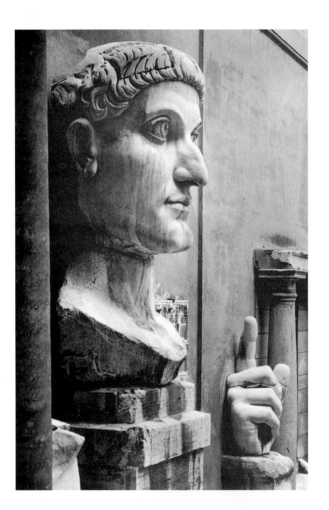

Constantine the Great, from the Basilica of Maxentius and Constantine, Rome. 325–26 CE Marble, height of head 8'6" (2.6 m). Palazzo dei Conservatori, Rome

These fragments came from a statue of the seated emperor. The original sculpture combined marble and probably bronze supported on a core of wood and bricks. Only a few marble fragments survive—the head, a hand, a knee, an elbow, and a foot. The body might have been made of either colored stone or of bronze on a scaffold of wood and bricks sheathed in bronze. This statue, although made of less expensive materials, must have been awe-inspiring. Constantine was a master of the use of portrait statues to spread imperial propaganda.

Constantine (fig. 6-31), found in the basilica, evidently served as a stand-in for the emperor and a reminder of his imperial power. Three brick-and-concrete barrel vaults of the side aisle still loom over the streets of modern Rome (fig. 6-32). The central hall was covered with groin vaults (see "Arch and Vault," page 141). The side aisles were covered with barrel vaults that acted as buttresses, or projecting supports, for the central groin vault and allowed generous window openings in the clerestory areas of the central aisle. A groin-vaulted porch extended across the short side and sheltered a triple entrance to the central hall. At the opposite end of the long axis of the hall was an apse nearly as wide as the nave, which acted as a focal point for the interior. The directional focus along a central axis from the entrance to the apse emphasized the imperial presence of the emperor, or his statue.

One of the last major pre-Christian Roman monuments to be constructed was a triumphal arch erected by the Senate to commemorate Constantine's defeat of Maxentius in 312 CE. This memorial, placed next to the Colosseum in Rome, took the

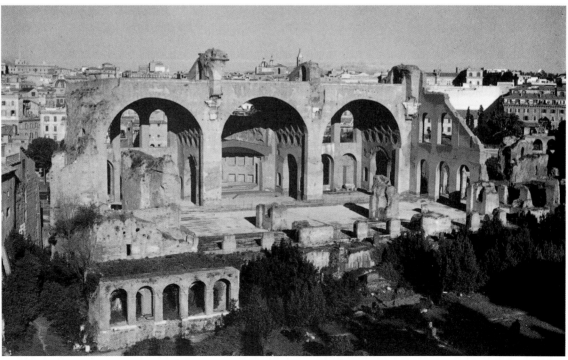

6-32 | **Basilica of Maxentius and Constantine**

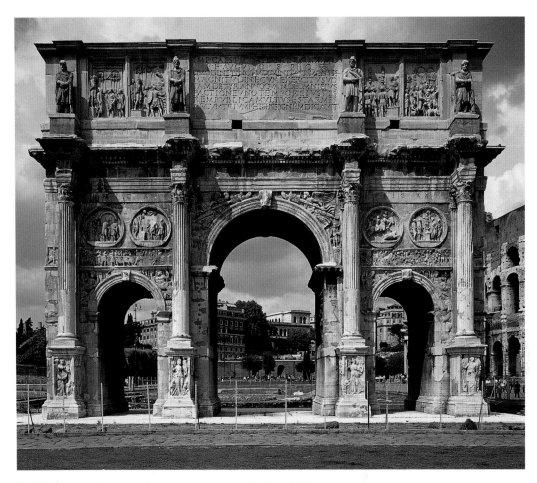

6-33 | **Arch of Constantine,** Rome. 312–15 CE (dedicated July 25, 315 CE)

This massive, triple-arched monument to Emperor Constantine's victory over Maxentius in 312 CE is a wonder of recycled sculpture. On the attic story, flanking the inscription over the central arch, are relief panels taken from a monument celebrating the victory of Marcus Aurelius over the Germans in 174 CE. On the attached piers framing these panels are large statues of prisoners made to celebrate Trajan's victory over the Dacians in the early second century CE. On the inner walls of the central arch (not seen here) are reliefs also commemorating Trajan's conquest of Dacia. Over each of the side arches are pairs of giant roundels taken from a monument to Hadrian (see fig. 6-25). The rest of the decoration is contemporary with the arch.

form of a huge triple arch (fig. 6-33) that dwarfs the nearby Arch of Titus (see fig. 6-13). Three barrel-vaulted passageways are flanked by columns on high pedestals and surmounted by a large attic story bearing a laudatory inscription indicating that the arch was dedicated to Constantine by the Senate and the Roman people. Some of the sculpture decorating it came from other monuments made for Constantine's illustrious predecessors, the "good emperors" Trajan, Hadrian, and Marcus Aurelius. The reused items in effect transferred to Constantine the virtues of strength, courage, and piety associated with these earlier emperors. New reliefs made for the arch recount the story of Constantine's victory and remind the viewers of his power and generosity. A panel above the left arch depicts his first public speech after he defeated Maxentius (see fig. 6-25). Toward the center of the panel, the emperor (his head is missing) stands on a temporary speaker's platform. He is flanked by standing officials and seated statues of Marcus Aurelius and Hadrian. In the background, the Basilica Julia and the Arch of Tiberius are to the left and the Arch of Septi-

mus Severus is to the right, identifying the site of the speech as the Republican Forum.

Although the new reliefs reflect the long-standing Roman fondness for depicting important events with realistic detail, in style and subject matter they contrast with the reused elements in the arch. The stocky, mostly frontal figures, each one resembling the next, are compressed into the foreground plane. The participants below the standing Constantine look so uniform that they seem to isolate "the new Augustus" and connect him visually with his illustrious predecessors on each side of him. This two-dimensional, hierarchical approach, with its emphasis on authority, ritual, and symbolism rather than outward form, was adopted by the emerging Christian Church. After 324 CE Constantine ruled as sole emperor until his death in 337. He made the port city of Byzantium the new Rome and renamed it Constantinople (modern Istanbul, in Turkey). After Constantinople was dedicated in 330, Rome, which had already ceased to be the seat of government in the West, further declined in importance.

BCE 3000	1500	1000

AEGEAN & GREECE

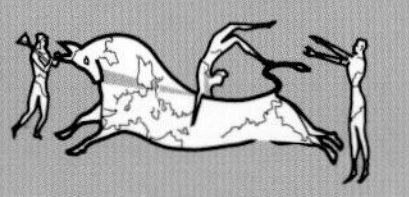

Bull Leaping c. 1450–1375

Dipylon vase c. 750

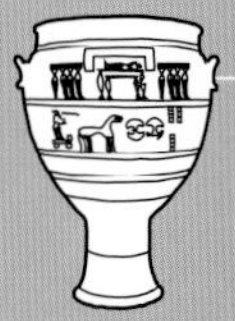

▲ MINOAN 3000–1400
▲ CYCLADIC 3000–1600

MYCENAEAN 1400–1100 ▲

GEOMETRIC 900–700 ▲

ETRUSCAN & ROMAN

L O O K I N G   B A C K   2

The Achievement of an Ideal

Today we no longer seek our ideals in the distant past, but until the twentieth century, many people in Europe and America considered classical Greek and Roman culture to constitute a "Golden Age" and Greek sculpture and architecture of the fifth century BCE to be the pinnacle of artistic achievement. Between the sixth and the fourth centuries BCE, the Greeks looked at their surroundings with intense interest, focusing on every detail from the acanthus leaf to the colonnaded temple, but especially the human figure.

This outburst of intellectual and aesthetic energy may have been connected to the new political system evolving in Greece. Especially in Athens, the first democratic form of government encouraged individuals to express their opinions, desires, and ideas. The importance of the individual may be associated with a new art focused on images of men and women. The ideal of individual freedom created an environment in which new ideas could flourish.

Ultimately, the Greek ideal of beauty can be summed up by such words as balance, order, and simplicity. Such standards spread from the Greek homeland through the western Mediterranean and permeated local cultures. Etruscans, Scythians, Persians, Egyptians, and others adapted and integrated Greek aesthetics into their own traditions. The Greeks touched these people through trade and colonies and later through Alexander the Great's empire.

The Romans, whose empire eventually supplanted the Greeks, had their own strengths—efficiency, practicality, a genius for organization—but they also appreciated Greek art and adapted it to their own uses. With sophisticated visual propaganda, Roman art served the state and imperial authority; at the same time, people so much like us—living in cities filled with law courts and office buildings, shopping and entertainment centers, sports arenas and swimming pools—did fit art into their lives.

Why have so many people in different times and places turned to the classical art of Greece and Rome for inspiration? Perhaps each in his or her own way respected and admired an art grounded in the intense study of nature and the human condition. The Greeks created their ideal of perfection through mathematical proportions and observation; the Romans achieved a realism based on actual appearances. While Greeks sought timeless images, Romans tried to capture the specific moment; both created works of art that formed an enduring ideal of excellence in the West.

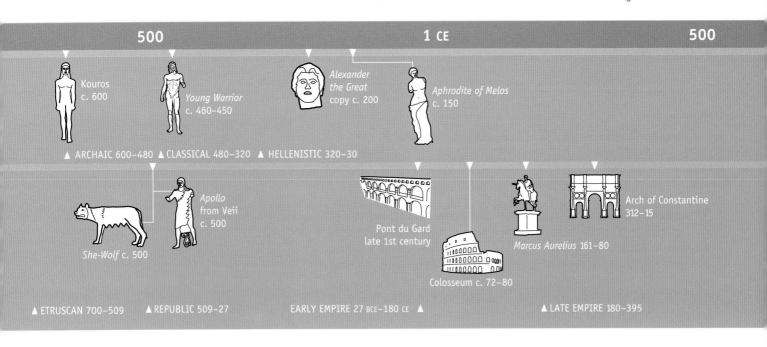

500   1 CE   500

Kouros
c. 600

Young Warrior
c. 460–450

Alexander
the Great
copy c. 200

Aphrodite of Melos
c. 150

▲ ARCHAIC 600–480 ▲ CLASSICAL 480–320 ▲ HELLENISTIC 320–30

Apollo
from Veii
c. 500

She-Wolf c. 500

Pont du Gard
late 1st century

Colosseum c. 72–80

Marcus Aurelius 161–80

Arch of Constantine
312–15

▲ ETRUSCAN 700–509   ▲ REPUBLIC 509–27   EARLY EMPIRE 27 BCE–180 CE ▲   ▲ LATE EMPIRE 180–395

Aegean, Greek, Etruscan, and Roman Art

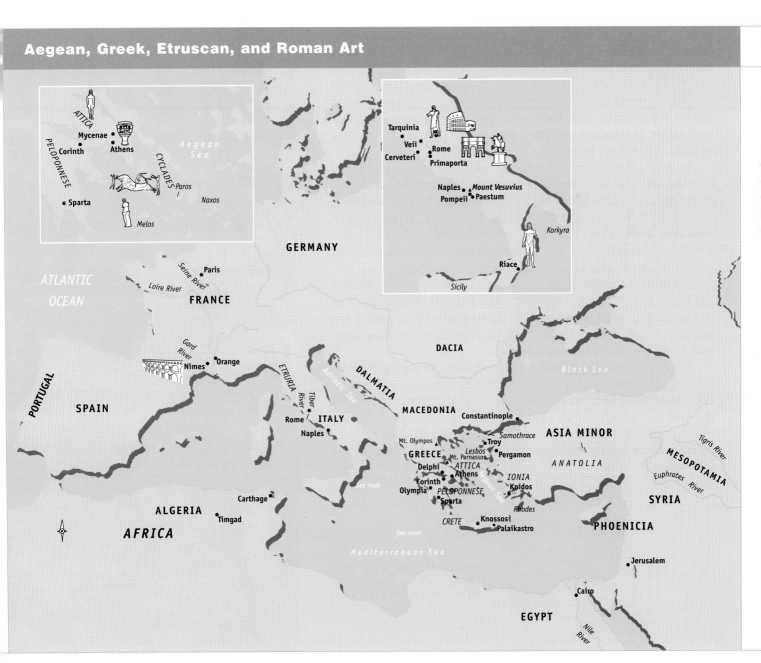

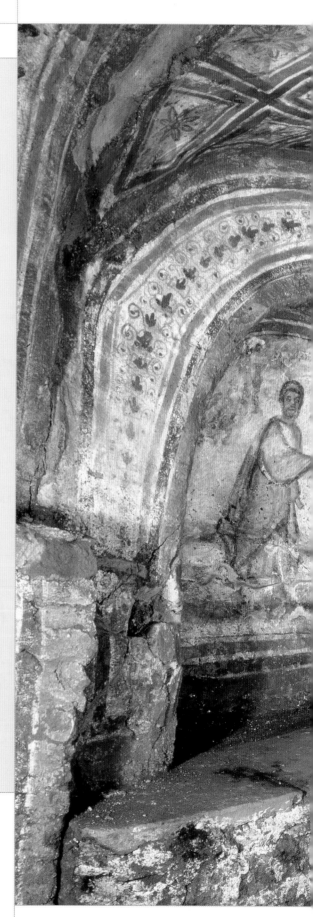

In a Roman catacomb painting, Peter, like Moses before him, strikes a rock with his staff and water flows forth (scene at left). Imprisoned in Rome after the arrest of Jesus, Peter converted his fellow prisoners and jailers to Christianity, but he needed water with which to baptize them. Miraculously a spring gushed forth at the touch of his staff. In spite of his all too human fragility, Peter became the rock (*petrus*) on which Jesus founded the Church. He was the first bishop of Rome, today's pope. In the niche seen on the right, two early Roman Christian martyrs, Felix (d. 274) and Adauctus (d. 303) join Christ, who holds a book emphasizing his role as teacher. By including Peter, Romans, and Roman martyrs, in the chamber's decoration, the early Christians, who dug this catacomb as a place for the dead, emphasized the importance of their city in Christendom.

In the star-studded heavens painted above, the face of Christ appears. The Greek letters alpha and omega, symbolizing the beginning and the end of earthly time, flank Christ. Christ has the aspect of a Greek philosopher, bearded and with long dark hair. The circle around his head (a halo) indicates his importance and his divinity.

In these catacomb paintings we see two of the major directions of Christian art—the narrative (educational) and the symbolic (or iconic). In the narrative image, which loosely illustrates the story of Saint Peter striking the rock, we find symbolic intent as well: the establishment of the Church and also the essential Christian rite of baptism. As a symbolic image, the painting symbolically expresses essential religious meaning rather than exact external appearance.

The other scene, Christ's face flanked by alpha and omega, the first and last letters of the Greek alphabet, offers a tangible expression of an intangible, non-narrative concept. The letters signify the beginning and end of time, and, combined with the image of Christ, symbolically represent an idea—without a narrative intent.

For the next thousand years, and throughout the history of Christian art, these two divergent tendencies will be apparent—the urge to tell a good story, with moral implications and educational values, and the symbolic image in which viewers find meaning through their store of information and belief. In the West, the didactic narrative achieves prominence; in the Eastern Orthodox Church, the symbolic image, the icon, reigns.

Cubiculum of Leonis, Catacomb of Commodilla, near Rome
Late 4th century. (See pages 170–71.)

Jewish, Early Christian, and Byzantine Art

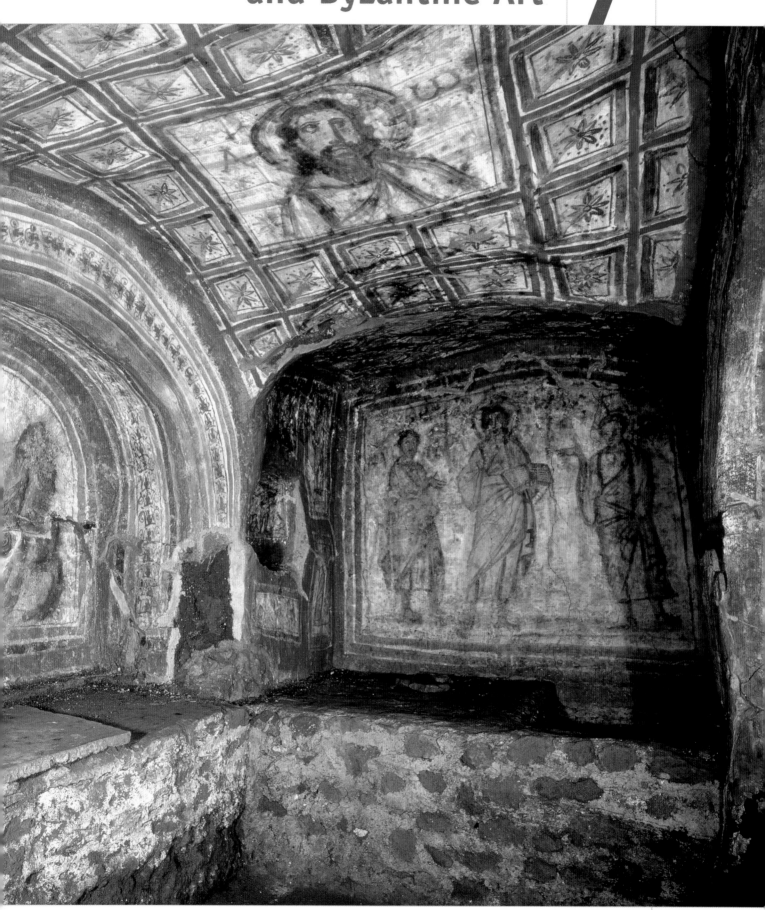

7

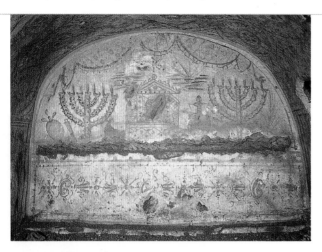

7-1 *Menorahs and Ark of the Covenant,* wall painting in a Jewish catacomb, Villa Torlonia, Rome. 3rd century. 3'11" x 5'9" (1.19 x 1.8 m)

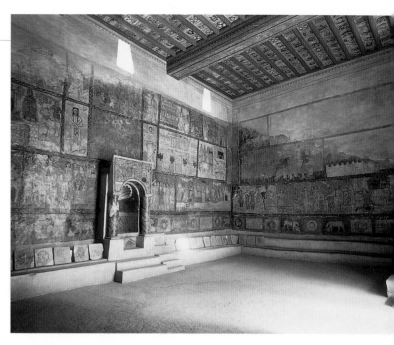

7-2 | **Wall with Torah niche,** from a house-synagogue, Dura-Europos Syria. 244–45. Tempera on plaster, section approx. 40' (12.19 m) long. Reconstructed in the National Museum, Damascus, Syria

Three religions that arose in the Near East dominate the spiritual life of the Western world: Judaism and Christianity, discussed in this chapter, and Islam, treated in Chapter 8. All three religions are monotheistic, meaning that their followers believe that only one god created and rules the universe. They are known as "religions of the book" because they have written records of God's will and words: the Hebrew Scriptures of the Jews; the Christian Bible, which includes both the Hebrew Scriptures as its Old Testament and the Christian New Testament; and the Muslim Koran, the word of God (Allah) revealed through the angel Gabriel to the prophet Muhammad. Each religion builds on the beliefs and traditions of the earlier. Traditional Jews believe that God made a covenant, or pact, with their ancestors and that they are God's chosen people. They await the coming of a savior, the Messiah, "the anointed one." Traditional Christians maintain that Jesus of Nazareth was that Messiah (the title *Christ* is derived from the Greek term meaning "Messiah"). They believe that God took human form, preached among men and women, was put to death on a cross, and then rose from the dead and ascended into heaven having established the Christian Church under the leadership of the apostles (his closest disciples). Muslims, while accepting the Hebrew prophets and Jesus as divinely inspired, believe Muhammad to be Allah's last and greatest prophet, through whom Islam was revealed some six centuries after Jesus' earthly lifetime.

Jewish, Christian, and Muslim art combine in varying degrees Greek, Roman, and Near Eastern themes and forms. Jews and Christians use the visual arts to educate their followers through narratives and to glorify their religious services through ornamental enrichment of buildings and books. Muslims also use ornamental forms and abstract styles but prefer words to images to convey meaning (see Map 3, page 231).

Judaism

The Jewish people trace their ancestry to a Semitic people called the Hebrews, who lived in the land of Canaan. Canaan, known from the second century CE by the Roman name of Palestine, was located between the Mediterranean Sea and the Jordan River. According to the Torah (the first five books of the Hebrew

Scriptures), God promised the patriarch Abraham that Canaan would be a homeland for the Jewish people (Genesis 17:8), a belief that remains important among Jews to this day.

Jewish settlement of Canaan probably began sometime in the second millennium BCE. According to Exodus, the second book of the Torah, the prophet Moses led the Hebrews out of slavery in Egypt to the promised land of Canaan. At one crucial point during the journey, Moses climbed alone to the top of Mount Sinai, where God gave him the Ten Commandments, the cornerstone of Jewish law. The Commandments, inscribed on tablets, were kept in a gold-covered wooden box, the Ark of the Covenant.

In the tenth century BCE, the Jewish king Solomon built a temple in Jerusalem to house the Ark of the Covenant. The Temple consisted of courtyards, a porch, a hall, and the holy of holies housing the Ark with its guardian **cherubim**. King Solomon sent to nearby Phoenicia for cedar, cypress, and sandalwood, and for a master craftsman to supervise the Temple's construction (II Chronicles 2:2–15). The Temple was the spiritual center of Jewish life.

In 586 BCE, the Babylonians, under King Nebuchadnezzar II, conquered Jerusalem. They destroyed the Temple, exiled the Jews, and carried off the Ark of the Covenant. When Cyrus the Great of Persia conquered Babylonia in 538 BCE, the Jews were permitted to return to Jerusalem and rebuild the Temple, but from that time forward Canaan existed primarily under foreign rule and eventually became part of the Roman Empire. In 70 CE Roman forces led by the future emperor, Titus, destroyed the Second Temple and Jerusalem (see Chapter 6).

Jews continued to live in dispersed communities throughout the Roman Empire. Most of the earliest surviving examples of Jewish art date from the Hellenistic and Roman periods. Six Jewish **catacombs**, or underground burial chambers, discovered just outside the city of Rome and in use from the first to fourth century CE, display wall paintings with Jewish themes. In one example, from the third century CE, two **menorahs**, or seven-branched

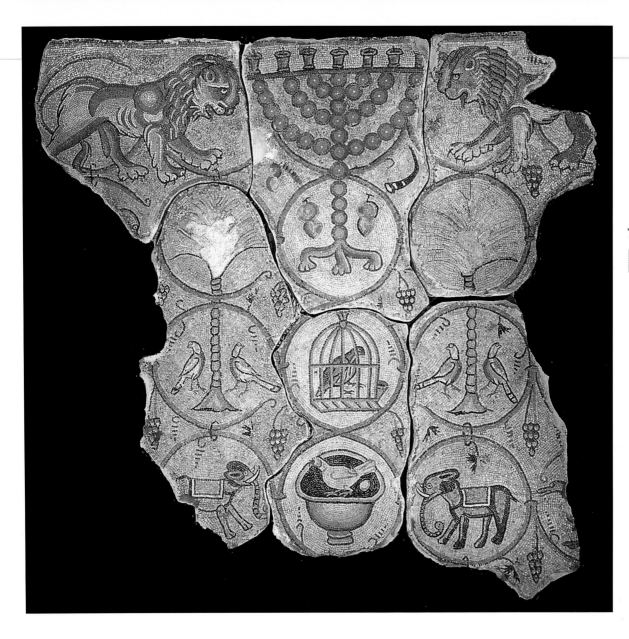

7-3

**Synagogue
floor,** Maon
c. 530. Mosaic
The Israel
Museum
Jerusalem

lamps, flank the long-lost Ark of the Covenant (fig. 7-1). The conspicuous representation of the menorah looted from the Second Temple of Jerusalem on the Arch of Titus in Rome (see fig. 6-13) kept the memory of these treasures alive. The menorah form probably derives from the ancient Near Eastern Tree of Life, symbolizing both the end of exile and the paradise to come.

Judaism has always emphasized religious learning. Jews gather in synagogues for study and worship; a synagogue can be any large room where the Torah scrolls are kept and read publicly. The destroyed Temple in Jerusalem had been a special, central holy place for all Jews, but synagogues could be constructed in any Jewish community. Some Jewish places of worship, or synagogues, were located in private homes, or in buildings originally constructed as homes. Far less Jewish art than Christian or Islamic art has survived, but a number of synagogues have been discovered or excavated. Their architecture and ornament reflect late Roman artistic traditions melded with specifically Jewish symbolism. In the Roman city of Dura-Europos, in modern Syria, excavators discovered a Jewish **house-synagogue**, or synagogue built within a private home; a Christian **house-church**; shrines to the Persian gods Mithras and Zoroaster; and temples to Roman gods. The first Dura-Europos synagogue consisted of an assembly hall, a separate alcove for women, and a courtyard. After a

remodeling of the building, completed in 244–45 CE, men and women shared the hall, and residential rooms were added. Two architectural features distinguished the assembly hall: a bench along its walls and a niche for the Torah scrolls (fig. 7-2). Scenes from Jewish history cover the walls of the synagogue at Dura-Europos. The story of Moses unfolds in a continuous narrative around the room. The vivid narrative follows the Roman tradition of historical representation; however, the frontal poses, strong outlines, and flat colors are pictorial devices that are associated with Near Eastern art.

The Dura-Europos synagogue had originally been built as a house, but Jews also built synagogues designed on the model of the ancient Roman basilica. A typical basilica synagogue had a central **nave**; an **aisle** on both sides, separated from the nave by a line of columns; a semicircular apse in the wall facing Jerusalem; and perhaps an atrium (courtyard) and porch, or **narthex**. A Torah was kept in a shrine in the apse.

Synagogues contained almost no **representational** sculpture because Jewish law forbade praying to images or idols. Paintings and mosaics, on the other hand, often decorated walls and floors. A fragment of a mosaic floor (fig. 7-3) from a sixth-century synagogue at Maon (Menois) features traditional Jewish symbols along with a variety of stylized plants, birds, and

ICONOGRAPHY OF THE LIFE OF JESUS

Iconography is the study of subject matter in art. It involves identifying both what a work of art represents—what it depicts—and the deeper significance of what is represented—its symbolic meaning. Stories about the life of Jesus, grouped in "cycles," form the basis of Christian iconography. What follows is an outline of those cycles and the main events of each.

The Incarnation Cycle and the Childhood of Jesus

This cycle comprises the events surrounding the conception and birth of Jesus.

The Annunciation: The archangel Gabriel informs the Virgin Mary that God has chosen her to bear his son. A dove represents the Incarnation, her miraculous conception of Jesus through the Holy Spirit.

The Visitation: The pregnant Mary visits her older cousin Elizabeth, pregnant with the future Saint John the Baptist. Elizabeth is the first to recognize and acknowledge the divinity of the child Mary is carrying.

The Nativity: Jesus is born to Mary in Bethlehem. The Holy Family—Jesus, Mary, and her husband, Joseph—is shown in a house, a stable, or, in Byzantine art, in a cave.

The Annunciation to the Shepherds and The Adoration of the Shepherds: An angel announces Jesus' birth to humble shepherds. They hurry to Bethlehem to honor him.

The Adoration of the Magi: The Magi, wise men from the East, follow a bright star to Bethlehem to honor Jesus as King of the Jews, presenting him with precious gifts—gold (symbolizing kingship), frankincense (divinity), and myrrh (death). In the European Middle Ages the Magi were identified as three kings.

The Presentation in the Temple: Mary and Joseph bring the infant Jesus to the Temple in Jerusalem, where he is presented to the highpriest. It is prophesied that Jesus will redeem humankind and that Mary will suffer great sorrow.

The Massacre of the Innocents and The Flight into Egypt: An angel warns Joseph that King Herod—to eliminate the threat of a newborn rival king—plans to murder all the babies in Bethlehem. The Holy Family flees to Egypt.

Jesus among the Doctors: In Jerusalem for the celebration of Passover, Joseph and Mary find the twelve-year-old Jesus in serious discussion with Temple scholars, a sign of his coming ministry.

The Public Ministry Cycle

In this cycle Jesus preaches and performs miracles (signs of God's power).

The Marriage at Cana: At his mother's request Jesus turns water into wine at a wedding feast, his first public miracle. Later the event was interpreted as a prefiguration of the Eucharist.

The Cleansing of the Temple: Jesus, in anger, drives money changers and animal traders from the Temple.

The Baptism: At age thirty Jesus is baptized by John the Baptist in the Jordan River. He sees the Holy Spirit and hears a heavenly voice proclaiming him God's son. His ministry begins.

Jesus and the Samaritan Woman at the Well: Jesus rests by a spring called Jacob's Well. Contrary to Jewish custom, he asks a local Samaritan woman for a drink of water.

The Miracles of Healing: Jesus performs miracles of healing—the Blind, the Possessed (mentally ill), the Paralytic, Lepers, and he also resurrects the dead.

The Miraculous Draft of Fishes: At Jesus' command Peter lowers the nets and catches so many fish that James and John have to help him bring them into the boat. Jesus promises the men that soon they will be "fishers of men."

Jesus Walking on the Water; Storm at Sea: The disciples, in a storm-tossed boat, see Jesus walking toward them on the water. Peter tries to go out to meet Jesus, but begins to sink, and Jesus saves him.

The Calling of Levi/Matthew: Passing by the customhouse, Jesus sees Levi, a tax collector, to whom he says, "Follow me." Levi complies, becoming the disciple Matthew.

The Raising of Lazarus: Jesus brings his friend Lazarus back to life four days after his death. Lazarus emerges from the tomb wrapped in his shroud.

Jesus in the House of Mary and Martha: Mary sits listening to Jesus while Martha prepares food. Mary represents the contemplative life and Martha, the active life. Jesus praises Mary.

The Transfiguration: Jesus reveals his divinity in a dazzling vision on Mount Tabor in Galilee as his closest disciples—Peter, James, and John—look on. A cloud envelops them, and a heavenly voice proclaims Jesus to be God's son.

The Tribute Money: Challenged to pay the temple tax, Jesus sends Peter to catch a fish, which has the required coin in its mouth.

The Delivery of the Keys to Peter: Jesus designates Peter as his successor, symbolically turning over to him the keys to the kingdom of heaven.

The Passion Cycle

This cycle contains events surrounding Jesus' death and resurrection. (*Passio* is Latin for "suffering.")

---

animals. Two lions of Judah flank a menorah. Beside it is a *shofar,* or ram's horn, blown on ceremonial occasions, and three *etrogs*, or citrons, used to celebrate the harvest festival of Sukkot. Palm trees refer to another Sukkot emblem, the *lulav*, a sheaf of palm, myrtle, and willow branches, and an etrog, used to symbolize the bounty of the earth and unity of all Jews. The variety of placid animals may symbolize the universal peace as prophesied by Isaiah (11:6–9; 65:25). The pairing of images around a central element, as in the birds flanking the palm trees, or the lions facing the menorah, is characteristic of Near Eastern art. In contrast, the grapevine, stylized until it is almost unrecognizable, forms circular **medallions** as a frame for the images.

In 395 the Roman Empire split permanently in two, becoming the Western (Roman) Empire, which collapsed in 476, and the Eastern, or Byzantine, Empire, which lasted until 1453, when it fell to the Ottoman Turks. By this time most Jews lived outside Palestine, in communities spread across the Middle East, North Africa, and Europe. Because their religious practice set them apart, and their numbers made them a minority, they faced special taxes, restrictions on the occupations they could enter, and sometimes

The Entry into Jerusalem: Jesus, riding an ass, and his disciples enter Jerusalem in triumph. Crowds honor them, spreading clothes and palm fronds in their path.

The Last Supper: During the Jewish Passover seder, Jesus reveals his impending death to his disciples. Instructing them to drink wine (his blood) and eat bread (his body) in remembrance of him, he lays the foundation for the Christian Eucharist (Mass).

Jesus Washing the Disciples' Feet: After the Last Supper, Jesus humbly washes the disciples' feet to set an example of humility. Peter, embarrassed, protests.

The Agony in the Garden: In the Garden of Gethsemane on the Mount of Olives, Jesus struggles between his human fear of pain and death and his divine strength to overcome them (*agon* is Greek for "contest"). The apostles sleep nearby, oblivious.

The Betrayal (The Arrest): Judas Iscariot, one of the disciples, accepts a bribe to point Jesus out to his enemies. Judas brings an armed crowd to Gethsemane. He kisses Jesus, a prearranged signal. Peter makes a futile attempt to defend Jesus from the Roman soldiers who seize him.

The Denial of Peter: Jesus is brought to the palace of the Jewish high priest, Caiaphas, to be interrogated for claiming to be the Messiah. Peter follows, and there he three times denies knowing Jesus, as Jesus predicted he would.

Jesus before Pilate: Jesus is taken to Pontius Pilate, the Roman governor of Judaea, and charged with treason for calling himself King of the Jews. He is sent to Herod Antipas, ruler of Galilee, who scorns him. Pilate proposes freeing Jesus but is shouted down by the mob, which demands that he be crucified. Pilate washes his hands before the crowd to signify that Jesus' blood is on its hands, not his.

The Flagellation (The Scourging): Jesus is whipped by his Roman captors.

Jesus Crowned with Thorns (The Mocking of Jesus): Pilate's soldiers torment Jesus. They dress him in royal robes, crown him with thorns, and kneel before him, hailing him as King of the Jews.

The Bearing of the Cross (The Road to Calvary): Jesus bears the cross from Pilate's house to Golgotha, where he is executed. Medieval artists depicted this event and its accompanying incidents in fourteen images known as the Stations of the Cross: (1) Jesus is condemned to death; (2) Jesus picks up the cross; (3) Jesus falls for the first time; (4) Jesus meets his grieving mother; (5) Simon of Cyrene is forced to help Jesus carry the cross; (6) Veronica wipes Jesus' face with her veil; (7) Jesus falls again; (8) Jesus admonishes the women of Jerusalem; (9) Jesus falls a third time; (10) Jesus is stripped; (11) Jesus is nailed to the cross; (12) Jesus dies on the cross; (13) Jesus is taken down from the cross; (14) Jesus is entombed.

The Crucifixion: The earliest representations of the Crucifixion are abstract, showing either a cross alone or a cross and a lamb. Later depictions include some or all of the following narrative details: two criminals (one penitent, the other not) are crucified on either side of Jesus; the Virgin Mary, John the Evangelist, Mary Magdalen, and other followers mourn at the foot of the cross; Roman soldiers torment Jesus—one extends a sponge on a pole with vinegar instead of water for him to drink, another stabs him in the side with a spear, and others gamble for his clothes; a skull identifies the execution ground as Golgotha, "the place of the skull," where Adam was buried. The association symbolizes the promise of redemption.

The Descent from the Cross (The Deposition): Jesus' followers take his body down from the cross. Joseph of Arimathea and Nicodemus wrap it in linen with myrrh and aloe. Also present are the grief-stricken Virgin, John the Evangelist, and sometimes Mary Magdalen, other disciples, and angels.

The Lamentation (Pietà): Jesus' sorrowful followers gather around his body. An image of the Virgin mourning alone with Jesus across her lap is known as a pietà (from the Latin *pietas,* "pity").

The Entombment: Jesus' mother and friends place his body in a nearby sarcophagus, or rock tomb. This is done hastily because of the approaching Jewish Sabbath.

The Descent into Limbo (The Harrowing of Hell): No longer in mortal form, Jesus, now called Christ, descends into limbo, or hell, to free deserving souls, among them Adam, Eve, and Moses.

The Resurrection (The Anastasis): Three days after his death, Christ walks out of his tomb while the soldiers guarding it sleep.

The Marys at the Tomb (The Holy Women at the Sepulchre): Christ's female followers—usually including Mary Magdalen and the mother of the apostle James, also named Mary—discover his empty tomb. An angel announces Christ's resurrection. The soldiers guarding the tomb look on, terrified.

Noli Me Tangere **("Do Not Touch Me"), The Supper at Emmaus, and The Doubting of Thomas:** Christ makes a series of appearances to his followers in the forty days between his resurrection and his ascension. He first appears to Mary Magdalen, as she weeps at his tomb. She reaches out to him, but he warns her not to touch him. In the Supper at Emmaus, he shares a meal with his apostles. In the Doubting of Thomas, Christ invites Thomas to touch the wound in his side to convince the doubting apostle of his resurrection.

The Ascension: Christ ascends to heaven from the Mount of Olives, disappearing in a cloud. His apostles, often accompanied by the Virgin, watch.

---

violent persecution. The history of Jewish art is fragmented because many artworks were destroyed when Jewish homes and synagogues were attacked and burned. The artworks that survive reflect the interplay of many styles, centuries, and regions.

Early Christianity

Christianity began with the life and teachings of Jesus of Nazareth, a Jew born sometime between 8 and 4 BCE and crucified at the age of thirty-three. Christians believe that Jesus was the son of God, born in a human body to a virgin woman, Mary, and resurrected after death. They believe in one God manifest in three Persons, a Trinity of Father (God), Son (Jesus Christ), and Holy Spirit. In later years Christians also began to acknowledge saints: devout individuals connected with verifiable miracles and canonized, or officially honored, by the Church for upholding and practicing Christian beliefs, often at the cost of martyrdom, or execution. Worshipers may ask the saints to intercede for them with God, but saints are not worshiped as gods in their own right.

The life of Jesus is described in the Christian New Testament, in the first four books, known as the Gospels (the Good News).

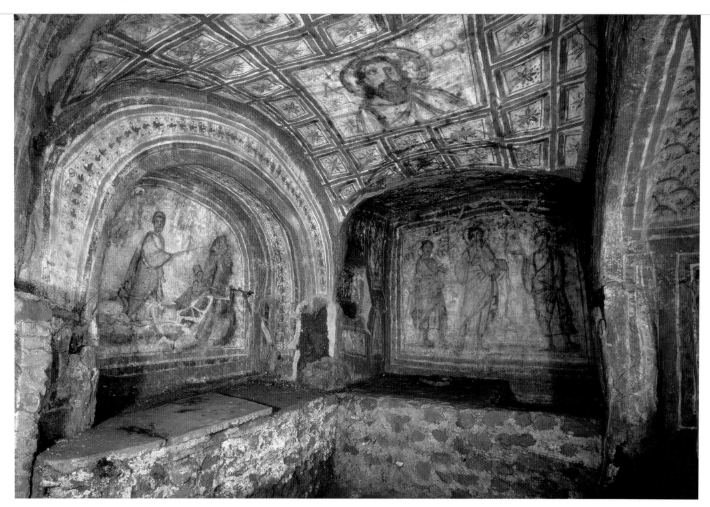

7-4 | *Cubiculum of Leonis, Catacomb of Commodilla,* near Rome. Late 4th century. (See pages 164–65.)

The Gospels relate that Jesus was a descendant of the Jewish royal house of King David and that he was born in Bethlehem in Judaea, where his mother, Mary, and her husband, Joseph, had gone to be registered in the Roman census. He grew up in Nazareth in Galilee, where Joseph was a carpenter. At the age of thirty, Jesus began his public ministry. He gathered about him a group of disciples, male and female; he preached love and charity, a personal relationship with God, the forgiveness of sins, and the promise of life after death. From his followers, he chose

twelve as his apostles to carry on his work after his death (see "Iconography of the Life of Jesus," pages 168–69).

Jesus limited his ministry primarily to Jews; his apostles, including Paul, who joined the group later, took Jesus' teachings to non-Jews. Despite sporadic persecutions, Christianity persisted and spread throughout the Roman Empire. The Roman emperor Constantine permitted the Christians freedom of worship with the Edict of Milan in 313 CE. By the end of the fourth century, Christianity had become the official religion of the empire, and non-Christians became the targets of persecution.

In Rome, even before their religion was recognized, Christians met in private houses for worship. Several private patrons also owned cemeteries and funeral basilicas. The congregations used the burial grounds as places to gather for worship, commemorative meals, and funeral rituals, and they excavated catacombs below ground for burials. The underground cemeteries, or catacombs consist of narrow passages and small burial chambers (the **cubiculum**) lined with rectangular burial niches (fig. 7-4). These niches were filled with stone sarcophagi or sealed with tiles or stone slabs. Painted walls and ceilings in catacombs provide some of the earliest examples of Christian art. The ceiling of a cubiculum, or small room, in the fourth-

transept

apse (hidden by transept)

gatehouse

clerestory

side aisles

narthex

atrium

fountain

7-5 **Reconstruction drawing of Old Saint Peter's,** Rome c. 320–27; atrium added in later 4th century. For plan see "Basilica-Plan and Central-Plan Churches," opposite.

Elements of Architecture

BASILICA-PLAN AND CENTRAL-PLAN CHURCHES

The forms of early Christian buildings were based on two **classical** prototypes: rectangular Roman basilicas (see figs. 6-31, 6-32) and round-domed structures—rotundas—such as the Pantheon (see figs. 6-22, 6-23). As in Old Saint Peter's in Rome (see fig. 7-5), **basilica-plan** churches are characterized by a forecourt, the **atrium**, leading to a porch, the **narthex**, spanning one of the building's short ends. Doorways—known collectively as the church's **portal**—lead from the narthex into a long central area called a **nave**. The high-ceiling nave is separated into **aisles** on either side by rows of columns. The nave is lit by windows along its upper story—called a **clerestory**—that rises above the side aisles' roofs. At the opposite end of the nave from the narthex is a semicircular projection, the **apse**. The apse functions as the building's symbolic core where the altar, raised on a platform, is located. Sometimes there is also a **transept**, a horizontal wing that crosses the nave in front of the apse, making the building T-shaped; this is known as a *Tau* plan. When additional space (a choir) separates the transept and the apse, the plan is called a **Latin cross**.

Central-plan buildings were first used by Christians as tombs, baptism centers, and shrines to martyrs. (The **Greek-cross plan**, in which two similarly sized "arms" intersect at their centers, is a type of central plan.) Instead of the longitudinal axis of basilican

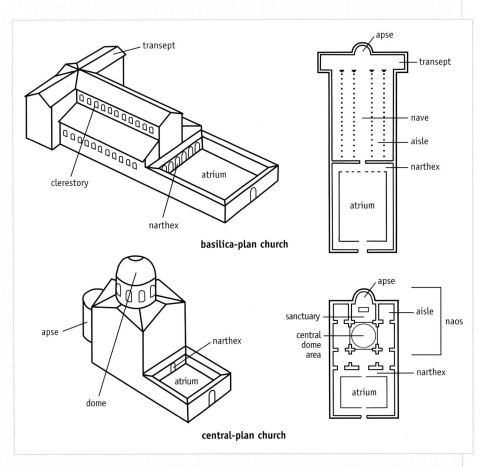

basilica-plan church

central-plan church

churches, which draws worshipers forward toward the apse, central-plan churches such as Ravenna's San Vitale (see figs. 7-14, 7-15) have a more vertical axis. This makes the **dome**, a symbolic "vault of heaven," a natural focus over the main worship area. Like basilicas, central-plan churches generally have an atrium, a narthex, and an apse. The naos is the space containing the central dome, sanctuary, and apse.

century catacomb of Commodilla is painted with a central medallion showing the face of Christ.

The era of religious toleration, which began with the Edict of Milan and Constantine's active support of Christianity, spurred the building of Christian churches and shrines. Constantine ordered a monumental basilica constructed at the place where Christians believed Saint Peter, the leader of Jesus' apostles, to be buried. Peter (d. c. 64 CE) had established the first Christian community in Rome. As the city's first bishop (spiritual and administrative leader of the Church), he was later recognized as the precursor of the popes—the heads of the Christian Church in the West. Old Saint Peter's Church (called "old" because it was completely replaced by a new building in the sixteenth century, see page 326) became the pope's church and came to signify his authority over all Christendom.

Old Saint Peter's Church (see "Basilica-Plan and Central-Plan Churches," above) included architectural elements arranged in a way that has characterized Christian basilica-plan churches ever since (fig. 7-5). A narthex across the width of the building protected the doorways, which opened into the nave and the four side aisles, two on each side of the nave. As in Roman secular basilicas, which inspired its design, a clerestory

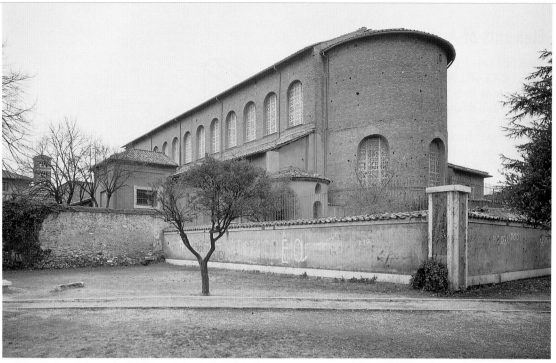

7-6

7-6 **Church of Santa Sabina,** Rome 422–32

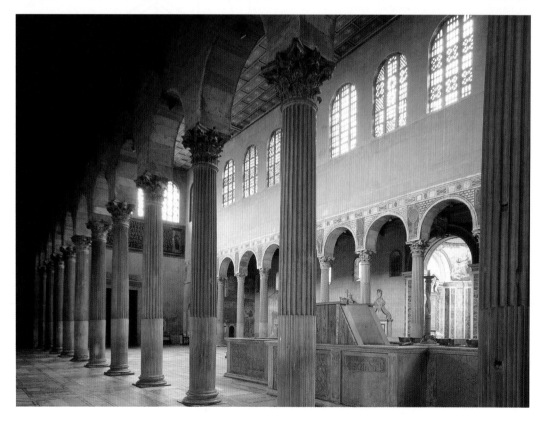

7-7 **Interior Church of Santa Sabina** View from the sanctuary to the entrance

with windows in the tall central nave lit the interior, and the nave was lined with columns supporting an entablature. At Old Saint Peter's, because of its size and double aisles, the columns of the side aisles supported a series of round arches. At the end of the nave and aisles was another special feature of Old Saint Peter's, a **transept**—a wing that crossed the nave and aisles at a right angle. The transept met the need for more space near the tomb of the saint. A large number of clergy and pilgrims gathered near the altar and tomb for elaborate rituals. Christians believed that Saint Peter's bones lay beneath the high altar; indeed early Christian and pagan catacombs did lie under the church. Clearly, Old Saint Peter's had to serve a variety of functions: it was a congregational church, a burial place, and a pilgrimage shrine containing the relics of Saint Peter. Old Saint Peter's could hold at least 14,000 worshipers, and it remained the largest of all Christian churches until the eleventh century.

Old Saint Peter's is gone, but some idea of its splendor can be gained from the basilicas of Santa Sabina and Santa Maria Maggiore, built in Rome in the fifth century. The Church of

Santa Sabina in Rome, constructed by Bishop Peter of Ilyria between 422 and 432, appears much as it did in the fifth century (fig. 7-6). The basic elements of the basilica church are clearly visible inside and out: a nave with side aisles lit by **clerestory** windows, ending in a rounded apse (compare Roman secular basilicas, such as the Basilica of Maxentius and Constantine, see fig. 6-32). Santa Sabina's exterior, typical of the time, is severe brickwork. In contrast, the interior displays a wealth of marble veneer and twenty-four fluted marble columns with Corinthian capitals acquired from a second-century building (fig. 7-7). The columns support round arches, creating a **nave arcade**, in contrast to a **nave colonnade**. The **spandrels** are inlaid with marble images of the chalice and paten (the plate that holds the bread)—the essential equipment for the **Eucharistic** rite that took place at the altar. The decoration of the upper walls is lost, and a paneled ceiling covers the rafter roof. The **triforium**, the blind wall between the arcade and the clerestory, typically had paintings or mosaics with scenes from the Old Testament or the Gospels.

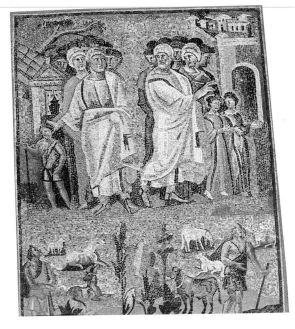

7-8 | ***Parting of Lot and Abraham,*** mosaic in the nave arcade, Church of Santa Maria Maggiore, Rome, 432–40. Panel approx. 4'11" x 6'8" (1.49 x 2.03 m)

Triforium mosaic panels still survive in the Church of Santa Maria Maggiore (Saint Mary the Great), which was built between 432 and 440. (The church was the first to be dedicated to the Virgin Mary after the Council of Ephesus awarded Mary the title Mother of God.)

Mosaics along the nave walls, in framed panels high above the worshipers, illustrate Old Testament stories of Jewish patriarchs and heroes whom Christians accepted as part of their own history. One mosaic, *Parting of Lot and Abraham* (fig. 7-8), illustrates a story told in the first book of the Old Testament (Genesis 13:1–12). The people of Abraham and his nephew Lot, dwelling together, had grown too numerous, so the two agreed to separate and lead their followers in different directions. On the right, Lot and his daughters turn toward Jordan, while Abraham and his wife stay in Canaan. This parting is meaningful to Christians since Abraham was the founder of the Jewish nation from which Jesus descended. The solid, three-dimensional rendering of the toga-clad foreground figures and the hint of perspective in the buildings reflect a continuation of the earlier

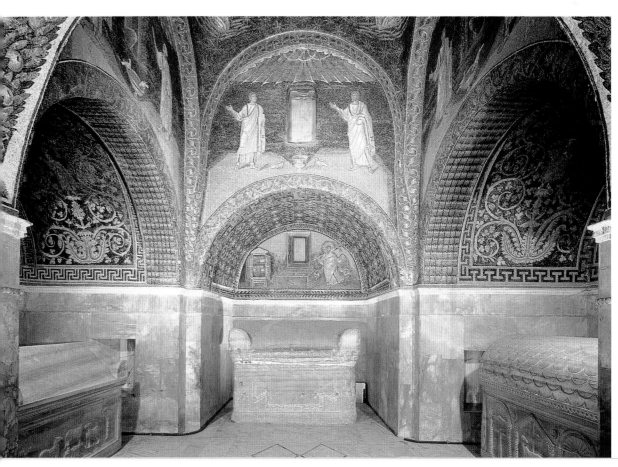

7-9

Mausoleum of Galla Placidia
Ravenna, Italy
c. 425–26
Eastern bays with sarcophagus niches and lunette mosaic of the *Martyrdom of Saint Lawrence*

Few images have such great appeal as the Good Shepherd, with associations at once loving, caring, protective, and strong (fig. 7-10). Originating in agrarian societies, the theme of the shepherd watching over a flock of sheep or carrying home a weak or lost lamb develops as a powerful and positive motif even in urban cultures. If today the Good Shepherd is thought of as a Christian symbol, it was not always conceived as such. Among ancient Greeks and Romans, Hermes could be represented as a shepherd carrying a lamb or calf, and Orpheus charmed the flocks and even defied death with his music. Jewish patriarchs measured their wealth in herds of sheep and camels, and one of the greatest and best known of the songs of King David envisions God as an all-providing shepherd (Psalm 23). Not surprisingly, Christians adopted this imagery for Jesus, who used it himself in his parables as an effective way to make God's love understandable to his listeners (Luke 15:3–7 and Matthew 18:12–14). According to John (10:10–11), Jesus called himself the good shepherd who lays down his life for his sheep. And so the imagery contributed to a common theme for Jews and Christians alike in both West and East.

By the fifth century, with Christianity relatively secure as an established religion, the artist might add, or the patron might request, specifically Christian symbols. In the Ravenna mosaic, Jesus sits with his sheep in a luxuriant landscape, like a young Orpheus. But his shepherd's crook has become a golden cross. Not dressed as a simple peas-

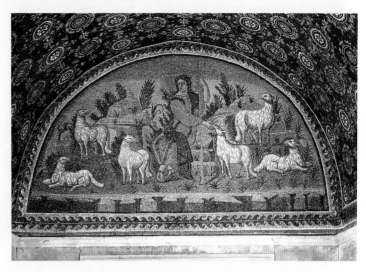

7-10 | **Good Shepherd,** mosaic in the lunette over the west entrance, Mausoleum of Galla Placidia, Ravenna, Italy c. 425–26

ant, he wears imperial robes of purple and gold and embodies the Byzantine ideal of majesty. Nearly a century had passed since the last official persecution of Christians, and at the time this mosaic was made, Christianity had been the official state religion for forty-five years. The patrons of the Ravenna mosaic chose to assert the glory of Jesus Christ in gold and purple mosaic, the richest medium of decoration known, and to present Jesus in the guise of a young emperor, an imperial image still imbued with pagan spirit but now glorying in the triumph of the new faith.

naturalistic style of Roman art, even as the sheen of the gold tesserae tends to flatten the forms and reduce the illusion of space.

By the time the Roman Churches of Santa Sabina and Santa Maria Maggiore were completed, Rome had lost its political, although not its spiritual, importance. The capital of the Western Roman Empire was moved to Milan in the late fourth century, and then to Ravenna at the beginning of the fifth century. Ravenna had an important naval base, Classis, and offered direct access by sea to Constantinople, the capital of the Eastern, or Byzantine, Empire. Ravenna became the capital of the Byzantine state in Italy.

One of the earliest surviving Christian structures in Ravenna is a small, cross-shaped chapel once attached to the church of the imperial palace. It is called the Mausoleum of Galla Placidia after one of the most remarkable women of the fifth century (although she was not buried there). Galla Placidia was the daughter of the Western Roman emperor, wife of the Gothic king, sister of Emperor Honorius, and mother of Emperor Valentinian. As regent for her son after 425, she ruled the Western Empire.

The vaults of the tiny chapel are richly decorated with mosaics, and panels of veined marble cover the walls below (fig. 7-9; see page 173). Floral designs derived from funeral garlands cover the four central arches, and the walls above them are filled with the figures of standing apostles gesturing like orators. Saint Lawrence, to whom the building was probably dedicated, is represented in the central **lunette** in figure 7-9. The saint holds a cross and gestures toward the metal grill on which he was literally roasted. At the left stands a tall cabinet containing the books of the Gospels, signifying the faith for which Lawrence was martyred.

In another lunette is a mosaic depicting the *Good Shepherd* (fig. 7-10). In this mosaic Jesus is a young adult wearing imperial robes. There is a halo, or circle of light, behind his head—a device artists used to distinguish rulers and holy personages from ordinary people. The rocky band at the bottom of the lunette scene, resembling a cliff face riddled with clefts, separates the divine image from worshipers. This visual device illustrates an increasing tendency in Christian art to differentiate the sacred and secular worlds.

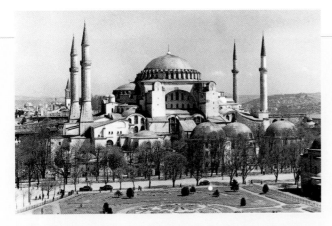

7-11 Anthemius of Tralles and Isidorus of Miletus. Church of Hagia Sophia, Istanbul, Turkey. 532–37. View from the southwest

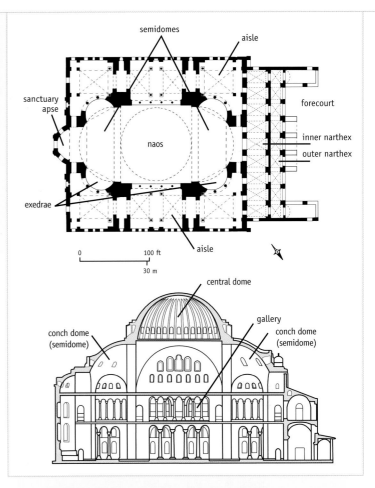

7-12 Plan and section of the Church of Hagia Sophia

Early Byzantine Art

During the fifth and sixth centuries, the Italian peninsula was invaded by the Visigoths, Vandals, and Ostrogoths—Germanic peoples from the north. Rome was sacked twice, in 410 and 455. The Western Roman Empire collapsed in 476, and Italy fell to the Ostrogoths.

During the same period, the Eastern Empire and its capital city of Constantinople flourished. Byzantine political power, wealth, and culture reached its height in the sixth century, under Emperor Justinian I (ruled 527–565), ably seconded by Empress Theodora (c. 500–548). At the height of its powers under Justinian, the Byzantine Empire included the areas that are now Greece, the Balkans, and Turkey; the Levant from Syria south to Arabia; Egypt; part of Spain; and a long strip along the Mediterranean coast of Africa. Justinian also reconquered Italy and Sicily from the Ostrogoths, establishing Ravenna as the administrative capital of Byzantine Italy.

In Constantinople, Justinian began a campaign of building and renovation, but little remains of his architectural projects or of the old imperial city. The Church of Hagia Sophia (Holy Wisdom) is a magnificent exception (fig. 7-11). Designed by two scholar-theoreticians, Anthemius of Tralles and Isidorus of

Miletus, it embodies both imperial power and Christian glory. Anthemius was a specialist in geometry and optics, and Isidorus was a specialist in physics who had studied vaulted construction. Their crowning achievement was the dome of Hagia Sophia, which provided a golden, light-filled canopy high above a processional space (fig. 7-12). Procopius of Caesarea,

Elements of Architecture

PENDENTIVES AND SQUINCHES

Pendentives and **squinches** are two methods of supporting a round dome or its drum over a square space. Pendentives are spherical triangles between arches that rise to form a circular opening on which the dome sits. Squinches are lintels supported on bracketlike constructions placed across the walls' upper corners. Because squinches create an octagon, which is close in shape to a circle, they provide a solid base for the dome. Byzantine builders experimented with both pendentives (as at Hagia Sophia, see fig. 7-13) and squinches. Elaborate squinch-supported domes became a hallmark of Islamic interiors.

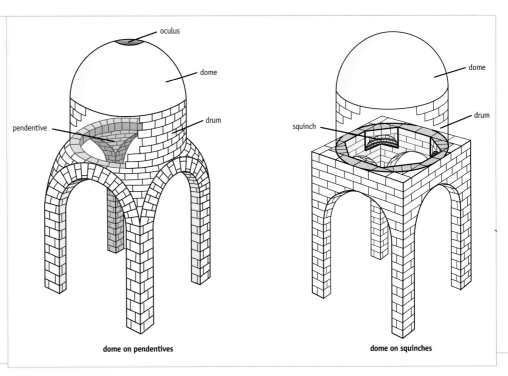

dome on pendentives   dome on squinches

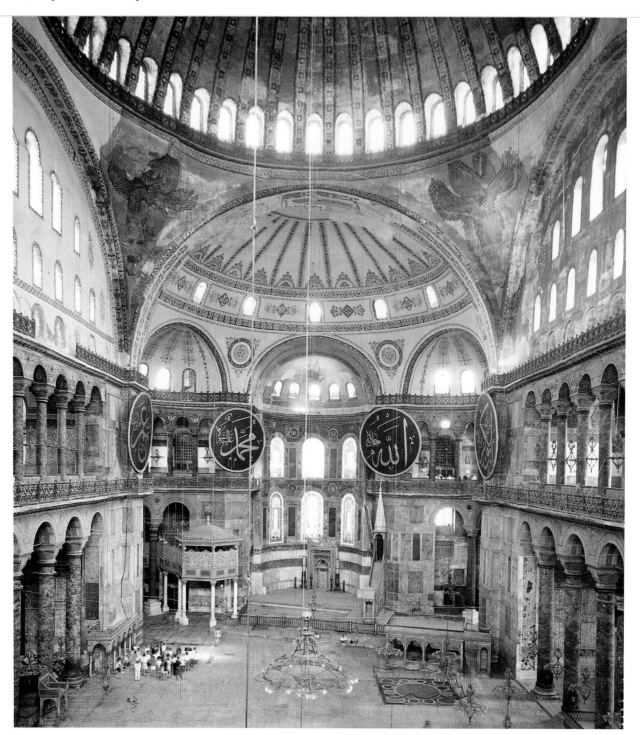

7-13

Church of Hagia Sophia

who chronicled Justinian's reign, claimed poetically that the dome seemed to hang suspended on a "golden chain from heaven." It was rumored that Hagia Sophia was constructed by angels, but mortal builders achieved the feat in only five years (532–537) (see "Pendentives and Squinches," page 175).

Hagia Sophia is based on a central plan with a dome inscribed in a square. To form a longitudinal nave, **conches**—semidomes—expand outward from the central dome to connect with the narthex on one end and the conch of the sanctuary apse on the other. This central core, called the **naos** in Byzantine architecture, is flanked by side aisles; above the aisles, galleries overlook the naos. The Byzantine church required **galleries** to accommodate female worshipers, who were not allowed to stand directly on the church floor.

The main dome of Hagia Sophia is supported on pendentives, triangular curving wall sections built between the four huge arches that spring from **piers** (large masonry supports) at the corners of the dome's square base (fig. 7-13). The origin of the dome on pendentives, which became the preferred method for supporting domes in Byzantine architecture, is obscure, but Hagia Sophia represents its earliest use in a major building. Unlike the Pantheon's dome, which rises as a solid form from a circular drum and opens with an oculus at the top (see fig. 6-24), the dome of Hagia Sophia has a band of forty windows around its base. This daring concept challenged architectural logic by weakening the integrity of the masonry but created the all-important circle of light that makes the dome appear to float.

Among the sixth-century Byzantine churches built outside of Constantinople, San Vitale in Ravenna and Sant'Apollinare in Classe were two of the most important structures. Both were commissioned by a local bishop, Ecclesius, when Italy was under Ostrogothic rule, but they were only completed after Justinian's conquest of Ravenna.

The Church of San Vitale was dedicated in 547 to the fourth-century Italian martyr, Saint Vitalis. Its design is basically a dome-covered octagon extended by eight **exedrae**, or semicircular **niches** (hollows or recesses in a wall or other architectural element) (fig. 7-14). A rectangular sanctuary and apse, flanked by circular rooms, project through one of the octagonal sides of the shell. A narthex once led to the palace.

The floor plan of San Vitale only begins to convey the effect of the complex, interpenetrating interior spaces of the church. The dome rests on eight large piers that frame the exedrae and the sanctuary. These two-story exedrae open through arches into outer aisles on the ground floor and into galleries on the second floor. They expand the circular central space physically and create an airy, floating sensation, reinforced by the liberal use of colored veined marble veneer and colored glass and gold tesserae in the surface decoration. In the vault over the altar, angels support the Lamb of God, and in the conch of the sanctuary apse, an image of Christ enthroned is flanked by Saint Vitalis and by Bishop Ecclesius, who presents a model of the church to Christ (fig. 7-15).

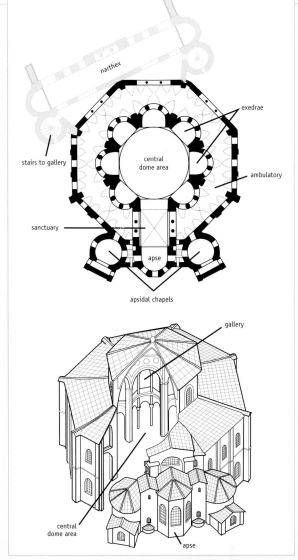

7-14 | **Plan and cutaway drawing of the Church of San Vitale**
Ravenna, Italy. 526–47

7-15

| **Church of San Vitale**
View across the central space toward the sanctuary apse with mosaic showing Christ enthroned and flanked by Saint Vitalis and Bishop Ecclesius

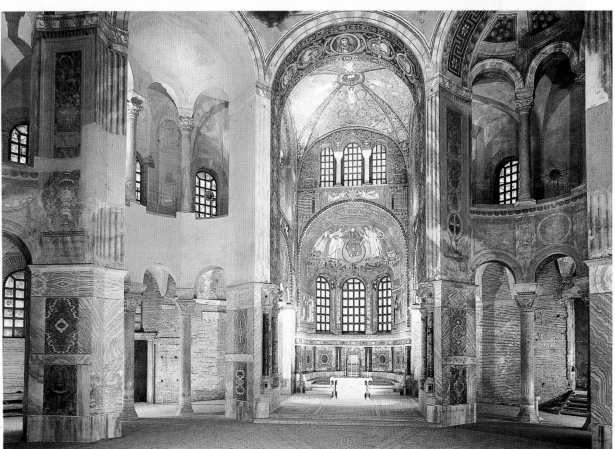

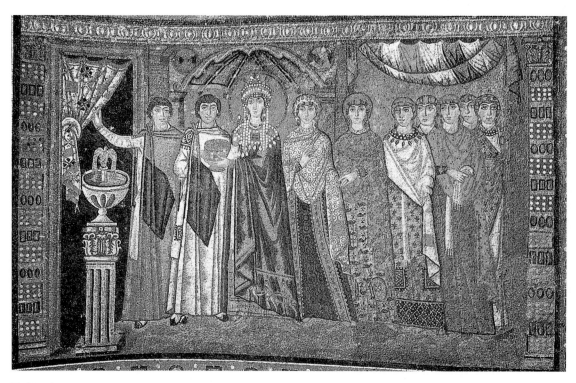

7-16 | ***Empress Theodora and Her Attendants,*** mosaic on south wall of the apse, Church of San Vitale
c. 547. 8'8" x 12' (2.64 x 3.65 m)

Theodora's head is adorned with a huge pearled crown and golden halo. Because of these ornaments, she
seems almost like a holy image. She may well have worn the extraordinary pearls in her ostentatious imperial
regalia as protection, for pearls were believed to be an antidote for poison and disease. Theodora died,
probably of cancer, in 548, only a year after the dedication of this church and its mosaics.

Justinian and Theodora may never have set foot in Ravenna, but two large mosaic panels that face each other across the apse make their presences known. Theodora, followed by her sisters and ladies of the court, carries a huge golden chalice, or cup, studded with jewels (fig. 7-16). She presents this as a precious offering to Christ—emulating the Magi, wise kings from the East, whom Christians believe brought valuable gifts to Jesus at his birth. The three Magi are depicted in the embroidered panel at the bottom of her purple robe. The chalice, in its function as a wine goblet, also represents an offering for the Mass, the religious ceremony performed during communal Christian worship. At the central core of the Mass, the ritual of Eucharist identifies the body and blood of Christ with the substances of bread and wine, which Jesus had instructed his followers to eat and drink in remembrance of him.

The empress and her ladies stand beside a fountain at the entrance to the women's gallery. The open door and curtain are classical **illusionistic** devices, but here the mosaicists deliberately avoided making them space-creating elements and instead turned them into flat two-dimensional patterns. Even nature plays tricks, for the figures cast no shadows but stand in pools of yellow light. By the sixth century, the early interest Christian artists had shown in capturing the appearance of the material world had given way to a newer, hieratic style: a formal, stately, and static mode of presenting religious imagery with which artists sought to convey a timeless, supernatural world.

The Church of Sant'Apollinare in Classe was consecrated two years after San Vitale, in 549. Designed on a simple basilica plan, its layout emphasizes the forward processional movement from the entrance to the semicircular apse at the end of the nave. In the grand mosaic that decorates the conch of the apse (fig. 7-17), a jeweled cross with the face of Christ at its center symbolizes the Transfiguration—the moment when Jesus revealed his divinity to the apostles Peter, John, and James (here represented as three sheep). The Hand of God reaches down from glowing clouds and the Old Testament prophets Moses and Elijah emerge from clouds at each side, symbolically linking the Old Testament with the New and

THE DEPICTION OF SPACE

In Western European art, the picture space appears to open out behind the picture plane (the image bearing surface). In Byzantine art, the picture space lies between the image and the viewer; that is, in front of the wall, panel, or parchment. It is an active space through which sight lines—like beams of light—move, joining image and viewer. This concept forces artists to create so-called "reverse perspective," in which lines perpendicular to the picture plane seem to spread apart. Images seem to move forward, away from the wall, rather than sink into a fictive space behind it. The possibility of intimate contact between the viewer and image gives Byzantine art great immediacy and power.

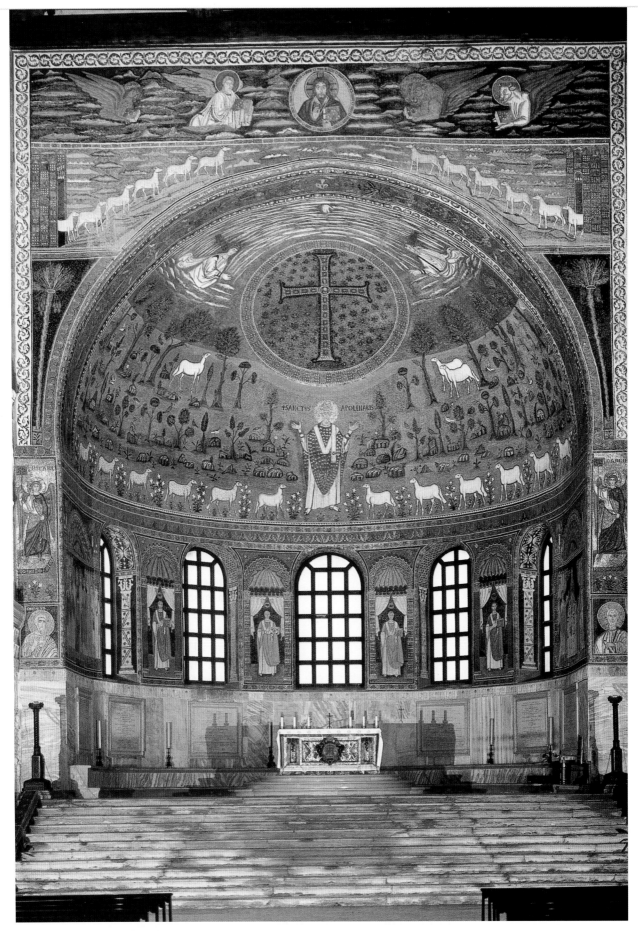

7-17 | ***The Transfiguration of Christ with Saint Apollinaris, First Bishop of Ravenna,*** mosaic in the apse Church of Sant'Apollinare in Classe, the former port of Ravenna (Classis), Italy. 533–49. Mosaic on the wall above the arch leading to the apse, 7th and 9th centuries

CHRISTIAN SYMBOLS

Symbols have always played an important part in Christian art. Some were devised just for Christianity, but most were borrowed from pagan and Jewish traditions and adapted for Christian use.

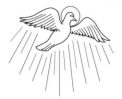

Dove

The Old Testament dove is a symbol of purity, representing peace when it is shown bearing an olive branch. In Christian art a white dove is the symbolic embodiment of the Holy Spirit.

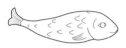

Fish

The fish was one of the earliest Christian symbols. The first letters of "Jesus Christ, Son of God, Savior" spelled "fish" in Greek. Because of its association with baptism in water, it came to stand for all Christians.

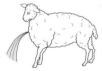

Lamb (Sheep)

The lamb, an ancient sacrificial animal, symbolizes Jesus' sacrifice on the cross as the Lamb of God, its pouring blood redeeming the sins of the world. A flock of sheep represents the apostles—or all Christians—cared for by their Good Shepherd, Jesus Christ.

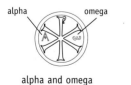

alpha and omega
I and X

Monograms

Alpha (the first letter of the Greek alphabet) and omega (the last) signify God as the beginning and end of all things. The initials *I* and *X* are the first letters of Jesus and Christ in Greek. The initials *XP*, known as the *chi rho*, were the first two letters of the word *Christos*. These emblems are sometimes enclosed by a halo or wreath of victory.

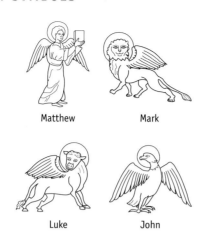

Matthew

Mark

Luke

John

Four Evangelists

The evangelists who wrote the New Testament Gospels are traditionally associated with the following creatures: Saint Matthew, a man (or angel); Saint Mark, a lion; Saint Luke, an ox; and Saint John, an eagle.

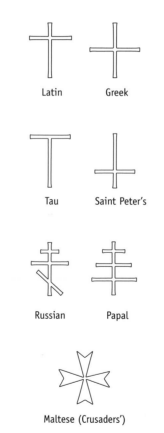

Latin

Greek

Tau

Saint Peter's

Russian

Papal

Maltese (Crusaders')

Cross

The primary Christian emblem, the cross, symbolizes the suffering and triumph of Jesus' crucifixion and resurrection as Christ. It also stands for Jesus Christ himself, as well as the Christian religion as a whole. Crosses have taken various forms, the two most common in Christian art being the Latin and the Greek.

attesting to the coming of the Messiah. Saint Apollinaris, the first bishop of Ravenna, is shown below the cross as an **orant**; the twelve lambs flanking him, and the twelve sheep emerging from the buildings represented on the wall above, represent Jesus' twelve apostles.

The mosaics on the wall above the apse were added in the seventh and ninth centuries. Christ, holding the Gospels, is portrayed with a cross inscribed in his halo, an indication of his sacrifice as a human being. He is flanked by figures symbolizing the Four Evangelists—Matthew, Mark, Luke, and John—the authors of the four Gospels. Saint Matthew is represented by an angel, Saint Mark by a lion, Saint Luke by an ox, and Saint John by an eagle (see "Christian Symbols," left).

Christians required large numbers of books for religious services, for public education, and for personal study and meditation. Until the invention of printing, all books were **manuscripts**—that is, they were written by hand on **parchment,** specially prepared animal skin. If they were decorated or illustrated, today we say that they were *illuminated*. During the Byzantine period and the European Middle Ages, many illuminated manuscripts were made in monasteries and convents, religious communities where devout men and women (monks and nuns) withdrew from the secular world to devote their lives to study and prayer.

The manuscript page (called a **folio**) illustrated in figure 7-18 comes from an illuminated manuscript of the Gospels signed by a monk named Rabbula and completed in February 586, at a monastery in Beth Zagba, Syria. It depicts crucial events from the life of Jesus. Both upper and lower illustrations incorporate the convention of narrative. The upper illustration tells the story of the Crucifixion. Jesus was said to be crucified in the company of two criminals, one penitent and the other not. As he died, he was tormented by Roman soldiers: one extending a sponge on a pole with vinegar instead of water for him to drink, another stabbing him in the side with a spear, and others gambling for his clothes. Jesus is dressed in a long purple robe, called a colobium, signifying royal status in the Byzantine world. Jesus' mother, the Virgin Mary, and Saint John the Evangelist watch the Crucifixion from the far left.

In the lower register, Jesus' empty tomb stands with open doors, proving that Christ rose from the dead. The soldiers guarding his burial place have fallen asleep. At left, an angel announces the Resurrection to the Marys, and at

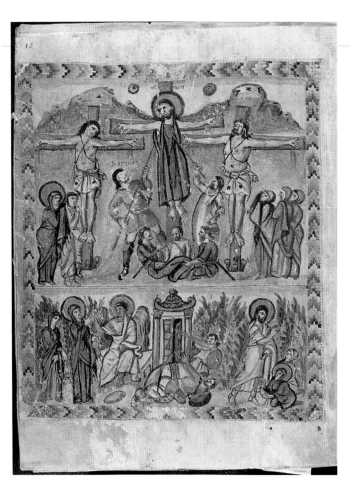

7-18 | Page with *The Crucifixion,* from the *Rabbula Gospels* from Beth Zagba, Syria. 586. 13¹/₄ x 10¹/₂" (33.7 x 26.7 cm). Biblioteca Medicea Laurenziana, Florence

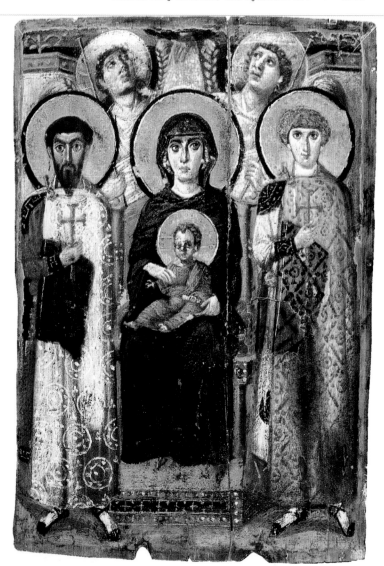

7-19 | *Virgin and Child with Saints and Angels,* icon, Monastery of Saint Catherine, Mount Sinai, Egypt. Second half of 6th century. Encaustic on wood, 27 x 18⁷/₈" (69 x 48 cm)

right, Jesus appears to female followers who came to his tomb. That events take place in an otherworldly setting is indicated by the lush foliage and glowing bands of color in the sky.

Many Eastern Christians prayed to Christ, Mary, and the saints while looking at images of them in manuscripts or on painted panels known as **icons**. Church doctrine toward the veneration of icons distinguished between idolatry—the worship of images—and the veneration of an idea or holy person depicted in a work of art. Icons were thus accepted as aids to meditation and prayer: the images were thought to act as intermediaries between worshipers and the holy personages they depicted.

In the eighth century, in a reaction against the veneration of images known as **iconoclasm**, conservative churchmen destroyed the icons. A few very beautiful examples survived in isolated places like the Monastery of Saint Catherine on Mount Sinai, Egypt. Among the finest is the *Virgin and Child with Saints and Angels* (fig. 7-19). The humble, earthly mother of Jesus, the Virgin Mary as Theotokos, bearer of God, was viewed as a powerful intercessor, or go-between, who could appeal to her divine Son for mercy on behalf of repentant Christians. She was also called the Seat of Wisdom, and many images of her, like this one, show her holding Jesus on her lap in a way that suggests that she has become an imperial throne for her son.

She is flanked by the Christian warrior-saints Theodore (left) and George (right)—legendary figures said to have slain dragons. Symbolically the warrior-saints represent the triumph of the Church over the "evil serpent" of paganism. The artist who painted the Christ Child, the Virgin, and the angels worked in an illusionistic, Roman-derived manner and created almost realistic figures. The male saints are much more stylized, and the artist barely hints at real bodies beneath the richly patterned textiles of their cloaks. From their emergence in early Byzantine art, icons play an increasingly important role in later periods.

Later Byzantine Art

The first great age of Byzantine art, which began with the reign of Justinian I in the sixth century, ended with a period of iconoclasm in the eighth century. In 726, Emperor Leo III decreed that all religious images were idols and should be destroyed. Innumerable examples of devotional art were demolished before this policy was reversed, first in 787 by Empress Irene and then finally in 843 by Empress Theodora. A second golden age of Byzantine art began in 867 under the leadership of an imperial

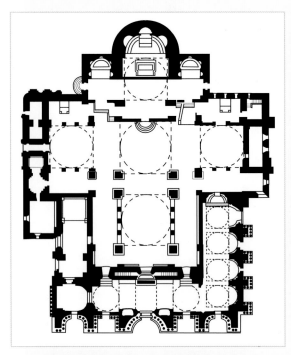

7-20 | **Plan of the Cathedral of San Marco**
Venice. Begun 1063

7-21 | **Cathedral of San Marco, Venice**
Present building begun 1063
View looking toward apse

This church is the third one built on the site. It was both the palace chapel of the doge and the *martyrium* that stored the bones of the patron of Venice, Saint Mark. This great multidomed structure, consecrated as a cathedral in 1807, has been reworked continually to the present day.

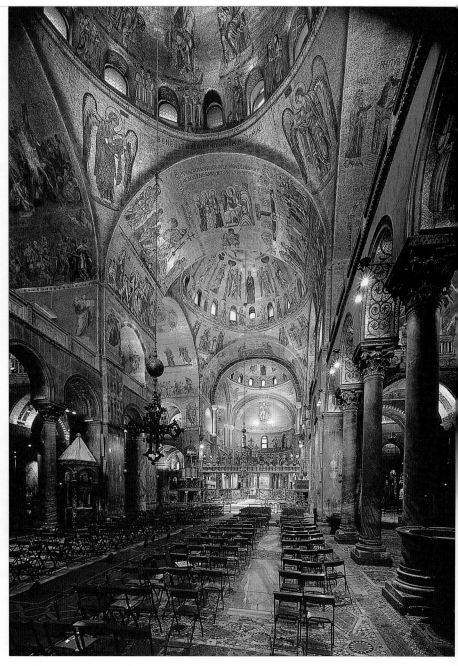

dynasty from Macedonia and lasted until Christian Crusaders from the West occupied Constantinople in 1204. Byzantine culture flourished once more in the fourteenth and early fifteenth centuries up to the time that Muslim Ottoman Turks conquered Constantinople in 1453.

While little Byzantine art survives from Constantinople, the northeastern Italian city of Venice holds rich treasures of middle and late Byzantine art. At the end of the tenth century, Constantinople granted Venice a special trade status that allowed its merchants to control much of the commercial exchange between western Europe and the Eastern Empire. With untold wealth flowing into the city's coffers, Venice's ruler, the doge, in 1063 commissioned a splendid church to replace an older chapel, holding the relics of the martyred patron saint of Venice, Saint Mark the Apostle. Venetian architects looked to the Byzantine domed church for inspiration, especially the no longer extant Church of the Holy Apostles in Constantinople. The plan of the Cathedral

of San Marco (fig. 7-20) is based on the Greek cross (a cross with four arms of the same length). Each of its five square units is covered with a great dome. Separated by barrel vaults and supported by pendentives, these domed compartments, covered with golden mosaics, produce a complex space in which each individual dome vies for attention in seeming competition with the high altar and choir (fig. 7-21). As at Hagia Sophia (see fig. 7-13), windows encircle the bases of the domes, and gold mosaics sweep over the vast spaces.

Although an outpost, Greece lay within the Byzantine Empire in the tenth and eleventh centuries. Two churches of the Monastery of Hosios Loukas (near Stiris) in Greece are excellent examples of later Byzantine architecture (fig. 7-22). The Katholikon (the major church) is a compact, central-plan structure. Pendentives fill the corners of the cubical core of the building; then squinches over the pendentives and barrel vaults form an octagonal base for the dome. The high central space

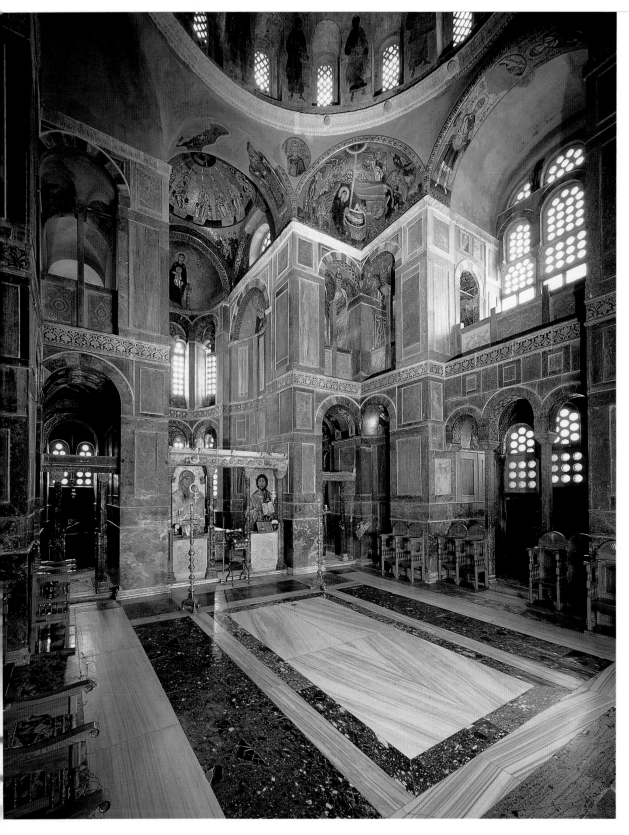

7-22

Central dome
and apse
Katholikon
Monastery of
Hosios Loukas
near Stiris
Greece. Early
11th century
and later

carries the eye of the worshiper upward into the main dome, which soars above a ring of tall arched windows. Abandoning the broad geometric forms of San Marco and Hagia Sophia, the builders of the Katholikon at Hosiso Loukas seem to revel in the complexity. Single, double, and triple windows create intricate and unusual patterns of light. The decorative program of mosaics and marble veneers further complicates the space. Visible in figure 7-22 are images of the Virgin and Child in the

apse, the Lamb of God surrounded by the Twelve Apostles in the sanctuary dome, and the Nativity in the pendentive (the mosaic of the Pantokrator in the central dome fell and was replaced by a painting). An icon screen (iconostasis) separates the sanctuary and the congregation.

As Constantinople turned its gaze to the east, Ukraine, Belarus, and Russia fell under its spell. These lands had been settled by Eastern Slavs in the fifth and sixth centuries, but later were ruled by Swedish Vikings (the Rus) who established headquarters in the upper Volga regions and in the city of Kiev. The first Christian member of the Kievan ruling family was Princess Olga (c. 890–969), who was baptized in Constantinople by the patriarch himself, with the Byzantine emperor as her godfather.

In the eleventh century Grand Prince Yaroslav (ruled 1019–1054) founded the Cathedral of Santa Sophia in Kiev. The finished building had double side aisles, five apses, a large central dome, and twelve smaller domes. The small domes were said to represent the twelve apostles gathered around Christ the Pantokrator, symbolized by the central dome. The central domed space of the **crossing** focuses attention on the nave and the main apse. The many individual bays, each of which is an almost independent vertical unit, create an often confusing and compartmentalized interior (fig. 7-23). The interior walls glow with lavish decoration: mosaics glitter from the central dome, the apse, and the arches of the crossing, and the remaining surfaces are painted with scenes from the lives of Christ, the Virgin, the apostles Peter and Paul, and the archangels.

The mosaics established an iconographical system that came to be followed in Russian Orthodox churches. The *Pantokrator* fills the center of the dome (not visible above the window-pierced drum in figure 7-23). At a lower level, the apostles stand between the windows of the drum, with the Four Evangelists in the pendentives. The Virgin Mary, arms raised in the traditional pose of prayer (an orant figure), seems to float in a golden heaven, filling half dome and upper wall of the apse. In the mosaic on the wall below the Virgin, Christ, appearing not once but twice, accompanied by

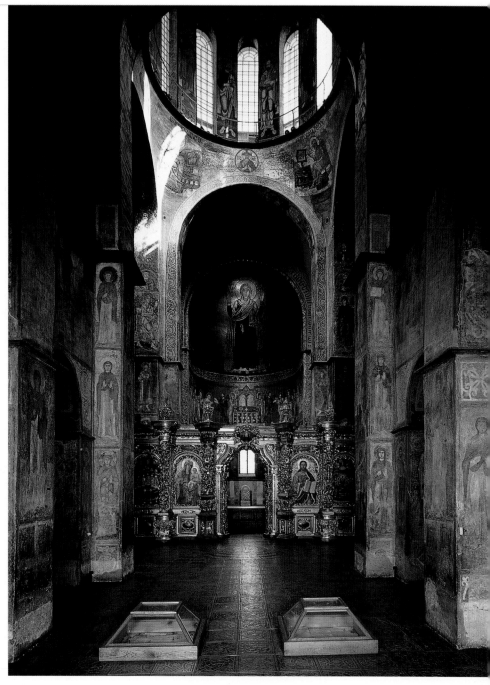

7-23   **Interior, Cathedral of Santa Sophia,** Kiev, Ukraine. 11th century and later

The view under the dome and into the apse does not convey the quality of the interior as an agglomeration of tall narrow spaces divided by piers whose architectural function is disguised or ignored by elaborate paintings.

angels who act as deacons, celebrates Mass at an altar under a canopy, a theme known as the Communion of the Apostles. He distributes communion to six apostles on each side of the altar. With this extravagant use of costly mosaic, Prince Yaroslav made a powerful political declaration of his own—and the Kievan church's—importance and wealth.

During the tenth, eleventh, and twelfth centuries, artists also produced luxury items for the Byzantine church and court, using precious materials such as silver and gold, jewels and **enamels**, and working them with impeccable skill and aesthetic sensibility. One of the prizes the Crusaders took back to Venice

in 1204 was a silver gilt-and-enamel icon of the archangel Michael (fig. 7-24). The angel's head and hands are executed in relief in the **repoussé** technique (pounded out from the back of the plate). Halo, wings, and garments are detailed in delicate **cloisonné** enamel, and the framing borders are inset with enamel roundels. (Cloisonné is produced by soldering fine wires in the desired pattern to a metal plate and then filling the cells—**cloisons**—with powdered colored glass. When the object is heated, the glass powder melts and fuses onto the surface of the metal to create small, jewel-like sections.) Although the angel is portrayed in timeless youthfulness, the dazzling patterns

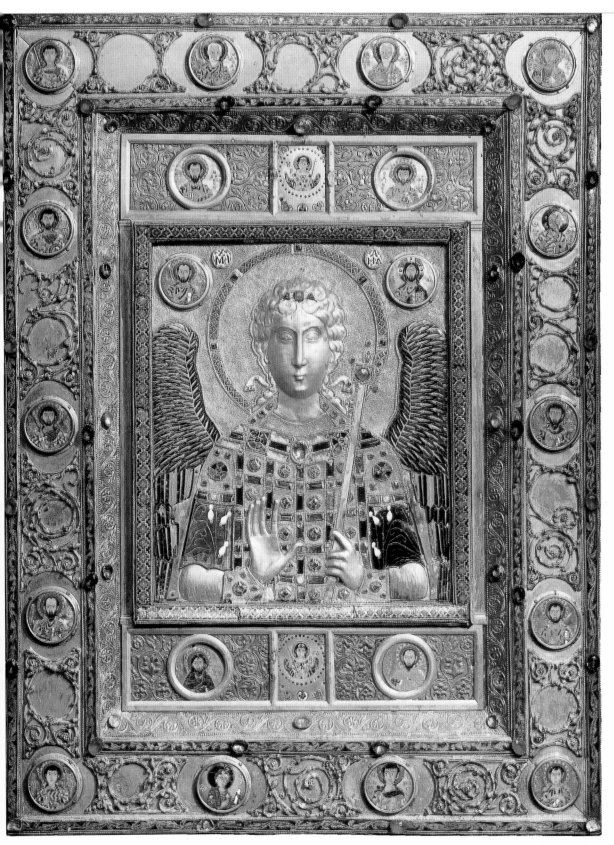

7-24

Archangel Michael, icon
10th century
Silver gilt and enamel, 19 x 14"
(48 x 36 cm)
Treasury of the Cathedral of San Marco, Venice

remove the image from the physical world. The sheer artistry of this icon seems to lift the image to a plane where light and color supplant form, and material substance becomes pure spirit.

A last great age of Byzantine art began after Crusaders, who occupied Constantinople in 1204, were expelled from the city in 1261. The patronage of emperors, wealthy courtiers, and the

Church stimulated renewed church building and renovation. In the early fourteenth century, an elaborately painted funerary chapel was added to the former Church of the Monastery of Christ in Chora, Constantinople (later a mosque and now a museum, Kariye Muzesi). A painting symbolic of the Resurrection of Christ, known as the *Anastasis*, is situated in the apse conch

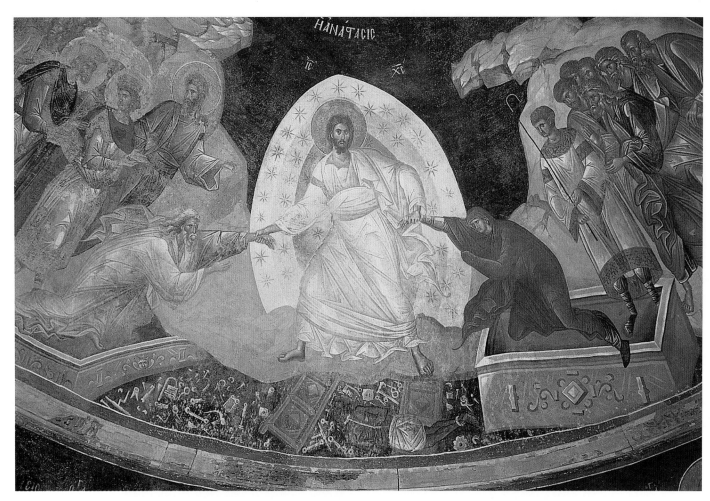

7-25 | ***Anastasis.*** Painting in the apse of Church of the Monastery of Christ in Chora (now Kariye djami, Istanbul, Turkey). c. 1315-21.
Swaan Photograph Collection, (96.P.21)

(fig. 7-25). Artists in western Europe usually depicted the Resurrection as the triumphant Christ emerging in glory from his tomb. The Eastern Church, as we see in this example, instead depicts Christ descending into hell to rescue Adam and Eve and other devout people from Satan. Christ, dressed in white, is backed by a star-studded **mandorla**, or almond-shaped light. He has trampled down the doors of hell; tied Satan into a helpless bundle; and shattered locks and chains, which lie scattered over the ground. He drags the elderly Adam and Eve from their open sarcophagi with such force that their bodies almost seem airborne.

This late Byzantine art coincided with a time of close commercial ties with Russia. After Constantinople's fall to the Ottoman Turks in 1453, leadership of the Orthodox Church shifted to Russia. Russian rulers declared Moscow to be the third Rome and themselves the heirs of Caesars (czars).

The practice of venerating icons continued in the Late Byzantine period. Many icons were believed to have been created miraculously and were thought to have magical protective and healing powers. A remarkable icon from this time is *The Old Testament Trinity (Three Angels Visiting Abraham)*, a large panel created between 1410 and 1420 by the famed artist-monk Andrey Rublyov (fig. 7-26). It was commissioned in honor of

the abbot Sergius of the Trinity-Sergius Monastery, near Moscow. The theme represents the dogma of the Trinity, which is a great challenge for artists. One solution used in late medieval works was to show three identical divine individuals—here, three angels—to suggest the idea of the Trinity. The subject was inspired by an Old Testament story of the Hebrew patriarch Abraham and his wife, Sarah, who entertained three strangers who were in fact God represented by three divine beings in human form (Genesis 18). Abraham and Sarah's home and the oak of Mamre are barely visible above the angels; their food becomes a chalice on an altarlike table. Rublyov conveys a sense of spirituality in this work by using Byzantine conventions, including simple contours, elongation of the body, and a focus on a limited number of figures.

Rublyov's icon clearly illustrates how Late Byzantine artists relied on mathematical conventions to create ideal figures, as did the ancient Greeks, thus giving their work remarkable consistency. Unlike the Greeks, who based their formulas on close observation of nature, Byzantine artists invented an ideal geometry to express a heavenly realm, and depicted human forms and features according to it. Here, as is often the case, the circle forms the underlying geometric figure, emphasized by the form of the haloed heads. Despite the formulaic, some-

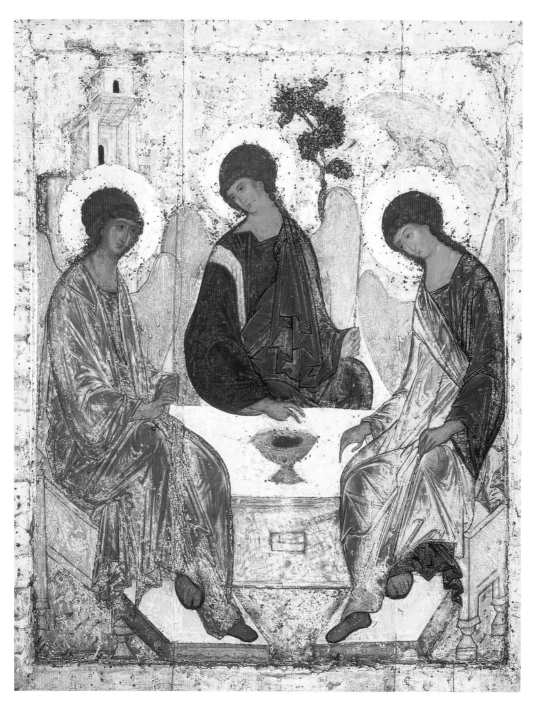

7-26   **Andrey Rublyov.** *The Old Testament Trinity (Three Angels Visiting Abraham)*, icon. c. 1410–20
Tempera on panel, 55½ x 44½" (141 x 113 cm). Tretyakov Gallery, Moscow

what uniform approach, talented artists like Rublyov managed to create a personal expressive style. He relied on typical conventions—simple contours, elongation of the body, and a focus on a limited number of figures—to capture the sense of the spiritual in his work, yet distinguished his art by imbuing it with a sweet, poetic ambience. In this artist's hands, the Byzantine style took on new life. The Byzantine tradition would

carry on in the art of the Eastern Orthodox Church and continues to this day in Russian icon painting. But in Constantinople, the three golden ages of Byzantine art—and the empire itself—came to a decisive end in 1453. When the forces of the Ottoman sultan Muhammad II overran the capital, the Eastern Empire became part of the Islamic world, with its own very rich aesthetic heritage.

Muslim artists and patrons held calligraphy in the highest esteem. Even writing equipment could be wonderfully decorated, and a pen box could become a prestigious possession. This pen box of polished brass, richly inlaid with precious silver, attests to the sophistication and wealth of its owner, Majd al-Mulk al-Muzaffar, a statesman and scholar and the governor of Khorasan, who died in 1221. The artist Shazi created exceptionally clear and elegant animated inscriptions in two different scripts—*kufic* and *naskhi*. To some letters he added duck heads and foliage, while in the rest of the inscription he embellished the vertical elements with human heads. Inscriptions on this pen box extol the virtues of the owner and wish him well.

As a "People of the Book," that is, those whose religion is revealed through sacred scriptures, Muslims had cause to honor fine writing. Since the Koran (Qur'an) is believed to be the word of God brought to Mohammed by the angel Gabriel, the words must be accurately preserved and deserve to be embellished. Consequently, calligraphy became the highest form of art in the Muslim world. Writing was not limited to books and documents but was used to adorn surfaces, from walls of buildings to curving brass candlesticks, and from silk textiles to glazed ceramics. As the most abstract of all the arts, calligraphy sometimes becomes so intricate that it seems to be a secret language. Mystics sometimes equated the creation of letters by scribes with the creation of human beings by God.

Formal kufic script (after Kufa, a city in Iraq) is blocky and angular, with strong upright strokes and long horizontals. In "foliated kufic," leaves and flowers seem to sprout from the terminals of the letters. Artists later created "animated" scripts, first by adding heads to upright strokes, and later by forming entire letters from figures. Kufic was used for inscriptions on buildings, on metal and wooden objects, and on textiles as well as for writing in ink on paper or vellum.

By the thirteenth century, scribes had developed several forms of cursive writing. Of the six major styles, one extraordinarily beautiful form, known as naskhi, was said to have been revealed and taught to scribes in a vision. Even those who cannot read Arabic can enjoy the beauty of the forms. The materials used by the scribes, especially the pens and the inks, had to be as perfect as the script. A pen box became a symbol of scholarly attainment.

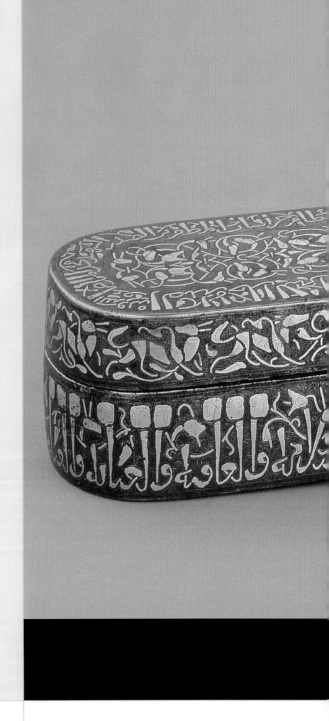

Shazi. Pen box, from Persia (Iran). c. 1210–11. Clasp side: brass inlaid with silver, copper, and black organic material, height 2" length 12⅝", width 2½" (5 x 31.4 x 6.4 cm). Freer Gallery of Art, Smithsonian Institution, Washington, D.C.

Purchase, (F1936.7)

(See pages 201–02 for side with inscription.)

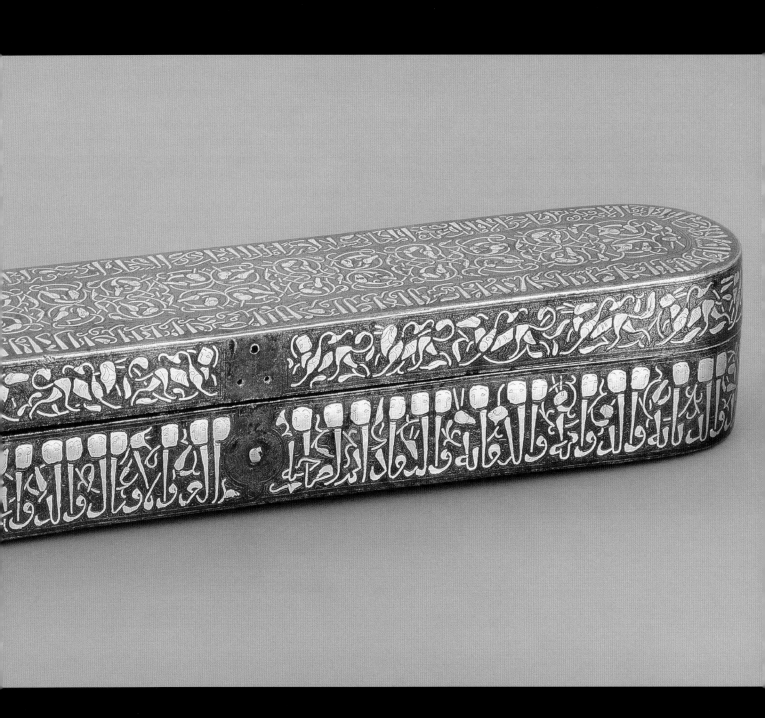

The religion called Islam (meaning "submission to [God's will]") originated in Arabia in the early seventh century. Under the leadership of its founder, the Prophet Muhammad (c. 570–632) and his successors, Islam spread rapidly, encompassing much of Africa, Europe, and Asia. Under four of Muhammad's closest associates, who assumed in turn the title of caliph (successor), Muslim armies conquered Persia (Iran), Egypt, and the Byzantine provinces of Syria and Palestine. The last of these caliphs, Ali (ruled 656–661), was succeeded by a rival, Muawiya (ruled 661–680), who founded the Umayyad dynasty. By the early eighth century, the aggressively expansionist Umayyads had reached India, conquered all of North Africa and Spain, and penetrated Europe to within 100 miles of Paris in France before being turned back. Today Islam is the world's fastest growing religion (see Map 3, page 231).

At first Islamic art reflected local traditions in art and architecture as diverse as Roman, Byzantine, and Persian. Because conservative Muslims discouraged the representation of figures, particularly in religious contexts, artists living in Islamic lands developed a rich vocabulary of nonfigural ornament, including complex geometric designs and the scrolling vines known outside the Islamic world as **arabesques**. They excelled in surface decoration, manipulating an infinite variety of highly controlled patterns and often highlighting the interplay between pure abstraction and organic form. For some people abstraction helps to free the mind from the contemplation of material form, opening it to the enormity of divine presence.

Art During the Early Caliphates

Arabic language and script have always held a unique place in Islamic society. As the language of the Koran (Qur'an), Arabic is a powerful unifying force within Islam. From the eighth through the eleventh centuries Arabic was the universal scholarly language in Muslim and Christian lands. Reverence for the Koran as the word of God extends by association to the act of writing. **Calligraphy**—the art of fine writing—is one of the glories of Islamic art.

The earliest formal script, called kufic (from the city of Kufa in modern Iraq), was angular and probably evolved from inscriptions on stone monuments. A page from a ninth-century Syrian

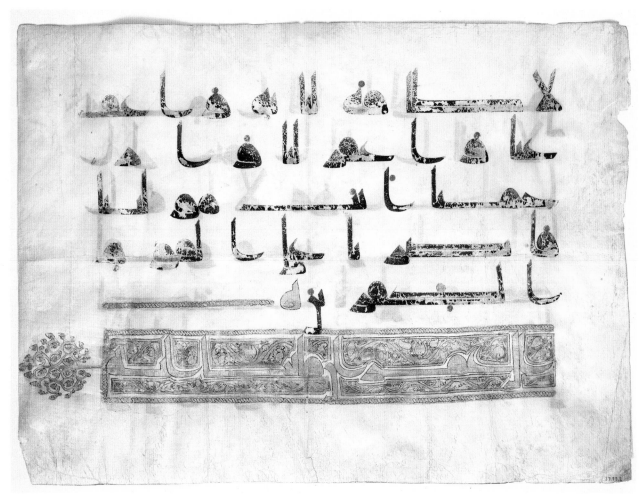

8-1 **Page from Koran** (*surah* II: 286 and title *surah* III) in kufic script, from Syria or Iraq. 9th century. Ink, pigments, and gold on vellum, 8⁵/₁₆ x 11¹/₂" (21.1 x 29.2 cm). The Metropolitan Museum of Art, New York
Rogers Fund, 1937 (37.99.2)

ISLAM AND THE PROPHET MUHAMMAD

Islam, meaning "submission [to the will of God]," originated in the Arabian peninsula in the seventh century. According to Islamic belief God (Allah) revealed his message to the archangel Gabriel who transmitted it to an Arab merchant, Muhammad. These revelations form the basis of the Islamic religion. Believers (Muslims) are those who submit to God and acknowledge Muhammad as his Prophet. Muslims also recognize earlier prophets—Moses, Abraham, Jesus—and share with Jews and Christians the belief in one God. Originally God's revelations were committed to memory and passed down orally, but after Muhammad's death an official transcription was made. The language of God—and the Koran ("recitation")—is Arabic.

The Prophet Muhammad was born about 570 in Mecca, a city in west-central Arabia. Mecca was the site of the Kaaba, an ancient, cube-shaped stone building believed to be the house Abraham built for God. Muhammad received his first revelations in 610 and soon thereafter was accepted as the Prophet of God by his friends and family. After failing to convert the local population, Muhammad and his companions were forced to emigrate in 622 to the oasis of Yathrib, which was renamed Medina, the [Prophet's] City. It is to this event, called the *hijra* (emigration), that Muslims date the beginning of their history. Muhammad regained control of Mecca in 630, and the inhabitants eventually accepted the new religion. The Kaaba in Mecca became Islam's sacred center, toward which Muslims around the world still face when praying. Muhammad died in Medina in 632. Only after his death was the Koran written down and assembled in 114 chapters, or *surahs*, each divided into verses, which make up the sacred scripture of Islam.

Muslims believe in a single, all-powerful God and in Muhammad as the last in the succession of true prophets. Islam also requires Muslims to follow the Five Pillars of Islam, sometimes symbolized by an open hand with five extended fingers. The most important pillar is the statement of faith, "There is no god but God and Muhammad is his messenger." The second pillar is ritual worship five times a day. (Muslims establish a direct, personal relationship with God through worship. The faithful prostrate themselves facing the Kaaba in Mecca.) The remaining pillars are charity to the poor, fasting during the month of Ramadan, and if possible, a pilgrimage to Mecca. Muslims participate in congregational worship and listen to a sermon at a **mosque** (prayer hall) on Friday.

The Prophet Muhammad and His Companions Traveling to the Fair, from a later copy of the *Siyar-i Nabi* (*Life of the Prophet*) of al-Zarir (14th century), Istanbul, Turkey. 1594
Pigments and gold on paper, 10⅝ x 15" (27 x 38 cm)
New York Public Library, New York
Spencer Collection

A sixteenth-century painting shows Muhammad traveling to a fair, accompanied by his father-in-law, Abu Bakr, and the warrior Ali, the husband of his daughter Fatima. After Muhammad's death, Abu Bakr became the first caliph, or successor to the Prophet. Ali became the fourth caliph. The power struggle that ended in Ali's death led to the division of Islamic communities into Sunni (traditional) and Shi'ite (followers of Ali) Muslims.

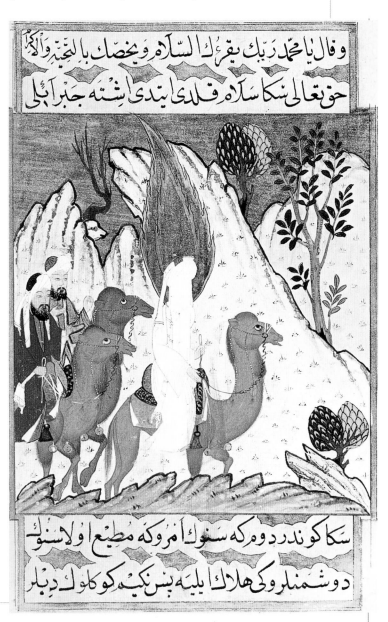

Koran exemplifies a style of kufic writing common from the eighth to tenth century (fig. 8-1). Red diacritical marks (pronunciation guides) accent the dark brown ink. Horizontal strokes are elongated, and fat-bodied letters are emphasized. This Koran is written on vellum, an especially fine parchment. Paper, a Chinese invention, was made in the Islamic world by the mid-eighth century but did not fully replace vellum and parchment until after the year 1000 (see "Indian Painting on Paper," page 214).

Under caliphs of the Umayyad dynasty (661–750) the political center of the Muslim world moved from the Arabian peninsula to the city of Damascus, in modern Syria. Inspired by the Roman and Byzantine architecture of the eastern Mediterranean, the Muslims became enthusiastic builders of shrines, **mosques**, and palaces. After Mecca and Medina, Jerusalem was the holiest site in Islam. In the center of the city rises the Haram al-Sharif (the Jewish temple mount), a rock outcrop that Muslims

8-2 **Dome of the Rock,** Jerusalem, Israel. Begun 692

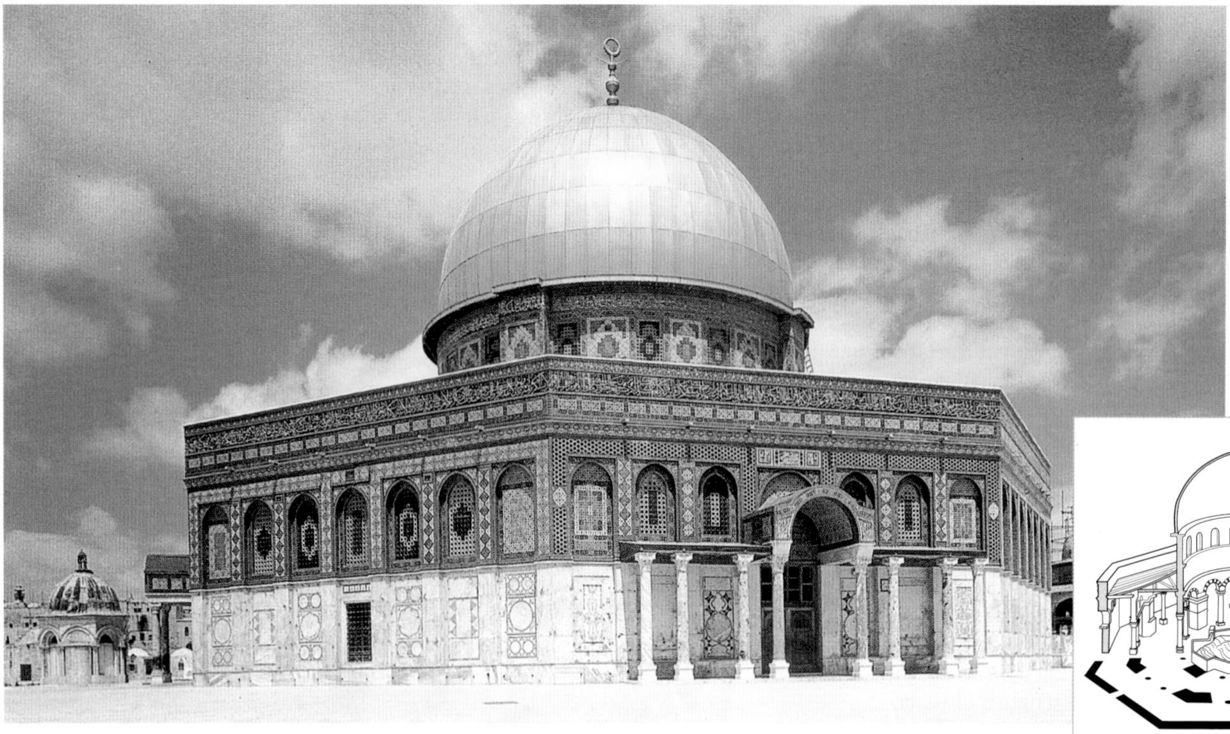

8-3

Cutaway drawing of the Dome of the Rock

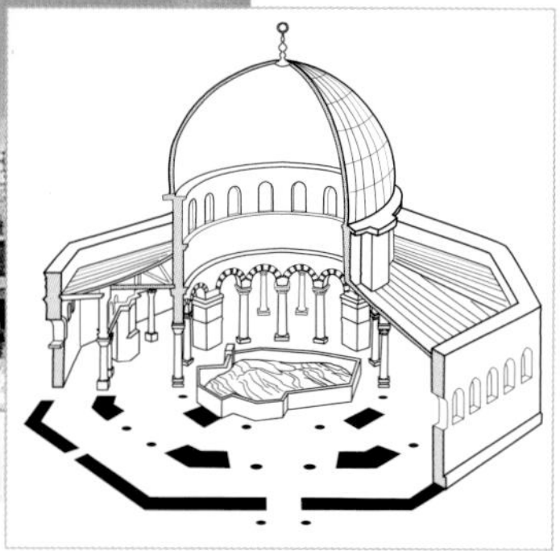

identify as the place from which Muhammad ascended to the presence of God on the Night Journey mentioned in chapter 17 of the Koran (fig. 8-2). The same rock face is also associated with the creation of Adam, the place where the patriarch Abraham prepared to sacrifice his son Isaac at the command of God, and the site of the temple of Solomon, making it important to Jews and Christians, as well as Muslims. In 692 the Umayyads constructed a shrine over the rock (fig. 8-3) using Syrian artisans trained in the Byzantine tradition. The Dome of the Rock is the oldest surviving Islamic building and is decorated on the interior with a mosaic frieze containing the earliest written text of the Koran. Its centralized octagonal plan is derived from both Byzantine and local Christian architecture. Muslim patrons and builders, however, delighted in complex mathematical forms; for example, the plan of the octagonal structure is based on the eight-pointed star, formed by two intersecting squares. The central space is covered by a dome on a tall drum supported by an arcade. Two concentric aisles enclose the rock (fig. 8-4).

Marble veneer at ground level and glass mosaics above decorate the building. Originally glass mosaics also covered the upper half of the octagon's outer walls. Although the lower part of the octagon walls retains its original white marble facings, inset with patterns in colored stone, they deteriorated over time. In the sixteenth century the Ottoman Sultan Suleyman ordered the mosaics replaced with magnificent, colorful ceramic tiles. Later Persian and Turkish builders used colorful tiles with consummate skill.

The Dome of the Rock is a special shrine. Mosques, in contrast, provide a place for regular public worship. Mosques (*masjid* in Arabic, a "place of prostration") may have several different plans (see "Mosque Plans," right), but they are usually entered through a courtyard, and they must have a large covered space to accommodate the community at Friday prayers. Mosques are oriented in the direction of Mecca (*qibla*), and worshippers arrange themselves in rows to pray facing Mecca. A niche called a **mihrab** identifies the *qibla* wall. The origin and significance of the *mihrab* are debated. A niche signifies a holy place in many religions: niches frame the sculpture of gods or ancestors in Roman architecture, form the shrine for the Torah scrolls in a synagogue, or the apse in a Christian Church. The *maqsura*, an enclosure in front of the *mihrab* for the ruler and other dignitaries, became a feature of the principal congregational mosque after an assassination attempt on a ruler. The *minbar*, or pulpit/throne, stands by the *mihrab* as a raised platform for the prayer leader and a symbol of his authority (for a fourteenth-century example, see fig. 8-12). The faithful gather for Friday prayers and listen to a sermon in the principal mosque of the city, called the Great Mosque or Friday Mosque (see fig. 8-10).

The earliest mosques were very simple, modeled on Muhammad's house with its courtyard and porticoes. The

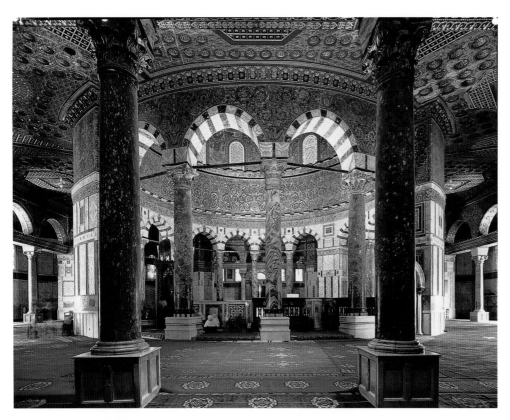

8-4

Dome of the Rock
Jerusalem, Israel
Interior. Begun 692

The gilt wooden beams
in the outer ambulatory
are not visible. The
carpets and ceiling are
modern but probably
reflect the original
patrons' intention.

Elements of Architecture

MOSQUE PLANS

The earliest mosques were **hypostyle halls** surrounding an open courtyard. Rows of closely spaced columns perpendicular to the **qibla** wall support a flat roof. The Great Mosque at Córdoba (see fig. 8-6) is typical.

The four-**iwan** mosque developed in Persia, and is seen in buildings like the Congregational Mosque at Isfahan (see fig. 8-11). *Iwans*—vaulted halls with monumental arched openings—faced each other across a central courtyard, and related structures spread out and behind the *iwans*.

Central-plan mosques, the last type to develop, were inspired by Istanbul's Byzantine architecture, such as the Church of Hagia Sophia in Istanbul (see fig. 7-13). The Selimiye Mosque in Edirne (see fig. 8-20) is characteristic. The large central dome permits the interior space to be uninterrupted by structural supports.

Plans are not to scale

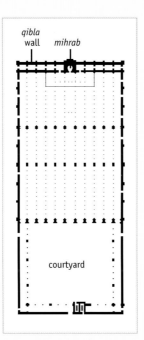

qibla wall   mihrab

courtyard

hypostyle mosque
Great Mosque, Córdoba

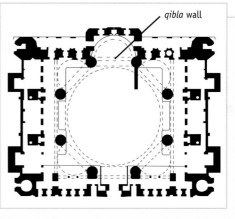

qibla wall

(*left*)
central-plan mosque
Selimiye Mosque, Edirne

(*right*)
four-*iwan* mosque
Congregational Mosque, Isfahan

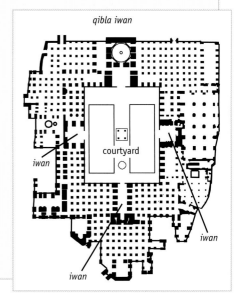

qibla iwan

courtyard

iwan

iwan

iwan

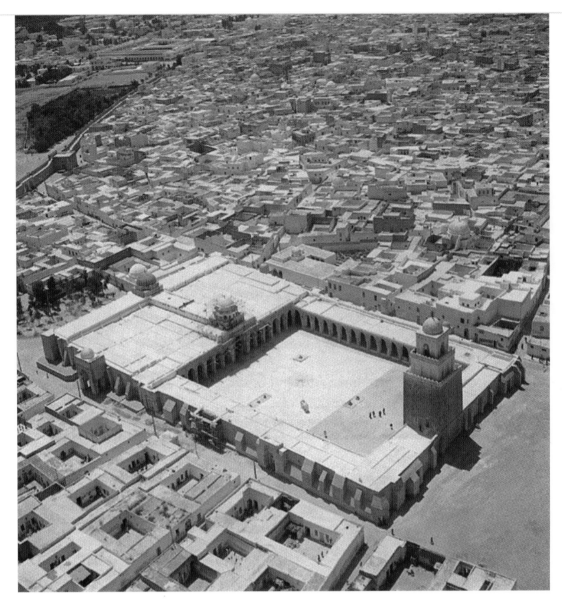

8-5 | **The Great Mosque.** Kairouan, Tunisia. 836–875

Prophet spoke to his followers from his raised seat. The Great Mosque of Kairouan, Tunisia (fig. 8-5), although built in the ninth century, reflects the early form of the mosque. Its large rectangular plan is divided between a courtyard and a hypostyle prayer hall with a flat roof. The system of repeated bays and aisles can easily be extended as the congregation grows in size. A huge tower (the **minaret**, from which criers call the faithful to prayer) rises opposite the *mihrab*. Later, one or more minarets came to symbolize Islam's presence in a city.

In 750, the Abbasids overthrew the Umayyads. Abbasid caliphs ruled the central and eastern lands of Islam until 1258 from their capitals at Baghdad and Samarra (in modern Iraq). Their long reign saw great achievements in medicine, mathematics, the natural sciences, philosophy, literature, music, and art.

While the Abbasids ruled the Muslim heartland, the Umayyads controlled the far West. In 750, when the Abbasid caliphs took power, a survivor of the Umayyad dynasty, Abd al-Rahman I, fled across North Africa into southern Spain (known as al-Andalus in Arabic). He established himself there as the provincial ruler, or emir (ruled 756–788). From a new capital at Córdoba, the Umayyads governed al-Andalus until 1031, first as emirs and then, beginning with Abd al-Rahman III (ruled 912–961), as caliphs. Iberian Umayyads set themselves up as equals to the Abbasids. Their court at Córdoba became a renowned center for scholars, scientists, poets, and musicians. They maintained close contacts not just with the Islamic world but also with European and Byzantine rulers.

The finest surviving example of Spanish Umayyad architecture (and the most accessible to Westerners) is the Great Mosque of Córdoba. This sprawling structure was begun on the site of a Christian church in 785 and was repeatedly enlarged. The marble columns and capitals in the first hypostyle prayer hall (fig. 8-6; see also "Mosque Plans," page 193) were recycled from the ruins of classical buildings in the region, formerly a wealthy Roman province. Two tiers of arches, one above the

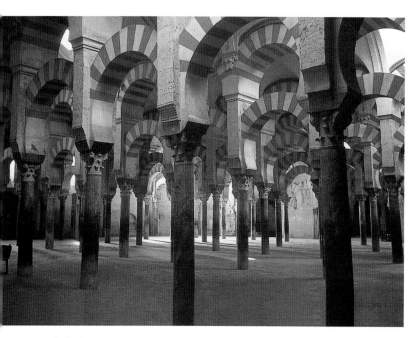

8-6 | **Prayer hall,** Great Mosque, Córdoba, Spain. Begun 785–86

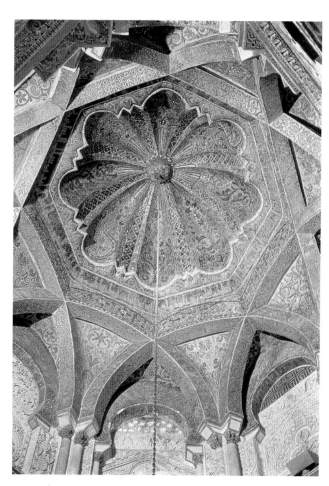

8-7 | **Dome in front of the *mihrab*,** Great Mosque. 965

other, surmount the columns. The double-tiered design increases the height of the interior space, stiffens the structure, and creates a light and airy impression. The distinctively shaped horseshoe arches—a form known from Roman times—came to be closely associated with Islamic architecture in the West. At the Great Mosque, these arches are distinguished by the alternation of pale stone voussoirs (wedge-shaped stone blocks) and red bricks. While the alternating colors and textures are decorative, the use of contrasting materials is also functional. The stone gives strength, and the brick lends flexibility and ease in achieving the circular form of the arch. Roman and Byzantine builders also used the technique, but usually in utilitarian structures like defensive walls. The Muslims saw the decorative possibilities of the technique and utilized it for purposes of ornamentation.

In the tenth century, Caliph al-Hakam II (ruled 961–976) commissioned luxurious renovations in the Great Mosque, including enlargements and a new *mihrab* with a richly decorated *maqsura*, the protected space for the ruler. In front of the *mihrab*, melon-shaped, ribbed domes seem to float over intersecting arches (fig. 8-7). The arches are placed diagonally over the corners of a space to provide a base for a dome whose surface is covered with arabesques, geometric motifs, and stylized vegetation and inscriptions. In conscious competition with the

Byzantines and the Abbasids, the Córdoban Umayyads employed mosaic decoration. Since the technique was not practiced in Spain, they acquired materials and the artisans from Byzantium to do the work.

Muslims in Spain had closer commercial and diplomatic associations with local Christians than with those in far-off Byzantium. After the Muslim conquest of Spain, Christians and Jews who did not convert to Islam but acknowledged the authority of the new rulers and paid the taxes required of non-Muslims were usually left free to follow their own religious practices. Christians in the Arab territories were called Mozarabs (from the Arabic *mustarib*, meaning "would-be Arab"). The conquest resulted in a rich exchange of artistic influences between the Islamic and Christian communities. Christian artists adapted many features of Islamic style to their traditional themes, creating a unique, colorful new style known today as Mozarabic.

In northern Spain, the antagonisms among Muslims, orthodox Christians, and the followers of various heretical Christian sects provided fertile material for theological debate. In the eighth century Beatus, abbot of the Monastery of San Martin at Liebana, defended the Christian position against heresy in influential commentaries on the New Testament Apocalypse (often combined with Jerome's commentary on the Old Testament Book

In a dazzling display of pure color, a peacocklike bird attacks a serpent. The painting is an **allegory** (representation of an abstract idea using specific objects or human figures) of the triumph of good over evil, Christ over Satan (fig. 8-8). The artists, who identified themselves as Emeterius and the nun Ende, painted in a style now called Mozarabic. Mozarabs were Christians living under Muslim rule in the Iberian peninsula; Mozarabic art combines Christian and Muslim styles. Christians and Muslims lived together not only in Spain, but also in the Holy Land, where Christians, Muslims, and Jews all laid claim to the same territory—especially to Jerusalem—as sacred to their faiths.

The dominance of decoration in Muslim art—pure line and color—over visual naturalism (where the physical appearance of the rendered image in nature is the primary inspiration) can be seen in the way the serpent is represented as a glittering, curling ribbon, and the bird as a series of red and yellow-bordered green shapes set against brilliant pen work. The tree, with its symmetrical pattern of branches, leaves, and birds seems plucked from a carpet. The illusion of nature, so prized in Greek and Roman art, has disappeared— replaced by a manner of expression based on decorative, geometric pattern. Yet the text tells us that the peacock represents Christ.

Some people argued that since God had chosen to take on a visible human shape, the representation of material forms must be justifiable, but others said that God spoke to Moses rather than revealing himself in material form (and through the archangel when communicating with Muhammad). Thus, words but not images should be treasured, glorified, and adorned. These different points of view led to dramatically different attitudes toward art. The natural and the decorative came together in the paintings by Emeterius and Ende in tenth-century Spain.

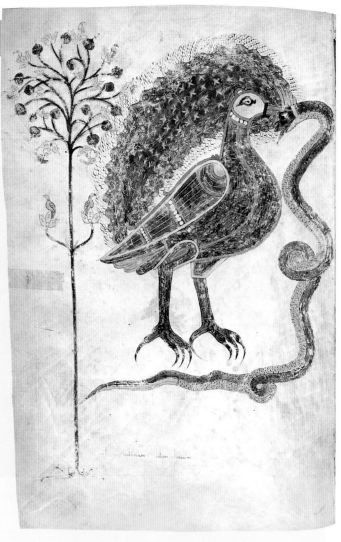

8-8 **Emeterius** and **Ende, with the scribe Senior. Page with *Battle of the Bird and the Serpent*** *Commentary on the Apocalypse* by Beatus and *Commentary on Daniel* by Jerome, made for Abbot Dominicus, probably at the Monastery of San Salvador at Tábara, León, Spain. Completed July 6, 975 Tempera on parchment, 15¾ x 10¼" (40 x 26 cm) Cathedral Library, Gerona, Spain
MS 7[11], fol. 18v

of Daniel). His description of the final fiery destruction of evil and the triumph of Christianity provided artists with a rich source of imagery when they copied and illuminated the text. A copy of Beatus's *Commentary*, according to its **colophon** (notes on the production at the end of a manuscript), was made for Abbot Dominicus under the direction of the scribe Senior, with paintings by Emeterius and the nun Ende, who finished the work in the year 975 in the monastery of San Salvador at Tabara, Leon. Ende—referred to in the colophon as "painter and servant of God"—is the first woman artist whose work is identified. Ende and Emeterius brilliantly illustrate a metaphorical description of the triumph of Christ over Satan (fig. 8-8).

Arabic calligraphy was used decoratively not only on architecture and in manuscripts but also on all kinds of functional objects, such as bowls and platters. Kufic-style letters decorate the ceramics made in the ninth and tenth centuries, even in distant centers like Nishapur (in modern northeastern Iran) and Samarkand (in modern Uzbekistan in Central Asia). Now known as Samarkand ware, these pieces are characterized by a clear lead glaze applied over a black inscription on a white, slip-painted ceramic ground (fig. 8-9). The script has been elongated to fill the bowl's rim, stressing the letters' verticality. The inscription translates: "Knowledge, the beginning of it is bitter to taste, but the end is sweeter than honey." Inscriptions on Samarkand ware provide a storehouse of such popular sayings and folk wisdom.

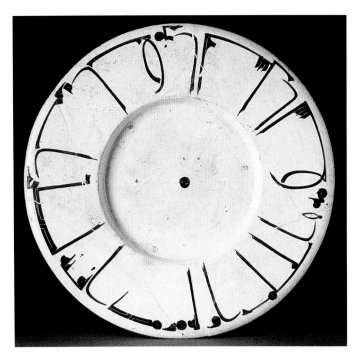

8-9 | **Bowl with kufic border,** Samarkand, Uzbekistan. 9th–10th century. Earthenware with slip, pigment, and glaze, diameter 14½" (37 cm). Musée du Louvre, Paris

The white ground of this piece imitated prized Chinese porcelains made of fine white kaolin clay. Samarkand was connected to the Silk Road (see Chapter 3), the great caravan route to China, and was influenced by Chinese culture.

Later Islamic Art

In the eleventh century, power in the Islamic world fell into the hands of more or less independent regional rulers. As the Abbasid caliphate disintegrated, one branch of the Seljuks, a Turkic people who converted to Islam in the tenth century, rose to power. They gained control of Persia in 1038–40 and took over the Abbasid capital city of Baghdad in 1055, where the Abbasids survived as token rulers until 1258. In 1071 Seljuk Turks defeated the Byzantine army and soon held most of the western Mediterranean including Anatolia (modern Turkey). In the west, Umayyad Spain broke up into small kingdoms centered around major cities such as Saragossa, Málaga, Granada, and Seville. They engaged in constant warfare with Christian armies, determined to expel them from the Iberian peninsula. This military action (or reconquest as the Christians call it) continued over a 400-year period, ending only in 1492 with the overthrow of the Nasrid dynasty in the Kingdom of Granada.

The Seljuk rulers proved themselves enlightened patrons of the arts. They built on a grand scale—mosques, *madrasas* (schools for advanced study), palaces, and hostels and trading stations for merchants. They adopted the Persian *iwan,* a vaulted open room (see "Mosque Plans," page 193), and they perfected a mosque/*madrasas* plan in which four *iwans* are arranged around a courtyard. The Great Mosque in the Seljuk capital of Isfahan (in modern Iran) has a four-*iwan* plan (fig. 8-10). The *qibla iwan* on the south was vaulted with *muqarnas* (nichelike cells) in the fourteenth century. The tall, slender minarets and brilliant blue tiles were added in the seventeenth century.

Tile work—another highlight of Islamic art—can be seen in a fourteenth-century tile mosaic *mihrab* originally from a

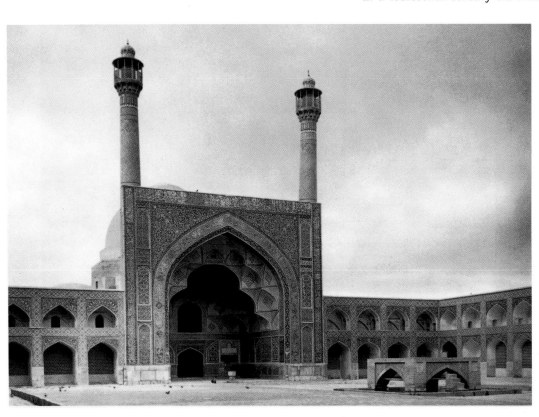

8-10 | **Courtyard, Masjid-i Jami** (Great Mosque), Isfahan Persia (Iran) 11th–18th century View from the northeast

8-11 | **Tile mosaic *Mihrab*, from the Madrasa Imami,** Isfahan, Persia (Iran). c. 1354 (restored). Glazed and cut ceramic, 11'3" x 7'6" (3.43 x 2.29 m). The Metropolitan Museum of Art, New York

Harris Brisbane Dick Fund (39.20)

One of the three Koranic inscriptions on this *mihrab* dates it to approximately 1354. Note the combination of decorated kufic (inner inscription) and cursive *muhaqqaq* (outer inscription) scripts. The outer inscription tells of the duties of believers and the heavenly rewards for the builders of mosques. The next (kufic) gives the Five Pillars of Islam. The center panel says: "The mosque is the house of every pious person."

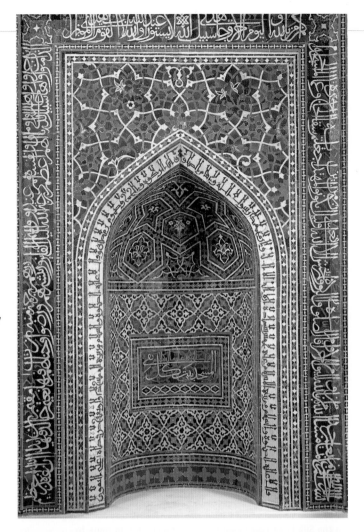

8-12 | ***Qibla* wall with *mihrab* and *minbar*,** main *iwan* (vaulted chamber) in a mosque, Sultan Hasan *madrasa*-mausoleum-mosque, Cairo Egypt. 1356–63

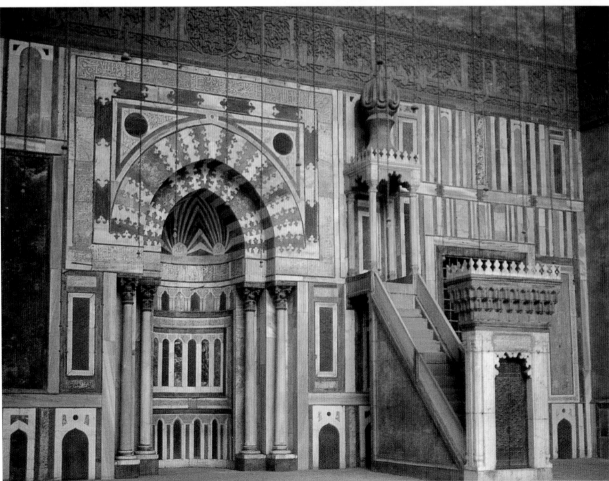

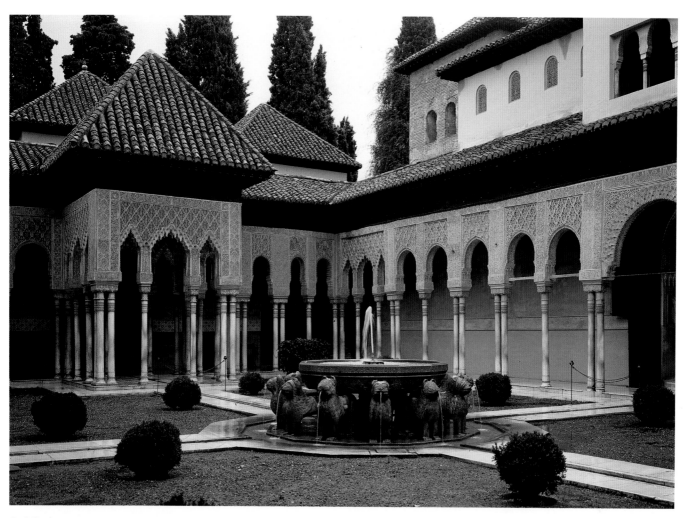

8-13 | **Court of the Lions,** Palace of the Lions (Palacio de los Leones), Alhambra, Granada, Spain. Begun c. 1380

Granada, with its ample water supply, had long been known as a city of gardens. The twelve stone lions in the fountain in the center of this court were salvaged from the ruins of an earlier palatial complex on the Alhambra hill. The earlier structure was begun in the late eleventh century by a high Granadan official of Jewish heritage named Samuel ibn Naghralla and completed by his son Yusuf in the early twelfth century. Commentators of the time praised this complex, with its pools, fountains, and gardens. No doubt it was a source of inspiration for the builders of the later palaces.

madrasa in Isfahan (fig. 8-11). More than 11 feet tall, it was made by painstakingly cutting each piece of tile, including the pieces making up the calligraphy on the curving surface of the niche and laying them side by side in mortar. The harmonious, dense patterns include organic and geometric forms that contrast with the inscriptions. The colors—white against turquoise and cobalt blue with accents of dark yellow and green—are characteristic.

In a *madrasa*-mausoleum-mosque complex built in the mid-fourteenth century by the Mamluk Sultan Hasan in Cairo, Egypt, *iwans* functioned as classrooms with students housed in neighboring rooms (fig. 8-12). The largest of the four *iwans* serves as the mosque for the entire complex. Hasan's domed tomb lies behind the *qibla* wall. The walls and vaults inside the mosque are plain except for a wide stucco frieze. Originally painted, this frieze combines calligraphy and intricate carved scrollwork. Marble panels cover the *qibla* wall and a double-arched *mihrab*. Slender columns support pointed arches. Marble inlays create blue, red, and white stripes on the voussoirs, a fanciful echo of the

brick and stone voussoirs of Umayyad architecture. The throne-like *minbar* at the right of the *mihrab* is of carved stone, although the door is elaborately carved wood.

Muslim architects also created luxurious palaces set in beautiful gardens, such as the well-preserved medieval palace in Granada, Spain. The Alhambra, a fortified hilltop palace complex, was the home of the Nasrids, who ruled the provinces of Almería, Málaga, and Granada from 1232 to 1492. The Alhambra gained its present form in the fourteenth century. The builders combined a fortress, royal residences, and city, including mosques, baths, servants' quarters, barracks, stables, workshops, and a mint. The Alhambra extends for about half a mile along the crest of a high hill overlooking Granada.

An especially luxurious section of the palace is the Palace of the Lions, a private retreat built by Muhammad V (ruled 1362–1391). At its heart is the rectangular Court of the Lions (fig. 8-13), named for a fountain whose basin is supported by stone lions. The patio is surrounded by small richly decorated rooms. Although the central courtyard is filled with sand today,

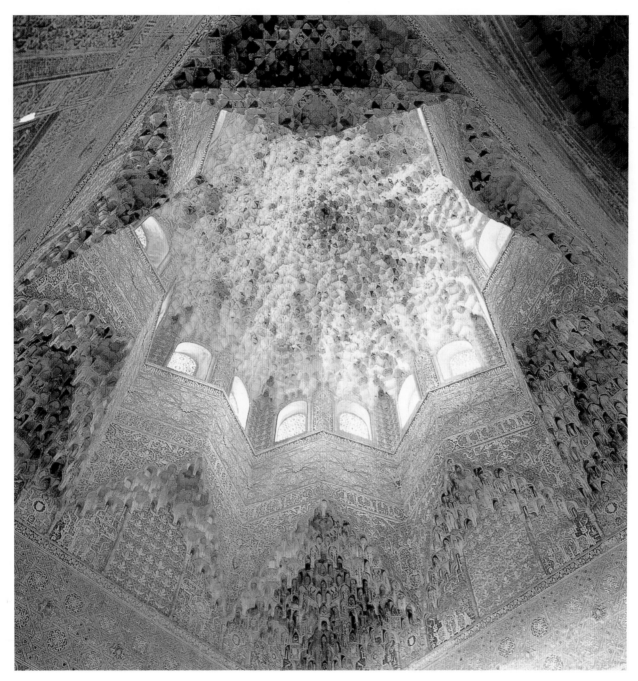

8-14 | *Muqarnas* **dome,** Hall of the Abencerrajes, Palace of the Lions

it was originally a sunken garden with raised fountains and waterways. Aromatic shrubs, flowers, and small citrus trees were planted between the water channels that radiate from the fountain and divide the courtyard into quarters evocative of the rivers of paradise. The architectural focus of the Alhambra was largely directed inward, toward these lushly planted courtyards, which embody the Muslim vision of paradise as a well-watered, walled garden. Indeed, the English word *paradise* comes from *pairidiz*, the old Persian term for an enclosed park.

Pavilions used for living and the performance of music and poetry open onto the Court of the Lions. One of these, the so-called Hall of the Abencerrajes, on the south side (probably a music room) is covered by a spectacularly intricate ceiling (fig. 8-14). The star-shaped dome rests on clusters of small squinches or nichelike cells (*muqarnas*) and a honeycomb of *muqarnas* also covers the dome. The effect is like architectural lace. Here the material form becomes an immaterial illusion of heavenly light.

In this cosmopolitan Islamic society not only palaces but portable objects made with exquisite craftsmanship were valued for their beauty and usefulness, and for the status they bestowed on their owners. Glass, made with the most ordinary

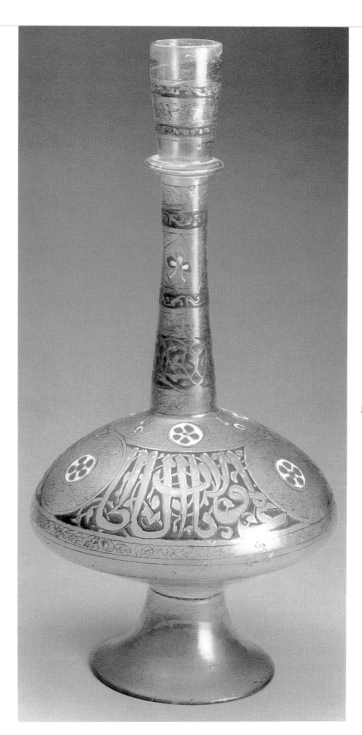

8-15 **Bottle,** from Syria. Mid-14th century. Blown glass with enamels and gilding, 19¹⁄₂" x 9³⁄₄" (49.7 x 24.8 cm). Freer Gallery of Art, Smithsonian Institution, Washington, D.C. Purchase, F1934.20

ingredients—sand and ash—is the most ethereal of materials. According to the twelfth-century poet al-Hariri, glass is "congealed of air, condensed of sunbeam motes, molded of the light of the open plain, or peeled from a white pearl" (cited in Jenkins, page 3). Glassmakers generally adapted earlier practices to new forms for the tools, and techniques of making glass have changed very little. A tall, elegant enameled bottle from the mid-fourteenth century exemplifies their skill in the application of enameled decoration in gold and various colors (fig. 8-15). Probably made in a Syrian workshop, it bears a large inscription in cursive script naming and honoring its owner, a sultan

from Yemen. The five-petaled red rosette is an insignia of the Yemeni dynasty.

Like glassmakers, metalworkers inherited the techniques of their Roman, Byzantine, and Sassanian predecessors, applying their artistic heritage to new forms. Educated leaders administering the lands for caliphs and emirs commissioned pieces in glass, metal, ivory, and precious stones. Personalized containers for pens, ink, and blotting sand became emblems of their class. According to its inscription, one such container, an inlaid brass box, belonged to Majd al-Mulk al-Muzaffar, the grand vizier (chief minister) of Khurasan in the early thirteenth century

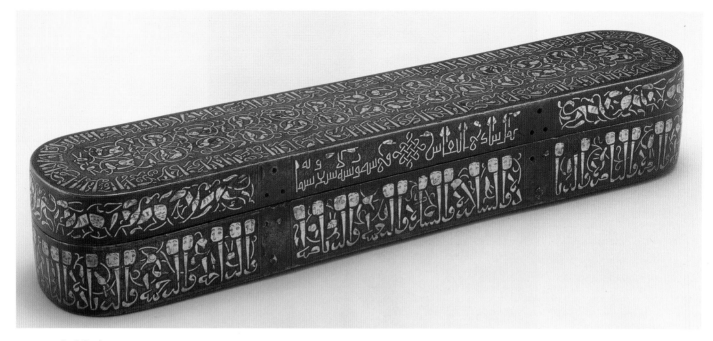

8-16 | **Shazi. Pen box,** from Persia (Iran). 1210–11. Side with inscription: brass inlaid with silver, copper, and black organic material, height 2", length 12⅝", width 2½" (5 x 31.4 x 6.4 cm). Freer Gallery of Art, Smithsonian Institution Washington, D.C.
Purchase (F1936.7)
(See pages 188–89 for clasp side.)

The inscriptions on the box include some twenty honorific phrases extolling its owner, Majd al-Mulk al-Muzaffar. The inscription in naskhi script on the lid calls him the "luminous star of Islam." The largest inscription, written in animated naskhi (an animated script is one with human or animal forms in it), asked twenty-four blessings for him from God. Shazi, the designer of the box, signed and dated it in animated kufic script on the side of the lid, making it one of the earliest signed works in Islamic art. Majd al-Mulk enjoyed his box for only ten years; he was killed by Mongol invaders in 1221.

(fig. 8-16). An artist named Shazi cast, engraved, embossed, and inlaid the box with consummate skill. Scrolls, interlacing designs, and human and bird heads enliven its calligraphic inscriptions. All these elements, animate as well as inanimate, seem to be engaged in a lively exchange. That a work of such quality was made of brass rather than a costlier metal may seem surprising. A severe silver shortage in the mid-twelfth century may have prompted the development of inlaid brass pieces like this one that used the more precious metal sparingly. Humbler plain brass ware would have been available in the marketplace to those of more modest means than the vizier.

The art of book production also flourished in Muslim countries. Islam's emphasis on the study of the Koran created a high level of literacy among both women and men in Muslim societies. Books on a wide range of secular as well as religious subjects were available, although even books copied on paper were fairly costly. Libraries, often associated with *madrasas*, were endowed by members of the educated elite. Books made for royal patrons had luxurious bindings and highly embellished pages, the result of workshop collaboration between noted calligraphers and illuminators. New scripts were developed for new literary forms.

In addition to religious works, scribes copied and recopied famous secular texts—scientific treatises, manuals of all kinds, fiction, and especially poetry. Painters supplied illustrations for these books, and they later created individual small-scale paintings—miniatures—that were collected by the wealthy and placed in albums. One of the great royal centers of miniature painting was at Herat (in modern Afghanistan). A school of painting and calligraphy was founded there in the early fifteenth century under the cultured patronage of the Timurid dynasty (1370–1507).

Prince Baysonghur held court in Herat. A great patron of painting and calligraphy, he commissioned superb illuminated manuscripts. The story of the Sassanian prince Bahram Gur, who married seven princesses, one for each night of the week, had been told in poems by the twelfth-century Persian mystic poet Nizami. The painting of *Bahram Gur with the Indian Princess in her Black Pavilion* illustrates the lyrical idealism that characterized the Timurid style (fig. 8-17). Although the scene takes place at night, the colors are clear and bright without a trace of shadow. The night sky with stars and moon and the two tall candles in the pavilion signal the viewer that night has fallen. The interior of the black pavilion is decorated with brilliant blue tiles, and through a central opening a garden in bloom can be seen. In the foreground a stream of silver water runs into a silver pool (however the silver has now tarnished to black). The viewpoint shifts: the pavilion, tiled walls and step, the huge pillow, and the items on trays are seen straight on, while the floor, pool, platform, and bed are seen from a **bird's-eye view**. Obviously, the artists delight-

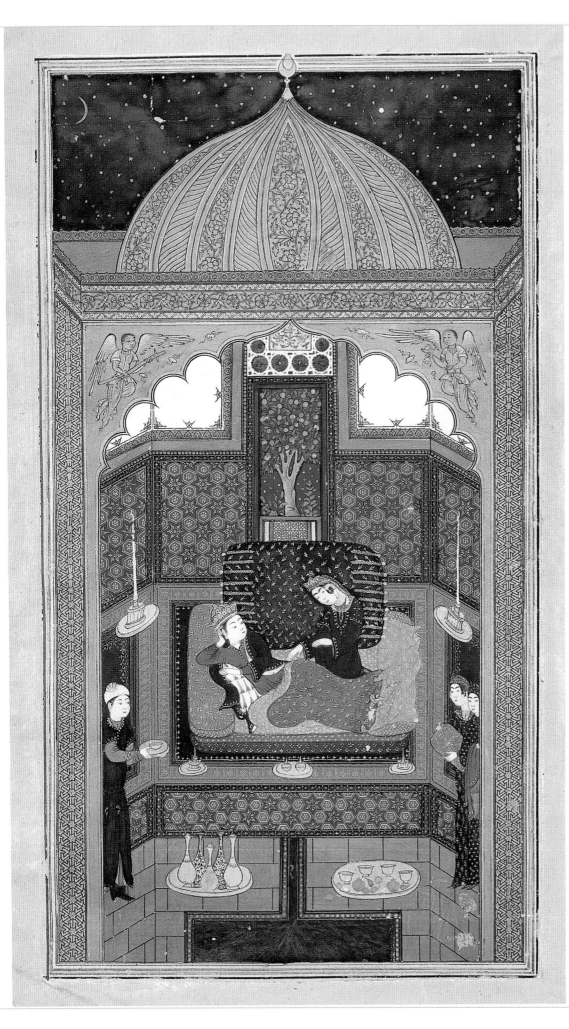

8-17

Bahram Gur with the Indian Princess in Her Black Pavilion
Folio 23 from a
Haft Paykar (*Seven Portraits*), by Nizami
15th century. Herat
Afghanistan. c. 1426
Color and gilt on
paper, height 8⁵/₈",
width 4⁵/₈"
(20.9 x 11.7 cm)
The Metropolitan
Museum of Art
New York

Gift of Alexander Smith
Cochran, 1913
(13.227.13)

stretching from Afghanistan to Delhi. Later Akbar (ruled 1556–1605), the third ruler, extended Mughal control over most of northern India. His grandson Shah Jahan (ruled 1628–1658) unified the empire.

Probably no one had more impact on the arts than the emperor Akbar. Known as a dynamic, humane, and just leader, Akbar loved the arts, especially painting. He created an imperial workshop of painters, which he placed under the direction of two artists from the Persian court. Learning from these masters, the Mughal painters soon transformed the lyrical, idealized Persian styles into a vigorous, naturalistic style.

One of the most famous and extraordinary works produced in Akbar's **atelier** is an illustrated manuscript of the *Hamza-nama*, a Persian classic about the adventures of Hamza, uncle of the Prophet Muhammad. Painted on cotton cloth, each illustration is more than 2½ feet high. The entire project gathered 1,400 illustrations into twelve volumes and took fifteen years to complete.

One illustration shows Hamza's spies scaling a fortress wall and surprising some men as they sleep (fig. 8-18). One man climbs a rope, another has already beheaded a figure in yellow and lifts his head aloft—realistic details characteristic of Mughal painting. The architecture, viewed from a slightly elevated vantage point, provides a three-dimensional setting, yet the sense of depth is boldly undercut by the flat geometric patterns of the tile work. The energy exuded by the large human figures is also characteristic of painting under Akbar—even the sleepers seem active. This robust naturalistic figure style contrasts with the decorative linear qualities derived from Persian painting.

Nearly as prominent as the architectural setting with its vivid human adventure is the sensuous landscape in the foreground, where monkeys, foxes, and birds inhabit a grove of trees that shimmer and glow against the darkened background. The treatment of the gold-edged leaves at first calls to mind the patterned geometry of the tilework, but a closer look reveals a skillful naturalism born of careful observation. Each tree species is carefully distinguished by the shape of its trunk and leaves and its overall form. Pink and blue rocks with lumpy, softly outlined forms add still further interest to this painting, whose every inch is full of intriguing details.

Mughal architects were the heirs to a 300-year-old tradition of Islamic building using arches and domes. (Earlier architecture in the subcontinent used primarily post-and-lintel construction.) The Mughals also benefited from the native virtuosity in stone carving. The Mughal style culminated in the most famous of all Indian Islamic structures, the Taj Mahal. The Taj Mahal is sited on the river bank at Agra in northern India. Built between 1632 and 1648, it was commissioned by the emperor Shah Jahan as a mausoleum for his wife. Shah Jahan may have taken a major part in overseeing the tomb's design and construction.

Visually, the Taj Mahal never fails to impress (fig. 8-19). As visitors enter through a monumental, hall-like gate, the tomb looms before them across a spacious garden set with long reflecting pools. Measuring some 1,000 by 1,900 feet, the garden is unobtrusively divided into quadrants planted with trees

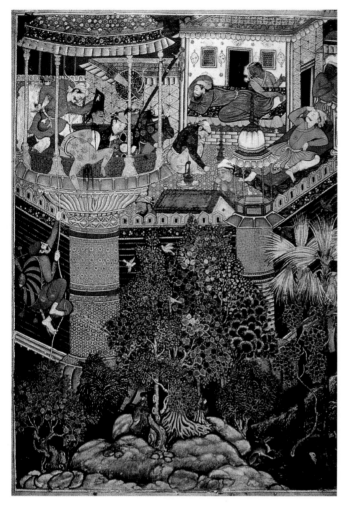

8-18 | **Page with *Hamza's Spies Scale the Fortress*** from the *Hamza-nama*, North India. Mughal period, Mughal, reign of Akbar, c. 1567–82 Gouache on cotton, 30 x 24" (76 x 61 cm) Museum of Applied Arts, Vienna

ed in the representation of intricate decorative details, especially the tiles, fabrics, and the garden foliage. The amorous couple and their servants with their round, impassive faces become part of the idealized world of Persian miniatures.

THE MUGHAL EMPIRE

Islam first touched the Indian subcontinent in the eighth century, when Arab armies captured a small territory near the Indus River. In the eleventh century the Turks began a war of conquest, and by the beginning of the thirteenth century Turkic dynasties ruled portions of the subcontinent from the northern city of Delhi. Although these early dynasties left their mark, it was in the sixteenth and seventeenth centuries that the Mughals made a lasting impression on Indian art.

The Mughals originally came from Central Asia. The first Mughal emperor, Babur (ruled 1526–1530) conquered an empire

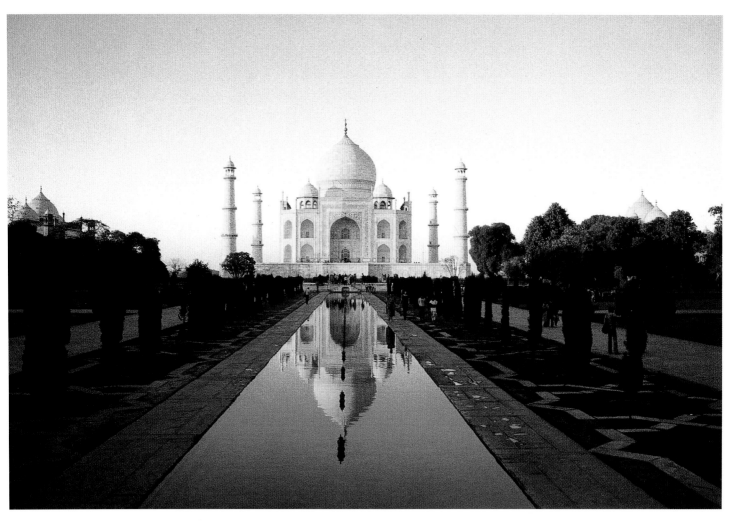

8-19 | **Taj Mahal,** Agra, India. Mughal period, Mughal, reign of Shah Jahan, c. 1632–48

and flowers and framed by broad walkways of stone inlaid in geometric patterns. In Shah Jahan's time, fruit trees and cypresses—symbolic of life and death—lined the walkways, and fountains played in the shallow pools. Truly, the senses were beguiled in this earthly evocation of paradise.

A lucid geometric symmetry pervades the entire design. Each facade of the main structure is identical, with a central *iwan* flanked by two stories of smaller *iwans*. By creating voids in the facades, these *iwans* contribute to the building's sense of weightlessness. The dome rises gracefully on its drum, allowing the swelling curves and lyrical lines of its beautifully proportioned, surprisingly large form to emerge with perfect clarity. Four minarets surround the central structure, each crowned with a pavilion. Traditional embellishments of Indian palaces, these pavilions quickly passed into the vocabulary of Islamic architec-

ture in India. Four more pavilions, this time on the roof, create a visual transition to the lofty dome.

The pristine surfaces of the Taj Mahal are embellished with utmost subtlety. The sides of the platform are carved in relief with a blind arcade motif, and carved relief panels of flowers adorn the base of the building. The portals are framed with verses from the Koran inlaid in black marble, while the spandrels are decorated with floral arabesques inlaid in colored semiprecious stones. Not strong enough to detract from the overall purity of the white marble, the embellishments enliven the surfaces of this impressive yet delicate masterpiece.

THE OTTOMAN EMPIRE

In the early fourteenth century the Ottoman Turks replaced the Seljuks in northwestern Anatolia. The Ottomans eventually

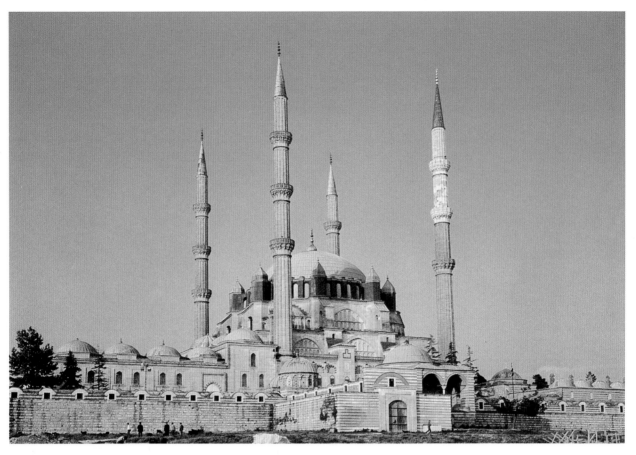

8-20 | **Sinan. Selimiye Cami (Mosque of Selim),** Edirne, Turkey. 1570–74

The minarets that pierce the sky around the prayer hall of this mosque, their sleek, fluted walls and needle-nosed spires soaring to more than 295 feet, are only 12½ feet in diameter at the base, an impressive feat of engineering. Only royal mosques were permitted multiple minarets, and more than two was highly unusual.

conquered most of the Eastern Mediterranean, Egypt, and the Sudan, as well as the Balkans in eastern Europe. In 1453 they captured Constantinople (renaming it Istanbul) and brought the Byzantine Empire to an end. The Church of Hagia Sophia (see fig. 7-11) became a mosque framed by graceful Ottoman minarets. The church's mosaics were destroyed or whitewashed over. The huge discs with the names of God, Muhammad, and the early caliphs were added to the interior in the mid-nineteenth century (see fig. 7-13). At present, Hagia Sophia is neither a church nor a mosque, but a state museum.

Inspired by this great Byzantine structure, Ottoman architects developed the domed, **central-plan** mosque (see "Mosque Plans," page 193). The finest example of this new form was the work of the architect Sinan (c. 1489–1588). Sinan began his career in the army and was chief engineer during the Ottoman campaign and siege of Vienna (1526–29). He rose through the ranks to become, in 1528, chief architect for Suleyman "the Magnificent," the tenth Ottoman sultan (ruled 1520–1566). Suleyman's reign marked the height of Ottoman power, and the sultan

sponsored a building program on a scale not seen since the days of the Roman Empire. Sinan's crowning accomplishment, completed about 1579, when he was over eighty, was a mosque he designed in the provincial capital of Edirne for Suleyman's son Selim II (ruled 1566–1574) (fig. 8-20). The gigantic hemispheric dome that tops this structure is more than 102 feet in diameter, larger than the dome of Hagia Sophia, as Sinan proudly pointed out. The dome crowns a building of great geometric complexity on the exterior and complete coherence on the interior, a space at once soaring and serene. In addition to the mosque, the complex housed a *madrasa* and other educational buildings, a burial ground, a hospital, and charity kitchens, as well as the income-producing covered market and baths. Framed by the vertical lines of four minarets and raised on a platform at the city's edge, the Selimiye mosque dominates the skyline.

A combination of abstract setting and realistic figures and details characterizes Ottoman manuscript painting. Painters often combined the decorative aspects of the painting with an intense religious feeling, as in the painting of Muhammad (see

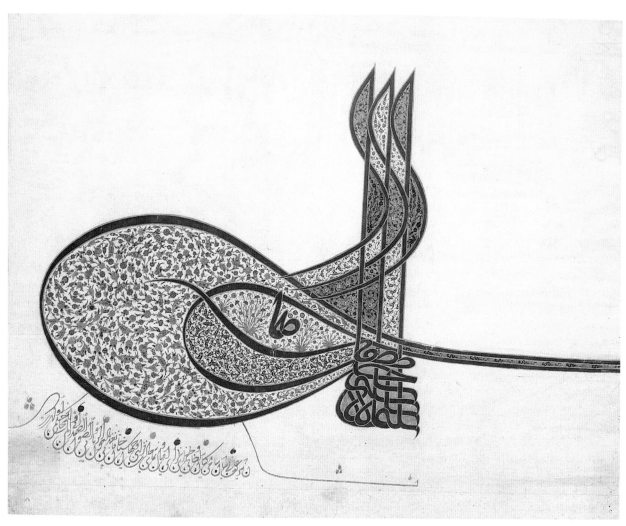

8-21 | **Illuminated *tughra* of Sultan Suleyman,** from Istanbul, Turkey. c. 1555. Ink, colors, and gold on paper, removed from a *firman* (official document) and trimmed to 20¹/₂ x 25³/₈" (52.1 x 64.5 cm). The Metropolitan Museum of Art, New York
Rogers Fund, 1938 (38.149.1)

"Islam and the Prophet Muhammad," page 191) where the Prophet appears as a white, wraithlike shadow under a flaming "halo," riding a realistic camel through a stylized landscape. At the Ottoman court of Sultan Suleyman in Istanbul, the imperial workshops produced even more remarkable illuminated manuscripts.

Following a practice begun by the Seljuks and Mamluks, the Ottomans put calligraphy to political use, developing the design of imperial ciphers—*tughras*—into a specialized art form. Ottoman *tughras* combined the ruler's name with the title Khan ("lord"), his father's name, and the motto "Eternally Victorious" into a monogram. Symbolizing the authority of the sultan, *tughras* appeared on seals, coins, and buildings, as well as on official documents. Suleyman issued hundreds of edicts, and a high court official supervised specialist calligraphers and illuminators who produced documents that required particularly elaborate *tughras*. The *tughra* shown here (fig. 8-21) is from a document endowing a charitable institution in Jerusalem that had been established by Suleyman's wife, Sultana Hurrem.

Tughras were drawn in black or blue ink with three long, vertical strokes (*tug* means "horsetail") to the right of two concentric horizontal teardrops. Decorative foliage patterns fill the spaces. *Tughras* required great skill to execute. The sweeping, fluid lines had to be drawn with perfect control according to set proportions, and a mistake meant starting over. The color scheme of the delicate floral **interlace** enclosed in the body of the *tughra* may have been inspired by Chinese blue-and-white ceramics, and similar designs appear on Ottoman ceramics and textiles. The Ottoman *tughra* is a sophisticated merging of abstraction with naturalism, boldness with delicacy, political power with informed patronage, and function—both utilitarian and symbolic—with adornment.

For many years the largest and most powerful political entity in the Islamic world, the Ottoman Empire lasted until the end of World War I. It was not until 1918 that the modern country of Turkey was founded in Anatolia, the former heart of the empire and the Arabic script used to write Ottoman was replaced by the Latin alphabet.

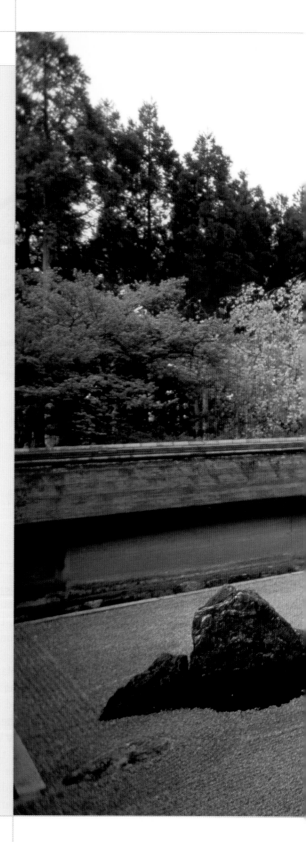

Elegant simplicity—profound and personal—was the result of disciplined meditation coupled with manual labor, as practiced in the Zen Buddhism introduced into Japan in the late twelfth century. Zen monasteries aimed at self-sufficiency. Monks were expected to be responsible for their physical as well as spiritual needs. Consequently, the performance of simple tasks—weeding the garden, cooking meals, mending garments—became occasions for meditation in the search for enlightenment. Zen monks turned to their gardens not as the focus of detached viewing and meditation but as the objects of constant vigilance and work—pulling weeds, tweaking unruly shoots, and raking the gravel of the dry gardens. This philosophy profoundly influenced Japanese art. An intimate relationship with nature pervades the later art of Asia, whether inspired by Buddhist, Hindu, or Shinto belief.

The dry landscape gardens of Japan (*karesansui*, literally "dried up mountains and water") exist in perfect harmony with Zen Buddhism. In front of the abbot's quarters in the Zen temple of Ryoan-ji, a flat rectangle of raked gravel, about 30 by 70 feet, surrounds fifteen stones of different sizes in islands of moss. The stones are set in asymmetrical groups of two, three, and five. Low, plaster-covered walls establish the garden's boundaries, but beyond the perimeter wall, maple, pine, and cherry trees add color and texture to the scene. Called "borrowed scenery," these elements are an important part of the design although they grow outside the garden.

Dry gardens began to be built in the fifteenth and sixteenth centuries in Japan. By the sixteenth century, Chinese landscape painting influenced the gardens' composition, and miniature clipped plants and beautiful stones re-created famous paintings of trees and mountains. Especially fine and unusual stones were even stolen and carried off as war booty, such was the cultural value of these seemingly simple places.

The Kyoto garden's design, as we see it today, probably dates from the mid-seventeenth century, since earlier written sources refer only to cherry trees, not to a garden. By the time this garden was created, such stone and gravel gardens had become highly intellectualized, abstract reflections of nature. This garden has been interpreted as representing islands in the sea, or mountain peaks rising above the clouds, perhaps even a swimming tigress with her cubs, or constellations of stars and planets. All or none of these interpretations may be equally satisfying— or irrelevant—to a monk seeking clarity of mind through contemplation.

Stone and gravel garden, Ryoan-ji
Kyoto. Muromachi period, c. 1480
(See pages 224, 226.)

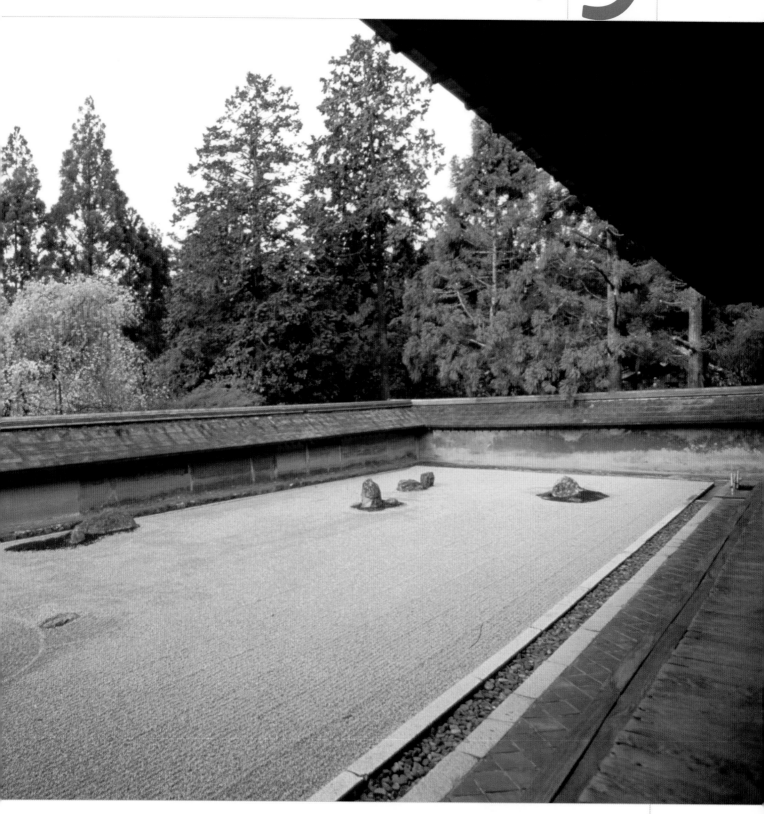

The long Indian Medieval period (c. 650–1526) was a time of transition in the South Asian subcontinent (see Map 3, page 231). Buddhism declined as a cultural force, while artistic achievements under Hinduism soared. The monumental architecture of Hindu temples was rich in symbolism and ritual function, with each region of India developing its own variation. Later Turkic people carried Islam to the subcontinent, and Muslim art added to the rich mix of styles on the Indian subcontinent, especially in the north. Islamic influence reached its height under the Mughals (1526–1857).

During roughly the same period that Hinduism began to displace Buddhism in India, Buddhism reached its height in China under the Tang dynasty (618–907) (see Chapter 3). Reaction to this flowering of a foreign religion on Chinese soil began during the late Tang and continued under the Song dynasty (960–1279), when openness to foreign influence gave way to greater cultivation of China's own traditions, including the revival of Confucianism. Landscape emerged as the most important theme and was used to express both philosophical and personal concerns.

Introduced from India by way of China and Korea, Buddhism was an important force in Japanese culture by the beginning of the Heian period (794–1185). New forms of Buddhism evolved: first Esoteric Buddhism and Pure Land Buddhism, and later, Zen. By the end of the fourteenth century, Zen Buddhism began to influence many aspects of Japanese life and culture, and soon Zen beliefs were expressed in sophisticated painting and calligraphy.

The South Asian Subcontinent

As Hinduism with its many gods and varied sects flourished in the Indian subcontinent, temple architecture developed rapidly. Local rulers rivaled each other in the building of temples to their favored deities—Shiva, Vishnu, and Devi the Great Goddess—until the middle of the thirteenth century when Hindu temples reached unparalleled heights of grandeur and complexity.

Hindu temples can be classified broadly into two types, northern and southern (fig. 9-1). The northern type, exemplified by the Kandariya Mahadeva temple (c. 1000 CE) dedicated to the god Shiva at Khajuraho in central India (fig. 9-2), is

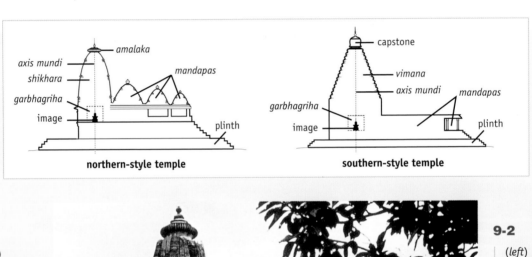

northern-style temple

southern-style temple

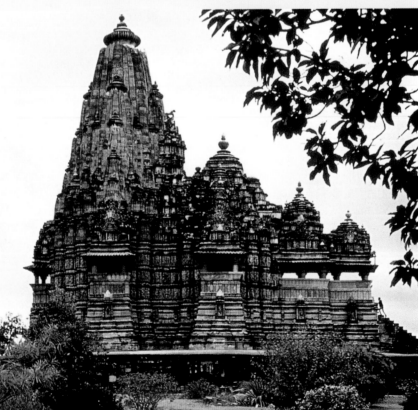

9-1

(*above*)
Schematic drawing of the two main Indian temple forms: northern style (left), and southern style (right)

9-2

(*left*)
Kandariya Mahadeva temple
Khajuraho Madhya Pradesh, India Chandella dynasty, Early Medieval period c. 1000 CE

chiefly distinguished by a superstructure called a ***shikhara***. The *shikhara* rises as a solid mass above the flat, stone ceiling of a windowless sanctuary, which houses an image of the temple's "resident" deity. Crowning the temple is a circular, cushionlike element, known as an *amalaka*. A **finial** leads the eye to the point where earthly and cosmic worlds are thought to join. An imaginary ***axis mundi*** (line connecting the center of the earth to the heavens) runs from the finial down through the temple and the image of the deity into the ground below. In this way the temple becomes a conduit between celestial realms and earth, a concept familiar from Buddhist stupas.

At the Kandariya Mahadeva temple, the *shikhara* is bolstered by the addition of many smaller *shikhara* motifs bundled around it. Below, the body of the temple is surrounded by porches on the sides and back. In the front (to the right in figure 9-2), a steep flight of stairs leads to a series of three halls, known as *mandapas*, preceding the sanctuary. The halls serve as a place for rituals, such as dances performed for the deity and for the presentation of offerings. The halls symbolically represent the second or Subtle Body stage of Shiva's threefold emanation—from Formless One (state of being), to Subtle Body (the world), to Gross Body (assistance for living beings).

The surface of the temple is so decorated with architectural motifs (miniature *shikharas*) and sculptured gods and goddesses that the lines of the architecture are almost obscured.

Another temple to Shiva, known as the Rajarajeshvara Temple (1003–10 CE), was built by the Chola ruler Rajaraja I (985–1014) as a thank offering for his many victories. Clarity of design, a formal balance of parts, and refined decor make the Rajarajeshvara Temple the supreme achievement of southern Hindu architecture (fig. 9-3). Rising to 216 feet, it was the tallest structure in India. Unlike the paraboloid shapes characteristic of northern temples, the southern temple uses horizontal and rectilinear forms. Its superstructure, called a ***vimana***, is a four-sided, hollow pyramid rising from a two-storied base articulated by large cornices; the halls at the front have flat roofs and enhance the sense of calm balance. Miniature shrines and figures decorate the *vimana* at every story and an octagonal dome-shaped capstone crowns the structure. This capstone is exactly above, and the same size as, the sanctuary thirteen stories below. It is meant to evoke the presence of the shrine as it points the viewer toward the cosmic sphere above.

During the Early Medieval period, when these temples were built, two major religious movements affected Hindu

9-3 | **Rajarajeshvara Temple to Shiva,** Thanjavur, Tamil Nadu, India. Chola dynasty, Early Medieval period, 1003–1010 CE

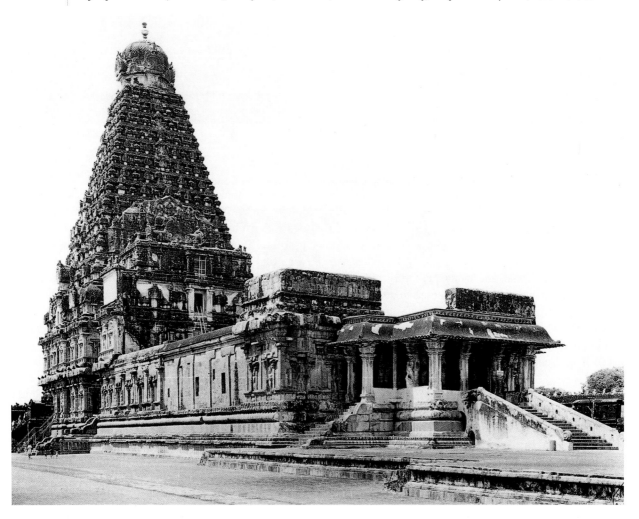

9-4 | *Nataraja: Shiva as Lord of Dance.* South India Chola dynasty, 11th century. Bronze, height 43⁷⁄₈" (111.4 cm). The Cleveland Museum of Art

© The Cleveland Museum of Art, 1998, Purchase from the J. H. Wade Fund, 1930.331

The fervent religious devotion of the *bhakti* movement was fueled in no small part by the sublime writings of a series of poet-saints who lived in the south of India. One of these poet-saints, Appar, who lived from the late sixth to mid-seventh century, wrote this tender, personal vision of the Shiva Nataraja. The ash the poem refers to is one of many symbols associated with the deity. In penance for having lopped off one of the five heads of Brahma, the first created being, Shiva smeared his body with ashes and went about as a beggar.

> If you could see
> the arch of his brow,
> the budding smile
> on lips red as the kovvai fruit,
> cool matted hair,
> the milk-white ash on coral skin,
> and the sweet golden foot
> raised up in dance,
> then even human birth on this wide earth
> would become a thing worth having.

(Translated by Indira Vishvanathan Peterson)

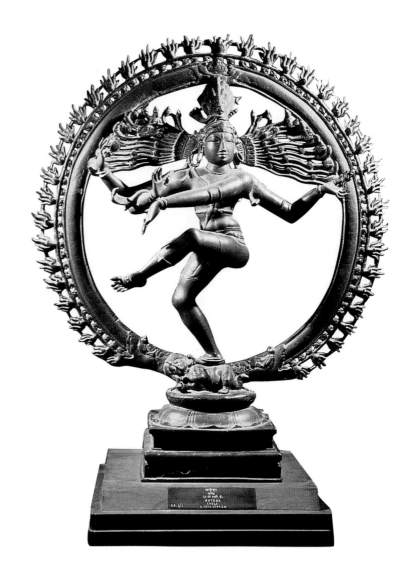

practice and its art: the tantric, or esoteric, movement primarily in the north and the *bhakti*, or devotional, movement primarily in the south. The *bhakti* movement, based on ideas expressed in ancient texts, especially the Bhagavad Gita, is concerned with the ideal relationship between humans and deities. *Bhakti* involves an intimate, personal, and loving relation with god, and the complete devotion and giving up of oneself to god. Inspired by *bhakti*, southern artists produced some of India's greatest and most humanistic work—the famous bronze sculptures. The movement profoundly influenced the Chola dynasty, rulers in the far south of India from the mid-ninth into the late thirteenth century.

Chola bronzes, such as this *Shiva Nataraja*, or *Lord of the Dance* (fig. 9-4), express the *bhakti* movement at its most fervent. No longer does the deity appear self-absorbed and introspective (see fig. 3-9). Instead, he generously displays himself to the devotee in full awareness of his benevolent powers. Dancing within a ring of fire, Shiva's extended left hand holds a spray of flames, emblematic of the destruction of the universe as well as of our ego-centered concepts. Shiva's back right hand holds a drum, whose ceaseless beat represents the unstoppable rhythms of creation and destruction, birth and death. With his right front hand, he makes the "have no fear" gesture. His left front arm, gracefully stretched across his body with the hand pointing to his raised foot and leg, symbolizes the promise of liberation. The earlier Hindu emphasis on ritual and the depiction of the gods' heroic feats is here subsumed into a pervasive and humanizing quality of grace.

The Hindu successors of the Chola continued the tradition of bronze sculpture in South India. The Shiva saint (see fig. 9) demonstrates the high level of achievement of the later artists.

The *bhakti* movement spread to North India during the ensuing Late Medieval period (c. 1200–1526) and flourished in the courts of local Hindu princes—the Rajputs, Indian warrior clans. This period also witnessed the incursion of Islam. The Muslim conquerors introduced Islamic architectural design to the subcontinent, but it was the Mughal dynasty that made the most lasting Islamic contribution to the art and architecture of India in painting (see fig. 8-18) and in buildings such as the Taj Mahal (see fig. 8-19).

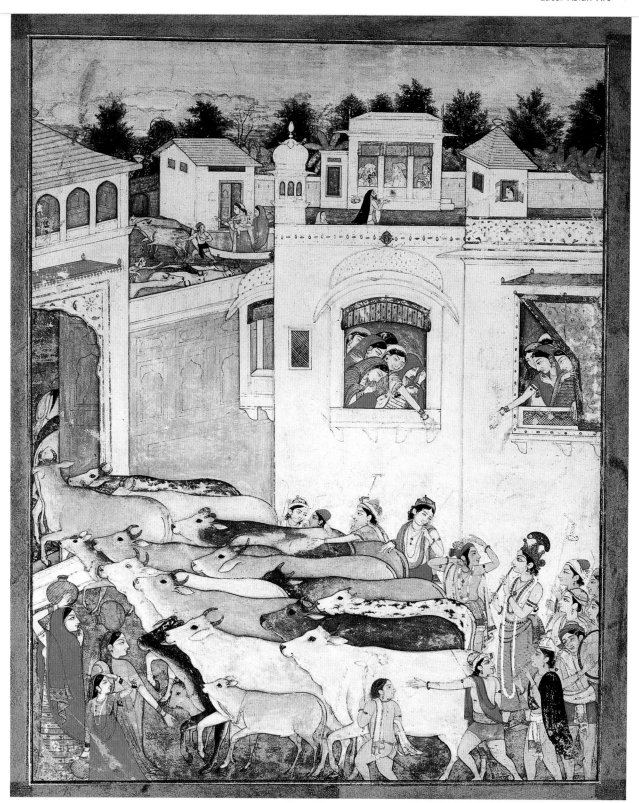

9-5 | ***The Hour of Cowdust.*** Indian, Pahari, c.1810-15. Kangra school, Pumjab Hills, Northern Indian. Attributed to The Family of Nainsukh. Opaque watercolor and gold on paper. 14¹⁵/₁₆" x 12⁹/₁₆" (38 x 31.9 cm).
Museum of Fine Arts, Boston, Denman W. Ross Collection. (#22.683)

RAJPUT PAINTING

Outside of the Mughal strongholds at Delhi and Agra, much of northern India was governed by local Hindu princes, descendants of the Rajput warrior clans, who were allowed to keep their lands in return for allegiance to the Mughals. Like the Mughals, Rajput rulers frequently established painting workshops at their courts. In Kangra, a large Rajput kingdom in the Punjab Hills,

the foothills of the Himalayas north of Delhi, a strong school of painting developed in the middle of the eighteenth century.

Inspired by a revival of the emotional *bhakti* movement, poets wrote of the love of the god Vishnu for human beings, metaphorically expressed as the love of Krishna for the cow maiden Radha. The *Hour of Cowdust* (fig. 9-5) depicts Krishna, who is living with the cowherds to escape the demons. Wearing

INDIAN PAINTING ON PAPER

Before the fourteenth century, most painting in India was made on walls or palm leaves. With the introduction of paper and the painting techniques adapted from Persia, later Indian artists produced jewel-toned paintings of unsurpassed beauty on paper. They used brushes made from the curved hairs of a squirrel's tail, arranged to taper from a thick base to a single hair at the tip. Their paint came from mineral and vegetable pigments, ground to a paste with water, then bound with a solution of gum from the acacia plant.

Artists frequently worked from a collection of sketches in a master painter's studio. Sometimes sketches were pricked with small holes, and wet color dabbed over the holes to transfer the drawing to a blank sheet beneath. The dots were connected into outlines, and the painting began. First, the painter applied a **wash**, or thin coat, of chalk-based white, which sealed the surface of the paper while allowing the underlying sketch to show through. Next, the artist filled the outlines with opaque color. When

the colors dried, the painting was placed face down on a smooth marble surface and burnished (rubbed) with a rounded agate stone. The indirect pressure against the marble polished the pigments to a high luster. Then outlines, details, and modeling were added with a fine brush. Raised details such as the pearls of a necklace were made with thick, chalk-based paint, each pearl a single droplet hardened into a tiny raised mound.

CLOSER LOOK

Frozen in timeless delight, carved in ivory against a golden ground where openwork, stylized vines with spiky leaves weave an elegant arabesque, loving couples dally under the arcades of a palace courtyard (fig. 9-6). Their huge eyes under heavy brows suggest the intensity of their gaze, and the artist's choice of the profile view shows off their long noses and thick lips. Their hair is tightly controlled; the men have huge buns and the women, long braids hanging down their backs. Are they divine lovers? After all, Krishna lived and loved on earth among the cow maidens. Or are we observing scenes of courtly romance?

The rich jewelry and well-fed bodies of the couples indicate a high station in life. Men as well as women have voluptuous figures—rounded buttocks and thighs, tummies hanging over jeweled belts, and sharply indented slim waists that emphasize seductive breasts. Their smooth flesh contrasts with the diaphanous fabrics that swath their plump legs, and their long arms and elegant gestures seem designed to show off their rich jewelry—bracelets, armbands, necklaces, huge earrings, and ribbons. Such amorous couples symbolize harmony as well as fertility.

The erotic imagery suggests that the box might have been a container for personal belongings such as jewelry, perfume, or cosmetics. In any event, the ivory relief is a brilliant example of South Indian secular arts.

9-6 | **Panel from a box.** Tamil Nadu, India, late 17th–18th century. Ivory backed with gilded paper 6 x 12³/₈ x ¹/₈" (15.2 x 31.4 x 0.3 cm). Virginia Museum of Fine Arts
The Arthur and Margaret Glasgow Fund. 80.171

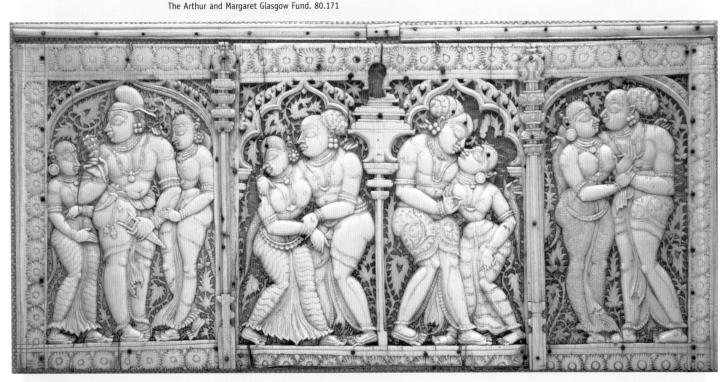

his peacock crown, garland of flowers, jewelry, and yellow garment, the blue-skinned god plays his flute as he returns to the village with his fellow cowherds and their cattle. All eyes are upon him for his music enchants all who hear it. Women with water jugs on their heads turn to look; others lean from windows to watch and call out to him. We are drawn into this charming village scene by the diagonal movements of the cows as they surge through the gate and into the courtyard beyond. Pink walls and white houses create a sense of space where we glimpse other villagers going about their work or peacefully sitting in their houses. A rim of dark trees softens the horizon, and a rose-tinted sky completes the aura of enchanted naturalism. The gentle, lyrical movement complements the idealism of the setting. The scene embodies the sublime purity and grace of the god, even in a humble setting.

South India had a rich and distinguished architectural and sculptural tradition, represented by the Rajarajeshvara Temple (see fig. 9-3) and the bronze dancing Shiva (see fig. 9-4). One of the most important states was Tamil Nadu in the eastern coastal plain. Inhabited by Tamil speakers (a Dravidian language, unlike the Sanskrit-based languages of the north), the region developed its own distinctive character with few outside influences.

The arts of Tamil Nadu are characterized by curvilinear rounded forms and the use of **gilding**, as seen here in an ivory panel (fig. 9-6). This ivory panel must have decorated a box—note the keyhole and the marks of nails in the borders. The delicate columns and pointed and scalloped arches of the architectural frames recall the inner courtyard of the palace in the capital city, Madurai, built in the middle of the seventeenth century (1646). Here Tirumala Nayak (1622–1662) lived and governed Tamil Nadu. The Nayak rulers commissioned sculpture and painting, but wood and ivory carving ranks among their artists' highest achievements.

The luxury arts—work in rock crystal, ivory and mother-of-pearl, metalwork, and jewelry—brought Indian fame to the craft arts, and beginning in the sixteenth century objects were made for export as well as local sale. Fine pieces were very important in daily life, but little scholarly work has been done on the decorative arts.

Sikhs took over the kingdom in 1826. The British followed in 1846, effectively ending distinctive local styles.

China

A period of confusion followed the fall of the Tang dynasty in 907. The Liao Dynasty (907–1125) exerted some semblance of power, but in fact was soon replaced by the Song dynasty (960–1279). In 1126, invaders from Manchuria defeated them and sacked the Song capital at Bian (present-day Kaifeng) and occupied much of the northern part of the country. Song forces withdrew southward and established a new capital at Hangzhou. The dynasty from this point on is known as Southern Song (1127–1279). The earlier years are called Northern Song (960–1126).

In spite of changing political fortunes artists continued to create splendid works. No hint of chaos or despair intrudes on the sublime grace and beauty of the *Seated Guanyin Bodhisattva*

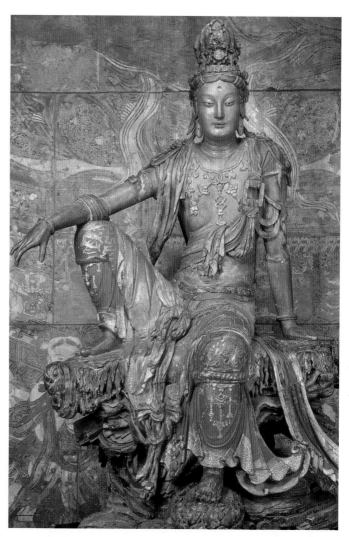

9-7 | ***Seated Guanyin Bodhisattva.*** Liao dynasty, 11th–12th century Wood with paint, height 95" (241.3 cm). The Nelson-Atkins Museum of Art Kansas City, Missouri
Purchase, Nelson Trust

(fig. 9-7). Bodhisattvas are enlightened beings who return to earth to help others achieve salvation; Guan-yin is the Bodhisattva of Infinite Compassion. Bodhisattvas are represented as young princes wearing royal garments and jewelry that represent their worldly but virtuous lives. Guan-yin appears in many guises; in this case as the Water and Moon Guan-yin he sits on rocks by the sea, in the position known as "royal ease." His right arm rests on his raised and bent right knee and his left arm and foot hang down, the foot touching a lotus blossom. The wooden figure was carved in the eleventh or twelfth century; however the painting and gilding date from the sixteenth century.

During the Song period, the martial vigor of the Tang and Liao gave way to a culture of increasing refinement and scholarship. It was a great period for the study of history, literature, and philosophy. Song philosophers revived Confucianism, drawing on both Buddhism and Daoism to provide Confucianism with a metaphysical basis, an all-embracing explanation of the universe. This new system of thought is called Neo-Confucianism. Neo-Confucianism teaches that the universe consists of two interacting

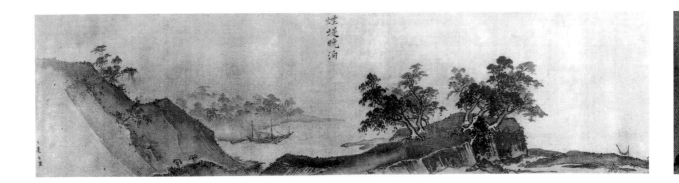

forces known as *li* (principle or idea) and *qi* (matter). All pine trees, for instance, consist of an underlying *li* we might call the "pine tree idea," brought into the world through *qi*, the living tree. All the *li* of the universe, including humans, are but aspects of an eternal first principle known as the Great Ultimate. The task of humans is to rid our *qi* of impurities through education and self-cultivation so that our *li* may achieve its oneness with the Great Ultimate.

Neo-Confucian ideas found visual expression in landscape painting. Northern Song artists studied nature closely to master its varied appearances—the way each species of tree grew, the distinctive character of rock formations, the changing of the seasons, the myriad birds, blossoms, and insects. This study was the artist's form of self-cultivation; mastering outward forms showed an understanding of the principles behind them. Yet despite the convincing representation of individual forms, the paintings do not record specific views. The artist's goal was to paint the eternal aspect of a mountain, for example, not to reproduce the particular appearance of a mountain. Over the centuries, landscape also became a vehicle for conveying human emotions, even for expressing one's deepest feelings.

One of the first great masters of Song landscape was Fan Kuan (active c. 990–1030), whose *Travelers among Mountains and Streams* is generally regarded as one of the great monuments in the history of Chinese art (fig. 9-8). The composition unfolds in three stages, comparable to the three acts of a drama. A low-lying group of rocks at the bottom establishes the extreme foreground, anticipating, on a small scale, the shape and substance of the mountains to come. In the middle ground, travelers and their mules enter from the right. We realize the discrepancies in relative scale—how small we are, how vast nature is! This middle ground, like the second act of a play, shows variation and development. Instead of a solid mass, the rocks here are separated into two groups by a waterfall. At right, the rooftops of a temple stand out above the trees.

Mist veils the transition to the background, so the mountain seems to loom up suddenly. This background area, almost twice as large as the foreground and middle ground combined, is the climactic third act of the drama. As our eyes begin their ascent, the mountain solidifies, its ponderous weight increasing as it billows upward. The whole painting summons the feeling of climbing a high mountain, leaving the human world behind to come face-to-face in a spiritual communion with the Great Ultimate.

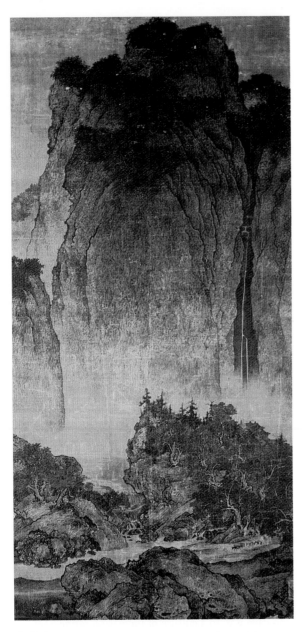

9-8 | **Fan Kuan.** *Travelers among Mountains and Streams*
Northern Song dynasty, early 11th century. Hanging scroll, ink and colors on silk, height 6'9¼"
(2.06 m). National Palace Museum, Taipei, Taiwan

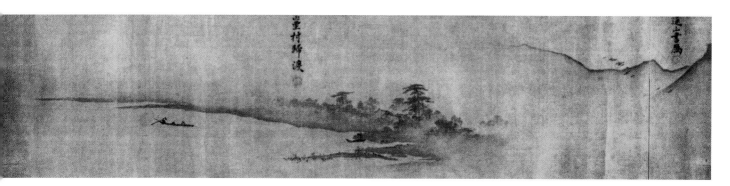

9-9   Xia Gui. *Detail of Twelve Views from a Thatched Hut.* Southern Song dynasty, early 13th century. Handscroll, ink on silk Height 11" (28 cm), length of extant portion 7'7¼" (2.31 m). The Nelson-Atkins Museum of Art, Kansas City, Missouri
Purchase, Nelson Trust (32–159/2)

The ability of Chinese landscape painters to let us wander freely through their recorded sites is closely linked to the absence of linear perspective as it has been understood in the West since the fifteenth century. Fifteenth-century European painters developed a "scientific" system for recording exactly the view that could be seen from a single, fixed vantage point (see "Renaissance Perspective Systems," page 289). The goal of Chinese painting is to show a totality beyond what we are normally given to see. If we can imagine the ideal viewpoint of Western painters as a photograph that shows only what can be seen from a fixed spot, we can imagine the ideal for Chinese artists as a video camera floating aloft in a balloon: distant, all-seeing, and mobile.

Landscape painting took a very different course after the fall of the Northern Song and the removal of the court to Hangzhou. The work of Xia Gui (c. 1180–1230), a member of a reestablished imperial painting academy, is representative of this change. His *Twelve Views from a Thatched Hut* (fig. 9-9), in sharp contrast to the majestic, austere landscapes of the Northern Song painters, presents an intimate and lyrical view of nature. In the surviving four of the twelve views that originally made up this long handscroll (narrow, horizontal painting), subtle ink washes describe a landscape veiled in mists. A few deft brushstrokes suffice to evoke fishermen at their work, trees laden with moisture, and two bent figures carrying their heavy loads along a path that skirts the hill. Simplified forms, stark contrasts of light and dark, asymmetrical compositions, and great expanses of blank space suggest a fleeting world that can be captured only in glimpses.

The highly cultivated audience that appreciated the subtle and sophisticated paintings of the Song was equally discerning in other arts, such as ceramics. Of the many types of Song ceramics, one of the most prized was Guan Ware, made mainly for imperial use (fig. 9-10). The form of this graceful vase flows without interruption from base to lip, but the potter intentionally allowed a pattern of irregular, spontaneous cracks to develop in the lustrous off-white glaze. This piece, with its careful interplay of ordered and unplanned elements, has an understated quality as eloquent as the blank spaces in Xia Gui's painting.

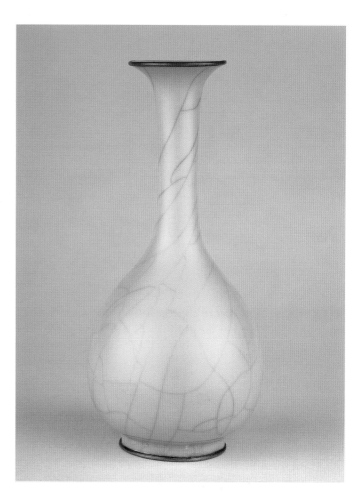

9-10   Guan Ware vase. Southern Song dynasty, 12-13th century. Stoneware with crackled glaze, height 6⅝" (18 cm).
Percival David Foundation of Chinese Art, London

In 1279, the Southern Song dynasty fell to the armies of the Mongol leader Kublai Khan, and China became part of the vast Mongol Empire. Kublai founded the Yuan dynasty (1279–1368), setting up his capital in the northeast, in what is now Beijing. The center of Chinese culture remained in the south, however, and southern Chinese scholars found themselves

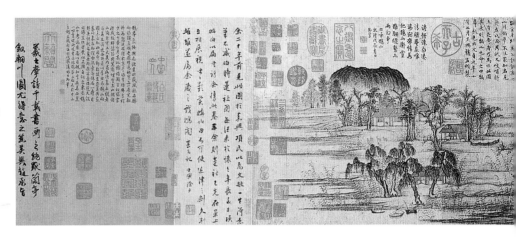

9-11 Zhao Mengfu. *Section of Autumn Colors on the Qiao and Hua Mountains.* Yuan dynasty, 1296. Handscroll, ink and color on paper, 11¼ x 36¾" (28.6 x 93.3 cm) National Palace Museum Taipei, Taiwan

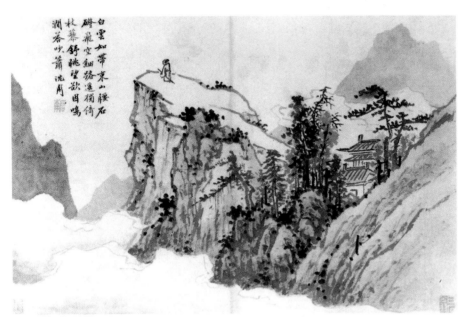

9-12 Shen Zhou. *Poet on a Mountain Top*, leaf from an album of landscapes; painting mounted as part of a handscroll, Ming dynasty, c. 1500. Ink and color on paper, 15¼ x 23¾" (38.1 x 60.2 cm). The Nelson-Atkins Museum of Art, Kansas City, Missouri Purchase, Nelson Trust (46–5½)

The poem at the upper left reads:

> White clouds like a belt encircle the mountain's waist
> A stone ledge flying in space and the far thin road.
> I lean alone on my bramble staff and gazing contented into space
> Wish the sounding torrent would answer to your flute.

(Translated by Richard Edwards, cited in *Eight Dynasties of Chinese Paintings*, page 185.)

Shen Zhou composed the poem and the inscription, written at the time he painted the album. The style of the calligraphy, like the style of the painting, is informal, relaxed, and straightforward—qualities that were believed to reflect the artist's character and personality.

alienated from the Mongol court. Denied normal access to the government positions for which they were educated, these scholars, known as the literati, searched for other outlets for their talents, including the arts.

The southerner Zhao Mengfu (1254–1322), a descendant of the imperial line of Song, is typical in this regard. Unlike many of his southern contemporaries, he eventually served the Yuan government in Beijing and was made a high official. Nevertheless, as a painter, calligrapher, and poet, he also produced works for cultivated southern literati. Zhao painted *Autumn Colors on the Qiao and Hua Mountains* (fig. 9-11) for a friend living in the south. The painting supposedly depicts the friend's ancestral home, Jinan, the present-day capital of Shandong province, in the north. However, the mountains are not painted in the naturalistic mode perfected before Zhao's time but rather in an archaic yet oddly elegant manner that recalls the art of the much earlier Tang dynasty. Through his painting, Zhao evoked a feeling of nostalgia, not only for his friend's distant homeland, but also for China's past.

This educated taste for archaic styles became an important aspect of **literati painting** in later periods. Also typical of the literati tradition are the unassuming brushwork, the subtle colors sparingly used, and even the intended audience—often a close friend. The literati painted not for public display but for each other. They favored **handscrolls**, **hanging scrolls**, or **album leaves**, which could easily be transported to show to friends or small gatherings (see "Formats of Chinese Painting," page 220).

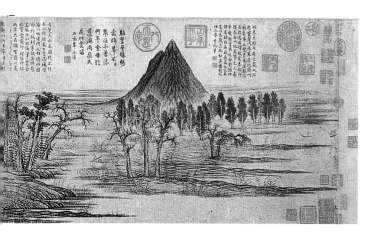

The contrast between the opulent display and the austere aesthetic ideals of the literati is a defining feature of Ming dynasty (1368–1644) painting. Whereas court painters revived academic traditions of the Song dynasty, many literati painters built on the styles created by their predecessors, the Yuan. One of the major literati artists of the Ming period is Shen Zhou (1427–1509), who spent most of his life in the southern city of Suzhou, far from the court in Beijing. Shen Zhou studied the Yuan painters avidly and tried to recapture their spirit in such works as *Poet on a Mountain Top* (fig. 9-12). Here the poet has climbed a mountain and surveys the landscape. Before his gaze, a poem hangs in the air, like a projection of his thoughts. Like the poem, the landscape is a vehicle for self-expression, having more to do with the artist's response to nature than with the physical world itself. With its perfect synthesis of poetry, calligraphy, and painting, and its harmony of mind and landscape, *Poet on a Mountain Top* represents the very essence of literati painting.

The cities of the south, such as Suzhou, where Shen Zhou painted, were full of newly wealthy merchants who collected paintings, antiques, and art objects. The court, too, was prosperous and patronized the arts on a lavish scale. In such a setting, the decorative arts thrived.

Like the Song dynasty before it, the Ming became famous the world over for its exquisite ceramics, especially **porcelain**. Porcelain is made from kaolin, an extremely refined white clay, and petuntse, a variety of the mineral feldspar. When properly combined and fired at a high temperature, the two materials fuse into a glasslike, translucent ceramic that is far stronger than it looks.

The porcelain flask in figure 9-13 came from the imperial kilns in Jingdezhen, in Jiangxi province, the most renowned center for porcelain in Ming China. The blue decoration—made from cobalt oxide, finely ground and mixed with water—was painted directly onto the unfired porcelain vessel in a technique known as **underglaze**. Next, the painter applied a white glaze over the blue designs. The piece was then fired, emerging from the kiln with its clear blue decoration set sharply against a snowy white background. The subtle shape, the refined yet vigorous decoration of dragons writhing in the sea, and the flawless **glazing** embody the high achievement of Ming artisans.

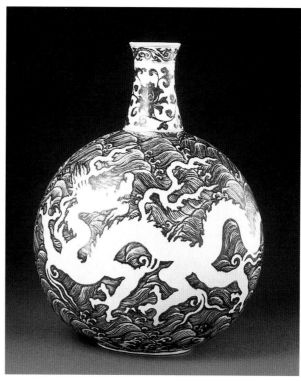

9-13 **Porcelain flask** with decoration in blue underglaze Ming dynasty, c. 1425–35. Palace Museum, Beijing

Dragons have featured prominently in Chinese folklore from earliest times—Neolithic examples have been found painted on pottery and carved in jade. In Bronze Age China, dragons came to be associated with powerful and sudden manifestations of nature, such as wind, thunder, and lightning. At the same time, dragons became associated with superior beings such as virtuous rulers and sages. With the emergence of China's first firmly established empire during the Han dynasty, the dragon was appropriated as an imperial symbol, and it remained so throughout Chinese history. Dragon sightings were duly recorded and considered auspicious. Yet even the Son of Heaven could not monopolize the dragon. During the Tang and Song dynasties the practice arose of painting pictures of dragons to pray for rain, and for Chan (Zen) Buddhists, the dragon was a symbol of enlightenment.

TECHNIQUE
Formats of Chinese Painting

Aside from wall paintings that decorated palaces, temples, and tombs, most Chinese paintings were done in ink and water-based colors on silk or paper (see **ink painting**). Finished works were usually mounted on silk as **handscrolls**, **hanging scrolls**, **albums**, or fans.

An album comprises a set of paintings of similar size, and usually of related subject matter, mounted in an accordion-fold book. Typically the paintings are square or rectangular, but fan paintings were sometimes collected in albums. Album-size paintings could also be mounted as a handscroll, a horizontal format generally about 12 inches high and anywhere from a few feet to dozens of feet long. More typically, however, a handscroll would be a single continuous painting, generally preceded by a panel giving the work's title and often followed by a long panel bearing colophons—inscriptions such as poems in praise of the work or comments by its owners over the centuries. Handscrolls were not meant to be displayed all at once, the way they are commonly presented today in museums. Rather, they were kept rolled up and only occasionally taken out for viewing. The viewer would unroll the scroll a couple of feet at a time, moving gradually through the entire scroll from right to left, lingering over favorite details.

Like handscrolls, hanging scrolls were not displayed permanently but were taken out for a limited time, whether a day, a week, or a season. Unlike a handscroll, however, the hanging scroll was viewed as a whole, unrolled and put up on a wall, with the wooden roller at the lower end acting as a weight to help the scroll hang flat.

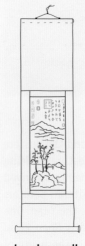

hanging scroll

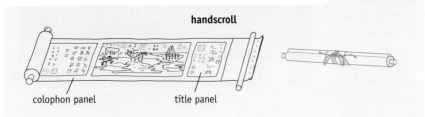

handscroll

colophon panel   title panel

Ming architects created the most important surviving example of traditional Chinese architecture: the Forbidden City, the imperial palace compound in Beijing (fig. 9-14). The basic plan of Beijing was the work of the Mongols, who laid out their capital city according to Chinese principles, creating a walled rectangle with gates oriented to the four cardinal directions and streets running north-south and east-west arranged on a grid. The palace enclosure occupied the center of the northern part of the city. Under the third Ming emperor (ruled 1402–1424) the Forbidden City was rebuilt as we see it today.

Visitors to the Forbidden City entered on the south and passed through the South Gate, the monumental U-shaped gate seen below in figure 9-14. Inside the gate, a bow-shaped canal spanned by five arched marble bridges crosses a broad courtyard. On the north side of the courtyard is the Gate of Supreme Harmony, opening into an even larger courtyard that houses three ceremonial halls raised on a broad platform. Classic examples of Chinese palace architecture, with brilliant yellow tile roofs and red lacquered columns, are the Halls of Supreme Harmony, Central Harmony, and Protecting

9-14

The Forbidden City, now the Palace Museum Beijing. Mostly Ming dynasty. View from the southwest

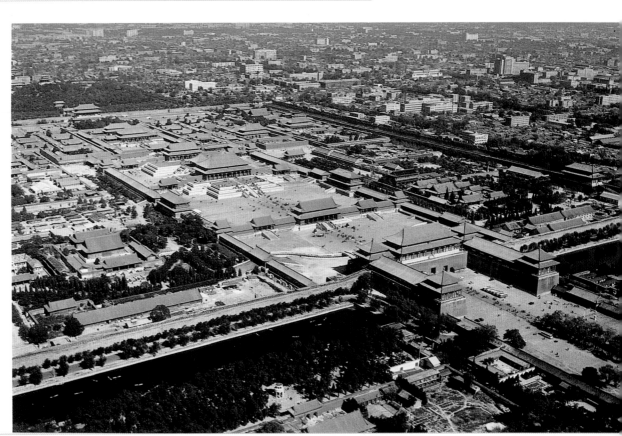

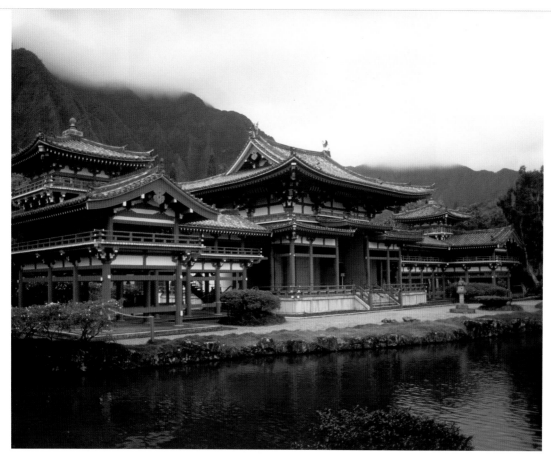

9-15

Byodo-in
Uji, Kyoto
Prefecture
Heian period
c. 1053

Harmony. In the first and largest, the Hall of Supreme Harmony, the emperor sat on his throne during important state occasions. He faced south, looking out toward his city and, by extension, his realm. His back was to the north, the source of evil spirits, not to mention military threats from non-Chinese peoples beyond the Great Wall.

Continuing on to the north in the Forbidden City, the visitor encounters an inner court that also has a progression of three buildings, this time more intimate in scale. In its directional orientation and symmetrical arrangement, the plan of the Forbidden City reflects ancient Chinese beliefs about the harmony of the universe and emphasizes the emperor's role as the Son of Heaven, whose duty was to maintain the cosmic order from his throne in the middle of the world.

Japan

In Japan, by the Heian period (794–1185), Buddhism was practiced throughout the land, although it did not completely supplant the country's indigenous religion, Shinto. Buddhism offers paradisiacal realms and enlightenment; Shinto, the intercession of the gods in the affairs of this world. Since these ideals did not fundamentally clash, modes of mutual accommodation were found. To this day, most Japanese see nothing inconsistent about having Shinto weddings and Buddhist funerals.

The generally peaceful Heian period was marked by a new cultural self-reliance on the part of the Japanese. Ties to China were severed in the mid-ninth century, and the imperial government was sustained by support from aristocratic families. During

these four centuries of splendor and refinement, two new schools of Buddhism became prominent: first, Esoteric (secret) Buddhism and later, Pure Land Buddhism.

In Esoteric Buddhism, the historical Shakyamuni Buddha became less important. Teaching centered instead on a universal or cosmic Buddha (called Dainichi, "Great Sun," in Japanese) of whom all other buddhas are emanations. Esoteric Buddhism gave rise to a huge pantheon of buddhas, bodhisattvas, and fierce guardian deities. The leisured aristocracy favored esoteric Buddhism whose network of deities, hierarchy, and ritual found a parallel in the elaborate social divisions of the Heian court.

Pure Land Buddhism came to prominence in the latter half of the Heian period, when a rising military class threatened the peace and tranquility of court life. In those uncertain years, many Japanese were ready for a form of Buddhism that would offer a means of salvation more direct than through the elaborate rituals of the Esoteric sects. Pure Land Buddhism taught that the Western Paradise (the Pure Land) of Amida (Amitabha) Buddha could be reached through faith alone. In its ultimate form, Pure Land Buddhism held that the mere chanting of a mantra—the phrase *Namu Amida Butsu* ("Hail to Amida Buddha")—would lead to rebirth in Amida's Pure Land, his Western Paradise. This doctrine, spread by traveling monks who took the chant to all parts of the country, has made Pure Land Buddhism the most popular form of Buddhism in Japan.

One of the most beautiful temples of Pure Land Buddhism is the Phoenix Hall at the Byodo-in (built c. 1053), located by the Uji River southeast of Kyoto (fig. 9-15). Originally the summer retreat of a powerful aristocrat, it was later converted into a

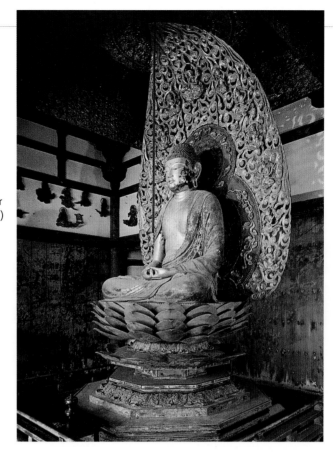

9-16 | Jocho. *Amida Buddha*
Byodo-in. Heian period
c. 1053. Gold leaf and lacquer
on wood, height 9'8" (2.95 m)

temple. The hall and its garden combine to evoke the palace of Amida in the Western Paradise. The lightness of its thin columns gives the Phoenix Hall a sense of airiness, as though the entire structure could easily rise up through the sky to the Western Paradise. In front of the hall is an artificial pond created in the shape of the Sanskrit letter *A*, the sacred symbol for Amida.

The Phoenix Hall's central image of Amida (fig. 9-16) was constructed out of individually carved blocks of wood by the master sculptor Jocho (d. 1057). This **joined-wood sculpture** method, developed by Jocho, allowed sculptors to create sculpture larger but lighter than those formerly carved from a single block of wood. Reflected in the water of the pond in front of it, the Amida image, heightened with gold leaf and **lacquer** (a hard, glossy surface varnish), seems to shimmer in its private retreat. The Buddha sits on an open lotus, a Buddhist symbol of purity. The flower's stem is an *axis mundi*, connecting the earthly and celestial realms. This timeless image exemplifies the compassion of the Buddha, who welcomes the souls of all believers to his paradise, nirvana.

While Buddhism dominated the Heian era, a refined secular culture also arose at court; it has never been equaled in Japan. A new system of writing in Japanese developed, known as *kana* script (see "Writing, Language, and Culture," right). With its simple, flowing symbols interspersed with more complex Chinese

WRITING, LANGUAGE, AND CULTURE

Written Chinese was the international language of scholarship in East Asia, much as Latin was in medieval Europe. Educated Koreans, for example, wrote almost exclusively in Chinese until the fifteenth century. In Japan, Chinese continued to be used for certain kinds of writing, such as philosophical and legal texts, into the nineteenth century.

When the Japanese first began to write, they borrowed Chinese characters, which they refer to as *kanji*. However, differences between the Chinese and Japanese languages made this system extremely unwieldy, so during the ninth century the Japanese developed two syllabaries (*kana*), *katakana* and *hiragana*, to transcribe the sounds of their own language. (A syllabary is a system in which each symbol stands for a syllable.) *Katakana*, now generally used for foreign words, consists of mostly angular symbols, while *hiragana*, which is used for Japanese words, has graceful, cursive symbols.

Below is a stanza of a poem written three ways. At the right, it appears in *katakana* glossed with the original phonetic value of each symbol. (Modern pronunciation has shifted slightly). In the center, the stanza appears in flowing *hiragana*. At left is the mixture of Chinese characters and *kana* that eventually became standard. This alternating rhythm of simple *kana* symbols and more complex Chinese characters gives a special flavor to Japanese calligraphy. In all three versions of the stanza, the text is written, like Chinese, in columns from top to bottom and across the page from right to left. Chinese and Japanese handscrolls also read from right to left.

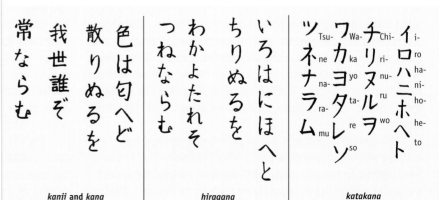

kanji and *kana*   *hiragana*   *katakana*

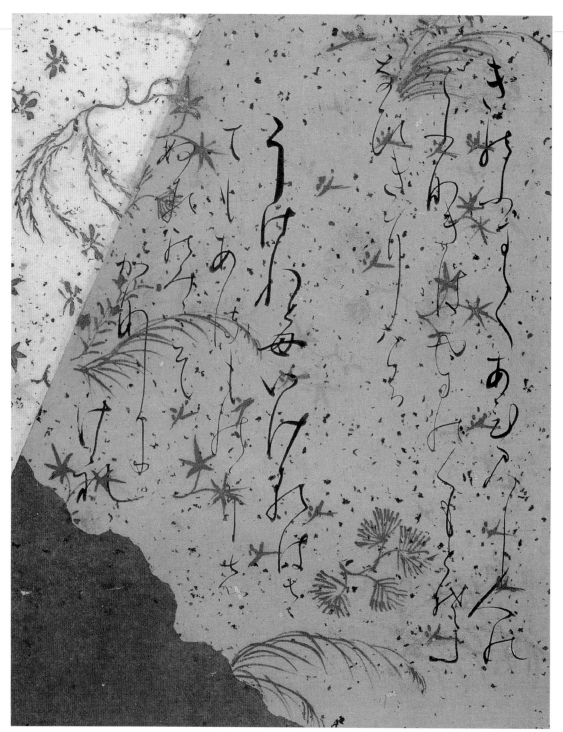

**Album leaf from
the *Ishiyama-gire***
Heian period, early 12th
century. Ink with gold
and silver on decorated
and collaged paper, 8 x
6³/₈" (20.3 x 16.1 cm)
Freer Gallery of Art
Smithsonian Institution
Washington, D.C.

characters, *kana* allowed Japanese writers to create a distinctive calligraphy quite unlike that of China.

Kana was used during the Heian period to write down a large body of literature, including many *tanka*, or five-line love poems. The poems of one famous Heian anthology, the *Thirty-Six Immortal Poets*, are still familiar to educated Japanese today. This anthology was produced in sets of albums, the *Ishiyama-gire*, which display elegantly written *tanka* on high-quality papers decorated with painting, **block printing**, scattered gold and silver, and sometimes paper **collage** (pasted colored papers).

The page shown here reproduces two *tanka* by the courtier Ki no Tsurayuki (fig. 9-17). Both poems express sadness for the loss of a lover, the first lamenting:

Until yesterday
I could meet her,
But today she is gone—
Like clouds over the mountain
She has been wafted away.

(Translated by Stephen Addiss)

The spiky, flowing calligraphy, the patterning of the papers, the rich use of gold, and the suggestion of natural imagery epitomize courtly Japanese taste.

The world's first known novel, *The Tale of Genji*, written in Japanese at the beginning of the eleventh century by Lady Murasaki, immortalizes the lifestyle of the Heian court. Underlying the story of the love affairs of Prince Genji and his

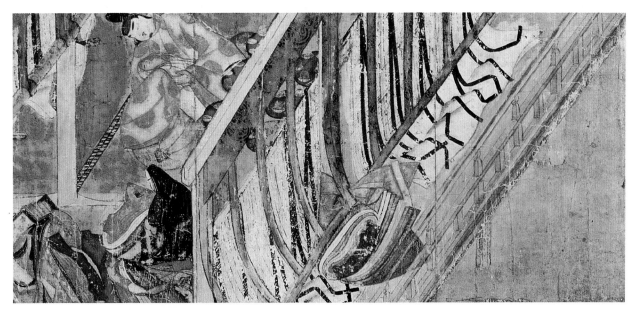

9-18 | **Scene from *The Tale of Genji*.** Heian period, 12th century
Handscroll, ink and colors on paper, 8⅝ x 18⅞" (21.9 x
47.9 cm). Tokugawa Art Museum, Nagoya

companions is the Japanese conception of fleeting pleasures
and ultimate sadness in life, an echo of the Buddhist view of
the vanity of earthly pleasures.

Among the earliest extant secular paintings from Japan are
illustrations for *The Tale of Genji*, done in the twelfth century by
unknown artists in a style sometimes described as "women's
hand." This style was characterized by emphasis on shapes rather
than lines, strong if sometimes muted colors, and asymmetrical
compositions in which interiors of buildings are viewed from
above through invisible, "blown-away" roofs. The painters convey feelings by colors and poses rather than through movement
or facial expressions. One evocative scene portrays a seemingly
happy Prince Genji holding a baby boy borne by his wife, Nyosan
(fig. 9-18). In fact, the baby was fathered by another court noble.
Since Genji himself has not been faithful to Nyosan, who appears
in profile below him, he cannot complain; meanwhile the true
father of the child has died, unable to acknowledge his only son.
The irony is even greater because Genji himself is the illegitimate
son of an emperor. Thus what should be a joyous scene has
undercurrents of sorrow. This is underscored visually by the
muted colors of Genji's clothing, which contrast with the bright
colors around him, and by the uncomfortable space he occupies.

The courtiers of the Heian era became so engrossed in their
own search for refinement that they neglected their responsibilities for governing the country. Clans of warriors, known as samurai, grew increasingly strong, and samurai leaders soon became
the real powers in Japan. The Kamakura era (1185–1392) began
when the samurai Minamoto Yoritomo (1147–1199) assumed

power in Japan as shogun (general-in-chief). He established a
military capital at the seaside town of Kamakura, far from Kyoto.
While paying respects to the emperor, Yoritomo kept both military and political power for himself. He thus began a tradition of
rule by shogun that lasted in various forms until 1868.

Toward the latter part of the Kamakura period, Zen Buddhism reached Japan from China. In some ways, Zen resembles
the original teachings of the historical Buddha in stressing that
individuals must achieve their own enlightenment through meditation, without the devotional practices or elaborate rituals promoted by other schools of Buddhism. In line with this emphasis
on self-reliance, Zen monks grow and cook their own food, clean
their temples, and are held as responsible for their own lives as
well as for their spiritual growth. This approach appealed to the
self-disciplined spirit of the samurai.

An abbot named Kao at an early Zen temple was a pioneer
in a kind of rough and simple painting in black ink that so
directly expresses the Zen spirit. In a remarkable portrait of a
monk sewing his robe (fig. 9-19), we are drawn into the activity
of the painting rather than merely sitting back and enjoying it
as a work of art. The almost humorous compression of the monk's
face, coupled with the position of the darker robe, focuses our
attention on his eyes, which then lead us out to his hand pulling
the needle.

By the beginning of the Muromachi period (1392–1568), Zen
dominated many aspects of Japanese culture. One of the most
renowned Zen creations in Japan, built during the Muromachi
era, is the "dry landscape garden" at the temple of Ryoan-ji in

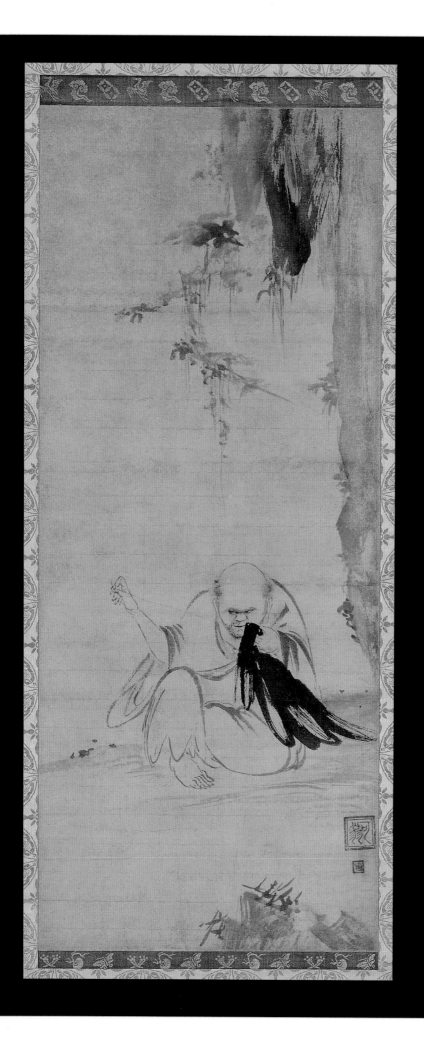

9-19

Attributed to Kao Ninga
Monk Sewing. Kamakura
period, early 14th century
Ink on paper, 32⅞ x 13¾"
(83.5 x 35.4 cm). The
Cleveland Museum of Art
John L. Severance Fund, 62.163

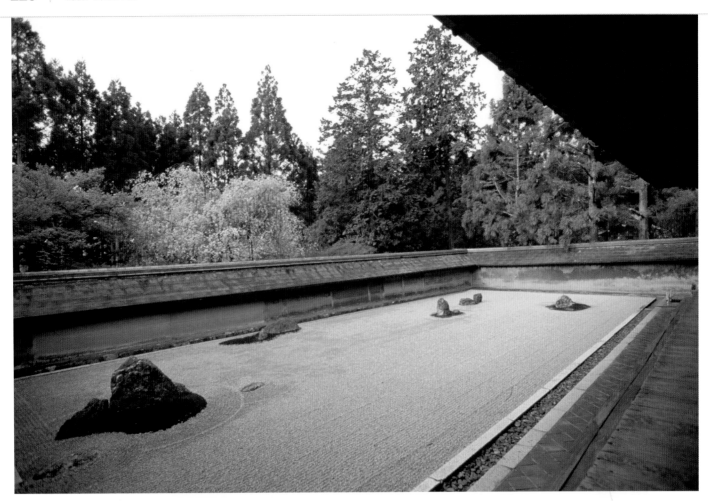

9-20 | **Stone and gravel garden, Ryoan-ji,** Kyoto. Muromachi period, c. 1480. (See pages 208–09.)

Kyoto (fig. 9-20). There is a record of a famous cherry tree at this spot, so the completely severe nature of the garden may have come about some time after its original founding in the late fifteenth century. Nevertheless, today the garden is celebrated for its serene sense of space and emptiness. The garden is only a part of the larger grounds of Ryoan-ji.

During the Momoyama period (1568–1603), civil wars swept through Japan, fought among samurai loyal to their own feudal lords rather than to the central government. Portuguese explorers and traders arrived, and with them European muskets and cannons, which soon changed the nature of Japanese warfare. In response to the new weapons, monumental fortified castles were built in the early seventeenth century. Many were sumptuously decorated, offering artists unprecedented opportunities to work on a grand scale. Large murals on *fusuma*—paper-covered sliding doors—were particular features of Momoyama design, as were folding screens with gold-leaf backgrounds. Temples, too, commissioned large-scale decorative paintings for rebuilding projects after the devastation of the civil wars.

Daitoku-ji, a celebrated Zen monastery in Kyoto, has a number of subtemples that are treasure troves of Japanese art. One, the Juko-in, features *fusuma* by Kano Eitoku (1543–1590). Eitoku was one of the most brilliant painters from the Kano school, a professional school of artists patronized by government leaders for several centuries. The illustration here shows two of

three walls of *fusuma* panels painted when the artist was in his mid-twenties (fig. 9-21). The subject to the left is a popular Kano-school theme of cranes and pines, both symbols of long life; to the right is a great gnarled plum tree, a symbol of spring and renewal. An island situated where two walls meet in a corner provides a focus for the outreaching trees. Ingeniously, it belongs to both compositions at the same time, thus uniting them into a single organic whole.

During the Momoyama period, there continued to be interest in the quiet, the restrained, and the natural. This introspective mood found expression in the tea ceremony. "Tea ceremony" is an unsatisfactory characterization of *cha no yu*, the Japanese ritual of preparing and drinking of tea, for which there is no counterpart in Western culture. The most famous tea master in Japanese history, Sen no Rikyu (1521–1591), conceived of the tea ceremony as an intimate gathering in which a few people would enter a small, rustic room, drink tea carefully prepared in front of them by their host, and quietly discuss the tea utensils or a work of art displayed for their enjoyment.

The age-old Japanese admiration for the natural and the asymmetrical is reflected in certain types of tea ceramics. A teabowl would be judged by such factors as how well it fit into the hands, how subtly its shape and texture appealed to the eye, and who had previously used and appreciated it. If a bowl had been given a name by a leading tea master, it was especially

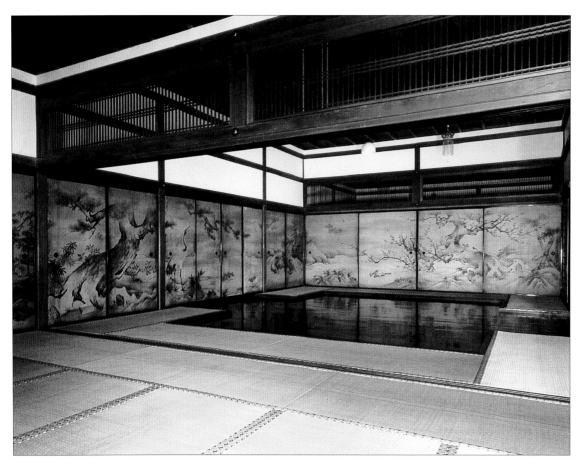

9-21

Kano Eitoku
Fusuma depicting
pine and cranes
(left) and plum tree
(right), from the
central room of the
Juko-in, Daitoku-ji
Kyoto. Momoyama
period, c. 1563–73
Ink and gold on
paper, height 5'9$^{1/8}$"
(1.76 m)

treasured by later generations. One of the finest teabowls extant was crafted by Hon'ami Koetsu (1558–1637). Named *Mount Fuji* after Japan's most sacred peak (fig. 9-22), it is an example of **raku**—a hand-built, low-fired ceramic developed especially for use in the tea ceremony. With its small foot, straight sides, slightly irregular shape, and crackled texture, this bowl exemplifies the entire ceremony. Merely looking at it suggests the feeling one would get from holding it, warm with tea, in one's hands.

During the Edo period (1603–1868), when the *Mount Fuji* bowl was made, peace and prosperity came to Japan at the price of an increasingly rigid and often repressive form of government. Zen Buddhism was replaced as the prevailing intellectual force by a form of Neo-Confucianism, the philosophy formulated in Song dynasty China that emphasized loyalty to the state. The government discouraged foreign ideas and foreign contacts, forbidding Japanese from traveling abroad and barring outsiders from Japan, with the exception of small Chinese and Dutch trading communities on an island off the southern port of Nagasaki.

Across Japan, and especially in the bustling new capital of Edo (modern Tokyo), people savored the delights of their peaceful society. Wealthy merchants patronized painters in the middle and later Edo period, and even artisans and tradespeople could purchase less costly works of art—above all, **woodblock prints**.

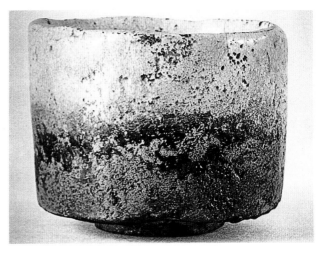

9-22   **Hon'ami Koetsu. Teabowl,** called *Mount Fuji*. Edo period, early 17th century. Raku ware, height 3$^{3/8}$" (8.5 cm). Sakai Collection, Tokyo

A specialized vocabulary developed to allow connoisseurs to discuss the subtle aesthetics of tea. A favorite term was *sabi*, which summoned up the particular beauty to be found in stillness or even deprivation. *Sabi* was borrowed from the critical vocabulary of poetry, where it was first established as a positive ideal by the early-thirteenth-century poet Fujiwara Shunzei. Other virtues were *wabi*, conveying a sense of great loneliness or humble and admirable shabbiness, and *shibui*, meaning plain and astringent.

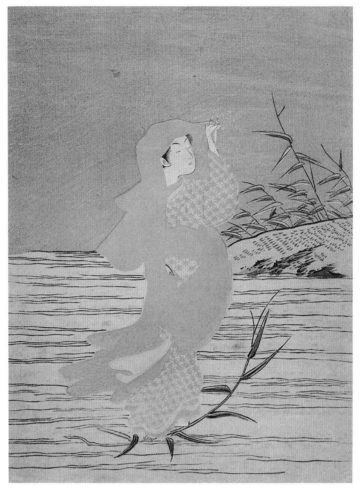

9-23 | **Suzuki Harunobu.** *Geisha as Daruma Crossing the Sea*
Edo period, mid-18th century. Color woodcut, 10⁷/₈ x 8¹/₄"
(27.6 x 21 cm). Philadelphia Museum of Art

Gift of Mrs. Emile Geyelin, in memory of Anne Hampton Barnes

Ukiyo-e ("pictures of the floating world"), as these prints are called in Japanese, represent the combined expertise of three people: the artist, the carver, and the printer. The artist supplied the master drawing for the print, executing its outlines in ink on tissue-thin paper. The carver pasted the drawing facedown on a hardwood block and cut around the lines with a sharp knife. The rest of the block was chiseled away, leaving the outlines standing in relief. This block, which reproduced the master drawing, was called the **key block**. If the print was to have several colors, the carver made a separate block for each color. A printer brushed water-based ink or color over the blocks, beginning with the key block; placed a piece of paper on top; and then rubbed with a smooth, padded device called a *baren* to make an impression. A publisher coordinated and funded the endeavor and distributed the prints to stores or itinerant peddlers.

The first artist to design **polychrome** prints was Suzuki Harunobu (1724–1770). One print that displays the charm and wit of Harunobu's art is *Geisha as Daruma Crossing the Sea* (fig. 9-23), in which a gracefully robed young woman is shown floating across the water on a reed. This is a playful reference to one of the legends about Bodhidharma, a semi-legendary Indian monk, known in Japan as Daruma, and recognized as the founder of the Zen tradition in China. Many paintings were made of this monk standing on a reed to cross the Yangzi River. To see a young woman rather than a grizzled Zen master peering ahead to the other shore must have greatly amused the Japanese populace. There was also another layer of meaning in this image because geishas (meaning "artists," traditional Japanese entertainers) were sometimes compared with Buddhist teachers or deities in their ability to bring earthly pleasure, akin to enlightenment, to humans.

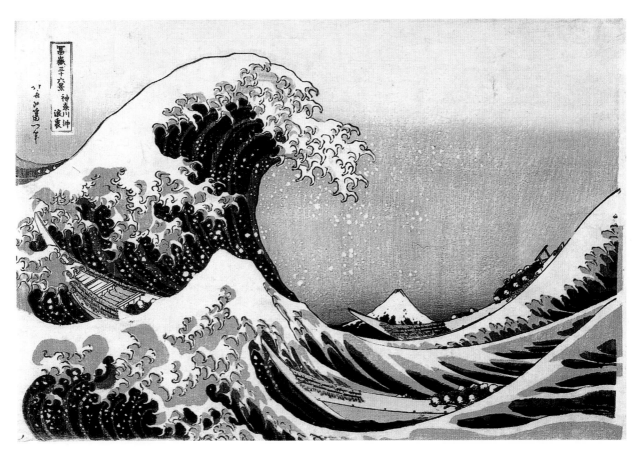

9-24 | **Katsushika Hokusai.** *The Great Wave off Kanagawa,* c. 1828. Edo period. Polychrome woodblock print on paper, 9⁷/₈" x 14⁵/₈" (25 x 37.1 cm). Honolulu Academy of Arts, Honolulu, Hawaii.
The James A. Michener Collection. (HAA 13,695)

Popular *ukiyo-e* subjects included courtesans and actors. One of the finest practitioners of the art at the end of the eighteenth century was Kitagawa Utamaro (1753–1806), whose *Woman at the Height of Her Beauty* has been discussed in the Introduction (see fig. 8). Beginning in the nineteenth century, landscapes, such as *Thirty-six Views of Fuji*, by Katsushika Hokusai (1760–1849), also became a popular subject for the makers of colored woodblock prints. The blocks were printed again and again until they were worn out. Then they were recarved and printed again.

The Great Wave (fig. 9-24) may be the most famous scene from the series *Thirty-six Views of Fuji*. The great wave rears up like a dragon with claws of foam, ready to crash down on the figures huddled in the boats below. Far in the distance rises Japan's most sacred peak, Mount Fuji, whose slopes, we

suddenly realize, swing up like waves and whose snowy crown is like foam—comparisons the artist makes clear in the wave nearest us, caught just at the moment of greatest resemblance.

When first seen in Europe and America, these and other Japanese prints were immediately acclaimed, and they strongly influenced late-nineteenth and early-twentieth-century Western art (see "Japonisme," page 448). Not only was the first book on Hokusai published in France, but the value of these prints as collectable works of art was recognized in the West before it was in Japan. Only within the past fifty years or so have Japanese museums and **connoisseurs** fully recognized the value of this originally "plebeian" form of art. In the twentieth century artists such as Roger Shimomura (see fig. 27) have rediscovered the power of the prints and incorporated the design in their own work.

100 CE	250	500	750

JEWISH, EARLY CHRISTIAN, BYZANTINE

Old Saint Peter's c. 320–27

Hagia Sophia 532–37

▲ EARLY CHRISTIAN c. 100–6TH CENTURY　　　▲ IMPERIAL CHRISTIAN 313–c. 6TH CENTURY　　　▲ EARLY BYZANTINE 527–867　　　LATER BYZANTINE 867–14

ISLAMIC

Dome of the Rock c. 687–91

Great Mosque at Córdoba 785–86

UMAYYAD DYNASTY 661–750 ▲　　　ABBASID DYNASTY 750–1258 ▲
EARLY CALIPHS 633–61 ▲　　　SPANISH UMAYYAD DYNASTY 756–1031 ▲

INDIA, CHINA, JAPAN

HEIAN 794–1185 ▲

L O O K I N G　B A C K　3

Giving Form to the Immaterial

People in widely different times and places have sought answers to the fundamental questions of life and death and in so doing have tried to explain their relationship to a spiritual world. The arts reflect their search for eternal truths. The exploration of the world of the intellect and imagination has often led artists toward an abstract or conceptual art rather than to naturalistic styles. Artists have adapted, rejected, or altered earlier styles as they created new modes of visual expression appropriate for their beliefs. The Greeks and Romans had imagined their gods in human form; earlier people, for example in Egypt and Mesopotamia, imagined terrifying composite deities. But Jews, Christians, and Muslims believed in a single unique God.

For Jews and Muslims God could not be given physical shape. God's word, rather than his likeness, held a position of primary importance for these "People of the Book." Muslim and Jewish artists raised the art of calligraphy (beautiful writing) to a level of exquisite sophistication and expressiveness. In China and Japan written words also had visual and aesthetic as well as linguistic significance. Using elegant calligraphy, scribes captured the sounds of language and made them permanent and visible as they gave ideas abstract shape with pen or brush and ink. Such linear abstractions were almost entirely divorced from nature. Meanwhile, Christian artists, while continuing to respect the Word, believed that God came to earth as a man. They created a powerful figurative art using human beings as expressive symbols.

Eternal truths as well as social ideas filtered through the imagination of these artists. Whether in the faces of Byzantine angels, in Muslim floral arabesques and witty human-headed script, or in mountains rising above the clouds in Chinese ink on silk, artists molded the images of the world into preconceived and simplified abstract forms. Patrons admired the combination of abstract form and technical skill, which might also be expressed in luxury arts, such as Chinese porcelain vases. The superficially rough and even accidental quality of a Japanese tea bowl appealed to a similar refined taste. In architecture, from the domes of Byzantium to the vaults of Santiago de Compostela and the gardens of the Alhambra, buildings also expressed both the spiritual and worldly aspirations of the people. Whether as small as a tea bowl or as large as the Church of Hagia Sophia, ultimately form captured spirit as men and women refined matter into works of art.

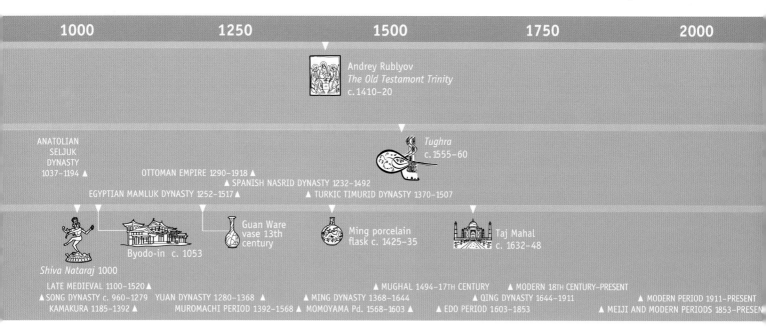

1000 **1250** **1500** **1750** **2000**

Andrey Rublyov
The Old Testamont Trinity
c. 1410–20

Tughra
c. 1555–60

ANATOLIAN
SELJUK
DYNASTY
1037–1194 ▲
OTTOMAN EMPIRE 1290–1918 ▲
▲ SPANISH NASRID DYNASTY 1232–1492
EGYPTIAN MAMLUK DYNASTY 1252–1517▲
▲ TURKIC TIMURID DYNASTY 1370–1507

Guan Ware
vase 13th
century

Ming porcelain
flask c. 1425–35

Taj Mahal
c. 1632–48

Byodo-in c. 1053

Shiva Nataraj 1000

LATE MEDIEVAL 1100–1520▲
▲ MUGHAL 1494–17TH CENTURY   ▲ MODERN 18TH CENTURY–PRESENT
▲SONG DYNASTY c. 960–1279 YUAN DYNASTY 1280–1368 ▲ ▲ MING DYNASTY 1368–1644 ▲ QING DYNASTY 1644–1911 ▲ MODERN PERIOD 1911–PRESENT
KAMAKURA 1185–1392 ▲ MUROMACHI PERIOD 1392–1568 ▲ MOMOYAMA Pd. 1568–1603 ▲ ▲ EDO PERIOD 1603–1853 ▲ MEIJI AND MODERN PERIODS 1853–PRESEN

Jewish, Early Christian, Byzantine, and Islamic Art

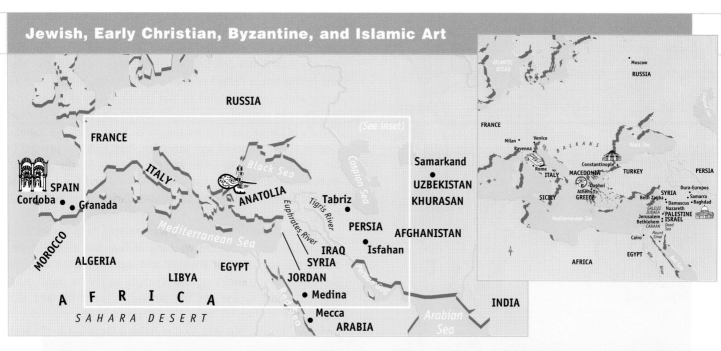

Later Asian Art

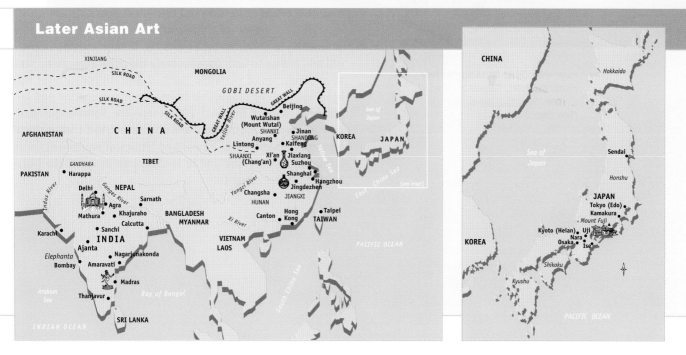

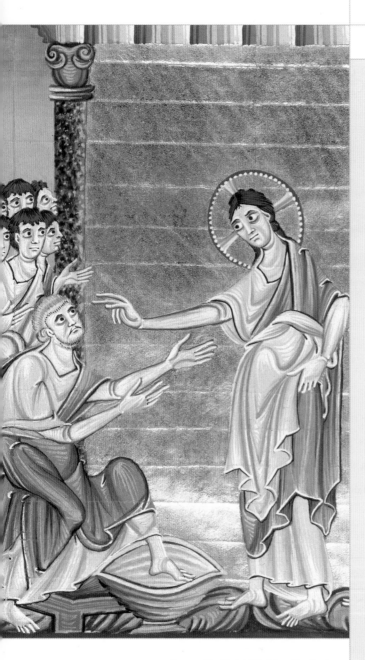

Page with *Christ Washing the Feet of His Disciples,* *Gospels of Otto III* c. 1000. Staatsbibliothek, Munich (See page 242.)

A dazzling golden light fills the interior of a fantastic building whose towers, basilicas, and domes balance precariously on a pair of green Roman columns. Framed within the columns, tall slender men gesture dramatically with long thin fingers. The scene depicts the moment when Jesus performs the ancient ritual of hospitality by washing the feet of his disciples, a humble courtesy described by Saint John (13:1–17). On the night before the Jewish feast of the Passover, Christ and his disciples gathered in Jerusalem. Rising from the meal (referred to as the Last Supper) and tying a towel around himself, Jesus washed their feet. As he performed this act of subservience and brotherly love, Peter tried to stop him, and in this image Peter has one foot reluctantly poised over the basin while Jesus explains to him the necessity of an act that will come to symbolize the forgiveness of sins and foreshadows Christ's ultimate sacrifice on the cross. Herein lies the foundation of Christian belief and salvation: God humbled himself to become a man and to suffer and die like one for the salvation of humankind. And yet, the cruciform halo and the lavish use of gold remind us that for Christians Christ alone is God and lord.

By the time this miniature was painted in a Gospel book around the year 1000, the Washing of Feet had come to symbolize the sacrament of Baptism and was associated with the sacrament of the Eucharist. The disciple on the far right undoing his sandal symbolizes the putting aside of sin and also recalls the traditional removing of shoes in the presence of divinity. The disciple next to him holds a large basin of water, placing unusual emphasis on the rite of purification. The two men give visual expression to Christ's example.

The iconography of this painting explains the importance of humility in Christian belief, that is, the subjugation of one's will and reason to God. Consequently the ritual came to be seen as a foundation of monastic spiritual life. Millennial fever may have inspired the production of images of subjugation and forgiveness. But for the next 200 years—the Romanesque period—emperors, kings, popes, and abbots lavished their material resources on churches, altars, and liturgical equipment in an attempt to glorify God and to re-create an image of the heavenly Jerusalem on earth.

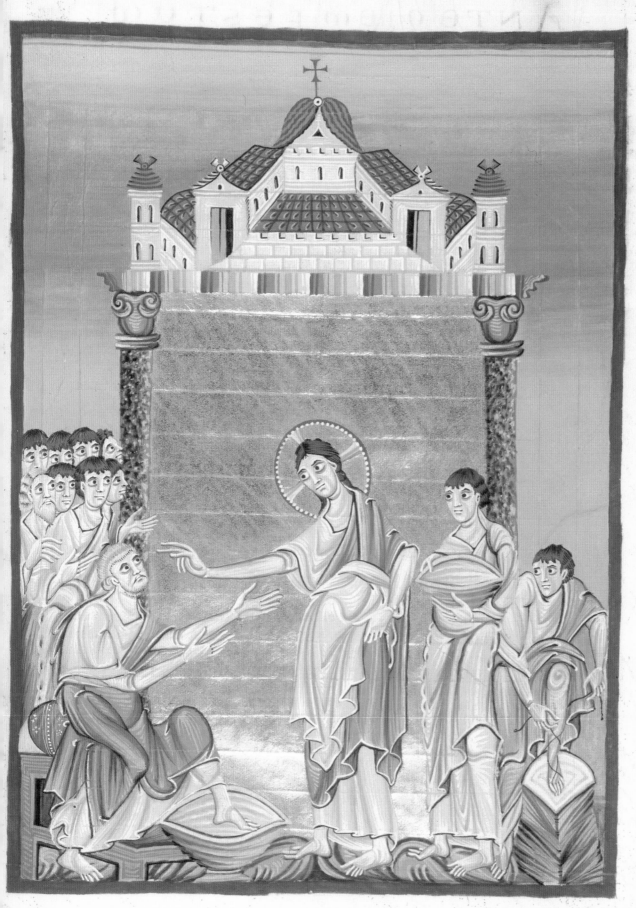

As Roman authority crumbled at the outset of the Middle Ages, political power in western Europe passed to the bishops as well as secular lords. The Church, as the repository of tradition and learning, provided intellectual as well as spiritual leadership. As patrons of the arts, clergymen sponsored the building of churches and the creation of equipment for use in Church ritual, including crosses, **reliquaries** (shrines for holy relics), and copies of sacred books. Secular leaders built manor houses and castles and commissioned the making of secular works of art such as jewelry, textiles, and armor, little of which survives. Stylistically, early medieval art reflects the fusion of Germanic and late Roman traditions in the former Western Empire, as well as the influence of both pre-Christian art from northern Europe and the Islamic art of Spain (see Map 4, page 285).

The fall of the Western Roman Empire in the fifth century left the Germanic peoples, including the Ostrogoths, Visigoths, Alemani, Angles, Saxons, and Franks, settled in many former Roman territories. The artists often worked in abstract geometric patterns inherited from the Bronze and Iron Ages (see fig. 6-29), and they also created the fantastic creatures seen in the **animal style**. The Gummersmark brooch (fig. 10-1), a large silver-gilt pin

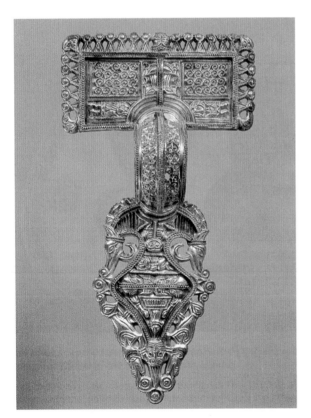

10-1 | **Gummersmark brooch,** Denmark. 6th century. Silver gilt Height 5³⁄₄" (14.6 cm). Nationalmuseet, Copenhagen

The faceted surface of this pin seems to seethe with abstract human, animal, and grotesque forms such as the eye-and-beak motif that frames the headplate, the man compressed between dragons just below the bridge element, and the pair of monster heads and crouching dogs with snapping tongues that frame the foot plate.

made in Denmark in the sixth century, displays an impressive array of generally symmetrical designs, emphasizing fantastic animal forms. Probably one of a pair, it was used to fasten a cloak around the wearer's shoulders. Individual **motifs** include spirals, birds, humans, and dragonlike animals so interlaced that one has to look carefully to identify them.

Christianity gained steadily in strength in the vacuum left by the collapse of the Roman Empire. The Church helped unify Europe's heterogeneous population, and Christianity spread into lands far from its Mediterranean origins, such as Ireland and eventually Scandinavia, which had never been ruled by Rome. In the eighth century, the German emperor Charlemagne sought to revive the glory of the Empire of Constantine and to reestablish an explicitly Christian regime in the West.

Western Europeans in the early medieval period looked with dismay on the rapid advance of Islam. The presence of Muslims in Spain from the eighth century on raised fears among Christians of further Islamic inroads into Europe. Muslim rulers were often tolerant of Christians and Jews in their territories. The Muslims were also "People of the Book." Monotheistic, they accepted Judaism and Christianity as forerunners of their own prophet, Muhammad. But western and northern European leaders were rarely so broad-minded. They viewed Muslims not only as unwanted foreigners but also as dangerous infidels. The Franks beat back the Muslim armies in the eighth century and so secured Europe to develop as a Christian land. By the end of the eleventh century Christians were on the offensive, mounting crusades against the Muslims in return.

Early Medieval Art in the British Isles and Scandinavia

Another clash of cultures had occurred in the British Isles (see pages 157–59). The Romans subjugated the native Celtic inhabitants of Britain in 43 CE but did not invade Ireland. During the period of Roman rule, which lasted until 406, Christianity took root in Britain and spread to Ireland. But after the fall of the Roman Empire, British chieftains took control, vying for dominance with the help of soldiers from continental Europe, thus giving rise to the legends of King Arthur and the Round Table. The Angles, Saxons, and Jutes from the Continent soon established kingdoms of their own, and the people under their rule adopted Anglo-Saxon speech and customs. Over the next 200 years, a new Anglo-Saxon and Hiberno-Saxon culture (*Hibernia* was the Roman name for Ireland) formed out of a fusion of these Celtic, Germanic, and Romanized British traditions.

Metalworking is one of the glories of Anglo-Saxon art. References to splendid jewelry and military equipment decorated with gold and silver fill Anglo-Saxon literature, such as the epic poem *Beowulf*. An early-seventh-century burial mound, excavated in the English region of East Anglia at a site called Sutton Hoo (*hoo* means "hill"), concealed a hoard of such treasures. The grave's still unidentified occupant was buried in an 86-foot-long ship. The vessel held weapons, armor, other equipment for the afterlife, and such luxury items as an exquisitely worked lid for a purse (fig. 10-2).

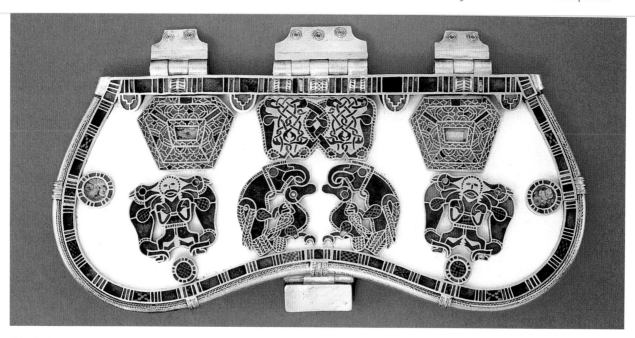

10-2 | **Purse cover,** from the Sutton Hoo burial ship, Suffolk, England. c. 615–25. Cloisonné plaques of gold, garnet, and checked millefiore enamel, length 8" (20.3 cm). The British Museum, London

Only the decorations on this purse cover are original. The lid itself, of a rich tan-colored ivory or bone, deteriorated and disappeared centuries ago, and the white backing is a modern replacement. The leather pouch has disintegrated but the coins in the purse survived.

10-3 | ***Chi Rho Iota* page,** Book of Matthew, *Book of Kells* probably made at Iona, Scotland. Late 8th or early 9th century. Tempera on vellum, 13 x 9½" (33 x 24 cm) The Board of Trinity College, Dublin

MS 58 (A.1.6.), fol. 34v

The Greek letters *chi rho iota* (*XPI,* or *chri*) form the abbreviation for *Christi,* the first word in the Latin sentence *Christi autem generatio,* meaning: "Now this is how the birth of Jesus Christ came about" (Matthew 1:18). The word *autem* appears as another Latin abbreviation resembling an *h,* which is followed by *generatio* written out. The text continues on the next page. Medieval scribes had to learn a long list of standard abbreviations for Latin words, which were used like modern shorthand to save time and space in transcribing long documents or copying texts. Scribes in the courts of popes and secular rulers were even given the official title of "abbreviator."

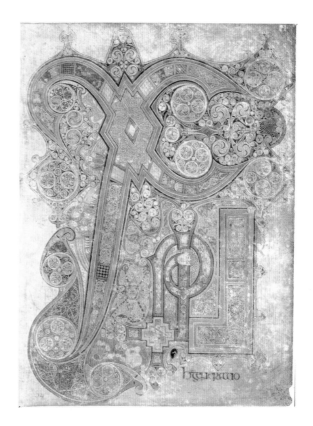

The purse lid is decorated with intricate **cloisonné** enamel, whose designs come from wide-ranging sources. **Animal interlace** forms the central piece. Growing out of the animal style popular in Scandinavia, animals (here two pairs of quadrupeds) stretch out into interwoven serpentine ribbons (compare with fig. 10-1). The pairs of animals flanking human figures at the lower right and left recall the "animal combat" theme prevalent throughout the ancient Near East (see fig. 2-8), and in another combat, Norse hawks with curved beaks and square eyebrows attack Celtic ducks. The rich blend of motifs on the purse represent a complex style that flourished in England and Ireland during the seventh and eighth centuries.

As Christianity spread through the islands Hiberno-Saxon scribes adapted pagan styles for large, lavishly decorated gospel books (see "The Medieval Scriptorium," page 237). The *Book of Kells,* one of the most original and inventive of the surviving Hiberno-Saxon Gospels, was probably made in the late eighth

century in a monastery on Iona, an island off the west coast of Scotland. The most celebrated folio (manuscript page) in the *Book of Kells* may be the one from the Gospel of Matthew that begins the account of Jesus' birth (fig. 10-3). The Greek letters *chi, rho,* and *iota* dominate the page. The letters create an irregularly shaped form that resembles a cluster of gold and enamel brooches. At first glance, the page seems filled with completely

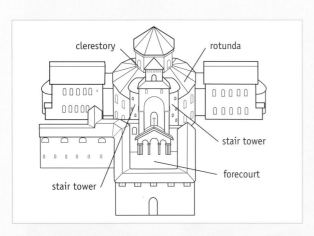

10-4 Reconstruction drawing of the Palace Chapel of Charlemagne, Aachen (Aix-la-Chapelle), Germany Constructed 792–805

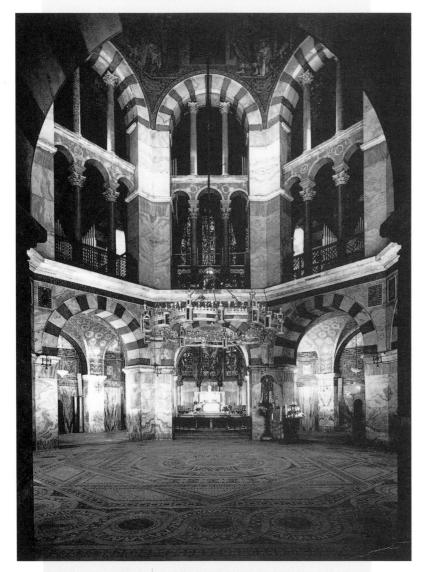

10-5 Palace Chapel of Charlemagne

abstract ornament, but hidden in the dense thicket of spirals and interlaces are human and animal forms. The curve of the *rho* in the center of the page ends in the head of a red-headed youth, possibly representing Christ. Three angels hold the left vertical edge of the *chi*, and below them, just to the right of the long stroke of the letter, an otter catches a salmon and pairs of cats capture mice. The cat-and-mouse scene signals the triumph of good (embodied in the cats) over evil (embodied in the mice who try to eat the host—the Communion wafer, the mystical body of Christ).

Even as monks finished the *Book of Kells*, Hiberno-Saxon culture came under threat from abroad. At the end of the eighth century, seafaring bands of Scandinavians known as Vikings began to appear on the coasts of the British Isles, lured by the wealth of church treasuries and fertile land. The monks of Iona retreated, taking their precious Gospels to the inland Irish monastery of Kells. The Vikings soon descended on the rest of Europe. Intermittently looting and destroying coastal and inland river communities, they were a terrifying presence in Europe for nearly 300 years. Viking bands settled in Iceland, Greenland, Ireland, England, France, Scotland, and Russia. About 1000 they even established a short-lived outpost in North America.

Carolingian Art

The Franks, another Germanic tribe, settled in northern Gaul (modern France) by the end of the fifth century. In 732 Frankish warriors turned back the Muslim invasion of Gaul, and their leaders established a dynasty of rulers known as the Carolingians, after their greatest member Charles the Great, called Charlemagne (ruled 768–814). Charlemagne consolidated an empire in continental Europe during the second half of the eighth century, which at its greatest extent encompassed modern France, western Germany, Belgium, Holland, Luxemburg, and even northeastern Spain. Charlemagne imposed Christianity, sometimes brutally, throughout this territory and promoted church reform through his support of the Benedictine order of monks and nuns. In 800, Pope Leo III (ruled 795–816) granted Charlemagne the title of emperor, declaring him the rightful successor to the first Christian Roman emperor, Constantine. This event served to reinforce Charlemagne's authority over his realm and strengthened the bonds between the papacy and secular government in the West.

To proclaim the glory of the new empire visually, Charlemagne's architects, painters, and sculptors turned to the two former Western imperial capitals, Rome and Ravenna, for inspiration. The chapel of Charlemagne's palace at Aachen (in Germany) served as the emperor's private chapel, the church of his imperial court, a **martyrium** to house the precious relics of saints, and, after Charlemagne's death, his mausoleum. The building has a central octagonal plan (fig. 10-4), as does the Church of San Vitale in Ravenna (see fig. 7-14); however, it lacks San Vitale's sophisticated structure. The core of the chapel building is a

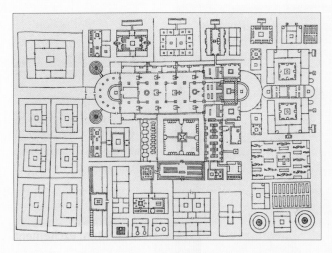

10-6 | **Plan of the Abbey of Saint Gall** (redrawn). c. 817
Original in red ink on parchment, 28 x 44¹/₂"
(71.1 x 112.1 cm). Stiftsbibliothek, St. Gallen
Switzerland, Cod. Sang. 1092

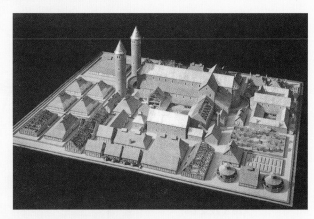

10-7 | **Model after the Saint Gall monastery plan**
(see fig. 10-6). Constructed by Walter Horn and
Ernst Born, 1965

soaring octagon, surrounded at the ground level by an **ambulatory** (passage) and ringed by a **gallery** (opening overlooking the **nave**) on the second floor (fig. 10-5). Alternating square and triangular **bays** convert the inner octagon to a sixteen-sided building. In the gallery, bays divided by diaphragm arches (arches supporting walls) support transverse barrel-vaulted bays. Columns and railings at the gallery level form a screen and reemphasize the flat, pierced walls of the octagon. These features create a powerful vertical visual movement from the floor of the central area to the top of the vault.

A new architectural feature created by Carolingian architects is the **westwork**, or monumental entrance. Above a projecting porch, a throne room and chapel face the apse, which gave the emperor an unobstructed view of the ceremonies at the high altar, and at the same time ensuring his privacy and safety. Twin stair towers flank this entrance complex and create a distinctive western facade. The vertical emphasis of the western towers and the equally upward rising thrust of the interior were northern contributions to Christian architecture, in marked contrast to the more horizontal forms of Roman and Early Christian basilicas.

Charlemagne turned to the Church to help stabilize his empire through religion and education. He looked to the Benedictine monks whom he called his "cultural army." The monks followed the *Rule for Monasteries*, written by Saint Benedict of Nursia (c. 480–c. 547), a set of practical guidelines for community life that combined work, prayer, and participation in religious services. To house such a community, in the ninth century, Abbot Haito of Reichenau developed an ideal plan for the layout of monasteries, which survives in the library of the Abbey of Saint Gall in modern Switzerland (fig. 10-6). The Saint Gall plan shows a basilican church with towers and both eastern and western apses to house altars and relics (fig. 10-7). The monks' quarters lie at the south, with dormitory, refectory (dining room),

THE MEDIEVAL SCRIPTORIUM

Today, presses can produce hundreds of thousands of identical copies of any book. In Europe in the Middle Ages, however, before the invention of printing from movable type in the mid-1400s, books were made by hand, one at a time, with pen, ink, brush, and paint. Each one was a time-consuming and expensive undertaking.

At first, medieval books were usually made by monks and nuns in a workshop called a **scriptorium** (plural, scriptoria), usually in a monastery or convent. As the demand for books increased, rulers set up palace workshops of both religious and lay scribes, supervised by scholars.

Before paper came into common use in the early 1400s, books were written on animal skin—either **vellum**, which was fine and soft, or **parchment**, which was heavier and shinier. The skins were cleaned and scraped to create a smooth surface that would absorb ink and paint, which also required time and experience to prepare. Many pigments—particularly blues and greens—were made from costly semiprecious stones. In luxury manuscripts artists also used gold in the form of gold leaf or gold paint.

Work on a book was often divided between scribes, who copied the text, and one or more artists, who painted illustrations, large initials, or other decorations. Although most books were produced anonymously, scribes and illustrators sometimes signed their work or provided background information in a **colophon** (notes on the book's production at the end of the manuscript).

The very earliest books were kept in the form of *rolls* for protection and storage, with the sheets pasted or stitched together. Today, the most common kind of book is the *codex*, in which a number of folded sheets are stitched together (a *gathering*). About 400 CE, the codex began to assume greater favor than other book forms in Europe. The scroll remained popular in Asia.

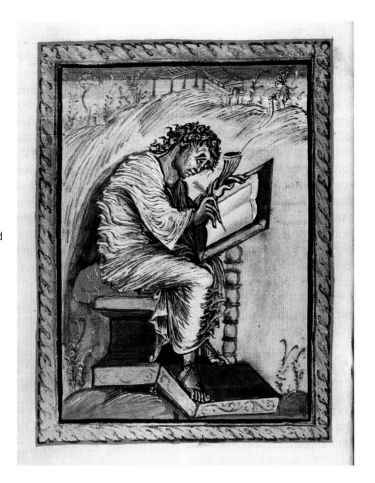

10-8

**Page with
Matthew the
Evangelist**
Book of Matthew
Ebbo Gospels
c. 816–40. Ink and
colors on vellum
10¹/₄ x 8³/₄"
(26 x 22.2 cm)
Bibliothèque
Municipale
Epernay, France
MS 1, fol.18v

and workrooms; at the east are the cemetery, hospital, and school for young monks and novices; and at the north stand the abbot's residence, guest quarters, and a hospice for the poor. Buildings for lay farm workers and shelter for animals surrounded this central core. So efficient and functional was this plan that Benedictine monasteries often still follow the layout today.

Although their principal duties consisted of prayer and liturgical services, monks and nuns also spent hours producing books. Scrupulously edited versions of key religious texts, written in a new, clear script, are among the lasting achievements of the Carolingian period. The monasteries of northeastern France became one of the centers of book production during the reign of Louis the Pious (ruled 814–840), Charlemagne's son and successor. A portrait of Saint Matthew from a gospel book made for Archbishop Ebbo of Reims, begun after 816 at the Abbey of Hautevillers near Reims, demonstrates the unique style that emerged there (fig. 10-8). The figure of Saint Matthew seems to vibrate with intensity. Even the acanthus leaves in the frame seem blown by a violent wind. The rapid, calligraphic style focuses attention on the evangelist's spiritual excitement as he hastens to transcribe the Word of God delivered by the angel (Matthew's symbol) in the upper-right corner. As if to echo the saint's turbulent emotions, the footstool tilts precariously, and the top of the desk seems about to detach itself from the pedestal. Following an ancient tradition, a portrait of the author introduces each Gospel, as a photograph on a book jacket flap introduces the author to the reader today.

Manuscripts such as the *Ebbo Gospels* represent an enormous investment in time, talent, and materials. Only a wealthy monastery could afford to slaughter the hundreds of sheep required for the parchment on which the books were written. Books were protected with heavy, leather-covered wooden, and sometimes jeweled, covers. One of the richest of these covers (fig. 10-9), probably made between 870–880 at one of the workshops of Charles the Bald (ruled 840–877), the son of Louis the Pious, combines jewels, pearls, and sculpture in gold. (Sometime before the sixteenth century the cover was added to a late-ninth-century Carolingian manuscript known as the *Lindau Gospels*.)

The Crucifixion scene on the front cover of the *Lindau Gospels* features gold figures in relief. They are formed by the repoussé technique, which we saw in the Byzantine icon of the archangel Michael (see fig. 7-24). Angels hover above the arms of the cross, and mourners twist in agony below. Over Jesus' head figures representing the sun and moon hide their faces. In contrast to these agitated figures the artist modeled Jesus in a rounded, naturalistic style that suggests a **classical** source. Christ stands in front of the cross—straight and wide-eyed with outstretched arms, announcing his triumph over death and welcoming believers into the faith. The jewels, polished to form cabochons (polished, not faceted, stones), are raised on tiny feet that allow light to penetrate and enhance their luster. The glowing colored jewels reminded the medieval believers of descriptions of the Heavenly Jerusalem.

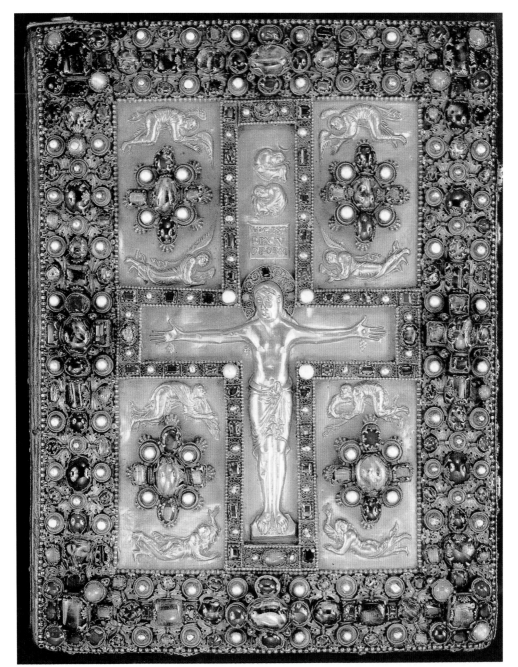

10-9

Crucifixion with Angels and Mourning Figures, outer cover, *Lindau Gospels*
c. 870–80
Gold, pearls, and gems
13³/₄ x 10³/₈"
(34.9 x 26.7 cm)
The Pierpont Morgan Library
New York
MS 1

Painting in Christian Spain

The Christian and Islamic worlds met in medieval Spain. When Muslim armies arrived in the early eighth century, Spain was governed by a Germanic people known as the Visigoths, who had ruled over the indigenous Spanish population since the fall of the Western Roman Empire. The Islamic conquest of Spain in 711 ended Visigothic rule. With some exceptions, the Muslims allowed Christians and Jews to follow their own religious practices. Christian artists adapted many features of Islamic style to fit their traditional themes, and soon developed a hybrid style known today as Mozarabic.

Writing biblical commentaries to refute heretical beliefs became a major task of the monasteries of northern Spain. The antagonisms among Muslims, orthodox Christians, and the followers of various heretical Christian beliefs provided fertile material for Spanish theologians. Beatus, the abbot of a monastery in the kingdom of Asturias on the northern coast, compiled an influential commentary on the Apocalypse, which describes the final and fiery destruction of the world before the Last Judgment and triumph of Christ. The scribe named Senior made a copy of Beatus's *Commentary on the Apocalypse* in the late tenth century at the Monastery of San Salvador at Tábara, in the Spanish kingdom of León. The illustrators were a monk named Emeterius and a nun named Ende, who signed herself "painter and servant of God." A full-page painting from this book (see fig. 8-8) illustrates Beatus's metaphorical description of the triumph of Christ over Satan. According to the text next to the illustration, a bird with a powerful beak and beautiful plumage

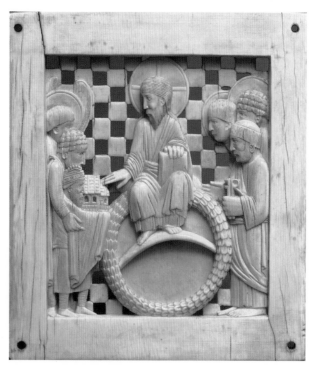

10-10 | *Christ Enthroned with Saints and Emperor Otto I*
one of a series of nineteen ivory plaques, known
as the *Magdeburg Ivories*. German or North Italian
c. 962–73. Ivory plaque, 5 x 4¹/₂" (12.7 x 11.4 cm)
The Metropolitan Museum of Art, New York
Gift of George Blumenthal, 1941 (41.100.157)

During the reign of Otto I, Magdeburg was on the edge of a buffer
zone between the Ottonian Empire and the pagan Slavs. In the
960s, Otto established a religious center there from which the
Slavs could be converted.

(Christ) covers itself with mud to trick the snake (Satan). Just
when the snake decides the bird is harmless, the bird swiftly
attacks and kills it. **Allegories** such as this were popular among
artists, writers, and theologians in the Middle Ages. Because
allegories translate abstract ideas into concrete events and
images, they communicate directly with people of almost any
level of education. The painters followed a time-honored Christian
tradition, for Jesus himself spoke to the people in parables.

The Ottonian Period

The heirs of Louis the Pious divided the Carolingian Empire
into three parts, setting the stage for the modern divisions of
Europe. The western portion eventually became France. In the
tenth century, control of the eastern portion of the empire,
which corresponded roughly to modern Germany, Switzerland, and Austria passed to a dynasty of Saxon rulers known
as the Ottonians, after its three principal figures, Otto I (ruled
936–973), Otto II (ruled 973–983), and Otto III (ruled
983–1002). Otto I gained control of Italy in 951; and the pope
crowned him emperor in 962. Thereafter Otto and his successors
dominated the papacy and appointments to other high Church
offices. This union of Germany and Italy under a German ruler
came to be known in the twelfth century as the Holy Roman
Empire. The Empire survived in modified form (having lost

most Italian territories by the sixteenth century) as the Habsburg Empire into the twentieth century.

An ivory panel shows Otto I presenting a model of the cathedral of Magdeburg to Christ (fig. 10-10). For all his earthly
power, Otto is a tiny figure in the company of Christ and the
saints, who include Saint Peter, holding the keys to heaven, and
Saint Maurice, who presents Otto to Christ. Saint Maurice was a
third-century Roman Christian commander of African troops
who is said to have suffered martyrdom for refusing to worship
in pagan rites. In the Middle Ages he was often represented as
a dark-skinned African. Christ, seated on a heavenly wreath, his
feet on the arc of the earth, graciously extends his hand to
receive the offering.

In the tenth and eleventh centuries, Ottonian artists in
northern Europe, drawing on Roman, Byzantine, and Carolingian
models, began a new tradition of large sculpture in wood and
bronze that would have a significant influence on later medieval
art. An important patron of architecture and sculpture was Bishop
Bernward of Hildesheim, Germany, who was himself a skilled
goldsmith. A pair of bronze doors made under his direction for
his Abbey Church of Saint Michael represents the most ambitious
and complex bronze-casting project since antiquity (fig. 10-11).
The inscription in the band running across the center of the
doors states that Bishop Bernward installed them in 1015.

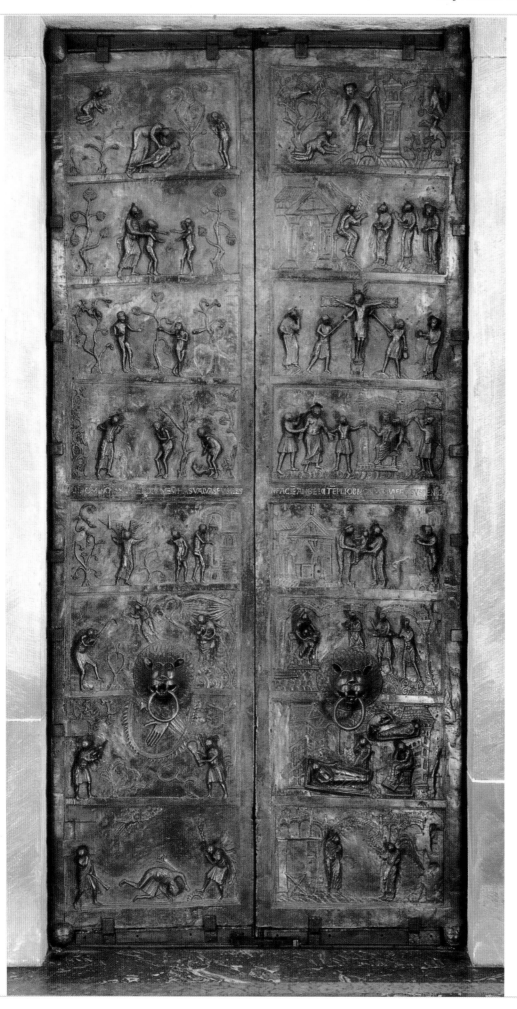

10-11

Bishop Bernward Doors made for the Abbey Church of Saint Michael Cathedral Museum Hildesheim Germany 1015. Bronze, height 16'6" (5 m)

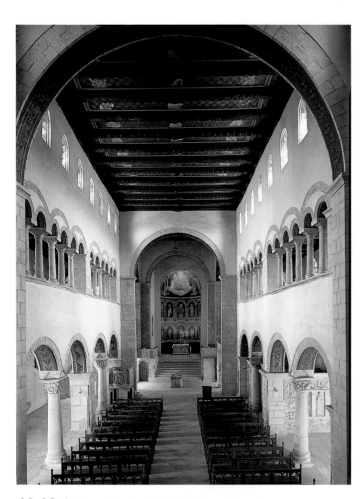

10-12 | Nave, Church of Saint Cyriakus, Gernrode

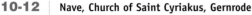

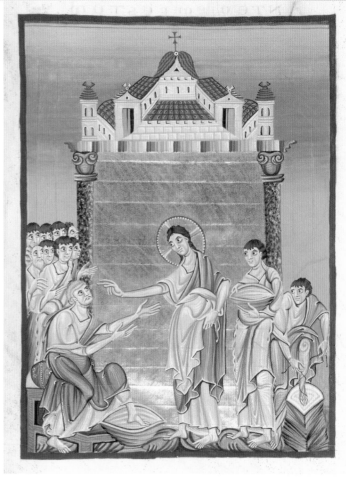

10-13 | Page with *Christ Washing the Feet of His Disciples*
Gospels of Otto III. c. 1000. Staatsbibliothek, Munich
(See pages 232–33.)

The doors, standing more than 16 feet tall, are decorated with Old Testament scenes on the left and New Testament scenes on the right. The Old Testament scenes read down from the top to the bottom panel; the New Testament narrative continues on the right, upward from the bottom panel (the Annunciation) to the top (*Noli me tangere*) (see "Iconography of the Life of Jesus," pages 168–69). In each pair of scenes, the Old Testament event can be interpreted as a prefiguration of the New Testament event. Such elaborate parallels characterize the Christian use of images. The third panel down, for example, shows on the left Adam and Eve picking the forbidden fruit of Knowledge in the Garden of Eden and thus bringing down on humankind the evils of sin, suffering, and death. This scene is paired on the right with the Crucifixion of Jesus, whose sacrifice was believed to have atoned for Adam and Eve's Original Sin. At the center of the doors six panels down, Eve and Mary sit side by side, holding their sons. Cain (who murdered his brother) and Jesus signify the opposition of evil and good, damnation and salvation.

Aristocratic women often held positions of authority in the Ottonian Empire, especially as abbesses. When Margrave Gero (provincial military governor) founded the convent of Saint Cyriakus, he made his widowed daughter-in-law the convent's first abbess, following the Ottonian policy of appointing relatives and close associates to important church offices. He began building the church of Saint Cyriakus (fig. 10-12) in 961. The church has a nave and **side aisles** with a tri-part elevation and a flat wooden ceiling. Rectangular piers interrupt the rows of columns in the nave arcade, creating a rhythmic effect more interesting than that of the uniform colonnades of earlier churches. At the gallery level six arches in three groups of two reinforce the rhythm. The two arches on the nave level surmounted by the six arches on the gallery level, surmounted in turn by three windows in the clerestory establish a vertical division. This seemingly simple architectural aesthetic, with its rhythmic alternation of heavy and light supports, its balance of rectangular and round forms, and its combination of horizontal and vertical movements, found full expression in the succeeding Romanesque style.

Like their Carolingian predecessors, monks and nuns created richly illuminated manuscripts, often subsidized by the secular rulers. Styles varied from place to place, depending on the traditions of the local scriptorium and the models available in each library. For example, the *Gospels of Otto III* (fig. 10-13), made in a German monastery about 1000, shows the inspiration of Byzantine art in the use of clear outline drawing, rich colors, and lavish amounts of gold. Otto III abandoned his German homeland, preferring to live in Rome. From his palace on the hill near the Early Christian Church of Santa Sabina

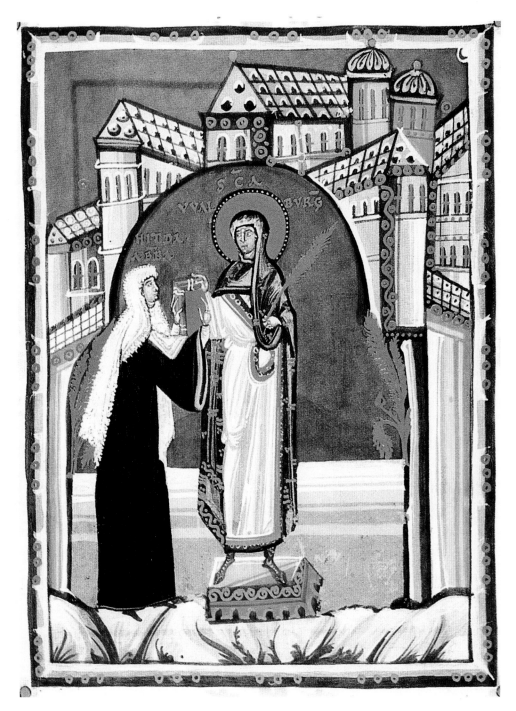

10-14

Presentation page with Abbess Hitda and Saint Walpurga, *Hitda Gospels*. Early 11th century. Ink and colors on vellum, 11³⁄₈ x 5⁵⁄₈" (29 x 14.2 cm) Hessische Landes- und Hochschulbibliothek Darmstadt, Germany

(see fig. 7-6) he could look out over the ruins of ancient Rome. The theme of Christian charity and humility represented by the painting showing Christ washing his disciples' feet contrasts with Otto's dream of imperial glory as well as the richness of the illuminated manuscript. The grandeur evoked by this intensely expressive style makes Ottonian painting one of the most splendid in all medieval art.

Elaborate architecture provides the setting for a very different image, the presentation page of a gospel book made for Abbess Hitda (d. 1041), of Meschede, near Cologne, in the early eleventh century (fig. 10-14). The abbess offers her book to Saint Walpurga, her convent's patron saint. The artist has arranged the architectural lines of the convent in the background to frame the figures and draw attention to the transaction. The size of the buildings underscores the abbess's position of authority. The foreground setting—a rocky, uneven strip of landscape—is meant to be understood as holy ground, separated from the rest of the world by golden trees and the huge arch-shaped aura that silhouettes Saint Walpurga. The simple contours of the stately figures give them a monumental quality that recalls Byzantine art.

The Ottonian court in Rome gave northern artists access to the artistic heritage of Italy, which they reinterpreted in light of their own local materials and techniques. From this groundwork during the early medieval period emerged the arts of European Romanesque culture.

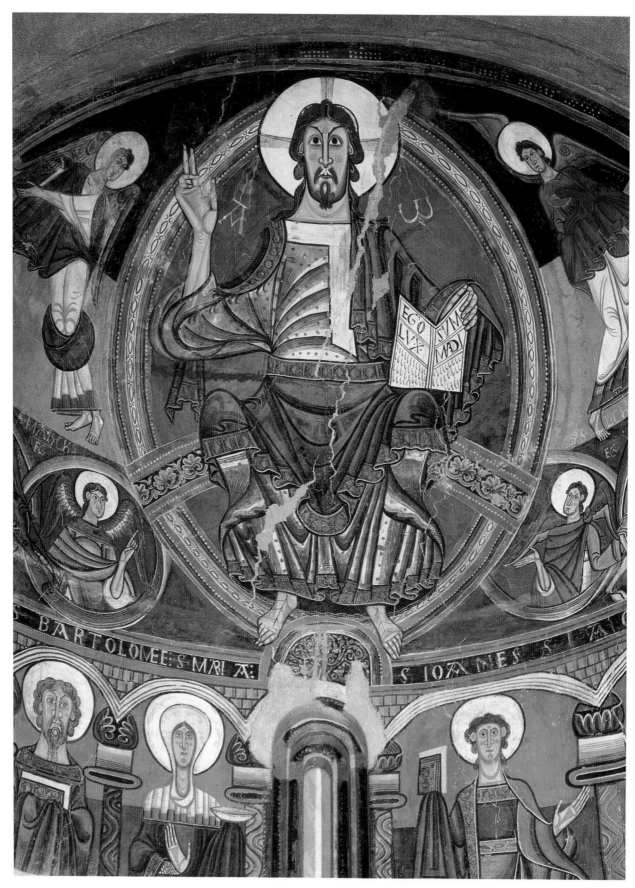

10-15 | ***Christ in Majesty,*** detail of apse painting from the Church of San Clemente, Tahull Lérida, Spain. c. 1123. Museu Nacional d'Art de Catalunya, Barcelona

The Romanesque Period

European society in the Early Middle Ages was predominantly agricultural, but during the Romanesque period villages grew into towns and trade began to revive. In some regions, a system governing social and political relations called feudalism evolved. In this system, land belonged to the ruler (kings claimed to hold their territories in trust from God), who granted some of this property to lesser noblemen, called vassals. In exchange, the vassal promised to the ruler his allegiance and military service, which usually included a troop of armed knights and warhorses. These vassals regranted portions of their land to vassals of their own under similar terms. Landless but free peasants living in villages performed farm work and other manual labor on the estates. At the same time, cities with populations of merchants and artisans arose outside the feudal system. Towns might have royal charters, since by granting charters to cities, kings could collect revenue and create an independent power base.

The nations we know today did not exist in medieval Europe, especially in Germany and Italy, where local rulers and towns resisted attempts by the successors of the Ottonians to impose a central authority. Although parts of these regions were called the Holy Roman Empire in the twelfth century, they remained politically fragmented until the nineteenth century. In France, where powerful dukes controlled the richest lands, the kings of the Capetian dynasty began to consolidate their authority from their personal stronghold around Paris. By the end of the twelfth century, they had laid the foundation for a powerful national monarchy, although southern France retained close linguistic and cultural ties to northern Spain. Meanwhile Normandy, a peninsula on the northern coast that had been settled by Vikings, became a powerful feudal duchy. In 1066, Duke William of Normandy (1035–1087) invaded England and, as William the Conqueror, he became that country's king. William replaced the Anglo-Saxon nobility with Norman nobles, and England began to emerge as a nation. In 1054, the Christian Church split into two major parts, the Roman Catholic Church, led by the pope in western Europe, and the Eastern Orthodox Church, led by the patriarch of Constantinople in the Byzantine Empire.

Forces also existed to unify people and broaden their horizons. The Church became an international force, as the pope and the patriarch acted as important players in European politics, often forging fruitful alliances with the political rulers. In 1095, Pope Urban II called for the first of several medieval Crusades to free Jerusalem and the Holy Land from Islamic rule. Although the Crusades were for the most part military failures, the Western crusaders' encounters with the sophisticated Byzantine and Islamic worlds created a demand for luxury goods from the East. More people traveled and made pilgrimages to the holy places of Christendom—especially Jerusalem, Rome, and Santiago de Compostela—despite undergoing dire material and physical hardships. Travel and trade led to the rise of an increasingly knowledgeable and urban society. Foreign contacts helped to nourish a period of intellectual and artistic ferment that has been termed the "twelfth-century renaissance," or rebirth of learning.

The art produced during the period of the eleventh and twelfth centuries is called *Romanesque* ("in the Roman manner").

A modern term first used to describe the romance languages, it eventually was used to define the appearance of eleventh- and twelfth-century architecture that had the solid masonry walls, rounded arches, and masonry vaults characteristic of ancient Roman building. The term *Romanesque* is now applied to all the arts produced from roughly the mid-eleventh through the twelfth century.

ARCHITECTURE AND MURAL PAINTING

In the eleventh and twelfth centuries, churches and monasteries multiplied across Europe. As one eleventh-century monk put it, the world was "clothed everywhere in a white garment of churches" (Radulphus Glaber, cited in Holt, page 18). A remarkable variety of artistic traditions, including Roman, Carolingian, Mozarabic, and Italo-Byzantine join with local styles to form the Romanesque style. An apse painting from the Church of San Clemente (fig. 10-15) in Tahull, in the Catalonian Pyrenees of northern Spain, shows these influences. The Romanesque artist has re-created an almost Byzantine Pantokrator—Christ as ruler and judge of the world. Byzantine features include the figure's frontal pose, the modeling of forms through the use of repeated colored lines of varying width and shades, and such iconographical features as the alpha and omega (the first and last letters of the Greek alphabet) and the depiction of Christ holding a book inscribed in Latin, "ego sum lux mundi" ("I am the light of the world"; John 8:12). The San Clemente Master, as the otherwise anonymous Tahull painter is known, borrowed elements from several styles. He adapted the Byzantine style to the local taste for geometry and simplicity of form, turning facial features and draperies into elegant patterns. The striped background is Mozarabic. The inventive detailing of the draperies with their crinkles and loops, as well as the mosaiclike intensity of the colors built up from many thin coats of paint, produce a refreshingly decorative feeling often found in Carolingian painting. The expressive figures of Evangelists, pointing toward Christ or interacting directly with the viewer, may have been inspired by southern French art, transmitted to the Pyrenees over pilgrimage routes.

Romanesque churches, like their early medieval predecessors, often have Early Christian basilica plans, but they featured significant structural innovations. Instead of wooden roofs, in some regions they were covered with stone barrel vaults or groin (sectional) vaults sometimes reinforced by powerful supporting arches called ribs. Masonry vaults enhanced the acoustical properties of the building and the effect of the Gregorian chant. They also provided some protection against fire. These new vaulting techniques permitted builders more flexibility in laying out interior space (see "Rib Vaulting," page 255). **Buttresses** (thick masses of masonry) reinforced walls at critical points and made taller buildings and masonry vaults possible. Towers emphasized both the **crossing** (where the nave and transept intersect) and the west facade, which contained the principal entrance to the church (and by extension, to the City of God, the Heavenly Jerusalem). The growth in popularity of the veneration of the relics of saints inspired people to make pilgrimages to the shrines, and in Europe the tombs of Saint Peter in Rome and Saint

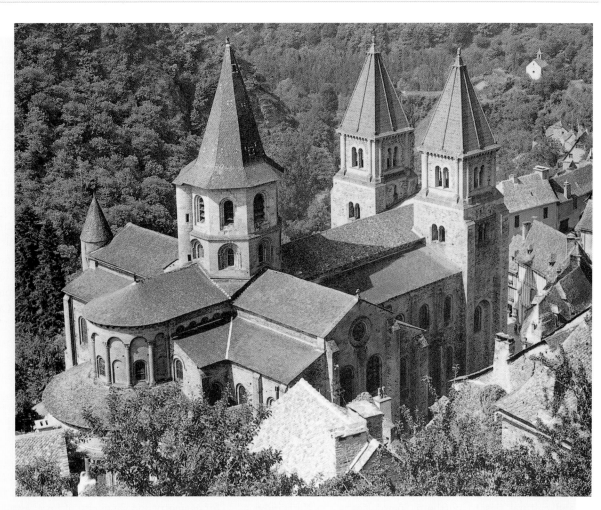

10-16

Abbey Church of Sainte-Foy
Conques
Rouergue, France
Mid-11th–12th
century. Western
towers rebuilt in
the 19th century;
crossing tower
rib-vaulted in the
14th century;
restored in the
19th century.
View from the
northeast

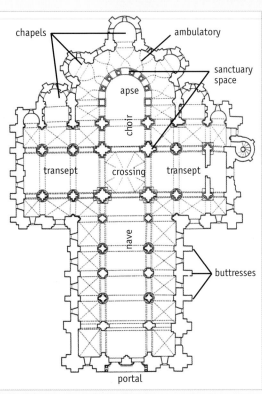

10-18 | **Plan of Abbey Church of Sainte-Foy**

James in Galicia rivaled the Holy Sepulchre in Jerusalem. The Cathedral of Saint James in Santiago de Compostela (see fig. 10) and churches like Sainte-Foy at Conques (fig. 10-16) represented a new design intended to accommodate the crowds.

The body of Saint James, the apostle to the Iberian Peninsula, lay in Spain, and one of the many later saints, an Early Christian child, Saint Foy (Saint Faith) could be venerated in the Abbey Church of Sainte-Foy at Conques in south-central France on the road to Compostela (fig. 10-17). There a golden reliquary contained her remains. To accommodate the many pilgrims the clergy constructed new, larger churches, beginning in the mid-eleventh century and continuing into the next century. The **cruciform** (cross-shaped) plan with a wide transept and long nave is typical of Romanesque pilgrimage churches (fig. 10-18). Portals, or large doorways, mark the entrances. At the east end, the sanctuary combines the choir, the apse containing the high altar, many chapels housing additional altars and relics, and a wide ambulatory, or walkway, which permitted the pilgrims to move freely from chapel to chapel.

On entering a church like the Cathedral of Santiago de Compostela, the viewer's attention is focused on the principal altar but is also to some extent drawn upward (see fig. 10). A ribbed barrel vault covers the high nave; the ribs continue the vertical line of the piers. In the upper-level galleries, half-barrel vaults, called **quadrant vaults**, help strengthen the building by carrying the outward thrust of the nave vault to the outer walls and buttresses. Above the

During the late Middle Ages, people in western Europe once again began to travel in large numbers as traders, soldiers, and Christians on pilgrimages. Pilgrims throughout history have journeyed to holy sites—the ancient Greeks to Delphi, early Christians to Jerusalem and to Rome, Muslims to Mecca—but in the eleventh century, pilgrimages to the holy places of Christendom dramatically increased.

As difficult and dangerous as these journeys were, rewards awaited the courageous travelers along the routes, even before they reached their destination. Pilgrims could stop along the way to venerate local saints through their relics and visit the places where miracles were believed to have taken place. Relics—bodies of saints, parts of bodies, or even things owned by saints—were thought to have miraculous powers, and they were kept in richly decorated reliquaries.

Having and displaying the relics of saints so enhanced the prestige and wealth of a community that people went to great lengths to acquire them, not only by purchase but also by theft. In the ninth century, for example, the monks of Conques stole the relics of the child martyr Saint Foy (Saint Faith) from her shrine at Saint-Agens. Such a theft was called holy robbery, for the new owners insisted that the saint had encouraged them because she wanted to move. The monks of Conques encased their relic—the skull of Saint Foy—in a jewel-bedecked gold statue whose head was made from a Roman parade helmet (fig. 10-17).

To accommodate the faithful and instruct them in Church doctrine, many monasteries on the major pilgrimage routes built large new churches and filled them with sumptuous altars, crosses, and reliquaries. Sculpture and paintings on the walls illustrated important religious stories and doctrines and served to instruct as well as fascinate the faithful. These awe-inspiring works of art and architecture, like most of what has come down to us from the Romanesque period, had a Christian purpose. One monk wrote that by decorating the church "well and gracefully" the artist showed "the beholders something of the likeness of the paradise of God" (cited in Theophilus, page 79).

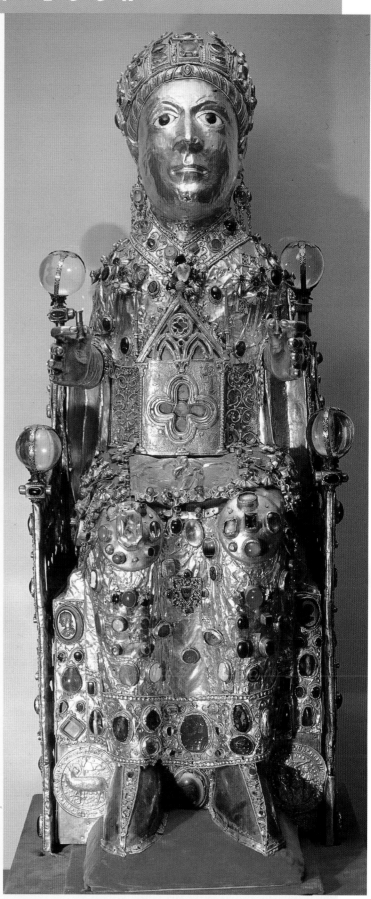

10-17 | **Reliquary statue of Saint Foy (Saint Faith),** made in the Auvergne region, France, for the Abbey Church of Conques, Rouergue, France. Late 9th to first half of 10th century. Gold repoussé and gemstones over wood core (incorporating a Roman helmet and Roman cameos; later additions 12th–19th centuries), height 33" (85 cm) Cathedral Treasury, Conques, France

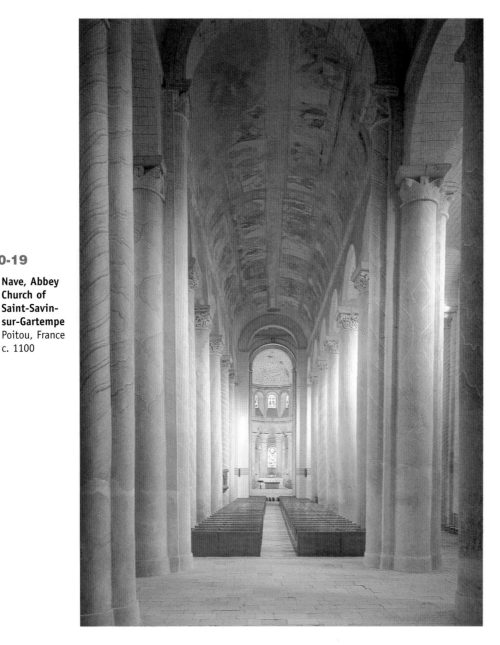

10-19

Nave, Abbey Church of Saint-Savin-sur-Gartempe
Poitou, France
c. 1100

church's square crossing, a windowed, octagonal **lantern** tower admits daylight. The light streaming in from the lantern and apse windows acted as a beacon, directing the worshipers' attention to the altar. The piers supporting the nave arcade have attached half-columns on all four sides, and for this reason are known as **compound piers**. Compound piers and ribbed vaults create spatial units or bays. The sculptural form they give to church interiors was a major contribution of Romanesque builders to architectural structure and aesthetics.

Richly painted decoration, most of it now faded or lost, covered the interior of Romanesque churches. As we have seen at Tahull, painting took the place of the expensive mosaics and marble veneers found in Early Christian and Byzantine buildings. At the Abbey Church of Saint-Savin-sur-Gartempe, in the Poitou region of western France (fig. 10-19), painted Old Testament scenes cover the entire length of the tunnel-like barrel vault. Scenes from the New Testament and from the

lives of two local saints, Savin and Cyprian, appear in the transept, ambulatory, and chapels. The nave columns are painted to resemble veined marble. Several artists or teams of artists worked in different parts of the church, and the painters used several different models. Some must have seen examples of Byzantine art; others may have had Carolingian or even Early Christian models. The paintings of the nave vault are filled with energetic figures, suggesting the work of Carolingian and Ottonian artists, like the narrative drama of the Hildesheim doors (see fig. 10-11).

SCULPTURE

Not just painting, but also sculptural decoration enriched medieval churches. Portal sculpture (located around and above the main entrances) was one of the most notable features of Romanesque architecture. The most important carving was located on the lintel, the **tympanum** (the semicircular area above the

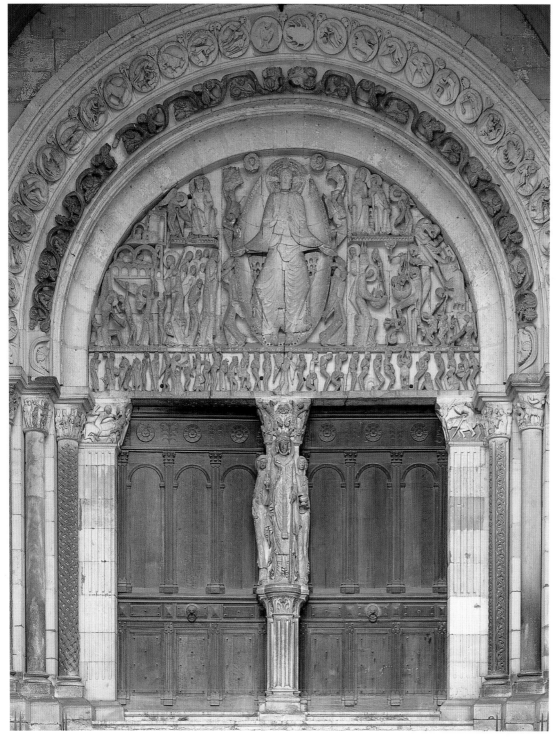

10-20

West portal
Cathedral
(originally
abbey church)
of Saint-Lazare
Autun
Burgundy, France
c. 1120–35/40

door lintel), the archivolts (the moldings that follow the contour of the arch), and the **trumeau** (the central supporting post) and jambs of the door. The tympanum above the west portal of the Cathedral of Saint-Lazare at Autun in France depicts the Last Judgment (fig. 10-20). Christ, enclosed in a mandorla (almond-shaped nimbus), presides in judgment over the cowering, naked figures of the resurrected humans at his feet. The damned writhe in torment at Christ's left (the sinister hand on the viewer's right) while the saved, praying, reach toward heaven on Christ's right. In the lintel, angels help other souls to rise from their

graves, while a pair of giant, pincerlike hands descends at the far right to snatch one of the damned into hell. Above these hands, in a scene reminiscent of the Egyptian Books of the Dead (see fig. 2-35), the archangel Michael oversees the weighing of souls on the scales of good and evil. Beneath Christ's feet we find the name Gislebertus.

Gislebertus may also have carved the pilaster capitals lining the nave and aisles of the church. The creation of lively narrative scenes within the geometric confines of column capitals (the "historiated capital") was an important Romanesque

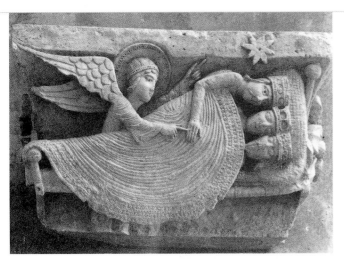

10-21 | *The Magi Asleep,* capital from the nave, Cathedral of Saint-Lazare. c. 1120–32. Musée Lapidaire, Autun

contribution to architectural decoration. One capital depicts the sleeping Magi (fig. 10-21). According to the Gospels, three Magi, or wise men, traveled from the East to bring gifts to the newborn Jesus and acknowledge him as King of the Jews. Medieval tradition identified the Magi as kings, and gave them the names Caspar, Melchior, and Balthasar. Gislebertus represents the eldest, Caspar, as bearded, Melchior with a mustache, and Balthasar, the youngest, as clean-shaven. An angel awakens the Magi and points to the Star of Bethlehem that will guide their journey. The sculptor's simultaneous use of two vantage points—the Magi and the head of the bed viewed from above and the angel and foot of the bed from the side—communicates the key elements of the story with wonderful economy and clarity. This capital, one of a series illustrating events related to the birth of Jesus, may have reminded worshipers that they were embarking on a metaphorically parallel journey to find Christ.

Reliquaries, altar frontals (a cover for the front of an altar), crucifixes, devotional images, and other sculpture once filled medieval churches. One form of devotional image that became increasingly popular during the later Romanesque period was that of the Virgin Mary holding the Christ Child on her lap, a type known as the Throne of Wisdom (see fig. 7-19). Mary becomes both a throne for Jesus and *Theotokos* (Greek for "bearer of God"). She is revered in the West from the twelfth century on as the nurturing, ever-merciful intercessor, second in heavenly power only to the Trinity. The well-preserved example in painted wood illustrated in figure 10-22 was made in the Auvergne region of France in the second half of the twelfth century. Mother and Child sit erect in a frontal pose, as rigid as they are regal, but appearing less remote than in earlier representations. Mary, seated on a thronelike bench, protectively supports

10-22 | *Virgin and Child in Majesty,* from Auvergne region France c. 1150–1200. Linen, gesso, and polychromy on walnut, height 31" (78.7 cm). The Metropolitan Museum of Art, New York
Gift of J. Pierpont Mongan, 1916 (16.32.194)

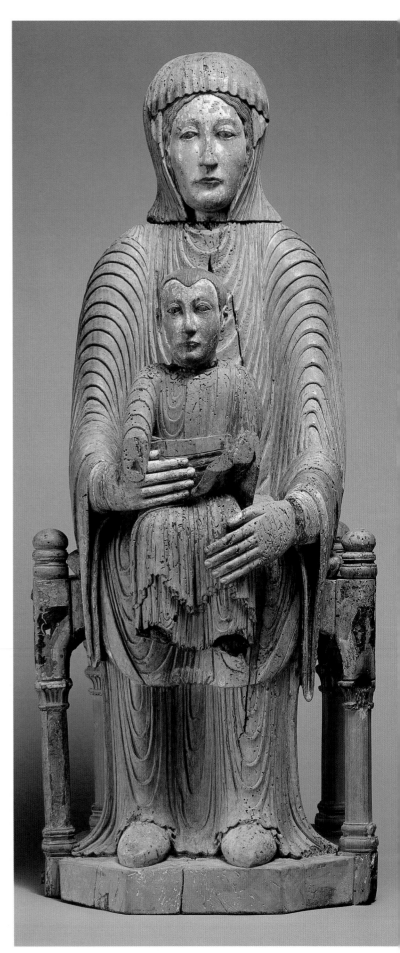

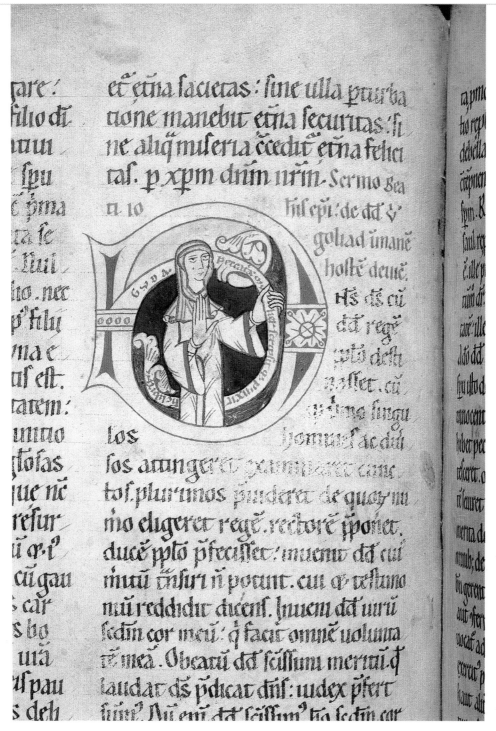

10-23

Page with self-portrait of the nun Guda, *Book of Homilies.* Early 12th century. Ink on parchment. Stadt- und Universitätsbibliothek Frankfurt, Germany

MS. Barth. 42, folio 110v

the Christ Child, who raises his (now missing) right hand in a blessing. Recent cleaning has revealed the colorful blues, reds, and cream colors of the original surface. The sweet, slightly pouting expressions and softly modeled faces are typical of Auvergne figures. Painted wood became an increasingly common medium in the Romanesque period as abbeys and churches with only limited means began commissioning hundreds of statues.

BOOKS AND EMBROIDERY

The output of books, like other arts, increased dramatically in the eleventh and twelfth centuries. Monastic **scriptoria**, or workshops, continued to be centers of production. In the Romanesque period, as earlier in the Middle Ages, women were involved in the production of books as authors, scribes, painters, and patrons. The Abbess Hitda had been a patron; the nun Guda, from Westphalia, was both a scribe and painter. In a book of homilies (sermons) she inserted her self-portrait into the letter *D* and signed the image "Guda, the sinful woman, wrote and illuminated this book" (fig. 10-23). A simple drawing with colors only in the background spaces, the importance of Guda's self-portrait lies in its demonstration that women were far from anonymous workers. Guda and other nuns played an important role in the production of books in the twelfth century, and this image is the earliest signed self-portrait by a woman in western Europe.

In England, book illumination flourished after the Norman conquest. The *Worcester Chronicle*, written by a monk named

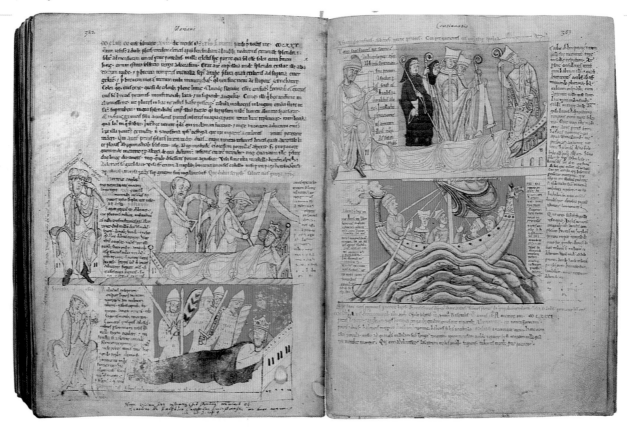

10-24 John of Worcester. Page with *Dream of Henry I, Worcester Chronicle,* Worcester, England. c. 1140. Ink and tempera on vellum, each page 12¾ x 9⅜" (32.5 x 23.7 cm). Corpus Christi College, Oxford

One of the most significant achievements of Henry I's father, William the Conqueror, was a comprehensive census of English property owners, the *Domesday Book*. Compiled into two huge volumes, this document was used to assess taxes and settle property disputes.

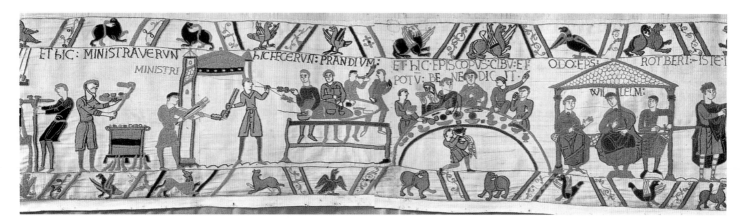

10-25 *Bishop Odo Blessing the Feast,* sections 47–48 of the *Bayeux Tapestry,* Norman-Anglo-Saxon embroidery from Canterbury Kent, England, or Bayeux, Normandy, France. c. 1066–82. Linen with wool embroidery, height 20" (50.8 cm). Centre Guillaume le Conquérant, Bayeux, France, by spcial permission of the City of Bayeux

A text running above the scenes describes the action. In this section servants (identified as *ministri*) are preparing the meal by roasting meat on spits over a grill. They pass the food to the warriors seated at table made by placing shields on trestles. At the head table Bishop Odo blesses the food, attended by a servant holding a basin and towel. At the right William the Conqueror (Willelm) confers with his two half-brothers, Bishop Odo (Odo epsi) and Robert (Rotbert) who holds a sword.

John, is the earliest known illustrated English history book (fig. 10-24). The pages shown here concern Henry I (ruled 1100–1135), the second of William the Conqueror's sons to sit on the English throne. The text relates a series of dreams the king had in 1130, in which his subjects demanded tax relief. The illustrations depict the King's dreams with energetic directness. On the first night, angry farmers confront the sleeping king; on the second, armed knights surround his bed, and on the third, monks, abbots, and bishops present their case. In the fourth illustration, the king travels in a storm-tossed ship and saves himself by promising God to rescind the increase for seven years. *The Worcester Chronicle* assured its readers that this story came from a reliable source, the royal physician Grimbald, who appears in the margins next to most scenes.

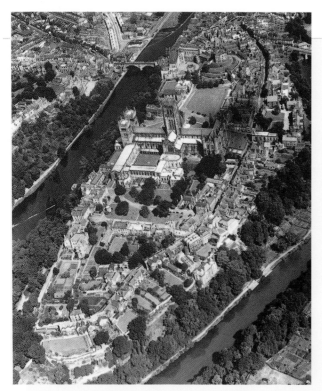

10-26 | (*left*) **Castle-monastery-cathedral complex, Durham**
Northumberland, England. c. 1075–1100s, plus later alterations and additions

Since 1837, the castle has housed the University of Durham (now joined with the University of Newcastle). The castle was added to and rebuilt over the centuries. The Norman portion extends to the left of the keep. The castle and cathedral share a parklike green. South of the cathedral (lower in the photograph), the cloister with chapter house, dormitory (now library), and kitchens are clearly visible. Houses of the old city cluster around the buildings as they would have in the earlier days. Trees, however, would not have been allowed to grow near the approaches to this fortified outpost against the Scots.

10-27 | (*right*) **Plan of Durham Castle**

In Norman times, the bishops of Durham lived in a three-story residence. An exterior staircase led from the courtyard (inner bailey) to a single undivided, multipurpose room on the middle floor occupied by the bishop and his principal servants (Constable's Hall and Tunstall's Gallery in the plan). Other people occupied humbler wood structures within the castle complex or outside its walls in the village that served it. The structures at the left date from Gothic times.

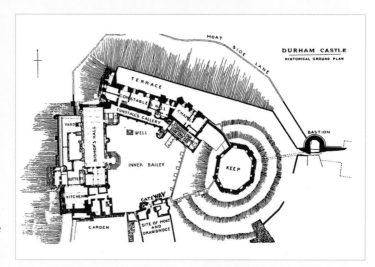

The best-known narrative work of Norman art is not a book but an **embroidered** wall hanging known as the *Bayeux Tapestry* (fig. 10-25). The work, which documents events surrounding the Norman Conquest of England in 1066, was embroidered in eight colors of wool on lengths of undyed linen, stitched together to form a hanging 230 feet long and 20 inches high. William the Conqueror's half brother Odo, Bishop of Bayeux in Normandy and Earl of Kent in southern England, may have commissioned the embroidery for his Cathedral's consecration in 1077. According to an inventory made in 1476, the embroidery decorated the nave of the church on the Feast of Relics.

The *Bayeux Tapestry* is a major political document, celebrating William's victory, validating his claim to the English throne, and promoting Odo's interests as a powerful leader himself. Recent research suggests that a Norman probably wrote the narrative, another specialist provided drawings, and women did the actual embroidery. The scene illustrated here shows Odo and the Norman knights feasting at a curved table on the eve of battle. At the left, attendants provide roasted birds on skewers, placing them on a makeshift table made from the knights' shields placed on trestles. A kneeling servant in the middle proffers a basin and towel so that the diners may wash their hands. A man seated next to Odo (the central figure) points impatiently to the next event, a council of war among three men of power: William, Odo, and a third man labeled "Rotbert," probably Robert of Mortain, another of William's half brothers.

CASTLES AND CHURCHES IN ENGLAND AND NORMANDY

Normans working in England and Normandy after the conquest of 1066 made major innovations in Romanesque architecture. Northerners were masters of carpentry. The great forests of northern Europe provided the materials for timber buildings of all kinds. Two forms of timber construction evolved: one that used stacked horizontal logs, notched at the ends, to form a rectangular building (the still-popular log cabin), and another in which vertical planks were set directly in the ground or into a sill (a horizontal beam). Typical buildings had a shingled, turf or thatched roof supported by interior posts. The same basic structure was used for almost all building types—on a large scale for palaces, assembly halls, and churches, on a small scale for huts and family homes, which were shared with domestic animals, including horses and cattle. As defense, people built massive earthworks topped with palisades. Subject to decay and fire, early timber buildings have largely disappeared, leaving only postholes and other traces in the soil.

When the British turned from timber architecture to stone, brick, and mortar, they associated the masonry building—whether church, feasting hall, or castle—with the power and glory of ancient Rome where those materials had been used. They also recognized the greater strength and resistance to fire of masonry walls. Monastic communities appreciated the acoustical properties of stone vaults. Not surprisingly, they soon began to

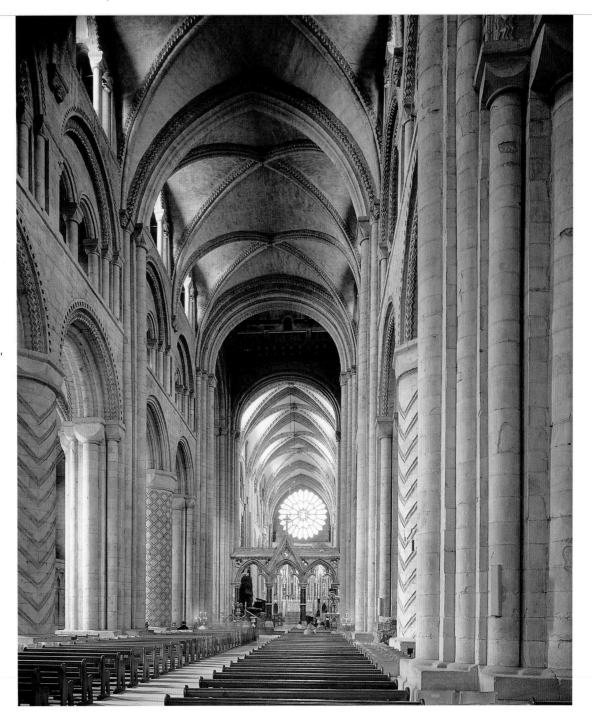

10-28

Nave of Durham Cathedral
Early 12th century
Original apses replaced by a Gothic choir 1242–c. 1280
Vault height 73' (22.2 m). View from the west

experiment with masonry vaults, as can be seen at Durham Castle and Cathedral in northeastern England.

Strategically located on England's northern frontier with Scotland, Durham grew after the Norman Conquest into a fortified complex with a castle, cathedral, monastery, and village (fig. 10-26; see page 253). The count-bishop held both secular and religious power, secure in his castle where the only way in and out was over a drawbridge and through a fortified gatehouse (fig. 10-27; see page 253). Beyond the gatehouse was the bailey, or castle yard. In times of danger, the defenders took up their battle positions along the ramparts overlooking a sheer cliff. The Wear River acted as a natural moat (in other places a water-filled ditch) since it looped around the high, rocky outcrop on which the castle-cathedral complex was built. If the walls failed them,

the defenders could retreat to the massive tower (the **keep**) next to the bailey. At Durham, a stone keep soon replaced an earlier timber tower on an earthen mound (the Norman "motte and bailey" or earthwork and palisade fort). Other buildings, including the living quarters and the great hall in which the bishops conducted their business, extended along the walls. The Norman chapel, located between the great hall and the keep, was built about 1075 and may have been the first stone structure in the compound.

Across the green from the castle, Durham Cathedral, begun by 1093, is one of the most impressive of all medieval buildings as well as one of the most original (fig. 10-28). Enormous compound piers alternating with circular piers supporting the nave arcade, gallery, and vaults still overwhelm the viewer. The round

Elements of Architecture

RIB VAULTING

Rib vaulting was one of the chief technical contributions of medieval builders. Rib vaults are a form of **groin vault** (see "Arch and Vault," page 141) in which the ridges (groins) formed by the intersecting vaults are supported by curved moldings called ribs. These ribs were structural as well as decorative. They were constructed first and supported the scaffolding while the vault was being built. They strengthened the joins and helped (although not as much as nineteenth-century architects believed) channel the vaults' outward thrust. Over time architects turned the ribs into an intricate masonry "skeleton," filled with an increasingly lightweight "skin," the web of the vault, or webbing.

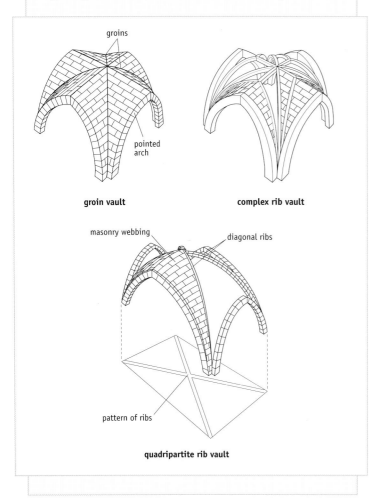

groins

pointed arch

groin vault

complex rib vault

masonry webbing

diagonal ribs

pattern of ribs

quadripartite rib vault

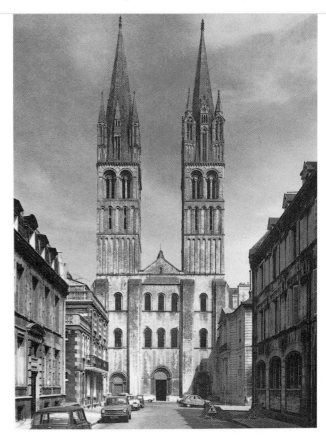

10-29 | **Church of Saint-Étienne,** Caen, Normandy, France Begun 1064; facade late 11th century; spires 13th century

churches such as Saint-Étienne at Caen, and then adopted by French masons at the beginning of the Gothic period.

In Normandy, William's monastery of Saint-Étienne in Caen, begun nearly a generation before Durham Cathedral, originally had a sophisticated wall design but a wooden roof. In the twelfth century the builders replaced the timber roof with a six-part ribbed masonry vault. The west facade of the church (fig. 10-29), probably built about 1096–1100, had soaring towers (the spires are thirteenth-century additions in the Gothic style). Tall wall buttresses divide the facade into three vertical sections, reflecting the interior division of nave and side aisles. At each window level **stringcourses**—horizontal moldings—suggest the three stories of the building's interior. A product of the logic so characteristic of the Normans, the design of the facade reflects the plan and the elevation of the church itself, an idea that would be adopted along with the emphasis on verticality by Gothic builders.

Gislebertus of Autun, the nuns Ende and Guda, and many anonymous women and men of the eleventh and twelfth centuries created a new art that—although based on the Bible and the lives of the saints—focused on human beings, their stories, and their beliefs. The artists worked on a monumental scale in painting, sculpture, and even embroidery, and their art moved from the cloister to the public walls of churches. While they emphasized the spiritual and intellectual concerns of the Christian Church, they also began to observe and record what they saw around them. In so doing they laid the groundwork for the art of the Gothic period.

piers are carved with **chevrons** (inverted V s), spiral fluting, and diamond patterns, and end in scalloped capitals. All of this ornamentation was originally painted.

The masons at Durham developed a new system of vaulting (see "Rib Vaulting," above). They modified the Romanesque ribbed groin vault by using two pairs of crisscrossing ribs in each bay. The complex patterns created by the ribs are visually compelling, and the diagonal lines of the ribs and the uniform height of the vaults unify the separate bays. The architects also experimented with rectangular rather than square bays. Between 1093 and 1133, the Durham builders developed a system of vaulting that was carried to the Norman homeland in France, perfected in

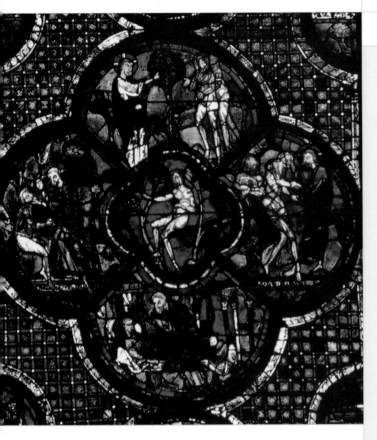

(*right*) Detail from **Genesis** and **The Parable of the Good Samaritan**, south aisle window, Chartres Cathedral c. 1210 Stained glass. (See page 263.)

(*above*) Detail from **The Life of Charlemagne** ambulatory window, Chartres Cathedral. c. 1225. Stained glass (See page 263.)

The Gothic style created by patrons, architects, and artists working together toward a super mundane goal dominated the aesthetic life of Europe for 400 years. By mid-twelfth century in western Europe, a combination of technological skill, material resources, and intellectual and spiritual motivation created an art and architecture that expressed the dedicated religious belief of the Christian community. Reformers might rant against ostentation, waste, and materialism but bishops, abbots, and civic leaders vied to build and decorate the largest, richest churches. Just as residents of twentieth-century American cities raced to erect higher and higher skyscrapers, so too the bishops of medieval western Europe competed in the building of cathedrals and parish churches with tall naves and soaring towers. The masons' skill in constructing high vaults supported on piers and designing window-filled walls—both stabilized by flying buttresses —created open, light-filled interior spaces. Meanwhile the glassmakers perfected the techniques of coloring and painting glass and filled ever-larger window openings with glowing images. Light passing through the stained-glass windows not only illuminated the wall but also changed the open space into a many-colored haze. Walls, objects, and even people seemed to dissolve—dematerializing into color. Truly, churches became the glorious jeweled houses of God.

Abbot Suger (1081–1151) in the Benedictine Abbey of Saint-Denis near Paris wrote of his experience in rebuilding his abbey church of Saint-Denis in the twelfth century. He described his visual and spiritual journey through the medium of pure colored light. Although Abbot Suger died before he was able to finish the work, he is remembered for his inspired departure from traditional building practice in order to achieve a truly radiant architecture. His innovations led to the widespread use of large stained-glass windows, such as those that bathe the inside walls of Chartres Cathedral with sublime washes of color. At Chartres Cathedral the Creation and Fall of Adam and Eve and the parable of the Good Samaritan in the south aisle window and Charlemagne from an ambulatory window remind us that the windows are actually monumental paintings. They are transparent and luminous murals filled with energetic figures activated with color and light.

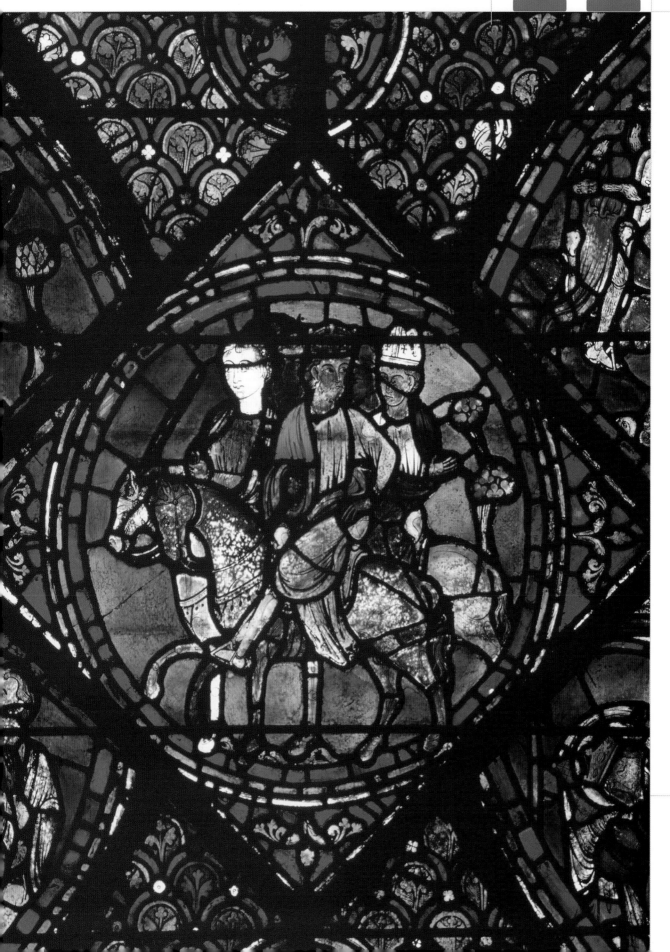

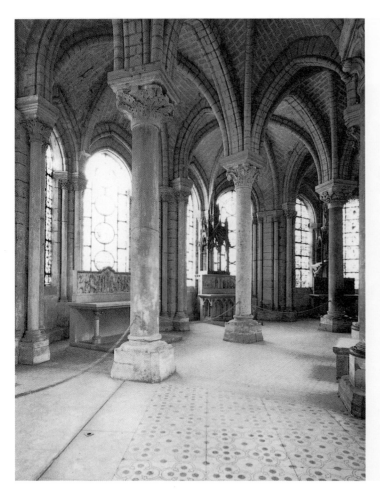

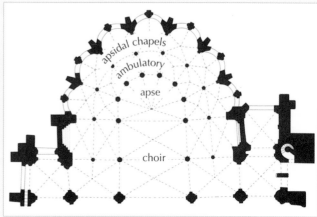

11-1 | **Ambulatory choir, Abbey Church of Saint-Denis**
Saint-Denis, Île-de-France, France

11-2 | **Plan of the sanctuary,** Abbey Church
of Saint-Denis. 1140–44

In the middle of the twelfth century, while builders throughout Europe were working in the Romanesque style, a distinctive new architecture known today as Gothic emerged in the Île-de-France, the French king's domain around Paris (see Map 4, page 285). The appearance there of the new style and building technique coincided with the emergence of the monarchy as a powerful centralizing force in France. From that point, the Gothic style spread, and it prevailed in western European art until about 1400, then lingered for another century in some regions. Unprecedented resources were devoted to Christian art in the late Middle Ages. Within 100 years an estimated 2,700 churches were built in the Île-de-France region around Paris alone. These new churches shimmered with **stained glass**, sumptuous altars, sculpture, crosses, and reliquaries, paid for by clergy, monarchs, aristocrats, and wealthy merchants. Private patrons commissioned innumerable other works of art for personal use as well, such as luxurious clothing, jewels, armor, and castles.

The term *Gothic* was introduced in the sixteenth century by the Italian artist and historian Giorgio Vasari, who disparagingly attributed the style to the Goths, the Germanic invaders who had destroyed the classical civilization of the Roman Empire that he and his contemporaries so admired. In its own day the Gothic style was simply called "modern art" or the "French style." As it spread from the Île-de-France, it gradually displaced Romanesque forms but took on regional characteristics inspired by those forms. England developed a distinctive national style,

which also influenced architectural design in continental Europe. The Gothic style was slow to take hold in Germany but ultimately endured there well into the sixteenth century. Italy proved more resistant to French Gothic elements, and by 1400, Italian artists and builders there sought a return to **classical** traditions. In the late fourteenth century, the various regional styles of Europe coalesced into what is known as the international Gothic style. Gothic architecture's elegant, soaring, light-filled interiors were adapted to all types of structures, including town halls, market buildings, residences, and Jewish synagogues, as well as Christian churches.

During the flowering of the Gothic style in the twelfth and thirteenth centuries, Europe enjoyed a period of vigorous growth. Towns gained increasing prominence, becoming important centers of artistic patronage and intellectual life. Urban universities and cathedral schools supplanted rural monastic schools as centers of learning. The first European university, at Bologna, Italy, was founded in the eleventh century, and soon important universities were established in Paris, Cambridge, and Oxford. Two new religious orders arose to serve the new urban population, the Franciscans and the Dominicans. The friars, as these monks were called, went out into the world to preach and minister to those in need, rather than confining themselves to monasteries.

Crusades and pilgrimages continued throughout the thirteenth century. One of the benefits of the resulting contact with the Byzantine and Islamic worlds was the European discovery of many literary works from classical antiquity. These writings, particularly those of Aristotle, promoted rational inquiry rather than faith as the path to truth, which, at first, seemed incompatible with Christian emphasis on faith and spirituality. The thirteenth-century scholar Thomas Aquinas finally brought together faith and reason—traditional belief and the new logic—in Scholastic philosophy, which has endured as a basis of Catholic thought to this day.

The artists and master builders, like the Scholastic thinkers, saw divine order in geometric relationships and expressed these in their art. Unlike their Romanesque predecessors, who used stylization and distortion to achieve emotional impact, thirteenth-century sculptors created more naturalistic forms that reflected the idealism and reasoned analysis of Scholastic thought. Gothic religious imagery, like Romanesque imagery, aimed to instruct and persuade the viewer; however, its effects are more varied and subtle, and it incorporates a wide range of subjects drawn from the natural world. In the Gothic church, Scholastic logic and the new naturalism intermingle with the mysticism of light and color to create for the worshiper a direct, emotional, ecstatic experience of the church as the embodiment of God's house, filled with divine light.

Gothic Art in France

The birth of the Gothic style took place in France against the backdrop of the growing power of the French monarchy. Europe's first Gothic structure is arguably the Abbey Church of Saint-Denis, which had great symbolic significance for the French crown. Located a few miles north of central Paris, it housed the tombs of many French kings, the royal regalia, and the relics of Saint Denis, the patron saint of France. Construction began on a new church in the 1130s under the supervision of Abbot Suger, leader of the Benedictine monastery there.

Abbot Suger was familiar with the latest architecture and sculpture of Romanesque Europe through his travels in France, the Rhineland, and Italy. He also turned for inspiration to the authority of Church writings, including treatises erroneously attributed to a first-century follower of Saint Paul named Dionysius, who identified radiant light with divinity. Through the centuries Dionysius had become confused with Saint Denis, so Suger, not unreasonably, adapted Dionysius's concept of divine luminosity to the redesign of the Abbey Church of Saint-Denis. When he began work on the **choir** after completing a magnificent Norman-inspired and structurally innovative facade, he created "a circular string of chapels" so that the whole church "would shine with the wonderful and uninterrupted light of most luminous windows, pervading the interior beauty" (cited in Panofsky, page 101).

The plan of the choir, built 1140–44, superficially resembles that of a Romanesque pilgrimage church (fig. 11-1); that is, the semicircular sanctuary is surrounded by an ambulatory from which radiate seven chapels of uniform size. All the architectural elements of the choir had already appeared in Romanesque buildings, including pointed arches, ribbed groin vaults springing from cylindrical piers, and **buttresses** to relieve stress on the walls and to permit larger window openings. The dramatic

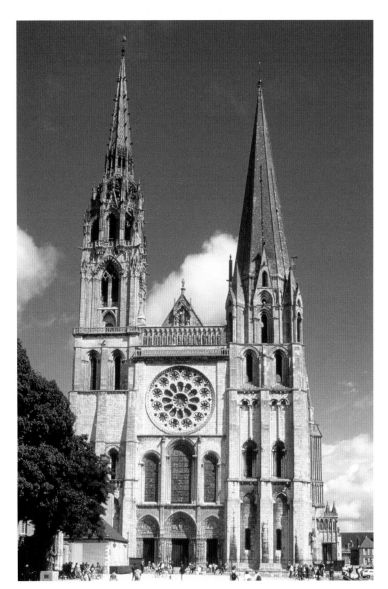

11-3   **West facade, Chartres Cathedral, the Cathedral of Notre-Dame Chartres,** France. c. 1134–1220; south tower c. 1160; north spire 1507–13

achievement of Suger's master mason was to combine these features into a fully integrated architectural whole that emphasized open, flowing space (fig. 11-2). Sanctuary, ambulatory, and chapels open into one another, and the walls give the impression of being made of stained glass rather than masonry. Windows allow light to flood the interior with color. Suger saw light and color as a means of illuminating the soul and uniting it with God. The Abbey Church of Saint-Denis initiated a period of competitive experimentation in the Île-de-France and surrounding regions that resulted in ever-taller churches enclosing increasingly larger interior spaces walled with ever-greater expanses of colored glass.

At the Cathedral of Notre-Dame in Chartres (fig. 11-3), southwest of Paris, masons built on the concepts pioneered at Saint-Denis. Chartres Cathedral, constructed in several stages beginning in the mid-twelfth century and extending into the mid-thirteenth, illustrates both the early and the mature Gothic

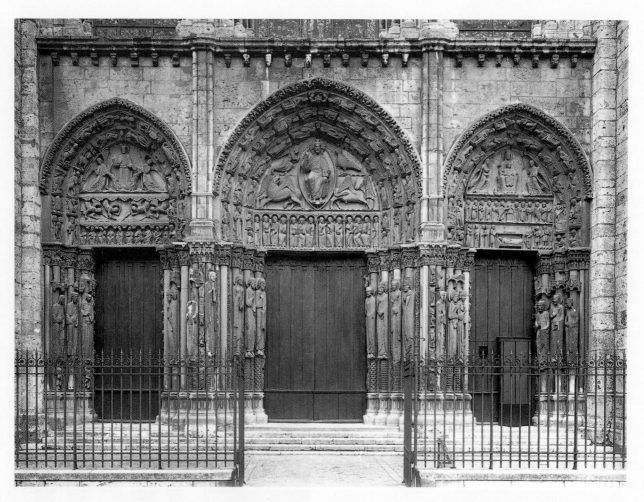

11-4 Royal Portal, west facade, Chartres Cathedral. c. 1145–55

11-5 Plan of Chartres Cathedral. c. 1194–1220

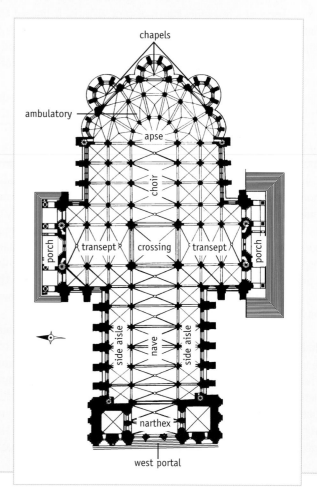

style. The facade survived a fire in 1194 and consequently represents a design contemporary with the church facade of Saint-Denis. Its three western doors—the so-called Royal Portal (fig. 11-4)—show Christ enthroned in majesty on the central **tympanum**, supported by his Old Testament precursors; Mary and the Christ Child at the right and the Ascension at the left. The sculptors pose their high-relief figures naturally and comfortably in the architectural setting. The erect, frontal **column statues** with their elongated proportions and vertical drapery echo the cylindrical shafts from which they seem to emerge. Their heads are finely rendered with idealized features.

In the rest of the building, constructed after 1194 (fig. 11-5), the master mason and his men brought together what were to become the typical Gothic structural devices: pointed arches and ribbed groin vaulting rising from **compound piers** over rectangular bays, supported by exterior flying buttresses, which permitted the masons to introduce huge windows into the upper walls (see "The Gothic Church," page 262). The **triforium** (series of arched openings under the clerestory) became a mid-level passageway overlooking the nave through an arcaded

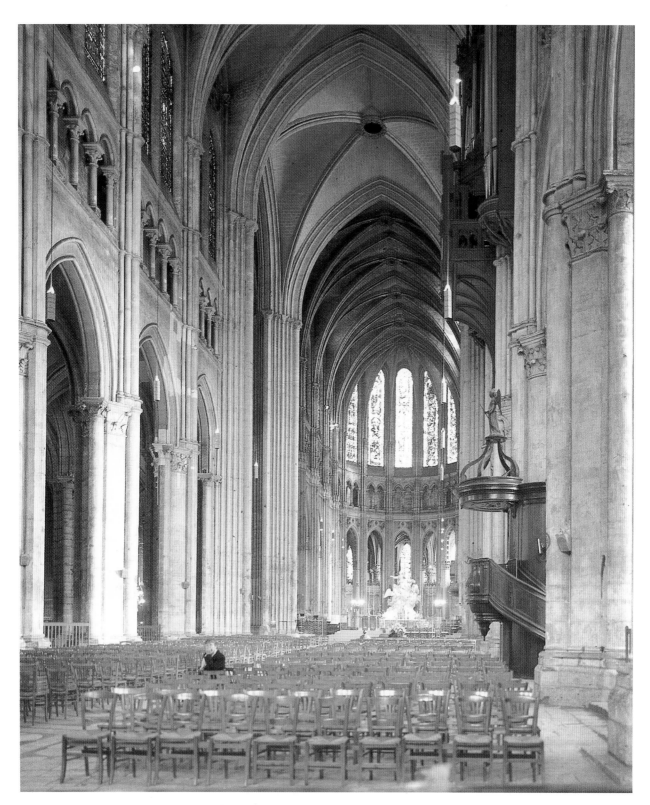

11-6 | **Nave, Chartres Cathedral.** c. 1200–20

screen, rather than a flat wall (as in a basilica) or a full gallery. At Chartres, the elegant glass and masonry shell encloses an enormous open space. The building has one of the widest naves in Europe (45½ feet) and vaults that soar 118–120 feet above the floor (fig. 11-6). The large and luminous clerestory is filled by tall, arched windows, composed of a pair of **lancents** surmounted by circular windows, or oculi. In a Romanesque church, the worshiper's gaze is mainly drawn forward toward the apse; at Chartres it is drawn upward as well, to the clerestory windows and the soaring vaults overhead.

Elements of Architecture

THE GOTHIC CHURCH

Most large Gothic churches in western Europe were built on the Latin-cross plan, with a projecting **transept** marking the transition from **nave** to **sanctuary**. The main entrance portal was generally on the west, the **choir** and **apse** on the east. A **narthex** led to the nave and **side aisles**. An **ambulatory** with radiating chapels circled the apse and facilitated the movement of worshipers through the church. Above the nave were a triforium passageway and windowed **clerestory**. Narthex, side aisles, ambulatory, and nave usually had **rib vaults** in the Gothic period. **Flying buttresses** help support the high rib-vaulted naves by carrying the outward thrust of the nave vaulting over the aisles to massive wall buttresses, which are freestanding above the aisle roofs. Church walls were decorated inside and out with arcades of round and pointed arches, engaged columns and colonnettes, and horizontal moldings called **stringcourses**. The roof was supported by a wooden framework. A spire or crossing tower above the junction of the transept and nave was usually planned, though often never finished. The **apsidal** chapels ringing the apse were often visible on the exterior, as were the buttress piers and flying buttresses that countered the outward thrusts of the interior vaults. Portal facades were customarily marked by high, flanking towers or gabled porches ornamented with **pinnacles** and finials. Architectural sculpture covered each portal's **tympanum, archivolts**, and **jambs**. A magnificent stained-glass rose window typically formed the centerpiece of the portal facades. Stained glass filled the tall, pointed **lancets**.

Chartres Cathedral

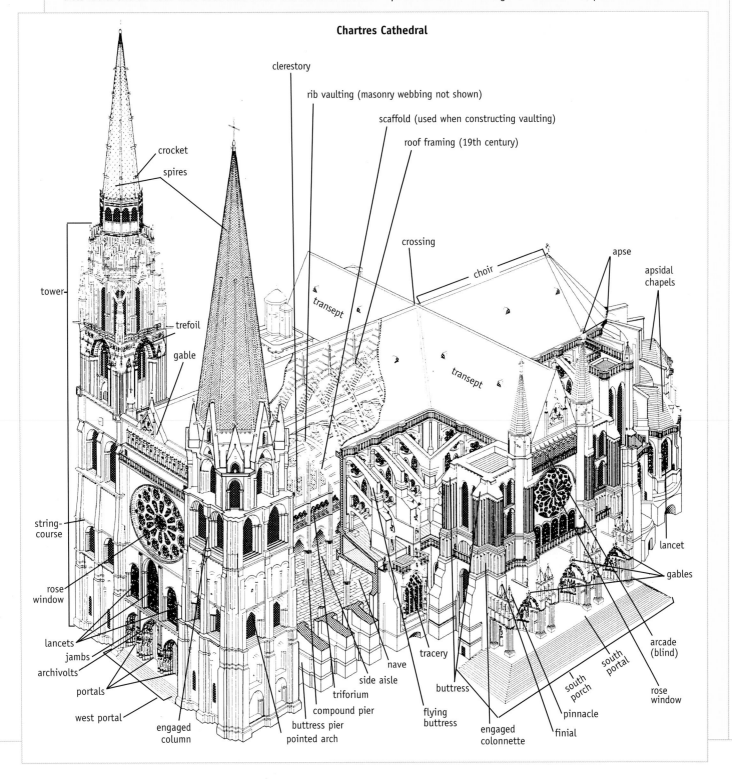

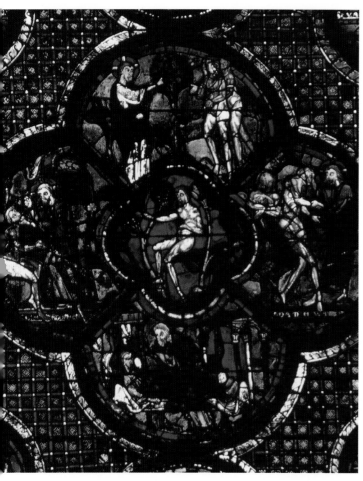

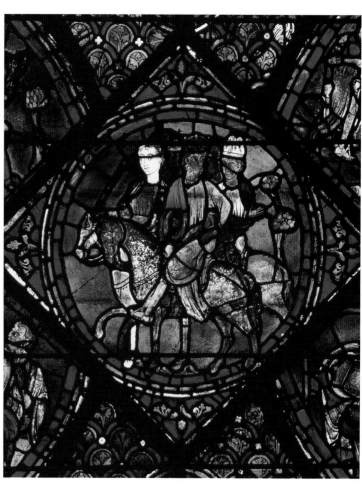

11-7 Detail from *Genesis* and *The Parable of the Good Samaritan* south aisle window, Chartres Cathedral. c. 1210. Stained glass (See page 257.)

11-8 Detail from *The Life of Charlemagne,* ambulatory window Chartres Cathedral. c. 1225. Stained glass. (See page 256.)

Chartres is unique among French Gothic buildings in that most of its stained-glass windows have survived (figs. 11-7, 11-8). The cathedral was famous for its glassmaking workshops, which by 1260 had installed about 22,000 square feet of stained glass. Most of the glass dates from between about 1210 and 1250. The Samaritan parable window illustrates the complexity of Gothic narrative art with an allegory on sin and salvation (see fig. 11-7). The window illustrates a biblical story about a traveling Samaritan who happens upon a stranger, beaten, robbed, and left for dead by thieves along the side of a road. The Good Samaritan is an allegory for Christ's redemption of humanity's sins. Adam and Eve's fall, as described in the Old Testament, introduced sin into the world, but Christ (the Good Samaritan) rescues humanity (the traveler) from sin (the thieves). Christ leads sinners into the Church just as the Good

Samaritan takes the wounded man to an inn (as seen in the bottom portion of the window). Other windows tell of saints and heroes like Charlemagne (see fig. 11-8).

The *Tree of Jesse* window in the west facade of the cathedral dates from the mid-twelfth century (fig. 11-9; see page 264). Jesse was the father of King David, who, according to the Gospels, was an ancestor of Mary and therefore of Jesus. A family tree literally connects Jesus with the house of David. At Chartres, Jesse is shown recumbent with the tree trunk growing from his body. In the branches above him appear four kings of Judea, Christ's royal ancestors, then the Virgin Mary, and finally Christ himself. Fourteen prophets stand in the half-moons flanking the tree. The glass is set within a rectilinear iron armature, visible as silhouetted black lines filled with blues and reds.

TECHNIQUE
Stained-Glass Windows

The basic technique for making colored glass has been known since ancient Egypt. It involves the addition of metallic oxides—cobalt for blue, manganese for red and purple—to a basic formula of sand and ash or lime that is fused at high temperature. Such "stained" glass was used on a small scale in church windows during the Early Christian period and in Carolingian and Ottonian churches. Colored glass sometimes adorned Romanesque churches, but the art form reached its height of sophistication and popularity in the cathedrals and churches of the Gothic era.

Making a stained-glass image was a complex and costly process. A designer first drew a composition on a wood panel the same size as the opening of the window to be filled, noting the colors of each of the elements in it. Glassblowers produced sheets of colored glass, then artisans cut individual pieces from these large sheets and laid them out on the wood template. Painters added details with enamel emulsion, and the glass was reheated to fuse the enamel to it. Finally, the pieces were joined together with narrow lead strips, called **cames**. The assembled pieces were set into iron frames that had been made to fit the window opening.

The colors of twelfth-century glass—mainly reds and blues with touches of dark green, brown, and orange yellow—were so dark as to be nearly opaque, and early uncolored glass was full of impurities. But the demand for stained-glass windows stimulated technical experimentation to achieve new colors and greater purity and transparency. The Cistercians adorned their churches with grisaille windows, painting foliage and crosses onto gray glass, and Gothic artisans developed a clearer material onto which elaborate narrative scenes could be drawn.

By the thirteenth century, many new colors were discovered, some accidentally, such as a sunny yellow produced by the addition of silver oxide. Flashing, in which a layer of one color was fused to a layer of another color, produced an almost infinite range of colors. Blue and yellow, for example, could be combined to make green. In the same way, clear glass could be fused to layers of colored glass in varying thicknesses to produce a range of hues from light to dark. The deep colors of early Gothic stained-glass windows gave them a saturated and mysterious brilliance. The richness of some of these colors, particularly blue, has never been surpassed. Pale colors and large areas of grisaille glass became increasingly popular from the mid-thirteenth century on, making the windows of later Gothic churches bright and clear by comparison.

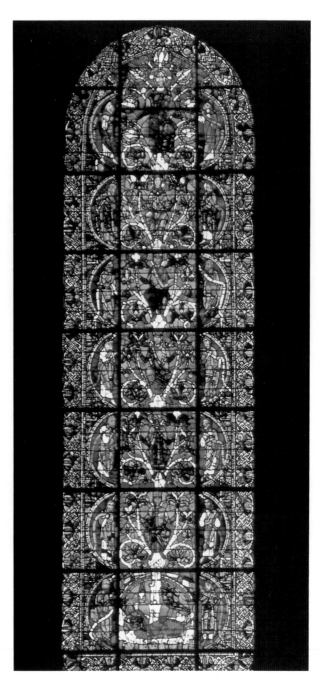

11-9 | *Tree of Jesse,* west facade, Chartres Cathedral c. 1150–70. Stained glass

The bishop of Paris could not be outdone by his fellow churchmen at the Abbey of Saint-Denis or the Cathedral of Chartres. The Benedictine abbey just north of Paris guarded the relics of Saint-Denis, the apostle to the Franks, but Paris was the preferred residence of the kings themselves as well as the administrative center of the diocese. As the location of the royal court and therefore the capital of France, Paris deserved an imposing, modern cathedral building. On a small island in the Seine River, where earlier churches already stood, Pope Alexander III set the corner stone for the new cathedral—known today as simply Notre-Dame—in 1163, and the building was essentially finished during the next hundred years (fig. 11-10).

Overlapping with the building of Chartres Cathedral was the construction of the Cathedral of Notre-Dame at Reims, where the kings of France were traditionally crowned. Construction began in 1211 and continued throughout the century. Artisans at each site borrowed from and influenced each other. The nave of Reims Cathedral, like Chartres, has a ribbed vault and a three-part elevation composed of a tall arcade, a triforium, and a windowed clerestory. In the west wall, the great **rose window** in the clerestory, a row of lancets at the triforium level, and windows over the portals replace the traditional stone of wall and tympana. A technique known as bar tracery, perfected at Reims, made possible this remarkable expanse of glass. In bar tracery,

CLOSER LOOK

Think of Gothic architecture. Chances are, the image that springs to mind is that of a soaring cathedral like Notre-Dame (Our Lady) of Paris (fig. 11-10). In fact, the Notre-Dame we see today began as an early Gothic building that bridged the period between Abbot Suger's rebuilding of the Abbey Church of Saint Denis and the thirteenth-century Chartres Cathedral. Begun in 1163, construction was far enough along for the altar to be consecrated twenty years later. The nave, rising to 115 feet dates to 1180–1200. The west facade, erected between 1200 and 1250, incorporated an earlier portal dedicated to Mary (Our Lady). By this time, the massive walls, buttresses, and six-part vaults, adopted from Norman Romanesque architecture, must have seemed very old-fashioned. After 1225, a new master modernized and lightened the building by reworking the clerestory with the large double-lancet and rose windows we see today. Notre-Dame may have had the first true flying buttresses (experts are still arguing) although those seen at the right of the photograph, rising dramatically to support the high vault of the choir, result from later Gothic remodeling. (The 290-foot spire over the crossing is the work of the nineteenth-century architect Eugene-Emmanuel Viollet-le-Duc, who followed the tradition of placing a tower or spire in this location.)

For all its spiritual and technological glory, the Cathedral Church of Notre-Dame of Paris barely survived the French Revolution. The revolutionaries decapitated the statues associated with deposed nobility and transformed the cathedral into a secular "Temple of Reason" (1793–95). Still, traditional Christians who continued to believe that Mary's church would be restored to her proved to be right, as Notre-Dame was soon returned to Christian use. Napoleon crowned himself emperor at its altar in 1804. In the twentieth century, Parisians celebrated the liberation of Paris from the Nazis in August 1944. Today boats filled with tourists glide under bridges that link the island where the cathedral stands with the Left Bank, the traditional students' and artists' quarter. Notre-Dame so resonates with life and history that it has become more than a house of worship and work of art; it is a symbol of Paris and part of the shared culture of humankind.

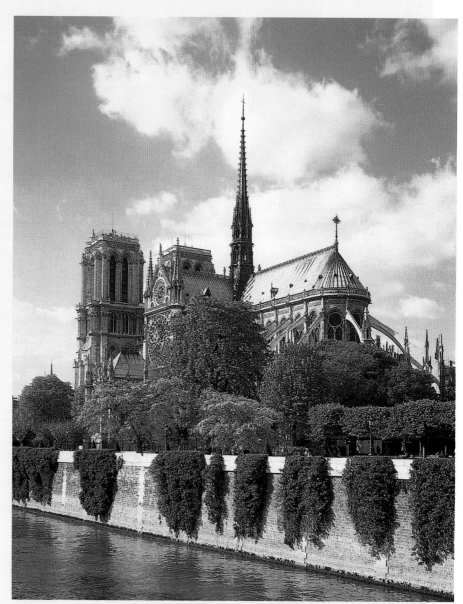

11-10 | **Cathedral of Nôtre-Dame,** view from the southeast. Paris, France. Begun 1163.
Swaan Photograph Collection, (96.P.21)

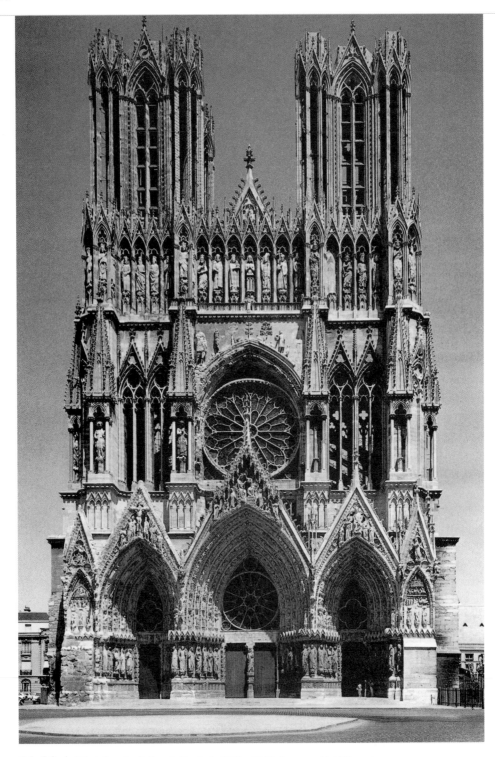

11-11 | **West facade, Reims Cathedral.** 1230s–1260; towers mid-15th century

The cathedral was restored in the sixteenth century and again in the nineteenth and twentieth centuries. During World War I it withstood bombardment by some 3,000 shells, an eloquent testimony to the skills of its builders. It was recently cleaned.

thin stone strips, called **mullions**, form a lacy frame for the glass, replacing the older practice in which glass was inserted directly into window openings. In Reims's western wall the glass is anchored visually by a masonry screen around the doorway. Here, ranks of carved Old Testament prophets and ancestors of Christ serve as moral guides for the newly crowned monarchs, who faced them after coronation.

A view of the magnificent west facade shows the massive gabled portals with their soaring peaks as well as the large stained-glass windows filling the portal tympana (fig. 11-11). In a departure from tradition, the imagery of the central portal focuses on Mary rather than Christ, a reflection of the growing popularity of Mary's cult. The enormous rose window, the focal point of the facade, fills the entire clerestory level. The towers

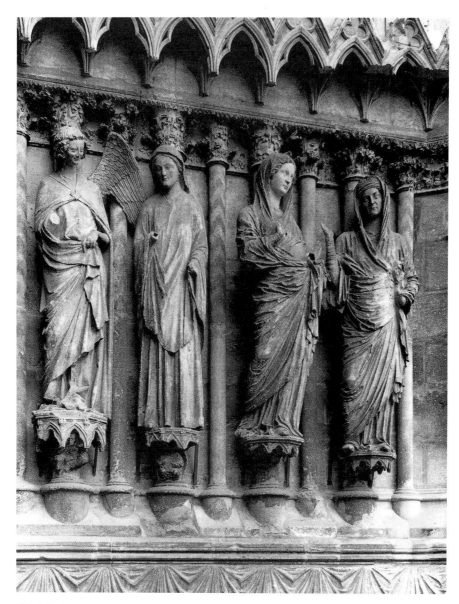

11-12 | *Annunciation* (left pair: archangel Gabriel c. 1255, Mary c. 1245) **and** *Visitation* (right pair: c. 1230), right side, central portal, west facade, Reims Cathedral

were later additions, as was the row of statues (the so-called Kings' Gallery) stretching across the facade at the base of the towers. The spires were never completed.

Different workshops and individuals worked at Reims over a period of several decades. A group of four figures from the central portal of the western front illustrates three of the styles of sculpture found at Reims (fig. 11-12). The subject of the pair on the right is the *Visitation*, in which Mary (left), pregnant with Jesus, visits her older cousin, Elizabeth (right), who is pregnant with Saint John the Baptist. These figures' sculptors, from the so-called Classical Shop, which was active in Reims about 1230–1235, drew on classical sources. The heavy figures have the same solidity seen in Roman sculpture (see fig. 6-9), and Mary's full face, wavy hair, and heavy mantle recall imperial portrait statuary. The figures seem to turn toward each other as if in conversation, their weight shifted to one leg creating a swaying posture.

The pair on the left in figure 11-12 illustrates the *Annunciation*, in which the archangel Gabriel (left) announces to Mary that she will bear Jesus. Mary's slight body, restrained gesture, and delicate features, already the work of a different master, contrast markedly with the bold tangibility of the figures to the right. Gabriel is the work of an artist known today as the Master of the Smiling Angels or the Saint Joseph Master, after his most famous sculptures at Reims. This artist, whose work began to appear in the middle of the thirteenth century, created tall, gracefully swaying figures whose aristocratic refinement became a guiding force in later Gothic sculpture and painting.

The architects of the royal palace chapel in Paris, called the Saint-Chapelle (built 1243–48), took the use of stained glass and interior sculpture to new heights. Constructed to house the French king Louis IX's prized collection of relics, the Sainte-Chapelle resembles a giant reliquary itself, one made of

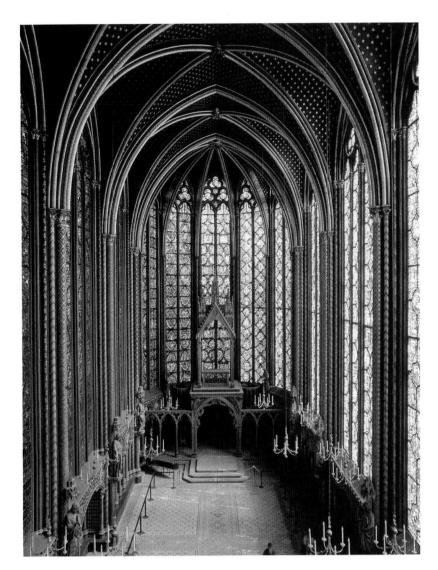

11-13 | **Interior, upper chapel, the Sainte-Chapelle,** Paris. 1243–48

Louis IX avidly collected relics of the Passion, some of which became available in the aftermath of the Crusaders' sack of Constantinople. Those that Louis acquired were supposedly the crown of thorns that had been placed on Jesus' head before the Crucifixion, a bit of the metal lance tip that pierced his side, the vinegar-soaked sponge offered to wet his lips, a nail used in the Crucifixion, and a fragment of the True Cross. The king is depicted in the Sainte-Chapelle's stained glass walking out barefoot to demonstrate his piety and humility when his treasures arrived in Paris.

stone and glass instead of gold and gems. Built in two stories, it has a ground-level chapel accessible from a courtyard and a private upper chapel entered from the royal residence. Entering this upper chapel is like emerging into a glowing jewel box (fig. 11-13). The ratio of glass to stone is higher here than in any other Gothic structure, for the walls have been reduced to clusters of slender painted **colonnettes** framing tall windows filled with brilliant colored glass. The stained glass illustrates narrative and symbolic scenes, including, among others, the Nativity and Passion (sufferings) of Christ, the life of Saint John the Baptist, and the story of King Louis's acquisition of his relics. This exquisite structure epitomizes a new Gothic

style known as *Rayonnant* (a French term meaning "radiant" or "radiating") because of its radiating bar tracery. The style is also sometimes called the Court style because of its association with the royal courts of Paris and London.

Besides carving the sculptural ornament for churches, Gothic sculptors also found a lucrative new outlet for their work in a growing demand for small religious statues intended for homes and personal chapels or as donations to favorite churches. Among the treasures of the Abbey Church of Saint-Denis is a silver-gilt image, slightly more than 2 feet tall, of a standing *Virgin and Child* (fig. 11-14). An inscription on the base bears the date 1339 and the name of Queen Jeanne d'Evreux, wife of

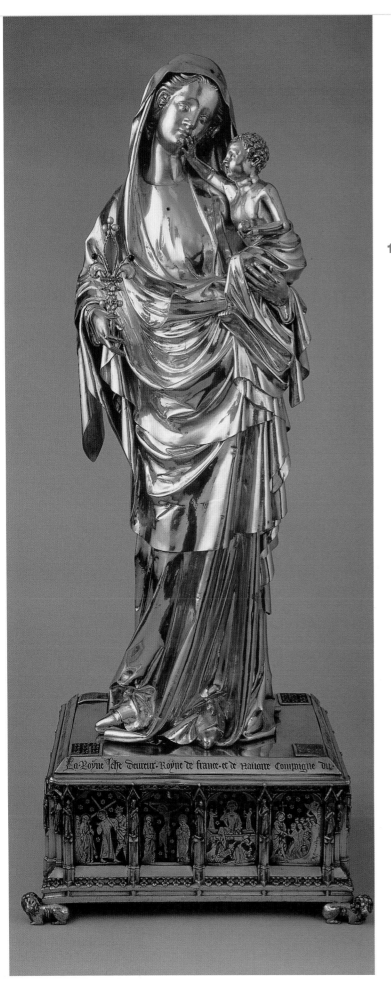

11-14 | ***Virgin and Child***
from the Abbey Church
of Saint-Denis. c. 1339
Silver gilt and enamel
Height 27¹/₈" (69 cm)
Musée du Louvre, Paris

Charles IV of France (ruled 1322–1328). The Virgin holds her son in her left arm, and supports her weight on her left leg, creating the graceful S-curve pose that was a stylistic signature of the period (see fig. 11-12). She holds a scepter topped with an enameled and jeweled lily, the heraldic fleur-de-lis of French royalty, and she originally had a crown on her head. The statue served as a reliquary for hairs said to come from Mary's head. Despite this figure's clear association with royalty, the Virgin's simple clothing and sweet, youthful face anticipates a type of the ideally beautiful mother that emerged in the later fourteenth and fifteenth centuries in northern France, Flanders, and Germany.

France gained renown in the thirteenth and fourteenth centuries not only for the new Gothic architecture and sculpture but also for painting and illustrated books. Books ranged from practical manuals for artisans to elaborate devotional works illustrated with exquisite miniatures. The production of high-quality manuscripts flourished in Paris during the reign of Louis IX, whose royal library was renowned. Queen Blanche of Castile, Louis's mother, served as regent of France (1226–1234) until he came of age. She and the

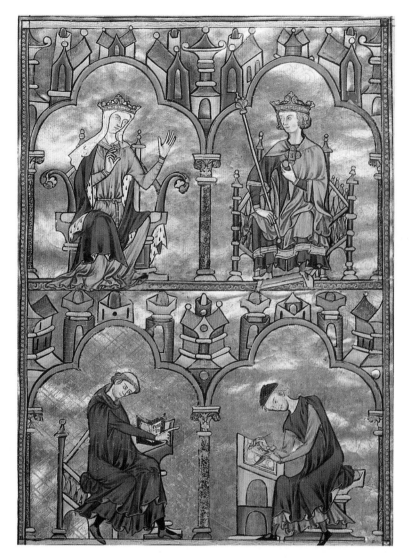

11-15 | Page with *Louis IX and Queen Blanche of Castile,* Moralized Bible, from Paris. 1226–34. Ink, tempera, and gold leaf on vellum, 15 x 10½" (38 x 26.6 cm). The Pierpont Morgan Library, New York
M.240, f.8

teenage king appear on the dedication page (fig. 11-15) of a Moralized Bible—one in which selected passages of the Old and New Testaments are paired to give an allegorical, or moralized, interpretation (see page 263). The royal pair sits against a solid gold background under trilobed arches. Below them a scholar-monk dictates to a scribe. The ornate thrones of Louis and his mother and the buildings atop the arches suggest that the figures sit inside a royal palace, and in fact it would not have been unusual for the queen to have housed the scholar, scribe, and illuminator while they were executing her commission. Interestingly only the slightly oversized heads of the queen and king preserve a sense of hierarchical scale. The scribe, in the lower right, is working on a page with a column of roundels for illustrations. This format of manuscript illustration—used on the pages that follow the Bible's dedication page—derives from stained-glass lancets with their columns of images in

medallions (see fig. 11-8). The illuminators also show their debt to stained glass in their use of glowing red and blue and reflective gold surfaces.

Beginning in the late thirteenth century, private prayer books became popular among those who could afford them. Such books came to be called Books of Hours because they contained special prayers to be recited at the eight canonical "hours," literally around the clock. Books of Hours were most commonly devoted to the Virgin, but they could be personalized for individual patrons with prayers to patron saints, a calendar of saints' church festivals, and other offices, such as that said for the dead.

A tiny, exquisite **Book of Hours** given by Charles IV to his wife, Queen Jeanne d'Evreux, shortly after their marriage in 1325 is the work of an illuminator named Jean Pucelle (fig. 11-16). Instead of the intense colors used by earlier illuminators, Pucelle

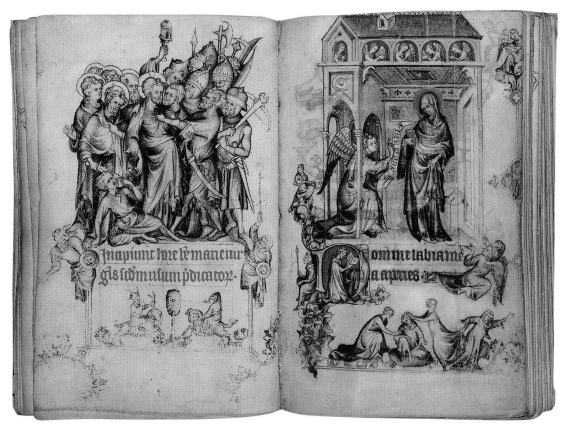

11-16 | Jean Pucelle. Pages with *Betrayal and Arrest of Christ,* folio 15v. (left) **and** *Annunciation,* folio 16r. (right)
Petites Heures of Jeanne d'Evreux, from Paris. c. 1325–28. Grisaille and color on vellum, each page 3½ x 2¼"
(8.2 x 5.6 cm). The Metropolitan Museum of Art, New York
The Cloisters Collection, 1954 (54.1.2)

This book was precious to the queen, who mentioned it in her will; she named its illuminator, an unusual tribute.

worked in a technique called **grisaille**—monochromatic painting in shades of gray—with delicate touches of color added. The pages shown here are part of a narrative cycle juxtaposing scenes from the Infancy and the Passion of Christ, a form known as the Joys and Sorrows of the Virgin. Here, the "Joy" of the *Annunciation* on the right is paired with the "Sorrow" of the *Betrayal and Arrest of Christ* on the left.

In the *Annunciation*, Mary receives the archangel Gabriel in her Gothic-style home, as rejoicing angels look on from windows under the eaves. Queen Jeanne appears in the initial below the Annunciation, kneeling before a lectern and reading from her Book of Hours. This inclusion of the patron in prayer within a scene, a practice that continued in monumental painting and sculpture in the fifteenth century, conveyed the idea that the scenes were "visions" inspired by meditation rather than records of historical events. In the Betrayal scene on the

left page, the traitorous disciple Judas Iscariot embraces Jesus, thus identifying him to soldiers who have come to seize him and setting in motion the events that lead to the Crucifixion. The spoof of military training sketched below, showing "knights" riding goats and jousting at a barrel stuck on a pole, is perhaps a comment on the lack of valor of the soldiers assaulting Jesus.

Both pages show Pucelle adapting the sculptural style of the French court to manuscript illustration. Softly modeled, voluminous draperies are gathered around tall, elegantly curved figures with curly hair and broad foreheads. Jesus on the left and Mary on the right stand in the swaying S-curve pose typical of Court style works, such as the *Virgin and Child* from Saint-Denis, commissioned by the same queen (see fig. 11-14). The earnest face of the *Annunciation* archangel resembles that of the angel Gabriel at Reims (see fig. 11-12).

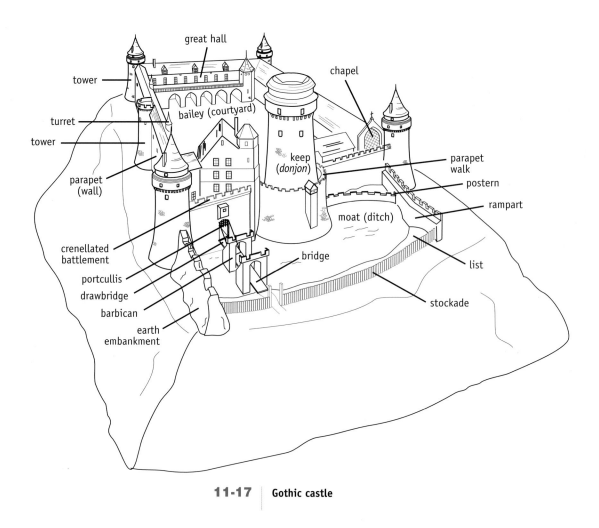

11-17 | **Gothic castle**

CASTLES

Although the Gothic style is most studied in religious architecture, it is also seen in such secular structures as castles, which during the turbulent Middle Ages became fortress-residences. Castles evolved during the Romanesque and Gothic periods from enclosed strongholds to elaborate fortified residential complexes (fig. 11-17). Since a castle needed a site that gave it a defensive, military advantage, the best sites were hilltops or cliffs along a river where the water formed a natural moat.

Medieval warfare consisted of long sieges. Castle defenses included ditches, or moats, and heavy walls and towers with stone battlements designed to shield defenders standing on **parapet** walks, which allowed the troops to repel attacks by shooting through notched crenellations. The most secure spot in the castle, and the final refuge of the defenders, was a massive tower called the *donjon* (France) or keep (England). Inside the walls a large courtyard (the bailey) provided space for living quarters including the great hall, stables, and the chapel. The castle was entered through a heavily defended gate that might include a drawbridge over the moat, an iron portcullis (a grating set into the doorway), and even a separate defensive structure around the portal called a barbican. All of these

elements, which seem so **picturesque** today, had both a military and a political function. Castles established an aura of power and wealth for a family.

By the end of the Middle Ages castles became luxurious residences, their military aspect often more symbolic than real. Private rooms for the ladies, for example, were added to the great hall. In the manuscript illumination (see fig. 20) the queen of France receives the author Christine de Pisan in a room with tapestry-hung walls, painted woodwork, and glass windows as well as magnificent furniture. Woven and **embroidered** textiles provided both insulation and enrichment. The use of heraldry (a symbolic language defining lineage) reinforced the depiction of power and feudal rights. Little secular art survives but embroideries such as the Chichester-Constable chasuble (a priest's vestment) (see fig. 11-21) suggest the finery worn by the queen and her ladies.

Beginning in the late thirteenth century, France began to suffer from overpopulation and economic decline. The plague followed in the fourteenth century, along with a devastating conflict with England known as the Hundred Years' War. Large-scale cathedral construction generally ceased, although the Gothic style continued to develop in smaller churches, municipal and commercial buildings, and private residences.

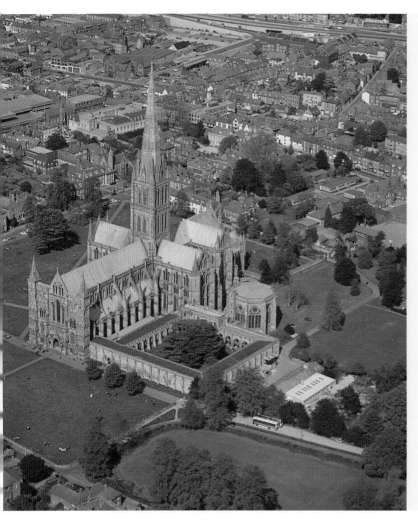

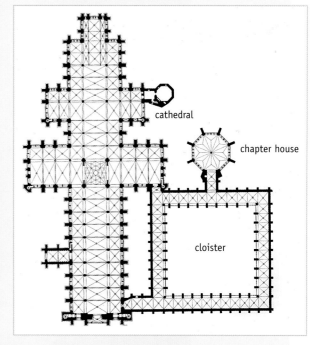

11-18 | **West facade, Salisbury Cathedral,** Salisbury Wiltshire, England. 1220–58; west facade 1265; spire c. 1320–30

11-19 | **Plan of Salisbury Cathedral**

Gothic Art in England

As the Gothic style spread outside of France, it not only became an international style in Europe but also took on innovative regional forms in the thirteenth and fourteenth centuries. In England, for instance, cathedral builders were less concerned with height than were their French counterparts, and they constructed long, broad naves, Romanesque-type galleries, and clerestory-level passageways. The English builders focused their decorative efforts on the cathedral walls, which retained a Romanesque solidity. Salisbury Cathedral, because its principal structure was built in a relatively short period of time (1220–58), has a consistency of style that makes it an ideal representative of English Gothic architecture (fig. 11-18). Typically English is the parklike setting (the cathedral close, or precinct) and attached **cloister** and chapter house for the cathedral clergy (fig. 11-19). Tier upon tier of blind **tracery** and arcaded niches underscore the width of the massive west facade. In contrast to French cathedral facades, which suggest the entrance to paradise with their mighty towers flanking deep portals, English facades like the one at Salisbury suggest a jeweled wall around paradise.

Many English churches were completed with splendid towers and spires in the fourteenth century. At Salisbury Cathedral, about 1320–30, Master Richard of Farleigh built a crossing tower with a spire rising to the extraordinary height of 400 feet. Taller than anything visualized by the original builders, the spire required extra buttressing and the builders added flying buttresses. The spire has such harmonious proportions that it seems the logical, and indeed inevitable, focal point of the architectural composition.

Before devastating plagues, including the Black Death, brought major building campaigns to a halt, the king's carpenter, William Hurley of London, designed and supervised the construction of a windowed tower, or **lantern**, at Ely Cathedral (1328–47) (fig. 11-20; see page 274). William constructed eight masonry piers, which form an octagon 72 feet in diameter. They carry a wooden superstructure where long ribs support an octagonal lantern closed by a star vault. Huge oak timbers 63 feet long and over 3 feet thick at the base stand on hammer beams cantilevered out from the walls and form the vertical members of the lantern. The Ely octagon is more than a technical achievement; it is one of the finest spatial designs produced in a period famed for the ingenuity of its builders. The ribs literally shape the space, sweeping the viewer's eyes upward through the streaming light from the lantern into the star of the vault.

Like the French, the English also made richly decorated books, but they became renowned throughout Europe for their

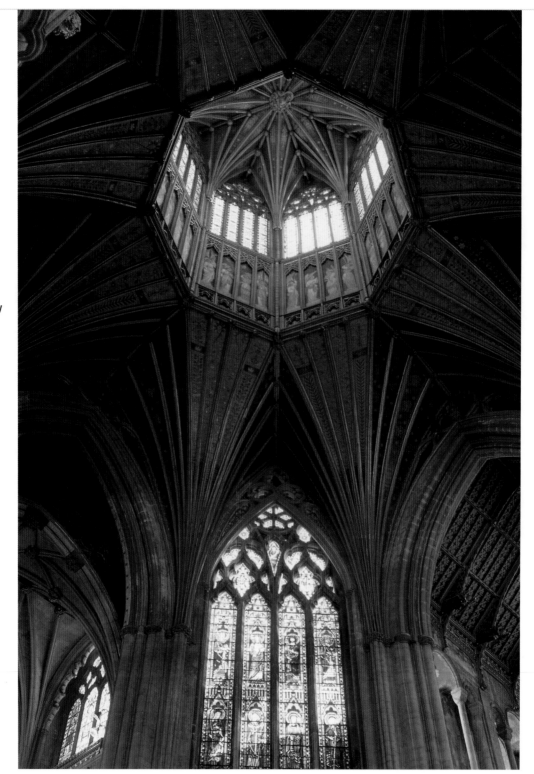

11-20

William Hurley
Lantern Tower
Ely Cathedral
Cambridgeshire
England
1328–47

pictorial needlework using colored silk and gold thread to create images as detailed as the painters produced in manuscripts. The art came to be called *opus anglicanum* (English work). The names of several prominent embroiderers are known, but in her own day no one surpassed Mabel of Bury St. Edmunds, who worked for King Henry III. She created both religious and secular pieces for him, and the grateful king paid her in money and rich gifts.

None of Mabel's work has been identified, but it must have resembled the embroidery seen on a chasuble—a garment worn by priests while celebrating the Mass—known as the Chichester-Constable chasuble (fig. 11-21). Here, the images are formed by fine gradations of colored silk as subtle as the finest painting. Three Marian scenes—the Annunciation, the Adoration of the Magi, and the Coronation of the Virgin—are arranged in three registers framed by cusped, crocketed S-shaped arches and twisting branches sprouting oak leaves with seed-pearl acorns. This vestment would have glinted in the candlelight amid the other treasures of the altar. So heavy did such gold and bejeweled garments become that their wearers often needed help to move.

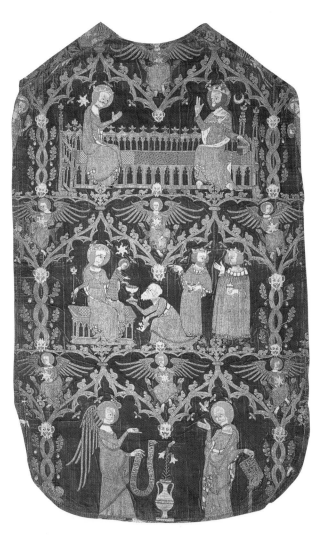

11-21 | *Life of the Virgin* (Chichester-Constable chasuble back from a set of vestments embroidered in *opus anglicanum*) from southern England. 1330–50. Red velvet with silk and metallic thread; length 5'1½" (1.64 m), width 30" (76 cm) The Metropolitan Museum of Art, New York

Fletcher Fund, 1927 (2.7 162.1)

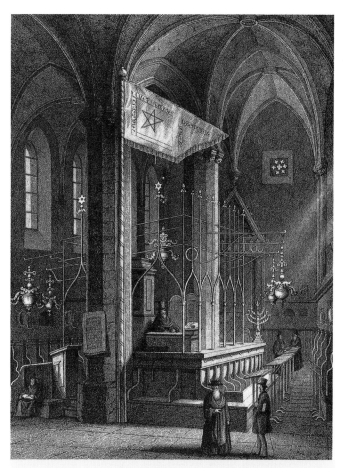

11-22 | **Interior, Altneuschul**, Prague, Bohemia (Czech Republic). c. late 13th century; later additions and alterations. Engraving from *Das Historisches Prag in 25 Stahlstichen*, 1864

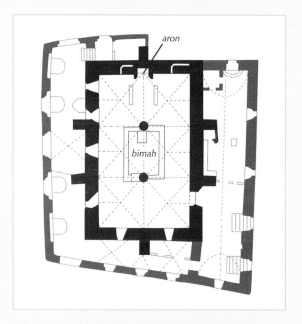

11-23 | **Plan of Altneuschul**

Gothic Art in the Germanic Lands

In Germany, a new type of Gothic church, the **hall church**, developed in the thirteenth century in response to the increasing importance of sermons within church services. The hall church featured a nave and **side aisles** with vaults of the same height, creating a spacious and open interior that could accommodate the large crowds drawn by charismatic preachers. The flexible design of these "great halls" was also widely adopted for civic and residential buildings and even by Jewish architects.

The oldest functioning synagogue in Europe, Prague's Altneuschul (Old-New Synagogue), was built in the style of a Gothic great hall, probably in the late thirteenth or fourteenth century (fig. 11-22). As in a hall church, the vaults of the synagogue are all the same height. But unlike a church, with its nave and side aisles, the Altneuschul has two central aisles with six bays (fig. 11-23). The bays have four-part vaulting with a decorative fifth rib.

The synagogue had two focal points, the *aron*, or shrine for the Torah scrolls, located on the east wall, toward Jerusalem, and a central raised reading platform called the *bimah*. The *bimah* can be seen in figure 11-23, straddling the two central bays. The interior of the synagogue was originally richly adorned with murals. Men worshiped and studied in the principal space; women were sequestered in annexes.

Gothic Art in Italy

The thirteenth century was a period of political division and economic expansion for the Italian peninsula and its neighboring islands. The papacy had emerged from its conflict with the Holy Roman Empire as a significant international force, but its temporal success weakened its spiritual authority and brought it into conflict with the growing power of the kings of France and England. In 1309, after the election of a French pope, the papal court moved from Rome to Avignon, in southern France. During the Great Schism of 1378 to 1417, there were two rival lines of popes, one in Rome and one in Avignon, each claiming legitimacy.

The prolonged conflict between the papacy and the empire created two political factions: the pro-papacy Guelphs and the pro-imperial Ghibellines. Northern Italy was dominated by several independent and wealthy city-states controlled by a few powerful families. Consequently, these cities were subject to chronic internal factional strife as well as conflict with one another.

Nevertheless, great wealth and a growing individualism promoted arts patronage in northern Italy. Artisans began to emerge as artists in the modern sense, both in their own eyes and the eyes of patrons. Although their methods and working conditions remained largely unchanged, they now belonged to powerful urban **guilds** and contracted freely with wealthy townspeople and nobles and with civic and religious bodies. Their ambitious, self-aware art reflects their economic and social freedom.

SCULPTURE

In the first half of the thirteenth century, Holy Roman Emperor Frederick II had fostered a classical revival at his court in southern Italy, a revival that stimulated a trend toward greater naturalism in Italian Gothic sculpture. A leading early exemplar of the trend was Nicola Pisano (active c. 1258–1278), who moved from the south to Tuscany at midcentury. An inscription on a freestanding marble pulpit (fig. 11-24) in the Pisa **Baptistry** identifies Nicola as a supremely self-confident sculptor. The inscription reads: "In the year 1260 Nicola Pisano carved this noble work. May so gifted a hand be praised as it deserves." The six-sided structure, open on one side for a stairway, is supported by columns topped with leafy Corinthian capitals. Standing figures and an angel flank Gothic trefoil arches. Three columns rest on the back of a shaggy-maned lion guarding its prey and the center column stands on crouching figures. The pulpits' panels illustrate New Testament subjects, each treated as an independent composition unrelated to the others. The sculptural treatment of the deeply cut, full-bodied

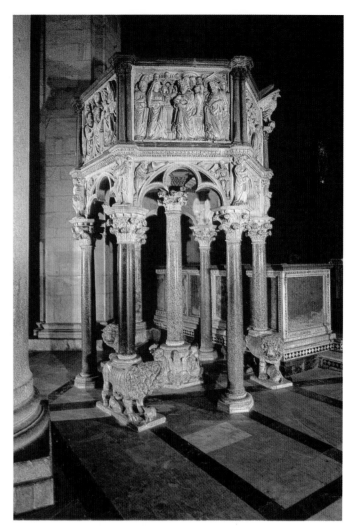

11-24 | **Nicola Pisano. Pulpit, Baptistry, Pisa.** 1260
Marble; height approx. 15' (4.6 m)

forms is almost classical, as are their heavy, placid faces; the congested layout and the use of hierarchical scale are not. The format, style, and technique of Roman sarcophagus reliefs —readily accessible in the burial ground near the cathedral— may have inspired the carving.

In 1330, another Italian sculptor, Andrea Pisano (active 1320s–1348, unrelated to Nicola), was awarded the prestigious commission for a pair of gilded bronze doors for the Florentine Baptistry of San Giovanni (fig. 11-25). Completed within six years, the doors are decorated with twenty-eight scenes from the life of Saint John the Baptist (San Giovanni) framed by barbed quatrefoils. The figures reflect the monumental classicizing style then current in Florence, but the overall effect of the repeated barbed quatrefoils is two-dimensional and decorative. The individual scenes are elegantly natural, and the figures' placement and modeling create a remarkable illusion of three-dimensionality. Surrounding the doors are lush vine scrolls filled with flowers, fruits, and birds, cast in bronze and applied to the doorway's lintel and jambs.

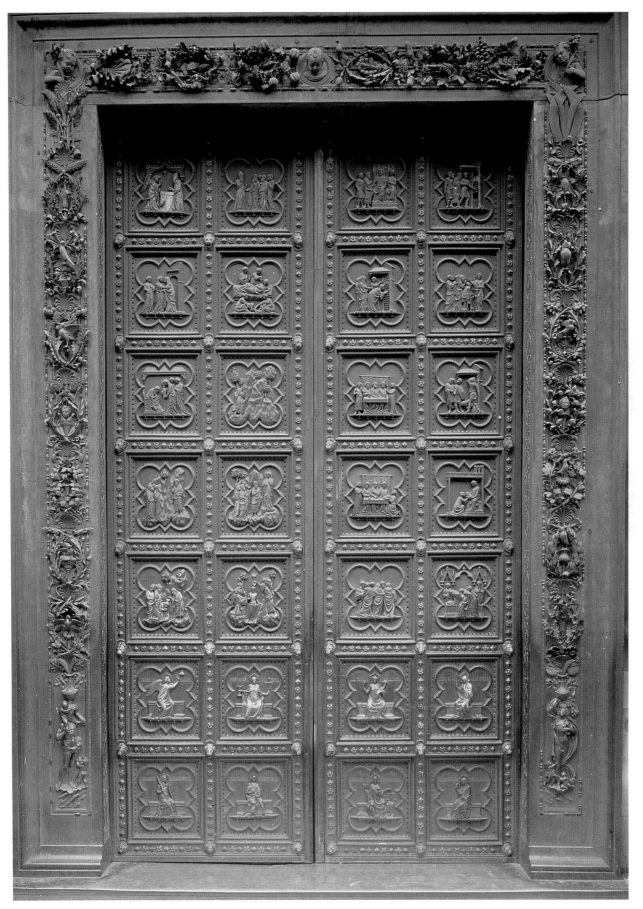

11-25 | **Andrea Pisano.** *Life of John the Baptist,* south doors, Baptistry of San Giovanni, Florence. 1330–36. Gilded bronze

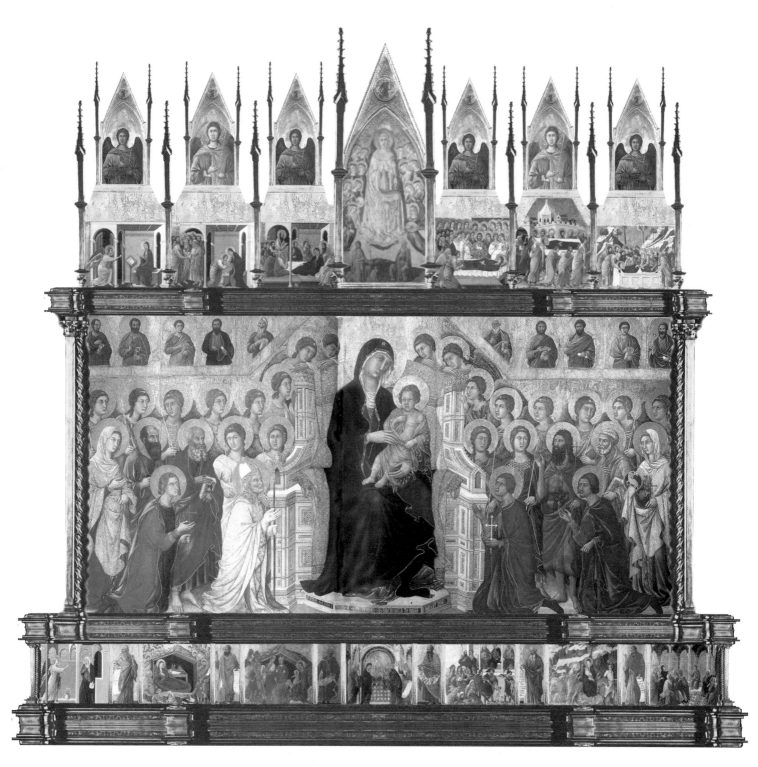

11-26 **Duccio de Buoninsegna.** Conjectural reconstruction of *Virgin and Child in Majesty (Maestà)*. Original location Siena Cathedral. 1308–11. Tempera and gold on wood. Main panel, 7' x 13' (2.13 x 4.12 m) and many small panels now in Museo dell'Opera del Duomo, Siena. Computerized reconstruction of the front by Sarah Loyd (from Hartt and Wilkins, page 127.)

Duccio's *Maestà Altarpiece* was removed from the cathedral's main altar in 1505. In 1771, the altarpiece was cut up to make it salable. Over the years, sections were dispersed, appearing later at auctions or in museums and private collections. The value of the panels remaining in Siena was finally recognized, and they were placed in the cathedral museum in 1878.

Cennini on Panel Painting

Cennino Cennini's Il Libro dell'Arte (The Handbook of the Crafts), a compendium of early-fifteenth-century Florentine artistic techniques, includes step-by-step instructions for making panel paintings. The wood for these paintings, he specified, should be fine-grained, free of blemishes, and thoroughly seasoned by slow drying.

The first step in preparing a panel for painting was to cover its surface with clean white linen strips soaked in a gesso made from gypsum, a task best done on a dry, windy day. Gesso provides a ground, or surface, on which to paint. Cennini specified that at least nine layers should be applied, with a minimum of two-and-a-half days' drying time between layers, depending on the weather. The gessoed surface should then be burnished until it resembled ivory. The artist could now sketch the composition of the work with charcoal made from burned willow twigs. At this point, advised the author, "When you have finished drawing your figure, especially if it is in a very valuable [altarpiece], so that you are counting on profit and reputation from it, leave it alone for a few days, going back to it now and then to look it over and improve it wherever it still needs something . . . (and bear in mind that you may copy and examine things done by other good masters; that it is no shame to you)" (cited in Thompson, page 75).

The final version of the design, he directed, should be inked in with a fine squirrel-hair brush, and the charcoal brushed off with a feather. Gold leaf was to be affixed on a humid day over a reddish clay ground called bole, and the tissue-thin sheets carefully glued down with a mixture of fine powdered clay and egg white and burnished with a gemstone or the tooth of a carnivorous animal. Punched and incised patterning was to be added later.

Italian painters at this time worked in a type of paint known as **tempera**, powdered pigments mixed most often with egg yolk, a little water, and an occasional touch of glue. **Apprentices** were kept busy grinding and mixing paints according to their masters' recipes, setting them out for more senior painters in wooden bowls or shell dishes. Cennini claimed that panel painting was a gentleman's job, but given its laborious complexity, that was wishful thinking. The claim does, however, reflect the rising social status of painters.

Cennini specified a detailed and highly formulaic painting process. Faces, for example, were always to be done last, with flesh tones applied over two coats of a light greenish pigment and highlighted with touches of red and white. The finished painting was to be given a layer of varnish to protect it and enhance its colors. Reflecting the increasing specialization that developed in the thirteenth century, Cennini assumed that an elaborate frame would have been produced by someone else according to the painter's specifications and brought fully assembled into the studio.

ITALIAN PANEL AND MURAL PAINTING

The elegant Court style seen in manuscript illustrations and embroideries also influenced Gothic **panel painting** (see "Cennini on Panel Painting," left). Large-scale paintings on wood panels made to stand behind and above the altar (altarpieces), began to appear in the twelfth century and proliferated throughout Europe in the thirteenth century.

Two very important schools of Italian Gothic painting emerged in Siena and Florence, rivals in this as in everything else. Siena's foremost painter was Duccio di Buoninsegna (active 1278–1318), whose synthesis of Byzantine and northern Gothic influences transformed the tradition in which he worked. Duccio and his studio assistants painted a huge altarpiece for Siena Cathedral, known as the *Maestà* (*Majesty*) *Altarpiece*, between 1308 and 1311. Creating this altarpiece was an arduous undertaking. The work was large—the central panel alone was 7 by 13 feet—and it had to be painted on both sides because the main altar stood in the center of the sanctuary. Because the *Maestà* was broken up in the eighteenth century, its power and beauty can only be imagined from scattered parts. The main scene, depicting the *Virgin and Child in Majesty* (fig. 11-26), was once accompanied above and below by narrative scenes from the *Life of the Virgin and the Infancy of Christ*. On the back were scenes from the *Life and Passion of Christ*. In this altarpiece, Duccio has combined a softened Italo-Byzantine figure style (an Italian adaptation of later Byzantine art) with the linear grace and easy relationship between figures and their settings characteristic of the Gothic art of France. This subtle blending of northern and southern elements can be seen in the haloed ranks around Mary's architectonic throne (which represents both the Catholic Church and its specific embodiment, Siena Cathedral). The central, most holy figures retain an iconic Byzantine solemnity and immobility, but those adoring them reflect a more naturalistic, courtly style that became the hallmark of the Sienese school for years to come. The ornate **punchwork**, or tooled designs in gold leaf, is also characteristically Sienese.

The enthusiasm with which the citizens of a city greeted a great painting or altarpiece demonstrates the power of the images it represented—as well as the association of the images with the glory of the city, but only rarely was it a testimony to the skill or fame of the artist. Duccio's completed altarpiece for Siena Cathedral was carried from his workshop to the cathedral in a joyous procession:

> On the day that it was carried to the [cathedral] the shops were shut, and the bishop conducted a great and devout company of priests and friars in solemn procession, accompanied by . . . all the officers of the commune, and all the people, and one after another the worthiest with lighted candles in their hands took places near the picture, and behind came the women and children with great devotion. And they accompanied the said picture up to the [cathedral], making the procession around the campo [square], as is the custom, all the bells ringing joyously, out of reverence for so noble a picture as is this (cited in Holt, page 69).

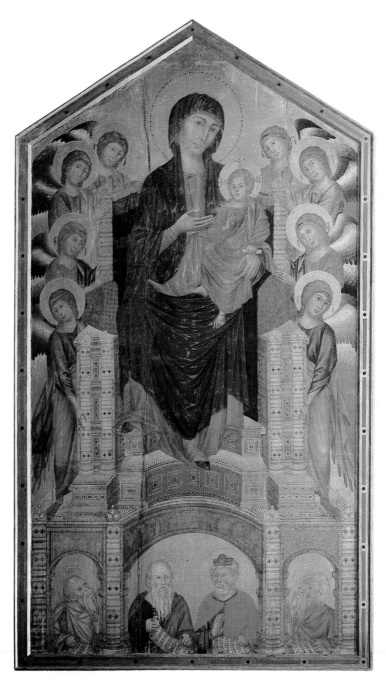

11-27 Cimabue. *Virgin and Child Enthroned,* from the Church of Santa Trinità, Florence. c. 1280. Tempera and gold on wood, 12'7¹/₂" x 7'4" (3.9 x 2.2 m). Galleria degli Uffizi, Florence

In Florence the transformation of the Italo-Byzantine style began somewhat earlier than in Siena. Duccio's Florentine counterpart was an older painter named Cenni di Pepi (active c. 1272–1302), better known by his nickname, Cimabue. Cimabue is believed to have painted the *Virgin and Child Enthroned* (fig. 11-27) in about 1280 for the main altar of the Church of the Santa Trinità (Holy Trinity) in Florence. At more than 11¹/₂ feet high, this enormous panel painting seems to have set a precedent for monumental altarpieces. Surrounded by saints, angels, and Old Testament prophets, Mary holds the infant Jesus in her lap and points to him as the path to salvation.

Cimabue employed Byzantine formulas in determining the proportions of the figures, the placement of their features, and even the tilts of their haloed heads. To render the draperies (and to suggest divinity), he used the Byzantine technique of highlighting the base color with thin lines of gold. Mary's huge throne, painted to represent gold with inset enamels and gems, provides an architectural framework for the figures. The vantage point suspends the viewer in space in front of the image, simultaneously looking down on the projecting elements of the throne and Mary's lap, but straight at the prophets at the base of the throne and the splendid winged seraphim who appear one above

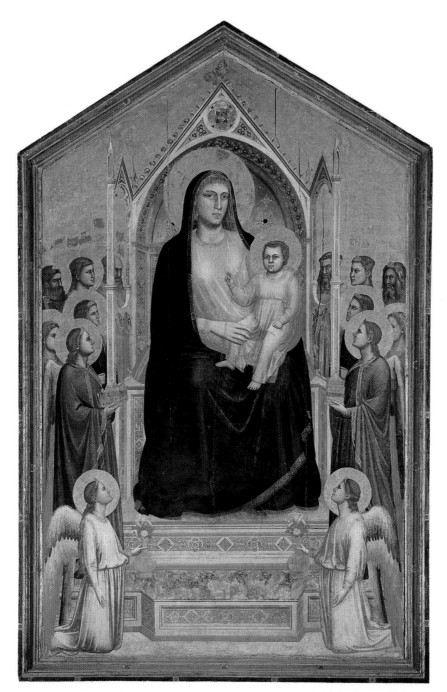

11-28   **Giotto di Bondone.** *Virgin and Child Enthroned,* from the Church of the
Ognissanti, Florence. c. 1310. Tempera and gold on wood, 10'8" x 6'8¼"
(3.53 x 2.05 m). Galleria degli Uffizi, Florence

another on either side. These spatial ambiguities, as well as subtle
asymmetries throughout the composition, the Virgin's thoughtful gaze, and the well-observed faces of the old men, are all
departures from tradition that serve to enliven the picture.

According to the sixteenth-century chronicler Georgio
Vasari, Cimabue discovered a talented shepherd boy, Giotto di
Bondone, and taught him how to paint. Then, "Giotto obscured
the fame of Cimabue, as a great light outshines a lesser." Vasari
also credited Giotto (active c. 1300–1337) with "setting art upon
the path that may be called the true one [for he] learned to draw
accurately from life and thus put an end to the crude Greek [i.e.,

Italo-Byzantine] manners" (trans. J. C. and P. Bondanella). The
painter and commentator Cennino Cennini (c. 1370–1440) (see
"Cennini on Panel Painting," page 279), writing in the late fourteenth century, was struck by the accessibility and modernity of
Giotto's art, which, though it retained traces of the "Greek manner," was moving toward the depiction of a humanized world
anchored in three-dimensional form.

Giotto shared his teacher's concern for spatial volumes,
solid forms, and warmly naturalistic human figures. Giotto's
1310 painting of the *Virgin and Child Enthroned* (fig. 11-28) for
the Church of the Ognissanti (All Saints) in Florence reflects

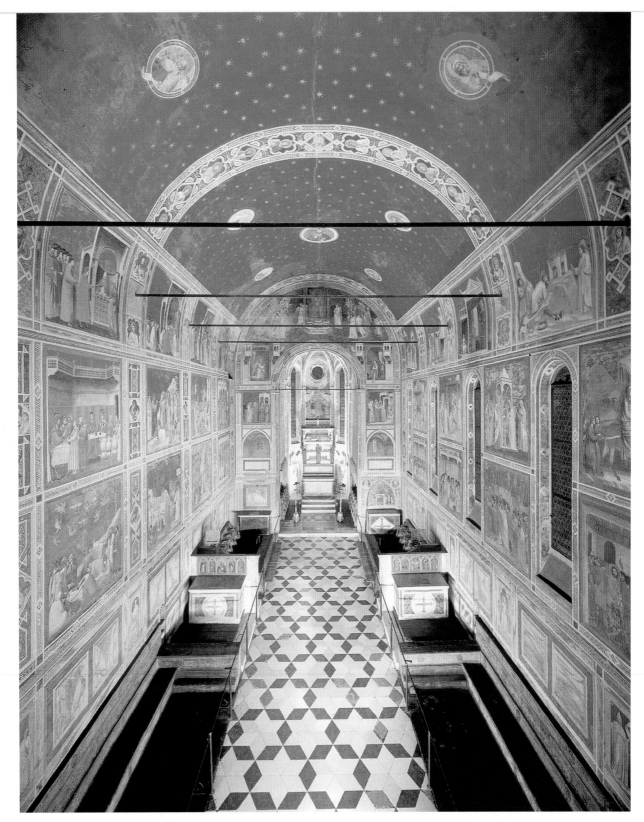

11-29 | **Giotto di Bondone. Frescoes, Arena (Scrovegni) Chapel,** Padua. View toward the east wall, 1305–06

Cimabue's influence in its largely symmetrical composition, the rendering of the angels' wings, and Mary's Byzantine facial type. Gone, however, are the Virgin's modestly inclined head and delicate gold-lined drapery; instead, light and shadow play across her substantial form. Figures even peer through openings in the throne canopy. This colossal Mary seems to overwhelm her slen-

der Gothic throne. Despite Giotto's retention of hierarchical scale and the formal, enthroned image type, he has created the sense that his figures are fully three-dimensional beings inhabiting real space.

Giotto's masterpiece is the frescoed interior of the Scrovegni family chapel in Padua (fig. 11-29), painted about

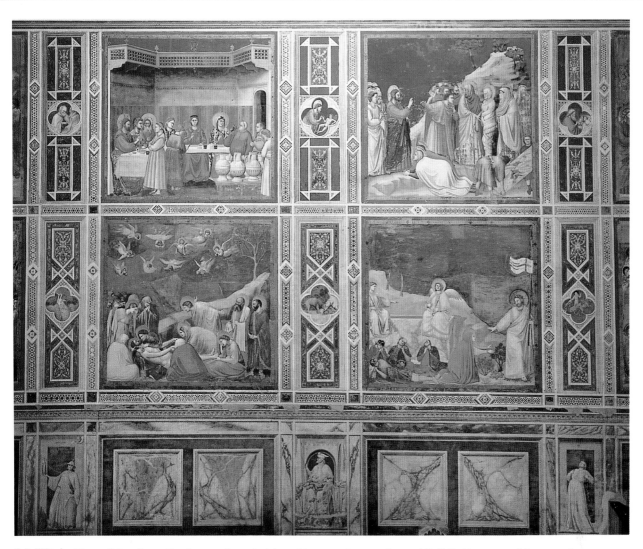

11-30 | **Giotto di Bondone.** *Marriage at Cana, Raising of Lazarus, Resurrection and Noli Me Tangere,* **and** *Lamentation* (clockwise from top left), frescoes on north wall of Arena Chapel, Padua

1305. The chapel (also known as the Arena Chapel because of its location near an ancient Roman arena) is a simple, barrel-vaulted room. Giotto covered the entrance wall with a scene of the *Last Judgment* and the sanctuary wall with the *Annunciation*. He subdivided the side walls with a dado of allegorical grisaille paintings of the *Virtues and Vices*, from which rise vertical bands containing quatrefoil portrait medallions. The medallions are set within a framework painted to resemble marble inlay and carved relief. The central band of medallions spans the vault, crossing a brilliant lapis blue, star-spangled sky in which large portrait disks float like glowing moons. Set into this framework are rectangular narrative scenes juxtaposing the life of the Virgin with that of Jesus. Both the individual scenes and the overall program display Giotto's genius for distilling a complex narrative into a coherent visual experience.

Both Giotto's narrative skills and his use of **typology**—in which earlier events presage later ones—are apparent in the paintings on the side walls (fig. 11-30). Events in the life of the Virgin Mary and in the ministry of Jesus are depicted in three registers that circle the room. In the section illustrated here, the first miracle, the event of Jesus' changing water to wine at the wedding feast at Cana (recalling that his blood will become the wine of the Eucharist, or communion), is followed by the raising of Lazarus (a reference to the Resurrection). Below, the lamentation over the body of Jesus by those closest to him leads to the Resurrection, indicated by angels at the empty tomb. Giotto rendered his bulky figures as pure color masses by painting the deepest shadows with the most intense **hues** and highlighting shapes with lighter shades mixed with white. These sculpturally modeled figures enabled Giotto to convey a sense of depth in both landscape and architectural settings. In his paintings Giotto conveys real human emotions that draw viewers into the scenes. This direct emotional appeal and the simplicity of the forms embody the new Francican values of personal devotion and service.

Sienese painting was a key contributor to the development of the mainstream of Gothic art in Europe, but Florentine painting, in the style originated by Giotto and kept alive by his pupils and their followers, was fundamental to the development of Italian Renaissance art over the next two centuries. With Giotto, art moved toward the depiction of a humanized world anchored in three-dimensional form.

500 CE	600	700	800	900

**EARLY MEDIEVAL,
ROMANESQUE, GOTHIC**

Palace Chapel
of Charlemagne
792–805

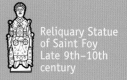

Reliquary Statue
of Saint Foy
Late 9th–10th
century

▲ CHRISTIAN SPAIN 500–

▲ BRITAIN/IRELAND 500–

SCANDINAVIAN VIKING 800–1100 ▲

CAROLINGIAN PERIOD 750–900 ▲

OTTONIAN PERIOD 900–1000 ▲

LOOKING BACK 4

Mission and Message

As the Roman Empire disintegrated, the Christian Church assumed an ever-greater social as well as spiritual role in Europe. Christian bishops replaced Roman provincial governors, and the pope, who had originally been the bishop of Rome, emerged as the new supreme leader of the Church. The idea of imperial Rome remained strong, both as a secular empire and as the headquarters of the Christian Church. Germanic warlords like Charlemagne allied themselves with the pope, and they used the arts to proclaim their power. Meanwhile, Jews and Muslims, perpetual outsiders in Europe's predominantly Christian society, nevertheless often lived at peace with their neighbors. In places like Spain and Sicily a rich exchange of intellectual and artistic influence took place. From this extraordinary amalgam—first the blending of ancient classical forms with the ornamental styles found in the hinterlands of the Roman Empire, namely Celtic and Germanic, then the mingling of Near Eastern abstract modes with the art of the West—there developed a new narrative and figurative art that was also richly decorative and expressive. For a thousand years artists created images in what we now call the medieval style.

The medieval artist worked in the service of God, and all the fruits of his or her labor were meant to glorify God (thus the anonymity of many medieval artists; the modern notion of the artist as an individual who can claim fame through his or her work would come later with the birth of the Renaissance). Inspired by biblical accounts of the jeweled walls of heaven and the golden gates of paradise, architect/builders labored to erect glorious dwelling places for God and the saints on earth. To capture the effects of light and color, they constructed ever-larger buildings with higher vaults, and thinner walls that permitted the insertion of huge windows. The glowing, back-lit colors of stained glass and the soft sheen of mural paintings dissolved the solid forms of masonry, while within the church the reflection of gold, enamels, and gems on altars and gospel books, on crosses and candlesticks, captured the splendor of paradise on earth. Subtle light and dazzling color created a mystical visual pathway to heaven as artists fulfilled their mission and gave tangible form to the unseen and unknowable.

Along with glorifying God, the single most important function of Christian art was to teach a largely illiterate populace. From the very beginning the Church recognized the educational and persuasive power of the visual arts. With figures and symbols they told the stories and explained complex ideas underlying their faith. In their earliest art, still seen in the catacombs of Rome, they depicted scenes of miracles and symbols of salvation. Using every medium—from bronze to ivory, from enamel to tempera paint—and working in every scale—from enormous stained glass windows to tiny book illustrations—artists proclaimed the Christian message. Even priestly vestments used at the altar carried embroidered religious messages. On the outside of churches, sculptors carved the portals and facades, like the church of Saint Lazare at Autun, with terrifying scenes of the Last Judgment. To the Medieval man or woman who could not read, art told of heaven's rewards and the horrors of hell.

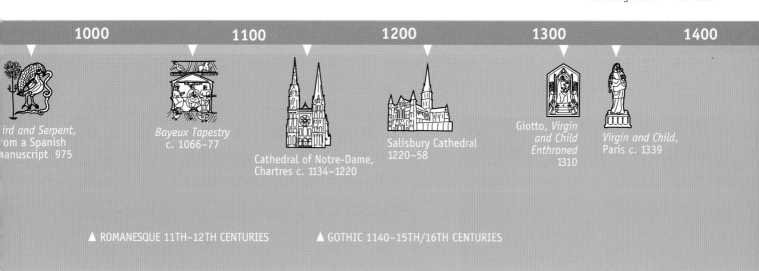

1000	1100	1200	1300	1400

ird and Serpent, om a Spanish anuscript 975

Bayeux Tapestry c. 1066–77

Cathedral of Notre-Dame, Chartres c. 1134–1220

Salisbury Cathedral 1220–58

Giotto, *Virgin and Child Enthroned* 1310

Virgin and Child, Paris c. 1339

▲ ROMANESQUE 11TH–12TH CENTURIES ▲ GOTHIC 1140–15TH/16TH CENTURIES

Early Medieval, Romanesque, and Gothic Art

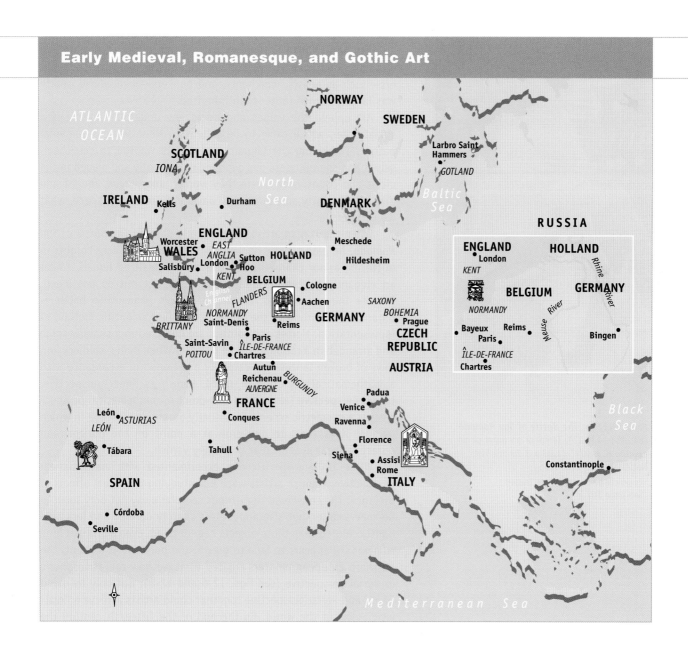

Paolo Uccello. *The Battle of San Romano*
(*details*) 1430s(?). Tempera on wood panel
approx. 6' x 10'7" (1.83 x 3.23 m). The
National Gallery, London
(See page 307.)

Fascinated by what they saw around them, fifteenth-century artists sought to observe and represent the material world. They and their patrons were guided by a new emphasis on humanist secular thinking, which placed value on science, reason, and the individual over intangible religious mysticism. A new social order emerged from this secular worldview in which social mobility replaced the static medieval feudal hierarchy dominated by the nobility and Church. Power was no longer the prerogative only of divinely sanctioned elites, but now lay in the hands of commoners—such as artists, merchants, and bankers—men whose wealth was largely earned rather than inherited.

Art upheld the values and worldview underpinning the new social order, which came to be called the Renaissance. Humanist patrons (including the Church) and artists wanted to see themselves and their possessions depicted realistically and placed in the cities and countryside where they worked and played, fought and died. They tacitly agreed on new ways of representing space, what we call perspective.

When the Italian artist Paolo Uccello painted *The Battle of San Romano*, he paid artistic homage to the old order where knights in glittering armor charge into battle riding idealized horses. Under an elegantly fluttering banner, knights battle but do not bleed. Despite these unnatural features, Uccello's pageantlike battle is organized according to the precepts of a new scientific method of representation. Horses and soldiers are depicted in a shallow stage and arranged in a rational spatial pattern. When dying, soldiers join rows of broken lances—all carefully positioned in accordance with a mathematical depiction of space, known as linear perspective. Linear perspective (also called one-point or mathematical perspective) is a geometric scheme for visually organizing a scene in which parallel lines seem to converge at a point on the horizon and objects appear ever smaller until they vanish.

While Italians like Uccello experimented with mathematical perspective, Flemish artists were also studying the visual effects of distance. They observed that things seen far away not only seem to become smaller, but also appear less sharply defined and less brilliantly colored than those objects near at hand. Even a brilliant blue summer sky appears to fade to gray at the horizon. As a result, the northern European painters created what we now call atmospheric or aerial perspective (see figs. 12-6 and 12-8). But only by using linear and aerial perspective together could artists achieve a "realistic" view of the world. By the end of the fifteenth century the visual mastery of the material world seemed complete; the rational and scientific had triumphed in both secular and religious art.

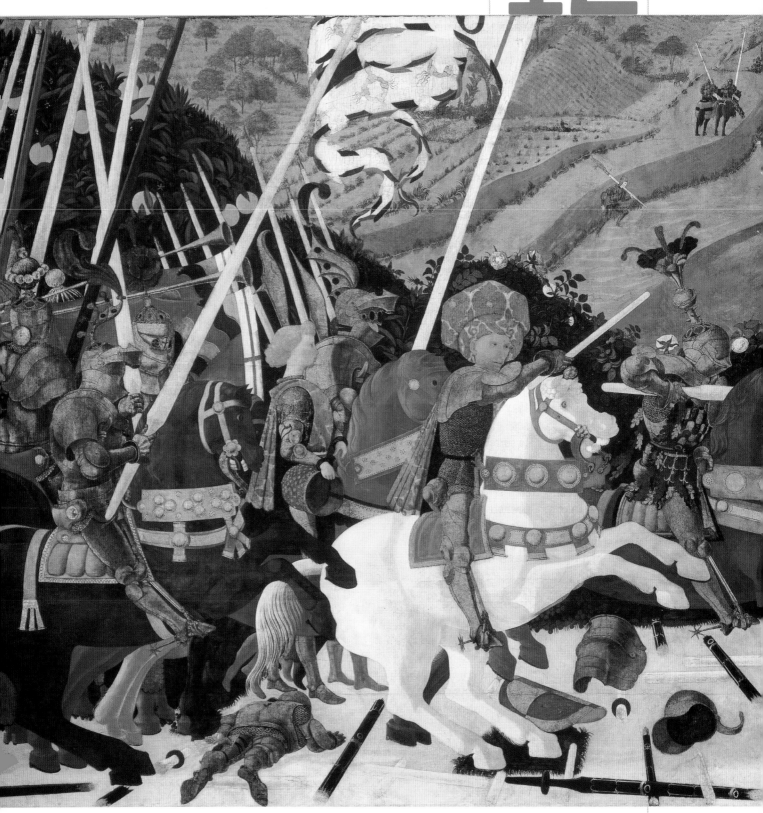

Discovery, not just physical but also intellectual discovery, was the guiding theme of the *Renaissance*, or "rebirth." During the Middle Ages, European scholars had studied the work of Greek and Roman philosophers, poets, rhetoricians, and historians. In the fifteenth and early sixteenth centuries, a group of scholars of antiquity, known as humanists, rediscovered the equally remarkable accomplishments of the ancient mathematicians, astronomers, geographers, physicians, naturalists, artists, and architects. Encouraged by these examples, Renaissance scholars and artists tried to understand, describe, and reproduce the appearance of the natural world in a rational and scientific way. In Italy, Renaissance artists developed a system known as **linear perspective** (see "Renaissance Perspective Systems," far right), which allowed them to represent three-dimensional reality convincingly, and architects revived features of classical architecture, including the classical orders, and borrowed designs and decorative motifs from ruins of Roman temples, triumphal arches, and tombs. Both painters and sculptors tried to portray the human body accurately, and they even depicted nude human beings in secular art for the first time since classical antiquity. The methods of seeing and reproducing the visual world that Renaissance artists revived prevailed across Europe as late as the nineteenth century. The Renaissance viewpoint survives in "realistic" art and in the conventions of popular art.

Renaissance Art in the Low Countries

Renaissance art followed slightly different paths in Italy and north of the Alps (see Map 5, page 383). The French Gothic style had never taken deep root in Italy, where artists continued to be influenced by Byzantine art and were surrounded by the ruins of Roman antiquity. Thus, the Italian Renaissance was less a reaction to the Gothic past than a return to a classical tradition that had never been completely forgotten.

In northern Europe, in contrast, where the Gothic style had emerged from native traditions, artists came to the Renaissance by way of an intense interest in the natural world. Gothic artists in France, Germany, and the Low Countries had depicted birds, plants, and animals with breathtaking accuracy in manuscript painting, textiles, and sculpture. In the fourteenth century, they enlarged on these developments by accurately portraying such things as reflections on water, steamy breath on a cold winter's day, and the sheen of a metal basin. In the fifteenth century, they learned to place these details convincingly in scenes from the material world. Similarly, fifteenth-century portraits seem astonishingly lifelike (see fig. 12-3), and even in religious paintings, saints and angels often seem to have distinct personalities (see fig. 12-5).

Throughout most of the fifteenth century, the artists of Flanders were considered the best in Europe. The art produced in the Low Countries and Burgundy during this period is commonly called *Flemish* because its greatest exponents lived in the province of Flanders (roughly equivalent to the western part of modern Belgium and a small area of northern France), part of the domain of the duke of Burgundy. Flanders, with its major seaport and commercial center at Bruges, was the commercial power of northern Europe, rivaling the Italian city-states of Florence and Venice.

The most outstanding exponents of the new Flemish style were Robert Campin (documented from 1406; d. 1444), Jan van Eyck (c. 1370/90–1441), and Rogier van der Weyden (c. 1399–1464). About 1425–28, Campin painted an altarpiece now known as the *Mérode Altarpiece* (fig. 12-1) after the name of its former owners. Its relatively small size—slightly more than 2 feet tall and about 4 feet wide with the **wings** open—suggests that it was made for a private chapel. Campin portrayed the Annunciation as if the Virgin lived in a Flemish home. Into this contemporary setting he brought normal household objects that could also be seen as religious symbols. The lilies on the table, for example, were a traditional element of Annunciation imagery symbolizing Mary's virginity. The hanging water pot and towel in the niche refer to Mary's purity and her sacred role as the vessel for the Incarnation of Christ. Such objects are often referred to as "hidden" symbols because they are treated as a normal part of the scene, but their religious meanings would have been understood by most contemporary viewers.

TECHNIQUE
Painting on Panel

Painting pictures on wood has an ancient history, and wood panels were particularly favored by European painters and their patrons in the fifteenth century for works ranging from enormous altarpieces to small portraits. First the wood surface was prepared to make it smooth and nonabsorbent. After being sanded, the panel was coated—in Italy with **gesso**, a fine solution of plaster, and in northern Europe with a solution of chalk. These coatings soaked in and closed the pores of the wood. Fine linen was often glued down over the whole surface or over the joining lines on large panels made of two or more pieces of wood. The cloth was then also coated with gesso or chalk.

Once the surface was ready, the artist could paint on it with **tempera** (see "Cennini on Panel Painting," page 279) or **oil paint**. Italian artists favored tempera, using it almost exclusively for panel painting until the end of the fifteenth century. Northern European artists preferred the oil technique that Flemish painters so skillfully exploited at the beginning of the century. In some cases, wood panels were first painted with oil, then given fine detailing with tempera, a technique especially popular for small portraits.

Tempera had to be applied in a very precise manner, because it dried almost as quickly as it was laid down. Shading had to be done with careful overlying strokes in tones ranging from white and gray to dark brown and black. Because tempera is opaque—light striking its surface does not penetrate to lower layers of color and reflect back—the resulting surface was **matte**, or dull, and had to be varnished to give it a sheen. Oil paint, on the other hand, took much longer to dry, and while it was still wet, changes could have been made easily. Oil could also be made translucent by applying it in very thin layers, called glazes. Light striking a surface built up of glazes penetrates to the lower layers and is reflected back, creating the appearance of glowing from within. In both tempera and oil the desired result in the fifteenth century was a smooth surface that betrayed no brushstrokes and somewhat resembled enamel.

TECHNIQUE
Renaissance Perspective Systems

In the fifteenth century, Italian humanists developed a system known as **linear**, or **mathematical perspective** that enabled artists to represent the visible world in a convincingly illusionistic way. The architect Filippo Brunelleschi first demonstrated the system about 1420, and the scholar and architect Leon Battista Alberti codified it in 1436 in his treatise *Della Pittura* (*On Painting*).

For Alberti, a picture's surface was a flat plane that intersected the viewer's field of vision at right angles. This highly artificial concept presumed a one-eyed viewer standing dead center at a prescribed distance from a work of art. From this fixed vantage point, everything would appear to recede into the distance at the same rate, shaped by imaginary lines called **orthogonals** that met at a single **vanishing point** on the horizon. The use of orthogonals replicated the optical illusion that things grow smaller and closer together as they get farther away from us.

Linear perspective has the advantage of making the pictorial space seem almost like an extension of the real space, creating a compelling, even exaggerated sense of depth (see fig. 12-18). In the course of the fifteenth century, however, many artists adopted multiple vanishing points, which gave their work a more relaxed, less tunnel-like feeling.

Meanwhile, in the north, artists such as Jan van Eyck (see fig. 12-2) continued to employ older visual systems known as **atmospheric** and **intuitive perspective**. In atmospheric perspective, variations in color and clarity convey the feeling of distance. In intuitive perspective, artists use visual devices, such as making background figures smaller, to convey spatial depth, but do not follow a consistent mathematical system of linear perspective.

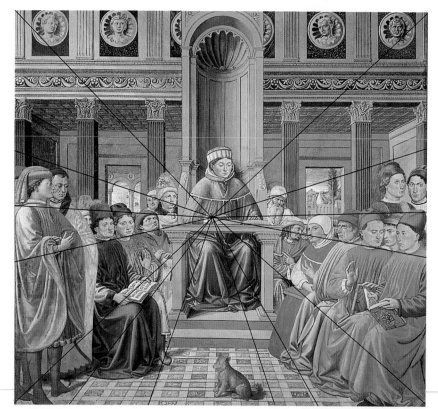

Benozzo Gozzoli
Saint Augustine Teaching in Rome
1464–65. Fresco
Church of Sant'Agostino
San Gimignano, Italy

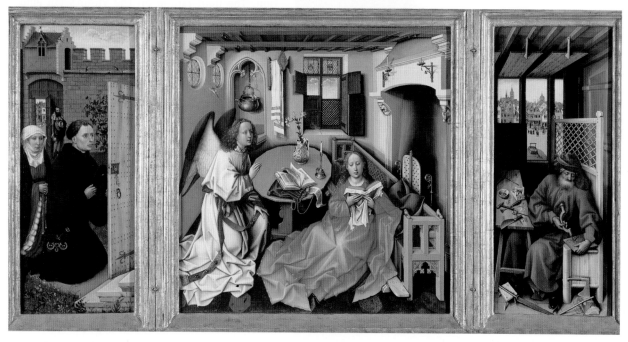

12-1 Robert Campin and assistants. *Mérode Altarpiece (Triptych of the Annunciation)* (open). c. 1425–28. Oil on wood Center 25¹/₄ x 24⁷/₈" (64.1 x 63.2 cm); each wing approx. 25³/₈ x 10⁷/₈" (64.5 x 27.6 cm). The Metropolitan Museum of Art, New York
The Cloisters Collection, 1956 (56.70)

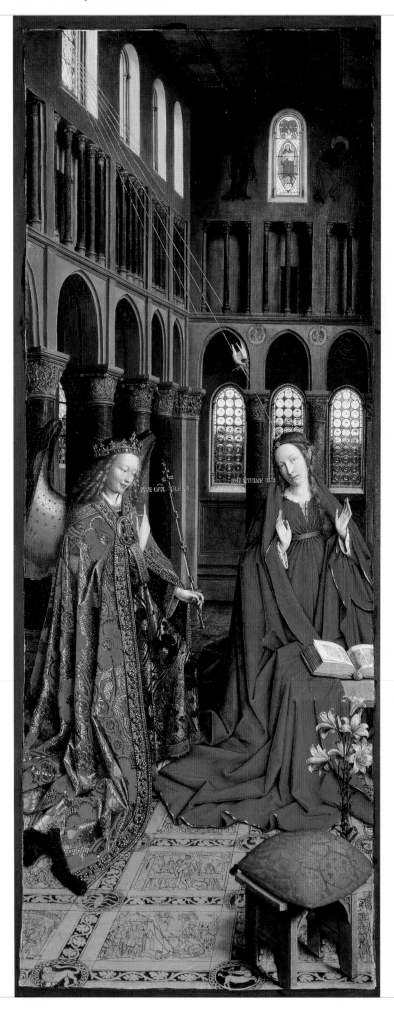

12-2 | **Jan van Eyck.** *The Annunciation.* c. 1434–36
Oil on canvas, transferred from wood panel,
painted surface 35³/₈ x 13⁷/₈" (90.2 x 34.1
cm). National Gallery of Art, Washington, D.C.
Andrew W. Mellon Collection (1937.1.39)

In the right-hand panel of the *Mérode Altarpiece*, the
mousetraps in Joseph's carpentry shop are a reference to
a passage written by the theologian Saint Augustine,
referring to Christ as the bait in a trap set by God to catch
Satan. In the left-hand panel, the altarpiece's donors
kneel in front of the open door of the house where the
Annunciation takes place, suggesting that the scene is a
vision induced by their prayers. Such a presentation, often
used by Flemish artists, allowed the donors of a religious
work to appear in the same space and time, and often on
the same scale as the figures of the saints represented. The
view out of Saint Joseph's window in the right panel, however, depicts a realistic Flemish street scene.

The complex treatment of light in the *Mérode Altarpiece* is an example of the innovation of the Flemish
painters. The strongest **illumination** comes from an
unseen source at the upper left in front of the **picture
plane** (picture surface), apparently the sun entering
through the miraculously transparent wall that allows
the viewer to observe the scene. More light comes from
the rear windows, and a few rays from the round window at left are a symbolic vehicle for the Christ Child's
descent. Jesus seems to slide down the rays of light joining God and Mary, carrying the cross of human salvation. The light falling on the Virgin's lap emphasizes
this connection.

Campin's contemporary Jan van Eyck was a court
painter to Philip the Good, duke of Burgundy, who was
the uncle of the king of France and one of the wealthi-
est and most sophisticated men in Europe. He made Jan
van Eyck one of his confidential employees and even
sent him on an embassy to Portugal. The duke was not
Jan's only patron. Civic leaders, town councils, and rich
merchants were also important art patrons in the Low
Countries, where cities were largely independent of the
landed nobility.

Jan's *Annunciation* (fig. 12-2), a small independent
panel, is an excellent example of the Flemish desire to
paint more than the eye can see and almost more than
the mind can grasp. We can enjoy the painting for its
visual characteristics—the drawing, colors, and arrangement of shapes—but we need information about the
painting's cultural context to understand it fully. The
Annunciation takes place in a richly appointed church,
not Mary's house, as we saw in Robert Campin's painting.
Gabriel, a richly robed youth with splendid multicolored
wings, has interrupted Mary's reading. The two figures
gesture gracefully upward toward a dove flying down

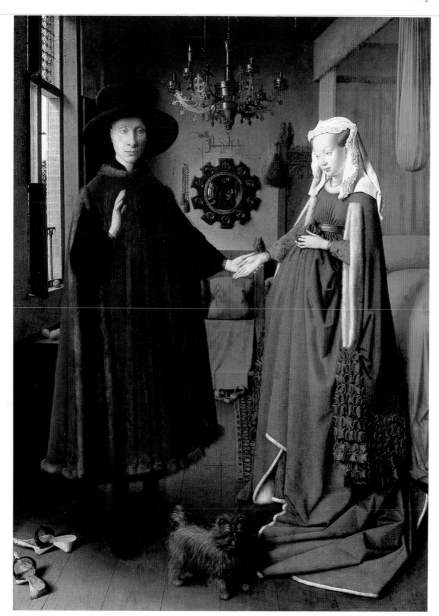

12-3   Jan van Eyck. *Portrait of Giovanni Arnolfini (?) and His Wife, Giovanna Cenami (?)*. 1434. Oil on panel, 33 x 22¹/₂" (83.8 x 57.2 cm). The National Gallery, London

Reproduced by courtesy of the Trustees

Jan is famous for his talent with the technique of painting with oil on wood panel—so much so that he is sometimes mistakenly called the "inventor" of oil painting. Oils had been known as a medium for several centuries but had been used for practical purposes, for example, for painting that would be exposed to the weather. Jan perfected the technique by building up his images in transparent oil layers, a procedure called glazing, using tiny, carefully applied brushstrokes to render detail.

through beams of gold. As the angel Gabriel tells the Virgin Mary that she will bear the Son of God, Jesus Christ, golden letters spell out the angel's greeting and Mary's response, "Hail, full of grace" and "Behold the handmaiden of the Lord." The story is recounted in the Gospel of Luke (1:26–38). In the painting every detail has a meaning. The dove symbolizes the Holy Spirit, the white lilies are symbols of Mary. The signs of the zodiac in the floor tiles indicate the traditional date of the Annunciation, March 25. The one stained-glass window representing God rises above the tree windows enclosing Mary and representing the Trinity of Father, Son, and Holy Spirit.

Jan's best-known painting today is an elaborate double portrait of a couple, traditionally identified as Giovanni Arnolfini and his wife Giovanna Cenami (fig. 12-3). Early interpreters suggested that this fascinating work represents a wedding or betrothal. Below the mirror on the back wall, the artist inscribed the words: *Johannes de eyck fuit hic 1434* ("Jan van Eyck was here 1434"). Normally, the signature on a work of art in fifteenth-century Flanders would have read, "Jan van Eyck made this." But Arnolfini married in 1447, thirteen years after the date on the wall. The painting evidently represents some form of formal contract since the mirror reflects two witnesses.

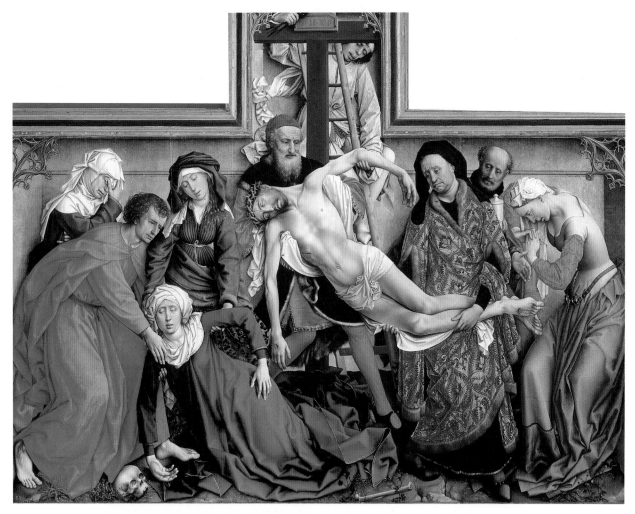

12-4 **Rogier van der Weyden.** *Deposition,* from an altarpiece commissioned by the Crossbowmen's Guild, Louvain, Brabant, Belgium c. 1442. Oil on panel, 7'2⁵/₈" x 8'7¹/₈" (2.2 x 2.62 m). Museo del Prado, Madrid

The people stand in the principal room of a house filled with impressive furniture, including a luxurious bed. (Recall the bed in the Queen of France's chamber in figure 20. The modern idea of rooms performing a single specific function did not yet exist.) The furnishings in Jan's painting may have hidden significance. The crystal prayer beads on the wall suggest the couple's piety; the dog is a symbol of fidelity; the single candle and the round mirror, the presence of God.

Another early Flemish artist, Rogier van der Weyden, maintained a large workshop in Brussels, attracting **apprentices** and assistants from as far away as Italy. Nevertheless, not a single existing work of art bears his name. The painting scholars use to establish the thematic and stylistic characteristics for Rogier's art is a large panel (more than 7 by 8 feet), depicting the Deposition, or removal of Christ's body from the cross (fig. 12-4). The central panel of an altarpiece, commissioned by the Louvain Crossbowmen's Guild sometime around 1442, once included other panels representing the Four Evangelists and Christ's Resurrection.

The Deposition was a popular theme in the fifteenth century because of its dramatic, personally engaging character. Here Jesus' suffering and death are made palpably real by the display of the lifesized corpse at the center of the composition. Rogier has arranged the figure in a graceful curve, framed by a jarringly angular pattern of arms, echoed by the form of the fainting Virgin. The highly emotional treatment of both mother and son encourages the viewer to identify with both of them. Red and white color accents focus attention on the main subject. The whites of the winding cloth and the tunic of the youth on the ladder set off Jesus' pale body, as the white veil wrapped like a turban and shawl emphasizes the ashen face of Mary. The solid, three-dimensional figures, compressed in a shallow space in front of a gilded wood backdrop, press toward the viewer, allowing no escape from their expressions of intense grief.

Many scholars see the emotional quality of Rogier's work as a tie with the Gothic past, but the intense feelings evoked by his painting can also be interpreted as an example of fifteenth-century humanistic concern for the individual. Although united by their sorrow, the mourning figures react in personal ways, from the intensity of Mary Magdalen wringing her hands in anguish at the right, to Saint John the Evangelist looking sorrowfully down at the Virgin, whom he supports on the left.

The extraordinary achievements of Robert Campin, Jan van Eyck, and Rogier van der Weyden attracted many followers. Petrus Christus (documented from 1444; d. c. 1475), who worked in Bruges beginning about 1444, probably came from the northern duchy of Brabant. In 1449, Christus painted one of his most admired works, *A Goldsmith in His Shop* (fig. 12-5). According to Christian legend, Eligius, a seventh-century ecclesiastic, a goldsmith and mintmaster for the French court, used his wealth to ransom Christian captives. Here he weighs a ring to determine its value, as a handsome couple looks on. The young people are dressed in the height of Burgundian court fashion. The woman wears a rich Italian brocade gown and jeweled headdress; the man, fur-lined black wool. A box of rings and many other treasures rest on a shelf in the background, affording us a remarkable view of a fifteenth-century goldsmith's wares.

As in Jan van Eyck's double portrait (see fig. 12-3), a convex mirror extends the viewer's field of vision, in this case showing two men on the street outside. The emphasis on everyday details is so strong that the presence of the saint seems more a pretext for a secular subject rather than an integral part of a religious scene. In fact, this painting provided the precedent for a long line of clearly secular pictures showing business people in their shops, which persisted well into the sixteenth century.

The painter Hugo van der Goes (c. 1440–1482) brought together the intellectualism of Jan van Eyck and the emotionalism of Rogier van der Weyden in an entirely new style. Hugo's major work was an exceptionally large altarpiece, more than 8 feet tall, commissioned by Tommaso Portinari for the family chapel in Florence and probably painted between 1474 and 1476 (fig. 12-6). Portinari, a Florentine living in Bruges, was the local manager

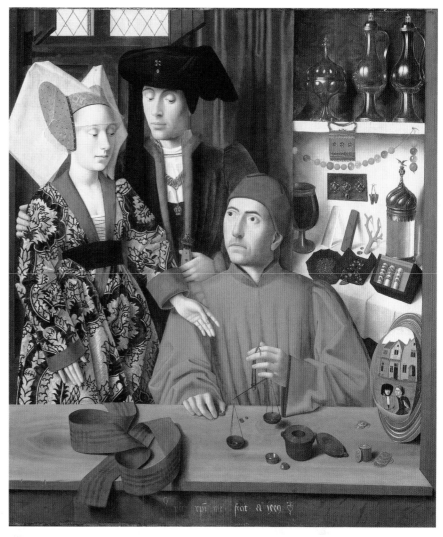

12-5 Petrus Christus. *A Goldsmith in His Shop, Possibly Saint Eligius.* 1449. Oil on wood, 38⅝ x 33½" (98 x 85 cm). The Metropolitan Museum of Art New York

Robert Lehman Collection, 1975 (1975.1.110)

12-6 Hugo van der Goes. *Portinari Altarpiece* (open). c. 1474–76. Tempera and oil on panel, center 8'3½" x 10' (2.53 x 3.01 m); wings each 8'3½" x 4'7½" (2.53 x 1.41 m). Galleria degli Uffizi, Florence

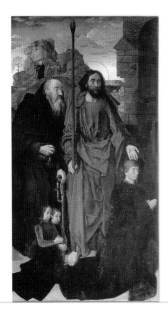
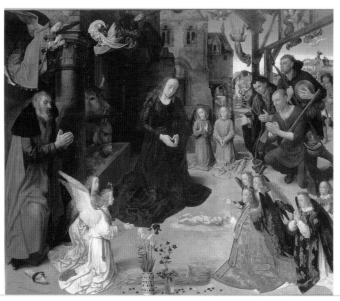
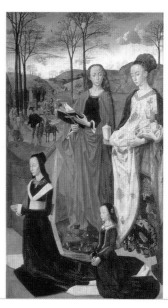

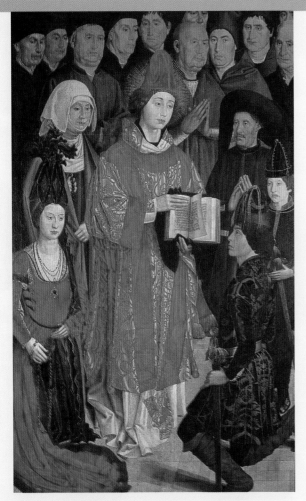

12-7   Nuño Gonçalvez. *Saint Vincent with the Portuguese Royal Family,* panel from the *Altarpiece of Saint Vincent.* c. 1471–81. Oil on panel, 6'9³/₄" x 4'2⁵/₈" (2.07 x 1.28 m). Museu Nacional de Arte Antiga, Lisbon

With furrowed brow and eyes fixed on a distant goal, Prince Henry the Navigator stands next to Saint Vincent, a patron saint of the royal house of Portugal, the city of Lisbon, and the Portuguese navigators (fig. 12-7). Prince Henry (1394–1460), the third son of King João I of Portugal, was a crusading soldier who fought against Islamic forces in North Africa; he was also a classical scholar, a prince and statesman, an intensely religious Catholic who wore a hair shirt beneath his clothes, and a remarkable catalyst of the Age of Exploration. Although he never journeyed on a voyage of discovery himself, he founded an observatory and a school for the study of geography and navigation and spent some forty years sponsoring the expeditions of mariners who explored the African coast in search of a sea route to India and the Far East. He was motivated by both the love of pure knowledge and a desire for riches to fill Portuguese coffers. He almost certainly believed the words of his personal motto, "the desire to do good."

of the bank owned by the powerful Medici family. He and his wife, Maria Baroncelli, kneel on the wing interiors with their three eldest children, accompanied by patron saints. The central panel represents the Adoration of the newborn Jesus by Mary and Joseph, a host of angels, and a few shepherds who have rushed in from the fields. Although the brilliant palette and meticulous accuracy recall Jan van Eyck, and the intense but controlled feelings suggest the emotional **content** of Rogier van der Weyden's works, the composition and interpretation of the altarpiece are entirely Hugo's. The monumental figures of Joseph, Mary, and the shepherds dominating the central panel are the same size as the patron saints on the wings; the Portinari family and the angels are small in comparison.

In the center of the composition, the Christ Child rests naked and vulnerable on the ground with rays of light emanating from his body. The source of this image was the visionary writing of the medieval Swedish mystic Bridget (declared a saint in 1391). Saint Bridget described Mary kneeling to adore the Child immediately after giving birth. The glass vessel in the foreground still life alludes to Christ's entry into Mary's womb without destroying her virginity, the way light passes through glass without breaking it. The three red carnations in the glass (barely visible here) may refer to the Trinity; the seven blue columbines symbolize the Virgin's future sorrows; and the violets scattered on the ground symbolize humility. The **majolica** (glazed earthenware) *albarelo,* or drug jar, a luxury ceramic imported from Spain, holds three irises—white for purity and purple for Christ's royal ancestry— and a red lily, representing the blood of Christ. Hugo's artistic vision goes far beyond this formal religious symbolism. For example, the shepherds, who stand in unaffected awe before the miraculous event, are among the most sympathetically rendered images of common people to be found in the art of this, or any, period.

FLEMISH-INFLUENCED ART OUTSIDE THE LOW COUNTRIES

The style of northern masters such as Hugo van der Goes and Jan van Eyck influenced many artists outside the Low Countries. Spanish and Portuguese painters quickly absorbed the new Flemish style to such an extent that the term Hispano-Flemish is applied to their works in the second half of the fifteenth century. Nuño Gonçalvez, a major artist connected with the court of Portugal, painted monumental figures with an intensity of detail and a richness of color that recalls the style of Jan van Eyck. Gonçalvez was renowned for his portraiture and for his virtuoso rendering of costumes and draperies. Sadly, the only paintings that are surely his own are six panels from a **polyptych** (multiple-panel work) discovered in the Lisbon Convent of Saint Vincent de Fora. The altarpiece may have been commissioned about 1471 for the chapel of Saint Vincent in Lisbon Cathedral and finished before the king's death in 1481. In one of the two largest panels (fig. 12-7), Saint Vincent, magnificent in red and gold vestments, appears with the Portuguese royal family and a row of courtiers. With the exception of the saint, whose features are idealized, all are portraits: at the right, in front of Saint Vincent, kneels King Alfonso V, while his young son and late uncle, Henry the Navigator, look on. At the left are Alfonso's wife and mother, their right

WOMEN ARTISTS IN THE LATE MIDDLE AGES AND THE RENAISSANCE

Since most formal apprenticeships were closed to women, medieval and Renaissance women artists learned their trade either from family members or in convents. Despite the obstacles, however, a few highly skilled women received major commissions. In the fourteenth century, Bourgot, the daughter of the miniaturist Jean le Noir, illuminated books for Charles V of France and Jean, duke of Berry. Christine de Pisan supported herself and her children by writing for these same patrons. She oversaw the production of her books and wrote of one artist named Anastaise, "who is so learned and skillful in painting manuscript borders and miniature backgrounds that one cannot find an artisan who can surpass her . . . nor whose work is more highly esteemed" (*Le Libre de la Cité des Dames*, I.41.4, translated by Earl J. Richards).

Also in the fourteenth century, Jeanne de Montbaston and her husband, Richart, worked together as book illuminators under the auspices of the University of Paris. After Richart's death, Jeanne continued the workshop and was sworn in as a *libraire* (publisher) by the university in 1343.

In the fifteenth century, women were admitted to the artists' guilds (professional organizations) in some cities, including the Flemish towns of Ghent, Bruges, and Antwerp. The painter Agnes van den Bassche of Ghent, for example, operated a painting workshop with her artist husband and became a free master of the painters' guild after his death. A study of the painters' guild of Bruges has shown that by the 1480s one-quarter of its members were female.

The position of women artists in Italy was not as strong as in Flanders. The humanists' emphasis on academic study rather than apprenticeship for artists, the tie between mathematics and the new linear perspective, and the emphasis on anatomical study—forbidden to women—and realistic figure drawing, prevented women from following careers in painting. Some women nevertheless learned from their fathers or husbands and helped in the family business.

Page with Thamyris, from Giovanni Boccaccio's *De Claris Mulieribus* (*Concerning Famous Women*). 1402. Ink and tempera on vellum. Bibliothèque Nationale, Paris

hands wrapped in rosary beads. Saint Vincent is clearly a vision, brought on by the intense prayer of the royal family. This altarpiece may have been created to commemorate a Portuguese crusade against the Muslims in Morocco undertaken in 1471 under Saint Vincent's flag.

In France, the Flemish style was particularly influential in manuscript illumination, a field in which women excelled (see "Women Artists in the Late Middle Ages and the Renaissance," above). Anastaise for example, who worked for Christine de Pisan, gained considerable renown. The painting of Christine presenting her manuscript to the Queen of France also serves to illustrate the luxurious woven and embroidered textiles in the royal apartments (see fig. 20).

At the beginning of the fifteenth century, the most famous northern illuminators were three brothers, Paul, Herman, and Jean, commonly known as the Limbourg brothers because they came from the region of Limbourg in the Low Countries. In the fifteenth century, people generally did not have family names, but were known instead by their first names, often followed by a reference to their place of origin, parentage, or occupation. For instance, Jan van Eyck means "Jan from [the town of] Eyck."

The Limbourg brothers are first recorded as apprentice goldsmiths in Paris about 1390. About 1404, they entered the service of the duke of Berry, for whom they produced their major work, the so-called *Très Riches Heures* (*Very Sumptuous Hours*), between 1413 and 1416. This Book of Hours included a calendar section with full-page paintings introducing each month. The subjects alternated between peasants' labors and aristocratic pleasures. In the *February* page, farm people relax before a blazing

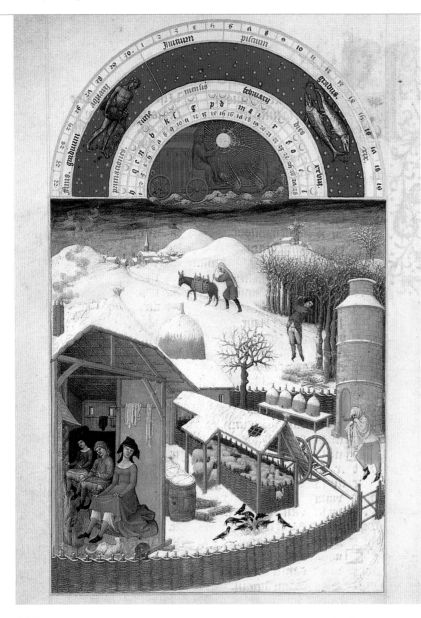

12-8 | **Paul, Herman, and Jean Limbourg. Page with *February, Très Riches Heures*** 1413–16. Musée Condé, Chantilly, France

The importance of textiles in the fifteenth century cannot be overemphasized. Major weaving centers arose in Brussels, Tournai, Arras, and in the Loire Valley, where Flemish and French artists produced outstanding tapestries that served both as sumptuous wall coverings and as a form of portable wealth. Indeed, the wealth of individuals can often be judged from the number of tapestries listed in their household inventories. The Christine de Pisan painting (see fig. 20) gives a good idea of the effect achieved by luxurious wall hangings.

One of the finest examples of tapestry of the period around 1500 is the Hunt of the Unicorn, probably made for Anne of Brittany whose initials AE hang on a cord from the fountain (fig. 12-9). The unicorn, a mythical horselike beast with a single horn, could be captured only by a young virgin, to whom it came willingly. The animal symbolized the Incarnation, with Christ as the unicorn captured by the Virgin Mary; in the secular world, the unicorn hunt became a metaphor for romantic love and a suitable subject for wedding tapestries. The unicorn's horn was believed to be an antidote for poison; thus, the unicorn here is shown dipping its horn into the stream and so purifying the water from the fountain.

The figures in the Unicorn tapestry appear in a dense forest, filled with flowers, with a distant view of a castle. The many birds and animals shown have symbolic meanings: the lion represents valor and faith; the stag, the Resurrection and protection against evil; rabbits, fertility; and dogs, fidelity. Among the birds, the pheasants perched on the fountain are emblems of human love and marriage, and the goldfinch is another fertility symbol. The plants, depicted with botanical accuracy, reinforce the theme of protective and curative powers: the strawberry stands for sexual love, the pansy for remembrance, the oak for fidelity, the holly for protection, and the orange for fertility. The tapestry captures the vision of the biblical Song of Songs (4:12–13): "You are an enclosed garden, my sister, my bride, an enclosed garden, a fountain sealed."

Renaissance Art in Italy

In the fifteenth century, Flemish art was so admired that many artists came to Flanders from abroad to study the work of the Flemish painters. Only at the end of the century did European patrons begin to favor the new styles of art and architecture developed in Italy beginning around 1400. At that time, Italian painters and sculptors, like their Flemish counterparts, began to move toward a greater precision in rendering the illusion of physical reality, building on the achievements of the great Florentine artist Giotto (see fig. 11-29). Rather than replicating the smallest details of appearance with perfect fidelity to

fire (fig. 12-8). Although many country people at this time lived in hovels, this farm looks comfortable and well maintained, with timber-framed buildings, a row of beehives, a sheepfold, and woven fences.

Most remarkably, the details of the painting convey the feeling of the cold winter weather: the breath of the bundled-up worker turning to steam as he blows on his hands; the leaden sky, bare trees, and soft snow. The painting clearly shows several Gothic conventions (seen, for example, in the *Petites Heures of Jeanne d'Evreux*, see fig. 11-16), which persisted in northern Renaissance art into the first half of the fifteenth century. These include the missing front wall of the house, the attention to detail, and the high placement of the **horizon line**. The integration of figures and animals into the landscape has been accomplished within the prevailing Gothic style, but on a more believable scale, with a landscape receding continuously from foreground to middleground to background.

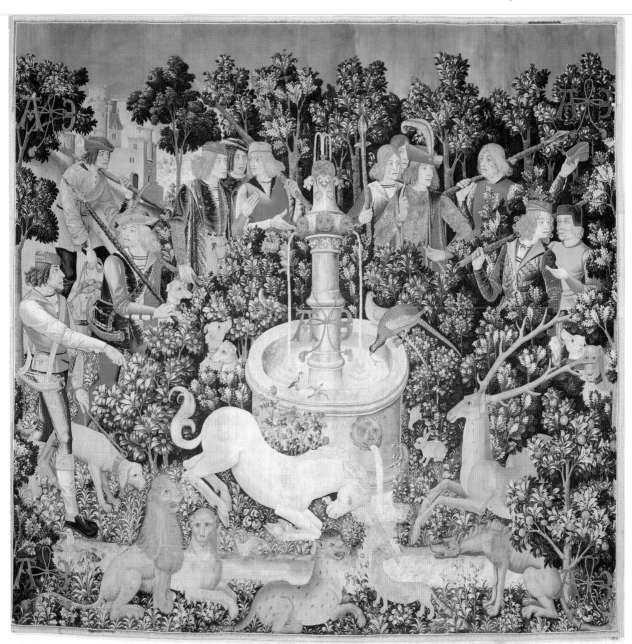

12-9 | ***The Unicorn is Found,*** from the Hunt of the Unicorn tapestry series. c. 1498–1500. Wool, silk, and metal threads (13–21 warp threads per inch), 12'1" x 12'5" (3.68 x 3.78 m). The Metropolitan Museum of Art, New York
Gift of John D. Rockefeller, Jr., 1937 (37.80.2)

The price of a tapestry depended on the materials used. Rarely was a fine, commissioned series woven only with wool; instead, tapestry producers enhanced it to varying degrees with silk, silver, and gold threads. The richest kind of tapestry was one made entirely of silk and gold. Because the silver and gold threads used silk wrapped with real metal, people later burned many tapestries in order to retrieve the precious materials. As a result of this practice, few French royal tapestries survived the French Revolution. Many existing works show obvious signs, however, that the metallic threads were painstakingly pulled out in order to preserve the tapestries.

nature, like the Flemings, Italian artists aimed instead at achieving anatomically correct but idealized figures—perfected, generic types—set within a rationally, rather than intuitively, defined space, organized through the use of linear perspective (see "Renaissance Perspective Systems," page 289). At the same time, Italian architects began to use mathematically derived design principles and the classical architectural orders to create buildings expressing the ideals of symmetry and restraint.

ARCHITECTURE AND SCULPTURE

Towering figures of early Renaissance art—the sculptor Donatello, the architect Brunelleschi, and the painter Masaccio—came from Florence, the birthplace of the Italian Renaissance. Donatello and Brunelleschi visited Rome together to study the physical remains of classical antiquity, and they integrated detailed knowledge of the past into their own highly original works. Donatello, born Donato di Niccolo Bardi

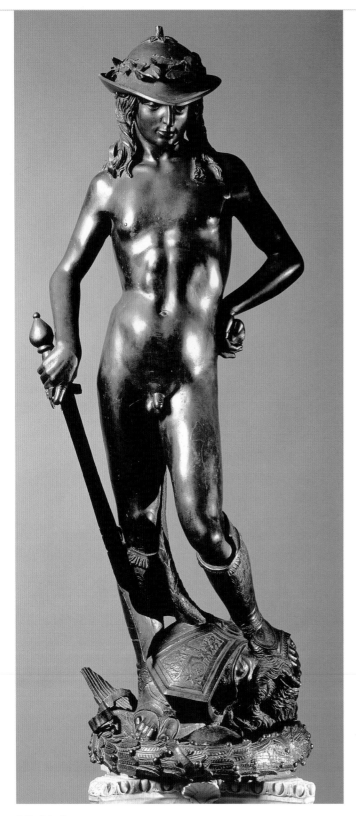

(c. 1386–1466), executed each commission as if it were a new experiment in expression. His sculpture is like an encyclopedia of techniques and ideas, with nearly every piece breaking new ground. For example, Donatello's rendition of the biblical hero David, who slew the giant Goliath with a stone from his slingshot, is the earliest known lifesize freestanding bronze nude in European art since antiquity (fig. 12-10). The sculpture was first recorded in 1469 in the courtyard of the palace owned by the ruling Medici family of Florence, where it stood on a base engraved with an inscription extolling Florentine heroism and virtue. Although the work clearly draws on the classical tradition of heroic nudity, this portrayal of a sensuous, adolescent boy in a jaunty hat and boots, standing on his enemy's severed head, is utterly original. David's angular pose, his underdeveloped torso, and the sensation of his wavering between childish interests and adult responsibility heighten his heroism in challenging and defeating the giant warrior.

Donatello influenced other artists both in and outside Florence. He worked for a decade in Padua, where he was called in 1443 to execute an equestrian statue commemorating the Venetian general Erasmo da Narni, nicknamed *Gattamelata* (Honeyed Cat) (fig. 12-11). The sources for this statue were two surviving Roman bronze equestrian portraits, one (now lost) in the north Italian city of Pavia, the other of the emperor Marcus Aurelius (see fig. 6-26) which the sculptor certainly saw and

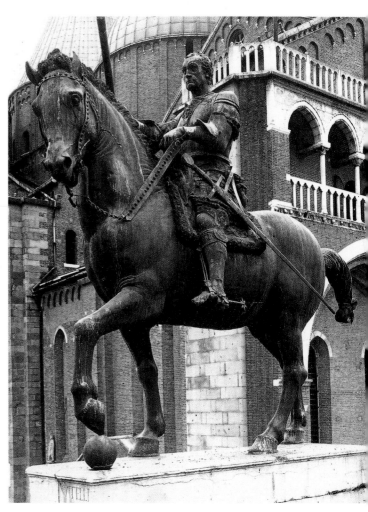

12-10 | **Donatello. *David.*** Dated as early as c. 1420 and as late as the 1460s. Bronze, height 5'2¼" (1.58 m). Museo Nazionale del Bargello, Florence

12-11 | **Donatello. Equestrian monument of Erasmo da Narni (Gattamelata),** Piazza del Santo, Padua. 1443–53. Bronze Height approx. 12'2" (3.71 m)

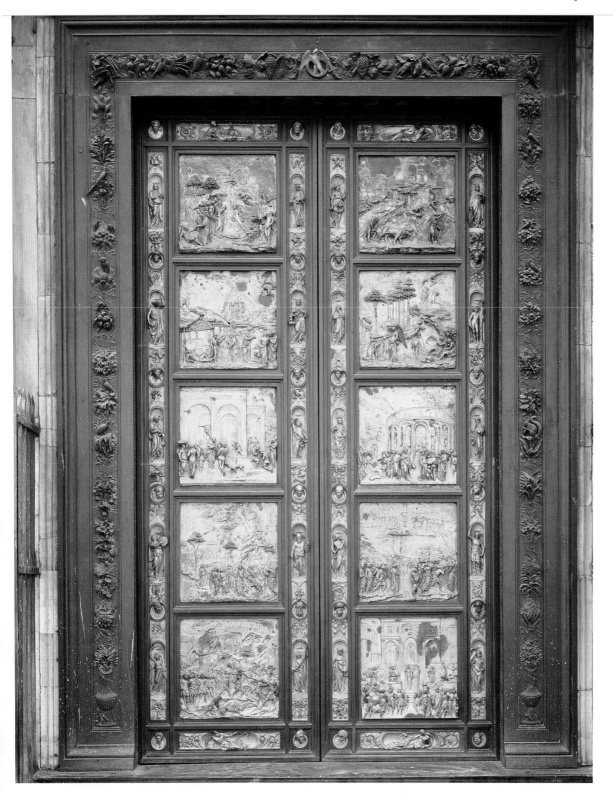

12-12

Lorenzo Ghiberti
Gates of Paradise
(East Doors)
Baptistry of San
Giovanni, Florence
1425–52. Gilt,
bronze, height 15'
(4.57 m). Museo
dell'Opera del
Duomo, Florence

probably sketched during his youthful stay in Rome. The completed monument, installed on a high base in front of the church dedicated to the beloved Italian Franciscan Saint Anthony, was the first large-scale bronze equestrian portrait since antiquity. Viewed from a distance, this man-animal juggernaut seems capable of thrusting forward at the first threat. Seen from up close, however, the man's sunken cheeks, sagging jaw, ropey neck, and stern but sad expression suggest a war machine now grown old and tired. Such **expressionism** was a recurring theme in Donatello's portrayals.

While Donatello was working in Padua, in Florence his rival Lorenzo Ghiberti (1381?–1455) gained the prestigious commission for a set of gilded bronze doors to be placed in the Baptistry facing the cathedral's west facade. Ghiberti's doors, installed in 1452, were reportedly said by Michelangelo to be worthy of being the Gates of Paradise (fig. 12-12). Overall gilding unifies the ten large, square reliefs. Ghiberti organized the space either by a system of linear perspective, approximating the one described by Alberti in his 1435 treatise on painting (see "Renaissance Perspective Systems," page 289), or by a series of arches or rocks or

12-13 | (*below*) **Filippo Brunelleschi. Dome of Florence Cathedral.** 1417–36; lantern completed 1471

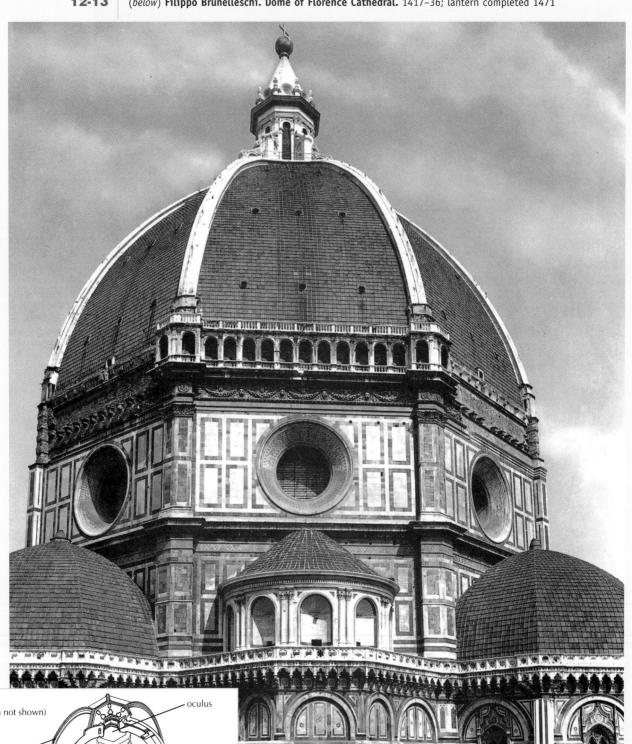

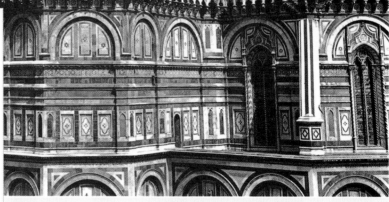

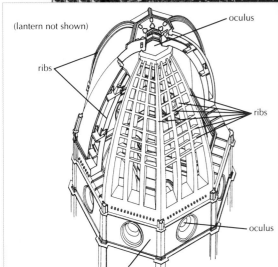

(lantern not shown)

oculus

ribs

ribs

oculus

drum

12-14 | (*left*) **Cutaway drawing of Brunelleschi's dome,** Florence Cathedral
Drawing by P. Sanpaolesi

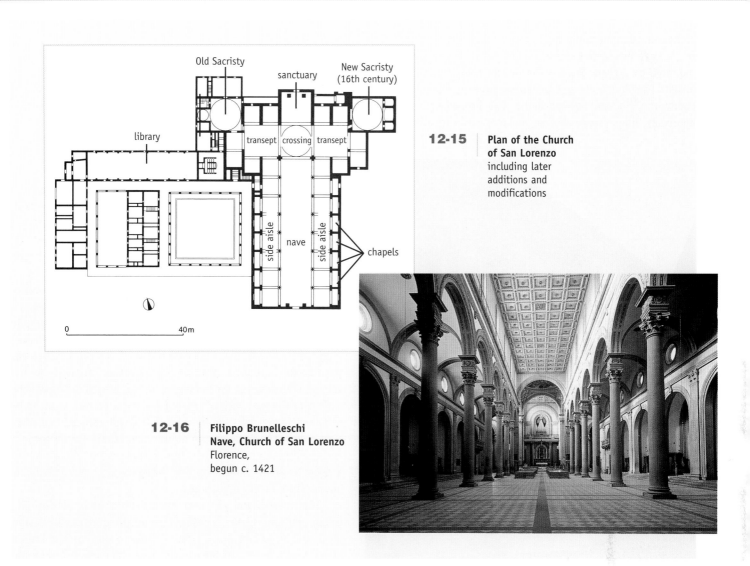

12-15 | **Plan of the Church of San Lorenzo** including later additions and modifications

12-16 | **Filippo Brunelleschi Nave, Church of San Lorenzo** Florence, begun c. 1421

trees leading the eye into the distance. Foreground figures are grouped in the lower third of the panel, while the other figures decrease gradually in size, suggesting deep space. In some panels, the tall buildings suggest ancient Roman architecture and illustrate the emerging antiquarian tone in Renaissance art.

Donatello's friend Filippo Brunelleschi (1377–1446), a young sculptor-turned-architect, was one of the major pioneers of Renaissance architectural design in Florence. His design for the vast dome of Florence Cathedral (fig. 12-13) was a great technical accomplishment. The dome was essentially a Gothic construction based on the pointed arch, using ribs to support the vault. It had an octagonal outer shell and a lower inner shell connected to the outer one through a system of arches and horizontal sandstone rings. Brunelleschi invented an ingenious structural system by which each portion of the dome reinforced the next one as it was built up layer by layer (fig. 12-14). When completed, this self-buttressed unit required no external support. The dome is still the source of immense local pride.

Brunelleschi also produced remarkably innovative plans for smaller projects. Around 1421 he was commissioned to rebuild the Church of San Lorenzo in Florence (fig. 12-15), and between 1419 and 1423 he built the Capponi Chapel in the Church of

Santa Felicità (see fig. 13-20). The Church of San Lorenzo is an austere basilica with a long nave flanked by single side aisles opening into shallow chapels. A short transept forming a square crossing anticipates the square sanctuary. Two **sacristies** (rooms housing ritual attire and vessels) project from the transept. Brunelleschi designed the Old Sacristy as a chapel and mausoleum for the Medici family; the New Sacristy was built in the sixteenth century.

Brunelleschi, like many Romanesque and Gothic builders before him, worked out his church plans on a module, or basic unit of measure, that could be multiplied or divided and applied to every element of the design. The result was a series of clear, rational interior spaces in harmony with one another. Unlike the Romanesque and Gothic system, however, the result was architecture on a human scale.

The nave of the church (fig. 12-16) has a flat ceiling inset with coffers, like a Roman basilica; a hemispherical dome on pendentives covers the crossing. Each nave arch springs from an **impost block**, or section of entablature, resting on slender Corinthian columns. With this arrangement, Brunelleschi managed to bend, without exactly breaking, the rules of classical architecture, in which piers, rather than columns, supported arches, and columns only supported entablatures (see fig. 6-12). In the side aisles, the arched openings to the chapels are surmounted by arched lunettes that mirror the shape of the nave arcade. The Church of San Lorenzo was an experimental building combining old and new elements, but Brunelleschi's rational approach, unique sense of order, and innovative incorporation of

classical motifs inspired later Renaissance architects, many of whom learned from his work firsthand by completing his unfinished projects.

Leon Battista Alberti (1404–1472), a humanist-turned-architect, wrote about his classical theories on art before ever designing a building. His various writings, including books on painting and sculpture and a ten-volume treatise on architecture, present the first coherent exposition of early Italian aesthetic theory. Like Brunelleschi, Alberti integrated classical forms into his works. In one of his relatively few actual building projects, a palace commissioned by the Rucellai family in Florence, Alberti dealt with one of the continuing challenges faced by Renaissance architects: the relationship (or more often, the lack of one) of a facade to the building behind it. He designed the facade—begun in 1455 but never finished—to be the unifying front for a planned merger of eight adjacent houses acquired by Giovanni Rucellai (fig. 12-17). The simple rectangular front suggests a single, cubical three-story building capped with an overhanging cornice. The stone blocks in the facade are lightly **rusticated** (left rough or textured), in a style derived from fortifications that was popular in Florentine town house exteriors. Inspired by the ancient Colosseum in Rome (see fig. 6-12), Alberti organized the surface of the wall with a horizontal-vertical pattern of pilasters and architraves that superimposed his free interpretation of classical orders: the Doric on the ground floor, Ionic on the second, and Corinthian on the third. Thus the Palazzo Rucellai provided a visual lesson for later architects in the use of classical elements and mathematical proportions.

The intellectual ferment surrounding architecture and urban planning in Renaissance Italy inspired artists to design ideal, and often imaginary, cities. The anonymous central Italian artist who painted an ideal city-center included a triumphal arch and a mini-Colosseum amid contemporary town houses (fig. 12-18). The octagonal church or baptistry in the right background suggests the influence of Alberti's theories. In his 1452 treatise *De re aedificatoria* (*On Architecture*), Alberti

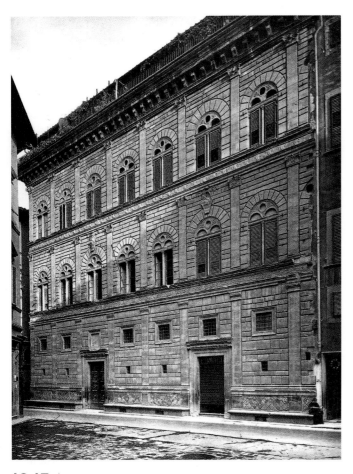

12-17 | Leon Battista Alberti. Palazzo Rucellai, Florence. 1455–70

12-18 | Anonymous. *View of an Ideal City.* c. 1500. Oil on panel, 30½" x 7'1⅝" (77.4 cm x 2.17 m) Walters Art Museum, Baltimore

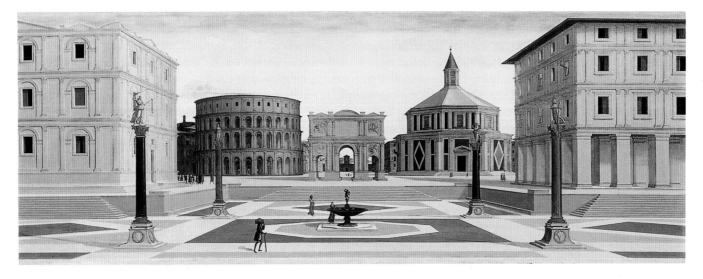

expressed his preference, based on his understanding of classical buildings such as the Pantheon, for churches that were either circular or polygonal, because "most things which are generated, made or directed by Nature are round." The streets in this view are unnaturally wide and clean—surely totally unlike the crowded and twisted alleyways that crisscrossed virtually all fifteenth-century cities. (Note the few tiny figures that walk through the ideal city.) The roofs of the houses are the same height, as Alberti recommended in a description of an ideal city. The Four Cardinal Virtues—Justice, Prudence, Patience, and Fortitude—stand on columns in the four corners of the square, a reminder of the dreams of Renaissance theorists, who predicted that ideal surroundings would bring out the best qualities in a city's people.

PAINTING

One of the major achievements of Italian Renaissance artists was the convincing integration of human figures into rational architectural settings. This accomplishment can be seen early on in the works of the Florentine artist Maso di Ser Giovanni di Mone Cassai (1401–1428), nicknamed Masaccio ("big, ugly Tom"). In his short career of less than a decade, he established a new direction in Florentine painting, much as Giotto had a century earlier. The exact chronology of his works is uncertain, and his fresco painting of the Trinity in the Church of Santa Maria Novella in Florence falls sometime between 1425 and 1428 (fig. 12-19).

The *Trinity* fresco was meant to give the illusion of a stone funerary monument and altar table set in a deep **aedicula** (framed niche) in the wall. Masaccio created the appearance of the niche through precisely rendered linear perspective in which the vanishing point lies on a horizon line at the eye level of an adult viewer just above the base of the cross. The niche itself resembles the architecture of San Lorenzo (see fig. 12-16). Thus, the painting demonstrates Masaccio's intimate knowledge of both Brunelleschi's perspective experiments (see "Renaissance Perspective Systems," page 289) and his architectural style. A consistent

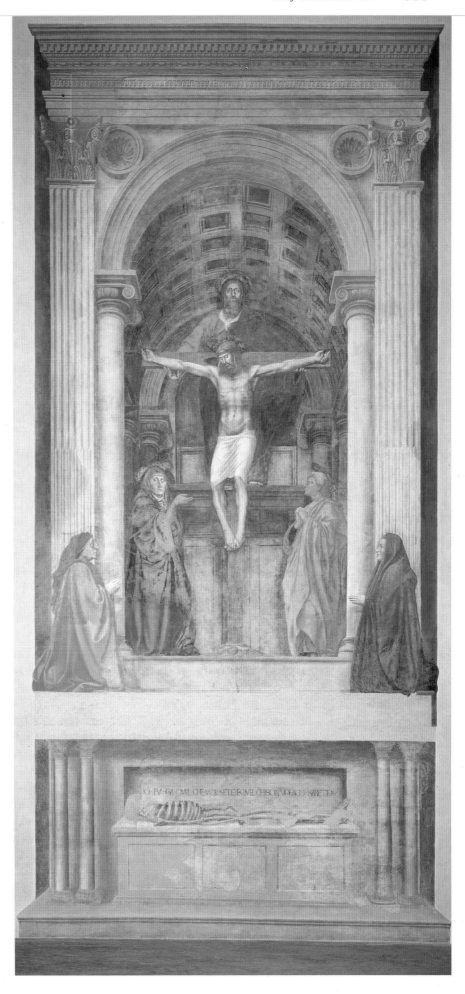

12-19   Masaccio. *Trinity with the Virgin Saint John the Evangelist, and Donors* fresco in the Church of Santa Maria Novella, Florence. c. 1426–27. 21' x 10'5" (6.4 x 3.17 m)

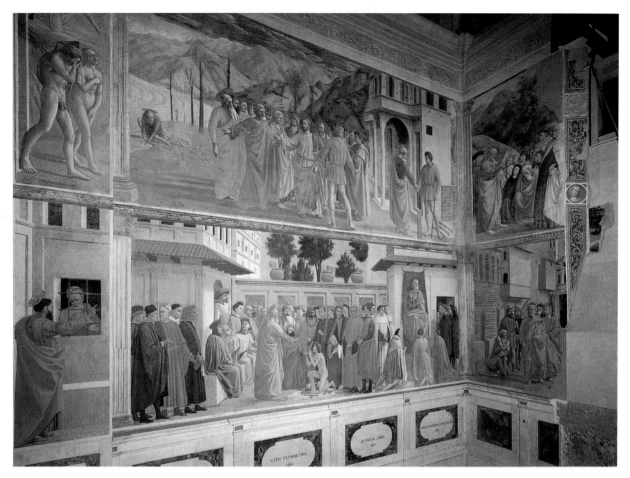

12-20 | **Interior of the Brancacci Chapel, Church of Santa Maria del Carmine,** Florence, with frescoes by Masaccio and Masolino (1424–27) and Filippino Lippi (c. 1482–84)

Reading from left to right in the upper register: *The Expulsion of Adam and Eve from Paradise* (Masaccio, 4 *giornate*), *Tribute Money* (Masaccio, 32 *giornate*), *Saint Peter Preaching* (Masolino, 9 *giornate*); and in the lower register: *Saint Paul Visiting Saint Peter in Prison* (Filippino Lippi, 3 *giornate*), *Saint Peter Raising the Son of the Ruler of Antioch* and *Saint Peter Preaching* (Masaccio and Filippino Lippi, 54 *giornate*), and *Saint Peter Healing with His Shadow* (Masolino, 10 *giornate*).

illumination, whose "source" seems to lie behind the viewer, models the figures and casts reflections on the coffers, or sunken panels, of the vault.

In Masaccio's painting, God the Father holds the cross on which Jesus hangs, while the dove of the Holy Spirit seems poised in downward flight between Jesus' tilted halo and the Father's head. Mary and Saint John the Evangelist stand at the foot of the cross, and outside the niche the donors kneel in prayer. Mary gazes calmly out at us, her raised hand presenting the Trinity. Below, in an open sarcophagus, is a skeleton, a grim reminder that death awaits us all and that our only hope is redemption and life in the hereafter through Christian belief. The inscription above the skeleton reads: "I was once that which you are, and what I am you also will be."

Masaccio's brief career reached its height in his collaboration with a painter known as Masolino (c. 1383–after 1435) on the fresco decoration of the Brancacci Chapel in the Church of Santa Maria del Carmine in Florence (fig. 12-20). The chapel was originally dedicated to Saint Peter and the frescoes illustrate events in his life. In the scene of the *Tribute Money* (fig. 12-21),

Masaccio illustrates an incident in which a collector of Jewish temple taxes demands payment from the apostle Peter, shown in the central group with Jesus and the other disciples (Matthew 17:24–7). Jesus instructs Peter to "go to the sea, drop in a hook, and take the first fish that comes up," which Peter does at the far left. In the fish's mouth, Peter finds a coin worth twice the tax demanded, which he gives to the tax collector at the far right.

Tribute Money is particularly remarkable for its use of both linear and **atmospheric perspective** to integrate the figures, architecture, and landscape into a consistent whole. The group of Jesus and his disciples forms a clear central focus, from which the landscape seems to recede naturally into the far distance. To create this illusion, Masaccio used linear perspective in the depiction of the house, and then reinforced it by diminishing the sizes of the barren trees and reducing Peter's size at the left. The lines of the house lead the viewer's eye to the head of Jesus, which the painter has placed at the vanishing point. A second vanishing point determines the position of the steps and stone rail at the right. The cleaning of the fresco revealed that the painting was done in thirty-two **giornate** (the freshly plastered

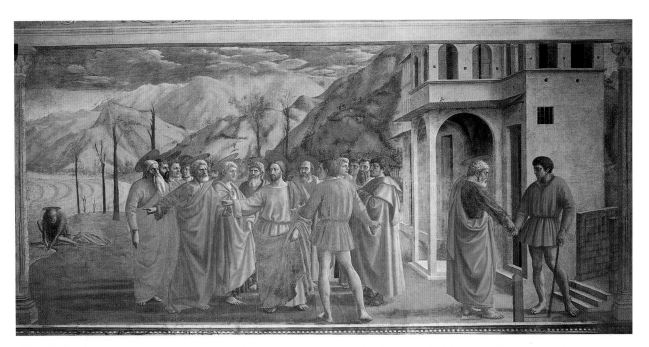

12-21 | **Masaccio.** *Tribute Money,* fresco in the Brancacci Chapel, Church of Santa Maria del Carmine, Florence. c. 1427
8'1" x 19'7" (2.46 x 6 m). (See fig. 12–20.)

Much valuable new information about the Brancacci Chapel frescoes was discovered during the course of a cleaning and restoration carried out between 1981 and 1991. Art historians now have a more accurate picture of how the frescoes were done and in what sequence, as well as which artist did what. One interesting discovery was that all of the figures in the *Tribute Money,* except those of the temple tax collector, originally had gold-leaf halos, several of which had flaked off. Rather than silhouette the heads against flat gold circles in the medieval manner, Masaccio conceived of the halo as a gold disk hovering in space above each head and subjected it to perspective foreshortening depending on the position of the figure.

day's work) and also that Masaccio used atmospheric perspective in the distant landscape, where mountains fade from grayish green to grayish white, and houses and trees on their slopes are loosely sketched.

The volumetric solidity of the foreground figures testifies to Masaccio's intimate knowledge of Roman sculpture as well as earlier Italian painters, such as Giotto. He **modeled** them with strong highlights and shadows. The figures cast their long shadows on the ground toward the left, implying a light source at the far right, as if the scene were lit by the actual window in the rear wall of the chapel. Not only does the lighting give the forms sculptural definition, but the colors vary in tone according to the strength of the illumination. Masaccio used a wide range of hues—pale pink, mauve, gold, seafoam green, apple green, and peach—and a sophisticated shading technique in which he used contrasting colors (for example, Andrew's green robe is shaded with red instead of darker green). When restorers cleaned the painting, they also discovered a wealth of linear details, especially in the settings, that had been obscured by dirt and overpainting. The landscape and buildings were much closer in appearance to the paintings by Masaccio's northern European contemporaries than previously thought. In contrast to the Flemish artists, however, Masaccio's figures exhibit the artist's study of classical sculpture and late Gothic painting, which he could have seen in fifteenth-century Florence.

Stylistic innovations take time to be fully accepted, and Masaccio's genius for depicting weight and volume, consistent lighting, and spatial integration was best appreciated by later generations of painters. Many important sixteenth-century Italian artists, including Michelangelo (see Chapter 13), studied and sketched from Masaccio's Brancacci Chapel frescoes. In the meantime, painting in Florence after Masaccio's death developed along lines somewhat different from that of the *Tribute Money* or *Trinity,* as other artists like Uccello (see fig. 12-23) experimented with their own ways of conveying the illusion of a believably receding space (see "Renaissance Perspective Systems," page 289).

The tradition of covering walls with paintings in fresco continued through the century. Between 1435 and 1445, the decoration of the Dominican Monastery of San Marco in Florence, where Fra Angelico served as the prior, was one of the most extensive projects. Born Guido di Pietro (c. 1395/1400–55) and known to his peers as Fra Giovanni da Fiesole, Fra Angelico (Angelic Brother) earned his nickname through his piety as well as his painting. He is documented as a painter in Florence in 1417–1418, and he continued to be a very active painter after taking his vows as a Dominican monk in nearby Fiesole between 1418 and 1421.

In the Monastery of San Marco, Fra Angelico and his assistants created a painting to inspire meditation in each monk's cell (forty-four in all), and they also added paintings to the chapter house and the corridors. At the top of the stairs in the north

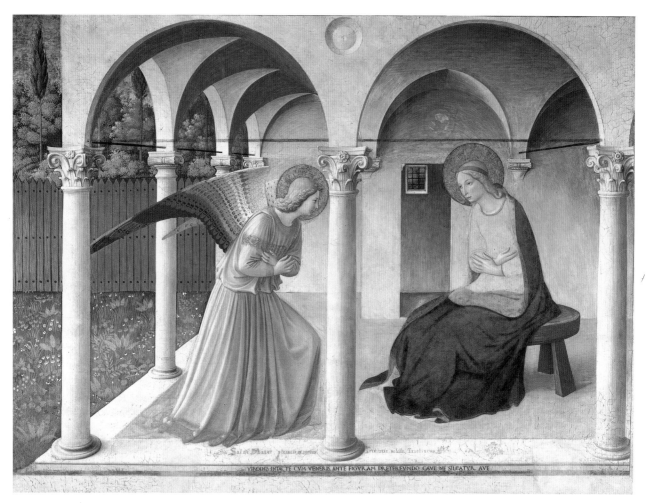

12-22 | **Fra Angelico.** *Annunciation,* fresco in north corridor, Monastery of San Marco, Florence, c. 1438–45. 7'1" x 10'6" (2.2 x 3.2 m)

The shadowed vault of the portico is supported by a wall on one side and by slender Ionic and Corinthian columns on the other, a new building technique being used by Brunelleschi in the very years when the painting was being created. The edge of the porch, the open door in the back wall, and the grilled window, drawn in linear perspective, establish a complex but ample space for the figures.

corridor Fra Angelico painted the scene of the Annunciation (fig. 12-22). Here the monks were to pause for prayer before going to their individual cells. The illusion of space created by the careful linear perspective seems to extend the stair and corridor out into a second cloister, the Virgin's home and verdant enclosed garden, where the angel Gabriel greets the modest, youthful Mary. The slender, graceful figures wearing flowing draperies assume modest poses. The natural light falling from the left models their forms and casts an almost supernatural radiance over their faces and hands. The scene is a vision that welcomes the monks to the most private areas of the monastery and prepares them to continue their meditations.

Pope Eugene IV summoned Fra Angelico to Rome in 1445, and the painter's assistants completed the frescoes in Florence. The pope may have hoped to make the painter a church official, the archbishop of Florence, but finally appointed the vicar of San Marco, Antonino Pierozzi, to the post in January 1446. When Pierozzi was proposed for canonization in the early sixteenth century, several people testified that Pope Eugene's first choice

for archbishop had been Fra Angelico, who declined the honor and suggested his Dominican brother Antonino. The world of art was left richer because of the choice, however, for Fra Angelico dedicated the last years of his life to his painting, including the pope's private chapel in the Vatican Palace.

At midcentury, when Fra Angelico was still painting his radiant visions of Mary and Jesus in the monastery of San Marco, a new generation of artists emerged. Thoroughly conversant with the theories of Brunelleschi and Alberti, they had mastered the techniques (and tricks) of depicting figures in a constructed architectural space. The creation of the more subtle nuances of landscape came later with the knowledge of Flemish painting and atmospheric or aerial perspective.

Some artists became specialists. The eccentric painter Paolo de Dono (1377–1475), called Paolo Uccello (Paul Bird), devoted his life to the study of linear perspective. Giorgio Vasari, the sixteenth-century artist and courtier who wrote the first history of art, devoted a chapter to Uccello, whom he described as a man so obsessed with the study of perspective that he neglected his

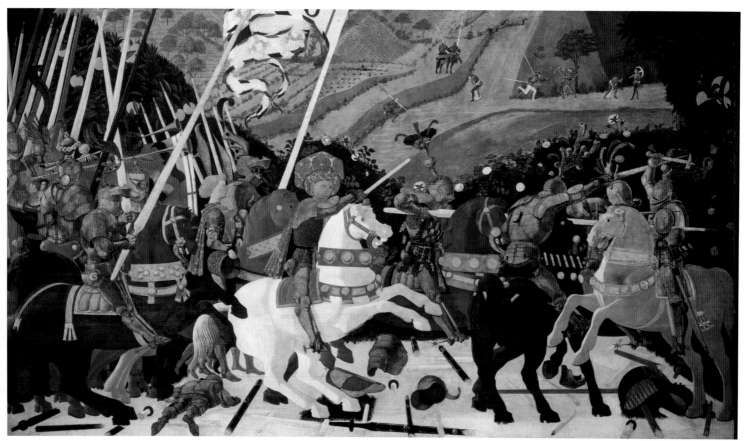

12-23 | **Paolo Uccello.** *The Battle of San Romano.* 1430s(?). Tempera on wood panel, 6' x 10'7" (1.83 x 3.23 m) (later cut down at the top)
The National Gallery, London

(See pages 286–87.)

The Florentine forces in the battle against the Sienese at San Romano were led by General Niccolo da Tolentino, a friend and supporter of the Medici, who died in the conflict. In the painting, the general charges onto the field on a white horse, accompanied by his page. He wears a red and gold hat and carries a general's baton; both serve to identify him in this action-packed scene.

painting, his family, and even his pet birds. Finally Uccello became, in Vasari's words, "solitary, eccentric, melancholy, and impoverished" (Vasari, *Lives of the Painters*, page 79). According to Vasari, Uccello's wife complained that he sat up drawing all night and when she called to him to come to bed he would say, "Oh, what a sweet mistress is this perspective!"

In three large paintings, Uccello recorded a battle won by the Florentine forces in 1432 (fig. 12-23). Together with their carved and gilded frames, the three paintings once formed a frieze in the Medici palace in Florence. Far from a realistic record of events, Uccello used the men, horses, and arms as devices to display the fashionable new perspective drawing. The broken lances and the downed knight in armor establish a three-dimensional grid leading back to the dense hedge and distant fields where soldiers continue to ravage the countryside.

In the second half of the century a younger generation of artists turned the walls of chapels and palaces into brilliant displays of the good life as it was lived by the rich and powerful citizens of the Italian city-states—Florence, Mantua,

Urbino, and elsewhere. The subject of the murals might be religious or historical, but patrons wanted to see themselves at work, at prayer, at play, surrounded by images of their neighbors, their families, their servants, their fine horses, and dogs—all the better to show off their jewelry, clothing, and household goods. The interest in material possessions, an interest that reformers claimed reached the point of obsession, is apparent in the dazzling display of wealth even in purportedly religious scenes.

No one captured the richness and elegance of the moment better than Benozzo Gozzoli (c. 1420–1497). He had learned his craft as an assistant to Fra Angelico in the Vatican, and in 1459 he won the commission to paint the private chapel in the Medici palace in Florence. Six years later in San Gimignano he painted the chancel of the Church of Sant'Agostino (Saint Augustine) with scenes from the life of the patron saint, the early bishop and Father of the Church (see illustration in "Renaissance Perspective Systems," page 289). The events take place in idealized, Florentine settings, rich in classical architectural detail. The fig-

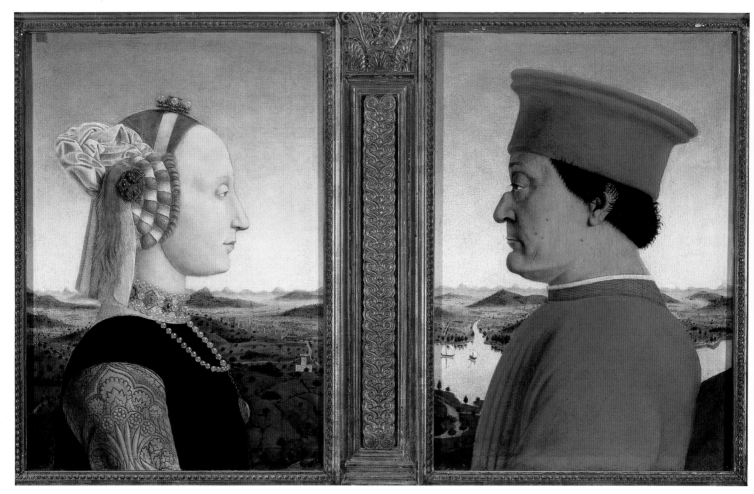

12-24 | Piero della Francesca. *Battista Sforza* (left) **and** *Federico da Montefeltro* (right). 1472–73. Oil on wood panel, each 18½ x 13" (47 x 33 cm). Galleria degli Uffizi, Florence

ures, all of whom wear fifteenth-century dress, depict events occurring hundreds of years earlier. As always, both painters and patrons saw history in contemporary terms. Well-dressed scholars listen to Augustine's instruction. They sit in neat rows, controlled as much by the laws of perspective as by the eloquence and logic of their teacher. Gozzoli's technical facility must have appealed to the wealthy middle-class merchants, bankers, and clerics who were his patrons.

An artist who was profoundly influenced by Masaccio was Piero della Francesca (c. 1406/12–1492). Born in the small Tuscan town of Borgo San Sepulcro, Piero worked in Florence in the 1430s. He knew current thinking in art and art theory—including Brunelleschi's system of spatial illusion and linear perspective, Masaccio's powerful modeling of forms and atmospheric perspective, and Alberti's theoretical treaties. Piero was one of the few practicing artists who also wrote about his own theories. Not surprisingly, in his treatise on perspective he emphasized the geometry and the volumetric construction of forms and spaces that were so apparent in his own work.

Commissions took Piero to the court of Federico da Montefeltro at Urbino. There, in 1472–73, he painted a pair of companion portraits of Federico and his recently deceased wife, Battista Sforza (fig. 12-24). Like portraits on Roman coins and

cameos, the figures are portrayed in strict profile, as remote from the viewer as icons. Piero emphasized the underlying geometry of the forms, rendering the figures with an absolute stillness. At the same time, his use of the northern technique of atmospheric perspective, with the landscape features becoming lighter and paler as they recede, resulted in a highly believable illusion of space. Piero used another northern European device in the harbor view near the center of Federico's panel: the water narrows into a river and leads the eye into the distant landscape. The portraits may have been joined as a **diptych** (a pair of panels), since the landscape appears continuous across the two panels. On the back of the panels, the couple rides in triumphant chariots through another continuous landscape.

Contrasting sharply with Piero's sober monumentality is the fluid, linear grace characteristic of the Florentine painter Sandro Botticelli (1445–1510). Botticelli's best-known works are paintings of mythological subjects, among them the *Birth of Venus* (fig. 12-25). The date of this painting is controversial, but it was probably made around 1484–86 for the private collection of Lorenzo de' Medici, who had become ruler of Florence in 1469.

Botticelli's *Birth of Venus*, whose central image, a type known as the modest Venus, is based on the antique statue of

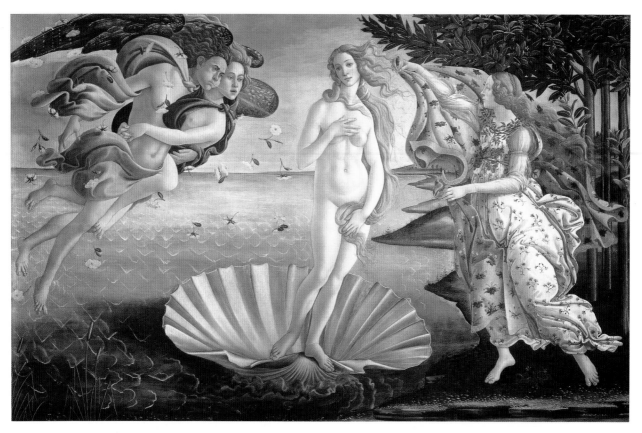

12-25 | **Sandro Botticelli.** *Birth of Venus.* c. 1484–86. Panel, 5'8⁷/₈" x 9'1⁷/₈" (1.8 x 2.8 m) Galleria degli Uffizi, Florence

Venus in the Medici collection (see fig. 7). The classical goddess of love and beauty, born of sea foam, floats ashore on a scallop shell gracefully arranging her hands and hair to hide—or enhance—her sexuality. Blown by the wind, Zephyr (and his love, the nymph Chloris), and welcomed by a devotee holding a garment embroidered with flowers, Venus arrives at her earthly home. The circumstances of this commission are uncertain, but it inspired Neoplatonic debate about the meaning of the "two Venuses"—one sacred, and one profane.

The meaning of Botticelli's mythological paintings is probably related to Neoplatonism, a philosophy favored by the Medicis. Cosimo de' Medici the Elder (1389–1464) had founded an academy in Florence devoted to the study of classical texts, especially the works of Plato and his followers, the Neoplatonists. Neoplatonism is highly complex, but basically it is characterized by a sharp opposition of the spiritual (the ideal or idea) and the carnal (matter that can be overcome by severe discipline and aversion to the world of the senses). Neoplatonists conceived of Venus, the goddess of love, as having two natures, one terrestrial and the other celestial. The first ruled over earthly, human love and the second over universal or divine love. For the Florentine Neoplatonists, the celestial Venus was a classical equivalent of the Virgin Mary.

In northern Italy, the Renaissance appeared first in Venice and in Padua, where both Giotto (in the fourteenth century) and Donatello (in the mid-fifteenth) had lived and worked. Donatello was working in Padua during the formative years of the young artist Andrea Mantegna (1431–1506). Mantegna absorbed the system of linear perspective used by Donatello and pushed it to its limits with his own radical perspective views and strongly foreshortened figures.

Mantegna's mature style is exemplified by the frescoes of the Camera Picta (Painted Room) in the Ducal Palace of Mantua. The artist decorated this tower chamber between 1465 and 1474 for Ludovico Gonzaga, the ruler of Mantua. On the vaulted ceiling, the artist painted a tour de force of perspective, a viewpoint called *di sotto in sù* (seen directly from below), which began a long tradition of illusionistic ceiling painting (fig. 12-26; see page 310). The room appears to be open to a cloud-filled sky through a large oculus in a simulated marble and mosaic-covered vault. On each side of a precariously balanced planter, three young women and an exotically turbaned African man peer over a marble railing. A fourth young woman in a veil looks dreamily upward. Joined by a large peacock, several winged **putti** (naked little boys) frolic around the **balustrade** (supports topped by a rail). Mantegna completed the decoration of the room with

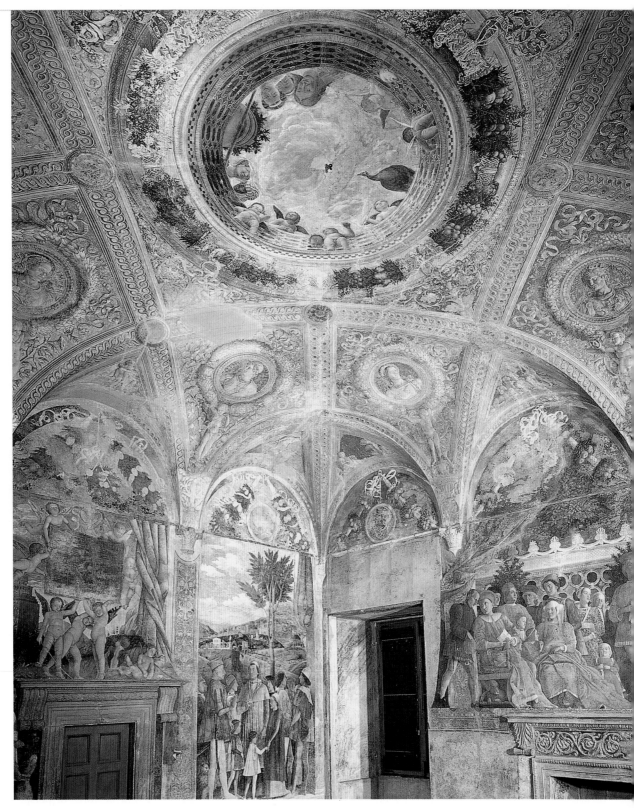

12-26

Andrea Mantegna Frescoes in the Camera Picta Ducal Palace Mantua 1465–74

murals featuring portraits of members of the Gonzaga family.

In the last quarter of the fifteenth century, Venice—once a center of Byzantine art—emerged as a major center of Renaissance painting. From the late 1470s on, Venetian artists embraced the oil medium for works on both panel and canvas. The most important of these painters were members of the Bellini family, Jacopo and his sons Gentile and Giovanni. Andrea Mantegna was also part of this circle, for he married one of Jacopo Bellini's daughters.

Giovanni Bellini demonstrates the intense investigation and recording of nature associated with the early Renaissance. His painting of *Saint Francis in Ecstasy* (fig. 12-27), painted in the 1470s, illustrates his command of an almost Flemish realism. The saint stands in communion with nature, bathed in early morning sunlight, his outspread hands showing the stigmata (the miraculous appearance of Christ's wounds on the saint's body). Francis had moved to a cave in the barren wilderness in his search for communion with God, but in this landscape, the fields blos-

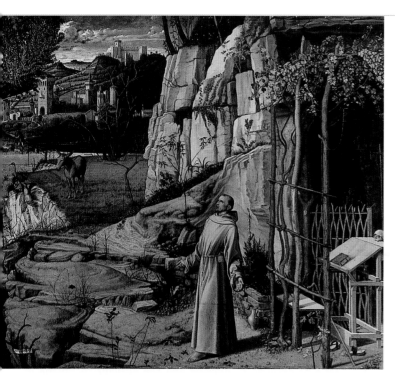

12-27   **Giovanni Bellini.** *Saint Francis in Ecstasy.* 1470s. Oil and tempera on wood panel, 49 x 55⁷/₈" (125 x 142 cm) The Frick Collection, New York

Copyright the Frick Collection, New York

som and flocks of animals graze. The grape arbor over his desk and the leafy tree toward which he directs his gaze add to an atmosphere of sylvan delight. True to fifteenth-century religious art, however, Bellini unites Old and New Testament themes to associate Francis with Moses and Christ: the tree symbolizes the burning bush; the stream, the miraculous spring brought forth by Moses; the grapevine and the stigmata, Christ's sacrifice. The crane and donkey represent

the monastic virtue of patience. The detailed realism, luminous colors, and symbolic elements suggest Flemish art, but the golden light suffusing the painting is associated with Venice, a city of mist, reflections, and above all, color. Giovanni's career spanned the second half of the fifteenth century, but he produced many of his greatest paintings in the early years of the sixteenth, when his work matured into a grand, simplified, idealized style.

Late in the fifteenth century, the city of Rome became a magnet for Renaissance artists. Pope Sixtus IV summoned the finest painters to decorate the walls of his newly built Sistine Chapel, among them Pietro Vannucci, called Perugino (c. 1445–1523). Perugino, who was active in Florence, came from near the town of Perugia in Umbria. In 1482, he painted the *Delivery of the Keys to Saint Peter* (fig. 12-28), an event not actually described in the Bible but suggested in Matthew 16:19. The event provided the justification for the supremacy of papal authority—Christ is shown giving the keys to the kingdom of heaven to the apostle Peter, the first bishop of Rome.

Delivery of the Keys is a remarkable study in linear perspective (see "Renaissance Perspective Systems," page 289). The clear demarcation of the paving stones of the piazza provides a geometric grid against which the figures stand like chess pieces on the squares. The figures and buildings are scaled to size according to their distance from the picture plane and modeled by a consistent light source from the upper left. Horizontally, the composition is divided between the foreground frieze of figures and the widely spaced background buildings, vertically by the open space at the center between Christ and Peter and by the symmetrical architectural forms on either side of this central axis. Perugino's

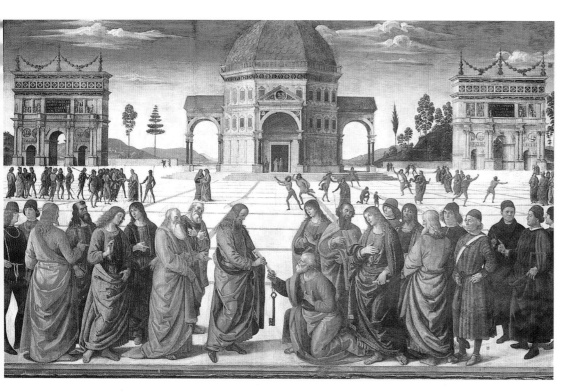

12-28

Pietro Perugino. *Delivery of the Keys to Saint Peter* fresco in the Sistine Chapel, Vatican, Rome 1482. 11'5¹/₂" x 18'8¹/₂" (3.48 x 5.70 m)

Modern eyes accustomed to gigantic parking lots would not find a large open space in the middle of a city extraordinary, but in the fifteenth century this great piazza was purely the product of artistic imagination. A real piazza this size would have been very impractical. In summer sun or winter wind and rain, such spaces would have been extremely unpleasant for a pedestrian population, but, more important, no city could afford such extravagant use of land.

painting is, among other things, a representation of Alberti's ideal city (see fig. 12-18), described in Alberti's treatise on architecture as having a "temple" (that is, a church) at the very center of a great open space raised on a dais and separate from any other buildings that might obstruct its view.

Printmaking in Renaissance Europe

The achievements of Renaissance painters, sculptors, and architects were disseminated across Europe through single-sheet prints and printed books. Printmaking emerged in Europe with the wider availability of paper and the development of the printing press at the end of the fourteenth century. The major types of prints produced during the Renaissance were **woodcuts** and **engravings** (see "Woodcuts and Engravings on Metal," below). In the beginning, woodcuts were often made by untrained artisans, but soon artists began to draw images for them to cut from the block. Engravings, on the other hand, seem to have developed from the metal-working techniques of goldsmiths and armorers.

The Florentine goldsmith and sculptor Antonio del Pollaiuolo (c. 1432–1498) may have intended his influential and only known print, *Battle of the Ten Nudes* (an engraving done about 1465–70), as a study in the human figure in action (fig. 12-29). The naked men fighting each other ferociously against a tapestry-like background of foliage seem to have been drawn from a single model in a variety of poses, many of which were taken from classical sources. Much of our fascination with the print lies in the way in which Pollaiuolo depicts the muscles of the male body reacting under tension.

The German painter Martin Schongauer, who learned engraving from his goldsmith father, was an immensely skillful print-

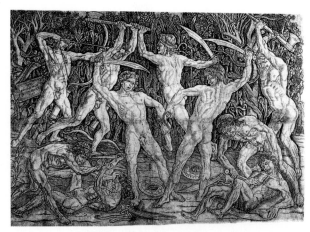

12-29 | **Antonio del Pollaiuolo.** *Battle of the Ten Nudes*
c. 1465–70. Engraving, 15⅛ x 23¼" (38.3 x 59 cm)
Cincinnati Art Museum, Ohio
Bequest of Herbert Greer French. 1943.118

maker who excelled in drawing and the difficult technique of shading from deep blacks to the faintest grays. One of his best-known prints today is the *Temptation of Saint Anthony*, engraved about 1480 to 1490 (fig. 12-30). Schongauer illustrated the original biblical meaning of temptation, expressed in the Latin word *tentatio*, as a physical assault rather than a subtle inducement. Wildly acrobatic, slithery, spiky demons lift Anthony off the ground to torment and terrify him in midair. The engraver intensified the horror of the moment by condensing the action into a swirling mass of figures beating, scratching, poking, tugging, and no doubt shrieking at the stoical saint, whose faith made him impervious to all.

TECHNIQUE
Woodcuts and Engravings on Metal

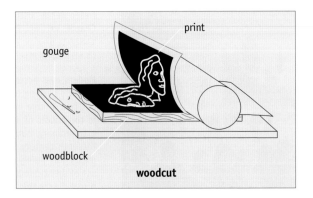

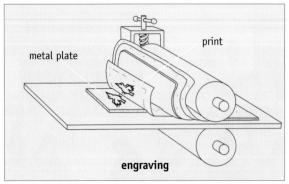

An artist making a **woodcut** draws a design on a smooth block of wood, then cuts away all the areas around the lines, leaving them in **high relief**. When the block's surface is inked and a piece of paper pressed down hard on it, the ink on the relief areas is transferred to the paper to create a reverse image.

Engraving on metal, in contrast, requires a technique called **intaglio**, in which lines are cut into the plate with tools called gravers or **burins**, while the surface remains flat. Ink is applied over the whole plate and forced down into the lines, after which the surface of the plate is carefully wiped clean. The ink in the recessed lines prints onto a sheet of paper pressed hard against the metal plate.

Whichever technique is used, the great advantage of printmaking is that woodblocks and metal plates can be used repeatedly to make nearly identical images.

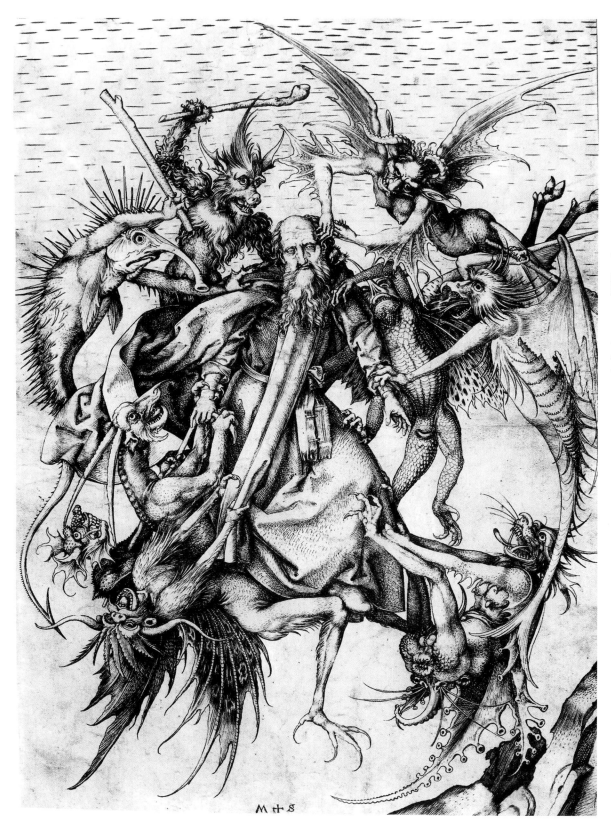

12-30

Martin Schongauer *Temptation of Saint Anthony* c. 1480–90 Engraving, 12¼ x 9" (31.1 x 22.9 cm). The Metropolitan Museum of Art New York

Rogers Fund, 1920 (20.5.2)

The prevalence of religious prints made for private devotion, whether simple woodcuts or highly sophisticated engravings like Schongauer's, are an important reminder that the rise of humanism did not signify a decline in the importance of Christianity. In fact, an intense spirituality, as well as the popular belief in things unseen, continued to inspire European artists in spite of the intellectual, social, geographic, and religious ferment sweeping over the continent.

In a single generation at the beginning of the sixteenth century, the painter Raphael (1483–1520), together with architect Donato Bramante (1444–1514), Michelangelo (1475–1564), and a few other artists, established a style often called the High Renaissance. Reason seemed to have triumphed. Artists and philosophers, each in their own way, combined Christian belief and ancient philosophy into a balanced, rational, humanistic system. Faith in human rationality and perfectibility seems to underlie Raphael's decoration of the private apartment of Pope Julius II, who ruled from 1503 to 1513. Raphael achieved a lofty style in keeping with papal ideals, but when he died at the age of thirty-seven on April 6, 1520, the grand moment was already passing; Luther and the Protestant Reformation were challenging papal authority.

Pope Julius II intended the Stanza della Segnatura, or Room of the Signature, to be his library and study. The paintings in the pope's library proclaimed that all human knowledge existed under the power of Divine Wisdom. Raphael retained the traditional organization of a library into divisions of theology, philosophy, the arts, and jurisprudence; and he created allegories to illustrate the themes. Churchmen discussing the sacraments represent theology (see fig. 13-4), while across the room ancient philosophers debate in the *School of Athens* (see fig. 13-5). Poetry and the arts are represented by Apollo and the Muses; and Justice, holding a sword and scales, assigns each his due.

Plato and Aristotle lead the *School of Athens*. They carry appropriate books, Plato holding the *Timaeus* and Aristotle the *Nicomachean Ethics*. Ancient representatives of the academic curriculum—Grammar, Rhetoric, Dialectic, Arithmetic, Music, Geometry, and Astronomy—surround them. The poet Sappho is the only woman in the room. She reclines against the (real) window frame among the Muses. Raphael included his own portrait among the onlookers in the *School of Athens* and signed the painting with his initials.

In this all-encompassing iconographic program, Raphael has created an ideal setting for papal activity. In backgrounds inspired by Roman antiquities, or Bramante's designs for the new church of Saint Peter, or in majestic landscapes with oak trees (a gracious reference to the pope's powerful della Rovere, "of the oak," family), monumental figures move with quiet dignity. Raphael's idealized forms are as grand as the ideas they represent. During his all too short career, Raphael established the standard of classical Renaissance art for the future.

Raphael. Stanza della Segnatura, Vatican, Rome
Right: *Philosophy* or *School of Athens* with Plato and Aristotle; left: (over the window) *Poetry and the Arts*, represented by Apollo and the Muses
1510–11. Fresco, 19 x 27' (5.8 x 8.2 m)
(See pages 319–20.)

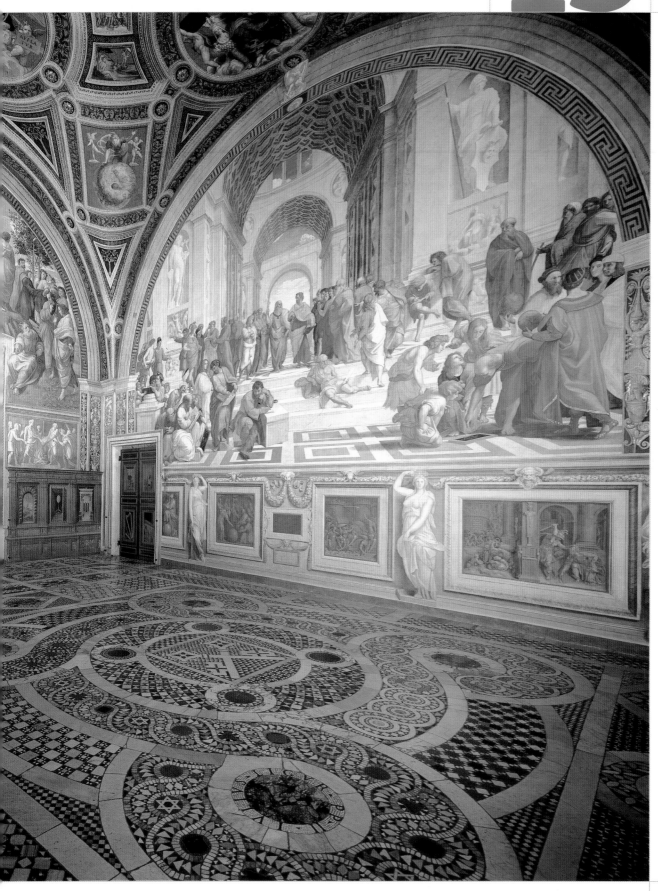

During the sixteenth century, the humanism of the early Renaissance underwent a radical shift. With its medieval roots and often uncritical acceptance of the authority of classical texts, Renaissance humanism slowly gave way to an intensified spirit of inquiry. This impulse led scholars to investigate the natural world around them, to conduct scientific and mechanical experiments, to explore lands in Africa, Asia, and the Americas previously unknown to Europeans, and even to question the authority of the pope and the Church hierarchy in a movement known as the Reformation. The influential writings and leadership of important reformers, especially Martin Luther (1483–1546) in Germany, led to the establishment of Protestant churches in northern Europe (see Map 5, page 383). In response, at the Council of Trent (1545–63), the Roman Catholic hierarchy formulated a program to counter the Reformation, which included the Inquisition with its special tribunals to root out heresy.

The effects of the Reformation on art were significant and sometimes even violent. Some Protestants considered religious imagery to be idolatrous and in some areas actually destroyed religious art and whitewashed church interiors. As a result, many artists turned to portraiture and other secular subjects to make their livings. In Catholic regions, people still venerated traditional images of Christ and the saints, but officials from the Church scrutinized works of art for heretical or profane subject matter.

As travel became easier and safer, artists became increasingly mobile, traveling from city to city and from one country to another; consequently, styles and techniques became less regional and more international. The materials artists worked with changed. Fresco painting was still common, but more and more artists painted with oil on canvas. They could produce oil paintings in their studios and easily transport and install them anywhere. Artists of stature became sought-after international celebrities, and their social status rose as painting, sculpture, and works of architecture came to be seen as liberal rather than manual arts.

Italian Art

The painting, sculpture, and architecture produced during the early sixteenth century reflect a self-confident humanism, an abiding admiration for classical forms, and a dominating sense of stability and order. These characteristics are found above all in the work of four towering figures: Leonardo da Vinci, Raphael Sanzio, Michelangelo Buonarotti, and Titian Vecelli. The achievements of these artists are so remarkable that nineteenth-century scholars called the period in Italy from c.1495 to the death of Raphael in 1520 the High Renaissance.

Leonardo da Vinci (1452–1519) received his training in Florence in the workshop of the painter and sculptor Verrocchio. Leonardo's fame as an artist is based on only a few known works of art, for his fertile mind jumped from one subject to another, and he seldom finished his projects. He had a passion for the study of mathematics, science, and engineering, and he compiled volumes of detailed drawings and notes on anatomy, botany, geology, meteorology, architectural design, and

THE VITRUVIAN MAN

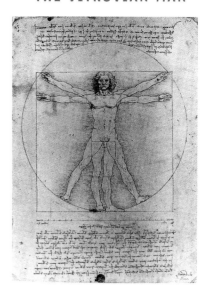

Leonardo da Vinci. *Vitruvian Man*
c. 1490. Ink, approx. 13$\frac{1}{2}$ x 9$\frac{5}{8}$" (34.3 x 24.5 cm). Galleria dell'Accademia Venice

Artists throughout history have turned to geometric shapes and mathematical proportions to seek the ideal representation of the human form. Leonardo da Vinci, and before him the first-century BCE Roman architect and engineer Marcus Vitruvius Pollio, equated the ideal man with both circle and square.

In his ten-volume *De architectura* (*On Architecture*), Vitruvius wrote: "For if a man be placed flat on his back, with his hands and feet extended, and a pair of compasses centered at his navel, the fingers and toes of his two hands and feet will touch the circumference of a circle described therefrom. And just as the human body yields a circular outline, so too a square figure may be found from it. For if we measure the distance from the soles of the feet to the top of the head, and then apply that measure to the outstretched arms, the breadth will be found to be the same as the height" (Book III, Chapter 1, Section 2). Vitruvius determined that the body should be eight heads high. Leonardo added his own observations in the reversed writing he always used for his notebooks when he created his well-known diagram for the ideal male figure, called the *Vitruvian Man*.

mechanics (see "The Vitruvian Man," above). At the court of Duke Ludovico Sforza of Milan, where he worked from 1482 or 1483 until 1498, he spent much of his time on military and civil engineering projects, including an urban renewal plan for the city. But at Duke Ludovico's request, Leonardo also created one of the defining monuments of Renaissance art: an image of the Last Supper painted on the wall of the refectory (dining room) in the Monastery of Santa Maria delle Grazie in Milan (fig. 13-1; see also fig. 19).

On one level, Leonardo painted a narrative, showing the moment when Jesus tells his companions that one of them will betray him. They react with shock, disbelief, and horror, presenting a study of human emotions. On another level, the *Last Supper* is replete with timeless symbolism. The disciples are arranged in four groups of three around the stable, pyramidal

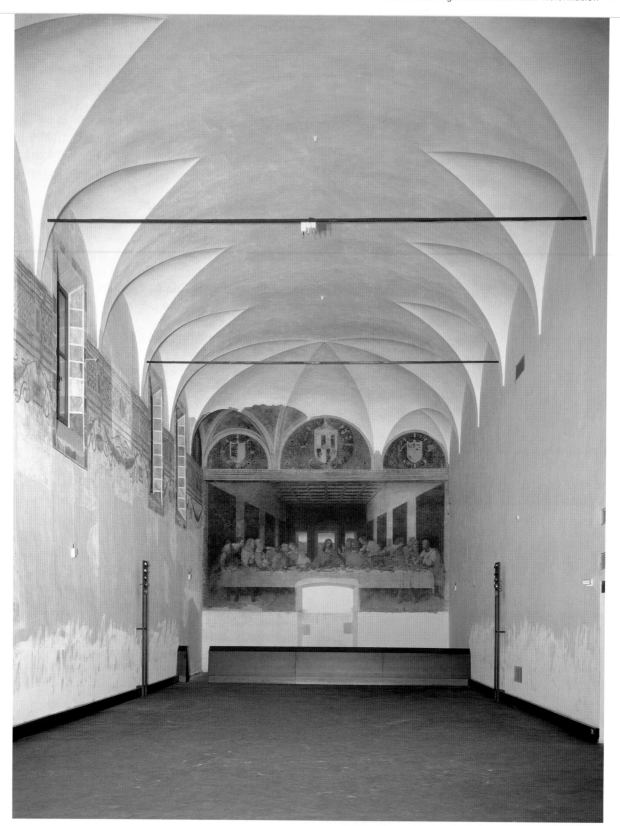

13-1 | Leonardo da Vinci. *Last Supper,* wall painting in the Refectory, Monastery of Santa Maria delle Grazie, Milan. 1495–98 Tempera and oil on plaster, 15'2" x 28'10" (4.6 x 8.8 m)

Instead of painting in fresco, Leonardo devised an experimental technique for this mural. Hoping to achieve the freedom and flexibility of painting on panel, he worked directly on dry *intonaco*—a thin layer of smooth plaster—with an oil tempera paint, whose formula is unknown. The result was disastrous. Within a short time, the painting began to deteriorate, and by the middle of the sixteenth century its figures could be seen only with difficulty. In the seventeenth century, the monks saw no harm in cutting a doorway through the lower center of the composition. Since then the work has barely survived, despite many attempts to halt its deterioration and restore its original appearance. The painting narrowly escaped complete destruction in World War II, when the refectory was bombed to rubble around its heavily sandbagged wall. The most recent restoration was finished in May 1999.

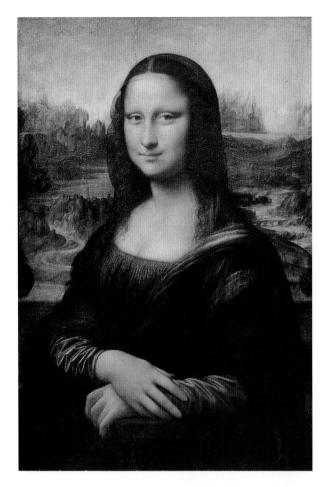

13-2 | Leonardo da Vinci. *Mona Lisa.* c. 1503–06. Oil on panel 30¼ x 21" (76.8 x 53.3 cm). Musée du Louvre, Paris

form of Jesus, who sits calmly in the middle of the general commotion. Leonardo placed Judas in the first triad to the left of Jesus, along with the young John the Evangelist and the elderly Peter. Judas, Peter, and John were each to play essential roles in Jesus' mission: Judas, to set in motion the events leading to the Crucifixion; Peter, to lead the Church after Jesus' death; and John, the visionary, to foretell the Second Coming of Christ and the Last Judgment in the Apocalypse. By arranging the disciples and architectural elements in four groups of three, Leonardo incorporated a medieval tradition of numerical symbolism—the three persons of the Trinity, the three Theological Virtues, the four Cardinal Virtues, the four seasons, and the four elements (earth, air, fire, and water).

The composition enhances the meaning of the painting. The scene is set in a stagelike space defined by the horizontals of table and coffered ceiling; the one-point linear perspective is emphasized by the tapestries on the side walls. These orthogonals, or perspective lines, converge on the head of Jesus where a triple window behind Jesus' head forms a natural halo of light. Leonardo modeled the figures in a rich **chiaroscuro** (light and shadow), which is somewhat obscured by the deterioration of the experimental medium, but now recaptured in a recent restoration.

In 1498, Leonardo left Milan and resettled in Florence. There he painted his renowned portrait *Mona Lisa* (fig. 13-2), between about 1503 and 1506. The subject may have been twenty-four-year-old Lisa Gherardini del Giocondo, the wife of a prominent Florentine merchant. The solid, pyramidal form of her half-length figure is silhouetted against distant mountains, whose desolate grandeur reinforces the mysterious atmosphere of the painting. Leonardo achieved this atmosphere and unified his compositions partly by covering them with a thin, lightly tinted varnish, which helped to create the effect of a smoky overall haze, or **sfumato**, a refinement of his masterful use of chiaroscuro. Because early evening light is likely to produce a similar effect naturally, he considered dusk the finest time of day and recommended that painters set up their studios in a courtyard with black walls and a linen sheet stretched overhead to reproduce the effects of twilight.

Mona Lisa's facial expression has been called "enigmatic" because her gentle smile is not accompanied by the warmth one would expect to see in her eyes. The contemporary fashion for plucked eyebrows and a shaved hairline to increase the height of the forehead adds to her arresting appearance. Perhaps most unsettling is the bold way her gaze has shifted toward the right to look straight out at the viewer. The implied challenge of her direct stare, contrasting with her apparent serenity, has made

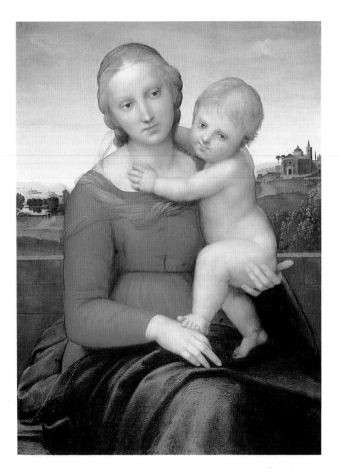

13-3 | Raphael. *The Small Cowper Madonna.* c. 1505. Oil on panel 23⅜ x 17⅜" (59.4 x 44.1 cm). National Gallery of Art Washington, D.C.
Widener Collection (42.9.57)

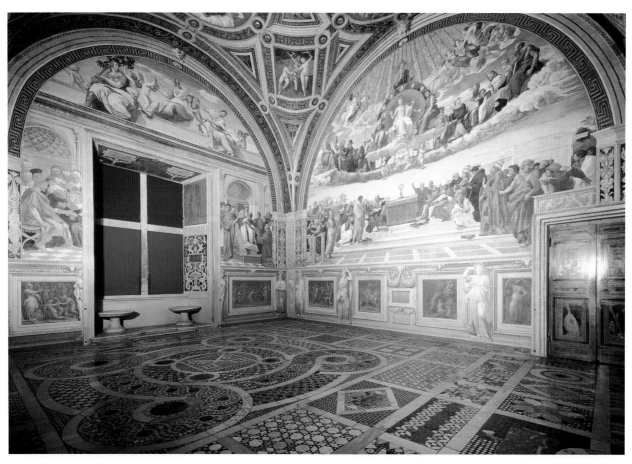

13-4 | Raphael. *Disputà,* fresco in the Stanza della Segnatura, Vatican, Rome. 1510–11. Fresco, 19 x 27' (5.8 x 8.2 m)

the *Mona Lisa* one of the most studied and written about, and best-known, paintings in the history of art.

Leonardo returned to Milan in 1508 and lived there until 1513. He also lived for a time in the Vatican at the invitation of Pope Leo X, but there is no evidence that he produced any art during his stay. In 1516, he accepted the French king Francis I's invitation to relocate to France as an adviser on architecture. He lived there until his death in 1519 (see page 338).

In 1504, Raphael (Raffaello Santi or Sanzio, 1483–1520) arrived in Florence from his native Urbino after studying in Perugia with the leading artist of that city, Perugino. Raphael soon achieved success in Florence. His paintings of the Virgin and Child, such as *The Small Cowper Madonna* (named for a modern owner) of about 1505 (fig. 13-3), brought him fame and attracted patrons. The monumental, pyramidal form of the Virgin and Child, the naturalistic draperies, and the rich, concentrated colors show that Raphael must have studied the work of Leonardo. However, the clear, even light that softly but solidly models the figures contrasts with the *sfumato* Leonardo favored. *The Small Cowper Madonna* recalls instead the atmospheric clarity and lovely colors of Perugino's paintings (see fig. 12-28).

In the distance on a hilltop, Raphael has painted a scene he knew well from his childhood, the domed Church of San Bernardino, two miles outside Urbino. The church contains the tombs

of the dukes of Urbino, Federico and Guidobaldo da Montefeltro, and their wives (see fig. 12-24). Donato Bramante (1444–1514), who worked in Urbino before settling in Rome in 1499, may have designed the church (see "Saint Peter's Basilica," page 326).

Raphael's greatest achievements came during a dozen years spent in Rome, where he arrived around 1509. As the fortunes of the ruling families of Florence and Milan fluctuated sharply because of political struggles, Rome rose to become the most active artistic and intellectual center in Italy. Pope Julius II began a campaign to rebuild Rome and the Vatican, and he put Raphael to work almost immediately decorating the papal apartments. In the library, Raphael painted the four branches of knowledge as conceived in the sixteenth century: theology (the *Disputà*, depicting the discussions concerning the true presence of Christ in the Communion bread), philosophy (the *School of Athens*), poetry and the arts (*Parnassus*, home of the Muses), and law, or jurisprudence (the *Cardinal Virtues under Justice*).

The shape of the walls and vault of the room itself inspired the composition of the paintings—the arc of clouds intersected by Christ's mandorla in the *Disputà*, for example, or the receding arches and vaults in the *School of Athens*. For all their serene idealism, the figures break classical conventions in their foreshortened **contrapposto** poses. In the *Disputà*, theologians and Church officials discuss the meaning of the Eucharist (fig. 13-4).

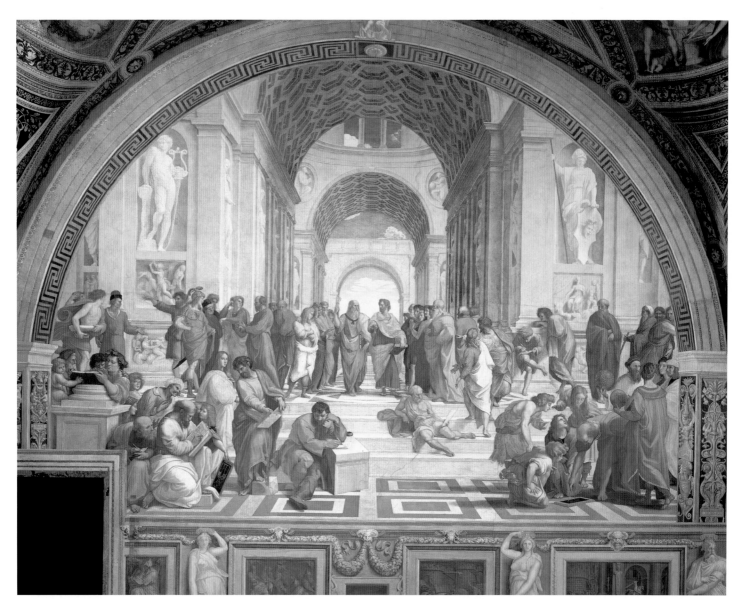

13-5 | **Raphael.** *School of Athens,* fresco in the Stanza della Segnatura, Vatican, Rome. 1510–11. 19 x 27' (5.79 x 8.24 m). (See pages 314–15.)

Raphael gave many of the figures in his imaginary gathering of philosophers the features of his friends and colleagues. Plato, standing immediately to the left of the central axis and pointing to the sky, was said to have been modeled after Leonardo da Vinci; Euclid, shown inscribing a slate with a compass at the lower right, was a portrait of Raphael's friend the architect Donato Bramante. Michelangelo, who was at work on the Sistine Ceiling only steps away from the *stanza* (room) where Raphael was painting his fresco, is shown as the solitary figure at the lower left center, leaning on a block of marble and sketching, in a pose reminiscent of the figures of sibyls and prophets on his great ceiling. Raphael's own features are represented on the second figure from the front group at the far right, as the face of a young man listening to a discourse by the astronomer Ptolemy.

Above them, the three persons of the Trinity, flanked by the apostles, fill the upper half of the painting. The consecrated Host in the monstrance (a vessel in which the Host is displayed), silhouetted against the sky, rests on the altar, where Pope Julius's name appears in the embroidered altar frontal.

Raphael's most outstanding achievement in these rooms was the *School of Athens* (fig. 13-5), painted during 1510–1511. The painting seems to summarize the ideals of the Renaissance papacy in its grand conception of harmoniously arranged forms and rational space, as well as the calm dignity of the figures. The viewer gazes at the scene through an illusionistic arch. The Classical

Greek philosophers Plato and Aristotle command center stage. At the left, Plato gestures toward the heavens as the ultimate source of his philosophy, while Aristotle, his outstretched hand palm down, seems to emphasize the importance of gathering empirical knowledge from observing the natural world. Looking down from niches in the walls are Minerva (on the right), the Roman goddess of wisdom, and Apollo (holding a lyre), the Greek and Roman god of sun, rationality, poetry, and music. Around Plato and Aristotle are mathematicians, naturalists, astronomers, geographers, and other philosophers. The scene, flooded with light from a single source, takes place in an immense barrel-vaulted interior

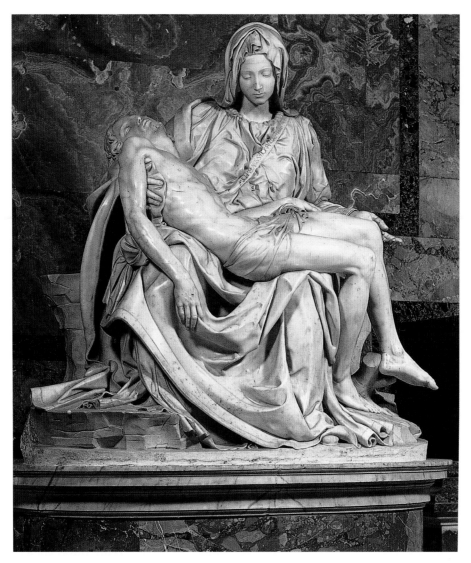

13-6 | **Michelangelo.** *Pietà,* from Old Saint Peter's. c. 1500. Marble, height 5'8½" (1.74 m)
Saint Peter's, Vatican, Rome

possibly inspired by the new design for Saint Peter's, which was being rebuilt on a plan by the architect Bramante. The grandeur of the building is matched by the monumental dignity of the philosophers themselves and the sweeping arcs of the composition, which link the figures in a dramatic unity.

Like many Renaissance artists, Raphael was a master of several arts. He provided **cartoons** (full-scale paintings or drawings to be used as models) for the tapestries in the Sistine Chapel. He was the director of all archaeological and architectural projects in Rome for the Medici pope, Leo X. When he died at age thirty-seven, he was given an impressive funeral and buried in the Pantheon. His death in 1520 marks the end of the classical phase of the High Renaissance in many people's view.

Michelangelo Buonarroti (1475–1564), like Raphael, spent part of his early career in Florence and later worked for Pope Julius II in Rome. Born in the Tuscan town of Caprese, Michelangelo grew up in Florence and was apprenticed at age thirteen to the painter Domenico Ghirlandaio. He soon joined the household of Lorenzo de Medici, the Magnificent, where he studied

sculpture with Bertoldo di Giovanni, a pupil of Donatello. Bertoldo worked primarily in bronze, and Michelangelo later claimed that he had taught himself to carve marble by studying the Medici collection of classical statues.

Michelangelo's major early work, at the turn of the century, was a **pietà**, commissioned by a French cardinal and installed as a tomb monument in Old Saint Peter's in the Vatican (fig. 13-6). Pietàs—works in which the Virgin supports and mourns the dead Jesus—had long been popular in northern Europe but were rare in Italian art at the time. Italians generally preferred the Lamentation, which includes all of Christ's followers. Michelangelo's image established a new theme in Italy. Michelangelo's Virgin is a very young, sweet-faced woman of heroic stature holding the smaller, smoothly modeled body of her grown son. The artist's compelling vision of beauty is meant to be seen up close at the statue's own level, so that the viewer can look into Jesus' face. Michelangelo carved his name prominently on the strap across the Virgin's breast. The twenty-five-year-old artist is said to have done this after the statue was finished, stealing into the church

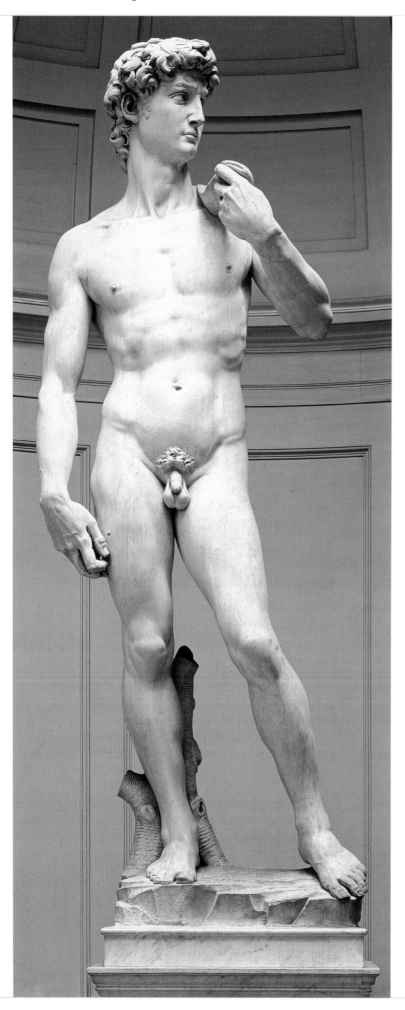

13-7 | Michelangelo. *David*
1501–04. Marble
Height 17' (5.18 m)
Galleria dell'Accademia
Florence

at night to provide the answer to the many questions about its creator.

Michelangelo traveled to the marble quarries at Carrara in central Italy to select the block from which to make this large work, a practice that he was to follow for nearly all of his sculpture. The choice of the stone was important to him because he envisioned the image as already existing within the marble and needing only to be "set free."

In 1501, Michelangelo accepted a commission for a statue of the biblical hero David (fig. 13-7) for an exterior buttress of the Florence Cathedral. When it was finished in 1504, the *David* was so admired that the Florentine city council placed it in the principal city square, next to the Palazzo della Signoria, the building housing the city's government. Although the statue embodies the antique ideal of the athletic, nude male, the emotional power of the facial expression and concentrated gaze is new. Unlike Donatello's bronze *David* (see fig. 12-10), this is not a triumphant hero with the head of the giant Goliath under his feet. Slingshot over his shoulder and a rock in his right hand, Michelangelo's *David* frowns and stares into space, seemingly preparing himself psychologically for the danger ahead. No match for his opponent in experience, weaponry, or physical strength, David represents the power of right over might. He was a perfect emblematic figure for the Florentines, who twice drove out the powerful Medici and reinstituted short-lived republics in the early years of the sixteenth century.

Michelangelo had a contract to make other statues for the cathedral, but in 1505 Pope Julius II arranged for him to come to Rome. The sculptor's first undertaking was the pope's future tomb, but Julius set this commission aside in 1506 and ordered Michelangelo to redecorate the ceiling of his private chapel in the Vatican, the Sistine Chapel (fig. 13-8). Julius's initial directions for the ceiling specified a simple architectural decoration; later he added the Twelve Apostles. When Michelangelo objected to the limitations of Julius's plan, the pope told him to paint whatever he liked. This Michelangelo presumably did, although he may have had advice from a theologian.

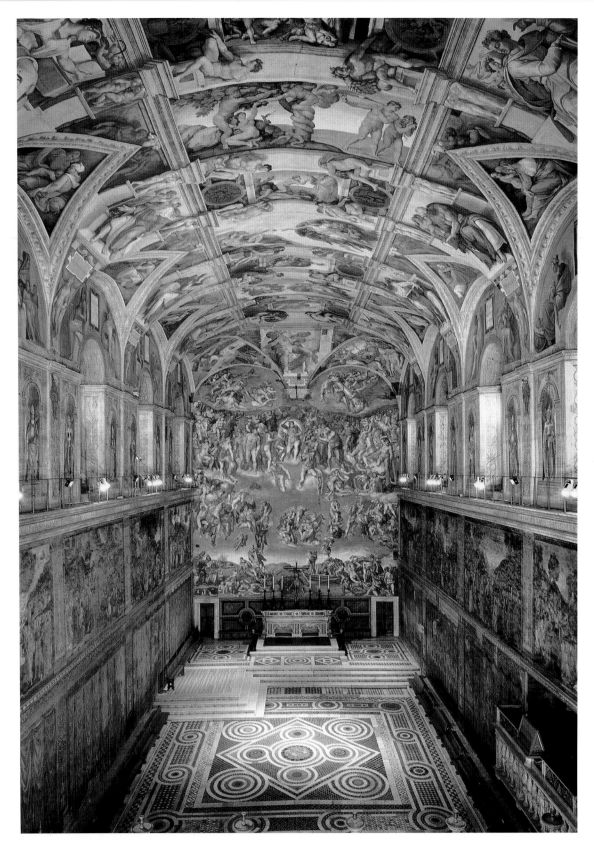

13-8 | **Interior, Sistine Chapel,** Vatican, Rome. Built 1475–81. Ceiling painted 1508–12; wall behind altar painted 1536–41

Named after its builder, Pope Sixtus (Sisto) IV, the chapel is slightly more than 130 feet long and about 43½ feet wide, approximately the same measurements recorded in the Old Testament for the Temple of Solomon. The floor mosaic was recut from stones used in the floor of an earlier papal chapel. The plain walls were painted in fresco between 1481 and 1483 with scenes from the life of Moses and the life of Christ by Perugino (see fig. 12-28), Botticelli, Ghirlandaio, and others. Below these are *trompe l'oeil* painted draperies, where Raphael's tapestries illustrating the Acts of the Apostles once hung. Michelangelo's famous ceiling frescoes begin with the lunette scenes above the windows (see fig. 13-9). On the end above the altar is his *Last Judgment*, finished in 1541 (see fig. 13-10).

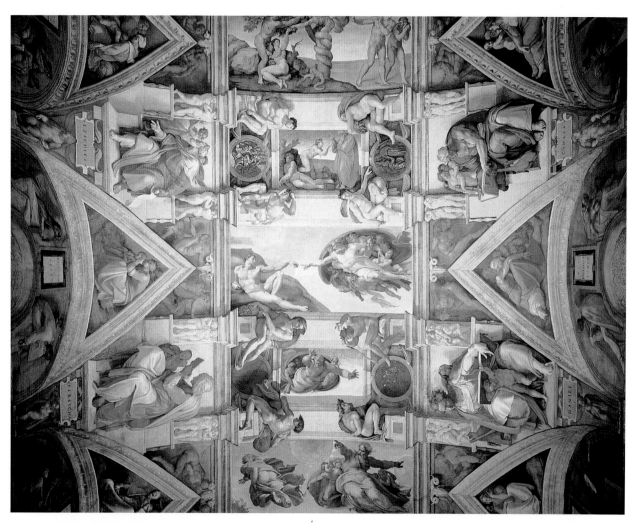

13-9 | **Michelangelo. Sistine Ceiling.** Top to bottom: *Expulsion* (center); *Creation of Eve* with *Ezekiel* (left) and *Cumaean Sibyl* (right); *Creation of Adam* (middle); *God Gathering the Waters* with *Persian Sibyl* (left) and *Daniel* (right); and *God Creating the Sun, Moon, and Plants*. Frescoes on the ceiling, Sistine Chapel. 1508–12

Michelangelo's design for the Sistine Ceiling consists of an illusionistic, painted architectural structure composed of a ribbed vault, and pilasters supporting a cornice (fig. 13-9). Figures of nude young men sit in a variety of poses on pedestals above this fictive cornice. Rising behind the youths the ribs of the vault divide the ceiling into compartments. The scenes in these compartments depict the Creation, the Fall of Man (the disobedience of Adam and Eve), and the story of Noah and the Flood, as told in Genesis. The triangular spandrels contain paintings of the ancestors of Jesus. Between the spandrels are figures of Old Testament prophets and classical sibyls (female prophets), who were believed to have foretold Jesus' birth.

Central on the ceiling is the Creation of Man, in which Michelangelo depicts the moment when God charges the languorous Adam with the spark of life. As if to echo the biblical text, Adam's heroic body and pose mirror those of God, in whose image he has been created. Directly below Adam is a youth grasping a bundle of oak leaves and giant acorns, which refer to Julius's family name (della Rovere, or "of the oak"), and possibly

also to a passage in the Old Testament prophecy of Isaiah (61:3): "They will be called oaks of justice, planted by the Lord to show his glory."

A quarter of a century later, Michelangelo again went to work in the Sistine Chapel, this time on the *Last Judgment*, painted between 1536 and 1541 on the large end wall behind the altar (fig. 13-10). Michelangelo, now entering his sixties, had complained of feeling old for years, yet he accepted this important and demanding task, which took him two years to finish. He painted a writhing swarm of resurrected humanity with the saved dragged from their graves and pushed up into a vortex of figures around Christ. Despite the efforts of several saints to save them at the last minute, the damned plunge toward hell on the right. To the right of Christ's feet is Saint Bartholomew, who in legend was martyred by being skinned alive, holding his flayed skin, the face of which is painted with Michelangelo's own distorted features. On the lowest level of the mural, directly above the altar, is the gaping, fiery Hellmouth, toward which the demonic boatman Charon propels his

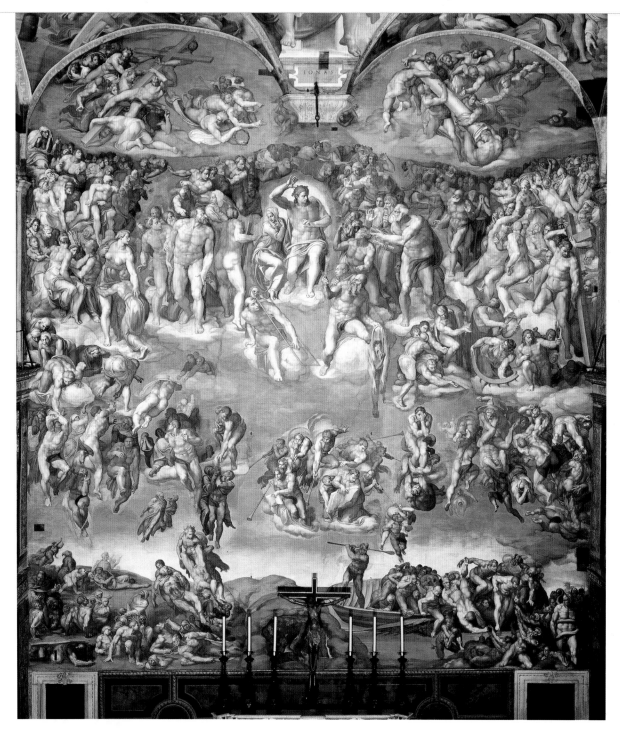

13-10 | **Michelangelo.** *Last Judgment,* Sistine Chapel, 1536–41. Fresco, 48 × 44' (encompassing approx. 190 square meters or 2,100 square feet of surface). Dark, rectangular patches left by the restorers (visible, for example, in the upper left and right corners) contrast with the vibrant colors of the chapel's frescoes. These dark areas show just how dirty the walls had become over the centuries before their recent cleaning.

craft on the River Styx, which encircles the underworld. The painting is a grim and constant reminder to the celebrants of the Mass—the pope and his cardinals—that ultimately they will be judged for their deeds.

Besides being a sculptor and painter, Michelangelo was also an architect of genius. More than thirty years after the completion of the Sistine Chapel ceiling in 1512, the artist took on his most important building commission, the rebuilding of Saint Peter's in Rome. The project had begun in 1506, when Pope Julius II made the astonishing decision to demolish the venerable but

crumbling Constantinian basilica over Saint Peter's tomb (see fig. 7-5). The pope appointed the architect Donato Bramante, who like Raphael came from Urbino, to design and build a magnificent new church. Bramante envisioned the new Saint Peter's as a central-plan building, a Greek cross (a cross with four arms of equal length) crowned with an enormous dome (see "Saint Peter's Basilica," page 326). The design was intended to continue the ancient Roman tradition of domed temples and round tombs; in Renaissance thinking, the central plan and dome also symbolized the perfection of God.

Elements of Architecture

SAINT PETER'S BASILICA

The original church of Saint Peter's was built in the fourth century CE by Constantine, the first Christian Roman emperor, to mark the grave of the apostle Peter, the first bishop of Rome and therefore the first pope. Because this site was considered one of the holiest in the world, Constantine's architect had to build a monumental structure both to house Saint Peter's tomb and to accommodate the large crowds of pilgrims who came to visit it. A huge terrace was cut into the side of the Vatican Hill in the midst of a cemetery across the Tiber River from the city. Here Constantine's architect erected a **basilica**, a type of Roman building used for law courts, markets, and other public gatherings. Like most basilicas, Saint Peter's had a **nave**, with flanking **side aisles** set off by **colonnades**, and an **apse**. To allow large numbers of visitors to approach the shrine, a **transept** was added. The rest of the church was, in effect, a covered cemetery, carpeted with the tombs of believers who wanted to be buried near the grave of the apostle. In front of the church was a walled **atrium**. When it was built, Constantine's basilica was one of the largest buildings in the world (interior length 368 feet, 112.17 m; width 190 feet, 57.91 m),

and for more than a thousand years it was the most important pilgrim shrine in Europe.

In 1506, Pope Julius II made the decision to demolish the Constantinian basilica, which had fallen into disrepair, and to replace it with a new building. That anyone, even a pope, had the nerve to pull down such a venerated building is an indication of the extraordinary sense of assurance of the age—and of Julius himself. To design and build the new church, the pope appointed Donato Bramante. The architect envisioned the new Saint Peter's as a grander version of the Tempietto, a small, round, domed shrine he had designed for the site of Saint Peter's martyrdom. His Greek-cross plan was intended to continue the ancient Roman tradition of domed temples and round **martyria**, which had been revived by Filippo Brunelleschi in Florence Cathedral (see fig. 12-13).

The deaths of both pope and architect in 1513–1514 put a temporary halt to the project. Successive plans by Raphael and others changed the Greek cross to a Latin cross in order to provide the church with a full-length nave. However, when Michelangelo was appointed architect in 1546, he returned to the Greek-cross plan. Michelangelo simplified

Bramante's design to create a single, unified space. The dome was finally completed some years after Michelangelo's death by the Baroque architect Giacomo della Porta, who retained Michelangelo's basic design but gave the dome a taller and slimmer profile.

By the early seventeenth century the needs of the basilica had changed. During the Counter-Reformation, the Church emphasized congregational worship, so more space was needed for people and processions. Moreover, it was felt that the new church should more closely resemble Old Saint Peter's and should extend over roughly the same area, including the ground covered by the atrium. In 1606, Pope Paul V commissioned the architect Carlo Maderno to change Michelangelo's Greek-cross plan to a Latin-cross plan. Maderno extended the nave to its final length of slightly more than 636 feet and added a Baroque facade (see fig. 14-2), thus completing Saint Peter's as it is today. Later in the seventeenth century, the sculptor and architect Gianlorenzo Bernini monumentalized the square in front of the basilica by surrounding it with a great colonnade.

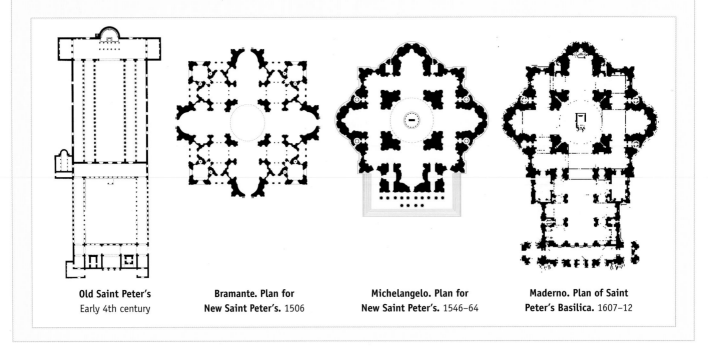

Old Saint Peter's
Early 4th century

Bramante. Plan for New Saint Peter's. 1506

Michelangelo. Plan for New Saint Peter's. 1546–64

Maderno. Plan of Saint Peter's Basilica. 1607–12

The deaths of Julius in 1513 and Bramante in 1514 halted the project temporarily. Successive plans by Raphael and others changed the Greek cross to a Latin cross in order to provide the church with a long nave. However, when Michelangelo was appointed architect in 1546, he returned to the Greek-cross plan, tearing down or canceling those parts of the previous design that he found without merit. Ultimately, Michelangelo transformed the building into a central-plan church of magnificent proportions and superhuman scale (fig. 13-11). Seventeenth-century additions and renovations dramatically changed the original plan of the church and the appearance of its interior (see fig. 14-1). However, Michelangelo's Saint Peter's can still be seen in the contrasting forms of the flat and angled walls and the three **hemicycles** (semicircular structures). Within this arrangement, the

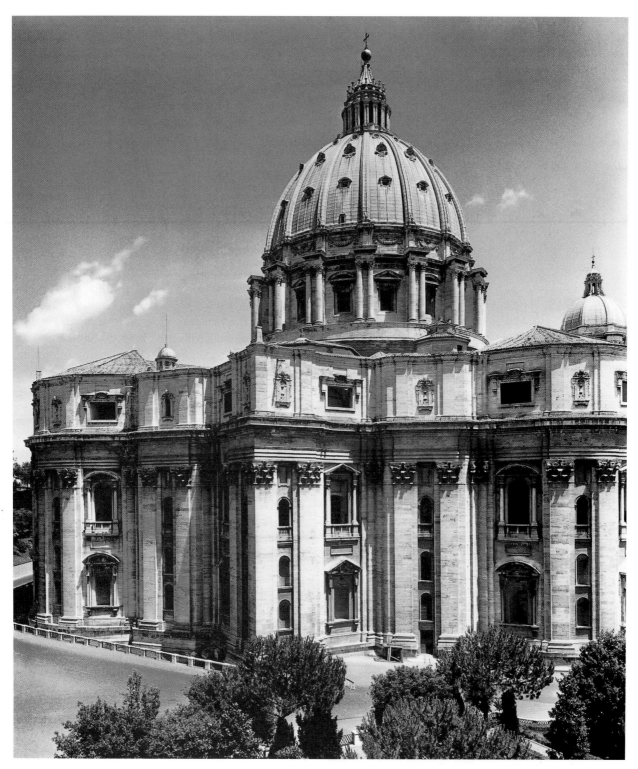

13-11 | **Michelangelo. Saint Peter's Basilica,** Vatican, Rome. c. 1546–64 (dome completed 1590 by Giacomo della Porta). View from the southwest

colossal pilasters (engaged columnar elements extending through two or more stories), **blind windows** (having no openings), and niches form the sanctuary of the church. How Michelangelo would have built the great dome is not known; most scholars believe that he would have made it hemispherical. The dome that was actually erected, by Giacomo della Porta in 1588–90, retains Michelangelo's basic design: it is a segmented dome with regularly spaced ribs, resting on a high drum with pedimented windows between paired columns, and surmounted by a tall lantern shaped like a circular temple. Della Porta raised the dome's height, narrowing its segmental bands and changing the shape of its openings.

Over the course of his lengthy career, Michelangelo continued to explore his art's expressive potential. In his late work, he

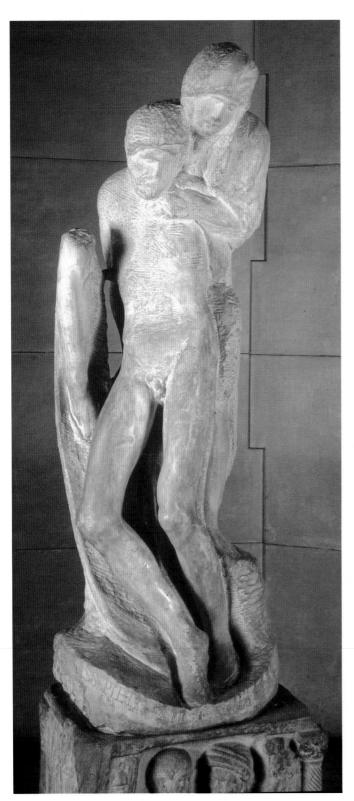

13-12 | **Michelangelo. *Pietà* (known as the *Rondanini Pietà*)**
1555–64. Marble, height 5'3³/₈" (1.61 m). Castello Sforzesco, Milan

Shortly before his death in 1564, Michelangelo resumed work on this sculpture group, which he had begun some years earlier. He cut down the massive figure of Jesus, merging the figure's now elongated form with that of the Virgin, who seems to carry her dead son upward toward heaven.

discovered new stylistic directions that would inspire succeeding generations of artists. Michelangelo was an intense man who alternated between periods of depression and frenzied activity. He was difficult and often arrogant, yet he was devoted to his friends and helpful to young artists (see fig. 13-23). He believed that his art was divinely inspired; later in life, he became deeply absorbed in religion and dedicated himself chiefly to religious works.

Michelangelo's last days were occupied by an unfinished composition now known, from the name of a modern owner, as the *Rondanini Pietà* (fig. 13-12). The *Rondanini Pietà* is the final artistic expression of a lonely, disillusioned, and physically debilitated man. In his youth, the stone had released the *Pietà* in Old Saint Peter's as a perfect, exquisitely finished work (see fig. 13-6), but this block resisted Michelangelo's best efforts to shape it. The ongoing struggle between artist and medium is nowhere more apparent than in this moving example of Michelangelo's often deliberately unfinished creations. In his late work, Michelangelo subverted Renaissance ideals of human perfectibility and denied his own youthful idealism, uncovering new forms that mirrored the tensions in Europe during the second half of the sixteenth century.

VENICE AND THE VENETO

In the last quarter of the fifteenth century, Venice emerged as a major artistic center. Venetian painters embraced the oil medium earlier than most other Italian artists, working with oil on both panel and canvas from the late 1470s on. Oil pigments were particularly suited to the Venetian climate and permitted the brilliant color and lighting effects created by Venice's most famous sixteenth-century painters: Titian, Tintoretto, and Veronese.

The early life of Titian (Tiziano Vecelli, c. 1478?–1576) is obscure. He supposedly began an apprenticeship as a mosaicist, then studied painting under the Venetian painters Gentile and Giovanni Bellini (see page 311). In 1507 Titian began working as an assistant to another Venetian artist, Giorgio da Castelfranco, called Giorgione (c. 1477–1510). Besides portraits, altarpieces, and frescoes, Giorgione made a few paintings showing figures placed in mysterious, intensely observed landscapes. Their meaning is uncertain, and scholars have theorized that Giorgione approached his work as many modern-day artists do, by selecting subjects in response to personal, private impulses, which he then expressed through his paintings.

The painting known as *Pastoral Concert* (fig. 13-13) is one of these mysterious paintings. Perhaps Giorgione began the painting and Titian completed it after Giorgione's death, or Titian, inspired by Giorgione, painted it alone. In this puzzling picture, two young men, one richly dressed, the other a barefoot peasant, relax in a verdant landscape. They seem almost oblivious to the two nude women beside them and the shepherd tending his flock in the background. While the meaning of the juxtaposition of the nude and clothed figures is obscure, in a general sense this scene of an outdoor concert evokes the romantic ideal of a lost golden age, some misty time in remote antiquity when people led

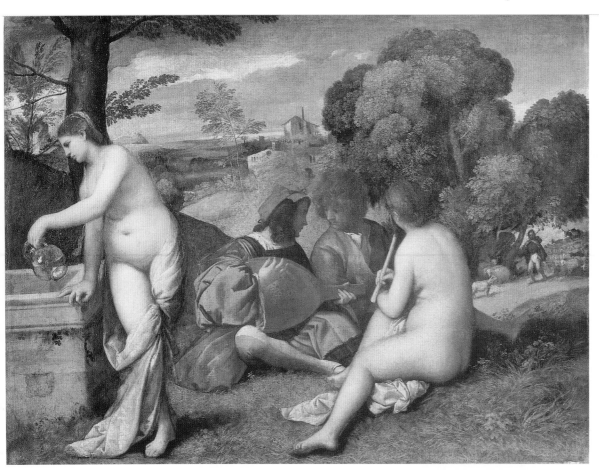

13-13

Titian
(formerly attributed to Giorgione)
Pastoral Concert
c. 1509–10
Oil on canvas
43¼ x 54⅜"
(109.9 x 132.1 cm)
Musée du Louvre
Paris

WOMEN PATRONS OF THE ARTS

In the sixteenth century, many wealthy women, from both the aristocracy and the merchant class, were enthusiastic patrons of the arts. Two English queens, the Tudor half sisters Mary I and Elizabeth I, glorified their combined reigns of half a century with the aid of court artists, as did most sovereigns of the period. The Habsburg princesses Margaret of Austria and Mary of Hungary presided over brilliant humanist courts when they were regents of the Netherlands. But perhaps the Renaissance's greatest woman patron of the arts was the marchesa of Mantua, Isabella d'Este (1474–1539), who gathered painters, musicians, composers, writers, and literary scholars around her. Married to Francesco II Gonzaga at age fifteen, she had great beauty, great wealth, and a brilliant mind that made her a successful diplomat and administrator. A true Renaissance woman, her motto was the epitome of rational thinking—"Neither Hope nor Fear." An avid reader and collector of manuscripts and books, she sponsored an edition of Virgil while still in her twenties. She also collected ancient art and objects, as well as works by contemporary Italian artists such as Botticelli, Mantegna, Perugino, Correggio, and Titian. Her *grotto*, or cave, as she called her study in the Mantuan palace, was a veritable museum for her collections. The walls above the storage and display cabinets were painted in fresco by Mantegna, and the carved-wood ceiling was covered with mottoes and visual references to Isabella's impressive literary interests.

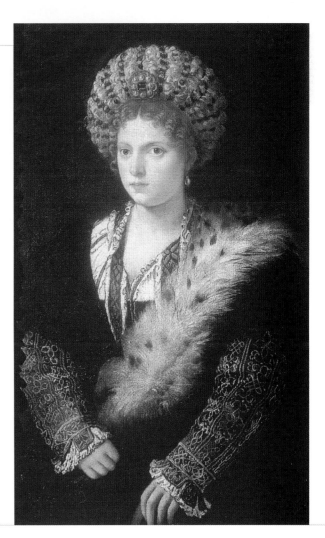

Titian. *Isabella d'Este.* 1534–36
Oil on canvas, 40⅙ x 25¼" (102 x 64.1 cm)
Kunsthistorisches Museum, Vienna

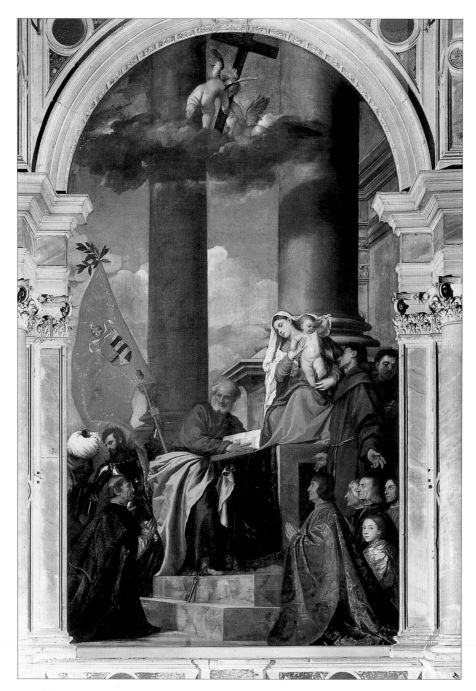

13-14 | **Titian. *Pesaro Madonna.*** 1519–26. Oil on canvas, 15'11" x 8'10" (4.85 x 2.69 m) Pesaro Chapel, Santa Maria Gloriosa dei Frari, Venice

a carefree pastoral life, a theme much loved by classical and early Renaissance poets. The subject also permitted Titian to display his incomparable talent for painting female nudes. The flesh seems to glow with an incandescent light. The relaxed pose of the seated woman with the pipe contrasts with the complicated stance of the woman at the well. Her tightly crossed legs and the swiveling twist of her body are impractical if her aim is to fill the glass pitcher but function admirably to focus the viewer's attention on the swelling forms of her stomach and thighs. The sensuous quality of this work suggests that Titian was as inspired by flesh-and-blood beauty as by any source from poetry or art.

Titian became official painter to the Republic of Venice in 1516. Three years later, the powerful Pesaro family commissioned him to paint an altarpiece for the Franciscan Church of Santa Maria Gloriosa dei Frari in Venice, a Madonna and Child surrounded by members of the Pesaro family (fig. 13-14). In the left foreground, Jacopo Pesaro, Bishop of Paphos, kneels directly in front of the Virgin. No doubt he merited this honored spot because he had led a Venetian army in victory over the Turks in 1502. A turbaned Turkish captive stands behind

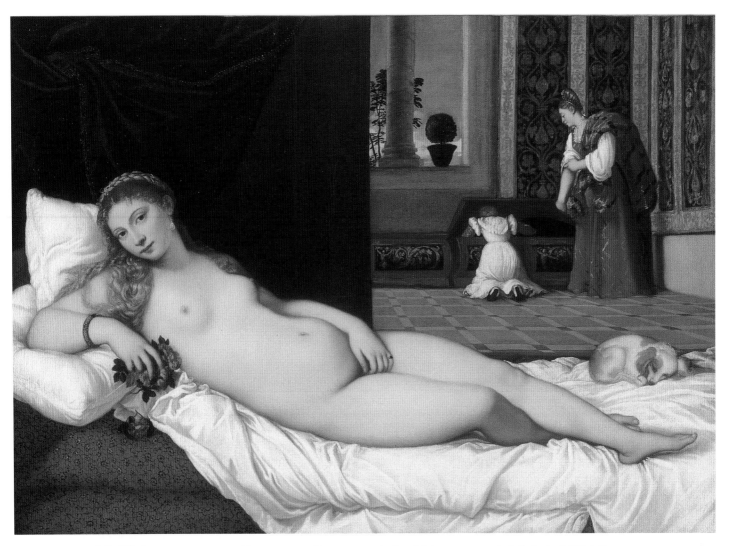

13-15 | Titian. *Venus of Urbino.* c. 1538. Oil on canvas, 3'11" x 5'5" (1.19 x 1.65 m). Galleria degli Uffizi, Florence

him, and a knight holds a banner incorporating the arms of Jacopo Pesaro and Pope Alexander VI. Saint Peter, a monumental figure with the key of heaven at his feet, looks approvingly at Jacopo, while Saint Francis, at right, gazes upward at the Christ Child. The grandeur of the scene, with its massive columns and marble staircase, enhances the power and glory of the Pesaros. No photograph can convey the vibrancy of the paint surfaces, which Titian built up in layers of pure colors, chiefly red, white, yellow, and black. The powerful intersecting diagonals of the composition reach from Jacopo Pesaro to the Virgin (innovatively placed off-center), and from the family at the right to the tilting banner at the upper left.

Titian's skill as a portrait painter led the most powerful and distinguished people of the time, including Emperor Charles V, to seek him out. Titian skillfully represented his sitters as they wanted to be remembered, at their best. The great humanist and patron of the arts, Isabella d'Este, was sixty years old when Titian painted her portrait, but he had studied an earlier portrait of the lady in order to capture her youthful beauty (see "Women Patrons of the Arts," page 329).

Paintings of nude reclining women became especially popular in sophisticated court circles, where male patrons could enjoy and appreciate the "Venuses" under the cloak of respectable classical mythology. Typical of such paintings is the Venus Titian painted about 1538 for the duke of Urbino (fig. 13-15). Here, a beautiful Venetian courtesan—whose gestures seem deliberately provocative—stretches languidly on her couch in a spacious palace, white sheets and pillows setting off her glowing flesh and golden hair. A spaniel, symbolic of fidelity, sleeping at her feet and maids assembling her clothing in the background lend a comfortable domestic air. The *Venus of Urbino* inspired artists as distant in time as Manet (see fig. 18-15).

Paolo Caliari (1528–1588), called Veronese after his home town of Verona, carried on Titian's vision of the glories of both Venice and the Church. Like Titian, Veronese employed elaborate architectural settings and costumes for religious images, but he also added still lifes, anecdotal vignettes, and other details unconnected with the main subject that proved immensely appealing to Venetian patrons. One of Veronese's most famous works is the painting now called *Feast in the House of Levi*

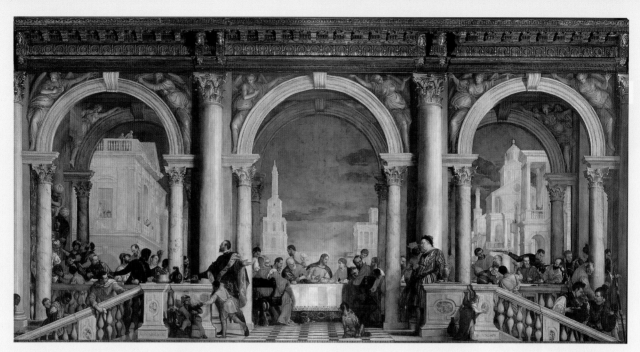

13-16 | **Veronese.** *Feast in the House of Levi,* from the Monastery of Santi Giovanni e Paolo, Venice. 1573. Oil on canvas 18'3" x 42' (5.56 x 12.8 m). Galleria dell'Accademia, Venice

According to the New Testament, Jesus revealed his impending death to his disciples during a seder, a meal celebrating the Jewish festival of Passover. This occasion, known to Christians as the Last Supper, and which, according to the Gospels, took place the evening before the Crucifixion, was a popular subject in sixteenth-century European art. But in 1573, when the painter Veronese delivered an enormous canvas of this subject to fulfill a commission (fig. 13-16), the Venetian clergy were shocked. Some were offended by the grandiose pageantry of the scene. Others protested the impiety of surrounding Jesus with a man picking his teeth, scruffy dogs, and foreign

soldiers. As a result of the furor, Veronese was called before the Inquisition. There he justified himself first by asserting that the picture actually depicted not the Last Supper, but rather the Feast in the House of Simon, a small dinner held shortly before Jesus' final entry into Jerusalem. He also noted that artists customarily invent details in their pictures and that he had received a commission to paint the piece "as I saw fit." His argument fell on unsympathetic ears, and he was ordered to change the painting. Later he sidestepped the issue by changing its title to that of another banquet, one given by the tax collector Levi, whom Jesus had called to follow him (Luke 5:27–32).

(fig. 13-16), painted for the Dominican Monastery of Santi Giovanni e Paolo, Venice. At first glance the true subject of this painting seems to be architecture, with the inhabitants of the space secondary to it. Beyond the enormous **loggia** (covered open-air gallery), entered through colossal triumphal arches, an imaginary city of white marble gleams in the distance. The size of the canvas allowed Veronese to make his figures realistically proportional to the architectural setting without losing their substance. His painting, *The Triumph of Venice,* in the Ducale Palace of Venice (see fig. 14) is equally glorious.

Jacopo Robusti (1518–1594), called Tintoretto ("little dyer") after his father's trade, carried Venetian Renaissance painting in

another direction. He is said to have been an apprentice in Titian's shop, where he proclaimed as his goal the combination of his master's color with the drawing of Michelangelo. The speed with which Tintoretto drew and painted was the subject of comment in his own time and of legends thereafter. He may have seemed to paint so rapidly because he employed a large workshop, which included other members of his family. Of his eight children, four became artists. His oldest child, Marietta Robusti, worked with him as a portrait painter, and two or perhaps three of his sons also joined the shop. Another daughter, famous for her needlework, became a nun. Marietta, in spite of her fame and many commissions, stayed in her father's shop until she died, at

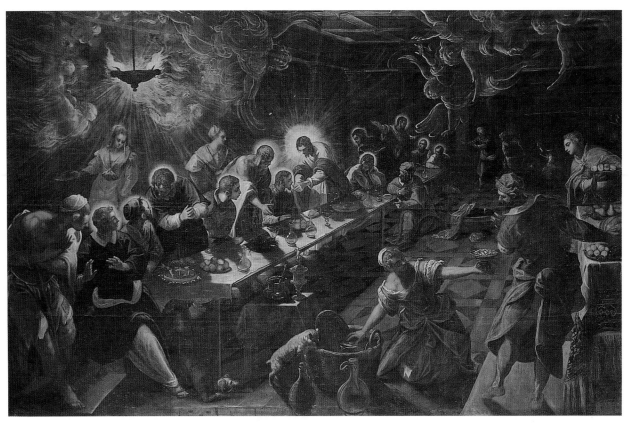

13-17 | **Tintoretto.** *Last Supper.* 1592–94. Oil on canvas, 12' x 18'8" (3.7 x 5.7 m) Church of San Giorgio Maggiore, Venice

Tintoretto often developed a composition by creating a small-scale model like a miniature stage set, which he populated with wax figures. He then adjusted the positions of the figures and the lighting until he was satisfied with the entire scene. Using a grid of horizontal and vertical threads placed in front of this model, he could easily sketch the composition onto squared paper for his assistants to recopy onto a large canvas. His assistants also primed the canvas, blocking in the areas of dark and light, before the artist himself, now free to concentrate on the most difficult passages, finished the painting.

the age of thirty. So skillfully did she capture her father's style and technique that today art historians cannot be certain which paintings are hers.

With his dynamic technique, strong colors, and bright highlights, Tintoretto created a pictorial mood of intense spirituality. The *Last Supper* (fig. 13-17), one of his last paintings, is filled with the kind of everyday details that Veronese also included, such as a servant kneeling by a basket of provisions, which is inspected by a curious cat. But these realistic elements are transformed by the plunging, off-center perspective and by the brilliant, otherworldly light emanating from Jesus and the disciples, which takes the place of traditional halos. Bands of angels swoop in from above as the supernatural and secular worlds become one. Compared with the timeless, rigorous geometry of Leonardo da Vinci's *Last Supper* (see fig. 13-1), Tintoretto's

composition is all sweeping motion and twisting, gesturing figures. The spectator is drawn irresistibly inward, caught up in the sacred drama.

Tintoretto painted the *Last Supper* and a companion painting, the *Gathering of Manna*, for the walls of the sanctuary of the church of San Giorgio Maggiore in Venice, designed by the architect Antonio Palladio (Andrea di Pietro, 1508–1580). Palladio began his career as a stonecutter in Padua, but became one of the foremost architects in Italy. After moving to Vicenza (in a region ruled by Venice), he became the protégé of a humanist scholar and amateur architect, Giangiorgio Trissino, with whom he made three trips to Rome. During these trips he made drawings of the ancient Roman remains.

Palladio's ability can best be seen in numerous villas (country houses) built early in his career. Around 1550 he

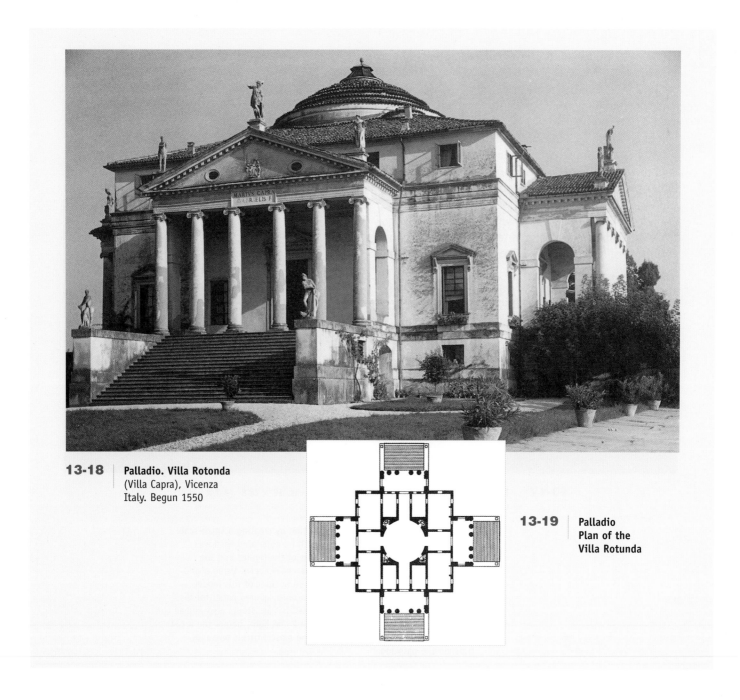

13-18 | **Palladio. Villa Rotonda**
(Villa Capra), Vicenza
Italy. Begun 1550

13-19 | Palladio
Plan of the
Villa Rotunda

started his most famous villa, just outside Vicenza (fig. 13-18), completed in 1569. Although most rural villas were working farms, Palladio designed this one as a retreat for relaxation. To afford views of the countryside, he placed an Ionic-order porch and a wide staircase on each face of the cubical building. Called the Villa Rotonda because it had been inspired by another round building, the Roman Pantheon (see fig. 6-22), the Rotonda became known as the Villa Capra after its purchase in 1591 by the Capra family. The plan (fig. 13-19) shows the geometrical clarity of Palladio's conception: a circle inscribed in a small square inside a larger square, with symmetrical rectangular rooms and identical rectangular projections from each of its faces. The use of a central dome on a domestic building was a daring innovation that effectively secularized the dome. The Villa Rotonda was the first of what was

to become a long tradition of domed palaces and houses, particularly in England and the United States, including Monticello, Thomas Jefferson's country house in Virginia (see fig. 17-10).

Mannerism in Italy and France

A new style, Mannerism, arose in Florence and Rome in the 1520s. Mannerism comes from the Italian word *maniera,* a term used in the sixteenth century to mean charm, grace, or even courtly behavior. It suggests art concerned with formal beauty for its own sake rather than idealized nature according to Renaissance conventions. **Mannerist** characteristics included figures with elongated proportions and enigmatic facial expressions, compositions with irrational special treatment, unusual colors and color juxtapositions, and obscure, unsettling, and often erotic imagery.

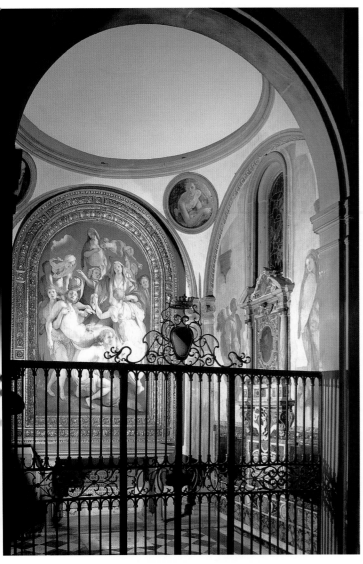

13-20 | **Capponi Chapel, Church of Santa Felicità,** Florence
Chapel by Filippo Brunelleschi, 1419–23; paintings by
Pontormo, 1525–28

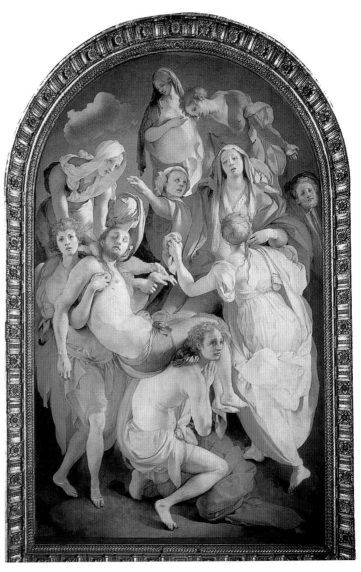

13-21 | **Pontormo.** ***Entombment.*** 1525–28. Oil on panel, 10'3" x
6'4" (3.12 x 1.93 m). Capponi Chapel, Church of Santa
Felicità, Florence

The first Mannerist painters emerged in Florence in the 1520s. The frescoes and altarpiece created by Jacopo da Pontormo (1494–1557) between 1525 and 1528 for the hundred-year-old Capponi Chapel in the Church of Santa Felicitá in Florence are clearly Mannerist in style (fig. 13-20). Open on two sides, the chapel creates the effect of a loggia in which frescoes depict the Annunciation. The altarpiece on the adjoining wall depicts the Entombment. In Pontormo's *Entombment*, the Virgin accepts the angel's message but also seems to have a vision of her future sorrow as she sees her son's body lowered from the Cross (fig. 13-21). Pontormo's ambiguous composition enhances the visionary quality of the painting. The rocky ground and cloudy sky give little sense of location in space, and some figures press into the viewer's space, while others seem to levitate or stand on a ring of boulders. Pontormo chose a moment just after Jesus' removal from the cross, when the youths who have lowered him have paused to regain

their hold. The emotional atmosphere of the scene is expressed in the odd poses and drastic shifts in scale, but perhaps most poignantly in the use of secondary colors, and colors shot through with contrasting colors, like iridescent silks. The palette is predominantly blue and pink with accents of olive green, gray, scarlet, and creamy white. The overall tone of the picture is set by the color treatment of the crouching youth, whose skintight bright pink shirt is shaded in iridescent, pale gray-green.

Pontormo's assistant at this time was Bronzino (Agnolo di Cosimo, 1503–1572), whose nickname means "Copper-Colored" (just as we might call someone "Red"). In 1540, Bronzino became the Medici court painter. Although he was a versatile artist who produced altarpieces, frescoes, and tapestry designs over his long career, he is best known today for his portraits in the courtly Mannerist style. Bronzino's virtuosity in rendering costumes and settings creates a rather cold and formal

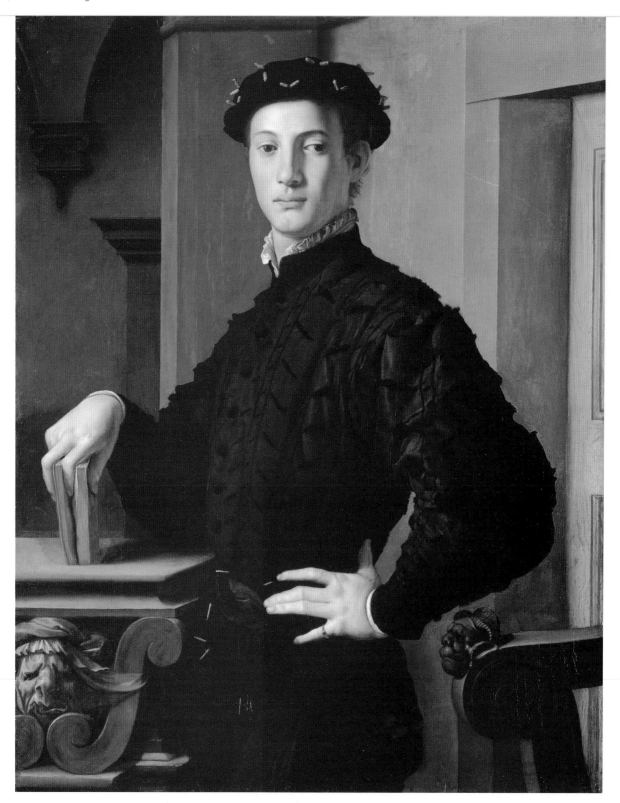

13-22 | **Bronzino. *Portrait of a Young Man.*** c. 1540–45. Oil on wood panel, 37⅝ x 29½" (95.5 x 74.9 cm). The Metropolitan Museum of Art, New York

The H. O. Havemayer Collection, Bequest of Mrs. H. O. Havemeyer, 1929 (29.100.16)

effect, but the self-contained demeanor of his subjects admirably conveys their haughty personalities. The *Portrait of a Young Man* (fig. 13-22) demonstrates Bronzino's characteristic portrayal of his subjects as intelligent, aloof, elegant, and self-assured. The youth toys with a book, suggesting his scholarly interests, but his walleyed stare creates a slightly unsettling effect and seems to associate his face with the carved masks that flank him.

Many sixteenth-century Italian artists continued to be inspired by the great leaders of the earlier generation—Leonardo da Vinci, Raphael, and Michelangelo—rather than adopting Mannerist principles. The father of the gifted portrait painter from Cremona, Sofonisba Anguissola (1528–1625), consulted Michelangelo about his daughter's artistic talents. In 1557, he asked Michelangelo for a drawing that she might copy and return

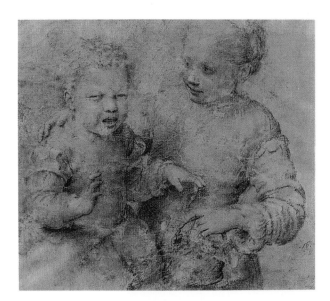

13-23 | Sofonisba Anguissola. *Child Bitten by a Crayfish*
c. 1558. Black chalk, 12³/₈ x 13³/₈" (31.5 x 34 cm)
Galleria Nazionale de Capodimonte, Naples

Anthony Van Dyck met Sofonisba in Palermo in
1624, where he sketched her and noted that she
was then 96 years old. He wrote that she advised
him on positioning the lights for her portrait. She
said that she did not want the light to be placed
too high because the strong shadows would bring
out her wrinkles. Clearly she was a lively woman and
a realist to the end.

Sofonisba was not the only talented Anguissola
daughter. Her sisters Elena, Lucia, Minerva, Europa,
and Anna were all painters, too. Only their brother,
Asdrubale, evidently lacked the family talent, but as
a member of the city council of Cremona he may
have had a political career.

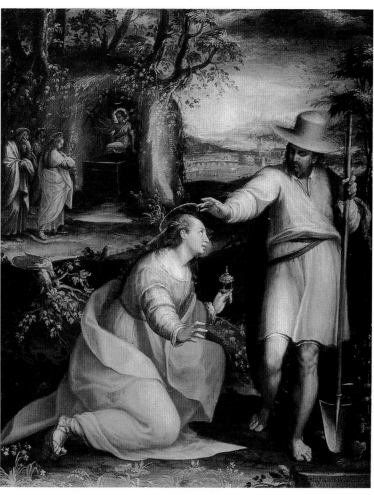

13-24 | Lavinia Fontana. *Noli Me Tangere.* c. 1581. Oil on canvas
47³/₈ x 36⁵/₈" (120.3 x 93 cm). Galleria degli Uffizi, Florence

it for the master's criticism. Michelangelo not only obliged but
also set another task for Sofonisba Anguissola: she was to send
him a drawing of a crying boy (see page 328). Michelangelo and
his contemporary, Leonardo da Vinci, were both intensely interested in the expression of human emotion, and both made many
drawings of faces showing specific emotional states.

Sofonisba Anguissola took the concept one step further. She
turned the assignment into an excuse for a charming **genre
scene**, or picture of everyday life. She drew a young boy, perhaps
her brother, wailing because a crayfish is biting his finger, while
a slightly older girl attempts to comfort him (fig. 13-23). The
sketch, with its naturalistic treatment of the two children, so
impressed Michelangelo that he gave it as a gift to his closest
friend. Within three years Sofonisba Anguissola became an official court painter to the queen of Spain, a post she held for twenty years. Unfortunately, most of her Spanish works were lost in
a seventeenth-century palace fire.

Another northern Italian, Lavinia Fontana (1552–1614), also
learned to paint from her father, a Bolognese follower of Raphael.
By the 1570s, she was a highly respected painter of narratives as
well as of portraits, the more usual field for women artists of the
time. Her success was so well rewarded, in fact, that her husband,
the painter Gian Paolo Zappi, gave up his own career to care for
their large family and help Lavinia by building frames for her
paintings. This situation was unusual even in Bologna, which
boasted some two dozen women painters as well as a number of
women scholars who lectured at the university in a variety of
subjects, including law.

While still in her twenties in 1581, Lavinia painted a *Noli Me
Tangere* (fig. 13-24), illustrating the biblical story of Christ
revealing himself for the first time to Mary Magdalen following
his Resurrection (Mark 16:9, John 20:17). The Latin title of the
painting means "Do not touch me," Christ's words when the Magdalen moved to embrace him, explaining to her that he now
existed in a new form somewhere between physical and spiritual.
According to the Gospel of John, Mary Magdalen at first mistook
Christ for a gardener, so Lavinia represented him with a broad-
brimmed hat and spade.

In 1603, Lavinia moved to Rome as an official painter to the
papal court. She also soon came to the attention of the Habsburgs, who paid large sums for her work. In 1611, she was honored with a commemorative medal portraying her in a bust as a

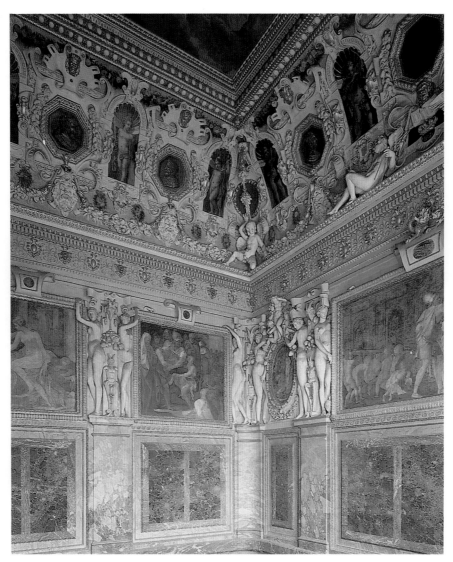

13-25 **Primaticcio. Stucco and wall painting**, Chamber of the duchess of Étampes
Château of Fontainebleau. 1540s

Primaticcio worked on the decoration of Fontainebleau from 1532 until his death
in 1570. During that time, he also commissioned and imported a large number of
copies and casts made from original Roman sculpture, including the *Apollo
Belvedere* in the Vatican gardens, the newly discovered *Laocoön* (see fig. 24), and
even the relief decoration on the Column of Trajan. These works provided an
invaluable visual source for the northern artists employed on the project.

dignified, elegantly coiffed woman on one side and as an
intensely preoccupied artist with rolled-up sleeves and wild,
uncombed hair on the other.

Painters from Italy carried the Mannerist style to France,
where King Francis I (ruled 1515–1547) was an important patron
of the arts and enthusiastic supporter of the Italian Renaissance
style. Francis even persuaded Leonardo da Vinci to join him at
Amboise in the Loire River valley of France, where the artist
spent the last two years of his life.

Having chosen as his primary residence a medieval hunting
lodge at Fontainebleau, Francis began transforming it in 1526 into
a grand country palace, or **château**. In 1530, the king appointed
a Florentine artist, the Mannerist painter Rosso Fiorentino

(1495–1540), as the first artistic director of the project. After
Rosso died, he was succeeded by his Italian colleague Francesco
Primaticcio (1504–1570), who spent the rest of his career at
Fontainebleau. Among Primaticcio's first projects was the redeco-
ration, in the 1540s, of the chambers of the king's official mistress, Anne, duchess of Étampes (fig. 13-25). The artist combined
the arts of woodworking, stucco relief, and fresco painting in his
complex but lighthearted and graceful interior design. The lithe
figures of his stucco nymphs recall Pontormo's painting style (see
fig. 13-21), with their elongated bodies and small heads. Their
spiraling postures and the bits of clinging drapery are playfully
sexual. The wall surface is almost overwhelmed with garlands,
mythological figures, and Roman architectural ornament, and the

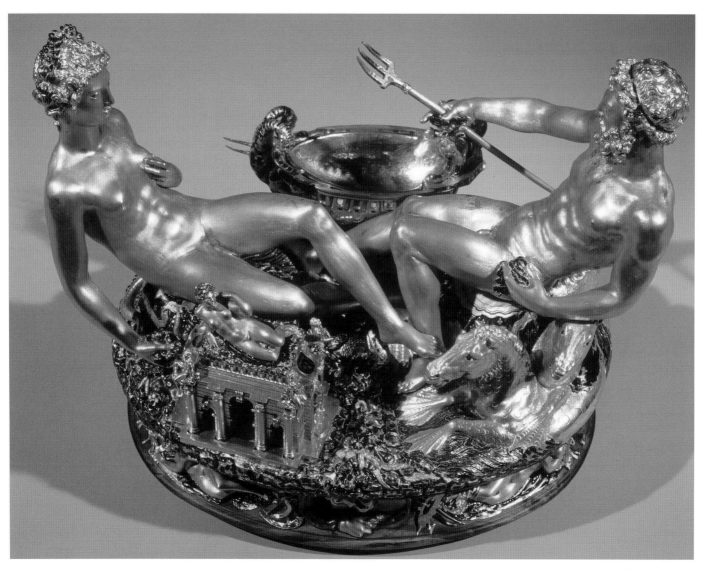

13-26 | **Benvenuto Cellini.** *Saltcellar of Francis I of France* (container for salt and pepper). 1540–43
Gold and enamel, 10½ x 13⅛" (26.67 x 33.34 cm). Kunsthistorisches Museum, Vienna

total visual effect is extraordinarily confident and joyous. The first School of Fontainebleau, as this Italian phase of the palace decoration is called, established a tradition of Mannerism in painting and interior design that spread to other centers in France and the Netherlands.

Italian craftspeople began to move north after the end of the fifteenth century, and the Fontainebleau treasury included some of the finest work of the Florentine goldsmith and sculptor Benvenuto Cellini (1500–1571). Cellini worked from just before 1540 to 1545 at Fontainebleau, where he made the famous *Saltcellar of Francis I* (fig. 13-26). This utilitarian table piece, dated 1540–43, was transformed into an elegant sculptural ornament through the artist's fanciful imagery and superb execution in gold and enamel. The Roman sea god, Neptune, representing the source of salt, sits next to a tiny boat-shaped container that carries the seasoning. Opposite him, a personification of the earth guards the plant-derived pepper, contained in the triumphal arch. The Seasons and the Times of Day on the base refer to both

daily meal schedules and festive seasonal celebrations. The two main figures, their poses mirroring each other's with one bent and one straight leg, lean out from the center at impossible angles; they are nevertheless connected and visually balanced by glances and gestures. Their supple elongated bodies and small heads reflect the Mannerist conventions.

The architect Giacomo Barozzi (1507–1573), called Vignola after his native town, worked with Primaticcio in France from 1541 to 1543. On his return to Italy, his work seems more expressive of Italian Renaissance than French Mannerist ideals. In Rome he designed the headquarters church for the Society of Jesus (the Jesuit Order), the Church of Il Gesù (Jesus). As conceived by Vignola, the church fit compactly into a city block, its interior essentially a hall for preaching, with shallow side chapels. Even the traditional Christian desire for an east-west-oriented building gave way to the practical considerations of theatrical oratory and urban space. After Vignola's death, Giacomo della Porta completed the church in 1584. The

Elements of Architecture

PARTS OF THE CHURCH FACADE

Giacomo da Vignola and Giacomo della Porta's facade for Il Gesù (see below), of about 1575–84, like Renaissance and Mannerist buildings, is firmly grounded in the clean articulation and vocabulary of classical architecture. Il Gesù's facade employs the **colossal order** and uses huge **volutes** to aid the transition from the wide lower stories to the narrow upper level. Verticality is also emphasized by the large double pediment that rises from the wide entablature and pushes into the transition zone between stories; by the repetition of triangular pedimental forms (above the **aedicula** window and in the crowning **gable**); by the rising effect of the volutes; and most obviously by the massing of upward-moving forms at the center of the facade. Cartouches, cornices, and **niches** provide concave and convex rhythms across the middle zone.

Giacomo da Vignola and
Giacomo della Porta
**Facade elevation of the Church
of Il Gesù**, Rome. c. 1575–84

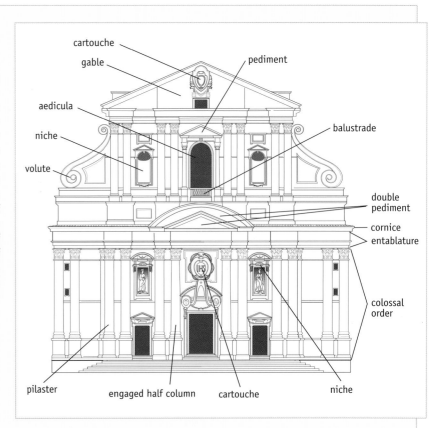

13-27 | **Giacomo da Vignola** and
Giacomo della Porta
**Church of Il Gesù
Facade,** Rome. Begun on
Vignola's design in 1568;
completed by della Porta
c. 1575–84

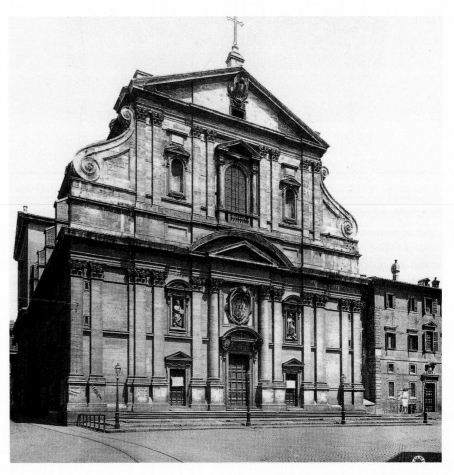

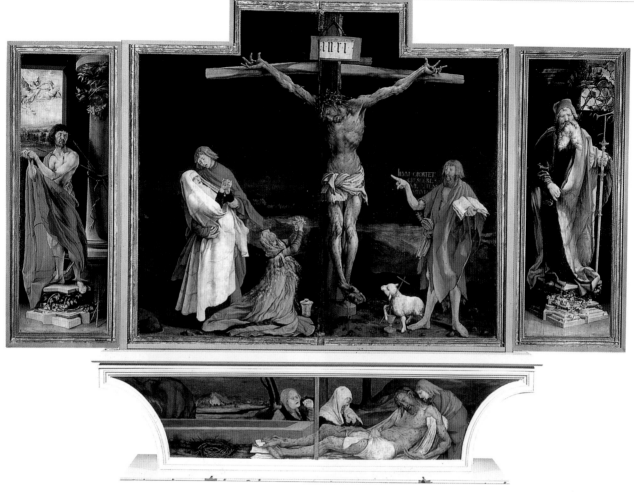

13-28   Matthias Grünewald. *Isenheim Altarpiece,* closed, from the Community of Saint Anthony, Isenheim, France. *Crucifixion* (center panel); *Lamentation* (predella); Saints Sebastian and Anthony Abbot (side panels). c. 1510–15. Oil on panel, center panels 9'9" x 10'9" (2.97 x 3.28 m); each wing 8'2" x 3'1/2" (2.49 x 0.93 m); predella 2'5½" x 11'2" (0.75 x 3.40 m) Musée d'Unterlinden, Colmar, France

simplicity and practical planning of the building, united with della Porta's dignified facade, influenced church design for more than a century.

The facade (fig. 13-27), planned by Vignola but altered by della Porta during construction, followed a design established by Renaissance architects. Paired colossal orders visually unite the first and second stories, while a second order is superimposed on the third story. Large volutes (scroll forms) ease the transition between the wide lower levels and the narrow third level by masking the sloping roofs of the side aisles (see "Parts of the Church Facade," left). The central axis of the building was stressed by gradually moving the orders on the lower level forward, from the relatively flat pilasters at the corners to the engaged half-columns at the center; by crowning the central door with a double pediment (a triangle inside a semicircle) that intrudes into the story above; and by enlarging the central window on the upper level.

German and English Art

Two very different artists, Matthias Gothardt, known as Matthias Grünewald (c. 1480–1528), and Albrecht Dürer (1471–1528) dominated the first decades of the sixteenth century in Germany.

Grünewald looked back to medieval German mysticism and emotionalism, while Dürer's intense observation of the natural world represented new interests in empirical observation, linear perspective, and a northern ideal of the human figure.

Grünewald is best known today for the wings he painted between 1510 and 1515 to protect the carved image of Saint Anthony in the *Isenheim Altarpiece* (fig. 13-28). The altarpiece had been made for the Community of Saint Anthony in Isenheim whose hospital specialized in diseases of the skin, including plague and leprosy. The altarpiece was thought to have healing properties, and viewing it was part of the treatment given to patients who entered the hospital.

The altarpiece, which had both fixed and movable wings, was displayed in different configurations depending upon the Church calendar. On normal weekdays, when it was closed, as illustrated here, viewers saw a shocking image of the Crucifixion in a darkened landscape, a Lamentation below, and lifesize figures of Saints Sebastian and Anthony Abbot standing like statues on pedestals at the sides. Grünewald represented in the most horrific detail the tortured body of Jesus covered with gashes from being beaten and pierced by the thorns used mockingly to form a crown for his head. Not only do his ashen color, open mouth,

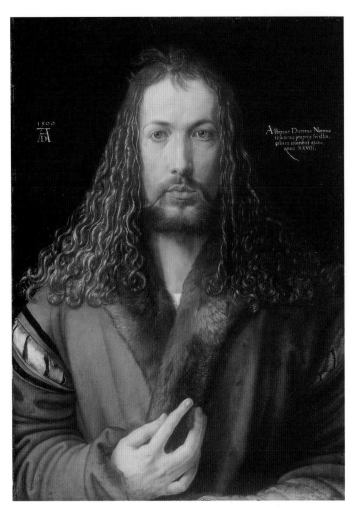

13-29 | Albrecht Dürer. *Self-Portrait.* 1500. Oil on wood panel 25⅝ x 18⅞" (65.1 x 48.2 cm). Alte Pinakothek, Munich

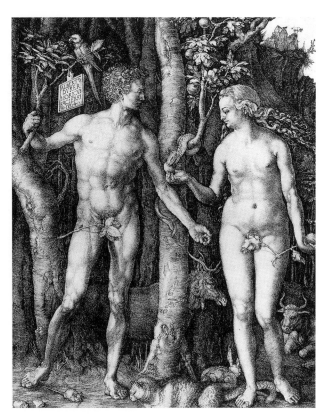

13-30 | Albrecht Dürer. *Adam and Eve.* 1504. Engraving 9⅞ x 7⅝" (25.1 x 19.4 cm). Philadelphia Museum of Art
Purchased: Lisa Nora Elkins Fund

and blue lips indicate that he is dead, but he also already appears to be decaying, an effect enhanced by the palette of putrescent greens, yellows, and purplish red. A ghostlike Virgin Mary has collapsed in the arms of an emaciated John the Evangelist, and Mary Magdalen has fallen in anguish to her knees. In the **predella**, or supporting platform, below, Jesus' bereaved mother and friends prepare his body for burial, a scene that must have been familiar indeed in the hospital. The saints on the wings serve as models for a life of Christian devotion and as intercessors for the sick and dying.

Grünewald's personal identification with the struggles of the peasants in the social and religious turmoil of the 1520s damaged his artistic career. After actively supporting the peasants, who, because of economic and religious oppression, rose up against their feudal overlords in the Peasants' War in 1525, he left Mainz and spent his last years in Halle, whose ruler was the chief protector of Martin Luther and a longtime patron of Grünewald's contemporary, Albrecht Dürer.

Albrecht Dürer (1471–1528), the leading Renaissance artist in Germany, was the son of a Nuremberg goldsmith and served apprenticeships in painting, stained-glass design, and printmaking. He became familiar with the latest developments in Italian

Renaissance art during two trips to Italy, in 1494–95 and 1505–06. He seems to have resolved to reform the art of his own country by publishing theoretical writings and manuals that discussed Renaissance problems of perspective, ideal human proportions, and the techniques of painting.

Dürer's first trip to Italy in 1494–95, clearly imparted to him both the Italian idealism associated with art there and the concept of the artist as an independent creative genius. In his self-portrait of 1500 (fig. 13-29), he represents himself as an idealized, even Christlike figure in a severely frontal pose, meeting the viewer's eyes like an icon. His rich fur-lined robes and flowing locks of curly hair create a monumental equilateral triangle, the timeless symbol of unity.

Dürer's early interest in Italian art and theoretical investigations continued in his 1504 engraving of *Adam and Eve* (fig. 13-30). These figures represent his first documented use of a canon of ideal human proportions. The nudes may have been based on Roman copies of Greek statues, probably known to him through prints or small sculpture in the antique manner. Although Dürer idealized the human figures, he recorded the flora and fauna of their setting with typically northern microscopic detail. Embedded in the landscape are symbols of the four humors: after Adam and Eve disobeyed God, they and their descendants became vulnerable to imbalances in body fluids that altered human temperament. An excess of black bile from the liver produced melancholy, despair, and greed; yellow bile caused

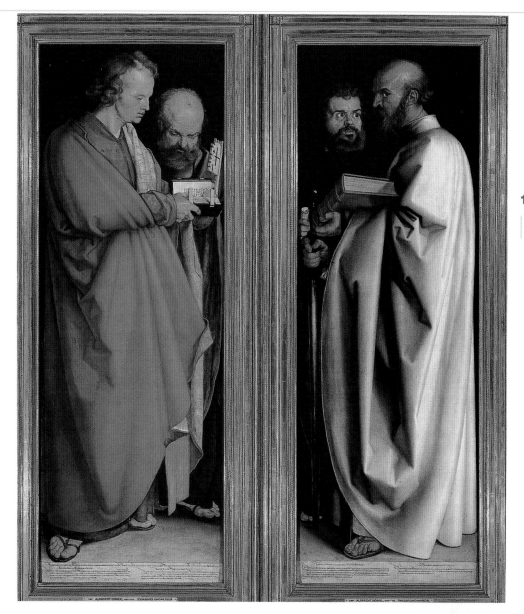

13-31

Albrecht Dürer
Four Apostles
1526. Oil on panel
Each panel 7'1/2" x
2'6" (2.15 x 0.76 m)
Alte Pinakothek
Munich

anger, pride, and impatience; phlegm in the lungs resulted in lethargy, disinterest, and a lack of emotion; and an excess of blood made a person unusually optimistic but also compulsively interested in the pleasures of the flesh. These four human temperaments are symbolized here by the melancholy elk, the choleric cat, the phlegmatic ox, and the sensual rabbit. The scurrying mouse is an emblem of Satan, and the parrot may symbolize false wisdom, since it can only repeat mindlessly what it hears. Dürer's pride in his engraving can be seen in the prominence of his signature—a placard bearing his full name and date hanging on a branch of the Tree of Life.

THE REFORMATION AND THE ARTS

Against a backdrop of broad dissatisfaction with financial abuses and lavish lifestyles among the clergy, religious reformers began to challenge specific Church practices and beliefs, especially Julius II's sale of indulgences (forgiveness of sins and insurance of salvation in return for a financial contribution) to finance the rebuilding of Saint Peter's. From their protests, the reformers came to be called Protestants, and their insistence on church reform gave rise to a movement called the Reformation.

Two of the most important reformers in the early sixteenth century were themselves Catholic priests and trained theologians: Desiderius Erasmus of Rotterdam (1466?–1536) in Holland and Martin Luther (1483–1546) in Germany. They questioned official Church teachings and the pope's supremacy, and they emphasized individual faith and turned to the Bible as the ultimate religious authority. The invention of movable type and the growing use of the printing press made the Bible and other Christian writings available to laypeople. These texts were translated into German so that they could be read by an increasingly literate public. The improved communications resulting from printed materials also allowed scholars throughout Europe to communicate with each other easily and added to the debates on religious matters. The Pope condemned Luther in 1521, and the Protestants broke away from Rome.

Religious upheavals and iconoclastic purges of religious images began to take a toll on artistic activity. Martin Luther, himself, never supported the destruction of religious art, and Dürer, who admired Luther's writings, may have painted a pair of large panels commonly referred to as the *Four Apostles* (fig. 13-31) in order to demonstrate that Protestant imagery was

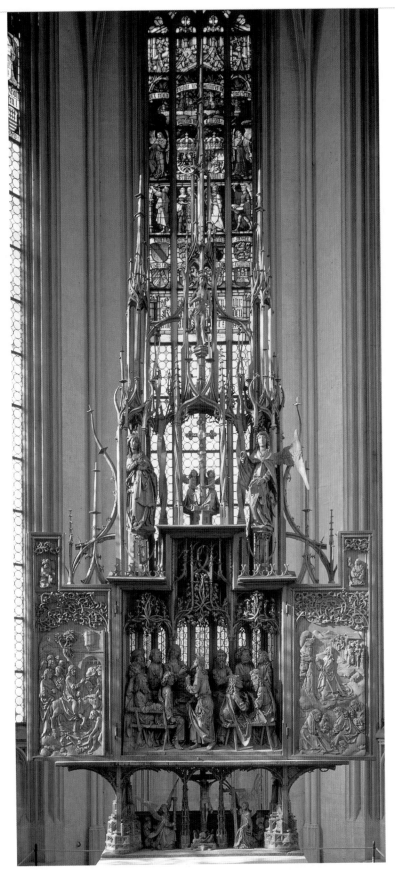

13-32 | **Tilman Riemenschneider.** *Altarpiece of the Holy Blood*
Last Supper (center); *Entry into Jerusalem* (left wing); *Agony in the Garden* (right wing); *The Annunciation* (upper figures), *The Resurrected Christ* (top-most figure). 1499–1505
Limewood, glass, height of tallest figure 39" (99.1 cm)
Height of altar 29'6" (9 m). Sankt Jakobskirche, Rothenburg ob der Tauber, Germany

possible. The paintings depict John, Peter, Paul, and Mark. On the left panel, the elderly Saint Peter, the first pope, seems to shrink behind the young Saint John, Luther's favorite evangelist. On the right panel, the Evangelist Mark is nearly hidden behind Saint Paul, whose teachings and epistles were greatly admired by the Protestants. Dürer presented the panels, painted in 1526, to the city of Nuremberg, which had already adopted Lutheranism (then almost synonymous with Protestantism) as its official religion.

German sculptors had to face even greater problems of theme and patronage than German painters, since their principal commissions had been for altarpieces and tombs. Nevertheless, they worked in every medium, and they produced some of their finest and most original work in the wood of the linden (limewood) tree, which grew abundantly in central and southern Germany. Tilman Riemenschneider (active 1483–1531) directed the largest sculpture workshop in Würzburg; he was also politically active in the city's government. Riemenschneider's work attracted patrons from other cities, and in 1501 he signed a contract for one of his major creations, the *Altarpiece of the Holy Blood,* for the Church of Saint James in Rothenburg. The most important relic in the church was a drop of what was believed to be Jesus' blood. The altarpiece was to be nearly 30 feet high. A specialist in carving shrines began work on the frame in 1499, while Riemenschneider provided the figures. The relative value their patrons placed on their contributions can be judged from the fact that the frame carver received fifty florins and Riemenschneider only sixty.

The main panel of the altarpiece represents the *Last Supper* (fig. 13-32). Like his Italian contemporary Leonardo da Vinci (see fig. 13-1), Riemenschneider depicted the moment of Jesus' revelation that one of his disciples would betray him. Unlike Leonardo, however, Riemenschneider composed his group with Jesus off-center at the left and the disciples crowded around him. Judas, at center stage, holds a money bag as a symbol of the thirty pieces of silver he received for his treachery. Jesus extends a morsel of food to Judas, signifying that he is the one destined to set in motion the events that will lead to Jesus' death (John 13:21–30). One apostle (John) points down toward the altar where the relic of the Holy Blood would have been displayed.

Rather than creating individual portraits, Riemenschneider repeated a limited number of types. His figures have large heads, prominent features, and elaborate hair treatments with thick wavy locks and deeply drilled curls. The muscles, tendons, and raised veins of hands and feet are especially lifelike, as are the pronounced cheekbones, sagging jowls, and baggy eyes. Voluminous draperies cover the slim figures; the deep folds and active patterning create strong highlights and dark shadows that unify the narrative and the intricate carving of the framework. Although earlier sculpture had been painted

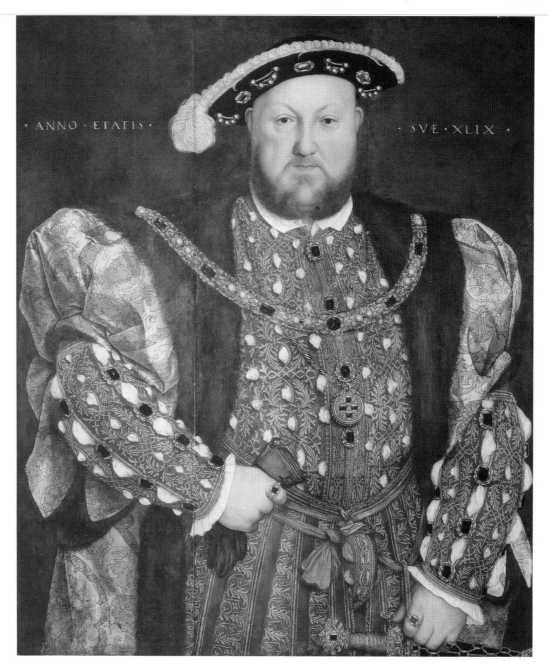

· ANNO · ETATIS ·   · SVÆ · XLIX ·

13-33 | **Hans Holbein the Younger.** *Henry VIII.* 1540. Oil on wood panel, 32½ x 29½" (82.6 x 75 cm) Galleria Nazionale d'Arte Antica, Rome

Holbein used the English king's great size to advantage for this official portrait, enhancing Henry's majestic figure with embroidered cloth, fur, and jewelry to create one of the most imposing images of power in the history of art. He is dressed for his wedding to his fourth wife, Anne of Cleves, on April 5, 1540.

and gilded, Riemenschneider introduced the use of a natural wood finish. The scene is set in a stagelike space with real windows in the back wall glazed with bull's-eye glass. Natural light from the church's windows illuminates the sculpture giving constantly changing effects, according to the time of day and the weather. Riemenschneider's career ended when his support of the 1525 Peasants' War led to his being fined and imprisoned. He survived, but created no more sculpture and died just six years later.

The successors of Grünewald and Dürer often had to compromise and to take drastic measures to navigate the radically changed German social and political scene. Some artists, like

Tilman Riemenschneider, found their careers at a standstill because of their sympathies for rebels and reformers. Others left their homes to seek patronage abroad because of their support for the Roman Catholic Church. Hans Holbein the Younger (1497–1543), born in Augsburg, spent much of his early career in Basel, Switzerland, but worked in Antwerp and London from 1526 to 1528 to escape religious turmoil. Although he had officially become a Protestant by 1532, harassment from reformers sent him once again to England, where he served as court painter to the Tudor monarch Henry VIII (ruled 1509–1547).

One of Holbein's official portraits of Henry (fig. 13-33) was painted about 1540. Although an inscription states that

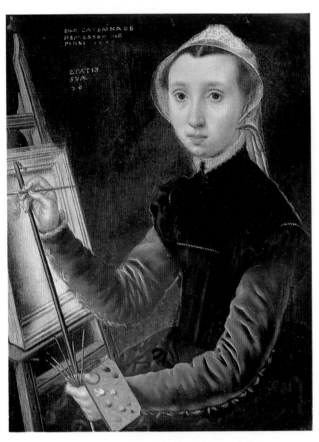

13-34 | **Caterina van Hemessen. *Self-Portrait.*** 1548. Oil on panel, 12¼ x 9¼" (31.1 x 23.5 cm). Öffentliche Kunstsammlung, Basel, Switzerland

This self-portrait of the artist at work provides a glimpse into an artist's studio and working methods. The panel on the easel already has its frame, against which the painter leans her painting stick—an essential painter's tool used to steady the hand while doing fine, detailed work. She holds a small rectangular palette, five brushes, and the painting stick in her left hand and, bracing her right hand on the stick, she sketches a head in the upper left hand corner of the panel.

Six years after she painted this self-portrait Caterina married Chretien de Morien, the organist of Antwerp Cathedral. At the death of their patron, Mary of Hungary, in 1558, the couple received a lifetime pension, and Caterina seems to have given up her painting career.

Henry is thirty-nine, Holbein used earlier sketches of the king's features. Henry's huge frame—he was well over 6 feet tall and had a 54-inch waist in his maturity—is covered by the latest style of dress, a short puffed-sleeved cloak of heavy brocade trimmed in dark fur, a narrow, stiff white collar fastened at the front, and a doublet slit to expose his silk shirt and encrusted with gemstones and gold braid. Henry was so fascinated by the elegant French king Francis I that he attempted to emulate and even surpass him in appearance. After Francis set a new style by growing a beard, Henry also grew one, as shown in this portrait. Just as Henry looked abroad so too the later Tudors favored Netherlandish, German, and French artists. A vigorous native school of painters did not emerge in England until the eighteenth century.

Netherlandish and Spanish Art

Politically the Netherlands and Spain were united under the Habsburg Empire during the sixteenth century. The art made there, however, followed several different directions. Some artists continued the styles of the late fifteenth century; others looked back to earlier Flemish painters for models; some became Mannerists in the Italian mode. A few artists, such as Hieronymus Bosch, were such individualists that they must be considered unique.

In paintings that reflect Renaissance roots in their quiet realism, Caterina van Hemessen (1528–1587) of Antwerp developed an illustrious international reputation. She learned to paint from her father, with whom she collaborated on large commissions. Her portraits typically depict the subject in three-quarter view, carefully including background elements that could be shown perspectivally, such as the easel in her *Self-Portrait* (fig. 13-34). In delineating her own features, Caterina presented a serious young person without personal vanity yet seemingly already self-assured about her artistic abilities. The inscription on the painting reads: "I Caterina van Hemessen painted myself in 1548. Her age 20."

Early in van Hemessen's career, she became a favored court artist of Mary of Hungary, regent of the Netherlands. When Mary ceased to be regent in 1556, the artist accompanied her to Spain, where Flemish painting had been popular since the fifteenth century. She arrived at the outset of the long reign of Philip II (ruled 1556–1598). Under Philip's direction, Spain halted the advance of Islam in the Mediterranean and secured control of most of the Americas. Despite enormous effort and expense, however, Philip could not suppress the revolt in the Spanish Netherlands, and his navy, the famous Spanish Armada, was destroyed by the English in 1588.

The Netherlandish artist Hieronymus Bosch (c. 1450–1516) created a world of fantastic imagery, often associated with medieval art, in paintings such as the *Garden of Earthly*

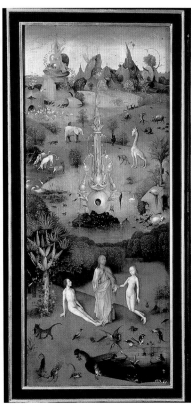
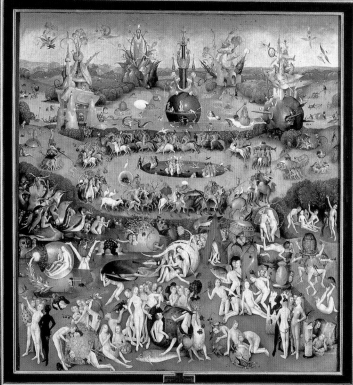
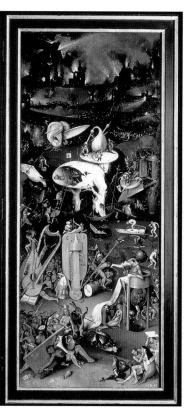

13-35 | **Hieronymus Bosch.** *Garden of Earthly Delights* (center); *Creation* (left wing); *The Damned* (right wing). c. 1505–15. Oil on wood panel, center panel 7'2¹/₂" x 6'4³/₄" (2.20 x 1.95 m), each wing 7'2¹/₂" x 3'2" (2.20 x 0.97 m). Museo del Prado, Madrid

This work was commissioned by an aristocrat for his Brussels town house, and the artist's choice of a triptych format, which suggests an altarpiece, may have been an understated irony. As a secular work, the *Garden of Earthly Delights* may well have inspired lively discussion and even ribald comment, much as it does today in its museum setting. Despite—or perhaps because of—its bizarre subject matter the triptych was copied in 1566 in tapestry versions, one (now in El Escorial, Madrid) for a cardinal and another for Francis I. At least one painted copy was made as well. Bosch's original triptych was sold at the onset of the Netherlands's revolt and sent in 1568 to Spain, where it entered the collection of Philip II.

Delights (fig. 13-35). There are many interpretations of the **triptych**. The subject seems to be based on the Christian belief in humanity's natural state of sinfulness. The imagery begins with the Creation of the World (on the wing exteriors, not shown), continues with the Creation of Adam and Eve on the left wing, and ends with the Last Judgment on the right. The fact that only the damned and not the saved are shown in the Judgment scene suggests that Bosch might have meant to suggest that damnation is the natural outcome of a life lived in ignorance and folly. The central panel illustrates the activities engaged in that condemn humanity, where seemingly harmless diversions such as games, romance, and music turn into sins such as lust, gluttony, and sloth. Luscious fruits—strawberries, cherries, grapes, and pomegranates—appear everywhere in the *Garden*, serving as food, as shelter, and even as

a boat. Herbalists believed these fruits enhanced desire and fertility. In the painting they also suggest that life is as fleeting and insubstantial as the taste of a strawberry.

The works of Hieronymus Bosch were so popular that the painter Pieter Bruegel the Elder (c. 1525–1569), nearly half a century later, began his career by imitating Bosch's work. Fortunately, Bruegel's talents went far beyond those of a copyist, and he soon developed his own style and themes. Working first in Antwerp and then in Brussels, he produced artfully composed works that reflected contemporary social, political, and religious conditions. Bruegel's inspiration came from visits to country fairs, where he sketched the farmers and townspeople who became the focus of both his religious and secular painting.

Cycles, or series, of paintings on a single allegorical subject such as the Times of Day, the Seasons, or the Five Senses

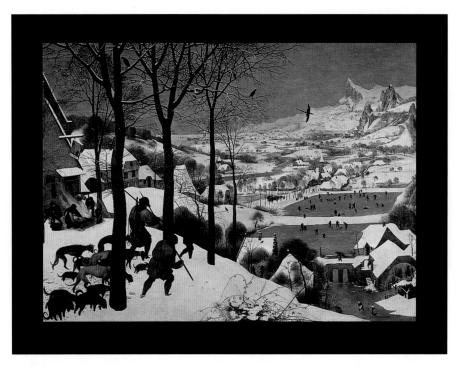

13-36 | **Pieter Bruegel the Elder.** *Hunters in the Snow.* 1565. Oil on panel 3'10¹/₂" x 5'3³/₄" (1.18 x 1.61 m). Kunsthistorisches Museum, Vienna

Between 1551 and 1554 Bruegel traveled through the Alps to Italy—to Rome, Naples, and all the way to Sicily. Unlike many Renaissance artists, he did not record the ruins of ancient Rome or the wonders of the Italian cities. Instead he seems to have been fascinated by the landscape, particularly the formidable jagged rocks and sweeping panoramic views of Alpine valleys, which he recorded in detailed drawings. Back home in his studio, he made an impressive leap of the imagination as he painted the flat and rolling lands of Flanders as broad panoramas, even adding imaginary mountains on the horizon.

became popular decorations in Flemish upper-class homes. Bruegel's *Hunters in the Snow* (fig. 13-36) of 1565 from a cycle of six panels representing the months, describes November and December. The artist captures the damp, cold winter weather much as his compatriots the Limbourgs did 150 years earlier (see fig. 12-8). In contrast to much Renaissance and Mannerist art, the subject matter in this painting appears neutral and realistic. The hunters slog stoically by, trailed by their dogs, while workers at an inn singe a pig in a fire before they finish the butchering. The viewer's eye, plunging across the wide valley toward the distant peaks, is deliberately slowed by the careful balance of the vertical tree trunks and the horizontal rectangles of frozen water.

As a depiction of Flemish life, this scene represents a relative calm before the storm. Two years after it was painted, the northern provinces of the Low Countries, which would eventually become the independent country of the Netherlands, began their struggle for independence from Spain. But even during the long years of political and social turmoil, which divided the Low Countries along religious lines, people found the resources to patronize artists.

As a serious art collector from an early age, Philip II supported artists in Spain and abroad throughout his realm. He did not, however, appreciate the works of the man who became one of Spain's most famous painters. This was the Greek painter Kyriakos (Domenikos) Theotokopoulos (1541–1614), who arrived in Spain in 1577 after working for ten years in Italy. El Greco ("the Greek"), as he was called, began his career as a Byzantine icon painter in his native Crete. He entered Titian's shop in Venice about 1566, but he soon moved to Rome. His mature style united the intense emotionalism seen in Byzantine religious art with rich color and loose brushwork reminiscent of Tintoretto. This pictorial vision ideally suited the needs of patrons in late-sixteenth-century Spain, which was undergoing a fervent religious revival.

In 1586, the artist was commissioned by the Orgaz family to paint a large canvas illustrating a local legend, the *Burial of Count Orgaz* (fig. 13-37). The fourteenth-century count had been a great benefactor of the Church, and at his funeral Saints Augustine and Stephen were said to have appeared and lowered his body into his tomb, while his soul was seen ascending to heaven. In El Greco's painting, an angel in the center lifts Orgaz's tiny

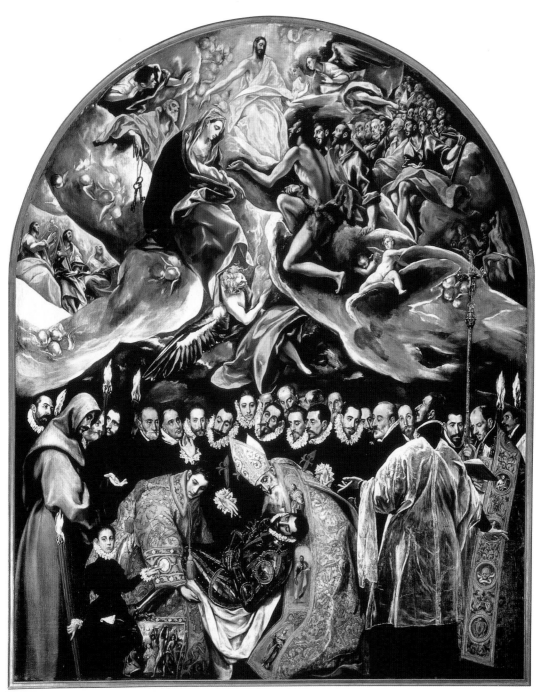

13-37 | El Greco. *Burial of Count Orgaz,* Church of Santo Tomé, Toledo, Spain. 1586
Oil on canvas, 16' x 11'10" (4.88 x 3.61 m)

ghostly soul as the miraculous burial takes place below. Portraits of local aristocrats and religious notables fill the background of the picture, which is painted, in the Mannerist tradition, without specific reference to the spatial setting (see fig. 13-21). El Greco placed his eight-year-old son at the lower left next to Saint Stephen and signed the painting on the boy's white kerchief. He may have put his own features on the man above Saint Stephen's head, the only one who looks straight out at the viewer.

El Greco distinguished between earth and heaven in this painting by elongating the heavenly figures and by creating a separate light source above in the figure of Christ, who sheds an otherworldly luminescence quite unlike the natural light below. The dramatic lighting effects and emotionalism of El Greco's work would be echoed by an increasing number of painters in the early seventeenth century, as European art entered the Baroque era.

Gianlorenzo Bernini. *Saint Teresa of Ávila in Ecstasy.* 1645–52. Marble Height of the group 11'6" (3.5 m) Cornaro Chapel, Church of Santa Maria della Vittoria, Rome (See page 354.)

In the Church of Santa Maria della Vittoria in Rome, the sixteenth-century Spanish mystic Teresa of Ávila swoons in ecstasy on a bank of billowing clouds. A youthful angel plucks open her robe, aiming a gilded arrow at her breast. Gilt bronze rays of supernatural light descend, even as actual light illuminates the figures from a hidden window above. This dramatic scene, created by Gianlorenzo Bernini (1598–1680) between 1645 and 1652, represents a famous vision described by Teresa, in which an angel pierced her body repeatedly with an arrow, transporting her to a state of ecstatic oneness with God.

The sculpture is an exquisite example of the emotional, theatrical style perfected by Bernini in response to the religious and political climate in Rome during the period of spiritual renewal known as the Counter-Reformation. Throughout Catholic Europe, painters as well as sculptors—Rubens, Caravaggio, Gaulli—created brilliant religious art. The Protestant Reformation of the sixteenth century was seen by many as an outgrowth of Renaissance humanism with its emphasis on rationality and independent thinking. In response the Catholic Church turned to the authoritarian position of the Middle Ages, a reaction supported by the new Society of Jesus founded by Ignatius Loyola (d. 1556, canonized 1622). In the "spiritual exercises" (1522–23) initiated by Saint Ignatius, Christians were enjoined to use all their senses to achieve appropriate emotional states as they reenacted (in their imaginations) the events on which they were meditating. They were to feel the burning fires of hell or the bliss of heaven, the lashing of the whips and the flesh-piercing crown of thorns. Art became an instrument of propaganda whose emotional appeal could lead the spectator to reinvigorated Christian belief.

The arts have always been used to convince or educate, nowhere more effectively than by the Catholic Church in the seventeenth century. To serve the educational mission of the revitalized and conservative Church, paintings and sculpture had to depict events and people accurately and clearly. To help worshippers achieve the emotional state of religious ecstasy, religious art depicted ecstatic states enhanced by light and miraculous masses of swirling drapery. Lascivious thoughts and the nude figure were prohibited, although today viewers find the sculpture of Saint Teresa charged with sexuality. For all its insistence on biblical accuracy, the Church approved of the supernatural mystical visions of saints like Teresa of Ávila (1515–1582, canonized 1622) who described her encounter with the angel with startling, physical clarity.

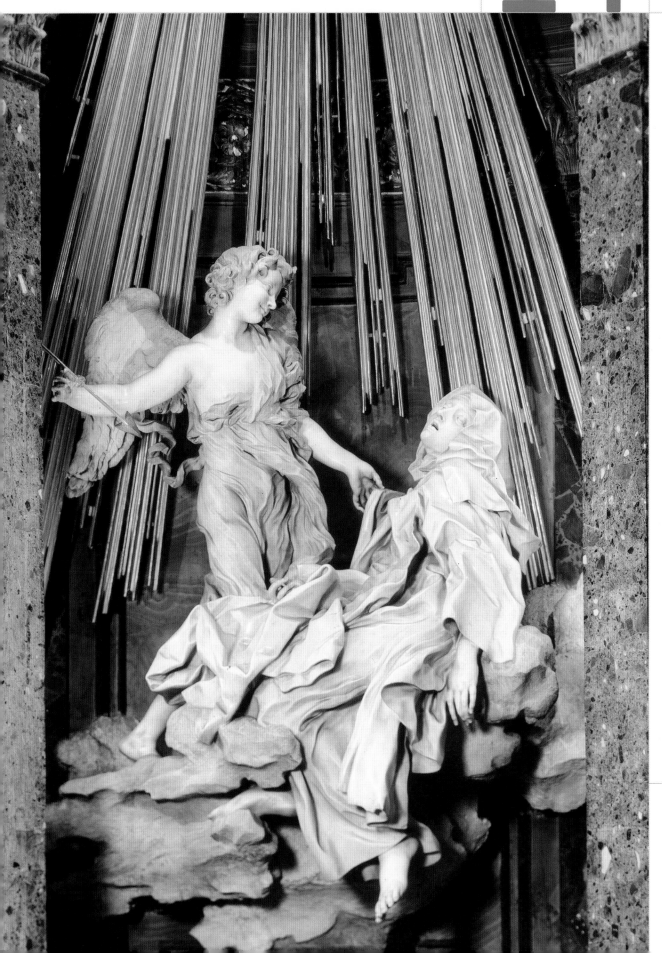

ernini's *Saint Teresa of Ávila in Ecstasy* is one of the great works of the Baroque, the prevailing artistic style in much of Europe in the seventeenth and early eighteenth centuries. Baroque features include the deliberate evocation of intense emotional responses in the viewer; the creation of dramatically lit, often theatrical compositions; the use of diverse media such as bronze and marble within a single artwork; and a spectacular technical virtuosity (all of which are seen on page 351; see also fig. 14-4). The Baroque also has its own version of classicism, a more emotional and dramatic variant of Renaissance ideals and principles. Baroque classicism featured idealization based on observation of the material world; balanced (although often asymmetrical) compositions; the sense of diagonal movement in space; rich, harmonious colors; and the inclusion of visual references to ancient Greece and Rome. Many Baroque artists achieved their ends through naturalism, the true-to-life depiction of the world that led to the popularity of portraiture, genre paintings (scenes from everyday life), still life (paintings of inanimate objects such as food, fruit, or flowers), and religious paintings featuring ordinary people and settings. Intense emotional involvement, naturalistic rendering, and classicism or classical references may exist in the same work. Many of the best examples of Baroque art combine all of these elements.

Late in the period, a refined Baroque manner known as the Rococo emerged. Developing in Italy at the beginning of the eighteenth century, this style soon spread into France, central Europe, and even Russia (see Map 5, page 383). The Rococo, characterized by fanciful architectural decoration, a light palette, and often a mood of playful melancholy, remained popular along with earlier Baroque styles until the rise of Neoclassicism in the third quarter of the eighteenth century.

Art for the Counter-Reformation Church: Italy

The patronage of the Church and the aristocratic families allied with the papacy—the Borghese, the Barberini, the Farnese—dominated Italian art from the late sixteenth to the late seventeenth century. A major program of the Counter-Reformation (the official Catholic reaction to the rise of Protestantism, see Chapter 13) was the use of art as propaganda. Churches whose splendid architecture was embellished with painting help convince the faithful of the power of traditional religion. In Rome, Pope Paul V (Borghese, 1605–1621) ordered the expansion and modernization of the new Saint Peter's Basilica. In 1606, he commissioned the architect Carlo Maderno (1556–1629) to add a longer nave and a new facade to Michelangelo's Greek-cross building, only a half century old (see "Saint Peter's Basilica," page 326). As congregational worship became important for both Catholics and Protestants, more space was needed. The new Saint Peter's more closely resembled the ancient basilica of Old Saint Peter's (see fig. 7-5) and its nave extended over roughly the same area.

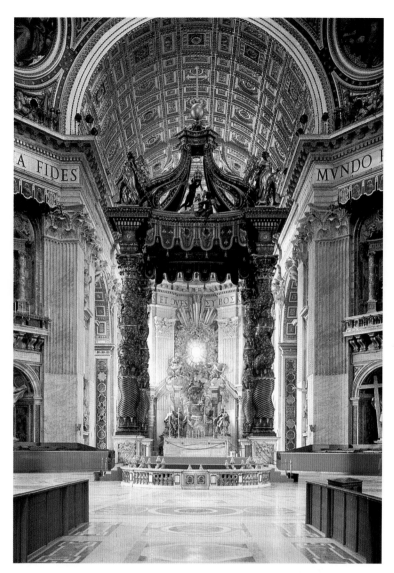

14-1 | Gianlorenzo Bernini. *Baldacchino.* 1624–33. Gilt bronze, height 100' (30.48 m). **Chair of Saint Peter** (visible at the back) 1657–66. Gilt bronze, marble, stucco, and glass. **Pier decorations.** 1627–41. Gilt bronze and marble. Located in the crossing of Saint Peter's Basilica, Vatican, Rome

When Urban VIII (Barberini, 1623–1644) was elected pope in 1623, he unhesitatingly gave the young Bernini the task of designing an enormous bronze **baldachin**, or canopy, for the main altar of Saint Peter's. The resulting *Baldacchino* (fig. 14-1), which stands about 100 feet high, exemplifies the Baroque tendency toward grandiose displays. Winding bronze vines decorate twisted columns inspired by columns legended to have come from Solomon's Temple in Jerusalem. The grapevines are an ancient symbol of the wine of the Eucharist. Thus, the columns combine symbolism from Judaism and Christianity; and in the view of Christian scholars, Solomon's Temple supports the Christian Church just as the Old Testament leads to the New. Crowning the structure is an orb and a cross representing the universe and the reign of Christ. The angels and putti, as well as the tasseled panels imitating textiles on the entablature, are all of bronze. These elements not only mark the tomb of Saint Peter but also serve as a tribute to Urban VIII and his family, the

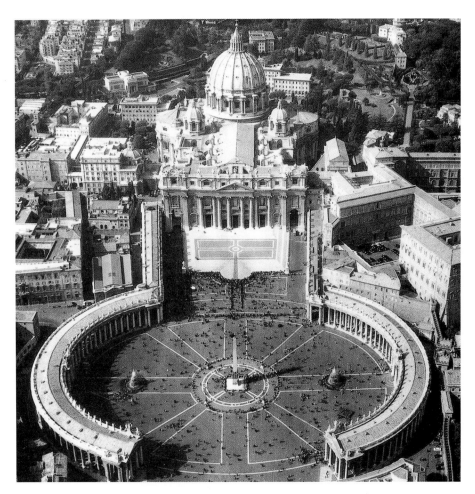

14-2 | **Gianlorenzo Bernini. Saint Peter's Basilica and Square.** Vatican, Rome
Carlo Maderno, facade 1607–15; Bernini, square designed c. 1656–57

Perhaps only a Baroque artist of Bernini's talents could have unified the many styles that come together in Saint Peter's Basilica. The visitor today does not see a piecing together of parts made by different builders at different times, starting with Bramante's original design for the building in the sixteenth century, but rather encounters a triumphal unity of all the parts in one coherent whole.

Barberini, whose emblems—honeybees, suns, laurel leaves—are prominently displayed.

Visible through the *Baldacchino* is the reliquary containing the throne of Saint Peter, an ancient wooden chair, encased in bronze. Known as the Chair of Saint Peter, it symbolizes the direct descent of Christian authority from the apostle Peter to the reigning pope. This belief was rejected by many Protestants and therefore deliberately emphasized in Counter-Reformation Catholicism. The chair is lifted upward by four theologians amid a surge of gilded clouds toward an explosion of angels, putti, and gilded rays of glory. These elements surround a stained-glass window depicting the dove of the Holy Spirit. The actual sunlight and the flickering candles, reflected and multiplied by the polished bronze, are a calculated part of the sculpture. Here Bernini has combined nature and art just as he did in the image of *Saint Teresa of Ávila in Ecstasy* (see pages 350–51).

When Maderno died in 1629, Saint Peter's Basilica was complete as we know it today. However, Bernini, Maderno's collaborator of five years, later designed and supervised the building of a colonnade to enclose the square in front of the church (fig. 14-2). The space that Bernini had to work with was irregular and already contained an Egyptian obelisk (moved there in 1586) and a fountain (to the right, made by Maderno in 1613), which had to be incorporated into the overall plan. In a remarkable design, Bernini framed the square with two enormous, curved covered walkways using giant Doric columns. These connect with two straight but diverging porticoes that lead up a slight incline to the two ends of Maderno's church facade. Later, in 1675, Bernini added a second matching fountain at the left of the obelisk, which serves to further define the vast space.

Bernini spoke of his conception as representing the "motherly arms of the church" reaching out to the world. He intended to build a third section of the colonnade closing the open side facing the church so that pilgrims, after crossing the Tiber River bridge and passing through the narrow streets, would suddenly emerge into the enormous open space in front of the church. Encountered this way, the great church, colonnade, and square, with its towering obelisk and monumental fountains, would have been an even more awe-inspiring sight.

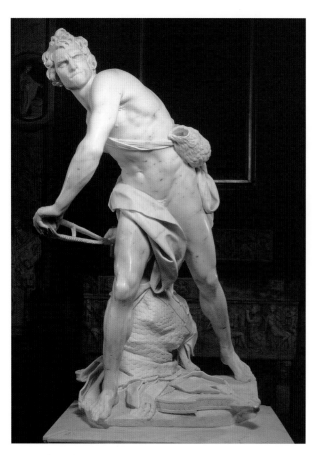

14-3 | Gianlorenzo Bernini. *David*. 1623. Marble, height 5'7" (1.7 m). Galleria Borghese, Rome

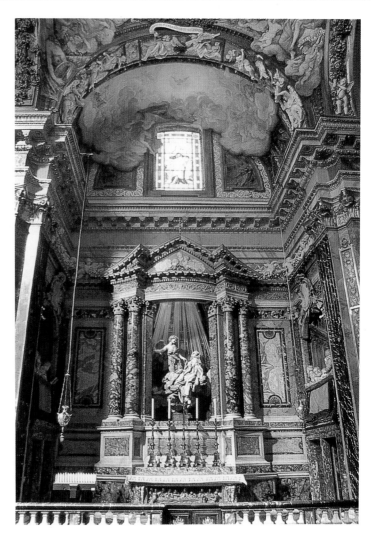

14-4 | Gianlorenzo Bernini. Cornaro Chapel, Church of Santa Maria della Vittoria, Rome. 1642–52. (See pages 350–51.)

Bernini began his career as a sculptor not as an architect, and continued to work in that medium throughout his career for both the papacy and private clients. His sculpture of *David* (fig. 14-3), made for the nephew of Pope Paul V in 1623, introduced a new type of three-dimensional composition that intrudes forcefully on the viewer's space. The young hero bends at the waist and twists far to one side, ready to launch the fatal rock. Unlike Donatello's introspective adolescent (see fig. 12-10) or Michelangelo's composed youth (see fig. 13-7), this more mature David, with his lean, sinewy body, is all tension and determination. His tightly clenched mouth and straining muscles echo his frame of mind, and the energetic figure activates its surrounding space by implying the presence of an unseen adversary.

Even after Bernini's appointment as Vatican architect in 1629, his large workshop enabled him to accept outside commissions, such as the decoration of the funerary chapel of Cardinal Federigo Cornaro in the Church of Santa Maria della Vittoria (fig. 14-4). For this project, carried out from 1642 to 1652, Bernini covered the walls of the tall, shallow chapel with colored marble panels and created the sculptural group of *Saint Teresa of Ávila in Ecstasy* (see pages 350–51) for a huge oval

niche above the altar. On the chapel's back wall, the curved ceiling surrounding the window appears to dissolve into a painted vision of clouds and angels, and on the side walls, kneeling against what appear to be balconies, are portrait statues of members of the Cornaro family. Two are reading from their prayer books; others converse; and one leans out from his seat, apparently to look at someone entering the chapel. Bernini's complex, theatrical interplay of the various levels of illusion in the chapel was imitated by sculptors throughout Europe.

Baroque illusionism reached its peak in ceiling decorations for churches, civic buildings, palaces, and villas. Many ceilings were covered entirely by **trompe l'oeil** (fool the eye) painting, but some were complex constructions combining architecture, painting, and stucco sculpture. A ceiling painted by Annibale Carracci (1560–1609) in the Roman palace of the powerful Farnese family is considered the major monument of early Baroque classicism. Commissioned to celebrate the wedding of Duke Ranuccio Farnese of Parma, it presents an exuberant mythological tribute to earthly love (fig. 14-5). Annibale, cofounder with his family of an art academy in Bologna, was assisted by his brother Agostino (1557–1602) on this spectacular project, painted

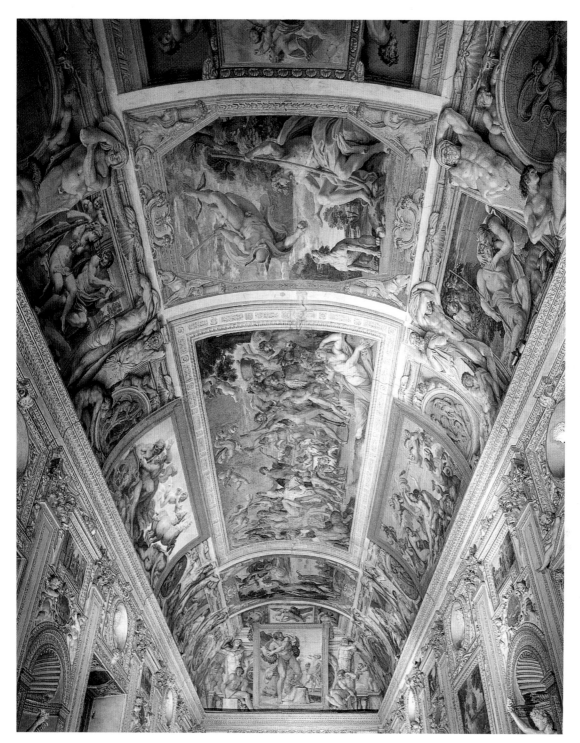

14-5 | **Annibale Carracci. Ceiling fresco of main gallery,** Palazzo Farnese, Rome. 1597–1601

at the turn of the century (1597–1601). The ceiling painting creates the illusion of framed paintings, stone sculpture, bronze medallions, and nude youths in an architectural framework, clearly inspired by Michelangelo's Sistine Ceiling (see figs. 13-8 and 13-9). But instead of Michelangelo's cool illumination and intellectual detachment, the Farnese Ceiling glows with a warm light that recalls the work of the Venetian painters Titian and Veronese. The primary image, set in the center of the vault, is *The Triumph of Bacchus and Ariadne*, a joyous procession cele-

brating the wine god's love for Ariadne, a mortal princess. The ceiling became famous almost immediately.

The Farnese family, proud of the gallery, were generous in allowing young artists to sketch the figures there, so that Annibale Carracci's great work influenced Italian art well into the seventeenth century. The classicism practiced at the academy and demonstrated in the Farnese palace ceiling produced a strong classical strain in Italian Baroque art, exemplified by the painting of Il Guercino (see fig. 15).

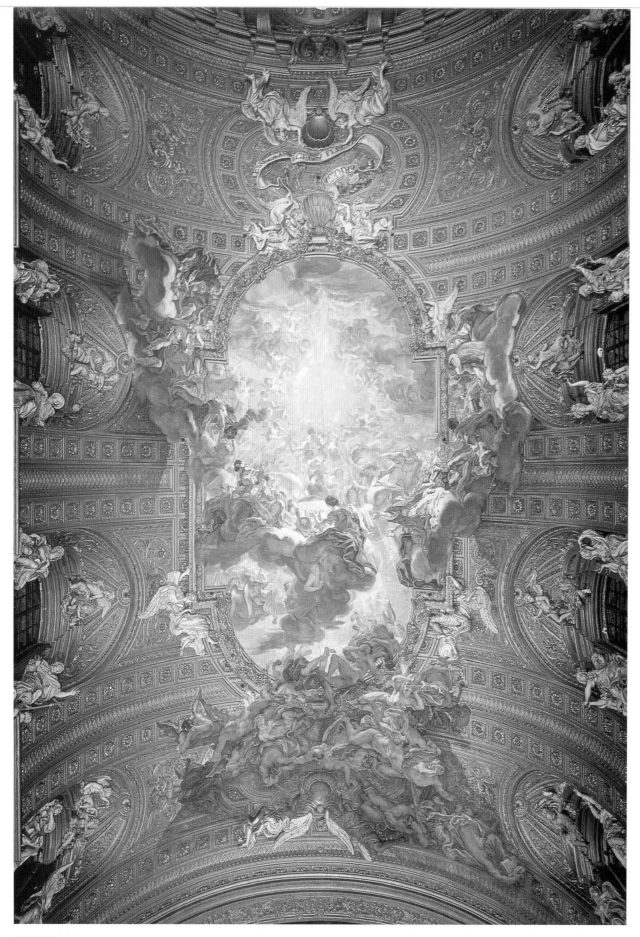

14-6 | **Giovanni Battista Gaulli.** *Triumph of the Name of Jesus,* ceiling fresco with stucco figures in the vault of the Church of Il Gesù, Rome. 1676–79

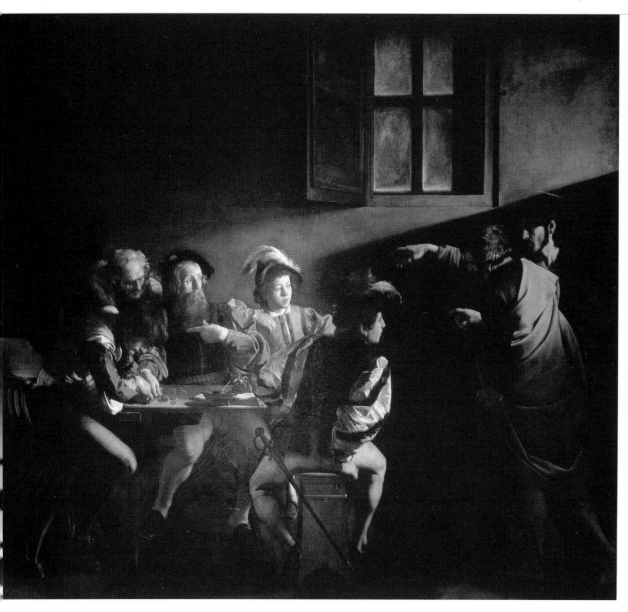

14-7

Caravaggio
*Calling of
Saint Matthew*
in the Contarelli
Chapel, Church
of San Luigi dei
Francesi, Rome
1599–1600
Oil on canvas
11'1" x 11'5"
(3.4 x 3.5 m)

Closer in spirit and style to Bernini's art, and the ultimate illusionistic Baroque ceiling is the *Triumph of the Name of Jesus* (fig. 14-6), which fills the vault of the nave of the Church of Il Gesù, mother church of the Society of Jesus (the Jesuits), in Rome (see fig. 13-27). The vault of Il Gesù had remained unpainted in the seventeenth century. Giovanni Battista Gaulli (1639–1709), also called Baciccio, created the ceiling we see today between 1676 and 1679. The artist had worked in his youth for Bernini, from whom he absorbed a Baroque taste for drama and spectacle.

Gaulli's astonishing creation went beyond anything that had preceded it. Architecture, sculpture, and painting combine to produce the illusion that clouds and angels have floated down through an opening in the church's vault. The whole composition, a Last Judgment, focuses off-center on the golden aura around the letters IHS (barely visible in figure 14-6), a Greek abbreviation for "Jesus," the holy name and symbol of the Jesuits. The elect rise toward the name of God and the damned plummet through the ceiling toward the nave floor. Sculptured angels, actual architectural moldings, and overlapping painted panels extend the frescoed images from the central vault. The

powerful and exciting appeal to the viewer's emotions and the total unity of visual effect have never been surpassed.

Not all Roman Baroque art was meant to overwhelm the viewer by sheer spectacle. Michelangelo Merisi (1571–1610), known as Caravaggio after his birthplace in northern Italy, introduced an intense new realism and a dramatic use of light and gesture to Italian Baroque art. After his arrival in Rome in 1592, Caravaggio painted for a small circle of sophisticated patrons. His subjects from the 1590s include still lifes and scenes featuring fortune-tellers, cardsharpers, and street urchins dressed as musicians or mythological figures. Most of his commissions after 1600 were for religious art, and reactions to these paintings were mixed. On occasion his powerful, sometimes brutal, naturalism was rejected by patrons as unsuitable to the subject's dignity. However, this very realism was closely allied with Counter-Reformation ideas of spirituality, including the meditations, or *Spiritual Exercises*, of Saint Ignatius Loyola (1491–1556), the founder of the Jesuit order. It was also connected to the populist theology of the preacher Filippi Neri, later canonized as Saint Philip Neri (1515–1595), who consciously strove to make Christian history and doctrine meaningful to common people.

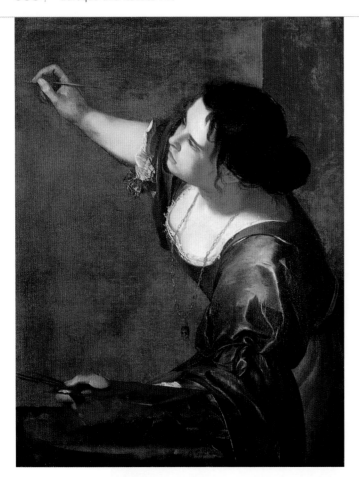

14-8 | Artemisia Gentileschi. *La Pittura,* a self-portrait. 1630. Oil on canvas, 38 x 29" (96.5 x 73.7 cm). The Royal Collection Windsor Castle, Windsor, England

of Design. Her paintings, like Caravaggio's, feature large figures set close to the picture plane and illuminated by the light source (often a lamp or candle) outside the picture that creates strong contrasts of light and dark.

In 1630 she painted *La Pittura*, an **allegory** on the art of painting (fig. 14-8). The image of a richly dressed woman, her hair loose, wearing a gold necklace with a mask pendant, follows the description of painting in *Iconologia* by Cesare Ripa, a popular source-book for images during the Baroque period. According to Ripa, wild hair denotes inspiration, the mask imitates the human face as painting imitates nature, and the gold chain symbolizes the continuous chain of relationships as each artist builds on the work of predecessors and carries this achievement into the future. Artemisia's allegory is also a self-portrait in which she commemorated her profession and paid tribute to her father and first teacher. After assisting her father in England, she eventually settled in Naples where she died in 1652.

Art for the Secular State: France

The princes of the Church were not the only patrons of the arts in the seventeenth century, which saw the growth of the nation-state and absolute monarchy. Kings and nobles realized that impressive buildings and splendid portraits could secure and enhance their status by surrounding them with an aura of power. Patronage of the arts became expected of an absolute monarch, and following the example of King Louis XIV of France, the rulers of Europe built and rebuilt their palaces, planted vast gardens, and spent fortunes on paintings, sculpture, and the decorative arts.

The early seventeenth century was a difficult period in France, marked by almost continuous foreign and civil wars. King Henry IV was assassinated in 1610, and the country endured a long regency during the youth of Henry's nine-year-old heir, Louis XIII (ruled 1610–1643). Louis XIV (ruled 1643–1715) also inherited the throne as a youth, beginning his personal rule only in 1661. An absolute monarch whose reign was the longest in European history, Louis XIV became known as *le Roi Soleil*, or "the Sun King." He was sometimes glorified in art through parallels drawn between him and the classical sun god, Apollo. In a 1701 portrait by the French court painter Hyacinthe Rigaud (1659–1743), the richly costumed monarch is revealed by an unseen hand pulling aside a billowing curtain (fig. 14-9). Showing off his elegant legs, of which he was quite proud, the sixty-three-year-old Louis XIV poses in a robe trimmed with gold fleurs-de-lis and white ermine and wears the high-heeled shoes he invented to compensate for his shortness. Despite the commanding pose and magnificent surroundings, the directness of the king's gaze and the realism of his aging face make him movingly human and testify to Rigaud's genius for portraiture.

Under Louis XIV's lavish patronage of the arts, the French court became the envy of every ruler in Europe. The Royal Academy of Painting and Sculpture, founded in 1648, maintained strict national control over the arts, and membership ensured an artist lucrative royal and civic commissions. Although the French Academy was not the first in Europe, none before it had exerted such dictatorial authority—an authority that lasted in France

Caravaggio painted one of his earliest religious commissions, the *Calling of Saint Matthew* (fig. 14-7; see page 357), during the years 1599–1600 for the private chapel of the Cointrel family (Contarelli in Italian) in the French community's church in Rome. The painting depicts the moment recorded in the Gospels when Jesus called the tax collector Levi to become one of his apostles (Mark 2:14, Matthew 9:9). Nearly hidden behind the beckoning Saint Peter, the gaunt-faced Jesus dramatically points toward Levi—who will become Saint Matthew—but who is now surrounded by overdressed young men in plumed hats, velvet doublets, and satin shirts. For all the naturalism of these figures, Caravaggio also used antique and Renaissance sources. Jesus' outstretched arm, for example, recalls God's gesture of giving life to Adam in Michelangelo's *Creation of Adam* on the Sistine Ceiling (see fig. 13-9). The future Saint Matthew responds by pointing to himself in surprise, a gesture emphasized by the stream of light entering the painting from a high, unseen source at the right. The dramatic contrast of light and dark is a heightened variant of chiaroscuro known as **tenebrism**, an invention of Caravaggio.

Caravaggio inspired an entire generation of painters with his tenebrist technique and his intense realism. One of his most successful Italian followers was Artemisia Gentileschi (1593–1652). Born in Rome, Artemisia first studied and worked under her father, an excellent though conservative artist. Later in Florence, she was elected at age twenty-three to the Florentine Academy

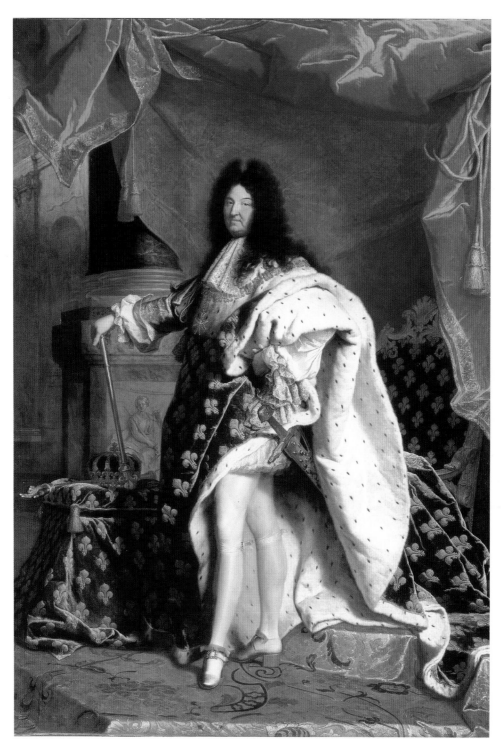

14-9   **Hyacinthe Rigaud. *Louis XIV.*** 1701. Oil on canvas
9'2" x 7'10½" (2.79 x 2.40 m). Musée du Louvre, Paris

until the late nineteenth century (see "Grading the Old Masters," page 360). Classicism enjoyed particular favor in the academy and permeates French Baroque painting, sculpture, and architecture. When the Royal Academy of Architecture was founded in 1671, its members developed guidelines for architectural design based on the belief that mathematics was the true basis of beauty, with Vitruvius (see "Vitruvian Man," page 316) and Palladio (see fig. 13-18) as their models.

In 1668, Louis XIV turned his attention to enlarging a small hunting lodge, a château built by Louis XIII at Versailles. The changes Louis XIV commanded consumed the energy of France's greatest painters, sculptors, designers, and architects for decades. For both political and sentimental reasons, the old Versailles château was left standing, and the new building went up around it under the direction first of Louis Le Vau (1612–1670) beginning in 1668, and then after his death, of

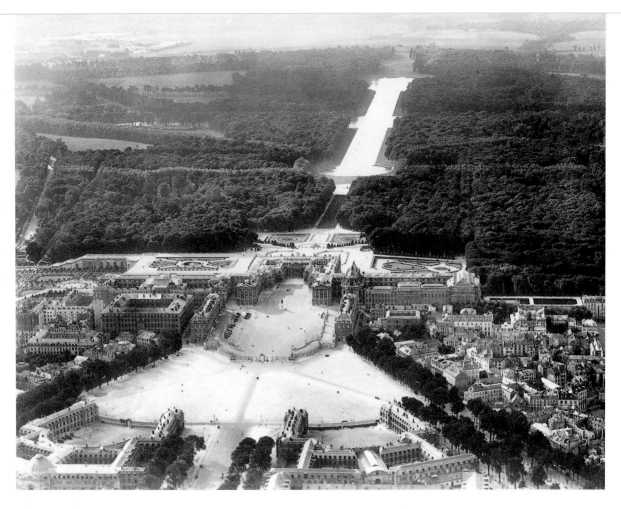

14-10

Louis Le Vau and **Jules Hardouin-Mansart. Palais de Versailles** Versailles France. Gardens by André Le Nôtre. 1668–85

Jules Hardouin-Mansart (1646–1708) (fig. 14-10). Concurrently, André Le Nôtre (1613–1700), who planned the gardens, turned the terrain around the palace into an extraordinary work of art, destined to have a powerful influence on urban as well as garden design. Neatly contained expanses of lawn and broad, straight vistas seem to stretch to the horizon, while the formal gardens immediately behind the palace are an exercise in precise geometry. From these gardens, terraces descend to shaped, wooded areas and the mile-long Grand Canal. Classically harmo-nious and restful in their symmetrical, geometric design, the Versailles gardens are Baroque in their vast size and extension into the surrounding countryside.

Residents and visitors to the château could admire the gardens from an arcaded rear terrace designed by Le Vau. In his renovations, Hardouin-Mansart enclosed this previously open space, turning it into an immense gallery known as the Hall of Mirrors (fig. 14-11). He lit the hall, which is about 240 feet long (73.15 m), with seventeen immense arched windows,

GRADING THE OLD MASTERS

The members of the French Royal Academy of Painting and Sculpture considered ancient classical art the standard by which contemporary art should be judged. By the 1680s, however, younger artists began to argue that modern art might equal and even surpass the art of the ancients. A debate also arose over the relative merits of drawing and color in painting. The conservatives argued that drawing was superior because it appealed to the mind, while color appealed to the senses. They saw the work of Nicolas Poussin as perfectly embodying the classical principles of subject and design. The young artists, who admired the vivid colors of Titian, Veronese, and Peter Paul Rubens, claimed that paint-ing should deceive the eye, and since color achieves this deception more convincingly than drawing, color should be valued over drawing. The two factions were called the *poussinistes* (in honor of Poussin) and the *rubénistes* (for Rubens).

The portrait painter and critic Roger de Piles (1635–1709) published his views in a series of pamphlets in which he took up the cause of the *rubénistes*. In *The Principles of Painting*, de Piles evaluated the most important painters on a scale of 0 to 20. He gave no score higher than 18, since no mortal could possibly achieve perfection. Caravaggio received the lowest grade, a 0 in expression and 6 in drawing, while Michelangelo and Leonardo both got a 4 in color and Rembrandt a 6 in drawing. Top grades (18) went to Titian for color, Rubens for composition, and Raphael for drawing and expression.

If we work out the "grades" using the traditional scale of 90% = A, 80% = B, and so forth, most of the painters we have studied don't do very well. Raphael and Rubens get A's; but no one seems to get a B, although Van Dyck might be considered close with a C plus. Poussin and Titian earn solid C's, while Rembrandt slips by with a C minus. Leonardo gets a D, and Michelangelo, Dürer, and Caravaggio all are resounding failures in de Piles's view. Tastes change, and someday our ideas may seem just as misguided as those of the academicians.

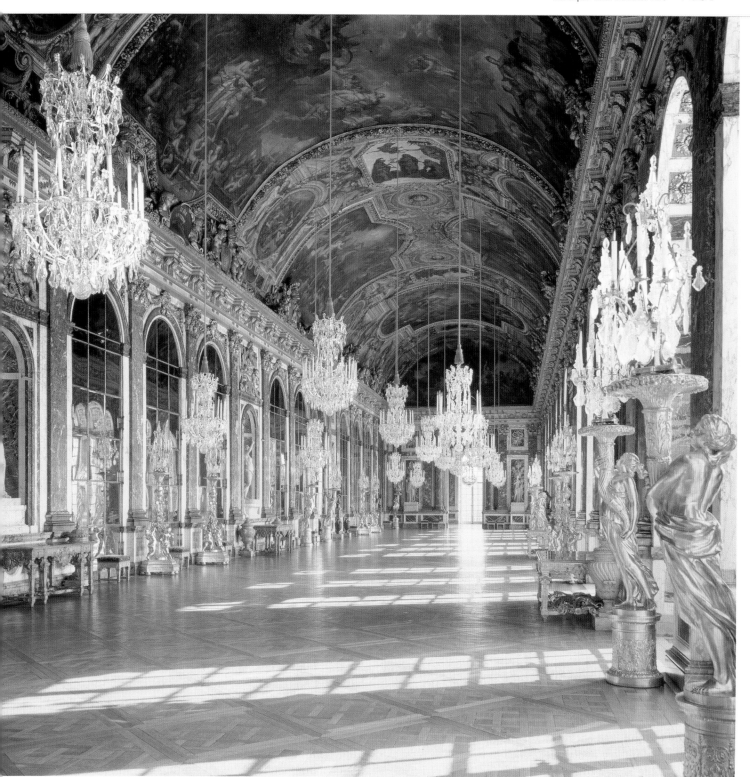

14-11 | **Jules Hardouin-Mansart** and **Charles Le Brun. Hall of Mirrors,** Palais de Versailles. Begun 1678

lining the opposite wall with Venetian glass mirrors—enormous-ly expensive in the seventeenth century—of exactly the same size and shape. The mirrors reflect the natural light from the win-dows and give the impression of an even larger space. In a trib-ute to Carracci's Farnese Ceiling (see fig. 14-5), the painter Charles Le Brun (1619–1690), a founding member of the Royal Academy of Painting and Sculpture, decorated the vaulted ceil-ing with paintings glorifying the reign of Louis XIV. The under-lying theme for the design and decoration of the palace was the glorification of the king as the sun god Apollo.

French seventeenth-century painting was much affected by developments in Italian art. The important painter Nicolas Poussin (1594–1665) worked for French patrons but pursued his career in Italy. As a dedicated classicist, he did not paint the landscape as he saw it but instead organized nature, build-ings, and figures into idealized compositions. Thus, Poussin's

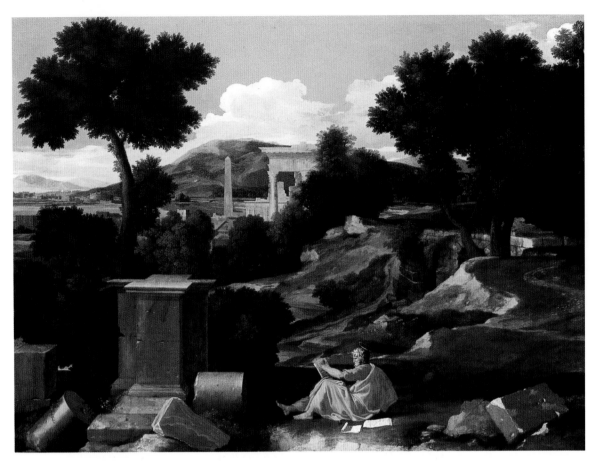

14-12   **Nicolas Poussin,** French, 1594-1665. ***Landscape with Saint John on Patmos.*** 1640. Oil on canvas, 39½" x 53¾" (100.3 x 136.4 cm).
The Art Institute of Chicago, A.A. Munger Collection, (1930.500)

Landscape with Saint John on Patmos (fig. 14-12), from 1640, appears orderly and admirably arranged. The artist has created a consistent perspective progression from the picture plane back into the distance through a clearly defined **foreground**, **middle ground**, and **background**. These zones are marked by alternating sunlight and shade, as well as by architectural elements in the Roman or Renaissance styles. Some of Poussin's landscapes are of identifiable sites, but this scene incorporates both real and imaginary buildings. In the middle distance are a ruined temple and an obelisk, while the round building set down in the distant city is Hadrian's tomb from Rome (barely visible here). Precisely placed trees, hills, mountains, water, and even clouds have a solidity of form that suggests architecture. The reclining Saint John, and his symbol, the eagle, to the right of him, seem almost incidental to this perfect landscape. The subject of Poussin's painting is in effect the balance and order of nature rather than the story of the saint. Poussin's classical style became the basis of French academic art.

The Habsburg Empire in Spain and Flanders

Spain's Habsburg kings in the seventeenth century—Philip III, Philip IV, and Charles II—presided over the political and economic decline of the Spanish Empire. Agriculture, industry, and trade all suffered, and there were repeated local rebellions, culminating in 1640, when Portugal reestablished its independence. Protestant England and the Dutch Republic were an increasingly serious threat to Spanish trade and colonial possessions, and what had seemed an endless flow of gold and silver from the Americas diminished.

In spite of economic decline, artists and writers created a "Golden Age" and one of the most brilliant painters of any age appeared on the scene. Diego Rodríguez de Silva y Velázquez (1599–1660) had entered the painters' guild of Seville in 1617. Like many artists in Spain and Spanish-ruled Naples in the early seventeenth century, at the beginning of his career he looked to the Italian Caravaggio. Velázquez painted taverns,

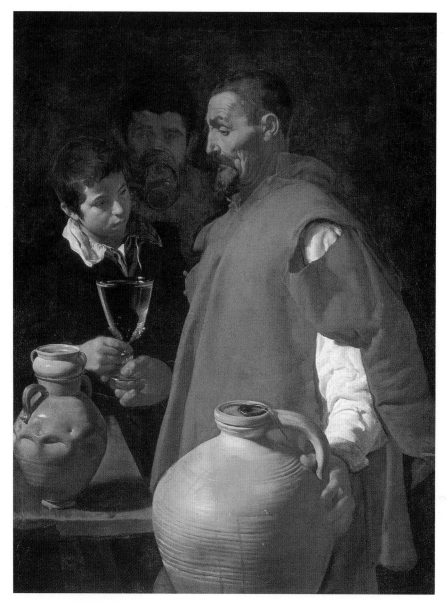

14-13 | Diego Velázquez. *Water Carrier of Seville.* c. 1619. Oil on canvas, 41½ x 31½" (105.3 x 80 cm). Wellington Museum, London

In the oppressively hot climate of Seville, Spain, where this painting was made, water vendors walked the streets selling their cool liquid from large clay jars like the one in the foreground. In this scene, the clarity and purity of the water are proudly attested to by its seller, who offers the customer a sample poured into a glass goblet. The jug contents were usually sweetened by the addition of a piece of fresh fruit or a sprinkle of aromatic herbs.

markets, or kitchens, showing ordinary people and still lifes of various foods and kitchen utensils. Velázquez sketched from life; for example the model for the *Water Carrier of Seville* (fig. 14-13), a painting of about 1619, was a well-known character in the city. The objects and figures in the painting, arranged with an almost mathematical rigor, allowed the artist to exhibit his virtuosity in rendering sculptural volumes and contrasting textures such as pottery, glass, hair, and fabric. All the elements in the picture are illuminated by dramatic

natural light in Velázquez's version of Caravaggio's tenebrism.

In 1623, Velázquez moved to Madrid, where he became courtier and official painter for the young Habsburg monarch Philip IV (ruled 1621–1665), a powerful position that he maintained until his death in 1660. The artist's style evolved significantly over his long career, stimulated in part by visits to Italy in 1629–31 and again in 1649–51.

Perhaps Velázquez's most striking and enigmatic work is the enormous multiple portrait, known as *Las Meninas*, or *The*

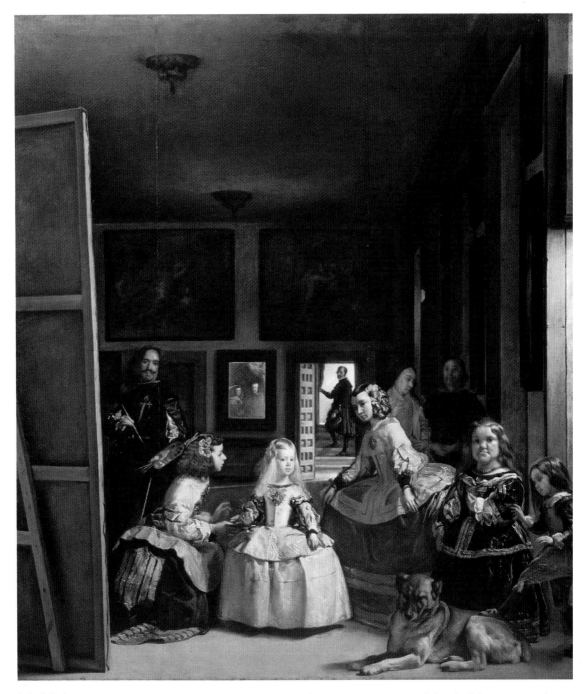

14-14 | Diego Velázquez. *Las Meninas (The Maids of Honor)*. 1656. Oil on canvas, 10'5" x 9'1/2" (3.18 x 2.76 m) Museo del Prado, Madrid

Maids of Honor, painted in 1656, near the end of the artist's life (fig. 14-14). Here, Velázquez draws the spectator directly into the complex composition. The viewer seems to stand in the space occupied by King Philip and his queen, whose reflections can be seen in the large mirror on the back wall. Velázquez himself is also present, brushes and palette in hand, beside a huge canvas. However, the central focus of the painting is on the royal couple's five-year-old daughter, the Infanta (Princess) Margarita. She is surrounded by her attendants, all of whom are identifiable portraits. In a bravura style of painting that fascinated the French Impressionist painters in the nineteenth

century (see fig. 18-19), Velázquez built up his forms with layers of loosely applied paint and finished off the surfaces with dashing highlights in white, lemon, and pale orange. His technique captures the appearance of light on surfaces, while on close inspection his forms dissolve into a complex maze of individual strokes of paint.

The sobriety and rigorous geometry of Velázquez's compositions contrast with later manifestations of Spanish Baroque art. In architecture, a profusion of ornament swept into fashion through the work of a family of architects and sculptors named Churriguera. The style, known as **churrigueresque,**

Elements of Architecture

THE BAROQUE CHURCH FACADE

In the seventeenth and eighteenth centuries architects reinterpreted the classical vocabulary of the Renaissance in ways that emphasized the power and grandeur of the church and state. Vigorously projecting and receding walls, columns, and pediments in the elevation and the profusion of sculptural ornament overall create an arresting theatrical display. Portals become special focal points where the vertical composition of doors and windows can become a lavish sculptural creation. By the eighteenth century buildings like Pedro de Ribera's Hospice of San Fernando in Madrid (see fig. 14-15) had a principal portal heavily encrusted with elaborate carved ornament. Carved stone swags seem to part like curtains to reveal a profusion of broken pediments and cornices, niches, cartouches, pilasters, foliage, figures, and finials. Elaborate late Baroque styles spread through the Habsburg territories and even reached the colonies in America.

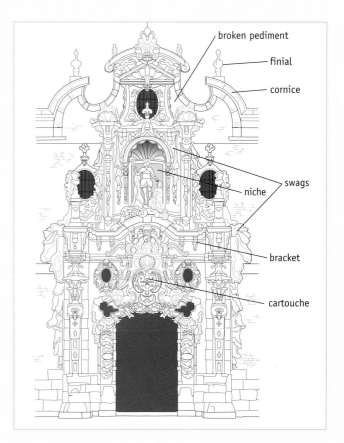

Pedro de Ribera. **Facade elevation of the Portal of the Hospicio de San Fernando,** Madrid. 1722

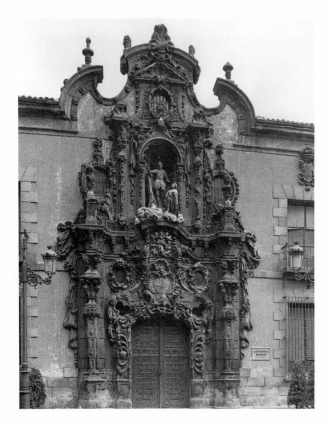

14-15 | Pedro de Ribera. **Portal of the Hospicio de San Fernando,** Madrid. 1722

found its most exuberant expression in the work of eighteenth-century architects such as Pedro de Ribera (c. 1638–1742). Ribera's 1722 facade for the Hospicio de San Fernando in Madrid concentrates an elaborate sculptural scheme on the portal (fig. 14-15). Like a huge altarpiece, the portal soars upward, breaking through the roofline into semicircular and triangular pediments. The structural forms of classical architecture are transformed into projecting and receding layers overlaid with foliage. Carved curtains loop back as if to reveal the doorway and central niche, which holds the figure of the hospital's patron saint. This florid style also inspired the architecture of the Spanish colonies of Mexico and Peru.

The Spanish Habsburgs also held Flanders during most of the Baroque period. After a period of relative autonomy under a Habsburg regent from 1598 to 1621 the country came under direct and often oppressive Spanish rule. In spite of the shift in political climate, artists of great talent flourished in Antwerp, the capital city and major art center, where the Spanish were enthusiastic patrons of the arts. The painting of Peter Paul Rubens (1577–1640) who worked for the Habsburgs

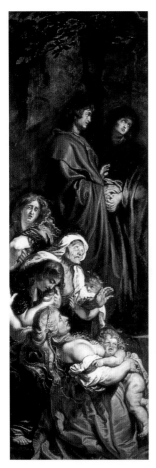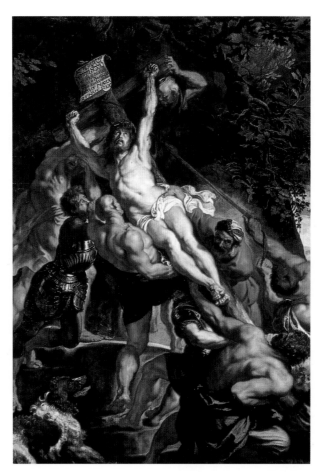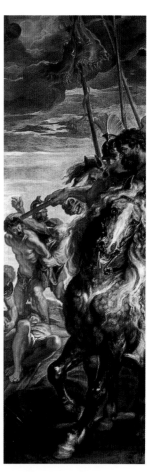

14-16 | **Peter Paul Rubens.** *The Raising of the Cross*, painted for the Church of Saint Walpurga, Antwerp, Belgium. 1609–10. Oil on canvas, center panel 15'1⁷/₈" x 11'1¹/₂" (4.62 x 3.39 m); each wing 15'1⁷/₈" x 4'11⁷/₈" (4.62 x 1.52 m). Cathedral of Our Lady, Antwerp

and other rulers, has become nearly synonymous with the Flemish Baroque style. Rubens was accepted into the Antwerp painters' guild at the age of twenty-one, and shortly thereafter, in 1600, he left for Italy, where he obtained a post with the duke of Mantua. Other than designs for court entertainment and occasional portraits, the duke never acquired a single original work of art by Rubens. Instead, he had him copy famous paintings in collections all over Italy to add to the ducal collection, and so inadvertently provided the young painter with an excellent education.

Rubens returned in 1608 to Antwerp, where he accepted employment from the Habsburg governors of Flanders. His first major commission was a large canvas triptych for the main altar of the Church of Saint Walpurga, *The Raising of the Cross* (fig. 14-16), painted in 1609–10. Unlike many earlier triptychs, where the wings contained related but independent images, Rubens extended the action and landscape of the central scene across all three sections. At the center, Herculean figures strain to haul upright the wooden cross with Jesus already stretched upon it. The followers of Jesus mourn at left, and indifferent soldiers on the right supervise the execution. In his paintings Rubens merges the drama and intense emo-

tion of Caravaggio with the virtuoso technique of Annibale Carracci, but he transforms these qualities into a distinctive personal style. The heroic nude figures, dramatic lighting effects, dynamic diagonal composition, and intense emotions show the artist's debt to Italian art, but the rich colors and the realism of the varied textures and forms reflect his native Flemish tradition.

Rubens's intelligence, courtly manners, and personal charm made him a valuable and trusted courtier to royal patrons, including Philip IV of Spain, Marie de' Medici of France, and Charles I of England. He became the first international superstar of the art world. In 1621, Marie de' Medici, widow of King Henri IV and regent for her young son, Louis XIII, asked Rubens to paint the story of her life. In twenty-one paintings, Rubens glorified her role in ruling France and also commemorated the founding of the Bourbon dynasty, which began with Henri IV. In Rubens's paintings the lives and political careers of Marie and Henri appear as one continuous triumph overseen by the Roman gods. In the painting depicting the royal engagement (fig. 14-17), Henri IV falls in love with Marie as he gazes at her portrait, shown to him by Cupid and the god of marriage, Hymen. The supreme Roman god, Jupiter, and his wife, Juno, look down

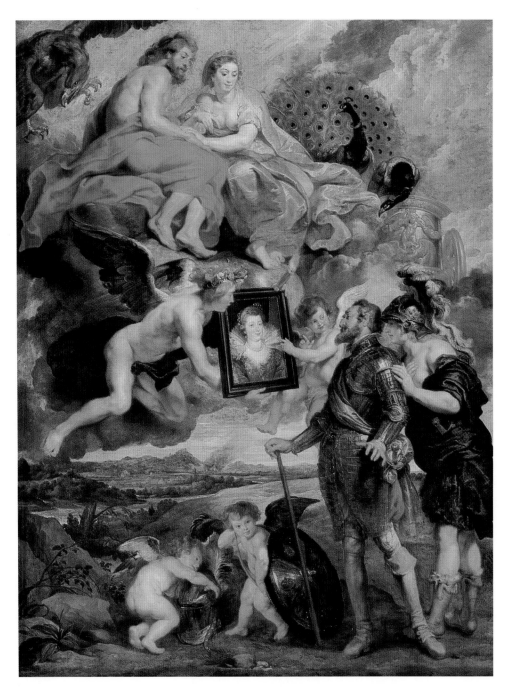

14-17 | **Peter Paul Rubens.** *Henri IV Receiving the Portrait of Marie de' Medici.* 1621–25. Oil on canvas, 12'11¹⁄₈" x 9'8¹⁄₈" (3.94 x 2.95 m). Musée du Louvre, Paris

approvingly from the clouds. Henri, silhouetted against a landscape in which the smoke of battle lingers, is encouraged by a personification of France to abandon war for love, as putti frolic with pieces of his armor. The sustained visual excitement of these enormous canvases makes them not only important works of art but political propaganda of the highest order.

Rubens, who accepted commissions from all over Europe, employed dozens of assistants as specialists in the painting of fruit and flowers, textiles, landscapes, even portraits. Using workshop assistants was standard practice among major artists, but Rubens was particularly efficient, and created something

close to a painting factory. Working from his detailed sketches, his assistants completed giant canvases suitable for palatial rooms. Among these assistants who were, or became, important painters in their own right are Jan Brueghel (see fig. 14-18) and Anthony van Dyck (see fig. 14-19).

Jan Brueghel (1568–1625), the grandson of Pieter Bruegel (see fig. 13-36) (Jan added the "h" to the family name) was Rubens's neighbor. The two artists frequently collaborated, Rubens rendering the figures and Brueghel creating allegorical settings for them. About 1617 Rubens and Brueghel painted five allegories on the theme of the senses for the rulers of the

CLOSER LOOK

Of the five paintings in the series of the *Senses*, painted for the Habsburg rulers, *Sight* (fig. 14-18) is the most splendid. It is almost an illustrated catalog of the ducal collection. Gathered in a huge vaulted room are paintings, sculpture, furniture, objects in gold and silver, and scientific equipment—all under the magnificent double headed eagle emblems of the Habsburgs. The viewer is encouraged to explore the painting *Sight* inch by inch, as if reading a book or a palace inventory. There on the table are Brueghel's copies of Rubens's portraits of Archduke Albert and Princess Isabel Clara Eugenia; another portrait of the duke is on the floor. Besides the portraits, we can find Rubens's *Daniel in the Lions' Den* (upper left corner), *The Lion and Tiger Hunt* (top center), and *The Drunken Silenus* (lower right) as well as the popular subject *Madonna and Child in a Wreath of Flowers* (far right), for which Rubens

painted the Madonna and Brueghel created the wreath. Brueghel also included Raphael's *Saint Cecilia* (behind the globe) and Titian's *Venus and Psyche* (over the door).

In the foreground, the classical goddess Venus attended by Cupid (both painted by Rubens) has put aside her mirror to contemplate Jan Brueghel's painting *Christ Healing the Blind*. Venus is surrounded by the equipment needed to see and to study: the huge globe at the right and the sphere with its gleaming rings at the upper left symbolize the extent of humanistic learning. In symbolism that speaks to viewers of our day as clearly as it did to those during Rubens's and Brueghel's day, the books and prints, ruler, compasses, magnifying glass, and the more complex astrolabe, telescope, and eyeglasses refer to those who look but do not see, that is, to spiritual blindness.

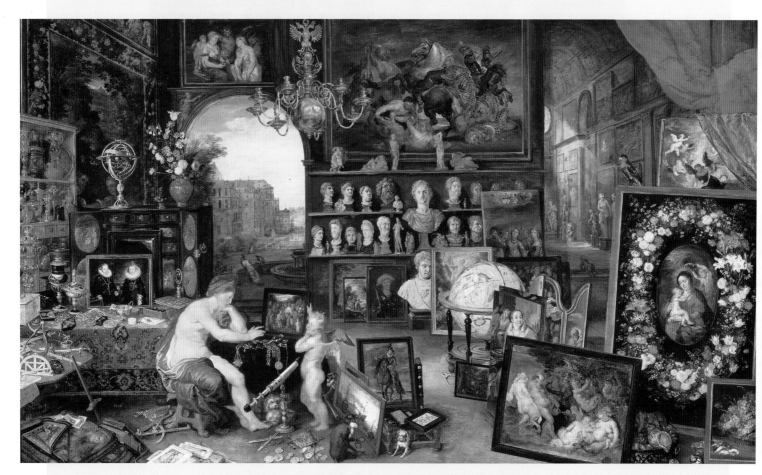

14-18 | **Jan Brueghel** and **Peter Paul Rubens.** *Sight*, from *Allegories of the Five Senses.* c. 1617–18. Oil on panel 25⅝ x 43" (65 x 109 cm). Museo del Prado, Madrid

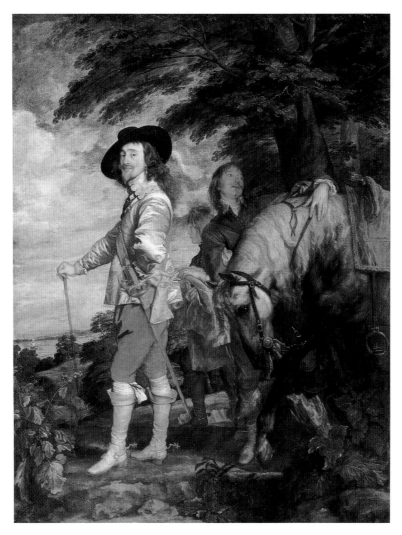

14-19

Anthony van
Dyck. *Charles I
at the Hunt*
1635. Oil on
canvas, 9 x 7'
(2.75 x 2.14 m)
Musée du
Louvre, Paris

Habsburg Netherlands, the Spanish princess Isabel Clara Eugenia and the Austrian archduke Albert. These rulers were great patrons of the arts and sciences and were friends of artists—especially Peter Paul Rubens (fig. 14-18).

Another of Rubens's collaborators, Anthony van Dyck (1599–1641), had an illustrious independent career as a portraitist. A precocious student at ten, he had his own studio and a roster of pupils at age sixteen, although he did not become a member of the Antwerp painters' guild until 1618, the year after he began his association with Rubens as a painter of heads. Later in his career, Van Dyck became court painter to Charles I of England, by whom he was knighted and given a studio, a summer home, and a large salary.

In *Charles I at the Hunt* (fig. 14-19) of 1635, Van Dyck was able, by clever manipulation of the setting, to portray the king truthfully and yet as a quietly imposing figure. Dressed casually for the hunt and standing on a bluff overlooking a distant view, Charles, who was in fact a very small person, is shown as being taller than his pages and even than his horse, since the animal has lowered its head, and its heavy body is partly off the canvas. The viewer's gaze is directed to his pleasant features, framed by his jauntily cocked hat. As if in decorous homage, the tree branches bow gracefully toward him, echoing the circular lines of the hat.

Protestant England

England and Scotland had been joined under a Stuart monarch since the death of the imposing Queen Elizabeth I (ruled 1558–1603), when James VI of Scotland ascended the English throne as James I (ruled 1603–1625). James's son, Charles I (ruled 1625–1649), was a better patron of the arts than he was a politician and king.

In 1615 King James I appointed the architect Inigo Jones surveyor-general and commissioned him to design a residence for his queen in Greenwich and a banqueting house for the royal palace of Whitehall in London. Jones (1573–1652) introduced Renaissance classicism to England. His architectural style was based on the work of the Renaissance architect Andrea Palladio (see Chapter 13). Jones had studied Palladio's buildings in Venice and owned a copy of the Italian architect's famous treatise, the *Four Books of Architecture*.

The Whitehall Banqueting House, constructed in 1619–22 to replace an earlier building destroyed by fire, exemplifies the understated elegance of Jones's interpretation of Palladian

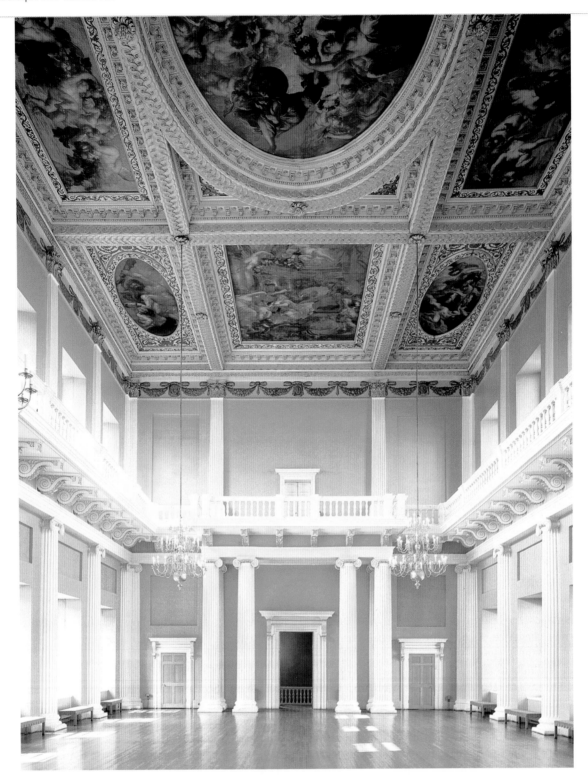

14-20 | **Interior, Banqueting House, Whitehall Palace.** Ceiling painting of the apotheosis of King James and the glorification of the Stuart monarchy by Peter Paul Rubens. 1630–35. The architect was Inigo Jones.

design. The Banqueting House was used for court entertainments and ceremonies (fig. 14-20). The building is one large hall with a balcony on the upper level, and antechambers at each end, one of which contains the entrance. Ionic pilasters suggest a colonnade but do not impinge on the ideal, double-cube space. In 1630, Charles I commissioned Peter Paul Rubens to decorate the ceiling. Jones had divided its flat surface into nine compartments, for which Rubens painted canvases glorifying the

reign of James I, with a classical apotheosis of the king and the Stuart dynasty. So proud was Charles of the pictures, installed in 1635, that, rather than allow the smoke of candles and torches to darken them, he moved the evening entertainments to an adjacent pavilion.

Religious and political tensions, particularly a conflict between Charles and the religious reformers known as Puritans, resulted in a series of civil wars, beginning in 1642.

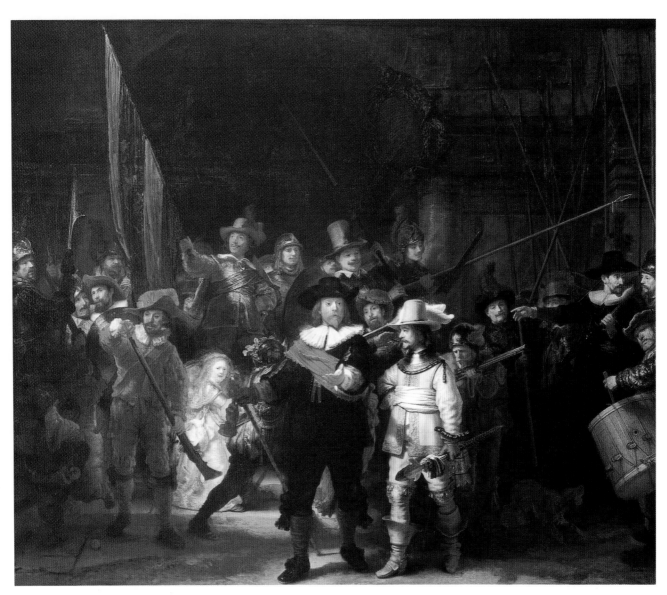

14-21 | Rembrandt van Rijn. *Captain Frans Banning Cocq Mustering His Company (The Night Watch).* 1642. Oil on canvas (cut down from the original size), 11'11" x 14'4" (3.63 x 4.37 m). Rijksmuseum, Amsterdam

Charles lost his throne, and his head, in 1649. Now in power, the Puritans, led by Oliver Cromwell as lord protector, stifled artistic expression. In 1660 the restoration of the Stuart dynasty under Charles II brought renewed patronage of foreign artists, especially portrait painters. In the eighteenth century, the Hanoverian kings, George I, II, and III, gave the name Georgian to art and architecture in the British Isles and the North American colonies.

The Protestant Netherlands

Spain recognized the sovereignty of the northern Netherlands in 1648. Even before this official recognition, the Dutch Republic, as the united northern provinces of the Low Countries were officially known, managed not only to maintain its hard-won freedom but to prosper. Dutch artists found many eager patrons among the prosperous middle-class citizens of Amsterdam, Leiden, Haarlem, Delft, and Utrecht.

The most important painter working in the Netherlands in the seventeenth century was Rembrandt van Rijn (1606–1669).

After studying painting in Amsterdam and Leiden and working as an artist in both cities, Rembrandt established a busy studio in Amsterdam. He continued his studies with close observation of the art of his predecessors, such as his analysis (see fig. 18) of Leonardo's *Last Supper* (see figs. 19, 13-1) as well as intense observation of the world around him. His repertoire included paintings and etchings of mythological subjects, religious scenes, and landscapes, but like many artists in Protestant Holland his primary source of income was portraiture.

In 1640 a civic guard company commissioned Rembrandt to create a large group portrait of its members for its new meeting hall. *Captain Frans Banning Cocq Mustering His Company* (fig. 14-21) was traditionally known as *The Night Watch* because a layer of dirt and old varnish obscured its colors in the nineteenth century so that viewers thought they saw a night scene. After recent cleaning and restoration, the painting glows with a natural golden light that sets afire the palette of rich colors—browns, blues, olive green, orange, and red—around a central

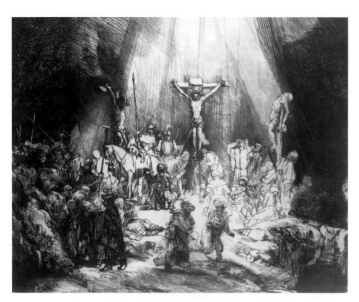

14-22 | **Rembrandt van Rijn.** *The Three Crosses* (first state) 1663. Drypoint and engraving. 15¹/₆ x 17³/₄" (38.5 x 45 cm). Rijksmuseum, Amsterdam

14-23 | **Rembrandt van Rijn.** *Self-Portrait* 1659. Oil on canvas, 33¹/₄ x 26" (84.5 x 66 cm). National Gallery of Art, Washington, D.C.
Andrew W. Mellon Collection (37.1.72)

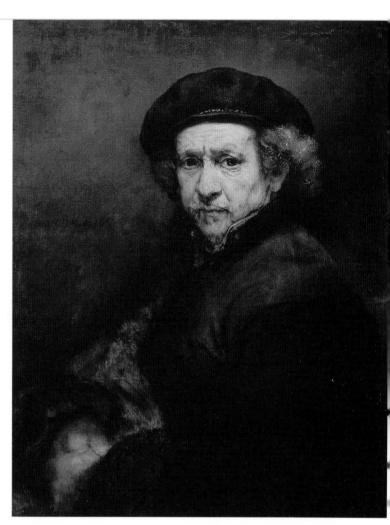

TECHNIQUE
Woodcuts and Engravings on Metal

Rembrandt was the first artist to popularize **etching** as a major form of artistic expression. In the etching process, a metal plate is coated on both sides with an acid-resistant resin that dries hard without being brittle. Then, instead of laboriously cutting the lines of the desired image directly into the plate, the artist draws through the resin with a sharp needle to expose the metal. The plate is then immersed in acid, which eats into the metal exposed by the drawn lines. By controlling the time the acid stays on different parts of the plate, the artist can make fine, shallow lines or heavy, deep ones. The resin covering the plate is removed before an **impression** is taken. If a change needs to be made, the lines can be "erased" with a sharp metal scraper. Not surprisingly, a complex image with a wide range of tones requires many steps.

Another technique for registering images on a metal plate is called **drypoint**. A sharp needle is used to scratch lines in the metal. In drypoint, however, the burr, or metal pushed up by the drypoint needle, is left in place. Unlike engraving where the burr is scraped off, both the burr and the groove hold the ink. To the unaided eye, the rich black appearance of the printed line is impossible to achieve with engraving or

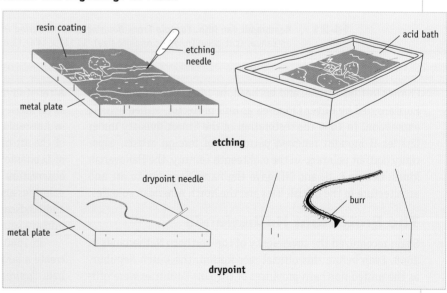

etching. Unfortunately, drypoint burr is fragile, and only a few prints—a dozen or fewer—can be made before it flattens and loses its character. Rembrandt's earliest prints were pure etchings, but later he enriched his prints with drypoint to achieve greater tonal richness.

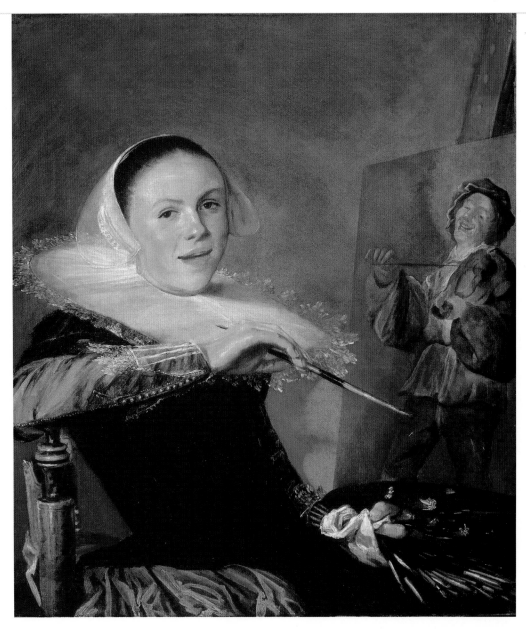

14-24

Judith Leyster
Self-Portrait. 1635
Oil on canvas, 29½
x 25¾" (74.9 x
65.4 cm). National
Gallery of Art
Washington, D.C.
Widener Collection
(49.6.1)

core of lemon yellow. As the company takes up its ranks, the crowd, including children, mill around. The surprising image of the running girl carrying a chicken with claws (*klauw* in Dutch) prominently displayed may be a pun on the name of the guns (*klover*) that gave the name Kloveniers to the company. The complex interactions of the figures and the vivid, individualized likenesses of the militiamen make this painting one of the greatest group portraits in European art.

Rembrandt also created profoundly moving religious art. His **etchings** and **drypoints** (see "Woodcuts and Engravings on Metal," left) were sought after, widely collected, and brought high prices even in his lifetime. As he grew older, Rembrandt seems to have experienced a deepening religious belief, perhaps based on his study of the Bible. In a series of states (versions) of his print the *Three Crosses*, Rembrandt tried to capture the moment during the Crucifixion, as described in the Gospels, when Jesus cried out, "Father, into your hands I commend my spirit" (Luke 23:46). We can follow Rembrandt's intellectual process through four successive stages from the relatively anecdotal depiction of the crosses and the surrounding crowd in the first

state (fig. 14-22) to the haunting blackness of the fourth and final state. As Jesus cries out, a mystical light illuminates the darkened scene. Mary, the apostles, and the Roman soldiers are captured and immobilized by the blinding light. Here Rembrandt has depicted the miracle of redemption and the power of God.

Rembrandt painted many self-portraits. These images became more searching as the artist aged and, like many of his paintings, expressed a personal, internalized spirituality new in the history of art. In a self-portrait of 1659 (fig. 14-23), the half-length figure and the setting merge in a rich, luminous chiaroscuro with the face and clasped hands emerging out of the darkness. A few well-placed brushstrokes suggest the physical tension in the fingers and the weariness of the soul in the deep-set eyes. Mercilessly analytical, the portrait depicts the furrowed brow, sagging flesh, and prematurely aged face (he was only fifty-three) of one who has suffered deeply but retained his dignity.

More typical of Dutch painters, Judith Leyster (c. 1609–1660) painted boisterous genre scenes categorized in their own time by descriptive titles such as "merry company" or "garden party." In her lively *Self-Portrait* of 1635 (fig. 14-24), Leyster

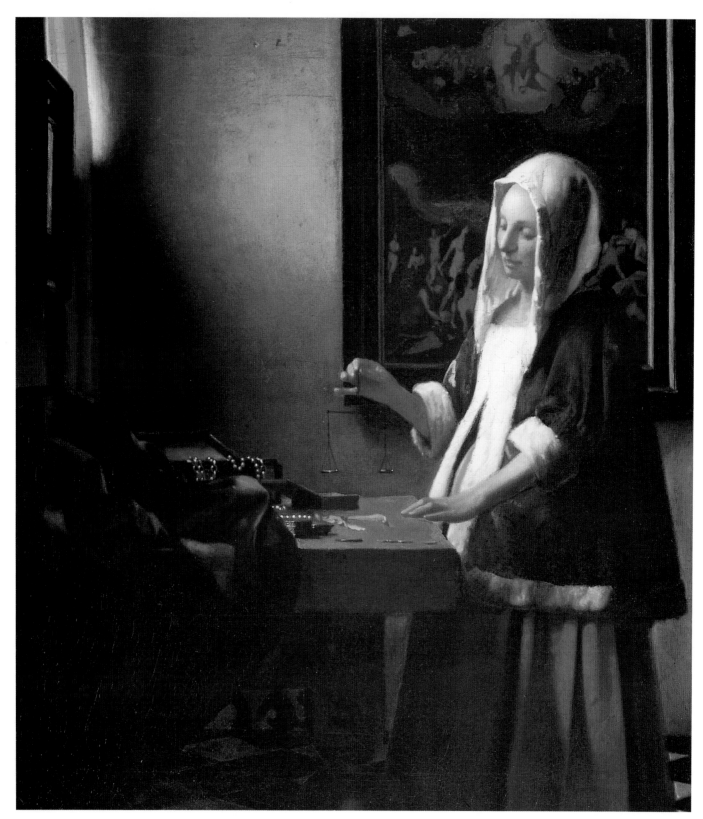

14-25 **Jan Vermeer.** *Woman Holding a Balance.* c. 1664. Oil on canvas, 16³/₄ x 15" (42.5 x 38.1 cm). National Gallery of Art, Washington, D.C. Widener Collection (42.9.97)

displays on her easel the type of work on which her popularity was based. The subject, a man playing a violin, may also be a visual pun on the painter's instruments, the palette and brush. To let the viewer immediately see the difference between her painted portrait and the painted painting, she varied her technique, executing the image on her easel more loosely. The narrow range of colors sensitively dispersed in the composition and the warm spotlighting are typical of Leyster's mature style.

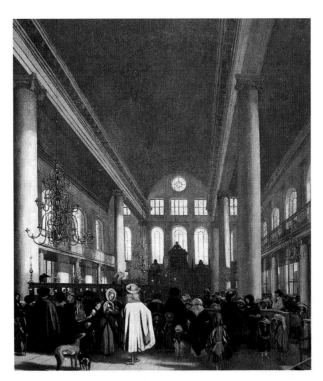

14-26 **Emanuel de Witte.** ***Portuguese Synagogue Amsterdam.*** 1680. Oil on canvas, 43½ x 39" (110.5 x 99.1 cm). Rijksmuseum, Amsterdam

Fund-raising for a new synagogue began in November 1670, with a pledge of 40,000 guilders (the finished building cost 164,365 guilders excluding the land). In 1671 Elias Bouman won the building competition; during the construction Daniel Stalpaert functioned as Amsterdam's official city architect, a post awarded to Bouman in 1681. The Sephardi community (Portuguese and Spanish Jews) in Amsterdam had about 2,300 members, most of whom were well-to-do merchants. Their new synagogue, with its classical architecture, Brazilian *jakaranda* wood furniture, and twenty-six brass chandeliers, was considered to be one of the notable sights of the city. The building was spared by the Nazis during World War II because the Germans planned to turn it into a museum of Jewish culture.

The art produced in the Netherlands of the seventeenth century shows that the Dutch delighted in depictions not only of themselves, but also of their country's landscape, cities, and domestic concerns. Jan Steen's *The Drawing Lesson* (see fig. 17) is typical of the beautifully painted scenes of daily life (genre paintings) that appealed to middle-class patrons of the arts.

Perhaps the greatest Dutch painter of contemporary life was Jan (Johannes) Vermeer of Delft (1632–1675). Vermeer produced few works. Many are enigmatic scenes of women in domestic settings, occupied with some cultivated activity such as writing, reading letters, or making music. Vermeer, a Catholic in a Protestant country, sometimes added a sobering religious reference to his work. Scholars of this period have noted that many of these works by Vermeer, like other Dutch genre paintings, contain apparently symbolic elements that suggest underlying meanings. For instance, Vermeer's *Woman Holding a Balance* (fig. 14-25) painted about 1664, once described in a sale simply as "a young lady weighing gold," can be understood straightforwardly as an exquisitely painted genre scene in which every object is carefully placed to achieve an overall balance and is illuminated by the clear, even light. However, the painting on the wall behind the young woman depicts the Last Judgment, suggesting that the empty balance in the woman's hand is more than a casual inclusion. The jewelry and coins on the table and the mirror on the wall were traditional elements in paintings with so-called ***vanitas*** subject matter, which stressed the fleeting nature of beauty, youth, and riches.

Another type of genre painting that achieved great popularity in the Baroque period was the architectural interior. These views seem to have been painted for their own special beauty, just as were exterior views of the land, cities, and harbors. Emanuel de Witte (c. 1617–1692) specialized in architectural painting in Delft and in Amsterdam. Many of his interiors, such as his *Portuguese Synagogue, Amsterdam* (fig. 14-26), are portraits of actual buildings. Today the painting is interesting not only as a work of art, but also as a record of seventeenth-century synagogue architecture and as evidence of Dutch religious tolerance in an age when Jews were often persecuted. The building is a rectangular hall with women's galleries on both sides, roofed by three wooden barrel vaults and lit by large glass windows. In de Witte's painting, the elegant couple in the foreground, the crowd, and the dogs suggest the size and popularity of the synagogue. The artist's shift of the straight-line viewpoint slightly to one side has created an interesting spatial composition, and strong contrasts of light and shade add dramatic movement to the simple interior.

The Dutch loved the peaceful, orderly beauty of their civilized countryside. Meindert Hobbema (1638–1709) in his painting, *Avenue at Middelharnis,* records the rational art of a

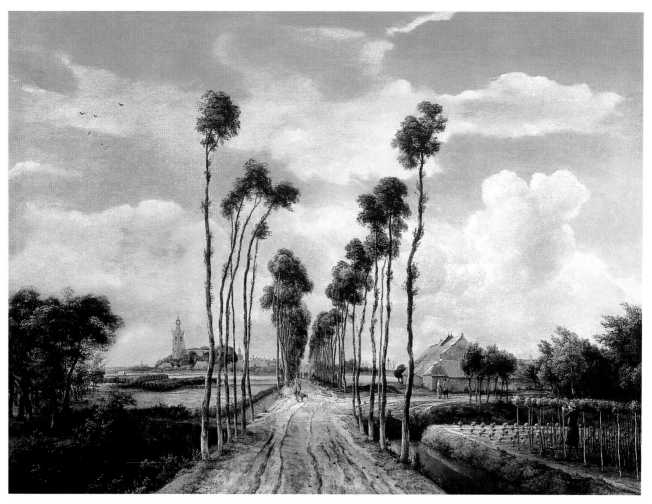

14-27 | Meindert Hobbema. *Avenue at Middelharnis.* 1689. Oil on canvas, 40¾ x 55½" (104 x 141 cm). The National Gallery, London

SCIENCE AND THE CHANGING WORLDVIEW

During the seventeenth and eighteenth centuries, some of the new discoveries of the natural world brought a sense of the grand scale of the universe without, while others focused more precisely on the complexity of the world within. As frames of reference expanded and contracted, artists found new ways to mirror these changing perspectives in their own works.

Francis Bacon (1561–1626) in England and René Descartes (1596–1650) in France established a new scientific method of studying the world by insisting on scrupulous objectivity and logical reasoning. Bacon proposed that facts be established by observation and tested by controlled experiments. Descartes argued for the deductive method of reasoning, in which a conclusion was arrived at logically from basic premises, the most fundamental of which was "I think, therefore I am."

In 1543, the Polish scholar Nicolaus Copernicus (1473–1543) published *On the Revolutions of the Heavenly Spheres*, which contradicted the long-held view that Earth is the center of the universe (the Ptolemaic theory) by arguing instead that Earth and other planets revolve around the Sun. The Church viewed the Copernican theory as a challenge to its doctrines and put Copernicus's work on its Index of Prohibited Books in 1616. At the beginning of the seventeenth century, Johannes Kepler (1571–1630), the court mathematician and astronomer to Holy Roman Emperor Rudolf II, demonstrated that the planets revolve around the Sun in elliptical orbits. Kepler noted a number of interrelated dynamic geometric patterns in the universe, the overall design of which he believed was an expression of divine order.

Galileo Galilei (1564–1642), an astronomer, mathematician, and physicist, was the first to develop a tool for observing the heavens, the telescope. His findings provided further confirmation of the Copernican theory, and after the teaching of that theory was prohibited by the Church, Galileo was tried for heresy by the Inquisition. Under duress, he publicly rejected his views, although at the end of his trial, according to legend, he muttered, "Nevertheless it [Earth] does move." As the first person to see the craters of the moon through a telescope, Galileo began the exploration of space that would culminate in the first human steps on the moon in 1969.

The new seventeenth-century science turned to the study of the very small as well as to the vast reaches of space. This included the development of the microscope, developed by the Dutch lens maker and amateur scientist Anton van Leeuwenhoek (1632–1723). Leeuwenhoek perfected grinding techniques and increased the power of his lenses far beyond what was required for a simple magnifying glass. Ultimately, he was able to study the inner workings of plants and animals and even see microorganisms. Early scientists learned to draw or depended on artists to draw the images revealed by the microscope for further study and publication. Not until the discovery of photography in the nineteenth century could scientists communicate their discoveries without an artist's help.

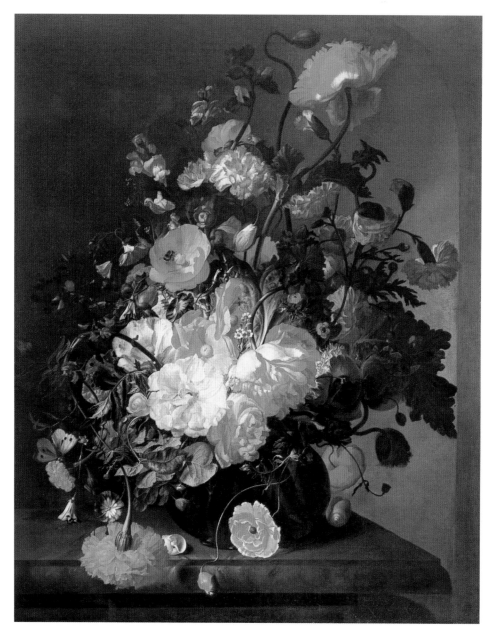

14-28 **Rachel Ruysch.** *Flower Still Life*. After 1700. Oil on canvas, 30 x 24" (76.2 x 61 cm)
The Toledo Museum of Art, Ohio
Purchased with funds from the Libbey Endowment. Gift of Edward Drummond Libbey

Flower painting was a much-admired specialty in the Netherlands of the seventeenth and
eighteenth centuries. Such paintings were almost never straightforward depictions of actual
fresh flowers. Instead, artists made color sketches of fresh examples of each type of
flower and studied scientifically accurate color illustrations in botanical publications.
Using their sketches and notebooks, in the studio they could compose bouquets of perfect
specimens of a variety of flowers that could never be found blooming at the same time.

country physically constructed by its people who reclaimed
the land from the sea (fig. 14-27). In contrast to the broad horizontal sweep of the land, Hobbema's compelling demonstration of one-point perspective draws the viewer into the picture
and down the rutted, sandy road toward the distant village of
Middelharnis.

Finally, still-life paintings—pictures of artfully arranged
everyday objects—were a particular specialty in the Dutch
Republic (see fig. 2). The Dutch were so proud of their artists'

still-life paintings that they presented one to the French queen
Marie de' Medici when she made a state visit to Amsterdam. One
of the most sought-after and highest-paid still-life painters in
Europe was Rachel Ruysch (1663–1750), who worked in Amsterdam (fig. 14-28). During her seventy-year career, she specialized
in **flower pieces**, or still-life paintings consisting predominantly of cut-flower arrangements (see "Art and Science," page 380).
Her works were highly prized for their sensitive, free-form
arrangements and their unusual and beautiful color harmonies.

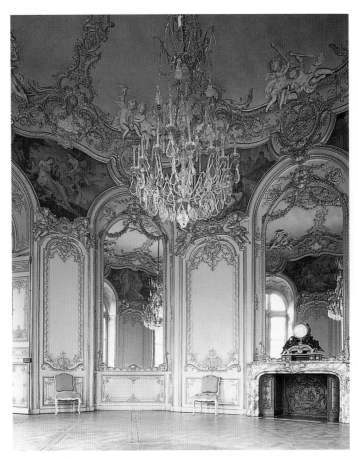

14-29 Germain Boffrand. *Salon de la Princesse,* Hôtel de Soubise,
Paris, France. Begun 1732.
Swaan Photograph Collection, (96.P.21)

The Rococo Style

The Rococo style is characterized by pastel colors, delicately
curving forms, dainty figures, and an apparently lighthearted
mood. The Rococo mode may be seen partly as a reaction at all
levels of society, even among kings and bishops, against the
Grand Manner of Baroque art, identified with the formality
and rigidity of seventeenth-century court life. The tendency
toward a lighter, more delicate style appeared in Italian painting and pastels about 1700. By the end of Louis XIV's reign in
1715, the Rococo style dominated French architectural decoration, and it quickly spread across Europe.

In France, the Rococo first appeared in the furnishings and
decoration of the elegant Parisian town houses that are known
in French as *hôtels*. The Salon de la Princesse in the Hôtel de
Soubise in Paris (fig. 14-29), designed by Germain Boffrand
beginning in 1732, is typical of French Rococo *hôtel* design of
the 1730s. The glitter of silver or gold against expanses of white
or pastel color, the visual confusion of mirror reflections, delicate ornament in sculpted stucco, carved wood panels called
boiseries, and inlaid wood designs on furniture and floors were
all part of the new look. In residential settings, pictorial themes
were often taken from classical love stories, and sculpted ornaments were rarely devoid of putti, cupids, and clouds. In these
elegant rooms, Parisian intellectuals gathered for conversation
and entertainments presided over by accomplished, educated
women of the upper class.

In Habsburg Germany and Austria, a major architectural project in the new Rococo style was the Residenz, a splendid palace
built for the prince-bishop of Würzburg from 1719 to 1744 by
Johann Balthasar Neumann (1687–1753). One of Neumann's
great triumphs of planning and decoration is the oval Kaisersaal,
or Imperial Hall (fig. 14-30). Although the clarity of the plan,
the size and proportions of the marble columns, and the large
windows recall the Hall of Mirrors at Versailles, the decoration of
the Kaisersaal, with its white-and-gold color scheme and its profusion of delicately curved forms, embodies the Rococo spirit.

Neumann's collaborator on the Residenz was a brilliant
Venetian painter, Giovanni Battista Tiepolo (1696–1770), who
began to work there in 1750. Tiepolo was acclaimed interna-
tionally for his confident and optimistic expression of the illusionistic fresco painting pioneered by such sixteenth-century
Venetians as Veronese (see figs. 14, 13-16). Tiepolo's work in the
Kaisersaal—three scenes glorifying the twelfth-century crusad-
er-emperor Frederick Barbarossa, who had been a patron of the
bishop of Würzburg—is a superb example of his architectural
painting. *The Marriage of the Emperor Frederick and Beatrice of
Burgundy* (seen on the vault at the far end of the hall in figure
14-30) is presented as if it were theater, with painted and gilded stucco curtains drawn back to reveal the splendor of an imperial wedding. Like Veronese's grand conceptions, Tiepolo's
spectacle is populated with an assortment of character types,
presented in dazzling light and sun-drenched colors.

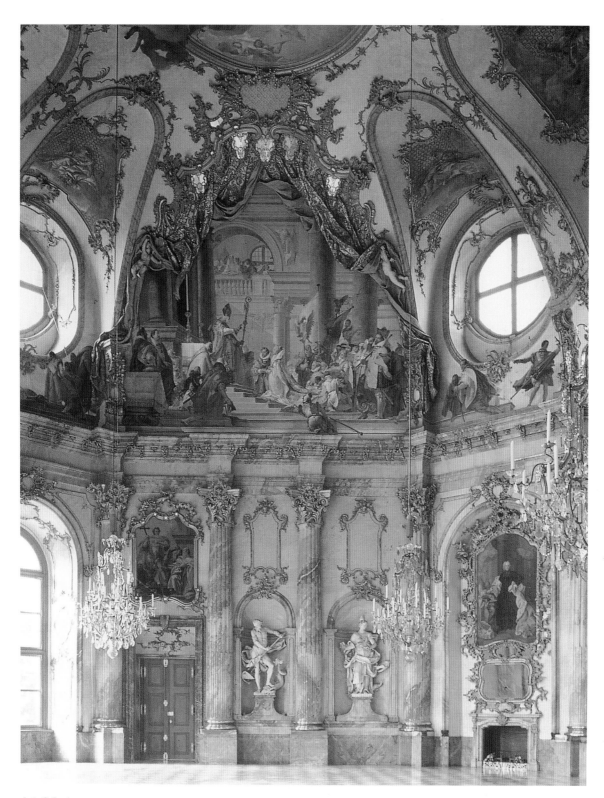

14-30 | **Johann Balthasar Neumann. Kaisersaal (Imperial Hall),** Residenz, Würzburg, Bavaria, Germany. 1719–44
Fresco decoration by Giovanni Battista Tiepolo. 1751–52

The Rococo style of painting emerged with the career of the French artist Jean-Antoine Watteau (1684–1721). Watteau worked for a time as a decorator of interiors. In 1717, he was elected to membership in the Royal Academy of Painting and Sculpture on the basis of a painting for which there was no established category. The academicians created a new classification for it, called the ***fête galante***, or elegant outdoor entertainment. The work he submitted, *The Pilgrimage to Cythera* (fig. 14-31, see page 380), depicted a dreamworld in which an assortment of beautifully dressed couples depart for, or perhaps take their leave from, the mythical island of love. The lush landscape, which has no more reality than a painted theater backdrop, would

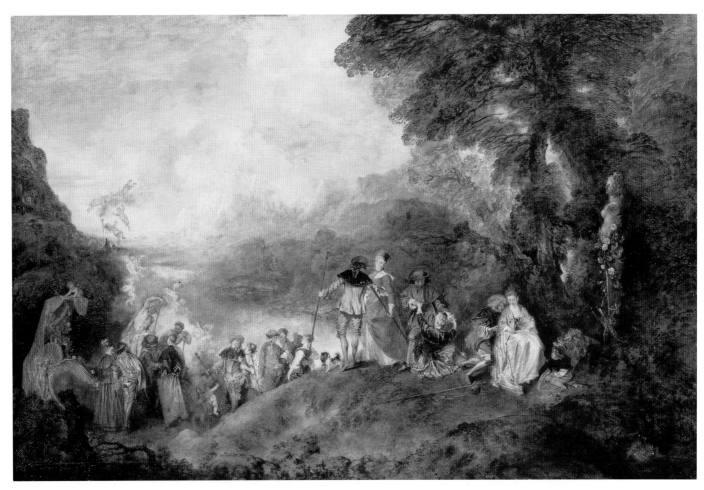

14-31 | Jean-Antoine Watteau. *The Pilgrimage to Cythera.* 1717. Oil on canvas, 4'3" x 6'4½" (1.3 x 1.9 m). Musée du Louvre, Paris

never soil the characters' exquisite satins and velvets, nor would a summer shower ever threaten them. This idyllic vision, with its overtones of wistful melancholy, had a powerful attraction in early-eighteenth-century Paris and soon charmed the rest of Europe.

Jean-Honoré Fragonard (1732–1806) carried the French Rococo fantasies that Watteau pioneered into the second half of the eighteenth century. Fragonard's most memorable work is a group of fourteen canvases commissioned about 1771 by Madame du Barry, Louis XV's mistress. *The Meeting* (fig. 14-32) shows a secret encounter between a young man and his sweetheart, who looks back anxiously over her shoulder to be sure she has not been followed while clutching the letter arranging the tryst. These marvelously free and seemingly spontaneous visions of lovers seem to explode in color and luxuriant vegetation. The rapid brushwork that distinguishes Fragonard's technique is at its freest and most lavish here. However, Madame du Barry rejected the paintings and commissioned another set in the newly fashionable Neoclassical style (see Chapter 17). Her view of Fragonard's ravishing visions as passé showed that the Rococo world was, indeed, at its end.

ART AND SCIENCE

Artists who worked with scientists (see "Science and the Changing Worldview," page 376) or carried on scientific investigations in their own right heralded the future. Before the invention of photography, scientists relied on painters to illustrate their work. Artist and scientist were seldom the same person, but Anna Maria Sibylla Merian (1647–1717) contributed to botany and entomology both as a researcher and as an artist. German by birth and Dutch by training, Merian was once described by a Dutch contemporary as a painter of worms, flies, mosquitoes, spiders, "and other filth." In 1699, Amsterdam subsidized Merian's research on plants and insects in the Dutch colony of Surinam in South America. She spent two years exploring the jungle and recording the insects there. On her return to Holland, she published the results of her research as *Dissertation in Insect Generations and Metamorphosis in Surinam,* illustrated with seventy-two large plates engraved after her watercolors (fig. 14-33).

Perhaps less daring but also "scientific" in her outlook, Rachel Ruysch made every flower in her still-life paintings a botanical study. Ruysch had learned botany as a girl, for her

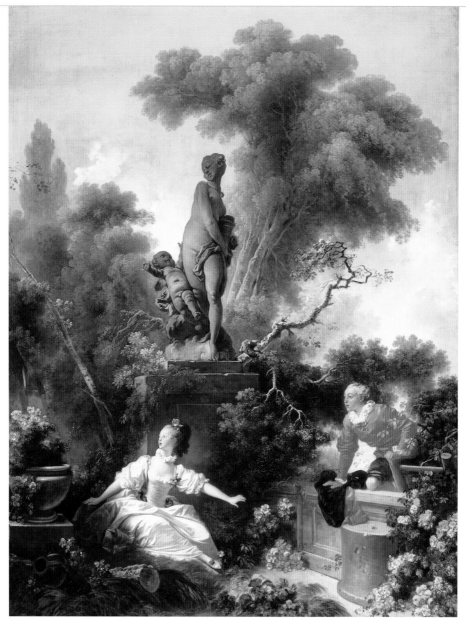

14-32

Jean-Honoré Fragonard. *The Meeting,* from *The Progress of Love.* 1771–73
Oil on canvas
10'5¼" x 7'5/8"
(3.18 x 2.15 m)
The Frick Collection
New York

father was a professor of anatomy and botany in Amsterdam. Although married with ten children, Ruysch never stopped painting. She achieved such fame in her lifetime that her paintings often brought higher prices than did work by Rembrandt. In her *Flower Still Life* (see fig. 14-28), painted after 1700, Ruysch created an asymmetrical arrangement of pale oranges, pinks, and yellows rising from the lower left to the top right of the picture, offset by the strong diagonal of the table edge. Ruysch often enlivened her compositions with reptiles or insects—in this case, two snail shells and a large gray moth—that give the paintings an unsettling feeling. Besides appreciating the beauty of such compositions, viewers could have seen the flaming tulip (the most expensive variety) as a warning against the vanity of pride and greed, just as the short life of the cut flowers reminded them of the fleeting nature of beauty and human life. In Protestant Holland, even art informed by science carried a moral message in the Baroque and Rococo periods.

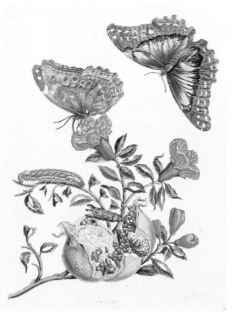

14-33

Anna Maria Sibylla Merian
Plate 9 from *Dissertation in Insect Generations and Metamorphosis in Surinam*
1719 (printed posthumously)
Bound volume of seventy-two hand-colored engravings (second edition)
18⅞ x 13" (47.9 x 33 cm)
National Museum of Women in the Arts. Washington, D.C.
Gift of Wallace and Wilhelmina Holladay

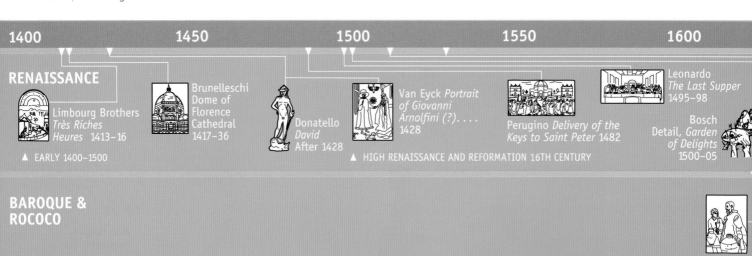

RENAISSANCE

Limbourg Brothers *Très Riches Heures* 1413–16

Brunelleschi Dome of Florence Cathedral 1417–36

Donatello *David* After 1428

Van Eyck *Portrait of Giovanni Arnolfini (?)....* 1428

Perugino *Delivery of the Keys to Saint Peter* 1482

Leonardo *The Last Supper* 1495–98

Bosch Detail, *Garden of Delights* 1500–05

▲ EARLY 1400–1500   ▲ HIGH RENAISSANCE AND REFORMATION 16TH CENTURY

BAROQUE & ROCOCO

Velázquez *Water Carri of Seville* c. 1619

BAROQUE c. END 16TH–17TH CENTURY ▲

L O O K I N G   B A C K   5

Exploration and Abundance

In the fifteenth, sixteenth, and seventeenth centuries in Europe—the Renaissance and Baroque periods—artists and scholars began to explore the natural world with the kind of intensity that their predecessor had devoted to heaven and hell. They studied human and animal anatomy, botany and geology, astronomy and mathematics, and many other subjects as well. In their desire to incorporate this new knowledge in works of art they created a naturalistic style that had not existed since the days of the Roman Republic. They invented systems of perspective that enabled them to create convincing illusions of three-dimensional objects in space on flat surfaces. In this endeavor, Italians took a theoretical, almost mathematical approach (linear perspective), while the Flemish, French, and others studied the effects of distance on the color and clarity of things (atmospheric or aerial perspective).

After this period of intense exploration in the fifteenth century, artists and architects turned to more literary studies, in part inspired by the Neoplatonic philosophy of the humanists. They studied classical art and architecture in their search for a canon of ideal beauty and in particular observed the ruins of ancient Rome, from which they borrowed such decorative details as acanthus scrolls, delicate moldings, and inscriptions with wonderfully clear letters. At the beginning of the sixteenth century, painting and sculpture seem to reflect and even rival the art of Greece in the fifth and fourth centuries BCE. Nevertheless, artists and patrons soon turned from the lofty ideals of Raphael and Michelangelo to the more easily appreciated grace and elegance of the Mannerist style. In the seventeenth and eighteenth centuries Baroque and Rococo artists represented human emotions with a new expressiveness.

Printed books began to replace manuscripts in the sixteenth century, creating an information explosion comparable to the revolution brought about by computer technology today. An increasingly literate public gained access not only to practical information but also to new ideas, while conservative elements in governments and the Catholic Church sought to control information. The examination of natural phenomena led to widespread questioning of authority and eventually to the movement both within and outside the established Church known as the Protestant Reformation. The most extreme Protestants declared the arts to be wasteful, frivolous, and even idolatrous.

The Roman Catholic Counter-Reformation of the sixteenth century turned to the arts to further its causes. By the seventeenth century, popes and cardinals commissioned art to glorify traditional religion and inspire the faithful, and artists covered walls and ceilings with splendid allegories of the triumph of the Church and intensely realistic martyrdoms of saints. The leaders of emerging national states in western Europe encouraged painters and sculptors to produce flamboyant portraits and glorified histories of their deeds, sometimes disguised by classical themes. Protestant Dutch burghers bought meticulously realistic paintings and prints of their prosperous countryside, peaceful cities, and affluent homes. Artists skillfully met the demands of their patrons, and in spite of religious and political controversy, the arts flourished in an increasingly informed and prosperous world.

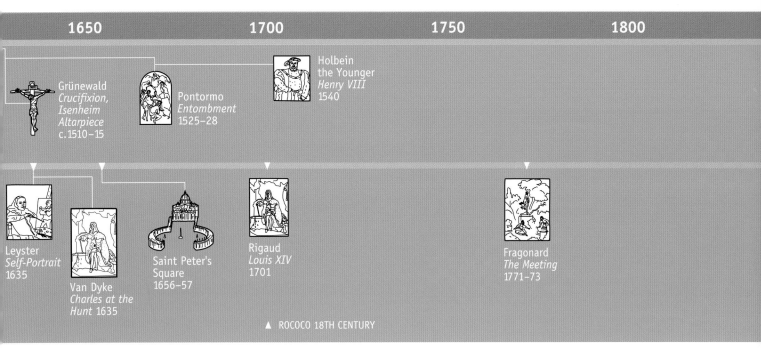

1650   1700   1750   1800

Grünewald
*Crucifixion,
Isenheim
Altarpiece*
c.1510–15

Pontormo
Entombment
1525–28

Holbein
the Younger
Henry VIII
1540

Leyster
Self-Portrait
1635

Van Dyke
*Charles at the
Hunt* 1635

Saint Peter's
Square
1656–57

Rigaud
Louis XIV
1701

Fragonard
The Meeting
1771–73

▲ ROCOCO 18TH CENTURY

Renaissance, Baroque, and Rococo Art

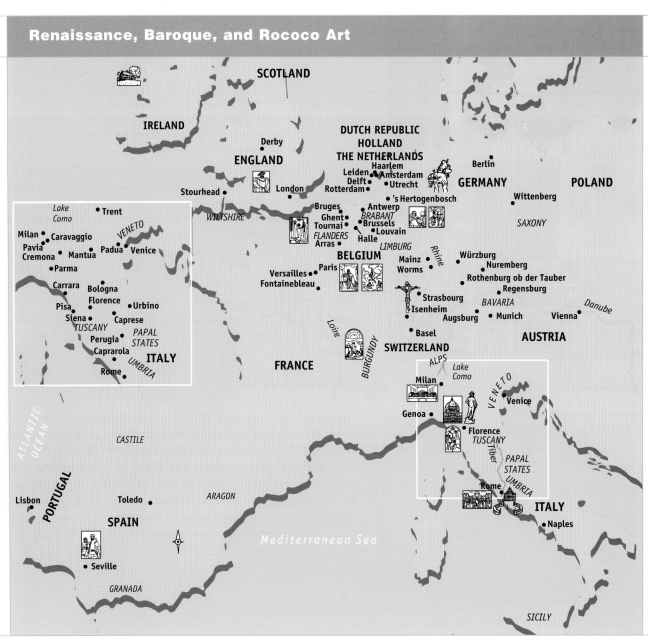

Tunic, from Peru. Inca, c. 1500 CE. Wool and cotton
35⅞ x 30" (91.1 x 76.2 cm). Dumbarton Oaks Research
Library and Collections, Washington, D.C.
(See page 393.)

The remarkable art and architecture of the Americas surprised the Spanish explorers when they arrived in Mexico in 1519 and in Peru in 1532. They found an especially high quality of urban planning, stonework, fiber arts, metalwork, and ceramics. The skill of Inca weavers, for example, continues to amaze us today. In Inca society fine textiles had both religious and political significance. Cloth was not only deemed a worthy gift to the gods, but was used to create the images of gods, and to wrap images made of precious metals. Cloth was also equated with wealth and power.

Felipe Guaman Poma de Ayala described the Conquest, indigenous population, and customs of the Inca in a handwritten and illustrated book written sometime before 1615. One of the 400 full-page illustrations shows the Inca king and his generals and officials dressed in knee-length tunics with checkerboard designs. The colorful tunics are more than mere clothing. Patterns may have signified rank, family, or a geographic location, and seem to have been standardized throughout the empire. The elaborate royal tunic seen here has a pattern made up of miniature tunics, conveying the ruler's domination over wearers of other types of tunics. Although the Incas never developed a writing system, clearly some kind of symbolic language is indicated in what today we "read" as an abstract design.

Inca textiles suggest that they were the products of a complex society. The production of the cloth required a settled agricultural community where wool (alpaca and vicuña) and cotton could be produced, cleaned, dyed, and spun into yarn. The weavers worked on simple back-strap looms using a wool weft on a cotton warp. Both men and women worked as weavers for the central government, and the finished cloth was collected and stored in warehouses throughout the empire. The people in effect paid taxes in textiles.

Inca textiles prove to be an interesting study of the effect of official policy, centralized power, and standardization of the fine arts. Weavers and other artists who worked for the state followed the official requirements in design, quality, and quantity. Individual creativity expressed itself within traditional uses of simple repeated geometric patterns arranged symmetrically. Patterns and colors identified the wearer's status and family or group membership; consequently, textiles played an important role in governing and identifying people in a far-flung empire. Heraldic trappings had a similar place in western Europe in the Middle Ages and Renaissance. Today, school or team colors and mascots still identify sports fans and inspire loyalty throughout the world.

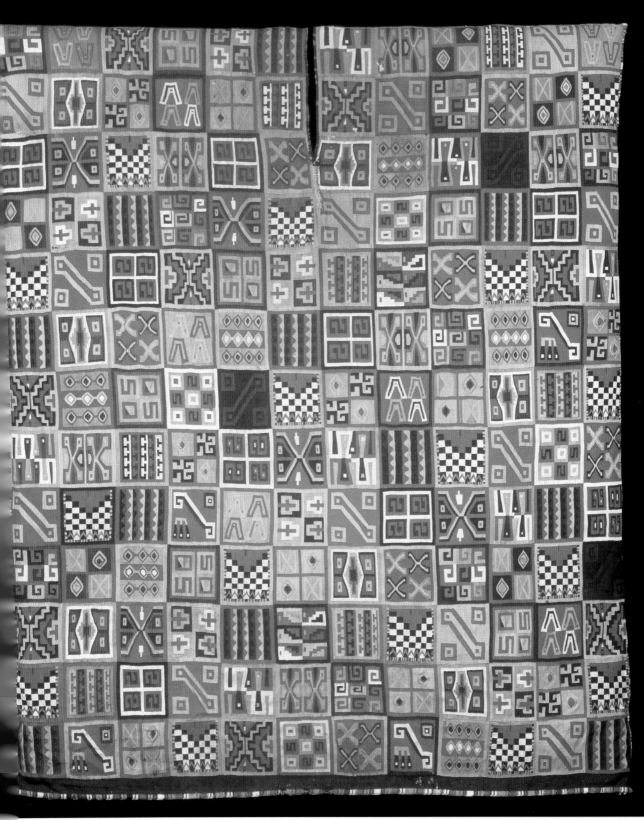

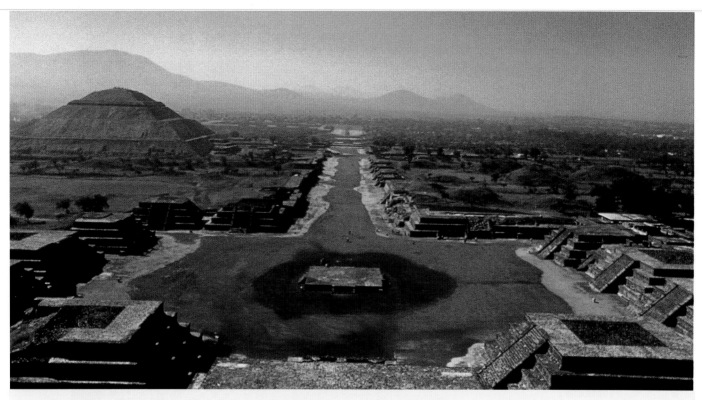

15-1 **Ceremonial center of the city of Teotihuacan**, Mexico. Teotihuacan culture, c. 500 CE

View from the Pyramid of the Moon down the Avenue of the Dead to the Ciudadela and the Temple of the Feathered Serpent. The Pyramid of the Sun is on the middle left.

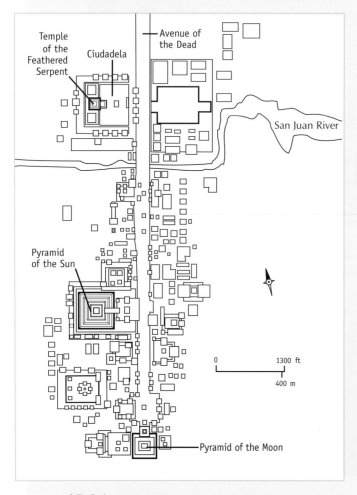

15-2 **Plan of the ceremonial center of Teotihuacan**

Human beings first arrived in North and South America during the last Ice Age, when glaciers trapped enough of the world's water to lower the level of the oceans and expose a land bridge between Asia and North America. Sometime before about 12,000 years ago, perhaps as early as 20,000 to 30,000 years ago, Paleolithic hunter-gatherers crossed over this land bridge and began to spread out into two vast, uninhabited continents.

Between 10,000 and 12,000 years ago, bands of hunters roamed most of North America; a few reached the southern end of South America by about 12,500 years ago. Although contact between Siberia and Alaska continued after the ice had retreated and rising oceans had flooded the Bering Strait, the people of the Western Hemisphere were essentially cut off from those of Africa and Eurasia until they were overrun by European invaders beginning in the late fifteenth century CE.

In this isolation, the people of the Americas experienced transformations similar to those that followed the end of the Paleolithic era elsewhere. In many regions, they developed an agricultural way of life, based on the cultivation of native plants: corn, beans, and squash. Other plants first domesticated in the Americas included potatoes, tobacco, cacao (chocolate), tomatoes, and avocados. As elsewhere, the shift to agriculture in the Americas was accompanied by population growth and, in some places, the rise of hierarchical societies and the appearance of ceremonial centers and towns with monumental architecture. Cities such as Teotihuacan in the Basin of Mexico rivaled those of Europe in size and splendor. The people of Mesoamerica—the region that extends from central Mexico to northern Central America—developed writing, a complex and accurate calendar, and a sophisticated system of mathematics. Central and South American peoples developed an advanced metallurgy and produced exquisite gold, silver, and copper jewelry. In the American Southwest, Native American people built multistoried, apartmentlike villages and cliff dwellings, as well as elaborate irrigation systems with canals (see Map 6, page 415).

The sudden incursion of Europeans from the fifteenth century onward had a dramatic and lasting impact on Native American people and their art. In some areas, highly advanced civilizations, such as those of the Aztec and Inca, were destroyed. In other regions, such as the North American plains, indigenous groups lost much of their land and saw their populations decimated yet retained their traditions and still exist as distinct cultural entities today.

Mesoamerica

Ancient Mesoamerica encompassed the area from north of the Basin of Mexico (the location of Mexico City) to modern Belize and parts of Honduras and El Salvador in Central America. The people of this physically diverse region, which included tropical rain forests and semiarid mountain plateaus, were linked by trade and cultural similarities. Among the shared features of the civilizations that arose in Mesoamerica were a complex calendrical system based on interlocking 260-day and 365-day cycles, a ritual ball game with religious and political significance, and aspects of monumental ceremonial building construction. Mesoamerican society was also sharply divided into elite and commoner classes.

Archaeologists have traditionally divided Mesoamerican history into three broad periods: the Formative or Preclassic (1500 BCE–250 CE), the Classic (250–900 CE), and the Postclassic (900–1521 CE). The Classic period brackets the time during which the Maya erected dated stone monuments. The term reflects the view of early scholars that the Classic period was a kind of golden age, the equivalent of the Classical period in ancient Greece (see Chapter 4). Although this view is no longer current and the periods are only roughly applicable to other parts of Mesoamerica, the terminology has endured.

The earliest known major Mesoamerican civilization, that of the Olmecs, emerged during the Formative period along the Gulf of Mexico. In the swampy coastal areas of the modern Mexican states of Veracruz and Tabasco, the Olmecs cleared farmland, drained fields, and raised earth mounds on which they constructed religious and political centers. They created monumental works of basalt sculpture, such as colossal heads (see fig. 1-17), altars, and seated figures. The Olmecs also established trade contacts throughout Mesoamerica, importing goods not found in the Gulf region, such as obsidian, iron ore, and jade. Writing and calendrical systems first appeared around 600 to 500 BCE in areas with strong Olmec influence.

By 200 CE, forests and swamps began to reclaim Olmec sites, but Olmec civilization had spread widely throughout Mesoamerica and was to have an enduring influence on its successors. As the Olmec centers of the Gulf Coast faded, the great Classic period

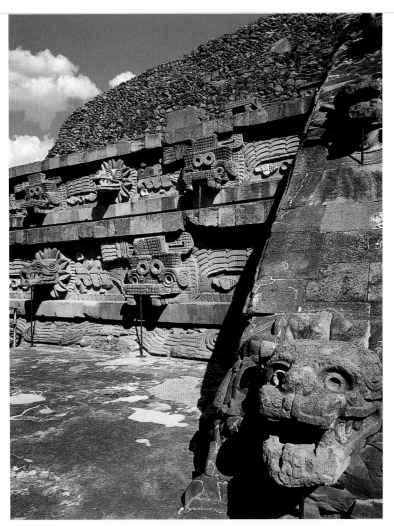

15-3 | **Temple of the Feathered Serpent, the Ciudadela,** Teotihuacan Mexico. Teotihuacan culture, c. 350 CE

centers at Teotihuacan in the Basin of Mexico as well as in the Maya region were beginning their ascendancy.

Located some 30 miles northeast of present-day Mexico City, Teotihuacan experienced a period of rapid growth early in the first millennium CE. By 200 CE it had emerged as a significant center of commerce and manufacturing, the first large city-state in the Americas. At its height, between 350 and 650 CE, Teotihuacan covered nearly 9 square miles and had a population of some 150,000, making it one of the largest cities in the world at that time (figs. 15-1, 15-2). One reason for its dominance was the control of the market for high-quality obsidian. This volcanic stone, made into tools and vessels, was traded for luxury items such as the green feathers of the quetzal bird, used for priestly headdresses, and the spotted fur of the jaguar, used for ceremonial garments.

The name *Teotihuacan* is an Aztec word meaning "The City (gathering place) of the Gods." The people of Teotihuacan worshiped many deities that were recognizably similar to those worshiped by later Mesoamerican people, including the Aztecs, who dominated central Mexico at the time of the Spanish Conquest. Among these are the Rain or Storm God (god of fertility, war, and sacrifice), known to the Aztecs as Tlaloc, and the Feathered Serpent, known to the Maya as Kukulcan and to the Aztecs as Quetzalcoatl.

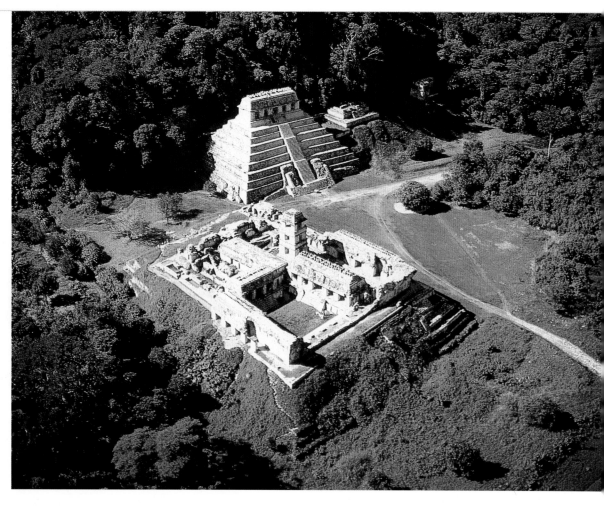

15-4

Palace (foreground) and Temple of the Inscriptions (tomb-pyramid of Lord Pacal), Palenque Mexico. Maya culture late 7th century CE

Teotihuacan's principal structures included the Pyramid of the Sun, the Pyramid of the Moon, and the Ciudadela, a vast sunken plaza surrounded by temple platforms (see fig. 15-2). The city's principal religious and political center, the Ciudadela could accommodate an assembly of more than 60,000 people. Its focal point was the pyramidal Temple of the Feathered Serpent. This seven-tiered structure exhibits the ***talud-tablero*** construction that is a hallmark of the Teotihuacan architectural style. The sloping base, or *talud*, of each platform supports a vertical *tablero*, or entablature, which is surrounded by a frame and filled with sculptural decoration. The Temple of the Feathered Serpent was enlarged several times, and as was characteristic of Mesoamerican pyramids, each completed enlargement enclosed the previous structure, like the concentric layers of an onion.

Archaeological excavations of earlier-phase *tableros* and a stairway balustrade have revealed painted heads of the Feathered Serpent, the goggle-eyed Rain or Storm God (or Fire God, according to some), and reliefs of aquatic shells and snails (fig. 15-3; see page 387). Their flat, angular, abstract style, typical of Teotihuacan art, is in marked contrast to the curvilinear style of Olmec art. The Rain God features a squarish, stylized head or headdress with protruding upper jaw, huge, round eyes originally inlaid with obsidian, and large, circular earspools. The fanged serpent heads, perhaps composites of snakes and other creatures, emerge from an aureole of stylized feathers. The Rain God and the Feathered Serpent may be symbols of regeneration and cyclical renewal, perhaps representing the alternating wet and dry seasons.

The homeland of the Maya people lay southeast of Teotihuacan. In southern Mesoamerica, which includes present-day Guatemala, the Yucatan peninsula, Belize, and the western part of Honduras and El Salvador, the Maya built imposing pyramids, temples, palaces, and administrative structures in densely populated cities. They developed the most advanced hieroglyphic writing in Mesoamerica and the most sophisticated version of the Mesoamerican calendrical system. In addition, they studied astronomy and the natural cycles of plants and animals, and they developed the mathematical concepts of zero and place value before they were used in Europe.

An increasingly detailed picture of the Maya has emerged from recent archaeological research and progress in deciphering their writing. It shows a society divided into competing centers, each with a hereditary ruler and an elite class of nobles and priests supported by a far larger class of farmer-commoners. Rulers established their legitimacy, maintained links with their divine ancestors, and venerated the gods through elaborate rituals, including ball games, bloodletting ceremonies, and human sacrifice. A complex pantheon of deities, many with several manifestations, presided over the Maya universe.

The Maya civilization, which emerged during the late Preclassic period (250 BCE–250 CE), reached its peak in the southern lowlands of Guatemala during the Classic period (250–900 CE), and shifted to northern Yucatan during the Postclassic period (900–1500 CE). In Palenque, a prominent city of the Classic period, the major buildings are grouped on high ground. A central group of structures includes the so-called Palace (possibly an administrative and ceremonial center as well as a residential structure), the Temple of the Inscriptions, and two other temples (fig. 15-4). Most of the structures in the three building complexes were commissioned by a powerful ruler, Lord Pacal (Maya for "shield"), who ruled from 615 to 683 CE, and his two sons, who succeeded him.

The Temple of the Inscriptions is a nine-level pyramid that rises to a height of about 75 feet. The consecutive layers probably reflect the belief, current among the Aztec and the Maya at the time of the Spanish Conquest, that the underworld had nine levels. Priests would climb the steep stone staircase on the exterior to reach the temple on top, which recalls the kind of pole-and-thatch houses the Maya still build in parts of Yucatan today. The roof of the temple was topped with a crest known as a **roof comb**, and its facade still retains much of its stucco sculpture. Inscriptions about Pascal's life carved inside the temple gave the structure its name.

In 1952, a Mexican archaeologist studying the Temple of the Inscriptions discovered a corbel-vaulted stairway beneath the summit shrine. This stairway descended almost 80 feet to a small subterranean chamber that contained the undisturbed tomb of Lord Pacal himself. The ruler, covered in jade ornaments, lay in a monumental sarcophagus with a lid carved in low relief that showed him balanced between the underworld and the earth. A stucco portrait of Lord Pacal found with the sarcophagus depicts him as a young man wearing a diadem of jade and feathers (fig. 15-5). His features reveal the characteristics of the Maya ideal of beauty: a sloping forehead and elongated skull (babies had their heads bound to produce this shape), a large curved nose (enhanced by an added ornamental bridge, perhaps of latex), and full lips. Traces of pigment indicate that this portrait, like much Maya sculpture, was colorfully painted.

As the focus of Maya civilization shifted northward in the Postclassic period, a northern Maya group called the Itzá rose to prominence. Their principal center, Chichén Itzá, which means "at the mouth of the well of the Itzá," flourished from the ninth to the thirteenth century CE, eventually covering about 6 square miles.

One of Chichén Itzá's most conspicuous structures is a massive, nine-level pyramid in the center of a large plaza with a stairway on each side leading to a square temple on the pyramid's summit (fig. 15-6). Sculptured Feathered Serpent heads embellish the base of the stairway. This structure is known today as the Castillo (Spanish for "castle"). At the spring and fall equinoxes, the rising sun casts an undulating, serpentlike shadow on the stairway balustrades that form a body for the serpent heads.

Sculpture at Chichén Itzá includes half-reclining figures known as **Chacmools** (fig. 15-6), which have the sturdy forms, proportions, and angularity of architecture. The Chacmools probably represent fallen warriors and were used to receive sacrificial offerings. They once typified Pre-Columbian sculpture for many Westerners.

Maya civilization was in decline by the time of the Spanish Conquest. By the end of the fifteenth century, a people known as the Aztecs controlled much of Mexico. Their rise to power had been recent and swift. Only 400 years earlier, according to their

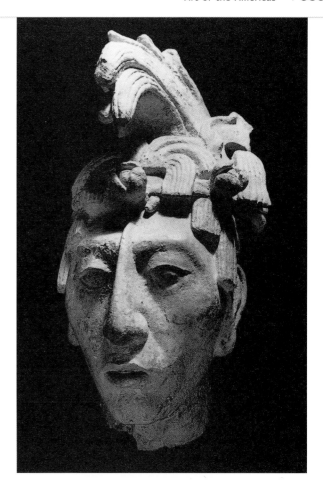

15-5 | **Portrait of Lord Pacal, from his tomb**
Temple of the Inscriptions. Late 7th century CE
Stucco, height 16⁷/₈" (43 cm)
Museo Nacional de Antropología, Mexico City

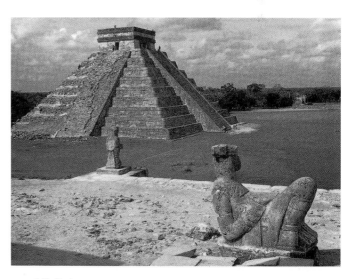

15-6 | **Castillo with Chacmool in foreground,** Chichén Itzá, Yukatan, Mexico. 9th-13th century.
Swaan Photograph Collection, (96.P.21)

own legends, they had been a nomadic people living on the shores of the mythical island called Aztlan somewhere to the northwest of the Basin of Mexico, where present-day Mexico City is located. They called themselves the *Mexica*, hence the name *Mexico*. The term *Aztec* derives from the word *Aztlan*.

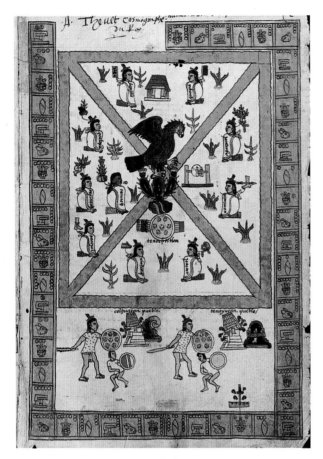

15-7 **The Founding of Tenochtitlan,** page from *Codex Mendoza*. Aztec, 1540s CE. Ink and paint on paper, 8⁷/₁₆ x 12³/₈" (21.4 x 31.4 cm). The Bodleian Library, Oxford MS. Arch Selden. A.1.fol. 2r

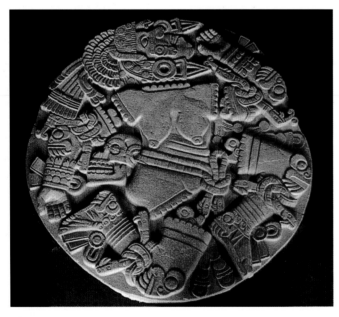

15-8 **The Moon Goddess, Coyolxauhqui.** Aztec, late 15th century CE Stone, diameter 11'6" (3.5 m)

This disk was discovered accidentally in 1978 by workers from a utility company who were excavating at a street corner in downtown Mexico City.

After a period of migration, the Aztecs arrived in the Basin of Mexico in the thirteenth century. There they eventually settled on an island in Lake Texcoco, where they had seen an eagle perching on a prickly pear cactus (*tenochtli*), a sign that Huitzilopochtli, their patron god, told them would mark the end of their wandering. They called the place Tenochtitlan (meaning "the prickly pear cactus on a stone"). The city was situated on a collection of islands linked by human-made canals.

In the fifteenth century, the Aztecs and their allies in a triple alliance began an aggressive campaign of expansion. The tribute they exacted from all over Central Mexico transformed Tenochtitlan into a glittering capital. As the Spanish conquistador Hernándo Cortés approached Tenochtitlan in November 1519, he and his soldiers marveled at the stone buildings, towers, and temples that seemed from a distance to rise from the water like a mirage.

Most Aztec books were destroyed in the wake of the Spanish invasion, but the work of Aztec scribes appears in several **codexes** (manuscripts) created after the Conquest. The first page of the *Codex Mendoza*, prepared for the Spanish viceroy in the 1540s, can be interpreted as an idealized representation of the city of Tenochtitlan (fig. 15-7). An eagle perched on a prickly pear cactus—the symbol of the city—fills the center of the page. Waterways surround the city and divide it into four quarters, which are further subdivided into wards, as represented by the seated figures. The victorious warriors at the bottom of the page represent early Aztec conquests over nearby cities.

Tenochtitlan had a sacred precinct, possibly symbolized in figure 15-7 by the structure (a temple or house) at the top of the page. The focal point of the precinct was the Great Temple, a 130-foot-high stepped pyramid with dual temples on top, one of which was dedicated to Huitzilopochtli (an Aztec patron-god associated with the sun and warfare) and the other to Tlaloc, the Mesoamerican god of rain and fertility. The Great Temple was an important site for ritual sacrifice. Victims climbed stairs on the exterior to the Temple of Huitzilopochtli at the summit, where several priests threw them over a stone and another quickly cut open their chests and offered their still-throbbing hearts to the gods. Their bodies were then rolled down the stairs and dismembered. Hundreds of severed heads were said to have been kept on a skull rack in the plaza of the sacred precinct.

The Aztecs believed that human actions, including bloodletting and human sacrifice, were vital to the continued existence of the universe. Huitzilopochtli, son of the Earth Mother Coatlicue, was thought to require sacrificial victims so that he could, in a re-creation of the events surrounding his birth, drive the stars and the moon from the sky at the beginning of each day. The stars were his half brothers, and the moon, Coyolxauhqui, was his half sister. According to the myth, when Coatlicue conceived Huitzilopochtli by placing a ball of feathers in her bosom as she was sweeping, Huitzilopochtli's jealous siblings conspired to kill her. When they attacked, Huitzilopochtli emerged from her body fully grown and armed, drove off his brothers, and destroyed his half sister, Coyolxauhqui. Aztec rituals re-created the mythic events surrounding his birth.

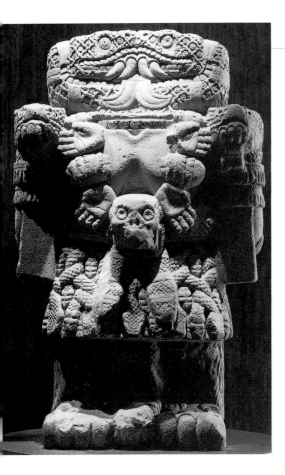

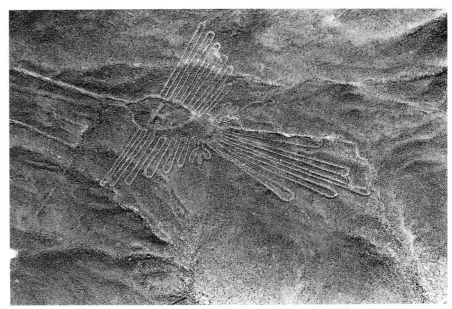

15-9 | ***The Mother Goddess, Coatlicue.*** Aztec, late 15th century CE. Stone, height 8'6" (2.59 m). Museo Nacional de Antropología, Mexico City

15-10 | **Earth drawing of a hummingbird,** Nazca Plain, southwest Peru. Nazca culture c. 100 BCE–700 CE. Length approx. 450' (137 m); wingspan approx. 200' (60.9 m)

A huge circular relief of Coyolxauhqui once lay at the foot of the Huitzilopochtli shrine, as if the enraged and triumphant god had cast her there like a sacrificial victim (fig. 15-8). Her torso is in the center, surrounded by her decapitated head and dismembered limbs. The rope belt around her waist is attached to a skull buckle. She wears bells on her cheeks, a magnificent feather headdress, and distinctive ear ornaments composed of disks, rectangles, and triangles. The sculpture is two-dimensional in concept, with a deeply cut background.

Inside the Temple of Huitzilopochtli, an imposing statue of Coatlicue (fig. 15-9), mother of Huitzilopochtli, stood high above the vanquished Coyolxauhqui. One of the conquistadors who arrived at the site in 1520 described seeing such a statue covered with blood. Coatlicue means "she of the serpent skirt," and this broad-shouldered figure with clawed hands and feet wears a skirt of twisted snakes. A pair of serpents, symbols of blood, rise from her neck to form her head. Around her neck hangs a necklace of sacrificial offerings—hands, hearts, and a dangling skull pendant. Despite its intricate surface, the sculpture's simple, bold, and blocky forms create a single visual whole. The colors with which it was originally painted would have heightened its dramatic impact.

The Spanish built their own capital, Mexico City, over the ruins of Tenochtitlan and built a cathedral on the site of Tenochtitlan's sacred precinct. The statue of Coatlicue was found near the cathedral during excavations there in 1792.

South America: The Central Andes

Like Mesoamerica, the central Andes of South America—primarily present-day Peru and Bolivia—saw the development of complex hierarchical societies with rich and varied artistic traditions. The area is one of dramatic contrasts. The narrow coastal plain sandwiched between the Pacific Ocean and the soaring Andes is one of the driest deserts in the world. Life here depends on the rich marine resources of the Pacific and the rivers that descend from the Andes. The Andes themselves are a region of snow-capped peaks, fertile river valleys, and high plateaus that support llamas, alpacas, vicuñas, and guanacos. The lush eastern slopes of the Andes descend to the tropical rain forest of the Amazon basin.

In the central Andes, the earliest evidence of monumental architecture dates to the third millennium BCE. Sites with ceremonial mounds and plazas were discovered near the sea, while early centers in the highlands consisted of multiroomed, stone-walled structures with sunken central fire pits in which ritual offerings were burned. Large, U-shaped ceremonial complexes with circular sunken plazas were built from the second millennium BCE. Some of the most enigmatic monumental constructions in Peru are the earthworks, or **geoglyphs**, first created by the people of the Nazca culture, who dominated the south coast of Peru from about 100 BCE to 700 CE. On great stretches of desert, the people literally drew in the earth. By removing a layer of dark gravel, they exposed the lighter underlying soil, then edged the resulting lines with stones. In this way, they created gigantic images, visible only from the air, including a hummingbird (fig. 15-10), a killer whale, a monkey, a spider, a duck, and other birds, plants, geometric patterns and straight, parallel lines that extend for up to 12 miles. The beak of the hummingbird in figure 15-10 consists of two parallel lines, each 120 feet long. Despite numerous theories, the purpose of these geoglyphs, which dwarf even the most ambitious modern environmental sculpture, is not known. Animals and plants in a similar style appear on a much smaller scale on multicolored pottery made by Nazca artisans.

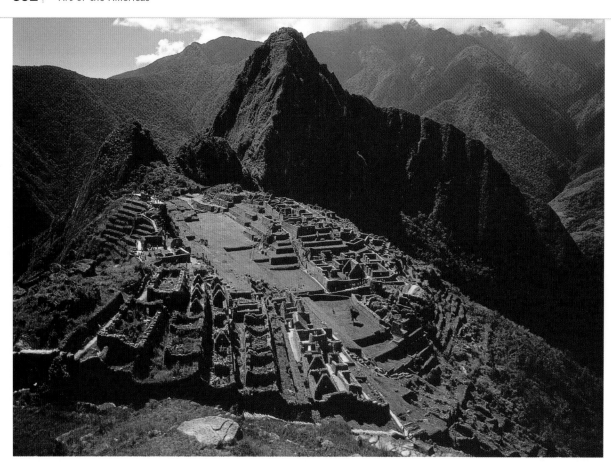

15-11

Machu Picchu
Peru. Inca
15th–16th
century CE

The largest state in the Andes region in the Pre-Columbian era was the Inca Empire. It extended for more than 2,600 miles along western South America, encompassing most of modern-day Ecuador, Peru, Bolivia, and northern Chile. The Inca called their empire the Land of the Four Quarters. At its center was their capital, Cuzco, "the navel of the world," located high in the Andes Mountains. The early history of the Inca people is obscure.

The Cuzco region had been under the control of the earlier Wari Empire, and the Inca state was probably one of many small competing kingdoms that emerged in the highlands in the wake of the Wari collapse. In the fifteenth century, the Inca, like the Aztecs in the Basin of Mexico, began suddenly and rapidly to expand. Through conquest, alliance, and intimidation, they subdued most of their vast domain by 1500. To hold together the linguistically and ethnically diverse empire, the Inca relied on an overarching state religion, a hierarchical bureaucracy, and various forms of labor taxation, satisfied by a set amount of time spent performing tasks for the state. To speed transport and communication, the Inca built nearly 15,000 miles of roads, with more than a thousand lodgings spaced a day's journey apart and a relay system of waiting runners to carry messages. In common with other Native American civilizations, the Inca had no draft animals or wheeled vehicles for transportation. Travelers went on foot, and llamas were used as pack animals.

Inca builders created stonework structures of great refinement and durability (see "Inca Masonry," left). The most spectacular surviving example is Machu Picchu (fig. 15-11). At 9,000 feet above sea level, the site straddles a ridge between two high peaks in the eastern slopes of the Andes. Machu Picchu's location, near the eastern limits of the empire, suggests that it may have been a frontier outpost. Its temples and carved sacred stones imply it may also have had an important religious function.

The production of textiles is an ancient art in the Andes. As one of the primary forms of wealth for the Inca, cloth was a

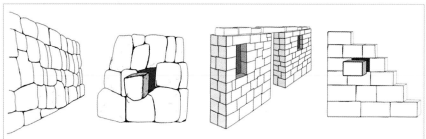

Elements of Architecture

INCA MASONRY

Working with the simplest of tools—mainly heavy stone hammers—and using no mortar, Inca builders created stonework of great refinement and durability, built-up terraces for growing crops, and structures both simple and elaborate, as well as roads that linked the empire together. At Machu Picchu (see fig. 15-11), all buildings and terraces within its 3-square-mile extent were made of granite, the hard stone indigenous to the site. Commoners' houses and some walls were constructed of irregular stones b and religious structures were erected using squared-off, smooth-surfaced stones laid in even rows. At a few Inca sites, the stones were boulder-size: up to 27 feet tall.

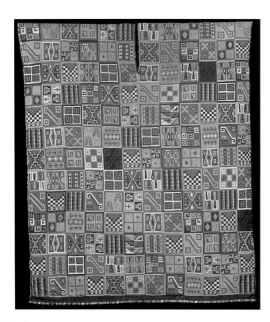

15-12 | **Tunic, from Peru. Inca,** c. 1500 CE. Wool and cotton, 35⁷/₈ x 30" (91.1 x 76.2 cm). Dumbarton Oaks Research Library and Collections, Washington, D.C. (See pages 384–85.)

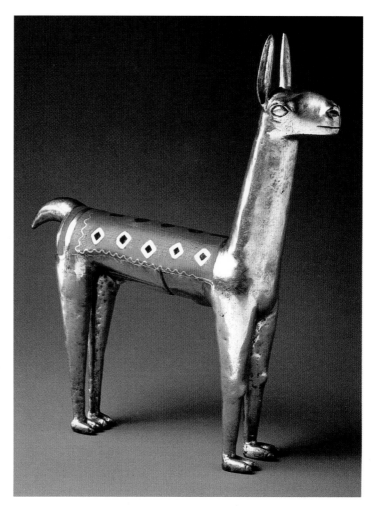

15-13 | **Llama, from Bolivia or Peru,** found near Lake Titicaca, Bolivia. Inka, 15th century CE. Cast silver with gold and cinnabar, 9" x 8¹/₂" x 1³/₄" (22.9 x 21.6 x 4.4 cm). Image #5003. Photo by American Museum of Natural History Library, New York

fitting offering for the gods (fig. 15-12). Fine garments were draped around golden statues, and complex images were woven of cloth. Garments also carried important symbolic messages. Their patterns and designs indicated, among other things, a person's ethnic identity and social rank. Each square in the tunic represents a miniature tunic, but the meaning of the individual patterns is not yet completely understood. The checkerboard pattern designated military officers and royal escorts. The four-part motifs may refer to the Land of the Four Quarters.

THE AFTERMATH OF THE SPANISH CONQUEST

Hernándo Cortés arrived off the eastern coast of Mexico from the Spanish colony in Cuba in 1519. He forged alliances with the Aztecs' enemies and, within two years, took Tenochtitlan. Over the next several years, Spanish forces subdued much of the rest of Mexico and established it as a colony of Spain. In 1532, Francisco Pizarro, following Cortés's example, led an expedition to South America. He and his men seized the Inca ruler Atahualpa, held him for a huge ransom in gold, then treacherously strangled him. They marched on to Cuzco and seized it in 1533.

The Spanish who conquered the Inca Empire were obsessed with amassing gold and silver. They melted down whatever they could find to enrich themselves and the royal coffers of Spain. The Inca, in contrast, valued gold and silver not as precious metals in themselves, but as symbols of the sun and the moon. Only a few small figures, buried as offerings, escaped the invaders' treasure hunt. A small llama was found near Lake Titicaca (fig. 15-13). To the Inca, the llama had a special connection with the sun, rain, and fertility. In Cuzco, a llama was sacrificed to the sun every morning and evening. Dressed in a red tunic and wear-

ing gold jewelry, this llama would be paraded through the streets during April celebrations. According to Spanish commentators, these processions included lifesize gold and silver images of llamas, people, and gods.

Native American populations in Mexico and Peru declined sharply after the Conquest because of the exploitive policies of the conquerors and the ravages of smallpox and other diseases, against which the indigenous people had no immunity. European missionaries suppressed local beliefs and practices and spread Roman Catholicism throughout the Americas.

In 1531, converts in Mexico gained their own patron saint when the Virgin Mary appeared as an Indian to an Indian named Juan Diego. Mary is said to have asked that a church be built on a hill where an Aztec Mother Goddess (see fig. 15-9) had once been worshiped. As evidence of this vision, Juan Diego brought flowers to the archbishop that the Virgin had caused to bloom, wrapped in a cloak. When he opened the bundle, the cloak bore the likeness of the Virgin Mary, in her guise as the Woman of the Apocalypse and the Virgin of the Immaculate Conception. The site of the vision was renamed Guadalupe, after the Guadalupe shrine in Spain, and became

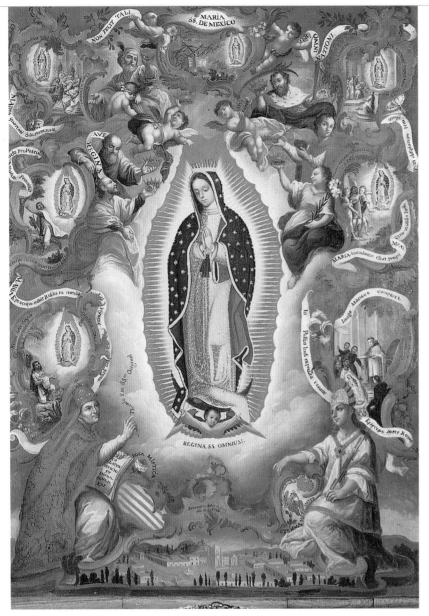

15-14 | Sebastián Salcedo. *Our Lady of Guadalupe,* 1779. Oil on copper, 25" x 19" (63.5 x 48.3 cm).

Denver Art Museum Collection: Funds contributed by Mr. and Mrs. George G. Anderman and an Anonymous Donor, 1976.56

At the bottom right is the female personification of New Spain (Mexico) and at the left is Pope Benedict XIV (ruled 1740–1758), who in 1754 declared the Virgin of Guadalupe to be the patron of the Americas. Between the figures, the sanctuary of Guadalupe in Mexico can be seen in the distance. The four small scenes circling the Virgin represent the story of Juan Diego and (at the top) three scenes of Mary's miracles. The six figures above the Virgin represent Old Testament prophets and patriarchs and New Testament apostles and saints.

a venerated pilgrimage center. In 1754, the pope declared the Virgin of Guadalupe to be the patron saint of the Americas (fig. 15-14). The pope recently made Juan Diego a saint.

North America

Compared with the densely inhabited agricultural regions of Mesoamerica and South America, much of North America remained sparsely populated before the arrival of Europeans in the fifteenth century. In the Northeast, people lived primarily by hunting, fishing, and gathering edible plants. In the

Southeast and in the lands drained by the Mississippi and Missouri river systems, agriculture emerged, and nomadic hunting and gathering gave way to more settled communities by 1000 BCE or possibly even earlier. Toward the end of the first millennium BCE, people in the Southwest of the present-day United States also began to adopt an agricultural way of life.

THE SOUTHEAST AND THE SOUTHWEST

In the fertile lands near the Ohio, Illinois, Mississippi, and Missouri Rivers, the people of the Adena, Hopewell, and Mississippian cultures cultivated maize (corn) and other crops. They began building monumental **earthworks** and burying their leaders with valuable grave goods sometime before 1000 BCE. Objects discovered in these burials show that the people of the Mississippi and Ohio Valleys traded widely with other regions. For example, burials of the mound-building Adena (1000 BCE–200 CE) and Hopewell (1500 CE) cultures contained jewelry made with copper imported from present-day Michigan's Upper Peninsula and silhouettes cut in sheets of mica from the Appalachian Mountains.

The Hopewell people made pipes of fine-grain pipestone carved with realistic representations of forest animals and birds, sometimes with inlaid eyes and teeth of freshwater pearls and bone. A pearl-eyed beaver crouching on a platform forms the bowl of a pipe found in present-day Illinois (fig. 15-15). As in a modern pipe, the bowl—a hole in the beaver's back—could be filled with dried leaves (the Hopewell may not have grown tobacco), the leaves lighted, and smoke drawn through a hole in the stem. A second way that these pipes were used was to blow smoke inhaled from another vessel through the pipe to envelop the animal carved on it. Hopewell pipes and pipestone have been found from Lake Superior to the Gulf of Mexico.

The people of the Mississippian culture (900–600 CE) continued the mound-building tradition of the Adena, Hopewell, and other early southeastern cultures. One of the most impressive Mississippian-period earthworks is the Great Serpent Mound, nearly 1/4-mile long, in present-day Ohio (fig. 15-16). Carbon-14 dating of wood charcoal samples from the mound suggests that the earthwork was built about 1070 CE. It was probably the work of the people of the Fort Ancient culture (900–1600 CE), a Mississippian group of the Ohio Valley. There have been many interpretations of the twisting snake form, especially the "head" at the highest point, an oval enclosure which some see as opening its jaws to swallow a huge egg formed by a heap of stones.

The Mississippian peoples built a major urban center known as Cahokia near the juncture of the Illinois, Missouri, and Mississippi Rivers (now East St. Louis, Illinois). Cahokia was founded about 900 CE, but most construction took place between about 900 and 1500. At its height, the city had a population of between

15-15 **Beaver effigy platform pipe,** from Bedford Mound Pike County, Illinois. Hopewell culture, c. 100–200 CE Pipestone, pearl, and bone, length 4¹/₂" (11.4 cm) Gilcrease Museum, Tulsa, Oklahoma

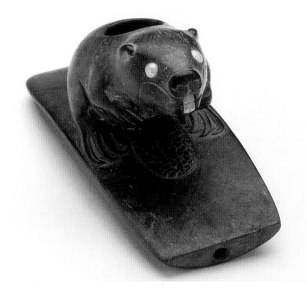

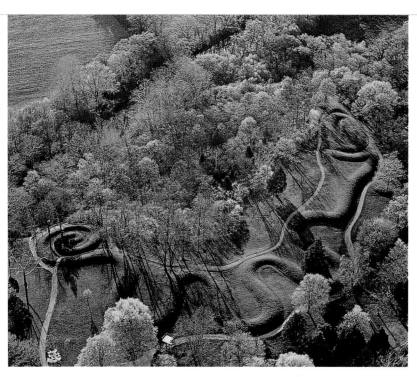

15-16 | **Great Serpent Mound,** Adams County, Ohio. c. 1070 CE Length 1,254' (328.2 m)

10,000 and 20,000 people, with another 10,000 in the surrounding countryside (fig. 15-17).

The most prominent feature of Cahokia is an enormous 100-foot earth mound called Monk's Mound covering 15 acres. A small, conical platform on its summit originally supported a wooden fence and a rectangular temple or house. Smaller rectangular and conical mounds in front of the principal mound surrounded a large, roughly rectangular plaza. The city's entire ceremonial center was protected by a stockade, or fence, of upright wooden posts—a sign of increasing warfare. In all, the walled enclosure contained more than 500 mounds, platforms, wooden enclosures, and houses. The various earthworks functioned as tombs and as bases for palaces and temples and also served to make astronomical observations. A conical burial mound, for example, was located next to a platform that may have been used for sacrifices.

Farming cultures were slower to arise in the arid southwestern region of what is now the United States. The Hohokam culture, centered in central and southern Arizona, emerged around 200 BCE and endured until sometime after 1200 CE. The Hohokam built

large-scale irrigation systems with canals made deep and narrow to reduce evaporation and lined with clay to reduce seepage. In the Four Corners region, where Colorado, Utah, Arizona, and New Mexico meet, the Anasazi (a Navajo word meaning "the ancient ones") adopted this irrigation technology to produce food for settled communities. Around 900 CE they began building elaborate, multistoried structures with many rooms for specialized purposes, including communal food storage and ritual. The Spaniards called the Rio Grande communities "pueblos" or towns. The descendants of the Anasazi, including the Hopi and Zuni, still occupy these pueblos and other areas. An early photographer, Timothy O'Sullivan, recorded Anasazi ruins in the Cañon de Chelley, in Arizona, while accompanying a geological expedition in 1873 (see fig. 18-10).

15-17 | **Reconstruction of central Cahokia** East St. Louis, Illinois. Mississippian culture, c. 1150 CE. Earth mounds and wooden structures; east-west length approx. 3 miles (4.84 km), north-south length approx. 2¹/₄ miles (3.63 km); base of great mound, 1,037 x 790' (316 x 241 m), height approx. 100' (30 m). Painting by William R. Iseminger

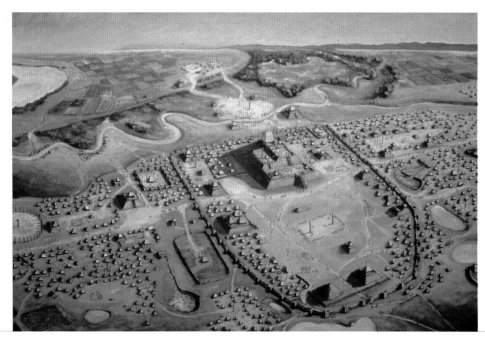

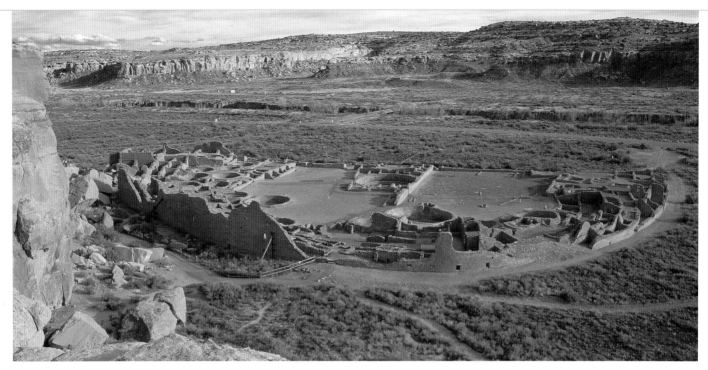

15-18 | **Pueblo Bonito, Chaco Canyon,** New Mexico. Anasazi culture, c. 900–1200 CE

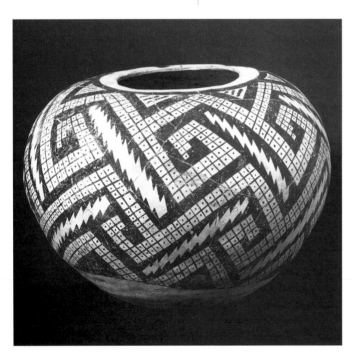

15-19 | **Seed jar. Anasazi culture,** c. 1150 CE. Earthenware and black-and-white pigment, diameter 14¹/₂" (36.8 cm) The St. Louis Art Museum, St. Louis, Missouri

Purchase: Funds given by the Children's Art Festival 175:1981

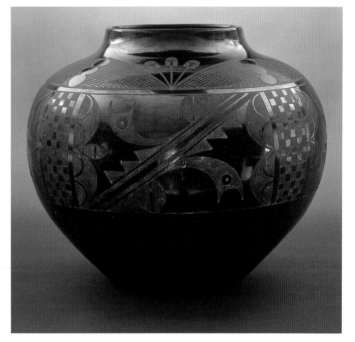

15-20 | **Maria Montoya Martínez** and **Julian Martínez. Black on black ceramic storage jar,** c. 1942. San Ildefonso Pueblo, New Mexico. Black on black ceramic. Ht. 18³/₄" (47.6 cm), diameter 22¹/₂" (57.1 cm).

Museum of Indian Arts and Culture/Laboratory of Anthropology, Museum of New Mexico, Santa Fe (Catalog #31959/12)

The largest known ancient Anasazi center is Pueblo Bonito in Chaco Canyon, New Mexico, which was built in stages from the tenth to mid-thirteenth century CE (fig. 15-18). This remarkable, D-shaped structure covered more than three acres. Some 800 rooms—including thirty kivas (subterranean circular rooms used as ceremonial centers)—rose four or five stories high. Its outer perimeter wall was 1,300 feet long. The sandstone masonry walls on the ground floor were 4 feet thick, and trunks of

ponderosa pines transported 50 miles were used for roof beams. As new rooms were added over time, older rooms lost access to natural light. Amazingly, all aspects of construction—including quarrying, timber cutting, and transport—were done without draft animals, wheeled vehicles, or metal tools.

Pueblo Bonito stood at the center of a trading network of wide, straight roads, in some places with curbs and paving. The builders made no effort to avoid topographic obstacles; when

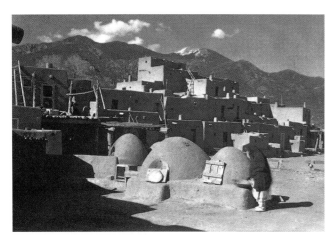

15-21 | **Taos Pueblo,** Tewa, Taos, New Mexico
Photographed by Laura Gilpin in 1947
Amon Carter Museum, Fort Worth, Texas
Laura Gilpin Collection (neg. # P1979.208.698)

they encountered cliffs, they ran stairs up them. This practice suggests that the roads served as processional routes in addition to practical thoroughfares.

Women were the potters in Anasazi society. In the eleventh century, these potters perfected a functional, aesthetically pleasing, coil-built earthenware, or ceramic fired at a low temperature. The wide-mouthed seed jar shown in figure 15-19 is painted with complex black-and-white checkerboard and zigzag patterns that conform to the body of the jar and, in spite of their angularity, enhance its curved shape. The intricate and inventive play of dark and light, positive and negative, suggests lightning flashing over a grid of irrigated fields.

The ceramic tradition of the Anasazi continues today among the Pueblo people of the Southwest. One of the best-known twentieth-century Pueblo potters is Maria Montoya Martínez (1881–1980) of San Ildefonso Pueblo. Inspired by prehistoric **blackware** pottery that was unearthed at nearby archaeological excavations, she and her husband, Julian Martínez (1885–1943), developed a distinctive new ware decorated with **matte** (nongloss) black designs on a lustrous black background (fig. 15-20). Their decorative patterns were inspired by both traditional Pueblo imagery and the then-fashionable Euro-American Art Deco style (see "'Primitivism' and Modernity," page 470).

Other traditional practices have survived today (see "Basketry," right). Some contemporary Pueblo villages, like those of their Anasazi forebears, consist of multistoried, apartmentlike dwellings built of adobe bricks rather than stone. One of these, Taos Pueblo, shown here in a 1947 photograph (fig. 15-21), is located in north-central New Mexico. The northernmost of the surviving Pueblo communities, Taos once served as a trading center between Plains and Pueblo peoples. It burned in 1690 but was rebuilt about 1700 and has been modified often since. Two complexes of great multifamily houses stand on either side of Taos Creek, rising up to five stories in a stepped fashion to form a series of roof terraces, where people could view the ceremonies in the plaza below.

THE EASTERN WOODLANDS AND THE GREAT PLAINS

When European settlement began in earnest in North America around the late 1500s to the early 1600s, forests stretched from the Hudson Bay to the Gulf of Mexico and from the Atlantic coast to the Mississippi River and Missouri River watersheds. Between this Eastern Woodlands region and the Rocky Mountains to the west lay an area of prairie grasslands now known as the Great Plains.

In the Eastern Woodlands, Native American peoples supported themselves by a combination of hunting and agriculture. Living together in villages, they cultivated corn, squash, and beans. They used waterproof birchbark to construct their homes and to make the watercraft known as the canoe. In the sixteenth century, one Eastern Woodlands group, the Iroquois, formed a powerful confederation of northeastern Native American nations

TECHNIQUE
Basketry

Basketry involves weaving reeds, grasses, and other materials to form containers. The three principal basket-making techniques are: coiling, or sewing together a spiraling foundation of rods with some other material; twining, or sewing together a vertical warp of rods; and plaiting, which involves weaving strips over and under each other. In North America the earliest evidence of basketwork, found in Danger Cave, Utah, dates to as early as 8400 BCE. Over the subsequent centuries basket makers developed basketry into an art form that combined utility with great beauty.

The coiled basket shown here was made by the Pomo of northern California. According to Pomo legend, the earth was dark until their ancestral hero stole the sun and brought it to earth in a basket. He hung the basket first just over the horizon, but, dissatisfied with the light it gave, he kept suspending it in different places across the dome of the sky. He repeats this process every day, which is why the sun moves across the sky from east to west. In the Pomo basket the structure of coiled willow and bracken fern root produces a spiral surface into which the artist worked sparkling pieces of clamshell, trade beads, and the soft tufts of woodpecker and quail feathers. Such baskets were treasured possessions, often cremated with their owners at death.

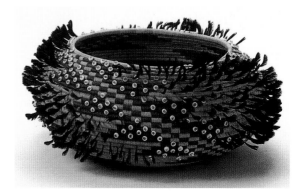

Feathered Bowl Wedding Basket. c. 1877. Pomo. Willow, bracken fern root, clamshell, trade beads, woodpecker and quail feathers. Height 5 1/2" (14 cm), diameter 12" (30.5 cm). Philbrook Museum of Art, Tulsa, Oklahoma
Gift of Clark Field (1948.39.37)

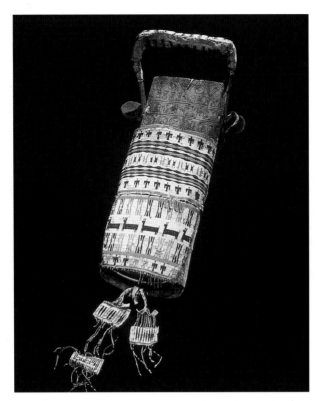

15-22 | **Baby carrier, from the Upper Missouri River area**
Eastern Sioux, 19th century. Board, buckskin, porcupine quill, length 31" (78.7 cm)
Smithsonian Institution Libraries, Washington, D.C.

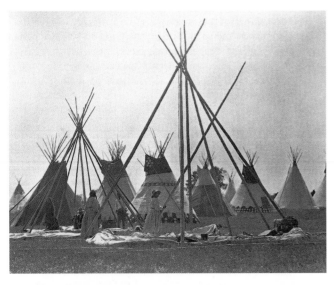

15-23 | **Blackfoot women raising a tepee**
Photographed c. 1900. Montana Historical Society
Helena

When packed to be dragged by a horse, the tepee served as a platform for transporting other possessions as well. Tepees were the property and responsibility of women. Blackfoot women could set up their tepees in less than an hour.

Men recorded their exploits in symbolic and narrative paintings on tepee covers and on buffalo-hide robes. They painted traditional symbols and decorative motifs at the bottom of the cover and filled the center section with personal images.

that played a prominent military and political role until after the American Revolution.

On the Great Plains, two differing ways of life developed, one nomadic—dependent on the region's great migrating herds of buffalo for food, clothing, and shelter—and the other sedentary and agricultural. Horses, introduced by Spanish explorers in the late seventeenth century, and later, firearms, made buffalo hunting vastly more efficient than before and attracted more people to the nomadic way of life.

As European settlers on the eastern seaboard began to turn forests into farms, they put increasing pressure on the Eastern Woodlands peoples, seizing their lands and forcing them westward. The resulting interaction of Eastern Woodlands artists with one another and with Plains artists led to the emergence of a Prairie style among numerous groups.

One distinctively Eastern Woodlands medium that found its way to the Plains was **quillwork** embroidery. Quillwork involved soaking porcupine and bird quills to soften them, then dyeing them, and working them into rectilinear, ornamental surface patterns on deerskin clothing and on birchbark artifacts like baskets and boxes. A Lakota legend recounts how a mythical ancestor, Doublewoman ("double" because she was both beautiful and ugly, benign and dangerous), appeared to a Lakota woman in a dream and taught her the art of quillwork. As this legend suggests, quillwork was a woman's art form. The Sioux cradle shown in figure 15-22 is richly decorated with symbols of protection and well-being, including bands of antelopes in profile and thunderbirds with their heads turned and their tails outspread. The thunderbird was an especially beneficent symbol, thought to be capable of providing protection against both human and supernatural adversaries. In some areas beadwork replaced quillwork in the nineteenth century when the women began to acquire colored glass beads through trade with Europeans. At first they imitated the patterns of quillwork, but by midcentury they began to incorporate European floral designs into their work.

The nomadic Plains peoples developed a light, portable dwelling known as a **tepee** (fig. 15-23), which was sturdily constructed to withstand the wind, dust, and rain of the prairies. Hides (later, canvas) covered a framework of poles to form an almost conical structure that leaned slightly in the direction of the prevailing wind. The flap-covered door and smoke hole (the opening at the top above the central hearth) usually faced away from the wind. Designed and built by women, the typical tepee required about eighteen buffalo hides, the largest about thirty-eight. An inner lining covered the lower part of the walls and part of the floor to protect the occupants from drafts. The women painted, embroidered, quilled, and beaded tepee linings, backrests, clothing, and equipment. But life and art on the Plains changed abruptly in the 1870s and 1880s when the transcontinental railway (1869) was completed and settlers killed off the buffalo, thereby destroying the Native American way of life.

THE NORTHWEST COAST

Before the arrival of European explorers, the Native American peoples comprising the First Nations of the Northwest Coast—

CLOSER LOOK

During the harsh winter season, when spirits are thought to be most powerful, many northern people seek spiritual renewal through their ancient rituals—including the potlatch and the initiation of new members into the prestigious Hamatsa Society. With snapping beaks and cries of *"Hap! Hap! Hap!"* ("Eat! Eat! Eat!"), Hamatsa, the people-eating spirit of the north, and his three assistants—horrible masked monster birds—begin their wild, ritual dance (fig. 15-24). The dancing birds threaten and even attack the Kwakwaka'wakw (Kwakiutl) people who gather for the Winter Ceremony. At this time, youths are captured, taught the Hamatsa lore, and then in a spectacular theater-dance performance are "tamed" and brought back into civilized life.

Afterwards, the masked bird dancers appear—first Raven-of-the-North-End-of-the-World, then Crooked-Beak-of-the-End-of-the-World, and finally the untranslatable Huxshukw, who cracks open skulls with its beak and eats the brains of its victims. Snapping their beaks, these masters of illusion enter the room backward, their masks pointed up as though the birds are looking skyward. They move slowly counterclockwise around the floor. At each change in the music they crouch, snap their beaks, and let out their wild cries of *"Hap! Hap! Hap!"* Essential to the ritual dances are the huge carved and painted wooden masks, articulated and operated by strings worked by the dancers. Among the finest masks are those by Willie Seaweed (1873–1967), a Kwakwaka'wakw chief (see fig. 15-25), whose brilliant colors and exuberantly decorative carving style determined the direction of twentieth-century Kwakwaka'wakw sculpture.

The Canadian government, abetted by missionaries, outlawed the Winter Ceremony and potlatches in 1885, claiming the event was injurious to health, encouraged prostitution, endangered children's education, damaged the economy, and was cannibalistic. But the Kwakwaka'wakw refused to give up their "oldest and best" festival—one that

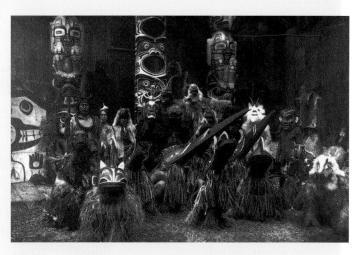

15-24 | **Hamatsa dancers,** Kwakwaka'wakw (Kwakiutl) Canada. Photographed 1914 by Edward S. Curtis

spoke powerfully to them in many ways, establishing social rank and playing an important role in arranging marriages. By 1936 the government and the missionaries, who called the Kwakwaka'wakw "incorrigible," gave up. But not until 1951 could the Kwakwaka'wakw people gather openly for Winter Ceremonies, including the initiation rites of the Hamatsa Society.

The photographer Edward S. Curtis (1868–1952) devoted thirty years to documenting the lives of Native Americans. This 1914 photograph shows participants in a film he made about the Kwakwaka'wakw. For the film, his Native American informant and assistant, Richard Hunt, borrowed family heirlooms and commissioned many new pieces from the finest Kwakwaka'wakw artists. Most of the pieces are now in museum collections. The photograph shows carved and painted posts, masked dancers (including those representing people-eating birds), a chief at the left (holding a speaker's staff and wearing a cedar neck ring), and spectators at the right.

among them the Tlingit of southern Alaska, the Haida of southern Alaska and the Queen Charlotte Islands, and the Kwakwaka'wakw (formerly called Kwakiutl) along the central Canadian coast, Alert Bay—lived on the Pacific coast of North America from southern Alaska to northern California. Their major food source was salmon from the region's many rivers. Harvested and dried, the fish could sustain large populations throughout the year.

People lived in extended family groups in large, elaborately decorated communal houses made of massive timbers and thick planks. Family groups claimed descent from a mythic animal or animal-human ancestor. Chiefs, who were in the most direct line of descent from the ancestor, validated their status and garnered prestige for themselves and their families by holding ritual feasts known as potlatches at which time they gave valuable gifts to the guests. Shamans, who were sometimes also chiefs, mediated between the human and spirit worlds.

The participants who danced in the Winter Ceremony of the Kwakwaka'wakw wore striking costumes and gigantic carved and painted masks. Among the most elaborate masks were those used by the elite Hamatsa society in their dances (fig. 15-24). The dancers, transformed into supernatural creatures, search for

15-25

Kwakwaka'wakw (Kwakiutl) Bird mask, from Alert Bay, Canada. Prior to 1951. Cedar wood, cedar bark, feathers, and fiber, 10 x 72 x 15" (25.4 x 183 x 38.1 cm). Collection of the Museum of Anthropology Vancouver, Canada

(A6120)

The name *Seaweed* is an Anglicization of the Kwakwaka'wakw name *Siwid*, meaning "Paddling Canoe," "recipient of paddling," or "Paddled To"—referring to a great chief to whose potlatches guests paddle from afar. Willie Seaweed was not only the chief of his clan, but a great orator, singer, and tribal historian who kept the tradition of the potlatch alive during years of government repression.

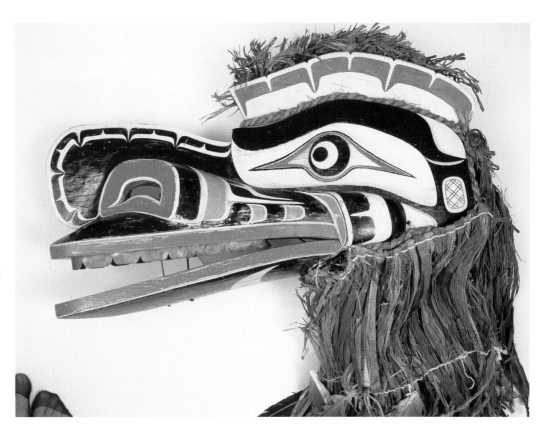

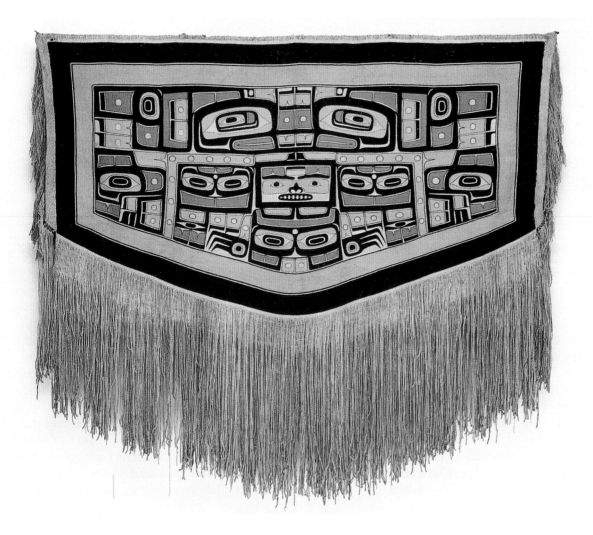

15-26

Chilikat blanket Tlingit, Canada. Before 1928 Goat hair and cedar bark fiber. L. 55⅛" (140 cm.), W. 63¾" (162 cm.)

Image #3804. Photo by American Museum of Natural History Library

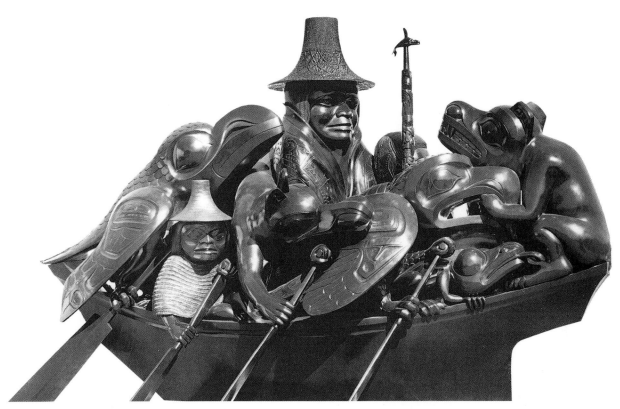

15-27 | Bill Reid. *The Spirit of Haida Gwaii.* Haida, 1991. Bronze approx. 13 x 20' (4 x 6 m). Canadian Embassy, Washington, D.C.

victims (fig. 15-25). By using strings inside the masks, they snap the beaks open and shut with spectacular effect.

Blankets and other textiles produced by the Tlingit had great prestige throughout the Northwest Coast (fig. 15-26). To weave the Chilkat blanket women followed complex designs painted on story boards made by men. They worked in three colors of mountain goat wool—natural, dyed black, and dyed mustard yellow. (Painters preferred a color scheme of black, white, and red and only later added yellow and blue-green.) Instead of using looms, the weavers hung **warp** (vertical) threads from a rod and twisted colored threads back and forth through the warp threads to make the pattern. The ends of the warp formed the fringe at the bottom of the blanket.

The designs are very complex and difficult to interpret. The stylized creature in the center of this blanket is perhaps a sea bear or a standing eagle with a bear as its body. The legs and claws are placed on either side of the blocky body. The images on the blanket consist of two basic elements: the ovoid (a slightly bent rectangle with rounded corners) and the **formline** (a continuous, shape-defining line). When the blanket is worn, its two-dimensional forms become three-dimensional, with the dramatic central figure curving over the wearer's back.

The contemporary Haida artist Bill Reid (1920–1998) sought to sustain and revitalize the traditions of his Haida ancestors' art in his work. Trained as a wood carver, painter, and jeweler,

Canadian Reid revived the art of carving dugout canoes and totem poles in the Haida homeland of Haida Gwaii—"Islands of the People"—known on maps today as the Queen Charlotte Islands. Late in life he began to create large-scale sculpture in bronze. With their black patina, these works recall traditional Haida carvings in argillite, a shiny black stone. One of them, *The Spirit of Haida Gwaii,* now stands outside the Canadian Embassy in Washington, D.C. (fig. 15-27). This sculpture, which Reid viewed as a metaphor for modern Canada's multicultural society, depicts a collection of figures from the natural and mythic worlds of the First Nations struggling to paddle forward in a canoe. The dominant figure in the center is a shaman wearing a spruce-root basket hat and Chilkat blanket. He holds a speaker's pole—a staff that gives him the right to speak with authority. In the prow, the place reserved for the chief in a war canoe, is the Bear. The Bear faces backward rather than forward, however, and is bitten by the Eagle, with formline-patterned wings. The Eagle, in turn, is bitten by the Seawolf. In the stern, steering the canoe, is the Raven, the trickster in Haida mythology. The Raven is assisted by Mousewoman, the traditional guide and escort of humans in the spirit realms. According to Reid, the work represents a "mythological and environmental lifeboat," where "the entire family of living things . . . whatever their differences, . . . are paddling together in one boat, headed in one direction."

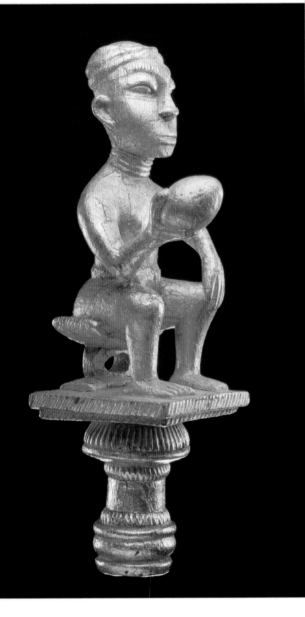

Kojo Bonsu (attributed). Finial of a spokesperson's staff (*okyeame poma*), from an Akan kingdom, Ghana Asante culture, 20th century. Wood and gold, height 11¼" (28.57 cm). Gold of Africa Museum, Cape Town (See page 411.)

A staff or rod is a nearly universal symbol of authority and leadership. In ancient Egypt, 5,000 years before Kojo Bonsu carved this Asante speaker's staff, a sculptor depicted King Narmer holding a mace (a weighted club, see fig. 2-14). The mace's symbolism emphasized his role as the mighty ruler who brought order to the lands watered by the Nile. Today in many colleges a ceremonial mace is still carried by the leader of an academic procession and placed in front of the speaker's lectern. Asante speakers who carry their image-topped staffs are part of this widespread tradition.

As in other societies throughout the world, art in Africa identifies those who hold important positions. Art validates their right to kingship, or their authority as representatives of the family or community, and communicates the rules for moral behavior that must be obeyed by all members of the society. The finial of this luxurious gold-covered spokesperson's staff belonged to the royal culture of one of the Akan kingdoms of Ghana, in West Africa. The Akan admire elegant speech. One of their adages is, "We speak to the wise man in proverbs, not in plain speech." Consequently their governing system includes the special post of Ruler's Spokesperson. Since about 1900 these advisers have carried staffs of office such as the one pictured here. The carved figure holding an egg illustrates a parable that may have multiple meanings when told by a witty owner. "Political power is like an egg," says an Akan proverb, "Grasp it too tightly and it will shatter in your hand; hold it too loosely and it will slip from your fingers."

Since the fifteenth century when the first Europeans explored Africa, quantities of artworks—such as this staff—have been shipped back to western museums of natural history or ethnography, where the works were first exhibited as curious artifacts of "primitive" cultures. Toward the end of the nineteenth century, however, profound changes in western thinking about art gradually led more and more people to appreciate the inherent aesthetic qualities of these unfamiliar objects and at last to embrace them fully as art. In recent years, scholars have further enhanced the world's vision of traditional African arts by exploring their rich meaning from the point of view of the people who made and used them. If we are to attempt to understand artwork such as this staff on its own terms, we must first take it out of the glass museum case where we usually encounter it and consider how it plays a vital role in the continuity of human life.

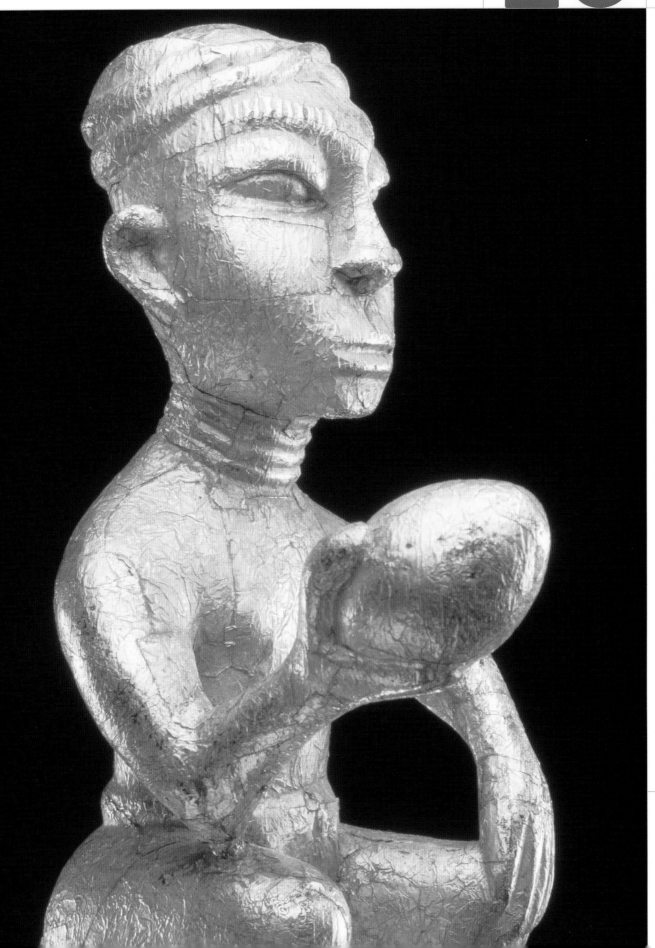

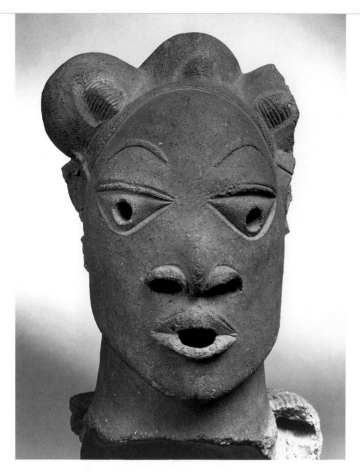

16-1 | **Head. Nok style,** from Nigeria. c. 500 BCE–200 CE. Terra cotta
Height 14¹³/₁₆" (36 cm). National Museum, Lagos, Nigeria

to the east. As the Saharan grasslands dried up, some of their inhabitants may have migrated to the Nile Valley region in search of arable land and pasture. Perhaps this migration, by greatly expanding the population of the valley, contributed to the tensions that resulted in the emergence of complex forms of social organization there.

Saharan people presumably migrated southward as well, into the Sudan, the broad belt of grassland that stretches across Africa south of the Sahara desert, bringing with them knowledge of agriculture and animal husbandry. Agriculture reached the Sudan by at least 3000 BCE, and knowledge of ironworking spread across the area toward the middle of the first millennium BCE.

Some of the earliest evidence of iron technology in sub-Saharan Africa comes from the so-called Nok culture, which arose in the western Sudan, in present-day Nigeria, as early as 500 BCE. The Nok people were farmers who grew grain and oil-bearing seeds; they were also smelters, using the technology for refining ore. In addition, they created the earliest known sculpture of sub-Saharan Africa, producing accomplished **terra-cotta** figures of human and animal subjects between about 500 BCE and 200 CE.

The Nok head shown here (fig. 16-1), slightly larger than lifesize, originally formed part of a complete figure. The triangular or D-shaped eyes are characteristic of Nok style and appear also on sculpture of animals. Each of the large buns of the elaborate hairstyle is pierced with a hole that may have held

Africa is a continent of enormous diversity. Geographically, it ranges from vast deserts to tropical rain forests, from flat grasslands to spectacular mountains and dramatic rift valleys. Human diversity in Africa is equally impressive. More than 1,000 major languages have been identified, representing a seemingly infinite variety of cultures, each with its own history, customs, and art forms (see Map 6, page 415). Africa is the site of one of the great ancient civilizations, that of Egypt (see Chapter 2), and North Africa later contributed prominently to the development of Islamic art and culture.

As we saw in Chapter 1, the history of African art begins in the Paleolithic era. Like prehistoric people around the world, early Africans painted and inscribed an abundance of images on the walls of caves and overhanging rocks. The mountains of the central Sahara have especially fascinating examples of rock art, with the earliest images dating from at least 8000 BCE. At that time, the Sahara was a great grassy plain, perhaps much like the game-park areas of modern East Africa. Vivid images of hippopotami, elephant, giraffe, antelope, and other animals incised into rock surfaces testify to the abundant wildlife that roamed the region.

By 4000 BCE, hunting had given way to herding as the Saharan climate became more arid. Remarkably lifelike paintings on rock surfaces from the herding period show scenes of cattle and the people who tended them. The desiccation of the Sahara coincided with the rise of Egyptian civilization along the Nile Valley

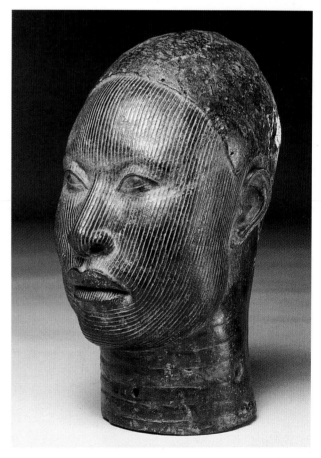

16-2 | **Head of a king (oni), from Ife,** Nigeria. Yoruba culture
c. 12th–15th century. Bronze, height 11⁷/₁₆" (29cm)
Museum of Ife Antiquities, Ife, Nigeria

ornamental feathers. Other Nok figures boast large quantities of beads and other prestige ornaments. Since none of these sculptures have been excavated by archaeologists, their original meaning and function is unknown.

The city of Ife, a sacred site for the Yoruba people, arose in the southern, forested part of present-day Nigeria by about 800 CE several centuries after the last Nok terra cottas were produced. Yoruba myth tells how at Ife the gods descended from heaven on iron chains to create the world. Remarkable, naturalistic works of sculpture were created in this sacred city between about 1050 CE and 1400 CE.

A lifesize bronze head of an *oni* (king) shows the extraordinary artistry achieved by Ife sculptors (fig. 16-2). The modeling of the flesh is extremely sensitive, especially around the nose and mouth. The eyes are strikingly similar in shape to those of some modern Yoruba, and the face is covered with decorative parallel scarification patterns (decorations made by scarring). Holes along the scalp apparently permitted the attachment of hair, a crown, or perhaps a beaded veil. The head might possibly have been attached to a wooden mannequin using the large holes at the base of the neck. The mannequin would have been dressed in a deceased *oni*'s robe used for display during his memorial services, or the heads might have held the sacred crowns of the *oni* during a vacancy of the throne.

Ife was the artistic parent of the great city-state of Benin, which arose some 150 miles to the southeast. According to oral histories, the earliest kings of Benin belonged to the Ogiso, or Skyking, dynasty. After a long period of misrule, however, the Edo people of Benin asked the *oni* of Ife for a new ruler. The *oni* sent Prince Oranmiyan, who founded a new dynasty in 1170 CE. Some two centuries later, the fourth king, or *oba*, of Benin decided to start a tradition of memorial sculpture like that of Ife. He sent to Ife for master metal casters. The practice of casting memorial heads for the shrines of royal ancestors of Benin is still in the hands of their descendants to this day.

Benin brass heads range from small, thinly cast, naturalistic images to large, thickly cast, highly stylized representations. The dating of these works is controversial, but many scholars have concluded that the smallest, most naturalistic heads were created during a so-called Early Period (1400–1550 CE), when Benin artists were still heavily influenced by those of Ife. The memorial heads grew increasingly stylized during the Middle Period (1550–1700 CE), becoming very large and heavy during the ensuing Late Period (1700–1897 CE), with angular, stylized features and an elaborate beaded crown (fig. 16-3). A similar crown is still worn by the present-day *oba*.

All of the heads include representations of coral-bead necklaces, which have been part of the royal costume from earliest times to the present day. In Late Period sculpture, the necklaces form a tall, cylindrical mass that obscures the chin and greatly adds to the weight of the sculpture. The increase in size and weight of Benin memorial heads over time may reflect the growing power and wealth of the *oba* deriving from Benin's expanding trade with Europe. Benin traded with Portugal from the late fifteenth century, first in ivory and forest products and later, tragically, in slaves. Commerce between Benin and Europe flourished

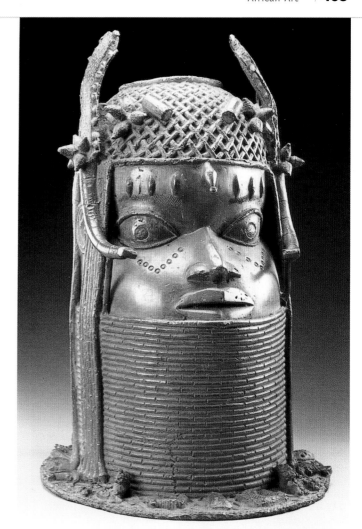

16-3 | **Head of an *oba* (king), from Benin,** Nigeria. Edo culture c. 1700–1897 CE (Late Period). Brass, height 17¾" (45 cm) Museum für Völkerkunde, Vienna/Musée Dapper, Paris

Almost all Benin metal sculpture was made by the **lost-wax casting** process (see page 10). Although Benin sculptures are popularly referred to as "bronze," other copper alloys such as brass were more common.

THE MYTH OF "PRIMITIVE" ART

The word *primitive* was once used by western art historians to lump together the art of Africa, the Pacific Islands, and North, South, and Central America before the arrival of Columbus. The term itself means "early," and its very use implies that these civilizations are frozen at an early stage of development.

How, then, did labels like *primitive* arise? Many historical attitudes were rooted in racism and colonialism. These usages were extended to the creations of the cultures, and "*primitive*" art became the dominant label for the cultural products of these people. Criteria previously used to label a people "*primitive*" included the use of so-called Stone Age technology, the absence of written histories, and the failure to build "great" cities. Yet the accomplishments of the people of Africa strongly belie this categorization: Africans south of the Sahara have smelted and forged iron since at least 500 BCE, and Africans in many areas made and used high-quality steel for weapons and tools. Many African people have recorded their histories in Arabic since at least the tenth century. The first European visitors to Africa admired politically and economically sophisticated urban centers such as Benin, Kilwa, Djenné, Great Zimbabwe, and Mbanza Kongo.

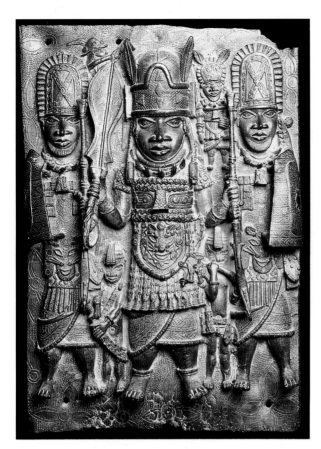

16-4 | *General and Officers*, **from Benin,** Nigeria. 17th century. Bronze, height 21" (53.5 cm). National Museum, Lagos, Nigeria

The general wears an elaborate, appliqué apron depicting the head of a leopard, and the flanking officers wear leopard pelts. Leopards were symbols of royalty in Benin. Live leopards were kept at the royal palace, where they were looked after by a special keeper. Water pitchers in the form of leopards were cast in bronze and placed on altars dedicated to ancestors. An engraving from a European travel book of the sixteenth century depicts a procession of courtiers in Benin led by a pair of magnificent leopards.

until 1897, when, in reprisal for the massacre of a party of trade negotiators, British troops sacked and burned the royal palace of Benin, sending the *oba* into an exile from which he did not return until 1914.

The metal sculpture of Benin is a royal art; only the *oba* could commission works in brass or bronze. Among the most remarkable visual records of court ceremonial life are the hundreds of bronze plaques, each about 2 feet square, that once decorated the walls and columns of the royal palace. The plaques, produced during the Middle Period, are sometimes in such high relief that the figures are almost freestanding. An exceptionally detailed example shows a general holding a spear in one hand and a ceremonial sword in the other (fig. 16-4). Flanking him, two officers brandish spears and shields. Their helmets indicate their rank. Above the tip of the general's sword is a small figure of a Portuguese soldier. Images of Europeans in African art help date such works, and provide a pictorial historical record of relations between African and European peoples.

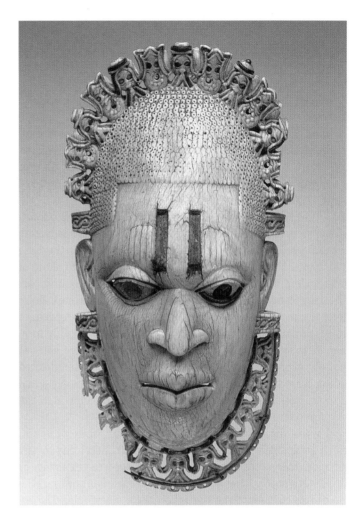

16-5 | **Pendant representing an** *iyoba*, **from Benin,** Nigeria. Edo culture, c. 1550 CE. Ivory, iron, and copper, height 9¼" (23.4 cm). The Metropolitan Museum of Art, New York
The Michael C. Rockefeller Memorial Collection, Gift of Nelson A. Rockefeller, 1972 (1978.412.323)

An *oba* also commissions important works in ivory. One example is a beautiful pendant that represents an *iyoba*, or queen mother (fig. 16-5). The *iyoba* is the mother of the king and ranked as one of the senior members of the court. This pendant may represent Idia, the first and best-known *iyoba*. She is particularly remembered for raising an army and using her magical powers to help her son Esigie (ruled 1504–1550 CE) defeat his enemies.

The pendant, a belt or hip ornament, was probably worn at the *oba*'s waist. There were originally iron inlays in the pupils and in the scarification patterns on the forehead. The *iyoba*'s necklace represents heads of Portuguese soldiers with beards and flowing hair. (The Portuguese also helped Esigie expand his kingdom.) In her crown, more Portuguese heads alternate with figures of mudfish, which in Benin iconography symbolized Olokun, the Lord of the Great Waters. Mudfish lived on the riverbanks, mediating between water and land, just as the *oba*, who was viewed as sacred, mediated between the human world and the supernatural world of Olokun.

Ife and Benin were but two of the many cities that arose in ancient Africa.

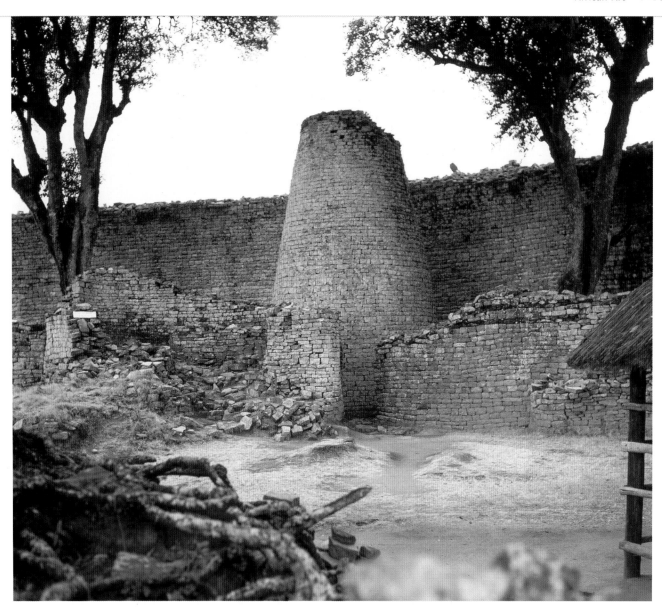

16-6 | **Conical Tower, Great Zimbabwe.** Before 1450 CE

Ife and Benin were but two of the many cities that arose in ancient Africa. Another example of an African city may be found in southeastern Africa where the Shona people constructed Great Zimbabwe. Zimbabwe was part of an extensive trade network along the Zambezi, Limpopo, and Sabi Rivers, which funneled gold, ivory, and exotic skins to coastal trading towns of the Swahili peoples between 1000 and 1500 CE. It is estimated that at the height of its power in the fourteenth century, Great Zimbabwe and its surrounding environs housed a population of more than 10,000 people. A large cache of goods containing items such as Portuguese medallions, Persian pottery, and Chinese porcelain testifies to the extent of trade at Great Zimbabwe.

The word *zimbabwe* derives from the Shona term for "venerated houses" or "houses of stone," and, indeed, much of Great Zimbabwe was built of stone. Scholars agree that the stone structures were constructed by the ancestors of the present-day Shona people, who still live in the region. Construction at the site took advantage of the enormous boulders abundant in the vicinity.

Masons used the uniform granite blocks that split naturally from the boulders to build a series of tall enclosing walls. As the artisans grew more skillful, they used dressed, or smoothly finished, stones and laid them in fine, level courses. Each enclosure defined a ritual space or surrounded dwellings made of adobe with conical thatched roofs.

The largest building complex at Great Zimbabwe is located in a broad valley below the hilltop enclosures. Known today as Imba Huru, or the Big House, it was probably a royal residence as well as a religious center. It is ringed by a massive masonry wall constructed without mortar. This wall is more than 800 feet long, 32 feet high, and 17 feet thick at the base. Inside the outer wall are numerous smaller stone enclosures and adobe platforms. A fascinating structure known simply as the Conical Tower (fig. 16-6) is some 18 feet in diameter and 30 feet high, and the tower was originally capped with three courses of ornamental stonework. Resembling a large version of a present-day Shona granary, it may have represented the good harvest and prosperity for which the ruler of Great Zimbabwe was held responsible.

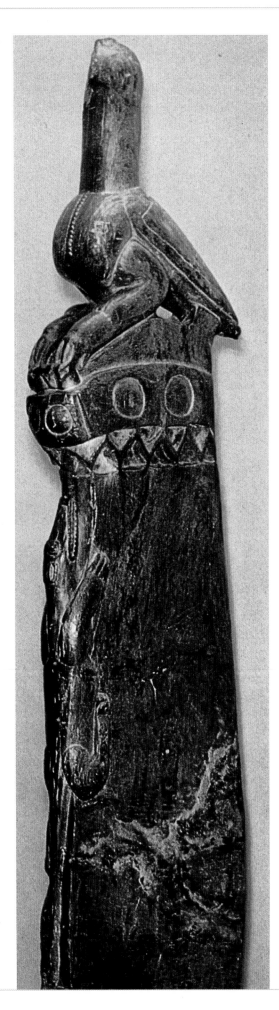

16-7 | **Bird, top part of a monolith, from Great Zimbabwe**
c. 1200–1400 CE. Soapstone, height 14½" (36.8 cm)
Great Zimbabwe Site Museum, Zimbabwe

Among the many interesting finds at Great Zimbabwe are a series of carved soapstone birds (fig. 16-7). The carvings, which originally crowned tall **monoliths,** refer to birds of prey, although they have toes instead of claws. Traditional Shona beliefs associate the king and his ancestors with an eagle called *shiri ye denga,* or "bird of heaven," who brings lightning, a metaphor for communication, between the heavens and earth. These soapstone birds may have depicted such messengers from the spirit worlds. As symbols of royalty, they expressed the king's power to mediate between his subjects and the supernatural world of spirits.

During the twentieth century, African sculptures—wood carvings of astonishing formal inventiveness and power—have found admirers the world over. Wood decays rapidly, however, and little wood sculpture from lands south of the Sahara remains from before the nineteenth century. As a result, much of ancient Africa's artistic heritage has probably been as irretrievably lost, as have, for example, the great monuments of wooden architecture of dynastic China. Yet the beauty of ancient African creations in such durable materials as terra cotta, stone, and bronze bears eloquent witness to the skill of ancient African artists and the splendor of the civilizations in which they worked.

African Art in the Modern Era: Living Traditions and New Trends

European exploration and subsequent colonization of the African continent brought its flourishing and diverse societies into sudden and traumatic contact with the "modern," largely European, world. European ships first visited sub-Saharan Africa in the fifteenth century, but for the next several hundred years, European contact with Africa was almost entirely limited to coastal areas, where trade, including the devastating slave trade, was carried out. During the nineteenth century, however, as the trade in slaves to the West was gradually eliminated, European explorers and Christian missionaries, such as Stanley Livingston, began to investigate the unmapped African interior. Drawn by the potential wealth of Africa's natural resources, European governments began to seek territorial concessions from African rulers. Diplomacy soon gave way to force, and, toward the end of the century, competition among rival powers fueled the so-called scramble for Africa, when European leaders raced to lay claim to whatever portion of the continent they were powerful enough to seize. By 1914, virtually all of Africa was under colonial rule.

In the years following World War I, nationalistic movements arose across Africa. From 1945 through the mid-1970s, one colony after another gained its independence, and the map of modern African nations took substantial shape. Many contemporary African artists today have come of age in a postcolonial culture that mingles American, European, and African elements. Drawing on these diverse influences, they have established a place in the lively international art scene along with their European, American, and Asian counterparts, and their work is shown as readily in Paris, Tokyo, and Los Angeles as it is in the African cities of Abidjan, Kinshasa, and Dakar.

In many West African cultures, fired ceramics are made exclusively by women. Among the Mande-speaking people of Mali, Burkina Faso, Guinea, and Ivory Coast, potters are *numumusow*, female members of *numu* lineages, and hold an important place in society. Women from these families may resolve disputes and initiate girls; their husbands, fathers, and sons are the sculptors and blacksmiths of the Mande.

Numumusow make a wide selection of vessels, including huge storage jars (fig. 16–8). The shapes of these pots reflect their intended use, from wide bowls and cooking pots to narrow-necked stoppered water bottles, from large storage vessels to small eating dishes. The *numumusow* form the soft and sticky clay by coiling and modeling with their fingers. They decorate their vessels by burnishing (polishing), engraving, or by adding pellets or coils of clay, or by coloring with slip (a wash of colored clay). The vessels are fired at low temperatures in a shallow pit or in the open: this produces a ware that can be used to cook over an open fire without breaking.

Even though most urban Africans use metal and plastic dishes and cookware today, large earthenware jars still keep water cool and clean in areas where refrigeration is expensive. In the past, water-storage jars were public display pieces, standing near the entrance to the house, where a guest would be offered a drink of cool water as an essential part of hospitality. Mande vessels for drinking water are often decorated with incised lines and molded ridges. On

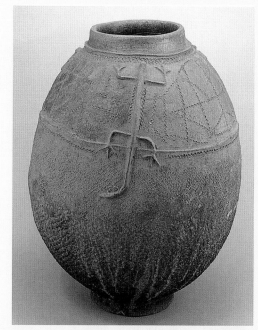

16-8 | **Jar,** from Mali. Bamana culture, 20th century
Earthenware, 23¹/₂ x 18³/₄" (59.7 x 47.6 cm)
The Nelson-Atkins Museum of Art, Kansas City
Missouri
Purchase: The George H. and Elizabeth O. Davis Fund

older wares, such as this example, raised images of figures or lizards might have referred to Mande myths or to philosophical concepts.

At the same time, other African artists have continued to create art objects which play a vital part in the spiritual and social life of their communities (fig. 16-8). The living arts of African cultures today, together with collections of African art in both Africa and the West, enable us to better understand the historic role of these enduring objects in the cycle of daily life.

Much traditional African art is devoted to dealings with the spirit world. Spirits are believed to inhabit the fields that produce crops, the rivers that provide fish, the bush and forests that are home to game, and the land that must be cleared in order to build a new village. A family, too, includes spirits—those of its ancestors as well as those of children yet unborn. In the blessing or curse of these myriad spirits lies the difference between success and failure in life. To communicate with these all-important spirits, some African societies usually rely on a specialist in ritual—a person known as a diviner who opens the lines of communication between the supernatural and human worlds (see fig. 13). Diviners use such techniques as prayer, sacrifice, offerings, magic, divination, and even the creation of images that give spirits a physical form.

Excellent examples of works made for centuries in central Africa are *minkisi* (singular, *nkisis*) of the Kongo and Songye peoples of the Democratic Republic of the Congo (formerly Zaire) to enforce ethical behavior and regulate power. The best known of these are the large wooden *minkonde* (singular, *nkonde*) figures, which bristle with nails, pins, blades, and other sharp objects (fig. 16-9; see page 410). A *nkisi nkonde* begins its life as a simple, unadorned wooden figure. It may be purchased from a carver at a market or commissioned by a diviner who is adept at diagnosing supernatural ills on behalf of a client or clients. Drawing on vast knowledge, the diviner prescribes certain magical/medicinal ingredients, called *bilongo*, that will help solve the client's problem. These *bilongo*, which may include human hair, nail clippings, and other animal, plant, or mineral ingredients, are added to the figure, either mixed with white clay and plastered directly onto the body or held in a packet suspended from the neck or waist.

The *bilongo* transform the *nkonde* into a living being with frightful powers, ready to attack the forces of evil on behalf of a human client. Each *bilongo* ingredient has a specific role in activating the figure. For example, the Kongo people admire the quickness and agility of a particular species of mouse. Tufts of this mouse's hair included in the *bilongo* ensure that the *nkisi nkonde* will act rapidly when its powers are activated.

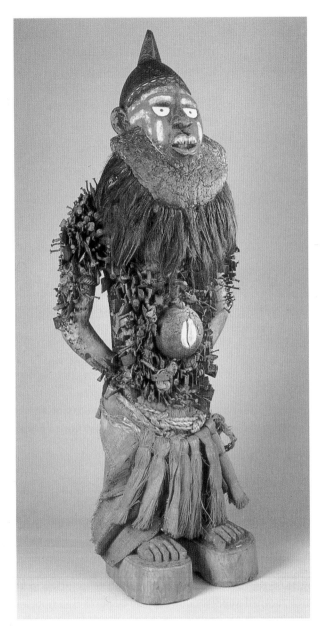

16-9 | **Power figure (*nkisi nkonde*),** from the Democratic Republic of the Congo (formerly Zaire). Kongo culture 19th century. Wood, nails, pins, blades, and other materials, height 44" (111.7 cm). The Field Museum Chicago
(# A109979Ac)

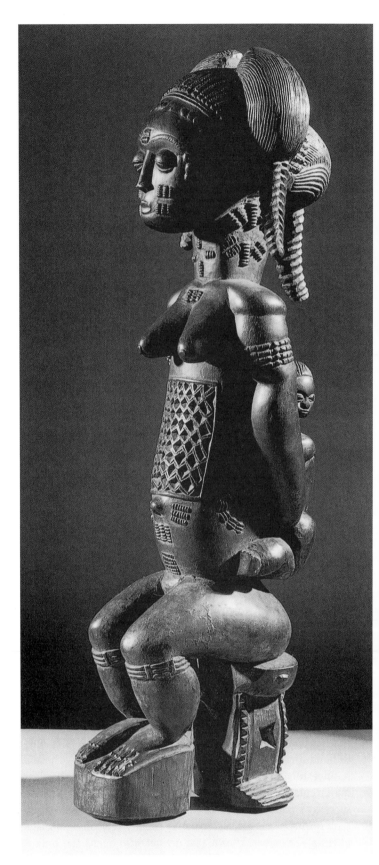

16-10 | **Spirit-spouse (*bloto bla*),** from Ivory Coast. Baule culture, early 20th century. Wood, height 17⅛": (43.5 cm).
The University Museum, University of Pennsylvania (neg. # S5-23115)

To mobilize the figure's powers, clients drive a nail or other pointed object into the *nkisi nkonde*, which may serve many private and public functions. Two warring villages might agree to end their conflict by swearing an oath of peace in the presence of the *nkonde* and then driving a nail into it to seal the agreement. A mother might invoke the power of the *nkonde* to heal her sick children. Two merchants might agree to a partnership by driving two small nails into the figure side by side and then make their pact binding by wrapping the nails together with a stout cord.

Another ongoing artistic tradition is found among the Baule people in the Ivory Coast. They believe that each of us lived in the spirit world, a parallel realm, before we were born. While there, we had a spirit spouse, whom we left behind when we entered this life. A person who has difficulty assuming his or her gender-specific role as an adult Baule—a man who has not married, for example, or a woman who has not borne children—may dream of his or her spirit spouse.

For such a person, the diviner may prescribe the carving of an image of the spirit spouse (fig. 16-10)—either a female figure (*blolo bla*) for a man or a male figure (*blolo bian*) for a woman. The figures display the most admired and desirable marks of beauty so that the spirit spouses may be encouraged to enter and inhabit them. The owner keeps the figure in his or her room, dressing it in beautiful textiles and jewelry, washing it, anointing it with oil, feeding it, and caressing it. The Baule hope that pleasing their spirit spouse (by caring for the sculpture) will restore balance to their human life.

Works of art in Africa, as in other continents, can be used to signify power in this world as well as in the spirit world. In an Akan kingdom of Ghana or the Ivory Coast, the spokesperson's staff indicates the eminence of the ruler's special advisers. In the finial of the staff on pages 402–03, the allegorical carving of the man holding an egg was probably made in the 1960s or 1970s by Kojo Bonsu. The son of a famous carver, Osei Bonsu, Kojo Bonsu lives in the Asante city of Kumasi and continues to carve prolifically. He decorated the staff with **gold leaf**, a sign of the object's importance. Gold was a major source of power for the Asante, who traded it for centuries, first across the Sahara to the Mediterranean world, and then directly to Europeans on the West African coast.

Yoruba kings manifested their power through the large, complex palaces in which they lived. In the traditional palace plan, the principal rooms once opened onto a veranda where elaborate figured posts supported the roof. Dense, highly descriptive figure carving also covered the doors. Perhaps the finest architectural sculptor of modern times was Olówè of Isè, who carved doors and veranda posts for rulers of the Ekìtì-Yoruba kingdoms in southwestern Nigeria.

The door of the royal palace in Ikéré illustrates Olówè's artistry (fig. 16-11). Its asymmetrical composition combines narrative and symbolic scenes in horizontal rectangular panels. Tall figures carved in profile end in heads facing out to confront the viewer. Their long necks and elaborate hairstyles make them appear even taller, unlike typical Yoruba sculpture, which uses shorter, more static figures. The figures are in such high relief

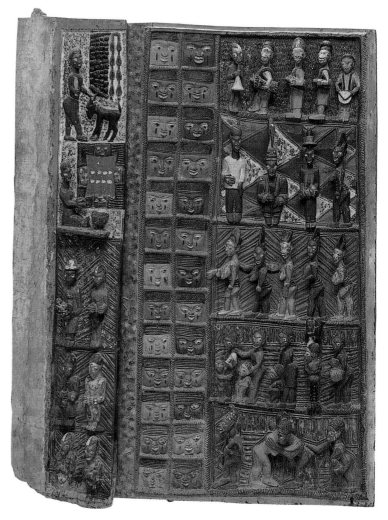

16-11   **Olówè of Isè. Door from Yoruba royal palace in Ikéré**
Nigeria. c. 1925. Wood, pigment, height 6'2⁷/₈" (1.9 m)
The Detroit Institute of the Arts

Acc. 1997.80 .A & .B. Gift of Bethea and Irwin Green in honor of the 20th anniversary of the Department of African, Oceanic and New World Cultures

Carvings illustrate scenes from palace life. At the left are scenes of divination and the use of a divination bowl. On the right side, the second register depicts the principal figures: a guard, the Ogoga (king) wearing his crown, and his principal wife wearing a European top hat and nursing a child.

that the upper portions are actually carved in the round. The figures move energetically against an underlying decorative pattern, and the entire surface of the door is also painted.

Olówè seems to have worked from the early 1900s until his death in 1938. He was famous throughout Yorubaland and called upon by patrons as distant as 60 miles from his home, even though few written records of his activities remain. An art historian, Philip Allison, wrote of meeting him and watching him work, and (echoing the praises of the Yoruba themselves) described Olówè carving the iron-hard African oak "as easily

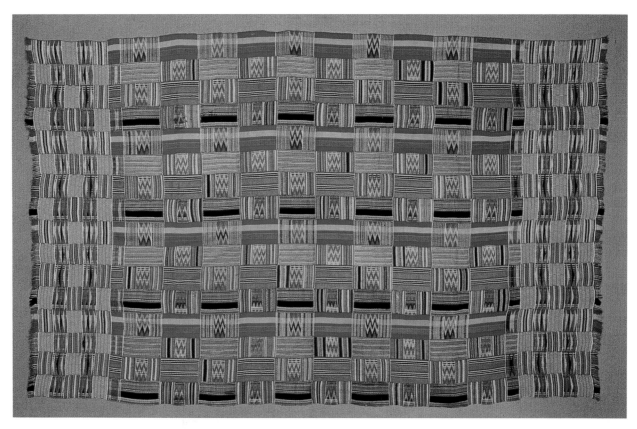

16-12 | *Kente* **cloth, from Ghana.** Asante culture, 20th century. Silk, 6'10⁹/₁₆" x 4'3⁹/₁₆" (2.10 x 1.31 m). National Museum of African Art and National Museum of Natural History, Washington, D.C.

Purchased with funds provided by the Smithsonian Collections Acquisition Program, 1983–85, EJ 10583

as [he would] a calabash [gourd]." Olówè also carved the divination bowl illustrated in the Introduction (see fig. 13).

Woven textiles, called **kente**, still signal status in the Akan kingdoms of Ghana (fig. 16-12). The pattern of the Asante *kente* cloth here, known as *oyokoman ogya da mu*—meaning "there is a fire between two factions of the Oyoko clan"—refers to the civil war that followed the death of the Asante king Osei Tutu in about 1730. Traditionally, only the king of the Asante was allowed to wear this pattern. Other patterns were reserved for members of the royal family or the court. Commoners who dared to wear a restricted pattern were severely punished.

Kente cloth is made on small, light looms that produce long, narrow strips of fabric. Asante weavers begin by laying out the long **warp** (vertical) threads in a brightly colored pattern. Today the threads are likely to be rayon. Formerly, however, they were silk, which the Asante produced by unraveling Chinese cloth obtained through European trade. **Weft** threads woven through the warp produce complex patterns, including double weaves in which the front and back of the cloth display different patterns. The long strips produced on the loom are then cut to size and sewn together to form large rectangles of finished *kente* cloth. In present-day Ghana, the wearing of *kente* and other traditional textiles is encouraged, and patterns are no longer restricted to a particular person or group.

In many communities, masquerades no longer occur, and Kongo peoples rarely dance with masks today. However, the Bwa people of central Burkina Faso still use masks to depict spirits in seasonal ceremonies. When young Bwa men and women are initiated into adulthood following the onset of puberty, they are taught about the world of nature spirits and about the wooden masks that represent them.

The initiates are first separated from younger playmates by older relatives who "kidnap" them and explain their disappearance in the community by saying that they have been devoured by wild beasts. The initiates are stripped of their clothing and made to sleep on the ground without blankets. Isolated from the community, they are taught about the spirit world invoked by the masks. Although they have seen these masks all their lives, they learn for the first time that they are made of wood and have been worn by their older brothers and cousins. They learn of the spirit each mask represents, and they memorize the story of each spirit's encounter with the founding ancestors of the clan. Returning to the community, the initiates display their new knowledge in a public ceremony. Each boy performs with one of the masks, in a dance that expresses the character and personality the mask represents. The girls, who are not allowed to wear the masks, sing the songs that accompany each one. At the end of the ceremony, the young men and women rejoin their families as adults, ready to marry, start farms, and begin families of their own.

Most Bwa masks depict spirits in human or animal shapes. Among the most spectacular masks, however, are abstract examples crowned with a tall, narrow plank, which represent spirits

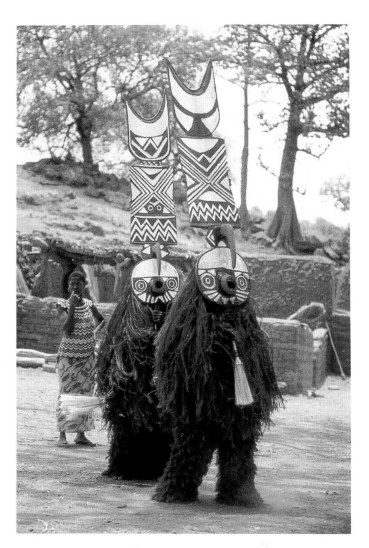

16-13 Two masks in performance, from Dossi
Burkina Faso. Bwa culture, 1984. Wood,
mineral pigments, and fiber, height
approx. 7' (2.13 m)

When the Bwa became targets of slave
raiders, they developed a new art form
in response to the threat; they created
imposing wooden masks like these as a
more powerful means of communicating
with protective spirits. (The new masks
replaced earlier ones made of leaves.)

that have taken neither animal nor human form (fig. 16-13). The
patterns of these abstract masks convey a message about the
proper moral conduct of life. The white crescent at the top
represents the quarter moon, under which initiations are held.
The large central X represents the scar that every initiated Bwa
wears. The horizontal zigzags at the bottom represent the path
of ancestors and symbolize adherence to traditional ways. The
hooked shape that projects in front of the face is said to
represent the beak of the hornbill, a bird associated with the
supernatural world and believed to be an intermediary between
the living and the dead.

Africa also has a rich tradition of funerary art—that of
Egypt is probably the best known in the West (see Chapter 2).
All over Africa, when death comes, special ceremonies and
rituals help the community to mourn. The death of a child is
a particularly traumatic event. The Yoruba people of Nigeria
have one of the highest rates of twin births in the world. The
birth of twins is a joyful occasion, yet it is troubling as well,
for twins are more delicate than single babies, and one or both
may well die. When a Yoruba twin dies, the parents consult a
diviner, who may tell them that an image of a twin, or *ere ibeji,*
must be carved.

The mother cares for the "birth" of this image by sending the
artist food while the image is being carved and gifts when it is
finished. Then she dances home, carrying the figure as she would
a living child, accompanied by the singing of neighborhood
women. She places the figure in a shrine in her bedroom and lav-
ishes care upon it, feeding it, dressing it richly, and anointing it
with cosmetic oils. The Yoruba believe that the spirit of a dead
twin thus honored may bring its parents wealth and good luck.

The female *ibeji* figures, which may be the work of the
Yoruba artist Akiode (d. 1936), radiate health and well-being
(fig. 16-14). Their beautiful, glossy surfaces and rings of fat indicate that they are well fed; breasts and other attributes signal
the mature adulthood that they might one day have achieved.
They represent hope for survival, for the future, and for prosperity. Figures such as these reflect the enduring cycle of life that
is such a vital part of African art.

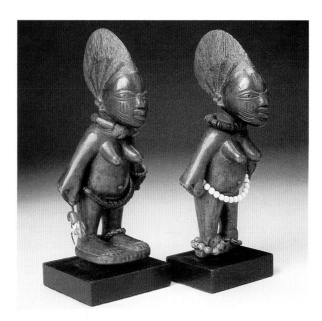

16-14 Twin figures (*ere ibeji*), from Nigeria. Yoruba
culture, 20th century. Wood, height 7⁷/₈" (20 cm)
The University of Iowa Museum of Art, Iowa City
The Stanley Collection

200 CE	400	600	800	1000

THE AMERICAS
▲ NAZCA c. 100 BCE–700 CE
▲ MAYA c. 250–1500
▲ CLASSIC PERIOD c. 250–900
▲ TEOTIHUACAN c. 350–650
▲ AZTEC c. 1300–1525
▲ INCA c. 1300–1537

Chacmool
9th–13th century

ANASAZI c. 750–1230 ▲
MISSISSIPPIAN c. 800–1500 ▲

POSTCLASSIC
PERIOD
c. 900–1300 ▲

Great Serpent Mound
c. 1070 CE

AFRICAN

Nok head
c. 500 BCE–200 CE

▲ NOK c. 500 BCE–200 CE
▲ URBAN CENTERS 3RD CENTURY–PRESENT

▲ IFE 800–PRESENT

LOOKING BACK 6

Art or Craft?

In many world cultures, the distinction between "fine art" and "craft" does not exist. The traditional Western academic hierarchy of materials—in which marble, bronze, oil, and fresco are valued more than terra cotta and watercolor—and the equally artificial hierarchy of subjects in which history painting, including religious history, stands supreme are irrelevant to non-Western art.

The indigenous peoples of Africa, the Americas, and the Pacific did not produce objects as works of art. In their eyes all pieces were utilitarian objects, adorned in ways necessary for their intended purposes. A work was valued for its effectiveness and for the role it played in society. Some, like a West African water jar, ease the burden of daily life, or, like a Sioux baby carrier, enrich mundane life with their aesthetic qualities. Others, such as Pomo baskets, commemorate important events. The function of a Hopewell pipe, an Inca tunic, or Ikéré palace doors may have conferred status on their owners or users through their material value or symbolic associations. And like art in all cultures, many pieces have had great spiritual or magical power. Such works of art cannot be fully comprehended or appreciated when they are seen only on pedestals or encased in glass boxes in museums or galleries. They must be imagined, or better yet seen, as acting in their societies. How powerfully might our minds and emotions be engaged if we saw Kwakwaka'wakw or Bwa masks functioning in religious drama, changing not only the outward appearance, but also the very essence of the individual.

At the beginning of the twentieth century, European and American artists broke away from the academic bias that extolled the classical heritage of Greece and Rome. They found new inspiration in the art—or craft, if you will—of many different non-European cultures. Artists explored a new freedom to use absolutely any material or technique that effectively challenged outmoded assumptions and opened the way for a free and unfettered delight in, and understanding of, Native American art as well as African and Pacific Island art. The intellectual community as well as collectors, dealers, and critics have come to appreciate the non-Western aesthetics and to treasure forgotten and ignored arts on their own terms. And the later twentieth- and twenty-first centuries' conception of art as a multimedia adventure has helped validate works of art once seen only in ethnographic collections and in the homes of private collectors. Today objects once called "primitive" are recognized as great works of art and acknowledged to be an essential dimension of a twenty-first-century worldview. The line between "art" and "craft" seems more artificial and less relevant than ever before.

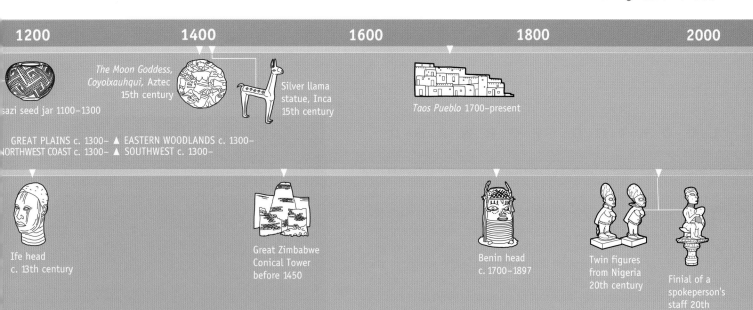

1200 — 1400 — 1600 — 1800 — 2000

...sazi seed jar 1100–1300

The Moon Goddess, Coyolxauhqui, Aztec 15th century

Silver llama statue, Inca 15th century

Taos Pueblo 1700–present

GREAT PLAINS c. 1300– ▲ EASTERN WOODLANDS c. 1300–
NORTHWEST COAST c. 1300– ▲ SOUTHWEST c. 1300–

Ife head c. 13th century

Great Zimbabwe Conical Tower before 1450

Benin head c. 1700–1897

Twin figures from Nigeria 20th century

Finial of a spokeperson's staff 20th century

▲ BENIN 1170–PRESENT

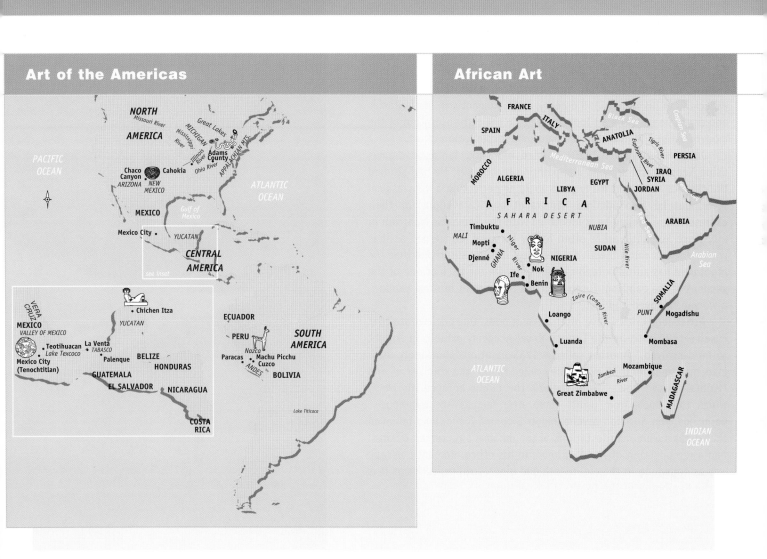

Art of the Americas

African Art

John Fuseli's painting *The Nightmare* (1781) forms a remarkable counterpoint to Bernini's sculpture of Saint Teresa (see pages 350–51). In both, a woman falls back in an ecstatic swoon; she is in the grip of the unconscious; and in each case the source of the vision or dream is personified, either by an angel in Saint Teresa or a succubus in the dreamer. The contrast of good and evil could not be clearer. What caused the woman's nightmare? What do the enigmatic containers on the table hold? Laudanum was a popular sleeping potion at the time. Is this a drug-induced vision? In *The Nightmare*, the world of fantasy, emotional excess, and escape through mind-altering substances create a sensational image with erotic overtones. In his painting, Fuseli bridges the artistic traditions of the late eighteenth and early nineteenth centuries. He is a Neoclassical master, especially in his figures and drapery, and a Romantic in his fantasies and erotic images. His art looks forward to the self-absorption of the modern artist and even to the commercial exploitation of art.

John Fuseli (1741–1825) painted his dark, fantastic dramas using Neoclassical drawing and painting techniques. He had studied the classics and spent many years in Rome perfecting a Neoclassical style, but he also admired Rembrandt and Caravaggio for their expressiveness. Today he is identified with the Romantic tradition in art. Since Romantic art is often highly personal, concerned as it is with emotions and subjective experience, it is not surprising that *The Nightmare* has autobiographical elements. On the back of one of the versions of the painting, Fuseli sketched the portrait of Anna Landolt, a woman he loved and lost.

Artists and critics have often been at odds. One critic wrote that Fuseli's 1780 entry in the London Royal Academy exhibition "ought to be destroyed." Another called a 1785 painting "shockingly mad, mad, mad, madder than ever." They called Fuseli "the Wild Swiss" and "Painter to the Devil." Nevertheless, the public enjoyed his work, which they knew from prints made after famous—or infamous—paintings. The Austrian psychoanalyst Sigmund Freud, who believed that dreams were manifestations of the dreamer's repressed desires, had a reproduction of *The Nightmare* in his office. Romantic escape was as appealing in the eighteenth and nineteenth centuries as it is at the beginning of the twenty-first century.

John Henry Fuseli. *The Nightmare.* 1781. Oil on canvas 39³/₄ x 49¹/₂" (101 x 126 cm). The Detroit Institute of Arts
Founders Society Purchase with funds from Mr. and Mrs. Bert L. Smokler and Mr. and Mrs. Lawrence A. Fleischmann

(See pages 432–33.)

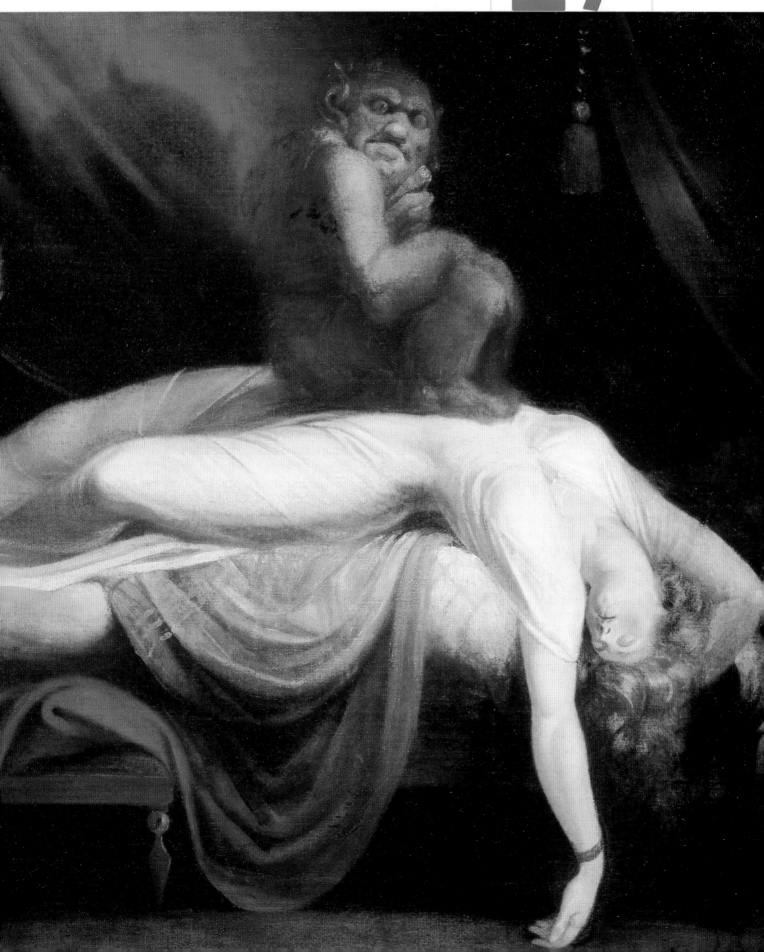

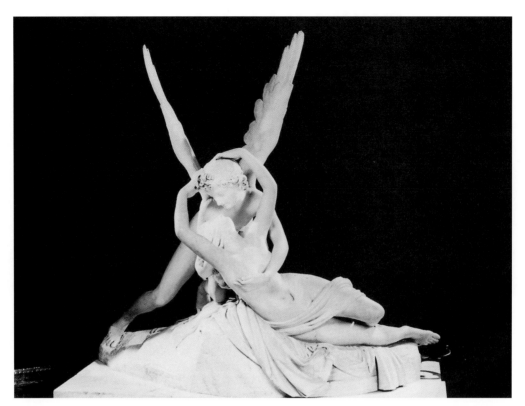

17-1 | Antonio Canova. *Cupid and Psyche.* 1787–93. Marble, 5'1" x 5'8⅛"
(1.55 x 1.73 m). Musée du Louvre, Paris

Cultural historians call the eighteenth century the Age of Enlightenment or the Age of Reason. Reason became the touchstone for evaluating nearly every civilized endeavor, including philosophy, art, and politics. By extension, nature, which was thought to embody reason, was invoked to corroborate the correctness—and goodness—of everything from political systems to architectural designs (see Map 7, page 529).

An optimistic and even reverential attitude toward scientific inquiry developed in the West during the eighteenth century, and this enthusiasm for scientific inquiry extended to historical and archaeological studies. Partly as a result of this new awareness of their history and partly stimulated by new discoveries in the excavations of Pompeii (see Chapter 6) and Herculaneum, two Roman cities buried by the first-century eruption of Mount Vesuvius, Neoclassicism emerged as the dominant style in art in the later years of the eighteenth century. Neoclassicism in art was characterized by subject matter borrowed from ancient Greece and Rome, stylistic dependence on antique sources, heroic nudity in sculpture and sometimes painting, classical orders in architecture, and the dominance of drawing over **painterly** effects in the visual arts. A persuasive moralism exalted virtues popularly attributed to Republican Rome: moral incorruptibility, patriotism, and courage. Playful Rococo tendencies gave way to a general longing for a noble and serious mode of expression.

Running parallel with Neoclassicism was another strain of expression called Romanticism. Romantic painting and sculpture often feature fantastic or literary themes, perhaps set in a remote time or place, and infused with a spirit of poetic fancy or melancholy. But Romanticism was less a specific style than an imaginative approach to art, centered in the strong subjective feelings of the artist. Many artworks at the end of the century combine elements of Neoclassicism and Romanticism.

The nineteenth century, in turn, has been called the Positivist Age. In the visual arts, the positivist spirit appears in the widespread rejection of Romantic subjectivism and imagination in favor of the accurate and apparently objective description of the ordinary, observable world. A new emphasis on descriptive accuracy, or **realism**, had its roots in the approach to art known as naturalism—in use since ancient times. Naturalist art that carried a socialist political message was at first described as realism. But by 1860 the term *realism* lost its political meaning and had become for most artists and critics simply a synonym for naturalism. In fact, the terms *realism* and *naturalism* are often used interchangeably.

Neoclassicism and Its Heritage

Eighteenth-century Italy, with its wealth of antique ruins, was the birthplace of the Neoclassic movement, led by Antonio Canova (1757–1822), the foremost Neoclassic sculptor in Europe. Born into a family of stonemasons near Venice, Canova settled in Rome in 1781, rapidly achieving such renown that critics compared him with Michelangelo. One of Canova's most admired works is the erotic mythological subject *Cupid and Psyche* (fig. 17-1). Condemned to a deathlike sleep by a jealous Venus, Psyche revives at Cupid's kiss. Here Canova combined a Romantic interest in emotion with a more typically

Neoclassical appeal to the senses of sight and touch. Cupid's wings offset the rounded forms of the two linked bodies, and the lustrous finish of the off-white marble skin is played against the textures of drapery and rocks. Although carved fully in the round, the figures are meant to be seen in an almost two-dimensional way, as a symmetrical series of interlocking triangles and ovals. The piece also recalls the ancient classical sculpture that attracted so many artists and scholars to Rome.

A trip through Europe to Italy—known as the "Grand Tour"—and a prolonged stay in Rome became an important part of the education of well-to-do people. Many countries established academies in Rome, which still flourish today as centers of study and research. The academies promoted classical principles in the arts, and artists and architects readily adopted the new classicism.

PORTRAIT PAINTING

In France a strong reaction against the Rococo had solidified during the 1760s and many French artists began to work in a classicizing mode. For some years they expressed their new sobriety in subject matter while still retaining Rococo forms and coloring. Marie-Louise-Élisabeth Vigée-Lebrun's 1787 portrait of the French queen, Marie Antoinette and her children,

Forty Years of Revolution: 1775–1815	
1775	First skirmishes of the American Revolution, Lexington and Concord, Massachusetts
1776	American Declaration of Independence
1781	Victory of the Americans over the English at Yorktown, New York
1787	Constitution of the United States signed
1789	Storming of the Bastille in Paris and beginning of the French Revolution; George Washington, first president of the United States, 1789–1797
1793	Execution of Louis XVI and Marie Antoinette in Paris
1799	Napoleon takes over French government
1801	Thomas Jefferson, third president of the United States (1801–1809)
1802	Napoleon becomes life consul; emperor, 1804
1808	Spanish war for independence (1808–14)
1812	Napoleon defeated in Russia; British-American War of 1812
1814	Napoleon abdicates and is exiled
1815	Return of Napoleon; defeat at Waterloo, second exile; Congress of Vienna divides up Europe
The end of an era: 1820, death of George III of England; 1821, death of Napoleon; 1826, death of Jefferson	

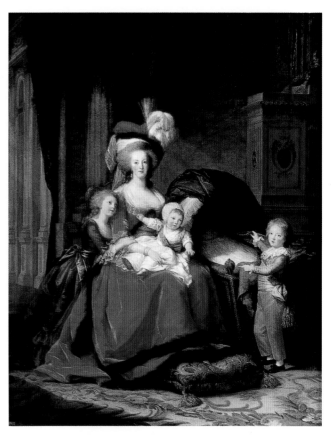

17-2 | **Marie-Louise-Élisabeth Vigée-Lebrun.** *Portrait of Marie-Antoinette with Her Children.* 1787. Oil on canvas, 9'1¼" x 7'5⅝" (2.75 x 2.15 m).
Château de Versailles et de Trianon

As the favorite painter to the queen, Vigée-Lebrun escaped from Paris with her daughter on the eve of the French Revolution of 1789 and fled to Rome. After a very successful self-exile working in Italy, Austria, Russia, and England, the artist finally resettled in Paris in 1804 at the invitation of Napoleon I and again became popular with Parisian art patrons. Over her long career, she painted around 800 portraits in a vibrant style that changed very little over the decades.

falls into this mode (fig. 17-2). Painted two years before the outbreak of the French Revolution spelled the end of the Bourbon monarchy, the court hoped that the queen's depiction as a devoted mother would counter her public image as immoral, extravagant, and conniving. Marie Antoinette's youngest son squirms on her lap, and her daughter leans affectionately against her. In a poignant touch, her eldest son points to the empty cradle of a recently deceased sibling. The image of Marie Antoinette as a loving mother surrounded by her children represented the ideal expounded by Enlightenment philosophers, especially the influential French-Swiss theorist Jean-Jacques Rousseau (1712–1778), who concluded that men and women should conform to the roles assigned to them by nature (i.e., biology), with women tending to the home and raising children, and men practicing learned professions, governing the state, and taking other active roles in public life.

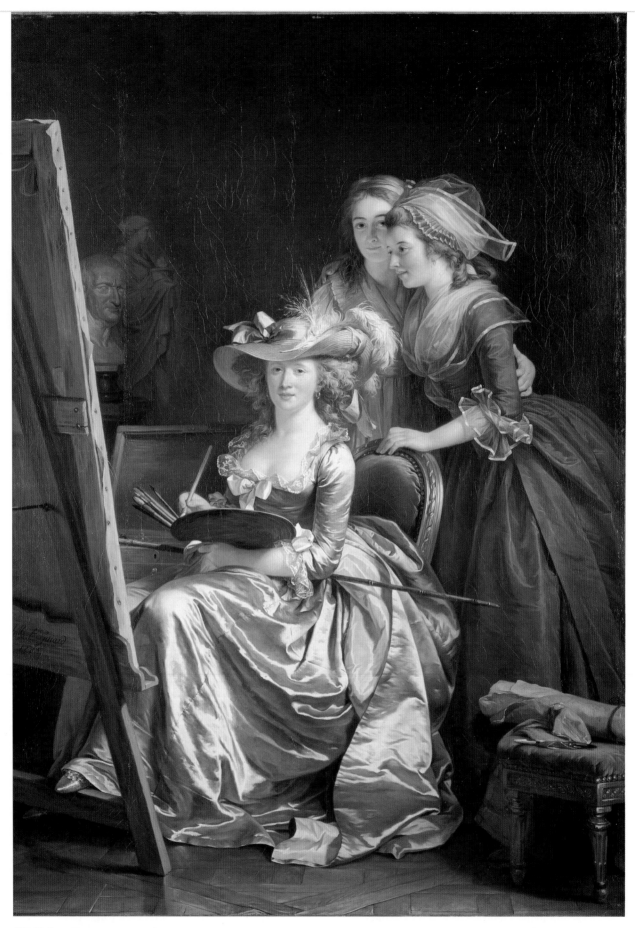

17-3 Adélaïde Labille-Guiard. *Self-Portrait with Two Pupils, Mademoiselle Marie Gabrielle Capet (1761–1818) and Mademoiselle Carreaux de Rosemond (d. 1788).* 1785. Oil on canvas, 6'11" x 4'11½" (2.11 x 1.51 m). The Metropolitan Museum of Art, New York

Gift of Julia A. Berwind. (53.2255)

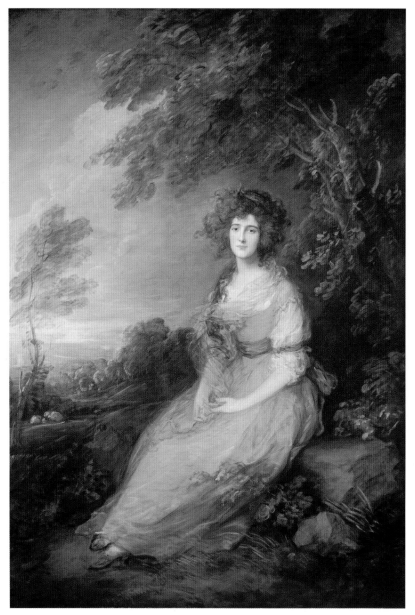

17-4

Thomas Gainsborough.
Portrait of Mrs. Richard Brinsley Sheridan. 1785-87.
Oil on canvas, 220 x 154 cm
(86⅝" x 60⅝").

National Gallery of Art, Washington, D.C., Andrew W. Mellon Collection, 1937.1.92.(92)/PA

Vigée-Lebrun (1755–1842) was one of the most famous portraitists in France in the last quarter of the eighteenth century. In 1783 she was elected to one of the four places in the French Academy available to women (see "Art Academies in the Eighteenth Century," page 422). Elected at the same time was Adélaïde Labille-Guiard (1749–1803), who in 1790 successfully petitioned to end the restriction on entry for women. Labille-Guiard's commitment to training and promoting the interests of women painters is reflected in her *Self-Portrait with Two Pupils* (fig. 17-3). Exhibited in 1785 at the **Paris Salon**, the biennial exhibition open to members of the French Academy, this monumental image of the artist at her easel was also meant to answer sexist rumors that her paintings had been painted by men. In a witty role reversal, the only male to be seen was her father, whose portrait bust is at her side. Labille-Guiard's self-portrait, like many other paintings produced in France just before the Revolution, is relaxed, elegant, and urbane.

In England at this time Thomas Gainsborough (1727–1788) achieved great success with paintings like his *Portrait of Mrs.*

Richard Brinsley Sheridan (fig. 17-4), which shows the professional singer and wife of the celebrated playwright seated informally outdoors. The distant landscape view and the use of a tree to frame the sitter's head recall Van Dyck (see fig. 14-19) but the formula is updated through feathery brushwork and a lighter palette. Gainsborough seems to identify the woman with the landscape, matching her windblown hair to the foliage of the tree overhead. The work illustrates one of the new values of the Enlightenment: the emphasis on nature and the natural as the sources of goodness and beauty.

In colonial North America, the taste of the settlers was generally conservative, and styles often lagged behind the European mainstream. John Singleton Copley (1738–1815), the stepson of an English immigrant painter-engraver, grew up to be North America's first painter of genius. Copley's sources of inspiration were meager, but his work was already drawing attention by the time he was fifteen. Copley's clients valued not only his excellent technique, but also his ability to dignify them while recording their features with unflinching realism. In his portrait of *Mrs.*

ART ACADEMIES IN THE EIGHTEENTH CENTURY

During the seventeenth century, the French government founded royal academies for the instruction and encouragement of artists and architects, writers, scientists, musicians, and dancers. In 1667 the Royal Academy of Painting and Sculpture began to mount occasional exhibitions of the members' recent work. These exhibitions came to be known as the Salons because they were held in the Salon d'Apollon (Salon of Apollo) in the Palais du Louvre. From 1737, the Salons were mounted every other year, with a jury of members selecting the works that would be shown. As the only public art exhibitions of any importance in Paris, the Salons were enormously influential in establishing officially approved styles and in molding public taste.

In England, the Royal Academy of Arts was different in that it was a private institution independent of any interference from the Crown. Founded in 1768, it had only two functions: to operate an art school and to hold two annual exhibitions, one of art of the past and the other of contemporary art, which was open to any exhibitor on the basis of merit alone. The Royal Academy continues to function in this way today.

Besides the influential French and British academies, other art academies, public and private, sprang up throughout Europe in the eighteenth century. They primarily welcomed male artists; the number of women members was often restricted or women were welcomed only as honorary members. In France only seven women were awarded the title of academician (full member) between 1648 and 1706, and then the Royal Academy declared itself closed to women. Nevertheless, four women had been admitted by 1770, when the men again became worried that women members would become "too numerous" and declared four women would be the limit at any one time. Women were not admitted to the Academy's school or allowed to compete for Academy prizes, both of which were nearly indispensable for professional success.

Women fared even worse at London's Royal Academy. After the Swiss painters Angelica Kauffmann and Mary Moser were named founding members in 1768, no other women were elected until 1922, and then only as associates. In a 1771–72 portrait of the London Academicians, Johann Zoffany showed the men grouped around two nude male models. Propriety prohibited the presence of women in this setting, so Zoffany painted the portraits of the female members hanging on the wall.

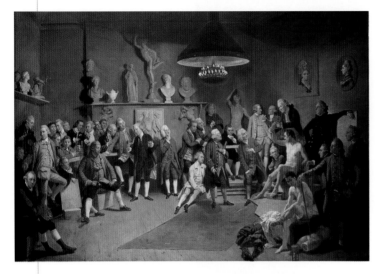

Johann Zoffany. *Academicians of the Royal Academy*
1771–72. Oil on canvas, 47½ x 59½" (120.6 x 151.2 cm)
The Royal Collection, Windsor Castle, New Windsor, England

Ezekiel Goldthwait (Elizabeth Lewis) (fig. 17-5), painted in 1771, Copley emphasized the sitter's prosperity by painting her dressed in a lace-trimmed silk dress and seated at a mahogany table. But her open, amiable features, strong, thick wrists, and large, capable hands show a lack of vanity and a commitment to hard work that seem to personify the spirit of Puritan New England.

Copley's talents so outdistanced those of his colonial contemporaries that he decided to travel abroad to enhance his career. In June 1774, he sailed for Europe, where he visited London, Paris, and Italy. The next year he settled in London where he spent the rest of his life. For over a century, many of the most talented artists of the young United States followed in Copley's footsteps, going to Europe to obtain the best training and to forward their careers.

MORALIZED GENRE PAINTING

Mrs. Sheridan and Mrs. Goldthwait were members of the growing middle class made up of newly prosperous merchants and professionals who had money to commission portraits, and they also helped to fuel the market for a type of painting known as moralized genre painting. Reformers argued that art should promote and support public virtue and integrity, and for this they favored a restrained, Neoclassical style.

British patrons tended to favor amusing and easily understandable satirical and moralizing scenes over high-minded history paintings with subjects drawn from mythology, the Bible, or classical literature. By doing so, they contradicted art theorists of their time and earlier, who had long considered **history painting** the highest form of artistic endeavor. Following the discontinuation of government censorship in 1695, there emerged in Britain a flourishing culture of literary satire, directed at a variety of political and social targets. The first painter inspired by the work of these novelists and essayists was William Hogarth (1697–1764). Hogarth believed art should contribute to the improvement of society, so about 1730, he began illustrating moralizing tales of his own invention in sequences of four to six paintings. He then reproduced the canvases as sets of prints for sale to the public, both to maximize his profits and to influence as many people as possible.

Hogarth's *Marriage à la Mode* series (1743–45) was inspired by an essay written by the English essayist and poet Joseph Addison promoting the concept of marriage based on love. The opening scene, *The Marriage Contract* (fig. 17-6), shows the gout-ridden Lord Squanderfield pointing proudly to his family tree as he arranges for his son to marry the daughter of a wealthy merchant. The merchant gains entry for his family into the aristocracy, while the lord gets the money he needs to complete his Palladian house, which is visible out the window. Sitting back to back are the loveless couple, who will be sacrificed for their fathers' pride and greed. The young Squanderfield admires himself in the mirror, while the lawyer Silvertongue whispers to the unhappy fiancée. Five more paintings show the progressively

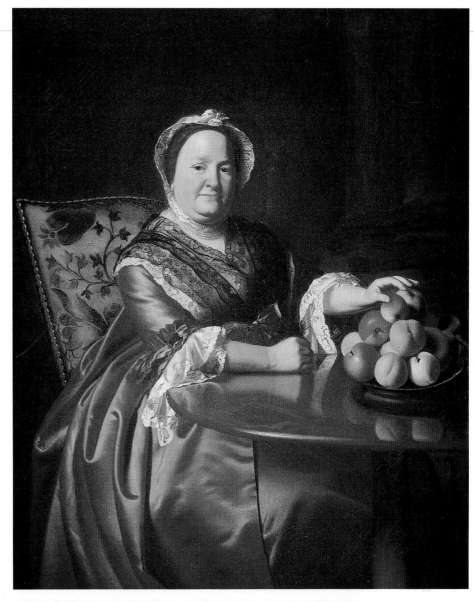

17-5

John Singleton Copley.
Mrs. Ezekiel Goldthwait
(Elizabeth Lewis).
1771. Oil on canvas,
50³/₈" x 40¹/₄" (128.0 x
102.2 cm).

Courtesy, Museum of Fine
Arts, Boston. Bequest of
John T. Bowen in memory of
Eliza M. Bowen, 1941 (41.84)

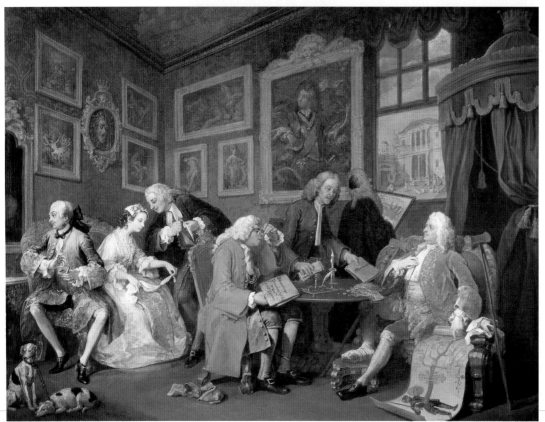

17-6

William Hogarth
The Marriage Contract
from *Marriage à la Mode*
1743–45. Oil on canvas
28 x 36" (71.7 x 92.3 cm)
The National Gallery
London

Reproduced by Courtesy
of the Trustees

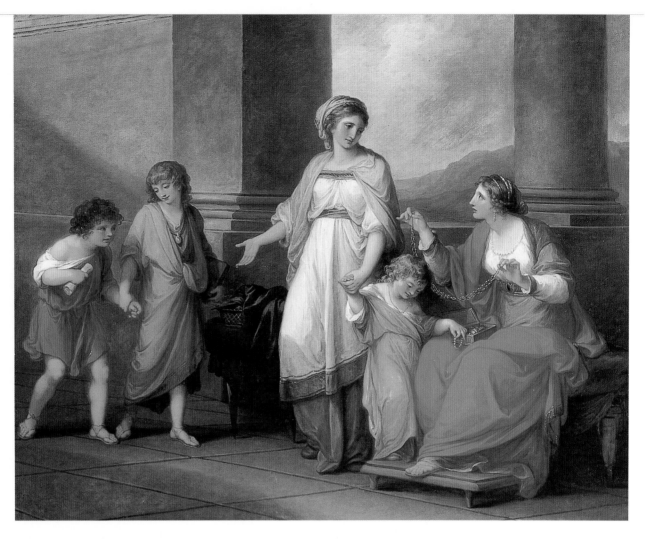

17-7

Angelica Kauffmann *Cornelia Pointing to Her Children as Her Treasures* 1785. Oil on canvas, 40 x 50" (101.6 x 127 cm) Virginia Museum of Fine Arts Richmond Virginia

The Adolph D. and Wilkins C. Williams Fund

disastrous results of such a union, culminating in murder and suicide. Stylistically, Hogarth's paintings combine the anecdotal realism of seventeenth-century Dutch genre painters (see fig. 17) with the nervous elegance of the Rococo style. His work became so popular that in 1745 he was able to give up portrait painting altogether, an art which he considered a deplorable form of vanity, and he devoted his time to moralizing satires.

The Italian-trained Swiss artist Angelica Kauffmann (1741–1807), a leading Neoclassical history painter, had been invited to Britain in 1766 by a wealthy client, and by 1768 she was one of only two women artists named among the founding members of the Royal Academy in London (see "Art Academies in the Eighteenth Century," page 422). In her painting *Cornelia Pointing to Her Children as Her Treasures* (fig. 17-7), Kauffmann illustrated both an incident from ancient Republican Rome and a moral lesson. A woman visitor had been showing Cornelia her jewels and then requested to see those of her hostess. In response, Cornelia gestured to her children and stated, "These are my jewels." The setting is classically simple, and the figures are based loosely on those found in Roman wall paintings. The sentiment, however—the glorification and idealization of the good mother—belongs unmistakably to the eighteenth century. Whatever their subject matter, many paintings reflected Enlightenment values, including an interest in social progress, an embrace of natural beauty, and faith in reason and science.

Science and technology provided artists with another new theme. In a series of paintings of scientific experiments, Joseph Wright of Derby (1734–1797) glorified the scientist as a modern wizard. In *An Experiment on a Bird in the Air-Pump* (fig. 17-8), a scientist looms over the scene. The dramatic chiaroscuro, which recalls Baroque religious painting (see fig. 14-7), suggests that science sheds light in a world of darkness and ignorance.

NEOCLASSICAL ARCHITECTURE IN ENGLAND AND NORTH AMERICA

While the Rococo style remained popular in continental architecture, a group of British professional architects and wealthy amateurs took a stance against what they saw as the immoral extravagance of the Italian Baroque. They advocated a return to the austerity and simplicity they saw in the architecture of Andrea Palladio (see figs. 13-18 and 13-19). They studied in Italy and then returned home to build magnificent Palladian villas set in extensive gardens on their country estates. In the art of garden design, the British could claim true originality. They created a style that contrasted sharply with the rigid formality of seventeenth-century gardens (see fig. 14-10) and with the classicism of their stately homes. Known throughout Europe as the English landscape garden, the sweeping lawns, winding paths, irregularly shaped pools and streams, and asymmetrically placed groves of trees imitated the appearance of the natural rural landscape, carefully and discreetly "improved" by human intelligence and skill.

An especially innovative British Neoclassical architect was the Scottish architect and interior designer Robert Adam (1728–1792). When he made the Grand Tour in 1754–58, Adam largely ignored the great Roman civic architecture and focused instead on the applied ornament of Roman domestic architecture. When he returned to London to set up an architectural firm with his two younger brothers, he brought with him drawings and prints that provided a complete inventory of ancient, decorative motifs, which he then modified to create his own elegant style. His designs proved ideally suited both to the evolving taste of wealthy clients and to the imperial aspirations of the new king, George III, whose reign began in 1760.

Adam achieved worldwide fame for his interior designs, such as the renovations he carried out between 1760 and 1769 for the Duke of Northumberland at his country estate, Syon House, near London. The opulent colored marbles, gilded relief panels, classical statues, spirals, garlands, rosettes, and gilded **moldings** are luxuriously profuse yet are restrained by the

CLOSER LOOK

An Enlightenment concern with developments in the natural sciences is seen in the dramatic depiction of *An Experiment on a Bird in the Air-Pump* (fig. 17-8) by Joseph Wright of Derby (1734–1797). Trained as a portrait painter, Wright made the Grand Tour in 1773–75 and then returned to the English Midlands to paint local society. Many of those he painted were the self-made entrepreneurs of the first wave of the Industrial Revolution, which was centered there in towns such as Birmingham. Wright belonged to the Lunar Society, a group of industrialists (including Josiah Wedgwood), mercantilists, and progressive nobles who met in Derby. As part of the society's attempts to popularize science, Wright painted a series of "entertaining" scenes of scientific experiments, including *An Experiment on a Bird in the Air-Pump*.

The eighteenth century was an age of rapid technological advances and the development of the air pump was among the most innovative scientific developments of the time. Although it was employed primarily to study the property of gases, it was also widely used to promote the public's interest in science because of its dramatic possibilities. In the experiment shown here, air was pumped out of the large glass bowl until the small creature inside, a bird, collapsed from lack of oxygen; before the animal died, air was reintroduced by a simple mechanism at the top of the bowl. In front of an audience of adults and children, a lecturer is shown on the verge of reintroducing air into the glass receiver. Near the window at the right, a boy stands ready to lower a cage when the bird revives. (The moon visible out the window is a reference to the Lunar Society.) By delaying the reintroduction of air, the scientist has created considerable suspense, as the reactions of the two girls indicate. Their father, a voice of reason, attempts to dispel their fears. The dramatic lighting not only underscores the life-and-death issue of the bird's fate but also suggests that science brings light into a world of darkness and ignorance. The lighting adds a spiritual dimension as well. During the Baroque era, such intimate lighting effects had been used for religious scenes (see fig. 14-7). Here science replaces religion as the great light and hope of humanity. This theme is emphasized through the devout expressions of some of the observers.

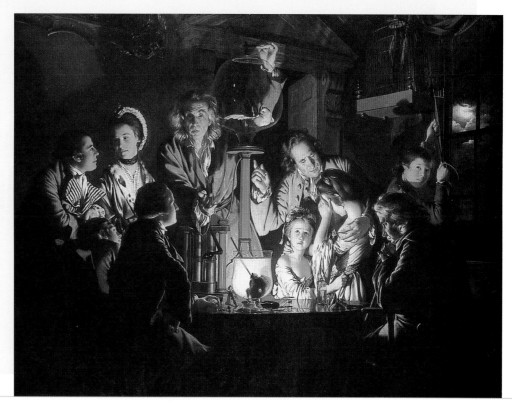

17-8 Joseph Wright. *An Experiment on a Bird in the Air-Pump*
1768. Oil on canvas
6 x 8' (1.83 x 2.44 m)
The National Gallery, London

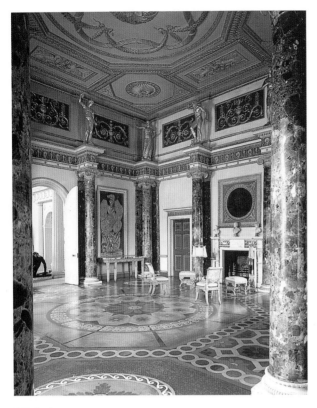

17-9 | **Robert Adam. Anteroom, Syon House,** Middlesex England. 1760–69

strong geometric order imposed on them (fig. 17-9). Adam's preference for bright pastel colors and small-scale decorative elements lightens the effect. Such interiors were designed partly as settings for the art collections of British aristocrats, which included antiquities as well as a range of Neoclassical painting, sculpture, and decorative arts.

Despite mounting hostilities with Britain from 1775 to 1781, American domestic architecture remained tied to developments in England. Neoclassicism became the dominant style in the United States during the Federal Period (1783–1830) that followed the colonies' victory in their War of Independence.

Thomas Jefferson (1743–1826), an enthusiastic amateur architect, designed his Virginia residence, Monticello, in a style influenced by British Palladian villas. His first house, built in the 1770s, was based on a design in Palladio's *Four Books of Architecture*. In 1785, Jefferson went to Paris as the American ambassador to France. There he discovered an elegant domestic architecture that made his home seem very provincial. When he returned in 1793, he completely redesigned Monticello, using French doors and tall narrow windows (fig. 17-10) and a balustrade above the unifying cornice to mask the second floor. Despite these French elements and his stated rejection of the British Palladian mode, the building's simplicity and combination of temple front and dome remain closer to English than to French buildings. Monticello is less grand than English stately homes because of its humbler building materials (brick with wooden trim, and columns formed of stuccoed and painted bricks), and its extended low-lying profile.

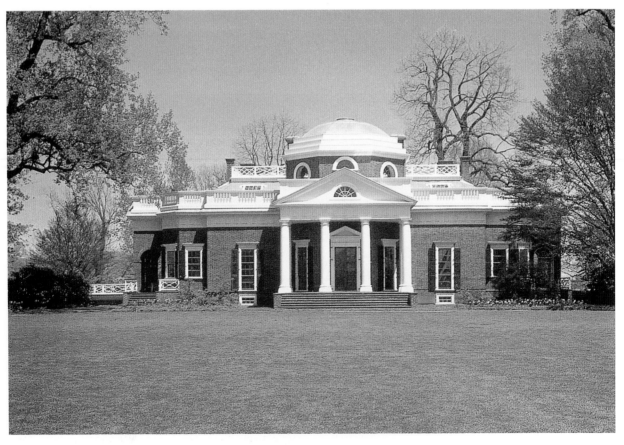

17-10 | **Thomas Jefferson. Monticello,** near Charlottesville, Virginia. 1770–84, 1796–1806

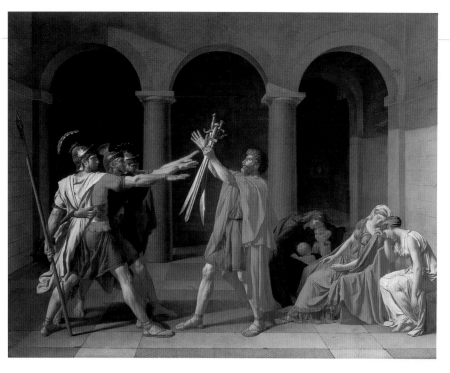

17-11 | **Jacques-Louis David**
Oath of the Horatii
1784–85. Oil on canvas
10'8⅜" x 14' (3.26 x
4.27 m). Musée du
Louvre, Paris

17-12 | **Jacques-Louis David.** *Napoleon Crossing
the Saint-Bernard.* 1800-01. Oil on canvas.
8'11" x 7'7" (2.7 x 2.3 m).
Chauteaux de Versailles et de Trianon

NEOCLASSICAL PAINTING IN FRANCE

In the 1770s, the French history painter Jacques-Louis David (1748–1825) developed a truly Neoclassical painting style. In 1774 David had won the Prix de Rome, a competitive scholarship for study in Italy awarded to the top graduating students from the French Academy's art school. During six years in Rome, David studied Raphael and Michelangelo, the Baroque classicism of Poussin and the Carracci, and above all, ancient Roman sculpture and frescoes. After his return to Paris he produced a series of severe, anti-Rococo paintings that extolled the antique virtues of moral incorruptibility, stoicism, courage, and patriotism. The first of these, painted as a royal commission, was the *Oath of the Horatii* of 1784–85 (fig. 17-11). David's painting was inspired by Pierre Corneille's seventeenth-century drama *Horace*. Somewhat surprisingly, however, David chose to depict an incident that is not part of the story in any known source: the Horatii taking an oath to fight to the death for Rome. The young men's father, Horace, standing at the center, administers the oath to his sons. To the right of him, Horace's daughter Camillia, who is betrothed to one of the Curatii, and his daughter-in-law Sabina, a Curatii herself, weep, knowing that whatever the outcome of the battle, they will inevitably lose someone dear to them. The energetic young men with their glittering swords are a powerful contrast to the swooning women already mourning the tragedy to come. The message of the finished painting—the value of putting patriotic duty above personal interests and even family obligations—is expressed with such clarity and power that it created a sensation when David exhibited it in Rome and Paris in early 1785.

David's *Oath* became an emblem of the French Revolution of 1789. Its harsh lesson in republican citizenship effectively captured the mood of the new leaders of the French state who came to power in 1793—especially the Jacobins, egalitarian democrats who abolished the monarchy and presided over the Reign of Terror in 1793–94. (The Reign of Terror was unprecedented for its murderous vengence. During one particularly bloodthirsty stretch, 1,376 individuals were guillotined in only 47 days.)

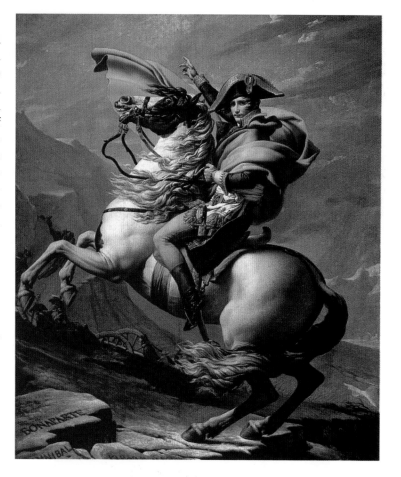

The initial French Republic ended in 1799 when the government was reorganized under Napoleon Bonaparte, a popular and successful general. After Napoleon was named emperor in 1804, David became his court painter. Even before that time, David produced canvases that turned Napoleon into a larger-than-life figure. *Napoleon Crossing the Saint-Bernard* (fig. 17-12), painted during 1800–01, is an idealized vision of a military campaign. David shows the future emperor leading his troops across the Alps into Italy. Although Napoleon actually made the crossing on

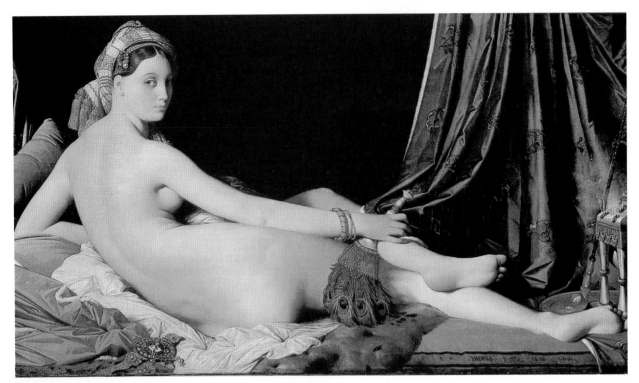

17-13

Jean-Auguste-Dominique Ingres. *Large Odalisque* 1814. Oil on canvas, approx. 35 x 64" (88.9 x 162.5 cm) Musée du Louvre, Paris

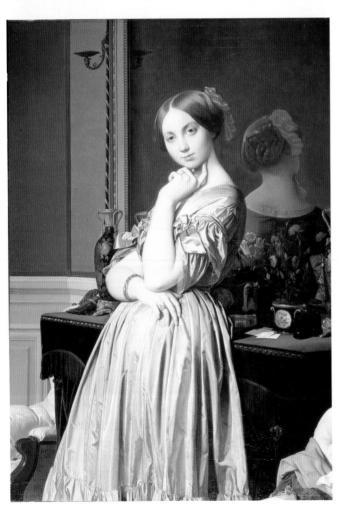

17-14 | Jean-Auguste-Dominique Ingres. *The Comtesse d'Haussonville.* Dated 1845. Oil on canvas, 51⁷/₈" x 36¹/₄" (131.8 x 92.1 cm). The Frick Collection, New York

a donkey, here he charges up the mountain on a rearing horse, past rocks incised with his name and the names of his heroic predecessors, Hannibal and Charlemagne. With its sweeping diagonals and flowing draperies, this painting of a contemporary event owes as much to the idealized Grand Manner of the Baroque as it does to Neoclassicism. When Napoleon fell from power in 1814, David moved to Brussels, where he died in 1825.

As the leading force in French painting during the Revolutionary and Napoleonic eras, David trained many young artists. Jean-Auguste-Dominique Ingres (1780–1867) was one of David's most talented pupils—he thoroughly absorbed his teacher's Neoclassical vision yet interpreted it in a new manner. Inspired by Raphael rather than by antique art, Ingres emulated the Renaissance artist's graceful lyricism, precise drawing, and idealized forms. Ingres won the Prix de Rome and lived in Italy from 1806 to 1824; he returned to Italy to serve as director of the French Academy in Rome from 1835 to 1841. As a teacher and theorist, Ingres became the most influential artist of his time.

Although Ingres, like David, fervently desired acceptance as a history painter, his paintings of literary subjects and contemporary events were less successful than his female nudes and erotically charged portraits of women, especially his numerous representations of the odalisque (a woman living in the woman's quarter of an *oda*, a Turkish house). The odalisque was considered a Romantic subject because of its exotic, non-Western source. In the *Large Odalisque* (fig. 17-13) of 1814, the look the woman levels at her master, while turning her naked body away from what we assume is his gaze, makes her simultaneously erotic and aloof. The cool blues of the couch and the curtain at the right heighten the effect of the woman's warm skin, while the tight angularity of the crumpled sheets accentuates the languid, sensual contours of her form. Although Ingres's commitment to fluid line and elegant postures was grounded in his Neoclassical training, he treated a number of Romantic themes (such as this odalisque) in a highly

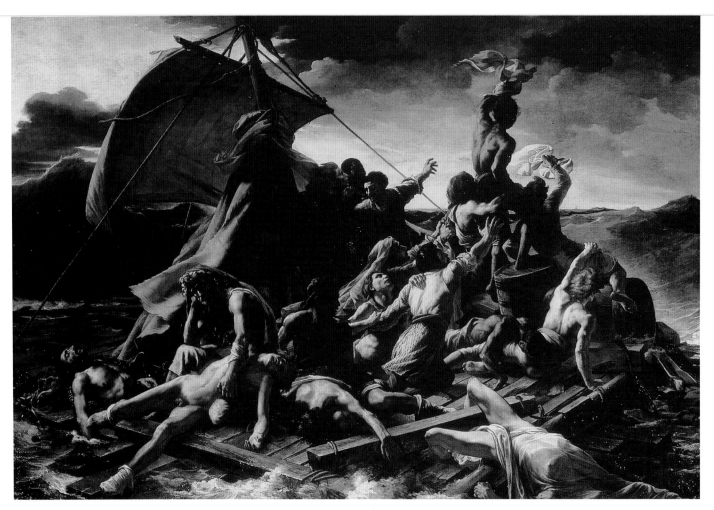

17-15 | Théodore Géricault. *Raft of the "Medusa."* 1818–19. Oil on canvas, 16'1" x 23'6" (4.9 x 7.16 m). Musée du Louvre, Paris

personal, almost **mannerist** fashion. Here the elongation of the woman's back (she seems to have several extra vertebrae), the widening of her hip, and her tiny, boneless feet are anatomically incorrect but aesthetically compelling.

Although Ingres complained that making portraits was a "considerable waste of time," he was unparalleled in rendering a physical likeness and the material qualities of clothing, hairstyles, and jewelry. In 1845 he painted a lifesize oil portrait of the Comtesse d'Haussonville (fig. 17-14). Ingres relies on outline to delineate the beautiful head and shoulders of the comtesse (also reflected in the mirror behind her) as well as the interior setting. Line is the undisputed means of definition; we are hardly aware of the physical medium of paint. As a teacher and theorist, Ingres established the taste of a generation. He helped to ensure the dominance of classicism over a strong subcurrent of Romanticism in France well into the nineteenth century.

Romanticism

Romanticism, already anticipated in French painting during Napoleon's reign, did not gain wide public acceptance until after 1830. In general, Romantic painting featured loose, fluid brushwork, strong colors, complex compositions, dramatic contrasts of light and dark, and expressive poses and gestures—all suggesting a revival of the more dramatic aspects of the Baroque. French Romantic artists not only drew upon literary sources but also

added the new dimension of social criticism. The Romantic style became identified with a type of social commentary in which the dramatic presentation was intended to stir public emotions, especially in the work of its chief exponents, Théodore Géricault (1791–1824) and Eugène Delacroix (1798–1863).

Géricault began his career painting works inspired by Napoleonic military campaigns. During a brief stay in Rome between 1816 and 1817, he studied the work of Michelangelo. Géricault returned to Paris determined to make a great painting of a contemporary event, and finally decided to treat the scandalous and sensational shipwreck of the "Medusa" (fig. 17-15). In 1816 a ship of colonists headed for Madagascar ran aground near its destination; its captain was an incompetent aristocrat appointed by the newly restored monarchy for political reasons. Because there were insufficient lifeboats, the captain ordered 152 passengers and crew onto a small raft, which tossed about on stormy seas for nearly two weeks before it was found. The fifteen survivors had subsisted for the last days of their horrific voyage on human flesh.

Géricault decided to show the moment when the survivors first spotted their rescue ship, but survival was not yet assured. The outstretched arms of the victims lead the viewer's eye to the climactic figure of an African held aloft by other men. He waves a cloth to attract the attention of a ship that is still only a speck on the horizon. Géricault's academic training underlies

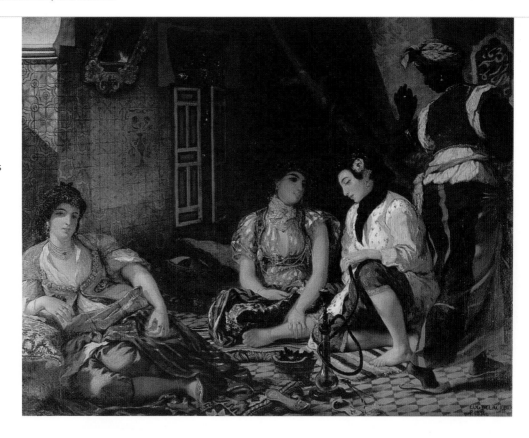

17-16

Eugène Delacroix
Women of Algiers
1834. Oil on canvas
5'10⅞" x 7'6⅛"
(1.8 x 2.29 m)
Musée du Louvre
Paris

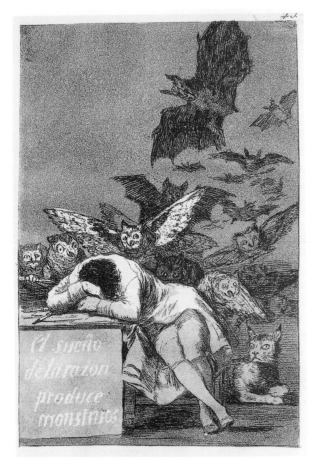

17-17 | Francisco de Goya. *The Sleep of Reason Produces Monsters,* from *Los Caprichos* (*The Caprices*), 1796-98. Series published 1799. Etching and aquatint. 8½" x 6" (21.6 x 15.2 cm).
Courtesy of The Hispanic Society of America, New York

the painting's organization as a series of interlocking triangles, through which he illustrates this human tragedy and injustice with indignant compassion.

At the Salon of 1819, Géricault showed his painting under the neutral title *A Shipwreck Scene*, perhaps to downplay its politically inflammatory aspects and to encourage appreciation of its larger philosophical theme—the eternal and tragic struggle of humanity against the elements. Most contemporary French critics interpreted the painting as a political commentary, however, with liberals praising it and royalists condemning it. Because the monarchy understandably refused to buy the canvas, Géricault exhibited *The Raft of the "Medusa"* commercially on a two-year tour of Ireland and England, where the London exhibition attracted more than 50,000 paying visitors.

Eugène Delacroix, who modeled for one of the nude victims on the raft, followed Géricault as the inspirational leader of the Romantic movement. Although Delacroix generally supported liberal political aims, his visit in 1832 to Morocco seems to have stirred his more conservative side. As enthralled as Delacroix was with the brilliant color and dignified inhabitants of North Africa, his attraction to the patriarchal political and social system is also evident in paintings such as *Women of Algiers* (fig. 17-16). This image of hedonism and passivity countered the contemporaneous demands of many French women for property reform, more equitable child-custody laws, and other egalitarian initiatives. The contrast in styles between Ingres's *Large Odalisque* (see fig. 17-13) and Delacroix's *Women of Algiers* points out the difference between the clear, linear, sculptural Neoclassical style and the diffuse, colorful, painterly, almost Baroque Romantic mode.

In Spain Francisco Goya y Lucientes (1746–1828) became a major figure in the Romantic movement. Goya began his career painting portraits and genre scenes, the latter used as tapestry

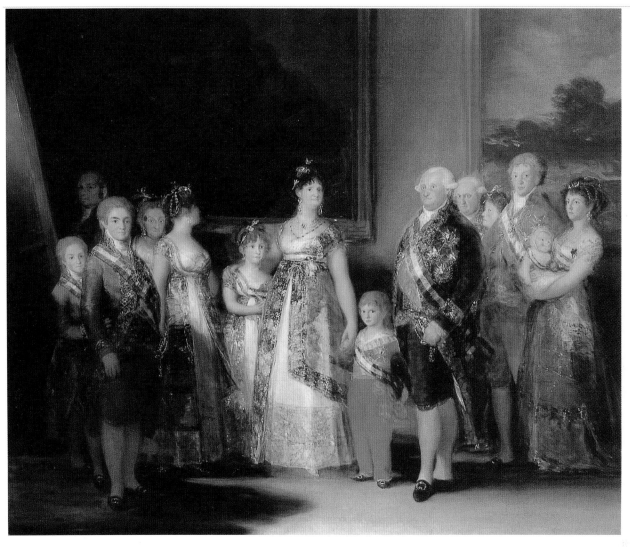

17-18

| Francisco Goya
Family of Charles IV
1800. Oil on canvas
9'2" x 11' (2.79 x 3.36 m)
Museo del Prado, Madrid

designs by the Royal Manufactory in Madrid. By the turn of the century, however, his study of Velázquez and Rembrandt began to be manifest in his work in freer brushwork, richer colors, and dramatic presentation.

In 1799 Goya published *Los Caprichos* (*The Caprices*), the first of several suites of etchings he created. These prints exhibit a bitter outlook that is absent from his earlier genre paintings and tapestry cartoons. Setting the tone for the eighty etchings is the print originally intended as its **frontispiece**, *The Sleep of Reason Produces Monsters* (fig. 17-17). Although the text published with the print sounds a hopeful note ("Imagination abandoned by reason produces impossible monsters; united with her, she is the mother of the arts and the source of their wonders"), the images are an angry attack on contemporary Spanish manners and morals that make Hogarth's satire (see fig. 17-6) seem tame.

The print shows a slumbering personification of Reason, behind whom lurk the dark creatures of the night—owls, bats, and a cat—that are let loose when Reason sleeps. The rest of the *Caprichos* enumerate the specific follies of Spanish life. Goya hoped that the series would show Spanish people the errors of their ways and reawaken them to reason. Although the premise is hopeful, Goya's portrait of human folly and cruelty is disturbing. Goya did not share the Enlightenment faith in the ultimate rationality and goodness of humanity. On the con-

trary, he believed that the violence, greed, and foolishness of his society had to be examined mercilessly if it were to be changed in any way.

Goya's large portrait of the *Family of Charles IV* (fig. 17-18) openly acknowledges the influence of Velázquez's *Las Meninas* (see fig. 14-14). Goya even places himself behind the easel on the left, just as Velázquez had in his painting. Unlike *Las Meninas*, however, Goya's painting is realistic rather than flattering—some see the painting as a cruel exposé of the royal family as common, ugly, and inept. Considering Goya's position as the principal court painter at the time of this royal commission, it is difficult to imagine the artist deliberately mocking his patrons. In fact, Goya made preparatory sketches for the painting, which the family apparently approved. The viewers who first saw the painting in 1800 would have found it striking not because it was demeaning but because its candid representation was refreshingly modern.

In 1808 Napoleon conquered Spain and placed his brother Joseph Bonaparte on its throne. Many Spaniards, including Goya, at first welcomed the French because they hoped for liberal reforms, but soon the government turned despotic. On May 2, 1808, a rumor spread in Madrid that the French planned to kill the royal family. The populace rose up and a day of bloody street fighting ensued. Hundreds of Spanish people were executed the following morning. The fighting soon

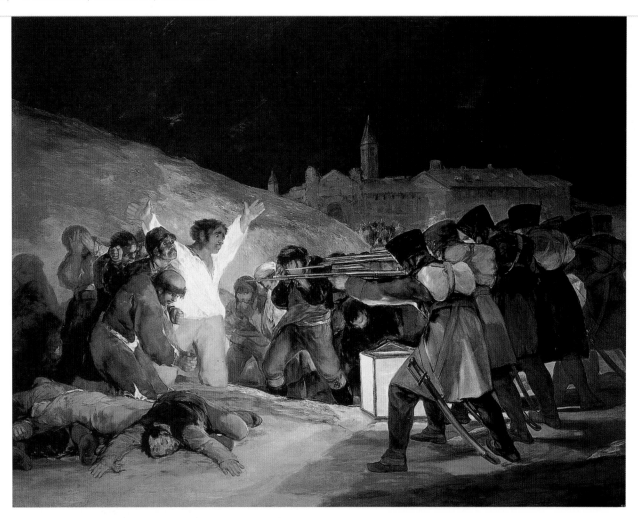

17-19 | Francisco Goya. *Third of May, 1808.* 1814–15. Oil on canvas, 8'9" x 13'4" (2.67 x 4.06 m). Museo del Prado, Madrid

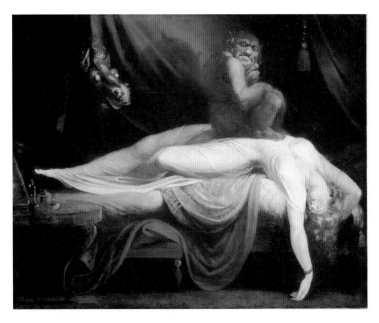

17-20 | **John Henry Fuseli. *The Nightmare.*** 1781. Oil on canvas 39¾ x 49½" (101 x 126 cm) The Detroit Institute of Arts

Founders Society Purchase with funds from Mr. and Mrs. Bert L. Smokler and Mr. and Mrs. Lawrence A. Fleischmann

(See pages 416–17.)

spread to the countryside, and for the next six years the Spanish conducted guerilla warfare against the French occupying forces, events recorded by Goya in another print series, *The Horrors of War*.

After the war, Goya made a pair of paintings to commemorate the events of May 2 and May 3. The more famous of the two paintings shows a French firing squad executing helpless Spanish prisoners in the predawn hours of May 3 (fig. 17-19). The violent gestures of the terrified rebels and the mechanical efficiency of the firing squad are like scenes from a nightmare. The man in the white shirt, confronting his faceless killer with outstretched arms suggesting the crucified Jesus, is an image of particular horror and pathos. When asked why he painted such a brutal scene, Goya responded: "To warn men never to do it again."

The Enlightenment's faith in reason and empirical knowledge was countered by Romanticism's celebration of the emotions and subjective forms of experience, as dramatized in Goya's *The Sleep of Reason Produces Monsters* (see fig. 17-17). This rebellion against reason led Romantic artists like John Henry Fuseli (1741–1825) to glorify the irrational side of human nature that the Enlightenment sought to deny. The Swiss Fuseli was raised in an intellectual household where originality, freedom of expression, and the imaginative power of the irrational were celebrated. His family and friends were inspired by British poetry

17-21 | John Constable. *The White Horse*
1819. Oil on canvas, 4'3¾" x 6'2⅛" (1.31 x 1.88 m). The Frick Collection, New York

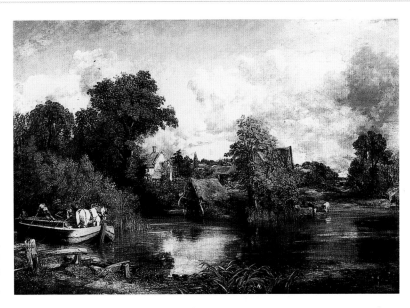

and by Shakespeare. Not surprisingly, after studying in Rome (1770–78) where he focused on Michelangelo rather than ancient classical art, Fuseli settled permanently in London. By the early 1780s, he began to make a reputation as a painter of the irrational and the erotic, with works such as *The Nightmare* (fig. 17-20).

ROMANTIC LANDSCAPE PAINTING

Romantic taste in England found a major outlet in landscape painting. By the early nineteenth century Romantic landscape painting generally took one of two forms—the naturalistic or the dramatic. The naturalistic style entailed closely observed representations of tranquil nature, meant to communicate reverence for the landscape as a spiritual precinct and to counteract the effects of industrialization and urbanization that were rapidly transforming it. The other—the dramatic—emphasized turbulent or fantastic natural scenery, often shaken by natural disasters such as storms and avalanches, and aimed to stir viewers' emotions and arouse a feeling of the **sublime**. John Constable (1776–1837), one of the two great landscape painters in England, specialized in naturalistic scenes of rural stability. The other, Joseph Mallord William Turner (1775–1851), focused on mood and drama.

The son of a successful miller, Constable claimed that the landscape of his youth in southern England had made him a painter before he ever picked up a brush. In spite of his training at the Royal Academy, where landscape was considered an inferior art, he was greatly impressed by the work of seventeenth-century Dutch landscapists, and theirs was the example he followed. Constable's *The White Horse* (fig. 17-21) of 1819 draws on his intense observation of every facet of the natural landscape, recorded in sketches he made on walking tours. As a storm passes away to the right, a farmer and his helpers ferry a workhorse across a river. Sunlight glistens off the water and foliage, an effect Constable achieved through tiny dabs of white paint.

Constable detested what he called "cold, trumpery stuff" and "bravura," by which he meant Romantic effects of drama and grandeur. Although he composed his paintings in his studio, he used sketches made on the site, insisting that art should be an objective record of things actually seen. The naturalistic stylistic current to which his pastoral idylls belong is sometimes referred to as Romantic naturalism. Constable made no reference to rural England's ongoing economic depression and civil unrest, or to the blight attending England's industrialization.

Turner, Constable's contemporary, imbued his early works with a pleasant, picturesque quality not far removed from Constable's, and he rapidly won public acclaim. At twenty-seven, Turner was elected a full member of the Royal Academy, and later he became a professor at the Royal Academy school. As Turner's personal style matured, the phenomena of colored light and atmospheric movement became the true subjects of

"AM I NOT A MAN AND A BROTHER?"

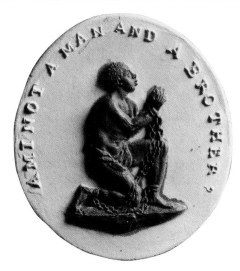

William Hackwood, for Josiah Wedgwood. *"Am I Not a Man and a Brother?"* 1787. Black-and-white jasperware 1⅜ x 1⅜" (3.5 x 3.5 cm). Wedgwood Museum Trust Limited, Barlaston, Staffordshire, England

For two centuries the name Wedgwood has been synonymous with fine English ceramics, especially tableware. But there was another side to Josiah Wedgwood. He was active in the international effort to halt the African slave trade and abolish slavery. To publicize the abolitionist cause, he asked the sculptor William Hackwood to design an emblem for the British Committee to Abolish the Slave Trade, formed in 1787. The compelling image created by Hackwood had the likeness of a black African man kneeling in chains, with the legend, "Am I Not a Man and a Brother?" Wedgwood sent copies of the medallion to Benjamin Franklin, the president of the Philadelphia Abolition Society, and to others in the movement. In the nineteenth century, the women's suffrage movement in the United States adapted the image by representing a woman in chains with the motto, "Am I Not a Woman and a Sister?"

A work of art as explicitly political as this was unusual in the eighteenth century. Nevertheless, artists in both Europe and America responded to the tumultuous social changes and political events with powerful and courageous works of art.

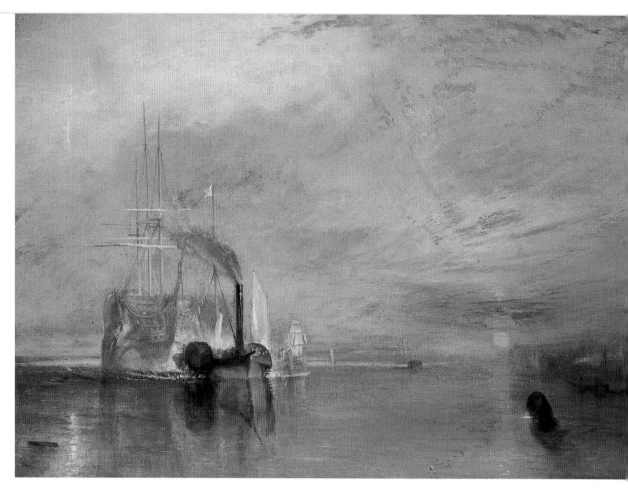

17-22

Joseph Mallord William Turner *The Fighting "Téméraire," Tugged to Her Last Berth to Be Broken Up* 1838. Oil on canvas, 35¼ x 48" (89.5 x 121.9 cm). The National Gallery London

his paintings. To the **academicians** his works increasingly looked like sketches or preliminary underpainting of unfinished canvases, but to his admirers, including Constable, they were "golden visions, glorious and beautiful," painted with "tinted steam."

Turner's *The Fighting "Téméraire," Tugged to Her Last Berth to Be Broken Up* (fig. 17-22) of 1838 is both a painting of a contemporary event and a study in the optical effects of the setting sun over water. The "Téméraire" had been the second-ranking British ship at the Battle of Trafalgar in 1805, a great British naval victory over the combined fleets of Spain and Napoleon's France. Some thirty-three years later, however, the ship was ready for the scrap heap, and Turner watched as it was towed away to be destroyed. Some have interpreted the scene as a symbol of the passing of the old order, the sailing ship literally and figuratively destroyed by the steam-engine-driven tug. The broad and painterly treatment of the sky, which Turner laid down largely with a palette knife, hints at the abstraction of his late works of the 1840s, in which land, sea, and sky dissolve into vaporous bursts of color and light.

Early Photography

The development of photography was a prime expression of the new, positivist interest in descriptive accuracy. Since the Renaissance, western people had been seeking a mechanical method for recording a scene. One early device was the **camera obscura** (Latin for "dark chamber"). It consisted of a darkened room or box with a lens on one side through which light passed and projected onto the opposite side an upside-down image of the scene,

which an artist then traced. In the nineteenth century photography was developed as a way to "fix"—that is, to make permanent—the visual impressions produced by a camera obscura, or camera, on light-sensitive material.

The first person to achieve this goal was the "gentleman inventor" Joseph-Nicéphore Niépce (1765–1833). Using metal-and-glass plates covered with a kind of light-sensitive asphalt called bitumen, and a camera, he succeeded around 1826 in making the first positive-image photographs. Later Niépce met Louis-Jacques-Mandé Daguerre (1787–1851), who, working with a lens maker, developed an improved camera. After Niépce's death in 1833, Daguerre, in 1835, discovered that an exposure to light of only twenty to thirty minutes would produce a latent image on a silver plate treated with iodine fumes, which could then be made visible through an after-process involving mercury vapor. By 1837 he had developed a method of fixing the image by bathing the plate in a strong solution of common salt after exposure. Daguerre's first picture of this type (**dagurreotype**), a still life of plaster casts and a framed drawing (fig. 17-23), makes the earliest claim for photography as an art form through its specifically "artistic" subject matter.

The 1839 announcement of Daguerre's invention prompted the English scientist William Henry Fox Talbot (1800–1877) to publish the results of his own work on what he called the **calotype** (from the Greek term for "beautiful image"). Fox Talbot's process, even more than Daguerre's, became the basis of modern photography because, unlike Daguerre's, which created a single, positive image, Talbot's calotype process produced a

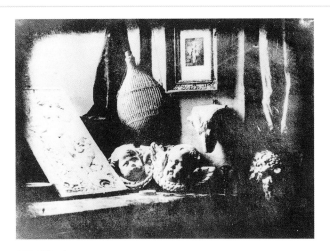

17-23 | **Louis-Jacques-Mandé Daguerre.** *The Artist's Studio*
1837. Daguerreotype, 6⁵/₈ x 8⁵/₈" (17 x 22 cm)
Société Française de Photographie, Paris

negative image from which an unlimited number of positives, or prints, could be made.

Beginning in the mid-1830s, Fox Talbot made negative copies of engravings, pieces of lace, and leaves by placing them on paper impregnated with silver chloride and exposing them to light. By the summer of 1835 he was using this chemically treated paper in both large and small cameras. Then, in 1840, he discovered, independently of Daguerre, that latent images resulting from exposure to the sun for short periods of time could be developed chemically. Applying the technique he had earlier used with engravings and leaves, Fox Talbot was able to make positive prints from the calotype negatives.

Fox Talbot's book *The Pencil of Nature* (issued in six parts, 1844–46) was the first book to be illustrated with photographs. The subjects of the photographs were often rural. In *The Open Door* (fig. 17-24) the photographer evoked an agrarian way of life that was fast disappearing. A traditional, handcrafted broom—of a type that mass production was beginning to make obsolete—rests against the doorway of a timeworn cottage. In an attempt at artfulness, the photographer carefully positioned the broom's handle to parallel the shadows on the door.

In 1851, Frederick Scott Archer, a British sculptor and photographer, took the final step in the development of early photography. Archer found that silver nitrate would adhere to glass if it was mixed with collodion, a combination of guncotton, ether, and alcohol used in medicinal bandages. When wet, this collodion-silver nitrate mixture needed only a few seconds' exposure to light to create an image. The result was a glass negative, from which countless positive proofs with great tonal subtleties could be made.

Once this practical photographic process had been invented, the question became how to make use of it. For some, photography was a convenience, replacing a live model; for others, it was a cheap substitute for, and therefore a threat to, the profession of painting, especially portraiture. Those in the sciences agreed on its value for recording data, but artists were less certain how to take advantage of it. Julia Margaret Cameron (1815–1879) was one of the pioneers of photography as an art form in its own right. Cameron's principal subjects were the great men of British arts, letters, and sciences, many of whom had long been family friends.

Cameron's portrait of the famous British historian Thomas Carlyle is deliberately slightly out of focus (fig. 17-25). By blurring details Cameron sought to call attention to the light that suffused her subjects—an artistic metaphor for creative genius. Carlyle's concentrated expression is so intense that the dramatic

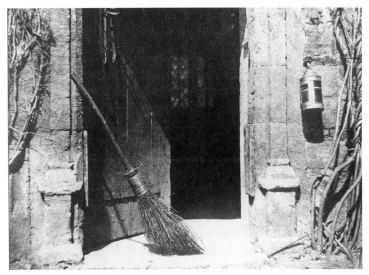

17-24 | **William Henry Fox Talbot.** *The Open Door.* 1843. Salt-paper print from a calotype negative. Science Museum, London
Fox Talbot Collection

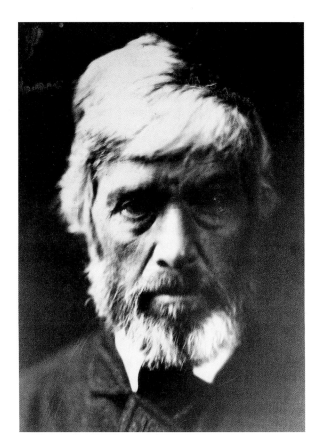

17-25 | **Julia Margaret Cameron.** *Portrait of Thomas Carlyle*
1863. Silver print, 10 x 8" (25.4 x 20.3 cm)
The Royal Photographic Society, London

TECHNIQUE
How Photography Works

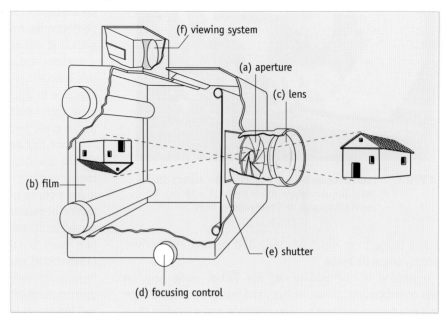

A camera is essentially a lightproof box with a hole, called an aperture (a), which is usually adjustable in size and which regulates the amount of light that strikes the film (b). The aperture is covered with a lens (c), which focuses (d) the image on the film, and a shutter (e), a kind of door that opens for a controlled amount of time, to regulate the length of time that the film is exposed to light—usually a small fraction of a second. In the example illustrated, the shutter is open, exposing the film to light. Modern cameras with viewfinders (f) and small single-lens reflex cameras are generally used at eye level, permitting the photographer to see virtually the same image that the film will "see."

Photography is based on the principle that certain substances are sensitive to light and react to light by changing **value**. In modern black-and-white photography, silver halide crystals (silver combined with iodine, chlorine, or other halogens) are suspended in a gelatin base to make an emulsion that coats the film (in early photography, before the invention of plastic, a glass plate was coated with a variety of emulsions). The film is then exposed. Light reflected off objects enters the camera and strikes the film. Pale objects reflect more light than do dark ones. The silver in the emulsion collects most densely where it is exposed to the most light, producing a "negative" image on the film. Later, when the film is placed in a chemical bath (developed), the silver deposits turn black, as if tarnishing. The more light the film receives, the denser the black tone created. A positive image is created from the negative in a darkroom—the film negative is placed over a sheet of paper that, like the film, has been treated to be light-sensitive, and light is directed through the negative onto the paper. Thus, a multiple number of positive prints can be generated from a single negative.

---

lighting of his hair, face, and beard almost seems to emanate from within. With regard to her medium Cameron said: "My aspirations are to ennoble Photography and to secure for it the character and uses of High Art by combining the real and ideal."

Naturalism and Realism in Europe

Painting of all types, whether academic or avant-garde, increasingly shared with photography an allegiance to factual accuracy. In the second quarter of the nineteenth century, innovative English artists such as Constable pioneered a naturalist credo that art should faithfully record ordinary life. In France this naturalistic current was represented by the Barbizon School, a group of painters working around the quiet village of Barbizon in the 1830s and 1840s. Academic jurors and conservative critics initially attempted to bar their naturalistic landscapes and rural scenes from the Salons, but after about 1850 the critical fortunes of the members of the Barbizon School soared. To those living in a rapidly urbanizing Europe, the image of a peaceful and contented country life began to grow in appeal.

Rosa Bonheur (1822–1899), though not a member of the Barbizon School, was one of the most popular French painters to address the taste for rural scenes. Bonheur's success in what was then a male domain owed much to the socialist convictions of her parents, who belonged to a radical utopian sect that believed in the equality of women. In order to achieve realistic depictions of the farm animals she loved, she read zoology books and made detailed studies in the countryside and in slaughterhouses. (To gain access to these all-male preserves, Bonheur had to get police permission to dress in men's clothing.)

Although Bonheur received some critical praise for her animal portraits in the 1840s, her success dates from the Salon of 1848, where she showed eight paintings and won a first-class medal. As a result, the government commissioned a work from her, *Plowing in the Nivernais: The Dressing of the Vines* (fig. 17-26). In this monumental painting, powerful beasts and workers offer a reassuring image of the continuity of agrarian life. The stately movement of men and animals reflects the kind of carefully balanced compositional schemes taught in the academy and echoes scenes of processions found in classical art. The painting's compositional harmony—the shape of the hill is answered by and continued in the general profile of the oxen and their handler on the right—as well as its smooth illusionism and conservative theme were very appealing to popular taste in England, the United States, and France. Bonheur became so famous that in 1865 she received France's highest award, membership in the Legion of Honor, becoming the first woman to be awarded its Grand Cross.

A defining moment in Realism as we understand it today grew out of the Revolution of 1848 in France. In February of that year, Parisian workers overthrew the monarchy and established the Second Republic (1848–51). Its founders' socialist goals, including collective ownership of the means of production and

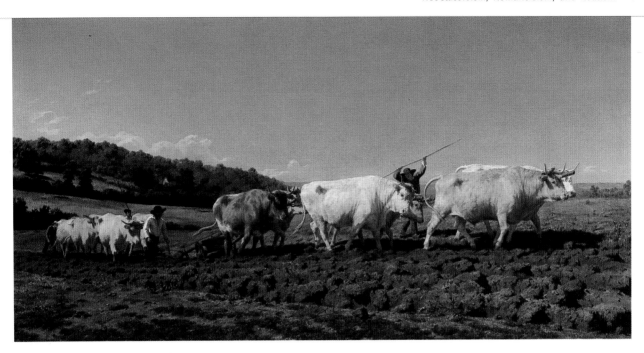

17-26 | **Rosa Bonheur. *Plowing in the Nivernais: The Dressing of the Vines.*** 1849. Oil on canvas, 5'9" x 8'8" (1.75 x 2.64 m) Musée d'Orsay, Paris

Bonheur was often compared with Georges Sand, a contemporary woman writer who adopted a male name as well as male dress. Sand devoted several of her novels to the humble life of farmers and peasants. Critics at the time noted that *Plowing in the Nivernais* may have been inspired by a passage in Sand's *The Devil's Pond* (1846) that begins: "But what caught my attention was a truly beautiful sight, a noble subject for a painter. At the far end of the flat ploughland, a handsome young man was driving a magnificent team [of] oxen."

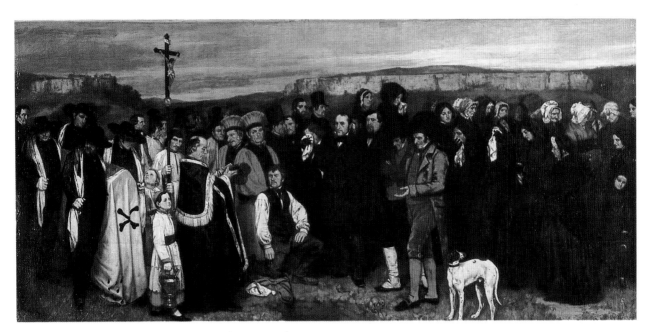

17-27 | **Gustave Courbet. *A Burial at Ornans.*** 1849. Oil on canvas, 10'2" x 21'8" (3.1 x 6.6 m) Musée d'Orsay

distribution, were abandoned when conservative factions won elections that summer. Fear of further disruptions continued to trouble many, while others, including the painter Gustave Courbet (1819–1877), became converts to the radicals' visions of social change.

Gustave Courbet was inspired by the events of 1848 to turn his attention to poor and ordinary people. Born and raised in Ornans near the Swiss border and largely self-taught as an artist, he moved to Paris in 1839. The street fighting of 1848 seems to

have radicalized him. Courbet proclaimed his new political commitment in three large paintings he submitted to the Salon of 1850–51. One of these, *A Burial at Ornans* (fig. 17-27), is a monumental canvas showing the funeral of Courbet's grandfather Oudot, who had died in 1847. Instead of arranging figures in a conventional pyramid that would indicate a hierarchy of importance, Courbet lined them up in rows across the picture plane— an arrangement he considered more democratic. The artist's respect and affinity for the people is expressed in the vast scale

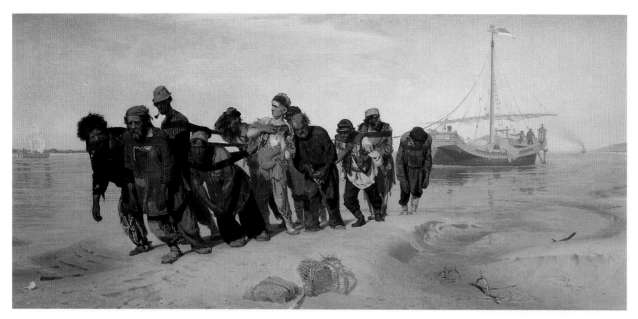

17-28 **Ilya Repin. *Bargehaulers on the Volga.*** 1870–73. Oil on canvas, 4'3¹/₁₆" x 9'2⁵/₈" (1.3 x 2.81 m). Russian State Museum St. Petersburg

of the work—a size ordinarily reserved for the depiction of major historical events. It is also shown in the way the mourners' genuine sorrow is contrasted with the apparent indifference of the two Church officials dressed in red behind the officiating priest. Conservative critics hated the work for its focus on common people and for its disrespect for traditional composition and standards of beauty.

Partly for convenience, Bonheur, Courbet, and the other country-life naturalists and Realists who emerged in the 1850s are sometimes referred to as the generation of 1848 (named for the year of the Revolution). Because he had liberal political views and sympathized with working-class people, the somewhat older Honoré Daumier (1808–1879) is grouped with this generation. Daumier believed that art and architecture must invent new forms and subject matter to speak to the realities of contemporary life (see fig. 26). He helped to usher in the new taste for realism through biting satires of academic art and its upper-middle-class audience. Daumier used the new medium of lithography, and the popular press to express his ideas in images that recall the power of Goya.

Artists of other western nations also embraced realism in the period after 1850. In Russia, for example, the plight of the peasantry captured the painters' attention. In 1861 the czar abolished serfdom, emancipating Russia's peasants from the virtual slavery they had endured on the large estates of the aristocracy. Two years later, a group of painters inspired by the emancipation declared their allegiance to the peasant cause and to freedom from the St. Petersburg Academy of Art, which had controlled Russian art since 1754. Rejecting what they considered the escapist "art for art's sake" **aesthetics** of the academy, the members of the group, calling themselves the Wanderers, dedicated themselves to bringing a socially relevant art to the people in traveling exhibitions.

Ilya Repin (1844–1930), who attended the St. Petersburg Academy and won a scholarship to study in Paris, joined the Wanderers on his return to Russia in 1878. He had painted a series of works illustrating the social injustices then prevailing in his homeland, the first and most famous of which was *Bargehaulers on the Volga* (fig. 17-28). The painting features a group of wretched peasants condemned to the brutal work of pulling ships up the Volga River. In order to heighten our sympathy for these workers, Repin placed a youth in the center of the group, a young man who will soon look as old and tired as his companions unless something is done to rescue him. In this way, the painting is a cry for action.

Painting in the United States

While Europe suffered through the Napoleonic Wars, the United States was entering an era of great optimism and expansion. The new country emerged from its war for independence from Britain with sufficient resources, technology, and entrepreneurs to move into the forefront of the industrialized world. Many nineteenth-century American painters, sculptors, and architects looked to Europe for their inspiration, but others found everything they needed in their native landscape and took pride in the American scene. These artists and their patrons tended to favor a detailed realism and local interests over high-minded Neoclassical scenes drawn from ancient history.

Before the advent of photography, artists played an important role in circulating knowledge about the natural world. One of America's most celebrated scientific naturalists was John James Audubon (1785–1851), a French immigrant who set out to record the birds of America in accurate watercolors. Like Merian (see fig. 14-33) before him, he reproduced his work in prints and published hand-colored impressions of them in portfolios. To support publication of his *Birds of America* (completed in 1839), Audubon sold paintings after his drawings to private collectors.

To complete his bird encyclopedia, Audubon traveled and sketched from Labrador to Florida, and southwest as far as Texas. Ultimately he made 435 watercolor studies of birds. Combining

17-29 John James Audubon. *Common Grackle,* **illustration for** *The Birds of America,* 1825. Watercolor, graphite, selective glazing. 23⁷/₈" x 18¹/₂" (61.22 x 47.44 cm). Collection of The New-York Historical Society, New York City (1863.17.007)

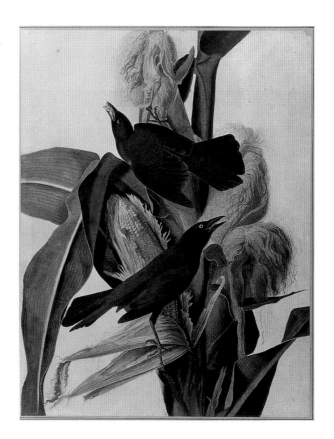

close observation with an artist's eye for design, he showed the birds in their natural habitats, often whimsically or dramatically. In his *Common Grackle* (fig. 17-29), these sleek and fearless birds are shown assaulting ears of corn.

The first major painter to live and work west of the Mississippi River was George Caleb Bingham (1811–1879), who sketched and painted scenes of everyday life along the river. With *Fur Traders Descending the Missouri* (fig. 17-30), painted about 1845 Bingham began an association with the newly formed American Art Union in New York. As a way to promote American painters, the Union purchased works for a flat fee, then reproduced prints of the paintings to be sold by subscription. *Fur Traders Descending the Missouri,* which Bingham sold to the Union for $25, is an idyllic scene of a French trapper and his son with their pet bear cub in a dugout canoe. As they glide through the early-morning stillness, the still-hidden sun tinges the clouds with rosy gold, and morning mists shroud the river landscape in mystery. Despite the peacefulness of the scene, there is an underlying ominous feeling. Branches and rocks stick out of the water, reminders of the hazards the boatmen faced, and the mysterious black shape of the chained bear mirrored in the glassy water surface produces an eerie effect reminiscent of the demon in Fuseli's *The Nightmare.* The images seem not only idealized but also nostalgic, for by now the independent French voyageurs who had opened the fur trade using canoes had been replaced by trading companies using larger, more efficient craft. Bingham's painting records a vanished way of life and celebrates the early stages of commerce on the frontier.

Bingham's idyllic visions of life in the West appeared just as America's open spaces began to face threats from industrial development and urbanization. The Industrial Revolution, the flurry of technological progress and mechanization that began in Europe in the mid-eighteenth century, reached the United States by the early nineteenth century. A transcontinental railroad was completed in 1869, and by the 1890s the frontier had disappeared. By the second half of the nineteenth century, both the United States and Europe were ready for a new art and the modern age.

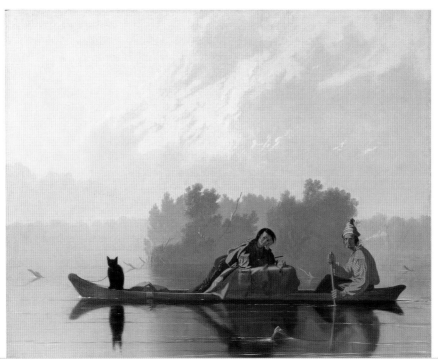

17-30

George Caleb Bingham *Fur Traders Descending the Missouri.* c. 1845 Oil on canvas, 29 x 36¹/₂" (73.7 x 92.7 cm) The Metropolitan Museum of Art, New York Morris K. Jesup Fund, 1933. (33.61)

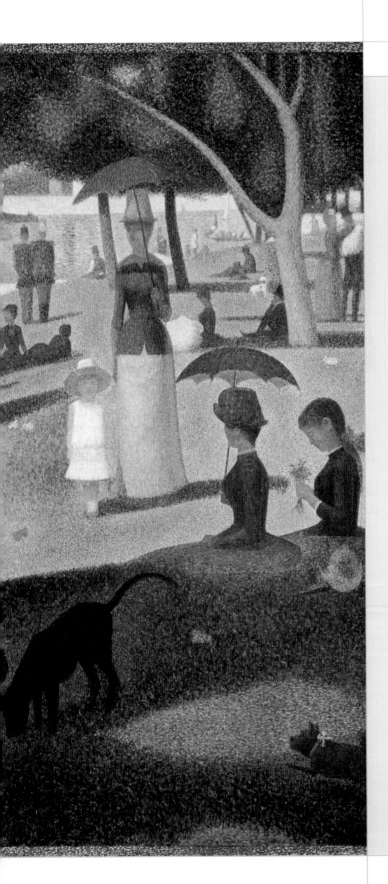

In his painted evocation *A Sunday Afternoon on the Island of La Grande Jatte*, Georges Seurat (1859–1891) took a typical Impressionist subject, weekend leisure activities, and gave it an entirely new interpretation. An avid reader of scientific color theory, Seurat applied his paint in small dots of pure color in the belief that when they are "mixed" in the eye—as opposed to being mixed on the palette—the resulting colors would be more luminous. He used upward-moving lines (seen in the angle of the coastline) and warm bright colors, presuming that these elements created "happy" paintings. During the months he spent visiting the island, he studied the individuals he found there and also the way the light fell on the figures and the landscape. Each character in the final painting—even the woman with the monkey—was based on his detailed observations at the original site.

The technique Seurat developed, known as pointillism, was an aspect of the Neo-Impressionist style—only one of many western European and American artistic styles that began at the end of the nineteenth century. The various styles, often consciously at odds with one another, are nevertheless grouped by writers and critics under the common label of "modernism." In many ways, modernism is an attitude, not a look. Beginning with Manet, the process of painting—the materials and their handling—assumed a much larger role in the work of art. Some of these styles were directed at self-expression, others at the suppression of human feeling. Many artists saw the need to communicate deep-felt social concerns. A sometimes unbridled utopianism often stood in direct counterpoint to the political crises of the age. Yet another group of artists saw the artwork as a unique experience in which the materials and process of painting, carving, or printmaking were primary, leading ultimately to abstraction.

Seurat's Parisians felt as much rain and cold as sun, and the popular island of La Grand Jatte must have been littered with picnic refuse by the time the crowds left on Sunday. But in his painting, Seurat makes it seem an island of perpetual tranquility and a place to escape from messy worldly problems. It is a perfect lazy day, and that feeling of relaxation is conveyed through the vivid warm colors and a composition of horizontals and verticals receding gently into the background. Is Seurat presenting his vision of an ideal society in his carefully calculated and formal representation of people in a sunny landscape? Or is he simply engaged in an intellectual exercise in the method of painting?

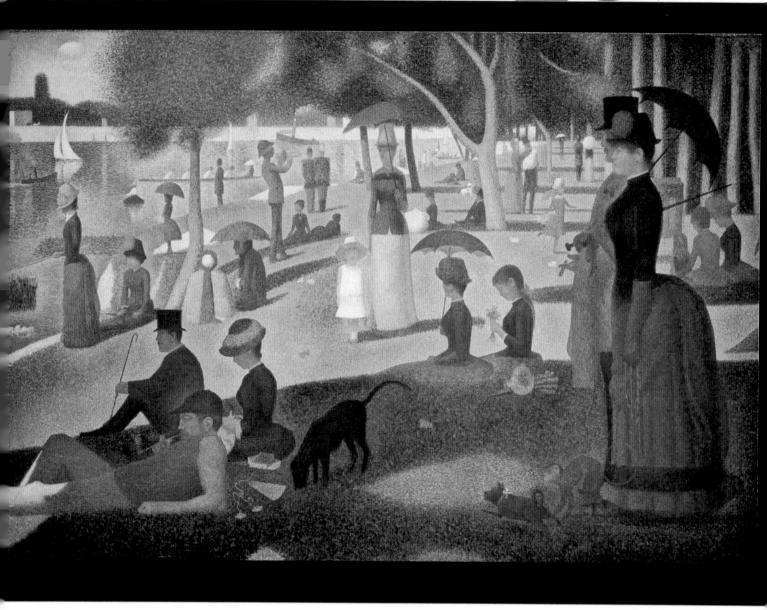

Georges Seurat. *A Sunday Afternoon on the Island of La Grande Jatte.* 1884–86. Oil on canvas, 6'9½" x 10'1¼" (2.07 x 3.08 m). The Art Institute of Chicago

Helen Birch Bartlett Memorial Collection

(See page 459.)

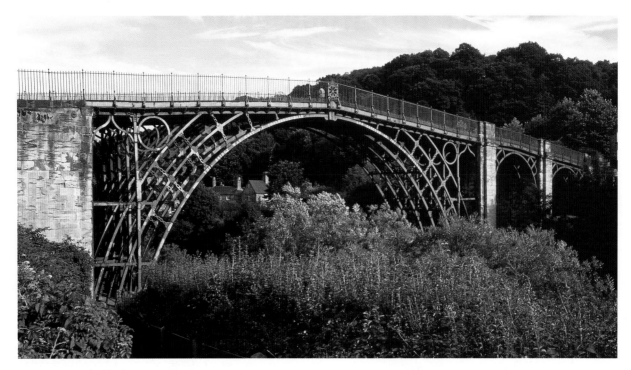

18-1 | **Abraham Darby III. The Severn River Bridge,** Coalbrookdale, England. Completed 1779

The Enlightenment set in motion powerful forces that would dramatically transform life in Europe and the United States during the nineteenth century (see Map 7, page 529). Great advances in manufacturing, transportation, and communications created new products for consumers and new wealth for entrepreneurs, fueling the rise of urban centers and improving living conditions for many. But this so-called Industrial Revolution also condemned masses of workers to poverty and catalyzed new political movements that sought to reform society. Animating these developments was the widespread belief in "progress" and the ultimate perfectibility of human civilization—a belief rooted deeply in Enlightenment thought.

Some scientific discoveries challenged traditional religious beliefs and affected social philosophy. Contrary to the biblical account of creation, Charles Darwin proposed that all life evolved from a common ancestor and changed through genetic mutation and natural selection, so that the best-adapted species survive while others become extinct. Religious conservatives attacked Darwin's account of evolution, which seemed to deny the divine creation of humans and even the existence of God.

Technological developments in agriculture and manufacturing displaced many owners of small farms and cottage industries who were forced to move to new factory and mining towns in search of employment. These industrial laborers suffered miserable working and living conditions. Socialist movements condemned the exploitation of laborers by capitalist factory owners and advocated communal or state ownership of the means of production and distribution. The most radical of these movements was Communism, which called for the abolition of private property. In 1848 Karl Marx and Friedrich Engels published the *Communist Manifesto*, which predicted the violent overthrow of the property-holding bourgeoisie (middle class) by the proletariat (working class) and the creation of a classless society.

Feminists struggled to improve the status of women and abolitionists worked to end slavery. The Americans Lucretia Mott and Elizabeth Cady Stanton held the country's first women's rights convention, in Seneca Falls, New York, in 1848. They called for the equality of women and men before the law, property rights for married women, the acceptance of women into institutions of higher education, the admission of women to all trades and professions, equal pay for equal work, and women's suffrage (achieved only in 1920). American suffragists were also active in the abolitionist movement, but slavery in the United States was only finally eliminated as a result of the devastating Civil War (1861–65). After the Civil War, the United States became a major industrial power, and the American Northeast underwent rapid urbanization, fueled by millions of immigrants from Europe seeking economic opportunities.

In the second half of the nineteenth century, positivist thinking influenced by objective, scientific inquiry is evident not only in the rejection of Romanticism and the growth of **realism** in art but also in the highly descriptive style of academic art, the application of new technologies in architecture, and in the last quarter of the century the Impressionist and Post-Impressionist painters' emphasis on light and the phenomenon of perception.

Architecture

Major works of public architecture in the nineteenth century tended to be based on historic models—a practice called **historicism,** which is the application of decorative motifs and styles from the past. The conventions of historicism were taught at the architecture school of the École des Beaux-Arts (School of Fine Arts) in Paris, an important training ground for

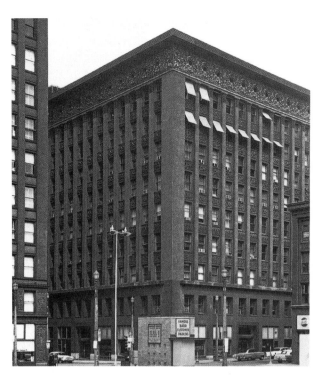

18-2 | **Louis Sullivan. Wainwright Building**
St. Louis, Missouri. 1890–91

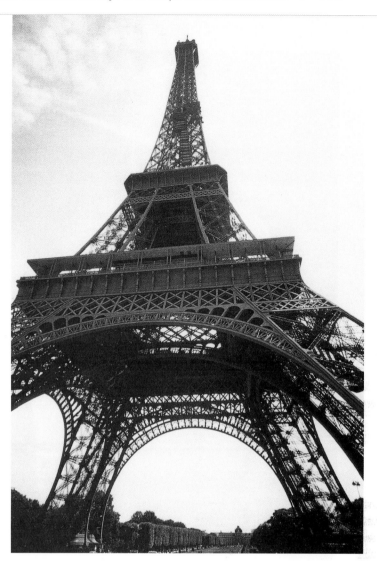

18-3 | **Gustave Eiffel. Eiffel Tower,** Paris. 1887–89

European and American architects. But while historicism and revival styles, such as Neoclassicism and Gothic Revival, were popular, modern conditions and materials had an increasing impact on construction. Building techniques introduced in the late eighteenth and first half of the nineteenth centuries ultimately led to an emphasis on structure and the abandonment of dependence on historic styles.

It was engineers rather than architects who had pioneered the use of the most important new building materials: cast iron, wrought iron, and steel. In England in 1776–79, Abraham Darby III built the first cast-iron bridge at an industrial site known as Coalbrookdale (fig. 18-1). In this groundbreaking use of structural metal on a large scale, iron replaced the heavy, hand-cut stone voussoirs used to construct earlier bridges. The skeletal structure desired by builders since the twelfth century was at last possible, enabling the qualities of light, space, and movement to be incorporated into building designs.

Iron-framed buildings, however, have a fatal susceptibility to fire. Exposed to intense heat, iron will warp, buckle, collapse, or melt altogether. The immediate solution was to encase the internal iron supports in fireproof materials and return to masonry sheathing. In the early 1860s the perfection of a technique for making inexpensive steel (an alloy of iron and carbon that is stronger and lighter than pure iron) introduced new architectural possibilities. Steel's light weight combined with strength made taller buildings feasible, as did the introduction of passenger elevators, the first of which was installed in the United States in 1857.

Steel was first used for buildings in 1884 by young Midwestern architects who are now grouped under the label, the Chicago School. Equipped with the new technologies and eager to escape from Beaux-Arts historicism, the Chicago School architects produced a new kind of building, the skyscraper. An early example of their work, and evidence of its rapid spread throughout the Midwest, is the Wainwright Building in St. Louis, Missouri (fig. 18-2), built by Louis Sullivan (1856–1924). Sullivan adapted the formal vocabulary and basic compositional rules of the Beaux-Arts tradition, dividing the ten-story office building into three parts—base, body, and crowning cornice—but he gave the building an entirely new vertical emphasis. The Wainwright Building is taller than it is wide; its governing verticals emphasize this height. The corner piers rise in uninterrupted lines to the cornice, their verticality echoed and reinforced by small piers between the windows, designed to suggest the steel framing beneath them.

While the Chicago School was looking for an American alternative to the Beaux-Arts tradition, its European counterparts had also been calling for an end to historicism and the invention of an architectural style appropriate to the modern age. The search would lead eventually to the frank acceptance of new industrial materials and techniques, like those that first appeared in structures such as the Eiffel Tower (fig. 18-3).

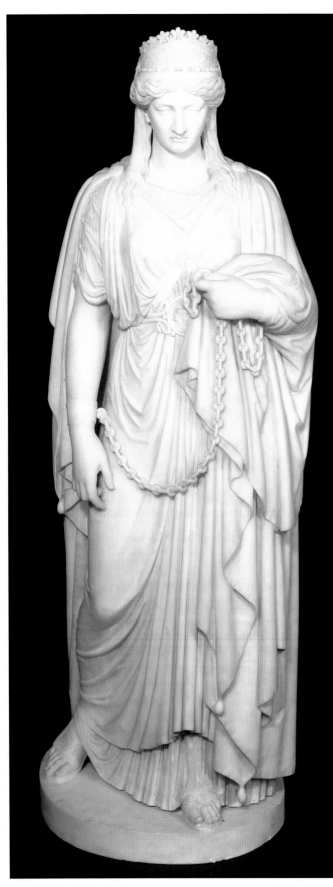

18-4 | **Harriet Hosmer.** *Zenobia in Chains.* 1859, Marble Height 4' (1.21 m). Wadsworth Atheneum, Hartford Connecticut

Gift of Mrs. Josephing M. J. Dodge

Gustave Eiffel (1832–1923), a civil engineer, built his famous tower for the Paris Universal Exposition of 1889. He won a competition for the design of a monument that would symbolize French industrial progress. Composed of iron latticework, the tower stands on four huge legs reinforced by trussed (braced) arches similar to those used in railway bridges. Passenger elevators allowed fairgoers to ascend to the top of what was then, at 984 feet (300 meters), the tallest structure in the world. Although the French public loved the tower, most architects, artists, and writers found it completely lacking in beauty. Monstrous, ugly, and useless were but a few of the words they used to describe it. They dolefully predicted that it would have a brutalizing effect on the future of architecture in Paris. (One response to this concern was the birth of Art Nouveau, a style stressing flowing curves and organic forms that attempted to be modern without losing a pre-industrial sense of beauty. (See pages 447–49.)

Academic Art

Historicism in nineteenth-century architecture had its counterpart in academic art: painting and sculpture that followed the conservative principles of the French Academy, which continued to exert enormous influence over artistic matters. Students at the École des Beaux-Arts and other academic institutions began their training by copying prints and plaster casts of classical and Renaissance sculpture; then they studied live models posed like classical sculpture. When, in the opinion of their teachers, they had developed sufficient technical skill and detailed knowledge of the human form to make actual paintings or works of sculpture, they were expected to recall their earlier immersion in classical art and "correct" ordinary nature to conform to classicism's higher ideal.

As a sequel to study at the Academy, or sometimes as an alternative to it, the young artists, and sculptors in particular, often visited or settled in Italy. Italy remained the wellspring of inspiration for artists (and for sculptors it was also the source of the materials and skilled workers needed to work the white marble, the material associated with classical sculpture). By the second half of the nineteenth century bustling artists' colonies in Rome and Florence even included women, whom the American author Henry James dubbed the "white, marmorean [marble] flock."

The most prominent of these women, Harriet Hosmer (1830–1908), had moved to Rome in 1852. Hosmer rapidly mastered the Neoclassical mode and began producing major exhibition pieces such as *Zenobia in Chains* (fig. 18-4). Neoclassical in form but Romantic in content, the sculpture represents an exotic historical subject calculated to appeal to the viewer's emotions. Zenobia, the heroic third-century queen of Palmyra, was defeated by the Romans and forced to march through the streets of Rome in chains. Hosmer presents her as a noble figure, resolute even in defeat. "I have tried to make her too proud to exhibit passion or emotion of any kind," wrote Hosmer of Zenobia, "not subdued, though a prisoner; but calm, grand, and strong within herself." Zenobia embodies an ideal of womanhood strikingly modern in its defiance of Victorian conventions of female submissiveness.

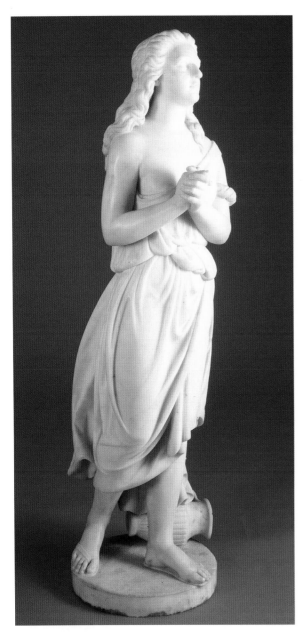

18-5 Edmonia Lewis. *Hagar in the Wilderness.* 1875
Marble, 52⅝ x 15¼ x 17" (133.6 x 38.7 x 43.2 cm)
Smithsonian American Museum, Smithsonian
Institution, Washington, D.C.

Edmonia Lewis (c.1843/45–after 1911) also moved to Rome to become a sculptor. Born in New York State to a Chippewa mother and an African-American father, Lewis was orphaned at the age of four and raised by her mother's people. With the help of abolitionists, she attended Oberlin College, the first college in the United States to grant degrees to women, and then moved to Boston. Her highly successful busts and medallions of abolitionist leaders and Civil War heroes financed her move to Rome in 1867, where she was welcomed into Hosmer's circle.

In Rome, Lewis continued to dedicate herself to the causes of human freedom, especially those involving women: "I have a strong sympathy for all women who have struggled and suffered," she said. *Hagar in the Wilderness* (fig. 18-5), for example,

tells the story of the Egyptian concubine of the biblical patriarch Abraham, given to him by his childless wife, Sarah, so that he might have a son. Hagar bore a son, Ishmael, but later the elderly Sarah also bore a son, Isaac. The jealous Sarah demanded that Abraham abandon Hagar and Ishmael and drive them out into the wilderness. When Hagar and Ishmael were dying from thirst in the desert, an angel provided water (Genesis 16:1–16; 21:9–21). Because of her African origins, Hagar represented for Lewis the plight and the hope of her entire race.

Neoclassical idealism remained a powerful force in both sculpture and painting well into the nineteenth century, but a new taste for descriptive accuracy gradually emerged. The bankers and businesspeople who came to dominate European and North American society and politics in the years in the second half of the nineteenth century were, as patrons, generally less interested in art that idealized than in art that brought the ideal down to earth.

Although the national academies throughout Europe continued to control both the teaching and the display of art in the second half of the nineteenth century, increasing numbers of artists rejected their precepts in favor of the naturalist credo that art should faithfully record ordinary life. Artists and patrons reflected the positivist values of the times (see page 442), although photography, with the camera's extraordinary ability to create an accurate record, may also have contributed to this shift in taste. The national academies soon embraced the new desire for highly detailed depiction of physical forms. By the 1860s the terms *Realism* and *naturalism* had lost their socialist political meanings (see page 436).

Even painters who treated subjects remote from contemporary life showed a growing interest in realistic detail. With a reporter's concern for the facts, Sir Lawrence Alma-Tadema carefully researched Greek history and archaeology for his 1868 painting, *Pheidias and the Frieze of the Parthenon, Athens* (see fig. 23), even recording the color applied to the sculpture frieze in defiance of earlier Neoclassical artists' delight in pure white marble. Compared with Neoclassical artists such as Jacques-Louis David (see fig. 17-11), Sir Lawrence and his contemporaries began to think of history more as a set of objective facts than as something from which to learn moral lessons.

REACTIONS AGAINST THE ACADEMY

Reaction against academic idealism began building at midcentury. In England seven young artists formed the Pre-Raphaelite Brotherhood in 1848 to counter what they considered the misguided practices of contemporary British art. Instead of the idealized Raphaelesque conventions taught at the Royal Academy, they advocated the naturalistic, descriptive approach to the human body and to nature used by earlier northern Renaissance masters. They also advocated moralizing subject matter in keeping with a long tradition in Britain, exemplified by Hogarth (see fig. 17-6), and they filled their paintings with the type of symbolism found in medieval art.

Dante Gabriel Rossetti (1828–1882), a leading member of the Pre-Raphaelite Brotherhood, looked to the Middle Ages for a spiritual beauty and meaning he found lacking in his own time. His

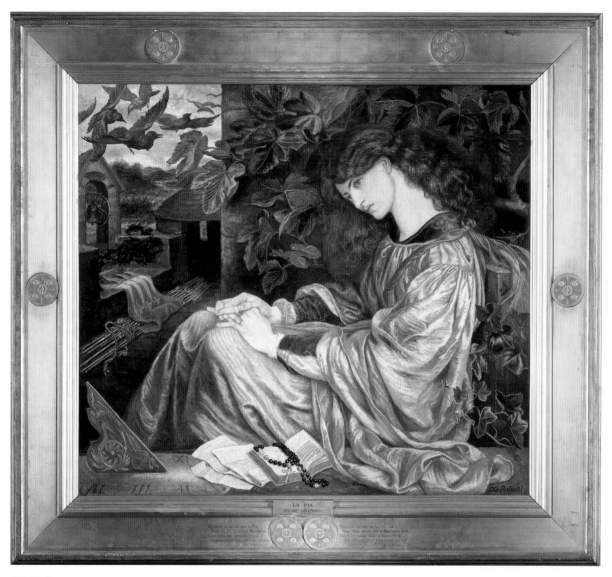

18-6 **Dante Gabriel Rossetti.** *La Pia de' Tolomei.* 1868–69. Oil on canvas, 41½ x 47½" (105.4 x 119.4 cm) Spencer Museum of Art, The University of Kansas, Lawrence

In addition to his work as a painter and poet, Rossetti created innovative and beautiful designs for picture frames, book bindings, wallpaper, and furniture, as well as architectural sculpture and stained glass. The gilded frames he designed for his pictures were intended to enhance their decorative effect and make their meaning clearer through inscriptions and symbols. The massive frame surrounding *La Pia de' Tolomei* features simple moldings on either side of broad, sloping boards, into which are set a few large roundels. The title of the painting is inscribed above the paired roundels at the lower center. On either side of them appear four lines from Dante's *Purgatory* spoken by the spirit of La Pia, in Italian at the left and in Rossetti's English translation at the right, which reads: "Remember me who am La Pia,—me/From Siena sprung and by Maremma dead./This in his inmost heart well knoweth he/With whose fair jewel I was ringed and wed."

painting *La Pia de' Tolomei* (fig. 18-6) had a personal relevance while at the same time illustrating an incident from Dante's *Purgatory*. La Pia (Pious One), wrongly accused of infidelity and locked up by her husband in a castle, is dying. The rosary and prayer book at her side refer to the piety from which she takes her name, while the sundial and ravens apparently allude to her impending death. Her continuing love for her husband, whose letters lie under the prayer book, is also symbolized by the evergreen ivy behind her; however, the luxuriant fig leaves that surround her are traditionally associated with lust and the Fall of Man and have no source in Dante's tale. In fact, the painting is not simply an idealized transcription of a text but a metaphor

for Rossetti's own unhappy situation. Jane Burden, Rossetti's model for this and many other paintings, was the wife of Rossetti's friend William Morris, but she had become Rossetti's lover. Here La Pia (Jane) fingers her wedding ring, a captive not so much of her husband as of her marriage.

William Morris (1834–1896) was less interested in painting than in design. His interest in handcrafts developed in the context of a widespread reaction against gaudy and shoddy industrially produced goods. After marrying Jane Burden in 1859 Morris set out to decorate their new home. Unable to find satisfactory furnishings, Morris, with the help of some friends, designed and made the furniture himself. He then founded a

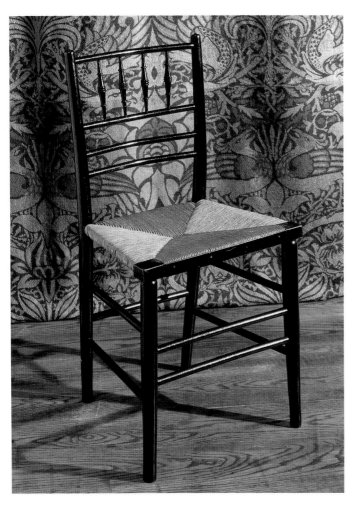

18-7 | (*foreground in photo*) **Philip Webb (?). Single chair from the Sussex range.** In production from c. 1865. Ebonized wood with rush seat, 32⅝ x 19⅜" (83.8 x 35.6 cm) Manufactured by Morris & Company. William Morris Gallery (London Borough of Waltham Forest)

(*background*) **William Morris. Peacock and Dragon curtain** 1878. Handloomed jacquard-woven woolen twill, 12'10½" x 11'5⅛" (3.96 x 3.53 m). Manufactured at Queen Square and later at Merton Abbey. Victoria and Albert Museum, London

Morris and his principal furniture designer, Philip Webb (1831–1915), adapted the Sussex range from traditional rush-seated chairs of the Sussex region. The handwoven curtain in the background is typical of Morris's fabric design in its use of flat patterning that affirms the two-dimensional character of the textile medium. The pattern's prolific organic motifs and soothing blue and green hues—the decorative counterpart to those of naturalistic landscape painting—were meant to provide relief from the stresses of modern urban existence.

decorating firm to produce a full range of medieval-inspired pieces. Although many of the furnishings offered by Morris & Company were expensive, one-of-a-kind items, others, such as the rush-seated chair illustrated here (fig. 18-7), were relatively cheap, intended to provide a handcrafted alternative to the vulgar excesses characteristic of industrial furniture. Concerned with creating a "total" environment in which architecture and décor were styled in harmony, Morris and his colleagues designed not only furniture but also stained glass, tiles, wall-

paper, and fabrics, such as the Peacock and Dragon curtain seen behind the Sussex chair in figure 18-7.

Morris inspired what became known as the Arts and Crafts Movement. As a socialist, his aim was to benefit not just a few wealthy clients but all of society. Morris recognized a wholesome social component in the skilled craftwork needed to produce handcrafts such as these. He sought to eliminate industrialization not only because he found factory-made products ugly but also because of mass production's deadening influence on the worker. With craftwork, he maintained, the laborer would acquire as much satisfaction from creating a fine piece as the consumer did using it. Morris saw the pre-industrial era as a model for economic and social reform.

Not all of those who participated in the revival of the decorative arts were committed to improving the conditions of modern life. Many, including the American expatriate James Abbott McNeill Whistler (1834–1903), saw in the Arts and Crafts revival simply another way to satisfy an elitist taste for beauty. In 1859 he moved from Paris to London, partly to distance himself from artists like Courbet, since the new vogue for Japanese art fueled in him a growing dissatisfaction with naturalism. Whistler had been one of the first to collect Japanese art when it became available in curio shops in London and Paris after the 1853 reopening of that nation to the West.

The simplified, elegant forms and subtle chromatic harmonies of Japanese art (see Chapter 9) had a profound influence on Whistler. In 1864 he exhibited three paintings that signaled his new direction. One of them, *Rose and Silver: The Princess from the Land of Porcelain* (see fig. 21, left wall), shows a Caucasian woman dressed in a Japanese robe and posed amid a collection of Asian artifacts. The work is Whistler's answer to the medieval costume pieces of the Pre-Raphaelites. What Whistler saw in Japanese objects was neither a preferable world nor a way to reform European decorative arts, but rather a model for painting. As the work's title—*Rose and Silver*—declares, Whistler attempted to create a formal, coloristic harmony. Thus, delicate organic shapes are shown against a rich orchestration of colors featuring silver and rose. By leaving his wet brushmarks visible, Whistler emphasized the paint itself over the depicted subject. Whistler's growing commitment to "art for art's sake," or an art of purely aesthetic values, culminated in the Peacock Room which he created to showcase his painting.

ART NOUVEAU

Whistler's commitment to "art for art's sake" anticipated a popular style known as Art Nouveau (New Art). The practitioners of Art Nouveau rejected the values of modern industrial society and sought new aesthetic forms that would retain a pre-industrial sense of beauty. Their ideas and style permeated all aspects of European art at the end of the nineteenth century. They applied fluid linear arabesques and organic forms to all aspects of design, drawing inspiration from ancient Celtic art and from nature—vines, snakes, flowers, and winged insects—whose delicate and sinuous forms were the basis of their graceful and attenuated linear designs. Following from this commitment to organic principles, they also sought to

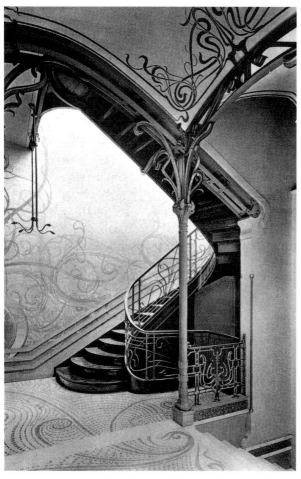

18-8 | **Victor Horta.** *Stairway, Tassel House,* Brussels. 1892–93

JAPONISME

Whistler's interest in Japanese art was part of a widespread fascination with Japan and its culture that swept across the West in the last half of the nineteenth century. The vogue began shortly after the U.S. Navy forcibly opened Japan to western trade and diplomacy in 1853. Soon, Japanese lacquers, fans, bronzes, hanging scrolls, kimonos, ceramics, illustrated books, and ***ukiyo-e*** (prints of the "floating world," the realm of geishas and popular entertainment) began to appear in western European specialty shops, art galleries, and even some department stores. French interest in Japan and its arts reached such proportions by 1872 that the art critic Philippe Burty gave this enthusiasm a name: ***japonisme***.

Japanese art (see Chapter 9) profoundly influenced western painting, printmaking, applied arts, and eventually architecture. The tendency toward simplicity, flatness, and the decorative evident in much painting and graphic art in the West between roughly 1860 and 1900 is probably the most characteristic result of that influence. Nevertheless, its impact was extraordinarily diverse. What individual artists took from the Japanese depended on their own interests. Thus, Whistler found encouragement for his decorative conception of art, while Edgar Degas discovered both realistic subjects and interesting compositional arrangements (see fig. 18-18), and those interested in the reform of late-nineteenth-century industrial design found in Japanese objects both fine craft and a smooth elegance lacking in the West. Some, like Vincent van Gogh, saw in the spare harmony of Japanese art and wares evidence of an idyllic society, which he considered a model for the West.

18-9

Antoni Gaudí Serpentine bench, Güell Park, Barcelona 1900–14

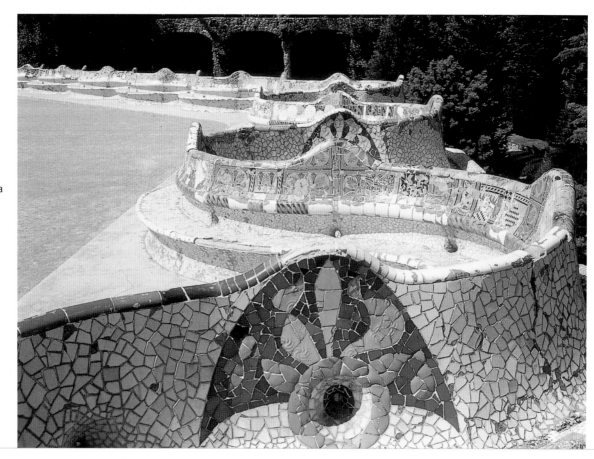

harmonize all aspects of design into a beautiful whole, as found in nature itself. In Italy this movement was known as Stile floreale (Floral Style) and Stile Liberty (after the Liberty department store in London); in Germany, Jugendstil (Youth Style); in Spain, Modernismo (Modernism); in France it had a number of names, including *moderne*. The name most used today came from a shop, La Maison de l'Art Nouveau (The House of the New Art), which opened in Paris in 1895.

The man who launched the Art Nouveau style of the 1890s was a Belgian architect, Victor Horta (1861–1947). In 1892 Horta received his first independent commission, to design Tassel House, a private residence in Brussels. The result, especially the house's entry hall and staircase (fig. 18-8), was strikingly original. Horta laid out the wall decoration, floor tile, and ironwork (used instead of stone or wood) in an intricate series of long, graceful curves to integrate interior design and architecture into an exquisite and unified whole.

Almost ten years before Horta's decorative ironwork at the Tassel House in Brussels, the Catalan architect Antoni Gaudí (1852–1926) was creating spectacular examples of Art Nouveau in Barcelona. Unlike his contemporaries, Gaudí attempted to introduce the organic principle into the very structure of his buildings. Much of his work, such as his residential complexes and churches in Spain, reflects his concern for integrating natural forms into daily life and for combining architecture, sculpture, and craft arts. In Güell Park, the ideal community he designed on the outskirts of Barcelona, a continuous, serpentine bench serves as a boundary wall for the public plaza (fig. 18-9). Like a strange flowering vine, the surface of the bench-wall glitters with a mosaic of broken pottery and tiles in homage to the long tradition of Moorish and Mudejar ceramic art in Spain. This is a national as well as a personal alternative to academic historicism and modern industrialization, reflecting Gaudí's affinity for the Iberian traditions as well as his concern for organic and harmonious surroundings.

ART IN THE UNITED STATES

In the United States, in contrast to the late Neoclassicism prevalent in sculpture, factual naturalism had an unbroken tradition in painting stretching back to Colonial portrait painters (see fig. 17-5). The advocates of realism had long considered it distinctly American and democratic, and the Civil War (1861–65) brought increasing attention to that most naturalistic of media—photography. The work of photographers came to public attention when Mathew B. Brady (1823–1896) gained permission from government officials to take a team and a darkroom wagon to the field of battle. Among his assistants was Timothy O'Sullivan, whose photographs of Western landscapes rival the finest paintings.

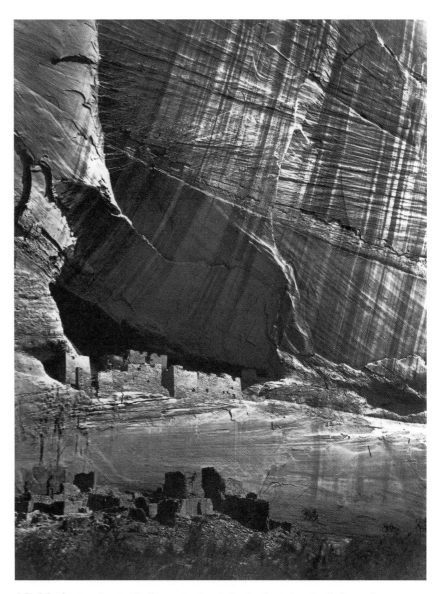

18-10 Timothy H. O'Sullivan. *Ancient Ruins in the Cañon de Chelley, Arizona* 1873. Albumen print. National Archives, Washington, D.C.

Timothy H. O'Sullivan (1840–1882) accompanied Western survey expeditions to make what were ostensibly documentary photographs; however, images like *Ancient Ruins in the Cañon de Chelley, Arizona* (fig. 18-10) are infused with a Romantic sense of awe before the grandeur of nature. The 700-foot canyon wall fills the composition, giving the viewer no clear vantage point and scant visual relief. The bright, raking sunlight across the rock face reveals little but the cracks and striations formed over countless eons. The image suggests not only the immensity of geological time but also humanity's insignificant place within it. Like the classical ruins that were a popular theme in European Romantic art and poetry, the Native American ruins suggest the inevitable passing of all civilizations. The four puny humans on the left, standing in this majestic yet barren place, reinforce the theme of human futility and insignificance. The melancholic sensibility that tinges *Ancient Ruins in the Cañon de Chelley, Arizona* may reflect the emotional impact of the Civil War.

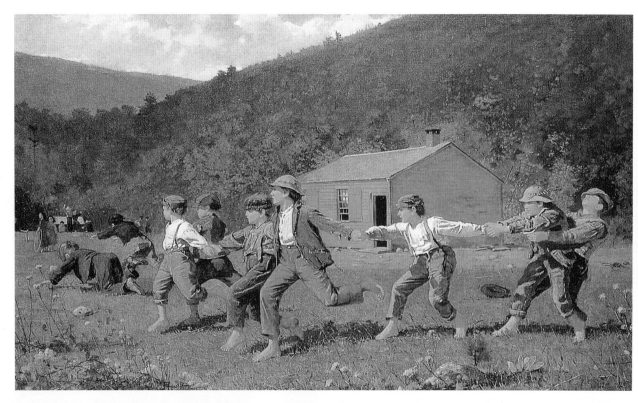

18-11

Winslow Homer. *Snap the Whip*
1872. Oil on canvas, 22¼ x 36½" (57.1 x 92.7 cm) The Butler Institute of American Art Youngstown Ohio

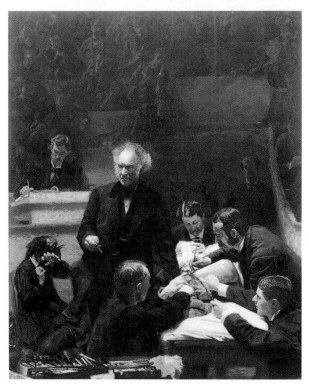

18-12 | **Thomas Eakins.** *The Gross Clinic.* 1875. 8' x 6'5" (2.44 x 1.96 m). Jefferson Medical College of Thomas Jefferson University, Philadelphia

In the shadows along the right-hand side of *The Gross Clinic* Eakins included a self-portrait, testimony to his personal knowledge of the subject. Eakins had studied anatomy, an interest that led him to photography, which he used both as an aid for painting and as a tool for studying the body in motion.

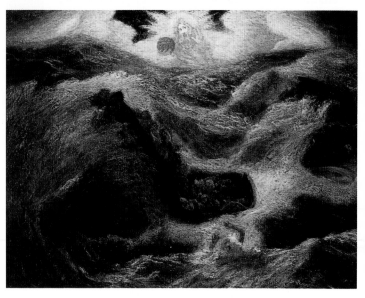

18-13 | **Albert Pinkham Ryder.** *Jonah.* c. 1885. Oil on canvas mounted on fiberboard, 27¼ x 34³/₈" (69.2 x 87.3 cm) National Museum of American Art, Smithsonian Institution Washington, D.C.
Gift of John Gellatly

Another artist who made his name recording the Civil War for the press was Winslow Homer (1836–1910). Homer believed that unadorned realism was the appropriate style for a democratic people. In 1866–67 he spent ten months in France, where the naturalist art he saw may have inspired the rural subjects that he painted when he returned. Works like *Snap the Whip* (fig. 18-11), with its depiction of boys playing outside a schoolhouse in the Adirondack Mountains, evoke the innocence of childhood and the imagined charms of a pre-industrial America

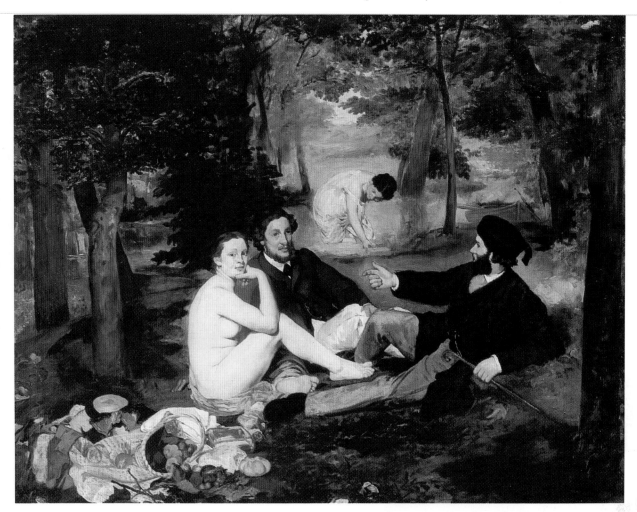

18-14

Édouard Manet
Le Déjeuner sur l'herbe (The Luncheon on the Grass)
1863. Oil on canvas, 7' x 8'8" (2.13 x 2.64 m)
Musée d'Orsay Paris

for an audience that was increasingly urbanized. Many of these paintings were reproduced as wood engravings for illustrated books and magazines.

The most uncompromising American naturalist of the era, Thomas Eakins (1844–1916), following an academic training in Philadelphia and Paris, spent six months in Spain, where he encountered the profound realism of Diego Velázquez (see fig. 14-13) and other seventeenth-century masters. After he returned to Philadelphia in 1870, he began painting frank portraits, often in everyday settings, whose lack of conventional charm generated little popular interest.

One work, *The Gross Clinic* (fig. 18-12), did attract attention: but of a negative kind. The painting was severely criticized and was refused exhibition space at the 1876 Philadelphia Centennial. *The Gross Clinic* shows Dr. Samuel David Gross performing an operation while young medical students look on. Beams of light highlight the representatives of science—a young medical student, the doctor, and his assistants. The light is not meant to stir emotions but to make a point: amid the darkness of ignorance and fear, modern science is the light of knowledge.

Some American artists of the late nineteenth century turned their backs on modern reality and escaped into the realms of myth, fantasy, and imagination. Some were also attracted to traditional literary, historical, and religious subjects, which they treated in unconventional ways to give them fresh meaning, as

did Albert Pinkham Ryder (1847–1917) in his dark and highly expressive interpretation of the biblical story of Jonah and the whale (fig. 18-13). Ryder depicted the moment when the terrified Old Testament prophet, thrown overboard by his shipmates, was about to be consumed by a great fish. The subject—being overwhelmed by hostile nature—and its dramatic treatment through dynamic curves and sharp contrasts of light and dark, and the intensity of the emotion expressed identify Ryder with both the Romantic tradition and the expressionist current that would gain greater momentum in the twentieth century.

Impressionism

In France the artists who matured around 1870 pushed the French realist tradition into new territory. Instead of treating themes that had engaged Courbet and the Barbizon painters—those of the working classes and rural life—they generally painted the upper middle class, the city, and leisure activities. Although many of these artists also painted the countryside, their point of view was usually that of a city person on holiday.

The leader of this loosely knit group was the painter Édouard Manet (1832–1883). The poet Charles Baudelaire, a close friend of Manet, called for an artist to be the painter of contemporary manners, "the painter of the passing moment and of all the suggestions of eternity that it contains." Manet seems to have responded by painting *Le Déjeuner sur l'herbe* (*The Luncheon on the Grass*) (fig. 18-14). When the jury for the official Salon of

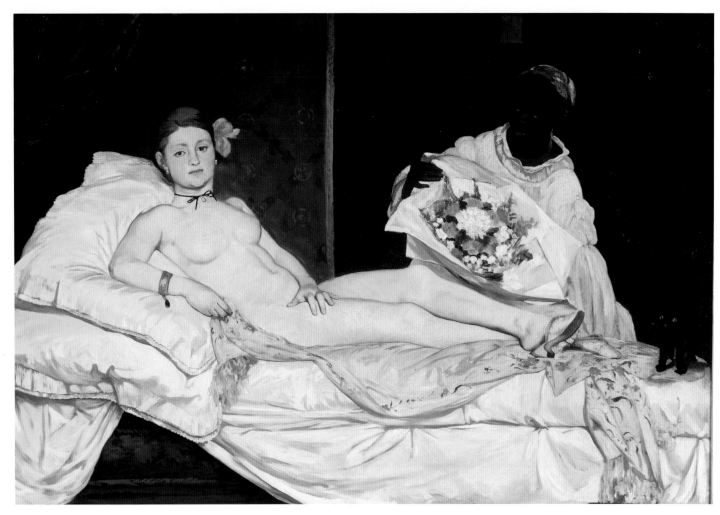

18-15 | **Édouard Manet.** *Olympia.* 1863. Oil on canvas, 4'3" x 6'2¼" (1.31 x 1.91 m). Musée du Louvre, Paris

1863 turned down nearly 3,000 works, including Manet's, a storm of protest erupted, prompting the French emperor Napoleon III to order an exhibition of the refused works called the Salon des Refusés (Salon of the Rejected Ones). In that exhibition, *Le Déjeuner sur l'herbe* provoked a critical avalanche that was a mixture of shock and bewilderment. Manet had ignored the basic tenets of academic painting. To a viewer used to traditional perspective and the rounded modeling of forms using gradations of shadow, the figures were jarring. Nor did critics understand why Manet had chosen the scandalous subject of well-dressed men relaxing with scantily clad women, although the artist had thought that his basic intent would be fairly obvious to viewers.

Today some critics see Manet as a painter of modern alienation; his figures are distant in both their physical and their psychological relationships. The man on the left gazes off absently while the nude turns her attention away from her companions and to the viewer. Moreover, her gaze makes us conscious of our role as outside observers—we, too, are estranged. Manet's rejection of warm colors for a scheme of cool blues and greens plays an important role, as do his flat, sharply outlined figures, which seem starkly lit because of the near absence of modeling. The figures are not integrated with their natural surroundings, as in the

paintings that inspired Manet, but seem to stand out sharply against them, as if cutouts seated before a painted backdrop (see "Artistic Allusions in Manet's Art," right).

Shortly after completing *Le Déjeuner sur l'herbe,* Manet painted *Olympia* (fig. 18-15), whose title alluded to a socially ambitious prostitute of the same name in a novel and play by Alexandre Dumas fils (the younger). Like *Le Déjeuner sur l'herbe, Olympia* was based on a painting by Titian (see fig. 13-15). At first, Manet appears to pay homage to its Venetian source in its subject matter and composition; however, Manet has made his modern counterpart the very antithesis of Titian's Venus. Whereas Titian's woman is curvaceous and softly rounded, Manet's is angular and flattened. Whereas Venus looks lovingly at the male spectator, Olympia appears coldly indifferent. Our relationship with Olympia is underscored by the reaction of her cat, who arches its back and seems to hiss. Manet has subverted the entire tradition of the accommodating female nude, for Olympia stares down on us, indicating that she is in the position of power. Not surprisingly, conservative critics heaped scorn on the painting when it was displayed at the Salon of 1865.

By the mid-1860s Manet had become the unofficial leader of a group of progressive artists and writers who gathered at

ARTISTIC ALLUSIONS IN MANET'S ART

Édouard Manet had in his studio a copy of *The Pastoral Concert*, a work in the Louvre then attributed to Giorgione and now attributed to both Titian and Giorgione (see fig. 13-13). His *Le Déjeuner sur l'herbe* (see fig. 18-14) was clearly inspired by *The Pastoral Concert*, a modern reply to its theme of ease in nature. Manet also adapted for his composition a group of river gods and a nymph from an engraving by Marcantonio Raimondi based on Raphael's *The Judgment of Paris*—an image that, in turn, looked back to classical reliefs. Manet's allusion to the engraving was apparent to some observers at the time, such as the critic Ernest Chesneau, who specifically noted this borrowing and objected to it.

With its deliberate allusions to Renaissance artworks, Manet's painting addresses not just the subject of figures in a landscape. It also addresses the history of art and Manet's relationship to it by encouraging the viewer to compare his painting with those that inspired it. To a viewer who has in mind the traditional perspective and the rounded modeling of forms of the two Renaissance works, the stark lighting of Manet's nude and the flat, cutout quality of his figures become all the more shocking. Thus, by openly referring to these exemplary works of the past, Manet emphasized his own radical innovations.

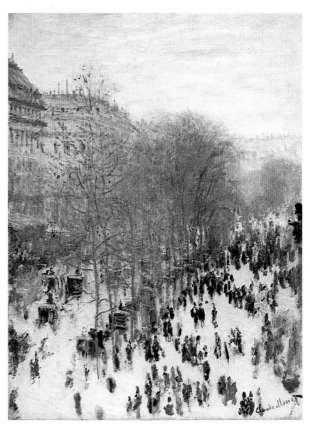

18-16   **Claude Monet.** *Boulevard des Capucines, Paris*
1873–74. Oil on canvas, 31¼" x 23¼" (79.4 x 59.1 cm). The Nelson-Atkins Museum of Art, Kansas City Missouri

Purchase: The Kenneth A. and Helen F. Spencer Foundation Acquisition Fund (F72-35)

the Café Guerbois in the Montmartre district of Paris. Among the artists who frequented the café were Monet, Degas, and Renoir who would soon exhibit together as the Impressionists. With the exception of Degas, who, like Manet, remained a studio painter, these artists began to paint outdoors, *en plein air* ("in the open air"), in an effort to record directly the fleeting effects of light and atmosphere. (*Plein air* painting was greatly facilitated by the invention in 1841 of portable tin tubes filled with premixed oil paint.)

In April 1874, Claude Monet, Berthe Morisot, Edgar Degas, Pierre-Auguste Renoir, Paul Cézanne, and others exhibited together in Paris as the Société Anonyme des Artistes Peintres, Sculpteurs, Graveurs, etc. (Corporation of Artists Painters, Sculptors, Engravers, etc.), usually shortened to Société Anonyme. While the exhibition received some positive reviews, it was attacked by conservative critics. Louis Leroy, writing in the comic journal *Charivari*, seized on the title of a painting by Monet, *Impression, Sunrise* (1872), and dubbed the entire exhibition *Impressionist*. While Leroy used the word to attack the paintings, Monet and many of his colleagues were pleased to accept the label, which spoke to their concern for capturing an instantaneous impression of a scene in nature. Seven more Impressionist exhibitions followed between 1876 and 1886, with the membership of the group varying slightly on each occasion. By the end of the century these independent exhibitions effectively ended the French Academy's centuries-old stranglehold on the display of art and thus on artistic standards.

Claude Monet (1840–1926), after some early efforts at *plein air* painting near his family home along the Normandy coast, developed his own technique of painting with strokes

and touches of pure color, intended to describe flowers, leaves, and waves, but also to register simply as marks of paint on the surface of the canvas. Monet's fully Impressionist pictures of the 1870s and 1880s, such as *Boulevard des Capucines, Paris* of 1873–74 (fig. 18-16), are made up almost entirely of flecks of color (Leroy sneeringly called them "tongue-lickings"). Using these discrete marks of paint, Monet recorded the shifting play of light on the surface of objects and the effect of that light on the eye, without concern for the physical character of the objects being represented. His decision to paint the street scene from an upper window enabled him to combine the high vantage point that he admired in Japanese prints with the direct observation of life associated with Impressionism.

The American painter Lilla Cabot Perry (1848–1933) recalled Monet telling her, "When you go out to paint, try to forget what objects you have before you—a tree, a house, a field, or whatever. Merely think, here is a little square of blue, here an oblong of pink, here a streak of yellow, and paint it just as it looks to you, the exact color and shape, until it gives your own naive impression of the scene before you." Two important ideas are expressed here. One is that a quickly painted oil sketch provides the most accurate record, a view that had been a part of academic training since the late eighteenth century. Sketches had been considered merely part of the preparation

18-17 **Berthe Morisot. *In the Dining Room.*** 1886. Oil on canvas, 24¹/₈" x 19³/₄" (61.3 x 50.2 cm).
National Gallery of Art, Washington, D.C., Chester Dale Collection, 1963.10.185.(1849)/PA

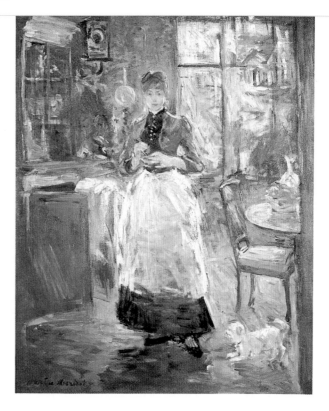

for the final work, and as a result, viewers did not see Monet's paintings as "finished." The second idea—that art benefits from a naive vision untainted by intellectual preconceptions—was a part of the naturalist and Realist traditions from which Monet's work evolved.

Monet's fellow Impressionist Berthe Morisot (1841–1895), who participated in seven of the Impressionists' eight exhibitions, had met Édouard Manet in 1868, and she married his brother Eugene in 1874. Unlike most women who gave up painting to devote themselves to domestic duties, Morisot continued painting, although she took as her subject the lives of bourgeois women. Her technique became increasingly loose and painterly over the course of the 1870s. In fact her vigorous and varied brushwork in *In the Dining Room* (fig. 18-17) calls attention to the act of painting itself. The palette of pastel colors and her lavish use of white are characteristic of her work. In her painting, Morisot sought an equality for women that she felt men refused to cede. Late in life she commented: "I don't think there has ever been a man who treated a woman as an equal, and that's all I would have asked, for I know I'm worth as much as they" (cited in Higonnet, page 19).

Unlike Morisot, not all of the painters who are grouped with the Impressionists (because they participated in some or all of the exhibitions organized by Monet and his friends) truly worked in an Impressionist style. The artist whose work most

severely tests the Impressionist label is Edgar Degas (1834 –1917). His friendship with Manet, whom he met in 1862, and with the Realist critics in his circle, led him gradually toward the depiction of contemporary life. After a period of painting psychologically probing portraits of friends and relatives, Degas turned in the 1870s to such Paris amusements as the music hall, opera, ballet, circus, and racetrack. Degas began to think of art

18-18

Edgar Degas. *The Rehearsal of the Ballet on Stage*
c. 1874. Pastel over brush-and-ink drawing on thin, cream-colored wove paper, laid on Bristol board, mounted on canvas, 21 x 28¹/₂" (53.3 x 72.3 cm). The Metropolitan Museum of Art, New York

Bequest of Mrs. H. O. Havemeyer Collection, Gift of Horace Havemeyer, 1929 (29.160.26)

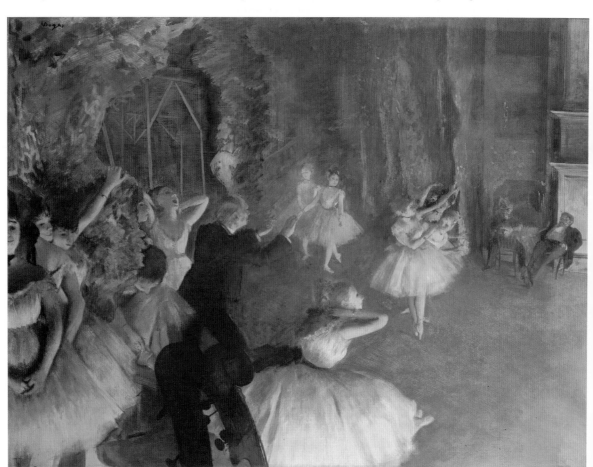

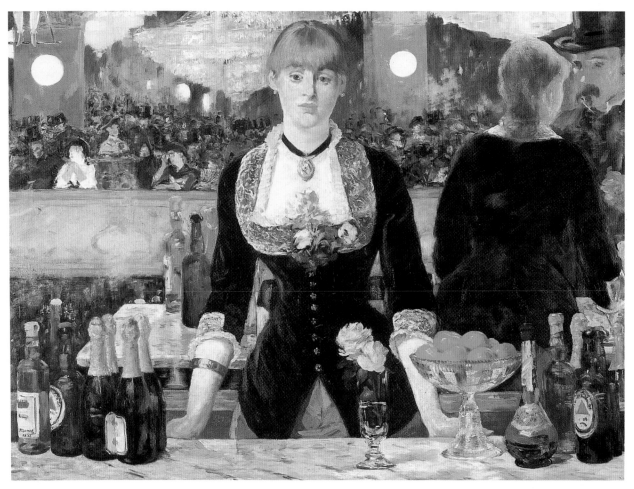

18-19   **Édouard Manet. *A Bar at the Folies-Bergère.*** 1881–82. Oil on canvas, 37³/₄ x 51¹/₆" (95.9 x 130 cm). Courtauld Institute Galleries, London
Home House Collection

less as a mirror held up to the world than as a lofty form of entertainment that employed realistic elements.

Degas was drawn to the ballet. From carefully observed studies of rehearsals and performances, he arranged his own visual choreography. *The Rehearsal of the Ballet on Stage* (fig. 18-18) is not a factual record of something seen but a careful contrivance, inspired partly by Japanese prints, intended to delight the eye (see "Japonisme," page 448). The rehearsal is viewed as if from an opera box close to the stage, creating an abrupt foreshortening of the scene emphasized by the dark scroll of the bass viol that juts up from the lower left.

It could be argued, based on such carefully arranged works as *The Rehearsal of the Ballet on Stage*, that Degas never truly adopted an Impressionist style. Other artists passed through an Impressionist phase but then went on to explore other ideas. In the years after 1880, in particular, a number of artists began to reconsider their earlier approaches or make important adjustments to them. Manet, for instance, had embraced his younger colleagues' brighter palette about 1870, but his late paintings, such as *A Bar at the Folies-Bergère* (fig. 18-19), contradict the happy aura of works such as Monet's boulevard or country scenes. Manet's painting revolves around one of the barmaids at the Folies-Bergère, a large nightclub with a series of bars arranged

around a vaudeville theater. A performer on a trapeze, whose legs can be seen at the upper left, entertains the crowd reflected in the mirror behind the bar.

On the marble bartop Manet has spread a glorious still life of liquor bottles, tangerines, and flowers, associated not only with the pleasures for which the Folies-Bergère was famous but also (formally) with the barmaid herself, whose wide hips, strong neck, and closely combed golden hair are echoed in the champagne bottles. The barmaid's demeanor, however, refutes these associations. Manet puts the viewer directly in front of her, in the position of her customer. From the front, the woman appears self-absorbed and downcast, but her mirrored reflection and that of her customer suggest a different story. In the reflection she leans toward the patron, whose intent gaze she appears to meet; the physical and psychological distance between them has vanished. Exactly what Manet meant to suggest by this juxtaposition has been much debated. One possibility is that he wanted to contrast the longing for happiness and intimacy with the disappointing reality of everyday existence.

LATER IMPRESSIONISM

In the years after 1880, Impressionism underwent what historians have termed a "crisis," as many artists grew dissatisfied

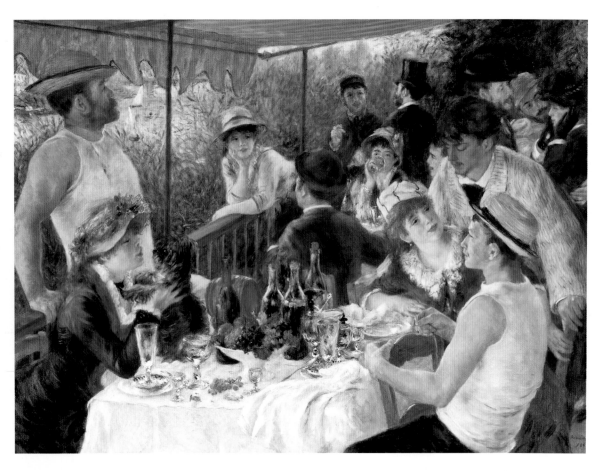

18-20

Pierre-Auguste Renoir *Luncheon of the Boating Party.* 1881
Oil on canvas
4'3" x 5'8"
(1.29 x 1.73 m)
The Phillips Collection
Washington
D.C.

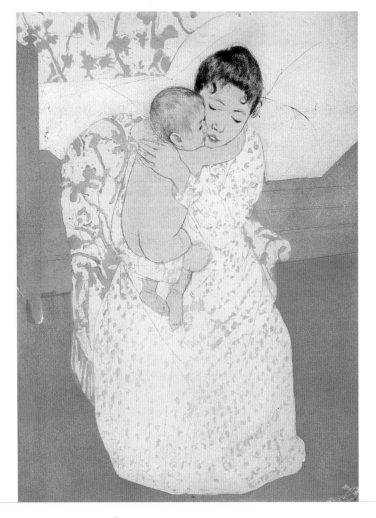

with their attempts to capture momentary perceptions through spontaneous brushwork and casual compositions. In response, they began to select subjects more carefully, work longer on their pictures, and develop styles that lent their imagery a greater sense of permanence and seriousness.

The artist most strongly affected by this crisis was Renoir, whose experience of the paintings of Raphael and other Old Masters on a trip to Italy in 1881 caused him to reconsider his commitment to painting fleeting impressions of modern life. Consequently, although he continued to use sensual brushwork and lush color, he began to present firmly modeled figures and relatively traditional compositions. In *Luncheon of the Boating Party* a variation on the traditional pyramidal structure advocated by the academies underlies the apparent informality of the summer scene (fig. 18-20). A small triangle whose apex is the woman leaning on the rail is set within a larger, somewhat looser one that culminates in the two men at the rear. Thus, instead of a moment quickly scanned in passing (an impression), Renoir created a more stable and permanent scene. Renoir has glamorized his young artist friends and their models, showing them in

18-21

Mary Cassatt. *Maternal Caress.*
1891. Drypoint and soft-ground etching, and aquatint. 14³/₄" x 10³/₄" (37.5 x 27.3 cm).
National Gallery of Art, Washington, D.C., Rosenwald Collection, 1963.10.255.(B-22323)/PR

18-22 | **Claude Monet. *Water Lilies.*** c. 1920. Oil on canvas, 6'5½" x 19'7½" (1.97 x 5.98 m)
The Museum of Modern Art, New York
Mrs. Simon Guggenheim Fund

attitudes of relaxed congeniality, smiling, chatting, and flirting. This idyllic image of a carefree age of innocence, a kind of paradise, nicely encapsulates Renoir's essential notion of art; he said, "For me a picture should be a pleasant thing, joyful and pretty."

Mary Cassatt (1845–1926), who, like Renoir, exhibited with the Impressionists, also moved toward a firmer handling of form and more classic subjects in the period after 1880. In the *Maternal Caress* (fig. 18-21), one of the many colored prints she produced in her later career, Cassatt offers a sensitive, modern response to the tradition of the Madonna and Child. The plump infant, apparently fresh from the bath, shares a tender moment with its adoring mother. The flat decorative patterns, simple contours, and sharply sloping floor derive from Japanese prints (see "Japonisme," page 448). Cassatt, like Degas, remained a studio painter, but her distaste for what she called the tyranny of the Salon jury system made her one of the Impressionist's, staunchest supporters.

By the early twentieth century, of the original group of artists designated as Impressionists, Monet remained closest to the original roots of the style, with its flickering brushstrokes designed to capture the passing moment. During the last two decades of his life (he died in 1926), Monet found endless enjoyment painting his gardens and his lily pond at Giverny, his country home. In most of his paintings of the lily pond, there is neither a horizon line nor a place for the viewer to stand. We are in the midst of the pool, between water and sky, adrift among floating blossoms and reflections of leaves and clouds (fig. 18-22). The largest of these water-lily canvases dwarf us, envelop us, even engulf us completely in what began as a single fleeting moment of time.

Post-Impressionism

The English critic Roger Fry coined the term *Post-Impressionism* in 1910 to identify a broad reaction against Impressionism in **avant-garde** painting of the late nineteenth and early twentieth centuries. Art historians recognize Paul Cézanne, Paul Gauguin, Vincent van Gogh, Georges Seurat, and Paul Signac as the principal Post-Impressionist artists; some also add Henri Toulouse-Lautrec. Each of these painters moved through an Impressionist phase and continued to use in his mature work the bright Impressionist palette. But each also came to reject Impressionism's emphasis on the spontaneous recording of light and color and instead sought to create art with a greater degree of formal order and structure. This goal led the Post-Impressionists to develop more abstract styles that would prove highly influential for the development of modernist painting in the early twentieth century.

Paul Cézanne's (1839–1902) radical stylistic innovations were instrumental in paving the way for twentieth century **abstraction.** Yet he was ignored or misunderstood in his own day by all but a few perceptive collectors and fellow artists. In the 1870s Cézanne discovered Impressionism and began the objective transcription of what he called his "sensations" of nature. Unlike the Impressionists, however, Cézanne did not seek to capture transitory effects of light and atmosphere but rather to create a sense of order in nature through a careful and methodical application of color that merged drawing and modeling into a single process. His professed aim was to "make of Impressionism something solid and durable, like the art of the museums."

Cézanne's tireless pursuit of his goal is exemplified in his paintings of Mont Sainte-Victoire, the view near his home in

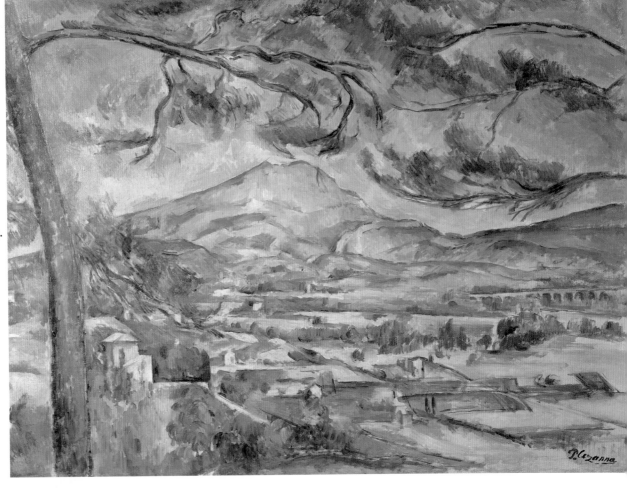

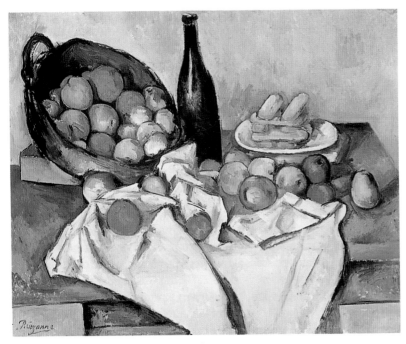

18-24 | Paul Cézanne. *Still Life with Basket of Apples.* 1890–94. Oil on canvas, 24³/₈ x 31" (61.9 x 78.7 cm). The Art Institute of Chicago
Helen Birch Bartlett Memorial Collection

Aix-en-Provence. The mountain (fig. 18-23) rises above the valley, which is dotted with houses and trees and is traversed at the far right by an aqueduct. Framing the scene at the left is an evergreen tree, which echoes the contours of the mountain, creating visual harmony between the two principal elements of the composition. The even lighting, still atmosphere, and absence of human activity in the landscape communicate a sense of timeless endurance, at odds with the Impressionists' interest in capturing a momentary aspect of the ever-changing world. Cézanne's handling of paint is more deliberate and constructive than the Impressionists' spontaneous and sometimes random brushwork. His strokes, which vary from short, parallel hatchings to sketchy lines to broader swaths of flat color, weave every element of the landscape together into a unified surface design. That surface design coexists with the effect of spatial recession that the composition simultaneously creates, generating a fruitful tension between the illusion of three dimensions "behind" the picture plane and the physical reality of its two-dimensional surface.

Although it is tempting to see in *Mont Sainte-Victoire* evidence of Cézanne's ultimate rejection of Impressionist **aesthetics** for an interest in solid form, this and works like it remain firmly grounded in the understanding of the individual brush mark as a record of the artist's immediate "sensation" of nature. In the middle section, for example, the solid rectangular strokes, generally applied according to a rigid grid of vertical and horizontal lines, nevertheless form dynamic and irregular contours. Cézanne used the "**passage** technique" in which shapes closed on one side are open on another so that they can merge with adjacent shapes (see "Cubism," pages 475–77). The merging of shapes along with the juxtaposition of warm and cool colors creates a spatial tension. The passage technique is heightened by the contradiction between the presumed depth of the landscape and the flat painted surface of the canvas that the viewer actually sees. Producing **nonrepresentational** art was never Cézanne's intention. Instead, he *abstracted* what he considered nature's deepest truth—its essential tension between permanence and change.

Spatial ambiguities of a different sort appear in Cézanne's late still lifes, in which many of the objects seem incorrectly drawn. In *Still Life with Basket of Apples* (fig. 18-24), for example, an apparently conventional studio arrangement of fruit, pastries, and wine bottle is, on closer examination, on the verge of collapse. As he shifts his viewpoint to capture every aspect of the objects, the bottle seems to tilt precariously on a tabletop whose two sides do not match. The folds of the white cloth add considerably to the work's instability; only the small tucks in the fabric prevent the apples from cascading to the floor. Such apparent inaccuracies are not evidence of Cézanne's incompetence, however, but of his willful disregard for the rules of traditional scientific perspective. Although scientific perspective mandates that the eye of the artist (and hence the viewer) occupy a fixed point relative to the scene being observed (see "Renaissance Perspective Systems," page 289), Cézanne studies different objects in a painting from slightly different positions. The composition as a whole, assembled from multiple sightings, is complex and dynamic. Instead of a faithful reproduction of objects in his still life paintings, Cézanne was re-creating and reconstructing nature.

Cézanne's Post-Impressionist colleagues Georges Seurat and Paul Gauguin held different beliefs—they saw art as a force for social commentary and even change. The word that came into general use to describe such art was *avant-garde*. Originally a military term for an advance unit, it was used in 1825 by a French socialist, the Comte de Saint-Simon, to refer to those artists whose visual expression would prepare people to accept the social changes he and his colleagues envisioned. The idea of producing a socially revolutionary art had briefly attracted such artists as Courbet, but the real popularity of this notion dates from the Post-Impressionist era.

Georges Seurat (1859–1891) was apparently one of the first in his generation to think of himself as an avant-garde artist. He devoted his energies to "correcting" Impressionism, which he found too intellectually shallow and too improvisational. In the mid-1880s he gathered around him a circle of young artists who became known as the Neo-Impressionists. (Neo-Impressionism refers primarily to a type of technique and theory involving vision and color, while Post-Impressionism refers mostly to a timeframe or era. Artists like Georges Seurat and

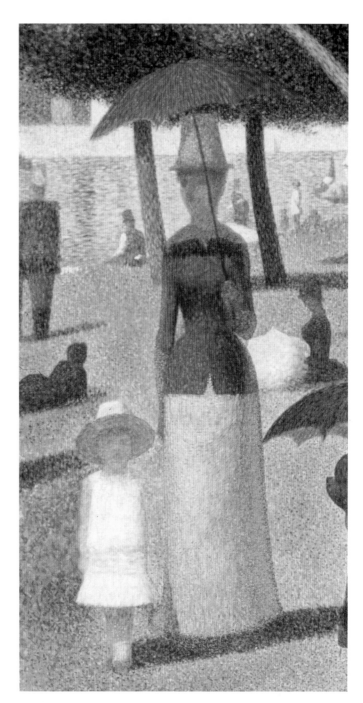

18-25 | Georges Seurat. Detail of *A Sunday Afternoon on the Island of La Grande Jatte*
(See pages 440–41.)

Paul Signac (see pages 462–63) fall into both categories.) Seurat belonged to a group of artists, intellectuals, and amateur scientists who were studying theories of vision, light, and color. Seurat applied their theories to his painting in a technique he called "divisionism" or "pointillism" (see page 463). The work that became the centerpiece of the new movement and made Seurat's reputation was *A Sunday Afternoon on the Island of La Grande Jatte* (fig. 18-25). Seurat first exhibited *La Grande Jatte* at the eighth and final Impressionist exhibition in 1886. The theme of weekend leisure is typically Impressionist, but the rigorous divisionist technique, the stiff formality of the figures,

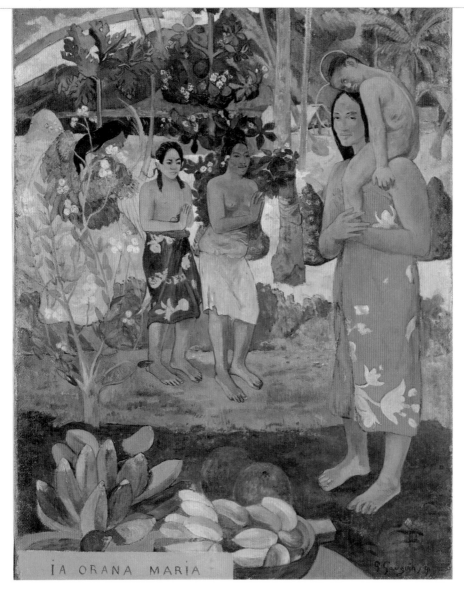

IA ORANA MARIA

18-26 | **Paul Gauguin.** *Ia Orana Maria (We Hail Thee Mary).* c. 1891–92. Oil on canvas 44³/₄ x 34¹/₂" (113.7 x 87.6 cm). The Metropolitan Museum of Art, New York
Bequest of Sam A. Lewisohn, 1951 (51.112.2)

held the opposite view. At the age of thirty-seven, Gauguin gave up a conventional existence as a Paris stockbroker and left his wife and five children to pursue a full-time painting career. Seeking to escape the corruption of modern life, he moved to Brittany, then to Panama, spent two months with Van Gogh in Arles in 1888, and then sailed for Tahiti in the South Pacific in 1891. He thought that he could find a pre-industrial paradise among the Tahitians, a people he and other Europeans imagined were childlike and close to nature. In fact native culture had nearly disappeared in this westernized French colony.

Before he left for the South Pacific, Gauguin found inspiration in the simplified drawing, flattened space, and anti-natural color of medieval stained glass, Breton folk art, and Japanese prints. He rejected Impressionism (although he had exhibited in the last four Impressionist exhibitions, 1880–86) because it neglected subjective feelings. Gauguin called his anti-Impressionist style *synthetism*, because it synthesized observation of the subject in nature with the artist's feelings about that subject, expressed through abstracted line, shape, space, and color.

The first picture Gauguin painted in Tahiti was *Ia Orana Maria* (*We Hail Thee Mary*) (fig. 18-26). Gauguin's new Mary was a strong Polynesian woman holding a contented and robust child. The warm, rich colors and decorative patterns in the painting underscore the message that life in this supposedly uncivilized world is sweet and harmonious. The fresh-plucked fruits on the table in the foreground, as well as the serene people, invite the viewer to leave a chaotic industrial society and enjoy the bounty of a primeval paradise.

Among the artists in Gauguin's circle before his departure for Tahiti was the Dutch painter Vincent van Gogh (1853–1890). Van Gogh had moved to Paris in 1886, where at first he came under the influence of the Impressionists and Neo-Impressionists. Soon he departed radically from Seurat's divisionist technique and applied his paint freely in multidirectional dashes of thick pigment, giving his pictures a greater sense of physical energy and a palpable surface texture.

Van Gogh shared Gauguin's desire for a simple, pre-industrial life, and the two planned to move to the south of France and establish a commune of like-minded artists. In the spring of 1888, Van Gogh moved to Arles, where the radiant sun and the lush farmland prompted him to create such dazzling images as his famous *Sunflowers* (fig. 18-27), painted in anticipation of his friend's arrival. When Gauguin finally joined Van Gogh, their

and the highly calculated geometry of the composition produce a solemn, abstract effect quite at odds with the casual naturalism of earlier Impressionism.

From its first appearance, the painting, with its curiously formal and stylized figures, gave rise to a number of conflicting interpretations. Contemporary accounts of the island indicate that on Sundays it was noisy, littered, and chaotic. Seurat knew how rowdy it could be because he spent months visiting the island and studying the people enjoying themselves there. He observed and sketched every man, woman, and child—from the distant sailors and oarsmen to the monkey and dogs in the foreground. By painting the island the way he did, Seurat may have intended to represent an ideal image of middle-class life and leisure—a model for a more civilized way of life in the modern city. The key perhaps lies in the composure of the two central figures, the mother and child around which the others move. The child, in particular, is a model of self-restraint. She may even represent Seurat's sense of the progress of human evolution, as obliquely suggested by the contrasting presence of the monkey in the right foreground.

Whereas Seurat seems to have believed that people were not civilized enough, the French painter Paul Gauguin (1848–1903)

constant quarrels led to violent confrontation and Gauguin's departure. Only a few close friends and his brother Theo stood by Van Gogh to the end. After a series of psychological crises that led to his hospitalization, Van Gogh shot himself in July 1890.

The paintings Van Gogh produced during the last year and a half of his life testify to his heightened emotional state. At the same time, they contributed significantly to the emergence of the expressionistic tradition, in which the intensity of an artist's feelings overrides fidelity to the actual appearance of things. One of the earliest examples of **expressionism** is *The Starry Night* (fig. 18-28), which Van Gogh painted from the window of his cell in a mental asylum. The sky, pulsating with exploding stars high above the quiet town, is clearly a record of what Van Gogh felt, not a record of what he saw. The painting may give expression to the then-popular idea that after death people journeyed to a star, where they continued their lives. Van Gogh wrote: "Just as we take the train to get to Tarascon or Rouen, we take death to reach a star." In the painting, a cypress tree, a traditional symbol of both death and eternal life, dramatically links the terrestrial world and the heavens.

Expressionism was one way to communicate the psychological impact of the modern world. Another artistic response was to capture the emotive energy of modern life, a tactic followed by Henri de Toulouse-Lautrec (1864–1901) in his paintings and prints (see "Lithography," page 462). From the late 1880s, Toulouse-Lautrec

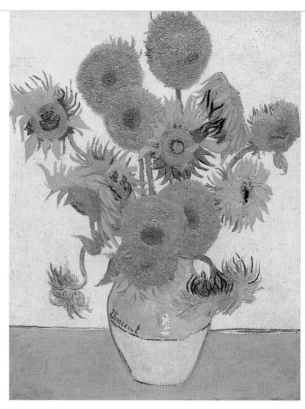

18-27 | **Vincent van Gogh.** *Sunflowers.* 1888. Oil on canvas 36¼ x 28¾" (92.1 x 73 cm). The National Gallery London

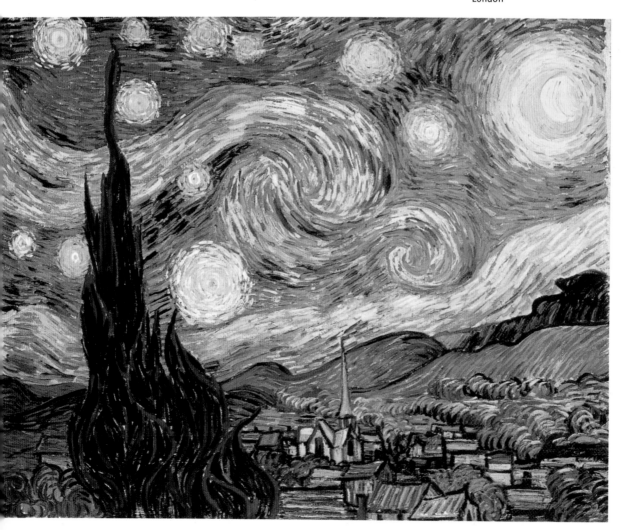

18-28

Vincent van Gogh. *The Starry Night.* 1889. Oil on canvas. 28¾" x 36¼" (73 x 92 cm). The Museum of Modern Art, New York. Acquired through the Lillie P. Bliss Bequest (472.1941)

often depict the sad reality of the festivities at the popular dance halls, and like Manet's paintings, they reveal the artist's sensitivity to a new kind of loneliness—the modern feeling of alienation.

Paul Signac (1863–1935), once seen as a follower of Seurat, emerged as an influential painter and the leading theorist in the Neo-Impressionist circle of the 1880s and 1890s that included the critic Félix Fénéon (1861–1944) and the eccentric amateur scientist Charles Henry (1859–1926). In Fénéon's view great art "sacrifices anecdote to arabesque, analysis to synthesis, fugitive to permanent" (Ferretti-Bocquillon, page 161). And this is precisely what Signac has done in his *Plane Trees, Place des Lices, Saint-Tropez, Opus 242* (fig. 18-30).

In 1888 Signac illustrated Charles Henry's *Chromatic Circle*, published as a monograph in 1890. His own book, *From Delacroix to Neo-Impressionism* (1899), in which he articulated the Neo-Impressionist aesthetic theory, is a landmark in the study of color and the appreciation of Delacroix. Signac was close to people who (in retrospect) became leading Post-Impressionists and expressionists—Van Gogh, Gauguin, Toulouse-Lautrec, and Henri Matisse (see Chapter 19)—and was one of the artists represented in the first exhibition held in the shop that gave its name to the Art Nouveau movement. In 1887 Signac had

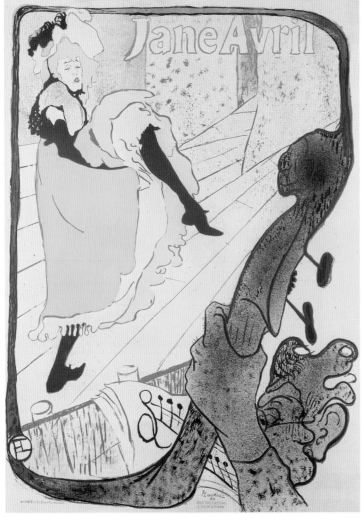

18-29   **Henri de Toulouse-Lautrec. *Jane Avril.*** 1893. Lithograph 50½ x 37" (129 x 94 cm). San Diego Museum of Art
The Baldwin M. Baldwin Collection

chronicled life in Montmartre, a part of Paris devoted to entertainment and inhabited by many who lived on the fringes of society.

Toulouse-Lautrec designed lithographic posters as advertisements for popular night spots and entertainers between 1891 and 1901. His portrayal of the café dancer *Jane Avril* (fig. 18-29) demonstrates the remarkable originality that he brought to an essentially commercial project. The composition juxtaposes the dynamic figure of the dancer onstage with the cropped image of a bass viol player and the scroll of his instrument. The bold foreshortening of the stage and the prominent placement of the bass in the foreground both suggest the influence of Degas (see fig. 18-18); however, Toulouse-Lautrec has extended the bass viol's head into a curving frame that surrounds Avril and connects her visually with her musical accompaniment. The radical simplification of form, suppression of modeling, flattening of space, and integration of blank paper into the composition all suggest the influence of Japanese woodblock prints (see "Japonisme," page 448). Meanwhile, the emphasis on curving lines and the harmonization of the lettering with the rest of the design connect the poster with Art Nouveau. Nevertheless Toulouse-Lautrec's images

TECHNIQUE
Lithography

Aloys Senefelder invented **lithography** in Bavaria, Germany, in 1796 and registered for an exclusive right to the process the following year. Lithography is a plano-graphic process—that is, the printing is done from a flat surface. It was the first wholly new printing process to be introduced since the fifteenth century, when the **intaglio**, or **incising**, process was developed.

Lithography, still popular today, is based on the natural antagonism between oil and water. The artist draws on a flat surface—traditionally, fine-grained stone—with a greasy, crayonlike instrument. The stone's surface is flooded with water, over which an oil-based ink is rolled. The ink adheres to the greasy areas but not to the damp ones. A sheet of paper is laid facedown on the inked stone. Blankets are laid over the paper to protect it from the scraper. The stone, paper, and protective blankets are then passed through a flatbed press. A scraper applies light pressure from above as the stone and paper pass under it, transferring ink from stone to paper, thus making lithography a direct method of creating a printed image. Francisco Goya, Honoré Daumier, and Henri de Toulouse-Lautrec exploited the medium to great effect.

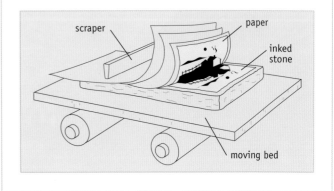

CLOSER LOOK

In the center of a park in Saint-Tropez an old man sits, framed by the undulating branches of the rows of plane trees (European sycamores) and the horizontal lines of the bench, the distant wall, and red-roofed buildings (fig. 18-30). The trees defy the regularity of the rows in which they were planted and seem to dance rhythmically. Paul Signac's painting of the Place de Lices reflects the avant-garde painter's interests in the abstract, decorative quality of Japanese prints and in the scientific study of light and perception. The subtle asymmetrical composition of dark branches seen against the setting sun recalls Hokusai's views of Mount Fuji (see fig. 9-24), and the brilliant contrasting purple/blue and yellow/orange paint, applied using the divisionist technique, reflect color theories being discussed in intellectual circles in Paris.

Artists like Seurat and Signac, whom in 1886 the critic Felix Fénéon dubbed Neo-Impressionists, knew Michel-Eugene Chevreul's 1839 "Law of the simultaneous contrast of colors." Chevreul (1786–1889) argued that not only do contrasting colors enhance each other's intensity, but adjacent objects also cast reflections of their own color onto their neighbors and create in them the effect of their complementary color. Fénéon described the phenomenon: "Two adjacent colors exert a mutual influence, each imposing its own complementary on the other; for green a purple, for red a blue green, for yellow an ultramarine, for violet a greenish yellow, for orange a cyan blue: contrast of hues. The lightest one becomes lighter; the darkest one darker: contrast of values." (cited in Ferretti-Bocquillon, page 160).

The backlit trees, the sun-dappled leaves, and the areas of dazzling light breaking up the shadows on the ground show that Seurat, Signac, and other Neo-Impressionists did not feel constrained to apply Chevreul's law systematically. They listened to people like the eccentric intellectual Charles Henry, who in 1889 devised a color wheel, which he called a chromatic circle, with ascending, assertive warm colors and descending, receding cool colors. In works illustrated by Signac, Henry studied the exact gradations of contrasting colors which placed side by side not only intensified each other's effect but, when used in small dots, "blend in the eye of the beholder" (a phenomenon known as optical mixture) and create a shimmering effect in the viewer's vision. Painters turned theory to practice and set down their hues in dots of pure color, next to one another, in what came to be known by various names: divisionism (the term preferred by Seurat), pointillism, and simply Neo-Impressionism. In theory, these juxtaposed dots would merge in the viewer's eye to produce the impression of other colors, which would be perceived as more luminous and intense than the same hues mixed on the palette. In fact, this optical mixture is never complete, for the dots of color tend to remain separate, giving Neo-Impressionist paintings a speckled appearance.

Signac sought to combine the ornamental quality he saw in Japanese art with the enduring quality of classical French landscape painting. He evidently liked the result he achieved in his painting of the park since he exhibited the work several times.

18-30 | **Paul Signac. *Place des Lices, Saint-Tropez.*** 1893. Oil on canvas 25³/₄" x 32³/₁₆" (65.4 x 81.8 cm). Carnegie Museum of Art, Pittsburgh. Acquired through the generosity of the Sarah Mellon Scaife Family (66.24.2)

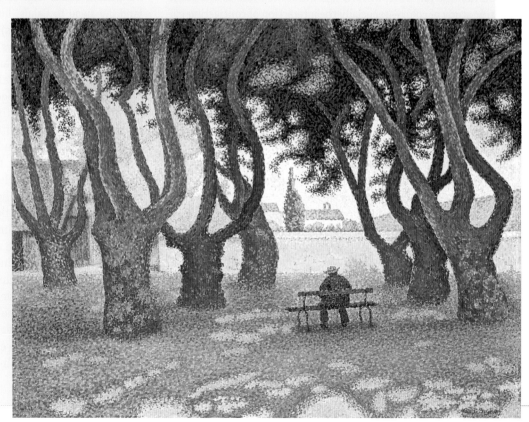

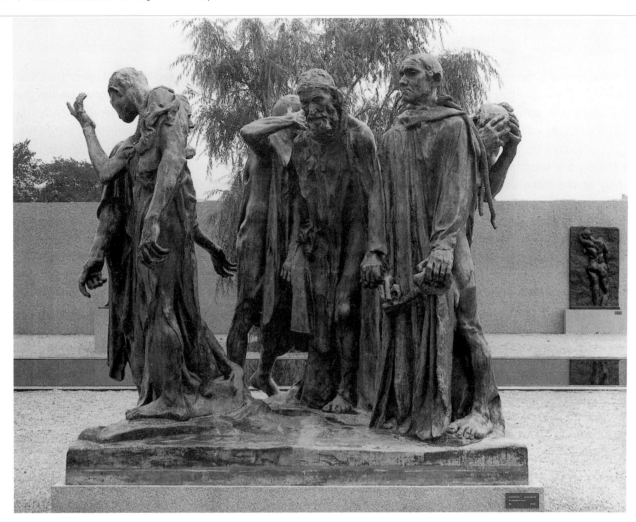

18-31 | **Auguste Rodin.** *Burghers of Calais.* 1884–86. Bronze, 6'10½" x 7'11" x 6'6" (2.1 x 2.4 x 2.0 m)
Hirshhorn Museum and Sculpture Garden, Smithsonian Institution, Washington, D.C.

befriended Van Gogh in Paris and introduced him to the scientific study of color—especially the interaction of contrasting colors—and he later visited Van Gogh in Arles.

An enthusiastic sailor, he divided his time between Paris and the coast, eventually acquiring a house in Saint-Tropez on the French Riviera. There he painted the harbor with its old houses and sailboats and only occasionally the people. His view of the Place des Lices is an homage to the light and color of the south—he gave it the musical title of *Opus 242*—and to the rhythms of the swaying plane trees, and only incidentally to humanity, in the guise of the man enjoying the park (see fig. 18-30).

Signac moved in the avant-garde intellectual and art circles of Paris, but he became enchanted by the landscape of the Mediterranean coast of France. He encouraged Matisse to come to the south. Fascinated by other painters' experiments with color, Seurat recognized Matisse's special talent (see pages 471–72).

LATE-NINETEENTH-CENTURY FRENCH SCULPTURE

The most successful and influential sculptor of the Post-Impressionist era was Auguste Rodin (1840–1917). His status as a major sculptor was confirmed in 1884, when he won the competition for a monument, commissioned by the city of Calais, to commemorate an event from the Hundred Years' War—the

Burghers of Calais (fig. 18-31). In 1347 King Edward III of England lay siege to Calais, but he offered to spare the city if six leading citizens (burghers) would surrender themselves to him for execution. Rodin shows the six volunteers—dressed in sackcloth with rope halters and carrying the keys to the city—marching out to what they assume will be their deaths. (Impressed by their courage, the king spared them.)

The officials in modern Calais were upset to find that their chosen sculptor produced not calm, idealized heroes but ordinary men in various attitudes of resignation and despair. Rodin expressively lengthened their arms, greatly enlarged their hands and feet, and swathed them in heavy fabric. He showed not only how they may have looked but also how they must have felt as they forced themselves to take one difficult step after another. Rodin's willingness to stylize the human body for expressive purposes was a revolutionary move that opened the way for the more radical innovations of later sculptors. He also planned to place the figures on a low base, almost at street level, to suggest to viewers that ordinary people like themselves were capable of noble acts. Rodin's removal of public sculpture from a high pedestal to a low base would lead, in the twentieth century, to the elimination of the pedestal itself and to the presentation of sculpture in the "real" space of the viewer (see fig. 20-42).

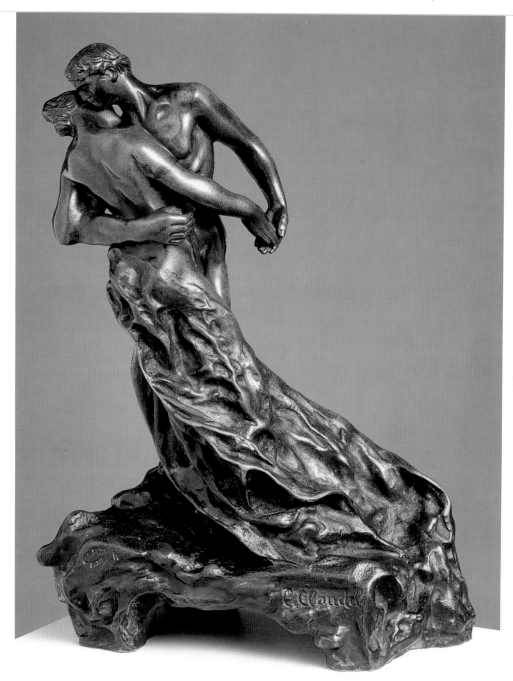

18-32 | **Camille Claudel.** *The Waltz.* 1892–1905. Bronze, 9⅞" (25 cm). Neue Pinakothek, Munich

Camille Claudel (1864–1943), an assistant in Rodin's studio who worked on the *Burghers of Calais*, was an accomplished sculptor whose work was overshadowed by the dramatic story of her life. Claudel formally began to study sculpture in 1879 and became Rodin's pupil four years later. After she started working in his studio, she also became his mistress—an often stormy relationship that lasted fifteen years. Both during and after her association with Rodin, Claudel enjoyed independent professional success, but she also suffered from psychological problems that eventually overtook her, and she spent the last thirty years of her life in a mental asylum.

Among Claudel's most celebrated works is *The Waltz* (fig. 18-32). The sculpture depicts a dancing couple, the man unclothed and the woman seminude, her lower body enveloped in a long, flow-ing gown. In Claudel's original conception, both figures were entirely nude, but she had to add drapery to the female figure after an inspector from the Ministry of the Beaux-Arts declared the piece to be indecent. The drapery proved to be a fortunate addition, for it conveys an illusion of fluent motion as the dancing partners whirl in space. The woman's swirling drapery recalls the fluid lines of Art Nouveau. Despite the closeness of the dancers there is little actual physical contact between them, and their facial expressions reveal no passion or sexual desire. After violating decency standards with her first version of *The Waltz*, Claudel perhaps sought in this new rendition to portray love as a union more spiritual than physical. It would remain for artists of the twentieth century to express emotions and ideas independent of the mundane physical world.

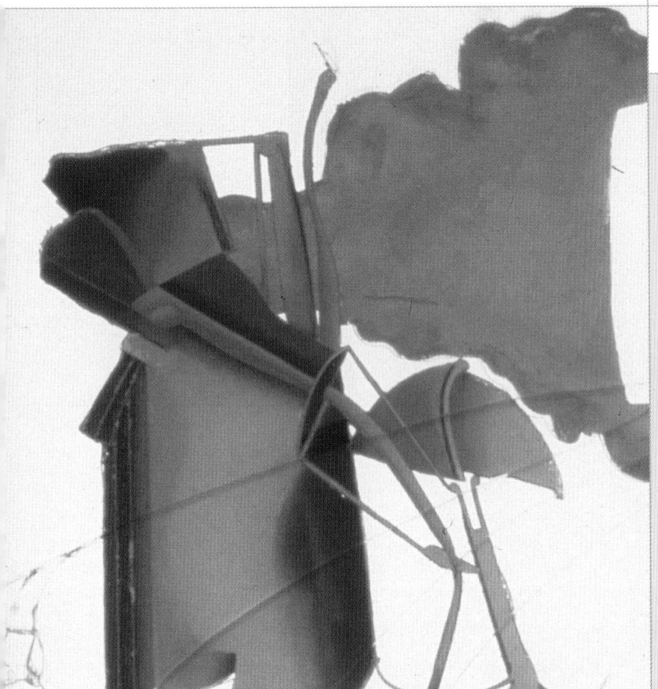

Marcel Duchamp. *The Bride Stripped Bare by Her Bachelors, Even (The Large Glass)*. 1915–23. Oil, varnish, lead foil, lead wire, and dust on two glass panels, 9'1¼" x 5'9¼" (2.77 x 1.76 m). Philadelphia Museum of Art

Bequest of Katherine S. Dreier

(See page 488.)

Marcel Duchamp (1887–1968) said he wanted to "put painting once again at the service of the mind," meaning that art is an intellectual process. He valued ideas more than the art object itself, and this new way of understanding art also liberated the creative process. Duchamp loved word play—poetry or puns—more than sequential communication, and he undermined the very idea of unique art objects with his "readymades." Readymades are found objects, ordinary manufactured items, like a bicycle wheel or snow shovel or a urinal (which he called *The Fountain;* see fig. 19-27) that became art simply because an artist selected them. Duchamp's radical concepts about art surfaced in all his works, especially his huge creation, *The Bride Stripped Bare by Her Bachelors, Even*. It is also known as *The Large Glass*. Although he worked on the piece for eight years, Duchamp only considered it finished after the nine-foot panel of glass, paint, and wire was accidentally shattered in 1926 and then put back together in 1936.

The complex clues to understanding the artwork and its title seem to be as equally important to Duchamp as the random accident that completed it. The Bride (detail, left) in the upper half of the glass controls the nine Bachelors below. Duchamp's notes on the piece, written between 1912 and 1915 leave paths to meaning as well as enigmas. "The Bride is basically a motor," Duchamp wrote, who runs on "love gasoline." Thus so she is also an image of female sexual desire. The Bride sends forth a cloud across the glass that Duchamp called "the Halo of the Bride" and her "Cinematic Blossoming," and she issues her "commands, orders, authorizations, etc." through the three squares of clear glass. Later critics suggested that the Bride is emitting a lovesick sigh.

In contrast, the Bachelors' portion of the glass (bottom half) contains recognizable objects drawn in linear perspective. Nine "malic" (Duchamp's word, "malelike") pieces at the left dangle from wires attached to seven cones which arch over a chocolate grinder. They are ready to be set in motion by a rectangular frame on elliptical gliders powered by a water wheel. Both water wheel and scissorlike rods are also linked to the chocolate grinder. At the right the three circular test patterns used by eye doctors hover as "Oculist Witnesses" to the thwarted consummation.

Duchamp believed that art was whatever the artist said it was and that the viewer was as important as the artist. As Calvin Tomkins in his biography *Duchamp* (page 12) wrote, "Duchamp has come to be considered a forerunner of Conceptual art, as well as Pop art, Minimal art, Performance art, Process art, Kinetic art, anti-form and Multimedia art, and virtually every postmodern tendency."

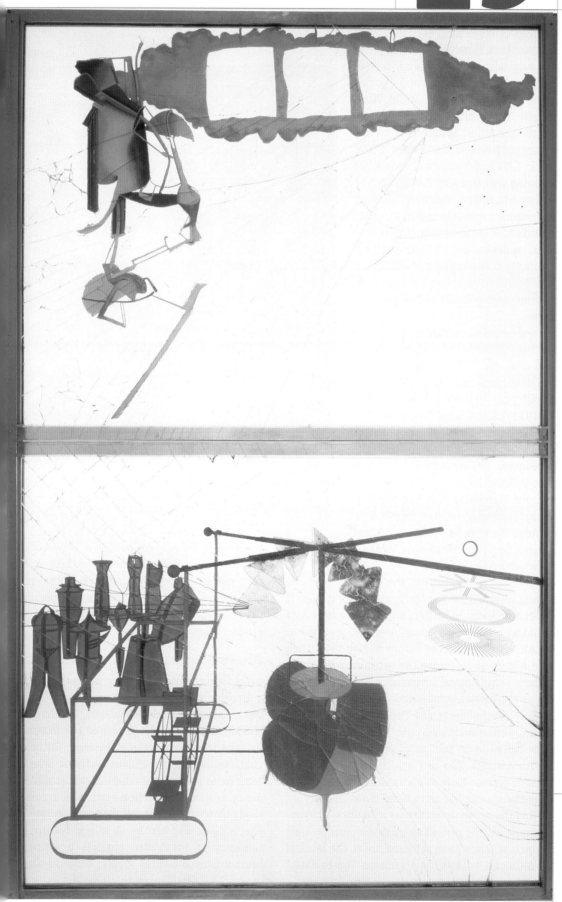

Considering the backdrop of politics, war, and technological change is critical to our understanding twentieth-century art. As that century dawned, many Europeans and Americans believed optimistically that human society would "advance" through the spread of democracy, capitalism, and technological innovation. However, the competitive nature of both colonialism and capitalism created great instability in Europe, and countries joined together in rival political alliances. World War I erupted in August 1914, initially pitting Britain, France, and Russia (the Allies) against Germany and Austria (the Central Powers). The United States entered the war in 1917 and contributed to an Allied victory the following year (see Map 7, page 529).

World War I significantly transformed European politics and economics, especially in Russia, which became the world's first Communist nation in 1917 when a popular revolution brought the Bolshevik (meaning "Majority") Communist party of Vladimir Lenin to power. In 1922 the Soviet Union, a Communist state encompassing Russia and neighboring areas, was created.

American and western European economies soon recovered from the war (with the exception of Germany whose economy was weakened by reparations the Allies demanded), but the 1929 New York stock market crash plunged the world into the Great Depression. In 1933 U.S. President Franklin D. Roosevelt responded with the New Deal, an ambitious welfare program meant to provide jobs and stimulate the American economy. Britain and France instituted state welfare policies during the 1930s as well. Elsewhere in Europe, the economic crisis brought to power right-wing totalitarian regimes: Benito Mussolini in Italy, Adolf Hitler in Germany, and General Francisco Franco in Spain. Meanwhile, in the Soviet Union, Joseph Stalin succeeded Lenin in 1924.

German aggression led in 1939 to the outbreak of World War II. The most destructive war in history, World War II claimed the lives of millions of soldiers and civilians from Asia to Europe, including 6 million European Jews who perished in the Nazi Holocaust. It ended first in Europe in May 1945, then in the Pacific in August 1945. During the two great wars of the twentieth century, technological innovations resulted in such deadly devices as the fighter bomber and the atom bomb. Yet dramatic scientific developments and improvements in medicine, agriculture, communications, and transportation also transformed the daily life of millions of people, especially in Europe and North America. The first analog and digital computers, designed to process huge amounts of data and perform advanced calculations, were also introduced in the 1930s.

Accompanying the momentous changes in politics, economics, and science were equally revolutionary developments in art and culture, which scholars have gathered under the label of "modernism." Although *modern* simply means "up-to-date,"

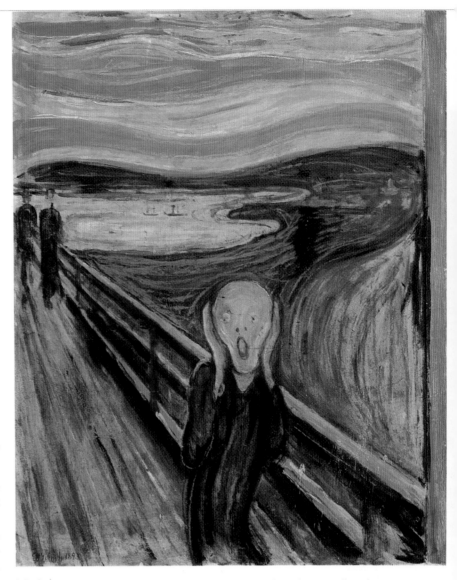

19-1 | **Edvard Munch.** *The Scream.* 1893. Tempera and casein on cardboard, 36 x 29" (91.3 x 73.7 cm). Nasjonalgalleriet, Oslo

the term *modernism* connotes a rejection of conventions and a commitment to radical innovation. Like scientists and inventors, modern artists engaged in a process of experimentation and discovery, seeking to explore new possibilities of creativity and expression in a rapidly changing world (see "Modernism," right).

Early Modern Tendencies in Europe

After 1900 the pace of artistic innovation increased, producing a dizzying succession of movements, or "isms," including Fauvism, Cubism, Futurism, Dadaism, and Surrealism. Each had a charismatic leader who promoted the movement's unique philosophy through written statements. Although modernism is characterized by tremendous aesthetic diversity, several broad tendencies mark many artists as modernist. Foremost is a tendency toward **abstraction**—art which communicates exclusively through such formal, nonrepresentational means as line, shape, color, and texture. A second feature of modernism is a tendency to emphasize physical processes through visible brushstrokes and chisel marks. A third feature is modernism's continual exploration of the nature of art itself through the adoption of new techniques and materials, including ordinary, "nonartistic" materials which break down distinctions between art and everyday life.

The rise of European and American modernism in the early twentieth century was driven by such exhibitions as the 1905 Salon d'Automn, ("Autumn Exhibition") in Paris, which launched the Fauve movement; the first exhibition of der Blaue Reiter group in Munich in 1911; and the 1913 New York Armory Show, the first large-scale introduction of European modernism to American audiences. In 1929 The Museum of Modern Art opened in New York; and state-supported museums dedicated to modern art also opened in major European capitals, such as Paris, Rome, and Brussels, signaling the transformation of modernism from an embattled fringe movement to officially recognized "high culture" (see "The High/Low Myth of Modernism," page 506).

Expressionism

From the Post-Impressionist period onwards, a great many artists assumed that the chief function of art was to express their intense feelings to the world. From Van Gogh and Gauguin—and even Ryder (see fig. 18-13) in the United States—the paths to **expressionism** were many and varied. An unforgettable image of modern alienation, *The Scream* (fig. 19-1), by the Norwegian painter and printmaker Edvard Munch (1863–1944), foretells the powerful emotions that will pervade the work of twentieth-century expressionist artists. Munch described the genesis of the painting in his diary: "One evening I was walking along a path. . . . I was tired and ill. . . . I sensed a shriek passing through nature. . . . I painted this picture, painted the clouds as actual blood." In the painting the scream emanates from a figure on a bridge and fills the landscape with clouds of "actual blood." The figure's skull-like head suggests the overwhelming anxiety that sought release in this primal scream. The expressive abstraction of form and color in the painting reflects the influence of Gauguin, whose work Munch had encountered shortly before he painted *The Scream*.

Another artist who found inspiration in Gauguin's formal simplicity and Edenic themes was Paula Modersohn-Becker (1876–1907). Living in the rustic village of Worpswede, an artist's colony in Germany, she became dissatisfied with the prevailing naturalist style. She made four trips to Paris between 1900 and her death in 1907 to see the latest developments in art. Her *Self-Portrait with an Amber Necklace* (fig. 19-2), painted in 1906, testifies to her assimilation of the innovations she

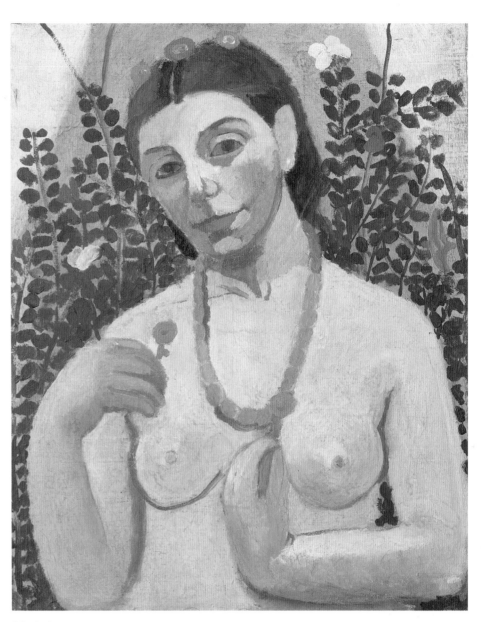

19-2   **Paula Modersohn-Becker.** *Self-Portrait with an Amber Necklace.* 1906. Oil on canvas 24 x 19³/₄" (61 x 50 cm). Öffentliche Kunstsammlung, Kunstmuseum, Basel Switzerland

MODERNISM

Like the word *Romanticism,* the term *modernism* has no agreed-upon definition, although it suggests the "art of the new." One traditional but still useful way of looking at modern art was popularized by the art historian Alfred H. Barr, director for many years at The Museum of Modern Art in New York. Barr saw two broad aesthetic directions in the work of modernist artists—loosely articulated, these are expressionism and formalism. Expressionism is the manipulation of visual elements in a work of art to convey intense feeling. Formalism is the aesthetic arrangement of shapes, colors, and forms. In a modernist artwork, both approaches may take precedence over the naturalistic or realistic representation of a subject. Expressionist and formalist currents may intermingle in modernist artworks, just as Neoclassical and Romantic currents did in an earlier period.

"PRIMITIVISM" AND MODERNITY

European nations began to colonize Africa in the late nineteenth century, and African objects were brought to Europe by soldiers, administrators, and adventurers. They displayed pieces like the Ngombe chair (see below) as trophies from the newly vanquished territories. Western artists believed that immersion in "primitive" aesthetics gave them access to a more authentic state of being, uncorrupted by civilization. Modernist "primitivism" drew its inspiration from the so-called primitive art of Africa, Pre-Columbian America, and Oceania, as well as the work of children, folk artists, and the mentally ill.

European artists, such as Pablo Picasso and Henri Matisse, and designers, such as Pierre Legrain (1889–1929), were inspired by the formal power of African art. The Ngombe chair is exemplary of African artistry. The rich surface decoration consists of European brass carpet tacks and darker iron tacks arranged in parallel lines and diamond patterns. Legrain adapted the simple, elegant forms of the chair to French taste.

Legrain's Africa-inspired pieces (see below right) appeared in the 1925 design exhibition, International Exposition of Modern Decorative and Industrial Arts, where the term *style moderne* was given to describe the new geometric simplicity that characterized many of the objects displayed there. The exposition helped launch a popular commercial style called *Art Deco* (a label coined in the late 1960s). The Art Deco label is loosely applied to describe variations on a modern design trend developed in Europe and the United States that visually defined the "Machine Age," the era between World War I and World War II.

Designers working in the Art Deco style drew upon a variety of sources. Like Legrain's chair, Art Deco objects and ornaments are characterized by angular or arched lines or forms rendered with an impersonal precision that recall the attributes of machines: flawless accuracy, speed, and automation. Ironically, many Art Deco objects that celebrate modern mechanization through their style are actually hand-crafted luxury items. Such is the case with Legrain's chair and many of the objects and ornaments displayed at the 1925 Paris exposition.

For many artists and designers active during the first half of the twentieth century, "primitivism" and modernity were not necessarily antithetical to each other. Modernization had connotations of a vigorous, new vitality—a youthful energy that, like the "primitive," possessed the power to renew western civilization and liberate it from old-fashioned attitudes that seemed to hamper its progress toward the future. "Primitive" art and modern machines, in many cases, were composed of simple, geometric forms—a fresh look that was perceived as appropriate to the new century.

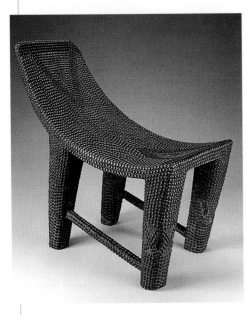

Chair, Ngombe artist, Democratic Republic of the Congo. Wood, brass, and iron tacks 25⅝" (65.1 cm). National Museum of African Art, Washington, D.C.
Museum Purchase, 90-4-1

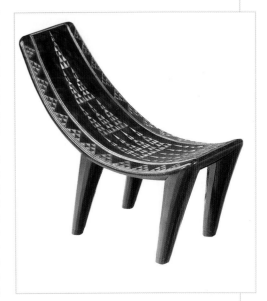

Pierre Legrain. Tabouret. c. 1923 Lacquered wood, horn, gilding, length 25¼" (64.1 cm). Virginia Museum of Fine Arts Richmond, Virginia
The Sydney and Frances Lewis Endowment Fund

saw in France. The basic shapes and simple outlines of the self-portrait—with its prominent eyes as well as its nudity, her body decorated only with flowers and a necklace—suggest that she may have seen African sculpture as well as Post-Impressionist painting. Standing before a screen of flowering plants and tenderly holding two small blooms, she shows herself at one with nature.

More deeply involved with the ills of society in the early modern period is Käthe Schmidt Kollwitz (1867–1945). Raised in a socialist household, she studied at the Berlin School of Art for Women and at a similar school in Munich. In 1891 she married a doctor who shared her leftist political views, and they settled in a working-class neighborhood in Berlin. Art for her

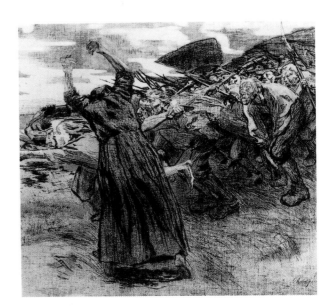

19-3 | **Käthe Schmidt Kollwitz. *The Outbreak,*** from the *Peasants' War* series. 1903. Etching. Staatliche Museen zu Berlin, Preussischer Kulturbesitz, Kupferstichkabinett

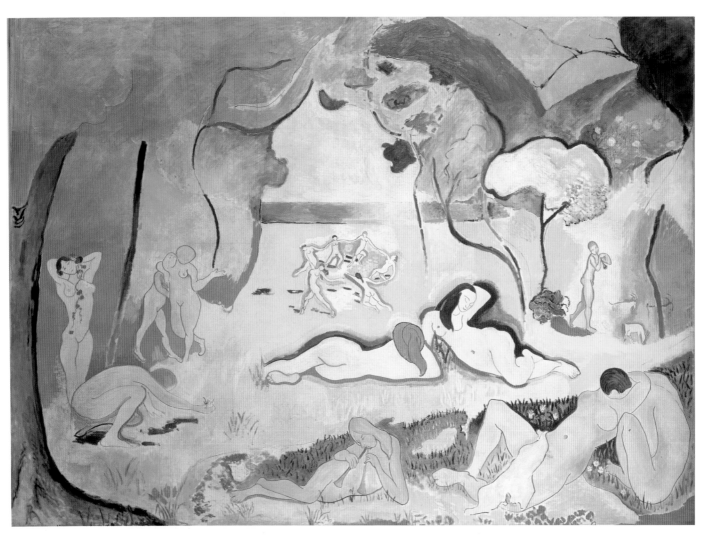

19-4 **Henri Matisse. *The Joy of Life.*** 1905–06. Oil on canvas, 5'8½" x 7'9¾" (1.74 x 2.38 m). The Barnes Foundation, Merion, Pennsylvania (BF 719)

was a political tool, and to reach as many people as possible, she became a printmaker.

Kollwitz hoped to win sympathy for working-class people. Between 1902 and 1908, she produced the *Peasants' War* series, seven etchings that depict events in the sixteenth-century peasant rebellion in a stark graphic style. In *The Outbreak* (fig. 19-3), Kollwitz takes full advantage of etching technique in order to express the peasants' emotive energy exploding against their oppressors. Raw and jagged lines scratched into the plate communicate the peasants' built-up fury from years of mistreatment. In the front, with her back to us, is Black Anna, the leader of the revolt. Kollwitz said that she modeled the figure of Anna after herself.

EXPRESSIONIST MOVEMENTS

Van Gogh, Ryder, Munch, Modersohn-Becker, Kollwitz, and others developed their personal visions in the 1880s and 1890s. Then in the years just before World War I many artists in France, Germany, and Russia turned to expressionist styles, formed groups of like-minded artists, and finally came to the notice of the critics and the public.

The first of these groups emerged in France around 1905. Henri Matisse (1869–1954) and his friends combined the dynamic brushwork of Van Gogh with bold primary colors, often applied directly from the tube. The effect was explosive—"like sticks of dynamite," the painter André Derain said—and won the style's practitioners the label of Fauves (French for "wild beasts," a derogatory name given by the critic Louis Vauxcelles). Dynamic brushwork heightened the energy of the brilliant colors, conveying a new intensity of visual experience.

Matisse's *The Joy of Life* (fig. 19-4) treats hedonistic pursuits in a pastoral realm animated by a bouquet of luscious colors. Naked revelers dance, make love, commune with nature, or simply stretch out in their idyllic glade by the sea. Colors freed from naturalistic constraints convey the joyous mood, as do the uninhibited figures. The brushwork, too, is softer and more careful, subservient to the pure sensuality of the color. The only movement is in the long, flowing curves of the trees and the sinuous contours of the nude bodies. These undulating rhythms, in combination with the relaxed poses of the two reclining women at the center, establish the quality of "serenity, relief from the stress of modern life"—the way Matisse characterized his work from this

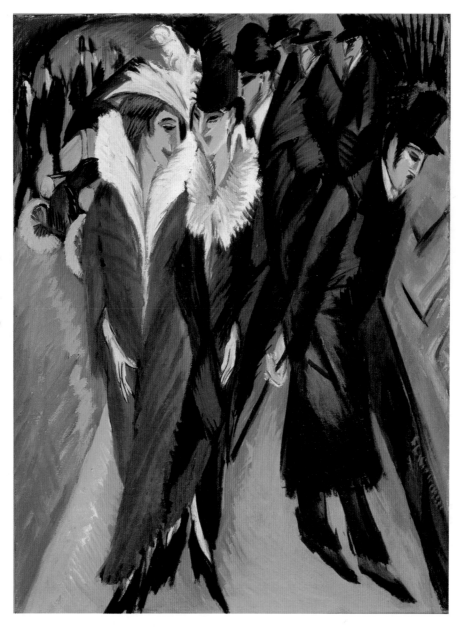

19-5

Ernst Ludwig Kirchner.
Street, Berlin. 1913.
Oil on canvas, 47½" x
37⅞" (120.6 x 91 cm).
The Museum of Modern Art,
New York. Purchase (274.39)

point. In an essay titled "Notes of a Painter," which Matisse published in 1908, he expressed his allegiance to "an art . . . devoid of troubling or depressing subject matter . . . a mental comforter, something like a good armchair in which to rest."

The German counterpart to Fauvism was die Brücke ("the Bridge"). In 1905, three architecture students at the Dresden Technical College, including Ernst Ludwig Kirchner (1880–1938), formed what they called a brotherhood. Members of the group admired the writings of the German philosopher Frederick Nietzsche. In *Thus Spoke Zarathustra*, Nietzsche used the metaphor of the bridge to explain how civilization is precariously balanced between two contradictory states of being in the evolutionary process—progress and degeneration, or modernity (the future) and barbarism (the past). Though tinged with pessimism, Nietzsche emphasized the process of human transformation and perceived in "primitive" states, such as childhood or the animal, possibilities for rebirth and renewal. These Nietzschean ideas punctuate the work of die Brücke artists before World War I.

For die Brücke artists, both modernity (as symbolized by the metropolis) and the "primitive" held connotations for regeneration—but could also signify and lead to de-evolution. They associated large urban centers with fresh creativity and new beginnings (see "'Primitivism' and Modernity," page 470). Yet the modern metropolis tended to breed a competitive climate that recalled a Darwinian struggle for the survival of the fittest. They believed that just below the surface of polite society seethed a barbarism on the verge of becoming unleashed. Die Brücke artists were both excited by and wary of this precarious balance.

Kirchner's *Street, Berlin* (fig. 19-5) captures this dynamic paradox. A crowd of sophisticated urbanites seem to speed to the foreground of the canvas. The immediacy of their hurried movement is conveyed through Kirchner's slashing brushstrokes and raw, vibrant colors. Although crowded together physically, the well-dressed men and women seem psychologically distant; they are inhuman manikins, rather than members of a community. Their angular, brittle shapes formally

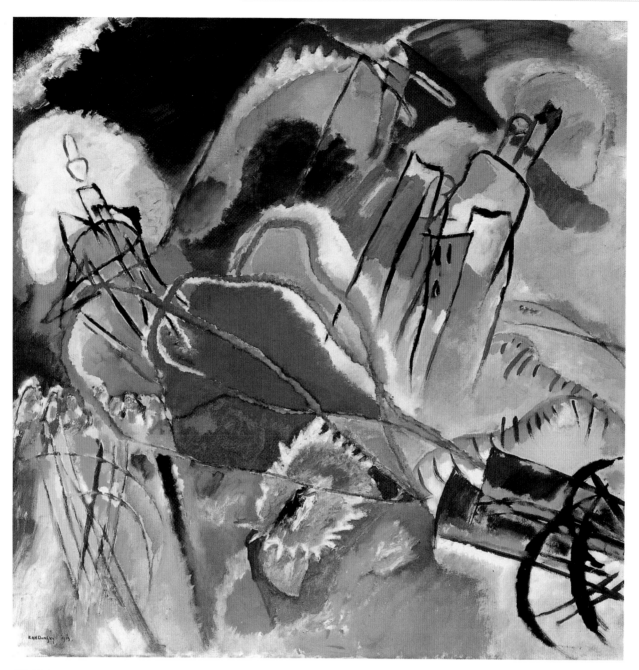

19-6 | **Vasily Kandinsky.** *Improvisation No. 30 (Cannons).* 1913. Oil on canvas, 43¼ x 43¼" (109.9 x 109.9 cm). The Art Institute of Chicago

Arthur Jerome Eddy Memorial Collection

underscore the message about modern alienation caused by the stress and friction of city living. In Kirchner's painting, the metropolis has become an emblem of the conflicting nature of modernity—it is new and energetic, but also can evoke the savagery masked by civilized behaviors.

The last major pre–World War I expressionist group to come out of the crucible of late-nineteenth-century painting formed in Munich around the Russian painter Vasily Kandinsky (1866–1944). In 1895, after seeing a Monet painting whose color moved him deeply, Kandinsky decided to devote himself to art. He left Moscow to study in Munich because of the research being done there on the effects of color and form on the human psyche. In 1911 Kandinsky organized der Blaue Reiter ("the Blue

Rider" or "Blue Knight"), a group of nine artists who shared his interest in the power of color. "The Rider" or "Knight" was the popular Russian name for the image of Saint George, mounted on a horse and slaying a dragon, that appeared on the Moscow city emblem. The horseman was blue because Kandinsky considered that color to be the male principle and to represent spirituality.

Millennial and apocalyptic imagery appeared often in Kandinsky's art in the years just prior to World War I. According to an ancient Russian tradition, revived around 1900, Moscow would be the capital of the world during the millennium, the thousand years of Christ's reign on earth that would follow the Apocalypse, as prophesied by Saint John the Evangelist. In *Improvisation No. 30 (Cannons)* (fig. 19-6), the firing cannons

19-7 | **Paul Klee.** *Hammamet with Its Mosque.* 1914. Watercolor and pencil on two sheets of laid paper mounted on cardboard, 8⅛ x 7⅝" (20.6 x 19.4 cm). The Metropolitan Museum of Art, New York
The Berggruen Klee Collection, 1984 (1984.315.4)

in the lower right combine with the intense reds, a blackened sky, and precariously leaning buildings and mountains to suggest a scene from the end of the world. Although sometimes thought to reflect fear of the coming war, the painting may instead be an ecstatic vision of the destructive prelude to the Second Coming of Christ. Kandinsky never expected his viewers to understand the symbolism of his forms, which at times intentionally border on the nonrepresentational. Instead, he intended to awaken their spirituality through the sheer force of color that explodes dramatically across the canvas.

The Swiss-born Paul Klee (1879–1940) is among the best-known artists associated with der Blaue Reiter, but his involvement with the group was never more than tangential. A 1914 trip to Tunisia inspired Klee's interest in the expressive potential of color. On his return, he painted a series of watercolors based on his memories of North Africa, among them *Hammamet with Its Mosque* (fig. 19-7). The play between geometric composition and irregular brushstrokes in this watercolor is reminiscent of Cézanne's work, which Klee had recently seen. The luminous colors and delicate washes (applications of dilute watercolor) result in a gently shimmering effect. The subtle modulations of red across the bottom, especially, are positively melodic. Klee, who played the violin and belonged to a musical family, seems to have wanted to use color the way a musician would use sound, not to describe appearances but to evoke subtle nuances of feeling. The theory that painting could be abstract and **nonrepresentational** like music was a prevailing idea among many European modernists, especially expressionists like Klee and Kandinsky. If notes, tunes, and melodies could evoke an emotive response, so could pure forms, colors, shapes, and lines.

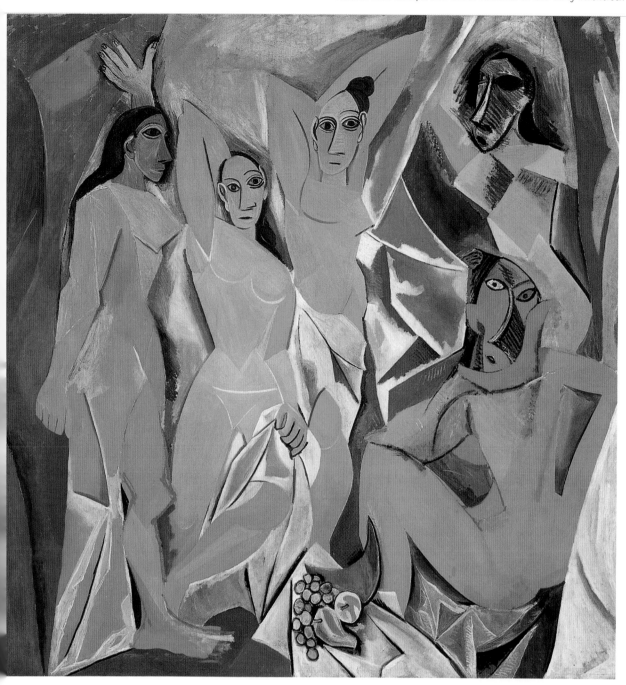

19-8

Pablo Picasso.
Les Demoiselles d'Avignon.
1907. Oil on canvas, 8' x 7'8" (2.43 x 2.33 m).
The Museum of Modern Art, New York, Acquired through the Lillie P. Bliss Bequest (333.1939)

Cubism

Both the splintered shapes in Kirchner's *Street, Berlin* (see fig. 19-5) and the flattened space and geometric blocks of color in Klee's *Hammamet* (see fig. 19-7) reflect the influence of Cubism, one of the most talked-about "isms" of twentieth-century art. Cubism was the joint invention of Pablo Picasso (1881–1973) and Georges Braque (1882–1963).

Picasso, born in Spain and educated in the art academies in Barcelona and Madrid, began to make frequent extended visits to Paris, where he moved early in 1904. Initially drawn to the socially conscious tradition in French painting that included artists such as Daumier (see fig. 26) and Toulouse-Lautrec (see fig. 18-29), Picasso went through an extraordinary and complex transformation between early 1905 and the winter of 1906–07. Wanting to produce art of greater formal and psychological strength, he began to study classical sculpture at the Louvre. In

1906 the Louvre installed a newly acquired collection of sculpture from Iberia (Spain and Portugal) that dated to the sixth and fifth centuries BCE. These archaic figures became the chief influence on his work for the next year. His interest in abstraction was reinforced by visits to Spain where he saw Catalan medieval art (see fig. 10-15) and also by African sculpture (see Chapter 16), which he saw in the ethnographic museum in Paris.

Picasso's wide-ranging studies culminated in 1907 in *Les Demoiselles d'Avignon* (fig. 19-8). The simplified features and wide, almond-shaped eyes of the three figures on the left reflect the Iberian influence, while the two figures at the right were inspired by African masks. The painting is Picasso's response to Matisse's *The Joy of Life* (see fig. 19-4), exhibited the year before, and to the French classical tradition, which to Picasso was embodied in Ingres's paintings of odalisques (see fig. 17-13). Picasso, however, substituted a bordello for a harem. The term

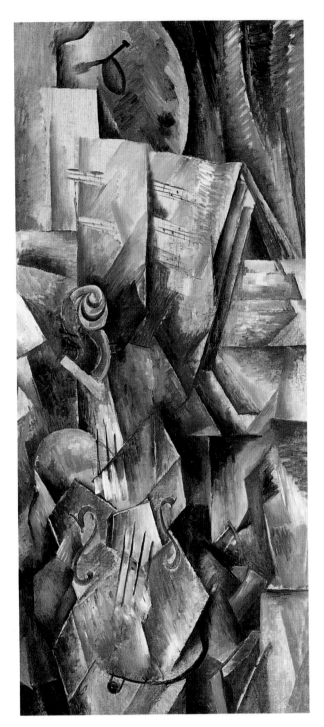

19-9 | **Georges Braque. *Violin and Palette.*** 1909–10. Oil on canvas, 36¹⁄₈ x 16⁷⁄₈" (91.8 x 42.9 cm). Solomon R. Guggenheim Museum, New York
(54.1412)

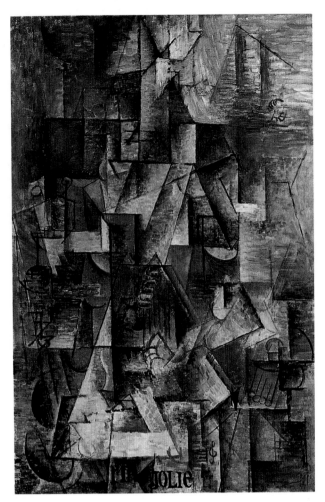

19-10 | **Pablo Picasso. *Ma Jolie Woman with a Zither or Guitar.*** 1911-12. Oil on canvas 39³⁄₈" x 25³⁄₄" (100 x 65.4 cm).
The Museum of Modern Art, New York. Lillie P. Bliss Bequest (176.1945)

In 1923 Picasso said, "Cubism is no different from any other school of painting. The same principles and the same elements are common to all. The fact that for a long time Cubism has not been understood . . . means nothing. I do not read English, [but] this does not mean that the English language does not exist, and why should I blame anyone . . . but myself if I cannot understand [it]?"

demoiselles is a euphemism for prostitutes, and Avignon refers not to the French town but to a street in the red-light district of Barcelona.

Picasso makes the viewer an uneasy participant in the painting. The fruit in the foreground rests on a surface that tilts boldly into the viewer's space, a perspective or angle that contradicts the angle at which the female figures are rendered. The women pose for and look directly at us, but they hardly present a con-

ventional picture of yielding femininity. The artist flattened the figures and transformed the entire space into a turbulent series of sharp curves and angles, conveying what one art historian has called "a tidal wave of aggression." Two women raise their arms in a traditional gesture of accessibility but contradict it with their hard, piercing gazes and firm mouths. Women, Picasso suggests, are not the gentle and passive creatures men would like them to be.

Picasso's friends were horrified by his new work. Matisse, for example, accused Picasso of making a joke of modern art and threatened to break off their friendship. Only one artist, the French painter Georges Braque, responded positively, and he saw in *Les Demoiselles d'Avignon* a potential that Picasso probably had not fully intended. Picasso was not consciously trying to break with the traditional western means of depicting space. Yet it was his formal innovation in this area that Braque responded to in this proto-Cubist work: Picasso, Braque observed, had flattened space, incorporated multiple perspectives within a single picture plane, and taken liberties with form much as Cézanne had in his late paintings (see fig. 18-24).

Braque carried the experiment further during 1908. In his landscape painting he reduced nature's complexity to its essential colors and basic geometric shapes. Matisse remarked on Braque's "little cubes," and the critic Louis Vauxcelles picked up the phrase and wrote that Braque "reduced everything to cubes." Thus the name Cubism was born. Braque's painting also pointed Picasso in a new direction, and soon the two artists had begun an intimate working relationship that lasted until Braque went off to war in 1914.

The move toward abstraction continued in a series of still-life paintings Braque and Picasso produced over the next two and a half years. In Braque's *Violin and Palette* (fig. 19-9) the gradual elimination of traditional pictorial space and the reduction of clearly recognizable subject matter is well under way. The still-life items are not arranged on a table using illusionistic depth but are placed in a shallow space parallel to the picture plane. None of the lines converge at a single point on an established "horizon." Using the **passage** technique developed by Cézanne (see page 459), Braque knit the various elements together into a single shifting surface of forms until he moved toward the complete disintegration of subject matter. Such paintings have been called Analytic Cubism because of the way the artists broke objects into parts as if to analyze them.

The works of 1911 and early 1912 reflect a different approach to the breaking up of forms and the flattening of pictorial space. Instead of simply fracturing an object, Picasso and Braque picked it apart and rearranged its elements. Remnants of the subject are evident throughout Picasso's *Ma Jolie* (fig. 19-10), for example, but any attempt to reconstruct the image of a woman with a stringed instrument would be misguided because the subject provided only the raw material for a formal composition. *Ma Jolie* is not a representation of a woman, a place, or an event—it is simply "pure painting." Picasso included a musical analogy—a treble clef and the words *Ma Jolie* ("My Pretty One"), a popular song—suggesting that the viewer should approach the painting the way one would a musical composition, either by simply enjoying the arrangement of its elements or by analyzing it, but not by asking what it represents.

A subtle tension between order and disorder is maintained throughout the painting. For example, the shifting effect of the surface, a delicately patterned texture of grays and browns, is regularized through the use of short, horizontal brushstrokes that firmly establish a grid and effectively counteract the surface flux. What at first may seem a random assemblage of lines and muted colors turns out to be a well-organized composition. The aesthetic satisfaction of such a work depends on the way chaos seems to resolve itself into order.

Works like *Ma Jolie* brought Picasso and Braque to the brink of total abstraction, but in the spring of 1912 they changed course and began to create works that suggested more clearly discernible subjects. This second major phase of Cubism is known as Synthetic Cubism because of the way the artists created motifs

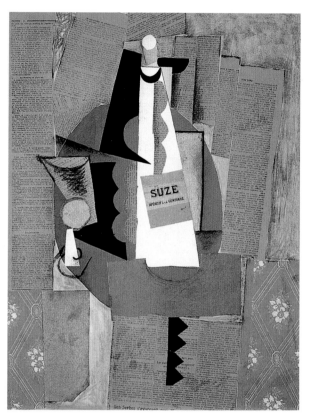

19-11 | **Pablo Picasso. *Glass and Bottle of Suze.*** 1912
Pasted paper, gouache, and charcoal, 25 3/4 x 19 3/4"
(65.4 x 50.2 cm). Washington University Gallery of
Art, St. Louis, Missouri
University Purchase, Kende Sale Fund, 1946

by combining simpler elements, as in a chemical synthesis. Picasso's *Glass and Bottle of Suze* (fig. 19-11), like many of the works he and Braque created from 1912 to 1914, is a **collage** (coller, "to glue" in French), a technique in which paper forms are pasted onto another surface. At the center, newsprint and construction paper suggest a tray or round table supporting a glass and a bottle of liquor with an actual label. In true Cubist mode, multiple perspectives are at work. We see simultaneously the top of the blue table, tilted toward us, and the side of a cup. The bottle stands on the table, its label facing us, while we can also see the round top of the bottle and the top of its cork, which are parallel with the angle of the table. Around this arrangement Picasso pasted larger pieces of newspaper and wallpaper. The elements together evoke not only a place, a bar, but also an activity—the viewer alone with a newspaper, enjoying a quiet drink.

The refuge from daily bustle that both art and quiet bars can provide was a central theme in the Synthetic Cubist works of Braque and Picasso. The two artists, however, used different types of newspaper clippings. Braque's clippings deal almost entirely with musical and artistic events, but Picasso often included references to political events that would soon shatter the peaceful pleasures these works evoke. In *Glass and Bottle of Suze* the newspaper clippings deal with the First Balkan War of 1912–13, which led to World War I.

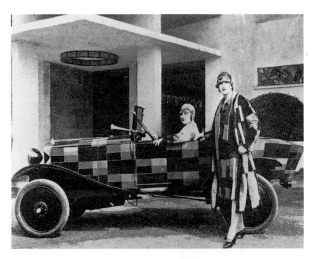

19-12 | **Sonia Delaunay-Terk. Clothes and customized Citroën B-12.** From *Maison de la Mode*, 1925

The term *Art Deco* derives from the 1925 International Exposition of Modern Decorative and Industrial Arts in Paris and refers to the kind of geometric style evident in many of the works on display, including Delaunay-Terk's clothing and fabric designs.

RESPONSES TO CUBISM

As the various phases of Cubism emerged from the studios of Braque and Picasso, it became clear to the art world that something of great significance was happening. The radical innovations upset the public and most critics, but the avant-garde saw in them the future of art. Even Matisse, the great lyrical colorist and Fauve, took a hard look at the new concept of space and form inaugurated by Picasso and Braque.

Even greater emphasis on color appeared in the radical painting of Robert Delaunay (1885–1941) and Sonia Delaunay-Terk (1885–1979), who took Cubism into a new, wholly different direction. Beginning in 1910, they began to fuse Fauvist color with Analytic Cubist form in works dedicated to the modern city and modern technology. The critic Apollinaire labeled the style Orphism (from Orpheus, the legendary Greek musician), implying an analogy between music and the new abstract style of painting. The Delaunays preferred to think of their work in terms of "simultaneity," a complicated concept connoting the collapse of spatial distance and temporal sequence into the simultaneous "here and now," and the creation of harmonic unity out of discordant elements.

Sonia Delaunay-Terk became a distinguished textile and fashion designer. Her greatest critical success came in 1925 at the International Exposition of Modern Decorative and Industrial Arts (see "'Primitivism' and Modernity," page 470). She decorated a Citroën sports car to match one of her textile designs (fig. 19-12). Her bold geometric patterns seemed to express the new modernity of the automobile age. Moreover, the small three-seater Citroën was specifically designed to appeal to the "new woman," who, like Delaunay-Terk, was more mobile, less tied to home and family, and less dependent on men than her predecessors.

In Italy, Cubism led to another twentieth-century "ism." Futurism emerged on February 20, 1909, when a Milanese literary magazine editor, Filippo Marinetti, published his "Foundation and Manifesto of Futurism" in a Paris newspaper. An outspoken attack against everything old, dull, "feminine," and safe, Marinetti's manifesto (declaration of principles) promoted the supposedly exhilarating "masculine" experiences of warfare and reckless speed to liberate Italy from its outworn past.

Among the artists and poets who gathered around Marinetti to create art forms for a revitalized Italy was Umberto Boccioni (1882–1916), whose major sculptural work, *Unique Forms of Continuity in Space* (fig. 19-13), seemed to epitomize a revitalized Italy. Cubist figure studies, which Boccioni saw in Paris in

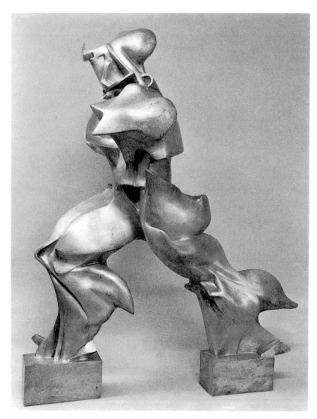

19-13 | **Umberto Boccioni. *Unique Forms of Continuity in Space.*** 1913. Bronze, 43⅞" x 34⅞" x 15¾".
The Museum of Modern Art, New York. Acquired through the Lillie P. Bliss Bequest (231.1948)

1911, inspired the exaggerated muscular curves and counter-curves of this powerful nude figure. Boccioni seems to have stretched and inflated the forms to express the figure's force and speed. The sculpture personifies the new Italian man envisioned by the Futurists, a strong male figure rushing headlong into the brave new Futurist world.

In Russia since the time of Peter the Great (ruled 1682–1725), the upper classes had turned to western Europe for cultural models. In 1898, two wealthy young men—Aleksandr Benois (1870–1960) and Serge Diaghilev (1872–1929)—launched the magazine *World of Art*, dedicated to international

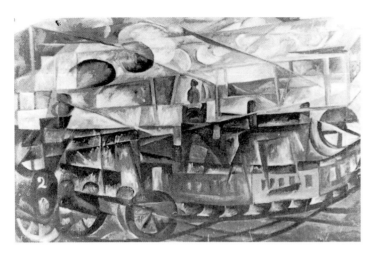

19-14 | **Natalia Goncharova. *Aeroplane over Train*.** 1913. Oil on canvas, 21⁵/₈ x 32⁷/₈" (55 x 83.5 cm). Kazan-skii Muzej Russia

art, literature, and music. The following year the World of Art group, centered in Russia's capital, St. Petersburg, held its first international art exhibition, including works by Degas, Monet, and Whistler. Diaghilev took an exhibition of contemporary Russian art to Paris in 1906 and three years later brought his ballet company, the Ballets Russes, to the French capital, where it enjoyed enormous success. Natalia Goncharova (1881–1962) designed costumes and sets for some of the most memorable Ballets: *Le coq d'or* (1914), *Night on Bald Mountain* (1923), and *Firebird* (1926).

Goncharova was one of the many Russian artists who adopted French styles with some ambivalence. She and her lifelong companion Mikhail Larionov (1881–1964) were torn between the desire to develop a native, characteristically Russian art and the wish to keep up with western European developments. Exposed to French and Italian art and also the Slavophile (pro-Russian) movement in Moscow, they created a new Russian style known as Cubo-Futurism. Goncharova's *Aeroplane over Train* (fig. 19-14) combines two styles—blocky Cubist shapes closely packed in a dynamic Futurist composition—and two symbols of technological advance—the train and the airplane. Because knowledge of Analytic Cubism and Futurism had arrived in Moscow almost simultaneously and had some superficial similarities, Russian artists tended to link them.

After Goncharova and Larionov left for Paris in 1915, their colleague Kazimir Malevich (1878–1935) emerged as the leading figure in the Moscow avant-garde. Indeed, Kazimir Malevich was the first Russian to go beyond Cubo-Futurism, and he did so spectacularly and unforgettably. Malevich is recognized as the modernist artist who produced the first truly nonrepresentational work of art. According to his later reminiscences, "in the year 1913, in my desperate attempt to free art from the burden of the object, I took refuge in the square form and exhibited a picture which consisted of nothing more than a black square on a white field." Malevich exhibited thirty-nine works in this radically new mode in St. Petersburg in the winter of 1915–16. One work, *Suprematist Painting (Eight Red Rectangles)* (fig. 19-15), consists simply of rectangles arranged

diagonally on a white painted ground. Malevich called this art "Suprematism," short for "the supremacy of pure feeling in creative art." By eliminating objects and focusing entirely on formal issues, Malevich intended to "liberate" the essential beauty of all great art. At the same time, he freed twentieth-century artists to explore the previously untapped potential of nonrepresentational forms.

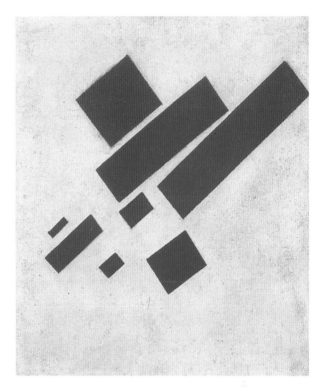

19-15 | **Kazimir Malevich. *Suprematist Painting (Eight Red Rectangles)*.** 1915. Oil on canvas, 22¹/₂ x 18⁷/₈" (57 x 48 cm). Stedelijk Museum, Amsterdam

Modernist Tendencies in the United States

At the end of the nineteenth century, American artists, led by the artist and teacher Robert Henri (1865–1929), sought a purely "American" style, free from both European academic conventions and the then dominant Impressionist style. In 1908, Henri organized an exhibition of paintings by artists who came to be known as The Eight. Because of their interest in depicting scenes of gritty urban life in New York City, five of them became known as members of the Ashcan School.

An outspoken opponent of the Ashcan School was the photographer Alfred Stieglitz (1864–1946) who chose a different approach in photographing the quintessentially modern city of New York. In *Spring Showers* (fig. 19-16; see page 480), he hid the new skyscrapers in an atmospheric haze, employing photography as a means to create purely aesthetic pleasure. The sanitation worker behind the tree makes no social statement; he is there only to balance the composition. The appeal of the photograph also depends on the contrast between the indefinite forms of the horse-drawn vehicles seen through the drizzle and the sharper foreground tree and fence.

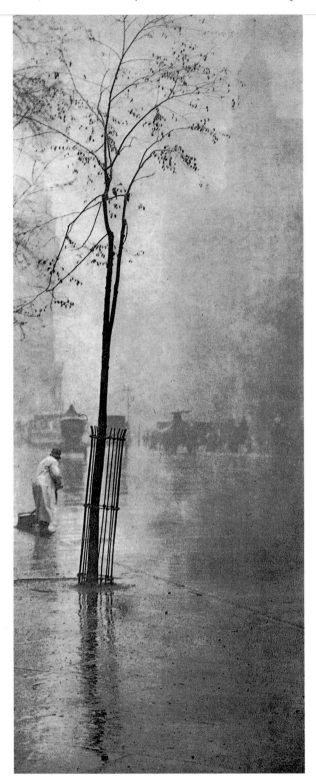

19-16 | **Alfred Stieglitz.** *Spring Showers.* 1901. The Art Institute of Chicago

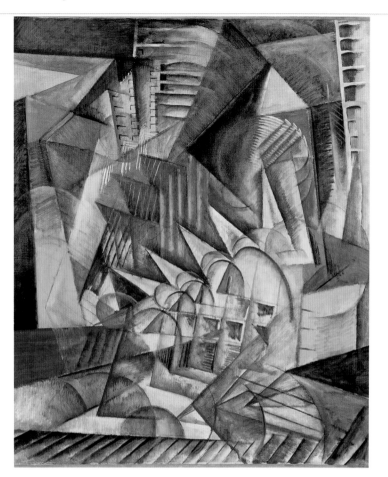

19-17 | **Max Weber.** *Rush Hour, New York.* 1915. Oil on canvas, 36¼" x 30¼" (92 x 76.8 cm).
National Gallery of Art, Washington, D.C. Gift of the Avalon Foundation, 1970.6.1.(2360)/PA

In 1905 Stieglitz opened a New York gallery where he exhibited contemporary art and photography, hoping to break down the artificial barrier between the two. Located at 291 Fifth Avenue, the Little Galleries of the Photo-Secession soon became known simply as 291 after its address. In collaboration with another American photographer, Edward Steichen (1879– 1973), who then lived in Paris, Stieglitz arranged exhibitions unlike any seen before in the United States, for he showed works by

Cézanne, Toulouse-Lautrec, Picasso, Braque, Matisse, Brancusi, and Rodin. The event that climaxed Stieglitz's pioneering efforts on behalf of European modernism (although he did not arrange it) was the "International Exhibition of Modern Art," held in 1913 at the 69th Regiment Armory in New York City, known as the Armory Show. The aim of the exhibition was to demonstrate how outmoded the views of the National Academy of Design were. The Armory Show also demonstrated how old-fashioned the American realistic approach to painting was.

Of the more than 1,300 works in the show, only about a third were by Europeans, but it was to these works that primary attention was paid. Critics claimed that Matisse, Kandinsky, Braque, and others were the agents of "universal anarchy." The American academic painter Kenyon Cox called them mere "savages." When a selection of works continued on to be shown in Chicago, civic leaders there called for a morals commission to investigate the show.

A number of younger artists, however, responded positively to the new art. Indicative of the work produced by Americans in the aftermath of the Armory Show is that of Max Weber (1881–1961). In the new climate established by the exhibition, he produced an American version of Cubo-Futurism, *Rush Hour, New York* (fig. 19-17). The tightly packed surface of angular and curvilinear elements suggests the noisy and crowded rush hour, but the harmonious colors—browns and gold with soft grays,

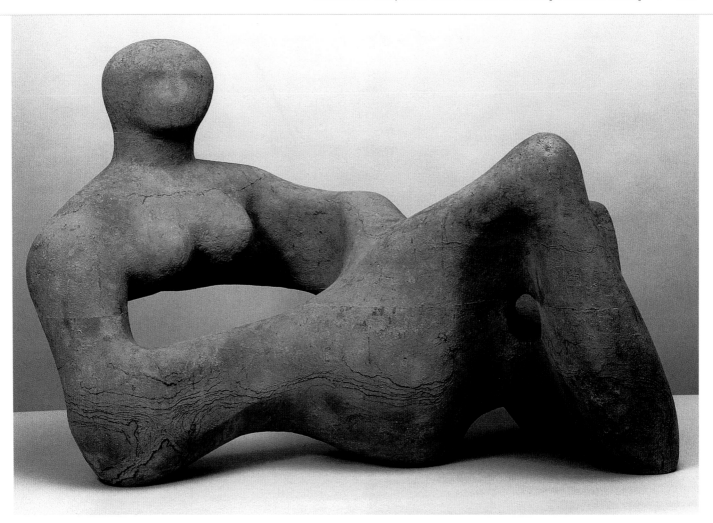

19-18 | Henry Moore. *Recumbent Figure.* 1938. Hornton stone, length 55" (141 cm). Tate Gallery, London

Originally carved for the garden of the architect Serge Chermayeff in Sussex, Moore's sculpture was situated next to a low-lying modernist building with an open view of the gently rolling landscape. "My figure looked out across a great sweep of the Downs, and her gaze gathered at the horizon," Moore later recalled. "The sculpture had no specific relationship to the architecture. It had its own identity and did not *need* to be on Chermayeff's terrace, but it so to speak *enjoyed* being there, and I think it introduced a humanizing element; it became a mediator between modern house and ageless land."

blues, and greens—undercut the hard-edged violence and emphasize the aesthetically pleasing formal composition.

The Armory Show marks an important turning point in the history of art in the United States. In the ten years after the Armory Show, Americans assimilated the most recent developments in European art. For the first time in their history, American artists at home began fighting their provincial status.

Art After World War I

The wars that ravaged Europe in the first half of the twentieth century had a profound effect on European artists and architects. After the Great War, as World War I was then known, members of artists' groups such as the Dutch de Stijl and the German Bauhaus sought the basis for a new civilization in severely rational beauty and order. The Dadaists and Surrealists, in contrast, celebrated subjectivity, intuition, and chance. In the United States, many artists retreated from European-inspired modernism into a focus on the American scene. Only in the late 1930s and 1940s did artists and architects fleeing Hitler's Europe renew American interest in nonrepresentational art. Abstract Expressionism, the

first modernist painting style of international importance developed in the United States, emerged during World War II and the immediate postwar period (see Chapter 20).

The dizzying array of "isms" that fragmented the European art world before World War I offered many formal options to postwar innovators. Some artists were even ready to reevaluate the classical tradition. In the late 1920s, the British sculptor Henry Moore (1898–1986) attempted to reinvigorate classicism with the strength and power of "primitive" art (see "The Myth of 'Primitive' Art," page 405, and "'Primitivism' and Modernity," page 470). The African, Oceanic, and Pre-Columbian art Moore saw at the British Museum had a powerful impact on his developing style. In the simplified forms of these "primitive" artists he discovered an intense vitality as well as a respect for the inherent qualities of the stone or wood from which the work is fashioned. In most of his own works of the 1920s and 1930s, Moore practiced direct carving in stone and wood as a way of pursuing the ideal of truth to material.

A central subject in Moore's art is the reclining female figure, such as *Recumbent Figure* (fig. 19-18), whose massive,

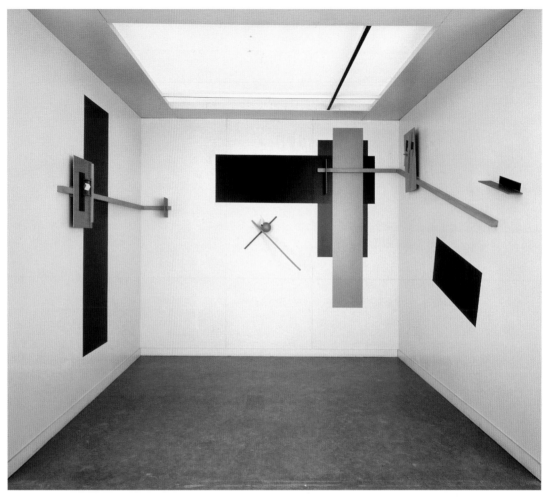

19-19 | **El Lissitzky. Proun space created for a Berlin art exhibition.** 1923, reconstruction 1965. Stedelijk Van Abbemuseum, Eindhoven, the Netherlands

simplified forms recall Pre-Columbian art. The carving reveals Moore's sensitivity to the inherent qualities of the stone, whose natural striations harmonize with the sinuous surfaces of the design. While certain elements of the body are clearly defined, such as the head and breasts, supporting elbow and raised knee, other parts flow together into an undulating mass more suggestive of a hilly landscape than of a human body. An open cavity penetrates the torso, emphasizing the relationship of solid and void fundamental to Moore's art. The sculptor wrote in 1937, "A hole can itself have as much shape-meaning as a solid mass."

In Russia, the most dynamic artistic achievements of the immediate postwar period came from avant-garde artists who enthusiastically supported the revolution: the overthrow of the czar in March, 1917, and the rise of the Bolsheviks (the radical socialists) under Vladimir Lenin in November 1917. The artists of the Russian Revolution were committed to the notion that the artist should leave the studio and "go into the factory, where the real body of life is made." The Constructivists, as they were known, envisioned politically engaged artists devoted to creating useful objects and promoting the aims of collective society.

One of the members of this socially visionary movement was an engineer, El Lissitzky (1890–1941). After the revolution, he taught architecture and graphic arts and soon came under the influence of a fellow professor, Kazimir Malevich. By 1919 he was using Malevich's formal vocabulary for propaganda posters and for artworks he called Prouns, an acronym for "Project for the Affirmation of the New." He made a Proun space for an exhibition in Germany (fig. 19-19). The engineered look is meant not merely to celebrate industrial technology but to encourage precise thinking among the viewers.

In the Netherlands the counterpart to the inspired **formalism** of Lissitzky was the de Stijl ("the Style") group, led by Piet Mondrian (1872–1944). The de Stijl movement was grounded in the conviction that there are two kinds of beauty: a sensual or subjective one and a higher, rational, objective, "universal" kind. In his mature works, Mondrian sought the essence of the second kind, eliminating representational elements because of their subjective associations and curves because of their sensual appeal. In paintings such as *Composition with Red, Blue, and Yellow* (fig. 19-20), he restricted his formal vocabulary to the three **primary colors** (red, yellow, and blue), the three neutrals (black, gray, and white), and horizontal and vertical lines. The two linear directions are meant to symbolize the harmony of a series of opposites, including male versus female, individual versus society, and spiritual versus material. For Mondrian the essence of

19-20

Piet Mondrian *Composition with Red, Blue, and Yellow* 1930. Oil on canvas, 20 x 20" (50.8 x 50.8 cm) Private collection

higher beauty was "dynamic equilibrium" achieved among the elements through the precise arrangement of color areas of different visual weight (the heavier weight of the red threatens to tip the painting to the right, but the placement of the tiny rectangle of yellow at the lower right prevents this imbalance by supporting the red's weight). Mondrian and his colleagues hoped that this style, based on ideas of balance and the resolution of conflict, would help to stabilize the viewer as well, "purifying" human-kind's chaotic natural instincts.

ARCHITECTURE BETWEEN THE WARS

Gerrit Rietveld (1888–1964) became the major architect and designer of the de Stijl movement. His famous Red-Blue Chair is shown here in the bedroom of the Schröder House (fig. 19-21) in Utrecht. Rietveld applied Mondrian's design aesthetic—the dynamic symmetry of rectangular planes of color—to the entire house and its built-in furnishings. Sliding partitions on the interior, the idea of the house's owner Truus Schröder-Schrader, allowed modifications in the spaces used for sleeping, working, and entertaining. Schröder-Schrader, a wealthy woman, wanted her home to suggest an elegant austerity, with the basic necessities sleekly integrated into a meticulously restrained whole.

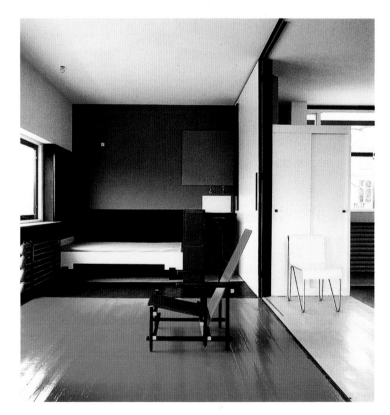

19-21 | **Gerrit Rietveld. Interior, Schröder House,** Utrecht, the Netherlands. 1924

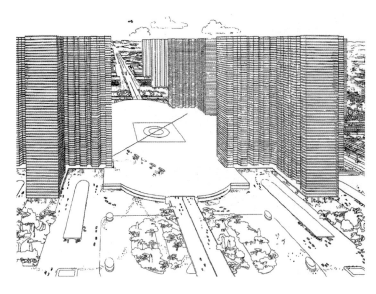

19-22 **Charles-Édouard Jeanneret (Le Corbusier)**
Plan for a Contemporary City of Three
Million Inhabitants. 1922
(From *Oeuvre complete*, 1910–29)

The skyscrapers Le Corbusier planned for the center of his city were intended to house offices, not residences. Residences would be in smaller suburban terraces of five-story houses around the periphery of the city. In 1925 Le Corbusier devised a similar plan for Paris, convinced that the center of the city needed to be torn down and rebuilt to accommodate automobile traffic. The Parisian street was a "Pack-Donkey's Way," he said. "Imagine all this junk . . . cleared off and carried away and replaced by immense clear crystals of glass, rising to a height of over six hundred feet!"

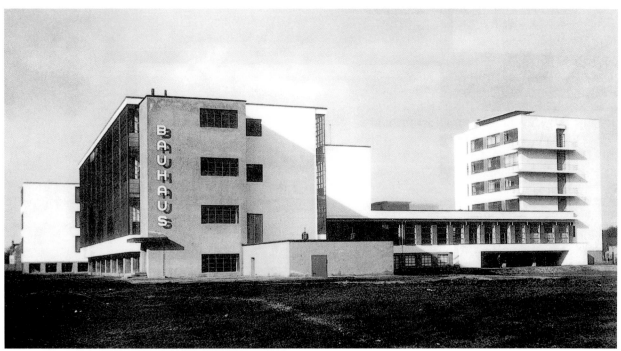

19-23 | **Walter Gropius. Bauhaus Building,** Dessau, Germany. 1925–26

One of the enduring contributions of the Bauhaus was **graphic design**. The sans serif letters of the building's sign not only harmonize with the architecture's clean lines but also communicate the Bauhaus commitment to modernity. Sans serif typography (that is, a typeface without serifs, the short lines at the end of the stroke of a letter) had been in use only since the early nineteenth century. A host of new sans serif typefaces was created in the 1920s.

Like the Dutch proponents of de Stijl, followers of a movement known as Purism, which developed in France, firmly believed in the power of art to change the world. The leading Purist figure was the Swiss-born Charles-Édouard Jeanneret (1887–1965), a largely self-taught architect and designer who moved to Paris in 1917. Three years later, Jeanneret, partly to demonstrate his faith in the ability of individuals to remake themselves, renamed himself Le Corbusier, a play on the French word for crow.

One of Le Corbusier's first major projects was his Plan for a Contemporary City of Three Million Inhabitants (fig. 19-22), which he exhibited in Paris in 1922. Le Corbusier envisioned for the future a city of uniform style, laid out on a grid, and dominated by skyscrapers (see "The Skyscraper," page 490), with wide traffic arteries that often passed below ground level. Large expanses of parkland would surround strictly functional buildings. The result, Le Corbusier thought, would be a new, clean, and efficient city filled with light, air, and greenery. Le Corbusier's vision had a profound effect on later city planning, especially in the United States.

The German counterpart to the total, rational planning envisioned by de Stijl and Le Corbusier was carried out at the Bauhaus school (loosely translated as "House of Building"). The Bauhaus (1919–33) was the brainchild of Walter Gropius (1883–1969), one of the founders of modernist architecture. Gropius, who belonged to several utopian groups, admired the spirit of the medieval building guilds, or *Bauhütten*, that had erected the great German cathedrals. He sought to revive their cooperative spirit and bring together modern art and industry by combining the schools of art and craft in the city of Weimar into a single institution. The Bauhaus moved to Dessau in 1925 and then to Berlin in 1932, but when the Nazis came to power in 1933, they closed the school (see "Suppression of the Avant-Garde in Germany," page 487).

At first the Bauhaus had no formal training program in architecture. Gropius felt that students needed to demonstrate proficiency in workshop courses before going on to study architecture. The workshops—which included pottery, metalwork, textiles, stained glass, furniture making, carving, and wall painting—were intended to teach both specific technical skills and basic design, based on the principle of learning through doing.

Gropius's design for the new Dessau Bauhaus, built in 1925–26 (fig. 19-23), frankly acknowledges the reinforced concrete, steel, and glass of which it is built. Gropius made no attempt to cover or decorate his building materials. Modern engineering methods made it possible to replace walls as massive structural supports with glass panels and to create light, airy spaces. The sans serif (without serifs) letters of the Bauhaus sign announce the functional ideals of the group.

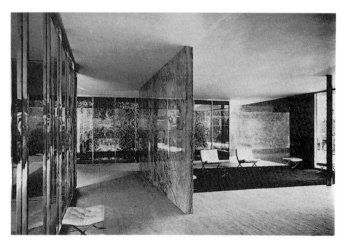

19-24 | **Ludwig Mies van der Rohe. Interior, German pavilion**
International Exposition, Barcelona, 1929

From 1930 until the Nazis closed it in 1933, the Bauhaus was directed by Ludwig Mies van der Rohe (1886–1969). Mies had a passion for realizing the subtle perfection of structure, proportion, and detail, using sumptuous materials such as travertine, richly veined marbles, tinted glass, and bronze. His abilities and interests are evident in the elegantly simple entrance pavilion to the German exhibit (fig. 19-24) that he designed for the 1929 Barcelona World's Fair. Slender piers support the floor and ceiling slabs while **curtain walls** (walls that

Elements of Architecture

THE INTERNATIONAL STYLE

After World War I, increased exchanges between modernist architects led to the development of a common formal language, transcending national boundaries, which came to be known as the International Style. The term gained wide currency as a result of a 1932 exhibition at The Museum of Modern Art in New York, "The International Style: Architecture Since 1922," organized by the architectural historian Henry-Russell Hitchcock and the architect and curator Philip Johnson. Hitchcock and Johnson identified three fundamental principles of the style.

The first principle was "the conception of architecture as volume rather than mass." The use of a structural skeleton of steel and ferroconcrete made it possible to eliminate load-bearing walls on both the exterior and interior. The building could now be wrapped in a skin of glass, metal, or masonry, creating an effect of enclosed space (volume) rather than dense material (mass). Interiors could now feature open, free-flowing plans providing maximum flexibility in the use of space.

The second principle was "regularity rather than symmetry as the chief means of ordering design." Regular distribution of structural supports and the use of standard building parts promoted rectangular regularity rather than the balanced axial symmetry of classical architecture. The avoidance of classical balance also encouraged an asymmetrical disposition of the building's components.

The third principle was the rejection of "arbitrary applied decoration." The new architecture depended upon the intrinsic elegance of its materials and the formal arrangement of its elements to produce harmonious aesthetic effects.

bear no weight but simply separate the inside from the outside or partition interior spaces) divide and enclose the spaces. Mies's design, based on the de Stijl conception of harmoniously balanced rectangles, resembles a Mondrian painting. Mies also designed furniture for the pavilion: a pair of elegantly simple, leather-cushioned, stainless-steel chairs for the king and queen of Spain to sit on during their official visit, as well as a number of stools for their entourage. Although the handmade originals were designed for ceremonial use, they were later mass-produced. The Barcelona Chair remains a status symbol in many homes and offices.

Business leaders embraced modernism in architecture. The so-called International Style seemed to epitomize the efficiency, standardization, and impersonality that had become synonymous with the modern corporation itself. But other architects and critics called for an architecture that would provide spiritual nourishment to those starved by the severity of the International Style. As early as 1900 Frank Lloyd Wright (1867–1959) advocated an "organic" approach that integrated architecture with nature. When asked what could be done to improve the modern industrial city, he bluntly responded: "Tear it down."

Wright's most famous architectural expression of his conviction that buildings ought to be a part of nature—in it, not simply

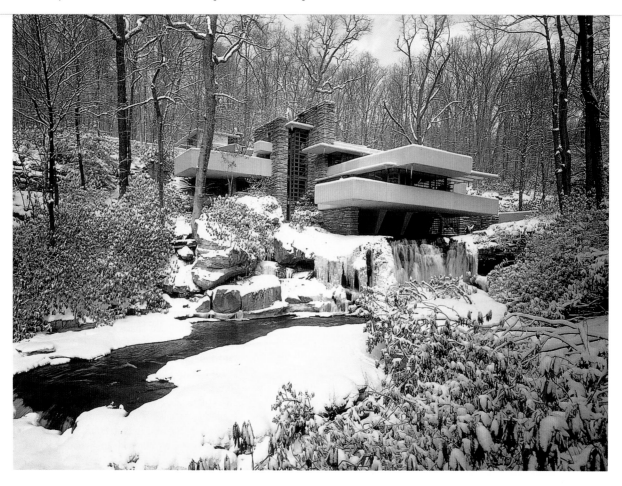

19-25

Frank Lloyd Wright. Edgar Kaufmann House, Fallingwater
Mill Run
Pennsylvania
1935–37

on it—is Fallingwater, in rural Pennsylvania (fig. 19-25). The site of this country house was notable for its waterfall and pool where the owners, the Edgar Kaufmann family, escaped to play and swim in the summer. Wright decided to build the house into the cliff over the pool, allowing the waterfall to flow around and under the house. In a daring engineering move, he **cantilevered** a series of broad terraces out from the cliffside, echoing the great slabs of rocks below. The rocks on which the family had once lounged by the waterfall became the hearthstone of the fireplace. Wright used long bands of windows and glass doors in order to offer spectacular views, uniting woods, water, and house.

DADA AND SURREALISM

Expressionist currents as well as the formalist aspects of modernism led to new styles during and after World War I. The Dada movement, which began with the opening of the Cabaret Voltaire in Zürich on February 5, 1916, was a remarkable manifestation of the disillusioned mood of the times. The cabaret's founders, the German actor and artist Hugo Ball (1886–1927) and his companion, Emmy Hennings, a nightclub singer, attracted a circle of avant-garde writers and artists who shared in Ball's and Hennings's disgust with bourgeois culture.

Ball's performance while reciting one of his sound poems, "Karawane" (fig. 19-26), reflects the spirit of the place. Ball encased his legs and body in blue cardboard tubes, and wore on his head a white-and-blue "witch-doctor's hat," as he called it. The huge gold-painted cardboard collar over his shoulders flapped when he moved his arms. Dressed in this manner, he slowly and solemnly recited the poem, which consisted entirely

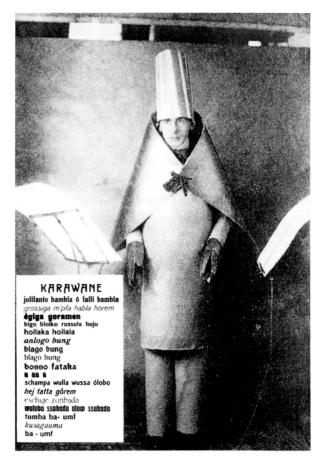

19-26 | Hugo Ball reciting the sound poem "Karawane"
Photographed at the Cabaret Voltaire, Zürich, 1916

SUPPRESSION OF THE AVANT-GARDE IN GERMANY

The 1930s in Germany witnessed a serious political reaction against avant-garde art and, eventually, a concerted effort to suppress it. One of the principal targets was the Bauhaus (see fig. 19-23), the art and design school founded in 1919 by Walter Gropius, where Paul Klee, Vasily Kandinsky, Josef Albers, Ludwig Mies van der Rohe, and many other luminaries taught. Through much of the 1920s the Bauhaus had struggled against an increasingly hostile and reactionary political climate. As early as 1924 conservatives had accused the Bauhaus of being not only educationally unsound but also politically subversive. To avoid having the school shut down by the opposition, Gropius moved it to Dessau in 1925, at the invitation of Dessau's liberal mayor, but left soon after the relocation. His successors faced increasing political pressure, as the school was a prime center of modernist practice, and the Bauhaus was again forced to move in 1932, this time to Berlin.

After Adolf Hitler came to power in 1933, the Nazi party mounted an aggressive campaign against modern art. In his youth Hitler himself had been a mediocre academic painter, and he had developed an intense hatred of the avant-garde. During the first year of his regime, the Bauhaus was forced to close for good. A number of the artists, designers, and architects who had been on its faculty—including Albers, Gropius, and Mies—immigrated to the United States.

The Nazis also launched attacks against the painters, whose often intense depictions of German soldiers defeated in World War I and the economic depression following the war were considered unpatriotic. Most of all, the treatment of the human form in these works, such as the expressionistic exaggeration of facial features, was deemed offensive. The works of these and other artists were removed from museums, while the artists themselves were subjected to public ridicule and often forbidden to buy canvas or paint.

As a final move against the avant-garde, the Nazi leadership organized in 1937 a notorious exhibition of banned works. The "Degenerate Art" exhibition was intended to erase modernism once and for all from the artistic life of the nation. Seeking to brand all the advanced movements of art as sick and degenerate, it presented modern artworks as specimens of human pathology; the organizers printed derisive slogans and comments to that effect on the gallery walls (see archival photograph, below). The 650 paintings, sculpture, prints, and books confiscated from German public museums were viewed by 2 million people in the four months the exhibition was on view in Munich and by another million during its subsequent three-year tour of German cities.

By the time World War II broke out, the authorities had confiscated countless works from all over the country. Most were publicly burned, though the Nazi officials sold much of the looted art at public auction in Switzerland to obtain foreign currency.

Among the many artists crushed by the Nazi suppression was Ernst Ludwig Kirchner, whose *Street, Berlin* (see fig. 19-5) was included in "Degenerate Art." The state's open animosity was a factor in his suicide in 1938.

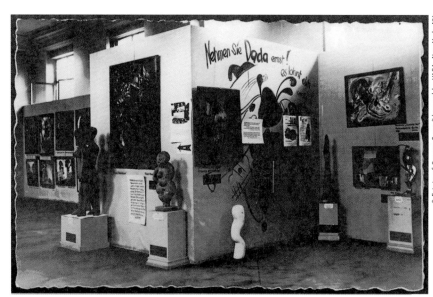

© Estate of George Grosz/Licensed by VAGA, New York, NY

Room 3 of "Degenerate Art" exhibition, Munich, 1937

of nonsense sounds. By retreating into sound alone, he avoided language, which he believed had been spoiled by the lies and excesses of journalism and advertising. But as was typical of Dada, this performance also had a playful element. Ball wanted to introduce the healthy play of children back into restricted adult lives. The flexibility of interpretation inherent in Dada extended to its name. In German the term signifies "baby talk"; in French it means "hobbyhorse;" in Russian, "yes, yes." The name and the movement could be defined as the individual wished.

The Dada movement first spread to New York and Barcelona; then to Berlin (1918), Cologne, and Paris. The leading figure in the New York group was the French artist Marcel Duchamp (1887–1968), who moved to New York in 1915. Duchamp and his friends maintained that art should appeal to the mind rather than to the senses.

Duchamp's cerebral approach is exemplified in his **readymades**, which were ordinary manufactured objects transformed into artworks simply through their selection by the artist. The most notorious readymade was the *Fountain* (fig. 19-27; see page 485), a porcelain urinal turned 90 degrees and signed with the pseudonym "R. Mutt," a play on the name of the fixture's manufacturer. Duchamp submitted the *Fountain* anonymously in 1917 to the first exhibition of the American Society of Independent Artists, open to anyone who paid a $6 entry fee. Duchamp, a founding member of the society, entered *Fountain* partly as a test. A majority of the society's directors declared that the *Fountain* was not a work of art, and, moreover, was indecent, so the piece was refused. Duchamp immediately resigned from the society.

Duchamp wrote, "The only works of art America has given are her plumbing and bridges." In a more serious vein, he added: "Whether Mr. Mutt with his own hands made the fountain or not has no importance. He CHOSE it. He took an ordinary article of life, placed it so that its useful significance disappeared under the new title and point of view—created a new thought for that

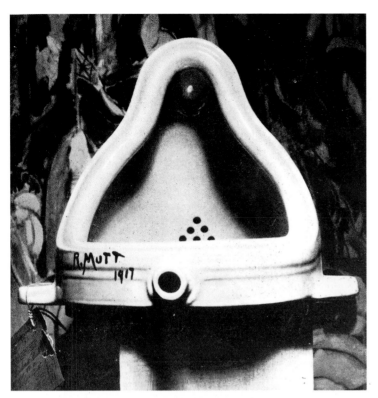

19-27 | **Marcel Duchamp.** *Fountain.* 1917. Porcelain plumbing fixture and enamel paint, height 24⁵/₈" (62.5 cm) Photographed by Alfred Stieglitz. Philadelphia Museum of Art

Louise and Walter Arensberg Collection

Stieglitz's photograph is the only known image of Duchamp's original *Fountain*, which mysteriously disappeared after it was rejected by the jury of the American Society of Independent Artists exhibition. Duchamp later produced several more versions of *Fountain* by simply buying new urinals and signing them "R. Mutt/1917."

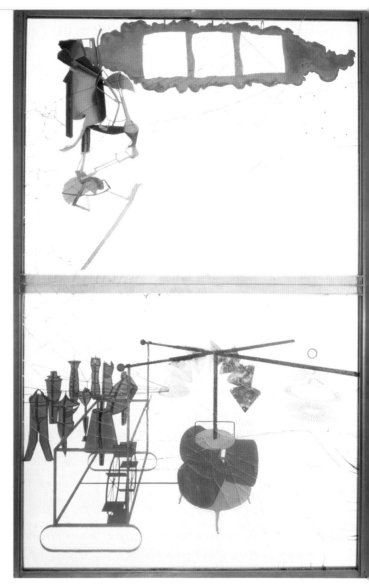

19-28 | **Marcel Duchamp.** *The Bride Stripped Bare by Her Bachelors, Even (The Large Glass).* 1915–23. Oil, varnish, lead foil, lead wire, and dust on two glass panels, 9'1¹/₄" x 5'9¹/₄"(2.77 x 1.76 m). Philadelphia Museum of Art

Bequest of Katherine S. Dreier (1952-98-1)

(See pages 466–67.)

object." Duchamp's philosophy of the readymade, succinctly expressed in these words, had a tremendous impact on later twentieth-century artists.

Duchamp's most intellectually challenging work is *The Bride Stripped Bare by Her Bachelors, Even* (fig. 19-28), also known as *The Large Glass*. Notes that Duchamp made while working on the piece confirm that it operates on several intellectual and aesthetic levels. Most fundamentally it is a pessimistic statement of the insoluble frustrations of male-female relations. Loaded with layers of irony, *The Large Glass* is also a statement about the role of chance in the creative process. For example, after sitting in storage for several years, some of the dust collected on its surface was glued permanently into place.

The successor to Dada was Surrealism, a movement founded by the French writer André Breton (1896–1966). Breton sought to free human behavior from the constrictions of reason and bourgeois morality. In 1924 he published his *Manifesto of Surrealism,* outlining his own view of Freud's theory that the human psyche is a battleground where the rational forces of the conscious mind struggle against the irrational, instinctual urges of the unconscious. Breton and his followers employed a

number of techniques for liberating the individual unconscious, including dream analysis, free association, **automatic writing**, word games, and hypnotic trances. Their aim was to help people discover the larger reality, or "surreality," that lay beyond conventional notions of what was real. Even artists such as Pablo Picasso, who was not actually part of the Surrealist group, profited from the approaches and techniques pioneered by the Surrealists. The expressive forms of *Guernica* (fig. 19-29)—fragmented, distorted, and evocative of much more than words can say—would not have been possible without the lessons of Surrealism.

Picasso created a nightmare scene of mechanized destruction coming from the heavens, as if humanity was caught in a modern-day Apocalypse. He created the mural-size painting for the Spanish Pavilion of the Paris Universal Exposition of 1937. In contrast, in the same exposition academic realism was the style

CLOSER LOOK

In April 1937, German pilots of the famous Condor Legion flying for the Spanish fascist leader General Francisco Franco bombed the Basque city of Guernica, killing more than 1,600 men, women, and children. Countries all over the globe were shocked by the world's first aerial bombing of civilians. The Spanish Civil War between Republicans and fascists had begun in 1936. Some historians, in retrospect, see this air attack as a prelude to World War II. Pablo Picasso, who was living in Paris at the time, reacted to the massacre by creating a painting (fig. 19-29) that has become a symbol of the brutality of war and humanity's struggle for freedom from oppression.

In a damning indictment of the fascists, Picasso painted *Guernica* as a stark, hallucinatory nightmare, focusing on its victims. He restricted his palette to black, gray, and white—the **tones** of the newspaper photographs that publicized the atrocity. Expressively distorted women, one holding a dead child and another in a burning house, wail in desolation at the carnage. The suffering Spanish Republic takes the form of a screaming horse, an image also taken to represent betrayed innocence. To the left is a bull, thought to symbolize either Franco or Spain. An electric light and a woman holding a lantern suggest Picasso's desire to reveal the event in all its horror.

The painting, commissioned by the short-lived Spanish Republican government for the Spanish pavilion at the world's fair in Paris in 1937, became a famous symbol of the inhumanity of fascism and war. (That same summer Hitler held the infamous exhibition of "degenerate art" in Munich; see "Suppression of the Avant-Garde in Germany," page 487.) During World War II, which Picasso spent in Paris, a Nazi officer showed him a reproduction of *Guernica* and asked, "Is that you who did that?" Picasso is said to have replied, "No, it is you."

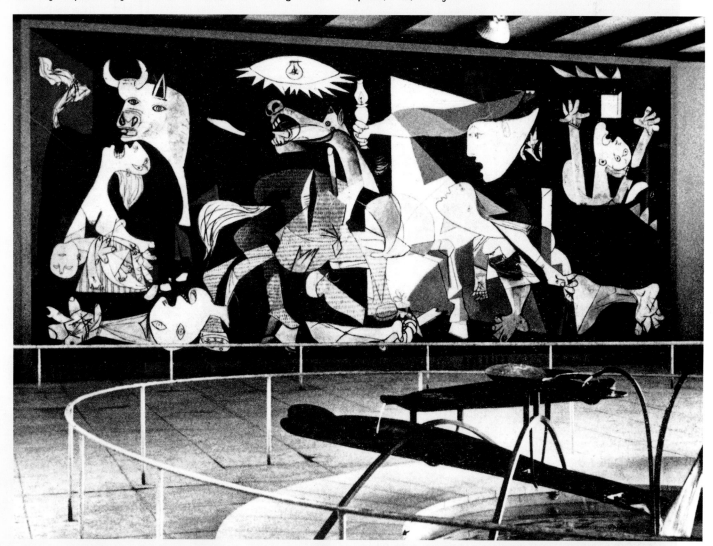

19-29 | **Pablo Picasso. *Guernica.*** 1937. Oil on canvas, 11'6" x 25'8" (3.5 x 7.8 m). Museo Nacional Centro de Arte Reina Sofía, Madrid. On permanent loan from the Museo del Prado, Madrid. Shown installed in the Spanish Pavillion of the Paris Exposition, 1937. In the foreground: Alexander Calder's *Fontaine de Mercure.* Mercury, sheet metal, wire rod, pitch, and paint, 44 x 115 x 77" (122 x 292 x 196 cm). Fundacio Joan Miró, Barcelona

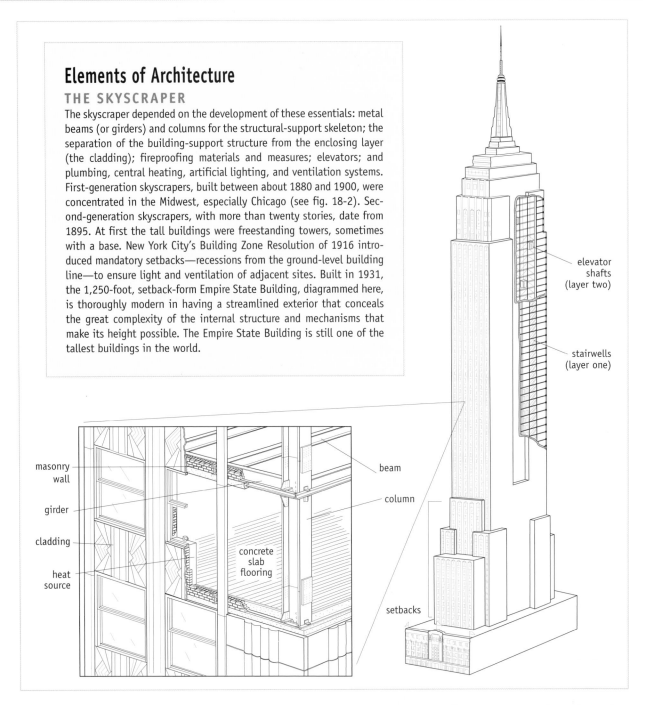

Elements of Architecture

THE SKYSCRAPER

The skyscraper depended on the development of these essentials: metal beams (or girders) and columns for the structural-support skeleton; the separation of the building-support structure from the enclosing layer (the cladding); fireproofing materials and measures; elevators; and plumbing, central heating, artificial lighting, and ventilation systems. First-generation skyscrapers, built between about 1880 and 1900, were concentrated in the Midwest, especially Chicago (see fig. 18-2). Second-generation skyscrapers, with more than twenty stories, date from 1895. At first the tall buildings were freestanding towers, sometimes with a base. New York City's Building Zone Resolution of 1916 introduced mandatory setbacks—recessions from the ground-level building line—to ensure light and ventilation of adjacent sites. Built in 1931, the 1,250-foot, setback-form Empire State Building, diagrammed here, is thoroughly modern in having a streamlined exterior that conceals the great complexity of the internal structure and mechanisms that make its height possible. The Empire State Building is still one of the tallest buildings in the world.

elevator
shafts
(layer two)

stairwells
(layer one)

masonry
wall

beam

girder

column

cladding

concrete
slab
flooring

heat
source

setbacks

of choice in the Soviet Pavilion; a factory worker with his hammer and a woman farm worker raising her sickle were represented as equal partners striding into the future. In 1944, Picasso joined the Communist Party, which later rejected his art.

Among the writers and artists around Breton was the Spanish painter and printmaker Salvador Dalí (1904–1989). Dalí contributed the "paranoiac-critical method" to Surrealist practice. In this approach, the sane man or woman cultivates the ability of the paranoiac to misread ordinary appearances

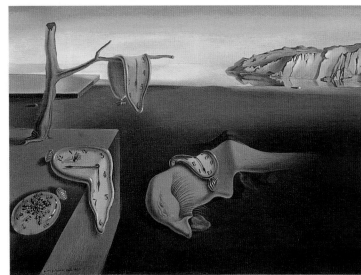

19-30 | Salvadore Dali. *Persistence of Memory*. 1931. Oil on canvas, 9½" x 13" (24.1 x 33 cm).
Museum of Modern Art, New York. (162.1934). Given anonymously

in order to free himself or herself from the shackles of conventional thought. Dalí demonstrated his method in *The Persistence of Memory* (fig. 19-30) by placing limp timepieces in a very realistic view of the Bay of Rosas near his birthplace in Catalonia.

According to Dalí, the idea of the soft watches came to him one evening after dinner while he was meditating on a plate of ripe Camembert cheese. One of the limp watches drapes over an amoebalike human head, its shape inspired by a large rock on the coast. The head, which Dalí identified as a self-portrait, appeared in several paintings and in combination with the limp watches, may express the anxiety Dalí felt concerning his own sexuality. Gala, Dalí's eventual wife, helped lessen his insecurities involving women, and later became an icon in his paintings. Another image of anxiety is the ant-covered watchcase at the lower left inspired by Dalí's childhood memories of seeing dead animals swarming with ants. Finally, Dalí chose a highly realistic style in order to make his irrational world seem more convincing and more unsettling.

In contrast, a blithe and playful spirit animates the painting of Joan Miró (1893–1983), another Catalan artist who exhibited on numerous occasions with the Surrealists, but never officially joined the group or shared its theoretical interests. In *Dutch Interior I* (fig. 19-31) Miró imaginatively paraphrased a seventeenth-century Dutch painting of a lute player serenading a young woman with a dog and cat on the floor. Miró playfully translated these elements into a **biomorphic** language of curving shapes and lines that evoke organic forms and seem to mutate before the viewer's eyes. The animated forms and cheerful colors create a giddy effect, counterbalanced by the crisply delineated shapes and tightly structured composition that reveal a high degree of formal control.

Miró gave a sense of movement to his painting, but the American sculptor Alexander Calder (1898–1976) actually introduced movement into art. Calder, an engineer, made contact with members of the Dada and Surrealist groups on visits to Paris in the 1920s and 1930s. He also visited Mondrian's studio, where he was impressed by the rectangles of colored paper that Mondrian had tacked up everywhere on the walls. What would it be like, he wondered, if the flat shapes were moving freely in space, interacting in not just two but three dimensions? The experience inspired Calder to begin creating mobiles, sculptures like his *Lobster Trap and Fish Tail* (fig. 19-32) in which the individual parts float and bob in response to shifting currents of air. At first, this mobile seems almost completely abstract, but Calder's title works on our imagination, helping us to find the oval trap awaiting unwary crustaceans at the right and the delicate wires at the left that suggest the backbone of a fish. The term *mobile*, which in French means both "moving body" and "motive," or "driving force," came from Calder's friend Marcel Duchamp, who no doubt relished the double meaning of the word.

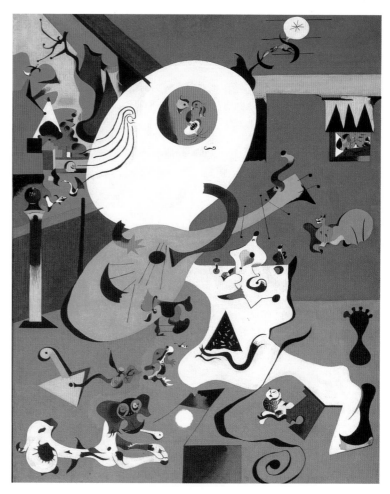

19-31 | Joan Miró. *Dutch Interior, I.* 1928. Oil on canvas, 36¹/8" x 28³/4" (91.8 x 73 cm).

The Museum of Modern Art, New York, Mrs. Simon Guggenheim Fund (163.1945)

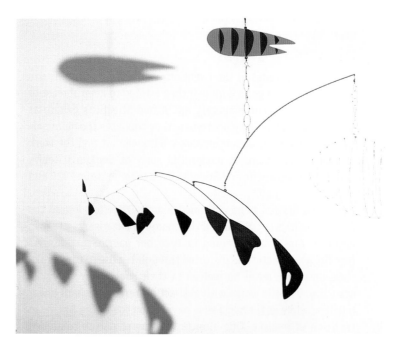

19-32 | Alexander Calder. *Lobster Trap and Fish Tail.* 1939. Hanging mobile of painted steel wire and sheet aluminum, height 8'6" (2.6 m).

The Museum of Modern Art, New York, Commissioned by the Advisory Committee for the stairwell of the Museum (590.1939.a-d)

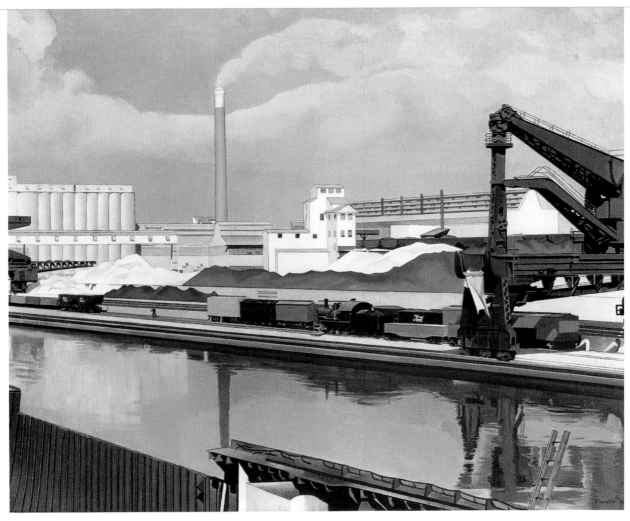

19-33 | **Charles Sheeler.** *American Landscape.* 1930. Oil on canvas 24" x 31" (61 x 78.7 cm).
The Museum of Modern Art, New York. Gift of Abby Aldrich Rockefeller (166.1934)

Art in North America Between the Wars

THE UNITED STATES

In the early decades of the twentieth century, American artists like Calder had to go to Europe if they wanted to keep abreast of developments in contemporary art. Alfred Stieglitz's gallery at 291 was one of the few places where they could see the more radical manifestations of contemporary European art and the work of pioneering American modernists such as Georgia O'Keeffe (1887–1986). O'Keeffe and Stieglitz lived together from 1920 and were married in 1924.

In her drawings and paintings Georgia O'Keeffe adopted the formal qualities of Cubism and the energy of Futurism to her own vision of America. Beginning in 1924 her paintings of flowers (see fig. 4), gigantic and distorted through her use of cameralike close-up views, recall Surrealism in their suggestion of female sexuality. O'Keeffe works with abstract patterns and sharp linear qualities while at the same time paying homage to the American tradition of realism. This intense scrutiny of nature combined with the use of the close-up also inspired the work of photographer Edward Weston (see fig. 3).

After World War I the United States entered a period of isolationism that lasted until the Japanese bombing of Pearl Harbor in 1941. In the 1920s and 1930s, the majority of American artists returned to realism and to paintings that chronicled American life. Urban and industrial subjects attracted the new realists who were inspired by photography, which during these same decades took as a subject the clean, abstract geometries of the factory and skyscraper.

A group of painters calling themselves Precisionists worked with simplified forms, crisply defined edges, smooth brushwork, and unmodulated colors. Although O'Keeffe shared important thematic and formal similarities with the work of the Precisionists she never claimed to be part of the group. The leading Precisionist artist was Charles Sheeler (1883–1965), who often based his paintings on his own photographs, many of which were made on commercial assignment. In 1927 Sheeler photographed the new Ford Motor Company plant at River Rouge, outside Detroit, Michigan. In 1930 he used the background of one of these photographs to make *American Landscape* (fig. 19-33), a panoramic scene of the River Rouge boat slip, ore storage bins, and cement plant that tells, among other things, about the transformation of raw materials into industrial goods. The title suggests that Sheeler was responding to the popular viewpoint that such factories demonstrated America's optimism in mechanization and belief in a better

19-34

Grant Wood.
American Gothic
1930. Oil on
beaverwood
29⁷/₈ x 24⁷/₈"
(74.3 x 62.4 cm)
The Art Institute
of Chicago

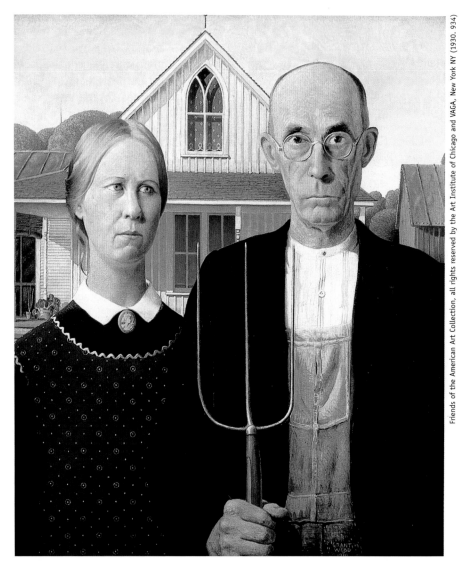

future. That he painted the work a year after the great stock-market crash of 1929, which began the Great Depression, suggests that the painting may be a testament to Sheeler's continuing faith in American industry and in its fundamental stability.

Sheeler's focus on a recognizable American subject, painted in a realistic style, allies his work to a broader tendency known as American Scene Painting, which flourished during the Great Depression. Struggling through economic distress and the agricultural catastrophe of the Dust Bowl, Americans turned their attention inward. Artists followed suit by painting indigenous subjects in an accessible realist style. American Scene painters energetically documented the lives and circumstances of the American people and the American land. While some produced images that confronted the depressed conditions of the present, others celebrated the myths and traditions of the American past or crafted optimistic images to provide hope for the future.

A generally optimistic attitude pervades the work of the Regionalists, a group of Midwestern American Scene painters led by Grant Wood (1891–1942) of Iowa, who focused on the farms and small-town life of the American heartland. Wood's *American Gothic* (fig. 19-34) is usually understood as a picture of a hus-

band and wife but was actually meant to show an aging Iowa farmer and his unmarried daughter (posed by Wood's dentist and sister). Wood pictures the stony-faced couple standing in front of their house, built in a Victorian style known as "Carpenter Gothic," which suggests the importance of religion in their lives. The farmer's pitchfork signifies his occupation while giving him a somewhat menacing air. The woman is associated with potted plants, seen behind her right shoulder, which symbolize traditionally feminine domestic and horticultural skills. Wood considered his painting to be a sincerely affectionate portrayal of the small-town Iowans he had grown up with—conservative, provincial, religious Midwesterners, descendants of the pioneers.

In spite of the largely positive visions of the Regionalists, the economic hardships of the Great Depression meant that many farmers faced bankruptcy, and rural regions suffered great poverty. In 1935, a newly established government agency, the Farm Securities Administration (FSA), began to hire photographers to document the problems of farmers and migrant workers. Dorothea Lange (1895–1965) played a major role in the formation of the FSA photography program. As a freelance photographer in San Francisco, Lange was touched by the struggles of the city's poor and unemployed, and she began to photograph their

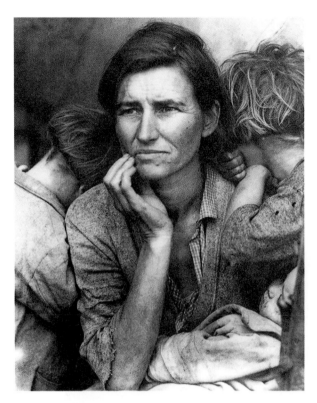

19-35 | Dorothea Lange. *Migrant Mother, Nipomo California.* February 1936. Gelatin-silver print Library of Congress, Washington, D.C.

plight. In 1934 she collaborated on a report on migrant farm laborers in California, which helped persuade state officials to build migrant labor camps. Her photographs influenced the federal government to include a photographic unit in the FSA, and Lange was hired as one of the unit's first photographers in 1935. Her most famous photograph is *Migrant Mother, Nipomo, Califor-*

nia (fig. 19-35). The woman in the picture is Florence Thompson, a thirty-two-year-old mother of ten children. Drawn and prematurely aged, she gazes past the viewer into an uncertain future. The fears of all disenfranchised people, perpetually shunted to the margins of society, seem crystallized in her worried face.

THE HARLEM RENAISSANCE

During World War I thousands of African Americans left the rural South for jobs in northern defense plants. The Great Migration, as it is known, created racial tensions over housing and employment that in turn fostered a concern for the rights of African Americans. African-American writers, artists, and musicians explored black experience and identity in what became known as the Harlem Renaissance. The intellectual Alain Locke, an influential voice in the 1920s Harlem Renaissance, encouraged younger black artists and writers to seek their contemporary cultural identity in their African and African-American heritage. In a 1925 essay titled "The New Negro" Locke urged for the transformation from older and negative models of the American black to one embracing a "new psychology" and "new spirit."

The first black artist to answer Locke's call was Aaron Douglas (1898–1979), a native of Topeka, Kansas, who moved to New York City in 1925 and rapidly developed an abstract style influenced by African art as well as the contemporary, hard-edged aesthetic of Art Deco (see "'Primitivism' and Modernity," page 470). In paintings such as *Aspects of Negro Life: From Slavery Through Reconstruction* (fig. 19-36), Douglas used schematic figures, silhouetted in profile with the eye rendered frontally as in ancient Egyptian art. He limited his palette to a few subtle hues, varying in value from light to dark and sometimes organized abstractly into concentric bands that suggest musical rhythms or spiritual emanations. This work, painted for the 135th Street

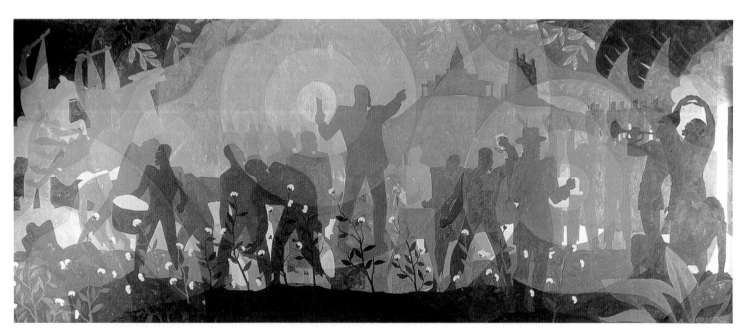

19-36 | Aaron Douglas. *Aspects of Negro Life: From Slavery Through Reconstruction.* 1934. Oil on canvas, 5' x 10'8" (1.5 x 3.25 m). Schomburg Center for Research in Black Culture, New York Public Library, Astor, Lenox, and Tilden Foundations

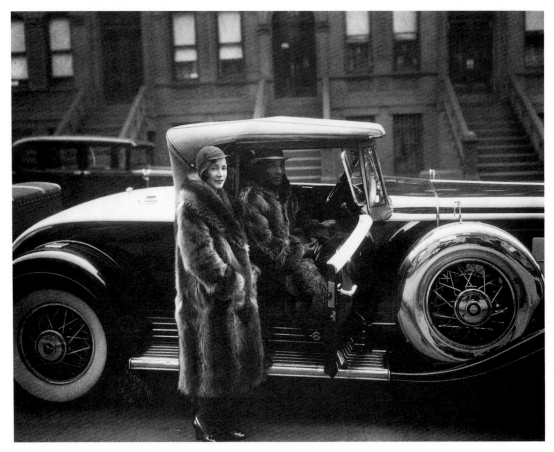

19-37 | James VanDerZee. Detail of *Couple Wearing Raccoon Coats with a Cadillac, Taken on West 127th Street, Harlem, New York.* 1932. Gelatin silver print

branch of the New York Public Library under the sponsorship of the Public Works of Art Project, was intended to awaken in African Americans a sense of their place in history. At the right, they celebrate the Emancipation Proclamation of 1863, which freed the slaves. Concentric circles issue from the Proclamation, which is read by a figure in the foreground. At the center of the composition, an orator, symbolizing black leaders of the Reconstruction era, urges black freed men, some still picking cotton, to cast their ballots, while he points to a silhouette of the U.S. Capitol on a distant hill. Concentric circles highlight the ballot in his hand. In the background the fearsome Ku Klux Klan, hooded and on horseback, invades from the left while at the right a jazz trumpeter heralds freedom. The heroic orator at the center of Douglas's panel remains the focus of the composition, inspiring contemporary viewers to continue the struggle for equality.

Like Douglas, photographer James VanDerZee (1886–1983) created positive images, as opposed to stereotypes, of African Americans that conveyed the sense of racial pride and social empowerment promoted by the "New Negro" movement. The largely self-taught VanDerZee maintained a studio in Harlem for nearly fifty years and specialized in portraits of the neighborhood's middle- and upper-class residents. His best-known photograph, *Couple Wearing Raccoon Coats with a Cadillac, Taken on*

West 127th Street, Harlem, New York (fig. 19-37), depicts the ideal "New Negro" man and woman: prosperous, confident, and cosmopolitan, thriving and living glamorously even in the midst of the Depression.

MEXICO

Prominent in the new Mexican mural movement was Diego Rivera (1886–1957), who had been living in Paris painting in the Synthetic Cubist style. In 1920–21 Rivera traveled in Italy to study the great frescoes of the Renaissance. On his return to Mexico he painted a series of monumental murals for Mexican government buildings, inspired by both Italian Renaissance art and the Pre-Columbian art of Mexico. In 1932 the Rockefeller family commissioned Rivera to paint a mural for the lobby of the RCA Building in Rockefeller Center in New York City on the theme "Man at the Crossroads Looking with Hope and High Vision to the Choosing of a New and Better Future." When Rivera, a Communist, provocatively included a portrait of Lenin in the mural, the Rockefellers canceled his commission, paid him his fee, and had the unfinished mural destroyed. In response to what he called an "act of cultural vandalism," Rivera re-created the mural in the Palacio de Bellas Artes in Mexico City, under the new title *Man, Controller of the Universe*

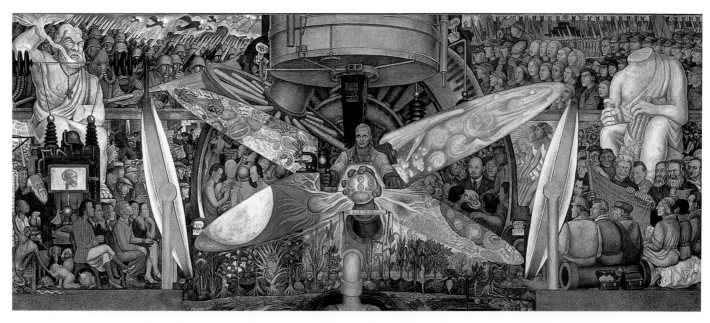

19-38 | **Diego Rivera. *Man, Controller of the Universe.*** 1934. Fresco, 15'9¹/₈" x 37'2¹/₂" (4.85 x 11.45 m). Museum del Palacio de Bellas Artes Mexico City

19-39

Frida Kahlo
The Two Fridas
1939. Oil on
canvas 5'8¹/₂" x
5'8¹/₂" (1.74 x
1.74 m) Museo de
Arte Moderno
Instituto Nacional
de Bellas Artes
Mexico City

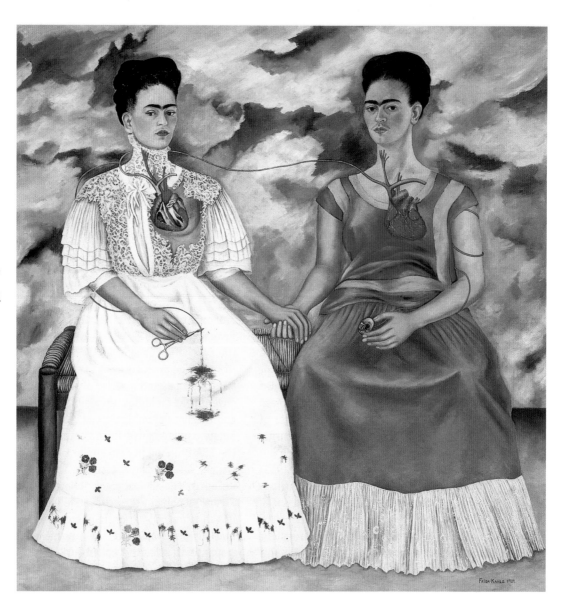

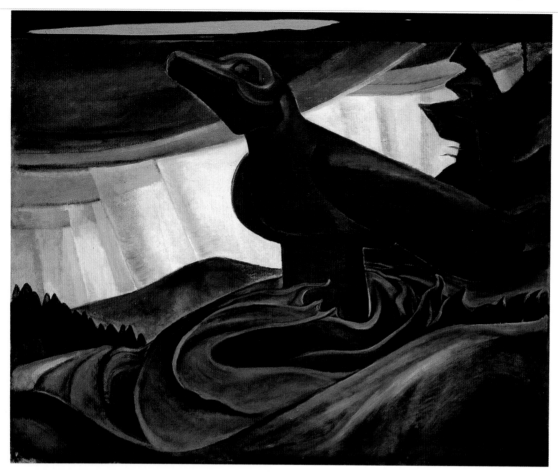

(fig. 19-38). At the center of the mural, a figure in overalls represents Man, who symbolically controls the universe through technology. Crossing behind him are two great ellipses that represent, respectively, the microcosm of living organisms as seen through the microscope at Man's right hand, and the macrocosm of outer space as viewed through the giant telescope above his head. Below, fruits and vegetables rise from the earth as a result of his agricultural efforts. To the viewer's right, Lenin joins the hands of several workers of different races; at the left, decadent capitalists debauch themselves in a nightclub. Rivera vengefully included in this section a portrait of the bespectacled John D. Rockefeller, Jr. At the sides of the mural Rivera contrasts the peaceful socialist workers with the militarism and labor unrest of the capitalist world.

While Rivera and other muralists painted public messages, other Mexican artists made more private, introspective statements through the medium of easel painting. André Breton claimed Frida Kahlo (1910–1954) to be a natural Surrealist, although she herself said: "I never painted dreams. I painted my own reality." That reality included her mixed German and Mexican ancestry. In *The Two Fridas* (fig. 19-39), Kahlo presented her two ethnic selves: the European one, in a Victorian dress, and the Mexican one, wearing a traditional Mexican skirt and blouse. The painting also reflects her stormy relationship with Diego Rivera. The two married in 1929 but were in the process of obtaining a divorce when Kahlo was painting *The Two Fridas* in 1939. She told an art historian at the time that the European image was the Frida whom Diego loved and the Mexican image was the Frida he did not. The two Fridas join hands and are linked by an artery

running between them. The artery begins at a miniature of Rivera as a boy held by the Mexican Frida and ends in the lap of the Europeanized Frida, who attempts without success to stem the flow of blood.

CANADA

The Bristish Columbian artist Emily Carr (1871–1945) lived in Vancouver, where she taught art and became a founding member of the British Columbia Society of Art. On a 1907 trip to Alaska she first saw the monumental carved poles of Northwest Coast Native Americans and resolved to document these "real art treasures of a passing race." Over the next twenty-three years Carr visited more than thirty native village sites across British Columbia, making drawings and watercolors, which became the basis for oil paintings.

As her art matured Carr developed a dramatic and powerfully sculptural style full of dark and brooding energy. An impressive example of such work is *Big Raven* (fig. 19-40), which Carr painted in 1931, based on a watercolor she made in 1912 in an abandoned village in the Queen Charlotte Islands. She had discovered a carved raven raised on a pole, the surviving member of a pair that had marked a mortuary house. In her autobiography Carr described the raven as "old and rotting," but in her painting the bird appears strong and majestic, thrusting dynamically above the swirling vegetation, a symbol of enduring spiritual power. Through its focus on a Native American artifact set in a recognizably northwestern Canadian landscape, Carr's *Big Raven* may be interpreted as an assertion of national pride comparable to the paintings of the Mexican muralists and the Harlem Renaissance.

"Cattle die. Kinfolk die. We all die. Only fame lasts," said the Vikings. Names remain. Polished black granite walls inscribed with thousands of names, reflect back the images of the living as they contemplate the memorial to the Vietnam War's (1965–73) dead and missing veterans. The idea is brilliant in its simplicity. The artist, Maya Ying Lin (b. 1960), combined two basic ideas: the minimal grandeur of long black granite walls and row upon row of names—the abstract and the intimate conjoined. The power of Maya Ying Lin's monument lies in its understatement. Flat, dark polished stone is engraved with the names of the dead—names so numerous that they lose individuality and become a surface texture. The wall is a statement of loss, sorrow, and the futility of war. Like a black mirror, it reflects back shadowy images of the mourners. It is a timeless monument to suffering humanity, faceless in sacrifice. Maya Ying Lin said, "The point is to see yourself reflected in the names."

One wall points to and reflects the George Washington Monument (constructed 1848–84). Robert Mills, the architect of many public buildings at the beginning of the nineteenth century, chose the obelisk, the time-honored Egyptian sun symbol, for his memorial to the nation's founder. The other wall leads the eye to the Neoclassical Lincoln Memorial. By incorporating the Washington and Lincoln monuments into the design, Lin's *Vietnam Veterans Memorial* reminds the viewer of sacrifices made in defense of liberty throughout America's history.

Until the modern era, most public art celebrated and commemorated political and social leaders and aspects of war: officers and soldiers—both victorious and slain—in large, freestanding monuments. The motives of those who have commissioned public art have ranged from civic pride, to the wish to honor heroes, to political propaganda, and social intimidation. Maya Ying Lin's memorial in Washington, D.C. to the American men and women who died in or never returned from the Vietnam War is among the most visited works of public art of the twenty-first century and is certainly among the most affecting war monuments ever conceived. As art critic Michael Kimmelman wrote in *The New York Times* (January 13, 2002, page 37), "Good art outlasts the events that prompted the artists to make it."

Maya Ying Lin. *Vietnam Veterans Memorial.* 1982. Black granite, length 500' (152 m). The Mall, Washington D.C. (See pages 525–26.)

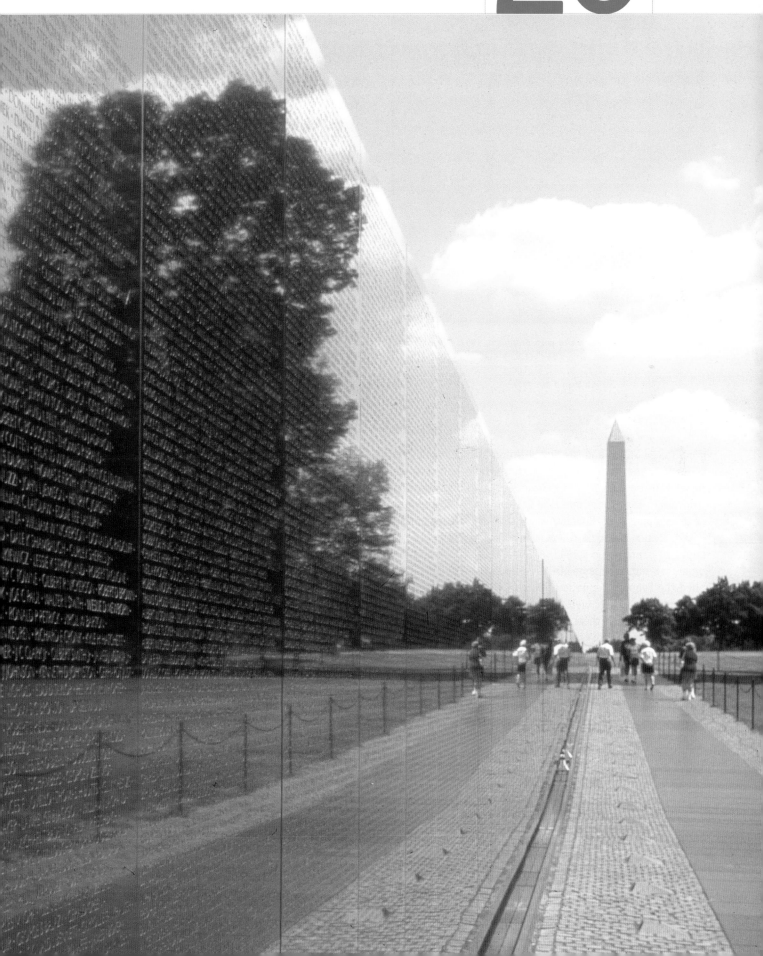

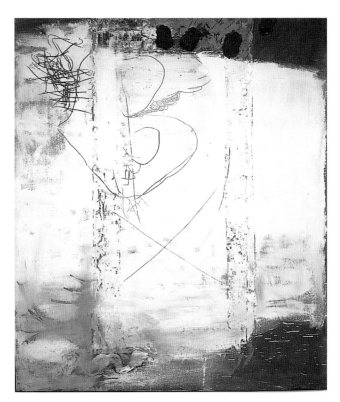

20-1 | Antoni Tàpies. *White with Graphism.* 1957. Mixed media on canvas, 6'3⁷/₈" x 5'8³/₄" (1.93 x 1.75 m). Washington University Gallery of Art, St. Louis, Missouri
Gift of Mr. and Mrs. Richard Weil, 1963

The United States and the Soviet Union emerged from World War II as the world's most powerful nations and soon were engaged in the Cold War. The Soviets set up Communist governments in Eastern Europe (the Eastern bloc) and supported the development of Communism elsewhere. Meanwhile the United States, through financial aid and political support, sought to contain the spread of Communism. A second huge Communist nation emerged in 1949 when Mao Tse-tung established the People's Republic of China. While the Soviet Union and the United States vied for world leadership, the old European states gave up their empires. The British led the way by withdrawing from India in 1947. Other European nations gradually granted independence to colonies in Asia and Africa (see Map 7, page 529).

In the 1980s, the Communist stronghold in Eastern Europe began to loosen and was virtually gone by 1990, effectively ending the Cold War. Formerly Communist republics turned to capitalism and many sought democratic reforms on social, economic, and political levels. This global capitalism increased the economic interdependence among all nations, and wealthy countries like the United States saw increasing prosperity. Despite this growth, the world seems smaller, thanks to remarkable advances in transportation and communication, including the Internet. With enhanced global communication has come increased awareness of the many grave problems that confront us at the dawn of the twenty-first century.

The "Mainstream" Crosses the Atlantic

The United States' stature after World War II as the most powerful democratic nation was soon reflected in the arts. American artists and architects assumed leadership in artistic innovation which by the late 1950s was acknowledged across the Atlantic, even in Paris. This dominance endured until around 1970, when the belief in the existence of an identifiable mainstream, or single dominant line of artistic development, began to wane (see "The Idea of the Mainstream," page 503).

Although realism dominated American art in the period between the two world wars, some artists of the period maintained an interest in the nonrepresentational styles of European art. In the 1930s ground-breaking exhibitions at The Museum of Modern Art in New York promoted European avant-garde art and so helped to pave the way for Abstract Expressionism, the dominant style of the late 1940s and 1950s in the United States.

America's living link with the modernist tradition in Europe was Hans Hofmann (1880–1966), a German-born teacher and painter who had come to the United States before World War II. The rise of fascism in Europe and the outbreak of World War II stranded people like Hofmann and led a number of prominent European artists and writers to move to the United States. By 1940 André Breton, Salvador Dalí, and Piet Mondrian were all living in New York. Although many of the émigrés kept to themselves, their very presence provoked fruitful discussions among American abstract artists.

After the war, in Europe the most distinctive approach to painting was called *art informel* ("formless" art) or Lyrical Abstraction or *tachisme* (*tache*, "spot" or "stain"). The artists reasoned that since the two world wars had discredited all notions of humanity as reasonable, they as artists had the duty to invent a new and more authentic concept of our species. They believed they were able to do so by returning to the origins of art as expressed in the simple, honest mark. One of the many artists who participated in this movement was the Catalan painter Antoni Tàpies (b. 1923). In works such as *White with Graphism* (fig. 20-1), he attempted to recover the primordial language of art with crudely drawn and incised marks on a white ground that recalled a prehistoric cave wall. Tàpies did not mean to communicate a particular message but rather to record the fundamental human urge for self-expression. In 1953, when he visited New York, he found that American artists were taking similar approaches to their art.

In New York, American artists, deeply affected by the ideas of Surrealism and the teaching of Hans Hofmann, began working in a style collectively called Abstract Expressionism. This term designates a wide variety of work produced between 1940 and roughly 1960. By the late 1940s, two major approaches to

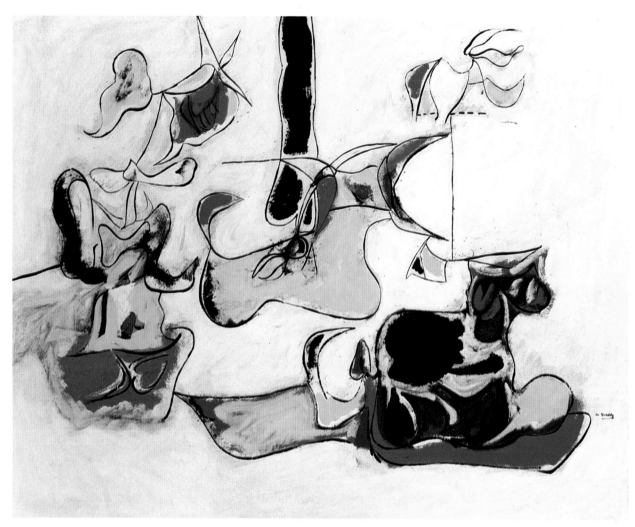

20-2 | **Arshile Gorky.** *Garden in Sochi.* c. 1943. Oil on canvas, 31 x 39" (78.7 x 99.1 cm). The Museum of Modern Art, New York
Acquired through the Lillie P. Bliss Bequest

abstract art emerged: action painting, or gesturalism, characterized by active paint handling, and Color Field painting, distinguished by broad sweeping fields of color. Because not all Abstract Expressionist work was either abstract or expressionistic, some art historians prefer to refer to the art simply as the New York School (see "The Idea of the Mainstream," page 503).

The Abstract Expressionists took from the Surrealists both a commitment to examining the unconscious and techniques for doing so. But whereas the European Surrealists had derived their notion of the unconscious from Sigmund Freud, many of the Americans subscribed to the thinking of Swiss psychoanalyst Carl Jung (1875–1961). His theory of the "collective unconscious" holds that beneath one's private memories is a storehouse of feelings and symbolic associations common to all humans.

One of the first artists to bring these influences together was Arshile Gorky (1904–1948), who was born in Armenia and emigrated to the United States in 1920. Converging in Gorky's mature work were his childhood memories of Armenia, his interest in Surrealism, and his attraction to Jungian ideas. These factors came together in the early 1940s in three paintings inspired by his memories of his father's garden in Sochi (fig. 20-2). In the

garden was a magical rock and a "Holy Tree" (the out-of-scale yellow shoes below the tree may refer to a pair of slippers his father gave him). Knowledge of autobiographical details is not necessary, however, for the fluid, **biomorphic** forms—derived from Miró (see fig. 19-31)—suggest vital life forces and signal Gorky's evocation of a universal, unconscious identification with the earth.

The most famous of the Jung-inspired Abstract Expressionists was the action painter Jackson Pollock (1912–1956). Undergoing Jungian analysis between 1939 and 1941, the alcoholic and self-destructive artist made little progress with his personal problems. The sessions greatly affected his work, however, giving him a new vocabulary of signs and symbols and a belief in the therapeutic role of art in society.

In the mid-1940s, Pollock replaced Jungian painted symbols with freely applied paint, working on large canvases spread out on the floor. He began to employ enamel house paints along with conventional oils sometime in the winter of 1946–47, dripping them onto his canvases with sticks and brushes using a variety of fluid arm and wrist movements. The result over the next four years was a series of graceful linear abstractions such as *Autumn*

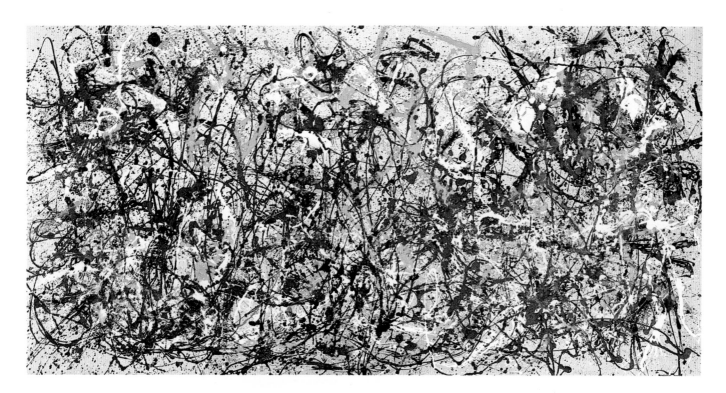

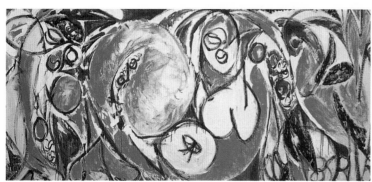

20-3 | (*above*) **Jackson Pollock. *Autumn Rhythm (Number 30)***
1950. Oil on canvas, 8'9" x 17'3" (2.66 x 5.25 m). The
Metropolitan Museum of Art, New York
George A. Hearn Fund, 1957 (57.92)

20-4 | (*left*) **Lee Krasner. *The Seasons.*** 1957. Oil on canvas
7'8³⁄₄" x 16'11³⁄₄" (2.36 x 5.18 m). Whitney Museum
of Art, New York
Purchased with funds from Frances and Sydney Lewis (by exchange),
the Mrs. Percy Uris Purchase Fund, and the Painting and Sculpture
Committee

Rhythm (Number 30) (fig. 20-3). Delicate skeins of paint effortlessly loop over and under one another in a mesmerizing pattern without beginning or end that spreads evenly across the surface of the canvas. As the titles of this and others of his paintings suggest, Pollock seems to have felt that in the free, unselfconscious act of painting he was giving vent to primal, natural forces.

In 1945 Pollock married Lee Krasner (1908–1984), a member of the original American Abstract Artists group and Hofmann's student. When Krasner began living with Pollock in 1942, she virtually stopped painting in order to devote herself to the conventional role of a supportive wife. Despite marital problems caused by Pollock's alcoholism, she continued to create significant works. After Pollock's death in an automobile crash in 1956, Krasner took over his studio and during the next year and a half produced a dazzling group of monumental gestural paintings (fig. 20-4), painted in bold sweeping curves that express not only her grief but also her identification with the forces of nature suggested by the bursting rounded forms.

In contrast to Pollock, who said that he found "pure harmony" when at work on his drip paintings, his contemporary Willem de

Kooning (1904–1997) insisted, "Art never seems to make me peaceful or pure." De Kooning was born in the Netherlands and immigrated to the United States in 1926. After a period of painting in a nonrepresentational mode, he shocked the New York art world in the early 1950s by returning to the figure with a series of paintings of women. The first of the series, *Woman I* (fig. 20-5), took him almost two years to paint. His wife, the artist Elaine de Kooning (1918–1989), said that he painted it, scraped it, and repainted it at least several dozen times. Part of de Kooning's dissatisfaction stemmed from the way his figure, inspired by conventionally pretty images of women seen in American advertising, kept veering away from those models. What emerges in *Woman I* is not the elegant companion of Madison Avenue fantasy but a powerful adversary, more dangerous than alluring. Only the soft pastel colors and luscious paint surface give any hint of de Kooning's original sources, and these qualities are nearly lost in the furious slashing of the paint.

De Kooning was committed to the highest level of aesthetic achievement historically set by great Western painters, and his paintings were a carefully orchestrated buildup of interwoven strokes and planes of color based largely on the example of

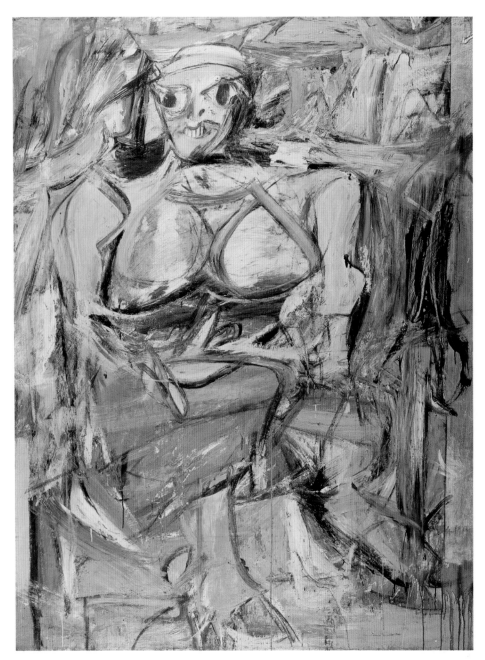

20-5

Willem de Kooning.
Woman I. 1950-52.
Oil on canvas, 6'3⁷/₈"
x 4'10".

The Museum of Modern
Art, New York. Purchase
(238.1948)

THE IDEA OF THE MAINSTREAM

A central conviction of modernist artists, critics, and art historians has been the existence of an artistic mainstream, the notion that some artworks are more important than others—not by virtue of their aesthetic quality but because they participate in the progressive unfolding of some larger historical purpose. This type of art has been extolled as representative of "high culture." According to this view, the overall evolutionary pattern is what confers value, and any art that does not fit within it, regardless of its appeal, can be for the most part ignored (see "The High/Low Myth of Modernism," page 506).

The first significant discussions of what constituted the modernist mainstream emerged after World War II, shaped by the critical writings of Clement Greenberg (1909–1994). Greenberg argued that modern art since Édouard Manet (see Chapter 18) involved the progressive disappearance of narrative, figuration, and pictorial space because art itself—regardless of what artists may have thought they were doing—was undergoing a "process of self-purification" in reaction to a deteriorating civilization.

Greenberg was famous for identifying Abstract Expressionism as the dominant style of the late 1940s and 1950s and championed the New York School of painting. Inspired in part by the artist Hans Hofmann's teaching, he demanded close analysis of the work of art and judgments based on visual perception alone—a methodology called **formalism** or formal analysis. However, belief in the concept of the mainstream gradually eroded; the reaction against Greenberg began in the 1970s. Because Greenbergian formalism omitted so much of the history of recent art, observers began questioning whether a single, dominant mainstream had ever existed. The extraordinary proliferation of art styles and trends after the 1960s greatly contributed to those doubts.

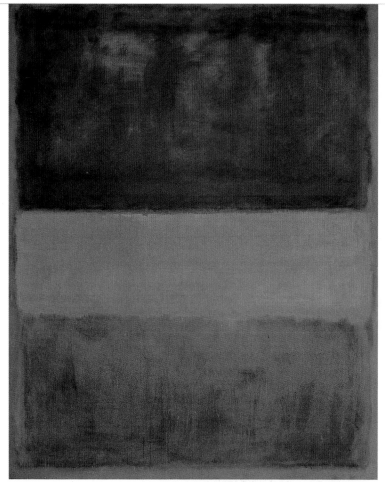

20-6 | **Mark Rothko.** *Brown, Blue, Brown on Blue.* 1953. Oil on canvas, 9'7¾" x 7'7¼" (2.97 x 2.34 m). The Museum of Contemporary Art, Los Angeles
The Panza Collection

Analytic Cubism (see figs. 19-9, 19-10). "Liquefied Cubism" is the way one art historian described them. The deeper roots of de Kooning's work, however, lie in the coloristic tradition of artists such as Titian and Rubens, who superbly transformed flesh into paint.

During the 1950s, de Kooning dominated the avant-garde in New York. Among the handful of modernist painters who resisted his influence was Mark Rothko (1903–1970), a pioneering Color Field painter who used large rectangles of color to evoke transcendent emotional states. In works such as *Brown, Blue, Brown on Blue* (fig. 20-6), Rothko consciously sought a profound harmony between the two divergent human tendencies that German philosopher Friedrich Nietzsche (1844–1900) called the Dionysian (after the Greek god of wine, the harvest, and inspiration) and the Apollonian (after the Greek god of light, music, and truth). The painting's rich color is its Dionysian element, the emotional and instinctive side of human nature, while the simple compositional structure underlying the coloristic virtuosity is its rational and disciplined Apollonian counterpart. Together they form a deeply satisfying unity, which hints at a momentary resolution of our fundamental human duality.

Elements from Color Field paintings like Rothko's intermingled with the gesturalism of action painting in the work of Helen Frankenthaler (b. 1928). Frankenthaler, like Pollock, worked on the floor, drawn to what she described as Pollock's "dancelike use of arms and legs." She produced a huge canvas, *Mountains and Sea* (fig. 20-7), in this way, working from watercolor sketches she had made in Nova Scotia. Instead of using thick, full-bodied paint, as Pollock did, Frankenthaler thinned her oils and applied them in washes that soaked into the raw canvas, producing an effect that resembles watercolor but also evokes Color Field painting. A few delicate contour lines suggest not only the mountains of the painting's title but also less translatable, dream-inspired Surrealistic forms.

The New York School also included talented sculptors such as David

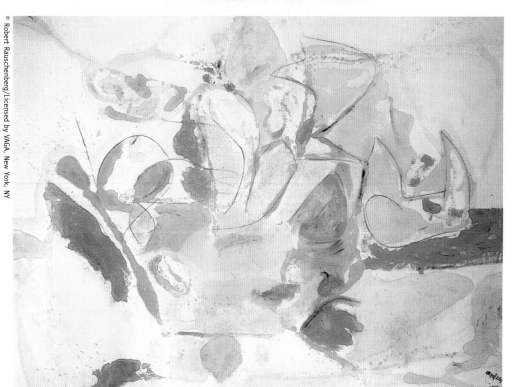

20-7 | **Helen Frankenthaler.** *Mountains and Sea.* 1952. Oil on canvas, 7'2¾" x 9'8¼" (2.20 x 2.95 m)
Collection of the artist on extended loan to the National Gallery of Art, Washington, D.C.

Smith (1906–1965). Smith learned metalworking as a welder and riveter at an automobile plant in his native Indiana. During the last five years of his life, Smith turned to formalism—a shift partly inspired by his discovery of stainless steel. Smith explored both the relative lightness and the beauty of steel's polished sur-

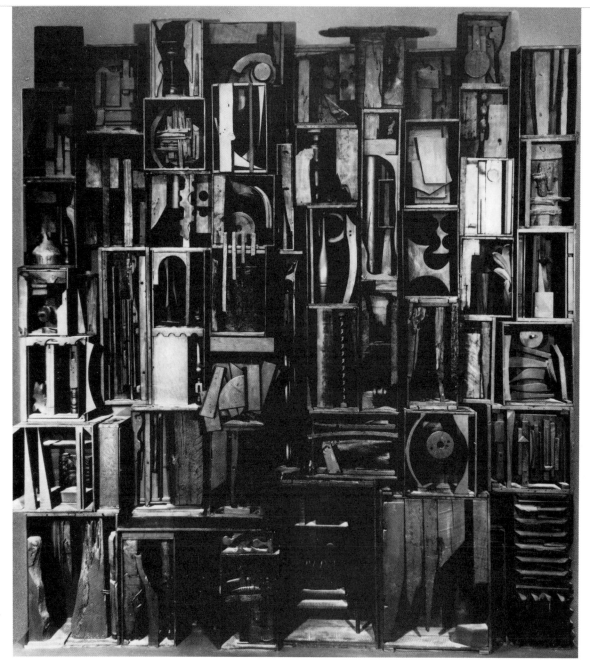

20-8

Louise Nevelson
Sky Cathedral
1958. Assemblage
of wood construction
painted black
11'3½" x 10'1¼" x
18" (3.44 m x 3.05
m x 45.7 cm). The
Museum of Modern
Art, New York
Gift of Mr. and Mrs.
Ben Mildwoff

faces in the Cubi series, monumental combinations of geometric units inspired by and offering homage to the formalism of Cubism. Like the Analytic Cubist works of Braque and Picasso, *Cubi XIX* (see fig. 5) presents a finely tuned balance of elements that, though firmly welded together, seem ready to collapse at the slightest provocation. The viewer's aesthetic pleasure depends on this tension and on the dynamic curvilinear patterns formed by the play of light over the sculpture's burnished surfaces. The *Cubi* works were meant to be seen outdoors, not only because of the effect of sunlight but also because of the way natural shapes and colors complement their inorganic form.

ASSEMBLAGE AND POP ART

By the end of the 1950s, many artists and critics were ready for a change from Abstract Expressionism. One alternative path was **assemblage**, that is, putting together disparate elements to construct a work of art. By 1950 Louise Nevelson

(1899–1988) had developed a Cubist-inspired version of assemblage that prefigured the Minimalist (stripped to essentials) focus on formal concerns. Prowling the streets of downtown Manhattan, she collected discarded packing boxes in which she would carefully arrange chair legs, broom handles, cabinet doors, spindles, and other wooden refuse. She painted her assemblages a matte black, both to obscure the identity of the individual elements and to integrate them formally.

After stacking several of these boxes together against a studio wall, Nevelson realized that the resulting accumulation made a more powerful effect than the individual units. One of her first monumental wall assemblages was *Sky Cathedral* (fig. 20-8). What she particularly liked about the new schema was the way it could transform ordinary space into another, higher realm— just as the prosaic elements she worked with had themselves been transformed into something finer. In order to complete this process, and to add a further poetic dimension, Nevelson first

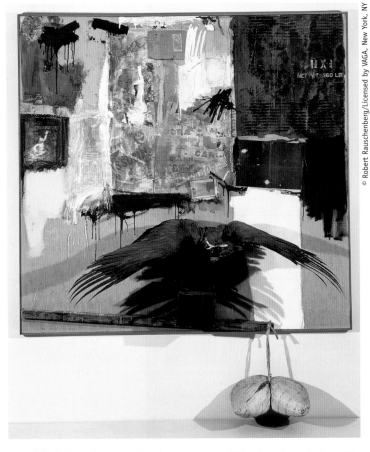

20-9 | **Robert Rauschenberg.** *Canyon.* 1959. Combine painting with oil, pencil, paper, metal, photograph, fabric, wood, on canvas, plus buttons, mirror, stuffed eagle, cardboard box, pillow, paint tube. 81³⁄₈" x 70 x 24".
Courtesy Sonnabend, New York. Baltimore Museum of Art. © Robert Rauschenberg/Licensed by VAGA, New York, NY

Avant-garde critics were not bothered by the fact that much of Rauschenberg's and the other assemblers' materials were drawn from popular culture. Many of the early-twentieth-century collagists, including Picasso and Braque, had worked with similar materials. However, critics such as Hilton Kramer (at *The New York Times*) and Thomas Hess (at *Artnews*) pointed out that whereas earlier artists had aesthetically coordinated such elements, transforming the crude materials of life into the finer ones of art, Rauschenberg and his associates left them in their raw, "unpurified" condition. In this view such works as this one were not art at all.

displayed *Sky Cathedral* bathed in soft blue light like moonlight. (An equally evocative use of assemblage can be seen in James Hampton's *Throne of the Third Heaven of the Nations' Millennium General Assembly*, see fig. 12)

Robert Rauschenberg (b. 1925) developed a distinctive style of assemblage by chaotically mixing painted and found elements in artworks he called "combines." *Canyon* (fig. 20-9), one of these combines, features an assortment of old family photographs (the boy with the upraised arm is Rauschenberg's son), public imagery (the Statue of Liberty), fragments of political posters (in the center), and various objects salvaged from the trash (the flattened steel drum at upper right) or even purchased or donated by friends (the stuffed eagle). The artist meant his work to be open to various readings, choosing material that each viewer might

THE HIGH/LOW MYTH OF MODERNISM

One of the prevailing ideals of the modernist avant-garde was to distance itself intellectually and aesthetically from the banalities of everyday, middle-class life—what was sometimes referred to as "lowbrow" culture.

"Low" culture, or kitsch, are labels applied to the habits, tastes, artifacts (mostly mass-produced), and amusements of ordinary, popular culture—that is, any cultural expression that falls outside the parameters of what was considered elite, or "high" culture (see "The Idea of the Mainstream," page 503). The term *kitsch* derives from the German word *verkitschen* (to make cheap). Mass-produced consumer goods have generally been given this label—a categorization that can sometimes have a pejorative connotation when such goods are compared to "high," or fine, art. (Kitsch is often considered a mark of vulgarity and "bad," or uneducated, taste.)

Boundaries between "high" and "low" began to blur when the Pop artists (see pages 507–10) of the early 1960s began to champion imagery culled from popular culture by putting it into the context of "high" art—similar to what Marcel Duchamp did when he exhibited a urinal as a work of art in 1917 and titled it *Fountain* (see Chapter 19). Postmodern artists (see page 513) continue to question and obscure distinctions between "high" and "low" as a way of repudiating and/or critiquing modernism.

interpret differently. Cheerfully accepting the chaos and unpredictability of modern urban experience, he tried to find artistic metaphors for it. "I only consider myself successful," he said, "when I do something that resembles the lack of order I sense."

In 1961 The Museum of Modern Art organized an exhibition titled "The Art of Assemblage." Rauschenberg was one of two major American artists included in the show; the other was his close friend Jasper Johns (b. 1930). Inspired by the example of Marcel Duchamp (see fig. 19-27), Johns produced conceptually challenging works that seemed to bear on issues raised in contemporary art. For instance, art historians and critics had praised the "nonhierarchical" or "allover" quality of so much Abstract Expressionist painting, particularly the late work of Pollock (see fig. 20-3). The target in *Target with Four Faces* (fig. 20-10), an emphatically hierarchical, organized image, can be seen as a response and a rebuttal to this position.

Target also has a psychological dimension that may stem from the artist's own anxieties and fears. Above the target are four faces, casts taken at different times from the same model. Cut off below eye level and thus made anonymous, they are as blank and empty as the target itself. The viewer can complete the process of depersonalization by closing the lid over the faces, obliterating the human presence. The work of Johns had a powerful effect on the artists who matured around 1960. His interest in Duchamp helped elevate that artist to a place of importance previously reserved for Picasso.

Not since Dada had the art world seen creations like the assemblages and **kinetic** sculptures (sometimes with moving parts) of Jean Tinguely (1925–1991). In his *Homage to New York*

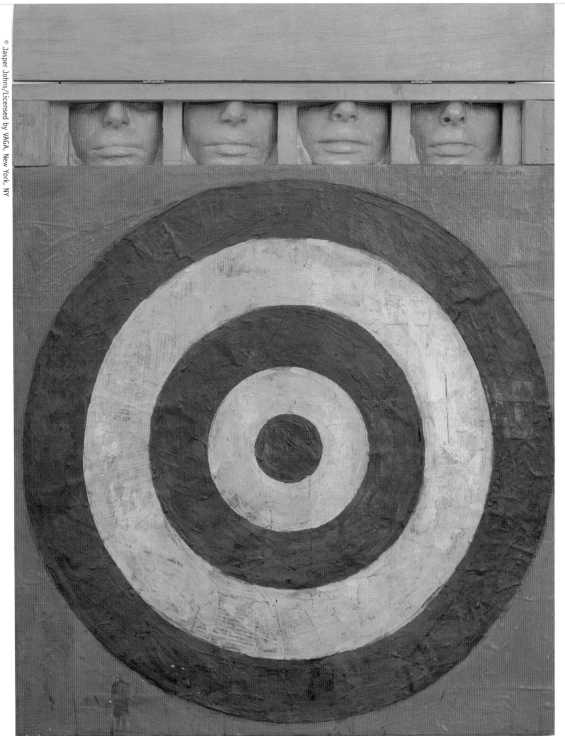

20-10

Jasper Johns. *Target with Four Faces.* 1955. Assemblage: encaustic on newspaper and cloth over canvas, surmounted by four tinted plaster faces in wood box with hinged front, overall, with box open. 33⅝" x 26" x 3" (85.4 x 66 x 7.6 cm).

The Museum of Modern Art, New York. Gift of Mr. and Mrs. Robert C. Scull (8.1958)

(fig. 20-11; see page 508), Tinguely, an anarchist, wanted to free the machine, to let it play. "Art hasn't been fun for a long time," he said. Like the creations of his Dada forebears, Tinguely's work was implicitly critical of an overly restrained and practical bourgeois mentality.

Pop art, as its name suggests, took its style and subject matter from popular culture: its sources were comic books, advertisements, movies, and television. Many critics were alarmed by Pop, fearful that it threatened the survival of both modernist art and high culture—meaning a civilization's most sophisticated, not its most representative, products (see "The High/Low Myth of Modernism," left). Such fears were not entirely unfounded.

The Pop artists' open acknowledgment of the powerful commercial culture contributed significantly to the eclipse, about 1970, of "standards" that had kept "high culture" safely insulated from "low."

Rauschenberg, with his conceptually intriguing use of subjects from ordinary life, helped open the way for Pop art. Even more attuned to popular culture, Roy Lichtenstein (1923–1997), used imagery he found in cartoons and advertisements. He adopted the print medium's heavy outlines and imitated the **Benday dots** used in offset printing. Although many people assume that he merely copied from the comics, in fact he made numerous subtle, important formal adjustments that tightened, clarified, and

On the evening of March 17, 1960, a distinguished group of guests, including Governor Nelson Rockefeller of New York, gathered in the sculpture garden of The Museum of Modern Art in New York City. Awaiting them was an unlikely construction titled *Homage to New York* (fig. 20-11) by the Swiss-born artist Jean Tinguely (1925–1991). The work was assembled from yards of metal tubing, several dozen bicycle and baby-carriage wheels, a washing-machine drum, an upright piano, a radio, several electric fans, a noisy old Addressograph machine, a bassinet, numerous small motors, two motor-driven devices that produced abstract paintings by the yard, several bottles of chemical inks, and various noisemakers. White paint covered everything except the crowning element—an inflated orange meteorological balloon.

The machine, designed to destroy itself when activated, was plugged in before the expectant guests. As smoke poured out of the machinery and covered the crowd, parts of the contraption broke free and scuttled off in various directions, sometimes threatening the onlookers. A device meant to douse the burning piano—which repeatedly played three notes—failed to work, and firefighters had to be called in. They extinguished the blaze and finished the work's destruction to boos from the crowd, which, with the exception of the museum officials present, had been delighted by the spectacle.

20-11 | **Jean Tinguely. Fragment from *Homage to New York*.** 1960. Painted metal, wood, and cloth, 6'-8¼" x 29⅝" x 7' 3⅞" (203.7 x 75.1 x 223.2 cm).
Self-destroying sculpture in the garden of the Museum of Modern Art, New York (227.1968). Gift of the artist.

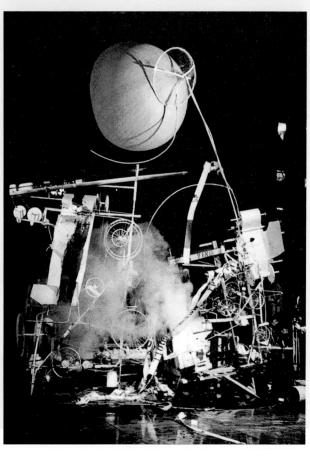

This new kind of art, dramatic but transitory, prefigured a question and answer raised by musician and philosopher John Cage (see page 512). Surveying art and music in 1961, he asked, "Where do we go from here," and his answer was, "Towards theater." Such questions about what art is and what role it plays in society have marked the richly innovative period since 1960.

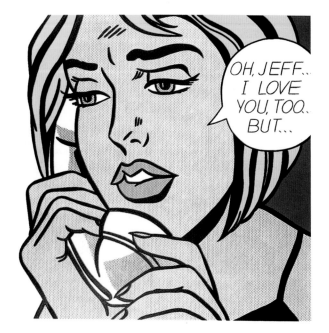

strengthened the final image. *Oh, Jeff . . . I Love You, Too . . . But . . .* (fig. 20-12) compresses into a single frame the soap opera story of two people who fall in love, face a crisis that temporarily threatens their relationship, and then live happily ever after. Lichtenstein reminds the grown-up viewer, however, that this plot is only an adolescent fiction; real-life relationships end with the "But . . . ".

Another Pop artist who veiled personal meditations behind the impersonal veneer of American popular imagery was Andy Warhol (1928?–1987). A successful commercial illustrator in New York City during the 1950s, Warhol grew envious of Rauschenberg's and Johns's emerging "star" status and decided in 1960 to pursue a career as an artist. His decision to focus on popular culture was more than a careerist move, however; it also allowed him to celebrate the middle-class social and material values he had

20-12 | **Roy Lichtenstein. *Oh, Jeff . . . I Love You, Too . . . But . . .*** 1964. Oil on Magna on canvas, 4 x 4' (1.22 x 1.22 m)
Private collection

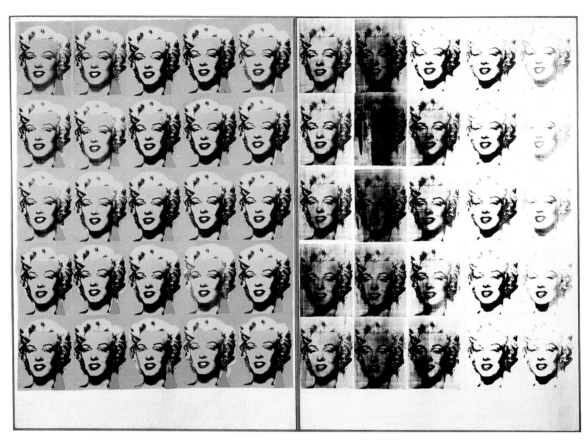

20-13 | **Andy Warhol. *Marilyn Diptych.*** 1962. Oil, acrylic, and silk screen on enamel on canvas, 6'8⅞" x 4'8⅝"
(2.05 x 1.44 m). Tate Gallery, London

absorbed growing up amid the hardships of the Great Depression.

Some of these values may be seen in the *Marilyn Diptych* (fig. 20-13), even in its industrial mode of production. The painting, produced in Warhol's studio called The Factory, is one of the first in which Warhol turned from hand painting to the assembly-line technique of silk-screening photo-images onto canvas, allowing him to produce many versions of the subject. Like so many Americans, Warhol was fascinated by American movie stars such as Marilyn Monroe. The strip of pictures in this work suggests the sequential images of film. Even the face Warhol portrays, taken from a publicity photograph (see "Appropriation," page 510), is not that of Monroe the person but of Monroe the star; Warhol was interested in her public mask, not in her personality or character. He borrowed the diptych format from the Byzantine **icons** of Christian saints he saw at the Greek Orthodox church services he attended every Sunday. By symbolically treating the famous actress as a saint, Warhol shed light on his own fascination with fame. Not only does fame bring wealth and transform the ordinary into the beautiful he implies, but it also confers, like holiness for a saint, a kind of immortality.

Swedish-born Claes Oldenburg (b. 1929) took both a more critical and a more humorous attitude toward his popular subjects than did Warhol and Lichtenstein. Oldenburg's humor—fundamental to his goal to reanimate a dull, lifeless culture—is most evident in such large-scale public projects as his Lipstick Monument for his alma mater, Yale University (fig. 20-14). The

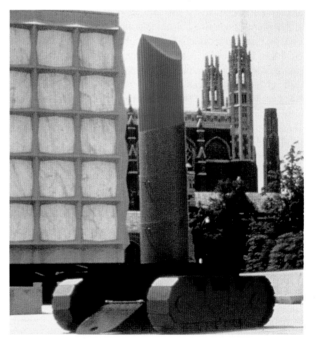

20-14 | **Claes Oldenburg. *Lipstick (Ascending) on Caterpillar Tracks.*** 1969, reworked 1974. Installed at Beinike Plaza, Yale University, New Haven Connecticut. Yale University Art Gallery
Gift of Colossal Keepsake Corporation

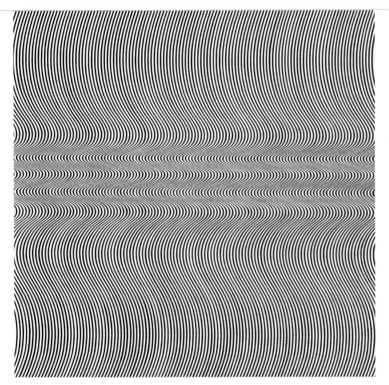

20-15 | **Bridget Riley.** *Current.* 1964. Synthetic polymer on board 58³/₈" x 58⁷/₈" (148 x 149 cm). The Museum of Modern Art New York

Philip Johnson Fund

APPROPRIATION

During the late 1970s and 1980s, appropriation (the presentation of a preexisting image as one's own) became a popular technique among postmodernists (see page 513) in both the United States and Western Europe. The borrowing of figures or compositions has been an essential technique throughout the history of art, but the emphasis had always been on changing or personalizing the source. A copy or reproduction was not considered a legitimate work of art until Marcel Duchamp changed the rules with his "readymades" (see fig. 19-27), insisting that the quality of an artwork depends not on formal invention but on the ideas that stand behind it. Duchamp's own sort of appropriations first inspired the Pop artists Andy Warhol and Roy Lichtenstein (see figs. 20-12 and 20-13), whose reuse of imagery from popular culture, high art, ordinary commerce, and the tabloids then helped point the way for the artists of the 1970s and 1980s.

Critics and historians now use the term *appropriation* to describe the activities of two distinct groups. To the first belong artists such as Betye Saar (see fig. 20-28) and Juane Quick-to-See Smith (see fig. 20-37), who combine and shape their borrowings in personal ways. These artists, along with earlier ones such as Robert Rauschenberg (see fig. 20-9), might be called **collage** appropriators. "Straight appropriators," on the other hand, are those who simply repaint or rephotograph imagery from commerce or the history of art and present it as their own.

The work of these artists is grounded in the ideas of the French literary critics known as the Post-Structuralists. In his essay "The Death of the Author" (1968), for example, Roland Barthes (1915–1980) argued that the meaning of a work of art depends not on what the author meant but on what the reader understands. Furthermore, he questioned the modernist notion of originality: of the author as a creator of an entirely new meaning. According to Barthes, the author merely recycles meanings from other sources.

late 1960s were marked by student demonstrations against the Vietnam War. By mounting a giant lipstick tube on tracks from a Caterpillar tractor, Oldenburg suggested a missile rising from a tank and simultaneously subverted the warlike reference by casting the missile in the form of a feminine cosmetic with erotic overtones. Oldenburg thus urged his audience, in the vocabulary of the time, to "make love, not war." The university, offended by the work's irreverent humor, made Oldenburg remove it. In 1974 he reworked *Lipstick (Ascending) on Caterpillar Tracks* in fiberglass, aluminum, and steel and donated it to the university, which this time accepted it.

MINIMALISM/POST-MINIMALISM AND OP ART

In contrast to the emphasis on content in Pop art, other styles that emerged in the wake of Abstract Expressionism focused on stripping all extra-artistic meanings from artworks and reducing them to their technical essentials. The most intense investigation of perception occurred in "optical art," popularly known as Op art, a kind of nonobjective art that used precisely structured patterns of lines and colors to affect visual perception. Paintings, such as *Current* (fig. 20-15) by the British artist Bridget Riley (b. 1931), consists of tightly spaced, parallel, curved lines, that produce an effect of fluctuating motion. As with many Op works, staring at the pattern may produce discomfort.

Other artists, including the sculptor Donald Judd (1928–1994), turned to a style known as Minimalism. Convinced that Abstract Expressionism had deteriorated into a set of techniques for faking both the subjective and the transcendent, around 1960 Judd began to search for an art free of falsehood. He decided that sculpture offered a better medium than painting for creating literal, matter-of-fact art. Rather than *depicting* shapes, which Judd thought smacked of illusionism and therefore fakery, he produced *actual* shapes. In search of simplicity and clarity, he soon evolved a formal vocabulary featuring identical rectangular

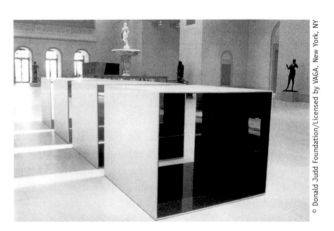

20-16 | **Donald Judd.** *Untitled.* 1969. Anodized aluminum and blue Plexiglas, each 3'11¹/₂" x 4'11⁷/₈" x 4'11⁷/₈" (1.2 x 1.5 x 1.5 m); overall 3'11¹/₂" x 4'11⁷/₈" x 23'8¹/₂" (1.2 x 1.5 x 7.2 m). The St. Louis Art Museum, St. Louis, Missouri

Purchase funds given by the Shoenberg Foundation, Inc.

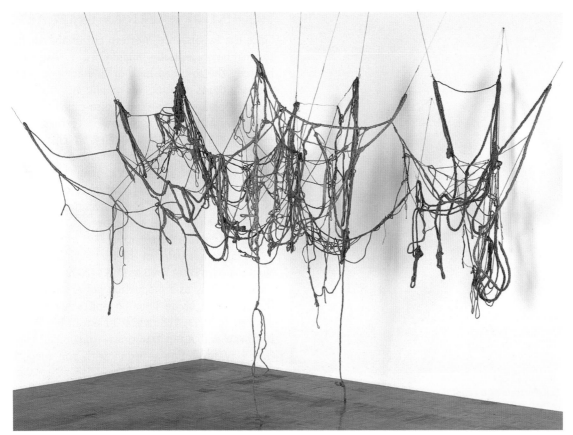

20-17

Eva Hesse. *Rope Piece*
1969–70. Latex over
rope, string and wire;
two strands, dimen-
sions variable. Whitney
Museum of American
Art, New York

Purchase, with funds from
Eli and Edythe L. Broad, the
Mrs. Percy Uris Purchase
Fund, and the Painting and
Sculpture Committee
(88.17a-b)

units arranged in rows and constructed of industrial materials, especially anodized aluminum and Plexiglas. *Untitled* (fig. 20-16) is a typical example of his mature work.

Approaches to Minimalism varied. Eva Hesse (1936–1970) countered the rigid prefabricated forms of Judd's Minimalism by incorporating malleable techniques such as sewing, lacing, and bandaging into her work. Instead of sleek surfaces, her work shows the actual process of art making. Her *Rope Piece* (fig. 20-17), for example, takes on a different shape and different dimensions each time it is installed. The work consists of several sections of rope, which Hesse and her assistant dipped in latex, knotted and tangled, and then hung from wires attached to the ceiling. The resulting linear web or "drawing in space" resembles a three-dimensional version of a poured painting by Jackson Pollock, and, like Pollock's work, it achieves a sense of structure despite its chaotic appearance. In the face of the severe exactitude of Minimalism, Hess provided an alternative in her choice of materials and in their inherent capacity for movement and change.

CONCEPTUAL AND PERFORMANCE ART

While Hesse and other Post-Minimalists made artworks whose mutability challenged the idea of the art object as static and durable, the artists who came to be known as Conceptualists pushed Minimalism to its logical extreme by eliminating the art object itself. This shift away from the aesthetic object toward the pure idea was largely inspired by the growing reputation of Marcel Duchamp and his assertion that making art should emphasize mental, rather than physical activity. The

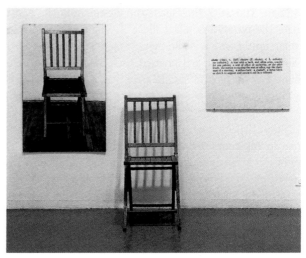

20-18 Joseph Kosuth. *One and Three Chairs.* 1965. Wood folding chair, photograph of chair, and photographic enlargement of dictionary definition of chair; chair 32³/₈ x 14⁷/₈ x 20⁷/₈" (82.2 x 37.8 x 53 cm); photo panel, 36 x 24¹/₈" (91.4 x 61.3 cm); text panel 24¹/₈ x 24¹/₂" (61.3 x 62.2 cm). The Museum of Modern Art, New York

Larry Aldrich Foundation Fund

most prominent American Conceptual artist was Joseph Kosuth (b. 1945), who abandoned painting in 1965 and began to work with language. His *One and Three Chairs* (fig. 20-18) presents an actual chair, a full-scale black-and-white photograph of the same chair, and a dictionary definition of the

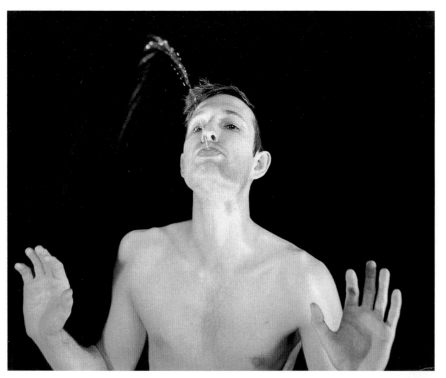

20-19 Bruce Nauman. *Self-Portrait as a Fountain*. 1966–67
Color photograph, 19³/₄ x 23³/₄" (50.1 x 60.3 cm)
Courtesy Leo Castelli Gallery, New York

word chair. The work thus leads the viewer from the physical chair to the purely linguistic ideal of "chairness" and invites the question of which is the most "real."

Some Conceptual artists used their bodies as an artistic medium and engaged in simple activities or performances that they considered works of art. In the late 1950s many artists fell under the spell of the musician and philosopher John Cage (1912–1992). Cage turned to everyday experience and pure chance in his compositions, and furthermore advocated the unity of the arts—including theater, music, and dance as well as the visual arts. Friends such as Allan Kaprow (b. 1927) gave up painting for loosely scripted, multimedia events they called **Happenings**. Meanwhile in Japan a group of artists produced similar dramatic displays they called **performance art**—for example, in *Hurling Colors* (not illustrated) they smashed bottles of paint on a canvas on the floor. In Paris Yves Klein (1928–1962), who after 1957 worked only in blue, which he considered the most spiritual color, produced *Anthropometries of the Blue Period* (not illustrated) in 1960. He covered three nude female models with blue paint and pressed them against large sheets of paper in an attempt to spiritualize the flesh. Klein's *Monotone Symphony*—twenty minutes of single notes followed by twenty minutes of silence—accompanied the performance.

Bruce Nauman (b. 1941), in 1966–67, made a series of eleven color photographs based on wordplay and visual puns. In *Self-Portrait as a Fountain* (fig. 20-19), for example, the bare-chested artist tips his head back, spurts water into the air, and, in the spirit of Duchamp, designates himself a work of art.

THE RISE OF AMERICAN CRAFT ART

Since the Renaissance, Western critics and art historians have generally maintained a distinction between the so-called high or fine arts—architecture, sculpture, painting, the graphic arts, and, more recently, photography—and the so-called minor or decorative arts—such as ceramics, textiles, glass, metalwork, furniture, and jewelry, which typically serve either a practical or an ornamental function. In the postwar decades, however, a number of artists began to push traditional craft mediums in new directions that blurred the conventional distinctions between fine and decorative art. Their work might best be called craft art.

A major innovator in the clay medium was the Montana-born Peter Voulkos (1924–2002), who after working briefly as a production potter came under the influence of de Kooning and other gestural painters in 1953. The radical American break from European and Asian traditions—sometimes called the "clay revolution"—began with the ruggedly

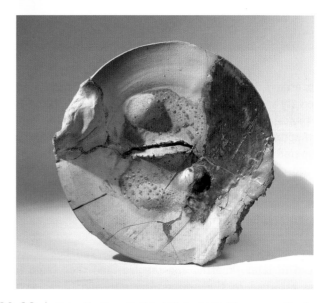

20-20 Peter Voulkos. *Untitled Plate*. 1962. Stoneware with glaze, gas fired, 16 ¹/₄" diameter.
Collection of the Oakland Museum, California. Gift of the Art Guild of The Oakland Museum Association, A62.87.4

sculptural ceramic works Voulkos produced in the mid-1950s. By the late 1950s Voulkos had abandoned the pot form altogether and was making large ceramic works spontaneously assembled from numerous wheel-thrown and slab-built elements, their surfaces often covered with bright, freely applied glazes or epoxy paint. In the early 1960s, Voulkos returned to traditional ceramic forms (fig. 20-20), but rendered them nonfunctional by tearing, gouging, and piercing them in the gestural fashion derived from Abstract Expressionism.

A comparable revolution in glass was initiated by Harvey Littleton (b. 1922), a professor at the University of Wisconsin.

In 1963, Littleton established the nation's first hot-glass studio program at the university, and other glass programs soon sprang up around the country. Many of them were led by Littleton's former students, including Dale Chihuly who established the famous Pilchuck Glass School in Seattle in 1971 (see fig. 16).

Like ceramics and glass, the use of fabric as a medium broke down the barriers between applied, or decorative, arts and fine art. Moreover, fabric had traditionally been utilized in crafts by women, an association that further distanced cloth materials and sewing crafts from the so-called fine arts. The innovative and unconventional role given fabric in works by Eva Hesse (see fig. 20-17) and Magdalena Abakanowicz (see fig. 20-32), for example, collapses the former limited perceptions about this medium.

Crafts or mediums traditionally associated with domesticity have also been elevated into a "high" art status by artists such as Wendell Castle (see page 520 and fig. 20-35), who created wood sculptures as well as sculptural furniture. Judy Chicago's *The Dinner Party* (see pages 516-17 and fig. 20-27) breaks all the boundaries by integrating painted porcelain, tile, and needlework in a dramatic installation.

Late Modernism/Postmodernism

Many Minimalists, inspired by the theories of art critics such as Greenberg (see "The Idea of the Mainstream," page 503), believed that art represented a pure realm outside ordinary existence and that the history of art followed a coherent, progressive trajectory culminating in modernism and abstraction. To most of the artists who came after them, by contrast, the concepts of artistic purity and the mainstream seemed naive. Critics and artists recognized that they lived in the midst of artistic **pluralism**, the acceptance of a variety of artistic intentions and styles. The generation that grew to maturity around 1970 had been the first to accept pluralism in its own right as a manifestation of our culturally heterogeneous age. The decline of the concept of modernism in the various arts was neither uniform nor sudden. Its gradual erosion occurred over a long period and was the result of many individual transformations. The many approaches to art that emerged at the end of the twentieth century are designated by the catchall term *postmodernism*. Although there is no universal agreement on what the term *postmodern* means, it involves rejection of the concept of the mainstream and recognition of artistic pluralism.

ARCHITECTURE

Modernism endured in architecture until about 1970. The stripped-down, rectilinear industrial vocabulary pioneered by such architects as Walter Gropius (see fig. 19-23) and Le Corbusier (see fig. 19-22) and known as the International Style dominated new urban construction in much of the world after World War II (see "Elements of Architecture: The International Style," page 485). Many of the finest examples of International Style architecture were built in the United States by Bauhaus architects, such as Walter Gropius and Mies van der Rohe, who escaped Nazi Germany and assumed prestigious positions at American schools of architecture and design.

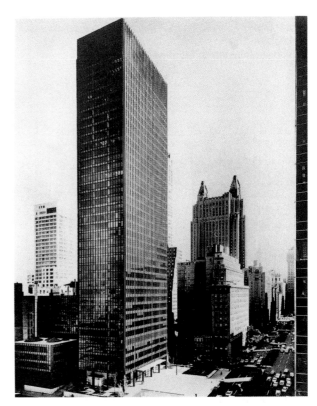

20-21 | **Ludwig Mies van der Rohe** and **Philip Johnson** **Seagram Building,** New York City. 1954–58

Mies designed schools, apartments, and office buildings, including the Seagram Building in New York City (fig. 20-21), which he designed with Philip Johnson (b. 1906). Mies's buildings are distinguished by his attention to detail. Because he had a large budget for the Seagram Building, he used custom-made bronze instead of standardized steel on the exterior. New York building codes required that the steel supports for the structure be encased in concrete, so the bronze beams are only ornamental stand-ins for the functional girders inside. Tall, narrow windows with discreet dark glass emphasize the skyscraper's height. Set back from the street, the building rises quickly and impressively off piers (metal or concrete columns that raise a building above ground level) from a sunlit plaza with reflecting pools, fountains, and, originally, beech trees.

Postmodernism manifested itself first in architecture, in the work of Robert Venturi (b. 1925). In the pioneering publication *Complexity and Contradiction in Architecture* (1966), Venturi argued that the problem with Mies van der Rohe and other International Style architects was their impractical unwillingness to accept the modern city for what it is: a complex, contradictory, and heterogeneous collection of "high" and "low" architectural forms (see "The High/Low Myth of Modernism," page 506). Taking these ideas further in the book *Learning from Las Vegas* (1972), he suggested that rather than turning their backs in disdain on ordinary commercial buildings, architects should get in "the habit of looking nonjudgmentally" at them. "Main Street is almost all right," Venturi observed. In buildings designed with

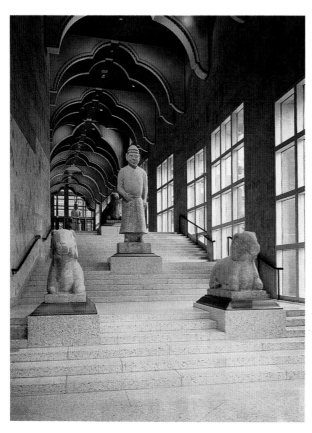

20-22 | **Robert Venturi** and **Denise Scott Brown. Stair Hall with Ming dynasty tomb figures**, The Seattle Art Museum. 1986–91

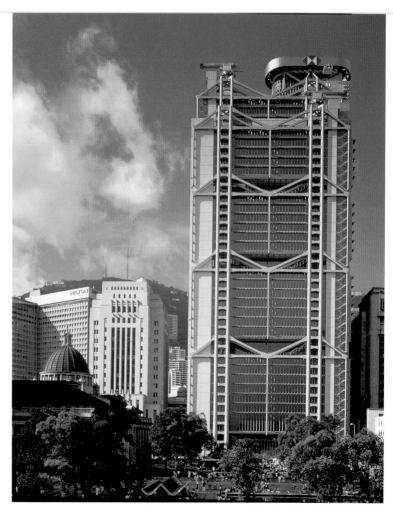

20-23 | **Norman Foster. Hongkong & Shanghai Bank, Hong Kong** 1979–86

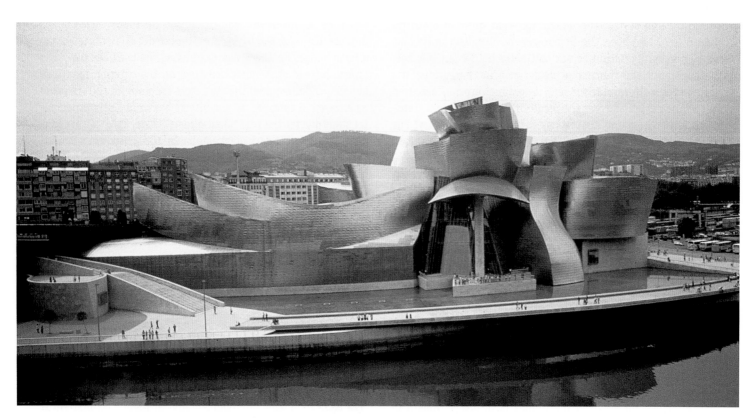

20-24 | **Frank O. Gehry. Guggenheim Museum, Bilbao,** Spain. 1993–97

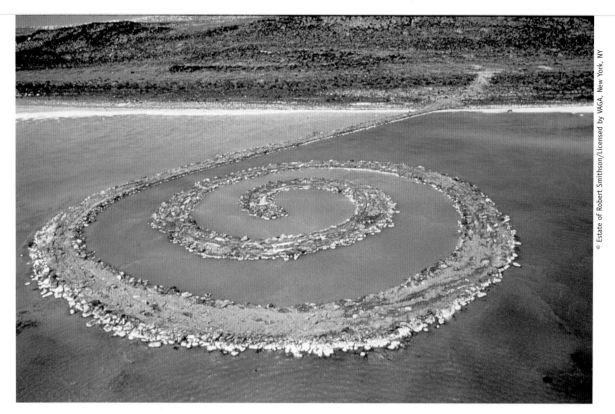

20-25 | **Robert Smithson.** *Spiral Jetty.* 1969–70. Black rock, salt crystal, and earth spiral, length 1,500' (457 m)
Great Salt Lake, Utah

Denise Scott Brown (fig. 20-22) the postmodern credo was fully established—as we "look backward at history and tradition to go forward; we can also look downward to go upward."

Another reaction to mid-century modernism in architecture, known as *High Tech*, is characterized by the expressive use of advanced building technology and industrial materials, equipment, and components. Among the most spectacular examples of High Tech architecture is the Hongkong & Shanghai Bank (fig. 20-23) by the English architect Norman Foster (b. 1935). Invited by his client to design the most beautiful bank in the world, Foster spared no expense in the creation of this futuristic forty-seven-story skyscraper. The rectangular plan features service towers at the east and west ends, eliminating the central service core typical of earlier skyscrapers such as the Seagram Building. The load-bearing steel skeleton, composed of giant masts and girders, is on the exterior. The individual stories hang from this structure, allowing for uninterrupted facades and open working areas filled with natural light.

The Toronto-born, California-based postmodernist Frank Gehry (b. 1929) was one architect who was willing to "look downward" at the chaotic heterogeneity of urban life as well as the architecture of the past. One of the most dramatic buildings created at the end of the twentieth century is his Guggenheim Museum for the Basque city of Bilbao, Spain (fig. 20-24). Although Gehry had made a reputation during the late 1970s and 1980s based on his use of vernacular forms and cheap materials, his guiding concern in Bilbao was to reconcile the client's needs with his own interest in sculptural form. The commission for the Guggenheim Museum Bilbao provided him with an extraordinary opportunity to realize that goal.

The Solomon R. Guggenheim Museum in New York had become one of the most famous museums in the world, as much for Frank Lloyd Wright's innovative architecture (see fig. 22) as for its collection of abstract art. Like Wright's spiraling design, Gehry's sprawling, organic plan resembles a living organism, like some gigantic metallic flower growing along the bank of the river. Gehry covered the building's complex steel skeleton with a thin skin of silvery titanium that shimmers gold or silver depending on the light. From many vantage points, however, the building also resembles a giant ship, a reference to the shipbuilding and port facilities so important to the economy of the northern Spanish city. Inside, the museum features a giant atrium, which both pays homage to Wright's famous design and attempts to outdo it in size and effect. In competing with Wright, Gehry said he meant to provide for the needs of the artists. "Artists want to be in great buildings," he claimed.

EARTHWORKS AND SITE-SPECIFIC ART

The Guggenheim Museum, Bilbao, both reflects and enhances its site, as Wright's "Fallingwater" had done earlier (see fig. 19-25). In the late 1960s and 1970s sculptors began to take art out of the marketplace and back to nature. They worked outdoors, using what they found at the site to fashion **earthworks** and calling this new category of art-making **site-specific** sculpture.

Robert Smithson (1938–1973) sought to illustrate what he called the "ongoing dialectic" in nature between constructive forces—those that build and shape form—and destructive forces—those that destroy it. *Spiral Jetty* (fig. 20-25), a 1,500-foot spiraling stone and earth platform extending into the Great Salt Lake in Utah, reflects these ideas. To Smithson, the salty

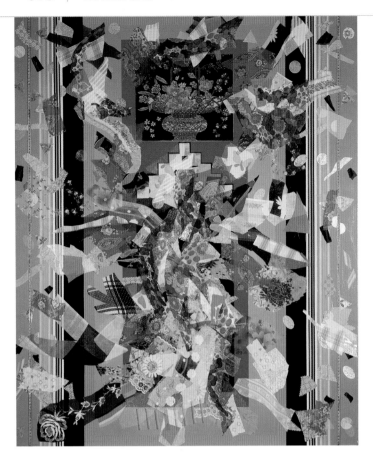

20-26 | Miriam Schapiro. *Personal Appearance #3.* 1973. Acrylic and fabric on canvas, 60 x 50" (152.4 x 127 cm) Private collection

waters and the algae of the lake suggested the primordial ocean where life began, and the abandoned oil rigs dotting the lakeshore brought to mind both prehistoric dinosaurs and some vanished civilization. He used the spiral because it is an archetypal shape that appears throughout the natural world, from galaxies to seashells. (The spiral attracted Frank Lloyd Wright for similar reasons.) Also, unlike modernist squares, circles, and straight lines, it is a "dialectical" shape, one that opens and closes, curls and uncurls endlessly. More than any other shape, it suggested to him the perpetual "coming and going of things." Algae turned the lake water into a harmony of ephemeral colors, and eventually the action of the water caused the earthwork to erode and disappear.

FEMINIST ART

The 1970s saw the rise of the feminist movement in the United States. In August 1970 (the fiftieth anniversary of the adoption of the Nineteenth Amendment to the Constitution, which guaranteed women the right to vote) women assessed their progress in various fields since 1920. They were disappointed by what they found. In the arts, women constituted half the nation's practicing artists, but only 18 percent of commercial New York galleries carried the work of any women at all. Of the 151 artists in the 1969 Whitney Annual, one of the country's most important exhibitions of the work of living artists, only 8 were women. Few women served as museum directors, and few achieved the rank of full professor in art history departments.

To focus more attention on women in the arts, feminist artists began organizing women's cooperative galleries. Feminist art historians, such as Eleanor Tufts, in her groundbreaking book *Our Hidden Heritage* (1974), and Linda Nochlin in essays, wrote about women artists. Nochlin, then a professor at Vassar College, helped inaugurate feminist art history with her 1971 essay "Why Have There Been No Great Women Artists?" (*Art News* LXIX, pages 22–39, 67–71). She argued that women had been denied the opportunity to achieve greatness by their exclusion from the male-dominated institutional systems of training, patronage, and criticism. Feminist curators and critics promoted the work of emerging women artists and long-neglected earlier ones. In 1972 Elizabeth Broun and Ann Gabhart broke new ground at the Walters Art Gallery in Baltimore with their exhibition, "Old Mistresses: Women Artists of the Past" (*Walters Art Gallery Bulletin* XXIV, no. 7, 1972), the first feminist exhibition in a major museum, followed by Ann Sutherland Harris and Linda Nochlin's exhibition, "Women Artists: 1550–1950" at the Los Angeles County Museum of Art in 1976–77.

In 1971, two feminist artists and teachers, Miriam Schapiro (b. 1923) and Judy Chicago (b. 1939), established the Feminist Art Program, dedicated to training women artists, at the California Institute of the Arts (CalArts). Schapiro championed the theory that women have a distinct artistic sensibility that can be distinguished from that of men, and hence a specifically feminine aesthetic. During the late 1950s and 1960s she made explicitly female versions of the dominant modernist styles, including reductive, hard-edged abstractions of the female form: large X-shapes with openings at their centers. In 1973 she created

20-27 | Judy Chicago. *The Dinner Party.* 1979. White tile floor inscribed in gold with 999 women's names; triangular table with painted porcelain, sculpted porcelain plates, and needlework. Mixed-media, 48" x 42" x 3' (122.9 x 42 x 91 cm). Collection of The Brooklyn Museum of Art. Gift of The Elizabeth A. Sackler Foundation

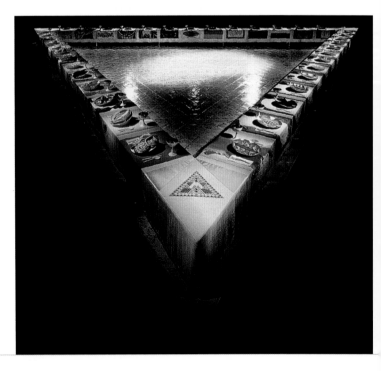

Personal Appearance #3 (fig. 20-26), using underlying hard edge rectangles and overlaying them with a collage of fabric and paper. She called her new technique *femmage* (from *female* and *collage*). By combining painting and fabrics, these works celebrate traditional women's craftwork. A founder of the P and D (Pattern and Decoration) movement, Schapiro said, "I dovetail my feminism with decoration" (cited in Gouma-Peterson, page 29). The formal and emotional richness of her work were meant to counter the Minimalist aesthetic of the 1960s, which Schapiro and other feminists considered typically male.

Judy Chicago assumed a leading role in the 1970s. Her *The Dinner Party* (fig. 20-27) is perhaps the best-known work of feminist art created in that decade. In 1970 she adopted the surname Chicago (from the city of her birth) to free herself from "all names imposed upon her through male social dominance." At CalArts, Chicago and Schapiro led a collective of twenty-one women students in the creation of *Womanhouse* (1971–72), a collaborative art environment, and from *Womanhouse* emerged *The Dinner Party* (1974–79). A complex, mixed-medium installation that fills an entire room, *The Dinner Party* speaks powerfully of the accomplishments of women throughout history. Five years of collaborative effort went into the creation of the work, involving hundreds of women and several men who volunteered their talents as ceramists, needle workers, and china painters to realize Chicago's designs.

The Dinner Party is composed of a large, triangular table, each side stretching 48 feet, which rests on a triangular platform covered with 2,300 triangular porcelain tiles. Chicago saw the equilateral triangle as a symbol of the equalized world sought by feminism and also identified it as one of the earliest symbols of the feminine. The porcelain "Heritage Floor" bears the names of 999 notable women from myth, legend, and history. Along each side of the table's three sides, thirteen place settings each represent a famous woman. The thirty-nine women honored include some that we have seen in this book, Hatshepsut (see fig. 2-24); Christine de Pisan (see fig. 20); Isabella d'Este (see page 329); Artemesia Gentileschi (see fig. 14-8); and Georgia O'Keeffe (see fig. 4).

Each place setting features a 14-inch-wide painted porcelain plate, ceramic flatware, a ceramic chalice with a gold interior, and an embroidered napkin, all set upon an elaborately decorated runner. The runners incorporate decorative motifs and techniques of stitching and weaving appropriate to the period with which each woman was associated. Most of the plates feature abstract designs based on female genitalia because, Chicago said, "that is all [the women at the table] had in common. . . . They were from different periods, classes, ethnicities, geographies, experiences, but what kept them within the same confined historical space" was the fact of their biological sex. Chicago thought it appropriate to represent the women through plates because they "had been swallowed up and obscured by history instead of being recognized and honored."

Chicago emphasized china painting and needlework in *The Dinner Party* to celebrate craft mediums traditionally practiced by women and to argue that they should be considered "high" art forms on par with painting and sculpture. This argument

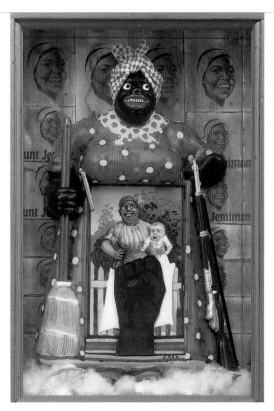

20-28 | Betye Saar. *The Liberation of Aunt Jemima.* 1972. Mixed media, 11¾" x 11⅞" x 2¾" (29.8 x 30.3 x 6.9 cm).

University Art Museum, University of California, Berkeley, Purchase with the aid of funds from the National Endowment of Arts (selected by The Committee for The Acquisition of Afro-American Art)

complemented her larger aim of raising awareness of the many contributions women have made to history, thereby fostering women's empowerment in the present.

Typical of those who achieved widespread recognition only with the arrival of the feminist movement is the Los Angeles-based, African-American sculptor Betye Saar (b. 1926), who constructed boxes of found objects. Saar's best-known work, *The Liberation of Aunt Jemima* (fig. 20-28) appropriates the derogatory stereotype of the cheerfully servile domestic servant and transforms it into an icon of militant black feminist power. Aunt Jemima holds a broom and pistol in one hand and a rifle in the other and stands behind a large clenched fist, the symbol of "black power." Saar's armed Jemima liberates herself not only from racial oppression but also from traditional gender roles that had long relegated black women to subservient positions.

A second generation of feminist artists in the 1980s tended to believe that the differences between the sexes were not intrinsic but "socially constructed." They argued that media images and other cultural forces worked against women to suit the needs of those in power. According to this view, young people learn how to behave from the role models they see heralded in magazines, movies, and other sources of mass culture. A major task of feminism and feminist art should be to resist the power of these forces.

In 1977 a leader of these later feminists, Cindy Sherman (b. 1954), began work on a series of black-and-white photographs of herself in various assumed roles. The images simulate

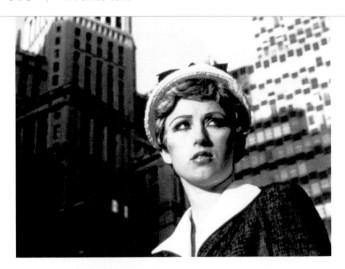

20-29 | **Cindy Sherman.** *Untitled Film Still.* 1978. Black-and-white photograph, 8 x 10" (20.3 x 25.4 cm). Courtesy Cindy Sherman and Metro Pictures, New York

stills from B-grade movies of the 1940s and 1950s. In one of these photographs Sherman plays a perplexed young innocent apparently recently arrived in a big city, its buildings looming threateningly behind her (fig. 20-29). The image suggests a host of films in which a similar character is overwhelmed by dangerous forces and is rescued by a hero. While Sherman's motives are complex, many observers have suggested that in these works she indicts Hollywood's stereotypical images of women and femininity by showing how one can "invent" oneself in a variety of roles.

PLURALISM

Despite declarations of the death of modernism by postmodern artists and critics, many artists remained committed to its central values of formal innovation and personal expression. A leading modernist painter is Elizabeth Murray (b. 1940), whose artistic breakthrough came in the late 1970s, when she began to work on irregularly shaped canvases. During the 1980s her canvases, now stretched over thick plywood supports, became increasingly complex and three-dimensional physical presences over whose swelling surfaces she painted abstracted figures and familiar objects. *Chaotic Lip* (fig. 20-30) is an enormous, organically shaped canvas with rounded lobes that radiate out in several directions. Her bold and colorful style is inspired simultaneously by "high" modernist art and "low" popular culture. She employs Cubist-style fragmentation, Fauvist color, Surrealist **biomorphism**, and gestural Abstract Expressionist paint handling, while also drawing inspiration from cartoons and animated films.

Much contemporary art (from c. 1970–present) implicitly acknowledges the exhaustion of the old modernist faith in modern innovation—and in what it implied about the "progressive" course of history—by reviving older styles. The names of these styles often begin with the prefix *neo*, denoting a new form of something that already exists, a typical postmodern position.

A number of shows in leading New York art galleries in 1980 signaled the emergence of Neo-Expressionism, the first of these revival styles. The emphasis on personal experience in feminist art helped to inspire a renewed interest in expressionism. About the same time, various European artists working in a similar vein

gained critical recognition in the United States. One was the German artist Anselm Kiefer (b. 1945). Kiefer sought to revisit his country's Nazi past and World War II. The burned and barren landscape in *Märkischer Heide* (fig. 20-31) evokes the ravages of war that the Brandenburg area, near Berlin, has frequently experienced. A road lures us into the landscape, a standard device used in landscape paintings since the seventeenth century. Kiefer's works compel viewers to ponder troubling historical and social realities, "in order," he said, "to understand the madness."

A great deal of recent avant-garde art has focused on the human body, which numerous postmodern critics have identified as an "object" subject to the operations of power as well as a "site" for the display and definition of race, class, gender, and sexual identity. One artist who has dealt extensively with the body as vulnerable yet enduring is the Polish sculptor Magdalena Abakanowicz (b. 1930). In the late 1960s she began producing large, woven, abstract works that soon gave way to figural pieces that challenged the conventional distinctions between craft and sculpture. Typical of her work is *Backs* (fig. 20-32), a composition of eighty headless, limbless, genderless, and hollow-front impressions made on a single mold over a five-year period. When shown in nature, as here, the figures appear to grow out of and form a part of the setting, a result of their organic shapes as well as their materials: coarse, brown, resin-impregnated burlap and

20-30 | **Elizabeth Murray.** *Chaotic Lip.* 1986. Oil on canvas, 9'9½" x 7'2½" x 1' (3.01 x 2.22 x 0.31 m). Spencer Museum of Art, The University of Kansas, Lawrence

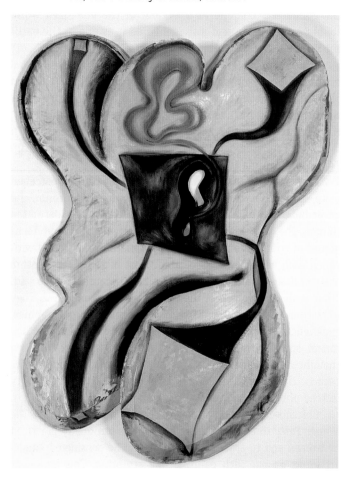

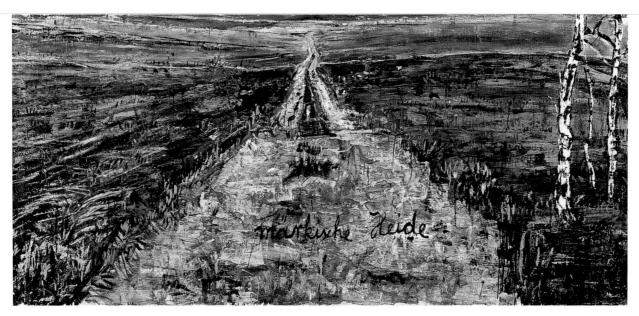

20-31 | **Anselm Kiefer.** *Märkischer Heide.* 1984. Oil, acrylic, and shellac on burlap, 3'10½" x 8'4" (1.18 x 2.54 m) Stedelijk Van Abbemuseum, Eindhoven, the Netherlands

Kiefer often incorporates words and phrases into his paintings that amplify their meaning. Here, the words *Märkischer Heide* ("Brandenburg Heath") evoke an old patriotic tune of the Brandenburg region, "Märkischer Heide, märkischer Sand," which Hitler's army adopted as a marching song.

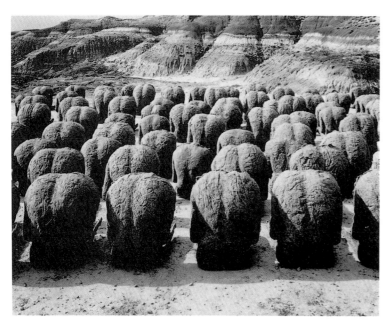

20-32 | **Magdalena Abakanowicz.** *Backs.* 1976–80. Burlap, twine, and resin, each piece approximately 25¾ x 21¾ x 23¾" (65.4 x 55.3 x 60.3 cm). Installed near Calgary, Canada, 1982. Collection of Museum of Modern Art, Pusan, South Korea

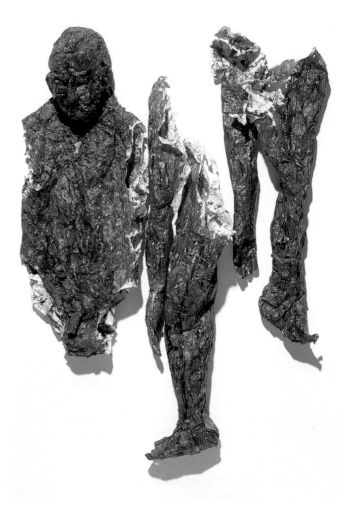

20-33 | **Kiki Smith.** *Untitled.* 1988. Ink on gampi paper, 48 x 38 x 7" (121.9 x 96.5 x 17.8 cm). The Art Institute of Chicago
Gift of Lannan Foundation (1997.121)

twine meant to resemble soil and roots. The anonymous figures appear to be both resigned to some awful fate and worshiping some unknown power.

A conscious rejection of the "pretty" has marked the production of numerous contemporary artists concerned with representing the base human body and its fluids, such as blood, vomit, and excrement. The American sculptor Kiki Smith (b. 1954) has thoroughly explored this territory in works such as *Untitled* (fig. 20-33). This disturbing sculpture,

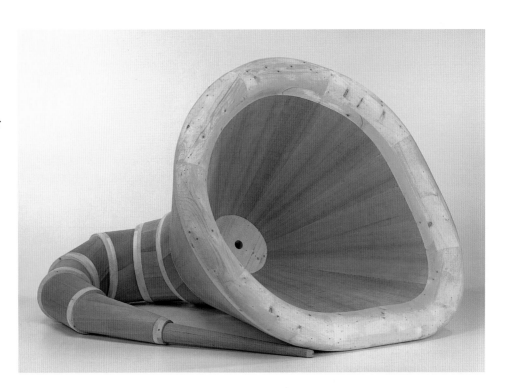

20-34

Martin Puryear
Plenty's Boast
1994–95. Red
cedar and pine
5'8" x 6'11" x
9'10" (1.73 x
2.11 x 1.35 m)
The Nelson-
Atkins Museum
of Art, Kansas
City, Missouri
Purchase of the
Renee C. Crowell
Trust

made of red-stained, tissue-thin gampi (Japanese paper made from fibers of a shrub), represents the flayed, bloodied, and crumpled skin of a male figure, torn into three pieces that hang limply from the wall. The body, once massive and vigorous, is now hollow and lifeless. The exposure of its interior suggests the loss of boundaries between the body and the environment.

Another artist devoted to the creation of evocative organic forms is the African-American sculptor Martin Puryear (b. 1941), whose early interest in biology marked an attraction to nature that would shape his mature aesthetic. Puryear's *Plenty's Boast* (fig. 20-34) does not represent anything in particular but suggests any number of things, including a strange sea creature or a fantastic musical instrument. Perhaps the most obvious reference is to the horn of plenty evoked in the sculpture's title. But the cone is empty, implying an "empty boast"—another reference to the title. The richness of the sculpture lies not only in its multiple metaphorical references (a postmodern trait), but also in its superbly crafted idiosyncratic yet elegant forms.

Puryear's impressive woodworking skills link his sculpture to the contemporary American craft art movement that has flourished in recent decades (see page 512–13). Another master of the medium of wood is Wendell Castle (b. 1932), who during the 1960s made highly original laminated wood furniture in an organic, sculptural style. In the late 1970s he changed direction and began carving technically demanding ***trompe l'oeil*** sculpture in wood. Related to the style known as Super Realism,

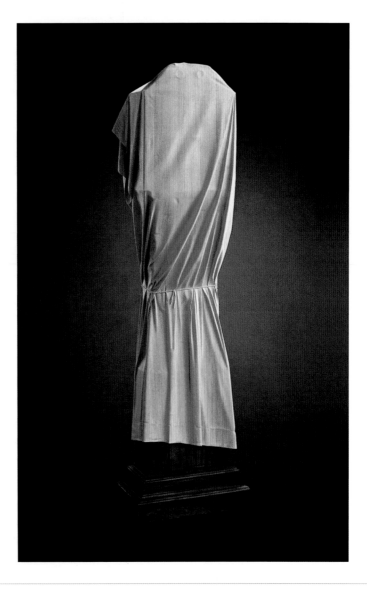

20-35 | **Wendell Castle. *Ghost Clock.*** 1985. Mahogany and bleached Honduras mahogany, 7'2¼" x 2'1½" x 1'3" (2.19 x 0.62 x 0.38 m). Renwick Gallery, Smithsonian American Art Museum, Washington, D.C.
Museum purchase through the Smithsonian Institution Collections Acquisition Program

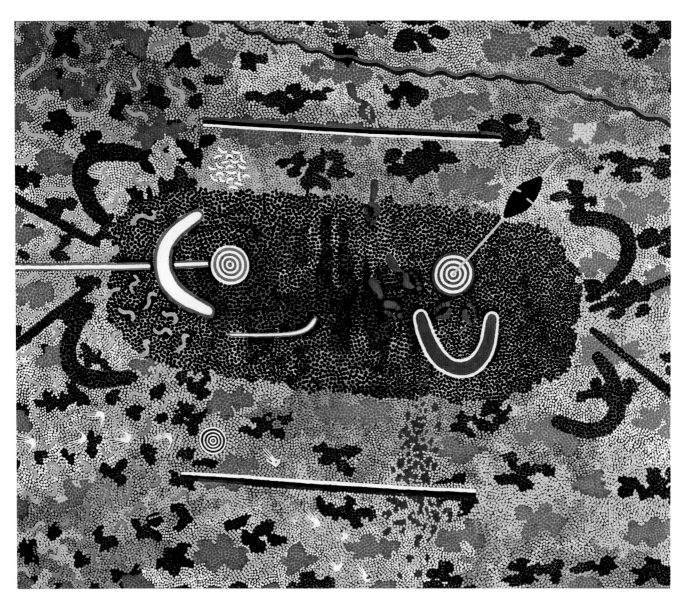

20-36 | **Clifford Possum Tjapaltjarri. *Man's Love Story*.** 1978. Papunya, Northern Territory, Australia. Synthetic polymer paint on canvas
6'11¾" x 8'4¼" (2.13 x 2.55 m). Art Gallery of South Australia, Adelaide
Visual Arts Board of the Australia Council Contemporary Art Purchase Grant, 1980

Castle's carvings represent everyday objects placed on or draped over furniture that he has built using traditional techniques. The impressively crafted *Ghost Clock* (fig. 20-35), which imitates an eighteenth-century clock, is covered by a *trompe l'oeil* sheet carved out of bleached mahogany. The sculpture's power comes not only from its astonishing illusionism but also its haunting imagery, evoking an anthropomorphic presence forever hidden beneath the shroud.

Modern American and European mediums and techniques have spread around the world. In Australia, for example, Aborigine artists adopted canvas and acrylic paint for rendering traditional imagery once associated with more ephemeral mediums like bark, sand, and body painting. Aborigines who were experts in sand painting—an ancient ritual art form that involves creating large colored designs on the ground—formed an art cooperative in 1971 in Papunya, in central Australia, and painting

soon became an economic mainstay in the region. Clifford Possum Tjapaltjarri (c. 1932–2002), a founder of the Papunya cooperative, gained an international reputation after an exhibition of his paintings in 1988. As in the technique of sand painting, he works with his canvas on the floor, using traditional patterns and colors (principally red and yellow ochers). His paintings, like *Man's Love Story* (fig. 20-36), may at first seem entirely abstract, but they actually convey complex myths, traditions, and social rules through stories.

Man's Love Story involves two mythical ancestors. One man came to Papunya in search of honey ants; the white U-shape on the left represents the man seated in front of a water hole with an ants' nest, represented by concentric circles. His digging stick lies to his right and white sugary leaves lie to his left. The straight white "journey line" represents his trek from the west. The second man, represented by the brown-and-white

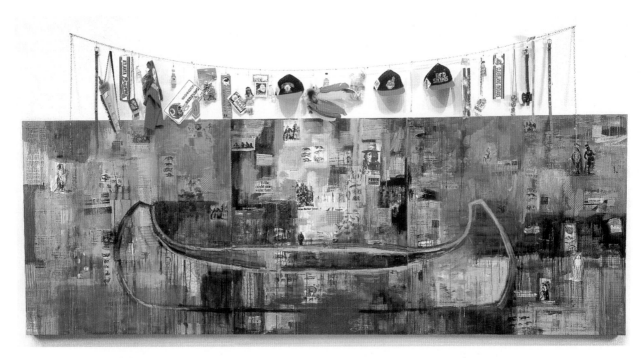

20-37 | **Jaune Quick-to-See Smith. *Trade (Gifts for Trading Land with White People).*** Salish-Cree-Shoshone, 1992. Oil and collage on canvas, 5' x 14'2" (1.52 x 4.32 m). Chrysler Museum of Art, Norfolk, Virginia

U-shaped form, came from the north, leaving footprints, and sat down by another water hole nearby. He began to spin a string made of human hair on a spindle (the form leaning toward the upper right of the painting) but he thought about the woman he loved, who belonged to a kinship group into which he could not marry. Distracted by her approach, he let his hair string blow away (represented by the brown flecks below him) and so lost all his work. Then four women (the dotted U-shapes) from the group into which he could marry came with their digging sticks and sat around the two men. A rich food supply surrounds them—wiggly shapes representing caterpillars and dots representing seeds. What seemed to be a richly decorative surface pattern is in fact a visual record of the ephemeral impressions left on the earth by the figures—their tracks, direction lines, and the U-shaped marks they left when sitting. Working carefully, dot by dot, the artist has captured the vast expanse and shimmering light of the arid landscape.

DECONSTRUCTION

Many artists since the 1980s have had an interest in the theory of deconstruction developed by French philosopher Jacques Derrida (b. 1930). Concerned mostly with the analysis of verbal texts, Derridean deconstruction holds that no text possesses a single, intrinsic meaning but rather its meaning is always "intertextual" —a product of its relationship to other texts—and is always "decentered," or "dispersed" along an infinite chain of linguistic signs whose meanings are themselves unstable. Deconstructivist art and architecture is, consequently, often "intertextual" in its use of design elements from other traditions, including modernism, and "decentered" in its denial of unified and stable forms.

ART WITH SOCIAL IMPACT

Artists may use the conventions of other cultures and still communicate with a Western audience more directly than Clifford Possom. As a major form of communication, the arts have always been used to drive home ideas, and since the nineteenth century artists have expressed their own ideas as well as those of their patrons. Roger Shimomura (b. 1939) turned painting and prints into powerful statements in a series based on his grandmother's diary. In his 1978 painting *Diary* (see fig. 27) he depicts his grandmother's record of the family's experience in an internment camp in Idaho. (American citizens of Japanese ancestry were forcibly confined in internment camps during World War II.) Shimomura painted his grandmother writing while he (the toddler) and his mother stand by an open door—a door that opens out to a barbed-wire-enclosed compound. Shimomura combined two formal traditions—the Japanese art of color woodblock prints (see figs. 9-23, 9-24) and American Pop art (see fig. 20-12)—to create a personal style that expresses his own dual heritage as it makes a powerful political statement.

Jaune Quick-to-See Smith (b. 1940), who was born on the Confederated Salish and Kootenai Reservation in western Montana and is enrolled there, also combines traditional and contemporary forms to convey political and social messages. During the United States' quincentennial celebration of Columbus's arrival in what came to be called the Americas (see Chapter 15), Quick-to-See Smith created paintings and collages that confronted viewers with their own, perhaps unwitting, stereotypes. In *Trade (Gifts for Trading Land with White People)* (fig. 20-37) a stately canoe floats over a richly colored and textured field, which on closer inspection proves to be a dense collage of clippings from

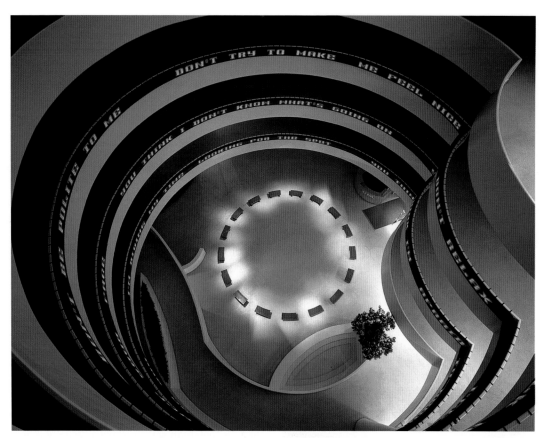

20-38 | **Jenny Holzer.** *Untitled (Selections from Truisms, Inflammatory Essays, The Living Series, The Survival Series, Under a Rock, Laments, and Mother and Child Text).* 1989. Extended helical tricolor LED electronic-display signboard; site specific dimensions, 16½" x 162' x 6" (41.9 cm x 49 m x 15.2 cm).
Solomon R. Guggenheim Museum, New York (89.326). Partial gift of the artist, 1989

Native American newspapers. On a chain above the painting hangs a collection of fake Indian trinkets (chicken feather headdresses, beaded belts, keyholders, necklaces) and demeaning mascot images for teams with names like the Atlanta Braves, the Washington Redskins, and the Cleveland Indians. Surely, the painting suggests, Native Americans could trade these goods to retrieve their lost lands, just as European settlers traded trinkets to acquire those lands in the first place. As Gerrit Henry wrote in *Art in America* (November 2001), Smith "looks at things Native and national through bifocals of the old and the new, the sacred and the profane, the divine and the witty."

INSTALLATION AND VIDEO ART

The issue of art's potential social mission and the desire to make art meaningful to a larger public took on a new prominence in the 1990s. Contemporary artists experimented with new media, such as video monitors to connect with modern audiences saturated by a media-oriented culture. Beginning in the early 1980s, Jenny Holzer (b. 1950) turned to some of advertising's more pervasive tools, including electronic signage, to reach out to people who do not go to galleries and museums. For example, using the Spectacolor board then in use in New York City's Times Square, she flashed a series of short, provocative messages. Holzer phrased her messages as one-liners suited to the reading habits

of Americans raised on advertising sound bites. Holzer's use of signage as a medium emphasizes the postmodern outlook that art consists of layers of "texts" (or meanings) that can be "read" (see "Deconstruction," left).

In a spectacular installation in 1989–90, Holzer wrapped her signboards in a continuous loop around the three-floor spiraling interior of Frank Lloyd Wright's Guggenheim Museum (fig. 20-38). The words moved and flashed in red, green, and yellow colored lights, surrounding the visitor with Holzer's unsettling declarations ("You are a victim of the rules you live by") and disturbing commands ("Scorn Hope," "Forget Truths," and "Don't Try to Make Me Feel Nice"). The installation also included, on the ground floor and in a side gallery, spotlighted granite benches carved with more of Holzer's texts. The juxtaposition of cutting-edge technology, lights, and motion with the static, hand-carved benches, evocative of antiquity and mortality, created a striking contrast fundamental to the expressive effect of the whole.

Installation artists often work with video, either using the video monitor itself as a visible part of their work or projecting video imagery onto walls, screens, or other surfaces. A pioneer video artist is the Korean-born, New York–based Nam June Paik (b. 1931), who proclaimed that just "as collage technique replaced oil paint, the cathode ray tube will replace the canvas." He began working with modified television sets in 1963

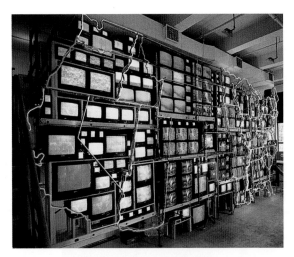

20-39 | Nam June Paik. *Electronic Superhighway: Continental U.S.* 1995. Installation: multiple television monitors, laser disk images, and neon, 15 x 32' (4.57 x 9.75 m). Holly Solomon Gallery, New York

and bought his first video camera in 1965. Since then, Paik has worked with live, recorded, and computer-generated images displayed on video monitors of varying sizes, which he often combines into sculptural ensembles such as *Electronic Superhighway: Continental U.S.* (fig. 20-39).

Electronic Superhighway is a site-specific installation created for the Holly Solomon Gallery in New York. Stretching across an entire wall, the work featured a map of the continental United States outlined in neon and backed by video monitors perpetually flashing with color and movement and accompanied by sound. The monitors within the borders of each state displayed images reflecting that state's culture and history, both distant and recent. The only exception was New York State, whose monitors displayed live, closed-circuit images of the gallery visitors, placing them in the artwork and transforming them from passive spectators into active participants.

Paik often uses rapid cuts and fast motion to evoke the ceaseless flow of images and information carried by electronic communication systems. By contrast, the California-based video artist Bill Viola (b. 1951) may employ extreme slow motion to heighten sensory awareness and induce a state of contemplation at odds with the fast-paced images of the mass media. Inspired by both Eastern and Western religions, Viola frequently addresses themes relating to birth, death, and spirituality. In *The Crossing* (fig. 20-40), two videos, projected simultaneously on either side of a 16-foot-high screen, show a casually dressed pale man on a dark set, approaching in slow motion. When his body almost fills the screen, he stops and stands impassively, facing the viewer. On one side of the screen, a small flame appears at the man's feet and gradually spreads to consume his entire body. On the other side, a trickle of water starts falling on his head, steadily increasing into a torrent that inundates him. Meanwhile, the amplified sounds of fire and water increase to a mighty roar. When the flames die down and the water subsides, the man has disappeared. What is perhaps most remarkable about this (illusionistic) annihilation is that the man does not physically resist but calmly accepts being engulfed by the elements, even stretching out his arms as if to welcome them. Viola's work dramatizes, among other things, the belief of many world religions—including Hinduism, Judaism, and Christianity—in the power of fire and water to purge and purify the human mind and soul.

While Viola's works resonate within a wide variety of cultural traditions, the photographic and video artist Shirin Neshat (b. 1957) addresses universal themes within the specific context of modern-day Islamic society. Neshat was studying art in California when revolution shook her native Iran in 1979. Returning to Iran in 1990, Neshat was shocked by the extent to which fundamentalist Islamic rule had transformed her

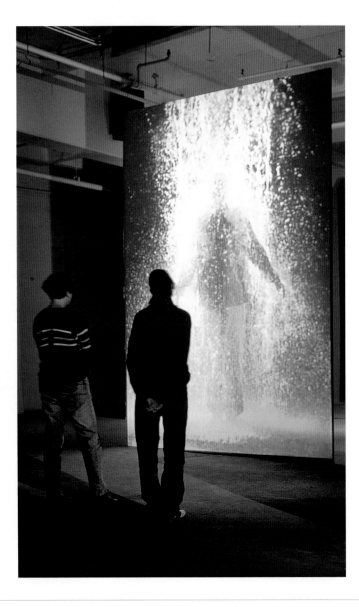

20-40 | Bill Viola. *The Crossing.* 1996. Video/sound installation with two channels of color video projected onto 16-foot-high screens, 10½ minutes. View of one screen at 1997 installation at Grand Central Market, Los Angeles. Bill Viola Studio

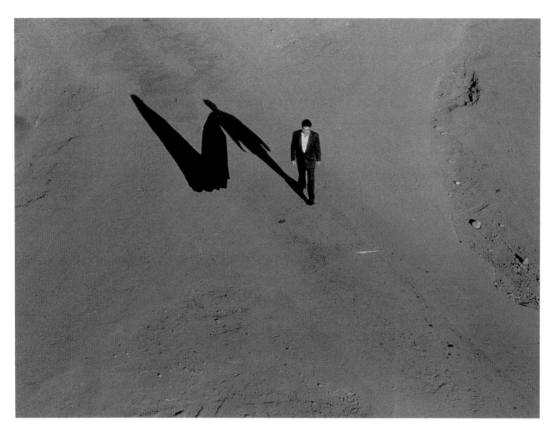

20-41

Shirin Neshat
Production still from
Fervor. 2000
Video/sound installation
with two channels of
black-and-white video
projected onto two
screens, 10 minutes
Courtesy Barbara
Gladstone Gallery

homeland, particularly through the requirement that women appear in public veiled from head to foot. Upon her return to the United States, Neshat began using the black *chador* (the enveloping veil) as the central motif of her work.

In the late 1990s Neshat began to make visually arresting and poetically structured videos that offer subtle critiques of Islamic society. *Fervor* (fig. 20-41), in Neshat's words, "focuses on taboos regarding sexuality and desire" in Islamic society that "inhibit the contact between the sexes in public. A simple gaze, for instance, is considered a sin. . . . " Composed of two separate video channels projected simultaneously on two large, adjoining screens, *Fervor* presents a simple narrative. In the opening scene, a black-veiled woman and jacket-wearing man, viewed from above, cross paths in an open landscape. Later, they meet again while entering a public ceremony where men and women are divided by a large curtain. On a stage before the audience, a bearded man fervently recounts (in Farsi, without subtitles) a story of seduction, and passionately urges his listeners to resist such sinful desires. As the audience begins to chant in response to his exhortations, the male and female protagonists grow increasingly anxious, and the woman eventually rises and exits hurriedly. *Fervor* ends with the man and woman passing each other in an alley, again without verbal or physical contact. Neshat concentrates on dualisms and divisions—between East and West, male and female, individual desire and collective law.

PUBLIC MEMORY AND ART: THE MEMORIAL

In recent years, art designed for public spaces rather than for museum walls or private collectors' homes has provoked many sensational controversies involving public funding, censorship, and individual rights.

The *Vietnam Veterans Memorial* (fig. 20-42), now widely admired as a fitting and moving testament to the Americans who died in that conflict, was originally a lightning rod for

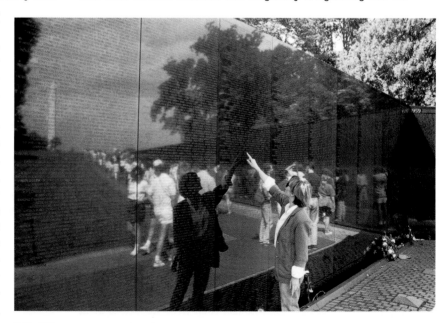

20-42   **Maya Ying Lin. *Vietnam Veterans Memorial.*** 1982. Black granite, length 500' (152 m). The Mall, Washington, D.C. (See pages 498–99.)

contention. The request for proposals for the design of the monument stipulated that the memorial be without political or military content, that it be reflective in character, that it harmonize with its surroundings, and that it include the names of the more than 58,000 dead and missing. In 1981 the Vietnam Veterans Memorial Fund awarded the commission to Maya Ying Lin (b. 1960), then an undergraduate in the architecture department at Yale University. Her Minimalist-inspired design called for two 200-foot-long walls (later expanded to almost 250 feet) of polished black granite, set into rising ground on the Mall in Washington, D.C. The names of the dead were to be incised into the stone in the order in which they died.

While construction was underway, several veterans groups asked that a realistic 8-foot sculpture of three soldiers on patrol be added toward the apex of the memorial and that a 50-foot flagpole also be raised. The veterans felt that in this way the survivors, too, would be honored. After much negotiation, a compromise provided that the additions would be made farther from the Lin design, at one entrance to the memorial grounds. In the end, the memorial as designed by Lin became one of the most compelling monuments in the United States. Quiet and solemn, it creates an understated encounter between the living, reflected in the mirrorlike polished granite, and the dead, whose names are etched into the black stone.

Art in public places often engages our intellect, educating or reminding us of significant events in history. Yet the most effective memorials also appeal to our emotions. Public memorials—art forms themselves—can be both a universal and intimate experience, addressing subjects that have entered our collective conscious as a nation, yet remain highly personal. The temporary light memorial to the victims of the World Trade Center disaster (fig. 20-43) followed this tradition of public memorial and at the same time broke new ground in the realm of public art.

Soon after the Twin Towers of the World Trade Center in New York City were destroyed on September 11, 2001, artists, architects, government officials, and ordinary citizens sought to create a meaningful testament that would serve several purposes. It was felt that a global statement against terrorism needed to be made and that the memorial should speak to the loss of lives as well as to the loss of innocence that occurred when such a prominent symbol of democracy was attacked on American soil.

Conceived and executed during the Cold War (see page 500), the World Trade Center reflected the United States' confidence in itself as a global power. The Twin Towers, two abstract blocks standing 110 stories tall, dominated the Manhattan skyline. Their ambitious height represented the last triumph of the International Style (see Chapter 19). While their simplistic and brute form was not well received by some critics, their sheer size left all in awe of this major engineering accomplishment. The Twin Towers became a symbolic gateway to Western democratic freedom, standing not far from another such symbol, the Statue of Liberty in New York City's harbor.

A public memorial to the World Trade Center, to what it represented, and to those who lost their lives, needed to be as monumental as the original buildings and the democratic values for which the Twin Towers had stood. The shock of seeing

20-43 **Digital rendering of the *Tribute in Light* memorial** by artists Julian LaVerdiere and Paul Myoda as it appears on the cover of *Art in America*, November 2001
Reprinted by permission of Brant Publications

This digital rendering illustrated on the cover of *Art in America* shows two towers of light shaped much like the original skyscrapers (1,368 and 1,362 feet; 417 and 415 meters tall) designed by American architect Minoru Yamasaki (1912–1986), completed 1973/80 and destroyed September 11, 2001. The idea for a light memorial was conceived separately in September 2001 by the architects John Bennett and Gustavo Bondevardi and the artists Paul Myoda and Julian LaVerdiere, who eventually joined together to include architect Richard Nash Gould and light fabricator Paul Marantz. The *Tribute in Light* beams, when illuminated March 11, 2002, were more transparent than this rendering, flickering in and out of sight as fog moved across the city skyline. Where the beams intersected with the clouds, puddles of light formed, appearing to open the heavens.

a terribly altered Manhattan skyline and the need to psychologically rebuild, fill the void, and heal the city while also mourn the loss of life and innocence played significant roles in shaping a public memorial. It was within this varied framework that the *Tribute in Light* memorial was conceived shortly after the September 11 attacks.

Six months after the tragedy, 88 mega bulbs (searchlights in the shape of $4\frac{1}{2}$-foot tall cannons) were amassed to form two distinct projectiles of light that would serve as giant votive candles for what became known as New York's "phantom limbs." The towers of light were built adjacent to the attack site, which at the time was still being excavated for victims' remains. Pointing seven miles into the sky, the two beams of light rose higher than the original towers they were made to represent, disappearing into the skies above Manhattan. Their beauty and power lay in their formal simplicity. Though ethereal and temporary, the lights were a testament to the enduring resiliency of the citizens of New York City, the United States, and the free world in the face of terrorism. The *Tribute in Light* was both personally poignant, especially for a population in mourning, but also politically powerful and confrontational in its symbolism. New York City, it proclaimed, would rebuild itself and its amputated skyline even while the sting of the terrorism was fresh and the area where the World Trade Center had stood—"ground zero"—was still being treated as a gravesite and crime scene.

Herbert Muschamp, architecture critic for *The New York Times*, wrote in March 2002 about the timeless effectiveness of a light memorial as public art: " . . . because of its neutrality, light can easily absorb a range of ideological connotations. . . . Ancient builders designed monuments to align sacred sites with the positions of sun and moon. The lightness of Gothic construction was inseparable from the biblical narratives inscribed in stained glass for the benefit of those who couldn't read. . . . Like the Statue of Liberty's torch and crown, the clear white radiance [of the *Tribute in Light*] enlightens the world, and New York's relationship to it." The lights were extinguished on April 14, 2002.

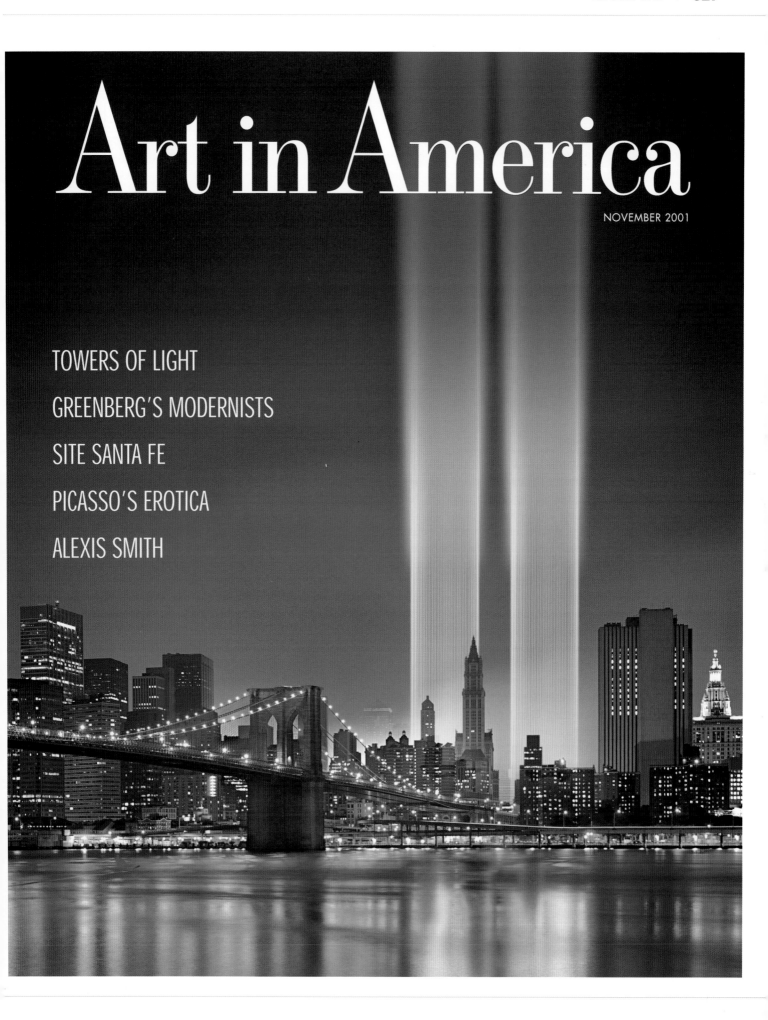

Art in America

NOVEMBER 2001

TOWERS OF LIGHT

GREENBERG'S MODERNISTS

SITE SANTA FE

PICASSO'S EROTICA

ALEXIS SMITH

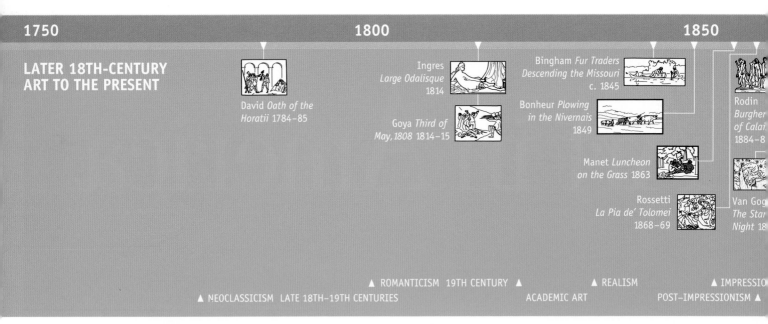

1750   1800   1850

LATER 18TH-CENTURY
ART TO THE PRESENT

David *Oath of the Horatii* 1784–85

Ingres *Large Odalisque* 1814

Goya *Third of May, 1808* 1814–15

Bingham *Fur Traders Descending the Missouri* c. 1845

Bonheur *Plowing in the Nivernais* 1849

Manet *Luncheon on the Grass* 1863

Rossetti *La Pia de' Tolomei* 1868–69

Rodin *Burgher of Calai* 1884–8

Van Gog *The Star Night* 18

▲ ROMANTICISM 19TH CENTURY ▲   ▲ REALISM   ▲ IMPRESSIO

▲ NEOCLASSICISM LATE 18TH–19TH CENTURIES   ACADEMIC ART   POST–IMPRESSIONISM ▲

LOOKING BACK 7

Point-Counterpoint

Science and technology defined and energized nineteenth- and twentieth-century culture. The examination of the material world, begun in the fifteenth century in the West, led to a continuous stream of new approaches to many activities, including the arts. The so-called scientific method—observe and collect evidence, analyze and evaluate data, propose and test hypotheses, and only then accept or reject the results—describes the approach of many artists in the previous two centuries just as aptly as it characterizes the orientation of scientists and leaders of business and industry.

Beginning in the nineteenth century, artists and art movements reacted to each other with accelerating vigor, as tastes swung back and forth between the poles of Neoclassicism and Romanticism. Somewhat later, the point-counterpoint relationship between Braque and Picasso, as they challenged and inspired each other in creating Cubist paintings, prints, and collages, exemplifies the way in which artists have proposed, tested, and revised their ideas and techniques. New technology also had a profound impact on how people made and saw art. Photography and cinema, video, and computers changed the way people visualize and understand the world.

As the twentieth century unfolded, art was increasingly influenced by and dependent on theoretical positions. In the late nineteenth century, the Impressionists claimed to respond to the visual world as objective organs of sight in order to scientifically record the light and color of the world on their canvases. Then, in reaction, others, such as Paul Cézanne, sought to reproduce solid forms or, like Vincent van Gogh, to capture emotional

states. Later, Surrealists emphasized the irrational, emotional, or the unconscious state. In contrast, Mondrian tried to become entirely rational, the embodiment of pure reason; his painting expressed a classical aesthetic. Art that was at least as much conceptual as it was visual came to the fore. Artists produced happenings, then performances, then eliminated the tangible work of art altogether. Some artists became active participants in highly untraditional methods, even turning themselves into works of art: Bruce Nauman, to name one, made himself into a fountain. For conceptual artists, such as Nauman, and performance artists, photography played a crucial role, documenting their temporary or time-based works. But even arguing factions could agree that in the modern and postmodern eras nearly every point of view has value. Postmodern artists could play with any and every style and medium—including the elimination of the physical object altogether—while also maintaining an ironic distance.

Even when artists have seemed to be more interested in intellectual exercise than in the physical object, the public has demonstrated its enduring love of beautifully made things by its robust attendance at museums and galleries. Certain styles and periods continue to captivate us: ancient Egypt, Impressionist and Post-Impressionist painting, old media made new, such as glass, goldsmithery, and the fiber arts, and art attached to intriguing personalities such as Andy Warhol's or Frida Kahlo's. It seems that our appreciation of the work of art as a superbly crafted object, an intellectually challenging encounter, and an aesthetically rewarding visual experience will outlast fads of taste and the seduction of technology.

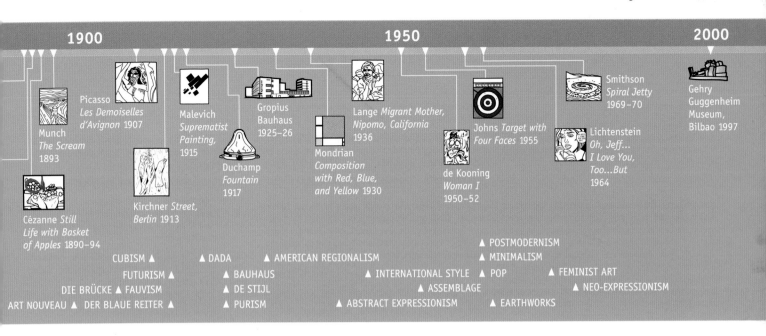

1900 1950 2000

Munch *The Scream* 1893

Picasso *Les Demoiselles d'Avignon* 1907

Malevich *Suprematist Painting,* 1915

Gropius *Bauhaus* 1925–26

Duchamp *Fountain* 1917

Mondrian *Composition with Red, Blue, and Yellow* 1930

Lange *Migrant Mother, Nipomo, California* 1936

de Kooning *Woman I* 1950–52

Johns *Target with Four Faces* 1955

Lichtenstein *Oh, Jeff... I Love You, Too...But* 1964

Smithson *Spiral Jetty* 1969–70

Gehry *Guggenheim Museum, Bilbao* 1997

Cézanne *Still Life with Basket of Apples* 1890–94

Kirchner *Street, Berlin* 1913

CUBISM ▲
FUTURISM ▲
DIE BRÜCKE ▲ FAUVISM
ART NOUVEAU ▲ DER BLAUE REITER ▲

▲ DADA
▲ BAUHAUS
▲ DE STIJL
▲ PURISM

▲ AMERICAN REGIONALISM
▲ INTERNATIONAL STYLE
▲ ASSEMBLAGE
▲ ABSTRACT EXPRESSIONISM

▲ POSTMODERNISM
▲ MINIMALISM
▲ POP
▲ EARTHWORKS

▲ FEMINIST ART
▲ NEO-EXPRESSIONISM

Neoclassicism, Romanticism, Realism, Later 19th-Century Art, and Modern and Contemporary Styles

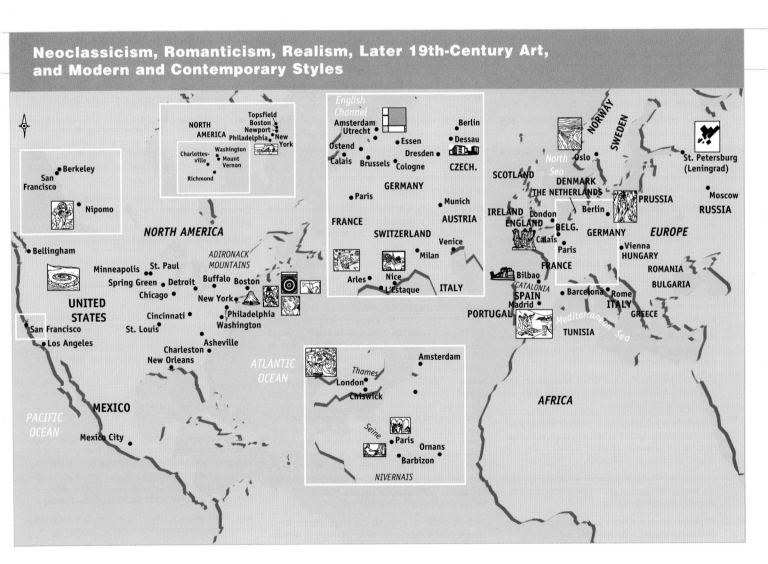

Glossary

abacus The flat slab at the top of a **capital**, directly under the **entablature**.

abstract, abstraction Any art that does not represent observable aspects of nature or transforms visible forms into a pattern resembling the original model. Also: the formal qualities of this process.

academy, academician An institutional group established for the training of artists. Most academies date from the Renaissance and after; they were particularly powerful state-run institutions in the seventeenth and eighteenth centuries. In general, academies replaced **guilds** as the venue where students learned the craft of art and were also provided with a complete education, including art theory and artistic rules. The academies helped artists to be seen as trained specialists, rather than as craftspeople, and promoted the change in the social status of the artist. An academician is an official academy-trained artist.

acanthus A leafy plant whose foliage inspired architectural ornamentation, used in the **Corinthian** and **Composite** orders and in the **relief** scroll known as the *rinceau*.

acropolis The citadel of an ancient Greek city, located at its highest point and consisting of temples, a treasury, and sometimes a royal palace. The most famous is the Acropolis in Athens, where the ruins of the Parthenon can be found.

adobe Sun-baked blocks made of clay mixed with straw. Also: the buildings made with this material.

aedicula (aediculae) A decorative architectural frame, usually found around a **niche**, door, or window. An aedicula is made up of a **pediment** and **entablature** supported by **columns** or **pilasters**.

aesthetics The philosophy of beauty.

aisle Passage or open corridor of a church, hall, or other building that parallels the main space, usually on both sides, and is delineated by a row, or **arcade**, of **columns** or **piers**. Called **side aisles** when they flank the **nave** of a church.

album A book consisting of blank pages (**album leaves**) on which typically an artist may sketch, draw, or paint.

allegory In a work of art, an image (or images) that illustrates an **abstract** concept, idea, or story, often suggesting a deeper meaning.

altar A tablelike structure where religious rites are performed. In Christian churches, the altar is the site of the rite of the **Eucharist**.

altarpiece A painted or carved panel or **winged** structure placed at the back of or behind and above an **altar**. Contains religious imagery, often specific to the place of worship for which it was made.

ambulatory The passage (walkway) around the **apse** in a **basilican** church or around the central space in a **centrally planned building**.

amphora An ancient Greek jar for storing oil or wine, with an egg-shaped body and two curved handles.

aniconic A representation without images of human figures.

animal interlace Decoration made up of interwoven animals or serpents, often found in Celtic and early northern European art. See **ribbon interlace**.

animal style A type of imagery used in Europe and western Asia during the ancient and medieval periods, characterized by animals or animal-like **forms** arranged in intricate patterns or combats.

apotheosis Deification of a person or thing. In art, often shown as an ascent to heaven or glory, borne by an eagle, angels, or **putti**.

apprentice A student artist or craftsperson in training. In a traditional system of art and craft training established under the **guilds** and still in use today, master artists took on apprentices (students) for a specific number of years. The apprentice was taught every aspect of the artist's craft, and he or she participated in the master's workshop or **atelier**.

appropriation Term used to describe an artist's practice of borrowing from another source for a new work of art. While in previous centuries artists often copied one another's figures, **motifs**, or **compositions**, in modern times the sources for appropriation extend from material culture to works of art.

apse, apsidal A large semicircular or polygonal (and usually **vaulted**) **niche** protruding from the end wall of a building. In a Christian church, it contains the **altar**. Apsidal is an adjective describing the condition of having such a semicircular or polygonal space.

aquatint A type of **intaglio** printmaking developed in the eighteenth century that produces an area of even **tone** without laborious **cross-hatching**. The aquatint is made by using a porous resin coating on a metal plate, which, when immersed in acid, allows an even, allover biting of the plate. The resulting printed image has a granular, textural effect.

aqueduct A trough to carry flowing water, if necessary, supported by **arches**.

arabesque A type of **linear** surface decoration based on foliage and **calligraphic forms**, usually characterized by flowing lines and swirling shapes.

arcade A series of arches, carried by **columns** or **piers** and supporting a common wall or **lintel**. In a **blind** arcade, the arches and supports are engaged (attached to the background wall) and have a decorative function.

arch In architecture, a curved structural element that spans an open space. Built from wedge-shaped stone blocks called **voussoirs**, which, when placed together and held at the top by a trapezoidal **keystone**, form an effective weight-bearing unit. Requires **buttresses** at either side to contain outward thrust caused by the weight of the structure. **Corbel arch**: arch or **vault** formed by **courses** of stones, each of which projects beyond the lower course until the space is enclosed; usually finished with a **capstone**. **Horseshoe arch**: an arch of more than a half-circle, often used in western Islamic architecture. **Ogival arch**: a pointed arch created by S-curves. **Relieving arch**: an arch built into a heavy wall just above a **post-and-lintel** structure (such as a gate, door, or window) to help support the wall above. Relieves some of the weight on the lintel by transferring the load to the side walls.

archaic smile The curved lips of an ancient Greek statue, usually interpreted as an attempt to animate the features.

architrave The bottom element of an **entablature**, beneath the **frieze** and the **cornice**.

archivolt Curved **molding** formed by the **voussoirs** making up an **arch**.

ashlar See **dressed stone**.

assemblage An artwork created by gathering and manipulating two- and/or three-dimensional found objects.

atelier The studio or workshop of a master artist or craftsperson, often including junior associates and **apprentices**.

atmospheric perspective See **perspective**.

atrium An unroofed interior courtyard in a Roman house, sometimes having a pool. Also: the open courtyard in front of a Christian church, or an entrance area in modern architecture.

attic story The top story of a building. In **classical** architecture, the level above the **entablature**, often decorated or carrying an inscription.

attribute The symbolic object or objects that identify a particular deity, saint, or personification in art.

automatism A technique whereby the usual intellectual control of the artist over his or her brush or pencil is forgone. The artist's aim is to allow the subconscious to create the artwork without rational interference. Also called **automatic writing**.

avant-garde A term derived from the French military word meaning "before the group," or "vanguard." Avant-garde denotes those artists or concepts of a strikingly new, experimental, or radical nature for the time.

axis mundi A concept of an axis of the world, which denotes important sacred sites and provides a link between the human and celestial realms. For example, in Buddhist art, the *axis mundi* can be marked by monumental freestanding decorated pillars.

background Within the depicted space of an artwork, the area of the image at the greatest distance from the **picture plane**.

bailey The outermost walled courtyard of a castle.

baldachin A canopy (whether suspended from the ceiling, projecting from a wall, or supported by **columns**) placed over an honorific or sacred space such as a throne or church **altar**.

balustrade A low barrier consisting of a series of short circular posts (called balusters), with a rail on top.

baptistry A building used for the Christian ritual of baptism. It is usually separate from the main church and often octagonal or circular in shape.

barrel vault See **vault**.

base Any support. Masonry supporting a statue or the **shaft** of a **column**.

basilica A large rectangular building. Often built with a **clerestory**, **side aisles** separated from the center **nave** by **colonnades**, and an **apse** at one or both ends. Roman centers for administration, later adapted to Christian church use. Constantine's architects added a tranverse aisle at the end of the nave called a **transept**.

bay A unit of space defined by architectural elements such as **columns**, **piers**, and walls.

beehive tomb A **corbel** vaulted tomb, conical in shape like a beehive, and covered by an earthen mound.

bell krater An ancient Greek bell-shaped vessel for mixing wine and water.

Benday dots In modern printing and typesetting, the dots that make up lettering and images. Often machine- or computer-generated, the dots are very small and closely spaced to give the effect of density and richness of **tone**.

biomorphic Adjective used to describe forms that resemble shapes found in nature. Also, a **style** in art characterized by biomorphic shapes is called **Biomorphism**.

bird's-eye view A view from above.

black-figure A style of ancient Greek pottery in which black figures are painted on a red clay ground.

blackware A ceramic technique that produces pottery with a primarily black surface. Blackware has both matte and glossy patterns on the surface of the wares.

blind window See **blind**.

blind Decorative elements attached to the surface of a wall, with no openings.

block printing A printed image, such as a **woodcut** or wood engraving, made from a carved wooden block.

bodhisattva A deity that is far advanced in the long process of transforming itself into a buddha. While seeking enlightenment or emancipation from this world (*nirvana*), bodhisattvas help others attain this same liberation.

Book of Hours A private prayer book, having a calendar, services for the canonical hours, and sometimes special prayers.

bracket, bracketing An architectural element that projects from a wall and that often helps support a horizontal part of a building, such as beams or the eaves of a roof.

bronze A metal made from copper alloy, usually mixed with tin. Also: any sculpture or object made from this substance.

burin A metal instrument used in **engraving** to cut lines into the metal plate. The sharp end of the burin is trimmed to give a diamond-shaped cutting point, while the other end is finished with a wooden handle that fits into the engraver's palm.

buttress, buttressing An architectural support, usually consisting of massive masonry built against an exterior wall to brace the wall and counter the thrust of the **vaults**. Transfers the weight of the vault to the ground. **Flying buttress**: An **arch** built on the exterior of a building that transfers the thrust of the roof vaults at important stress points through the wall to a detached buttress **pier** leading to the wall buttress.

cairn A pile of stones or earth and stones that served both as a prehistoric burial site and as a marker of underground tombs.

calligraphy The art of highly ornamental handwriting.

calotype The first photographic process utilizing negatives and paper positives. It was invented by William Henry Fox Talbot in the late 1830s.

came (cames) A lead strip used in the making of leaded or **stained-glass** windows. Cames have an indented vertical groove on the sides into which the separate pieces of glass are fitted to hold the design together.

camera obscura An early cameralike device used in the Renaissance and later for recording images of nature. Made from a dark box (or room) with a hole in one side (sometimes fitted with a lens), the camera obscura operates when bright light shines through the hole, casting an upside-down image of an object outside onto the inside wall of the box.

canon Established rules or standards.

canon of proportions A set of ideal mathematical ratios in art based on measurements of the human body.

cantilever A beam or structure that is anchored at one end and projects horizontally beyond its vertical support, such as a wall or **column**. It can carry loads throughout the rest of its unsupported length. Or a bracket used to carry the **cornice** or extend the eaves of a building.

capital The sculpted block that tops a **column**. According to the conventions of the orders, capitals include different decorative elements. See **order**. Also: a historiated capital is one displaying a narrative.

capstone The final, topmost stone in a **corbel** arch or **vault**, which joins the sides and completes the structure.

cartoon A full-scale drawing used to transfer the outline of a design onto a surface (such as a wall, canvas, or panel) to be painted, carved, or woven.

cartouche A frame for a **hieroglyphic** inscription formed by a rope design surrounding an oval space. Used to signify a sacred or honored name. Also: in architecture, a decorative device or plaque used for inscriptions or epitaphs.

caryatid A sculpture of a draped female figure acting as a **column** supporting an entablature.

catacomb An underground burial ground consisting of tunnels on different levels, having **niches** for urns and **sarcophagi** and often incorporating rooms (**cubiculae**).

cathedral The principal Christian church in a diocese, built in the bishop's administrative center and housing his throne (*cathedra*).

cella The principal interior room in a Greek or Roman temple within which the cult statue was usually housed. Also called the **naos**.

centering A temporary structure that supports a masonry **arch** and **vault** or **dome** during construction until the mortar is fully dried and the masonry is self-sustaining.

central-plan building Any structure designed with a primary central space surrounded by symmetrical areas on each side. For example, Greek-cross plan (equal-armed cross).

Chacmool In Mayan sculpture, a half-reclining figure probably representing an offering bearer.

château (châteaux) A French country house or residential castle. A château fort is a military castle incorporating defensive works such as towers and battlements.

cherub (cherubim) The second-highest order of angels. Popularly, an idealized small child, usually depicted naked and with wings.

chevet In a French church the space beyond the **transepts** consisting of **apse**, **ambulatory**, and radiating chapels.

chevron A decorative motif made up of repeated inverted Vs; a zigzag pattern.

chiaroscuro An Italian word designating the contrast of dark and light in a painting, drawing, or print.

Chiaroscuro creates spatial depth and **volumetric** forms through gradations in the intensity of light and shadow.

choir The section of a Christian church reserved for the clergy or the religious, either between the **crossing** and the **apse** or in the **nave** just before the crossing, screened or walled and fitted with stalls (seats). Also an area reserved for singers.

churrigeresque An elaborate style of Baroque architecture and ornament seen in Spain, Portugal, and Latin America, named after the Spanish architect José Benito de Churriguera (1665–1725).

Classical A term referring to the art and architecture of ancient Greece between c. 480–320 BCE.

classical, classicism Any aspect of later art or architecture reminiscent of the rules, **canons**, and examples of the art of ancient Greece and Rome. Also: in general, any art aspiring to the qualities of restraint, balance, and rational order exemplified by the ancients. Also: the peak of perfection in any period.

clerestory The topmost zone of a wall with windows in a **basilica** extending above the **aisle** roofs. Provides direct light into the central interior space (the **nave**).

cloisonné An enamel technique in which metal wire or strips are affixed to the surface to form the design. The resulting areas (**cloisons**) are filled with **enamel** (colored glass).

cloister An open space, part of a monastery, surrounded by an **arcaded** or **colonnaded** walkway, often having a fountain and garden, and dedicated to nonliturgical activities and the secular life of the religious. Members of a cloistered order do not interact with outsiders.

codex (codices) A book, or a group of manuscript pages (**folios**), held together by stitching or other binding on one side.

coffer A recessed decorative panel that is used to reduce the weight of and to decorate ceilings or **vaults**. The use of coffers is called coffering.

coiling A technique in basketry. In coiled baskets a spiraling structure is held in place by another material.

collage A technique in which cutout paper forms (often painted or printed), and/or found materials, are pasted onto another surface. Also: an image created using this technique.

colonnade A row of **columns**, supporting a straight **lintel** (as in a porch or **portico**) or a series of **arches** (an **arcade**).

colonnette A small **column** attached to a **pier** or wall.

colophon The data placed at the end of a book listing the book's author, publisher, **illuminator**, and other information related to its production.

colossal order See **order**.

column An architectural element used for support and/or decoration. Consists of a rounded vertical **shaft** placed on a **base** topped by a decorative **capital**. May follow the rules of one of the architectural **orders**. Although usually freestanding, columns can be attached to a wall (engaged).

column statue A column carved to depict a human figure.

complementary color The primary and secondary colors across from each other on the color wheel (red and green, blue and orange, yellow and purple). When juxtaposed, the intensity of both colors increases.

Composite order See **order**.

composition The arrangement of **formal elements** in an artwork.

compound pier A **pier** or large **column** with **shafts**, **pilasters**, or **colonnettes** attached to it on one or all sides.

conch A half-**dome**.

concrete A building material developed by the Romans, made primarily from lime, sand, cement, and rubble mixed with water. Concrete is easily poured or **molded** when wet and hardens into a particularly strong and durable stonelike substance.

cone mosaic An early type of surface decoration created by pressing colored cones of baked clay into prepared wet plaster.

connoisseurship A term derived from the French word *connoisseur*, meaning "an expert," and signifying the study and evaluation of art based on formal, visual, and stylistic analysis. A **connoisseur** studies the **style** and technique of an object to deduce its relative quality and possible maker. This is done through visual association with other, similar objects and styles. See also **contextualism**.

content When discussing a work of art, the term can include all of the following: its subject matter; the ideas contained in the work; the artist's intention; and even its meaning for the beholder.

contextualism A methodological approach in art history which focuses on the cultural background of an art object. Contextualism utilizes the literature, history, economics, and social developments (among other things) of a period, as well as the object itself, to explain the meaning of an artwork. See also **connoisseurship**.

contrapposto A twisting body position. Also: a way of representing the human body so that its weight appears to be borne on one leg.

corbel, corbeling A roofing and arching technique in which each course of stone projects inward and slightly beyond the previous layer (a corbel) until the uppermost corbels meet. Results in a high, nearly pointed **arch** or **vault**. A corbel table is a table supported by corbels.

corbel arch See **arch**.

corbeled vault See **vault**.

Corinthian order See **order**.

cornice The uppermost section of a **Classical entablature**. More generally, a horizontally projecting element found at the top of a building wall or **pedestal**. A raking cornice is formed by the junction of two slanted cornices, most often found in **pediments**.

course A horizontal layer of stone used in building.

crenellation Alternating high and low sections of a wall, giving a notched appearance and creating permanent defensive shields in the walls of fortified buildings.

cross-hatching A technique primarily used in printmaking and drawing, in which a set of parallel lines (hatching) is drawn across a previous set, but from a differing (usually right) angle. Cross-hatching gives a great density of **tone** and allows the artist to create the illusion of shadows efficiently.

cross vault See **vault**.

crossing The juncture of the **nave** and the **transept** in a church, often marked on the exterior by a tower or

dome.

cruciform A term describing anything that is cross-shaped, as in the cruciform plan of a church.

cubiculum (cubicula) A small private room for burials in the **catacombs**.

cuneiform writing An early form of writing with wedge-shaped marks; impressed into wet clay with a **stylus**, primarily by ancient Mesopotamians.

curtain wall A wall in a building that does not support any of the weight of the structure. Also: the free-standing outer wall of a castle, usually encircling the inner **bailey** (yard) and **keep** (primary defensive tower).

cycle A series of images depicting a story or theme intended to be displayed together, and forming a visual narrative.

cyclopean construction A method of building utilizing huge blocks of rough-hewn stone. Any large-scale, **monumental** building project that impresses by sheer size. Named after one-eyed giants of legendary strength from Greek myths.

cylinder seal A small cylindrical stone decorated with **incised** patterns. When rolled across soft clay or wax, the resulting raised pattern or design (**relief**) served as an identifying signature.

dado (dadoes) The lower part of a wall, differentiated in some way (by a **molding** or different color) from the upper section.

daguerreotype An early photographic process named for Louis-Jacques Mondé Daguerre. A daguerreotype was a positive print made on a light-sensitized copper-plate.

diptych Two panels of equal size, usually decorated with paintings or **reliefs**, and hinged together.

dolmen A prehistoric structure made up of two or more large (often upright) stones supporting a large, flat, horizontal slab or slabs.

dome A round **vault**, usually over a circular space. Consists of a curved masonry vault of shapes and cross sections that can vary from hemispherical to bulbous to ovoidal. May use a supporting vertical wall (**drum**), from which the vault springs, and may be crowned by an open space (**oculus**) and/or an exterior **lantern**. When a dome is built over a square space, an intermediate element is required to make the transition to a circular drum. There are two types: A dome on **pendentives** (spherical triangles) incorporates **arched**, sloping intermediate sections of wall that carry the weight and thrust of the dome to heavily **buttressed** supporting **piers**. A dome on **squinches** uses an arch built into the wall (squinch) in the upper corners of the space to carry the weight of the dome across the corners of the square space below. A half-dome or conch may cover a semicircular space.

Doric order See **order**.

dressed stone Highly finished, precisely cut blocks of stone laid in even **courses**, creating a uniform face with fine joints. Often used as a facing on the visible exterior of a building, especially as a **veneer** for the **facade**. Also called **ashlar**.

drillwork The technique of using a drill for the creation of certain effects in sculpture.

drum The wall that supports a **dome**. Also: a segment of the circular **shaft** of a **column**.

drypoint An **intaglio** printmaking process by which a metal (usually copper) plate is directly inscribed by

means of a pointed instrument (**stylus**). The resulting design of scratched lines is inked, wiped, and printed. Also: the print made by this process.

earthworks Artwork and/or sculpture, usually on a large scale, created by manipulating the natural environment. Also: the earth walls of a fort.

echinus A cushionlike circular element found below the **abacus** of a **Doric capital**. Also: a similarly shaped **molding** (usually with egg-and-dart **motifs**) underneath the **volutes** of an **Ionic** capital. (Egg-and-dart is a **motif** used in decorative **molding**, and is made up of an alternating pattern of round (egg) and downward-pointing, tapered (dart) elements.)

edition A single printing of a book or print. An edition includes only what is printed at a particular moment, usually pulled from the same press by the same publisher.

elevation The arrangement, proportions, and details of any vertical side or face of a building. Also: an architectural drawing showing an exterior or interior wall of a building.

embroidery The technique in needlework of decorating fabric by stitching designs and figures with threads. Also: the material produced by this technique.

enamel A technique in which powdered glass is applied to a metal surface in a decorative design. After firing, the glass forms an opaque or transparent substance that is fixed to the metal background. Also: an object created with enamel technique. See **cloisonné**.

enamelwork See **enamel**.

engaged column See **column**.

engraving An **intaglio** printmaking process of inscribing an image, design, or letters onto a metal or wood surface from which a print is made. An engraving is usually drawn with a sharp implement (**burin**) directly onto the surface of the plate. Also: the print made from this process.

entablature In the **Classical orders**, the horizontal elements above the **columns** and **capitals**. The entablature consists of, from top to bottom, a **cornice**, **frieze**, and **architrave**.

entasis A slight swelling of the **shaft** of a Greek **column**. The optical illusion of entasis makes the column appear from afar to be straight.

etching An **intaglio** printmaking process, in which a metal plate is coated with acid-resistant resin and then inscribed with a **stylus** in a design, revealing the plate below. The plate is then immersed in acid, and the design of exposed metal is eaten away by the acid. The resin is removed, leaving the design etched permanently into the metal and the plate ready to be inked, wiped, and printed.

Eucharist The central rite of the Christian Church, from the Greek word "thanksgiving." Also known as the Mass or Holy Communion, it is based on the Last Supper. According to traditional Catholic Christian belief, consecrated bread and wine become the body and blood of Christ; in Protestant belief, bread and wine symbolize the body and blood.

exedra (exedrae) In architecture, a semicircular **niche**. On a small scale, often used as decoration, whereas larger exedrae can form interior spaces.

expressionism Terms describing a work of art in which forms are created primarily to evoke subjective emotions rather than to portray objective reality.

facade The face or front wall of a building.

fête galante A subject in painting depicting well-dressed people at leisure in a park or country setting. It is most often associated with eighteenth-century French Rococo painting.

finial A knoblike architectural decoration usually found at the top point of a spire, **pinnacle**, canopy, or **gable**. Also found on furniture.

flower piece Any painting with flowers as the primary subject; a **still life** of flowers.

flying buttress See **buttress**.

folio A large sheet of paper, which, when folded and cut, becomes four separate or **parchment** pages in a book. Also: a page or leaf in a **manuscript** or book; more generally, any large book.

foreground Within the depicted space of an artwork, the area that is closest to the **picture plane**.

foreshortening The illusion created on a flat surface in which figures and objects appear to recede or project sharply into space. Accomplished according to the rules of **perspective**.

form In speaking of a work of art or architecture, the term refers to purely visual components: line, color, shape, texture, mass, spatial qualities, and **composition**—all of which are called **formal elements**.

formalism, formalist An approach to the understanding, appreciation, and valuation of art based almost solely on considerations of **form**. This approach tends to regard an artwork as independent of its time and place of making.

formline In Native American works of art, a line that defines a space or **form**.

forum A Roman town center; site of temples and administrative buildings and used as a market or gathering area for the citizens.

fresco A painting technique in which water-based pigments are applied to a surface of wet plaster (called *buon fresco*). *Fresco a secco* is created by painting on dried plaster. **Murals** made by both these techniques are called frescoes.

frieze The middle element of an **entablature**, between the **architrave** and the **cornice**. Usually decorated with sculpture, painting, or **moldings**. Also: any continuous flat band with **relief** sculpture or painted decorations.

frontispiece An illustration opposite or preceding the title page of a book. Also: the primary **facade** or main entrance **bay** of a building.

fusuma Sliding doors covered with paper, used in an East Asian house. *Fusuma* are often highly decorated with paintings and colored **backgrounds**.

gable The triangular wall space found on the end wall of a building between the two sides of a pitched roof. Also: a triangular decorative panel that has a gablelike shape.

gallery In church architecture, the story found above the side aisles of a church, usually open to and overlooking the **nave**. Also: in secular architecture, a long room, usually above the ground floor in a private house or a public building, used for entertaining, exhibiting pictures, or promenading. Also, *galleria*.

genre A type or category of artistic form, subject, technique, **style**, or **medium**.

genre scene A term used to loosely categorize paintings depicting scenes of everyday life, including (among others) domestic interiors, parties, inn scenes, and street scenes.

geoglyphs Earthen designs on a colossal scale, often created in a landscape as if to be seen from an aerial viewpoint.

geometric A period in Greek art from about 1100 to 600 BCE; the art is characterized by patterns of rectangles, squares, and other **abstract** shapes. Also: any **style** or art using primarily these shapes.

gesso A ground made from glue, gypsum, and/or chalk forming the ground of wood panel or the priming layer of a canvas. Provides a smooth surface for painting.

gesturalism Painting and drawing in which the brushwork or line visibly records the artist's physical gesture at the moment the paint was applied or the lines laid down. Associated especially with expressive styles, such as Zen painting and Abstract Expressionism.

gilding The application of paper-thin gold leaf or gold pigment to an object made from another **medium** (for example, a sculpture or painting). Usually used as a decorative finishing detail.

giornata (giornate) Adopted from the Italian term meaning "a day's work," a *giornata* is the section of a fresco plastered and painted in a single day.

glazing An outermost layer of vitreous liquid (**glaze**) that, upon firing, renders ceramics waterproof, and forms a decorative surface. In painting, a technique particularly used with oil **mediums** in which a transparent layer of paint (**glaze**) is laid over another, usually lighter, painted or glazed area.

gold leaf Paper-thin sheets of hammered gold that are used in **gilding**.

graffiti Decorative drawings scratched on rocks, walls, or objects. Also: drawings and/or text of an obscene, political, or violent nature.

Grand Manner A grand and elevated **style** of painting popular in the eighteenth century in which the artist looked to the ancients and to the Renaissance for inspiration.

granulation A technique for decorating gold in which tiny balls of the precious metal are fused to the main surface in a pattern.

graphic arts A term referring to those arts that are drawn or printed and that utilize paper as primary support.

graphic design A concern in the visual arts for shape, line, and two-dimensional patterning, often especially apparent in works including typography and lettering.

Greek-cross plan See **central-plan building**.

grid A system of regularly spaced horizontally and vertically crossed lines that gives regularity to an architectural **plan**. Also: in painting, a **grid** enables designs to be enlarged or transferred easily.

grisaille A painting executed primarily in shades of gray.

groin vault See **vault**.

groundline The solid baseline that indicates the ground plane on which the figure stands. In ancient representations, such as those of the Egyptians, the figures and the objects are placed on a series of groundlines to indicate depth (space in **registers**).

grout A soft cement placed between the **tesserae** of a **mosaic** to hold the design together. Also used in tiling.

guild An association of craftspeople. The medieval guild had great economic power, as it controlled the selling and marketing of its members' products, and it provided economic protection, political solidarity, and training in the craft to its members. The painters' guild was usually dedicated to Saint Luke, their patron saint.

half-barrel vault See **vault**.

handscroll A long, narrow, horizontal painting or text (or combination thereof) common in Chinese and Japanese art and of a size intended for individual use. A handscroll is stored wrapped tightly around a wooden pin and is unrolled for viewing or reading.

hanging scroll In Chinese and Japanese art, a vertically oriented painting or text mounted within sections of silk. At the top is a semicircular rod; at the bottom is a round dowel. Hanging scrolls are kept rolled and tied except for special occasions, when they are hung for display, contemplation, or commemoration.

haniwa Pottery forms (cylinders, human figures, and buildings) that were placed on top of Japanese tombs or burial mounds.

Happening An art form developed in the 1960s incorporating performance, theater, and visual images. A happening was organized without a specific narrative or intent; with audience participation, the event proceeded according to chance and individual improvisation.

hemicycle A semicircular interior space or structure.

henge A circular area enclosed by stones or wood posts set up by Neolithic peoples. It is usually bounded by a ditch and raised embankment.

hieratic In painting and sculpture, a formalized **style** for representing rulers or sacred or priestly figures.

hieratic scale The use of different sizes for significant or holy figures and those of the everyday world to indicate importance. The larger the figure, the greater the importance.

hieroglyphs Picture writing; words and ideas rendered in the form of pictorial symbols.

high relief See **relief sculpture**.

historicism The strong consciousness of and attention to the institutions, themes, **styles**, and forms of the past, made accessible by historical research, textual study, and archeology.

history painting Paintings based on historical, mythological, or biblical narratives. Once considered the noblest form of art, history paintings generally convey a high moral or intellectual idea and are often painted in a grand pictorial **style**.

hollow-casting See **lost-wax casting**.

horizon line A horizontal "line" formed by the implied meeting point of earth and sky. In **linear perspective**, the **vanishing point** or points are located on this "line."

horseshoe arch See **arch**.

house-church A Christian place of worship located in a private home.

house-synagogue A Jewish place of worship located in a private home.

hue Pure color. The saturation or intensity of the hue depends on the purity of the color. Its **value** depends on its lightness or darkness.

hydria A large ancient Greek and Roman jar with three handles (horizontal ones at both sides and one vertical at the back), used for storing water.

hypostyle hall A large interior room characterized by

many closely spaced **columns** that support its roof.

icon An image in any material representing a sacred figure or event in the Byzantine, and later the Orthodox, Church. Icons were venerated by the faithful, who believed them to have miraculous powers to transmit messages to God.

iconoclasm The banning or destruction of **icons** and religious art. Iconoclasm in eighth- and ninth-century Byzantium and sixteenth- and seventeenth-century Protestant territories arose from differing beliefs about the power, meaning, function, and purpose of imagery in religion.

iconography The study of the significance and interpretation of the **subject matter** of art.

idealization A process in art through which artists strive to make their **forms** and figures attain perfection, based on pervading cultural values or their own mental image of beauty.

illumination A painting on paper or **parchment** used as illustration and/or decoration for **manuscripts** or **albums**. Usually done in rich colors, often supplemented by gold and other precious materials. The illustrators are referred to as illuminators. Also: the technique of decorating manuscripts with such paintings.

illusionism, illusionistic An appearance of reality in art created by the use of certain pictorial means, such as **perspective** and **foreshortening**. Also: the quality of having this type of appearance.

impost, impost block A block, serving to concentrate the weight above, imposed between the **capital** of a **column** and the springing of an **arch** above.

impression Any single printing of an **intaglio** print (**engraving**, **drypoint**, or **etching**). Each and every impression of a print is by nature different, given the possibilities for variation inherent in the printing process, which requires the plate to be inked and wiped between every impression.

incising A technique in which a design or inscription is cut into a hard surface with a sharp instrument.

ink painting A monochromatic **style** of painting developed in China using black ink with gray **washes**.

inlay A decorative process in which pieces of one material are set into the surface of an object fashioned from a different material.

intaglio Term used for a technique in which the design is carved out of the surface of an object, such as an engraved seal stone. In the **graphic arts**, intaglio includes **engraving**, **etching**, and **drypoint**—all processes in which ink transfers to paper from **incised**, ink-filled lines cut into a metal plate.

interlace A type of **linear** decoration in which ribbonlike bands are **illusionistically** depicted as if woven under and over one another.

intuitive perspective See **perspective**.

Ionic order See **order**.

iwan A large, **vaulted** chamber with a **monumental arched** opening on one side.

jamb In architecture, the vertical element found on both sides of an opening in a wall, and supporting an **arch** or **lintel**.

japonisme A **style** in nineteenth-century French and American art that was highly influenced by Japanese art.

joined-wood sculpture A method of constructing large-scale wooden sculpture developed in Japan. The entire work is constructed from smaller hollow blocks, each individually carved and assembled when com-

plete. The joined-wood technique allowed the production of larger sculpture, as the multiple joints alleviate the problems of drying and cracking found with sculpture carved from a single block.

kente A woven cloth made by the Ashanti peoples of Africa. *Kente* cloth is woven in long, narrow pieces in complex and colorful patterns, which are then sewn together.

key block A key block is the master block in the production of a colored **woodcut**, which requires different blocks for each color. The key block is a flat piece of wood with the entire design carved or drawn on its surface. From this, other blocks with partial drawings are made for printing the areas of different colors.

keystone The topmost **voussoir** at the center of an arch, and the last block to be placed. The pressure of this block holds the arch together. Often of a larger size and/or decorated.

keep Principal tower in a castle.

kiln An oven designed to produce the high temperature for the baking, or firing, of clay.

kinetic art Artwork that contains parts that can be moved either by hand, air, or motor.

kore (*korai*) An archaic Greek statue of a young woman.

kouros (*kouroi*) An archaic Greek statue of a young man or boy.

kylix A shallow Greek vessel or cup, used for drinking, with a wide mouth and small handles near the rim.

lacquer A hard, glossy surface varnish. Lacquer can be layered and manipulated or combined with pigments and other materials for various decorative effects.

lancet A tall narrow window crowned by a sharply pointed **arch**, typically found in Gothic architecture.

lantern A turretlike structure situated on a roof, **vault**, or **dome**, with windows that allow light into the space below.

Latin-cross plan A cross-shaped building plan, incorporating a long arm (**nave**) and three shorter arms.

linear, linearity An emphasis on line, as opposed to mass or color.

linear perspective See **perspective**.

lintel A horizontal element of any material carried by two or more vertical supports to form an opening.

literati painting A **style** of painting that reflects the taste of the educated class of East Asian intellectuals and scholars. Aspects include an appreciation for the antique, small scale, and an intimate connection between maker and audience.

lithograph A print made from a design drawn on a flat stone block with greasy crayon. Ink is applied to a wet stone and, when printed, adheres only to the greasy areas of the design.

loggia Italian term for a covered open-air **gallery**. Often used as a corridor between buildings or around a courtyard, loggias usually have **arcades** or **colonnades**.

lost-wax casting A method of casting metal, such as bronze, by a process in which a wax mold is covered with clay and plaster, then fired, melting the wax and leaving a hollow form. Molten metal is then poured into the hollow space and slowly cooled. When the hardened clay and plaster exterior shell is removed, a solid metal form remains to be smoothed and polished.

low-relief See **relief sculpture**.

lunette A semicircular wall area, framed by an **arch** over a door or window. Can be either plain or decorated.

madrasa An Islamic institution of higher learning, where teaching is focused on theology and law.

majolica Pottery painted with a tin **glaze** that, when fired, gives a lustrous and colorful surface.

mandorla An almond-shaped area in which a sacred figure, such as Christ, is represented.

mannerist A sophisticated, elegant **style** characterized by elongated **forms**, irrational spatial relationships, unusual colors and lighting effects, and exquisite craft. These traits are associated with the style called Mannerism of the sixteenth century.

manuscript A handwritten book or document.

martyrium (martyria) In Christian architecture, a church, chapel, or shrine built over the grave of a martyr or the site of a great miracle.

mastaba A flat-topped, one-story building with slanted walls over an ancient Egyptian underground tomb.

mathematical perspective See **perspective**.

matte A smooth surface without shine or luster.

mausoleum A **monumental** building used as a tomb. Named after the tomb of Mausolos erected at Halikarnassos around 350 BCE.

medallion Any round ornament or decoration. Also: a large medal.

medium (mediums) In general, the material from which any given object is made. In painting, the liquid substance in which pigments are suspended.

menorah A Jewish lamp-stand with seven or nine branches; the nine-branched menorah is used during the celebration of Hanukkah. Representations of the seven-branched menorah, once used in the Temple of Jerusalem, became a symbol of Judaism.

metope The carved, painted, or plain rectangular spaces beween the **triglyphs** of a **Doric frieze**.

middle ground Within the depicted space of an artwork, the area that takes up the middle distance of the image. See also **foreground**.

mihrab A recess or **niche** that distinguishes the wall oriented toward Mecca (*qibla*) in a mosque.

minaret A tall slender tower on the exterior of a mosque from which believers are called to prayer.

minbar A high platform or pulpit in an Islamic mosque.

modeling In painting, the process of creating the illusion of three-dimensionality on a two-dimensional surface by use of light and **shade**. In sculpture, the process of **molding** a three-dimensional form out of a malleable substance.

molding A shaped or sculpted strip with varying contours and patterns. Used as decoration on architecture, furniture, frames, and other objects.

monolith A single stone, often very large.

monumental A term used to designate a project or object that, whatever its physical size, gives an impression of grandeur.

mosaic Images formed by small colored stone or glass pieces (**tesserae**), affixed to a hard, stable surface.

mosque An edifice used for communal Muslim worship.

motif Any recurring element of a design or composition. Also: a recurring theme or subject in artwork.

mudra A symbolic hand gesture in Buddhist art that denotes certain behaviors, actions, or feelings.

mullion A slender vertical element or **colonnette** that divides a window into subsidiary sections.

multiple-point perspective See **perspective**.

muqarna The transition between decorative flat and rounded surfaces; usually found on the **vault** of a **dome**.

mural Wall-like. A large painting or decoration, done either directly on the wall or separately and affixed to it.

naos The principal room in a temple or church. In ancient architecture, the **cella**. In a Byzantine church, the **nave** and **sanctuary**.

narthex The vestibule or entrance porch of a church.

naturalism, naturalistic A **style** of depiction in which the physical appearance of the rendered image in nature is the primary inspiration. A naturalistic work appears to record the visible world.

nave The central **aisle** of a **basilica**, two or three stories high and flanked by aisles, and defined by the nave **arcade** or nave **colonnade**.

necropolis A large cemetery or burial area, literally a city of the dead.

niche A hollow or recess in a wall or other solid architectural element. Niches can be of varying size and shape, and may be intended for many different uses, from display of objects to housing of a tomb.

niello A metal technique in which a black sulfur alloy is rubbed into fine lines **engraved** into a metal (usually gold or silver). When heated, the alloy becomes fused with the surrounded metal and provides contrasting detail.

nonrepresentational **Abstract** art that does not attempt to reproduce the appearance of objects, figures, or scenes in the natural world. Also called **nonobjective art**.

obelisk A tall, four-sided stone **shaft**, hewn from a single block, that tapers at the top and is completed by a pyramidion. A sun symbol erected by the ancient Egyptians in ceremonial spaces (such as entrances to temple complexes). Today used as a commemorative monument.

oblique perspective See **perspective**.

oculus (oculi) In architecture, a circular opening. Oculi are usually found either as windows or at the apex of a **dome**. When at the top of a dome, an oculus is either open to the sky or covered by a decorative exterior **lantern**.

ogival arch See **arch**.

oil painting Any painting executed with the pigments floating in a **medium** of oil. Oil paint has particular properties that allow for greater ease of working (among others, a slow drying time, which allows for corrections, and a great range of relative opaqueness of paint layers, which permits a high degree of detail and luminescence).

one-point perspective See **perspective**.

openwork Decoration, such as **tracery**, with open spaces incorporated into the pattern.

orant The representation of a standing figure praying with outstretched and upraised arms.

order A system of proportions in **Classical** architecture that includes every aspect of the building's **plan**, ele-

vation, and decorative system. **Composite**: a combination of the Ionic and the Corinthian orders. The **capital** combines **acanthus** leaves with **volute** scrolls. **Corinthian**: the most ornate of the orders, the Corinthian includes a **base**, a fluted column **shaft** with a capital elaborately decorated with acanthus leaf carvings. Its **entablature** consists of an **architrave** decorated with **moldings**, a **frieze** often containing sculptured **reliefs**, and a **cornice** with dentils. **Doric**: the column shaft of the Doric order can be fluted or smooth-surfaced and has no base. The Doric capital consists of an undecorated **echinus** and **abacus**. The Doric entablature has a plain architrave, a frieze with **metopes** and **triglyphs**, and a simple cornice. **Ionic**: the column of the Ionic order has a base, a fluted shaft, and a capital decorated with volutes. The Ionic entablature consists of an architrave of three panels and moldings, a frieze usually containing sculpted relief ornament, and a cornice with dentils. **Tuscan**: a variation of Doric characterized by a smooth-surfaced column shaft with a base, a plain architrave, and an undecorated frieze. A **colossal order** is any of the above built on a large scale, rising through several stories in height and often raised from the ground by a **pedestal**.

orthogonal Any line running back into the represented space of a picture perpendicular to the imagined **picture plane**. In **linear perspective**, all orthogonals converge at a single **vanishing point** in the picture and are the basis for a **grid** that maps out the internal space of the image. An orthogonal **plan** is any plan for a building or city that is based exclusively on right angles, such as the grid plan of many modern cities.

pagoda An East Asian **reliquary** tower built with successively smaller, repeated stories. Each story is usually marked by an elaborate projecting roof.

painterly A **style** of painting which emphasizes the techniques and surface effects of brushwork (also color, light, and **shade**).

palette A handheld support used by artists for the storage and mixing of paint during the process of painting. Also: the choice of a range of colors made by an artist in a particular work, or typical of his or her style.

panel painting Any painting executed on a wood support. The wood is usually planed to provide a smooth surface. A panel can consist of several boards joined together.

parapet A low wall at the edge of a balcony, bridge, roof, or other place from which there is a steep drop, built for safety. A parapet walk is the passageway, usually open, immediately behind the uppermost exterior wall or battlement of a fortified building.

parchment A writing surface made from treated skins of animals. Very fine parchment is known as **vellum**.

Paris Salon The annual display of art by French artists in Paris during the eighteenth and nineteenth centuries. Established in the seventeenth century as a venue to show the work of members of the French Academy, the Salon and its judges established the accepted official **style** of the time.

passage In painting, passage refers to any particular area within a work, often those where **painterly** brushwork or color changes exist. Also: a term used to describe Paul Cézanne's technique of blending adjacent shapes.

passage grave A prehistoric tomb under a **cairn**, reached by a long, narrow, slab-lined access passageway or passageways.

pedestal A platform or **base** supporting a sculpture or other monument. Also: the block found below the

base of a **classical column** (or **colonnade**), serving to raise the entire element off the ground.

pediment A triangular **gable** found over major architectural elements such as **Classical** Greek **porticoes**, windows, or doors. Formed by an **entablature** and the ends of a sloping roof or a raking **cornice**. A similar architectural element is often used decoratively above a door or window, sometimes with a curved upper **molding**. A broken pediment is a variation on the traditional pediment, with an open space at the center of the topmost angle and/or the horizontal **cornice**.

pendentive The concave triangular section of a **vault** that forms the transition between a square or polygonal space and the circular base of a **dome**.

performance art An artwork based on a live, sometimes theatrical performance by the artist.

peristyle A surrounding **colonnade** in Greek architecture. A peristyle building is surrounded on the exterior by a colonnade. Also: a peristyle court is an open colonnaded courtyard, often having a pool and garden.

perspective A system for representing three-dimensional space on a two-dimensional surface. **Atmospheric perspective**: A method of rendering the effect of spatial distance by subtle variations in color and clarity of representation. **Intuitive perspective**: A method of giving the impression of recession by visual instinct, not by the use of an overall system or program. **Oblique perspective**: An intuitive spatial system in which a building or room is placed with one corner in the picture plane, and the other parts of the structure recede to an imaginary **vanishing point** on its other side. Oblique perspective is not a comprehensive, mathematical system. **One-point** and **multiple-point perspective** (also called **linear**, **scientific**, or **mathematical perspective**): A method of creating the illusion of three-dimensional space on a two-dimensional surface by delineating a **horizon line** and multiple **orthogonal** lines. These recede to meet at one or more points on the horizon (called vanishing points), giving the appearance of spatial depth. Called scientific or mathematical because its use requires some knowledge of geometry and mathematics, as well as optics. **Reverse perspective**: A Byzantine perspective theory in which the orthogonals or rays of sight do not converge on a vanishing point in the picture, but are thought to originate in the viewer's eye in front of the picture. Thus, in reverse perspective the image is constructed with orthogonals that diverge, giving a slightly tipped aspect to objects.

pictograph A highly stylized depiction serving as a symbol for a person or object. Also: a type of writing utilizing such symbols.

picture plane The theoretical spatial plane corresponding with the actual surface of a painting.

picturesque A term describing the taste for the familiar, the pleasant, and the pretty, popular in the eighteenth and nineteenth centuries in Europe. When contrasted with the **sublime**, the picturesque stood for all that was ordinary but pleasant.

pier A masonry support made up of many stones, or rubble and concrete (in contrast to a column **shaft**, which is formed by a single stone or a series of **drums**), often square or rectangular in plan and capable of carrying very heavy architectural loads. See also **compound pier**.

pietà A devotional subject in Christian religious art. After the Crucifixion the body of Jesus was laid across the lap of his grieving mother, Mary. When others are present the subject is called the Lamentation.

pilaster An engaged **columnar** element that is rectangular in format and used for decoration in architecture.

pinnacle In Gothic architecture, a steep pyramid decorating the top of another element such as a **buttress**. Also: the highest point.

plaiting In basketry, the technique of weaving strips of fabric or other flexible substances under and over each other.

plan A graphic convention for representing the arrangement of the parts of a building.

plinth The slablike base or pedestal of a column, statue, wall, building, or piece of furniture.

pluralism A social structure or goal that allows members of diverse ethnic, racial, or other groups to exist within the society while continuing to practice the customs of their own divergent cultures. Also: an adjective describing the state of having many valid contemporary styles available at the same time to artists.

podium A raised platform that acts as the foundation for a building, or as a platform for a speaker.

polychromy The multicolored painted decoration applied to any part of a building, sculpture, or piece of furniture.

polyptych An **altarpiece** constructed from multiple panels, sometimes with hinges to allow for movable **wings**.

porcelain A type of extremely hard and fine ceramic made from a mixture of kaolin and other minerals. Porcelain is fired at a very high heat, and the final product has a translucent surface.

portal A grand entrance, door, or gate, usually to an important public building, and often decorated with sculpture.

portico In architecture, a projecting roof or porch supported by **columns**, often marking an entrance.

post-and-lintel construction An architectural system of construction with two or more vertical elements (posts) supporting a horizontal element (lintel).

predella The lower zone, or base, of an **altarpiece**, decorated with painting or sculpture related to the main **iconographic** theme of the altarpiece.

primary colors Blue, red, and yellow, the three colors from which all others are derived.

pronaos The enclosed vestibule of a Greek or Roman temple, found in front of the cella and marked by a row of **columns** at the entrance.

proscenium The stage of an ancient Greek or Roman theater. In modern theater, the area of the stage in front of the curtain. Also: the framing **arch** that separates a stage from the audience.

provenance The history of ownership of a work of art from the time of its creation to the present.

punchwork Decorative designs that are stamped onto a surface, such as metal or leather, using a punch (a handheld metal implement).

putto (putti) A plump, naked little boy, often winged. In classical art, called a cupid; in Christian art, a **cherub**.

pylon A massive gateway formed by a pair of tapering walls of oblong shape. Erected by ancient Egyptians to mark the entrance to a temple complex.

qibla The mosque wall oriented toward Mecca indicated by the *mihrab*.

quadrant vault See **vault**.

quillwork A Native American decorative craft technique. The quills of porcupines and bird feathers are dyed and attached to material in patterns.

raku A type of ceramic pottery made by hand, coated with a thick, dark **glaze**, and fired at a low heat. The resulting vessels are irregularly shaped and glazed and are highly prized for use in the Japanese tea ceremony.

readymade An object from popular or material culture presented without further manipulation as an artwork by the artist.

realism A term first used in Europe around 1850 to designate a kind of **naturalism** with a social or political message, which soon lost its didactic import and became synonymous with naturalism.

red-figure A style of ancient Greek vase painting made in the sixth and fifth centuries BCE. Characterized by red-clay-colored figures on a black **background**.

register A device used in systems of spatial definition. In painting, a register indicates the use of differing **groundlines** to differentiate layers of space within an image. In sculpture, the placement of self-contained bands of **reliefs** in a vertical arrangement. In printmaking, the marks at the edges used to align the print correctly on the page, especially in multiple-block color printing.

relic See **reliquary**

relief sculpture A sculpted image or design whose flat background surface is carved away to a certain depth, setting off the figure. Called high or low (bas) relief depending upon the extent of projection of the image from the background. Called sunken relief when the image is modeled below the original surface of the background, which is not cut away.

relieving arch see **arch**.

reliquary A container, often made of precious materials, used as a repository for sacred **relics** (venerated objects associated with a saint or martyr).

repoussé A technique of hammering metal from the back to create a protruding image. Elaborate **reliefs** are created with wooden armatures against which the metal sheets are pressed and hammered.

representational Any art that attempts to depict an aspect of the external, natural world in a visually understandable way.

reverse perspective See **perspective**.

ribbon See **ribbon interlace**.

ribbon interlace A linear decoration made up of interwoven bands.

rib vault See **vault**.

roof comb In a Mayan building, a masonry wall along the apex of a roof that is built above the level of the roof proper. Roof combs support the highly decorated false **facades** that rise above the height of the building at the front.

rose window A round window, often filled with **stained glass**, with **tracery** patterns in the form of wheel spokes. Large, elaborate, and finely crafted, rose windows are usually a central element of the **facade** of French Gothic cathedrals.

rosette A round or oval ornament resembling a rose.

rotunda Any building (or part thereof) constructed in a circular (or sometimes polygonal) shape, usually producing a large open space crowned by a **dome**.

roundel Any element with a circular format, often placed as a decoration on the exterior of architecture.

rustication In building, the rough, irregular, and unfinished effect deliberately given to the exterior facing of a stone edifice. Rusticated stones are often large and used for decorative emphasis around doors or windows or across the entire lower floors of a building.

sacristy In a Christian church, the room in which the priest's robes and the sacred vessels are housed. Sacristies are usually located close to the **sanctuary** and often have a place for ritual washing.

sanctuary A sacred or holy enclosure used for worship. In ancient Greece and Rome, consists of one or more temples and an **altar**. In Christian architecture, the space around the altar in a church called the chancel or presbytery.

sarcophagus (sarcophagi) A rectangular stone coffin. Often decorated with **relief** sculpture.

scientific perspective See **perspective**.

scriptorium (scriptoria) A room in a monastery for writing or copying **manuscripts**.

sculpture in the round Three-dimensional sculpture that is carved free of any background or block.

sfumato In painting, the effect of haze in an image. Resembling the color of the atmosphere at dusk, *sfumato* gives a smoky effect.

shade Any area of an artwork that is shown through various technical means to be in shadow. **Shading**: the technique of making such an effect.

shaft The main vertical section of a **column** between the **capital** and the **base**, usually circular in cross section.

shikhara In the architecture of northern India, a conical (or pyramidal) structure found atop a Hindu temple.

side aisle See **aisle**.

site-specific sculpture A sculpture commissioned and designed for a particular spot.

slip A mixture of clay and water applied to a ceramic object as a final decorative coat. Also: a solution that binds different parts of a vessel together, such as the handle and the main body.

spandrel The area of wall adjoining the exterior curve of an **arch** between its springing and the **keystone**, or the area between two arches, as in an **arcade**.

squinch An **arch** or **lintel** built over the upper corners of a square space. Allows a circular or polygonal **dome** to be more securely set above the walls, and converts the space to an octagon.

stained glass Molten glass is given a color that becomes intrinsic to the material. Additional colors may be fused to the surface (flashing). Stained glass is most often used in windows, for which small pieces of differently colored glass are precisely cut and assembled into a design, held together by **cames**. Additional painted details may be added to create images.

stela (stelae) A stone slab placed vertically and decorated with inscriptions or **reliefs**. Used as a grave marker or memorial.

still life A type of painting that has as its subject inanimate objects (such as food, dishes, fruit, or flowers).

stringcourse A continuous horizontal band, such as a **molding**, decorating the face of a wall.

stucco A mixture of lime, sand, and other ingredients into a material that can be easily molded or modeled. When dry, produces a very durable surface used for covering walls or for architectural sculpture and decoration.

stupa In Buddhist architecture, a bell-shaped or pyramidal religious monument, made of piled earth or stone and containing sacred **relics**.

style A particular manner, **form**, or character of representation, construction, or expression typical of an individual artist or of a certain school or period.

stylization; stylized A manner of representation that conforms to an intellectual or artistic idea rather than to **naturalistic** appearances.

stylobate In **Classical** architecture, the stone foundation on which a temple stands.

stylus An instrument with a pointed end (used for writing and printmaking), which makes a delicate line or scratch. Also: a special writing tool for **cuneiform** writing with one pointed end and one triangular wedge end.

subject matter See **content**.

sublime A concept, thing, or state of exceptional and awe-inspiring beauty and moral or intellectual expression. The sublime was a goal to which many nineteenth-century artists aspired in their artworks. See **picturesque**.

sunken relief See **relief sculpture**.

swag A decorative device in architecture or interior ornament (and in paintings) in which a loosely hanging garland is made to look like flowers or gathered fabric.

talud-tablero A design characteristic of Mayan architecture at Teotihuacan in which a sloping *talud* at the base of a building supports a wall-like *tablero*, where ornamental painting and sculpture are usually placed.

tempera A painting **medium** made by blending egg or egg yolks with water, pigments, and occasionally other materials, such as glue.

tenebrism The use of strong **chiaroscuro** and artificially illuminated areas to create a dramatic contrast of light and dark in painting.

tepee A portable dwelling constructed from hides (later canvas) stretched on a structure of poles set at the base in a circle and leaning against one another at the top. Tepees were typically found among the nomadic Native Americans of the North American plains.

terra cotta A **medium** made from clay fired over a low heat and sometimes left unglazed. Also: the orange-brown color typical of this medium.

tessera (tesserae) The small piece of stone, glass, or other object that is pieced together with many others to create a **mosaic**.

tint The dominant color in an object, image, or pigment.

tondo A painting or **relief** of circular shape.

tone The overall degree of brightness or darkness in an artwork. Also: saturation, intensity, or **value** of color and its effect.

torana In Indian architecture, an ornamented gateway **arch** in a temple, usually leading to the **stupa**.

tracery The stone or wooden bars in a window, screen, or panel, that support the form and often create an elaborate decorative pattern.

transept The arm of a **cruciform** church, perpendicular to the **nave**. The point where the nave and **transept** cross is called the **crossing**. Beyond the crossing lies the **sanctuary**, whether **apse**, **choir**, or **chevet**.

triforium The element of the interior **elevation** of a church, found directly below the **clerestory** and consisting of a series of arched openings. The triforium can be made up of openings from a passageway or **gallery** or can be a plain or decorated wall.

triglyph Rectangular blocks between the **metopes** of a **Doric frieze**. Identified by the three carved vertical grooves, which approximate the appearance of the ends of wooden beams.

triptych An artwork made up of three panels. The panels may be hinged together so the side segments (**wings**) fold over the central area.

triumphal arch A freestanding, massive stone gateway with a large central **arch**, built as urban ornament and/or to celebrate military victories (as by the Romans).

trompe l'oeil A manner of representation in which the appearance of natural space and objects is re-created with the express intention of fooling the eye of the viewer, who may be convinced that the subject actually exists as three-dimensional reality.

trumeau A **column**, **pier**, or **post** found at the center of a large **portal** or doorway, supporting the **lintel**.

tunnel vault See **vault**.

Tuscan order See **order**.

twining A basketry technique in which short rods are sewn together vertically. The panels are then joined together to form a vessel.

tympanum In **Classical** architecture, the vertical panel of the **pediment**. In medieval and later architecture, the area over a door enclosed by an **arch** and a **lintel**, often decorated with sculpture or **mosaic**.

typology In Christian **iconography**, a system of matching Old Testament figures and events and even some **classical** and other secular sources to New Testament counterparts to which they were seen as prefigurements.

ukiyo-e A Japanese term for a type of popular art that was favored from the sixteenth century, particularly in the form of color **woodblock** prints. *Ukiyo-e* prints often depicted the world of the common people in Japan, such as courtesans and actors, as well as landscapes and myths.

undercutting A technique in sculpture by which the material is cut back under the edges so that the remaining form projects strongly forward, casting deep shadows.

underglaze Color or decoration applied to a ceramic piece before glazing.

value The darkness or lightness of a color (**hue**).

vanishing point In a **perspective** system, the point on the **horizon line** at which **orthogonals** meet. A complex system can have multiple vanishing points.

vanitas An image, especially popular in Europe during the seventeenth century, in which all the objects symbolize the transience of life. *Vanitas* paintings are usually of **still lifes** or **genre** subjects.

vault An **arched** masonry structure that spans an interior space. **Barrel** or **tunnel vault**: an elongated or continuous semicircular vault, shaped like a half-cylinder. **Groin** or **cross vault**: a vault created by the intersection of two barrel vaults of equal size which creates four side compartments of identical size and shape. **Quadrant** or **half-barrel vault**: as the name suggests, a half-barrel vault. **Rib vault**: ribs (extra masonry) demark the junctions of a groin vault. Ribs may function to reinforce the groins or may be purely decorative. **Corbeled vault**: a vault made by projecting courses of stone. See also **corbeling**.

vellum A fine animal skin prepared for writing and painting. See **parchment**.

veneer In architecture, the exterior facing of a building, often in decorative patterns of fine stone or brick. In decorative arts, a thin exterior layer of finer material (such as rare wood, ivory, metal, and semiprecious stones) laid over the form.

verism A **style** in which artists concern themselves with capturing the exterior likeness of an object or person, usually by rendering its visible details in a finely executed, meticulous manner.

volumetric A term indicating the concern for rendering the impression of three-dimensional volumes in painting, usually achieved through **modeling** and the manipulation of light and shadow (**chiaroscuro**).

volute A spiral scroll, as seen on an **Ionic capital**.

votive figure An image created as a devotional offering to a god or other deity.

voussoirs The oblong, wedge-shaped stone blocks used to build an **arch**. The topmost voussoir is called a **keystone**.

wall painting See **mural**.

ware A general term designating pottery produced and decorated by the same technique.

warp The vertical threads in a weaver's loom. Warp threads make up a fixed framework that provides the structure for the entire piece of cloth, and are thus often thicker than weft threads. See also **weft**.

wash A diluted watercolor or ink. Washes may be applied to drawings or prints to add **tone** or touches of color.

weft The horizontal threads in a woven piece of cloth. Weft threads are woven at right angles to and through the warp threads to make up the bulk of the decorative pattern. In carpets, the weft is often completely covered or formed by the rows of trimmed knots that form the carpet's soft surface. See also **warp**.

westwork The monumental, west-facing entrance section of a Carolingian, Ottonian, or Romanesque church. The exterior consists of multiple stories between two towers; the interior includes an entrance vestibule, a chapel, and a series of **galleries** overlooking the **nave**.

wing A side panel of a **triptych** or **polyptych** (usually found in pairs), which was hinged to fold over the central panel. Wings often held the depiction of the donors and/or subsidiary scenes relating to the central image.

woodblock print A print made from a block of wood that is carved in **relief** or **incised**.

woodcut A type of print made by carving a design into a wooden block. The ink is applied to the plate with a roller. As the ink remains only on the raised areas between the carved-away lines, these carved-away areas and lines provide the white areas of the print. Also: the process by which the woodcut is made.

x-ray style In Aboriginal art, a manner of representation in which the artist depicts a figure or animal by illustrating its outline as well as essential internal organs and bones.

ziggurat In Mesopotamia, a tall stepped tower of earthen materials, often supporting a shrine.

Selected Bibliography

General

Adams, Laurie Schneider. *Art across Time*. New York: McGraw-Hill, 1999.

Anderson, Richard L. *Art in Small-Scale Societies*. 2nd ed. Englewood Cliffs, N.J.: Prentice Hall, 1989.

Andrews, Malcolm. *Landscape and Western Art*. Oxford History of Art. Oxford: Oxford Univ. Press, 1999.

Bearden, Romare. *A History of African American Artists: From 1792 to the Present*. New York: Pantheon, 1993.

Berlo, Janet Catherine, and Lee Ann Wilson. *Arts of Africa, Oceania, and the Americas: Selected Readings*. Englewood Cliffs, N.J.: Prentice Hall, 1993.

Brownston, David M., and Ilene Franck. *Timelines of the Arts and Literature*. New York: HarperCollins, 1994.

Chadwick, Whitney. *Women, Art, and Society*. 2nd rev. & exp. ed. New York: Thames and Hudson, 1997.

Chipp, Herschel Browning. *Theories of Modern Art: A Source Book by Artists and Critics*. California Studies in the History of Art. Berkeley: Univ. of California Press, 1984.

Cole, Bruce, and Adelheid Gealt. *Art of the Western World: From Ancient Greece to Post-Modernism*. New York: Summit, 1989.

Crouch, Dora P. *A History of Architecture: Stonehenge to Skyscrapers*. New York: McGraw-Hill, 1985.

Dictionary of Art, The. 34 vols. New York: Grove's Dictionaries, 1996.

Encyclopedia of World Art. 16 vols. New York: McGraw-Hill, 1972–83.

Ferguson, George Wells. *Signs and Symbols in Christian Art*. New York: Oxford Univ. Press, 1967.

Fleming, John, Hugh Honour, and Nikolaus Pevsner. *The Penguin Dictionary of Architecture*. 5th ed. New York: Penguin, 1998.

Gardner, Helen. *Gardner's Art through the Ages*. 10th ed. Ed. Richard G. Tansey and Fred S. Kleiner. Fort Worth: Harcourt Brace College, 1996.

Griffiths, Antony. *Prints and Printmaking: An Introduction to the History and Techniques*. 2nd ed. London: British Museum Press, 1996.

Hall, James. *Dictionary of Subjects and Symbols in Art*. Rev. ed. New York: Harper & Row, 1979.

Harris, Ann Sutherland, and Linda Nochlin. *Women Artists: 1550–1950*. Los Angeles: Los Angeles County Museum of Art, 1976.

Harrison, Charles, and Paul Wood, eds. *Art in Theory, 1900–1990: An Anthology of Changing Ideas*. Cambridge, Mass.: Blackwell, 1992.

Heller, Nancy G. *Women Artists: An Illustrated History*. 3rd ed. New York: Abbeville, 1997.

Holt, Elizabeth Gilmore, ed. *A Documentary History of Art*. 3 vols. New Haven, Conn.: Yale Univ. Press, 1986.

Honour, Hugh, and John Fleming. *The Visual Arts: A History*. 6th ed. New York: Abrams, 2002.

Hornblower, Simon and Antony Spawforth. *The Oxford Classical Dictionary*. 3rd ed. Oxford: Oxford University Press, 1996.

Hughes, Robert. *American Visions: The Epic History of Art in America*. New York: Alfred Knopf, 1997.

Hults, Linda C. *The Print in the Western World: An Introductory History*. Madison: Univ. of Wisconsin Press, 1996.

Janson, H. W., and Anthony F. Janson. *History of Art*. 6th rev. ed. New York: Abrams, 2003.

Jeffrey, Ian. *Photography: A Concise History*. London: Thames and Hudson, 1981.

Jones, Lois Swan. *Art Information and the Internet: How To Find It, How to Use It*. Phoenix: Oryx Press, 1999.

Kemp, Martin. *The Oxford History of Western Art*. Oxford: Oxford Univ. Press, 2000.

Kostof, Spiro. *A History of Architecture: Settings and Rituals*. 2nd ed. Rev. Greg Castillo. New York: Oxford Univ. Press, 2000.

Langer, Suzanne. *Feeling and Form*. Upper Saddle River, N.J.: Prentice Hall, 1990.

Livingstone, E. A. *The Concise Oxford Dictionary of the Christian Church*. Oxford: Oxford Univ. Press, 2000.

McConkey, Wilfred J. *Klee as in Clay: A Pronunciation Guide*. 3rd ed. Lantham, Md.: Madison Books, 1992.

Minor, Vernon Hyde. *Art History's History*. Upper Saddle River, N.J.: Prentice Hall, 2001.

Nelson, Robert S. and Richard Shiff, eds. *Critical Terms for Art History*. Chicago: Univ. of Chicago Press, 1996.

Pohl, Frances. *Framing America: A Social History of American Art*. New York: Thames and Hudson, 2002.

Preble, Duane, Sarah Preble, and Patrick Frank. *Artforms: An Introduction to the Visual Arts*. 6th ed. New York: Longman, 1999.

Roberts, Helene, ed. *Encyclopedia of Comparative Iconography: Themes Depicted in Works of Art*. 2 vols. Chicago: Fitzroy Dearborn, 1998.

Roth, Leland M. *Understanding Architecture: Its Elements, History, and Meaning*. New York: Icon Editions, 1993.

Rothberg, Robert I., Theodore K. Rabb, eds. *Art and History: Images and Their Meaning*. Cambridge: Cambridge Univ. Press, 1988.

Sed-Rajna, Gabrielle. *Jewish Art*. Trans. Sara Friedman and Mira Reich. New York: Abrams, 1997.

Slatkin, Wendy. *Women Artists in History: From Antiquity to the Present*. 3rd ed. Upper Saddle River, N.J.: Prentice Hall, 1997.

Stangos, Nikos. *The Thames and Hudson Dictionary of Art and Artists*. Rev. exp. & updated ed. World of Art. New York: Thames and Hudson, 1994.

Steer, John, and Antony White. *Atlas of Western Art History: Artists, Sites and Movements from Ancient Greece to the Modern Age*. New York: Facts on File, 1994.

Stokstad, Marilyn. *Art History*, 2nd ed. New York: Abrams, 2002.

Sutton, Ian. *Western Architecture: From Ancient Greece to the Present*. World of Art. New York: Thames and Hudson, 1999.

Thacker, Christopher. *The History of Gardens*. Berkeley: Univ. of California Press, 1979.

Trachtenberg, Marvin, and Isabelle Hyman. *Architecture, from Prehistory to Postmodernity*. 2nd ed. New York: Abrams, 2002.

Tufts, Eleanor. *Our Hidden Heritage: Five Centuries of Women Artists*. New York: Paddington, 1974.

Walker, John A. *Design History and the History of Design*. London: Pluto, 1989.

West, Shearer, ed. *The Bulfinch Guide to Art History: A Comprehensive Survey and Dictionary of Western Art and Architecture*. Boston: Little, Brown and Co., 1996.

Wilkins, David G., Bernard Schultz, and Katheryn M. Linduff. *Art Past/Art Present*. 4th ed. Upper Saddle River, N.J.: Prentice Hall, 2000.

Chapter 1 Art Before the Written Word

Bahn, Paul G. *The Cambridge Illustrated History of Prehistoric Art*. Cambridge: Cambridge Univ. Press, 1998.

Blocker, H. Gene. *The Aesthetics of Primitive Art*. Lantham, Md.: Univ. Press of America, 1994.

Castleden, Rodney. *The Making of Stonehenge*. London: Routledge, 1993.

Chauvet, Jean-Marie, Eliette Brunel Deschamps, and Christian Hillaire. *Dawn of Art: The Chauvet Cave*. New York: Abrams, 1996.

Chippindale, Christopher. *Stonehenge Complete*. New York: Thames and Hudson, 1994.

Flood, Josephine. *Archaeology of the Dreamtime: The Story of Prehistoric Australia and Its People*. Rev. ed. New Haven, Conn.: Yale Univ. Press, 1990.

Kenrick, Douglas Moore. *Jomon of Japan: The World's Oldest Pottery*. London and New York: Kegan Paul International, 1995.

Laing, Lloyd Robert, and Jennifer Laing. *Ancient Art: The Challenge to Modern Thought*. Dublin: Irish Academic, 1993.

Layton, Robert. *Australian Rock Art: A New Synthesis*. New York: Cambridge Univ. Press, 1992.

Leroi-Gourhan, André. *The Dawn of European Art: An Introduction to Paleolithic Cave Painting*. Trans. Sara Champion. Cambridge: Cambridge Univ. Press, 1982.

Lhote, Henri. *The Search for the Tassili Frescoes: The Story of the Prehistoric Rock-Painting of the Sahara*. 2nd ed. Trans. Alan Houghton Brodrick. London: Hutchinson, 1973.

Lloyd, Seton, and Hans Wolfgang Muller. *Ancient Architecture*. New York: Rizzoli, 1986.

Oliphant, Margaret. *The Atlas of the Ancient World: Charting the Great Civilizations of the Past*. New York: Simon & Schuster, 1992.

Price, T. Douglas and Gray M. Feinman. *Images of the Past*. 3rd ed. Mountain View, Calif.: Mayfield, 2000.

Ruspoli, Mario. *The Cave of Lascaux: The Final Photographs*. New York: Abrams, 1987.

Sanders, N. K. *Prehistoric Art in Europe*. 2nd ed. Pelican History of Art. New Haven: Yale Univ. Press, 1995.

Sura Ramos, Pedro A. *The Cave of Altamira*. Ed. Antonio Beltran. New York: Abrams, 1999.

Wilcox, A. R. *The Rock Art of Africa*. London: Croon Helm, 1984.

Chapter 2 The Art of Mesopotamia and Egypt

Aldred, Cyril. *Egyptian Art in the Days of the Pharaohs, 3100–320 B.C.* World of Art. London: Thames and Hudson, 1980.

Amiet, Pierre. *Art of the Ancient Near East*. Trans. John Shepley and Claude Choquet. New York: Abrams, 1980.

Andrews, Carol. *Ancient Egyptian Jewelry*. New York: Abrams, 1991.

Arnold, Dieter. *Temples of the Last Pharaohs*. New York: Oxford Univ. Press, 1999.

Bierbrier, Morris. *Tomb-Builders of the Pharaohs*. London: British Museum, 1982.

Bottero, Jean. *Mesopotamia: Writing, Reasoning, and the Gods*. Trans. Zainab Bahrani and Marc Van De Mieroop. Chicago: Univ. of Chicago Press, 1992.

Collon, Dominique. *Ancient Near Eastern Art*. Berkeley: Univ. of California Press, 1995.

Egyptian Art in the Age of the Pyramids. New York: Metropolitan Museum of Art, 1999.

Egyptian Book of the Dead, The: The Book of Going Forth by Day: Being the Papyrus of Ani (Royal Scribe of the Divine Offerings). Trans. Raymond O. Faulkner. San Francisco: Chronicle, 1994.

Frankfort, Henri. *The Art and Architecture of the Ancient Orient*. 5th ed. Pelican History of Art. New Haven: Yale Univ. Press, 1996.

Haywood, John. *Ancient Civilizations of the Near East and the Mediterranean*. London: Cassell, 1997.

James, T. G. H., and W. V. Davies. *Egyptian Sculpture*. Cambridge, Mass.: Harvard Univ. Press, 1983.

Kozloff, Arielle P., and Betsy M. Bryan. *Egypt's Dazzling Sun: Amenhotep III and His World*. Cleveland: Cleveland Museum of Art, 1992.

Lehner, Mar. *The Complete Pyramids*. New York: Thames and Hudson, 1997.

Malek, Jaromir. *Egyptian Art*. Art & Ideas. London: Phaidon, 1999.

Martin, Geoffrey Thorndike. *The Hidden Tombs of Memphis: New Discoveries from the Time of Tutankhamun and Ramesses the Great*. London: Thames and Hudson, 1991.

Mellaart, James. *The Earliest Civilization of the Near East*. London: Thames and Hudson, 1965.

Menu, Bernadette. *Ramesses II: Greatest of the Pharoahs*. Discoveries. New York: Abrams, 1999.

Montet, Pierre. *Everyday Life in Egypt in the Days of Ramesses the Great*. Trans. A. R. Maxwell-Hysop and Margaret S. Drower. Philadelphia: Univ. of Pennsylvania Press, 1981.

Reeves, C. N. *The Complete Tutankhamun: The King, the*

Tomb, the Royal Treasure. London: Thames and Hudson, 1990.

Roaf, Michael. *Cultural Atlas of Mesopotamia and the Ancient Near East.* New York: Facts on File, 1990.

Robins, Gay. *The Art of Ancient Egypt.* Cambridge, Mass.: Harvard Univ. Press, 1997.

Saggs, H. W. F. *Civilization before Greece and Rome.* New Haven, Conn.: Yale Univ. Press, 1989.

Smith, William Stevenson. *The Art and Architecture of Ancient Egypt.* 3rd ed. Rev. William Kelly Simpson. Pelican History of Art. New Haven: Yale Univ. Press, 1998.

Tiarditti, Francesco, and Araldo De Luca. *Egyptian Treasures from the Egyptian Museum in Cairo.* New York: Abrams, 1999.

Wilkinson, Richard H. *Reading Egyptian Art: A Hieroglyphic Guide to Ancient Egyptian Painting and Sculpture.* London: Thames and Hudson, 1992.

Winstone, H. V. F. *Howard Carter and the Discovery of the Tomb of Tutankhamun.* London: Constable, 1991.

Wolkstein, Dianne, and Samuel Noah Kramer. *Inanna: Queen of Heaven and Earth.* New York: Harper & Row, 1983.

Chapter 3 Early Asian Art

Arts of China. 3 vols. Tokyo: Kodansha International, 1968–70.

Barnhart, Richard M. *Three Thousand Years of Chinese Painting.* New Haven: Yale Univ. Press, 1997.

Berkson, Carmel. *Elephanta: The Cave of Shiva.* Princeton, N.J.: Princeton Univ. Press, 1983.

Chandra, Pramod. *The Sculpture of India, 3000 B.C.–1300 A.D.* Washington, D.C.: National Gallery of Art, 1985.

Clunas, Craig. *Art in China.* Oxford History of Art. Oxford: Oxford Univ. Press, 1997.

Craven, Roy C. *Indian Art: A Concise History.* Rev. ed. World of Art. New York: Thames and Hudson, 1997.

Ebrey, Patricia Buckley. *The Cambridge Illustrated History of China.* Cambridge: Cambridge Univ. Press, 1996.

Eck, Diana L. *Darsan: Seeing the Divine Image in India.* 3rd ed. Chambersburg, Pa.: Anima, 1998.

Elisseeff, Danielle, and Vadime Elisseeff. *Art of Japan.* Trans. I. Mark Paris. New York: Abrams, 1985.

Errington, Elizabeth, and Joe Cribb, eds. *The Crossroads of Asia: Transformation in Image and Symbol in the Art of Ancient Afghanistan and Pakistan.* Cambridge, Eng.: Ancient India and Iran Trust, 1992.

Fong, Wen, ed. *The Great Bronze Age of China: An Exhibition from the People's Republic of China.* New York: Metropolitan Museum of Art, 1980.

Harle, James C. *The Art and Architecture of the Indian Subcontinent.* 2nd ed. Pelican History of Art. New Haven: Yale Univ. Press, 1994.

Kurata, Bunsaku. *Horyu-ji, Temple of the Exalted Law: Early Buddhist Art from Japan.* New York: Japan Society, 1981.

Lee, Sherman E. *A History of Far Eastern Art.* 5th ed. New York: Abrams, 1994.

——. *China, 5,000 Years: Innovation and Transformation in the Arts.* New York: Solomon R. Guggenheim Museum, 1998.

Martynov, Anatolii Ivanovich. *Ancient Art of Northern Asia.* Urbana: Univ. of Illinois Press, 1991.

Mason, Penelope. *History of Japanese Art.* New York: Abrams, 1993.

Paine, Robert Treat, and Alexander Soper. *Art and Architecture of Japan.* 3rd ed. Pelican History of Art. Harmondsworth, Eng.: Penguin, 1981.

Pearson, Richard. *Ancient Japan.* Washington, D. C.: Sackler Gallery, 1992.

Sickman, Lawrence, and Alexander Soper. *Art and Architecture of China.* Pelican History of Art. Harmondsworth, Eng.: Penguin, 1971.

Stanley-Baker, Joan. *Japanese Art.* Rev. & exp. ed. World of Art. New York: Thames and Hudson, 2000.

Sullivan, Michael. *The Arts of China.* 4th ed. exp. & rev. Berkeley: Univ. of California Press, 1999.

Thorp, Robert L., and Richard Ellis Vinograd. *Chinese Art and Culture.* New York: Abrams, 2001.

Tregear, Mary. *Chinese Art.* Rev. ed. World of Art. New York: Thames and Hudson, 1997.

Varley, H. Paul. *Japanese Culture.* 4th ed. Updated & exp. Honolulu: Univ. of Hawaii Press, 2000.

Watanabe, Yasutada. *Shinto Art: Ise and Izumo Shrines.* Trans. Robert Ricketts. Heibonsha Survey of Japanese Art, vol. 3. New York: Weatherhill, 1974.

Weiner, Sheila L. *Ajanta: Its Place in Buddhist Art.* Berkeley: Univ. of California Press, 1977.

Whitfield, Roderick, and Anne Farrer. C*aves of the Thousand Buddhas: Chinese Art from the Silk Route.* London: British Museum, 1990.

Chapter 4 Art of the Aegean World

Adam, Robert. *Classical Architecture: A Comprehensive Handbook to the Tradition of Classical Style.* New York: Abrams, 1991.

Ashmole, Bernard. *Architect and Sculptor in Classical Greece.* Wrightsman Lectures. New York: New York Univ. Press, 1972.

Avery, Catherine, ed. T*he New Century Handbook of Greek Mythology and Legend.* New York: Appleton-Century Crofts, 1972.

Barber, R. L. N. *The Cyclades in the Bronze Age.* Iowa City: Univ. of Iowa Press, 1987.

Beard, Mary, and John Henderson. *Classical Art: From Greece to Rome.* Oxford History of Art. Oxford: Oxford Univ. Press, 2000.

Biers, William. *The Archaeology of Greece: An Introduction.* 2nd ed. Ithaca: Cornell Univ. Press, 1996.

Boardman, John. *Greek Art.* 4th ed. Rev. and exp. World of Art. London: Thames and Hudson, 1997.

——. *Greek Sculpture: The Archaic Period: A Handbook.* World of Art. New York: Oxford Univ. Press, 1991.

——. *Greek Sculpture: The Classical Period: A Handbook.* London: Thames and Hudson, 1985.

Cartledge, Paul, ed. *The Cambridge Illustrated History of Ancient Greece.* Cambridge Illustrated History. Cambridge: Cambridge Univ. Press, 1998.

Fitton, J. Lesley. *Cycladic Art.* 2nd ed. London: British Museum, 1999.

Francis, E. D. *Image and Idea in Fifth-Century Greece: Art and Literature after the Persian Wars.* London: Routledge, 1990.

Fullerton, Mark. D. *Greek Art.* Cambridge: Cambridge Univ. Press, 2000.

Higgins, Reynold. *Minoan and Mycenean Art.* Rev. ed. World of Art. New York: Thames and Hudson, 1997.

Hurwit, Jeffrey M. *The Art and Culture of Early Greece 1100–480 B.C.* Ithaca, N.Y.: Cornell Univ. Press, 1985.

——. *The Athenian Acropolis: History, Mythology, and Archaeology from the Neolithic Period to the Present.* Cambridge: Cambridge Univ. Press, 1999.

Jenkins, Ian. *The Parthenon Frieze.* Austin: Univ. of Texas Press, 1994.

Kunze, Max. *The Pergamon Altar: Its Rediscovery, History, and Reconstruction.* Berlin: Staatliche Museem zu Berlin, Antikensammlung, 1991.

Lagerlof, Margaretha Rossholm. *The Sculptures of the Parthenon: Aesthetics and Interpretation.* New Haven: Yale Univ. Press, 2000.

Lawrence, A. W. *Greek Architecture.* 5th ed. Rev. R. A. Tomlinson. Pelican History of Art. New Haven: Yale Univ. Press, 1996.

Osborne, Robin. *Archaic and Classical Greek Art.* Oxford History of Art. Oxford: Oxford Univ. Press, 1998.

Pedley, John Griffiths. *Greek Art and Archaeology.* 2nd ed. New York: Abrams, 1998.

Preziosi, Donald and Louise Hitchcock. *Aegean Art and Architecture.* Oxford History of Art. Oxford: Oxford

Univ. Press, 1999.

Spivey, Nigel. *Greek Art.* Art & Ideas. London: Phaidon Press, 1997.

Stewart, Andrew F. *Greek Sculpture: An Exploration.* 2 vols. New Haven, Conn.: Yale Univ. Press, 1990.

Chapter 5 The Spread of Greek Art and Culture

Aruz, Joan, ed. *The Golden Deer of Eurasia: Scythian and Sarmatian Treasures from the Russian Steppes.* New Haven: Yale Univ. Press, 2000.

Brendel, Otto J. *Etruscan Art.* 2nd ed. Pelican History of Art. New Haven: Yale Univ. Press, 1995.

De Grummond, Nancy T. and Brunilde S. Ridgway. *From Pergamon to Sperlonga: Sculpture in Context.* Berkeley: Univ. of California Press, 2000.

Ferrier, R. W., ed. *Arts of Persia.* New Haven, Conn.: Yale Univ. Press, 1989.

Fildes, Alan. *Alexander the Great: Son of the Gods.* Los Angeles, Calif.: J. Paul Getty Museum, 2002.

Kunze, Max. *The Pergamon Altar: Its Rediscovery, History, and Reconstruction.* Berlin: Staatliche Museen zu Berlin, Antikensammlung, 1991.

Pang, Tina. *Treasures of the Eurasian Steppes: Animal Art from 800 B.C. to 200 A.D.* New York: Ariadne Galleries, 1998.

Pollitt, J. J. *Art in the Hellenistic Age.* Cambridge: Cambridge Univ. Press, 1986.

Porada, Edith. *The Art of Ancient Iran: Pre-Islamic Cultures.* Art of the World. New York: Crown, 1965.

Reeder, Ellen D., ed. *Scythian Gold: Treasures from Ancient Ukraine.* New York: Abrams in association with the Walters Art Gallery and the San Antonio Museum of Art, 1999.

Roux, Georges. *Ancient Iraq.* 3rd ed. London: Penguin, 1992.

Smith, R. R. R. *Hellenistic Sculpture: A Handbook.* World of Art. New York: Thames and Hudson, 1991.

Spivey, Nigel. *Etruscan Art.* World of Art. New York: Thames and Hudson, 1997.

Sprenger, Maja, and Gilda Bartolini. *The Etruscans: Their History, Art, and Architecture.* New York: Abrams, 1983.

Webster, T. B. L. *The Art of Greece: The Age of Hellenism.* Art of the World. New York: Crown, 1966.

Chapter 6 Art of the Roman Republic and Empire

Bianchi Bandinelli, Ranuccio. *Rome: The Centre of Power: Roman Art to A.D. 200.* Trans. Peter Green. Arts of Mankind. London: Thames and Hudson, 1970.

Breeze, David John. *Hadrian's Wall.* 4th ed. London: Penguin, 2000.

Brown, Peter. *The World of Late Antiquity: A.D. 150–750.* New York: Norton, 1989.

Christ, Karl. *The Romans: An Introduction to Their History and Civilization.* Berkeley: Univ. of California Press, 1984.

D'Ambra, Eve. *Roman Art.* Cambridge: Cambridge Univ. Press, 1998.

Dunabin, Katherine M. D. *Mosaics of the Greek and Roman World.* Cambridge: Cambridge Univ. Press, 1999.

Elsner, Jaś. *Imperial Rome and Christian Triumph: The Art of the Roman Empire, A.D. 100–450.* Oxford History of Art. Oxford: Oxford Univ. Press, 1998.

Gabucci, Ada. *Ancient Rome: Art, Architecture, and History.* Eds. Stefano Peccatori and Stephano Zuffi. Trans. T. M. Hartman. Los Angeles, Calif.: J. Paul Getty Museum, 2002.

——, ed. *The Colosseum.* Los Angeles, Calif.: J. Paul Getty Museum, 2002.

Grant, Michael. *Art in the Roman Empire.* London: Routledge, 1995.

Guilland, Jacqueline, and Maurice Guilland. *Frescoes in the Time of Pompeii.* New York: Potter, 1990.

Heintze, Helga von. *Roman Art.* New York: Universe, 1990.

L'Orange, Hans Peter. *The Roman Empire: Art Forms and*

Civic Life. New York: Rizzoli, 1985.

MacDonald, William L. *The Architecture of the Roman Empire: An Introductory Study.* Rev. ed. 2 vols. Yale Publications in the History of Art. New Haven, Conn.: Yale Univ. Press, 1982.

———. *The Pantheon: Design, Meaning, and Progeny.* Cambridge, Mass.: Harvard Univ. Press, 1976.

———, and John A. Pinto. *Hadrian's Villa and Its Legacy.* New Haven: Yale Univ. Press, 1995.

Packer, James E., et al. *The Forum of Trajan in Rome: A Study of Its Monuments.* 2 vols., portfolio and microfiche. California Studies in the History of Art; 31. Berkeley: Univ. of California Press, 1997.

Pollitt, J. J. *The Art of Rome, c. 753 B.C.–337 A.D.: Sources and Documents.* Englewood Cliffs, N.J.: Prentice Hall, 1966.

Ramage, Nancy H., and Andrew Ramage. *Roman Art: Romulus to Constantine.* 2nd ed. Upper Saddle River, N.J.: Prentice Hall, 1996.

Strong, Donald. *Roman Art.* 2nd. rev. & annotated ed. Pelican History of Art. New Haven: Yale Univ. Press, 1995.

Vitruvius, Pollio. *Ten Books on Architecture.* Trans. Ingrid D. Rowland. Cambridge: Cambridge Univ. Press, 1999.

Chapter 7 Jewish, Early Christian, and Byzantine Art

Age of Spirituality: Late Antique and Early Christian Art, Third to Seventh Century. New York: Metropolitan Museum of Art, 1979.

Cioffarelli, Ada. *Guide to the Catacombs of Rome and Its Surroundings.* Rome: Bonsignori, 2000.

Cormack, Robin. *Byzantine Art.* Oxford History of Art. Oxford: Oxford Univ. Press, 2000.

Cutler, Anthony. *The Hand of the Master: Craftsmanship, Ivory, and Society in Byzantium (9th–11th Centuries).* Princeton, N.J.: Princeton Univ. Press, 1994.

Demus, Otto. *Mosaic Decoration of San Marco, Venice.* Ed. Herbert L. Kessler. Chicago: Univ. of Chicago Press, 1988.

Evans, Helen C., and William D Wixon, eds. *The Glory of Byzantium.* New York: Abrams, 1997.

Kleinbauer, W. Eugene. *Saint Sophia at Constantinople: Singulariter in Mundo.* Dublin, N.H.: William L. Bauhan, 1999.

Krautheimer, Richard. *Early Christian and Byzantine Architecture.* 4th ed. Pelican History of Art. Harmondsworth, Eng: Penguin, 1986.

Lowden, John. *Early Christian and Byzantine Art.* Art & Ideas. London: Phaidon, 1997.

Mainstone, R. J. *Hagia Sophia: Architecture, Structure and Liturgy of Justinian's Great Church.* London: Thames and Hudson, 1988.

Manicelli, Fabrizio. *Catacombs and Basilicas: The Early Christians in Rome.* Florence: Scala, 1981.

Mark, Robert, and Ahmet S. Cakmak. *Hagia Sophia from the Age of Justinian to the Present.* Cambridge: Cambridge Univ. Press, 1992.

Matthews, Thomas F. *The Art of Byzantium.* London: Calmann and King Ltd., 1999.

Milburn, R. L. P. *Early Christian Art and Architecture.* Berkeley: Univ. of California Press, 1988.

Rutgers, Leonard Victor. *Subterranean Rome: In Search of the Roots of Christianity in the Catacombs of the Eternal City.* Leuven: Peeters, 2000.

Simson, Otto Georg von. *Sacred Fortress: Byzantine Art and Statecraft in Ravenna.* Chicago: Univ. of Chicago Press, 1948.

Snyder, James. *Medieval Art: Painting, Sculpture, Architecture, 4th–14th Century.* New York: Abrams, 1989.

Stevenson, James. *The Catacombs: Rediscovered Monuments of Early Christianity.* Ancient Peoples and Places. London: Thames and Hudson, 1978.

Stokstad, Marilyn. *Medieval Art.* 2nd ed. Boulder: Westview, 2004.

Teteriatnikov, Natalia. *Mosaics of Hagia Sophia, Istanbul: The Fossati Restoration and the Work of the Byzantine Institute.* Washington, D.C.: Dumbarton Oaks Research Library and Collection, 1998.

Vio, Ettore and Eunio Concina. *The Basilica of St. Mark in Venice.* New York: Riverside, 1999.

Webb, Matilda. *The Churches and Catacombs of Early Christian Rome: A Comprehensive Guide.* Brighton, G.B.: Sussex Academic Press, 2001.

Weitzmann, Kurt. *Late Antique and Early Christian Book Illumination.* New York: Braziller, 1977.

Chapter 8 Islamic Art

Asher, Catherine B. *Architecture of Mughal India.* New York: Cambridge Univ. Press, 1992.

Atasoy, Nurhan. *Splendors of the Ottoman Sultans.* Ed. and trans. Tulay Artan. Memphis, Tenn.: Lithograph, 1992.

Atil, Esin. *The Age of Sultan Suleyman the Magnificent.* Washington, D.C.: National Gallery of Art, 1987.

Beach, Milo Cleveland. *Mughal and Rajput Painting.* New York: Cambridge Univ. Press, 1992.

Blair, Sheila S., and Jonathan M. Brown. *The Art and Architecture of Islam 1250–1800.* New Haven, Conn.: Yale Univ. Press, 1994.

Brend, Barbara. *Islamic Art.* Cambridge, Mass.: Harvard Univ. Press, 1991.

Dodds, Jerrilynn D., ed. *al-Andalus: The Art of Islamic Spain.* New York: Metropolitan Museum of Art, 1992.

Dye, Joseph M. *The Arts of India.* Richmond, Va.: Virginia Museum of Fine Arts/Philip Wilson Publishers, 2001.

Frishman, Martin, and Hasan-Uddin Khan. *The Mosque: History, Architectural Development and Regional Diversity.* London: Thames and Hudson, 1994.

Grabar, Oleg. *The Alhambra.* Cambridge, Mass.: Harvard Univ. Press, 1978.

———. *The Mediation of Ornament.* A. W. Mellon Lectures in the Fine Arts. Princeton, N.J.: Princeton Univ. Press, 1992.

———. *Mostly Miniatures: An Introduction to Persian Painting.* Princeton, N.J.: Princeton Univ. Press, 2000.

———, and Richard Ettinghausen. *The Art and Architecture of Islam, 650–1250.* Penguin History of Art. New Haven: Yale Univ. Press, 2001.

Irwin, Robert. *Islamic Art in Context: Art, Architecture, and the Literary World.* Perspectives. New York: Abrams, 1997.

Khatibi, Abdelkebir, and Mohammed Sijelmassi. *The Splendour of Islamic Calligraphy.* Rev. and exp. ed. New York: Thames and Hudson, 1996.

Koran, The. Rev. ed. Trans. N. J. Dawood. London: Penguin, 1993.

Nou, Jean-Louis. *Taj Mahal.* Text by Amina Okada and M. C. Joshi. New York: Abbeville, 1993.

Pal, Pratapaditya. *Court Paintings of India, 16th–19th Centuries.* New York: Navin Kumar, 1983.

——— et al. *Romance of the Taj Mahal.* Los Angeles: Los Angeles County Museum of Art, 1989.

Schimmel, Annemarie. *Calligraphy and Islamic Culture.* New York: New York Univ. Press, 1983.

Welch, Stuart Cary. *The Emperors' Album: Images of Mughal India.* New York: Metropolitan Museum of Art, 1987.

———. *India: Art and Culture, 1300–1900.* New York: Metropolitan Museum of Art, 1985.

Chapter 9 Later Asian Art

Addiss, Stephen. *The Art of Zen: Painting and Calligraphy by Japanese Monks, 1600–1925.* New York: Abrams, 1989.

Andrews, Julia Frances. *Painters and Politics in the People's Republic of China, 1949–79.* Berkeley: Univ. of California Press, 1994.

Barnhart, Richard M. *Painters of the Great Ming: The Imperial Court and the Zhe School.* Dallas, Tex.: Dallas Museum of Art, 1993.

Billeter, Jean François. *The Chinese Art of Writing.* New York: Skira/Rizzoli, 1990.

Blurton, T. Richard. *Hindu Art.* Cambridge, Mass.: Harvard Univ. Press, 1993.

Clunas, Craig. *Pictures and Visualities in Early Modern China.* Princeton, N.J.: Princeton Univ. Press, 1997.

Eight Dynasties of Chinese Painting: The Collections of the Nelson Gallery-Atkins Museum, Kansas City, and the Cleveland Museum of Art. Cleveland: Cleveland Museum of Art; Bloomington: Indiana University Press, 1980.

Fang, Jing Pei. *Treasures of the Chinese Scholar: Form, Function, and Symbolism.* Ed. J. May Lee Barrett. New York: Weatherhill, 1997.

Fisher, Robert E. *Buddhist Art and Architecture.* World of Art. New York: Thames and Hudson, 1993.

Fong, Wen C. and James C. Y. Watt. *Possessing the Past: Treasures from the National Palace Museum, Taipei.* New York: Metropolitan Museum of Art, 1997.

Forrer, Matthi. *Hokusai.* New York: Rizzoli, 1988.

Guth, Christine. *Art of Edo Japan: The Artist and the City, 1615–1868.* Perspectives. New York: Abrams, 1996.

Hayashiya, Tatsusaburo, Masao Nakamura, and Seizo Hayashiya. *Japanese Arts and the Tea Ceremony.* Trans. and adapted by Joseph P. Macadam. Heibonsha Survey of Japanese Art, vol. 15. New York: Weatherhill, 1974.

Hickman, Money L. *Japan's Golden Age: Momoyama.* New Haven: Yale Univ. Press, 1996.

Khanna, Balraj, and Aziz Kurtha. *Art of Modern India.* London: Thames and Hudson, 1998.

Liu, Laurence G. *Chinese Architecture.* New York: Rizzoli, 1989.

Losty, Jeremiah P. *The Art of the Book in India.* London: British Library, 1982.

Merritt, Helen and Nanako Yamada. *Guide to Modern Japanese Woodblock Prints, 1900–1975.* Honolulu: Univ. of Honolulu Press, 1995.

Mitchell, George. *The Royal Palaces of India.* London: Thames and Hudson, 1994.

Munroe, Alexandra. *Japanese Art after 1945: Scream Against the Sky.* New York: Abrams, 1994.

Murase, Miyeko. *Iconography of the Tale of Genji: Genji Monogatari Ekotoba.* New York: Weatherhill, 1983.

———. *Masterpieces of Japanese Screen Painting: The American Collections.* New York: Braziller, 1990.

Ng, So Kam. *Brushstrokes: Styles and Techniques of Chinese Painting.* San Francisco: Asian Art Museum of San Francisco, 1993.

Rowland, Benjamin. *Art and Architecture of India: Buddhist, Hindu, Jain.* Pelican History of Art. Harmondsworth, Eng.: Penguin, 1977.

Seo, Audrey Yoshiko. *The Art of Twentieth-Century Zen: Paintings and Calligraphy by Japanese Masters.* Boston: Shambala, 1998.

Sullivan, Michael. *Art and Artists of Twentieth-Century China.* Berkeley: Univ. of California Press, 1996.

———. *Symbols of Eternity: The Art of Landscape Painting in China.* Stanford: Stanford Univ. Press, 1979.

Thompson, Sarah E., and H. D. Harootunian. *Undercurrents in the Floating World: Censorship and Japanese Prints.* New York: Asia Society Gallery, 1992.

Till, Barry. *The Arts of Meiji Japan, 1868–1912: Changing Aesthetics.* Victoria, B.C.: Art Gallery of Victoria, 1995.

Tillotson, G. H. R. *The Rajput Palaces: The Development of an Architectural Style, 1450–1750.* New York: Oxford Univ. Press. 1999.

Vainker, S. J. *Chinese Pottery and Porcelain: From Prehistory to the Present.* London: British Museum, 1991.

Watson, William. *The Arts of China, 900–1620.* Pelican History of Art. New Haven: Yale Univ. Press, 2000.

Weidner, Marsha, ed. *Latter Days of the Law: Images of Chinese Buddhism, 850–1850.* Lawrence: Spencer Museum of Art, Univ. of Kansas, 1994.

Yu, Zhuoyun, comp. *Palaces of the Forbidden City.* Trans. Ng Mau-Sang, Chan Sinwai, and Puwen Lee. New York: Viking, 1984.

Chapter 10 Early Medieval and Romanesque Art

Alexander, J. J. G. *Medieval Illuminators and Their Methods of Work.* New Haven, Conn.: Yale Univ. Press, 1992.

Andrews, Francis B. *The Mediaeval Builder and His Methods.* New York: Barnes & Noble, 1993.

Backhouse, Janet, D. H. Turner, and Leslie Webster. *The Golden Age of Anglo-Saxon Art, 966–1066.* Bloomington: Indiana Univ. Press, 1984.

Branner, Robert. *Manuscript Painting in Paris during the Reign of Saint Louis: A Study of Styles.* California Studies in the History of Art. Berkeley: Univ. of California Press, 1977.

Braunfels, Wolfgang. *Monasteries of Western Europe: The Architecture of the Orders.* Trans. Alistair Laing. New York: Thames and Hudson, 1993.

Brown, Michelle. *Understanding Illuminated Manuscripts: A Guide to Technical Terms.* Malibu, Calif.: J. Paul Getty Museum in association with the British Library, 1994.

Cahn, Walter. *Romanesque Bible Illumination.* Ithaca, N.Y.: Cornell Univ. Press, 1982.

———. *Romanesque Manuscripts: The Twelfth Century.* 2 vols. Survey of Manuscripts Illuminated in France. London: H. Miller, 1996.

Calkins, Robert C. *Medieval Architecture in Western Europe: From A.D. 300–1500.* Iv. + laser optical disc. New York: Oxford Univ. Press, 1998.

———. *Monuments of Medieval Art.* New York: Dutton, 1979.

Conant, Kenneth John. *Carolingian and Romanesque Architecture, 800–1200.* 3rd ed. Pelican History of Art. Harmondsworth, Eng.: Penguin, 1973.

Diebold, William J. *Word and Image: An Introduction to Early Medieval Art.* Boulder, Colo.: Westview Press, 2000.

Dodwell, C. R. *Pictorial Arts of the West 800–1200.* Pelican History of Art. New Haven: Yale Univ. Press, 1993.

Duby, Georges. *Sculpture: The Great Art of the Middle Ages from the Fifth to the Fifteenth Century.* New York: Skira/Rizzoli, 1990.

Evans, Angela Care. *The Sutton Hoo Ship Burial.* Rev ed. London: British Museum, 1994.

Farr, Carol. *The Book of Kells: Its Function and Audience.* London: British Library, 1997.

Fitzhugh, William W. and Elisabeth I. Ward, eds. *Vikings: The North Atlantic Saga.* Washington, D.C.: Smithsonian Institution Press, 2000.

Forsyth, Ilene H. *The Throne of Wisdom: Wood Sculptures of the Madonna in Romanesque France.* Princeton, N.J.: Princeton Univ. Press, 1972.

Grape, Wolfgang. *The Bayeux Tapestry: Monument to a Norman Triumph.* New York: Prestel, 1994.

Harbison, Peter. *The Golden Age of Irish Art: The Medieval Achievement, 600–1200.* London: Thames and Hudson, 1998.

Hubert, Jean, Jean Porcher, and W. F. Volbach. *Carolingian Renaissance.* Arts of Mankind. New York: Braziller, 1970.

Kennedy, Hugh. *Crusader Castles.* Cambridge: Cambridge Univ. Press, 1994.

Kenyon, John. *Medieval Fortifications.* Leicester: Leicester Univ. Press, 1990.

Kubach, Hans Erich. *Romanesque Architecture.* History of World Architecture. New York: Electa/Rizzoli, 1988.

Labarge, Margaret Wade. *A Small Sound of the Trumpet: Women in Medieval Life.* London: Hamilton, 1990.

Laing, Lloyd. *Art of the Celts.* World of Art. New York: Thames and Hudson, 1992.

Mentre, Mirelle. *Illuminated Manuscripts of Medieval Spain.* New York: Thames and Hudson, 1996.

Myer-Harting, Henry. *Ottonian Book Illumination: An Historical Study.* 2 vols. 2nd rev. ed. London: Harvey Miller, 1999.

Megaw, Ruth, and Vincent Megaw. *Celtic Art: From Its Beginnings to the Book of Kells.* New York: Thames and Hudson, 1989.

Nees, Lawrence. *Early Medieval Art.* Oxford History of Art. Oxford: Oxford Univ. Press, 2003.

Nordenfalk, Carl Adam Johan. *Early Medieval Book Illumination.* New York: Rizzoli, 1988.

Petzold, Andreas. *Romanesque Art.* Perspectives. New York: Abrams, 1995.

Radding, Charles M., and William W. Clark. *Medieval Architecture, Medieval Learning: Builders and Masters in the Age of Romanesque and Gothic.* New Haven, Conn.: Yale Univ. Press, 1992.

Schapiro, Meyer. *Romanesque Art.* New York: Braziller, 1977.

Sekules, Veronica. *Medieval Art.* Oxford History of Art. Oxford: Oxford Univ. Press, 2001.

Stalley, R. A. *Early Medieval Architecture.* Oxford History of Art. Oxford: Oxford Univ. Press, 1998.

Stoddard, Whitney. *Art and Architecture in Medieval France: Medieval Architecture, Sculpture, Stained Glass, Manuscripts. The Art of the Church Treasuries.* New York: Harper & Row, 1972.

Stokstad, Marilyn. *Medieval Art.* 2nd ed. New York: Westview Press, 2004.

Stones, Alison, and Jeanne Krochalis, Paula Gerson, and Annie Shaver-Crandell. *The Pilgrim's Guide: A Critical Edition.* 2 vols. London: Harvey Miller, 1998.

Wieck, Roger S. *Time Sanctified: The Book of Hours in Medieval Art and Life.* New York: Braziller, 1988.

Williams, John. *The Illustrated Beatus: Corpus of the Illumination of the Commentary on the Apocalypse.* London: Harvey Miller, 1994.

Wilson, David M. *Anglo-Saxon Art: From the Seventh Century to the Norman Conquest.* London: Thames and Hudson, 1984.

———. *The Bayeux Tapestry: The Complete Tapestry in Color.* New York: Random House, 1985.

———, and Ole Klindt-Jensen. *Viking Art.* 2nd ed. Minneapolis: Univ. of Minnesota Press, 1980.

Year 1200, The. 2 vols. New York: Metropolitan Museum of Art, 1970.

Zarnecki, George. *The Art of the Medieval World: Architecture, Sculpture, Painting, the Sacred Arts.* New York: Abrams, 1975.

Chapter 11 Gothic Art

Andrews, Francis B. *The Medieval Builder and His Methods.* New York: Barnes and Noble, 1993.

Armi, C. Edson. *The "Headmaster" of Chartres and the Origins of "Gothic" Sculpture.* University Park: Pennsylvania State Univ. Press, 1994.

Bony, Jean. *French Gothic Architecture of the 12th and 13th Centuries.* California Studies in the History of Art. Berkeley: Univ. of California Press, 1983.

Borsook, Eve, and Fiorella Superbi Gioffredi. *Italian Altarpieces, 1250–1550: Function and Design.* Oxford: Clarendon, 1994.

Camille, Michael. *The Medieval Art of Love: Objects and Subjects of Desire.* New York: Abrams, 1998.

———. *Gothic Art: Glorious Visions.* Perspectives. New York: Abrams, 1996.

———. *The Gothic Idol: Ideology and Image Making in Medieval Art.* Cambridge New Art History and Criticism. Cambridge: Cambridge Univ. Press, 1989.

Chelazzi Dini, Giulietta, Alessandro Angelini, and Bernardina Sani. *Sienese Painting: From Duccio to the Birth of the Baroque.* New York: Abrams, 1997.

Chiellini, Monica. *Cimabue.* Trans. Lisa Pelletti. Florence: Scala, 1988.

Coldstream, Nicola. *Medieval Architecture.* Oxford History of Art. Oxford: Oxford Univ. Press, 2002.

Cole, Bruce. *Giotto and Florentine Painting, 1280–1375.* New York: Harper & Row, 1975.

Crosby, Sumner McKnight. *The Royal Abbey of Saint-Denis from Its Beginnings to the Death of Suger, 475–1151.* Yale Publications in the History of Art. New Haven, Conn.: Yale Univ. Press, 1987.

Erlande-Brandenburg, Alain. *Gothic Art.* Trans. I. Mark Paris. New York: Abrams, 1989.

———. *Notre Dame de Paris.* New York: Abrams, 1998.

Favier, Jean. *The World of Chartres.* Trans. Francisca Garvie. New York: Abrams, 1990.

Grodecki, Louis. *Gothic Architecture.* Trans. I. Mark Paris. History of World Architecture. New York: Electa/Rizzoli, 1985.

———, and Catherine Brisac. *Gothic Stained Glass, 1200–1300.* Ithaca, N.Y.: Cornell Univ. Press, 1985.

O'Neill, John Philip., ed. *Enamels of Limoges, 1100–1350.* Trans. Sophie Hawkes, Joachim Neugroschel, and Patri-

cia Stirneman. New York: Metropolitan Museum of Art, 1996.

Panofsky, Erwin. *Abbot Suger on the Abbey Church of St.-Denis and Its Art Treasures.* 2nd ed. Ed. Gerda Panofsky-Soergel. Princeton, N.J.: Princeton Univ. Press, 1979.

———. *Gothic Architecture and Scholasticism.* Latrobe, Penn.: Archabbey, 1951.

Pevsner, Nikolaus, and Priscilla Metcalf. *The Cathedrals of England.* 2 vols. Harmondsworth, Eng.: Viking, 1985.

Sauerlander, Willibald. *Gothic Sculpture in France, 1140–1270.* Trans. Janet Sandheimer. London: Thames and Hudson, 1972.

Scott, Kathleen L. *Later Gothic Manuscripts, 1390–1490.* 2 vols. A Survey of Manuscripts Illuminated in the British Isles; 6. London: Harvey Miller, 1996.

Simson, Otto Georg von. *The Gothic Cathedral: Origins of Gothic Architecture and the Medieval Concept of Order.* 3rd ed. Bollingen Series. Princeton, N.J.: Princeton Univ. Press, 1988.

Smart, Alastair. *The Dawn of Italian Painting, 1250–1400.* Ithaca, N.Y.: Cornell Univ. Press, 1978.

White, John. *Art and Architecture in Italy, 1250 to 1400.* 3rd ed. Pelican History of Art. Harmondsworth, Eng.: Penguin, 1993.

———. *Duccio: Tuscan Art and the Medieval Workshop.* New York: Thames and Hudson, 1979.

Williamson, Paul. *Gothic Sculpture 1140–1300.* Pelican History of Art. New Haven: Yale Univ. Press, 1995.

Wilson, Christopher. *The Gothic Cathedral: The Architecture of the Great Church, 1130–1530.* New York: Thames and Hudson, 1990.

Chapter 12 Early Renaissance Art

Adams, Laurie Schneider. *Italian Renaissance Art.* Boulder, Colo.: Westview Press, 2001.

Ainsworth, Maryan Wynn. *Petrus Christus: Renaissance Master of Bruges.* New York: Metropolitan Museum of Art, 1994.

Ahl, Diane Cole, ed. *The Cambridge Companion to Masaccio.* New York: Cambridge Univ. Press, 2002.

Alexander, J. J. G. *The Painted Page: Italian Renaissance Book Illumination, 1450–1550.* New York: Prestel, 1994.

Ames, Lewis Francis. *The Intellectual Life of the Early Renaissance Artist.* New Haven: Yale Univ. Press, 2000.

Art and Politics in Late Medieval and Early Renaissance Italy, 1250–1500. South Bend, Ind.: Univ. of Notre Dame Press, 1990.

Baxandall, Michael. *Painting and Experience in Fifteenth-Century Italy: A Primer in the Social History of Pictorial Style.* Oxford: Clarendon, 1972.

Campbell, Lorne. *Renaissance Portraits: European Portrait-Painting in the 14th, 15th, and 16th Centuries.* New Haven, Conn.: Yale Univ. Press, 1990.

Cavallo, Adolph S. *The Unicorn Tapestries at the Metropolitan Museum of Art.* New York: The Metropolitan Museum of Art; Abrams, 1998.

Chastell, Andre. *French Art: The Renaissance, 1430–1620.* Paris: Flammarion, 1995.

Christiansen, Keith. *Andrea Mantegna: Padua and Mantua.* New York: Braziller, 1994.

———, Laurence B. Kanter, and Carl Brandon Strehlke. *Painting in Renaissance Siena, 1420–1500.* New York: Metropolitan Museum of Art, 1988.

Circa 1492: Art in the Age of Exploration. Washington, D.C.: National Gallery of Art, 1991.

Cole, Bruce. *Italian Art, 1250–1550: The Relation of Renaissance Art to Life and Society.* New York: Harper & Row, 1987.

———. *Masaccio and the Art of Early Renaissance Florence.* Bloomington: Indiana Univ. Press, 1980.

Cuttler, Charles D. *Northern Painting from Pucelle to Bruegel: Fourteenth, Fifteenth and Sixteenth Centuries.* New York: Holt, Rinehart and Winston, 1973.

Freeman, Margaret B. *The Unicorn Tapestries.* New York: Metropolitan Museum of Art, 1976.

Hartt, Frederick, and David G. Wilkins. *History of Italian*

Renaissance Art: Painting, Sculpture, Architecture. 5th ed. New York: Abrams, 2003.

Heydenreich, Ludwig Heinrich. *Architecture in Italy, 1400 to 1600.* Rev. Paul Davies. Pelican History of Art. New Haven: Yale Univ. Press, 1996.

Huizinga, Johan. *The Autumn of the Middle Ages.* Trans. Rodney J. Payton and Ulrich Mammitzsch. Chicago: Univ. of Chicago Press, 1996.

Krautheimer, Richard. *Ghiberti's Bronze Doors.* Princeton, N.J.: Princeton Univ. Press, 1971.

Lane, Barbara G. *The Altar and the Altarpiece: Sacramental Themes in Early Netherlandish Painting.* New York: Harper & Row, 1984.

McCorquodale, Charles. *The Renaissance: European Painting, 1400–1600.* London: Studio Editions, 1994.

Pacht, Otto. *Early Netherlandish Painting: From Rogier van der Weyden to Gerard David.* Ed. Monika Rosenauer. Trans. David Britt. London: Harvey Miller, 1997.

———. *Van Eyck and the Founders of Early Netherlandish Painting.* Ed. Maria Schmidt-Dengler. Trans. David Britt. London: Miller, 1994.

Panofsky, Erwin. *Early Netherlandish Painting: Its Origins and Character.* 2 vols. Cambridge, Mass.: Harvard Univ. Press, 1966.

Paolucci, Antonio. *The Origins of Renaissance Art: The Baptistry Doors, Florence.* New York: George Braziller, 1996.

Saalman, Howard. *Filippo Brunelleschi: The Buildings.* University Park: Pennsylvania State Univ. Press, 1993.

Snyder, James. *Northern Renaissance Art: Painting, Sculpture, the Graphic Arts from 1350 to 1575.* New York: Abrams, 1985.

Verdon, Timothy and John Henderson, eds. *Christianity and the Renaissance: Image and Religious Imagination in the Quattrocento.* Syracuse, N.Y.: Syracuse Univ. Press, 1990.

Welch, Evelyn S. *Art and Society in Italy, 1350–1500.* Oxford History of Art. Oxford: Oxford Univ. Press, 1997.

Chapter 13 Art of the High Renaissance and Reformation

Aikema, Bernard, ed. *Renaissance Venice and the North: Crosscurrents in the Time of Bellini, Dürer, and Titian.* New York: Rizzoli, 2000.

Algranti, Gilberto, ed. *Titian to Tiepolo: Three Centuries of Italian Art.* New York: Rizzoli/St. Martin's Press, 2002.

Andrews, Lew. *Story and Space in Renaissance Art: The Rebirth of Continuous Narrative.* New York: Cambridge Univ. Press, 1995.

Bambach, Carmen. *Drawing and Painting in the Italian Renaissance Workshop: Theory and Practice, 1300–1600.* Cambridge: Cambridge Univ. Press, 1999.

Baxandall, Michael. *The Limewood Sculptors of Renaissance Germany.* New Haven, Conn.: Yale Univ. Press, 1980.

Bier, Justus. *Tilman Riemenschneider, His Life and Work.* Lexington: Univ. of Kentucky Press, 1984.

Blunt, Anthony. *Art and Architecture in France: 1500–1700.* 5th ed. Rev. Richard Beresford. Pelican History of Art. New Haven: Yale Univ. Press, 1999.

Boucher, Bruce. *Andrea Palladio: The Architect in His Time.* New York: Abbeville, 1994.

Brown, Jonathan. *Painting in Spain, 1500–1700.* Pelican History of Art. New Haven: Yale Univ. Press, 1998.

Brown, Patricia Fortini. *Art and Life in Renaissance Venice.* Perspectives. New York: Abrams, 1997.

Burroughs, Charles. *The Italian Renaissance Palace Facade: Structures of Authority, Surfaces of Sense.* Cambridge: Cambridge Univ. Press, 2002.

Cole, Alison. *Virtue and Magnificence: Art of the Italian Renaissance Courts.* Perspectives. New York: Abrams, 1995.

Dixon, Annette, ed. *Women Who Ruled: Queens, Goddesses, Amazons in Renaissance and Baroque Art.* London: Merrell; Ann Arbor, Mich.: University of Michigan Museum of Art, 2002.

Emison, Patricia A. *Low and High Style in Italian Renaissance Art.* New York: Garland Publishing, 1997.

Farago, Claire J. *Reframing the Renaissance: Visual Culture*

in Europe and Latin America, 1450–1650. New Haven: Yale Univ. Press, 1995.

Field, Judith Veronica. *The Invention of Infinity: Mathematics and Art in the Renaissance.* Oxford: Oxford Univ. Press, 1997.

Freedberg, S. J. *Painting in Italy, 1500 to 1600.* 3rd ed. Pelican History of Art. New Haven, Conn.: Yale Univ. Press, 1993.

Graham-Dixon, Andrew. *Renaissance.* Berkeley: Univ. of California Press, 1999.

Grössinger, Christa. *Picturing Women in Late Medieval and Renaissance Art.* New York: St. Martin's Press, 1997.

Harbison, Craig. *The Mirror of the Artist: Northern Renaissance Art in Its Historical Context.* Perspectives. New York: Abrams, 1995.

Hayum, André. *The Isenheim Altarpiece: God's Medicine and the Painter's Vision.* Princeton Essays on the Arts. Princeton, N.J.: Princeton Univ. Press, 1989.

Heydenreich, Ludwig H. *Leonardo: "The Last Supper."* Art in Context. London: Allen Lane, 1974.

Huizinga, Johan. *Waning of the Middle Ages: A Study of the Forms of Life, Thought, and Art in France and the Netherlands in the XIVth and XVth Centuries.* Garden City, N.Y.: Doubleday, 1954.

Jacobs, Fredrika Herman. *Defining the Renaissance Virtuosa: Women Artists and the Language of Art History and Criticism.* Cambridge: Cambridge Univ. Press, 1997.

Jestez, Bertrand. *The Art of the Renaissance.* Trans. Mark Paris. New York: Abrams, 1995.

Landau, David, and Peter Parshall. *The Renaissance Print: 1470–1550.* New Haven, Conn.: Yale Univ. Press, 1994.

Lotz, Wolfgang. *Architecture in Italy, 1500–1600.* Rev. Deborah Howard. Pelican History of Art. New Haven: Yale Univ. Press, 1995.

Manca, Joseph. *Moral Essays on the High Renaissance: Art in Italy in the Age of Michelangelo.* Lanham, Md.: Univ. Press of America, 2001.

Mann, Nicolas and Luke Syson, eds. *The Image of the Individual: Portraits in the Renaissance.* London: British Museum Press, 1998.

Martineau, Jane, and Charles Hope, eds. *The Genius of Venice, 1500–1600.* New York: Abrams, 1984.

McHam, Sarah Blake, ed. *Looking at Italian Renaissance Sculpture.* Cambridge: Cambridge Univ. Press, 1998.

Murray, Linda. *The High Renaissance and Mannerism: Italy, the North, and Spain, 1500–1600.* World of Art. London: Thames and Hudson, 1995.

Murray, Peter. *Renaissance Architecture.* History of World Architecture. Milan: Electa, 1985.

Olson, Roberta J. M. *Italian Renaissance Sculpture.* World of Art. New York: Thames and Hudson, 1992.

Paoletti, John T., and Gary M. Radke. *Art in Renaissance Italy.* 2nd ed. New York: Abrams, 2002.

Partridge, Loren W. *The Art of Renaissance Rome, 1400–1600.* New York: Abrams, 1996.

Perlingieri, Ilya Sandra. *Sofonisba Anguissola: The First Great Woman Artist of the Renaissance.* New York: Rizzoli, 1992.

Pietrangeli, Carlo et al. *The Sistine Chapel: The Art, the History, and the Restoration.* New York: Harmony, 1986.

Poeschke, Joachim. *Michelangelo and His World: Sculpture of the Italian Renaissance.* Trans. Russell Stockman. New York: Abrams, 1996.

Pope-Hennessy, Sir John. *Italian High Renaissance and Baroque Sculpture.* 3rd ed. Oxford: Phaidon, 1986.

Rosand, David. *Painting in Cinquecento Venice: Titian, Veronese, Tintoretto.* Rev. ed. Cambridge: Cambridge Univ. Press, 1997.

Rowland, Ingrid D. *The Culture of the High Renaissance: Ancients and Moderns in Sixteenth-Century Rome.* Cambridge: Cambridge Univ. Press, 1998.

Shearman, John. *Mannerism.* Harmondsworth, Eng.: Penguin, 1967.

Tavernor, Robert. *Palladio and Palladianism.* World of Art. New York: Thames and Hudson, 1991.

Tinagli, Paola. *Women in Italian Renaissance Art: Gender, Representation, and Identity.* New York: St. Martin's

Press, 1997.

Turner, Richard. *Renaissance Florence: The Invention of a New Art.* Perspectives. New York: Abrams, 1997.

Vasari, Giorgio. *The Lives of the Artists.* Trans. Julia Conaway Bondanella and Peter Bondanella. New York: Oxford Univ. Press, 1991.

Williams, Robert. *Art, Theory, and Culture in Sixteenth-Century Italy: From Techne to Metatechne.* Cambridge: Cambridge Univ. Press, 1997.

Wohl, Hellmut. *The Aesthetics of Italian Renaissance Art: A Reconsideration of Style.* Cambridge: Cambridge Univ. Press, 1999.

Chapter 14 Baroque and Rococo Art

Ackley, Clifford S. *Printmaking in the Age of Rembrandt.* Boston: Museum of Fine Arts, 1981.

Age of Caravaggio, The. New York: Metropolitan Museum of Art, 1985.

Alpers, Svetlana. *The Making of Rubens.* New Haven: Yale Univ. Press, 1995.

Berger, Robert W. *Versailles: The Chateau of Louis XIV.* Monographs on the Fine Arts. University Park: Pennsylvania State Univ. Press, 1985.

Blunt, Anthony, et al. *Baroque and Rococo Architecture and Decoration.* New York: Harper & Row, 1982.

Boucher, Bruce. *Italian Baroque Sculpture.* World of Art. New York: Thames and Hudson, 1998.

Brown, Christopher. *Scenes of Everyday Life: Dutch Genre Painting of the Seventeenth Century.* London: Faber & Faber, 1984.

Brown, Jonathan. *The Golden Age of Painting in Spain.* New Haven, Conn.: Yale Univ. Press, 1991.

———, and Carmen Garrido. *Velasquez: The Technique of Genius.* Hew Haven: Yale Univ. Press, 1998.

Earls, Irene. *Baroque Art: A Topical Dictionary.* Westport, Conn.: Greenwood Press, 1996.

Franits, Wayne E., ed. *The Cambridge Companion to Vermeer.* Cambridge: Cambridge Univ. Press, 2001.

Haak, Bob. *The Golden Age: Dutch Painters of the Seventeenth Century.* Trans. and ed. Elizabeth Willems-Treeman. New York: Abrams, 1984.

Held, Julius Samuel, and Donald Posner. *17th- and 18th-Century Art: Baroque Painting, Sculpture, Architecture.* Library of Art History. New York: Abrams, 1971.

Kiers, Judikje, et al. *Glory of the Golden Age: Dutch Art of the 17th Century.* Amsterdam: Waanders, Rijksmuseum, 2000.

———, and Fieke Tissink. *Golden Age of Dutch Art: Painting, Sculpture, Decorative Art.* London: Thames and Hudson, 2000.

Kubler, George, and Martin Soria. *Art and Architecture in Spain and Portugal and Their American Dominions, 1500–1800.* Pelican History of Art. Harmondsworth, Eng.: Penguin, 1959.

Lagerlof, Margaretha Rossholm. *Ideal Landscape: Annibale Caracci, Nicolas Poussin, and Claude Lorrain.* New Haven, Conn.: Yale Univ. Press, 1990.

Liedtke, Walter, Michael C. Plomp, and Axel Rüger. *Vermeer and the Delft School.* New York: Metropolitan Museum of Art, New Haven: Yale Univ. Press, 2001.

McTighe, Sheila. *Nicolas Poussin's Landscape Allegories.* Cambridge: Cambridge University Press, 1996.

Minor, Vernon Hyde. *Baroque and Rococo: Art & Culture.* New York: Abrams, 1999.

Norberg-Schulz, Christian. *Baroque Architecture.* New York: Rizzoli, 1986.

Olson, Todd. *Poussin and France: Painting, Humanism, and the Politics of Style.* New Haven: Yale Univ. Press, 2002.

Pizzamiglio, Gilberto and Manlio Brusatin., eds. *The Baroque in Central Europe: Places, Architecture, and Art.* Venice: Marsilio, 1992.

Plax, Julie Anne. *Watteau and the Cultural Politics of 18th-Century France.* New York: Cambridge Univ. Press, 2000.

Slive, Seymour. *Dutch Painting 1600–1800.* Pelican History of Art. New Haven: Yale Univ. Press, 1995.

Stratton-Pruitt, Suzanne L., ed. *Cambridge Companion to Velasquez.* Cambridge: Cambridge Univ. Press, 2002.

Sutton, Peter. *The Age of Rubens*. Boston: Museum of Fine Arts, 1993.

Tomlinson, Janis. *From El Greco to Goya: Painting in Spain, 1561–1828*. New York: Abrams, 1997.

Vergara, Alexander. *Rubens and His Spanish Patrons*. Cambridge: Cambridge Univ. Press, 1999.

Vlieghe, Hans. *Flemish Art and Architecture, 1585–1700*. Pelican History of Art. New Haven: Yale Univ. Press, 1998.

Welu, James A., and Pieter Biesboer, eds. *Judith Leyster: A Dutch Master and Her World*. New York: Yale Univ. Press, 1993.

Westerman, Mariët. *Art and Home: Dutch Interiors in the Age of Rembrandt*. Denver, Colo.: Denver Art Museum; Netherlands: Waanders, 2001.

——. *A Worldly Art: The Dutch Republic 1585–1718*. Perspectives. New York: Abrams, 1996.

White, Christopher. *Rembrandt as an Etcher: A Study of the Artist at Work*. 2nd ed. New Haven: Yale Univ. Press, 1999.

——, and Quentin Buvelot. *Rembrandt by Himself*. London: National Gallery Publications, 1999.

Wine, Humphrey. *Claude: The Poetic Landscape*. London: National Gallery Publications, 1994.

Wintermute, Alan. *Watteau and His World: French Drawing from 1700–1750*. New York: Rizzoli/St. Martin's Press, 1999.

Wittkower, Rudolf. *Art and Architecture in Italy, 1600 to 1750*. 3 vols. 6th ed. Rev. Joseph Conners and Jennifer Montagu. Pelican History of Art. New Haven: Yale Univ. Press, 1999.

Chapter 15 Art of the Americas

Archuleta, Margaret, and Rennard Strickland. *Shared Visions: Native American Painters and Sculptors in the Twentieth Century*. Phoenix: Heard Museum, 1991.

Benson, Elizabeth P., and Beatriz de la Fuente, eds. *Olmec Art of Ancient Mexico*. Washington, D. C.: National Gallery of Art, 1996.

Berlo, Janet Catherine, and Ruth B. Phillips. *Native North American Art*. Oxford History of Art. Oxford: Oxford Univ. Press, 1998.

Bringhurst, Robert. *The Black Canoe: Bill Reid and the Spirit of Haida Gwaii*. Seattle: Univ. of Washington Press, 1991.

Broder, Patricia Janis. *Earth Songs, Moon Dreams: Paintings by American Indian Women*. New York: St. Martin's Press, 1999.

Coe, Michael D., et al. *The Olmec World: Ritual and Rulership*. Princeton, N.J.: Princeton Univ. in association with Abrams, 1995.

Coe, Ralph. *Lost and Found Traditions: Native American Art 1965–1985*. Ed. Irene Gordon. Seattle: Univ. of Washington Press, 1986.

Crandall, Richard C. *Inuit Art: A History*. Jefferson, N.C.: McFarland, 2000.

Fane, Diane. *Converging Cultures: Art and Identity in Spanish America*. New York: Brooklyn Museum in association with Abrams, 1996.

Feest, Christian F. *Native Arts of North America*. Updated ed. World of Art. New York: Thames and Hudson, 1992.

Grimes, John B., Christian F. Feest, and Mary Lou Curran, eds. *Uncommon Legacies: Native American Art from the Peabody Essex Museum*. New York: American Federation of the Arts; Seattle; London: in association with the Univ. of Washington Press, 2002.

Jonaitis, Aldona, ed. *Chiefly Feast: The Enduring Kwakiutl Potlatch*. Seattle: Univ. of Washington Press, 1991.

Krumnine, Mary Louise Elliot, and Susan C. Scott, eds. *Art and the Native American: Perceptions, Reality, and Influences*. University Park, Pa.: Pennsylvania State Univ., 2001.

MacDonald, George F. *Haida Art*. Seattle: Univ. of Washington Press, 1996.

McQuinton, Don. *Visions of the North: Native Art of the Northwest Coast*. San Francisco: Chronicle Books, 1995.

Mauer, Evan M. *Visions of the People: A Pictorial History of Plains Indian Life*. Minneapolis: Minneapolis Institute of Arts, 1992.

Meuli, Jonathan. *Shadow House: Interpretations of Northwest Coast Art*. Amsterdam, The Netherlands: Harwood Academic Publishing, 2001.

Mexico: Splendors of Thirty Centuries. New York: Metropolitan Museum of Art, 1990.

Miller, Mary Ellen. *The Art of Mesoamerica: from Olmec to Aztec*. 3rd ed. World of Art. London: Thames and Hudson, 2001.

Monroe, Dan L. et al. *Gifts of the Spirit: Works of Nineteenth-Century and Contemporary Native American Artists*. Salem, Mass.: Peabody Essex Museum, 1996.

Pasztory, Esther. *Pre-Columbian Art*. New York: Cambridge Univ. Press, 1998.

——. *Aztec Art*. New York: Abrams, 1983.

Penny, David. *Native Arts of North America*. Trans. Peter Snowden. Paris: Terrail, 1998.

——. *Art of the American Indian Frontier: The Chandler-Pohrt Collection*. Detroit: Detroit Institute of the Arts, 1992.

Rasmussen, Waldo, Fatima Bercht, and Elizabeth Ferrer. *Latin American Artists of the Twentieth Century*. New York: Museum of Modern Art, 1993.

Reno, Dawn E. *Contemporary Native American Artists*. Brooklyn: Alliance Publishing, 1995.

Schobinger, Juan. *The Ancient Americans: A Reference Guide to the Art, Culture, and History of Pre-Columbian North and South America*. Trans. Carys Evans Corrales. Armonk, N.Y.: Sharp Reference, 2001.

Trimble, Stephen. *Talking with the Clay: The Art of Pueblo Pottery*. Santa Fe: School of American Research Press, 1987.

Vincent, Gilbert Tapley. *Masterpieces of American Indian Art: From the Eugene and Clare Thaw Collection*. New York: Abrams, 1995.

Wood, Nancy C. *Taos Pueblo*. New York: Knopf, 1989.

Chapter 16 African Art

Abiodun, Rowland, Henry J. Drewal, and John Pemberton III, eds. *The Yoruba Artist: New Theoretical Perspectives on African Arts*. Washington, D.C.: Smithsonian Institution, 1994.

Adler, Peter, and Nicholas Barnard. *African Majesty: The Textile Art of the Ashanti and Ewe*. New York: Thames and Hudson, 1992.

Astonishment and Power. Washington, D.C.: National Museum of African Art, Smithsonian Institution, 1993.

Bacquart, Jean-Baptiste. *The Tribal Arts of Africa*. New York: Thames and Hudson, 1998.

Bargna, Ivan. *African Art*. Trans. Jacqueline A. Cooperman. Rev. Michael Thompson. Milano, Italy: Jaca Book; Wappingers' Falls, N.Y.: Antique Collector's Club, 2000.

Barley, Nigel. *Smashing Pots: Feats of Clay from Africa*. London: British Museum, 1994.

Bassani, Ezio. *African Art and Artifacts in European Collections: 1400–1800*. Ed. Malcolm McLeod. London: British Museum, 2000.

Beckwith, Carol and Angela Fisher. *African Ark: People and Ancient Cultures of Ethiopia and the Horn of Africa*. New York: Abrams, 1990.

Ben-Amos, Paula. *The Art of Benin*. Rev. ed. Washington, D.C.: Smithsonian Institution Press, 1995.

Biebuyck, Daniel P. *Lega Culture: Art, Initiation, and Moral Philosophy among a Central African People*. Berkeley: Univ. of California Press, 1973.

Blauer, Ettagale. *African Elegance*. New York: Rizzoli, 1999.

Blier, Suzanne Preston. *Ritual Arts of Africa: The Majesty of Form*. Perspectives. New York: Abrams, 1998.

Cole, Herbert M. *Icons: Ideals and Power in the Art of Africa*. Washington, D.C.: National Museum of African Art, Smithsonian Institution, 1989.

D'Azevedao, Warren L. *The Traditional Artist in African Societies*. Bloomington: Indiana Univ. Press, 1989.

Drewal, Henry, and John Pemberton III. *Yoruba: Nine Centuries of African Art and Thought*. New York: Center for African Art, 1989.

Garlake, Peter S. *Early Art and Architecture of Africa*. Oxford History of Art. Oxford: Oxford Univ. Press, 2002.

——. *The Hunter's Vision: The Prehistoric Art of Zimbabwe*. Seattle: Univ. of Washington Press, 1995.

Gilfoy, Peggy S. *Patterns of Life: West African Strip-Weaving Traditions*. Washington, D.C.: National Museum of African Art, Smithsonian Institution, 1992.

Harris, Michael D. *Transatlantic Dialogue: Contemporary Art In and Out of Africa*. Chapel Hill, N.C.: Univ. of North Carolina; Seattle: Univ. of Washington Press, 1999.

Kasfir, Sidney Littlefield. *Contemporary African Art*. World of Art. London: Thames and Hudson, 2000.

Mark, John, ed. *Africa, Arts and Cultures*. London: British Museum, 2000.

Martin, Phyllis, and Patrick O'Meara, eds. *Africa*. 3rd ed. Bloomington: Indiana Univ. Press, 1995.

Mbiti, John S. *African Religions and Philosophy*. 2nd ed. Oxford: Heinemann, 1990.

McNaughton, Patrick R. *The Mande Blacksmiths: Knowledge, Power and Art in West Africa*. Bloomington: Indiana Univ. Press, 1988.

McClusky, Pamela. *Art from Africa: Long Steps Never Broke a Back*. Seattle: Seattle Art Museum; Princeton, N.J.: Princeton Univ. Press, 2002.

Meyer, Laure. *Art and Craft in Africa: Everyday Life, Ritual, and Court Art*. Paris: Terrail, 1995.

Murray, Jocelyn, ed. *Cultural Atlas of Africa*. New York: Facts on File, 1998.

Neyt, François. *Luba: To the Sources of the Zaire*. Trans. Murray Wyllie. Paris: Editions Dapper, 1994.

Perrois, Louis, and Marta Sierra Delage. *The Art of Equatorial Guinea: The Fang Tribes*. New York: Rizzoli, 1990.

Phillips, Tom. *Africa: The Art of a Continent*. London: Prestel, 1996.

Roy, Christopher D. *Art and Life in Africa: Selections from the Stanley Collection*. Iowa City: Univ. of Iowa Museum of Art; Seattle: Univ. of Washington Press, 1992.

Schildkrout, Enid, and Curtis A. Keim. *African Reflections: Art from Northeastern Zaire*. Seattle: Univ. of Washington Press, 1990.

Schuster, Carl, and Edmund Carpenter. *Patterns That Connect: Social Symbolism in Ancient & Tribal Art*. New York: Abrams, 1996.

Sieber, Roy. *African Furniture and Household Objects*. Bloomington: Indiana Univ. Press, 1980.

——, and Roslyn Adele Walker. *African Art in the Cycle of Life*. Washington, D.C.: National Museum of African Art, Smithsonian Institution, 1987.

Stepan, Peter. *Africa*. Trans. John Gabriel and Elizabeth Schwaiger. London: Prestel, 2001.

Thompson, Robert Ferris. *Face of the Gods: Art and Altars of Africa and the African Americas*. New York: Museum for African Art; Munich: Prestel, 1993.

Visonà, Monica Blackmun, et al. *A History of Art in Africa*. New York: Abrams, 2000.

Vogel, Susan. *Africa Explores: 20th Century African Art*. New York: Center for African Art, 1991.

Walker, Roslyn A. *Olówè of Isè: A Yoruba Sculptor to Kings*. Washington, D.C.: National Museum of African Art, Smithsonian Institution, 1998.

Whittington, Michael E. *Earth, Fire, and Spirit: African Pottery and Sculpture*. Charlotte, N.C.: Mint Museum of Art, 1998.

Willett, Frank. *African Art: An Introduction*. Rev. ed. World of Art. New York: Thames and Hudson, 1993.

Chapter 17 Neoclassicism, Romanticism, and Realism

Barger, M. Susan, and William B. White. *The Daguerreotype: Nineteenth-Century Technology and Modern Science*. Washington, D.C.: Smithsonian Institution, 1991.

Berger, Martin A. *Man Made: Thomas Eakins and the Construction of Gilded Age Manhood*. Berkeley: Univ. of California Press, 2000.

Boime, Albert. *Magisterial Gaze: Manifest Destiny and American Landscape Painting*. Washington, D.C.: Smithsonian Institution Press, 1991.

———. *Art in an Age of Bonapartism, 1800–1815*. Chicago: Univ. of Chicago Press, 1990.

Clark, T. J. *The Absolute Bourgeois: Artists and Politics in France, 1848–1851*. Berkeley: Univ. of California Press, 1999.

———. *Image of the People: Gustave Courbet and the 1848 Revolution*. Berkeley: Univ. of California Press, 1999.

Clarke, Graham. *The Photograph*. Oxford History of Art. Oxford: Oxford Univ. Press, 1997.

Conrads, Margaret C. *Winslow Homer and the Critics: Forging a National Art in the 1870s*. Princeton, N.J.: Princeton Univ. Press in association with the Nelson-Atkins Museum of Art, 2001.

Cooper, Wendy A. *Classical Taste in America 1800–1840*. Baltimore: Baltimore Museum of Art, 1993.

Denis, Rafael Cordoso, and Colin Trodd. *Art and the Academy in the Nineteenth Century*. New Brunswick, N.J.: Rutgers Univ. Press, 2000.

Des Cars, Laurence. *The Pre-Raphaelites: Romance and Realism*. New York: Abrams, 2000.

Eisenman, Stephen. *Nineteenth-Century Art: A Critical History*. London: Thames and Hudson, 1994.

Grinsby, Darcy Grimaldo. *Extremeties: Painting Empire in Post-Revolutionary France*. New Haven: Yale Univ. Press, 2002.

Hemingway, Andrew, and William Vaughn. *Art in Bourgeois Society, 1790–1850*. Cambridge: Cambridge Univ. Press, 1998.

Irwin, David. *Neoclassicism*. London: Phaidon, 1997.

Johns, Christopher, M. S. *Antonio Canova and the Politics of Patronage in Revolutionary and Napoleonic Europe*. Berkeley: Univ. of California Press, 1998.

Lucie-Smith, Edward. *American Realism*. New York: Abrams, 1994.

Malpas, James. *Realism*. Cambridge: Cambridge Univ. Press, 1997.

Manners and Morals: Hogarth and British Painting, 1700–1760. London: Tate Gallery, 1987.

Mitchell, Timothy. *Art and Science in German Landscape Painting, 1770–1840*. New York: Oxford Univ. Press, 1993.

Monneret, Sophie. *David and Neoclassicism*. Trans. Chris Miller and Peter Snowdon. Paris: Terrail, 1999.

Needham, Gerald. *19th-Century Realist Art*. New York: Harper & Row, 1988.

Nesterova, Yelena. *The Itinerants: The Masters of Russian Realism: Second Half of the 19th and Early 20th Centuries*. Trans. Paul Williams and Jovan Nicolson. Bournemouth: Parkstone; St. Petersburg: Aurora, 1996.

Newhall, Beaumont. *The History of Photography: From 1839 to the Present*. 5th ed. Rev. New York: Museum of Modern Art, 1997.

Novotny, Fritz. *Painting and Sculpture in Europe, 1780–1880*. 2nd ed. Pelican History of Art. New Haven: Yale Univ. Press, 1995.

Prettejohn, Elizabeth. *Rossetti and His Circle*. New York: Stewart, Tabori & Chang, 1998.

Pultz, John. *Body and the Lens: Photography, 1839 to the Present*. Perspectives. New York: Abrams, 1995.

Ribeiro, Aileen. *Ingres in Fashion: Representations of Dress and Appearance in Ingres's Images of Women*. New Haven: Yale Univ. Press, 1999.

Roberts, John. *The Art of Interruption: Realism, Photography, and the Everyday*. Manchester, N.Y.: Manchester Univ. Press, 1998.

Rosenblum, Naomi. *A World History of Photography*. 3rd ed. New York: Abbeville Press, 1997.

Rosenblum, Robert, and H. W. Janson. *19th-Century Art*. New York: Abrams, 1984.

Roworth, Wendy Wassyng. *Angelica Kauffman: A Continental Artist in Georgian England*. London: Reaktion, 1992.

Rykwert, Joseph, and Anne Rykwert. *Robert and James Adam: The Men and the Style*. New York: Rizzoli, 1985.

Schaaf, Larry J. *Out of the Shadows: Herschel, Talbot and the Invention of Photography*. New Haven, Conn.: Yale Univ. Press, 1992.

Sewell, Darrel. *Thomas Eakins*. Philadelphia, Pa.: Philadelphia Museum of Art in association with Yale Univ. Press,

New Haven, 2001.

Stoichita, Victor, and Anna Maria Coderch. *Goya: The Last Carnival*. London: Reaktion, 1999.

Taylor, Joshua C., ed. *Nineteenth-Century Theories of Art*. Berkeley: Univ. of California Press, 1987.

Todd, Pamela. *Pre-Raphaelites at Home*. New York: Watson-Guptill, 2001.

Toman, Rolf, ed. *Neoclassicism and Romanticism: Architecture, Sculpture, Painting, Drawing, 1750–1848*. Trans. Paul Aston, Peter Barton, and Eileen Martin. Cologne: Könemann, 2000.

Valkenier, Elizabeth Kridl. *Ilya Repin and the World of Russian Art*. New York: Columbia Univ. Press, 1990.

Vaughan, William. *Romanticism and Art*. World of Art. New York: Thames and Hudson, 1994.

———, and Francoise Cachin. *Arts of the 19th Century*. 2 vols. New York: Abrams, 1998.

Viscomi, Joseph. *Blake and the Idea of the Book*. Princeton, N.J.: Princeton Univ. Press, 1993.

West, Alison. *From Pigalle to Préault: Neoclassicism and the Sublime in French Sculpture, 1760–1840*. Cambridge: Cambridge Univ. Press, 1998.

Wolf, Bryan Jay. *Romantic-Revision: Culture and Consciousness in Nineteenth-Century American Painting and Literature*. Chicago: Univ. of Chicago Press, 1986.

Chapter 18 Later Nineteenth-Century Art in Europe and the United States

Adams, Steven. *The Barbizon School and the Origins of Impressionism*. London: Phaidon, 1994.

Adler, Kathleen. *Impressionism*. New York: Yale Univ. Press, 1999.

Baudelaire, Charles. *The Painter of Modern Life, and Other Essays*. 2nd ed. Trans. and ed. Jonathan Mayne. London: Phaidon, 1995.

Berger, Klaus. *Japonisme in Western Painting from Whistler to Matisse*. Trans. David Brit. Cambridge Studies in the History of Art. Cambridge: Cambridge Univ. Press, 1992.

Bocquillon-Ferretti, Marina. *Signac, 1863–1935*. New York: Metropolitan Museum of Art; New Haven: Yale Univ. Press, 2001.

Boime, Albert. *The Academy and French Painting in the Nineteenth Century*. London: Phaidon, 1971.

Bretell, Richard R. *Modern Art, 1851–1929: Capitalism and Representation*. Oxford History of Art. Oxford: Oxford Univ. Press, 1999.

Broude, Norma. *World Impressionism: The International Movement, 1860–1920*. New York: Abrams, 1990.

———. *Impressionism: A Feminist Reading: The Gendering of Art, Science, and Nature in the Nineteenth Century*. New York: Rizzoli, 1991.

Butler, Ruth. *Rodin: The Shape of Genius*. New Haven: Yale Univ. Press, 1993.

Callen, Anthea. *The Art of Impressionism: Painting Technique and the Making of Modernity*. New Haven: Yale Univ. Press, 2000.

Clark, T. J. *The Painting of Modern Life: Paris in the Time of Manet and His Followers*. Rev. ed. Princeton, N.J.: Princeton Univ. Press, 1999.

Cumming, Elizabeth, and Wendy Caplan. *Arts and Crafts Movement*. World of Art. New York: Thames and Hudson, 1991.

Denvir, Bernard. *Chronicle of Impressionism: A Timeline History of Impressionist Art*. Boston: Little, Brown, 1993.

———. *Post-Impressionism*. World of Art. New York: Thames and Hudson, 1992.

———. *The Impressionists First Hand*. World of Art. New York: Thames and Hudson, 1991.

———. *The Thames and Hudson Encyclopedia of Impressionism*. World of Art. New York: Thames and Hudson, 1990.

Dorra, Henri., ed. *Symbolist Art Theories: A Critical Anthology*. Berkeley: University of California Press, 1994.

Duncan, Alastair. *Art Nouveau*. World of Art. New York: Thames and Hudson, 1994.

Garb, Tamar. *Bodies of Modernity: Figure and Flesh in Fin-

de-Siècle France*. New York: Thames and Hudson, 1998.

Gibson, Michael. *Symbolism*. Köln: Taschen, 1995.

Hamilton, George Heard. *Painting and Sculpture in Europe, 1880–1940*. 6th ed. Pelican History of Art. New Haven: Yale Univ. Press, 1993.

Hargrove, June, ed. *The French Academy: Classicism and Its Antagonists*. Newark: Univ. of Delaware Press, 1990.

Herbert, Robert L. *Impressionism: Art, Leisure, and Parisian Society*. New Haven: Yale Univ. Press, 1988.

———. *Seurat: Drawings and Paintings*. New Haven. Yale Univ. Press, 2001.

Higonnet, Anne. *Berthe Morisot's Images of Women*. Cambridge, Mass.: Harvard Univ. Press, 1992.

Hornberg, Cornelia. *Vincent Van Gogh and the Painters of the Petit Boulevard*. New York: St. Louis Art Museum/Rizzoli, 2001.

Kelder, Diane. *The Great Book of French Impressionism*. 2nd ed. New York: Artabras, 1997.

Machotka, Pavel. *Cezanne: Landscape into Art*. New Haven: Yale Univ. Press, 1996.

Medina, Joyce. *Cezanne and Modernism: The Poetics of Painting*. Albany, N.Y.: State Univ. of New York Press, 1995.

Nochlin, Linda. *Representing Women*. New York: Thames and Hudson, 1999.

Nord, Phillip. *Impressionists and Politics: Art and Democracy in the Nineteenth Century*. London: Routledge, 2000.

O'Gorman, James F. *Three American Architects: Richardson, Sullivan, and Wright, 1865–1915*. Chicago: Univ. of Chicago Press, 1991.

Post-Impressionism: Cross-currents in European and American Painting, 1880–1906. Washington, D.C.: National Gallery of Art, 1980.

Roos, Jane Mayo. *Early Impressionism and the French State, 1866–1874*. Cambridge: Cambridge Univ. Press, 1996.

Rubin, James Henry. *Impressionism*. London: Phaidon, 1999.

Schapiro, Meyer. *Impressionism: Reflections and Perceptions*. New York: George Braziller, 1997.

Smith, Paul. *Seurat and the Avant-Garde*. New Haven: Yale Univ. Press, 1997.

———. *Impressionism: Beneath the Surface*. Perspectives. New York: Abrams, 1995.

Stansky, Peter. *Redesigning the World: William Morris, the 1880s, and the Arts and Crafts*. Princeton, N.J.: Princeton Univ. Press, 1985.

Thomson, Belinda. *Impressionism: Origins, Practice, Reception*. New York: Thames and Hudson, 2000.

———. *Post-Impressionism*. Cambridge: Cambridge Univ. Press, 1998.

Walther, Ingo F. *Vincent Van Gogh: The Complete Paintings*. New York: Taschen, 1997.

———. *Impressionist Art, 1860–1920*. Trans. Michael Hulse. New York: Taschen, 1997.

West, Shearer. *Fin-de-Siècle: Art and Society in an Age of Uncertainty*. Woodstock, N.Y.: Overlook Press, 1993.

Chapter 19 Modern Art: Europe and North America in the Early Twentieth Century

Alcantara, Isabel, and Sandra Egnolff. *Frida Kahlo and Diego Rivera*. New York: Prestel, 1999.

Antliff, Mark. *Cubism and Culture*. London: Thames and Hudson, 2001.

Arnason, H. H., and Marla F. Prather. *History of Modern Art: Painting, Sculpture, Architecture, Photography*. 4th ed. New York: Abrams, 1998.

Art into Life: Russian Constructivism, 1914–32. New York: Rizzoli, 1990.

Barron, Stephanie, ed. *Degenerate Art: The Fate of the Avant-Garde in Nazi Germany*. Los Angeles: Los Angeles County Museum of Art, 1991.

Behr, Shulamith. *Expressionism*. New York: Cambridge Univ. Press, 1999.

Blake, Peter. *No Place Like Utopia: Modern Architecture and the Company We Kept*. New York: Knopf, 1993.

Bois, Yve Alain. *Matisse and Picasso*. Paris: Flammarion, Kimball Art Museum, 1998.

Brown, Milton W. *The Story of the Armory Show: The 1913

Exhibition That Changed American Art. 2nd ed. New York: Abbeville, 1988.

Castleman, Riva, ed. *Art of the Forties.* New York: Museum of Modern Art, 1991.

Caws, Mary Ann, ed. *Surrealist Painters and Poets: An Anthology.* Cambridge, Mass.: MIT Press, 2001.

Corn, Wanda. *The Great American Thing: Modern Art and National Identity, 1915–1935.* Berkeley: Univ. of California Press, 1999.

Craven, Wayne. *American Art: History and Culture.* New York: Abrams, 1994.

Curtis, James. *Mind's Eye, Mind's Truth: FSA Photography Reconsidered.* Philadelphia: Temple Univ. Press, 1989.

Curtis, Penelope. *Sculpture, 1900–1945: After Rodin.* Oxford History of Art. Oxford: Oxford Univ. Press, 1999.

Dachy, Marc. *The Dada Movement, 1915–1923.* New York: Skira/Rizzoli, 1990.

Droste, Magdalena. *Bauhaus, 1919–1939.* Köln: Tachen, 1990.

Dube, Wolf-Dieter. *Expressionists.* Trans. Mary Whittall. World of Art. New York: Thames and Hudson, 1998.

Elger, Dietmar. *Expressionism: A Revolution in German Art.* Köln: Taschen, 1998.

Ferrier, Jean Louis. *The Fauves: The Reign of Color.* Paris: Terrail, 1995.

———, ed. *Art of Our Century: The Chronicle of Western Art, 1900 to the Present.* New York: Prentice Hall, 1989.

Folgarait, Leon. *Mural Painting and Social Revolution in Mexico, 1920–1940: Art of the New Order.* New York: Cambridge Univ. Press, 1998.

Freeman, Judi. *The Fauve Landscape.* Los Angeles: Los Angeles County Museum of Art, 1990.

Giedion, Sigfried. *Walter Gropius: Work and Teamwork.* New York: Dover, 1992.

Golding, John. *Paths to the Absolute: Mondrian, Malevich, Kandinsky, Pollock, Newman, Rothko, and Still.* Princeton, N.J.: Princeton Univ. Press, 2000.

Gray, Camilla. *Russian Experiment in Art, 1863–1922.* Rev. and enl. ed. by Marian Burleigh-Motley. New York: Thames and Hudson, 1986.

Green, Christopher. *Picasso's Les demoiselles d'Avignon.* Cambridge: Cambridge Univ. Press, 2001.

———. *Art in France, 1900–1940.* Pelican History of Art. New Haven: Yale Univ. Press, 2000.

Greenough, Sarah et al. *Modern Art and America: Alfred Stieglitz and His New York Galleries.* Washington, D.C.: National Gallery of Art; New York: Bullfinch, 2000.

Haiko, Peter, ed. *Architecture of the Early XX Century.* Trans. Gordon Clough. New York: Rizzoli, 1989.

Hammacher, A. M. *Modern Sculpture: Tradition and Innovation.* Enl. ed. New York: Abrams, 1988.

Harrison, Charles, Francis Frascina, and Gill Perry. *Primitivism, Cubism, Abstraction: The Early Twentieth Century.* New Haven, Conn.: Yale Univ. Press, 1993.

Haskell, Barbara. *The American Century: Art and Culture, 1900–1950.* New York: Whitney Museum of American Art, 1999.

Herbert, James D. *Fauve Painting: The Making of Cultural Politics.* New Haven, Conn.: Yale Univ. Press, 1992.

Hunter, Sam, John Jacobus, and Daniel Wheeler. *Modern Art: Painting, Sculpture, Architecture.* 3rd rev. ed. New York: Abrams, 2000.

Lane, John R., and Susan C. Larsen. *Abstract Painting and Sculpture in America 1927–1944.* Pittsburgh: Museum of Art, Carnegie Institute, 1984.

Levine, Neil. *The Architecture of Frank Lloyd Wright.* Princeton, N.J.: Princeton Univ. Press, 1996.

Lewis, Samella S. *African American Art and Artists.* Rev. ed.

Berkeley: Univ. of California Press, 1994.

Lloyd, Jill. *German Expressionism: Primitivism and Modernity.* New Haven: Yale Univ. Press, 1991.

Murray, Joan. *Canadian Art of the Twentieth Century.* Toronto: Dundurn, 1999.

Naumann, Francis M. *Making Mischief: Dada Invades New York.* New York: Whitney Museum of Art in association with Abrams, 1996.

Nesbitt, Peter T., and Michelle DuBois. *Over the Line: The Art and Life of Jacob Lawrence.* Seattle: Univ. of Washington Press, 2000.

Neumann, Eckhard, ed. *Bauhaus and Bauhaus People.* New York: Van Nostrand Reinhold, 1993.

Overy, Paul. *De Stijl.* World of Art. New York: Thames and Hudson, 1991.

Patton, Sharon. *African-American Art.* Oxford History of Art. Oxford: Oxford Univ. Press, 1998.

Powell, Richard. *Black Art and Culture in the Twentieth Century.* New York: Thames and Hudson, 1997.

Rickey, George. *Constructivism: Origins and Evolutions.* Rev. ed. New York: George Braziller, 1995.

Rosenblum, Robert. *Cubism and Twentieth-Century Art.* Rev. ed. New York: Abrams, 1984.

Rubin, William. *Picasso and Braque: Pioneering Cubism.* New York: Museum of Modern Art, 1989.

Spector, Jack. *Surrealist Art and Writing, 1919–1939.* New York: Cambridge Univ. Press, 1997.

Stich, Sidra. *Anxious Visions: Surrealist Art.* New York: Abbeville, 1990.

Tomkins, Calvin. *Duchamp: A Biography.* New York: H. Holt, 1996.

Udall, Sharyn Rohlfsen. *Carr, O'Keeffe, Kahlo: Places of Their Own.* New Haven: Yale Univ. Press, 2000.

Weiss, Jeffrey S. *The Popular Culture of Modern Art: Picasso, Duchamp, and Avant-Gardism.* New Haven: Yale Univ. Press, 1994.

Whitfield, Sarah. *Fauvism.* World of Art. New York: Thames and Hudson, 1996.

Whitford, Frank. *The Bauhaus: Masters and Students by Themselves.* Woodstock, N.Y.: Overlook Press, 1993.

Woodham, Jonathan M. *Twentieth-Century Design.* Oxford History of Art. Oxford: Oxford Univ. Press, 1997.

Chapter 20 Art Since 1945

Anfam, David. *Abstract Expressionism.* World of Art. New York: Thames and Hudson, 1990.

Atkins, Robert. *Artspeak: A Guide to Contemporary Ideas, Movements, and Buzzwords.* New York: Abbeville, 1990.

Archer, Michael. *Art Since 1960.* 2nd ed. New York: Thames and Hudson, 2002.

Batchelor, David. *Minimalism.* New York: Cambridge Univ. Press, 1997.

Bolton, Richard, ed. *Culture Wars: Documents from the Recent Controversies in the Arts.* New York: New Press, 1992.

Broude, Norma, and Mary D. Garrard. *The Power of Feminist Art: The American Movement of the 1970s, History and Impact.* New York: Abrams, 1994.

Deepwell, Katy. *Women Artists and Modernism.* New York: St. Martin's Press, 1998.

Dormer, Peter. *Design Since 1945.* World of Art. New York: Thames and Hudson, 1993.

Ferguson, Russell, ed. *Discourses: Conversations in Postmodern Art and Culture. Documentary Sources in Contemporary Art.* Cambridge, Mass.: MIT Press, 1990.

Fineberg, Jonathan. *Art Since 1940: Strategies of Being.* Rev. ed. New York: Abrams, 2000.

Goldberg, Rose Lee. *Performance Art: From Futurism to the*

Present. Rev. ed. London: Thames and Hudson, 2001.

Gouma-Peterson, Thalia, and Miriam Schapiro. *Shaping the Fragments of Art and Life.* New York: Abrams, 1999.

Hanhardt, John G. *The Worlds of Nam June Paik.* New York: Guggenheim Museum, 2000.

Hays, K. Michael, and Carol Burns, eds. *Thinking the Present: Recent American Architecture.* New York: Princeton Architectural, 1990.

Hertz, Richard. *Theories of Contemporary Art.* 2nd ed. Englewood Cliffs, N.J.: Prentice Hall, 1993.

Hoffman, Katherine. *Explorations: The Visual Arts Since 1945.* New York: HarperCollins, 1991.

Kingsley, April. *The Turning Point: The Abstract Expressionists and the Transformation of American Art.* New York: Simon & Schuster, 1992.

Kuspit, Donald B. *Clement Greenberg, Art Critic.* Madison: Univ. of Wisconsin Press, 1979.

Livingstone, Marco. *Pop Art: A Continuing History.* New York: Abrams, 1990.

Lucie-Smith, Edward. *Art in the Eighties.* Oxford: Phaidon, 1990.

Madoff, Steven Henry. *Pop Art: A Critical History.* Berkeley: Univ. of California Press, 1997.

McCarthy, David. *Pop Art.* New York: Cambridge Univ. Press, 2000.

Meyer, James, ed. *Minimalism.* New York: Cambridge Univ. Press, 1997.

Morgan, Robert C. *Conceptual Art: An American Perspective.* Jefferson, N.C.: McFarland, 1994.

Phillips, Lisa. *The American Century: Art and Culture, 1950–2000.* New York: Whitney Museum of American Art, 2000.

Rosen, Randy, and Catherine C. Brawer, comps. *Making Their Mark: Women Artists Move into the Mainstream, 1970–85.* New York: Abbeville, 1989.

Ross, Clifford. *Abstract Expressionism: Creators and Critics, An Anthology.* New York: Abrams, 1990.

Rush, Michael. *New Media in Late 20th-Century Art.* World of Art. New York: Thames and Hudson, 1999.

Rushing, Jackson W. III. *Native American Art in the Twentieth Century: Makers, Meanings, and Histories.* London: Routledge, 1999.

Sandler, Irving. *American Art of the 1960's.* New York: Harper & Row, 1988.

———. *The New York School: The Painters and Sculptors of the Fifties.* New York: Harper & Row, 1978.

Sayre, Henry M. *The Object of Performance: The American Avant-Garde Since 1970.* Chicago: Univ. of Chicago Press, 1989.

Shapiro, David, and Cecile Shapiro. *Abstract Expressionism: A Critical Record.* New York: Cambridge Univ. Press, 1990.

Smith, Jaune Quick-to-See, and Harmony Hammond. *Women of Sweetgrass: Cedar and Sage.* New York: American Indian Center, 1984.

Taylor, Paul, ed. *Post-Pop Art.* Cambridge, Mass.: MIT Press, 1989.

Wagner, Anne Middleton. *Three Artists (Three Women): Modernism and the Art of Hesse, Krasner, and O'Keeffe.* Berkeley: Univ. of California Press, 1996.

Waldman, Diane. *Collage, Assemblage, and the Found Object.* New York: Abrams, 1992.

Weaver, Mike, ed. *The Art of Photography, 1939–1989.* London: Royal Academy of Arts, 1989.

Wheeler, Daniel. *Art Since Mid-Century: 1945 to the Present.* Englewood Cliffs, N.J.: Prentice Hall, 1991.

Word as Image: American Art, 1960–1990. Milwaukee: Milwaukee Art Museum, 1990.

Index

Page numbers in *italics* refer to illustrations.

A

Abakanowicz, Magdalena, 513, 518–19, *519*
Abbot Suger: and Abbey Church of Saint-Denis, 256, 259; *Chalice of Abbot Suger*, *19*, 19–20
Abstract Expressionism, 481, 500–5; in ceramics, 512, *512*; reaction to, 506, *507*
abstraction, 14, 16, 513; by Cézanne, 459; Lyrical, 500; in modernism, 468; in Upper Paleolithic art, 33
academic idealism, 444–45; reactions against, 445–47
Acropolis of Athens, 26, 98, 108–14; Erechtheion at, 112, *112*; model of, *109*; Parthenon at. *See* Parthenon (Athens)
Adam and Eve (Dürer), *342*, 342–43
Adam, Robert, 425–26, *426*
additive sculpture, 8
adoration: of the Magi, 168; of the shepherds, 168
"A.D." Painter, 104, *104*
advertisements, by Toulouse-Lautrec, 462, *462*
Aegean art, 88–117
aerial perspective. *See* atmospheric perspective
Aeroplane over Train (Goncharova), 479, *479*
Aesop, 99
African-American artists: feminist, 517, *517*; and Harlem Renaissance, 494, 494–95. *See also specific artists, e.g.,* Puryear, Martin
African art, 402–13, 414–15, *415*; early, 404–8; influence of, 414, 470, 494; modern, 408–13
Age of Enlightenment (Reason), 418
Agnes van den Bassche, 295
Agony in the Garden, 169
Akan kingdom, 402, *402*, 403, 411
Akhenaten and His Family, *62*, 63
Akiode, 413
Akkadian art, 49, *49*
Albers, Josef, 487
Alberti, Leon Battista, 289, 299, *302*, 302–3; influence of, 306, 308, 312
album leaves (book pages): Chinese, 218, 220; Japanese, 223, *223*
Alexander the Great, 115, 117, *117*, 118, 120, 121, 162; death of, 129; defeat of Persians, 128, *128*
Alexander the Great (Lysippos), 117, *117*
Alexander the Great Confronts Darius III at the Battle of Issos (Helen of Egypt or Philoxenos), 134–35, *135*, 136
Alhambra, *199*, 199–200, *200*
Allegories of the Five Senses (Breughel and Rubens), 368, *368*
allegory, 196, 240; of Gentileschi, 358
Alma-Tadema, Sir Lawrence, 26, *26*, 445
Altamira cave painting, 36, *36*
Altarpiece of Saint Vincent (Gonçalvez), *294*, 294–95
Altarpiece of the Holy Blood (Riemenschneider), 344, *344*
Altneuschul (Prague), *275*, 275–76
America(s), *415*; art of, 384–401, 414–15; Central, 387; first inhabitants of, 386; North. *See* North American art; South, 387, 391–94
American Abstract Artists, 502
American Art Union, 439
American Gothic (Wood), 493, *493*
American Landscape (Sheeler), 492, 492–93
American Revolution, 419
American Scene Painting, 493, *493*
American Society of Independent Artists, 487
Amida Buddha (Jocho), 222, *222*
"Am I Not a Man and a Brother?" (Hackwood), 433, *433*
amphora, Greek, 103, 103–4
Analytic Cubism, 476, 477, 479, 505; de Kooning and, 504
Anasazi, 395–97, *396*
Anastase, 25, 295
Anastasis, 169; depictions of, 185–86, *186*, 283, *283*
Anastasis, 185–86, *186*
Ancient Ruins in the Cañon de Chelley, Arizona (O'Sullivan), 395, 449, *449*
Andrea di Pietro. *See* Palladio, Antonio
Andrea Pisano, 276, *277*
Anglo-Saxon metalworking, 234–35, *235*

Anguissola, Sofonisba, 336–37, *337*
animal images: Minoan, 92, *94*; Scythian, 125
animal interlace, Anglo-Saxon, 235, *235*
animal style, Gummersmark brooch in, 234, *234*
Annunciation, 168
Annunciation (Fra Angelico), 306, *306*
Annunciation (Master of the Smiling Angels/Saint Joseph Master), 267, *267*, 271
Annunciation (Pucelle), 271, *271*
Annunciation of the Shepherds, 168
Annunciation, The (Van Eyck), *290*, 290–91
Annunciation, Triptych of the (Campin), 289, 290
Anthemius of Tralles, 175, 175–76, *176*
anthropologists, 27
Anthropometries of the Blue Period (Klein), 512
Anu Ziggurat, 44, 45, 46
Apadana (Audience Hall), 128, *128*, 129
Aphrodite, 100
Aphrodite of Knidos (Praxiteles), 116–17, 131
Aphrodite of Melos, 130, *130*, 131
Apollinaire, 478
Apollo, 100; depictions of, *121*, 121–22, 155–56, *156*, 161, 314, 320, *338*
Apollo, *121*, 121–22
Apollo Belvedere, 338
arabesques, 190
Ara Pacis (Altar of Augustan Peace), *143*, 143–44; *Imperial Procession from*, 144, *144*
arcades, 141, 142
arch(es), 11, *11*; of Constantine, 160–61, *161*; corbel, 11, *11*, *97*; relieving, 97, *97*; round, 141, *141*, 142; of Titus, 147, 147–49, *148*, 161, 167
archaeologists, 27
Archangel Michael, 184–85, *185*, *267*
Archer, Frederick Scott, 435
architectura, De (*On Architecture*) (Vitruvius), 316
architectural decoration, Rococo, *378*, 378–80, *379*
architectural orders: Greek, 100, *100*; Roman, 146, 147, *147*
architectural sculpture, 8
architecture, 8; American, 426, 442–44; Anasazi, 396; ancient Greek, 99, 108–14, 162; Baroque, 352–53, 359–61, 364–65; beauty in, 18–19, *19*; Carolingian, 236–38; Chinese, 81–82, 220–21; early Christian, 170–74; early Renaissance, 288, 297, 301–3; early Shinto, 84, *84*; Egyptian, 56; English, 253–55, 424–26; European, 442–44; French Royal Academy of, 359; Gothic, 258–68, 273, 526; High Renaissance, 325–27, 333–34; Inca, 392, *392*; Islamic, 192–95; Italian, 297, 301–3; Japanese, 84–85, *221*, 221–22, *222*; Maya, 388–89; megalithic, 38–40; Mesoamerican, 387–89; Mississippian, 395, *395*; Mughal, 204–5, *205*; Mycenaean, *96*, 96–98, *97*; Nazca, 391; Neoclassical, 424–26; Neolithic, 37–40; Ottoman, 206, *206*; Ottonian, 242; Postmodern, 513–15; Pueblo, 397; Roman, 139–42, 145–49, 152–55, 158–61; Romanesque, 245–48, 253–55; Shona, 407; space-spanning construction devices in, 11, *11*; Sumerian, 45; two-dimensional representation of, 9; Upper Paleolithic, 34; between World Wars, 483–86
Arch of Constantine, 160–61, *161*
Arch of Titus, 147, 147–49, *148*, 161, 167
Arena Chapel (Giotto), 282, 282–83, *283*
Ares, 100
Aristarete, 116
Aristotle: on art, 14, 15; in *School of Athens* (Raphael), 314, 314–15, 320, *320*
Ark of the Covenant, 166; catacomb wall paintings of, *166*, 167
Armory Show of 1913, 469, 480, 481
aron, *275*, 276
art: defining, 14; destruction of, 27–28; "fine art" vs "craft," 414; restoration of, *27*, 27–28, *28*; as team effort, 23; understanding need for, 19–22; viewers of, 29
art academies: in 18th century, 422; women artists in, 422, *422*. *See also specific academies, e.g.,* Royal Academy of Painting and Sculpture (France)
Art Deco, 470, *478*; influence of, 494

Artemis Slaying Actaeon (Pan Painter), *105*, 106–7
Artemis, Temple of, 100–1, *101*
art history, 26–27
Art in America, 2001 cover of, *527*
art informel, 500
artists: African-American, 494, 494–95, 517, *517*; historical view of, 22–24; of Middle Kingdom Egypt, 59; patrons of, 24–26; during Reformation and High Renaissance, 316; as scientists, 380–81, *381*; women. *See* women artists. *See also specific artists, e.g.,* Klee, Paul
Artist's Studio, The (Daguerre), *435*
Art Nouveau, 444, 447–49, 462, 465
Arts and Crafts Movement, 447
Asante art, 402, *402*, 403, 411, 412, *412*
Ascension, The, 169
Ashcan School, 479
Asian art: early, 67–85; later, 208–29. *See also specific Asian countries, e.g.,* Japanese art
Aspects of Negro Life: From Slavery Through Reconstruction (Douglas), 494, 494–95
assemblage, 8, 9, *505*, 505–7, *506*, *507*, 508. *See also* collage
Assurbanipal and His Queen in the Garden, *51*, 51–52
Assyrian art, *51*, 51–52, 53, 120
Athanadoros of Rhodes, 27, 28
Athena, 100, *116*; temple of. *See* Parthenon (Athens)
Athena Attacking the Giants (Pergamene frieze), 133–34, *134*
Athena Nike, Temple of, 112–14, *113*
Athena Parthenos, Temple of. *See* Parthenon (Athens)
Athens: Acropolis of, 26, 98, 108–14, *109*, *112*. *See* Parthenon (Athens)
atmospheric perspective, 7, *7*, 286, 289, 382; by Masaccio, 305; by Piero, 308
atrium, Etruscan, 123
attributed to, defined, 8
Audubon, John James, 438–39, *439*
Augustus Caesar, 142, *142*, 143–45, *145*
Augustus of Primaporta, 142, *142*, 143, 144, 149
Aulus Metellus, 138, 139
Australian Aboriginal art, *521*, 521–22
Autumn Colors on the Qiao and Hua Mountains (Zhao Meng-fu), 218, 218–19
Autumn Rhythm (Number 30) (Pollock), 501–2, *502*
avant-garde, 459; Nazi suppression of, 487, *487*
Avenue at Middelharnis (Hobbema), 375–77, *376*
axis mundi, 71
Aztec art, 389–91

B

baby carrier, Sioux, 398, *398*, 414
Babylon, ancient, 125, *125*, *126*
Bacchus, 151, 151–52
Baciccio. *See* Gaulli, Giovanni Battista
background, 6, *6*
Backs (Abakanowicz), 518–19, *519*
Bacon, Francis, 376
Bahram Gur with the Indian Princess in Her Black Pavilion, 202–4, *203*
Baldacchino (Bernini), *352*, 352–53
Ballet Russes, 479
Ball, Hugo, *486*, 486–87
balloon frame, 11, *11*
Bamana culture, 409, *409*
Baptism, The, 168
Baptistry of San Giovanni, doors of, *299*, 299–301
Bar at the Folies-Bergère, A (Manet), 455, *455*
Barbizon School, 436, 451
Barcelona Chair, 485
Bargehaulers on the Volga (Repin), 438, *438*
Baroque art, 350–81, 382; in France, 6, 358–62; in Italy, 6, 352–58
barrel vault, 141, *141*
Basilica Nova, 153, 158–60, *160*
Basilica of Maxentius and Constantine, 153, 158–60, *160*, 173
Basilica Ulpia, 152–53, *153*
basketry, North American, 397, *397*, 414

Battista Sforza (Piero), 308, *308*
Battle of San Romano, The (Uccello), 286, *286*, 287, 307, *307*
Battle of the Bird and the Serpent (page from *Commentary on the Apocalypse*) (Emeterius, Ende, and Senior), 196, *196*, 239–40
Battle of the Ten Nudes (Pollaiuolo), 312, *312*
Baudelaire, Charles, 451
Bauhaus, 481; architecture of, *484*, 484–85, *485*, 513; Nazi suppression of, 487
Bauhaus Building (Dessau), *484*, 485
Baule art, *410*, 411
Bayeux Tapestry, *252*, 253
bay system, of construction, 82
beadwork, Native American, 398
Bearing of the Cross, 169
Beatus, 195–96, 239–40
beauty, defining, 14–19
Beaux-Arts, École des, 442–43, 444
Bellini, Gentile, 310, 328
Bellini, Giovanni, 310–11, *311*, 328
Bellini, Jacopo, 310
Benin art, 10, *10*, 405, 405–6, *406*
Bennett, John, 526, *527*
Benois, Aleksandr, 478–79
Berlin School of Art for Women, 470
Bernini, Gianlorenzo, 326, 350, *350*, *351*, *352*, 352–53, *353*
Bertoldo di Giovanni, 321
Betrayal, The (The Arrest), 169
Betrayal and Arrest of Christ (Pucelle), 271, *271*
bhakti movement, 212, 213
Big Raven (Carr), 497, *497*
bimah, *275*, 276
biomorphic language: of Gorky, 501; of Miró, 491
Bingham, George Caleb, 439, *439*
Birds of America (Audubon), 438–39, *439*
Birth of Venus (Botticelli), 308–9, *309*
Bishop Bernward Doors, 240–42, *241*
Bishop Odo Blessing the Feast (section of *Bayeux Tapestry*), *252*, 253
Bison (Altamira cave painting), *36*
black-figure painting, Greek, *103*, 104, *104*
Blackfoot Nation, *398*
blackware pottery, *396*, 397
blankets, Chilkat, *400*, 401
Blaue Reiter, der, 473–74
blolo bla (spirit spouse), *410*, 411
Boccaccio, Giovanni, 295
Boccioni, Umberto, 478, *478*
Bodhisattva (Indian wall painting), 73
bodhisattvas, 69, 73, *74*; Chinese Northern Song image of, 215, *215*
Boffrand, Germain, 378, *378*
Bondevardi, Gustavo, 526, *527*
Bonheur, Rosa, 436, *437*
Bonsu, Kojo, 402, *402*, *403*, 411
Bonsu, Osei, 411
Book of Homilies, 251, *251*
Book of Hours, 270; by Limbourg brothers, 295–96, *296*; by Pucelle, 270–71, *271*
Book of Kells, 235; *Chi Rho Iota* page of, *235*, 235–36
books: Aztec, 390; French Gothic, 269–71, *270*, *271*; Islamic, 202–4, *203*; medieval production of, 237, 238; and medieval scriptorium, 237; printed, 382; Romanesque, 251, 251–52, *252*. *See also* illuminated manuscripts
Books of the Dead, 64, 65
Bosch, Heironymus, 346–47, *347*
Botticelli, Sandro, 308–9, *309*, 323
bottle, enameled glass, 201, *201*
Bouman, Elias, *375*
Boulevard des Capucines, Paris (Monet), 453, *453*
Bourgot, 295
bowl: divination, 20, *20*, 409, *411*; with kufic border, *197*
box: Celtic openwork, 157–58, *159*; Islamic pen, 188, *188–89*, 201–2, *202*
brackets, architectural, 81–82
Brady, Mathew B., 449

Bramante, Donato, 314, 319; and Saint Peter's, 314, 321, 325, *326*, 326, *353*; in *School of Athens* (Raphael), *320*
Brancacci Chapel, in Church of Santa Maria del Carmine, *304*, 304–5, *305*
Brancusi, Constantin, 480
Braque, Georges, 475, *476*, 476–77, 505, 528; collage by, *506*; shown in United States, 480
brass sculpture, Benin, 10, *10*, 405, *405*, 406, *406*
Breton, André, 488, 497, 500
Bride Stripped Bare by Her Bachelors, Even, The (Duchamp), 466, *466*, *467*, 488, *488*
British Columbia Society of Art, 497
British Isles: early medieval art in, 234–36; England. *See* England; Romanesque book illumination in, 251, 251–52, *252*; Romans in, 157, 234
bronze: Etruscan, *120*, 121; Greek, 98, *99*, 107, 107–8, *108*, 114; hollow-casting of, 107; Ottonian, 240–42, *241*
Bronze Age: Aegean, 90, 91; Chinese, 76–77; European, *40*, 40–41; late, Mycenaean art in, 91, 95–98
Bronze Foundry, A (Foundry Painter), 105, *105*
Bronzino, 335–36, *336*
Broun, Elizabeth, 516
Brown, Blue, Brown on Blue (Rothko), 504, *504*
Brown, Dennis Scott, 514
Bruegel, Pieter the Elder, 347–48, *348*
Brueghel, Jan, 367–69
Brunelleschi, Filippo, 289, 297, 300, *301*, 301–2; influence of, 303, 306, 308, 326
Buddha: early Chinese sculpture of, 79, 79–80; early Indian images of, 71–72, *72*; early Japanese painting of, 85, *85*; marks of, 73
Buddha and Attendants, 72, *72*
Buddhism, 69; in early China, 79, 79–80, 81; Esoteric, 221; in India, 69–73, 210; in Japan, 84–85, 221; Pure Land, 221; symbols of, 73
Bull Jumping, 92, *94*
Burden, Jane, 446, *446*
Burghers of Calais (Rodin), 464, *464*, 465
Burial at Ornans, A (Courbet), 437, 437–38
Burial of Count Orgaz (El Greco), 348–49, *349*
burins, in printmaking, 312
Burkina Faso, art of, 412–13, *413*
Burty, Phillippe, 448
buttresses, 141, *141*, 245; flying, 262
Bwa art, 412–13, *413*, 414
Byodo-in, Phoenix Hall at, *221*, 221–22
Byzantine art: churches in, *175*, 175–78, *176*, *177*, *179*, *182*, 182–84, *183*, 184; depiction of space in, 178; early, 174–81; icons in, 164, 181, *181*, 184–85, *185*, 186–87, *187*, 509; later, 181–87; mosaics in, *178*, 178–80, *179*

C

Cabaret Voltaire (Zürich), 486, *486*
Café Guerbois, 453
Cage, John, 508, 512
Cahokia, 394–95, *395*
cairn, 39
Cairo, Egypt: Sultan Hasan *madrasa*-mausoleum-mosque of, 199
Calder, Alexander, 489, *491*, 491, *492*
California Institute of the Arts (CalArts), 516, 517
calligraphy, 230; Arabic, 188, *188–89*, 190, 196, 230; Chinese, 81, *81*; Ottoman, 207, *207*
Calling of Levi/Matthew, 168
Calling of Saint Matthew (Caravaggio), 357, *358*
calotype, 434–35
Camel Carrying a Group of Musicians (ceramic sculpture), *80*
camera obscura, 434
camera, operation of, 436
Cameron, Julia Margaret, 435–36, *436*
Campin, Robert, 288–90, *289*, *293*
Canadian art, between World Wars, 497, *497*
Canova, Antonio, *418*, 418–19
cantilever, 11, *11*
Canyon (Rauschenberg), 506, *506*
Capponi Chapel, in Church of Santa Felicità, 301, 335, *335*

Caprichos, Los (*The Caprices*) (Goya), 430, 431
capstone, 39; of Mycenaean tomb, *96*, 97
Captain Frans Banning Cocq Mustering His Company (*The Night Watch*) (Rembrandt van Rijn), 371, 371–73
Caravaggio, 357, 357–58; influence of, 360, 362–63, 416
Carolingian art, 236–38
Carracci, Agostino, 354
Carracci, Annibale, 354–55, *355*, 361; influence of, 427
Carr, Emily, 497, *497*
cartoons, 8; by Raphael, 321
caryatids, 112, *112*
Cassatt, Mary, 456, 457
Castillo (Chichén Itxá, Mexico), 389, *389*
casting, 8; hollow, 107; lost-wax, 8, 10, *10*, 405
castles, 272; of England, 253, 253–55; of Gothic France, 272, *272*
Castle, Wendell, 513, *520*, 520–21
catacomb wall paintings: Christian, 164, *164–65*, *170*, 170–71; Jewish, *166*, 166–67
cathedrals, 171. *See also specific cathedrals, e.g.*, Santa Sophia, Cathedral of
cave and rock paintings, 86; African, 404; Indian, 72–73; meaning of prehistoric, 36; Neolithic, 37, *37*; technique of, 35; Upper Paleolithic, 30, *30–31*, *34*, 34–36, *35*, *36*
ceiling decorations: Baroque, 354–55, *355*, *356*, 357, 361; in Sistine Chapel, 322–24, *323*, *324*, 355
Cellini, Benvenuto, 339, *339*
Celtic art, 157–58, *159*
Cenni di Pepi. *See* Cimabue
Cennini, Cennino, 279, 281
Central America, 387
ceramic glazes, Chinese, 80, 80–81
ceramics: Anasazi, *396*, 397; Arabic calligraphy on, 196, *197*; Chinese, 80, 80–81, 217, *217*, 219, *219*; in *The Dinner Party*, 516, 517; Greek, *103*, 103–5, *104*, *105*; Japanese, 227, *227*, 230; Minoan, 94, *94*; Paleolithic, 36, *37*; porcelain, 219, *219*; used by Gaudi, *448*, 449; West African, 409, *409*. *See also specific types of ceramic wear, e.g.*, hydria
Cézanne, Paul, 453, 457–59, *458*, 528; influence of, 474, 477; shown in United States, 480
Chacmools, 389, *389*
chair: Barcelona, 485; by Morris & Company, 447, *447*; Ngombe, 470, *470*; by Rietveld, 483, *483*
chakra, 73
Chalice of Abbot Suger, *19*, 19–20
cha no yu, 226–27
Chaotic Lip (Murray), 518, *518*
Charioteer, 107, *107*
Charlemagne, 236, 284; depiction in Chartres Cathedral, 256, *256*, 263; Palace Chapel of, *236*, 236–37
Charles I at the Hunt (Van Dyck), 369, *369*
Chartres Cathedral, *259*, 259–63, *262*; nave of, 261, *261*; plan of, *260*; royal portal of, 260, *260*; stained-glass windows of, 256, *256*, *257*, 263, *263*, *264*
Chauvet cave paintings, 30, *30–31*, 35, *35*
Chermayeff, Serge, *481*
chest ornament, Egyptian, 59, *59*
Chevreul, Michel-Eugene, 463
chiaroscuro, in *Last Supper*, 318
Chicago, Judy, 513, *516*, 517
Chicago School, 443
Chichester-Constable chasuble, 272, *274*, *275*
Chihuly, Dale, 22, 23, 24, 513
Child Bitten by a Crayfish (Anguissola), 337, *337*
china painting, in *The Dinner Party*, *516*, 517
Chinese art: early, 76–82; Ming period of, *219*, 219–21, *220*, 514; Song period of, 215, 215–17, *216*, *217*, 219; Yuan period of, 217–18, 219
Chi Rho Iota (page of *Book of Kells*), *235*, 235–36
Christ Enthroned with Saints and Emperor Otto I (from Magdeburg Ivories), 240, *240*
Christian art, 166, 230, 284; early, 164, *164–65*, 169–74; symbols in, 180
Christianity, 234
Christians
    early Eastern, 181, *181*

Eastern Orthodox, 245

Eastern Orthodox Church: icons of, 164, 184–85, *185*, 186–87, *187*

Protestant, 316, 343, 382

Roman Catholic, 284; in Americas, 393–94; Counter-Reformation of, 350, 352–58, 382; following Reformation, 350; during Reformation, 316; during Romanesque period, 245

Christine de Pisan, 25, *25*, 295, 296

Christine Presenting Her Book to the Queen of France, 25, *25*, 295, 296

Christ in Majesty (San Clemente Master), *244*, 245

Christus, Petrus, 293, *293*

Christ Washing the Feet of His Disciples (from *Gospels of Otto III*), 232, *232*, 233, *233*, 242, *242*, 243

Chromatic Circle (book) (Henry), 462, *463*

Church: medieval, 234; split of, 245. *See also* Christians

church(es), 284; Baroque, 352–53, *353*, 365; basilica-plan, 171, *171*; Byzantine, *175*, 175–78, *176*, *177*, *179*, *182*, 182–84, *183*, *184*; central-plan, 171, *171*; cruciform, 246; Early Christian, *170*, *171*, 171–73, *172*, *173*, 174; early Renaissance, *300*, *301*, 301–3; facade of, 340, *340*; Gothic, *256*, 258–68, *262*, 275; hall, 275; High Renaissance, 325–27, *326*, *327*, 333–34; Mannerist, 339–41, *340*; Romanesque, 253–55, *254*, *255*, 273; traditional usage and abbreviations for, 171. *See also specific churches, e.g.*, Old Saint Peter's Church

churrigueresque, 364–65

Cimabue, *280*, 280–81; as Giotto's teacher, 281–82

Citroën B-12, decorated by Delaunay-Terk, 478, *478*

Ciudadela (Teotihuacan, Mexico), *387*, 388

Claris Mulieribus, De (*Concerning Famous Women*) (Boccaccio), 295

classical idealism, 17; of French Baroque art, 359, 360, 361; Medici Venus and, 7, 17, *17*

Classical Shop, of Gothic sculpture, 267

Claudel, Camille, 465, *465*

"clay revolution," 512

Cleansing of the Temple, 168

cloisonné enamel, Anglo-Saxon, 235, *235*

Coatlicue, 390, 391, *391*

Codex Mendoza, 390, *390*

Cogul rock-shelter painting, 37, *37*

coins, Persian, 126–27, *127*

Cold War, 500

collage, 9; contemporary Native American, *522*, 522–23; Cubist, 477, *477*, *506*; feminist, *516*, 517. See also assemblage

colophon, 237

color, 5

Color Field painting, 501, 504, *504*

Column of Trajan, *338*

Colusseum (Rome), 145–46, *146*

Commentary on the Apocalypse (Beatus), 195–96, 239; *Battle of the Bird and the Serpent* page from, 196, *196*, 239–40

Commodus as Hercules, 157, *157*

Common Grackle (Audubon), 439, *439*

Complexity and Contradiction in Architecture (book) (Venturi), 513

Composite order, 147, *147*

composition, 5, 6

Composition with Red, Blue, and Yellow (Mondrian), 482–83, *483*

Comtesse d'Haussonville, The (Ingres), *428*, 429

Conceptual art, *511*, 511–12

Concerning Famous Women (*De Claris Mulieribus*) (Boccaccio), 295

concrete, reinforced, 11, *11*

cone mosaics, 45, 45–46

Confucianism: Chinese revival of, 210, 215–16; in early China, 77, 78–79, 81

Congregational Mosque at Isfahan, 193, *193*, 198

Conical Tower, 407, *407*

connoisseurship, 26–27

Constable, John, 433, *433*, 434, 436

Constantine the Great, 160, *160*

Constructivists, 482, *482*

contemporary art, 518

content, 6

contexts, of art work, 6

Copernicus, Nicolaus, 376

Copley, John Singleton, 421–22, *423*

corbel arch, 11, *11*; of Lion Gate, *97*

corbelled vaults, Mycenaean, *96*, 96–97

Córdoba: Great Mosque at, 193, *193*, 194–95, *195*; Islamic rule of, 194

Corinthian order, 100, *100*; capital of, 17, *17*

Cornelia Pointing to Her Children as Her Treasures (Kauffmann), 424, *424*

Corporation of Artists Painters, Sculptors, Engravers, etc., 453

Cosimo, Agnolo di. *See* Bronzino

Counter-Reformation, 350

Counter-Reformation art, 382; in Italy, 352–58

Couple Wearing Raccoon Coats with a Cadillac, Taken on West 127th Street, Harlem, New York (VanDerZee), 495, *495*

Courbet, Gustave, *437*, 437–38, 447, 451, 459

courses of stone, Mycenaean, *96*, 96–97

Court style, of Gothic architecture, 268

Cox, Kenyon, 480

Coyolxauhqui, 390, *390*, 391

Craft art: postwar American, *512*, 512–13; vs "fine art," 414

Crete, Minoan, 90–95

cross, as Christian symbol, 180

crossing, in church architecture, 245

Crossing, The (Viola), 524, *524*

Crucifixion with Angels and Mourning Figures (cover of *Lindau Gospels*), 238, *239*

Crucifixion, The, 169

Crucifixion, The (illuminated manuscript folio), 180–81, *181*

cruciform churches, 246

Cubiculum of Leonis, Catacomb of Commodilla, 164, *164–65*, *170*, 170–71

Cubism, 475–79, 528; Analytic, *476*, 477, 479, 504, 505; influence of, 505; and O'Keeffe, 492; responses to, 478–79; Synthetic, 477, *477*, 495

Cubi XIX (David Smith), 6, 16, *16*, 29, 505

Cubo-Futurism, 479; American version of, *480*, 480–81

cuneiform script, 45

Cupid and Psyche (Canova), *418*, 418–19

Current (Riley), 510, *510*

curtain walls, 485

Curtis, Edward S., 399, *399*

cutaway drawings, 9, *9*

Cycladic art, ancient, 90

cyclopean masonry, of Mycenaean tombs, 96

cylinder seals, Sumerian, 48–49, *49*

D

Dadaism, 481, 486, 486–88; influence of, 506, 507

dagger blade, Mycenaean, *95*, 95–96

Daguerre, Jacques-Mandé, 434, 435, *435*

Daitoku-ji temple (Kyoto, Japan), 226

Daoism, in early China, 78

Darby, Abraham, III, 443

daric, 126–27, 127

Darius and Xerxes Receiving Tribute (Apadana relief), 128, *129*

Darwin, Charles, 442

Daumier, Honoré, 28–29, *29*, 462, 475

David (Bernini), 354, *354*

David (Donatello), 298, *298*, 322, 354

David (Michelangelo), 322, *322*, 354

David, Jacques-Louis, 427, *427*, 445

da Vinci, Leonardo. *See* Leonardo da Vinci

Deconstructivist art, 522

decorative arts, 8; by Morris & Company, 447, *447*; postwar American, *512*, 512–13

Degas, Edgar, 448, 453, *454*, 454–55, 479; influence of, 462

"Degenerate Art" exhibition (1937), 487, *487*, 489

Déjeuner sur l'herbe, Le (*The Luncheon on the Grass*) (Manet), 451, 451–52

de Kooning, Elaine, 502

de Kooning, Willem, 502–4, *503*; influence of, 512

Delacroix, Eugène, 430, *430*; influence of, 462

Delaunay, Robert, 478

Delaunay-Terk, Sonia, 478, *478*

Delivery of the Keys to Peter, The, 168

Delivery of the Keys to Saint Peter (Perugino), 311, 311–12

della Porta, Giacomo: Church of Il Gesù completed by, 339–41, *340*; Saint Peter's Basilica completed by, 326, 327, *327*

Demeter, 100

Democratic Republic of the Congo, 409–11, *410*

Demoiselles d'Avignon, Les (Picasso), 475, 475–76

demotic writing, 45

Denial of Peter, The, 169

de Piles, Roger, 360

Deposition (Weyden), 292, *292*

der Blaue Reiter, 473–74

de Ribera, Pedro, 365, *365*

Derrida, Jacques, 522

Descartes, René, 376

Descent from the Cross, The (The Deposition), 169

Descent into Limbo, The (The Harrowing of Hell), 169

de Stijl movement, 481, 482, 484

Devi, 76

Devil's Pond, The (Sand), 437

de Witte, Emanuel, 375, *375*

Diaghilev, Serge, 478–79

diagonal perspective, 7, *7*

Diary (Minidoka Series #3) (Shimomura), 29, *29*

die Brücke, 472–73

Diego, Juan, 393–94, *394*

diminution, 7

Dinner Party, The (Chicago), 513, *516*, 517

Dionysos, 100; depiction of, *115*, 115–16

Disputà (Raphael), 319, 319–20

Dissertation in Insect Generations and Metamorphosis in Surinam (Merian), 380; *Plate 9* from, *381*

divergent perspective, 7, *7*

divination bowl (Olówè of Isè), 20, *20*, 409, *411*

divisionism, 459, 460, 463; *See also* pointillism

dolmen, 39

Dome of the Rock, 192, *192*, 193

Donatello, 297–98, *298*; influence of, 309, 321

Donato di Niccolo Bardi. *See* Donatello

Dono, Paolo de. *See* Uccello, Paolo

Doric order, 100

Doubting of Thomas , The, 169

Douglas, Aaron, 494, 494–95

dove, as Christian symbol, 180

dragons, in Chinese folklore, *219*

dramatic style, of Romantic landscape paintings, 433, *434*

drawing, 8

Drawing Lesson, The (Steen), *22*, 23, 375

Dream of Henry I (page from *Worchester Chronicle*), 252, *252*

Dresden Technical College, 472

dressed stone, 91

drypoint, 8, 372, *372*; by Rembrandt, 372, 373

Duccio di Buoninsegna, *278*, 279

Duchamp, Marcel, 466, *466*, 467, 487–88, *488*, 506; influence of, 466, 491, 506, 511, 512

Dumas fils, Alexandre, 452

Dürer, Albrecht, 341, *342*, 342–43, *343*, 360

Durham Castle (England), 253, *254*

Durham Cathedral (England), *254*, 254–55

Dutch art. *See* Netherlands

Dutch Interior I (Miró), 491, *491*

dwellings: Etruscan, 123; Neolithic, 38, *38*; Roman, 139–42, *140*; Upper Paleolithic, 34, *34*

Dying Gallic Trumpeter (Epigonos?), *132*, 133, 136

E

Eakins, Thomas, *450*, 451

earthworks, 9; Mississippian, 394, 395, *395*; Postmodern, *515*, 515–16

Easter Island, megalithic figures on, 41, *41*

Eastern Orthodox Church, 245; icons of, 164, 184–85, *185*, 186–87, *187*

Ebbo Gospels, 238; *Matthew the Evangelist* page of, 238, *238*

École des Beaux-Arts, 442–43, 444

Edgar Kaufmann House (Wright), 486, *486*, 515

Edo culture, *405*, 405–6, *406*

Egyptian art, 52–65, 162, 528; Early Dynastic and Old Kingdom period of, 52–58; Late Period in, 65; Late Period of, 65; Middle Kingdom period of, 58–59; New Kingdom period of, 59–65; symbols in, 57

Eiffel, Gustave, 443, 444

Eiffel Tower, *443*, 443–44
Eight, The, 479
Eirene, 116
Electronic Superhighway: Continental US (Paik), 524, *524*
elevations, 9, *9*
El Greco, 348–49, *349*
Ely Cathedral (England), 273, *274*
embroidery: Gothic, 273–74, *275*; quillwork, 398, *398*; Romanesque, *252*, 253
Emeterius, 196, *196*, 239–40
Empire State Building, 490, *490*
Empress Theodora and Her Attendants, 178, *178*
enamel: cloisonné, 235, *235*; on Islamic glass, 201, *201*
Ende, 196, *196*, 239–40, 255
Engels, Friedrich, 442
England: after World War I, *481*, 481–82; architecture of, *253*, 253–55, 424–26; churches of, 253–55; Gothic art in, 273–74; landscape gardens of, 424–25; Neoclassical art in, 421, *421*; Romantic art in, *433*, 433–34, *434*
engravings, 8; Renaissance, *312*, 312–13, *313*, 342–43, *343*
Entombment (Pontormo), 335, *335*
Entombment, The, 169
ephemeral art, 9; earthworks as, 394, 395, *395*, *515*, 515–16; Happenings as, 512, 528; performance art as, 512, *512*, 528; video art as, 523–25, *524*, *525*, 528
Epidauros theater, *129*
Epigonos, *132*, 133
Equestrian Monument of Erasmo da Narni (Gattamelata) (Donatello), *298*, 298–99
Erechtheion (Mnesikles), 112, *112*
ere ibeji (twin figures), 413, *413*
Eros, 100
erotic imagery, southern Indian, 214, *214*
etchings, 372, *372*; by Kollwitz, 470, *471*; by Rembrandt, 372, 373
Eternal Shiva, 75, 75–76
Etruscan art, 120, *120*, 121–24, 139, 162
Europe: Bronze Age in, *40*, 40–41; early 20th century, 468–79; following World War I, 481–92; incursion into Americas, 387; Islam in, 234; late 19th century, 442–65; Renaissance printmaking in, *312*, 312–13, *313*; since World War II, 500; and World War I, 468, 481. *See also specific countries, e.g.,* Italian art
Exekias, 102–3, *103*
Experiment on a Bird in the Air-Pump, An (Wright of Derby), 424, *425*, *425*
expressionism, 7, 469–74; Abstract, 481, 500–505, 506, *507*, 512, *512*; Neo-, 518, *519*; in photography, 15; of Van Gogh, 461

F

Factory, The, 509
Fallingwater (Wright), 486, *486*, 515
Family of Charles IV (Goya), 431, *431*
Fan Kuan, 216, *216*
Farm Securities Administration (FSA) photographs, 493–94, *494*
Farnese palace ceiling (Annibale Carracci), 354–55, *355*, 361
Fauve movement, 469, 471–72
Feast in the House of Levi (Veronese), 331–32, *332*
feathered bowl wedding basket, Pomo, *397*, 397
Feathered Serpent, Temple of the (Teotihuacan, Mexico), *387*, 388
Federico da Montefeltro (Piero), 308, *308*
feminist art, *516*, 516–18, *517*, *518*
femmage, *516*, 517
Fénéon, Félix, 462, *463*
Fervor, production still from (Neshat), 525, *525*
fête galante, 379
feudalism, 245
fiber art(s): Asante, 412, *412*; of Delaunay-Terk, 478, *478*; in *The Dinner Party*, *516*, 517; early, 53; embroidery as, *252*, 253, 273–74, *275*, 398, *398*; Inca, 384, *384*, 385, 392–93, *393*; postwar American, 513; prehistoric, 53; tapestry as, *252*, 253, 296, *297*, 321, *323*; Tlingit, 400, *401*
Fighting "Téméraire," Tugged to Her Last Berth to Be Broken Up, The (Turner), *434*, 434
figurines: ancient Greek, *98*, 99; Chinese, *80*, 80–81; Cycladic, *90*, 91; "goddess," 34; Kongo, 409–11, *410*; Upper Pale-
olithic, 32, 32–34, *33*; "Venus," 34; Yoruba, 413, *413*
"fine art" vs "craft," 414
fish, as Christian symbol, 180
Flagellation, The, 169
flask, porcelain, Chinese, 219
Flemish art: and Habsburg Empire, 365–69; Hispano-, *294*, 294–95; outside Low Countries, 294–96; Renaissance, 288–94
Flight into Egypt, The, 168
Florence: churches of, *299*, 299–302, *300*, *301*, *303*, 303–5, *304*, *305*, 322, 326, 335, *335*; monastery in, 305–6, *306*
Florence Cathedral, 322; dome of (Brunelleschi), *300*, 301, 326
Florentine painting: Gothic, 280–83; Renaissance, 307–9
flower pieces, Dutch, 7, *14*, 14–15, 29, 377, *377*, 380–81
Flower Piece with Curtain (Van der Spelt and Mieris), 7, *14*, 14–15, 29
Flower Still Life (Ruysch), 377, *377*, 381
flying buttresses, 262
"follower of," defined, 8
Fontainebleau, Château of, *338*, 338–39
Fontaine de Mercure (Calder), 489
Forbidden City, the (Palace Museum Beijing), 220, 220–21
foreground, 6, *6*
foreshortening, 7, *7*
form, 5–6
formal elements, 5–6
formalism, 469, 503; of David Smith, 505–6
formalistic style, 7
forum, 152
Forum Romanum and Imperial Forums, *153*
Foster, Norman, *514*, 515
"Foundation and Manifesto of Futurism" (Marinetti), 478
Founding of Tenochtitlan, The (page from *Codex Mendoza*), 390, *390*
Foundry Painter, 105, *105*
Fountain (Duchamp), 487–88, *488*, 506
Four Apostles (Dürer), 343, *343*
Four Books of Architecture (Palladio), 426
Fra Angelico, 305–6, *306*
Fra Giovanni da Fiesole. *See* Fra Angelico
Fragonard, Jean-Honoré, 380, *381*
frames: Cennini and, 279; by Rossetti, 446
France: architecture between World Wars, 484, *484*; Baroque art in, 6, 358–62; Flemish art influencing, 295; Gothic art in, 259–72; Mannerism in, 338–41; medieval book production in, 238, *239*; Neoclassical art in, 419, 419–21, *420*, *427*, 427–29, 428
Frankenthaler, Helen, 504, *504*
freestanding sculpture, 8
French Academy, in Rome, 428
French Revolution, 419; of 1789, 427; of 1848, 436–37
frescoes, 8; early Renaissance, 303–6, *304*, 309–10, *310*, *311*, 311–12; by Giotto, *282*, 282–83, *283*; by Michelangelo, 322–25, *323*, *324*, *325*
Freud, Sigmund, 416
From Delacroix to Neo-Impressionism (book) (Signac), 463
Fry, Roger, 457
fukabachi (cooking pots), Paleolithic, 36, *37*
functional art, 8, 414
funerary art: African, 413, *413*; Greek, *98*, 99, *105*, 106–7
funerary complex: Djoser's, 54; at Giza, *57*
funerary temple, Egyptian, 56, 60, *60*
furnishings: chairs as, 447, *447*, 470, *470*, 483, *483*, 485; by Morris & Company, 447, *447*
Fur Traders Descending the Missouri (Bingham), 439, *439*
Fuseli, John Henry, 416, *416–17*, 432, 432–33, 439
fusuma, 226, *227*
Futurism, 478, *478*, 479; O'Keeffe and, 492

G

Gabhart, Ann, 516
Gainsborough, Thomas, 421, *421*
Gaius Octavius. *See* Augustus Caesar
Galileo Galilei, 376
Garden in Sochi (Gorky), 501, *501*
Garden of Earthly Delights (Bosch), 346–47, *347*
gardens: English landscape, 424–25; Japanese dry landscape, 208, *208–9*, 224–26, *226*; of Versailles, 360, *360*
Garden Scene (Roman wall painting), 151, *151*
Gates of Paradise (Ghiberti), *299*, 299–301
Gathering of Manna (Tintoretto), 333
Gaudi, Antoni, 448, 449
Gauguin, Paul, 457, 459, *460*, 460–61, 469; influence of, 469; Signac and, 462
Gaulli, Giovanni Battista, 356, 357
Gehry, Frank O., 25, *514*, 515
Geisha as Daruma Crossing the Sea (Suzuki Harunobu), 228, *228*
Gemma Augustea, 144–45, *145*
General and Officers (Edo culture), 406, *406*
generation of 1848, 438
Genesis and *The Parable of the Good Samaritan* (from Chartres Cathedral), 256, *257*, 263, *263*
Gentileschi, Artemisia, 358, *358*
geoglyphs, Nazca, 391, *391*
George Washington Monument (Mills), 498
Géricault, Théodore, 429, 429–30
German art: architecture between World Wars, 484, 484–85, *485*; Gothic churches, 275; Renaissance, 341, 341–45, *342*, *343*, 344
gesso, 288
gesturalism, 501
Ghiberti, Lorenzo, 299, 299–301
Ghirlandaio, Domenico, 321, *323*
Ghost Clock (Castle), 520, *521*
Giacomo Barozzi. *See* Vignola, Giacomo da
Giangiorgio Trissino, 333
Gian Paolo Zappi, 337
Giorgio da Castelfranco. *See* Giorgione
Giorgione, 328, 453
Giotto di Bondone, 281, 281–83, *282*, *283*; influence of, 296
Giovanni Francesco Barbieri. *See* Guercino, Il
Gislebertus of Autun, 249, *249*, 250, *250*, 255
Giza: Great Pyramids at, 56, *57*, 86; Great Sphinx at, 13, *13*, 14, 24
glass
  Islamic, 200–201, *201*
  postwar American, 513
  stained-, 264; of Chartres Cathedral, 256, *256*, *257*, 263, *263*, *264*; of Reims Cathedral, 264–66
Glass and Bottle of Suze (Picasso), 477, *477*
"goddess" figurines, 34
Gogh, Vincent van. *See* Van Gogh, Vincent
goldsmiths: high Renaissance, 339, *339*; Inca, 393, *393*
Goldsmith in His Shop, Possibly Saint Eligius, A (Christus), 293, *293*
Gonçalvez, Nuño, *294*, 294–95
Goncharova, Natalia, 479, *479*
Good Shepherd (from Mausoleum of Galla Placidia), 174, *174*
Gorky, Arshile, 501, *501*
Gospels of Otto III (medieval illumination), 232, *232*, 233, *233*, 242, *242*, 243
Gothardt, Matthias. *See* Grünewald, Matthias
Gothic art, 256–83, 526; in England, 273–74; in France, 259–72; in Germanic lands, 275, 275–76; in Italy, 276–83
Gould, Richard Nash, 527
Goya y Lucientes, Francisco, 430, 430–32, *431*, *432*, 462
Gozzoli, Benozzo, 289, 307–8
graffiti, Roman, 37
granulation, Minoan use of, 94–95, *95*
graphic arts. *See* printmaking
graphic design, by Bauhaus, 484
Great Depression, 468
Great Mosque (Córdoba), 193, *193*, 194–95; dome in, 195, *195*; prayer hall of, 194–95, *195*
Great Mosque (Isfahan), 197, *197*
Great Mosque (Kairouan, Tunisia), 194, *194*
Great Pyramids at Giza, 56, *57*, 86
Great Serpent Mound, 394, *395*
Great Sphinx, 13, *13*, 14, 24
Great Stupa, 70, *70*, 71, *71*
Great Temple of Amun, *60*, 61, *61*
Great Wave, The (Katsushika Hokusai), 229, *229*
Great Wild Goose Pagoda, 82, *82*
Great Zimbabwe, *407*, 407–8, *408*
Greek architectural orders, 100, *100*
Greek art, 98–117, 162; Archaic period of, 99–105; Classical

period of, 108–15; Early Classical or Transitional period of, 106–8; geometric style of, *98*, 99; "Golden Age" of, 108–15; Hellenistic, 129–35; late Classical period of, 115–17; as naturalistic, 14; spread of, 119–35; women artists of, 116, *116*

Greek gods, 100; Roman counterparts of, 138, 139. *See also* specific gods, e.g., Apollo

Greenberg, Clement, 503, 513

grisaille, 271, *271*

groin vault, 141, *141*, 255, *255*

Gropius, Walter, *484*, 485, 487, 513

Gross Clinic, The (Eakins), *450*, 451

ground plane, 6, *6*

grout, 152

Grünewald, Matthias, *341*, 341–42

Guan Ware vase, 217, *217*

Guda, 255; self-portrait of, 251, *251*

Güell Park (Gaudi), *448*, 449

Guercino, Il, *22*, 22–23

Guernica (Picasso), *489*

Guggenheim Museum: in Bilbao, Spain (Gehry), 25, *514*, 515; in New York (Wright), 25, *26*, 515, 523, *523*

Guido di Pietro. *See* Fra Angelico

Gummersmark brooch, 234, *234*

H

Habsburg Empire, 240, 362–69; in Spain, 362–65

Hackwood, William, 433, *433*

Hades, 100

Hadrian Hunting Boar and Sacrificing to Apollo, 155–56, *156*, 161

Hadrian's Wall, 157, 158

Haft Paykar (*Seven Portraits*) (Nizami), 202, *203*

Hagar in the Wilderness (Lewis), 445, *445*

Hagesandros, 27, *28*

Hagia Sophia, Church of (Istanbul) (Anthemius of Tralles and Isidorus of Miletus), *175*, 175–76, *176*, 182, 193, 230; as mosque, 206

Haida people, 399, 401, *401*

hall church, 275

Hamatsa, 399

Hamatsa dancers, 399, *399*

Hammamet with Its Mosque (Klee), *474*, 474, 475

Hampton, James, 20, *20*, 22, 506

Hamza-nama, 204, *204*

Hamza's Spies Scale the Fortress (from *Hamza-nama*), 204, *204*

Handbook of the Crafts, The (*Il Libro dell'Arte*) (Cennini), 279

handscroll, 8; Chinese, 220, *220*; Japanese, 224

hanging scrolls, 8; Chinese, 218, 220, *220*

haniwa, 83, *83*

Happenings, 9, 512, 528

Haram al-Sharif, 191–92

Hardouin-Mansart, Jules, 360, *360*, 361

Harlem Renaissance, 494, *494*–95

Harmony in Blue and Gold (Whistler), 25, *25*, 447

Harris, Ann Sutherland, 516

Harvest Scene (Egyptian tomb painting), 59, *59*

Hasan *madrasa*-mausoleum-mosque, Sultan, *198*, 199

Hatshepsut funerary temple, 60, *60*

Helen of Egypt, 116, 134, *135*

Hellenistic art, 129–35

Hennings, Emmy, 486

Henri, Robert, 479

Henry, Charles, 462, *463*

Henry IV Receiving the Portrait of Marie dé Medici (Rubens), 366–67, *367*

Henry the Navigator, Prince, 294, *294*

Henry VIII (Holbein the Younger), *345*, 345–46

Hephaistos, 100

Hera I, Temple of, *99*, 99–100

Herakles, 100

Heraklitos, 136, *136*–37, 152, *152*

Hermes, 100, 174; depiction of, *115*, 115–16

Hermes and the Infant Dionysos (followers of Praxiteles), *115*, 115–16

Hesse, Eva, 511, *511*, 513

Hestia, 100

Hiberno-Saxon art, *235*, 235–36

hieratic writing, 45

hieroglyphs, 45, *45*

high relief, 8

High Tech architecture, *514*, 515

Hinduism, 76; in China, 210; in early India, 73–76; in Medieval India, 210

Hindu temples, 210–11; northern-style of, *210*, 210–11; southern-style of, *210*, 211, 215

hiragana, 222, *222*

Hispano-Flemish art, 294, *294*–95

historicism, 442–43, 444

history painting, 422

Hitchcock, Henry-Russell, 485

Hitda Gospels, 243, *243*

Hobbema, Meindert, 375–77

Hofmann, Hans, 500, 502, 503

Hogarth, William, 422–24, *423*, 431

Hohokam culture, 395

Hokusai, Katsushika, 229, *229*, 463

Holbein the Younger, Hans, *345*, 345–46

Holly Solomon Gallery (New York), 524, *524*

Holy Roman Empire, 240

Holzer, Jenny, 523, *523*

Homage to New York (Tinguely), 506–7, 508, *508*

Homer, 96

Homer, Winslow, *450*, 450–51

Hon'ami Koetsu, 227, *227*

HongKong & Shanghai Bank (Foster), *514*, 515

Hopewell people, 394; pipe from, 394, *395*, 414

horizon line, 7, *7*

Horrors of War, The (series) (Goya), 432

Horse and Sun Chariot (Bronze Age sculpture), *40*, 40–41

Horta, Victor, *448*, 449

Horyu-ji temple, 84–85, *85*

Hosmer, Harriet, 444, *444*

Hospicio de San Fernando (Madrid), 365, *365*

Hôtel de Soubise, Salon de la Princesse in (Boffrand), *378*, 378

Hour of Cowdust (Rajput painting), *213*, 213–15

House of M. Lucretius Fronto, *150*, 150–51

House of Pansa (Pompeii), 140, *140*

House of the Silver Wedding (Pompeii), 140, *140*

houses. *See* dwellings

hue, 5

Hugo van der Goes, 293, *293*–94

Huitzilopochtli, 390

Human-Headed Winged Lion (*Lamassu*) (Assyrian art), 51, *51*

humanism, 286, 288, 292, 382

humors, four, 342–43

Hungry Tigress Jataka (Japanese lacquer painting), 84–85, *85*

Hunters in the Snow (Bruegel the Elder), 348, *348*

Hurling Colors, 512

hydria, Greek, 104, *104*, 116, *116*

hypostyle hall: in Great Temple of Amun, 61, *61*; in Hatshepsut funerary temple, 60

I

Iaia, 116

Ia Orana Maria (*We Hail Thee Mary*) (Gauguin), 460, *460*

iconoclasm, 181

iconography, 6, 26; of life of Jesus, 168–69

icons, Byzantine, 164, 181, *181*, 184–85, *185*, 186–87, *187*, 509

ideal, 16–17

Ideal City with a Fountain and Statues of the Virtues (Anonymous), *302*, 302–3

idealism: academic, 444–47; classical, 7, 17, *17*, 359, 360, 361

idealization, 7, 14

Ife, Nigeria, 404, 405

Il Gesù, Church of (Rome), 339–41, *340*, 356, 357

Iliad (Homer), 96

illuminated manuscripts, 8, 180–81, *181*; Flemish, 295–96; Islamic, 202–4, *203*; Ottoman, *191*, 206–7; Ottonian, *242*, 242–43, 243; Romanesque, 251, *251*–52, 252. *See also* books

Imba Huru (Big House), 407

Impressionism, 451–57, 528; later, 455–57; Post-Impressionism compared, 457, 458–59

Impression, Sunrise (Monet), 453

Improvisation No. 30 (*Cannons*) (Kandinsky), 473, *473*–74

Inanna, 45–46, *46*, 125, 127. *See also* Ishtar

Inca Empire, *392*, 392–93, 414; fiber arts from, 384, *384*, *385*, 392–93, *393*; Spanish conquest of, 393

Incarnation Cycle of Jesus, 168

incense burner, early Chinese, 78, *78*

incising, 462

Indian art: Chola dynasty and, 18, *18*, 212, *212*; early, 68–76; Medieval, 210, *210*; Mughal dynasty and, 212, 213; and paper painting, *213*, 213–15

Indian subcontinent. *See* Indian art

Indus Valley civilization, *68*, 69

Ingres, Jean-Auguste-Dominique, *428*, 428–29, 430, 475

Initiation of Rites of the Cult of Bacchus, *151*, 151–52

ink painting, Japanese, 224, *225*

Inner Shrine (Shinto architecture), 84, *84*

Inscriptions, Palace and Temple of the, *388*, 388–89

installation art, 523–25

intaglio, 312, 462

intensity, 5

intention, of artists, 6

"International Exhibition of Modern Art" (1913), 480, 481

International Exposition of Modern Decorative and Industrial Arts (1925), 470, 478, *478*

International Style, 485, 513, *513*, 526

intertextual art, 522

In the Dining Room (Morisot), 454, *454*

intuitive perspective, 7, *7*, 289

Ionic order, 100, *100*

Ironworking: in architecture, 443; early, 404, *404*

Iroquois, 397–98

Isabeau, Queen of France, 25, *25*

Isabella d'Este, 329

Isabella d'Este (Titian), 329, 331

Isenheim Altarpiece (Grünewald), *341*, 341–42

Isfahan: Congregational Mosque of, 193, *193*; Great Mosque (Masjid-i Jami) of, 197, *197*; Madrasa Imami of, 197–99, *198*

Ishiyama-gire (*Thirty-six Immortal Poets*), 223, *223*

Ishtar, 125, 127. *See also* Inanna

Ishtar Gate, 125, *126*, 127

Isidorus of Miletus, *175*, 175–76, *176*, 182, 193, 230

Islam, 190, 191, 284; in medieval Europe, 234

Islamic art, 166, 188–207; early caliphates period of, 190–96; later, 197–207; during Mughal empire, *204*, 204–5, 205

Italian art: Baroque, 6, 352–58; early Renaissance, 296–312; Futurism, 478, *478*; Gothic, 276–83; High Renaissance, 316–34, 495; Mannerism, 334–41; Neoclassical, *418*, 418–19

Itxá art, 389, *389*

ivory: Benin, 406, *406*; Ottonian, 240, *240*

Ivory Coast, 410, 411

iwans, 193, *193*; of Sultan Hasan *madrasa*-mausoleum-mosque, *198*, 199

J

Jacopo Robusti. *See* Tintoretto

Jane Avril (Toulouse-Lautrec), 462, *462*

Japanese art: early, 82–85; Edo era of, 17–18, *18*, 227–29; Heian period of, 210, 221, 221–24; influence on European art, 447, 448, 455, 457, 462, 463; Kamakura era of, 224, *225*; Muromachi period of, 224–27

japonisme, 229, 448

jars: Anasazi, *396*, 397; Bamana, 409, *409*

Jeanneret, Charles-Édouard. *See* Le Corbusier

Jefferson, Thomas, 334, 426, *426*

Jerusalem: Entry into, 169; mosques in, 191–92

Jesus of Nazareth: Among the Doctors, 168; childhood of, 168; Crowned with Thorns, 169; in the House of Mary and Martha, 168; iconography of life of, 168–69; Before Pilate, 169; and the Samaritan Woman at the Well, 168; Walking on the Water, 168; Washing the Disciples' Feet, 169

jewelry: Egyptian, 59, *59*

Jewish art, 166, 230; early, *166*, 166–69, *167*

Jocho, 222, *222*

Johns, Jasper, 506, *507*, 508

Johnson, Philip, 485, 513

joined-wood sculpture, Japanese, 222, *222*

Jomon vessel, 36, *37*

Jonah (Ryder), *450*, 451

Jones, Inigo, 369–70, *370*
Joy of Life, The (Matisse), *471*, 471–72, 475
Judd, Donald, *510*, 510–11
Judgment before Osiris (from a Book of the Dead), *64*, 65
Judgment of Paris, The (Raphael), 453
Jugendstil. *See* Art Nouveau
Julius Caesar, 142, 143
Jung, Carl, 501

K

ka, 54
Kaaba, 191
Kahlo, Frida, *496*, 497, 528
Kalypso, 116
kana script, Japanese, *222*, 222–23
Kandariya Mahadeva temple, 210, *210*, 211
Kandinsky, Vasily, *473*, 473–74, 487; shown in United States, 480
kanji characters, 222, *222*
Kano Eitoku, *fusuma* by, 226, *227*
Kao Ninga, 224, *225*
Kaprow, Allan, 512
"Karawane" (poem) (Ball), *486*, 486–87
katakana, 222, *222*
Katholikon (Greece), 182–83, *183*
Kauffmann, Angelica, 422, 424, *424*
Kelper, Johannes, 376
kente cloth, *412*, 412
key block, in *ukiyo-e* prints, 228
keystone, *141*, 142
Khafre (Egyptian sculpture), 55
Kiefer, Anselm, 518, *519*
kiln, Etruscan use of, 121
Kirchner, Ernst Ludwig, *472*, 472–73, 475, 487
kitsch, 506
Klee, Paul, *474*, 474, 475, 487
Klein, Yves, 512
Knossos palace complex, 91–92, *92*, 94, *94*
Kollwitz, Käthe Schmidt, *470*, 470–71
Kongo art: figurines, 409–11, *410*; masks, 412–13, *413*
Koran, 191; page of, *190*, 190–91
kore(ai), 101, *102*; Etruscan knowledge of, 122
Kosuth, Joseph, *511*, 511–12
kouros(oi), 101, *102*, 102–3, 107; Etruscan knowledge of, 122
Krasner, Lee, 502, *502*
krater, Greek, *98*, 99, *105*, 106–7
Krishna, 213, 213–15
Kritios Boy (Greek statue), *106*, 107, 114
kufic script, 188, 190–91; on ceramics, 196, *197*; on page of Koran, *190*, 190–91
kurgans, 124
Kwakwaka'wakw people, *399*, 399–401, *400*, 414
kylix, Greek, *105*, 105
Kyoto, Japan: Byodo-in, *221*, 221–22; Daitoku-ji temple in, 226; Ryoan-ji temple in, 208, *208–9*, 224–26, 226

L

Labille-Guiard, Adélaïde, *420*, 421
lacquer paintings, Japanese, 84–85, *85*
Lagash votive statue, 49–51, *50*
Lakota, 398
lamb, as Christian symbol, 180
Lamentation (Giotto), *283*
Lamentation, The (Pietà), 169, 321; by Giotto, 283; by Michelangelo, 321, 321–22, 328, *328*
landscape gardens: English, 424–25; Japanese dry, 208, *208–9*, 224–26, 226
landscape painting: Chinese, 216–17, *216–17*; French Baroque, 362, *362*; Neo-Expressionist, 518, *519*; Romantic, *433*, 433–34, *434*
Landscape with Saint John on Patmos (Poussin), 361–62, *362*
Lange, Dorothea, 493–94, *494*
Laocoön and His Sons, 7, *27*, 27–28, *28*, 134, 136, *338*
Lapith Fighting a Centaur (Parthenon frieze), 110, 111
Large Glass, The (Duchamp). See *Bride Stripped Bare by Her Bachelors, Even, The* (Duchamp)
Large Odalisque (Ingres), *428*, 428–29, 430, 475
Larionov, Mikhail, 479
Lascaux cave paintings, *35*, 35–36

Last Judgment (Michelangelo), 323, 324–25, *325*
Last Supper (Riemenschneider), 344, *344*
Last Supper (Tintoretto), 333, *333*
Last Supper, The, 169, *332*
Last Supper, The (Leonardo da Vinci), 23–24, *24*, 316–18, *317*, 333, 344, 371
Last Supper, The (Rembrandt), *23*, 23–24
La Venta Olmec carved head (megalithic art), *41*, 41
LaVerdiere, Julian, 526, *527*
Lavinia Fontana, *337*, 337–38
Learning from Las Vegas (book) (Venturi), 513
le Brun, Charles, 361, *361*
Le Corbusier, 484, *484*, 513
Leeuwenhoek, Anton van, 376
Legrain, Pierre, 470, *470*
Le Nôtre, André, 360
Leonardo da Vinci, 22, *24*, 316, 316–19, *317*, *318*, 333, 337, 338; grading of, 360; influence of, 23–24, 319, 336, 371
Leroy, Louis, 453
Le Vau, Louis, 359, 360, *360*
Lewis, Edmonia, 445, *445*
Leyland, Frederick, 25, *25*
Leyster, Judith, *373*, 373–74
Liberation of Aunt Jemima, The (Saar), 517, *517*
Libro dell'Arte, Il (*The Handbook of the Crafts*) (Cennini), 279
Lichtenstein, Roy, 507–8, *508*, 509
Life of Charlemagne, The (from Chartres Cathedral), 256, *256*, *263*
Life of John the Baptist (Andrea Pisano), 276, *277*
Life of the Prophet (*Siyar-i Nabi*) (al-Zarir), 191
Life of the Virgin (from Chichester-Constable chasuble), 275
lighting effect(s): in religious paintings, *357*, 358, 425; symbolizing benefits of science, 425, *425*, 451; tenebrism as, 358, 363
Limbourg brothers, 295–96, *296*
Lin, Maya Ying, 498, *498–99*, 525, 525–26
Lincoln Memorial, 498
Lindau Gospels, 238, *239*
line, 5
linear perspective, 7, *7*, 286, 288, 289, 382; by Masaccio, 304; by Perugino, 311
Lion Gate, *97*, 97–98
Lion-Human, 32, 32–33
Lippi, Filippino, 304
Lipstick (Ascending) on Caterpillar Tracks (Oldenburg), *509*, 509–10
Lissitzky, El, 482, *482*
literati painting, of China, 218–19, *218–19*
lithography, 8, 462; of Toulouse-Lautrec, 462
Little Galleries of the Photo-Secession, 480
Littleton, Harvey, 513
Lives of the Most Excellent Italian Architects, Painters, and Sculptors (book) (Vasari), 26
llama, gold, 393, *393*
Lobster Trap and Fish Tail (Calder), *491*, 491
Locke, Alain, 494
Los Angeles County Museum of Art, 516
lost-wax casting, 8, 10, *10*, 405
lotus flower, as Buddhist symbol, 73
lotus throne, 73
Louis IX and Queen Blanche of Castile (from Moralized Bible), 270, *270*
Louis XIV (Rigaud), 358, *358*
Louis XIV of France, 358, 359
Louvre, The, 475
low relief, 8
Luncheon of the Boating Party (Renoir), *456*, 456–57
Luncheon on the Grass, The (*Le Déjeuner sur l'herbe*) (Manet), 451, 451–52
lyre, Sumerian, 47, *47*, 48
Lyrical Abstraction, 500
Lysippos, 115, 117, 131; *Alexander the Great* by, 117, *117*

M

Mabel of Bury St. Edmunds, 274
mace, 402
Machine Age, 470
Machu Picchu, Peru, 392, *392*
Maderno, Carlo, 353; Saint Peter's Basilica expansion by, 326,

326, 352
madrasa, 197
Madrasa Imami of Isfahan, 197–99, *198*
Maestà Altarpiece (Duccio), *278*, 279
Magdeburg Ivories, 240, *240*
Magi Asleep, The (from Cathedral of Saint-Lazare), 250, *250*
Maids of Honor, The (*Las Meninas*) (Velázquez), 363–64, *364*
mainstream art, 503; from United States, 500–13
Ma Jolie (Picasso), *476*, 477
Malevich, Kazimir, 479, *479*, 482
Man and Centaur, *98*, 99
Man, Controller of the Universe (Rivera), 495–97, *496*
mandala, 73
Manet, Édouard, 440, *451*, 451–53, 454, 455, *455*, 462; allusions in art by, 453; Greenberg on, 503; influences on, 331, 452
Manifesto of Surrealism (Breton), 488
Man's Love Story (Tjapaltjarri), *521*, 521–22
Mantegna, Andrea, 309–10, *310*, *310*, 329
Mantua, Ducal Palace of, 309–10, *310*
Marantz, Paul, 526, *527*
Marcus Aurelius, 156, *156*, 298–99
Marietta Robusti, 332–33
Marilyn Diptych (Warhol), *509*, 509
Marinetti, Filippo, 478
Market Woman, *130*, 131
Märkischer Heide (Kiefer), 518, *519*
Marriage à la Mode (series) (Hogarth), 422–24, *423*
Marriage at Cana (Giotto), *283*, 283
Marriage at Cana, The, 168
Marriage Contract, The (Hogarth), 422, *423*
Marriage of the Emperor Frederick and Beatrice of Burgandy, The (Tiepolo), 378, *379*
Marshals and Young Women (Parthenon frieze), *110*, 111
Martínez, Julian, 396, 397
Martínez, Maria Montoya, 396, 397
Martyrdom of Saint Lawrence (Mausoleum of Galla Placidia mosaic), *173*, 174
martyrium, 236
Marx, Karl, 442
Marys at the Tomb, The (The Anastasis), 169
Masaccio, 297, *303*, 303–5; influence of, 308
masks: Bwa, 412–13, *413*, 414; of Kwakwaka'wakw people, *399*, 399–401, *400*, 414
Maso di Ser Giovanni di Mone Cassai. *See* Masaccio
Masolino, 304, *304*
masonry, Inca, 392, *392*
mass, 5
Massacre of the Innocents, The, 168
Master of the Smiling Angels (Saint Joseph Master), 267, *267*
Maternal Caress (Cassatt), *456*, 457
mathematical perspective. *See* linear perspective
Matisse, Henri, *471*, 471–72; and Cubism, 477; influence of African art on, 470; Picasso and, 475, 476, 478; shown in United States, 480; Signac and, 462, *463*
Matthew the Evangelist (page from *Ebbo Gospels*), 238, *238*
Mauryan lion capital, 70, *70*
mausoleum: of Galla Placidia, *173*, 174, *174*; of Qin Shihuangdi, 66, *66*, *67*, 77, 77–78; of Sultan Hasan, 198, 199
Maya art, 388, *388*, 388–89, *389*
meanings, of art, 6
Mecca, 191
Medici, Marie dé, 366–67, *367*
Medici Venus, 7, 17, *17*; as copy of *Aphrodite of Knidos*, 116, 131
medieval art, 233–55, 284
Medina, 191
medium, 8–9
Medusa (Greek pedimental sculpture), 100–101, *101*
megalithic architecture, Neolithic, 38–40
memorial(s), 525–26; Lincoln, 498; *Tribute in Light* as, 526, *527*; Vietnam Veterans Memorial, 143, 498, *498–99*, 525, 525–26
Meninas, Las (*The Maids of Honor*) (Velázquez), 363–64, *364*; influence of, 431
Menkaure and His Wife, Queen Khamerernebty (Egyptian sculpture), 55–56, *56*
Menorahs and Ark of the Covenant, *166*, 166–67

Merian, Maria Sibylla, 380, *381*, 438
Merisi, Michelangelo. *See* Caravaggio
Mérode Altarpiece (Campin), 288–90, *289*
Mesoamerica, 386–87; ancient, 41, *41*, 387–91
Mesopotamian art, 43–52
metalworking: Benin, 10, *10*, 405, *405*, 406, *406*; Islamic, 201–2, *202*; Minoan, 94–95, *95*
Mexican art, between World Wars, 495–97
Mexico, Spanish conquest of, 393
Michelangelo Buonarotti, 314, 316, 321–28; *David* by, 322, *322*; on Gates of Paradise, 299; grading of, 360; influence of, 332, 336–37, 355, 427; influences on, 28, 305; *Last Judgment* by, 324–25, *325*; *Pietà* by, *321*, 321–22; *Rondanini Pietà* by, 328, *328*; Saint Peter's Basilica by, 325, *326*, 326–27, 327; in *School of Athens* (Raphael), *320*; Sistine Chapel ceiling by, 322–24, *323*, *324*, 355
middle ground, 6, *6*
Middle Kingdom Egypt, 58–59
Mieris, Frans van, 7, *14*, 14–15, 29
Mies van der Rohe, Ludwig, 485, *485*, 487, 513, *513*
Migrant Mother, Nipomo, California (Lange), 494, *494*
mihrab, 192; tile work on, 197–99, *198*
Mills, Robert, 498
mimesis, 14, 15, 16
Mimis and Kangaroo (prehistoric rock art), 34, *34*
minarets, 194, *194*; of Selimiye mosque, *206*
minbar, 198
Minerva, in *School of Athens* (Raphael), 320
miniature painting, 8
Minimalism, 505, *510*, 510–11, *511*, 513; feminist reaction against, 517
Minoan art, 90–95
Miracles of Healing, The, 168
Miraculous Draft of Fishes, The, 168
Miró, Joan, 491, *491*
Mississippian culture, 394–95, *395*
mixed medium, 9
M. Lucretius Fronto, house of, *150*, 150–51
Mnesikles, Erechtheion by, 112, *112*
moai (megalithic figures), 41, *41*
mobiles, by Calder, 491, *491*
Mocking of Jesus, The, 169
modeling, of Roman mosaic, 135
moderne. *See* Art Nouveau
modernism, 440, 467–97, 513, 528; definition of, 469; high/low myth of, 506; late, 513, 518
Modernismo. *See* Art Nouveau
Modersohn-Becker, Paula, *469*, 469–70
Mona Lisa (Leonardo da Vinci), 318, *318*–19
Monastery of Christ, Church of the (Chora), 185–86, *186*
Monastery of Hosios Loukas (Greece), 182–83, *183*
Monastery of San Marco, 305–6, *306*
Monastery of Santa Maria delle Grazie, 316, *317*
Mondrian, Piet, 482–83, *483*, 528; influence of, 491, 500
Monet, Claude, *453*, 453–54, 455, 457, *457*, 479; influence of, 473
Monk Sewing (Kao), 224, *225*
Monk's Mound, 395, *395*
monochromatic, 5
monograms, as Christian symbol, 180
Monotone Symphony (Klein), 512
Montbaston, Jeanne de, 295
Montbaston, Richart de, 295
Monticello (Jefferson), 334, 426, *426*
Mont Sainte-Victoire (Cézanne), 457–58, *458*
monumental architecture: of central Andes, 391, *391*; Neolithic, 38–40
monumental sculpture, 8
Moon Goddess, Coyolxauhqui, The, 390, 391
Moore, Henry, 481, 481–82
Moralized Bible, 270, *270*
moralized genre paintings, 422–24, *423*, *424*, *425*
Morisot, Berthe, 453, 454, *454*
Morris & Company, 447, *447*
Morris, William, 446–47
mosaics: cone, 45, 45–46; early Byzantine, *178*, 178–80, *179*; early Christian, *173*, 173–74, *174*; in mosques, 195, 197–99, *198*; Roman, 135, 136, *136*–37, 152, *152*; Sumerian, 45, 45–46; on synagogue floor, *167*, 167–68

Moser, Mary, 422
mosques, 191, 192–93; central-plan, 193, *193*, 206, *206*; four-iwan, 193, *193*, 197, *197*; hypostyle, 193, *193*, 194, *194*, 195; in Jerusalem, 191–92; mosaic art in, 195, 197–99, *198*; plans for, 193
Mother Goddess, Coatlicue, The, 391, *391*, 393
Mott, Lucretia, 442
Mountains and Sea (Frankenthaler), 504, *504*
Mount Fuji (Hon'ami Koetsu), 227, *227*
Mozarabic, 195, 196, 239
Mrs. Ezekiel Goldthwait (Elizabeth Lewis) (Copley), 421–22, *423*
Mughals, 204, 204–5, *205*
Muhammad, Prophet, 191, *191*
mummies, 55
Munch, Edvard, *468*, 469
muqarnas dome (Palace of the Lions), 200, *200*
murals: Romanesque, *244*, 245–48, *248*. *See also* frescoes; wall paintings
Murray, Elizabeth, 518, *518*
Museum of Modern Art, The (New York), 469, 485, 506, 508, *508*
museums: as patrons, 25–26. *See also specific museums, e.g.,* Solomon R. Guggenheim Museum (Wright)
Musicians and Dancers, 123, *123*
Mycenaean art, in late Bronze Age, 91, 95–98
Myoda, Paul, 526, *527*

N

Nanchan Temple, *81*, 81–82
Nanna Ziggurat, 46
Napoleon Crossing the Saint-Bernard (David), *427*, 427–28
narrative images: in Christian art, 164
naskhi script, 188
Nataraja: Shiva as Lord of Dance, 212, *212*, 215
National Academy of Design, 480
Native American art: contemporary, 522, 522–23; Eastern, 397–98; of Great Plains, 397–98; influence of, 414, 497, *497*; of Northwest coast, 398–401; prior to European introduction, 394–401; Southeastern, 394–97; Southwestern, 394–97
Native Americans: Iroquois as, 397–98; Lakota as, 398; Sioux as, 398, *398*, 414
Nativity, The, 168
naturalism, 7, 14, 418, 445; of Greek Early Classical or Transitional period, 106–7; in late-19th-century France, 436–38; in late-19th-century United States, 449; of Roman Republican period, 139, 144; Romantic, 433, *433*
Nauman, Bruce, 512, *512*, 528
Nebuchadnezzar's throne room, 125, *126*, 127
necropolis, 55
needlework, in *The Dinner Party*, 516, 517
Nefertiti (sculpture), 63, *63*
Neo-Babylonian art, 120, 125, *125*, *126*
Neoclassicism, 416, *416*–17, 418–29, 528; Romanticism and, 428–29, 469
Neo-Confucianism, 210, 215–16
Neo-Expressionism, 518, *519*
Neo-Impressionism, 440, 459, 460, 462, 463
Neolithic art, 36–41
Neolithic settlements: in Mesopotamia, 44; in Scotland, 37–38, *38*
Neoplatonism, 309
Neshat, Shirin, 524–25, *525*
Netherlandish art, 346, 346–48, *347*, *348*
Netherlands: after World War I, 482–83, *483*; flower pieces from, 7, *14*, 14–15, 29, 377, *377*, 380–81; Protestant, 371–77, 380–81, 382
Neumann, Johann Balthasar, 378, *379*
Nevelson, Louise, 505, 505–6
New Basilica (Basilica Nova), 153, 158–60, *160*
New Kingdom Egypt, 59–65, *60*, 61
"New Negro" movement, 495
New York School, 501–5; Greenberg on, 503; sculptors of, 504–5
New York School, painters of, 501–4
Ngombe chair, 470, *470*
Niépce, Joseph-Nicéphore, 434
Nietzsche, Frederick, 472, 504

Nigeria, Yoruba people of, 20, *20*, *404*, 405, *411*, 411–12, 413, *413*
Nightmare, The (Fuseli), 416, *416*–17, 432, 433, 439
Night Watch, The (Captain Frans Banning Cocq Mustering His Company) (Rembrandt van Rijn), *371*, 371–73
Nike (Victory) Adjusting Her Sandal (from Temple of Athena Nike), 113, 113–14
Nike (Victory) of Samothrace (marble), 118, *119*, 131, 131–33
Nizami, 202, *203*
nkisi nkonde (power figure), Kongo, 409–11, *410*
Nochlin, Linda, 516
Noir, Jean le, 295
Nok culture, *404*, 404–5
Noli Me Tangere ("Do Not Touch Me"), 169
Noli Me Tangere (Giotto), *283*
Noli Me Tangere (Lavinia), 337, *337*
nonobjective art. *See* nonrepresentational art
nonrepresentational art, 6, 16, 474; first works of, 479
Normandy: churches of, 255, *255*
North American art, 394–401
   of Canada, 497, *497*
   early 20th century, 466–97
   of Mexico, 495–97
   by Native Americans: contemporary, 522, 522–23; Eastern, 397–98; of Great Plains, 397–98; influence of, 414, 497, *497*; of Northwest coast, 398–401; prior to European introduction, 394–401; Southeastern, 394–97; Southwestern, 394–97
   Neoclassical, 421–22, *423*
   prior to European influx, 394–401
   of United States: 19th century, 438–39, *439*, 442–65, 449–51; modernist, 479–81; Neoclassical, 426, *426*, 449; realistic, 438–39, *439*; since World War II, 500
   between World Wars, 492–97
"Notes of a Painter" (essay) (Matisse), 472
Notre-Dame (traditional usage and abbreviationis), 171
Notre-Dame, Cathedral of (Chartles). *See* Chartres Cathedral
Notre-Dame, Cathedral of (Paris), 264, 265, *265*; in Paris history, 265
Notre-Dame, Cathedral of (Reims), 264–67, *266*, *267*
numerical symbolism, 318

O

Oath of the Horatii (David), *427*, 427
Octopus Flask, 94, *94*
Oh, Jeff...I Love You, Too...But (Lichtenstein), 508, *508*
oil painting, 288; Van Eyck and, *291*; in Venice, 328
O'Keeffe, Georgia, *15*, 15–16, 492
Oldenburg, Claes, 509, 509–10
Old Kingdom Egypt, 52–58
Old Saint Peter's Church (Vatican), *170*, 171–72, 326; *Pietà* in, *321*, 321–22; plan for, *326*; rebuilding of, 325–27
Old Testament Trinity, The (Three Angels Visiting Abraham) (Rublyov), 186–87, *187*
Olmec art, 387; La Venta carved head, 41, *41*
Olodumare, 20
Olówè of Isè, 20, *20*, *411*, 411–12
Olympia (Manet), 452, *452*
Olympias, 116
On Architecture (De architectura) (Vitruvius), 316
On Architecture (De re aedificatoria) (Alberti), 302–3
One and Three Chairs (Kosuth), *511*, 511–12
one-point perspective. *See* linear perspective
On the Revolutions of the Heavenly Spheres (Copernicus), 376
Op art, 510
Open Door, The (Talbot), 435, *435*
openwork box lid, Celtic, 157–58, *159*
"optical art," 510
opus anglicanum, 274, *275*
Orpheus, 174
Orphism, 478
orthogonals, 7, *7*
Osiris, 64–65; in Books of the Dead, *64*, 65; Tutankhamun as, 64, *64*–65
O'Sullivan, Timothy, 395, 449, *449*
Ottoman empire, 205–7, *206*, *207*
Ottonian art, 240, 240–43
Our Hidden Heritage (book) (Tufts), 516
Our Lady of Guadalupe (Salcedo), 394, *394*

Outbreak, The (Kollwitz), *470*, 471
overlapping, 7, *7*

P

Pacal, Lord: portrait of, *389*; tomb-pyramid of, *388*, 388–89
Padua: Renaissance painting in, 309–10
Pagoda, Great Wild Goose, 82, *82*
Paik, Nam June, 523–24, *524*
painting, 8
   cave and rock, 86; African, 404; Indian, 72–73; meaning of
      prehistoric, 36; Neolithic, 37, *37*; technique of,
      35; Upper Paleolithic, 30, *30–31*, *34*, 34–36, *35*, *36*
   china, *516*, 517
   Chinese landscape, 216–17, *216–17*
   Color Field, 501, 504, *504*
   early Japanese, 85, *85*
   history, 422
   ink, 224, *225*
   lacquer, 84–85, *85*
   landscape, 216–17, *216–17*, 362, *362*, 433, *433–34*, *434*,
      518, *519*
   literati, 218–19, *218–19*
   miniature, 8
   moralized genre, 422–24, *423*, *424*, *425*
   Neoclassical, 419–24, 425, 427–29
   oil, 288, *291*, 328
   panel, 8, 279–83, 288
   on paper, *213*, 213–15
   photography inspiring, 492
   plein air, 453
   portrait, 149, *149*, 419, 419–22, 422
   Renaissance, 303–12
   sand, *521*, 521–22
   still-life, 377, *377*, 459
   in United States, 438–39, *439*
   vase, *103*, 103–5, *104*, *105*, 116, *116*
   wall, 8; catacomb, 164, *164–65*, *166*, 166–67, *170*, 170–71;
      of early India, 72–73, *74*; Etruscan, 123, *123*; Minoan,
      92, *93*, 94, *94*; prehistoric. See cave and rock paintings;
      Roman, 149, 149–52, *150*, 151
Palace Chapel of Charlemagne, 236, *236–37*
Palace Museum Beijing (the Forbidden City), *220*, 220–21
Palace of the Lions (Alhambra), 199; Court of the Lions at,
   199, 199–200; Hall of the Abencerrajes at, 200, *200*
Palacio de Bellas Artes, 495–97, *496*
Palazzo Rucellai (Alberti), 302, *302*
Palenque, Mexico, *388*, 388–89, *389*
palette, 5
Palette of Narmer, 52, 52–54, 402
palettes, 52, *52–54*
P and D (Pattern and Decoration) movement, 517
panel painting, 8; Cennini on, 279; Italian Gothic, 279–83;
   technique of, 288
Pan Painter: *Artemis Slaying Actaeon*, *105*, 106–7
Pansa, House of (Pompeii), 140, *140*
Pantheon, *154*, 154–55, 155; Alberti on, 303; Hagia Sophia
   compared, 176; Villa Rotunda influenced by, 334
Paolo Caliari. *See* Veronese
paper, 191; Indian painting on, *213*, 213–15
parchment, 191, 237
Paris exposition of 1925. See International Exposition of
   Modern Decorative and Industrial Arts (1925)
Paris Salon, 421
Paris Universal Exposition of 1937, 488–90
Parrhasios, 14
Parthenon (Athens), 26, 88, *88–89*, 108–11, *109*; east pedi-
   ment of, *110*, 111; *Lapith Fighting a Centaur* from, *110*,
   111; *Marshals and Young Women* from, *110*, 111; *Procession* from, *110*, 111, 114, 144
Parting of Lot and Abraham (Santa Maria Maggiore mosaic),
   173, 173–74
passage graves, 39, *39*
passage technique, 459, 477
Passion Cycle, 168–69
Pastoral Concert, The (Titian and Giorgione), 328–30, *329*, 453
patrons, 24–26; individual, 24–25; institutional, 25–26; monarchs as, 358

Peacock and Dragon curtain: by Morris, 447, *447*
Peacock Room (Whistler), 25, *25*, 447
Peasants' War (series) (Kollwitz), *470*, 471
pectoral (chest ornament), Egyptian, 59, *59*
pen box: Islamic, 188, *188–89*, 201–2, *202*
Pencil of Nature, The (Talbot), 435
pendant: Benin, 406, *406*; Minoan, 95
pendentives, 175
People and Animals (rock-shelter painting), 37, *37*
Peplos Kore, *102*, 103, 114
Performance art, 9, 512, *512*, 528
Pergamene art, *132*, *133*, 133–34, 134; altar to Zeus, *133*,
   133–34, *134*, 144
Perikles, 26, *26*
period style, 6
peristyle court: of New Kingdom Egypt, 61; at Temple of
   Hera I, *99*
Perry Lilla Cabot, 453
Persepolis, 128, *128*, *129*
Persian art, 120–21, 125–28, 162
Persistence of Memory, The (Dali), *490*, 491
Personal Appearance #3 (Schapiro), *516*, 516–17
perspective, 6, 289, 382; atmospheric, 7, *7*, 286, 289, 305,
   308; diagonal, 7, *7*; divergent, 7, *7*; intuitive, 7, *7*, 289;
   linear, 7, *7*, 286, 288, 289, 304, 311, 382; vertical, 7, *7*
Perugino, Pietro, 311, 311–12, 323; influence of, 319
Pesaro Madonna (Titian), *330*, 330–31
Petites Heures de Jeanne d'Evreux (Pucelle), 270–71, *271*, 296
Pheidias, 26, *26*
Pheidias and the Frieze of the Parthenon, Athens (Alma-Tade-
   ma), 26, *26*, 445
Philosophy or The School of Athens (Raphael), 314, *314–15*
Philoxenos, 134, *135*
Phoenicians, 120
Phoenix Hall, at Byodo-in, *221*, 221–22, *222*
photography, 8, 15, 436, 528; early, 434–36; early-20th-cen-
   tury American, 493–94, *494*, 495, *495*; of Farm Securities
   Administration (FSA), 493–94, *494*; late-19th-century
   American, 449; paintings inspired by, 492
Pia dé Tolomei, La (Rossetti), 446, *446*
Picasso, Pablo, 475–77, *476*, 489, 490, 505, 528; African art
   as influence on, 470, 475; collage by, *506*; influence of,
   506; shown in United States, 480; Surrealism and, 488,
   489
pictographs, 45; and Chinese characters, 81
pictorial depth, 6
picture plane, 6, *6*
picture space, 6, *6*
Piero della Francesca, 308, *308*
Pietà (Michelangelo), 321, 321–22
Pietàs. *See* Lamentation, The (Pietà)
Pilchuck Glass School, 513
Pilgrimage to Cythera, The (Watteau), 379–80, *380*
pipe, Hopewell, 394, *395*, 414
Pisano, Nicola, 276, *276*
Pittura, La (Gentileschi), 358, *358*
Plane Trees, Place des Lices, Saint-Tropez, Opus 242 (Signac),
   462, 463, *463*
Plan for Contemporary City of Three Million Inhabitants (Le
   Corbusier), *484*, 484
plans, in architectural graphics, 9, *9*
Plato, 114; on beauty, 16–17; in *School of Athens* (Raphael),
   314, *314–15*, 320, *320*
Platonic ideal, 16–17
plein air painting, 453
Plenty's Boast (Puryear), 520, *520*
Pliny the Elder, 107, 116, 139
Plowing in the Nivernais: The Dressing of the Vines (Bonheur),
   436, *437*
pluralism, 513
Poet on a Mountain Top (Shen Zhou), *218*, 219
Poetry and the Arts (Raphael), *314–15*
pointillism, 440, *440*, *441*, 459, 463. See also divisionism
Pollaiuolo, Antonio del, 312, *312*
Pollock, Jackson, 501–2, *502*, 504, 506, 511
polychromy, 5
Polydoros, 27, 28
Polykleitos, *114*, 114–16
Pomo, 397, *397*, 414

Pompeii, 140, *140*; wall paintings of, 149, 149–52, *150*, 151
Pont du Gard, *141*, 141–42
Pontormo, Jacopo da, 335, *335*, 338
Pop art, 506, 507–10
porcelain, of Chinese Ming period, 219, *219*
Porch of the Maidens (Mnesikles), 112, *112*
Portinari Altarpiece (Hugo), 293, 293–94
portrait heads: Egyptian, 63, *63*; Greek, 6, 117, *117*; Roman,
   6, 148, 149
Portrait of a Young Man (Bronzino), 336, *336*
Portrait of Giovanni Arnolfini and His Wife, Giovanna Cenami
   (Van Eyck), 291, 291–92
Portrait of Marie Antoinette with Her Children (Vigée-Lebrun),
   419, *419*
Portrait of Mrs. Richard Brinsley Sheridan (Gainsborough),
   421, *421*
Portrait of Thomas Carlyle (Cameron), 435–36, *436*
portrait painting: Neoclassic and Romantic, 419, 419–22, 422;
   Roman, 149, *149*
Portugal, Hispano-Flemish art of, 294, *294–95*
Portuguese Synagogue, Amsterdam (de Witte), 375, *375*
Portunus, 139, *139*
Poseidon, 100
Positivist Age, 418
post-and-lintel construction, 11, *11*, 38; of Lion Gate, 97, *97*
Post-Impressionism, 457–65, 528
Post-Minimalism, 511, *511*
Postmodernism, 506, 513–27, 528
pottery. *See* ceramics
poussinistes, 360
Poussin, Nicolas, 360, 361–62, *362*; influence of, 427
power figure (*nkisi nkonde*), Kongo, 409–11, *410*
Prague, Altneuschul in, *275*, 275–76
Praxiteles, 115, 116–17, 131
Precisionists, 492, 492–93
Pre-Columbian art: Moore and, 482; Rivera and, 495
prehistoric art, 31–41; fiber art, 53; naming of, 34
Pre-Raphaelite Brotherhood, 445–46
Presentation in the Temple, The, 168
primary hue, 5
Primaticcio, Francesco, 338, 338–39
"primitive" art, 405, 414; Moore and, *481*, 481–82
primitivism, 470
Princess from the Land of Porcelain, The (Whistler), 25, *25*,
   447
Principles of Painting, The (de Piles), 360
printmaking, 8
   engravings, 8, *312*, 312–13, *313*, 342–43, *343*
   etchings, 8, 372, *372*, 373, *470*, 471
   in Renaissance Europe, *312*, 312–13, *313*, 342–43, *343*
   woodblock, 8; Japanese, 17–18, *18*, 227–29, *228*, 229, 455,
      457, 462, 463; Renaissance, 312, *312*
Procession (Parthenon frieze), *110*, 111, 114, 144
Processional Way (Babylon), 125, 127
"Project for the Affirmation of the New" (Prouns), 482, *482*
Prophet Muhammad and His Companions Traveling to the Fair,
   The (al-Zarir), 191, *191*
Protestant Netherlands, 371–77, 380–81, 382
Protestant Reformation, 316, 343, 382
Prouns, 482, *482*
Public Works of Art Project, 495, *495*
Pucelle, Jean, 270–71, *271*
Pueblo Bonito, 396, *396*
Pueblo communities, 395–96, *396*, *397*
pulpit, Italian Gothic, 276, *276*
punchwork, Sienese, *278*, 279
Punitavati (Karaikkalammaiyar), 18, *18*, 212
Pure Land Buddhism, 221; temples of, *221*, 221–22, *222*
Purism, architecture of, *484*, 484
purse cover, from Sutton Hoo burial ship, 234–35, *235*
Puryear, Martin, 520, *520*
pylon of Ramesses II, 61, 61–63
pyramid(s), 56; Great, 56, *57*; King Djoser's, *54*, 55; King
   Khufu's, 56, *57*; Maya, *388*, 388–89, *389*

Q

qibla wall, 192, *193*, 198
Qin Shihuangdi, 77; terra-cotta soldiers in tomb of, 66, *66*,
   67, *77*, 77–78, 86

Queen Nefertari Making an Offering to Isis (Egyptian tomb painting), *62*, 63
Queen Tiy (Egyptian portrait head), 63, *63*
Quick-to-See Smith, Jaune, *522*, 522–23
quillwork embroidery, Native American, 398, *398*

R

Raft of the "Medusa" (Géricault), *429*, 429–30. *See also Shipwreck Scene, A*
Raimondi, Marcantonio, 453
Raising of Lazarus (Giotto), 283, *283*
Raising of Lazarus, The, 168
Raising of the Cross, The (Rubens), 366, *366*
Rajarajeshvara Temple, 211, *211*, 215
Rajput painting, 213–15
raku ceramics, 227, *227*
Ramesses II, 61, 61–63
Raphael Sanzio, 314, *314–15*, 316, *318*, *323*; grading of, 360; influence of, 336, 337, 427, 428, 453; and Saint Peter's, 326
Rauschenberg, Robert, 506, *506*, 507, 508
Rayonnant architectural style, 268
ready-mades, 487–88, *488*
re aedificatoria, De (On Architecture) (Alberti), 302–3
realism, 7, 418; in United States, 449–51, *492*, 492–93, *493*, 500
Realism, 445; 19th-century French, 436–38
Recumbent Figure (Moore), *481*, 481–82
Red-Blue Chair (Rietveld), 483, *483*
Red Canna (O'Keeffe), *15*, 15–16
red-figure decoration, Greek, 104–5, *105*, 106–7
reductive sculpture, 8
Reformation art, 343–46, 382
Regionalists, *493*, 493
regional style, 6–7
Rehearsal of the Ballet on Stage, The (Degas), *454*, 455
Reid, Bill, 401, *401*
Reims Cathedral, 264–67, *266*; sculpture at, *267*
reinforced concrete, 11, *11*
relics: of Christian saints, 247, *247*, *268*, 269; in stupas, 70–71
relief, 8; of Han emperor's shrine, 79, *79*; sunken, 8, *62*
relieving arch: of Lion Gate, 97, *97*
reliquaries, 234; French Gothic, 269, *269*; in Horyu-ji temple, 84; Romanesque, 247, *247*
Rembrandt van Rijn, *23*, 23–24, 360, *371*, 371–73, *372*; influence of, 416, 431
Renaissance art: early, 286–313, 382; high, 314–49, 382; in Italy, 296–312; in Low Countries, 288–96; in Venice, 328–34
Renaissance perspective. *See* linear perspective
Renoir, Pierre-Auguste, 453, *456*, 456–57
Repin, Ilya, 438, *438*
representational art, 6
Residenz, Kaisersaal of (Bavaria) (Neumann), 378, *379*
restoration, of art, *27*, 27–28, *28*
Resurrection (Giotto), 283, *283*
Resurrection of Jesus, 169; depictions of, 185–86, *186*, 283, *283*
Riace Warriors, 107–8, *108*, 114
rib vaulting, 255, *255*
Riemenschneider, Tilman, *344*, 344–45
Rietveld, Gerrit, 483, *483*
Rigaud, Hyacinthe, 358, *358*
Riley, Bridget, 510, *510*
rituals, and art, *19*, 19–20, *20*
Rivera, Diego, 495–97, *496*
Road to Calvary, 169
rock paintings. *See* cave and rock paintings
Rococo art, 350–81, 424
rod. *See* staff
Rodin, Auguste, 464, *464*, 465; shown at Stieglitz's gallery, 480
Roman architectural orders, 147, *147*
Roman art, 137–63, 162; copying Greek art, 136, *136–37*; Early Empire period of, 143–45; Empire period of, 145–52; "Good Emperors" period of, 152–57; Greek art influencing, 135; Late Empire period of, 158–61; Republican period of, 139–42
Roman Catholic Church, 284; in Americas, 393–94; Counter-

Reformation of, 350, 352–58, 382; following Reformation, 350; during Reformation, 316; during Romanesque period, 245
Romanesque art, 233–55
Roman gods: as counterparts of Greek gods, 138, 139. *See also specific gods, e.g.,* Bacchus
Romanticism, 416, *416–17*, 429–34, 469, 528; Neoclassicism and, 428–29, 469
Rome: churches of, 171, *172*, 172–74, *173*, 339–41, *340*, 350, *350*, *351*, 352–55, 354, *354*, *356*, 357; Colusseum of, 145–46, *146*; French Academy in, 428; Renaissance painting in, 311–12; Vatican in. *See* Vatican
Rondanini Pietà (Michelangelo), 328, *328*
Room of the Signature (Stanza della Segnatura) (Vatican), 314, *314–15*
Rope Piece (Hesse), 511, *511*
Rose and Silver: The Princess from the Land of Porcelain (Whistler), 25, *25*, 447
rose windows, of Reims Cathedral, 264, 266, *266*
Rossetti, Dante Gabriel, 445–46, *446*
Rosso Fiorentino, 338
Rothko, Mark, 504, *504*
round arch, 141, *141*, 142
roundels, Roman, 155–56, *156*
Rousseau, Jean-Jacques, 419
Royal Academy of Architecture (France), 359
Royal Academy of Arts (England), 422, *422*, 433; reactions against, 445–47
Royal Academy of Painting and Sculpture (France), 358–59, 360, 361, 421, 422, 427, 444
rubénistes, 360
Rubens, Peter Paul, 360, 365–69, *366*, *367*, *368*, 370, *370*; influence of, 504
Rublyov, Andrey, 186–87, *187*
Rue Transonian, Le 15 Avril 1834 (Daumier), 28–29, *29*
Rush Hour, New York (Weber), *480*, 480–81
Russia: after World War I, 482, *482*; realism in, 438, *438*. *See also* Soviet Union
Ruysch, Rachel, 377, *377*, 380–81
Ryder, Albert Pinkham, *450*, 451, 469

S

Saar, Betye, 517, *517*
Saint Augustine Teaching in Rome (Gozzoli), 289
Saint Cyriakus, Church of (Gernrode), 242, *242*
Saint-Denis, Abbey Church of (France), 19–20, 256, *258*, 259; reliquary from, 268–69, *269*
Sainte-Chapelle (Paris), 267–68, *268*
Sainte-Foy, Abbey Church of (France), 246, *246*
Saint-Étienne, Church of (France), 255, *255*
Saint Foy (Saint Faith): Abbey Church of, 246, *246*; reliquary statue of, 247, *247*
Saint Francis in Ecstasy (Giovanni Bellini), 310–11, *311*
Saint Francis of Assisi, Basilica of (Italy), 28
Saint Gall, Abbey of (Switzerland), 237, 237–38
Saint James, Cathedral of the (Santiago de Compostela, Spain), 18–19, *19*, 246–48
Saint Joseph Master (Master of the Smiling Angels), 267, *267*
Saint-Lazare, Cathedral of (France), 249, 249–50, *250*, 284
Saint Luke Displaying a Painting of the Virgin (Il Guercino), *22*, 22–23
Saint Michael, Abbey Church of (Germany), 240; bronze doors of, 240–42, *241*
Saint Peter, 164, 169
Saint Peter's Basilica (Vatican), 314, 321, 326; baldachin for, *352*, 352–53; expansion of, 352; Old, *170*, 171–72, *321*, 321–22, 325–27, *326*; rebuilding of, 325–27; square of, 353, *353*
Saint-Savin-sur-Gartempe, Abbey Church of (Poitou, France), 248, *248*
Saint-Simon, Comte de, 459
Saint Teresa of Ávila in Ecstasy (Bernini), 350, *350*, *351*, 352, 353, 354
Saint Vincent with the Portuguese Royal Family (Gonçalvez), *294*, 294–95
Salcedo, Sebastian, 394, *394*
Salisbury Cathedral (England), 273, *273*
Salon d'Automn of 1905, 469
Salon des Refusés, 452

Saltcellar of Francis I of France (Cellini), 339, *339*
Samarkand ware, 196, *197*
San Clemente, Church of (Tahull, Spain), *244*, 245, 248
sanctuaries, for Greek gods, 99
Sand, Georges, 437
sand painting, Australian Aboriginal, *521*, 521–22
San Giovanni, Baptistry of (Florence), *299*, 299–301
San Lorenzo, Church of (Florence), 301, 301–2, 303
San Marco, Cathedral of (Venice), 182, *182*
San Marco, Monastery of (Florence), 305–6, *306*
sans serif typography, 484
Santa Felicitá, Church of (Capponi Chapel) (Florence), 301, 335, *335*
Sant'Agostino, Church of (Italy), 289, *289*, 307–8
Santa Maria del Carmine, Church of (Florence), *304*, 304–5, 305
Santa Maria della Vittoria, Church of (Rome), 350; Cornaro Chapel in, 354, *354*; *Saint Teresa of Ávila in Ecstasy* in, 350, *350*, *351*, 352, 353, 354
Santa Maria delle Grazie, Monastery of (Milan), 316, *317*
Santa Maria Maggiore, Church of (Rome), 171, *172*; mosaic in, *173*, 173–74
Santa Maria Novella, Church of (Florence), 303, *303*
Sant'Apollinare, Church of (Ravenna, Italy), 178–80, *179*
Santa Sabina, Church of (Rome), *172*, 172–73
Santa Sophia, Cathedral of (Kiev), 184, *184*
San Vitale, Church of (Ravenna, Italy), 177, *177–78*, 178
Sappho, 99; in *School of Athens* (Raphael), 314
sarcophagus(i): Etruscan, 123–24, *124*; of Tutankhamun, 64, *64–65*
saturation, 5
Satyricon (Petronius), 136
Scandinavia, early medieval art in, *234*, 234–36
Schapiro, Miriam, *516*, 516–17
Scholastic philosophy, 259
Schongauer, Martin, 312, 313, *313*
school, defined, 8
School of Athens or Philosophy (Raphael), 314, *314–15*, 319, *320*, 320–21
Schröder House (Rietveld), 483, *483*
Schröder-Schrader, Truus, 483
science: of 17th century, 376, 380–81; of 18th century, 376, 380–81, 418, 528
scientific perspective. *See* linear perspective
Scourging, The, 169
Scream, The (Munch), *468*, 469
script: cuneiform, 45; *kana*, 222, 222–23; seal, 81
scriptoria: medieval, 237; Romanesque, 251
Scrovegni Chapel (Giotto), *282*, 282–83, *283*
sculpture, 8; Baroque, 354; Benin, 10, *10*, 405, *405*, 406, *406*; French Gothic, 267, *267*, 268–69, *269*; Italian Gothic, 276; Italian Renaissance, 297–301; kinetic, 506; Maya, 389, *389*; Minimalist, *510*, 510–11, *511*; Neoclassic and Romantic, 418, 418–19, 444, 444–45; of New York School, 504–5, *505*; Nok, 404, 404–5; Ottonian, 240; Post-Impressionist, 464, 464–65, *465*; Reformation, 344, 344–45; Roman, 155–56, *156*, 157, *157*; Romanesque, 248–51, *249*; Shona, 408; site-specific, 515, 515–16; Yoruba, 404, 405, 413, *413*
sculpture in the round, 8; *Seated Harp Player* as, *90*, 91
Scythian art, 120, *124*, 124–25, 162
Scythian stag (shield plaque), *124*, 124–25
Seagram Building (Mies), 513, *513*, 515
seals: of Indus Valley, *68*, 69; Sumerian cylinder, 48–49, *49*; on Wang Xizhi's calligraphy, 81, *81*
seal script, 81
Seasons, The (Krasner), 502, *502*
Seated Guanyin Bodhisattva, 215, *215*
Seated Harp Player, *90*, 91
Seaweed, Willie, 399, *400*
secondary colors, 5
sections, in architectural graphics, 9, *9*
seed jar, Anasazi, *396*, 397
Self-Portrait (Caterina van Hemessen), 346, *346*
Self-Portrait (Dürer), 342, *342*
Self-Portrait (Leyster), 373, 373–74
Self-Portrait (Rembrandt van Rijn), *372*, 373
Self-Portrait as a Fountain (Nauman), 512, *512*, 528
Self-Portrait with an Amber Necklace (Modersohn-Becker),

469, 469–70

Self-Portrait with Two Pupils, Mademoiselle Marie Gabrielle Capet (1761–1818) and Mademoiselle Carreaux de Rosemond (d.1788) (Labille-Guiard), *420*, 421

Selimiye Cami (Mosque of Selim) (Sinan), 193, 206, *206*

Senefelder, Aloys, 462

Senior, 196, 239

Sen no Rikyu, 226

serpentine bench (Gaudi), *448*, 449

settlements, Neolithic, 37–38, *38*, 44

Seurat, Georges, 440, *440*, 441, 457, *459*, 459–60, 463

Seven Portraits (Haft Paykar) (Nizami), 202, *203*

Severn River Bridge (Darby), *442*, 443

sfumato, in *Mona Lisa*, 318

Shazi, pen box by, 188, *188–89*, 201–2, *202*

Sheeler, Charles, *492*, 492–93

sheep, as Christian symbol, 180

Shen Zhou, *218*, 219

Sherman, Cindy, 517–18, *518*

She-Wolf, *120*, 121

shikhara, 211

Shimomura, Roger, 29, *29*, 229

Shinto, 83–84

Shipwreck Scene, A (Géricault), *429*, 429–30. *See also* Raft of the Medusa

Shiva, *75*; and *bhakti* movement, 212, *212*, 215; temples honoring, 75, *75*–76, 210, *210*, 211, *211*

Shiva saint, 18, *18*, 212

Shona art, 408, *408*

Siena Cathedral, *278*, 279

Sienese painting, 8, *278*, 279, 283

Sight (Breughel and Rubens), 368, *368*, 369

Signac, Paul, 457, 459, 462–64, *463*

silk, making of, 80

Silk Road, 80

Silver Wedding, House of the (Pompeii), 140, *140*

simultaneity, 478

Sinan, 193, 206, *206*

Sioux, 398, *398*, 414

Sistine Chapel (Vatican), 323; ceiling of, 322–24, *323*, *324*, 355; *Delivery of the Keys to Saint Peter* in, *311*, 311–12; *Last Judgment* in, 323, 324–25, 325; tapestries for, 321, *323*

site-specific sculpture, *515*, 515–16

Siyar-i Nabi (Life of the Prophet) (al-Zarir), *191*

sketches, 8

Sky Cathedral (Nevelson), *505*, 505–6

skyscrapers, 443, *443*, 490, *490*; High Tech, *514*, 515; of Le Corbusier, *484*; by Mies, 513, *513*

Slavophile movement, 479

Sleep of Reason Produces Monsters, The (Goya), *430*, 431, 432

slip, Greek, 104

Small Cowper Madonna, The (Raphael), *318*, 319

small scale sculpture, 8

Smith, David, 6, 16, *16*, 29, 505–6

Smith, Kiki, 519, *519*–20

Smithson, Robert, *515*, 515–16

Snap the Whip (Homer), *450*, 450–51

soapstone sculpture, Shona, 408, *408*

social context, art and, 21–22

Société Anonyme des Artistes Peintres, Sculpteurs, Graveurs, etc., 453

sociopolitical intentions, in art, 28–29

Socrates, 114

Solomon R. Guggenheim Museum (Wright), 25, *26*, 515, 523, *523*

Sosos, 136, 152

South America, 387, 391–94; Machu Picchu in, 392, *392*; Spanish conquest of, 393

South asian art. *See* Indian art

Soviet Union: after World War I, 490; since World War II, 500. *See also* Russia

space, 5; Byzantine depiction of, 178; depicting recession in, 5, 7, *7*; picture, 6, *6*

space-spanning construction devices, 11, *11*

spacial attributes, 5

Spain: Civil War of, 489, *489*; Habsburg Empire in, 362–65; medieval Christian, 239–40; Mexico invaded by, 389, 390, 391; Napoleonic rule of, 419, 431–32, *432*; Neoclassicism

of, 430–32

spandrels, 141, *141*

Spear Bearer (Doryphorus) (Polykleitos), *114*, 114–16, 136, 142

sphinx: at Giza, 13, *13*, 14, 24; of Taharqo, *65*

spinning, early, *53*

Spiral Jetty (Smithson), *515*, 515–16

spiral shape, 516

Spirit of Haida Gwaii, The (Reid), 401, *401*

spirit spouse (*blolo bla*), *410*, 411

Spoils from the Temple of Solomon, 148

Spring Showers (Stieglitz), 479, *480*

squinches, 175

staff, 402; Asante speaker's, 402, *402*, *403*

stained-glass windows, 264; of Chartres Cathedral, 256, *256*, *257*, 263, *263*, *264*; of Reims Cathedral, 264–66

Stair Hall of Seattle Art Museum (Venturi and Brown), *514*

Stalpaert, Daniel, 375

Standing Buddha (sculpture), 72, *72*

Stanton, Elizabeth Cady, 442

Stanza della Segnatura (Room of the Signature) (Vatican, Rome), 314, *314–15*

Starry Night, The (Van Gogh), 461, *461*

statues: Egyptian, *55*, 55–56, *56*; French Gothic, 268–69, *269*; Greek, 101–3, *106*, *107*, 107–8, *108*, *114*, 114–17, *115*, *117*, 130, *130*; reliquary, 247, *247*, 269, *269*

steel, architectural, 11, *11*, 443

Steen, Jan, 22, *23*, 375

Steichen, Edward, 480

Stela of Hammurabi, 50, 51

Stela of Naramsin, 49, *49*

Stieglitz, Alfred, 479–80, *480*, 492

Stile floreale. *See* Art Nouveau

Stile Liberty. *See* Art Nouveau

still-life paintings: by Cézanne, *458*, 459; Dutch, *7*, *14*, 14–15, *29*, 377, *377*, 380–81

Still Life with Basket of Apples (Cézanne), *458*, 459

Stonehenge, 39, *39*–40, 86

storage jar, Anasazi, *396*, 397

St. Petersburg Academy of Art, 438

Street, Berlin (Kirchner), *472*, 472–73, 475, 487

stucco, Etruscan, 123

studies, 8

stupa(s), 70–71, *71*; Great, 70, *70*, 71, *71*; pagodas compared, 82

style, 6–8

stylistic analysis, 6

stylus, 45

subject matter, 6

Succulent (Weston), 15, *15*

Suicide of Ajax, The (Exekias), 102–3, *103*

Suleyman "the Magnificent," Sultan, 206, 207; *tughra of*, 207, *207*

Sullivan, Louis, 443, *443*

Sumerian art, 45–49

Sunday Afternoon on the Island of La Grande Jatte, A (Seurat), 440, *440*, 441, *459*, 459–60

Sunflowers (Van Gogh), 460, *461*

sunken relief, 8, *62*

Super Realism, *520*, 520–21

Supper at Emmaus, The, 169

Suprematism, 479

Suprematist Painting (Eight Red Rectangles) (Malevich), *479*

Surrealism, 481, 488–91, 528; Abstract Expressionism and, 500, 501; Frankenthaler and, 504; Kahlo and, 497; O'Keeffe and, 492

suspension works, 11, *11*

Suzuki Harunobu, 228, *228*

symbolic image. *See* icons, Byzantine

symbols, 6

synagogue(s), 167; Gothic, *275*, 275–76; mosaic floor of, *167*, 167–68; with Torah niche, *166*

Synthetic Cubism, 477, *477*, 495

Syon House renovations (Adam), 425–26, *426*

T

tabouret, by Legrain, *470*, *470*

tachisme, 500

Taj Mahal, 204–5, *205*, 212

Talbot, William Henry Fox, 434–35

Tale of Genji, The, 223–24, *224*

talud-tablero construction, 388

Tamamushi Shrine, 84–85, *85*

Tamil Nadu, art of, *214*, 215

Taos Pueblo, 397, *397*

tapestries, *297*; Flemish, 296, *297*; Norman, *252*, 253; for Sistine Chapel, 321, *323*

Tàpies, Antoni, 500, *500*

Target with Four Faces (Johns), 506, *507*

Tassel House (Horta), 448

tea ceremony, Japanese, 226–27, *227*, 230

tempera, 279, 288

Tempietto shrine (Bramante), 326

temples: Buddhist, *81*, 81–82, 84–85, *85*, *221*, 221–22, *222*; Egyptian, 60, *60*, 61, *61*; Etruscan, 122, *122*; Greek, 99–101, 108–14; Hindu, *75*, 75–76, 210, 210–11, *211*, 215; Maya, *388*, 388–89; Roman, 139, *139*; Sumarian, 44, 45; Zen, 208, *208–9*, 224–26, *226*

Temptation of Saint Anthony (Schongauer), 312, *313*

tenebrism, 358, 363

Tenochtitlan, 390, 393

Teotihuacan art, 387–88; ceremonial center in, *386*; Ciudadela in, *387*, 388

tepee, Native American, 398

terra-cotta sculpture: Etruscan, *121*, 121–22; Nok style, *404*, 404–5; from Qin mausoleum, 66, *66*, *67*, *77*, 77–78, 86

tesserae, 152

textile art. *See* fiber art(s)

textile production: early, *53*

texture, 5

Thamyris, 295

theaters, ancient Greek, 129, *129*

Third of May, 1808 (Goya), 432, *432*

Thirty-six Immortal Poets (Ishiyama-gire), 223, *223*

Thirty-six Views of Fuji (Katsushika Hokusai), 229; *The Great Wave* from, 229, *229*

Three Crosses, The (Rembrandt van Rijn), 372, *373*

three-dimensional art, 8–9

Throne of the Third Heaven of the Nations' Millenium General Assembly (Hampton), 20, *20*, 506

Thus Spoke Zarathustra (Nietzsche), 472

Tiepolo, Giovanni Battista, 378, *379*

tile work, Islamic, 197–99

Timarete, 116

Tinguely, Jean, 506–7, 508, *508*

Tintoretto, 332–33, *333*, 348

Titian Vecelli, 316, 328–31, *329*, *330*, *331*; influence of, 331, 332, 348, 360, 452, 453, 504

Ti Watching a Hippopotamus Hunt, 58, *58*

Tjapaltjarri, Clifford Possum, 521, *521*–22

Tlaloc, 390

Tlingit people, 399, *400*, 401

tomb(s)

    Egyptian, 54, *54*, 56–58, *57*, *58*, 59, *59*

    of the Lionesses, 123, *123*

    mastaba as, 54, 56, 58, *58*

    mausoleum(s): of Galla Placidia, *173*, 174, *174*; of Qin Shi huangdi, 66, *66*, *67*, *77*, 77–78; of Sultan Hasan, *198*, 199

    Mycenaean, *96*, 96–97, *97*

    Neolithic, 39, *39*

    pyramid(s), 56; Great, 56, *57*; King Djoser's, *54*, 55; King Khufu's, 56, *57*; Maya, *388*, 388–89, *389*

    of the Reliefs, burial chamber of, *122*, 123

tornana(s), 71; of Great Stupa, 71, *71*

Toulouse-Lautrec, Henri de, 457, 461–62, *462*, 475, 480

Trade (Gifts for Trading Land with White People) (Quick-to-See Smith), *522*, 522–23

Transfiguration of Christ with Saint Apollinaris, First Bishop of Ravenna, The, 178–80, *179*

Transfiguration, The, 168

Travelers among Mountains and Streams (Fan Kuan), 216, *216*

"Treasury of Atreus," *96*, 96–97, *97*

Tree of Jesse (from Chartres Cathedral), *263*, 264

Très Riches Heures (Very Sumptuous Hours) (Limbourg brothers), 295–96, *296*

Tribute in Light, 526, *527*

Tribute Money (Masaccio), 304–5, *305*

Tribute Money, The, 168
Trinity with the Virgin, Saint John the Evangelist, and Donors (Masaccio), *303*, 303–4
Triptych of the Annunciation (Campin), *289*, 290
Triumph of the Name of Jesus (Gaulli), *356*, 357
Triumph of Venice, The (Veronese), *21*, 21–22, 24, 332
trompe l'oeil, 152; Postmodern, *520*, 520–21
trusses, 11, *11*
Tufts, Eleanor, 516
tughras, 207; of Sultan Suleyman, 207, *207*
tunic, Inca, *384*, 385, *385*, 392–93, *393*, 414
Turner, Joseph Mallord William, 433–34, *434*
Tuscan order, 147, *147*
Tutankhamun, 63; funerary mask of, 42, *42*, *43*; sarcophagus of, 64, *64–65*; tomb of, 64
Twelve Views from a Thatched Hut (Xia Gui), *216–17*, 217
twin figures (*ere ibeji*), 413, *413*
two-dimensional art, 8; in representation of architecture, 9
Two Fridas, The (Kahlo), *496*, 497
291, (Stieglitz's gallery), 480, 492
typography, sans serif, *484*
typology, of Giotto, 283

U

Uccello, Paolo, 286, *286*, 287, 306–7, *307*
ukiyo-e prints, 227–29, *228*
Unicorn is Found, The (from Hunt of the Unicorn tapestry series), 296, *297*
Unique Forms of Continuity in Space (Boccioni), 478, *478*
United States: 19th-century art in, 438–39, *439*, 442–65, 449–51; modernism in, 479–81; Neoclassicism in, *426*, 426, 449; realistic art in, 438–39, *439*; since World War II, 500
Unswept Floor, The (Heraklitos), *136*, 136–37
Untitled (Judd), *510*, 511
Untitled (Kiki Smith), *519*, 519–20
Untitled Film Still (Sherman), *518*, 518
Untitled Plate (Voulkos), *512*, 512
Untitled (Selections from Truisms, Inflammatory Essays, The Living Series, The Survival Series, Under a Rock, Laments, and Mother and Child Text) (Holzer), 523, *523*
Upper Paleolithic art, *32*, 32–36, *33*
Utamaro, Kitagawa, 17–18, *18*, 23, 229

V

value, 5
van der Spelt, Adriaen, 7, *14*, 14–15, 29
VanDerZee, James, 495, *495*
van Dyck, Anthony, 360, 369, *369*, 421
van Eyck, Jan, 288, 289, *290*, 290–92, *291*, 293, 294, 295
van Gogh, Theo, 461
van Gogh, Vincent, 448, 457, 460–61, *461*, 469, 528; Signac and, 462, 463
van Hemessen, Caterina, 346, *346*
vanishing points, 7, *7*
vanitas subject matter, 375
Vannucci, Pietro. *See* Perugino, Pietro
Vasari, Giorgio, 26, 306–7
vase: Guan Ware, 217, *217*; Sumarian, 46, *46*
Vase Painter and Assistants Crowned by Athena and Victories, A, 116, *116*
vase painting, Greek, *103*, 103–5, *104*, 105; depiction of, 116, *116*
Vatican
    Saint Peter's Basilica at. *See* Saint Peter's Basilica (Vatican)
    Sistine Chapel at, *323*; ceiling of, 322–24, *323*, *324*, 355; *Delivery of the Keys to Saint Peter* in, *311*, 311–12; *Last Judgment* in, *323*, 324–25, *325*; tapestries for, 321, *323*
    Stanza della Segnatura in, 314, *314–15*, *319*, 319–21, *320*
vault, 11, *11*; barrel, 141, *141*; corbelled, *96*, 96–97; groin, 141, *141*, 255, *255*; rib, 255, *255*
Vauxalles, Louis, 471, 477
Velázquez, Diego Rodrigues de Silva y, 362–64, *363*, *364*; influence of, 431
vellum, 191, 237
Venice: High Renaissance art in, 328–34; Renaissance painting in, 310–11
Venturi, Robert, 513–15, *514*

Venus, 34, 308–9; depictions of, 7, 17, *17*, 34, 116, 130, *130*, 131, 308–9, *309*, 331, *331*, 452
Venus de Milo (marble), 130, *130*
"Venus" figurines, 34
Venus of Urbino (Titian), 331, *331*, 452
Venus of Willendorf. See Woman from Willendorf
Vermeer, Jan (Johannes), *374*, 375
Veronese, *21*, 21–22, 24, 331–32, *332*, 333, 360
Versailles, Palais de, 359–61, *360*; Hall of Mirrors in, 360–61, *361*
vertical perspective, 7, *7*
Very Sumptuous Hours (*Très Riches Heures*) (Limbourg brothers), 295–96, *296*
video art, 523–25, *524*, *525*, 528
Vietnam War, responding to, 510
Vietnam Veterans Memorial (Maya Ying Lin), 143, 498, *498–99*, *525*, 525–26
Vigée-Lebrun, Marie-Louise-Élisabeth, 419, 422
Vignola, Giacomo da, 339–41, *340*
Vikings, 236
Villa Capra (Palladio), 334, *334*
Villa of Livia (Primaporta), 151, *151*
Villa of the Mysteries (Pompeii), 151, 151–52
Villa Rotunda (Palladio), 334, *334*
Viola, Bill, 524, *524*
Violet Persian Set with Red Lip Wraps (Chihuly), 22, 23
Violin and Palette (Braque), *476*, 477
Virgin and Child (from Abbey of Saint-Denis), 268–69, *269*, 271
Virgin and Child Enthroned (Cimabue), 280, 280–81
Virgin and Child Enthroned (Giotto), 281, 281–82
Virgin and Child in Majesty, 250, 250–51
Virgin and Child in Majesty (*Maestà*) (Duccio), 278, 279
Virgin and Child with Saints and Angels, 181, *181*
Vishnu, 76, 213
Visitation (from Reims Cathedral), 267, *267*
Visitation, The, 168
Vitruvian Man (Leonardo da Vinci), 316, *316*
Vitruvius Pollio, Marcus, 122, 316, 359
volume, 5
votive statues: of Gudea, 49–51, *50*; Sumerian, 46–47, *47*–48
Voulkos, Peter, 512, *512*

W

Wainwright Building (Sullivan), 443, *443*
wall hanging, Romanesque embroidered, *252*, 253
wall paintings, 8
    catacomb, 164, *164–65*, *166*, 166–67, *170*, 170–71
    of early India, 72–73, *74*
    Etruscan, 123, *123*
    Minoan, 92, *93*, 94, *94*
    prehistoric, 36, 86; African, 404; Indian, 72–73; Neolithic, 37, *37*; technique of, 35; Upper Paleolithic, 30, *30–31*, 34, 34–36, *35*, *36*
    Roman, 149, 149–52, *150*, *151*
Walters Art Gallery (Baltimore), 516
Waltz, The (Claudel), 465, *465*
Wanderers, the, 438
Wang Xizhi, 81, *81*
Warhol, Andy, 508–9, *509*, 528
warp, in Asante weaving, 412
Water Carrier of Seville (Velázquez), 363, *363*
Water Lilies (Monet), 457, *457*
Watteau, Jean-Antoine, 379–80, *380*
weaving, early, 53
Webb, Philip, 447
Weber, Max, *480*, 480–81
Wedgwood, Josiah, 433
weft, in Asante weaving, 412
Weston, Edward, 15, *15*, 492
westwork, 237
Weyden, Rogier van der, 288, 292, *292*, 293, 294
Whistler, James Abbott McNeill, 25, *25*, 447, 479
Whitehall Banqueting House, 369–70, *370*
White Horse, The (Constable), 433, *433*
White Temple, 44, 45
White with Graphism (Tàpies), 500, *500*
"Why Have There Been No Great Women Artists?" (essay) (Nochlin), 516

William Hurley Lantern Tower, of Ely Cathedral, 273, *274*
Woman at the Height of Her Beauty (Utamaro), 17–18, *18*, 229
Woman from Brassempouy, 32, 33, *33*
Woman from Willendorf, 33, *33*
Woman Holding a Balance (Vermeer), *374*, 375
Womanhouse (Chicago and Schapiro), 517
Woman I (Willem de Kooning), 502, *503*
Woman Spinning (Assyrian tablet), 53
women: and beauty, *17*, 17–18, *18*; in Ottonian Empire, 242; as patrons of the arts, 329
women artists: of ancient Greece, 116, *116*; in art academies, 422, *422*; feminist, *516*, 516–18, *517*, *518*; of High Renaissance, 336–38, *337*; of late Middle Ages and Renaissance, 295, *295*; Mozarabic, 196; of Romanesque period, 251; studying in Italy, 444, 444–45. *See also specific artists, e.g.,* O'Keefe, Georgia
Women at a Fountain House ("A.D." Painter), 104, *104*
Women of Algiers (Delacroix), 430, *430*
woodblock prints, 8; Japanese, 17–18, *18*, 227–29, *228*, *229*, 455, 457, 462, 463; Renaissance, 312, *312*
Wood, Grant, 493, *493*
wood sculpture: African, 408; Japanese, 222, *222*; Postmodern, 513, 520, *520*; Yorbua, 20, *20*, 411, 411–12
Worcester Chronicle (John of Worchester), 251–52, *252*
"workshop of," defined, 8
World of Art (magazine), 478–79
World of Art group, 479
World's Fair: of 1929 in Barcelona, 485; of 1937 in Paris, 488–90
World Trade Center tribute, 526, *527*
World War I, 468, 481; European art after, 481–92; North American art after, 492–97
World War II, 468; art since, 499–527
Wright, Frank Lloyd, 25, *26*, 485–86, *486*, 515, 516, 523
Wright of Derby, Joseph, 424, 425, *425*
writing: demotic, 45; hieratic, 45; origins of, 45

X

Xia Gui, *216–17*, 217

Y

Yamasaki, Minoru, 526, *527*
Yoruba art, 20, *20*, *404*, 405, 411, 411–12, 413, *413*
Young Flavian Woman, 148, 149
Young Girl Gathering Crocus Flowers (Minoan wall painting), 92, *93*
Young Warrior, 107–8, *108*
Young Woman Writing, 149, *149*

Z

Zen Buddhism, Japanese, 22, 208, 210, 224–26, *226*, *228*
Zenobia in Chains (Hosmer), 444, *444*
Zeus, 100; Pergamon altar to, *133*, 133–34, *134*, 144
Zeusis, 14
Zhao Mengfu, 218, *218–19*
ziggurats, 44, 45, 46, *46*
Zoffany, Johann, 422, *422*

Credits

Artist Copyrights

15, bottom: © 2003 The Georgia O'Keeffe Foundation/ Artists Rights Society (ARS), New York:; 22, bottom: © Dale Chihuly; 26, left: © 2003 Frank Lloyd Wright Foundation/ Artists Rights Society (ARS), New York; 463: © 2003 Artists Rights Society (ARS), New York/ ADAGP, Paris; 466 (detail), 467: © 2003 Artists Rights Society (ARS), New York/ ADAGP, Paris/ Estate of Marcel Duchamp; 468: © 2003 The Munch Museum/ The Munch-Ellingsen Group/ Artists Rights Society (ARS), New York; 470, bottom: © 2003 Artists Rights Society (ARS), New York/ VG Bild-Kunst, Bonn; 471: © 2003 Succession H. Matisse, Paris/ Artists Rights Society (ARS), New York; 472: Ernst Ludwig Kirchner, © by Dr. Wolfgang & Ingeborg Henze-Ketterer, Wichtrach/Bern; 473: © 2003 Artists Rights Society (ARS), New York/ ADAGP, Paris; 474: © 2003 Artists Rights Society (ARS), New York/ VG Bild-Kunst, Bonn; 475: © 2003 Estate of Pablo Picasso/ Artists Rights Society (ARS), New York; 476, left: © 2003 Artists Rights Society (ARS), New York/ ADAGP, Paris; 476, right: © 2003 Estate of Pablo Picasso/ Artists Rights Society (ARS), New York; 477: © 2003 Estate of Pablo Picasso/ Artists Rights Society (ARS), New York:; 478, left: © L & M Services B.V. Amsterdam 20010515; 479, right: © 2003 Artists Rights Society (ARS), New York/ ADAGP, Paris; 481: Reproduced by permission of © The Henry Moore Foundation; 482: © 2003 Artists Rights Society (ARS), New York/ VG Bild-Kunst, Bonn; 483, top: © 2003 Mondrian/ Holtzman Trust/ Artists Rights Society (ARS), New York ; 483, bottom: © 2003 Artists Rights Society (ARS), New York/ Beeldrecht, Amsterdam ; 484, top: © 2003 Artists Rights Society (ARS), New York/ ADAGP, Paris/ FLC; 485: © 2003 Artists Rights Society (ARS), New York/ VG Bild-Kunst, Bonn; 486, top: © 2003 Frank Lloyd Wright Foundation/ Artists Rights Society (ARS), New York; 488 left, right: © 2003 Artists Rights Society (ARS), New York/ ADAGP, Paris/ Estate of Marcel Duchamp; 489: © 2003 Estate of Pablo Picasso/ Artists Rights Society (ARS), New York © 2003 Estate of Alexander Calder/ Artists Rights Society (ARS), New York; 490: © 2003 Salvador Dali, Gala-Salvador Dali Foundation/ Artists Rights Society (ARS), New York ; 491, top: © 2003 Succesión Miró/ Artists Rights Society (ARS), New York/ ADAGP, Paris; 491, bottom: © 2003 Estate of Alexander Calder/ Artists Rights Society (ARS), New York; 495: © Donna Mussenden VanDerZee; 496 top, bottom: © 2003 Banco de México Diego Rivera & Frida Kahlo Museums Trust, Av. Cinco de Mayo No. 2, Col. Centro, Del. Cuauhtémoc 06059, Mexico, D.F.; 500: © 2003 Artists Rights Society (ARS), New York/ ADAGP, Paris; 501: © 2003 Estate of Arshile Gorky/ Artists Rights Society (ARS), New York; 502 top, bottom: © 2003 The Pollock-Krasner Foundation/ Artists Rights Society (ARS), New York:; 503: © 2003 The Willem de Kooning Foundation/ Artists Rights Society (ARS), New York; 504, top: © 1998 Kate Rothko Prizel & Christopher Rothko/ Artists Rights Society (ARS), New York; 504, bottom: © Helen Frankenthaler; 505: © 2003 Estate of Louise Nevelson/ Artists Rights Society (ARS), New York; 507: © Jasper Johns/Licensed by VAGA, New York, NY; 508, top: © 2003 Artists Rights Society (ARS), New York/ ADAGP, Paris; 508, bottom: © Estate of Roy Lichtenstein; 509, top: © 2003 Andy Warhol Foundation for the Visual Arts/ Artists Rights Society (ARS), New York; 509, bottom: © The Claes Oldenburg Studio; 510, top: © Bridget Riley, Courtesy of the Karsten Schubert Gallery, London; 511, top: Reproduced with the permission of the Estate of Eva Hesse, Gallerie Hauser & Wirth, Zurich; 511, bottom: © 2003 Joseph Kosuth/ Artists Rights Society (ARS), New York; 512, top: © 2003 Bruce Nauman/ Artists Rights Society (ARS), New York; 512, bottom: © Peter Voulkos; 513: © 2003 Artists Rights Society (ARS), New York/ VG Bild-Kunst, Bonn; 514, top left: © Robert Venturi & Denise Scott-Brown; 514, top right: Courtesy of Foster and Partners, London; 516, top: © Miriam Schapiro; 516, bottom: © Judy Chicago, 1979; 518, top: Courtesy Cindy Sherman; 518, bottom: © Elizabeth Murray, Reproduced courtesy of the artist, Paula Cooper Gallery, New York; 519, top: © Anselm Kiefer, Courtesy of the Gagosian Gallery, New York; 519, bottom left: © Magdalena Abakanowicz, Courtesy Marlborough Gallery, New York; 519, bottom right: © 2004 Kiki Smith, reproduced courtesy of the Artist; 520, top: © Martin Puryear, Courtesy McKee Gallery, New York; 520, bottom: © 1985 Wendell Castle ; 522: Reproduced courtesy of the artist, Jaune Quick-to-See Smith; 523: © 2003 Jenny Holzer/ Artists Rights Society (ARS), New York; 524, top: © Nan June Paik, Courtesy Holly Solomon Gallery, New York; 524, bottom: © Bill Viola Studio; 525, top: © Shirin Neshat, Courtesy Barbara Gladstone Gallery, NY; 527: © Paul LaVerdiere and Paul Myoda.

Credits and Copyrights

13: Roger Wood/ CORBIS; 14: Photograph © 2003 The Art Institute of Chicago, All Rights Reserved; 15, top: © 1981 Center for Creative Photography, Arizona Board of Regents16: Tate Gallery, London/ Art Resource, N.Y.; 17, left: Archaeological Museum, Epidaurus/ Hellenic Ministry of Culture/ Archaeological Receipts Fund / TAP Service, Athens, Greece; 17, right: Scala/ Art Resource, New York; 18, left: William Bridges Thayer Memorial/ Spencer Museum of Art; 18, right: © The Nelson Gallery Foundation; 19, left: © Achim Bednorz, Köln; 19, right: © 2003 Board of Trustees, National Gallery of Art, Washington, D.C.; 20, top: Art Resource, N.Y.; 20, bottom: Photo by Franko Khoury; 21: Scala/ Art Resource, N.Y.; 22, top left: © The Nelson Gallery Foundation; 22, top right: © The J. Paul Getty Museum, Malibu, California; 23: Photograph © 1983 The Metropolitan Museum of Art; 24: Ghigo Roli/ INDEX, Firenze; 26, left: Photo by David Heald, 1993/ © The Solomon R. Guggenheim Foundation, N.Y.; 27: Hirmer Fotoarchiv, Munich; 29: Giraudon/ Art Resource, N.Y.; 30-31: © Jean Clottes/ SYGMA, N.Y.; 33, right: Sisse Brimberg/ National Geographic Society Image Collection; 33, left: Erich Lessing/ Art Resource, N.Y.; 34, right: Photo E. Brandl, Courtesy AIATSIS Pictorial Collection; 35, left: © Jean Clottes, SYGMA, N.Y.; 35 bottom, 36: Sisse Brimberg/ National Geographic Society Image Collection; 37, bottom: Institut Amatller d'Art Hispanic, Barcelona; 38, bottom: Ministry of Public Buildings and Works, Edinburgh. Crown Copyright Reserved; 39, right: Office of Public Works, Dublin; 39, bottom: Aerofilms, Borehamwood, Herts, UK; 41, left: George Gerster/Comstock, Inc.; 41, right: James Balog/ StockPhoto, New York; 42: Griffiths Institute, Ashmolean Museum, Oxford, UK; 43: Scala/Art Resource, N.Y.; 46, top: Hirmer Fotoarchiv, Munich; 46, bottom: Erwin Böhm, Mainz, Germany; 47, top: Courtesy of The Oriental Institute, The University of Chicago; 49, top: All rights reserved, The Metropolitan Museum of Art, New York; 49, bottom: Réunion des Musées Nationaux, Paris/Art Resource, N.Y.; 50, left: Photo by D. Arnaudet/Réunion des Musées Nationaux, Paris/Art Resource, N.Y.; 50, right: Photo by Herve Lewandowski/Réunion des Musées Nationaux, Paris/Art Resource, N.Y.; 51, top: Photograph © 1981 The Metropolitan Museum of Art; 51, bottom: © The British Museum, London,; 52: Erich Lessing/ Art Resource, N.Y.; 53: Photo by Herve Lewandowski/ Réunion des Musées Nationaux, Paris/ Art Resource, N.Y.; 54: The Image Bank/ Getty Images; 55: Araldo de Luca/ INDEX, Firenze; 57, top: Hirmer Fotoarchiv, Munich; 58: LaJoux/Arthephot; 59, top: Nina M. Davies, Ancient Egyptian Paintings, Volume I, University of Chicago/Oxford University Press, 1936, Plate VII; 59, bottom: Photograph © 1983 The Metropolitan Museum of Art; 60, top: Peter Clayton; 61, top: Jean Vertut Archive, Issy-les-Moulineaux; 61, bottom: Wim Swaan, New York; 62, top: Photo by Guillermo Aldana/ Getty Conservation Institute, Marina del Rey; 62 bottom, 63 left, right: Bildarchiv Preussischer Kulturbesitz, Berlin; 64-65: Araldo de Luca/ INDEX, Firenze; 64 bottom, 65: © The British Museum, London; 66, 67: O. Louis Mazzatenta/ National Geographic Image Collection; 68: © Roto Smeets De Boer NV; 70, top: Jean-Louis Nou; 70, bottom: Richard Todd; 71, right: Gene Markowski; 72, left: Richard Todd; 74: Photograph by Benoy K. Behl, Bombay; 75, top: Asian Art Archives, University of Michigan; 75, bottom: From Martin Hürlimann, India: The Landscape, the Monuments and the People, N.Y., B. Westermann, 1928, fig. 131.; 77: China Pictorial Publications, Beijing; 78: Cultural Relics Publishing House, Beijing; 79, top: Cultural Relics Publishing House, Beijing; 79, bottom: © Wolfgang Kaehler, Bellevue, WA; 80, 81 bottom, 82: Cultural Relics Publishing House, Beijing; 84: Yoshio Watanabe, Tokyo; 85, top: Mr. Junkichi Mayuyama, Tokyo; 85, bottom: Benrido, Tokyo; 88-89: © Studio Kontos, Athens; 90: Photograph © 1996 The Metropolitan Museum of Art; 92: Courtesy McRae Books, Florence; 93: Ch. Doumas, "The Wall Paintings of Thera," Idryma Theras-Petros M. Nomicos, Athens, 1992; 94 top, bottom, 95 top: © Studio Kontos, Athens; 95, bottom: Nimatallah/ Art Resource, N.Y.; 96, bottom: The Conway Library, Courtauld Institute of Art, London; 97, top: © Studio Kontos, Athens; 97, bottom: Deutsches Archaeologisches Institut, Athens; 98, top: Photograph © 1996 The Metropolitan Museum of Art; 98, bottom: Photograph © 2002 The Metropolitan Museum of Art; 99, top: Canali Photobank, Milan; 101 top, bottom: Deutsches Archaeologisches Institut, Athens; 102, left: Photograph © 1997 The Metropolitan Museum of Art; 102, right: © Studio Kontos, Athens; 103: Laboratoires Photographiques Devos, Boulogne sur Mer; 105, top: Bildarchiv Preussischer Kulturbesitz, Berlin; 106 left, right: Hirmer Fotoarchiv, Munich; 107: © Studio Kontos, Athens; 108 left, right: Scala/Art Resource, N.Y.; 109, bottom: © Studio Kontos, Athens; 110, top: K. Papaioannou, The Art of Greece, Harry N. Abrams, Inc., 1989/(Éditions Mazenod, Paris, 1972), page 400-401 top; 110, center: Hirmer Fotoarchiv, Munich; 111: Photo by Herve Lewandowski/ Réunion des Musées Nationaux, Paris/ Art Resource, N.Y.; 112, top: Alison Frantz Collection, American School of Classical Studies, Athens; 112, bottom: Hirmer Fotoarchiv, Munich; 113: Ministry of Culture/Archaeological Receipts Fund (TAP Service), Athens; 114: Archivi Alinari, Florence; 115, 116: Hirmer Fotoarchiv, Munich; 118, 119: Réunion des Musées Nationaux, Paris/ Art Resource, N.Y.; 120: Gabinetto Fotografico Nazionale, Rome; 121: Canali Photobank, Milan; 122, bottom: Scala/ Art Resource, N.Y.; 123: Soprintendenza Archeologica all'Etruria Meridionale, Tarquinia, Italy; 124, top: Hirmer Fotoarchiv, Munich; 124, bottom: Boltin Picture Library; 126: Bildarchiv Preussischer Kulturbesitz, Berlin; 128: Courtesy of The Oriental Institute, The University of Chicago; 129, top: Courtesy of The Oriental Institute, The University of Chicago; 130, left: Photo by D. Arnaudet/ J. Schormans/ Réunion des Musées Nationaux, Paris/Art Resource, N.Y.; 130, right: All rights reserved, The Metropolitan Museum of Art; 131: Service Photographique de la Réunion des Musées Nationaux, Paris; 132: Araldo De Luca, Rome; 132: Araldo De Luca/ INDEX, Firenze; 133: Bildarchiv Preussischer Kulturbesitz, Berlin; 134: Erich Lessing/ Bildarchiv Preussischer Kulturbesitz, Berlin; 135: Archivi Alinari, Florence; 136-137: Monumenti Musei e Gallerie Pontificie, Vatican City (Rome); 138,139 top: Canali Photobank, Milan; 140, bottom: Luciano Pedicini/ Archivo Dell'Arte/INDEX, Firenze; 142: Monumenti Musei e Gallerie Pontificie, Vatican City (Rome); 143: Michael Larvey, Austin, Texas; 144: Fototeca Unione, Rome; 146, top: Fotocielo, Rome; 146, bottom: Fototeca Unione, Rome; 147: A. Vasari/Index, Firenze; 148, top: Erich Lessing/ Art Resource, N.Y.; 148, bottom: Alinari/Art Resource, N.Y.; 149: Gemeinnützige Stiftung/Leonard von Matt, Switzerland; 150,151 top: Scala/ Art Resource, N.Y.; 151, bottom: Luciano Pedicini/ Archivio Dell'Arte/ INDEX, Firenze; 152: Monumenti Musei e Gallerie Pontificie, Vatican City (Rome); 153: Fototeca Unione, Rome; 154: Canali Photobank, Milan; 155, bottom: Bapier/ Artephot, Paris; 156, top: © Foto Vasari/ INDEX, Firenze; 156, bottom: Canali Photobank, Milan; 157: Araldo de Luca/ INDEX, Firenze; 158: Brian Brake/John Hillelson Agency, London; 160, top: Deutsches Archaeologisches Institut, Rome; 160, bottom: Fototeca Unione, Rome; 161: Araldo de Luca/ INDEX, Firenze; 164-165: © Pontifcia Commissione de Archeologia Sacra, Rome/ Index, Firenze; 166, left: Ludovico Canali/Pontificia Commissione di Archeologia Sacra, Rome, Italy; 166, right: R. Percheron/ Artephot, Paris; 167: David Harris, Jerusalem; 170: © Pontifcia Commissione de Archeologia Sacra, Rome/ Index, Firenze; 172 top, bottom: Nimatallah/ INDEX, Firenze; 173 top, bottom, 174: Canali Photobank, Milan; 175, left: GEKS, New York; 176: Wim Swaan, New York; 177, bottom: Scala/ Art Resource, N.Y.; 178, 179: Scala/ Art Resource, N.Y.; 181, left: Donato Pineider, Florence; 181, right: Nikos Kontos, courtesy of Ekdotike Athenon, Athens; 182 right, 183, 184: Photo by Bruce White/ Copyright © 1997 The Metropolitan Museum of Art; 185: Mario Carrieri Fotografo, Milan; 186: Research Library, The Getty Research Institute, Los Angeles; 187: Sovfoto/ Eastfoto; 190: Photograph © 1994 The Metropolitan Museum of Art; 192, right: A.F. Kersting, London; 193, top: © 1992 Saïd Nuseibeh Photography, San Francisco; 194: © Roger Wood/ CORBIS; 195, left: Comstock, Inc.; 195, right: Raffaello Bencini, Florence; 196: Oroñoz Fotografos, Madrid; 197, top: Réunion des Musées Nationaux, Paris/ Art Resource, N.Y.; 197, bottom: Imperial Embassy of Iran, Washington, D.C. (as it were); 198, top: Photograph © 1982 The Metropolitan Museum of Art; 198, bottom: Ronald Sheridan's "Ancient Art & Architecture Collection, London"; 199: Dagli Orti/ The Art Archive; 200: Peter Sanders Photography, Chesham, Bucks, UK; 203: Photograph © 1994 The Metropolitan Museum of Art; 204: Asian Art Archives, University of Michigan; 205: Wim Swaan, New York; 207: Photograph © 1986 The Metropolitan Museum of Art; 208-209: © Michael S. Yamashita/ CORBIS; 210, bottom: Asian Art Archives, University of Michigan; 211: Institute of American Indian Studies; 212: © Henri & Anne Stierlin, Geneva; 213: Courtesy, Museum of Fine Arts, Boston. Reproduced with permission. © 2003 Museum of Fine Arts, Boston. All Rights Reserved; 214: Katharine Wetzel/ © The Virginia Museum of Fine Arts; 215: Robert Newcombe/ © 1993 The Nelson-Atkins Museum of Art; 217 top, 218: Photo by Robert Newcombe; 220, bottom: Palace Museum, Beijing/ Wan-go Weng Inc. Archive; 221: © Wolfgang Kaehler/ CORBIS; 222, top: Sakamoto Manschichi Photo Research Library, Tokyo; 225: © 2003 The Cleveland Museum of Art; 226: © Michael S. Yamashita/ CORBIS; 227, top: Sakamoto Manschichi Photo Research Library, Tokyo; 227, bottom: Stephen Addiss, Midlothian, VA; 234: Kit Weiss, Copenhagen, Denmark; 235, top: © The British Museum; 235, bottom: The Green Studio Limited, Dublin, Ireland; 236, bottom: Foto Ann Münchow, Aachen, Germany; 237, right: Fotowerkstatte, Cologne, Germany; 238: Bibliothèque Nationale de France, Paris; 239: The Pierpont Morgan Library/ Art Resource, N.Y.; 240: Photograph © 1986 By The Metropolitan Museum of Art; 241: Frank Tomio, Dom- und Diözesan-

Text Copyrights

Single PC License Agreement and Limited Warranty

READ THIS LICENSE CAREFULLY BEFORE OPENING THIS PACKAGE. BY OPENING THIS PACKAGE, YOU ARE AGREEING TO THE TERMS AND CONDITIONS OF THIS LICENSE. IF YOU DO NOT AGREE, DO NOT OPEN THE PACKAGE. PROMPTLY RETURN THE UNOPENED PACKAGE AND ALL ACCOMPANYING ITEMS TO THE PLACE YOU OBTAINED THEM [[FOR A FULL REFUND OF ANY SUMS YOU HAVE PAID FOR THE SOFTWARE]]. *THESE TERMS APPLY TO ALL LICENSED SOFTWARE ON THE DISK EXCEPT THAT THE TERMS FOR USE OF ANY SHAREWARE OR FREEWARE ON THE DISKETTES ARE AS SET FORTH IN THE ELECTRONIC LICENSE LOCATED ON THE DISK:*

1. GRANT OF LICENSE and OWNERSHIP: The enclosed computer programs <<and data>> ("Software") are licensed, not sold, to you by Pearson Education, Inc. publishing as Prentice Hall ("We" or the "Company") and in consideration [[of your payment of the license fee, which is part of the price you paid]] [[of your purchase or adoption of the accompanying Company textbooks and/or other materials,]] and your agreement to these terms. We reserve any rights not granted to you. You own only the disk(s) but we and/or our licensors own the Software itself. This license allows you to use and display your copy of the Software on a single computer (i.e., with a single CPU) at a single location for <u>academic</u> use only, so long as you comply with the terms of this Agreement. You may make one copy for back up, or transfer your copy to another CPU, provided that the Software is usable on only one computer.

2. RESTRICTIONS: You may <u>not</u> transfer or distribute the Software or documentation to anyone else. Except for backup, you may <u>not</u> copy the documentation or the Software. You may <u>not</u> network the Software or otherwise use it on more than one computer or computer terminal at the same time. You may <u>not</u> reverse engineer, disassemble, decompile, modify, adapt, translate, or create derivative works based on the Software or the Documentation. You may be held legally responsible for any copying or copyright infringement that is caused by your failure to abide by the terms of these restrictions.

3. TERMINATION: This license is effective until terminated. This license will terminate automatically without notice from the Company if you fail to comply with any provisions or limitations of this license. Upon termination, you shall destroy the Documentation and all copies of the Software. All provisions of this Agreement as to limitation and disclaimer of warranties, limitation of liability, remedies or damages, and our ownership rights shall survive termination.

4. LIMITED WARRANTY AND DISCLAIMER OF WARRANTY: Company warrants that for a period of 60 days from the date you purchase this SOFTWARE (or purchase or adopt the accompanying textbook), the Software, when properly installed and used in accordance with the Documentation, will operate in substantial conformity with the description of the Software set forth in the Documentation, and that for a period of 30 days the disk(s) on which the Software is delivered shall be free from defects in materials and workmanship under normal use. The Company does not warrant that the Software will meet your requirements or that the operation of the Software will be uninterrupted or error-free. Your only remedy and the Company's only obligation under these limited warranties is, at the Company's option, return of the disk for a refund of any amounts paid for it by you or replacement of the disk. THIS LIMITED WARRANTY IS THE ONLY WARRANTY PROVIDED BY THE COMPANY AND ITS LICENSORS, AND THE COMPANY AND ITS LICENSORS DISCLAIM ALL OTHER WARRANTIES, EXPRESS OR IMPLIED, INCLUDING WITHOUT LIMITATION, THE IMPLIED WARRANTIES OF MERCHANTABILITY AND FITNESS FOR A PARTICULAR PURPOSE. THE COMPANY DOES NOT WARRANT, GUARANTEE, OR MAKE ANY REPRESENTATION REGARDING THE ACCURACY, RELIABILITY, CURRENTNESS, USE, OR RESULTS OF USE, OF THE SOFTWARE.

5. LIMITATION OF REMEDIES AND DAMAGES: IN NO EVENT, SHALL THE COMPANY OR ITS EMPLOYEES, AGENTS, LICENSORS, OR CONTRACTORS BE LIABLE FOR ANY INCIDENTAL, INDIRECT, SPECIAL, OR CONSEQUENTIAL DAMAGES ARISING OUT OF OR IN CONNECTION WITH THIS LICENSE OR THE SOFTWARE, INCLUDING FOR LOSS OF USE, LOSS OF DATA, LOSS OF INCOME OR PROFIT, OR OTHER LOSSES, SUSTAINED AS A RESULT OF INJURY TO ANY PERSON, OR LOSS OF OR DAMAGE TO PROPERTY, OR CLAIMS OF THIRD PARTIES, EVEN IF THE COMPANY OR AN AUTHORIZED REPRESENTATIVE OF THE COMPANY HAS BEEN ADVISED OF THE POSSIBILITY OF SUCH DAMAGES. IN NO EVENT SHALL THE LIABILITY OF THE COMPANY FOR DAMAGES WITH RESPECT TO THE SOFTWARE EXCEED THE AMOUNTS ACTUALLY PAID BY YOU, IF ANY, FOR THE SOFTWARE OR THE ACCOMPANYING TEXTBOOK. BECAUSE SOME JURISDICTIONS DO NOT ALLOW THE LIMITATION OF LIABILITY IN CERTAIN CIRCUMSTANCES, THE ABOVE LIMITATIONS MAY NOT ALWAYS APPLY TO YOU.

6. GENERAL: THIS AGREEMENT SHALL BE CONSTRUED IN ACCORDANCE WITH THE LAWS OF THE UNITED STATES OF AMERICA AND THE STATE OF NEW YORK, APPLICABLE TO CONTRACTS MADE IN NEW YORK, AND SHALL BENEFIT THE COMPANY, ITS AFFILIATES AND ASSIGNEES. THIS AGREEMENT IS THE COMPLETE AND EXCLUSIVE STATEMENT OF THE AGREEMENT BETWEEN YOU AND THE COMPANY AND SUPERSEDES ALL PROPOSALS OR PRIOR AGREEMENTS, ORAL, OR WRITTEN, AND ANY OTHER COMMUNICATIONS BETWEEN YOU AND THE COMPANY OR ANY REPRESENTATIVE OF THE COMPANY RELATING TO THE SUBJECT MATTER OF THIS AGREEMENT. If you are a U.S. Government user, this Software is licensed with "restricted rights" as set forth in subparagraphs (a)-(d) of the Commercial Computer-Restricted Rights clause at FAR 52.227-19 or in subparagraphs (c)(1)(ii) of the Rights in Technical Data and Computer Software clause at DFARS 252.227-7013, and similar clauses, as applicable.

Should you have any questions concerning this agreement or if you wish to contact the Company for any reason, please contact in writing: Social Sciences Media Editor, Prentice Hall, One Lake Street, Upper Saddle River, NJ 07458.